HANDBOOK OF WORLD EXCHANGE RATES, 1590–1914

Handbook of World Exchange Rates, 1590–1914

MARKUS A. DENZEL
University of Leipzig, Germany

ASHGATE

Published by
Ashgate Publishing Limited
Wey Court East
Union Road
Farnham
Surrey, GU9 7PT
England

Ashgate Publishing Company
Suite 420
101 Cherry Street
Burlington
VT 05401-4405
USA

www.ashgate.com

British Library Cataloguing in Publication Data
Denzel, Markus A.
    Handbook of World Exchange Rates, 1590–1914.
    1. Foreign exchange rates – History. 2. Economic history – 1600–1750. 3. Economic history –
    1750–1918. I. Title
    332.4'56'09-dc22

Library of Congress Cataloging-in-Publication Data

Library of Congress Control Number: 2010931187

ISBN   9780754603566

inted and bound in Great Britain by
PG Books Group, UK

PREFACE

When, in 1983, my academic teacher and mentor Jürgen Schneider, who held the Chair of Economic and Social History at the Otto-Friedrich-University of Bamberg at that time, started with his team to systematically collect exchange rates and money rates, and to process these data electronically, finally publishing this material, it was "the aim of the project ... to create data manuals presenting, area-wide and comprehensively, the monetary circumstances of the respective region under study."[1] Several projects, promoted by the Deutsche Forschungsgemeinschaft, produced a database covering the majority of the exchange rates and money rates available worldwide for the period between the late 17th century and 1951, the year before the appearance of the International Financial Statistics, with their extensive exchange rate quotations. Thus it was the central aim of this edition to act as an English anthology presenting the most important exchange rate series in the form of a handbook. After a work of more than six years, this edition can now be presented, allowing the inclusion of numerous additions compared to the original database.

On retirement in 2002, Jürgen Schneider withdrew from the project, leaving it to the editor to develop the concept, and to introduce and publish this volume. Because of both this fact and in recognition of our always trustful and fruitful collaboration over almost twenty years, I feel I must express my sincere thanks to my mentor and friend Jürgen Schneider for all he did for me: without him I would not have found my way into economic history and without him this volume would not have been realized.

During the past eight years numerous colleagues and friends accompanied the development of this volume, supporting me with many questions and strengthening my point of view that it was an essential work: Jean-François Bergier (†), Peter Bernholz (Basel), Wim Blockmans (Leiden), Andrea Bonoldi (Trento), Leonid Borodkin (Moscow), Sushil Chaudhuri (Calcutta), Murat Çizakça (Kuala Lumpur), Rainer Cunz (Hannover), Antonio Di Vittorio (Bari), Dennis O. Flynn (Stockton, Ca.), Hans-Jürgen Gerhard (Hardegsen), Rainer Gömmel (Regensburg), Gabriel Imboden (Brig), Karl Heinrich Kaufhold (Göttingen), Niklot Klüßendorf (Marburg),

---

1   Oskar SCHWARZER / Petra SCHNELZER, Quellen zur Statistik der Geld- und Wechselkurse in Deutschland, Nordwesteuropa und dem Ostseeraum im 18. und 19. Jahrhundert, in Wolfram FISCHER / Andreas KUNZ (eds.), *Grundlagen der historischen Statistik von Deutschland. Quellen, Methoden, Forschungsziele*, Opladen 1991, pp. 175-191, here p. 176 (translated from German).

Martin Körner (†), Andrea Leonardi (Trento), John J. McCusker (San Antonio, Tx.), John Munro (Toronto), Bogdan Murgescu (Bucharest), Jürgen Nautz (Vienna), Patrick Karl O'Brien (London), Horst Pietschmann (Hamburg), Hans Pohl (Bonn), Şevket Pamuk (Istanbul), Om Prakash (Delhi), Philipp R. Rössner (Leipzig), Peter Spufford (Cambridge), Herman Van der Wee (Leuven), Margarete Wagner-Braun (Bamberg), Angelika Westermann (Kiel), Ekkehard Westermann (Rantrum) and Harald Witthöft (Siegen).

Conclusions resulting from the research work for this volume have been presented and discussed at many international conferences, such as the international symposium "Dinero, moneda y crédito. De la Monarquía Hispánica a la Integración Monetaria Europea" in Madrid (1999), the 22nd Settimana di Studi of the Istituto Internazionale di Storia Economica "F. Datini" in Prato (2000), the 13th International Economic History Congress in Buenos Aires (2002), the international workshop "Russia and Western Countries" in Moscow (2003), the 20th International Congress of Historical Sciences in Sydney (2005), the Congreso de la Asociación Española de Historia Económica in Santiago de Compostela (2005), the Deutscher Historikertag in Kiel (2005) and at the 14th International Economic History Congress in Helsinki (2006). Sincere thanks go to all colleagues who shared in making this volume as good as possible with their suggestions and contributions to discussion.

It is thanks to Dr John Smedley, Ashgate Publishing Limited, that the publication of this volume became a reality. He was taken with the project after the first conversation I had with him, and then he waited patiently for its eventual completion. In addition, I am indebted to my dear colleagues and friends Dennis O. Flynn and Patrick Karl O'Brien for establishing contact with him. I am grateful to all members of the staff of Ashgate Publishing Limited, especially Kirsten Weissenberg, and freelance copy-editor Elizabeth Teague for all their endeavours in producing the volume.

The publication of this book in English was possible only with a large amount of translation work and numerous discussions with Dr Angela Schröder (Göttingen), Dr Klaus U. Hachmeier (Frankfurt am Main) and Alexandra Holzhey MA (Leipzig). Dr Schröder prepared the rough version of many introductory texts of the single country chapters, Dr Hachmeier translated parts of the Introduction, and Mrs Holzhey provided the final version of the whole volume. I thank all translators very sincerely, above all Mrs Holzhey, who did the translation work alongside her role as my assistant when I held the Chair for Social and Economic History at the University of Leipzig.

My warmest thanks, however, go to my dear wife Alexandra, who has accompanied the exchange rate project since 1993, supported me on several archive visits and was, last but not least, a reliable co-worker on the data input throughout.

I dedicate this book to my academic teacher, mentor and friend Jürgen Schneider.

Markus A. Denzel
Leipzig and Bolzano, January 2010

CONTENTS

INTRODUCTION

How to use this *Handbook*

The introductions to the different exchange markets or countries covered by this *Handbook* are structured uniformly; they include:
– a list of the sources used for the documentation of the exchange rate quotations of the relevant exchange market(s). Each list is followed by text in brackets that gives that period of time covered by the respective source. Sometimes single (printed) sources are quoted in an abbreviated form, whereas the source will be given in full in the references;
– the indication of the concordance, i.e. where the relevant (detailed) exchange rate series can be found in *Währungen der Welt* or in the volumes of the *Historische Statistik von Deutschland*;
– a short history of those currencies in which the documented exchange rates of one single exchange market are quoted in the *Handbook*. These short sections are, where applicable, based on previous works of the author, and they consider only the most important facts of currency history as far as they are necessary for understanding the documented exchange rate series;[2]
– a description of the way exchange rates of respective exchange markets documented in the *Handbook* were originally quoted;
– a list of exchange rate series that were excluded from this *Handbook* for the reasons mentioned above. They can be found in *Währungen der Welt* or in the volumes of the *Historische Statistik von Deutschland*;
– a short presentation of both the development of a country's exchange market(s) whose quotations are documented in this *Handbook* and their importance within

---

1 George CLARE, The A.B.C. of the Foreign Exchanges, *The Institute of Bankers* 13/II (1892), pp. 121–149, esp. pp. 142f.

2 The statements regarding currency history are not intended to provide elaborate discussions of currency history and currency politics. A more detailed description of the history of each currency would go beyond the scope of this *Handbook*.

the international cashless payments system. For practicability, these presentations are revised versions of introductory paragraphs the author published in German in previous editions of *Währungen der Welt* or in the volumes of the *Historische Statistik von Deutschland*;

– a list of references to the books and articles that have been used throughout the *Handbook*. Due to the abundance of literature on currency history and currency politics, the list cannot claim to be exhaustive.

1. Objectives and Concept of the *Handbook*

Research on international exchange rates and cashless payments has been one of the 'classical' topics in monetary and currency history. On the one hand, this was due to the need to explain systematically the mechanisms and possibilities of cashless payments to merchants and entrepreneurs, which had already been practised for centuries with varying intensity; Francesco Balducci Pegolotti's *Practica della mercatura* is the earliest example.[3] Merchant manuals highly specialized in the needs of cashless payments since the 17th century give emphatic evidence of this.[4] On the other hand, the intention was to explain more clearly the mechanisms of international payments in the late 19th and early 20th centuries. This aim became even stronger in relation to the 1920s, because the inter-war period was a time of economic experiments and hitherto unknown inflationary processes.[5] In addition to handbooks giving surveys of cashless payments at, for example, the Asian exchange markets,[6] there are also detailed case studies from this period that investigate single-payment relations of international importance.[7] For this purpose, exchange rate quotations were sought and compiled in data series in order to construct a sufficient database for this financial and currency research. Such data series, however, were usually limited to the most important exchange relations of a country and did not result – apart from a few exceptions[8] – in a systematic collection of historical exchange rate quotations.

Without examining the extensive research, its different tendencies and the resul-

---

3   Francesco Balducci PEGOLOTTI, *La pratica della mercatura*, ed. Alan EVANS, Cambridge (Mass.) 1936 (repr. New York 1970).

4   Markus A. DENZEL / Jean Claude HOCQUET / Harald WITTHÖFT (eds.), *Kaufmannsbücher und Handelspraktiken vom Spätmittelalter bis zum beginnenden 20. Jahrhundert / Merchant's Books and Mercantile Pratiche from the Late Middle Ages to the Beginning of the 20th Century*, Stuttgart 2002.

5   Last but not least, this becomes apparent from extensive systematic compilations of exchange rates, e.g. Emil DIESEN, *Exchange Rates of the World / Cours de changes du monde / Devisen-Kurse der Welt / Verdens Valutakurser, January 1st 1914 – December 31st 1921*, 2 vols., Christiania 1923.

6   William F. SPALDING, *Eastern Exchange, Currency and Finance*, London ²1918; Walter MAHLBERG, *Über asiatische Wechselkurse*, Leipzig ²1920.

7   E.g. Arthur H. COLE, Statistical Background of the Crisis Period 1837–42, *Review of Economic Statistics* 10 (1928), pp. 182–195; idem, The New York Money Market of 1843 to 1862, *Review of Economic Statistics* 11 (1929), pp. 164–170.

ting literature on the history of exchange rates, of currencies and of their influence on economic policy and economic development – which would go beyond the scope of this book – the main emphasis is on the production of data handbooks on money and exchange rates. Extensive surveys of historical exchange rate series have not been presented as far as World War II, when economic historians increasingly acknowledged the benefits and the necessity of statistical foundations for their research. According to my knowledge, the compilation of the Paris exchange rates during the last decades of the 18th century, published by Jean Bouchary in 1937, represents the oldest of such handbooks.[9] The next one covered Neapolitan exchange rates during the 'long' 17th century, published by Luigi de Rosa in 1955,[10] whereas Henri Lapeyre had presented an overview of the quotations on the Lyons fairs from the second half of the 16th century two years earlier.[11] Valentín Vazquez de Prada's survey of the Antwerp quotations from 1558 up to 1606[12] followed, as did José Gentil da Silva's detailed documentation of the exchange rates of the Genoese Bisenzone fairs from 1552 until 1722.[13] Numerous other publications of these and the following decades integrated more or less extensive tables with exchange rate quotations of one or more exchange markets into their respective studies without solely concentrating on this matter and giving handbook-like overviews of more than one exchange market, however.[14] The first to take this step was John J. McCusker with his handbook *Money and Exchange in Europe and America, 1600–1775*, which systematically combines transatlantic exchange rate quotations with all involved important exchange markets and their respective monetary backgrounds from the 17th century to the American Revolution.[15] Peter Spufford worked on a more extensive research subject in his *Handbook of Medieval Exchange* by listing and commenting on all important European and Levant currencies as well as money and exchange markets

---

8   E.g. F.L. HO, An Index of Foreign Exchange Rates, 1898–1926, *Chinese Economic Journal* (1928), pp. 1–40.

9   Jean BOUCHARY, *Le marché des changes de Paris à la fin du XVIIIe siècle (1778–1800) avec des graphiques et le relevé des cours*, Paris 1937.

10   Luigi DE ROSA, *I cambi esteri del Regno di Napoli dal 1591 al 1707*, Napoli 1955.

11   Henri LAPEYRE, *Une famille de marchands: les Ruiz*, Paris 1953, pp. 464–471.

12   Valentín VAZQUEZ DE PRADA, *Lettres marchandes d'Anvers*, Paris 1960/61, vol. I, pp. 270–325.

13   José GENTIL DA SILVA, *Banque et crédit en Italie au XVIIe siècle*, Paris 1969, vol. II, pp. 102–239.

14   Some examples that are remarkable for their rich data are: S.J. BUTLIN, *Foundations of the Australian Monetary System 1788–1851*, Melbourne 1953 (Sydney [2]1968); Astrid FRIIS / Kristof GLAMANN, *A History of Prices and Wages in Denmark 1660–1800*, vol. I, London – New York – Toronto 1958; Charles ISSAWI (ed.), *The Economic History of Iran 1800–1914*, Chicago – London 1971; J.T.M. VAN LAANEN, *Money and Banking 1816–1940* (= P. CREUTZBERG / J.T.M. VAN LAANEN (eds.), *Changing Economy in Indonesia. A Selection of Statistical Source Material from the Early 19th Century up to 1940*, vol. 6), The Hague 1980; Charles ISSAWI, *The Economic History of Turkey 1800–1914*, Chicago 1981; S.J. BUTLIN, *The Australian Monetary System 1851 to 1914*, [Sydney] 1986; Henry ROSEVEARE (ed.), *Markets and Merchants of the Late Seventeenth Century. The Marescoe–David Letters 1668–1680*, New York 1987; Jennifer NEWMAN, 'A Very Delicate Experiment'. British Mercantile Strategies for Financing Trade in Russia, 1680–1780, in Ian BLANCHARD / Anthony GOODMAN / Jennifer NEWMAN (eds.), *Industry and Finance in Early Modern History. Essays Presented to George Hammersley on the Occasion of his 74th Birthday*, Stuttgart 1992, pp. 116–141.

15   John J. McCUSKER, *Money and Exchange in Europe and America, 1600–1775. A Handbook*, London – Basingstoke 1978.

from the end of the 12th century up to 1500.[16]

These two standard works of economic history substantially determined the direction and conception of further documentation of money and exchange rates in the following years. In Canada, for instance, Alan Bruce McCullough compiled exchange rates of the Canadian exchange markets in a study on *Money and Exchange in Canada to 1900*.[17] In Switzerland a team headed by Martin Körner compiled a handbook on money rates in Switzerland from the 17th and 18th centuries.[18] Within the scope of the programme *Historische Statistik von Deutschland* (*Historical statistics of Germany*) financed by the Deutsche Forschungsgemeinschaft (German Research Association), the German Jürgen Schneider and his team set out in 1983 to document money and exchange rates of German and Northwest European financial markets in the 19th century. Within about ten years this project was followed by several further ones that gradually produced documentation and research on almost all internationally important exchange markets in the whole world from the 17th up to the middle of the 20th century. This was the starting point of the collection of 11 volumes of *Währungen der Welt* (*Currencies of the World*) (abbreviation: *WdW*)[19] and the two relevant volumes of the collection of *Quellen und Forschungen zur Historischen Statistik von Deutschland* (*Sources and Research on Historical Statistics of Germany*) (abbreviation: *HStD*).[20] Mainly following in concept McCusker's handbook and, consequently, his methodological approach, the studies of Jürgen Schneider's team became increasingly oriented in their scope towards Spufford's *Hand-*

---

16   Peter SPUFFORD, *Handbook of Medieval Exchange*, London 1986.

17   Alan Bruce MCCULLOUGH, *Money and Exchange in Canada to 1900*, Toronto – Charlottetown 1984.

18   Martin KÖRNER / Norbert FURRER / Niklaus BARTLOME with assistance of Thomas MEIER / Erika FLÜCKIGER, *Währungen und Sortenkurse in der Schweiz / Systèmes monétaires et cours des espèces en Suisse / Sistemi monetari e corsi delle specie in Svizzera 1600–1799*, Lausanne 2001.

19   Jürgen SCHNEIDER / Oskar SCHWARZER / Friedrich ZELLFELDER (eds.), *Währungen der Welt I: Europäische und nordamerikanische Devisenkurse 1777–1914*, 3 vols., Stuttgart 1991; Jürgen SCHNEIDER / Oskar SCHWARZER / Markus A. DENZEL (eds.), *Währungen der Welt II: Europäische und nordamerikanische Devisenkurse 1914–1951*, Stuttgart 1997; idem (eds.), *Währungen der Welt III: Geld und Währungen in Europa im 17. Jahrhundert*, Stuttgart 1994; Jürgen SCHNEIDER / Oskar SCHWARZER / Friedrich ZELLFELDER / Markus A. DENZEL (eds.), *Währungen der Welt IV: Asiatische und australische Devisenkurse im 19. Jahrhundert*, Stuttgart 1992; Jürgen SCHNEIDER / Oskar SCHWARZER / Markus A. DENZEL (eds.), *Währungen der Welt V: Asiatische und australische Devisenkurse im 20. Jahrhundert*, Stuttgart 1994; Jürgen SCHNEIDER / Oskar SCHWARZER / Friedrich ZELLFELDER / Markus A. DENZEL (eds.), *Währungen der Welt VI: Geld und Währungen in Europa im 18. Jahrhundert*, Stuttgart 1992; Jürgen SCHNEIDER / Oskar SCHWARZER / Markus A. DENZEL (eds.), *Währungen der Welt VII: Lateinamerikanische Devisenkurse im 19. und 20. Jahrhundert*, Stuttgart 1997; idem (eds.), *Währungen der Welt VIII: Afrikanische und levantinische Devisenkurse im 19. und 20. Jahrhundert*, Stuttgart 1994; Markus A. DENZEL (ed.), *Währungen der Welt IX: Europäische Wechselkurse vor 1620*, Stuttgart 1995; idem (ed.), *Währungen der Welt X: Geld- und Wechselkurse der deutschen Messeplätze Leipzig und Braunschweig (18. Jahrhundert bis 1823)*, Stuttgart 1994; idem (ed.), *Währungen der Welt XI: Nordwestdeutsche und dänische Wechselkurse vom ausgehenden 17. Jahrhundert bis 1914*, Stuttgart 1999. Henceforth, the volumes of *Währungen der Welt* will be cited with the abbreviation *WdW* followed by the number of the respective volume.

20   Jürgen SCHNEIDER / Oskar SCHWARZER (eds.), *Statistik der Geld- und Wechselkurse in Deutschland (1815–1913)* (= *Historische Statistik von Deutschland*, vol. XII), St. Katharinen 1990; idem / Petra SCHNELZER (eds.), *Statistik der Geld- und Wechselkurse in Deutschland und im Ostseeraum (18. und 19. Jahrhundert)* (= *Historische Statistik von Deutschland*, vol. XII), St. Katharinen 1993. Henceforth, the volumes of *Historische Statistik von Deutschland* will be cited with the abbreviation *HStD* followed by the number of the respective volume (i.e. either *XI* or *XII*).

book, which was chronologically followed by *Währungen der Welt IX*, despite greater gaps in the source material. During recent years I have added the previous documentations and extended them to exchange markets so far neglected and worked out a means to present the theoretical and empirical development of the international cashless payment system[21] using earlier research on cashless payments as a basis.[22]

This *Handbook* is based mainly on the already-published material in *Währungen der Welt* and – to a smaller extent – on the data in *Historische Statistik von Deutschland*, and it documents exchange rate quotations between different exchange markets from the end of the 16th century up to World War I. So, not exclusively, but especially from the perspective of cashless payments, the analysed period covers an era of economic history that was mainly determined by Northwestern Europe and the markets there – above all the 'world financial centres' of Amsterdam and later London – and the institutions of payments developed or improved there, for example the stock exchange, the endorsement, and the discount. In the wake of the European expansion and the emergence of the world economy, the techniques and media of the European cashless payment system were brought from Northwestern Europe to many parts of the world outside Europe as well,[23] so that Northwest European merchants and trading companies as well as the political powers of this region have played a central role within this distribution process from the 17th century. Thus the *Handbook* covers the period from the point when the centre of the European economy shifted from the Mediterranean region to the Atlantic coast until the end of the first (liberal) phase of the world economy at the beginning of World War I.[24]

This *Handbook* aims to be much more than a simple reprint of already known

---

21 Esp. Markus A. DENZEL, Wechselplätze als territoriale Enklaven an der europäischen Peripherie: Von der Anbindung zur Integration von Finanzmärkten im System des bargeldlosen Zahlungsverkehrs (Spätmittelalter bis beginnendes 20. Jahrhundert), in Hartmut ZWAHR / Uwe SCHIRMER / Henning STEINFÜHRER (eds.), *Leipzig, Mitteldeutschland und Europa. Festgabe für Manfred Straube und Manfred Unger zum 70. Geburtstag*, Beucha 2000, pp. 545–560, or in French: Les places de change de la périphérie européenne considérées comme des enclaves territoriales: de l'association à l'intégration des marchés financiers dans le système de paiement par virements (bas Moyen Age – début du 20ᵉ siècle), in Paul DELSALLE / André FERRER (eds.), *Les enclaves territoriales aux Temps Modernes (XVIᵉ–XVIIIᵉ siècles). Actes du Colloque de Besançon*, Besançon 2000, pp. 209–232; idem, Der Beitrag von Messen und Märkten zum Integrationsprozeß des internationalen bargeldlosen Zahlungsverkehrssystems in Europa (13.–18. Jahrhundert), in Simonetta CAVACIOCCHI (ed.), *Fiere e mercati nella integrazione delle economie europee, secc. XIII–XVIII. Atti della "Trentaduesima Settimana di Studi" 8–12 maggio 2000 sotto l'Alto Patronato del Parlamento Europeo con il patrozinio del prof. Romano Prodi, Presidente della Commissione Europea*, Prato 2001, pp. 819–835; idem, Bargeldloser Zahlungsverkehr im europäischen Überseehandel von der Europäischen Expansion bis zum Ersten Weltkrieg, *Jahrbuch für europäische Überseegeschichte* 2 (2002), pp. 71–103; idem, The European Bill of Exchange. Its Development from the Middle Ages to 1914, in Sushil CHAUDHURI / Markus A. DENZEL (eds.), *Cashless Payments and Transactions from the Antiquity to 1914*, Stuttgart 2008, pp. 153–194; idem, *Das System des bargeldlosen Zahlungsverkehrs europäischer Prägung vom Mittelalter bis 1914*, Stuttgart 2008.

22 Esp. Markus A. DENZEL, *"La Practica della Cambiatura". Europäischer Zahlungsverkehr vom 14. bis zum 17. Jahrhundert*, Stuttgart 1994; idem, Die Integration Deutschlands in das internationale Zahlungsverkehrssystem im 17. und 18. Jahrhundert, in Eckart SCHREMMER (ed.), *Wirtschaftliche und soziale Integration in historischer Sicht. Arbeitstagung der Gesellschaft für Sozial- und Wirtschaftsgeschichte in Marburg 1995*, Stuttgart 1996, pp. 58–109.

23 Until the Iberian overseas possessions gained independence, cashless payment transactions on the basis of the bill of exchange played no important role there; see p. ciii.

24 Cf. Hans POHL, *Aufbruch der Weltwirtschaft. Geschichte der Weltwirtschaft von der Mitte des 19. Jahrhunderts bis zum Ersten Weltkrieg*, Stuttgart 1989, p. 25.

data. On the one hand, the English synopsis is intended to make the material available to the non-German-speaking scientific community as well. On the other hand,
three significant modifications have been made to the original concept to improve
the use of the data and to present just one manageable handbook for the historian's
everyday work instead of presenting a huge number of single volumes.

First, only yearly averages are documented instead of monthly rates, which was
the case for the German volumes. As the experience with the practical part of the
work on the previous edition shows, these yearly averages are sufficient for historical research until around 1914. In order to answer questions that require more detailed material, i.e. monthly rates, one can refer to the German edition. Last but not
least, this is also the (practical) reason why this *Handbook* ends with the beginning
of World War I in July 1914. For the period of World War I, the interwar period,
World War II and the immediate post-war years, it would probably be necessary to
have at least monthly, if not daily, rates to answer questions regarding the development of currencies and payments.[25] Therefore the *Handbook* does not include the
decades from August 1914 until around 1951, as it was done in *Währungen der
Welt*.

Second, this *Handbook* concentrates almost exclusively on international exchange relations, in contrast to the previous edition. This means both that quotations
between two exchange markets made in the same currency were as far as possible
excluded, and that quotations of only one exchange market were always documented in relation to every currency area. There are only exceptional cases where it seemed necessary to understand the international cashless payment system with its economic and especially commercial and monetary implications: in particular, the quotations within the British Empire in pounds sterling could not be ignored, since they
demonstrate the payment relations between the British overseas possessions or colonies and London, which became closer and closer. But even the quotations between
the most important financial markets of the integrating economic region of the USA
are worth documenting for the period when this integration in the field of cashless
payments was still imperfect. In other cases, there were documented quotations on
only the most important exchange market of a currency area. For France, e.g., quotations were available only for Paris, but despite some exceptions no quotations were
documented for Bordeaux, Marseille, Lyons, Montpellier or other French exchange
markets because of the only small differences between those quotations. When currency standardizations took place, as mainly in Italy or Germany in the 1860s or early 1870s, just the quotations for or on the most important exchange market were documented, sometimes even with a delay, after the exchange rate quotations had been
adjusted to the new common currency. A few exceptions to this rule will be explained below.

Third, this edition – unlike the previous ones – will document only one quotation series of one exchange market on another. The increasing differentiation of several terms or usances from the 18th century has meant that the number of parallel
series has grown significantly. In the 19th century, the overseas markets in particular

---

25   Moreover, this would be a reasonable approach for the years of extreme inflation during the pe-
     riod documented, esp. the years of the assignate's inflation in Revolutionary France, which were
     analysed by BOUCHARY, *Le marché des changes de Paris*.

quoted London, with up to six and in some cases with even more usances, among which only one series was selected for documentation.

Now, it is not only possible to correct errors found in the previous editions, but also to complete and enlarge their data series by including recently found source material. This refers especially to exchange rate quotations of Saint Petersburg, Riga, Leghorn and Smyrna in the 18th century and Montevideo, Adelaide (South Australia) and the Persian markets in the 19th century as well as those of the Canadian markets between the mid-18th century and 1914.

In the following sections this *Introduction* deals with more general problems of cashless payment transactions and the exchange rate quotations documented here. Section 2 details the (types of) sources used and how they were prepared for this *Handbook*. Section 3 analyses the function of the bill of exchange, the most important medium of cashless payment in Europe, throughout the research period, the mechanisms of cashless payment transactions and the 'European' type of bill of exchange, which was brought into all parts of the economically relevant world during the centuries covered. This last aspect will be completed by a theoretical and empirical analysis of the system of international cashless payments from the Middle Ages to World War I in Section 4.[26]

2. From the Sources to this Edition of the Exchange Rate Series

The exchange rate quotations presented here were taken mainly from four types of source:

1. Exchange rate currents and price currents, the oldest type of commercial and financial journals that cover mostly one or at most two pages,[27] are the main source

---

26 Prior attempts of that kind failed primarily due to insufficient base data. Cf. Michael Peter ZERRES, *Die Wechselplätze. Eine Untersuchung der Organisation und Technik des interregionalen und internationalen Zahlungsverkehrs Deutschlands in der ersten Hälfte des 19. Jahrhunderts*, Zürich – Frankfurt/Main – Thun 1977, esp. pp. 210–213.

27 Cf. John J. MCCUSKER / Cora GRAVESTEIJN, *The Beginnings of Commercial and Financial Journalism. The Commodity Price Currents, Exchange Rate Currents, and Money Currents of Early Modern Europe*, Amsterdam 1991; John J. MCCUSKER, The Italian Business Press in Early Modern Europe, in Simonetta CAVACIOCCHI (ed.), *Produzione e commercio della carta e del libro, secc. XIII–XVIII*, Prato 1992, pp. 797–841 (repr. in John J. MCCUSKER [ed.], *Essays in the Economic History of the Atlantic World*, London – New York 1997, pp. 117–144); idem, The Business Press in England before 1775, *The Library: Transactions of the Bibliographical Society*, 6th ser., VIII (1986), pp. 205–231 (repr. in MCCUSKER [ed.], *Essays*, pp. 145–176); idem, The Role of Antwerp in the Emergence of Commercial and Financial Newspapers in Early Modern Europe, in *La ville et la transmission des valeurs culturelles au bas Moyen Âge et aux Temps Modernes / Die Städte und die Übertragung von kulturellen Werten im Spätmittelalter und in die Neuzeit / Cities and the Transmission of Cultural Values in the Late Middle Ages and Early Modern Period. Actes / Abhandlungen / Records*, Bruxelles 1996, pp. 303–332; idem, Information and Transaction Costs in Early Modern Europe, in Rainer GÖMMEL / Markus A. DENZEL (eds.), *Weltwirtschaft und Wirtschaftsordnung. Festschrift für Jürgen Schneider zum 65. Geburtstag*, Stuttgart 2002, pp. 69–83.

for exchange rate quotations of the European and Levant markets for the period between the late 16th and the early 19th centuries. Usually dated exactly, they report on the quotations of an exchange market at a certain date. Exchange rate currents of many different kinds also represented the solidity of a stock market or an exchange market. Thus doubtful, fragmentary and less approved quotations were omitted as far as possible.[28]

2. Moreover, exchange rate quotations can be found in commercial and financial journals from the 18th century, but especially during the 19th and early 20th centuries, i.e. in price currents, shipping lists or registers with numerous pages and also in 'normal', i.e. non-specialized, newspapers with a business section.[29] In this section, daily rates are also included. They are usually given in tables, similarly to the older exchange rate currents. Such journals and newspapers can be found from at least the mid-19th century for almost all commercial metropolises in the world, although some of these exchange rate quotations were quoted more extensively, more exactly and regularly than others. *The Economist*, published in London, was undoubtedly the most important commercial and financial journal from the perspective of exchange rate quotations, because it was the medium by which not only London's quotations were published but also those of the most important exchange markets from all over the world. Therefore a large part of the non-European quotations on London could be found in London's *Economist*. During the 19th and early 20th centuries, the commercial and financial journals of the overseas markets increasingly listed the quotations of several overseas banks. Usually these bank quotations did not differ fundamentally from one another in their amount.[30] In most cases it was usual to put the different quotations together in one table, i.e. they were 'standardized' before publication. In individual cases, however, several tables were also printed with the quotations of different overseas banks, as can be seen particularly in the case of the Mauritius exchange rate quotations.

3. Official or quasi-official exchange rate quotations of stock exchanges or (central) banks were used to a smaller extent than expected, mainly for two reasons: on the one hand, such official quotation lists are often incomplete, i.e. they show only some of the exchange partners that were actually quoted regularly on a financial market and whose quotations appear, therefore, in local commercial and financial journals as well. This holds, for example, for both the *Cours du Change à Paris sur les principaux places étrangères* quoted by the Banque de France or the official quotations of the Madrid stock exchange stating only those exchange rates that should be regarded as the most important ones concerning the editing institution. On the other hand, the official quotations were not always daily rates but sometimes monthly rates so that they fit the research concept only to a limited extent. Therefore

---

28   For London see Jacob M. PRICE, Notes on Some London Price-Currents, 1667–1715, *Economic History Review*, sec. ser. 7 (1954/55), pp. 240–250; for Germany see Ernst BAASCH, Aus der Entwicklungsgeschichte des Hamburger Kurszettels, *Bank-Archiv* 5 (1905/06), pp. 8–11.

29   Cf. Oskar SCHWARZER / Petra SCHNELZER, Quellen zur Statistik der Geld- und Wechselkurse in Deutschland, Nordwesteuropa und dem Ostseeraum im 18. und 19. Jahrhundert, in Wolfram FISCHER / Andreas KUNZ (eds.), *Grundlagen der Historischen Statistik von Deutschland. Quellen, Methoden, Forschungsziele*, Opladen 1991, pp. 175–191.

30   Walter BRANDT, Kurs- und Kreditsicherung der Überseebanken, *Zeitschrift für Handelswissenschaft und Handelspraxis* (1913/12), pp. 362–367, esp. p. 363.

such official quotations of stock exchanges or (central) banks are only referred to if there is a lack of alternative sources. Stock exchange markets were, nonetheless, less important for quotations at the non-European exchange markets than in Europe, because those quotations were mainly done by overseas banks, as shown above. Official reports on quotations like that of the Camara Syndical dos Corretores de Fundos Públicos, which cover a longer period, are available only in the case of Rio de Janeiro.[31]

4. Finally, official quotations of political institutions are included, especially those of the British colonial governments, which can be found in the *Blue Books* of the Colonial Acts. As the official quotations of stock exchanges or (central) banks, government quotations often list only the main exchange rate of a colony, i.e. the one on the financial centre of the mother country, London.[32] Daily rates were not quoted in the *Blue Books* at all and monthly rates were usually quoted only in the economically more powerful colonies, e.g. the Cape Colony, New South Wales or the Straits Settlements. In most instances, only yearly rates are available. The same can be observed with the official exchange rate statistics of the colonial governments in Netherlands India[33] or in the Indochinese Union.[34] These government quotations were used for the documentation of the exchange rate series only if none of the other three mentioned types of sources was available for the documented period.

Additionally, it is often necessary to refer to exchange rate series that can already be found in the literature. The underlying sources include all types of sources mentioned here. So the use of such series follows the outlined premises as well. We can distinguish between quotation series already published by contemporaries, e.g. the series of the different markets in the Baltic Sea region in the 18th century[35] or of Brazil in the early 19th century,[36] and those series that have been compiled from the sources only during the recent decades. In addition, a vast number of single quotations were included, i.e. quotations that partly date back to exchange rate currents printed in contemporary merchant manuals and other publications or to scattered information in literature on commercial or currency history.

In this context, contemporary merchant manuals need to be mentioned as a special type of source material very suitable for research in the field of cashless payments. There are only a few cases where original quotations or even complete printed exchange rate currents can be found in these sources, but the analysis of quotati-

---

31 Camara Syndical dos Corretores de Fundos Públicos da Capital Federal (ed.), *Relatorio da Camara Syndical dos Corretores de Fundos Públicos da Capital Federal ...*, Rio de Janeiro 1898–1915.

32 Cape Town represents an example for this statement. According to the *Blue Books* it quoted only London, but there is a commercial journal that also mentions quotations on Amsterdam, France, Calcutta, Madras and Bombay, although it is available only for a few years.

33 *Staat van de wisselkoers van Java op Nederland en Engeland. Handelingen van de Tweed Kamer der Staaten General 1852/52 II*, Annex VIII, B6, The Hague 1852.

34 *Administration des monnaies et des médailles, Rapport au Ministre des Finances*, Paris 1916, pp. 138–145.

35 E.g. John Jepson ODDY, *European Commerce ...*, London 1805, or J.G. CANZLER, *Nachrichten zur genauern Kenntniß der Geschichte, Staatsverwaltung und ökonomischen Verfassung des Königreichs Schweden*, Erster Theil, Dresden 1778.

36 Horace E. SAY, *Histoire des relations commerciales entre la France et le Brésil*, Paris 1839, pp. 297–300.

ons of single exchange markets allow statements both on other markets with which
an exchange market had regular exchange relations and on the extent to which it was
integrated into the international payment system.[37]

This kind of source material is absolutely vital for investigating the international
cashless payment system,[38] if there are exchange markets that lack either sufficient

---

37   The following merchant manuals have mainly been used for this work: M[artin] V[AN] VELDEN,
     *Fondament van de Wisselhandeling: Onderrichtingh ghevende van alle voornaemste Wisselen
     van Christenrijck, so van Trates, Remessen, vergelijcking van prysen, verscheyden comissien, te
     vormen, voegen ende calcula van baet of schade te maecken naer den cours, die te oordeelen,
     ende naer gelegentheyd van tijdt of plaets te konnen scheyden*, Amsterdam 1629; [2]1647 (in Ger-
     man: *Underricht der Wechsel-Handlung*, Frankfurt 1669); Johann Christian HERBACH, *Einlei-
     tung zum Gründlichen Verstand der Wechsel-Handlung ...*, Nürnberg 1716; idem, *Verbesserte
     und Viel-vermehrte Wechsel-Handlung ...*, Nürnberg 1726; idem, *Europäische Wechselhand-
     lung ...*, Nürnberg 1756/57; [Marcus Rudolf Balthasar] G[ERHARDT] (ed.), *Johann Christian
     Nelkenbrechers Taschenbuch eines Banquiers und Kaufmanns ...*, Berlin [2]1769; idem (ed.), *Jo-
     hann Christian Nelkenbrechers Taschenbuch eines Banquiers und Kaufmanns ...*, Berlin [4]1775;
     Jürgen Elert KRUSE, *Allgemeiner und besonders Hamburgischer Contorist*, Hamburg [4]1782;
     M[arcus] R[udolf] B[althasar] GERHARDT sen. (ed.), *Nelkenbrechers Taschenbuch der Münz-
     Maaß- und Gewichtskunde für Kaufleute*, Berlin [7]1793; idem (ed.), *Nelkenbrechers Taschenbuch
     der Münz- Maaß- und Gewichtskunde für Kaufleute*, Berlin [8]1798; Patrick KELLY, *The Universal
     Cambist and Commercial Instructor; Being a General Treatise on Exchange ...*, 2 vols., London
     1811; J.S.G. OTTO (ed.), *J.C. Nelkenbrechers allgemeines Taschenbuch der Münz-, Maaß- und
     Gewichtskunde für Banquiers und Kaufleute*, Berlin [11]1815; idem (ed.), *J.C. Nelkenbrechers
     allgemeines Taschenbuch der Münz-, Maaß- und Gewichtskunde für Banquiers und Kaufleute*,
     Berlin [12]1817; Johann Philipp SCHELLENBERG (ed.), *J.C. Nelkenbrechers allgemeines Taschen-
     buch der Münz-, Maaß- und Gewichtskunde für Banquiers und Kaufleute*, Berlin [13]1820;
     P[atrick] KELLY, *The Universal Cambist and Commercial Instructor ...*, 2 vols., London [2]1821,
     repr. 1835; J[ohann] H[einrich] D[aniel] BOCK / Carl CRÜGER (eds.), *J.C. Nelkenbrechers allge-
     meines Taschenbuch der Münz-, Maaß- und Gewichtskunde für Banquiers und Kaufleute. Auf's
     neue herausgegeben und mit vielen Handelsplätzen Amerika's und Asien's, desgl. mit den Usan-
     cen der Staatspapiere vermehrt*, Berlin [14]1828; J[ohann] H[einrich] D[aniel] BOCK (ed.), *J.C.
     Nelkenbrechers allgemeines Taschenbuch der Münz- Maaß- und Gewichtskunde für Banquiers
     und Kaufleute*, Berlin [15]1832; Christian NOBACK, *Vollständiges Handbuch der Münz-, Bank- und
     Wechsel-Verhältnisse aller Länder und Handelsplätze der Erde*, Rudolstadt 1833; F. WOLFF
     (ed.), *J.C. Nelkenbrecher's allgemeines Taschenbuch der Maaß-, Gewichts- und Münzkunde,
     der Wechsel- Geld- und Fondscourse u.s.w. für Banquiers und Kaufleute*, Berlin [16]1842; Chris-
     tian NOBACK / Friedrich NOBACK, *Vollständiges Taschenbuch der Münz-, Maass- und Gewichts-
     Verhältnisse, der Staatspapiere, des Wechsel- und Bankwesens und der Usanzen aller Länder
     und Handelsplätze*, 2 parts, Leipzig 1851; idem, *Münz-, Maass- und Gewichtsbuch. Das Geld-,
     Maass- und Wechselwesen, die Kurse, Staatspapiere, Banken, Handelsanstalten und Usanzen
     aller Staaten und wichtigern Orte*, Leipzig 1858; H. SCHWABE (ed.), *J.C. Nelkenbrecher's allge-
     meines Taschenbuch der Münz-, Maaß- und Gewichtskunde, der Wechsel-, Geld- und Fonds-
     Curse u.s.w.*, Berlin [19]1871; C. NEUBAUER (ed.), *J.C. Nelkenbrecher's Taschenbuch für Kauf-
     leute, II part: Münz-Tabelle*, Berlin [20]1877; Friedrich NOBACK, *Münz-, Maass- und Gewichts-
     buch. Das Geld-, Maass- und Gewichtswesen, die Wechsel- und Geldkurse, das Wechselrecht
     und die Usanzen*, Leipzig [2]1877; Ernst JERUSALEM (ed.), *J.C. Nelkenbrecher's Taschenbuch für
     Kaufleute. I. Abth.: Taschenbuch der Münz-, Maass- und Gewichtskunde, der Wechsel-, Geld-
     und Fonds-curse u.s.w. für Kaufleute*, Berlin [20]1890; Otto SWOBODA, *Die kaufmännische Arbi-
     trage. Eine Sammlung von Notizen und Usancen sämmtlicher Börsenplätze für den praktischen
     Gebrauch*, Berlin [7]1889; idem, *Die kaufmännische Arbitrage. Eine Sammlung von Notizen und
     Usancen sämtlicher Börsenplätze der Welt*, ed. Adolf SANDHEIM, Berlin [11]1902; idem, *Die Arbi-
     trage in Wertpapieren, Wechseln, Münzen und Edelmetallen. Handbuch des Börsen-, Münz- und
     Geldwesens sämtlicher Handelsplätze der Welt*, ed. Max FÜRST, Berlin [12]1905; idem, *Die Arbi-
     trage in Wertpapieren, Wechseln, Münzen und Edelmetallen. Handbuch des Börsen-, Münz- und
     Geldwesens sämtlicher Handelsplätze der Welt*, ed. Max FÜRST, Berlin [13]1909; idem, *Die Arbi-
     trage in Wertpapieren, Wechseln, Münzen und Edelmetallen. Handbuch des Börsen-, Münz- und
     Geldwesens sämtlicher Handelsplätze der Welt*, ed. Max FÜRST, Berlin [14]1913; idem, *Die Arbi-
     trage in Wertpapieren, Wechseln, Münzen und Edelmetallen. Handbuch des Börsen-, Münz- und
     Geldwesens sämtlicher Handelsplätze der Welt*, ed. Max FÜRST, Berlin [16]1924/25; idem, *Die Ar-
     bitrage in Wertpapieren, Wechseln, Münzen und Edelmetallen. Handbuch des Börsen-, Münz-
     und Geldwesens sämtlicher Handelsplätze der Welt*, ed. Eduard WAGON, Berlin [17]1928.

exchange rate data or any data at all.[39]

The following methodical principles were applied in order to document the exchange rates extracted from the types of source material and also from the literature mentioned above:

1. Usually, only exchange rates were documented, but not money rates, i.e. quotations that refer to bills of exchange but not to the exchanging of coins. Money rates (for coins or banknotes) were only documented if it could be proved that they had been quoted on a certain place instead of exchange rates, or if they were indispensable for the understanding of the monetary history of the respective country or exchange market. Money rates were documented, for instance, if exchange rates had been quoted in inflationary paper money in order to understand the changing relations between hard currency (gold or silver coins) and paper currency.

2. All exchange rate quotations to be published were dated exactly, i.e. they were intended to be daily rates. Average rates – monthly or yearly rates – were only used if a data series was of interest due to a special quoting or exchange market, and no daily rates were available.

3. All exchange rates were throughout converted into decimal price quotations, i.e. into the currency that was the most important unit of account at a certain exchange market at a certain point in time. This 'intervention' in the original data is necessary to ensure a fast and direct comparability of the different exchange rate series. Therefore this step was the most important one of the whole process, because it converts non-decimal quotations into decimal rates and quantity quotations into price quotations, i.e. special types of quotations that might seem strange to the user of the *Handbook*; for example quotations in or for % premium or discount with reference to a fixed rate have been converted.[40] In order to ensure understanding of the different conversions, the original quotations are listed in a table in each chapter's introductory paragraph, as mentioned above, allowing the reader to convert quotations that may be found in the future and to insert them in the material given here.

4. If a quotation is stated with a fluctuation margin or one (or more) quotations for both buying and selling rates, the average value was calculated and documented. However, quotations from overseas in particular still differed a great deal during the

---

38 Cf. Markus A. DENZEL, Kaufmannshandbücher als Quellengattung zur europäischen Überseegeschichte im 19. und frühen 20. Jahrhundert, in Thomas BECK et al. (eds.), *Überseegeschichte – Beiträge der jüngeren Forschung. Festschrift anläßlich der Gründung der Forschungsstiftung für vergleichende europäische Überseegeschichte 1999 in Bamberg*, Stuttgart 1999, pp. 120–136; idem, Handelspraktiken als wirtschaftshistorische Quellengattung vom Mittelalter bis in das frühe 20. Jahrhundert. Eine Einführung, in idem / HOCQUET / WITTHÖFT (eds.), *Kaufmannsbücher und Handelspraktiken / Merchant's Books and Mercantile Pratiche*, pp. 11–45.

39 Empirical studies have successfully verified these findings. Cf. DENZEL, Integration Deutschlands, pp. 58–109; idem, Die Integration ostmittel-, ost- und südosteuropäischer Städte in die internationalen Zahlungsverkehrsverbindungen im 19. und beginnenden 20. Jahrhundert, *Südost-Forschungen* 55 (1996), pp. 45–73; idem, Die Integration der Schweizer Finanzplätze in das internationale Zahlungsverkehrssystem vom 17. Jahrhundert bis 1914, *Schweizerische Zeitschrift für Geschichte* 48 (1998), pp. 177–235; idem, Kolonialstädte als Finanzplätze vom 18. Jahrhundert bis 1914. Das asiatische Wechselnetz und seine Anbindung an das europäisch-internationale Zahlungsverkehrssystem, in Horst GRÜNDER / Peter JOHANEK (eds.), *Kolonialstädte – Europäische Enklaven oder Schmelztigel der Kulturen?*, Münster 2001, pp. 225–259.

40 For the concept of converting different exchange rates, see Oskar SCHWARZER, Eine EDV-gestützte Forschungskonzeption zur Bearbeitung historischer Geld- und Wechselkurse, in *WdW I/I*, pp. 180–196.

19th century, so "the market rates quoted for buying and selling London bills normally showed large differences – of 6 per cent. in India and 3–4 per cent in China".[41] It
will be noted if only buying or selling rates were documented because of the available sources, as in the case of some exchange rate series between Asian and Australian exchange markets.

   5. Wherever possible, one daily rate was listed for each month, preferably taken
from the beginning of the relevant month. If there were quotations only from the
middle or the end of a month available, they were used likewise. Therefore only a
maximum of twelve quotations per year was stated, from which a yearly average
was calculated. The number of single quotations that were used for calculating the
yearly average is stated in the tables in brackets. The same rules were applied when
monthly rates had to be used for the calculation. In exceptional cases yearly rates
from the literature had to be used, marked by an (y) (= yearly).

   6. If sources provide quotations for different usances on a quoted exchange market, the most common usance for this exchange relation will then be used. If it is impossible to determine the most common one, the shortest usance will be used, i.e.
the highest ('most expensive') quotation will be documented. Information about the
different usances can be found in the list of abbreviations for usances.

3. The Medium and the Mechanisms of Cashless Payment: The (European) Bill of Exchange

The bill of exchange was the European merchants' medium of cashless payment
between the Middle Ages and the 20th century regardless of whether they were active in Europe or overseas. No doubt there were certain forms of cashless payment in
various pre-modern and non-European cultures and economic regions. Here, I have
chosen to refer to

   – the *syngraphe*, adopted by the Romans from Greek law, and the *chirogra-
     phum*;[42]
   – the Arabic *suftadja* (draft)[43] or *sakk* (order of payment);[44]
   – the *hundwîs* or *hoondees* of the Indian merchants;[45]
   – the Armenian *awak*, *zmei awak* or *hndvi*;[46]
   – the Chinese *Shansi bills*[47] or corresponding Japanese papers.

It remains highly questionable among researchers if and to what extent non-European papers can be compared to the European bill of exchange.[48] The *bill obligatory*
(or *handschryft*), common in Northwestern Europe and in the Baltic Sea area in late
medieval times, corresponded to the bill of exchange from the financial point of

---

41   A.S.J. BASTER, The Origins of the British Exchange Banks in China, *Economic History* (1934/
     1), pp. 140–151, esp. p. 144.

42   Both were documents of claims with the debtor committing in written form to paying a certain
     amount of money. They are supposed to have also served for the transaction of payments from
     one place to another; Carl Samuel GRÜNHUT, *Wechselrecht*, vol. 1, Leipzig 1897, pp. 22f.

view. By the end of the 16th century the bill obligatory was replaced by the bill of exchange as an international credit instrument in the Netherlands, England and later also in the Baltic Sea area, although the bill obligatory kept its great importance within the respective regions.[49] However, the following statements are exclusively restricted to the European bill of exchange coming from Italy and its exchange rates.[50]

---

43   "The *suftadja* is a banking instrument used in a monetary system and an economic life very different from that of the Christian West. ... The *suftadja*, a banking instrument totally distinct from the bill of exchange, was a transaction in which three persons took part and the repayment of the loan was established in the same kind of money originally paid. The *suftadja* was often followed by endorsement." Eliahu ASHTOR, Banking Instruments between the Muslim East and the Christian West, *Journal of European Economic History* 1 (1972), pp. 553–573, esp. p. 572; cf. ibid., pp. 562–565. On the contrary, Alfred E. LIEBER, Eastern Business Practices and Medieval European Commerce, *Economic History Review* 21 (1968), pp. 230–243, esp. p. 233 speaks of the *suftadja* "as a draft which was sometimes also a true bill of exchange", yet without explaining in detail what he understands about a "true bill of exchange". Abraham L. UDOVITCH, Bankers without Banks: The Islamic World, in [CHIAPPELLI, Fredi (ed.),] *The Dawn of Modern Banking*, New Haven – London 1979, pp. 255–273, esp. p. 263, describes the *suftadja* as "a letter of credit or a bill of exchange". Cf. idem, Commercial Techniques in Early Medieval Islamic Trade, in David S. RICHARDS (ed.), *Islam and the Trade of Asia. A Colloquium*, London – Colchester 1970, pp. 37–62, esp. p. 54.

44   "The *sakk* – this is the word that gave origin to cheque in the European languages – is a genuine cheque, that is to say an order of payment made through the banker with whom the drawer has an account; ... In using the cheque, the Muslims were actually using an instrument inherited from the Byzantines; an instrument already widespread in Egypt and some centuries before the Arab conquest." ASHTOR, *Banking Instruments*, p. 555. Not convincing is G. JAKOB, Die ältesten Spuren des Wechsels, *Westasiatische Studien* (1925), pp. 280f., who mentions the *sakk* as being equal to a bill of exchange.

45   *Hoondees* were a form of promissory notes that could be cashed in at their place of destination. Occasionally, there were *hoondee* quotations partially with commission charges and such *hoondees* could be discounted and endorsed. "A hoondee may be defined as a written order – usually unconditional – made by one person on another for the payment, on demand or after a specific time, of a certain sum of money to a person named therein"; L.C. JAIN, *Indigenous Banking in India*, London 1929, p. 71, quoted in Amiya Kumar BAGCHI, Money and Credit as areas of Conflict in Colonial India, in B. CHANDRA (Organizer), *Typology of Colonial Economic Development* (= *Eighth International Economic History Congress, Budapest 1982, B6*), Budapest 1982, pp. 28–35, esp. pp. 32f. Also, Celsa PINTO, *Trade and Finance in Portuguese India. A Study of the Portuguese Country Trade 1770–1840*, New Delhi 1994, pp. 71f. Cf. e.g. Irfan HABIB, The Monetary System and Prices, in Tapan RAYCHAUDHURI / Irfan HABIB (eds.), *The Cambridge Economic History of India, vol. 1: c. 1200–c. 1750*, Cambridge 1982, pp. 360–381, esp. pp. 362f.; idem, Merchant Communities in Precolonial India, in James D. TRACY (ed.), *The Rise of Merchant Empires. Long-Distance Trade in the Early Modern World, 1350–1750*, Cambridge 1990 (1993), pp. 371–399, esp. pp. 391–394; Om PRAKASH, The Cashless Payment Mechanism in Mughal India: The Working of the Hundi Network, in Sushil CHAUDHURI / Markus A. DENZEL (eds.), *Cashless Payments and Transactions from the Antiquity to 1914*, Stuttgart 2008, pp. 131–137; Sushil CHAUDHURI, No Ready Money? No Problem! The Role of Hundis (Bills of Exchange) in Early Modern India, c. 1600–1800, in ibid., pp. 139–151.

46   "These were interest bearing loans, usually fixed-term, repayable to a third party in a different place, and they could involve four of more persons: the drawee, the drawer, any representative of his, and the one who took the profit or his proxy. ... These loans gave rise to the establishment of a sort of promissory note distinct from a bill of exchange and called *barat*." Michel AGHASSIAN / Kéram KÉVONIAN, The Armenian Merchant Network: Overall Autonomy and Local Integration, in Sushil CHAUDHURI / Michel MORINEAU (eds.), *Merchants, Companies and Trade. Europe and Asia in the Early Modern Era*, Cambridge 1999, pp. 74–94, esp. p. 85. At the same time, the authors emphasize that "the widespread use of bills of exchange needs to be put into the Irano-Indian context, although even then it shows peculiarities." Ibid.

3.1 The European Bill of Exchange and its Development in Italy
in the Era of the Commercial Revolution

Following the expansion of trade, the Mediterranean navigation and the monetized economics in Europe during the time of the Crusades, it became increasingly neces-

47 The *Shansi bills* were a kind of bills of exchange drawn by the Shansi bankers, who were few in number (Beijing had only five Shansi bankers in 1900), but with their widespread credit connections they proved to be the most important agents in payments among Chinese merchants. These *Shansi bills* had an intermediate position between the bill of exchange and the letter of credit. If a merchant bought them with cash from a banker, they had the character of a bill of exchange; if they were bought on credit, one could rather speak of a letter of credit. The form of these bills was a 'triple bill', which means that the document consisted of three parts, the first a means of control for the banker, the second for the recipient and the third for the client; the document was cut in two after issue and the parts were handed to the persons involved. Both the banker and the recipient were responsible for encashing it, but the client was free of any responsibility. Acceptance was as obsolete as an order clause, as it was not an order but a bearer paper. Hence, such bills were put into circulation without any kind of endorsement and the bearer could not claim for recourse against the former bearer or the issuer. The liability went so far that in the case of bankruptcy of the original issuer the bills had to be cashed. The payments were mutually safeguarded by contracted current accounts. Sui-lu KU, *Die Form bankmäßiger Transaktionen im inneren chinesischen Verkehr mit besonderer Rücksicht des Notengeschäfts*, Hamburg 1926, pp. 40–44.

48 Amiya Kumar BAGCHI, Anglo-Indian Banking in British India: From the Paper Pound to the Gold Standard, *Journal of Imperial and Commonwealth History* 13 (1985), pp. 93–108, esp. p. 93 calls the *hoondee* an "Indian-style bill of exchange"; John CRAWFURD, A Sketch of the Commercial Resources and Monetary and Mercantile System of British India, with Suggestions for their Improvement, by Means of Banking Establishments (1837), in K[irti] N. CHAUDHURI (ed.), *The Economic Development of India under the East India Company 1814–58. A Selection of Contemporary Writings*, Cambridge 1971, pp. 217–316, esp. p. 291, "native bill of exchange"; CHAUDHURI, *Bengal*, p. 98 note 139, illus. before p. 99; Dietmar ROTHERMUND, *Indiens wirtschaftliche Entwicklung. Von der Kolonialherrschaft bis zur Gegenwart*, Paderborn et al. 1985, pp. 17, 45; Tapan RAYCHAUDHURI, Inland Trade, in idem / HABIB (eds.), *Cambridge Economic History of India*, vol. 1, pp. 325–359, esp. p. 346; David L. WHITE, *Competition and Collaboration. Parsi Merchants and the English East India Company in 18th Century India*, New Delhi 1995, p. 19.

49 The bill obligatory was similar to the *instrumentum ex causa cambii* (proven to have existed in England since the end of the 12th century). It was a payment promise rathern than an obligatory request for payment, and met the needs of the travelling merchants visiting fairs in the Netherlands until the 17th century. There were only two or three people involved in such deals: first, the merchant who borrowed the money and wanted to pay it back at the next fair, second, the merchant who lent the money and wanted to get it back at the next fair in person or via an agent, third, possibly the lender's representative who would collect the payment; John H. MUNRO, Art. "Inhaberschuldschein", in Michael NORTH (ed.), *Von Aktie bis Zoll. Ein historisches Lexikon des Geldes*, München 1995, pp. 172–174; idem, Die Anfänge der Übertragbarkeit: Einige Kreditinnovationen im englisch-flämischen Handel des Spätmittelalters (1360–1540), in Michael NORTH (ed.), *Kredit im spätmittelalterlichen und frühneuzeitlichen Europa*, Köln – Wien 1991, pp. 39–69, esp. pp. 46f.; M.M. POSTAN, Private Financial Instruments in Medieval England, *Vierteljahresschrift für Sozial- und Wirtschaftsgeschichte* 23 (1930), pp. 26–75, esp. pp. 27–42; Michael NORTH, Banking and Credit in Northern Germany in the Fifteenth and Sixteenth Centuries, in *Banchi pubblici, banchi privati e monti di pietà nell'Europa preindustriale. Amministrazione, tecniche operative e ruoli economici*, Genova 1991, vol. II, pp. 809–826, esp. pp. 819–822; G. DE MALYNES, *Consuetudo vel lex mercatoria, or The Ancient Law-Merchant*, London 1622 (repr. Amsterdam 1979), pp. 95–103.

50 Even here, the sources mentioned only one quotation for indigenous payment papers on non-European financial markets: *The Calcutta Weekly Gazette or Civil, Military and Commercial Register* published a list with *hoondee* quotations of Calcutta (Course of Hoondean) from January 12th 1840, quoting almost exclusively Madras, Bombay, Poona and Hyderabad as well as Hindustan cities at the border of the Punjab, including a few cities from the neighbouring Rajput countries and Madhya Pradesh, which seems to describe basically the entire monetary transaction rayon of that time; cf. DENZEL, Kolonialstädte, pp. 244f.

sary for merchants who worked also for the European-wide acting Papal Curia[51] to develop mechanisms for providing liquidity, whenever and wherever there was no or only little coined or uncoined precious metal available. So the new means of cashless payment started to emerge in Europe in the second half of the 12th century, probably in Genoa.[52] At first, the *lettres de foire* of the Champagne fairs[53] and the *instrumentum ex causa cambii* were developed. These means of cashless payment were combined instruments of credit and money transfer and served, thus, for the financing of exports as well as for transferring money without recourse to expensive and risky transfers of precious metals. They were developed by Italian, most likely Genoese merchants, especially for itinerant merchants travelling to the international Champagne fairs, "the forcing house for the development of bill of exchange,"[54] and they were notarially certified. So they were payment obligations or promises in the form of a debt certificate written by a notary. These early exchange contracts differ from the younger bill of exchange more in form than in function.[55] Moreover, only two or three people were included in these cashless transactions:

- the merchant, who raised a credit – for example in Genoa – and had his debt certificate and promise of repayment certified notarially;
- the merchant or creditor, who lent the money and could request repayment; and
- possibly the creditor's representative at a certain fair, who could receive the payment in place of the creditor himself.

As the merchant who had promised repayment at a certain fair used to travel there himself, he did not need a representative of his own who would effect the payment in his place.[56]

The situation changed when merchants started to settle at a certain town, stayed in their offices and instructed a trusted person, an agent or a partner to look after their obligations at fairs in other places.[57] With this person they would send, along with the formal notarial contract, an informal letter of advice (*littera*) as an order of

---

51 Yves RENOUARD, *Les relations des papes d'Avignon et des compagnies commerciales et bancaires de 1316 à 1378*, Paris 1941; Arnold ESCH, Bankiers der Kirche im Großen Schisma, *Quellen und Forschungen aus italienischen Archiven und Bibliotheken* 46 (1966), pp. 277–398; Markus A. DENZEL, *Kurialer Zahlungsverkehr im 13. und 14. Jahrhundert. Servitien- und Annatenzahlungen aus dem Bistum Bamberg*, Stuttgart 1991; idem, Kleriker und Kaufleute. Polen im kurialen Zahlungsverkehrssystem des 14. Jahrhunderts, *Vierteljahrschrift für Sozial- und Wirtschaftsgeschichte* 82 (1995), pp. 305–331; Rudolf HIESTAND, Bologna als Vermittlerin im kurialen Zahlungsverkehr zu Beginn des 13. Jahrhunderts. Eine übersehene Rolle der frühen Universitäten, in ibid., pp. 332–349.

52 At least we can find the definitely largest number of sources for cashless payment in Genoese archives of that time.

53 Cf. L. GOLDSCHMIDT, Die Geschäftsoperationen auf den Messen der Champagne (Les divisions des foires de Champagne), *Zeitschrift für das Gesammte Handelsrecht* 40 (N.F. 25) (1892), pp. 1–32, esp. p. 27.

54 SPUFFORD, *Handbook*, p. xxxi.

55 "In my opinion, the *instrumentum ex causa cambii* is undoubtedly the prototype of the bill of exchange, for it fulfilled exactly the same function. True, the *instrumentum* took the form of a promise to pay, whereas the bill of exchange is an order to pay, but this distinction, being purely formal, is more superficial than real"; Raymond DE ROOVER, New Interpretations of the History of Banking, in Julius KIRSHNER (ed.), *Business, Banking and Economic Thought in Late Medieval and Early Modern Europe. Selected Studies of Raymond de Roover*, Chicago – London 1974, pp. 200–238, esp. p. 203.

payment, which then evolved into the actual bill of exchange.[58] This development was supported by the fact that the emerging net of agents and correspondents, who knew each other personally, made notarial certification obsolete. "A rich network of international commercial correspondents ... extended to cover the entire economic and geographical area dominated by the Italian merchant bankers, and it was this that gave them the unrivalled possibilities for remitting to or drawing from any one place to any other."[59] The 'informal' bill of exchange was much easier to handle and less expensive than the former methods of payment. At first and in the 13th and 14th centuries it provided financial transactions only, and thus liquidity between two places and this usually only inside one trading company, for example between the merchant and his agent. This means was called *lettera di pagamento*. Since the 14th century such bills also circulated outside a single trading company between different merchants and different companies: the bill of exchange or the so-called *lettera di cambio* in its proper sense was generated, which became the most important means of cashless payment transactions and credit instrument for providing liquidity in the centres of trade and finance of the Italian merchant bankers, superseding the former means of cashless payment transactions.[60] The most important difference between the *letters de foires* and the *instrumentum ex causa cambii*, on the one hand, and the bill of exchange, on the other, was that the first constitutes a payment promise or obligation whereas the other is a payment order with the issuer of the bill ordering a third person at another place to settle a debt in his place.[61]

There were two elements fundamental for the exchange business: first, the *permutatio pecuniae absentis cum praesenti*; and, second, the *distantia* or *differentia loci*, i.e. the parties' difference in place and the exchange of the currency due to the underlying difference in coins that became manifest in the exchange rate. If one of the two elements was not given – especially the difference in place – an exchange transaction could not be effected, as the merchants would have been guilty of usury,

56   John H. MUNRO, Art. "Instrumentum Ex Causa Cambii", in NORTH (ed.), *Von Aktie bis Zoll*, pp. 174f.; Raymond DE ROOVER, *L'évolution de la lettre de change, XIV–XVIII siècles*, Paris 1953, pp. 23–42; R.D. FACE, Techniques of Business in Trade between the Fairs of Champagne and the South of Europe in the 12th and 13th Centuries, *Economic History Review* 2nd ser. 10 (1957/58), pp. 427–438. In the 11th and 12th centuries notarial certification was often necessary due to the basic fact that not all merchants were capable of reading and writing; cf. Alfred WENDEHORST, Wer konnte im Mittelalter lesen und schreiben?, in Johannes FRIED (ed.), *Schulen und Studien im sozialen Wandel des hohen und späten Mittelalters*, Sigmaringen 1986, pp. 9–33, esp. p. 28.

57   Raymond DE ROOVER, *Money, Banking and Credit in Medieval Bruges. Italian Merchant-Bankers, Lombards and Money-Changers. A Study in the Origins of Banking*, Cambridge (Mass.) 1948, p. 51.

58   MUNRO, Art. "Instrumentum Ex Causa Cambii", p. 175. Cf. Raymond DE ROOVER, Le contrat de change depuis la fin du treizième siècle jusqu'au début du dix-septième, *Revue belge de philologie et d'histoire* 25/1–2 (1946/47), pp. 111–128; idem, Précisions sur l'histoire de la lettre et du contrat de change (d'après des documents inédits des Archivs Datini à Prato), *La vie économique et sociale* 23 (1952), pp. 44–67; Georg SCHAPS, *Zur Geschichte des Wechselindossaments*, Stuttgart 1892, p. 9.

59   Alfonso LEONE, Some Preliminary Remarks on the Study of Foreign Currency Exchange in the Medieval Period, *Journal of European Economic History* 12 (1983), pp. 619–629, esp. p. 620.

60   DE ROOVER, *Lettre de change*, pp. 38–45; Markus A. DENZEL, Art. "Wechsel, Wechsler, Wechselbrief", in *Lexikon des Mittelalters*, vol. VIII, Zürich et al. 1997, columns 2086–2089.

61   John H. MUNRO, Art. "Wechsel", in NORTH (ed.), *Von Aktie bis Zoll*, pp. 413–416, esp. p. 413.

which was seen as a mortal sin against natural law in the 13th century, in addition to being against the commandment of charity.[62] It was only after the 13th century, after theologians had placed emphasis on the difference of coins as being essential, and resulting from the difference in place, that the bill of exchange was considered to be a harmless means of (cashless) payment compared to the canonical ban on interest-bearing loans. Even the Church itself liked to use the bill of exchange; for the merchant's 'work' had to be paid because the money had to be transported and exchanged. So the profit that was hidden behind the exchange rate or the premium could be justified according to canon law in some degree. Since the *Tractatus de usuris* by the Franciscan Alexander Lombardus or Alexander of Alessandria (died 1314) at the latest, the *cambium* was no longer regarded as *mutuum* but as *permutatio pecuniae*, being no longer associated with the problem of usury. All subsequent leading theologians accepted this opinion.[63] In contrast to this, theologians rejected the term *cambium reale* or *cambium verum* regarding local exchanges, as these missed the difference in place and thus the necessity of money transport. Still, the Bologna Law of Bills from 1569, ratified by Pope Pius V (1566–1572), and his bull from 1570 forbade such local exchanges.[64]

In general, a bill of exchange contained the following pieces of information:[65]
(1) the three or four persons involved in the transaction:
   – the issuer of the bill, the drawer or drafter who receives money from the remitter. Because of receiving money the issuer was also called the taker or *prenditore*;
   – the addressee named in the bill or the drawee (*trattario*) who had to pay the bill (hence also payer or *pagatore*). The drawee became the acceptor after accepting the bill of exchange by signing it. If the acceptance was denied, i.e. if the drawee 'protested', the bill was dishonoured. If the bill was sent to a different place than the drawee's residence, it was said to be 'domiciled' to this third place (bills of exchange that were domiciled to one of the important bill markets were considered safe and easily to handle);
   – the beneficiary of the bill (*beneficiario*), who had to present the bill to the drawee (hence he was also named presenter) and to whom the drawee had to pay the face value of the bill (*payee*);
   – the deliverer or remitter (*rimettente*), who paid the issuer money for the bill he received from him (hence also *datore*).

---

62 Jacques LE GOFF, *Wucherzins und Höllenqualen. Ökonomie und Religion im Mittelalter*, Stuttgart 1988.

63 Raymond DE ROOVER, The *cambium maritimum* Contract According to the Genoese Notarial Records of the Twelfth and Thirteenth Centuries, in David HERLIHY / Robert S. LOPEZ / Vsevolod SLESSAREV (eds.), *Economy, Society, and Government in Medieval Italy. Essays in Memory of Robert L. Reynolds*, Kent (Ohio) 1969, pp. 15–33, esp. pp. 28f. Cf. also Álonzo M. HAMELIN, *Un traité de morale économique au XIVe siècle: Le tractatus de Usuris de Maître Alexandre d'Alexandrie*, Louvain 1962, pp. 179–185; Raymond DE ROOVER, Les doctrines économiques des scholastiques: à propos du traité sur l'usure d'Alexandre Lombard, *Revue d'histoire ecclésiastique* 59 (1964), pp. 854–866, esp. pp. 858–860; idem, The Scholastics, Usury, and Foreign Exchange, *Business History Review* 41 (1967), pp. 257–271.

64 GRÜNHUT, *Wechselrecht*, vol. 1, pp. 27, 35f., 49–51.

65 Concerning the following terms cf. Friedrich ZELLFELDER, Glossar, in *WdW I/I*, pp. 197–207.

Figure 1: Exchange Transaction with Four Parties Participating[66] .

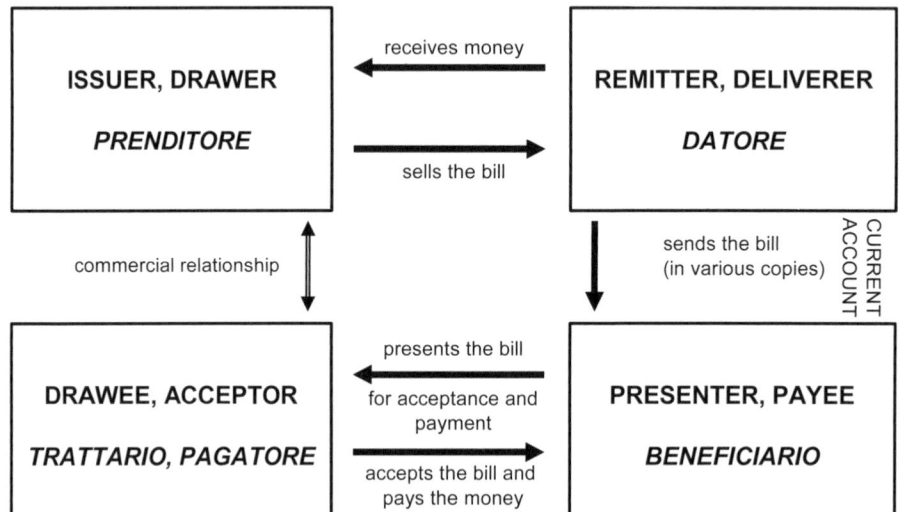

In a three-person-bill, the functions of the beneficiary and the remitter were usually joined in one person, which is why the modern Italian language also translates remitter by *beneficiario*.

(2) the sum of money over which the bill of exchange was issued;

(3) the currency in which the value of the bill had to be repaid, the exchange rate and the possible coinage in which the payment had to be effected;

(4) the usance or the term of the bill:[67] the usance, derived from the Italian *usanza*, usually meant the commercial custom at a place. Concerning cashless payment transactions, it determined the due date, i.e. the day of expiration of the bill of exchange and, thus, the timeframe during which the credit was granted within the transaction. The duration of bills varied between the different markets as well as the partners concerned, depending on the time of turnover between the two markets. Often the duration was extended to enlarge the *distancia temporis* caused by the *distancia loci* and, thus, widened the credit line. Until the 18th century, the terms of bills of exchange were accordingly set as 'uso' or '2 uso' or '2½ uso', meaning that the traditional duration of bills between two markets could be extended (or shortened). A merchant's knowledge of the traditional *uso* between two places was taken for granted. Usually, a distinction was made between dato bills and sight bills. Dato bills were to be repaid after a certain duration following the date of issuing (after date, *à date, dato fatta*), whereas the term

---

66   Cf. Spufford, *Handbook*, p. xxxii; Denzel, *"Practica"*, p. 90.

67   Cf. also Reinhold C. Mueller, Art. "Usance", in North (ed.), *Von Aktie bis Zoll*, p. 403; Markus A. Denzel, "Zeit ist Geld". Usancen-'Systeme' im bargeldlosen Zahlungsverkehr nach italienischen Kaufmannsnotiz- und -handbüchern des 14. und 15. Jahrhunderts, *Scripta Mercaturae* 29/2 (1995), pp. 96–111.

for the repayment of sight bills started after the drawee had seen (i.e. accepted) the bill (after sight, *à vue*, *vistà*). The bill at sight was a special type of sight bill. It had to be paid immediately following its presentation. When effecting cash-less payments at fairs it was common practice to determine the term of a bill to the next or next-but-one fair. In the 17th century it became common with almost all bills of exchange (with the exception of 'fair bills' and bills at sight) to admit some days of extra time to pay – the number of days varying for each market – meaning that a bill did not have to be repaid until a few days later than

(5) the date the bill of exchange was issued; and, finally,

(6) the signature of the issuer.

In principle, it is possible to determine two fields where transactions with bills of exchange were of great importance. The first was merchandise trade, where the bill of exchange was used as a means of payment and credit. The second was credit alone, when only money was sent and no connection to any trade in goods existed.

Figure 2: Exchange Transaction with Four Parties Participating in Connection with a Goods Credit[68].

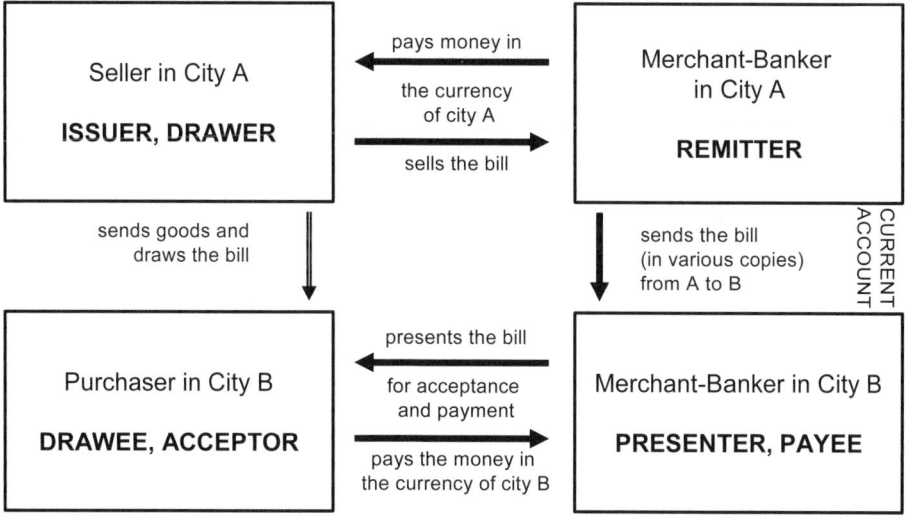

In the first case, a seller in city A could have sent goods to a purchaser in city B and drawn a bill of exchange on him.[69] This meant that the seller instructed the purchaser to pay the amount he owed to the payee (*beneficiario*) within a certain time and in a certain currency in city B. Here, the seller corresponded to the taker or drawer

---

68   Cf. DENZEL, *"Practica"*, p. 90.

69   Concerning the following, cf. DE ROOVER, *Lettre de change*, pp. 43–47; MUNRO, Art. "Wechsel", pp. 413f.; Raymond DE ROOVER, Cambium ad Venetias. Contribution to the History of Foreign Exchange, in KIRSHNER (ed.), *Business, Banking and Economic Thought*, pp. 239–259, esp. p. 241.

(*prenditore, traente*), the purchaser to the payer or drawee (*pagatore, trattario*). From the 16th century the drawn *littera di cambio* was called *tratte* (from the Italian: *tracta*[70] or *tratta*).[71] In order to receive the money as soon as possible, the exporter would have sold the bill of exchange to a local trading partner against cash in the currency of city A, who thus allowed the seller a credit, indirectly financing the selling of the goods to the purchaser. In this way the seller regained liquidity for further trading and did not have to wait for the payment of the purchaser in a couple of weeks. By declaring that he had received the money from the buyer of the bill of exchange, the issuer also declared that the payee instead of himself was to receive the sum of money over which the bill was issued. He also gave a guarantee for the cashing of the bill and was, thus, responsible for the payee receiving the equivalent amount at the other place.[72] Then the buyer of the bill, the deliverer or remitter (*datore, rimettente*), sent the original bill of exchange and – to be safe – possibly various copies and an accompanying letter (advice letter) to the payee,[73] with whom he held an open account. The remitter or even the issuer sent the first copy of the bill, the *secunda* – sometimes also accompanied by a letter of advice – to the drawee.[74] The payee would then accredit the remitter with the amount over which the bill of exchange was issued (redeemed debts, for example) or would effect a re-exchange (*recambium*) by buying a bill of exchange that had to be paid in city A and that had been issued in favour of the original remitter. In this case the payee would present the bill of exchange to the purchaser for him to accept. The purchaser would accept his obligation to pay, writing the word *accettata* (or *vista* or *vista et accettata*), the date and his signature on the back of the bill and, thus, becoming the acceptor. In the late Middle Ages and early modern times the formal acceptance of bills of exchange negotiated beside fairs could be omitted as those bills often did not reach their place of destination until shortly before the day of settlement due to the difficulties in communication and travel. Thus the presentation of the bill often went along with demanding the payment. If a bill was presented for acceptance, this could also be done orally. The word of the acceptor meant among merchants as much as a written acceptance.[75] All mutual obligations were settled with the acceptor's payment (or the accrediting of the account) to the presenter according to the local or agreed duration (usance) of the bill. So the acceptor had enough time to sell his import and to acquire the money needed for the settlement of the bill of exchange.

---

70 Cf. Schaps, *Geschichte*, p. 10.

71 Florence Edler, *Glossary of Medieval Terms of Business. Italian Series 1200–1600*, Cambridge (Mass.) 1934 (repr. New York 1970), p. 154.

72 Grünhut, *Wechselrecht*, vol. 1, p. 33.

73 Such an advice letter could also have the form of an order of payment or cheque, as Heers found out for Genoa: since the 14th century the use of a *polizza* next to a bill of exchange was usual, "un véritable cheque" or "un véritable mandat de *paiement*; le tiré doit effectivement payer la somme portée sur le papier. Le plus souvent, c'est un ordre de *virement* adressé au scribe d'une banque privée ou au notaire d'un des registres de San Giorgio. ... Rares sont les cas où le chèque est à l'origine d'une manipulation monétaire; il s'accompagne presque toujours d'une « scritta in banco »." Jacques Heers, *Gênes au XVe siècle. Activité économique et problèmes sociaux*, Paris 1961, p. 74.

74 Cf. Grünhut, *Wechselrecht*, vol. 1, pp. 64f.; Raban von Canstein, *Lehrbuch des Wechselrechts*, Berlin 1890, pp. 16–18.

75 Grünhut, *Wechselrecht*, vol. 1, p. 67.

The advantage of this method of payment was that the seller did not have any lack of liquidity, the purchaser could buy the goods on credit, both the seller of the goods and the payee were paid in local currency, and the payment was made without expensive and dangerous transportation of precious metals. Moreover, possible differences in exchange rates between the two cities could be used profitably. Taking into consideration that the issuer of the bill often had a current account with the drawee, the issuer would in fact only sell his demand for a certain amount of money when selling the bill of exchange. As a result, his account with the payee was accredited with this respective amount. If this was impossible, the payee would have to give him credit. This is how the fundamental ideas of the acceptance credit were formed as early as at the end of the Middle Ages, with the bank house as the acceptor guaranteeing the cashing of the bill of exchange for the issuer.[76]

Figure 3: Exchange Transaction with Three Parties Participating in Connection with Money Transfer[77].

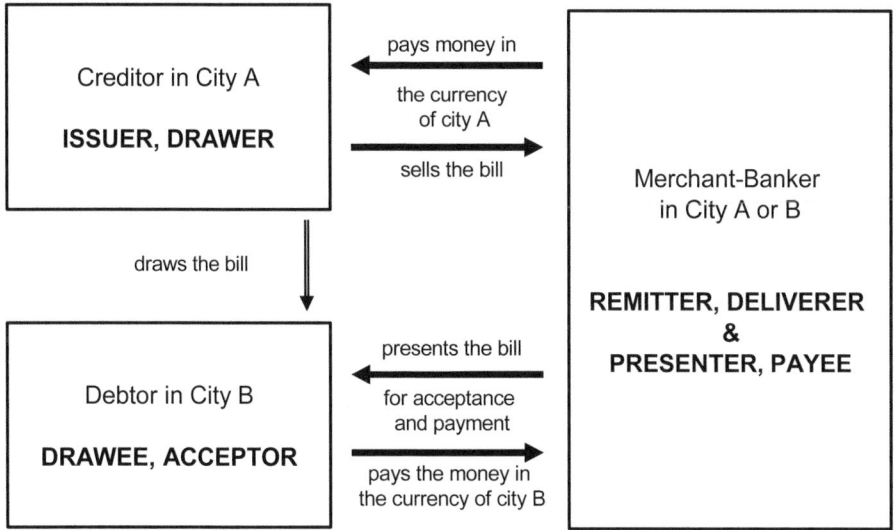

In the second case the transaction could serve only to send money. Mostly, only three people were involved in such a transaction, as the remitter and the payee could be the same person who would receive the issuer's (i.e. the creditor's) money from the drawee (i.e. the debtor).[78]

Even if the merchant issued a bill of exchange in favour of himself, meaning that the drawee and the remitter were one person, there were still only three people involved in the transaction.[79] The remitter could also sell the bill in order to send

---

76 MUNRO, Art. "Wechsel", p. 414.
77 Cf. DENZEL, *"Practica"*, p. 83.
78 Idem, Art. "Wechsel, -brief, Wechsler", column 2087.

money to another city, i.e. directly to the payee.[80]

The bill of exchange could fulfil four functions: first, it was a safe way to send money; second, it was a means of payment in trade; third, it functioned as a source of credit in lending money by issuing a bill of exchange (*dare a cambio*) and when selling a bill of exchange in foreign currencies on credit (*cambi a credenza*); fourth, one could benefit from the differences in exchange rates in different places (arbitrage transaction).[81] The chance and the risk of possible profits and losses of the exchange when issuing bills back and forth were of great concern to the merchants. Consequently, issuer and drawee would often agree on exchange rates that were higher than the mint parity or the 'usual local' rate for *cambium manuale*. According to Raymond de Roover, this difference in rates is to be seen as a hidden interest or profit. As long as this practice bore risk and uncertainty one could avoid ecclesiastic and secular bans on usury, which was – again according to de Roover – the overall and fundamental significance of bills of exchange. The risk consisted in the fact that exchange rates could change in the short or long term due to currency depreciation and appreciation, changes in the balance of payments, speculative trading of bills or changes in interest rates before the re-exchange could take place.[82]

A special form of the bill transaction was the dry exchange (*cambium siccum*) – "a loan dressed up as an exchange transaction"[83]– with the transfer of money being not the basis of the bill transaction, since no payment was made at the due date of the bill. Instead of this, the drawee (often equal to the payee) issued a bill of re-exchange (*recambium*) or the payee bought another bill of exchange with the money he had received from the first bill transaction, when the original remitter was called the new payee. On the due date this new payee could then achieve a higher sum than he had paid in the first transaction due to a possible change in exchange rates. A sequence of various re-exchanges between two cities without transferring any money could prolong a merchant's credit for however long his creditor was willing to renew the bill. The interest was the creditor's 'payment' for him, continually providing liquidity consisting of the difference between the exchange rates. There are examples from the early 14th to the 17th centuries of interest rates up to 12–14%.[84] The Church and the theologians regarded this type of bills of exchange as morally dubious, as there was in fact no difference in place but only a *distancia temporis*, and

---

79   "... si remittens ipse litteras cambiales exigit"; I.F. LEBKÜCHNER, *De valore cambii in Imperio*, Diss. Erlangae 1765, pp. x–xi. Cf. also DE ROOVER, *Lettre de change*, p. 44: "le preneur et le payeur étaient souvant une même personne". Cf. DENZEL, *"Practica"*, pp. 91–93. For examples see HEERS, *Livre de comptes*, p. 346.

80   MUNRO, Art. "Wechsel", p. 415. Cf. DENZEL, *"Practica"*, p. 94.

81   Jacques LE GOFF, *Kaufleute und Bankiers im Mittelalter*, Frankfurt/Main – New York 1993 (Paris 1956), pp. 33f., 70–77. It seems pointless to ask which of these functions was the most important, the transfer or the credit instrument. For this problem see the detailed discussion in SPUFFORD, *Handbook*, pp. xxxvii–xlix. Cf. Reinhold C. MUELLER, The Spufford Thesis on Foreign Exchange: The Evidence of Exchange Rates, *Journal of European Economic History* 24 (1995), pp. 121–129.

82   MUNRO, Art. "Wechsel", p. 415. For a critical comment on de Roover, cf. John H. MUNRO, Bullionism and the Bill of Exchange in England, 1272–1663: A Study in Monetary Management and Popular Prejudice, in [Fredi CHIAPPELLI (ed.),] *The Dawn of Modern Banking*, New Haven – London 1979, pp. 169–239, esp. pp. 170–172.

83   DE ROOVER, Cambium ad Venetias, p. 242.

the bill transaction was used as a means of providing funds that yielded ecclesiasti-
cally forbidden interest and of speculating on the unpredictable changes in exchange
rates. Nonetheless, it remained a used trading practice. From the economic point of
view the dry exchange provided the opportunity to receive a credit via bill transactions while the creditor could cancel the credit at any time by refusing the renewing
of the bill of exchange.[85]

Raymond de Roover explained the connection between the bill of exchange and
the bill of re-exchange in a fictitious example of a bill transaction between London
and Antwerp using real exchange rates from 1564.

Figure 4: Exchange and Re-Exchange Transaction[86].

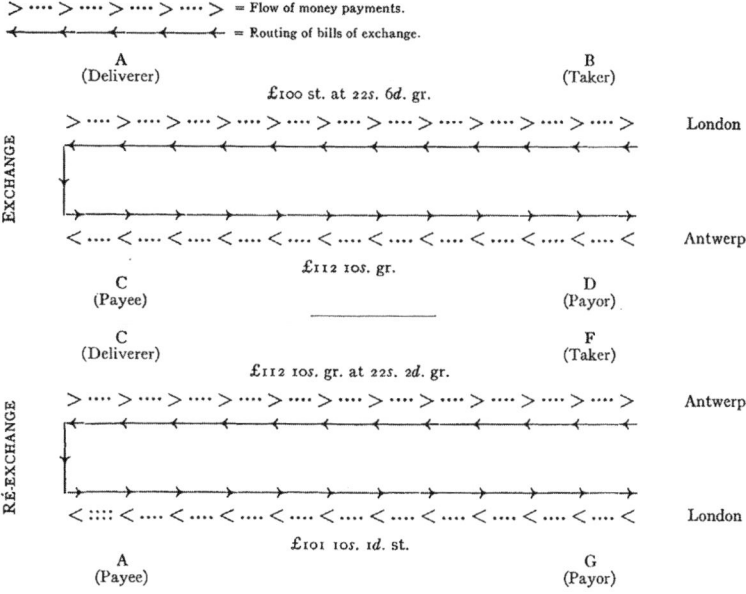

The deliverer, A, in London, having £100 st. [sterling] to spare, decides to buy a bill on Antwerp
at the prevailing rate of 22s. 6d. gr. [groot, Flemish money] per pound sterling. B, the taker,
needs £100 st. in London, but he does not have the sum available, though he has money coming

---

84 This practice can be interpreted as extortion only when the exchange rates had been fixed by the
    participants prior to the drawing of the (first) credit, e.g. when eliminating market risk. Cf. for
    the Late Middle Ages Reinhold C. MUELLER, *The Venetian Money Market. Banks, Panics, and
    the Public Debt, 1200–1500* (= *Money and Banking in Medieval and Renaissance Venice*, vol. I),
    Baltimore – London 1997, pp. 317–337.

85 GRÜNHUT, *Wechselrecht*, vol. 1, pp. 50s.; Reinhold C. MUELLER, Art. "Trockenwechsel", in
    NORTH (ed.), *Von Aktie bis Zoll*, pp. 398f.; Raymond DE ROOVER, What is Dry Exchange? A
    Contribution to the Study of English Mercantilism, in KIRSHNER (ed.), *Business, Banking and
    Economic Thought*, pp. 183–199; idem, Il trattato di fra Santi Rucellai sul cambio, il monte
    comune e il monte delle doti, in *Archivio Storico Italiano* 111 (1953), pp. 3–41, esp. pp. 29–34.

86 Idem, What Is Dry Exchange?, p. 189 (Chart I).

to him in Antwerp. A and B will easily come to terms by exchanging money for a bill on Antwerp. In return for a loan of £100 st. B makes out a bill, payable at usance in Antwerp by his agent D, in favor of A's agent, C, for the value received from A, the deliverer or banker. When this bill matures at the end of one month, C collects from D the sum of £112 10s. gr. or the equivalent of £100 st. at 22s. 6d. gr. A, the banker in London, now has a balance of £112 10s. gr. standing to his credit in Antwerp. Instead of keeping this money idle, he instructs his agent, C, to seek out a taker and to remit the sum of £112 10s. gr. to London by exchange. In pursuance of these instructions, C buys from F a usance bill on London at 22s. 2d. gr. per pound sterling and sends it for collection to A, the original deliverer in London. When this bill matures, A collects £101 10s. 1d. st. or the equivalent of £112 10s. gr. at 22s. 2d. gr. per Pound Sterling. ... By thus keeping his money running on the exchange, A has made a profit of £1 10s. 1d. st. in two months, or a return of about 9 per cent a year.[87]

Of course, such a double transaction was also possible if the payee and payer in the first part were the same person. This person would then function in the *recambium* as both deliverer and taker.

Figure 5: Dry-Exchange Transaction[88].

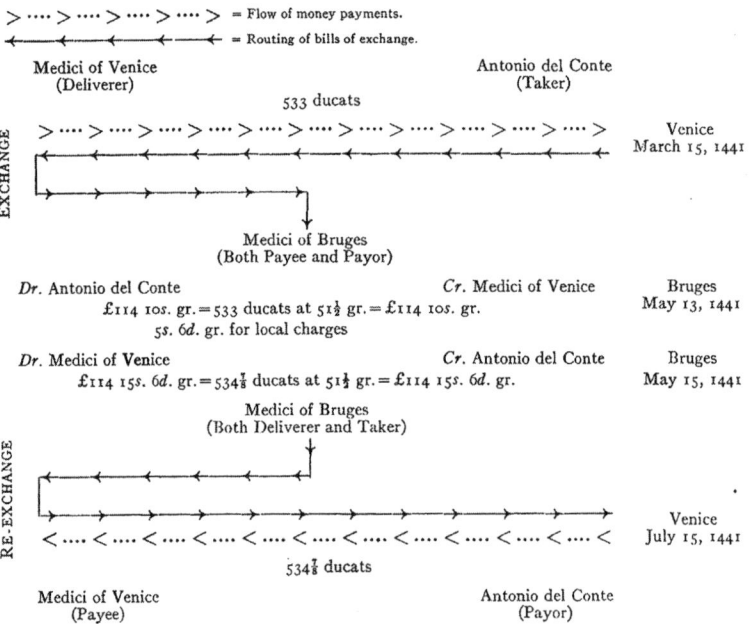

Such a bill still involved the customary four parties, but two of them were fused in the same person. Bills of this sort were fairly common in the Middle Ages. They usually read 'Pay to yourselves' (Pagate a voi medesimi) instead of 'Pay to So-and-So.' The use of this formula

---

87   Ibid., p. 188. For more numeric examples of (Genoese) *recambium* transactions see HEERS, *Gênes*, pp. 79–88.

88   DE ROOVER, *What Is Dry Exchange?*, p. 196 (Chart II).

frequently, but not always, indicated a transaction involving dry exchange. Bills thus payable 'to yourselves' did not give rise to any money payments but were usually settled by a transfer in the books of the payee, who was also the payer. Generally he wrote the amount stated in the bill to the debit of the taker and to the credit of the deliverer or the lender.[89]

Another form of the *cambio fittizio*, the fictitious bill of exchange transaction, was the *cambio con la ricorsa*, an agreement made between the participating parties that came to play a more important role with the Church's growing disapproval of the *cambia sicca*. The *ricorsa* that developed on the international exchange fairs of the 16th and 17th centuries was similar to the dry exchange in so far as it also was a hidden credit with uncertain profit or interest, but differed significantly from the *cambium siccum* as the repeated exchange back and forth, being an investment for the creditor and a credit for the debtor, was a binding agreement between the participating parties. The exchange rate for the re-exchange was also fixed in accordance with the existing exchange rates in order to guarantee a profit for the creditor (remitter). When processing such a *ricorsa* transaction the *cambista* or exchange banker instructed his colleague on the exchange fair to 'pay to himself' and to draw a bill of exchange on the first *cambista*, who then again paid himself on the due date. The exchange back and forth could be repeated a number of times each year, depending on the various exchange fairs that took place. Thus *ricorsa* exchanges served to cover up extortion in credit business, allowed quick drawing of credits and offered a profit-bearing investment with an average interest of 12–14% to capital owners. Nonetheless, the *ricorsa* exchange was approved by the Church, as it implied a *recambium* really taking place.[90]

There were three essential premises for all exchange transactions: a trusting personal relationship between the participating partners, the opportunity to sue for the payment of the bill of exchange in court if necessary and the existence of current accounts between the remitter and the presenter. In order to ensure that at least one copy of the bill of exchange reached the payee, the bill was issued in numerous copies (*prima, secunda, tertia*, etc.) that were sent to the different persons involved in the transaction.

The development of the bill of exchange revolutionized payments in Europe:

> No longer did every prospective purchaser or returning vendor need to carry with him large and stealable quantities of precious metals, whether in coin, or in marks of silver, or ounces of gold, depending on the trading area. Instead a manager could send and receive remittances from his factors and agents by bills of exchange without moving around Europe himself. This transformation of the methods of trade, which enabled a merchant to manage an international business without leaving his own home city, was so racial that de Roover christened it 'the commercial revolution of the thirteenth century'.[91]

---

89 Ibid., p. 195.

90 Idem, *Lettre de change*, pp. 79–81; Giulio MANDICH, *Le pacte de ricorsa et le marché italien des changes au XVIIe siècle*, Paris 1953; GRÜNHUT, *Wechselrecht*, vol. 1, pp. 81f.; Reinhold C. MUELLER, Art. "Ricorsa", in NORTH (ed.), *Von Aktie bis Zoll*, pp. 344f. Cf. Aldo DE MADDALENA, Affaires et gens d'affaires lombards sur les foires de Bisenzone. L'exemple des Lucini (1579–1619), *Annales. Économies – Sociétés – Civilisations* 22 (1967), pp. 939–990.

91 SPUFFORD, *Handbook*, pp. xxx-xxxi. Cf. idem, *Money and its Use in Medieval Europe*, Cambridge 1988, pp. 262f.: "The bill of exchange and the oral precursor of the cheque, rather than the florin or the grosso, were the really radical and important developments in the means of payment associated with the commercial revolution of the thirteenth century."

According to John Munro, the bill of exchange was "the most important achievement in the history of economics" and contributed greatly to the reduction of the international transfer of precious metals in Europe.[92]

3.2 The Innovations in Cashless Payments in the 16th and 17th Centuries: Endorsement and Discount – and their Consequence: The Decline of the International Exchange Fairs

With the bill of exchange as the medium of cashless payment transactions, a safe way of sending money and a source of credit had been developed, but a new problem arose: whereas coins or unminted precious metals could be transferred without any problems from one person to another, it was impossible to transfer a bill of exchange in either way. In late medieval times the bill of exchange was bound to the presenter mentioned in the document and only he could cash in the bill.[93] Thus it was impossible to transfer a bill to a person who was not involved in the exchange transaction, for Roman, Germanic, Islamic and Canon law did not allow the transfer of any kind of credit instrument.[94] This problem was solved primarily by using the big international fairs, where the merchants – either personally or via their representatives – gathered together in one place at certain times of the year representing a platform for the settlement of international payments:[95] At the Champagne fairs[96] and later at the Geneva fairs, the Castilian fairs, the Lyons fairs and, finally, at the Genoese Bisenzone fairs international payments were settled mainly during the fair business through the settlement of accounts. Provided that the creditor of the bill of exchange was at the same time the debtor of another bill, creditor and debtor would mutually write off their debts in the participating merchants' accounting books, i.e. all claims and debts were settled in a circle ('giro') of transfer and resulting compensation if there were, ideally, equally high debts.[97] Unsettled balances could then be transferred to the next fair using a bill of exchange, and the security of the payment of bills was guaranteed by the fair court.[98] This form of settling of payments doubt-

---

92   MUNRO, Art. "Wechsel", p. 415.

93   Peter OPITZ, *Der Funktionswandel des Wechselindossaments*, Berlin 1967, p. 31.

94   Harold J. BERMAN, *Recht und Revolution. Die Bildung der westlichen Rechtstradition*, Frankfurt/Main 1991 (Engl. 1983), p. 553.

95   Cf. DE ROOVER, *Lettre de change*, p. 65: "le caractère international du marché monétaire n'est pas un phénomène nouveau, puisqu'il remonte au temps des foires de Champagne."

96   At the Champagne fairs the settlement of accounts was fully developed as early as 1180; FACE, Techniques, pp. 428, 437; Jürgen SCHNEIDER, Messen, Banken und Börsen (15.–18. Jahrhundert), in *Banchi pubblici*, vol. I, pp. 133–169, esp. p. 135. Cf. also GOLDSCHMIDT, Geschäftsoperationen, pp. 30f.

97   VON CANSTEIN, *Lehrbuch*, pp. 26f.; GRÜNHUT, *Wechselrecht*, vol. 1, pp. 76–80; SCHNEIDER, Messen, Banken und Börsen, pp. 138f.; idem, Hat das Indossament zum Niedergang der Wechselmessen im 17. und 18. Jahrhundert beigetragen?, in Michael NORTH (ed.), *Geldumlauf, Währungssysteme und Zahlungsverkehr in Nordwesteuropa 1300–1800. Beiträge zur Geldgeschichte der späten Hansezeit*, Köln – Wien 1989, pp. 183–193, esp. p. 188.

98   Jürgen SCHNEIDER, Innovationen und Wandel der Beschäftigtenstruktur im Kreditgewerbe vom Spätmittelalter bis zur Mitte des 19. Jahrhunderts, in Hans POHL (ed.), *Innovationen und Wandel der Beschäftigtenstruktur im Kreditgewerbe. Erstes wissenschaftliches Kolloquium des Instituts für bankhistorische Forschung e.V. am 20. Juni 1986 in München*, Frankfurt/Main 1988, pp. 21–39, esp. p. 23; DENZEL, *"Practica"*, p. 97.

less had its climax during the Lyons fairs and at the Genoese exchange fairs of Bisenzone: in Lyons the central settlement of accounts was supported by the mediation of fair bankers keeping the merchants' money depots and opened current accounts. As the fair bankers also had current accounts with each other, payments could simply be made by crediting and debiting the respective accounts.[99] The Lyons fairs, just as the younger Bisenzone fairs, provided for a special unit of account, the *écu de marc* or the *scudo di marche* respectively, in relation to which all other traded currencies were set, thus significantly simplifying the settlement of payments.[100] The mechanisms of cashless settlement of claims were refined at the Bisenzone fairs,[101] which were founded exclusively for trading bills and without any trade in goods at all, so that they can be called "foire[s] de change par excellence".[102]

One can state in general that the opportunity of a concentrated, international settlement of claims several times a year without having to issue a new bill of exchange for every new transaction led to a concentration of cashless payments at these international fairs, so that they became the most important, even though not permanent, finance markets in Europe at their respective time. It was last but not least due to the great importance of the international fairs for cashless payment in late medieval Europe and of the 16th century that the contemporary legal literature made a difference between *cambia feriarium* (*nundinalia*) or *regularia* on the one hand and *cambia platearum* (*platealia*) or *irregularia* on the other,[103] i.e. the exchange business at the fairs was regarded as usual and bills of exchanges traded aside from fairs as exceptional.

An important innovation for the transferability of bills of exchange was the so-called endorsement, a notice written on the back (*in dosso* or *in dorso*) of a bill that enabled a person not yet part of the exchange transaction to present the bill. With the help of endorsing, the claim included in the bill of exchange was transferred to another person, which was determined by the signature *in dosso*.[104] By endorsement, the bill of exchange became a negotiable paper among merchants, almost like paper money:[105]

---

99 Marc BRÉSSARD, *Les foires de Lyon au XVe et XVIe siècles*, Paris 1914, pp. 279f.; SCHNEIDER, Messen, Banken und Börsen, pp. 138f.

100 Giuseppe FELLONI, Un système monétaire atypique. La monnaie de marc dans les foires de change génois, XVIe–XVIIIe siècle, in John DAY (ed.), *Études d'histoire monétaire, XIIe–XIXe siècles*, Lille 1984, pp. 249–262; Jürgen SCHNEIDER, Die Bedeutung von Kontoren, Faktoreien, Stützpunkten (von Kompanien), Märkten, Messen und Börsen im Mittelalter und Früher Neuzeit, in Hans POHL (ed.), *Die Bedeutung der Kommunikation für Wirtschaft und Gesellschaft. Referate der 12. Arbeitstagung der Gesellschaft für Sozial- und Wirtschaftsgeschichte vom 22.–25.4.1987 in Siegen*, Stuttgart 1989, pp. 37–63, esp. pp. 52f.; DENZEL, *"Practica"*, pp. 304, 315.

101 Pierre RACINE, Messen in Italien im 16. Jahrhundert: Die Wechselmessen von Piacenza, in Hans POHL (ed.), *Frankfurt im Messenetz Europas – Erträge der Forschung* (= Rainer KOCH, *Brücke zwischen den Völkern – Zur Geschichte der Frankfurter Messe*, vol. I), Frankfurt/Main 1991, pp. 155–170, esp. pp. 156–161, 168f.; DA SILVA, *Banque et crédit*, pp. 80–82; Giulio MANDICH, Delle fiere genovesi di cambi particolarmente studiate come mercati periodici di credito, *Revista di storia economica* 4 (1939), pp. 257–276; Claudio MARSILIO, *Dovè il denaro fa denaro. Gli operatori finanziari genovesi nelle fiere di cambio del XVII secolo*, Novi Ligure 2008.

102 DA SILVA, *Banque et crédit*, p. 12.

103 GRÜNHUT, *Wechselrecht*, vol. 1, p. 62.

104 Markus A. DENZEL, Art. "Indossament", in NORTH (ed.), *Von Aktie bis Zoll*, pp. 165f., esp. p. 165.

Figure 6: Exchange Transaction with Endorsement[106].

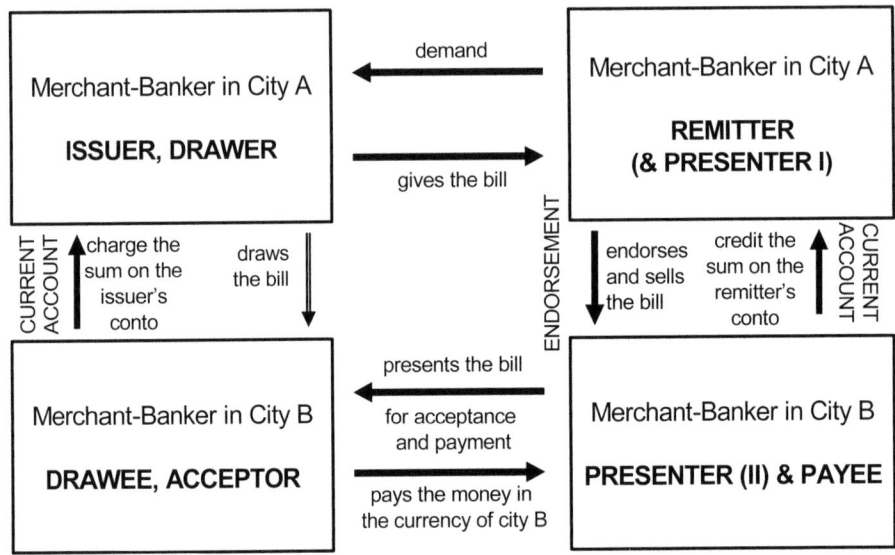

"Now bills of exchange became not only more easily transferable, but also negotiable; in other words, the bearer had a greater financial security than the previous bearer, who remained jointly responsible for payment without being a surety in the strictly legal sense."[107] Just as the bill of exchange itself, the endorsed bill developed – probably in accordance with other endorsed papers – among innovative merchants in Italy,[108] which can be proved from at least the beginning of the 15th century.[109] A forerunner of the endorsement[110] was the order clause providing the transfer of credit papers and promissory notes from the end of the 14th century. If he was not sure that the payee could receive the repayment personally, a merchant could, nonetheless, make the paper payable to a bearer, representative or an authorized person by adding their name to the order clause as early as in the mid-12th century.[111] "Examples of these first, still primitive, forms of endorsement, applied to bills and cheques in the

---

105 SCHNEIDER, Innovationen und Wandel, p. 31; idem, Indossament, p. 189. Cf. DE ROOVER, *Lettre de change*, pp. 83f.

106 Cf. DENZEL, *"Practica"*, p. 102.

107 Herman VAN DER WEE, Monetary, Credit and Banking Systems, in Edwin E. RICH / Charles H. WILSON (eds.), *The Economic Organization of Early Modern Europe* (= *The Cambridge Economic History of Europe*, vol. V), Cambridge et al. 1977, pp. 290–392, esp. p. 329.

108 OPITZ, *Funktionswandel*, p. 36.

109 Federigo MELIS, Una girata cambiaria del 1410 nell'Archivio Datini di Prato, *Economia e storia* 5 (1958), pp. 412–421; Henri LAPEYRE, Une lettre de change endossée en 1430, *Annales. Économies, sociétés, civilisations* 13 (1958), pp. 260–264; Raymond DE ROOVER, Le marché monétaire au moyen âge et au début des temps modernes, *Revue historique* 94 (1970), pp. 34f.; HEERS, *Gênes*, pp. 88–96. Cf. SPUFFORD, *Handbook*, pp. xxxi, xxxiii.

110 On the development of endorsement from older methods of transfer, cf. SCHAPS, *Geschichte*, pp. 39–85.

south, were found for Venice (1386), Prato (1394–1410), Florence (1430–1494), Genoa (1459), Lyons (1519, 1537, 1547), Seville (1537), Medina del Campo (1561 [and following years]).”[112] In the 15th century bills of exchange could be endorsed only once (not a few times) and for the real act of endorsing the presence of both the drawee as well as the new and the former payee was necessary. Such transfers were valid only within one city or territory as legal certainty for the transfer of claims could not yet be guaranteed.[113]

Endorsement gained greater economic importance in connection with another innovative institution, the – in contrast to the fairs – year-round bourse. Trade with fungible goods – the bill of exchange was such a good – did not develop in Italy but in Northwestern Europe and here especially in the respective leading mercantile centres, in Bruges and from the second half of the 15th century in Antwerp. During the second half of the 16th century, the merchant bankers (and later the private bankers) needed increasingly to extend their use of endorsements, offering the opportunity to buy endorsed bills of exchange in order to resell them at this *marché permanent*, i.e. the New Stock Exchange in Antwerp that opened in 1531.[114]

In contrast to this, endorsing was rather limited in Italy, because the *campsores* had taken upon themselves the responsibility for arranging cashless payments. It also reduced the number of bills of exchange payable at the big international trade and exchange fairs, i.e. it reduced the volume of cashed bills, because endorsing reduced issuing new bills of exchange in principle. Thus the fair places and fair bankers protested the longest and hardest against allowing endorsements or at least repeated endorsement, as the practice of endorsing would have broken their monopoly in trading with bills of exchange at fairs for ever. Before its introduction only they could present bills for acceptance and settlement of accounts. This situation had two very important consequences for cashless payment transactions. First, the importance of fairs, especially of exchange fairs, whose existence was based on the settlement of accounts, fell significantly and permanently, for merchants no longer had to turn to

---

111 John H. MUNRO, Art. “Inhaber-Klausel”, in NORTH (ed.), *Von Aktie bis Zoll*, pp. 171f.; idem, Übertragbarkeit, *passim*; Bernhard KIRCHGÄSSNER, Zur Geschichte und Bedeutung der Order-Klausel am südwestdeutschen Kapitalmarkt im 14. und 15. Jahrhundert, in Jürgen SCHNEIDER (ed.), *Wirtschaftskräfte und Wirtschaftswege. Festschrift für Hermann Kellenbenz, vol. I: Mittelmeer und Kontinent*, Stuttgart 1978, pp. 373–386; NORTH, Banking and Credit, p. 820. According to GRÜNHUT, *Wechselrecht*, vol. 1, p. 90, it was already supposed to be possible to add an order clause to promissory notes in antiquity.

112 VAN DER WEE, Monetary, Credit and Banking Systems, p. 328 ann. 2. Cf. also Raymond DE ROOVER, *The Rise and Decline of the Medici Bank (1397–1494)*, Cambridge (Mass.) 1963, pp. 137–140; Henri LAPEYRE, Las origins del endorso de lettras de cambio en España, in *Moneda y credito: Revista de economica* 52 (1952). Concerning the “cheque”, see Marco SPALLANZANI, A Note on Florentine Banking in the Renaissance: Orders of Payment and Cheques, *Journal of European Economic History* 7 (1978), pp. 145–168, esp. pp. 145f.: “By the XIVth century [the cheque] had taken on its full form, being distinct from both orders which a client would normally give to a banker by means of a letter, and from the more specific order to make payments to the client’s agent (*mandato all’incasso*). It was in this period that the cheque took on the characteristics typical of an instrument of payment with full power to extinguish debts with third parties. It is well known that these cheques, which were generally drafted on small slips of paper, have nearly all been destroyed and that virtually all the surviving examples come from Tuscany, particularly from Prato thanks to the Datini Archives.”

113 Jacques HEERS, *Le livre de comptes de Giovanni Piccamiglio homme d’affairs génois, 1456–1459*, Paris 1959, pp. 352, 356; DENZEL, Art. “Indossament”, p. 165.

114 SCHNEIDER, Messen, Banken und Börsen, p. 144.

the fair bankers for cashing bills of exchange and settling accounts. The decline of the exchange fairs and the total loss of their function and their fair bankers was irreversible and the endorsing merchant took over their activities. Second, the importance of the bill of exchange issued apart from at fairs grew for balancing payments, since the bill offered wider opportunities for circulation than the fair bill had ever had via the settlement of accounts.[115] The fundamental differences between the two types of balancing payments were four: first, the bill of exchange itself could be transferred by endorsement, whereas the settling of accounts could only transfer the claims resulting from the bills. Second, endorsement meant a written notice for the bill of exchange, whereas accounts could only be settled on the basis of the fair notebooks (*scartafacci*). Third, both payable bills and bills not yet payable could be endorsed, whereas the settlement of accounts was possible only with bills of exchange that were due for payment. Fourth, endorsement included the endorser's liability to the acceptant of the endorsed bill of exchange (endorsee), whereas the settlement of accounts excluded any kind of recourse as every participant had to be regarded as equally solvent.[116]

Only scarcely used during the 16ᵗʰ century,[117] the practice of endorsing at the Antwerp stock exchange led to its distribution throughout Northwestern Europe in the 17ᵗʰ and early 18ᵗʰ centuries: "This innovation was transferred to Amsterdam by the Portuguese Jews and various Protestants expelled from Antwerp in 1585 and was perfected with the establishment of the Amsterdam Wisselbank in 1609."[118] Unlike the Italian banks, the existing and developing stock exchanges and exchange banks accepted endorsed bills of exchange. Stock exchanges were founded in Amsterdam in 1530, in London in 1554/71 (the Royal Exchange), in Hamburg in 1558, in Cologne in 1566, in Danzig in 1593, in Bremen in 1614, in Berlin in 1685 etc. Exchange banks were established in Amsterdam in 1609 – the famous *Wisselbank* – then in Middelburg in 1616, in Hamburg in 1619, in Delft in 1621, in Rotterdam in 1635. In Danzig an exchange bank following the Amsterdam model was planned by Dutch immigrants but was never realized.[119] The more endorsing became important in the decades between 1610 and 1640, the more the importance of the fair bill declined. At the end of the Genoese era – as Fernand Braudel called it – the Bisenzone fairs underwent an emphatic process of decline. From the second half of the 17ᵗʰ century endorsing became accepted in large parts of Western and Central Europe according to the respective exchange regulations (*Wechselordnungen*), so in Hamburg, in Amsterdam in 1651, in France in 1673,[120] in Augsburg in 1665 or in 1707/16 respec-

---

115 Idem, Indossament, pp. 189–192; DENZEL, Art. "Indossament", p. 166; GRÜNHUT, *Wechselrecht*, vol. 1, pp. 12, 95f.

116 SCHAPS, *Geschichte*, pp. 44f.

117 According to Hans POHL, *Die Portugiesen in Antwerpen (1567–1648). Zur Geschichte einer Minderheit*, Wiesbaden 1977, p. 217, endorsement was rarely used in Antwerp at the beginning of the 17ᵗʰ century.

118 Larry NEAL, The Finance of Business During the Industrial Revolution, in R. FLOUD / D. McCLOSKEY (eds.), *The Economic History of Britain since 1700, vol. I: 1700–1860*, Cambridge ²1994, pp. 151–181, esp. p. 159.

119 Maria BOGUCKA, La lettre de change et le crédit dans les échanges entre Gdansk et Amsterdam dans la premier moitié du XVIIᵉ siècle, in Herman VAN DER WEE / Vladimir A. VINOGRADOV / Grigorii G. KOTOVSKY (eds.), *Fifth International Conference of Economic History, Leningrad 1970*, vol. IV, The Hague – Paris – New York 1976, pp. 31–41, esp. p. 38.

tively, in Frankfurt am Main in 1666, in Sweden in 1671, in Breslau in 1672, in Denmark and Norway in 1681, in Leipzig in 1682, in Brunswick in 1686 (limited again to only four endorsements in 1715), in Nuremberg in 1700, in Danzig in 1701, in the electorate of Brandenburg in 1709, in Prussia in 1724, but in Austria not until 1763.[121] The exchange places of the Holy Roman Empire, in particular, reflected the different exchange regulations that came into force in the individual cities, following one another relatively quickly in arguing over endorsements: endorsements were forbidden, for example, in Frankfurt am Main in 1620 and in 1635, but the 1666 regulation allowed it (confirmed in 1739). Following the Frankfurt example, Nuremberg forbade endorsement even in 1647, but the *giro* or endorsement was allowed there in 1654 and, finally, the multiple endorsement in 1700.[122] Later exchange regulations give the reason for the final approval of multiple endorsements; this instrument was then widely used in many other places and could no longer be forbidden for competitive reasons.[123] During the 18th century endorsing was a widely regarded common mercantile attribute, whereas the Italian exchange markets (Venice, the Bolzano fairs, the Bisenzone fairs at Novi, Naples and Florence) ruled out at least multiple endorsing because the *campsores* would otherwise have lost their function.[124] Nevertheless, bills were doubtless endorsed in some cases.[125] Endorsing appeared in Italy as a 'variety' of the *girata* that must have emerged around 1600. The *girata* did not differ from endorsing in function, but in the fact that it was not written on the back but on the front of the bill.[126] The term *girata* or its derivatives respectively – *giro* (instead of endorsement) and *girieren* (instead of to endorse) – were spread also in the Holy Roman Empire in the first half of the 17th century, last but not least through the Bolzano fairs,[127] so that these Italian terms are found rather of-

---

120 It was already common in France to endorse bills before the *Ordonnance du commerce*, probably since the 1680 ban on *billets en blanc*, which were papers with the name of the creditor left open in order to provide for unrestricted circulation; SCHAPS, *Geschichte*, pp. 123f. For the fair business in Lyons restrictions were made in 1678: Bills of exchange from Venice and Bolzano could not be endorsed at all, those from Novi (Bisenzone fairs) and other Italian cities, from Germany, Switzerland and Piedmont could be endorsed only once; GRÜNHUT, *Wechselrecht*, vol. 1, pp. 97–99 note 21. Cf. also SCHAPS, *Geschichte*, p. 125.

121 Ibid., pp. 145–150, 185; SCHNEIDER, Messen, Banken und Börsen, p. 169; GRÜNHUT, *Wechselrecht*, vol. 1, pp. 97–99 note 21. Concerning England, cf. James Steven ROGERS, *The Early History of the Law of Bills and Notes. A Study of the Origins of Anglo-American Commercial Law*, Cambridge 1995, p. 170.

122 SCHAPS, *Geschichte*, pp. 146–148; GRÜNHUT, *Wechselrecht*, vol. 1, pp. 97–99 note 21; SCHNEIDER, Messen, Banken und Börsen, pp. 150f.

123 GRÜNHUT, *Wechselrecht*, vol. 1, pp. 97–99 note 21. Cf., for example, Franz WALDER, *Das Wechselrecht der Reichsstadt Augsburg*, Erlangen 1922, p. 58.

124 Ja[c]ques SAVARY, *Le parfait négociant ou instruction générale pour ce qui regarde le Commerce de toute sorte de Marchandises, tant de France, que des Pays Étrangers*, Genève 1676, P. II, liv. 2, ch. 4, pp. 482, 487; Jacques DUPUYS DE LA SERRA, *L'art des lettres de change suivant les plus célèbres places d'Europe*, Paris 1693, p. 12f.; VON CANSTEIN, *Lehrbuch*, p. 33; SCHAPS, *Geschichte*, pp. 88–94, 107; GRÜNHUT, *Wechselrecht*, vol. 1, pp. 97–99 note 21; SCHNEIDER, Messen, Banken und Börsen, p. 152.

125 This is already proven for the beginning of the 17th century; DE ROOVER, *Lettre de change*, p. 153 (Doc. 8). Cf. SCHAPS, *Geschichte*, pp. 107f.

126 Francesco FERRARA, *La girata della cambiale*, Roma 1935; G. CASSANDRO, Vicende storiche della lettera di cambio, in *Bolletino storico del Banco die Napoli* IX–XII/1, 1955/56; idem, Art. "Cambiale", in *Enciclopedia del Diritto* V, Varese 1959, p. 836; SCHAPS, *Geschichte*, pp. 39f. Cf. SCHNEIDER, Messen, Banken und Börsen, p. 150; idem, Indossament, p. 193.

ten in the exchange regulations of the 17th and 18th centuries.[128]

Similar to endorsement or its Italian 'variety', the *girata*, the discount became the second important innovation of cashless payment transactions in the late 16th and the 17th centuries: discount means interest subtracted in advance, when a credit paper – e.g. a bill of exchange – was repaid before the due date.[129] Thus, to discount a bill of exchange meant to sell it before the date it is due for cashing under subtraction of interest, which could have been considered usury due to the canonical ban on taking interest:[130]

> The first example of modern discount in Antwerp was found in the Kitson Papers and related to the discounting of a writing obligatory in 1536. It was still an exceptional occurrence. The creditor usually kept the writings obligatory and bills of exchange in his portfolio until the due date. If the creditor suddenly needed cash, he would ask one or more debtors to repay their debt earlier with a *rabat* (rebate): this was still the old procedure that had already been in common use in the Middle Ages (the traditional discount). … The writings obligatory usually had a long term to run, sometimes up to 12 months or more, so that the need for quick cashing was often quite sharply felt. However, the general introduction of the bill of exchange into northwest Europe was also to foster the discounting of bills.[131]

Among the merchants of Antwerp discounting spread in the second half of the 16th century but did not develop into a usual business practice until the end of that century. During the 17th century, discounting was established beside endorsement in Northwestern Europe – and especially in England.[132] "Modern discount banking had thus become a fact of economic life."[133]

3.3 The Bill of Exchange as the Dominant Means of International Payment in Europe (17th to 19th Century)

"Bills of exchange were the dominant means of international payment in the seventeenth century, and their exchange rate was the effective rate of exchange for most commercial activity."[134] With endorsement and discount, the stock exchange as the place of trade and the exchange regulations as the legal safeguarding, cashless pay-

---

127 Markus A. DENZEL, *Die Bozner Messen und ihr Zahlungsverkehr (1633–1850)*, Bozen 2005, pp. 87–89.

128 SCHNEIDER, Messen, Banken und Börsen, p. 150.

129 Ibid., p. 153; John H. MUNRO, Art. "Diskont", in North (ed.), *Von Aktie bis Zoll*, pp. 85–87, esp. p. 85.

130 SPUFFORD, *Handbook*, p. xxxi.

131 VAN DER WEE, Monetary, Credit and Banking Systems, pp. 329f.

132 MUNRO, Art. "Diskont", p. 86. As early as during the 17th century goldsmith-bankers in England already discounted promissory notes, bills of exchange and even exchequer bills, although the transfer of such papers by endorsing them was not legally protected until the *Promissory Notes Act* from 1704. Cf. ROGERS, *Early History*, pp. 177–186; SCHAPS, *Geschichte*, pp. 178–180. Cf. also SCHNEIDER, Messen, Banken und Börsen, p. 154; Herman VAN DER WEE, *The Growth of the Antwerp Market and the European Economy (14th–16th Centuries), vol. II: Interpretation*, The Hague 1963, p. 349; idem, Monetary, Credit and Banking Systems, pp. 330f. Cf. also BRÉSSARD, *Foires de Lyon*, p. 281: "L'escompte fut pratiqué d'une manière courante à Lyon entre banquiers et marchands."

133 VAN DER WEE, Monetary, Credit and Banking Systems, p. 331.

134 Stephen QUINN, Gold, Silver, and the Glorious Revolution: Arbitrage between Bills of Exchange and Bullion, in *Economic History Review* 49/3 (1996), pp. 473–490, esp. p. 474.

ment transactions had gained a dynamic in Western and Central Europe since the close of the 17th century that flourished during the 18th century without any principal innovations. The mature mechanisms of cashless payments helped to raise the number of completed transactions, to accelerate their completion and to extend the range of the participants. A large number of merchants became merchant bankers not only in the big financial centres, but also in smaller country towns. This was the basis for the emergence of private bankers, finding its first climax, for example, in the Haute Banque Parisienne,[135] because merchant bankers specialized in banking when they owned a sufficient amount of capital. In the banking business they could definitely realize faster capital turnover than in commodity trading, which was of a quite long-drawn-out nature. Thus private banks developed from the former merchant-banking houses. Up to the mid-18th century as many as 30 private banks emerged in London alone and up to the early 19th century there were another 40.[136]

The individual element within the expansion of cashless payment transactions can be traced in the example of the, compared to international standards rather small, trading and banking house Amman in the little town Schaffhausen in Switzerland. The present exchange copy books give proof of more than 1,000 issuers from more than 320 cities, market towns and larger villages, situated in different parts of Western and Central Europe, in a few cases also in Southern Europe and Russia as issuing places for those bills of exchange that passed through the trading and banking house at one point or another. Generally, these bills of exchange reached Amman through a series of endorsements – sometimes up to eleven. The participants of these bill transactions often included – apart from various endorsers – only three parties: the issuer, the drawee and, as the third party, the banker financing the deal as remitter and presenter at the same time, as was often common in earlier centuries. Thus, if Amman bought commodities from a business partner at the French Atlantic Coast, the partner drew a bill of exchange on him, then Parisian bankers of Swiss origin, predominantly Tourton & Baur, Thellusson, Necker & C[ie] and Sellont & C[ie], acted as remitters and at the same time as presenters of the bill, which meant that they took up the bill of exchange from the merchant who sold the commodities at the Atlantic Coast and received their money, or a corresponding value, as another bill of exchange for example from Amman. Since this type of transactions in commodities was thus financed by Parisian bankers, and granted Amman at least a short-term credit in this way, Amman only seldom received bills of exchange sent to him directly by the supplier of the goods.[137] There are many examples from other parts of Europe giving proof of this development.[138]

---

135 Cf. Herbert LÜTHY, *La Banque protestante en France de la révocation de l'Édit de Nantes à la Révolution, t. II: De la banque aux finances (1730–1794)*, Paris 1961.

136 Michael NORTH, *Das Geld und seine Geschichte. Vom Mittelalter bis zur Gegenwart*, München 1994, p. 139.

137 Markus A. DENZEL, Die Geschäftsbeziehungen des Schaffhauser Handels- und Bankhauses Amman 1748–1779. Ein mikroökonomisches Fallbeispiel, in *Vierteljahrschrift für Sozial- und Wirtschaftsgeschichte* 89, 2002, pp. 1–40; idem, Geldwesen und Zahlungsverkehr in regionalen und internationalen Zusammenhängen in der Alten Schweiz. Das Fallbeispiel des Schaffhauser Kaufmann-Bankiers Amman (um 1750–1781), in Pascal LADNER / Gabriel IMBODEN (eds.), *Alpenländischer Kapitalismus in vorindustrieller Zeit. Vorträge des siebenten internationalen Symposiums zur Geschichte des Alpenraums*, Brig 2004, pp. 55–99.

There appeared an essential innovation that made cashless payment even safer for these merchant bankers: the acceptance credit developing into a new form of short-term international credits in Amsterdam since the end of the 17th century. By accepting a bill of exchange drawn on him, a banker could then assume future payment obligations of a debtor, mostly an importer, who had settled his obligations with another exporter using a bill of exchange. The importer then asked his bank to declare that it honoured the bill on its due date, which it was not obliged to do if the importer did not have a sufficient amount of money deposited at the bank. This bank acceptance provided security for the issuer or remitter of the bill as well as ensuring that the exporter would receive their money. Moreover, the bill could be discounted much more easily as the discounting bank basically took over the role of the creditor from the exporter by guaranteeing the cashing of the bill of exchange. For a long time during the 18th century, the financial market of Amsterdam financed not only Dutch foreign trade on the basis of acceptance credits but also often the trade of other Northwest European cities (especially London, Hamburg and Bordeaux) and of other locations of the Baltic Sea area.[139] During the 19th century the acceptance credit gained outstanding importance:

> For as foreign trade grew and as the bill of exchange became its modal means of payment, the London discount market acquired a new function, that of accepting bills on behalf of clients, often external to the British Isles. Certain of the London private banks came to accept for a commission bills on behalf of clients. … When such a bill fell due for payment it would be paid by the accepting house, which in turn was reimbursed by its client. This acceptance business, carried on mainly by a group of the London merchant banks, became an integral part of the London discount market and 'the bill on London' a reputable form of payment in international trade.[140]

This can be put down to the fact that invoices for international and especially intercontinental trade were settled quite regularly in pounds sterling, even if other European merchants were participating in the deal. This process went so far that it was even used when two German companies traded with each other. When converting a price from pounds sterling into mark, in Hamburg an exchange rate was used that

---

138 E.g. Kurt SAMUELSSON, International Payments and Credit Movements by the Swedish Merchant-Houses, 1730–1815, *Scandinavian Economic History Review* 3 (1955), pp. 163–202; Vasilij V. DOROŠENKO / Elisabeth HARDER-GERSDORFF, Ost-Westhandel und Wechselgeschäfte zwischen Riga und westlichen Handelsplätzen: Lübeck, Hamburg, Bremen und Amsterdam (1758/59), *Zeitschrift des Vereins für Lübeckische Geschichte und Altertumskunde* 62 (1982), pp. 120–147; Elisabeth HARDER-GERSDORFF, Zwischen Riga und Amsterdam: die Geschäfte des Herman Fromhold mit Frederik Beltgens & Comp., 1783–1785, in *The Interactions of Amsterdam and Antwerp with the Baltic Region, 1400–1800. De Nederlanden en het Oostzeegebied, 1400–1800. Papers presented at the 3rd International Conference of the Association Internationale d'Histoire des Mers Nordiques de l'Europe (Utrecht 1982)*, Leiden 1983, pp. 171–180; eadem, Aus Rigaer Handlungsbüchern (1783–1785): Geld, Währung und Wechseltechnik im Ost-West-Geschäft der frühen Neuzeit, in Eckart SCHREMMER (ed.), *Geld- und Währung vom 16. Jahrhundert bis zur Gegenwart. Referate der 14. Arbeitstagung der Gesellschaft für Sozial- und Wirtschaftsgeschichte vom 9. bis 13. April 1991 in Dortmund*, Stuttgart 1993, pp. 105–120; eadem, *Zwischen Rubel und Reichstaler. Soziales Bezugsfeld und geographische Reichweite des Revaler Wechselmarktes (1762–1800)*, Lüneburg 2000; Bertil ANDERSSON, Early History of Banking in Gothenburg Discount House Operations 1783–1818, *Scandinavian Economic History Review* 31 (1983), pp. 50–67.

139 Helma HOUTMAN-DE SMEDT, Art. "Akzeptkredit", in NORTH (ed.), *Von Aktie bis Zoll*, pp. 20f.

140 W.M. SCAMMEL, The London Discount Market: The Later 19th Century, in Ranald C. MICHIE (ed.), *The Development of London as a Financial Centre, vol. 2: 1850–1914*, London – New York 2000, pp. 151–177, esp. p. 154.

was fixed half a penny above the lowest level fixed at the Hamburg stock exchange for bills on London. Similar transactions in other European currencies were normally only settled, if they were pure commission business.[141]

The growing speed in transacting cashless payments is reflected both in the shortened time of turnover of bills of exchange noted with the current prices and in the acceptance of a shorter term as a second listing next to the traditional (longer) term. Whereas the usance of bills of exchange often depended on the time needed for transporting the bill – the usance of a bill of exchange from Amsterdam on Danzig being, for example, 40 days, on Königsberg 41 days – or a certain usance had become common over generations of merchants, the quotation for bills on sight became more frequent and more important during the 18th century. Thus Amsterdam introduced an at-sight quotation on London around the turn of the 17th to the 18th century and one on Paris in 1721. Starting in 1720, London differentiated within its quotations on Amsterdam between at-sight bills and longer-running bills (2 or 2½ months); an additional quotation for sight bills on Paris was introduced in 1721. In Hamburg an additional quotation for bills at short sight was introduced only for bills on Amsterdam, the most important partner for bills of exchange. The same was done for bills on London only in 1801, when the English metropolis surpassed the Dutch in importance from the perspective of Hamburg.[142] In the 18th century German bills of exchange with a term of fewer than eight days were called bills at short sight, whereas bills at long sight had a term that surpassed the usual usance of a bill market, meaning that they ran 'over uso'.[143]

In return, some usances of bills of exchange were prolonged in contemporary exchange rate currents, extending the credit term. This process could be interpreted as a growth of trust in the respective business partner. Hamburg, for example, lengthened its term for bills of exchange on Vienna from a four-week dato to a six-week dato; the one for bills on Prague was also extended from a four-week dato to a six-week dato about ten years later. In 1775/76 the usance for bills on Iberian cities (Madrid, Cádiz, Lisbon) was extended from a two-month dato to three-month dato. In return, the usance for bills on Hamburg was lengthed in Vienna in 1770 from two weeks after sight to a six-week dato, the one for bills on London from two weeks after sight to a two-month dato.[144] These examples demonstrate that the traffic and transport conditions had improved, allowing calculation with fixed dates after issuing bills of exchange and avoiding trusting in a certain term after sight – whenever this had supposedly occurred.

The listed usances of the exchange rate currents continued to change in the two noted tendencies during the 19th century. Hamburg is an example: the Hamburg exchange rate quotations listed Paris, Bordeaux, Saint Petersburg, London, Amsterdam and Antwerp with a two-month term far into the 19th century; only the Iberian places were listed with three months since 1775/76. In 1844 the commerce deputation asked the Senate to lengthen the term for bills of exchange to three months, but

---

141 Wilhelm FRIEDRICH, Die Technik des Zahlungs-Verkehrs im Export mit China, *Zeitschrift für handelswissenschaftliche Forschung* 4 (1910), pp. 340–350, esp. pp. 341, 346.

142 *HStD XII*, passim.

143 Cf. ZELLFELDER, Glossar, p. 206.

144 *HStD XII*, passim; *WdW VI*, S. 210–215; *WdW I/III*, pp. 309–326.

it disagreed about the merchants' interest in conceding longer-term credits to their foreign business partners. It was only when the commerce deputation stated that their request reflected the given situation that the Senate granted it partially in 1846. The terms for bills of exchange for most of the named places were lengthened, although those for Amsterdam and Antwerp had to be kept until 1856 and those for Germany and Austria until 1869, because small merchant houses, especially those trading mainly within Central Europe, had, by contrast, lengthened their main trading partners' credits.[145] The understanding of 'at short sight' and 'at long sight' changed fundamentally in Germany during the 19th century: in around 1859 one considered a usance of mostly two to three weeks (usually 14 days after sight) as 'at short sight'; a bill with a longer term was 'at long sight'.[146]

3.4 The Transfer of the European Techniques of Cashless Payment Overseas (16th to 19th Century)

With the help of endorsement and discount, the bill of exchange had become a popular negotiable paper developing into 'international money'.[147] But the use of the bill was limited: it remained a financing instrument of European merchants, as Raymond de Roover had already stressed for the 16th century: "la lettre de change au XVIᵉ siècle ne circulait au-delà des limites de la Chrétienté latine."[148]

In the course of European expansion, however, the operating range of European merchants also grew regarding cashless payments: they brought their instruments and techniques into the non-European areas in which they were economically interested and carried out their exchange transactions there and from there with Europe (almost) as fast as if they were in Europe. This holds especially for the neo-European colonies, as John J. McCusker described it for the British colonies in North America: "In negotiating bills on the mother country, colonists followed the forms and procedures common to European Exchange. Bills were drawn, presented, and protested in much the same way between Philadelphia and London as between Amsterdam – or, better, Dublin – and London."[149] The same holds for Canada, Australia, New Zealand, the numerous colonies in the Caribbean and later also for Africa. Often European remitters served as creditors for the whole transaction, but there are also many examples of the reversed situation, i.e. when an overseas merchant banker granted a European merchant a credit, as often happened in trading tobacco from Maryland to London, for example: "The ability of the London importer to pay the Baltimore exporter in a bill of exchange depended … on the willingness of the Baltimore merchant banker, who had to accept the bill, to extend credit to the London merchant banker."[150] Here the bill of exchange could also serve only as a mere sour-

---

145 BAASCH, Entwicklungsgeschichte, p. 10.
146 Cf. ZELLFELDER, Glossar, p. 206.
147 Markus A. DENZEL / Oskar SCHWARZER, Art. "Wechsel", in NORTH (ed.), *Von Aktie bis Zoll*, pp. 416f., esp. p. 416.
148 DE ROOVER, *Lettre de change*, p. 65.
149 McCUSKER, *Money and Exchange*, p. 120.
150 NEAL, The Finance of Business, p. 159.

ce of credit for the European (!) merchant banker; so "the bill of exchange became the major source of credit for British merchants engaged in the growing trade with the North American colonies".[151]

In contrast to North America, in Latin America the bill of exchange did not similarly develop into a means of payment, for it was unnecessary. Until the end of the colonial era, payments from the Spanish colonies as well as from Brazil to Europe could be made by transferring precious metals. Moreover, the natives' European suppliers requested immediate payment for their delivered goods. Bills of exchange and *préstamos marítimos* served only to a very limited extent for financing colonial trade, especially between Spanish merchants, ship owners, factors and the Casa da Contratación.[152] A Spanish merchant banker could draw a bill of exchange on an American merchant, who promised to pay the amount to a local factor or agent of the European issuer. But such exchange transactions were – due to the great distance and risk – connected with an unusually high premium, so that they occurred only rarely.[153] Within the Spanish American colonial empire, transactions of cashless payments were often made with the help of so-called *libranzas*, which could be endorsed and thus traded; their acceptance was limited to the American market, though, normally only to a single vice-kingdom.[154]

The bill of exchange reached Asia primarily via the Northwest European East India companies, which used this instrument for transactions both among their posts in the area of the Indian Ocean and, on the other hand to Europe. Although it was possible in the Portuguese Estado da India to draw money *a câmbio* if needed at the beginning of the 17th century, this was not a 'classic' bill of exchange transaction, but rather 'emprunts contractés', contractually secured lending of money with a fixed interest rate, which was put in the form of a bill of exchange.[155] These kinds of 'bills' were probably nothing else but interest-bearing promissory notes with a questionable negiotiability, that served (alone?) for acquiring money.

---

151 Ibid., p. 160.

152 Antonio-Miguel BERNAL, *La financiación de la Carrera de Indias (1492–1824). Dinero y crédito en el comercio colonial español con América*, Sevilla – Madrid 1992, especially capítulo I; idem, Crédito, financiación y beneficio en el comercio colonial español a través de los cambios y préstamos marítimos (ss XVI–XVII), in José CASAS PARDO (ed.), *Economic Effects of the European Expansion, 1492–1824*, Stuttgart 1992, pp. 39–76; Enrique OTTE, Letras de cambio de América, *Moneda y credito* 145 (1978), pp. 57–66; idem, Träger und Formen der wirtschaftlichen Erschließung Lateinamerikas im 16. Jahrhundert, *Jahrbuch für Geschichte von Staat, Wirtschaft und Gesellschaft Lateinamerikas* 4 (1967), pp. 226–266, esp. pp. 245f.

153 According to Thomás DE MERCADO the following courses were quoted in Seville in around 1570 for 100 pesos: on Santo Domingo 111 pesos, on México 118 pesos, on Panama 118 pesos; on Peru 133 pesos and on Chile 154 pesos; Thomás DE MERCADO, *Summa de tratos, y contrados*, Sevilla 1571, part 2, fol. 69[v] (cited from MCCUSKER, *Money and Exchange*, p. 299 note 135); André-E. SAYOUS, Les changes de l'Espagne sur l'Amérique au XVIe siècle, *Revue d'économie politique* 41 (1927), pp. 1417–1443.

154 Guillermo CÉSPEDES DEL CASTILLO, *América Hispánica (1492–1898)*, Barcelona 1983, p. 155; Hans POHL, *Die Wirtschaft Hispanoamerikas in der Kolonialzeit (1500–1800)*, Stuttgart 1996, p. 205f.; Murdo J. MACLEOD, Aspects of the Internal Economy of Colonial Spanish America: Labour; Taxation; Distribution and Exchange, in Leslie BETHELL (ed.), *The Cambridge History of Latin America, vol. II: Colonial Latin America*, Cambridge et al. 1984, pp. 219–264, esp. pp. 262–264. On Mexico in the ending colonial era, cf. D.A. BRADING, *Miners and Merchants in Bourbon Mexico 1763–1810*, Cambridge 1971, pp. 100–102.

155 Vitorino MAGALHÃES-GODINHO, *L'économie de l'empire portugais au XVe et XVIe siècles*, Paris 1969, p. 649.

As the opportunity remained limited for Europeans to draw a credit at the – otherwise highly developed – Asian financial markets, the Dutch Vereenigte Oostindische Compagnie (VOC) and the English East India Company (EIC) turned to other sources of credit: the companies started to issue money orders and bills of exchange in Asia that were payable by the companies' responsible offices in Europe:[156]

Figure 7: *Assignatië* Transaction between Asia and Europe[157].

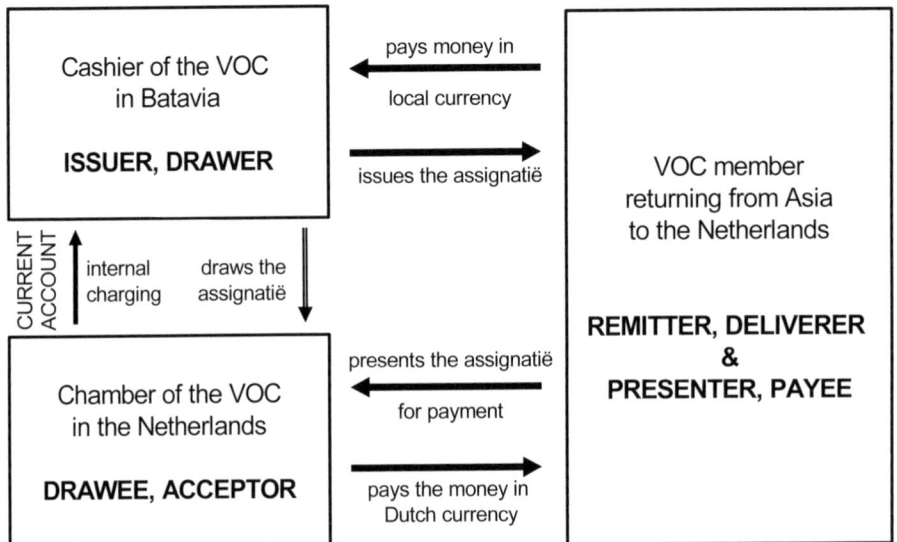

Thus the VOC had, since 1620, provided its members with the opportunity to deposit their money with an authorized cashier[158] of the VOC before returning to the Netherlands from Asia. The cashier would issue them a so-called *assignatië* over the deposited value, which an office in the Netherlands would then cash. This *assignatië* can be interpreted as a sort of three-person bill of exchange considering that in this case the function of the remitter and the presenter has merged in the person of the VOC member, who deposited his cash in Batavia, i.e. the member bought a bill of exchange and presented it in the Netherlands to reclaim his money. In opposition to bills of exchange, the VOC agency in the Netherlands paid interest on the *assignatië* amounting in general to 4% between 1664 and 1735.[159] From this point of view the

---

156 K[irti] N. CHAUDHURI, *The Trading World of Asia and the English East India Company 1660–1760*, Cambridge et al. 1978, p. 165.

157 Cf. Markus A. DENZEL, Zur Finanzierung des europäischen Asienhandels in der Frühen Neuzeit: Vom Zahlungsausgleich im Gewürzhandel zum bargeldlosen Zahlungsverkehr, in idem (ed.), *Gewürze in der Frühen Neuzeit: Produktion, Handel und Konsum. Beiträge zum 2. Ernährungshistorischen Kolloquium im Landkreis Kulmbach 1999*, St Katharinen 1999, pp. 37–69, esp. p. 54.

158 Until the mid-18th century only the general government in Batavia and the governments and agencies in Ceylon and at the Cape of Good Hope, later also those in Bengal, Surat, and on the Coromandel Coast functioned as offices for the issuing of *assignatiës*.

transaction was more a kind of deposit banking with different locations of depositing and reclaiming. In addition, the whole transaction was settled within the company itself and bears a resemblance to the use of the *letteras di pagamento* within Italian companies of the 13th and 14th centuries. Thus it is not surprising that contemporary directors of the VOC spoke rather of '*assignatië*' than of '*wissel*'.[160]

Indications for transactions of cashless payments between different agencies of the EIC in Bengal can also be found, with bills of exchange and letters of credit, from 1651. In order to transfer money to Europe, the EIC members used 'bills of exchange', which probably bore a high similarity to the VOC's *assignatië*.[161] But next to the three-person bills of exchange one can also find bills with four participating parties, as the first recorded bill of exchange transaction from Canton to London proves.[162] Since the 1760s the importance of the bills of exchange issued by the EIC, the so-called Company's bills, grew for settling payments between China on the one hand and London or India on the other. Between 1773 and 1780/84 it was even possible for the European East India companies to use their local branches for a kind of 're-exchange' from Europe to Calcutta due to a growing accumulation of capital. The directors of the VOC bought bills of exchange from English–Dutch bank houses, which they drew on their agency in Calcutta. The agents of the VOC in Bengal could then cash these bills of exchange on sight.[163] The other East India companies, of course, participated in the profit-bearing transactions of cashless payment with other local companies in the Indian Ocean area and with Europe.[164] Thus the money order and bill of exchange became an often and regularly used instrument for cash-

---

159 Om PRAKASH, Financing the European Trade with Asia in the Early Modern Period: Dutch Initiatives and Innovations, *Journal of European Economic History* 27 (1998), pp. 331–356, esp. pp. 337f.; Femme S. GAASTRA, The Exports of Precious Metal from Europe to Asia by the Dutch East India Company, 1602–1795, in John F. RICHARDS (ed.), *Precious Metals in the Later Medieval and Early Modern Worlds*, Durham (NC) 1983, pp. 447–475, esp. p. 461; idem, Private Money for Company Trade. The Role of the Bills of Exchange in Financing the Return Cargoes of the VOC, *Itinerario. European Journal of Overseas History* 18 (1994), pp. 65–76, esp. pp. 66–68; idem, De Vereenigde Oost-Indische Compagnie in de zeventiende en achttiende eeuw: de groei van een bedrijf. Geld tegen goederen. Een structurele verandering in het Nederlands-Aziatisch handelsverkeer, *Bijdragen en mededelingen betreffende de geschiedenis der Nederlanden* 91 (1976), pp. 249–272, esp. pp. 256–260.

160 Idem, Die Vereinigte Ostindische Compagnie der Niederlande – Ein Abriß ihrer Geschichte, in Eberhard SCHMITT / Thomas SCHLEICH / Thomas BECK (eds.), *Kaufleute als Kolonialherren: Die Handelswelt der Niederländer vom Kap der Guten Hoffnung bis Nagasaki 1600–1800*, Bamberg 1988, pp. 1–89, esp. p. 54. Cf. also Arent POL, Tot gerieff van India. Geldexport door de VOC en de muntproduktie in Nederland, 1720–1740, *Jaarboek voor munt- en penningkunde* 72 (1985), pp. 65–195, esp. p. 90.

161 Sus[h]il CHAUDHURI, *Trade and Commercial Organization in Bengal 1650–1720. With Special Reference to the English East India Company*, Calcutta 1975, pp. 102, 106, 118–120, 122.

162 Source: Hosea Ballou MORSE, *The Chronicles of the East India Company Trading to China 1635–1834*, Oxford 1926, vol. V, p. 102; reprinted in Louis DERMIGNY, *La Chine et l'Occident. Le commerce à Canton au XVIII° siècle 1719–1833*, Paris 1964, T. II, p. 762 note 2.

163 PRAKASH, Financing the European Trade, pp. 339f.; GAASTRA, Private Money, p. 73. According to PRAKASH, the fourth Dutch and English War prevented any further transactions from 1870 on; according to GAASTRA, the financial downfall of the VOC in 1784 was responsible for the drastic decline of such business transactions covering a total of nearly 12.8 million guilder between 1773 and 1785.

164 For the Danish *Asiatisk Kompagni*, for example, see Martin KRIEGER, *Kaufleute, Seeräuber und Diplomaten. Der dänische Handel auf dem Indischen Ozean (1620–1868)*, Köln – Weimar – Wien 1998, pp. 137f., 153f., 165, 167, 195.

less payment because it was used first by the East India companies and later more or less widely spread by private European businessmen or interlopers in the Asian trade. Exchange transactions in Asian–European or internal Asian payments served primarily as a direct source of liquidity: "The bills represented only a mechanism facilitating the transfer of purchasing power from Europe to Asia."[165] In general, bills of exchange were not used for commercial credit transactions,[166] as commodities were normally not paid for directly with a bill of exchange.[167] One would rather acquire cash with the help of a bill, using it to pay for the bought goods since local producers and intermediaries depended on receiving precious metal. One can state for the 19th century that "bills of exchange were known in Asia, but were not as commonly used in European–Asian trade as in European–American trade."[168]

Figure 8: Exchange Transaction between Overseas and Europe[169].

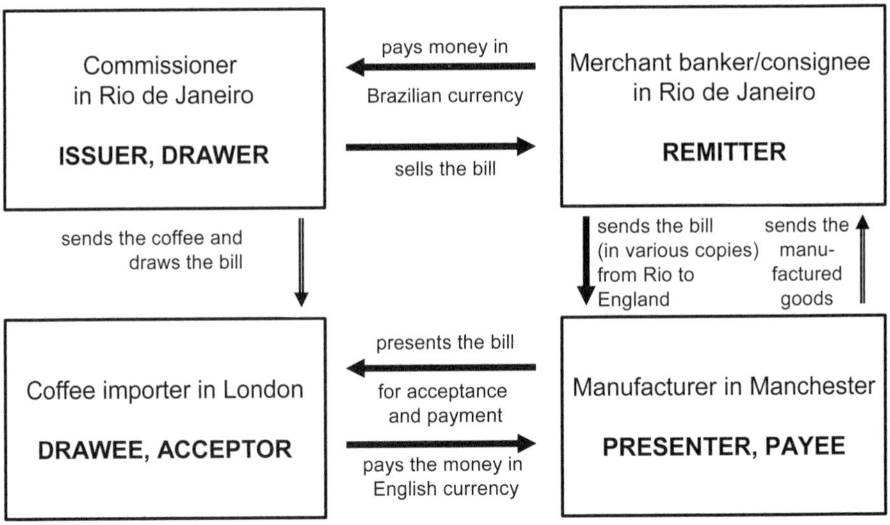

A vivid example of an exchange transaction between overseas and Europe in the first half of the 19th century is given by Horace Emile Say in his *Histoire des relations commerciales entre la France et le Brésil* from 1839.[170] A coffee importer in London asked a commissioner in Rio de Janeiro to send him a certain amount of

---

165 PRAKASH, Financing the European Trade, p. 341.

166 If there was, for example, a commercial credit transaction of a private agency, the above description of participants in the four-person bill of exchange would have been different. In this case the EIC occupied the position of the remitter and presenter attempting the cashless transfer of money from India or China to Europe and, at the same time, financing the private merchants' overseas trade.

167 KRIEGER, *Kaufleute*, S. 154.

168 Jacob M. PRICE, Transaction Costs: A Note on Merchant Credit and the Organization of Private Trade, in James D. TRACY (ed.), *The Political Economy of Merchant Empires*, Cambridge 1991, pp. 276–297, esp. p. 288.

169 Cf. DENZEL, Finanzplätze, Wechselkurse und Währungsverhältnisse in Lateinamerika, p. 3.

coffee and instructed him to draw a bill of exchange over the respective debt on his name (drawee). The commissioner would then issue the bill of exchange (drawer) and send the coffee and the original copy of the bill, the so-called *prima* or *tratte*, to London; the second copy of the bill of exchange, the *secunda* or *rimesse*, was sold in Rio de Janeiro after discounting to another merchant (remitter), who was in business relationship with England. This person could be a consignee who received factory goods from Manchester and had to pay for them. Instead of paying in cash, i.e. sending cash to Manchester, the consignee bought the *rimesse* from the coffee commissioner with the sales revenues or accredited his account with the agreed amount. Now the commissioner had cash (or a credit) at his disposal for new business operations. The buyer of the bill sent the *rimesse* to the producer in Manchester, who then presented the bill after its due date to the coffee importer in London. The last person, the drawer (acceptor), accepted the bill of exchange and paid the producer the amount over which the bill was issued in cash or he accredited his account with the respective amount. The money needed for cashing the exchange claim or accrediting the account had been earned in the meantime by selling the coffee. Thus all mutual obligations and claims could be settled.

The advantages of the exchange transaction have not changed since the Middle Ages: first, the business offered the opportunity to effect payments without the risky and expensive sending of precious metals (insurance costs, for example). If a bill of exchange was lost during its transportation, there were always other existing copies (*tertia, quarta*) that could document the mutual claims. Second, two credit deals took place: the European importer was not forced to pay instantly for the goods received. Instead of this, he had time to earn the money by selling the goods and to pay the bill of exchange; on the other hand, the overseas consignee also did not pay for the goods received from Manchester until the agreed term. Third, the respective recipient of the money was paid in his currency, i.e. the one he needed for new business operations in his country, pounds sterling in England, for instance, or milreis in Brazil. This was of great interest, especially for English exporters, because they used to revert to a compensation deal with overseas products in order to receive their money if they were not paid in sterling, bearing unpredictable risks for the desired revenues. Whether payments for goods sent overseas were really effected with bills of exchange (*rimesse*) or via the flow of commodities depended on the discretion of the European trading house and on the respective market situation.[171] Finally, the issuer of the bill of exchange would receive his money immediately by selling the *rimesse* without having to wait for payments from London, which would not have been effected until the due date of the bill. In this case the issuer had liquidity at his

---

170 SAY, *Histoire des relations commerciales*, pp. 101–104. This analysis of Say's example can also be found in Jürgen SCHNEIDER, *Handel und Unternehmer im französischen Brasiliengeschäft 1815–1848. Versuch einer quantitativen Strukturanalyse*, Köln – Wien 1975, p. 67. On cashless payment between Europe and overseas, its instruments and modalities, cf. Rolf WALTER, Wechsel, Pari, Kurs und ihre Bedeutung für das Überseegeschäft des 19. Jahrhunderts, *Scripta mercaturae* 16/1 (1982), pp. 55–78.

171 Cf. Rolf WALTER, Die nordwesteuropäische Wirtschaft in mikroökonomischer Perspektive: Das Beispiel Hasenclever, in Michael NORTH (ed.), *Nordwesteuropa in der Weltwirtschaft 1750–1950 / Northwestern Europe in the World Economy 1750–1950*, Stuttgart 1993, pp. 291–307, esp. pp. 296–304.

disposal that he could use for new business operations. This was a decisive factor for an overseas exporter: "the foreign exporter, who has consigned or sold produce to us, prefers to *draw* on London rather than have us remit. In so doing he finds a double advantage: – the advantage, namely, of getting his money at once by selling the bill, and the advantage of securing the best price for it by negotiating it himself. The foreign importer, too, who has to pay for the goods he has bought, would rather do so, by *remitting* to London than by allowing us to draw upon him."[172]

This resulted in the noteworthy fact that all overseas trading places quoted London, but the reverse rates on London were exceptionally quoted until World War I, as "the exchanges between England and other countries are controlled from the side, and ... we in London have practically neither part nor say in the matter. The rate of exchange, for example, between England and the United States, is fixed in New York; between England and Brazil, in Rio; ... There may be exceptions, of which the Indian Exchange is the most notable, but that is the general rule."[173] Of course this statement disregards that the credit system connected with cashless payment transactions was often much more difficult as, e.g., Stanley Champman described it for the transatlantic trade between the USA and Great Britain during the 1830s.[174]

3.5 From the Bill of Exchange to the Telegraphic Transfer and to the Cheque (from about 1850 to 1914)

"With the dramatic improvement in world communications, accompanied by the growth in numbers and expertise of financial intermediaries and institutions, a new era was coming into being after the mid-nineteenth century."[175] Although the 19th century's new means of transportation – steamboat and railroad – had reduced the time for the transportation of bills of exchange, the decisive progress regarding cashless payments did not set in until the appearance of the telegraph: the electronic telegraph made telegraphic money orders or transfers possible, i.e. telegraphic banking transactions, allowing depositing and cashing on the very same day between remote regions of the world.[176] Both developments taken together led not only to a harmonization of the usances of cashless payments everywhere but also to a significant shortening of the usances of intercontinental payments. The first result holds especially for Europe, where long-term bills of exchange were listed in general at 30

---

172 CLARE, The A.B.C. of the Foreign Exchanges, pp. 73–84, esp. p. 78.

173 Ibid., p. 79.

174 Stanley C. CHAPMAN, *The Rise of Merchant Banking*, London – Boston – Sydney ²1985, p. 109.

175 R.C. MITCHIE, *The London and New York Stock Exchanges 1850–1914*, London et al. 1987, p. 154.

176 Cf. Jorma AHVENAINEN, *The Far Eastern Telegraphs. The History of Telegraphic Communications between the Far East, Europe and America before the First World War*, Helsinki 1981; idem, Telegraphs, Trade and Policy. The Role of the International Telegraphs in the Years 1870–1914, in Wolfram FISCHER / R. Marvin McINNIS / Jürgen SCHNEIDER (eds.), *The Emergence of a World Economy 1500–1914. Papers of the IX International Congress of Economic History, 2 parts*, Stuttgart 1986, part II, pp. 505–518; idem, The Role of Telegraphs in the 19th Century Revolution of Communications, in Michael NORTH (ed.), *Kommunikationsrevolutionen. Die neuen Medien des 16. und 19. Jahrhunderts*, Köln – Weimar – Wien 1995, pp. 73–80; Robert BOYCE, *Submarine Cables as a Factor in Britain's Ascendancy as a World Power, 1850–1914*, in ibid., pp. 81–99.

or at 90 days towards the end of the 19th century.[177] The second applies to the traffic between India and Great Britain after the opening of the Suez Canal in November 1869. The result was a reduction of the standard usance of six months' sight to four months' sight or six months' dato since the beginning of the 1870s, certainly by the 1880s. Moreover, the common usance between the USA and Great Britain of 60 days' sight was reduced to ten days' sight in 1876 after the installation of the third overseas cable; after the early 1880s sight drafts became predominant.[178] Exchange rates for telegraphic transfers were set up in important overseas places, for example, from Calcutta and Shanghai on London from 1878, from New York from 1879, from Hongkong from 1880, from Bombay from 1883, from Yokohama from 1894 and from Australia from 1906.[179] In addition:

> Even as early as 1877 the *Economist* drew attention to the fact that telegraphic transfers and international coupons were replacing the overseas bill of exchange as a means of payment. That the overseas bill of exchange was able to rise to predominance from 1860 and remain the important staple of the discount market down to the interwar years; that, even in face of speedier forms of payment, the bill on London and those who administered it enjoyed in the period 1870–1914 their golden age, was partly due to the enormous growth in the volume of trade in that period which served to obscure longer-term influences, but no doubt also to the basic utility, safety and convenience inherent in this process of payment for those who engaged in foreign trade.[180]

It was especially the installation of a special category of 'telegraphic transfer' or 'cable transfer' in the New York exchange rate currents on London from December 1879, on Paris, Amsterdam and the German Empire from the beginning of 1909 that was the economic consequence from the growing transatlantic trade and the resulting – mostly cashless – payments between the USA and Europe. In the era of the telegraph, worldwide reactions to changing rates on the exchange markets were a matter only of hours and minutes. "By about 1880, the principal financial centers of the world were in telegraphic contact and thereafter the system was refined and extended, with both transmission times and costs falling substantially. By 1908, on the London–New York route, a telegram could be sent, and a reply to it received, within 2.5 minutes. Furthermore, with the introduction of the London–Paris telephone in 1891, the ultimate in instantaneous and continuous contact was achieved."[181] The faster and more reliable communication became, the shorter became the usual usances in the system of cashless payment transactions.

Regarding the exchange rate currents of overseas places, this development led to an enlargement of the number of rates listed on European exchange partners by listing sometimes as many as six different usances. Around the turn of the 20th century Sydney had listed rates on London for 30, 60, 90 and 120 days after sight in addition to quotations for sight bills and telegraphic transfers. In around 1900, Hong Kong listed quotations on London for six and four months as well as for 30 days after sight

---

177 Cf. ZELLFELDER, Glossar, p. 206.
178 Shizuya NISHIMURA, *The Decline of Inland Bills of Exchange in the London Money Market 1855–1913*, Cambridge 1971, p. 39; L.E. DAVIS / J.R.T. HUGHES, A Dollar-Sterling Exchange, 1803–1895, *Economic History Review* sec. ser. 13 (1960/61), pp. 52–78, esp. p. 59.
179 *WdW I/I*, pp. 334f., 342, 349, 368; *WdW IV*, pp. 107f., 179, 239f., 254f., 329.
180 SCAMMEL, The London Discount Market, p. 155.
181 Ranald C. MICHIE, The Invisible Stabliser: Asset Arbitrage and the International Monetary System since 1700, *Financial History Review* 15 (1998), pp. 5–26, esp. p. 14.

and also for sight bills and telegraphic transfers.[182] These examples could easily be continued. Table 1 shows typical payment locations within intercontinental trade during the years prior to World War I.

Table 1: Typical Payment Locations within Intercontinental Trade, c. 1910[183]

British India, Western and Eastern Africa, Australia	30, 60, 90, 120 days
Netherlands India, Straits Settlements	30, 60, 90, 120 days up to 6 months
South Africa	60, 90, 120 days up to 6 months
China, Japan	3 months, but 2, 4 and 6 months as well
Northern Africa, Levant	4 to 9 months
Central America, West Indies	4, 6 to 9 months
South America	3, 4, 6, 9, 12 months, but especially 3 and 6 months

But, "where bills were used [only] as instruments of financing foreign trade, there may not have been such a drastic reduction of usance as from sixty days to nil (cable transfers)."[184] Such bills of exchange had served in principle

> to settle debts between financial markets without the need to continually transport precious metals. Unfortunately, not all trade led to the creation of bills of exchange, while there were also major imbalances in timing and location. For instance, there was a seasonal marked trend in international trade, with primary producing nations exporting at harvest time but importing throughout the year, leading to serious shortages of bills in different directions at different times of the year. The solution to this was the finance bill (or banker's draft or cheque), through which credit was extended, at a cost, until payment could be made.[185]

In Great Britain, in particular, a cheque was interpreted during great parts of the 19th century as a bill of exchange drawn on a bank and payable at sight.[186] Generally, one may regard a cheque as a "formal bank depot order on sight", "through which the issuer instructs his bank to pay upon deliverance of the document the therein recorded amount to a third person".[187] It was not until the 17th century that the cheque as a depot order given by a private person to his bank, which is first recorded as having occurred in 14th-century Italy, became relevant in Antwerp and Amsterdam with the so-called *kassiers*, whose "written *orderbrieffes* or *assignatiës* acted as cheques. Like bills of exchange, they were endorsable and thus might pass, as means of pay-

---

182 *WdW IV*, pp. 99–108, 234–240, 323–329.

183 According to BRANDT, Kurs- und Kreditsicherung der Überseebanken, p. 363.

184 NISHIMURA, *The Decline of Inland Bills of Exchange*, pp. 39f.

185 Ibid.

186 SWOBODA [1913], p. 360; Dieter ZIEGLER, Art. "Scheck", in NORTH (ed.), *Von Aktie bis Zoll*, pp. 354f., esp. p. 353. Cf. Ernst SEYD, *Das London Bank-, Check- und Clearinghouse-System nebst Winken für seine Einführung in Deutschland*, translated into German according to the 3rd English edition by Otto SJÖSTRÖM, Leipzig 1874, pp. 17f.: "In its interior the cheque is not even a bill of exchange, but a regular money order of one person to transfer a certain amount to another, arisen through common use and valid under certain rules," but "the cheque is the same thing as a due bill of exchange, as far as it is already due when issued."

187 Ibid.

ment, from hand to hand. Their *kassierskwitantiën* (goldsmith notes), receipts to their depositors, equally became negotiable by endorsement. They could take the form of promises to (re)pay the sum deposited. Such promises became gradually payable to bearer."[188] These papers finally had their breakthrough in England and Scotland in the 18th century:

> L'usage du chèque est très-répandu dans tous les pays anglais et plus particulièrement à Londres et en Écosse. Dans ces pays, la caisse du négociant est tenue par son banquier, sur lequel il dispose par un chèque chaque fois qu'il a un payement à faire et auquel il remet les chèques qu'il a reçus en payement, de telle sorte que le chèque est, en quelques sorte, la monnaie courante du commerce. ... A Londres, le chèque est généralement présenté et recouvré le jour même, soit par le voie ordinaire, soit par une compensation entre banquiers à la *clearing house*.[189]

The London Bankers' Clearing House, dating back to 1770, was used by the clearing banks, as its members, to mutually settle bills of exchange; later cheques were also presented to them. It served at the same time as a model for the introduction of clearing or giro systems in other states:

> The giro traffic of the early Prussian Bank has been totally remodeled. Instead of the old incomplete system, a new one has been set, that does not only offer the giro customers of the Reichsbank the conveniences and commodities of the English banks, but also allows for the possibility to send and receive payments throughout the entire territory of the Reichsbank free of charge. Entire Germany has become one (sic!) giro-market on which payments between the giro customers of the Reichsbank can be settled without any costs or difficulties by merely signing the amount over from one account to another.[190]

The importance of British cheque transactions rose when the circulation of banknotes was limited by Peel's Bank Act in 1844 and thus caused a shortage of legal tender for the growing number of business transactions. At the instigation of the British banks of issue and with the help of the highly efficient clearing system, the cheque became the most important British means of business payments, surpassing even legal tender and the inland bill in this function,[191] while federal fiscal regulations – for example the high stamp tax on cheques and bills of exchange in Germany and France – hindered the spread of cheque transactions in continental Europe.[192] Moreover, the cheque's credit factor was much lower than that of the bill's, for the cheque was supposed to be cashed immediately at the place of payment. That is why the cheque did not play much of a role in international exchange rate quotations at this time – in contrast to the interwar period.[193] In 1880 cheque transactions were still

---

188 Pit DEHING / Marjolein 'T HART, Linking the Fortunes: Currency and Banking, 1550–1800, in Marjolein 'T HART / Joost JONKER / Jan Luiten VAN ZANDEN (eds.), *A Financial History of The Netherlands*, Cambridge 1997, pp. 37–63, esp. p. 43.

189 *Dictionnaire universel théorique et pratique du commerce et de la navigation, tome I: A–G*, Paris 1859, pp. 639f., esp. p. 639. On the clearing-house system, cf. SEYD, *Das London Bank-, Check- und Clearinghouse-System*, pp. 24–35.

190 *Verwaltungsbericht der Reichsbank für das Jahr 1876*, Berlin 1877, p. 6.

191 ZIEGLER, Art. "Scheck", p. 353. "The decline in the domestic bill which had become marked in the seventies continued and was intensified towards the end of the century by the rapid decline in the number of private banks. By 1914 the volume of domestic bills drawn and passing through the market was insignificant. The domestic bill which had brought the discount market into being and shaped its institutions had virtually disappeared." SCAMMEL, The London Discount Market, p. 160.

192 ZIEGLER, Art. "Scheck", p. 354.

193 Cf. *WdW II*, passim.

mostly limited to Great Britain in the form of a national money order made by a private person to a banking house with which the person had business relations. Starting in the 1890s, and especially after around 1910, cheque quotations can increasingly be found in international exchange rate currents.[194] The most important cheque quotation found so far are those from London on Paris (beginning in 1877), from Zurich on London (from 1884 onwards) and from Constantinople on London, Paris, Vienna and Berlin (1894–1911), as well as to a certain degree the Copenhagen exchange rate currents starting in 1881 (*a-vista* listings).[195]

Although the cheque as well as the sight credit gained increasing importance within domestic trade and Great Britain's industries, the bill of exchange of the London merchant banks remained essential for international capital movements.[196] Bills of exchange in London and the entire British Empire differed from one another according to the following criteria:

  – the type of bill of exchange: clean or blue bills (bills between two or more merchants) or financial bills, which were drawn on stock banks;
  – the usance: time bills (bills at longer sight) or sight bills (bills at sight);
  – the quality: banker's bills or commercial bills.[197]

Especially for overseas bill transactions of the second half of the 19th century, exchange rate currents made a difference between different bill qualities; i.e. the drawee's financial standing depended on the securities presented with the bill (insurance policies, etc.). In Asia this differentiation was made as early as the early 20th century. Particularly in intercontinental payment transactions, "the export houses ... were forced at many times to give their drawings to the banks for the handing over shipping documents, under the showing of granted credits and in general under giving all kinds of material and moral guarantees; the import houses would only accept bills of exchange on very limited terms."[198] Regarding bill transactions of the British Empire – i.e. from the different colonies to London – the exchange rate currents differentiated between Government or Treasury bills, Navy bills, mercantile or private bills as early as in the 19th century, while, in general, the exchange rate quotations became lower and lower from one type of bills to the others. Mauritius, Cape Town or West African places were quoted with differences between exchange rates of up to 3% and only sometimes higher.[199] Thus the following types of exchanges could be found at the big Asian financial centres between the late 19th and the early 20th century:[200]

  – *documents* or *documentary bills*, distinguishing between documents against payment (the so-called *d/p drafts*) and documents against acceptance (the so-

---

194 Cf. ZELLFELDER, Glossar, p. 206.

195 *WdW I/II*, pp. 27f.; *WdW I/III*, pp. 236f.; *WdW VIII*, pp. 112, 116, 119–121; *WdW XI*, pp. 29f., 43f., 53f., 62–69. On the peculiarities of the *a-vista* listing in Copenhagen, see Chapter 9.

196 NORTH, *Das Geld*, p. 162f.

197 Cf. ZELLFELDER, Glossar, pp. 198f.

198 NOBACK [1877], S. 767. On the importance of documents in international settlement of payments also cf. Oskar SCHWARZER with Markus A. DENZEL / Friedrich ZELLFELDER, Das System des internationalen Zahlungsverkehrs, in *WdW I/I*, pp. 1–34, esp. p. 4.

199 *WdW IV*, pp. 276–279; *WdW VIII*, p. 76–88.

200 BRANDT, Kurs- und Kreditsicherung der Überseebanken, p. 363; FRIEDRICH, Die Technik des Zahlungs-Verkehrs, pp. 341–343, 348.

called *d/a drafts*). In both cases the European exporter would draw a corresponding bill of exchange on the overseas importer when shipping the goods, adding the so-called 'documents', usually three ocean bills of lading, an excerpt from the shipping insurance and the bill, all in duplicate. Usually, the overseas bank in Europe paid this bill to the exporter when the goods were delivered. In the case of a d/p draft, the importer did not receive the commodities until the repayment of the money to the overseas bank's office overseas; in the case of a d/a draft, he received them on acceptance; the Indian merchants preferred the latter. Beside paying the price of the goods, the merchant had also to pay interest for the period between when the exporter had received the payment and the likely day of arrival of the corresponding amount in Europe. The exporter, however, did not get any discount;

- *clean bills* or *drafts* (i.e. finance bills), subdivided into *bank bills* and *credits* depending on whether they were drawn on overseas (exchange) banks[201] or were based on a customer credit;
- *telegraphic* or *cable transfers*.

In New York a distinction was made between clean bills on London, as between banker's and commercial bills, sometimes also between 'best' or 'prime banker's' (bills) i.e. bills drawn from overseas on the Bank of England, and 'good banker's' (bills) (from 1871 to 1880), 'first class credits' or 'prime commercial' (bills) and 'good commercial' (bills) (from 1867 to 1880) respectively. The reliability of the companies on which bills were drawn determined subdivision into the categories best/prime, good or those without any additional remark.[202] Documentary bills and cable transfers were listed as further categories.[203] The practice in Valparaiso was similar.

This development led also to an increase in the number of quotations on European exchange partners in the exchange rate currents of the overseas places, ending in the Americas in the first decade of the 20th century and in Asia with the end of World War I.

---

201 BASTER, British Exchange Banks in China, pp. 140–151. For Germany see Richard HAUSER, *Die deutschen Überseebanken*, Jena 1906; Richard ROSENDORFF, Die deutschen Banken im überseeischen Verkehr, *Schmollers Jahrbuch für Gesetzgebung, Verwaltung und Volkswirtschaft* 28 (1904), pp. 93–134; idem, Le développement des banques allemands à l'étranger, *Revue économique internationale* 1 (1906), pp. 45–105.

202 COLE, Foreign-Exchange Market, pp. 401–403.

203 For details see Chapter 14.

4. Money and Exchange:
European Currency Systems as the Dominant Monetary Systems in the International Payments System

This chapter follows a Euro-centred perspective. This is inevitable, because the countries involved in the international exchange system used almost exclusively European currencies or currencies on a European basis as a result of the political and/or economic influence of European colonial powers. Exceptions to this rule were India with the rupee, Persia with the kran and parts of China (especially Shanghai), which carried out their international cashless payments on the basis of the tael system. All other non-European countries used European (trade) coins and currency units respectively at least for their international transactions, or they followed those examples. The introductory paragraphs to the exchange rates of the respective countries contain references to local coins or currency systems in non-European countries, such as the Indian, Persian and Chinese tael system or the Japanese system before the establishment of the yen.

4.1 European Currency Systems from the Middle Ages up to c. 1870

The medieval and early modern systems of accounting and currency in Europe have their basis mainly in the early 4th-century currency system of Diocletian and Constantine, which was modified by the Carolingian currency reform of 793/94. From then on the libra or pondus was fixed at 20 solidi or 240 denari.[204] Many economically potential nuclei of medieval and early modern Europe generally used this system for accounting and tried either to adapt their own coins, minted under different designations, directly to this system or at least to relate them to it, such as France as well as England, the Netherlands, Northern Italy, parts of Southern Italy and the Christian part of Spain. In the Holy Roman Empire the libra–solidus system competed against different mark systems, representing the basic principles of the regional currency systems in Northern and Eastern Europe. Further examples of particular uses at the fringe of this European economic nucleus can be found in Southern Italy, with the ounces (*onzas*) consisting of 30 tari at 20 grani and in some parts of the Iberian Peninsula, above all in Castile, with maravedis at 10 dineros representing a survival of the Islamic era prior to the Reconquista.[205] As a result, Charlemagne's system became the basic relation for both the currencies becoming established over the centuries and the corresponding specifications differing regionally because of consistently slight variations of the pound and ounce weights.[206]

---

204 Cf. Harald WITTHÖFT, *Münzfuß, Kleingewichte, pondus Caroli und die Grundlegung des nordwesteuropäischen Maß- und Gewichtswesens in fränkischer Zeit*, Ostfildern 1984, especially pp. 38–40.

205 Markus A. DENZEL, Art. "Währungssystem", in NORTH (ed.), *Von Aktie bis Zoll*, pp. 409–411; Michael NORTH, Art. "Währung", in *Lexikon des Mittelalters*, vol. VIII, München 2002, columns 1924f.; cf. SPUFFORD, *Handbook*, p. xxii.

206 See DENZEL, Art. "Währungssystem", p. 410.

Table 2: Divisions of the Pound in the Middle Ages[207].

France	1 livre	= 20 sols (sous)	= 240 deniers
Italy	1 lira	= 20 soldi	= 240 denari
Catalonia, Aragon, Valencia	1 libra	= 20 sueldos	= 240 dineros
England	1 pound	= 20 shillings	= 240 pence
Netherlands	1 pond	= 20 shillings	= 240 groot
Holy Roman Empire	1 pfund	= 20 schillinge	= 240 pfennige

The libra–solidus system, however, lost its importance only with the introduction and the establishment of the decimal system during the 19th century (in Great Britain as late as 1971), but numerous more or less different coinages masked its recognition. Nevertheless, it remained the basis for accounting and exchange rate fixing in many parts of Western and Southern Europe, because money of account emerged together with the Carolingian reform of 793/94, since the libra was regarded as a unit of account of 20 solidi and the solidus as a unit of account of 12 denari. Although 240 denari no longer corresponded to the libra (pondus) in real weight from the 9th century, the relation 240 denari = 1 libra was kept for accounting. Since the 13th century, coins were minted that were of the same value as the previous money of account of the libra–solidus system,[208] namely at first silver grosso coins of 12 denari or 1 solidus respectively, and from the mid-13[th] century gold coins of 20 solidi or grossi or 1 libra respectively.[209] In 1252 Florence started to mint golden li[b]ra coins, the fiorino d'oro (at 3.537 grammes), followed by Genoa's genovino and Venice's ducato.[210] The first silver coin with a value of one counted pound was the lira tron minted in Venice since 1472, followed by the Tyrolean guldiner minted since 1484/86 and equal to one gulden in gold at 60 kreuzer or 240 pfennige (= denari).[211]

The most important extension of the existing systems took place during the 16th century with the gradual introduction of high-value silver coins in different European countries which should be at least initially of the same value as previous gold coins. In the Holy Roman Empire the *reichsthaler* (rixdollar) emanated from the guldiner, becoming a sort of archetype for thaler coinages in many other European countries: not only in Spain during the 15th century (the real de a ocho from 1497, called 'peso' in America), in the Netherlands during the 16th century (since 1538), in England (the crown since 1551), in Denmark and Sweden, but also in Savoy (first under the reign of Philibert II [1497–1504] but mainly since 1566), Genoa (1507), Milan (by 1551), Venice (1562), Florence (1568), in the Kingdom of Naples (1586) and in the Papal States (1588), with the different thaler coinages of the Italian states

---

207 According to BRANDT, Kurs- und Kreditsicherung der Überseebanken, p. 363.

208 Cf. SPUFFORD, *Money and Its Use*, passim.

209 Rainer METZ, Art. "Rechengeldsystem", in NORTH (ed.), *Von Aktie bis Zoll*, pp. 330–333, esp. pp. 330f.; DENZEL, *"Practica"*, p. 63.

210 R.S. LOPEZ, Back to Gold, 1252, in *Economic History Review* 9 (1956/57), pp. 219–240.

211 Named after the doge Nicolò Tron reigning in these years (1471–1473). Guido A. NEGRIOLLI, Monete venete nel Trentino e nell'Alto Adige, in *Archivio per l'Alto Adige* 33 (parte prima) (1938), pp. 653–668, esp. pp. 656–658; METZ, Art. "Rechengeldsystem", p. 331.

called tallero, ducatone (large ducat), scudo or piastra.[212] France (the Écu blanc in 1641), the Ottoman Empire (between 1687 and 1691) and the Russian Empire (the silver rouble of 100 kopecks in 1704) started to mint thaler or large silver coins only during the 17th and 18th centuries.[213]

Even though large silver coins and the numerous gold coins represented the most important means of payment for honouring debts resulting from bill transactions, monies of account were generally used to settle those transactions:

> A money of account is ... a scale, a measure. It makes possible the classification of prices and creates a continuous procedure. It is a unit of measurement for gold coin, silver, billon ... or copper; it brings them into a valid relationship with one another and itself becomes part of that relationship. ... 'Imaginary' currencies were part of everyday life across the whole of Europe. ... All prices, all accounting systems (even the most rudimentary) and all contracts – or at least almost all – were formulated in terms of an accounting unit, that is to say in a money which was 'not necessarily represented by metal currency', but which acted as a measure for the coin in circulation. ... why these apparent complications? They existed simply because they proved to be unavoidable, because they rounded off the monetary system and gave it coherence. A metal coin 'of full weight which rings true' represented so many grams of gold and silver: that is, of a commodity – bullion – of which the price varied like that of any other mechandise. Doubtless, governments always endeavoured to have a real money which corresponded to the accounting unit (which, indeed, originally had also been a real coin). But as a result of the fluctuations in the price of precious metals it was necessary to readjust constantly the intrinsic weights of this money, so as to keep the current coins in line with the money of accounts. ... As a result, the circulation soon consisted of coins which often differed considerably in weight, fineness, stamp, wear and tear, or illegal clipping (which often meant that they had to be weighted).[214]

Therefore, large parts of the exchange rates were quoted in different forms of money of account from the Middle Ages.[215] Not only those monies of account that had been established at international fairs but also those that became the basis for settling accounts in (public) banks of supra-regional importance attained special significance often reaching out beyond the quoting exchange market. In both cases the money of account served both to facilitate mutual clearings among merchants of different provenance who used to settle their accounts in different currency and money systems, and to supply the merchants' desire for safety because the establishment of a money of account as a medium of exchange dispossessed the governments to a large extent of the opportunity to undertake monetary experiments. Consequently, the development of a money of account system at a fair or within a bank meant that the respective institution was able to gain considerably more prestige, also improving its reputation among the merchants.

---

212 Konrad SCHNEIDER, Art. "Taler", in NORTH (ed.), *Von Aktie bis Zoll*, pp. 389–391; Dietrich KLOSE, Italienische Taler (Tallero, Scudo, Ducatone, Piastra), in Wolfgang HEß / Dietrich KLOSE (eds.), *Vom Taler zum Dollar 1486–1986*, München 1986, pp. 88f.; idem, Der spanische Taler (Peso), in ibid., pp. 93f.; idem, Niederländische Taler, in ibid., pp. 97–100; idem, Die Crown in Großbritannien, in ibid., pp. 103f.

213 Idem, Frankreich: Écu blanc und Laubtaler, in ibid., pp. 133f.; idem, Jefimok und Rubel, in ibid., pp. 136f.

214 Fernand BRAUDEL / Frank C. SPOONER, Prices in Europe from 1450 to 1750, in Edwin E. RICH / Charles H. WILSON (eds.), *The Economy of Expanding Europe in the Sixteenth and Seventeenth Centuries* (= *The Cambridge Economic History of Europe*, vol. IV), Cambridge et al. 1967, pp. 378–486, esp. pp. 378f.

215 E.g. Peter SPUFFORD, *Monetary Problems and Policies in the Burgundian Netherlands 1433–1496*, Leiden 1970, pp. 13–28.

Those fairs with an international reputation featured consistently a relatively stable money of account system throughout the period under investigation. At the 16th century Lyons fairs, for example, a differentiation was made between accounting in marc d'or (following the example of the older Geneva fairs), écu de marc d'or (= 1/65 marc d'or) or écu d'or au soleil. The écu de marc d'or at 3.08 grammes of fine gold was used as the most important clearing unit after 1533.[216] Following the example of the Lyons fairs, the exchange rates at the Genoese 'Bisenzone' fairs were quoted in the unit of account 'scudi (d'oro) di marche'. Since 1594/95 the value of the scudi (d'oro) di marche had resulted from the average weight of the seven internationally circulating gold coins from Antwerp, Spain, Genoa, Venice, Florence, Piacenza and Naples, being, therefore, independent of single national currencies. Whenever payments in cash were necessary to settle a balance, they were expressed in scudi di marche but executed in scudi d'oro (in oro), with the ratio of 100:101 of the scudi di marche to the average troy weight of the scudi d'oro remaining unchanged between 1552 and 1763.[217] The Bisenzone fairs' money of account influenced both the exchange fairs the Venetians had established in Verona in around 1630 and later in Murano, as well as even to some parts of the exchange rate quotations and the accounting at the Bolzano fairs. There, two systems of money of account developed: the moneta giro during the 17th century and the the valuta della fiera during the second half of the 18th century.[218] But also at the German fairs of international relevance, various systems of monies of account became important. In Frankfurt am Main, for example, the so-called 'Wechselgeld' (exchange money) was introduced in 1585 and endured with some changes until well into the 19th century. At the Leipzig fairs it became usual to settle accounts in 'Konventions-Wechselzahlung' after 1763. Generally, it has to be stated that systems of money of account were established at fairs only if they developed into centres of cashless payment transactions. If, however, they remained pure or mainly goods fairs, the development of a system of money of account did not happen because it was simply unnecessary, as, for instance, in Brunswick. In around 1577 Frankfurt am Main was primarily a reloading point for goods, evolving into an exchange market only during the early 1580s under the influence of French and Dutch immigrants who brought with them new techniques for banking and payment business, last but not least the use of an exchange money (introduced 1585).[219]

Similar to the big international fairs, a particular money of account developed in important supra-regional public banks, which represented a sort of bank money in which the bank kept its books and rendered its accounts, thus converting payments or clearings among merchants settling their transactions via this bank into this parti-

---

216 Helma HOUTMAN-DE SMEDT / Herman VAN DER WEE, Die Entstehung des modernen Geld- und Finanzwesens Europas in der Neuzeit, in Hans POHL (ed.), *Europäische Bankengeschichte*, Frankfurt/Main 1993, pp. 73–173, esp. p. 106.

217 Ibid., p. 110; DENZEL, *"Practica"*, pp. 315f.; Giuseppe FELLONI, All'apogeo dell fiere genovesi: Banchieri ed affari di cambio a Piacenza nel 1600, in *Studi in onore di Gino Barbieri. Problemi e metodi di Storia ed Economica*, vol. II, Pisa 1983, pp. 883–901.

218 DENZEL, *Die Bozner Messen*, pp. 97–114.

219 Hans-Peter ULLMANN, Der Frankfurter Kapitalmarkt um 1800: Entstehung, Struktur und Wirken einer modernen Finanzierungsinstitution, *Vierteljahrschrift für Sozial- und Wirtschaftsgeschichte* 77 (1990), pp. 75–92, esp. p. 77. Cf. LAPEYRE, *Les Ruiz*, p. 294; DENZEL, *"Practica"*, p. 325.

cular money of account. The bank money of the Venetian Banco della Piazza di Rialto (founded in 1597), for example, became legal tender for cashless payments in 1593, when all bills of exchange had to be encashed or settled at this bank. When the Amsterdam Wisselbank, Hamburg's Banco and Nuremberg's Banco Publico had been established, modelled on the Venetian example, the following stable bank monies and monies of account were established there: the guilder banko in Amsterdam,[220] in Hamburg the rixdollar or the mark banko respectively, and in Nuremberg the guilder current (gulden kurant) as bank monies and monies of account.

Last but not least, the establishment of monies of account was a result of the creeping inflation of the 16th century, i.e. of the gradual debasement of token coins by adding copper, in economic history known as the 'price revolution', although seen from a different perspective. During the 16th century price revolution(s) were almost a pan-European phenomenon; they could be found – despite strong regional and temporal differences – in the Holy Roman Empire, in Spain, in France and in many Italian regions.[221] I refrain from analysing the background of the price revolution in 16th-century Europe and, above all, the impact of American precious metal on the different European economies discussed in the respective literature.[222] Nevertheless, it must be emphasized that, despite its individual causes in the respective regions, the increasing stamping of copper coins since the late 16th century at the latest took place against the common background of silver production declining worldwide. This finding resulted again mainly from the dramatic decline of silver production in Spanish America and the resultant lesser exports to Europe from the last decade of the 16th century. Silver exports clearly increased again only from 1660. Altogether, the European supply of precious metals worsened to a considerable extent during the first half of the 17th century in comparison to the 16th century.[223] It was this fact, together with the decision of the princes to use their coinage prerogative in order to gain additional income that led to an increased use of copper as coin metal in different European countries. Three examples of this 17th-century "copper era" – as Michael North called it[224] – may suffice for illustration.

Spain was the first country to change to increased copper coinage, minting millions of debased vellón coins in different phases between 1599 and 1660 (1599–1606, 1617–1619 and 1621–1626), which were recoined, up- and devalued several times from the 1630s. Counterfeited vellón coins imported from abroad enforced the drain of full-weight Spanish gold and silver coins further, so that the whole cash cycle performed in copper from the 1630s represented a heavy burden on payment

---

220 Concerning the Netherlands, for example, H. VAN WERVEKE, Monnaie de compte et monnaie réelle, in *Revue belge de philologie et d'histoire* 13 (1934), pp. 123–152.

221 E.g. Pierre VILLAR, *Gold und Geld in der Geschichte. Vom Ausgang des Mittelalters bis zur Gegenwart*, München 1984 (French edition: *Or et monnaie dans l'histoire, 1450–1920*, Paris 1972), pp. 131–174; Renate PIEPER, *Die Preisrevolution in Spanien (1500–1640). Neuere Forschungsergebnisse*, Stuttgart 1985; Hans-Jürgen GERHARD, Ursachen und Folgen der Wandlungen im Währungssystem des Deutschen Reiches 1500–1625. Eine Studie zu den Hintergründen der sogenannten Preisrevolution, in SCHREMMER (ed.), *Geld und Währung*, pp. 69–84.

222 As a survey, cf. NORTH, *Das Geld*, pp. 93–96.

223 John J. TEPASKE, New World Silver, Castile and the Philippines 1590–1800, in John F. RICHARDS (ed.), *Precious Metals in the Later Medieval and Early Modern Worlds*, Durham (N.C.) 1983, pp. 425–445.

224 NORTH, *Das Geld*, p. 97.

transactions alone because of the weight and amount of coins to be transported. This economically unsustainable situation ended only with the currency reform of 1680.[225]

In France and in the Holy Roman Empire a phase of currency debasement and dramatically increased copper minting also started during the first decade of the 17th century, developing in the Holy Roman Empire into the infamous 'see-saw period' ('Kipper-and-Wipper era') with regionally highly differing occurrences. From the 16th century the silver price was rising due to falling outputs of the Central European mining areas. Although this price increase took place quite slowly, the rixdollar was traded higher and higher since it was not connected to any fixed nominal coin. This nuisance was caused, first, by the inadequate imperial monetary system, i.e. the wrong relation between rixdollar and token coins; second, by a permanent worsening of the standard of coinage, i.e. the number of coins made of a certain unit of precious metal permanently rising in order to satisfy the increasing demand for small cash; third, by leasing many mints to mercenary businessmen; fourth, by an inadequate control of coinage and, finally, by the emperor himself, who did not take any steps to improve the situation because of his weak political position. It was not only merchants and money changers having good coins recoined into bad coins on a grand scale, but also businessmen making their profits by maintaining a mint who thrived on this situation. As a result, the decisive upturn of the rixdollar course set in precisely between 1602 and 1612 and the inflationary spiral went on rotating faster and faster during the last decade prior to the Thirty Years' War. The silver price and with it the rixdollar course got out of control when the Thirty Years' War began, because the war entailed enormous financial expenses for paying the troops. The so-called 'Kipper-and-Wipper era' (1619–23), being marked by a plentiful issue of debased small change (also called die lange Münze, the 'long coins'), set in in the Habsburg countries only after the Battle of White Mountain (Schlacht am Weißen Berge) on November 8th 1620, followed by the reintegration of Bohemia into the Habsburg possessions. In 1623 – right in the middle of the war – a reversion to more stable monetary conditions set in, even though the rixdollar's value was no longer connected to the silver price but it was attached with a certain value, as all the other nominal coins were. So the collection of those 'long coins' and the negotiations with the creditors who had given credits in 'long coins' extended over several years.[226] Nevertheless, debasing a currency remained a reliable instrument for financing extraordinary public expenditures even in later decades. The Emperor Leopold I

---

225 Fernando SERRANO MANGAS, El papel del vellón, in Antonio M. BERNAL (ed.), *Dinero, moneda y crédito en la Monarquía Hispánica. Actas del Simposio Internacional "Dinero, moneda y crédito. De la Monarquía Hispánica a la Integración Monetaria Europea", Madrid, 4–7 de mayo de 1999*, Madrid 2000, pp. 567–573; Richard GAETTENS, *Geschichte der Inflationen. Vom Altertum bis zur Gegenwart*, München ²1957, pp. 59–72; NORTH, *Das Geld*, pp. 97–99.

226 Heinz MOSER / Heinz TURSKY, *Corpus Nummorum Tirolensium. Die Münzen Kaiser Rudolfs II. aus der Münzstätte Hall in Tirol 1602–1612*, Rum bei Innsbruck 1986, pp. 41f.; idem, Die Münzstätte Hall in Tirol, in Heinz MOSER / Helmut RIZZOLLI / Heinz TURSKY (eds.), *Tiroler Münzbuch. Die Geschichte des Geldes aus den Prägestätten des alttirolischen Raumes*, Innsbruck 1984, pp. 61–194, esp. pp. 123, 129. Cf. GAETTENS, *Geschichte der Inflationen*, pp. 84, 93; Fritz REDLICH, *Die deutsche Inflation des frühen Siebzehnten Jahrhunderts in der zeitgenössischen Literatur: Die Kipper und Wipper*, Köln – Wien 1972; Paul W. ROTH, Die Kipper- und Wipperzeit in den Habsburgischen Ländern, 1620 bis 1623, in SCHREMMER (ed.), *Geld- und Währung*, pp. 85–103.

(1658–1705) used it, for example, to finance the war against the Ottoman Empire in 1659, resulting in a clearly inflationary process within the Habsburg Monarchy during the 1660s.[227]

Sweden may serve as the final example of the rising issue of copper coins. As a result of increased copper output, Sweden coined copper from 1625. This happened many times after Sweden had entered the Thirty Years' War in 1630, with copper plates, the so-called 'kopparplåtmynt', subdivided into values between 1 and 10 dalers representing the dominant current money in circulation until 1700. Because these copper plates could weigh up to 20 kilograms and were therefore very unmanageable, and copper prices were subject to heavy fluctuations, the Stockholm Banco was founded in 1656, to follow the example of Amsterdam's Wisselbank. From 1668 it was managed under the direct control of the Swedish Estates (therefore called Rikets Ständers Bank); later this bank became the Sveriges Riksbank. Accordingly, the Stockholm Banco first issued banknotes in 1661, the so-called 'kreditivsedlar', intended to help monetary circulation.[228]

Michael North calls the 18th century the "era of currency reforms".[229] The reforms of coins and currency taking place in many European states represent the background of this estimation and can be traced back to the increasing acceptance of gold as a currency metal. Serving as the prime example for this development, England concluded the so-called Methuen contract with Portugal in 1703. Consequently, the inflow of gold from Brazil via Portugal to the British Isles increased heavily since large gold deposits had been discovered in today's Minas Gerais between 1693 and 1695. The Brazilian gold led to a reorientation of the British coinage away from silver and towards gold, so that Great Britain gradually changed to a gold standard as early as the 18th century. France, however, established a double standard of gold and silver when stabilizing its monetary conditions with the 1726 coinage reform: a new louis d'or (louis aux lunettes) and a new silver écu (écu aux lauriers) was introduced to overcome the disordered situation after John Law's monetary experiment with paper money during the 1720s. This double standard became characteristic of the French monetary conditions of the late 18th and 19th centuries outlasting in the long run even the confusions of the assignat paper money during the early years of the French Revolution. Double standards were also introduced in many Italian states as a result of currency reforms during the 18th century as, for example, in Venice (in 1722, 1733), Genoa (in 1745, 1759, 1792), Savoy (in 1755) and Milan (in 1778). The aims of all these currency reforms were both to start the production of copper token coins and to align the coinage to the gold–silver ratio by reducing the high part of gold within the circulation of money by upvaluing silver. Moreover, it was intended to reduce the number of nominal coins and mint standardized nominal coins in the different states. Thus one can assume that there were already beginnings

---

227 MOSER / TURSKY, Die Münzstätte Hall in Tirol [1984], pp. 134–140.

228 T. LINDGREN, The First Swedish Bank Notes, in *Revue international d'histoire de la banque* (1968), pp. 402–408; Oskar SCHWARZER / Markus A. DENZEL / Petra SCHNELZER, Geld- und Wechselkurse in Deutschland und im Ostseeraum (18. und 19. Jahrhundert), in *HStD XII*, pp. 2–43, esp. pp. 26f. Cf. also *Sveriges Riksbank 1668–1924. Bankens Tillkomst och Verksamhet*, Stockholm 1931, especially p. 141.

229 NORTH, *Das Geld*, p. 121.

of monetary standardization within Italy long before the Risorgimento.[230] In Spain there was also a currency reform standardizing the coinage in 1716 by prohibiting individual coinages in different parts of the country. Then a distinction was introduced within the circulation of money between the high-value moneda nacional of the Spanish-American possessions and the low-value moneda provincial of the 'province' of Spain, which was why exchange rates in Spain itself were throughout quoted in money of account during the 18th century. The peseta, a double real provincial, became the external sign of the standardized currency within the 'province' of Spain, replacing the maravedí as unit of account during the 19th century.[231]

In contrast to these standardizing tendencies in Western and Southern Europe, the monetary systems of the Holy Roman Empire developed in different directions in the course of the Austro–Prussian dualism: The Habsburg Hereditary Lands introduced a new 20-gulden standard in 1750, the so-called Konventionsfuß according to the Münzkonvention between Austria and the Electorate of Bavaria of 1753. The Konventionsthaler resulting from this currency reform and the Kronenthaler respectively coined in the Austrian Netherlands from 1790 became the dominant means of payment, together with the French louis aux lunettes (Schild-Louisd'or) and the écu aux lauriers (Laubthaler) in the Habsburg Hereditary Lands and beyond it in the whole West and South of the Empire. Under the direction of Johann Philipp Graumann, however, Brandenburg-Prussia introduced a new current dollar under the designation 'rixdollar' in 1750 based on a 14-thaler standard, the so-called Graumann standard of coinage. After an experiment with low-value war coins during the Seven Years' War (1756–1763), the Graumann standard of coinage of 1750 was reintroduced in 1764. Apart from the special developments of the monetary and currency system of the Hanseatic cities (especially in Hamburg and Bremen), the following simplified statement can be made: since the second half of the 18th century there was a monetary dualism within the Holy Roman Empire characterizing the development of money and currency in Germany until the German Empire was founded in 1871.

There was another direction to development of the 18th century that resulted in multiple currency reforms: several European states experimented with the introduction of paper money, regularly ending in more or less heavy inflation, with only one single exception. As early as the 1660s the Sveriges Riksbank was the precursor of this development. It was the first to begin issuing banknotes for a few years. During the 18th century the issue of bank notes was normally a result of shortages within public finances as a consequence of wars. Shortly after the issue a forced exchange was often imposed on the respective national paper money, so that its acceptance

---

230 John J. McCusker / James C. Riley, Money Supply, Economic Growth, and the Quantity Theory of Money: France 1650–1788, in Eddy H.G. van Cauwenberghe / Franz Irsigler (eds.), *Münzprägung, Geldumlauf und Wechselkurse / Minting, Monetary Circulation and Exchange Rates. Akten des 8th International Economic History Congress, Section C 7 (Budapest 1982)*, Trier 1984, pp. 265–289; Carlo M. Cipolla, *Le avventure della lira*, Milano 1958, pp. 73–75; Ugo Tucci, Monete e riforme monetarie nell'Italia del settecento, in *Rivista storica italiana* 98 (1986), pp. 78–119; Giuseppe Felloni, *Il mercato monetario in Piemonte nel secolo XVIII*, Milano 1968, pp. 139–167, 233–246; North, *Das Geld*, pp. 121–124.

231 Earl J. Hamilton, *War and Prices in Spain, 1651–1800*, Cambridge (Mass.) 1947, pp. 56f.; North, *Das Geld*, p. 124.

among the people became obligatory. Together with the fast-rising expenditures, this was why the value of such paper money rapidly declined below par, which also held for France and its issue of paper money following the Système Law (1716–1720) after the lost War of the Spanish Succession and of assignates during the French Revolution (1790–1796). In Sweden the so-called transport sedlar (transport bills) had been issued as early as 1701; these were generally used for payment transactions from the late 1730s and were followed by the banko sedlar and the riksgäld sedlar after the insolvency of the issuing Sveriges Riksbank in 1776. In Denmark banknotes of the Kurantbanken had been issued since 1737; these were also a means of payment convertible to precious metal for only a few years. In Austria the Banco-zettel of the Vienna Stadtbanco (from 1762) became more and more wide-spread passing into the Wiener Währung (Vienna currency) that became obligatory from 1800 as a result of the French Revolutionary Wars.[232] From 1768/69 the banco rouble or assignat rouble served as means of payment in Russia, and from 1786 also as national paper money. In Spain vales reales were issued as a consequence of war since 1780.[233]

The notes of the Bank of England were the only exception to this development. They were issued only in moderation, in comparison with the continent, so that these notes enjoyed a good reputation in Great Britain and became an increasingly important means of payment. From 1708 there was no other bank with more than six participators, other than the Bank of England, allowed to issue banknotes in England and Wales. That was why most of the private banks of issue remained comparatively small enterprises, which could not compete with the Bank of England. These country banks were founded mainly in the country, where there were no notes of the Bank of England circulating during the second half of the 18th century, and they mobilized the rural population's savings for the London capital market. It was only in the course of the French Revolutionary Wars during the 1790s that the English bank and currency system, which had weathered the heavy speculation crisis of the South Sea Company (the so-called South Sea Bubble of 1719/20), got into such severe difficulties that the bank's obligation to cash the notes had to be suspended until 1820/23. This did not lead to a national bankruptcy in Great Britain – unlike in Austria.[234] Generally, it was not until 1815 that most of the European states, having issued paper money during the 18th century, were successful in damming the flood of paper money little by little – even though not always for a long time.[235]

In post-Napoleonic Europe there were two central development directions characterizing monetary policy: first, steps were taken to harmonize different currencies within economic areas that were becoming increasingly integrated; and, second, there was a move to implement the gold standard following the example of Great Britain. Because this second step was of an importance reaching far beyond the European borders, it will be dealt with in a separate section (see Section 4.3).

The first development direction can be observed within the German Confedera-

---

232 Ibid., pp. 130–138.
233 Pedro TEDDE DE LORCA, *El Banco de San Carlos (1782–1829)*, Madrid 1988.
234 NORTH, *Das Geld*, pp. 133–135.
235 Ibid., p. 138.

tion. In 1834 seven parallel standards of coinage existed there besides the currency area of the Habsburg Monarchy, and each of these could again include different monetary systems. The variety of currencies and circulating coins within Germany was regarded an important barrier to trade and economic integration. This was why the Coinage Confederation of Southern Germany (Süddeutscher Münzverein) was founded in Munich in 1837, only a few years after the foundation of the German Customs Union (Zollverein) in 1834. As a consequence, Southern Germany had a widely standardized monetary system and a joint currency area based on the standard of coinage of 24½ guilders per mark of Cologne, which had been in use before. The next step was the Coin Treaty of Dresden from July 30th 1838, establishing a fixed relation between the guilder South German current and the thaler Prussian current (with a standard of coinage of 14 thaler per mark of Cologne). Being valid in all contractual states, a new coin, the so-called 'Vereinsmünze' (union coin), documented this relation: 1 Vereinsmünze = 2 thaler Prussian current = 3½ guilders South German current. After 1838 most of the other German states sooner or later joined the Coin Treaty of Dresden, with the exceptions of Hamburg, Bremen, Lübeck, both Mecklenburgs and Schleswig–Holstein. Finally, the Coin Treaty of Vienna of 1857 achieved the unification of the currency areas of the Coin Treaty of Dresden and the Habsburg Monarchy (as well as of Liechtenstein) using the metric pound at 500 grammes instead of the traditional mark as the basis of the coin weight. From then on, 30 thaler or 45 guilders Österreichische Währung (Austrian currency) or 52½ guilders South German current was to be coined out of one metric pound. At the same time, the Prussian thaler coin became, together with the 'Doppeltaler' (double thaler) of 1838 a union coin, called the 'Vereinstaler' (union thaler), expanding its validity area to Southern Germany and Austria. Austria and Liechtenstein, however, resigned from the Coin Treaty of Vienna as early as in 1867, after the War of 1866. In Germany, a definitive standardization of currency and coinage was achieved only after the Constitution of the German Empire in 1871 by gradually introducing a new standard currency, the mark Reichswährung (imperial currency), until 1876, which eliminated at the same time six different currency systems remaining in four currency areas.[236]

The currency standardization in Italy, the second nation state constituted at this time, proceeded within a considerably shorter period. Consequently, the lira currency (lira nuova) of the Kingdom of Piedmont–Sardinia, being equal to the French franc, was imposed on all Italian states attached to the Piedmontese state in the course of the Risorgimento. The first part of the standardization process took place within the Kingdom of Piedmont–Sardinia itself by eliminating the currency of the former Republic of Genoa in 1816/26 and introducing the lira nuova also on Sardinia in 1842/43.[237] In 1859/60 the currencies of all Italian states belonging to the Kingdom of Piedmont–Sardinia or Kingdom of Italy were changed to the Piedmontesian lira

---

236 Hans-Jürgen GERHARD, Vom Leipziger Fuß zur Reichsgoldwährung. Der lange Weg zur "deutschen Währungsunion" von 1871/76, in Reiner CUNZ (ed.), *Währungsunionen. Beiträge zur Geschichte überregionaler Münz- und Geldpolitik*, Hamburg 2002, pp. 249–290, esp. pp. 273–286; Bernd SPRENGER, Harmonisierungsbestrebungen im Geldwesen der deutschen Staaten zwischen Wiener Kongreß und Reichsgründung, in SCHREMMER (ed.), *Geld und Währung*, pp. 121–142; idem, *Das Geld der Deutschen. Geldgeschichte Deutschlands von den Anfängen bis zur Gegenwart*, Paderborn et al. ³2002, pp. 152–161.

nuova. A new currency unit, the lira italiana, was proclaimed for the whole Kingdom of Italy on July 17th 1861, which was of equal value to the previous Piedmontese lira nuova. On August 24th 1862 a law for the standardization of specie followed
to supersede previous ways of accounting within the old currency units. After Venetia, Mantua and the remaining parts of the Papal States had been incorporated on
September 3rd 1868 and October 13th 1870 respectively, the validity of the new uniform currency of Italy as a whole was extended to these areas.[238]

Finally, Switzerland also arrived at standardized coinage and currency conditions, but not before the mid-19th century. During the period of the Ancien Régime a
variety of different currencies characterized the Swiss territory. Even though
Switzerland was quite small, the situation resembled that of the Holy Roman Empire
because the cantons had the right to mint and issue coins.[239] A first attempt to standardize currencies had been made with a new common currency unit, the Schweizerfranken (Swissfranc), during the period of the Helvetic Republic (1798–1803),
but a currency and coinage reform was only enforced between 1849 and 1852 after
the constitution of the Swiss Confederation in 1848 and the end of cantonal sover-
eignty. Similar to the Piedmontese lira nuova or the lira italiana, the Swiss franc
(Schweizer Franken) was introduced as the common coinage and currency unit
equal to the French franc in 1849/50.[240]

Furthermore, currency agreements among states that were not confederated
within superordinate institutions as, for instance, the Deutsche Bund, led to a harmonization of currencies. During the 19th century those monetary unions were arranged
both in Scandinavia and in the Latin countries of Europe, which followed France regarding their economic and/or monetary policy. Thus the Latin Monetary Union was
arranged between France, Belgium, Italy and Switzerland in 1865. Without any official arrangement, Piedmont–Sardinia (1816), Belgium (1832), Switzerland (1850/
60) and Italy (1861/62) had adopted the French double standard based on the French
franc, the franc Germinal of 1803, under country-specific designations. Since the
silver token coins of the different currencies had been of different fineness, fluctuating exchange rates and speculative trade had often occurred. Consequently, the Latin Monetary Union was intended to avoid these developments. France dominated
the decisions on coinage and currency, such as the decision to maintain the double
standard instead of introducing the gold standard, because of the sheer supremacy of
the Paris capital market within the countries involved. For this reason the 1865 treaty in effect carried forward this supremacy. The aims of this union were to establish
a united circulation of coins, facilitate mutual payment transactions and reduce exchange rate fluctuations. Until the official end of the union in 1926, however, these
aims could only partially be achieved, particularly since Italy pursued a largely inde-

---

237 Giuseppe FELLONI, Monete e zecche negli Stati Sabaudi dal 1816 al 1860, *Archivio economico
   dell'unificazione italiana* II 2 (1956).

238 R. DE MATTIA, *L'unificazione monetaria italiana*, Torino 1959; Markus A. DENZEL, Die währungspolitische Einigung Italiens: Italienische Wechselplätze zwischen 1815 und 1861, in *WdW
   I/I*, pp. 82–104, esp. pp. 97f.

239 Martin KÖRNER, Zum Problem der Währungsvielfalt in der Schweiz, in VAN CAUWENBERGHE /
   IRSIGLER (eds.), *Münzprägung, Geldumlauf und Wechselkurse*, pp. 219–236.

240 Markus A. DENZEL, Vom "Schweizerfranken" zum "schweizer Franken" (1798–1860), in *WdW
   I/I*, pp. 72–81, esp. pp. 72–78.

pendent monetary policy often directed against the union itself. Although the union was very attractive to other countries during the first years of its existence – Greece (with its drachma in 1868), the Papal States (with its Papal lira in 1866/67), Romania (with its leu in 1868), Spain (with its peseta), Finland (with its markka) and later on Bulgaria (with its lew) and Serbia (with its denar) adopted the union's standard of coinage without becoming formal members – from the 1890s it existed only on paper.[241]

In contrast to the Latin Monetary Union, the Scandinavian Monetary Union proved far more successful until 1914. Officially it existed until 1933. With the Treaty of December 18th 1872, Sweden, Norway and Denmark formed a monetary union establishing a new, standardized and – for the first time – decimal monetary system based on gold, the crown of 100 öre. Unlike the area of the Latin Monetary Union, the coin circulation within the Scandinavian Monetary Union had already developed to an advanced state and the involved economies were quite convergent before the conclusion of the contract in 1872. The Scandinavian Monetary Union intended to create a wider currency area, to facilitate payment transactions and to stabilize exchange rates. The most important measure supporting these aims was the agreement between the central banks of the three countries involved from 1885. According to this agreement, the three countries mutually granted themselves three months' credit free of interest and commission in order to settle balances so that the drain of gold and coins could be restricted. Thanks to the well-coordinated discount policy and the partners' willingness to carry out the necessary adjustments, the Scandinavian Monetary Union functioned successfully and the original parity between the three currencies persisted until 1914.[242]

4.2 European Currency Systems and Trade Coins in the Non-European Regions of the World from the European Expansion up to c. 1870

In the wake of the European expansion the monetary systems of single European countries gained importance that reached far beyond Europe. Basically, two different development directions can be distinguished: on the one hand, certain coins became important as so-called world trade coins, i.e. they were specially produced for international trade and exported into certain world regions as a means of payment. On the other hand, the different European powers, in the course of building up colonies or overseas possessions, usually imposed their monetary systems on those overseas territories belonging to the respective European country. This held, for instance, for the Spanish and Portuguese Viceroyalties in America as well as for the English colonies in North America, Australia, New Zealand and – from the 19th century – in Africa. France and the Netherlands also imposed their monetary systems on their overseas possessions. India represents the most important exception: here, no European power was successful in implementing its monetary system. Instead, the Europeans had to adopt the Indian monetary system, which could maintain a certain

241 Friedrich ZELLFELDER, Der Lateinische Münzbund: Grundlagen, Entstehung und Scheitern, in ibid., pp. 105–121, esp. pp. 110ff.
242 Idem, Art. "Skandinavische Münzunion", in NORTH (ed.), Von Aktie bis Zoll, pp. 367f.

independence even after its connection to the pound sterling as a result of the 1893 reforms.[243]

Apart from the European possessions in China since the second half of the 19th century, which play a specific role from the perspective of monetary history, the implementation of the monetary system of the respective 'colonial power' was usually successful.[244] This implementation sometimes caused great difficulties requiring multiple measures such as the British government's "periodic attempts to impose some uniformity on the empire, attempted to establish a common monetary system throughout the empire by encouraging the use of British coinage" since the 1820s.[245] The 'mother countries', however, were not always successful in having the same money in circulation in their overseas possessions as they had at home. Instead of this, the system of the 'mother country' was often officially used for accounting, such as pounds, shillings and pence in the British colonies in North America, whereas token money of one's own or from neighbouring world regions was used as payment, such as paper money of the single colonies and Spanish dollars from Spanish America in the North American colonies.[246] This was also the most important reason for the dollar currencies becoming accepted as currency units and means of payment in the United States of America and later on also in Canada, in contrast to sterling currency.

The introduction of originally European coins overseas was above all successful in regions without a distinctive indigenous monetary culture or a competing European colonial power. This held for Australia, New Zealand and most of the African possessions. Even in Africa, however, a 'new' colonial power could only with difficulty substitute European monetary systems already established: for instance, it took many decades until the Dutch monetary system of the Cape Colony was replaced by a 'newer' British one. When the German Empire started to act as a colonial power in Africa, it was sometimes very difficult to establish the German monetary system in place of the older British system. Even though accounting in mark Reichswährung (imperial currency) was introduced in Togo as early as August 1st 1887, British token money dominated in this protectorate until the first decade of the 20th century. It was not until 1900 that the German means of payment became accepted, particularly since German small change was lacking before 1907.[247] The situation in Africa during the 19th and 20th centuries is, by the way, an excellent example of the fact that

---

243 Cf. Anton ARNOLD, *Das indische Geldwesen unter besonderer Berücksichtigung seiner Reformen seit 1893*, Jena 1906.

244 Canada was an important exception of this development.

245 McCULLOUGH, *Canada*, p. 92.

246 For a summary of the development of paper money in the colonies see John J. McCUSKER, Colonial Paper Money, in Eric P. NEWMAN / Richard G. DOTY (eds.), *Studies on Money in Early America*, New York 1976, pp. 94–104.

247 Markus A. DENZEL, Geldwesen und Zahlungsverkehr in den deutschen Schutzgebieten (bis 1914). Eine währungshistorische Skizze mit Problemaufriß für künftige Forschungen, in Thomas BECK / Marília DOS SANTOS LOPES / Christian RÖDEL (eds.), *Barrieren und Zugänge. Die Geschichte der europäischen Expansion. Festschrift für Eberhard Schmitt zum 65. Geburtstag*, Wiesbaden 2004, pp. 322–342, esp. p. 326. Cf. Karl-Dieter SEIDEL, *Die deutsche Gesetzgebung seit 1871. Münzen – Papiergeld und Notenbanken mit den Münzverträgen der deutschen Staaten im 19. Jahrhundert*, München 1973, pp. 133f.; Günther MEINHARDT, *Die Geldgeschichte der ehemaligen deutschen Schutzgebiete 2: Togo*, Dortmund 1956, pp. 12, 14, 16, 22.

the dominance of the European currency did not mean its exclusive use. The indigenous commodity money, which was at least used for local retail trade and sometimes also for regional trade, was tariffed like foreign trade coins such as gold dust and cowries in the Windward Districts of the British Gold Coast or palm oil in the German protectorate of Cameroon.[248] This was absolutely necessary because the colonial powers were usually unsuccessful in supplying an adequate volume of small cash for their possessions, having already strongly influenced the distribution of Spanish dollars and their fractions as well as of paper money in North America.

When the colonies or overseas possessions became independent, the previous monetary system was either continued partly with changed coin designations (as in the Spanish and Portuguese possessions in Latin America, in Australia and South Africa) or it was modified in accordance with the respective economic needs (as in the United States of America and Canada). Using the monetary problems resulting from the American Revolutionary War as a starting point, the young United States tried to harmonize the previous monetary systems of each state following the British example by establishing the Spanish or Mexican dollar, the most important trade coin of the North American and the Caribbean region, as the model of a standardized US currency unit.

Representing a novelty, the new US currency oriented itself towards the most important trade coin of America in modern times, the Spanish peso or dollar. It was minted in Mexico, which was why it had been also called the Mexican dollar since the 18th century. As early as the 16th century the Spanish or Mexican dollar had gained importance as an international trade coin far beyond the Spanish possessions in America, such as in the Caribbean, in the English colonies in North America or in Portuguese Brazil. There, it was known under the designation 'pataca' or 'patacão', being differently valued in the unit of account reís (480 reís in 1643, 640 reís in 1676, 800 reís in 1734 or 960 reís in around 1800).[249] The Spanish peso, however, functioned as international trade coin not only in America and Asia but also in the Ottoman Empire and in bordering African regions. It was as early as the 16th century that the Spanish real de a ocho (= peso) had stimulated the coinage of specific thaler coins in Italy (see above). Via the Italian trading towns, the peso also diffused in the Ottoman Empire, particularly because payment transactions with this world region were mainly conducted predominantly on the basis of cash money. Consequently, the peso obtained under the designation piastra the function of an international trade coin in the whole of Northern Africa, in the Levant, in Arabia, Abyssinia and far into the Sahara region. The Dutch Löwenthaler (lion dollar) became another international trade coin of this region in 1576 similar to the Austrian Marie Theresa thaler in 1753, developing into the most important trade coin of the whole Orient from the late 18th century.[250]

---

248 Markus A. DENZEL, Zahlungsverkehr, Wechselkurse und Währungsverhältnisse von Britischen Besitzungen in Afrika (1822–1931), in *WdW VIII*, pp. 1–29, esp. pp. 11, 14; idem, Geldwesen und Zahlungsverkehr in den deutschen Schutzgebieten, p. 325.

249 Dietrich KLOSE, Der spanische Piaster als Welthandelsmünze und die von ihm abgeleiteten Großsilbermünzen, in HEß / KLOSE (Bearb.), *Vom Taler zum Dollar*, pp. 187–190, esp. pp. 188f.; Markus A. DENZEL, Art. "Dollar", in NORTH (ed.), *Von Aktie bis Zoll*, pp. 87f.

250 KLOSE, Der spanische Piaster als Welthandelsmünze, p. 187.

Large quantities of Spanish dollars from both Europe and the Levant reached the Indian Ocean area, Southern and East Asia and even Australia during the late 18ᵗʰ century. Moreover, the so-called Current dollar, a money of account on Mauritius and in the whole Indian Ocean area, can be traced back to the Spanish dollar. The Philippines with Manila developed into an important transfer centre exchanging Spanish dollars against Chinese commodities, with silver having twice the value in China than in America. Although innumerable pesos had been melted down into silver bullion before in China, Spanish dollars established even as circulating money in Southern China and in several coast towns. When China ran short of the old Spanish American dollars during the 19ᵗʰ century, resulting in an inflated value for these dollars, great quantities of Mexican dollars entered the Asian sphere from 1854 via the China trade originating in California. After attempts to establish English or Indian money in Hong Kong had failed, the so-called British dollar or Hong Kong dollar was minted in Hong Kong between 1866 and 1868 both in the tradition of accounting and paying in Spanish and Mexican dollars and following the example of the Mexican dollar already in use there. The same held for the New British dollar or British Trade dollar minted in Bombay from 1895. In the Straits Settlements (Singapore, Malacca, Penang) the Straits Settlements dollar replaced the Mexican dollar in 1903/04. In the Chinese coast towns, at least, it remained usual to settle accounts and transact payments in Mexican dollars until the interwar period and as many as approximately 400 millions of Mexican dollars are said to have been circulating or hoarded in China in around 1910. The dollar had become so important that, despite serious reservations, the imperial government had to allow the provincial governors in 1890 to mint Chinese silver dollars, the so-called dragon dollars, depicting a Chinese dragon. In 1911 the Chinese government established the Silver dollar (*yuan*) as the national currency unit. Japan also followed the example of the Mexican dollar when introducing its new currency, the yen of 100 sen, in 1871. The Mexican dollar had already been used for foreign trade and international payment transactions during the first years after the opening up of Japan to the West. Finally, the Spanish dollar became approved as an authorized medium of circulation in Australia's Botany Bay in 1791, but it never became accepted since the coins were drained out of the country because of its chronic balance of trade deficit.²⁵¹

The US dollar, the most important 'spin-off' of the Spanish-Mexican dollar, itself became an example many currencies followed, for instance the currencies of the British colony of Canada (from 1864/67 dominion; with the US dollar as a circulating coin and the formal introduction of accounting in dollars and cents in 1857), of Panama, the Dominican Republic of Guatemala, Liberia, the Kingdom of Hawaii and on Cuba from 1899. However, the attempt failed to create a US coin for foreign trade, the US Trade dollar, between 1873 and 1885 in order to replace the Mexican dollar within the East Asian trade. As a result, the US Trade dollar lost all im-

---

251 Markus A. DENZEL, Die Adaption 'europäischer Währungssysteme' in China und Japan im 19. und beginnenden 20. Jahrhundert. Zur Durchsetzung des Dollar-Systems im ostasiatischen Raum, in Harald WITTHÖFT with Karl Jürgen ROTH, *Acta Metrologiae Historicae V: 7. Internationaler Kongreß des Internationalen Komitees für Historische Metrologie (CIMH) 25.–27. September 1997 in Siegen)*, St. Katharinen 1999, pp. 227–254; KLOSE, Der spanische Piaster als Welthandelsmünze, pp. 189f.

portance within international payment transactions after the drop of silver prices in 1877.[252] Finally, France also issued trade dollars following the example of the Mexican dollar. The so-called piastres de commerce, minted from 1885, were to replace the Mexican dollar in Indochina, similar to the British attempts in Malaysia.[253]

The Albertthaler (or Albertusthaler) of the Spanish Netherlands, the Löwenthaler of the Austrian Netherlands and above all the Austrian Marie Theresa thaler represent further trade coins of international relevance. The Löwenthaler (*Leeuwendaalder*), issued from 1575, is the oldest among these trade coins and was the first independently issued coin of the Spanish Netherlands. Because all thaler coins were equally valued in the Levant, the Löwenthaler with its relatively low silver content was primarily exported there since the mid-17th century. Until the early 19th century they circulated in the Levant under the Turkish designation *arslan* ('lion') or under the Arab designation *abu kelb* ('father of the dog' since the Arabs regarded the lion as a dog). It was only during the 18th century that first the Spanish dollars and then the Maria Theresa thaler replaced them as the most important trade coin.[254] Even though the Löwenthaler also circulated in Central and Eastern Europe, the Albertthaler (patagon or zilveren dukaat) was of much more importance in this area from the late 17th century. Being issued in the so-called Burgundian standard of coinage with a slightly lower silver content than the rixdollar it was imitated in many Central European territories from 1670. Moreover, the Albertthaler became not only the most important trade coin of the coastal towns and areas of the Baltic Sea region until far into the Russian Empire since the 17th century as a result of the important Dutch trade with the Baltic Sea region, but it was also used as unit of account in many towns such as Riga.[255]

Marie Theresa thaler were Austrian thaler coins, issued in the Convention standard (i.e. 10 thaler for one mark of Cologne fine silver) depicting Empress and Queen Maria Theresa. These coins were in such great demand in the Levant that the Austrian trade with them was very profitable, especially when in 1776 everybody was allowed to have Marie Theresa thaler coined from silver in different mints and to export them freely into the Orient. Because of their wide acceptance in the Levant, these Convention thaler, being especially minted for the trade, were later coined with Marie Theresa's portrait, even after her death in 1780. Being mainly exported via Leghorn, Trieste and Marseille, i.e. important ports for the Levant trade, they are said to have been used as means of payment for coffee in Yemen as early as around 1770. As with the Albertthaler many European states often imitated the Maria Theresa thaler. As early as the 18th century they circulated in the whole Ottoman Empire and in Arabia.[256] Arab merchants brought them along the North African coast as far as the Azores, Central Africa and Ethiopia, along the East African coast to Zanzibar, Mozambique and India (even though they were normally melted down

252 Ibid., p. 190; idem, *Der amerikanische Dollar*, in HEß / KLOSE (Bearb.), *Vom Taler zum Dollar*, pp. 202f.; DENZEL, Art. "Dollar", pp. 87f.; A. PIATT ANDREW, *The End of the Mexican Dollar*, in *Quarterly Journal of Economics* 18/3 (1904), pp. 321–356.

253 KLOSE, *Der spanische Piaster als Welthandelsmünze*, p. 190.

254 Idem, *Niederländische Taler*, pp. 98f.

255 Dietrich KLOSE, *Albertus-Taler in Deutschland und im Ostseegebiet*, in HEß / KLOSE (Bearb.), *Vom Taler zum Dollar*, pp. 129f.; KLOSE, *Niederländische Taler*, p. 99.

there), and, finally, even to Java. In the Balkan region the Marie Theresa thaler circulated until the end of Ottoman rule in the respective country and sometimes even
longer than that, for instance in Bosnia and Herzegovina at least until 1878 or in
Greece until 1882.[257] Marie Theresa thaler were quoted in the money and exchange
rate currents of the most important European export ports such as Leghorn and Trieste; in Trieste with some interruptions as recently as 1914.[258]

4.3 The International Gold Standard System (from c. 1870 up to 1914)

Great Britain was the only European country with a gold standard until 1870. In existence during the 18th century, gold currency was officially introduced with the act
of June 22nd 1816 defining gold as the only legal tender for consolidating the currency after the Napoleonic Wars. Moreover, the obligation of the Bank of England to
redeem notes in the respective amount of gold, suspended in 1797, was re-esta-
blished in 1821 guaranteeing again the convertibility of the circulating paper money.
There were two reasons for the British model of a gold currency becoming accepted
in the long run in Europe and the world, in comparison with the silver standard or at
least the double standard of nearly all other countries such as France. This can be
traced back, first, to Great Britain's industrial, commercial and financial power to
offer worldwide financial services and, second, to the fact that there were no restrictions within the money and capital transactions of Great Britain. Thus the pound
sterling became the most important currency of the world during the 19th century,
with more than two-thirds of total world trade being transacted in this currency during the late 19th century.[259] Conducting a large part of its foreign trade with Great
Britain, Portugal connected its currency to the gold standard as early as 1854. The
gradual transition of more and more countries to the gold standard was based on the
discovery of gold in California in 1848, in Australia in 1851/53 and in South Africa
and Alaska in the 1890s.[260]

     With gold reducing in price in comparison to silver as a result of its increased
supply since the 1850s, the actual price relation between these metals shifted mainly
in countries with a double standard currency based on an officially fixed gold–silver
ratio such as France (1:15.5). Large quantities of gold, for example, were imported
into France. Because it was overvalued there, it was exchanged for silver, which was
then exported to Asia and above all to India. Also, the four countries oriented towards the French franc, i.e. France (franc), Belgium (Belgian franc), Italy (lira) and
Switzerland (franken or franc), used debased silver coins to buy adequately valued

---

256 "The Muskat trader sells locally in rupees or [Maria Theresa] dollars, usually payable in instal-
     ments concluded in about three months." Report on the Conditions and Prospects of British
     Trade in Oman, Bahrain and Arab Ports in the Persian Gulf, in *Great Britain. Accounts and Pa-
     pers* 1905, 85, pp. 2–4, cited in Charles ISSAWI (ed.), *The Economic History of the Middle East,
     1800–1914. A Book of Readings*, Chicago 1966, p. 310.

257 Dietrich KLOSE, Der Maria-Theresien-Taler, in HEß / KLOSE (Bearb.), *Vom Taler zum Dollar*,
     pp. 195–199, esp. pp. 195–197.

258 *WdW I/II*, pp. 228, 449f.

259 Michael COLLINS, *Money and Banking in the UK*, London 1988, pp. 124–126.

260 NORTH, *Das Geld*, pp. 145f.

coins in neighbouring countries in order to sell the latter at a profit. Consequently, these four countries following the franc founded a confederation, the so-called Latin Monetary Union, in 1865 in order to tackle the problem of the continuous drain on silver. Within this union, France, the economically and politically most powerful partner, enforced its ideas of keeping the double standard although the three remaining countries preferred a transition to the gold standard. It was during the International Currency Conference at the World Exhibition in Paris in 1867 that the gold standard was regarded as having definitely better prospects of making a contribution to a worldwide harmonization of currencies.[261]

When the silver price dropped dramatically during the early 1870s as a result of an increase in production after silver had been discovered in the Rocky Mountains (Nevada), this gave reason for many European states to accept the gold standard. The newly founded German Empire, the most powerful industrial and commercial nation of the Continent, was the first of these states to establish the gold standard in 1873 (limping gold standard), representing the starting point for many smaller countries to follow suit. In the very same year Denmark and Sweden founded the Scandinavian Monetary Union, which incorporated Norway in 1875. The Netherlands introduced the gold standard in 1875/76. As a consequence, the countries of the Latin Monetary Union came under such heavy monetary pressure that they all accepted the limping gold standard during the 1880s, except Italy. Finally, Austria–Hungary and the Russian Empire joined this group during the 1890s. So all neighbouring countries of the German Empire and Great Britain had established the gold standard one after the other, following the example of the most powerful industrial and commercial nations of Europe with whom they maintained their most important commercial and financial relations. Countries that had established the (limping) gold standard sold their silver at the world market, with the result that, first, more and more countries felt impelled to establish the gold standard for monetary considerations and, second, the silver price was continually dropping since the 1870s. According to Barry Eichengreen, however, the latter aspect should not be overestimated.[262]

Because of increasingly powerful countries adopting the gold standard, the system of the so-called 'classic gold standard' developed during the 1870s as an internationally accepted system of payment settlement (see Table 3).[263]

> The classic gold standard was characterised by three principles: convertibility of gold, exchange rate stability and balance of payments adjustment. Whereas the governments had only to ensure gold convertibility, exchange rate stability and balance of payments adjustment emerged auto-

261 Ibid., pp. 146f.; Barry EICHENGREEN, *Vom Goldstandard zum Euro. Die Geschichte des internationalen Währungssystems*, Berlin 2000, p. 33.

262 Ibid., pp. 35f. Cf. also Guilio M. GALLAROTTI, The Scramble for Gold: Monetary Regime Transformation in the 1870s, in Michael D. BORDO / Forrest CAPIE (eds.), *Monetary Regimes in Transition*, Cambridge 1993, pp. 15–67.

263 The literature on the gold standard is enormous. Hence, only some essential works will be cited, presenting the state of research: A.G. FORD, *The Gold Standard 1880–1914. Britain and Argentina*, Oxford 1962; Marcello DE CECCO, *Money and Empire. The International Gold Standard, 1890–1914*, Oxford 1974; Barry EICHENGREEN (ed.), *The Gold Standard in Theory and History*, New York 1983; Ian M. DRUMMOND, *The Gold Standard and the International Monetary System 1900–1939*, Basingstoke 1987; Michael D. BORDO / Ronald MACDONALD, Violations of the "Rules of the Game" and the Credibility of the Classical Gold Standard, 1880–1914, in National Bureau of Economic Research (ed.), *Working Paper 6115*, Cambridge (Mass.) 1997; EICHENGREEN, *Vom Goldstandard zum Euro.*

matically, if seen from a theoretical point of view. … In the case of two countries the process of adjustment can theoretically be described as follows: falling prices in the home country raise exports and, as a consequence, lead to an active trade balance. The resulting surplus of foreign currency lowers the exchange rate, which after reaching the gold import point leads to an import of gold into the home country and, thus, increases the money supply. As one result, interest rates fall with the consequence of capital exports to the foreign country where higher interest rates are paid. Now, the exchange rate rises again deteriorating the balance of trade. Moreover, the previously mentioned increase of the money supply increases prices in the home country and exports decline. Therefore, both the interest rate mechanism and the price mechanism work towards a balance of trade equilibrium. The process of adjustment in the foreign country proceeds in the same direction: In the foreign country from which gold is exported the money supply shrinks and prices decline. This causes a rise of exports and, thereby, a contribution to the adjustment process in the trade balance. Capital movements responding very fast to changes of interest rates play a very important role in connection with the functioning of the system, as they are the basis for the very important stabilising speculation. According to this theory, the expected adjustments mechanisms should lead to an equilibrium in the balance of trade and to stability of prices.[264]

Table 3: The Transition to the Gold Standard[265].

Year	Country
1816 (by law)	Great Britain
1854	Portugal
1862	Uruguay
1871/76	Germany
1873	Sweden, Denmark, Norway, Belgium, France
1875	Italy, the Netherlands
1877	Finland
1885	Egypt
1890	Romania
1891	Tunis
1892/1900	Austria–Hungary
1895	Chile
1896	Costa Rica
1897	Russia, Japan
1899	India
1900	USA, Ecuador
1902	Siam
1903	Colombia
1904	Panama
1905	Mexico

---

264 Margarete WAGNER-BRAUN, Commercial Integration during the Era of the Classic Gold Standard, in Markus A. DENZEL (ed.), *From Commercial Communication to Commercial Integration. Middle Ages to 19th Century*, Stuttgart 2004, pp. 249–271, esp. p. 263. Cf. also W. SCAMMELL, The Working of the Gold Standard, in EICHENGREEN (ed.), *The Gold Standard*, pp. 103–120; EICHENGREEN, *Vom Goldstandard zum Euro*, pp. 45–50.

265 POHL, *Aufbruch der Weltwirtschaft*, pp. 247f.

Extensive stability of exchange rates can also be observed in the countries adopting the gold standard. Moreover, for most of the countries the reason for joining this system was to stabilize the exchange rates of their own currency. One should avoid speaking, however, of 'fixed rates', which happens very often in scientific literature, because the exchange rates among the countries that had adopted the gold standard were not fixed by any kind of order, but fluctuated slightly around the respective gold parity between two currencies.

During the early 20th century the gold standard system experienced its zenith, even though not all national currency systems resembled or even equalled one another at that time. Table 4 shows this.

Table 4: The Different Types of Gold Standard Currencies after c. 1880[266]

		Domestic money circulation:	
		mainly gold coins	gold, silver, token coins, bank notes
Monetary reserves:	gold	Great Britain, Germany, France, United States	Belgium, Switzerland
	mainly foreign exchange	Russian Empire, Australia, South Africa, Egypt	Austria–Hungary, Japan, the Netherlands, the Scandinavian Monetary Union, all other British dominions and overseas possessions
	solely foreign exchange		the Philippines, India, Latin American countries

Only Great Britain, Germany, the USA and France, the four most important industrial nations of that time, had a real gold standard, i.e. either the current coins circulating in the country were gold coins or the circulating banknotes and token coins were convertible into gold. France's gold standard was a limping standard since silver remained legal tender even though it was no longer coined. Similar to Belgium, Switzerland and the Netherlands, French banknotes could be converted into gold (or silver) coins only by official order and in the USA the gold standard was restricted until 1900 by legal regulations such as the Bland Allison Act of 1878 and the Sherman Act of 1890. In contrast to this, notes, silver coins and token coins circulated in the other countries of the gold standard system and could be converted into gold at fixed prices. For this purpose the central or state banks hoarded a fixed stock of gold reserves in different compositions often consisting of foreign exchange reserves such as British Treasury bills or bank deposits in London. This practice considerably supported, by the way, the dominant position of the London financial market within the whole financial system during the era of the gold standard. On the contrary, the London financial market and the Bank of England were of such great importance for maintaining the stability of the gold standard system that other countries supported the Bank of England during the years of crisis in 1890 and 1907.[267]

---

266 Ibid., p. 40.
267 Ibid., pp. 39–42, 61.

A combination of many factors led both to the gold standard's zenith during the last years before World War I and to a successful coping with the crises on the international financial markets such as that of 1907, managing, at the same time, to compensate for institutional deficiencies such as the lack of central banks in most of the non-European countries such as the USA until 1913.[268] During a time of relative peace and economic prosperity the openness of the markets and thus the expanding and increasingly multilateral trade not only supported the effectiveness of the gold mechanism but were also supported by the gold standard system. One of the most important fundamentals for the functioning of this system was Great Britain's unique position within the world economy, which helped to level out its balance of payments and made its pound sterling the key currency of the international payments system. The result of all these combined factors was the high stability of the exchange rates, the most obvious feature, representing a special exception of the whole period between the Middle Ages and 1914 and functioning as a real global payment system for only a few years.[269] With the outbreak of World War I, more and more countries left this system within a short time and suspended its mechanisms and basic premises, above all the guarantee to redeem notes in gold. During the interwar period the international payments system did not return to the gold standard of the period before 1914, despite multiple attempts.

4.4 Different Patterns of Quoting Exchange Rates

The discussion above proves that precious metal was the basis of payment transactions during the whole period of investigation, just as it had been in the ancient world and the Middle Ages. Absolute metallism was originally based on the principle of barter economy and acted on the assumption that monetary metals had a fixed value. It was replaced by the moderate metallism during the 17th century, allowing bank and governmental notes or token coins to be used for common monetary transactions in order to facilitate them. It was especially during the 19th century that bank and government notes gradually started to replace fully valued means of payment in precious metal, although such 'compensatory means of payment' demanded to be redeemable in gold. In this context it was of secondary interest which precious metal a currency was based on (silver, gold and sometimes copper), particularly, since this depended mainly on the availability of the respective precious metal. The slow establishment of gold as the only currency metal, finally ending only during the 19th century with the significant gold findings in California, Australia and Alaska, demonstrates this relationship. In many cases, a currency could also be based on two currency metals, normally silver and gold (bimetallism), where there was reluctance to abandon gold coins, although there was insufficient gold available to adopt the gold standard.[270]

---

268 It was only in this year that the Federal Reseve System was established, although it played a limited role in the period examined here, which ends in 1914. Cf. G. GORDON, Clearinghouses and the Origin of Central Banking in the United States, *Journal of Economic History* 45/2 (1985), pp. 277–283.

269 EICHENGREEN, *Vom Goldstandard zum Euro*, pp. 66f.

From this perspective of precious metals, the parity between two coins based on their fineness or their 'intrinsic value' expressed their real ratio of precious metal value. Thus the par of exchange between two financial markets with currencies based on the same precious metal could be calculated as the ratio between the fineness of current monies. If the precious metal bases differed, i.e. if one country followed the gold standard and the other the silver standard, exchange rates became additionally subject to the fluctuating prices of precious metals at the respective markets for them. This aspect becomes particularly apparent with the fluctuations of exchange rates of silver standard countries such as India, China or Persia in contrast to the gold-based pound sterling in the era of the classical gold standard. If one (or both) of the involved countries used paper money, the par of exchange could only be determined theoretically and only in relation to the then imaginary gold or silver currency backing the paper money.[271] Such exchange rate fluctuations, resulting from the changing valuation of precious metal or paper money on the international markets, represented the main risk of overseas trade for many European merchants.[272]

So, one can agree with Raymond de Roover, "An exchange rate is a price, the price set upon a foreign currency. Like other prices, it was set by supply and demand, that is, competitive bids, unless someone succeeded in rigging the market and in manipulating the rate to his advantage. Governments might try to do so occasionally, which does not mean that they always succeeded."[273] Basically, exchange rate quotations can be distinguished into direct and indirect quotations. Direct quotations refer to a certain currency common on the quoting exchange market A for a certain amount of currency units being used on the quoted exchange market B. On the contrary, indirect quotations are given on the quoting exchange market A in currency units of the quoted exchange market B for a certain amount of currency units of A that were fixed in B. Paris, for instance, quoted Madrid during the 18th century in French currency for 1 Peso de cambio (direct quotation), whereas London was quoted there in pence sterling for 1 écu of 3 livres tournois (indirect quotation).

Both direct and indirect quotations could be given in per cent premium or discount. This practice was particularly used if both the quoting and the quoted exchange market used the same currency such as the quotation among the exchange markets within France, Spain, the USA or the exchange markets of the Latin Monetary Union. The respective premium or discount was related to 1 or 100 currency units on one of the exchange markets. Nevertheless, a quotation in per cent premium or discount could also be done in relation to a fixed par of exchange, as was done on the exchange markets of the US Atlantic coast quoting on London. Similar quotations in per cent premium or discount on a fixed par of exchange also existed in Hava-

---

270 ZELLFELDER, Glossar, p. 203.

271 WALTER, Wechsel, Pari, Kurs, p. 62; ZELLFELDER, Glossar, p. 204. For parities of European currencies of around 1850 and 1913, see Jürgen SCHNEIDER / Oskar SCHWARZER, Währungsparitäten in Europa um 1850/1913, in Wolfram FISCHER (ed.), *Europäische Wirtschafts- und Sozialgeschichte von der Mitte des 19. Jahrhunderts bis zum Ersten Weltkrieg* (= idem et al. [eds.], *Handbuch der europäischen Wirtschafts- und Sozialgeschichte*, vol. 5), Stuttgart 1985, pp. 778f.

272 Hermann SCHUMACHER, Die Organisation des Fremdhandels in China, *Jahrbuch für Gesetzgebung, Verwaltung und Volkswirtschaft im Deutschen Reich* 23 (1899), pp. 259–293, esp. p. 275.

273 Raymond DE ROOVER, *The Bruges Money Market around 1400*, Brussels 1968, p. 27.

na[274] and in the Indian Ocean area, for instance on Mauritius: "The old habit of treating the rupee as 2s. sterling survives in the local method of quoting the exchanges
on London on the basis of a nominal par of 100 rupees = 10l., and adding the requisite number of rupees 'per cent premium'."[275] Exchange rate quotations among the
Indian exchange markets could also be given in annas (not per cent!) premium or
discount per 1 rupee with 1 anna = 1/16 rupee.

5. The Cashless Payments System and Its Exchange Markets from the 16ᵗʰ Century up to 1914[276]

5.1 Theoretical and Methodical Reflections on the Integration within the System of Cashless Payment Transactions

"A financial centre could be of local, national or regional importance in the general
services it provided, but of international importance in one particular area."[277] The
distinction between the *integration* of a certain exchange place or financial market
on the one hand *into* the up to 1870 solely European-centred international system of
cashless payments of a certain period of time, and on the other hand the *linking* of a
place *to* this system represents the central theoretical and methodical theme of this
chapter:

> In most cases, the *linking* can be seen as the 'early stage' and precondition of *integration* of
> exchange markets into the already existing payment system. This gradual process, often too dif-
> ficult to comprehend in detail due to the lack of sources, can be called *integrative process*: a
> process whose final result is *integration*, i.e. the complete integration of a certain exchange mar-
> ket into the particular payment system of a certain time.[278] The criteria for the *integration* are a
> (relatively) extended network of international exchange rate quotations administered by this
> exchange market, as well as equally extensive exchange rate quotations on this market, and
> finally the regularity of domestic and foreign quotations, whereas the (relatively) regular
> exchange relation to one or only a few foreign exchange markets constitutes a *linking*. The *linked*
> exchange market can use the mediation of the other one, which in this case functions as an inter-

---

274 DENZEL, Finanzplätze, Wechselkurse und Währungsverhältnisse in Lateinamerika, pp. 90–95.

275 Robert CHALMERS, *History of Currency in the British Colonies*, London 1893 [repr. Colchester
     1972], p. 368; cf. ibid., p. 361; SWOBODA [1889], p. 432.

276 The following chapter represents a slightly revised and enlarged version of one of the author's
     contributions already published in another context: Markus A. DENZEL, The System of Cashless
     Payment as a Basis for the Commercial Integration of Europe and the World, in idem (ed.), *From
     Commercial Communication to Commercial Integration*, pp. 199–248.

277 Ranald C. MICHIE, General Introduction: The Rise of a Global Financial Centre – the City of
     London since 1700, in idem (ed.), *The Development of London as a Financial Centre, vol. I:
     1700–1850*, London – New York 2000, pp. vii–xxxii, esp. p. viii. Cf. newly Reinhard H.
     SCHMIDT / Michael H. GROTE, Was ist und was braucht ein "bedeutender Finanzplatz"?, in
     *Europäische Finanzplätze im Wettbewerb. 27. Symposium des Instituts für bankhistorische For-
     schung e.V. am 16. Juni 2004 im Hause der Deutschen Bundesbank, Hauptverwaltung Frankfurt
     am Main* (= *Bankhistorisches Archiv. Zeitschrift zur Banken und Finanzgeschichte*, Beiheft 45),
     Stuttgart 2006, pp. 11–27.

mediary, for his own transactions with another; i.e. a third party in such a way this third party uses it itself and also to effect exchange business with the linked market.[279]

Regarding this integrative process as a model, it can be considered as a sequence involving different steps that can not always be distinguished clearly from one another, often as the result of frequently lacking relevant sources. My recent research suggests a useful differentiation between at least two fundamental aspects of this integrative process. Accordingly, the first is to be found in Europe and at its peripheries, in the Baltic Sea area, the Russian Empire and the Levant or the Ottoman Empire respectively; the second proposes that non-European possessions or areas are influenced by Europeans with European cashless payment techniques being introduced gradually. While the integrative process within Europe had already started with the development of cashless payment transactions techniques in the course of the Commercial Revolution of the 12th and 13th centuries, the integrative process of the financial markets within the non-European area started – with some remarkable exceptions in North America, the Caribbean and South and East Asia – only in the late 18th century, a period from which considerably more extensive and secure data have passed down to us than from the beginnings of this process in Europe. Consideration of the development of the European-shaped international cashless payment system within non-European regions allows us to reconstruct different phases or stages of this process of integration in a more subtly differentiated manner than would be possible for Europe, where, as a rule, this is only possible for particular peripheries at certain times.[280]

The integrative process in Europe (model 1). On the European continent, North and Central Italy represented the system's core. These commercial and financial centres or the merchant bankers working there were mutually integrated, a fact already acknowledged by the close linkage mentioned in Pegolotti's *Pratica della Mercatura* from the first half of the 14th century. The development of this system of cashless payment transactions from the Italian core can be understood in this way: cities lying outside this integrated core and functioning as exchange places were bound to this core.[281] Thus, not only was the technique of cashless payment transac-

---

278 The term 'integration', as used here, differs from its use by other economic historians, cf. among others Larry NEAL, Integration of International Capital Markets: Quantitative Evidence from the Eighteenth to Twentieth Centuries, *Journal of Economic History* 45 (1985), pp. 219–226; idem, The Integration and Efficiency of the London and Amsterdam Stock Markets in the Eighteenth Century, *Journal of Economic History* 47 (1987), pp. 97–115; Eric S. SCHUBERT, Innovations, Debts, and Bubbles: International Integration of Financial Markets in Western Europe, 1688–1720, *Journal of Economic History* 48 (1988), pp. 299–306; idem, Arbitrage in the Foreign Exchange Markets of London and Amsterdam during the 18th Century, *Explorations in Economic History* 26 (1989), pp. 1–20; Marie-Thérèse BOYER-XAMBEU / Ghislain DELEPLACE / Lucien GILLARD, A la recherche d'un âge d'or des marchés financiers: Intégration et efficience au XVI-IIe siècle, *Cahiers d'économie politique* 20/21 (1992), pp. 33–65.

279 Translated from: DENZEL, Integration Deutschlands, pp. 59f. Cf. idem, Integration ostmittel-, ost- und südosteuropäischer Städte, pp. 45–48; idem, Integration der Schweizer Finanzplätze.

280 Idem, Les places de change, *passim*.

281 From the perspective of the exchange system, cities linked in this way to the new system, either at the particular 'periphery' or in the course of European expansion into non-European countries, can be considered as enclaves in a region not yet bound to the European international system of cashless business payments, since these enclaves were normally found in areas characterized by payment transactions based upon precious metals.

tions spread, but the core of the system was extended simultaneously. These new exchange places, linked to the core, were forerunners in applying new technologies within payment transactions (as well as in the trade of goods), and they were also centres of a new supra-regional or even intercontinental communication. Therefore these exchange markets were focal points of a 'modern' development within the tertiary sector and contributed greatly and essentially to the linking as well as to the integration of 'their' region into the European and later worldwide network of payment transactions. In principle, no changes took place within this integration process between the end of the Middle Ages and the early 20th century.

What steps can be distinguished within this integration process? At the beginning of any linking of a 'new' exchange place to the central area of international cashless payments, 'contact' is established, i.e. an exchange relation is recognizable by an exchange rate quotation to at least one financial market that already belongs to a centre within a system of cashless payment transactions and that is consequently already integrated into this system (*type 1*). This 'exchange rate quotation on at least one financial market' has to be understood to mean that exchange rate quotations were probably established on two or more places lying in the core at the same time or in a series within a short time period; every 'new' exchange place has to be observed individually, since every one had its own simultaneous exchange rate quotations. The regularity, the intensity and partly also the duration of exchange relations of new exchange places to different financial markets of the centre was different throughout; they changed often in the course of the years and should, therefore, undergo a more detailed investigation. Since investigations are based on available sources, further research is almost impossible for European conditions at the end of the Middle Ages as well as for the early modern times, because they do not allow precise statements about subtleties of this process of integration.

A second stage is achieved if such exchange relations of the 'new' exchange place on already integrated financial markets of the central area became more steady, in particular when exchange rates were quoted relatively regularly over a longer period of time (at least over some years, or decades) on a particular constant group of exchange markets (*type 2*). Although still outside the core of the system of cashless payment transactions, the former 'new' exchange place can be regarded as established and, thus, as already closely bound to the international system. In the case of financial places of a particular European periphery, this stage often continued for a long period of time, sometimes for more than two centuries. During this stage, the integration process could still be unsuccessful and the place could suffer from disintegration. This occurred particularly when a change of political authority forced merchants as upholders of this system politically as well as economically to break off relations with the core of the system, for example if they were compelled to emigrate or if the trade existing behind cashless payment transactions declined due to military incidents.

An even closer linking is achieved by the exchange market if at least one market integrated in the core area starts to quote this exchange market. Initially, it quotes the place most often irregularly or only temporarily, and later on more regularly (*type 3*). Moreover, it was also possible that two or more already integrated places bound the exchange place closer and closer to the core, each of them with a different

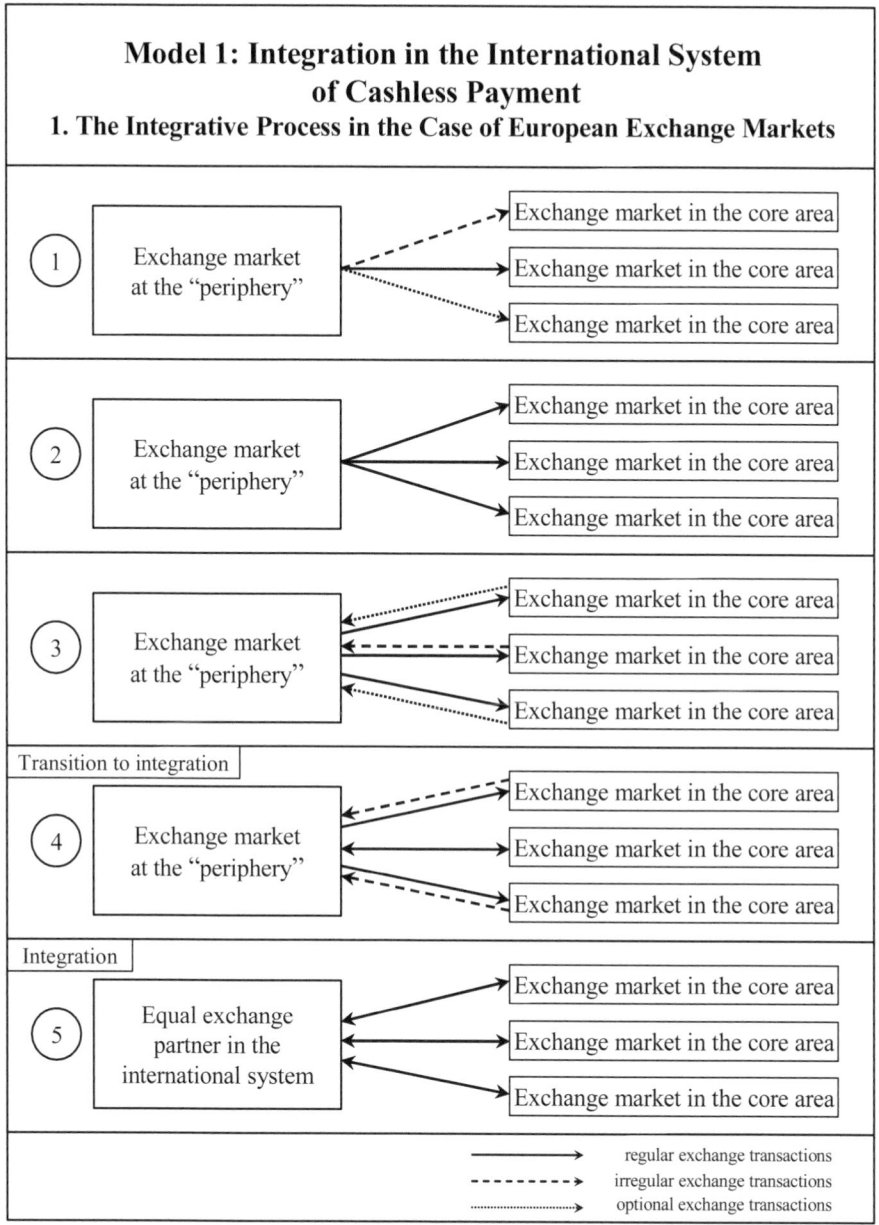

Model 1: Integration in the International System of Cashless Payment
1. The Integrative Process in the Case of European Exchange Markets

intensity. The transition to integration was accomplished only if at least one exchange market of the core area quoted regularly the exchange place previously on the periphery (other places perhaps still irregularly) (*type 4*). This transition to integration could result in a complete integration, characterized by several central exchange markets of the core area quoting regularly on the former 'new' exchange market and, as a result, accepting it as a partner of equal rank, thereby integrating it into the international system of cashless payment transactions (*type 5*). Thus this exchange market became part of the core area, which in consequence was extended, since the whole hinterland of the new integrated financial market was integrated into the international system at the same time, and every exchange market offered financial services – in this case within the domain of cashless payments – not only for the respective city itself, but also for its hinterland, whose size most often cannot be determined by the sources but which could contain large areas.

One aspect is left unconsidered from the chosen international perspective: the development of regional subsystems. In Europe and also on the European periphery, this process took place exclusively at the regional level, that is, within a country or a geographically relatively restricted area, for instance within the Kingdom of Naples or the Two Sicilies, or within the Netherlands, Spain, France or Germany respectively. While regional subsystems also developed in non-European regions between countries, subcontinents and even between continents (see below), such a complex and geographically vast subsystem could, in contrast, not develop within the European international cashless payment transactions and its periphery – last but not least because of its small spatial size – however, this was possible within individual countries. The Levant and the Black Sea region, which will be considered separately, held a position in between.

The integrative process in the non-European regions (model 2)[282]. In the non-European regions, the first and central exchange relation of all emerging exchange places was established as the central exchange market of the 'mother country', expressing the 'classical' economic relationship of dependency of non-European territories on their mother country.[283] From this it becomes clear that – concerning the techniques of payment transactions – the mother country or the merchants and bankers respectively were financing the trade with their non-European territories on their own exchange market(s) and, thus, granted credit to their economically subordinate overseas business partners. The exchange transaction was effected in such a way that, as a rule, bills of exchange were drawn only by European merchants or planters in the non-European country at merchants or bankers of the mother country[284] (which could have the effect of establishing an exchange rate quotation in the colony); this occurred only in exceptional cases the other way around (and was even less often documented in the exchange rate currents of European financial places by means of exchange rate quotations). Owing to this exchange relation to the central financial market of the mother country, a linking of the Europeans within the non-European territories to the entire European-based international cashless payment system was established. The background of this situation is of fundamental importance: to get one's bill of exchange accepted, the drawer had to draw the bill in the

---

282 Cf. DENZEL, Kolonialstädte als Finanzplätze, pp. 228–239; idem, Bargeldloser Zahlungsverkehr im europäischen Überseehandel, 73–80.

283 Cf. MCCUSKER, *Money and Exchange*, p. 120.

284 The bill which was primarily used was therefore the 'draft', while remittances were used less; cf. MAHLBERG, *Wechselkurse*, p. 21 for the non-European exchange business at the beginning of the 20th century.

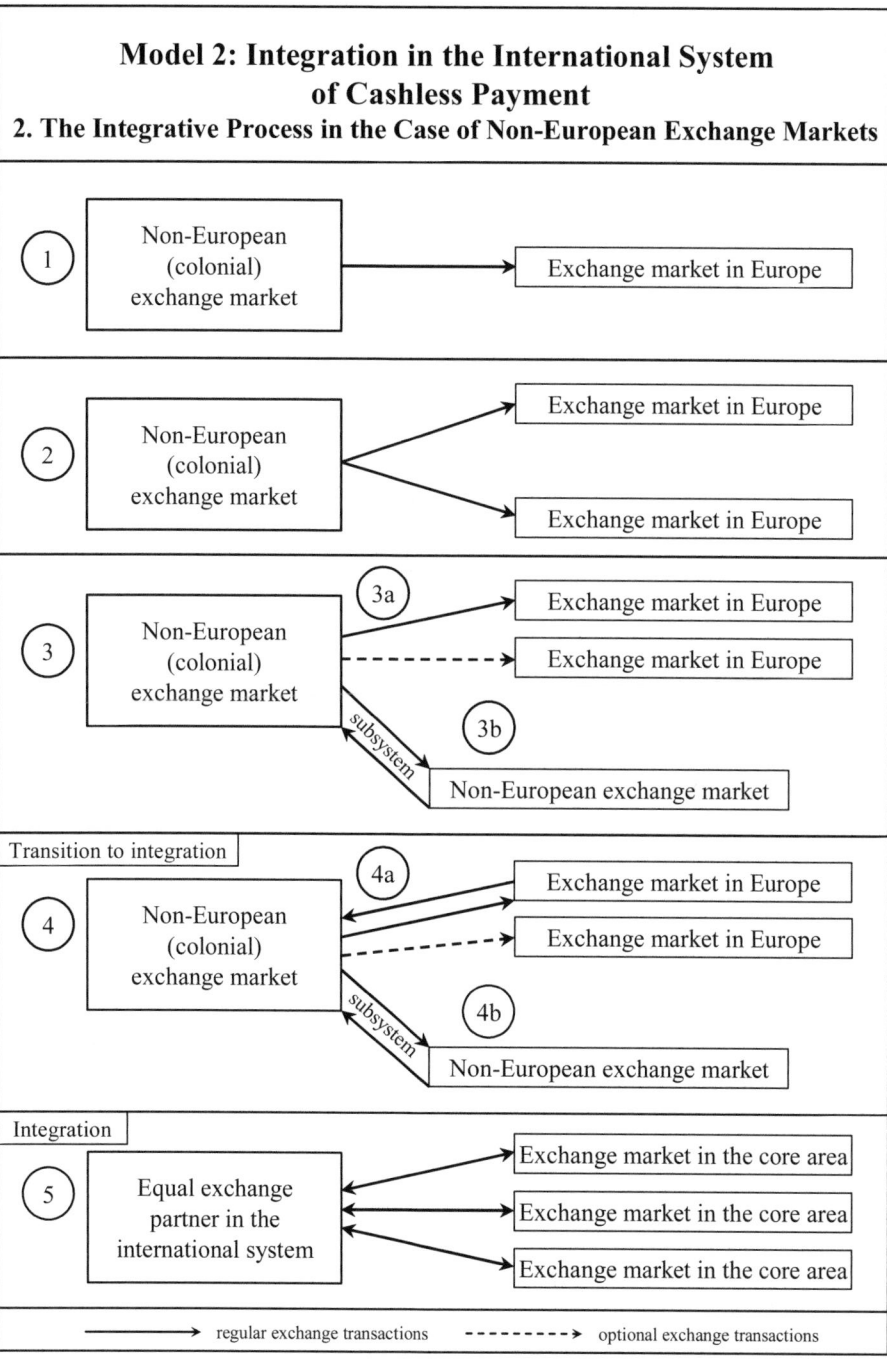

**Model 2: Integration in the International System
of Cashless Payment
2. The Integrative Process in the Case of Non-European Exchange Markets**

1. Non-European (colonial) exchange market → Exchange market in Europe

2. Non-European (colonial) exchange market → Exchange market in Europe / Exchange market in Europe

3. Non-European (colonial) exchange market
   - 3a → Exchange market in Europe
   - → Exchange market in Europe
   - 3b subsystem → Non-European exchange market

Transition to integration

4. Non-European (colonial) exchange market
   - 4a ↔ Exchange market in Europe
   - → Exchange market in Europe
   - 4b subsystem → Non-European exchange market

Integration

5. Equal exchange partner in the international system
   - → Exchange market in the core area
   - ↔ Exchange market in the core area
   - → Exchange market in the core area

—————→ regular exchange transactions   - - - - - - - ➤ optional exchange transactions

currency demanded by the drawee, most often in the currency of the mother country, although he himself could sell it within the non-European possession only in the currency of the colony: thus he himself took the risk, since the European exporter gave an invoice only in his own European currency. He accepted bills of exchange from the non-European territories in European currency as a payment for his exported goods, although those bills drawn in non-European currencies, i.e. the currency of a certain colony, were usually rejected.[285] This 'classical' relationship (*type 1*) within the cashless payment transaction between an overseas possession and the central financial market of the mother country was very often the only exchange relation of a non-European city within the whole period of investigation.

An evident enhancement of *type 1* occurred within the cashless payment transactions from a non-European possession to Europe when non-European partners were linked to the system due to exchange relations with two or more European exchange markets. This could be the result of two or more occupations of the colony between different colonial powers, so that the 'new' colonial power was quoted in addition to the traditionally quoted exchange market of the 'old' mother country. This fact can be observed in the French and Dutch colonies, which were taken over by Great Britain in the wake of the Napoleonic Wars, for instance in the Colony of the Cape of Good Hope, on Mauritius or in British Guyana. Furthermore, an overseas territory could start relationships with other financial markets of the mother country out of economic interests in order to gain trading advantages, especially during the 19th and the early 20th centuries.

In particular, the exchange rate quotation on London from all overseas territories of all European colonial powers in the 19th and 20th centuries should be mentioned here, since both London as 'financial centre of the world' at that time and the pound sterling as 'key currency of the world' enjoyed outstanding importance within cashless payments. As a result, an exchange rate quotation on London seemed to be economically necessary in all non-European territories apart from that quotation on the mother country. The orientation of an overseas possession towards two European financial centres (*type 2*) was an exceptional situation or a transitional stage after changes to rules or in the framework of further expansion of exchange relations. That is why it was most often relatively short-lived.

Beside those relations between non-European territories and Europe, more and more regionally developing exchange networks emerged within individually large economic areas, for example in Eastern and Southern Asia, in the Caribbean or in North America. By means of this qualitative innovation, we can detect closer economic connections within the (cashless) payment system and also between these regions, since the demand for cashless payments within a non-European region emerged only when non-European colonies became more independent and started to maintain payment connections among themselves and/or with local merchants;[286] these payment transactions were not required to be cashless. Within this integration process, we must again distinguish between the linking of an alternating intensity of individual exchange places to the regional system (*type 3a*) on the one hand and of

---

285 Cf. ibid., pp. 6f.
286 Cf. ibid., p. 6.

the complete integration of these exchange places into the regional system (*type 3b*) on the other. From the perspective of the European-dominated international cashless payment system, such a regional system should be considered as a kind of subsystem, which is to a large extent economically dependent on the financial capacity of European trading and banking houses. By now, external places were bound closer and closer to the whole international payment system itself as well as to the individual subsystem. At last, these places could be integrated into these systems, all of the hierarchies of the system being subject to perpetual change. Within the framework of this process, proper financial centres can emerge as intermediaries of the trade and of payment transactions between local and European merchants (or the other way round) and operate between various subsystems or hierarchies of different systems.

The last step to be examined here is the transition from the linking to the integration into the international payment system: this transition occurred by means of regular quotation of the financial centre of the mother country at the non-European exchange place. During this stage, connections of the non-European exchange place to other exchange places of the international system, and also exchange connections to regional subsystems were possible – either at the stage of linking (*type 4a*) or at that of integration (*type 4b*). The more variously the relationships to exchange markets of the international system were designed, the closer became the linking of the non-European exchange place to the international system. The integration process was finally completed with the non-European financial market being integrated into the international system, a stage at which the non-European and the European financial places acted as partners of equal rank with regular and mutual exchange rate quotations.

5.2 The Development in Europe from the Middle Ages up to c. 1870

As has already been indicated, the integrative process in Europe during the medieval and partly also during the early modern period can only be understood fragmentarily, since normally only the conclusion of this process, i.e. the integration into the cashless payment system, is visible by means of available sources. Sources that show a detailed course of the integrative process are only sufficiently available from the end of the 17th century. In the case of these 'younger' exchange places, which could usually be found at the former periphery of the European cashless payment system – e.g. in the Holy Roman Empire (among others Leipzig, Breslau, Vienna, Berlin), in the Ottoman Empire (Constantinople, Smyrna), in the Baltic Sea region (e.g. Stockholm) or in the Russian Empire (particularly Saint Petersburg) – this process can be reconstructed in a more detailed way than in the case of the 'older' or traditional exchange markets in Italy, Western and Central Europe, which by the 17th century had already been completely integrated in the system. The integrative process, which Europe was passing through between the Middle Ages and the 19th century, can be divided up into four stages.

Stage 1: The Mediterranean-centred cashless payment system of the 14th and 15th centuries[287]. For the first time, a certain network of exchange relations becomes tangible in Pegolotti's *Pratica della mercatura* from around 1340[288] – a network with a relatively high density within Italy, the motherland of cashless payment transactions based on the bill of exchange. In addition, this central area of Italy was associated – first via the fairs in the Champagne[289] – with Northwestern Europe (Bruges, London, Paris), the Iberian Peninsula, Northern Africa (Tunis) and the Levant (Rhodes, Famagusta, Alexandria, Crete, Constantinople, Pera and Caffa). According to contemporary merchant manuals,[290] relationships within Italy had expanded further about one century afterwards, and those to Northwestern Europe and to the Iberian east coast were clearly strengthened as well. Furthermore, it is remarkable that direct exchange connections existed now between Northwestern Europe and the Tyrrhenian Sea region, with the Geneva fairs playing the role of an important intermediary.[291] With regard to the above-mentioned model 1, this fact can be interpreted to mean that the exchange markets of Northwestern Europe and of the Iberian Peninsula, which had only been linked to the system via Italian exchange places around the middle of the 14th century, were completely integrated into the system (*type 5*): Merchants from Northwestern Europe and from the Iberian Peninsula could effect cashless payments without using the Italian exchange markets as intermediaries, as already carried out by Francesco di Marco Datini in around 1400.[292]

The Levant was excluded from this triangle between Italy, the east coast of the Iberian Peninsula and Northwestern Europe, which together now represented the central area of the European payment system.[293] There, exchange relations exceeded *type 1* at least in part. As suggested by exchange rate quotations in merchant manuals, it must still be considered doubtful to what extent the relatively regular exchange rate quotations from Italian places existed with their partners in the east (*type 3*, perhaps even *type 4*), since there are no detailed series of exchange rates as evidence. However, the development of regionally restricted subsystems seems to be more doubtful and would be expected at most between Constantinople, Pera and Caffa, and maybe between Chios and Rhodes.[294]

---

287 Cf. DENZEL, *"Practica"*, chapters 3 and 4; Peter SPUFFORD, Financial Markets and Money Movements in the Medieval Occident, in *Viajeros, peregrinos, mercaderes en el Occidente Medieval. XVIII semana de estudios medievales*, Navarra 1991, pp. 201–216.

288 PEGOLOTTI, *La pratica della mercatura*, cap. XLV and passim.

289 Scontration was developed here, which made it possible to settle accounts between merchants.

290 Giovanni-Francesco PAGNINI DELLA VENTURA, *Della decima e di varie altre gravezze imposte dal commune di Firenze, Della moneta e della mercatura de' Fiorentini fino al secolo XVI*, 4 vols., Lisbona – Lucca 1765/66, vol. IV: *La Pratica della Mercatura scritta de Giovanni di Antonio da Uzzano nel 1442*; Franco BORLANDI (ed.), *El Libro di Mercatantie et Usanze de' Paesi*, Torino 1936. Cf. LEONE, Some Preliminary Remarks.

291 Cf. Jean-François BERGIER, *Genève et l'économie européenne de la Renaissance*, Paris 1963.

292 Cf. DE ROOVER, *Lettre de change*, p. 45; Iris ORIGO, *"Im Namen Gottes und des Geschäfts". Lebensbild eines toskanischen Kaufmanns der Frührenaissance. Francesco di Marco Datini 1335–1410*, München 1985 (English edition: 1957, repr. 1963), pp. 130-132; DENZEL, *"Practica"*, pp. 89–91.

293 For the following, cf. idem, Wechselplätze als territoriale Enklaven, pp. 550–552.

294 Cf. also Michel MOLLAT, *Der königliche Kaufmann. Jacques Cœur oder der Geist des Unternehmertums*, München 1991 (French edition: 1988), p. 208.

All these relationships in the context of the European payment system fell victim to a process of disintegration after the Ottoman Empire's advance in the eastern Mediterranean world and in the Black Sea area, which becomes apparent with the taking of Constantinople and the fall of the Byzantine Empire in 1453. In the following decades, these relationships became clearly weaker, and if they still existed, they were used only by a few European trading-houses. A completely different development can be observed at the western periphery of the cashless payment system. In Pegolotti's day, cashless payments existed from Seville with Florence, Barcelona, and probably with Genoa and Majorca (*type 2*).[295] Merchant manuals from the middle of the 15th century provide evidence only for exchange rate quotations from Genoa at Seville,[296] which can probably be considered as being related to the comparatively large colony of Genoese merchants in Seville (*type 3*).[297]

Stage 2: The shift of the main focus of the cashless payment system from the Mediterranean area to the Atlantic coast in the 16th and early 17th century. In the wake of the early European expansion in the 15th century, the way was prepared to bring the Mediterranean-centred European cashless payments system gradually to a new development: from the late 15th century on, the countries and seaports of the Atlantic coast reached a pan-European economic importance. Functioning as departure and destination points in shipping and transport, they became centres of new intercontinental communication.[298] Not only through the influx of precious metals from the New World, with its consequence for the state and war finances of the Spanish crown, but also with the Portuguese trade in spices and other Asian treasures, the Atlantic regions gained in economic worth to a much higher degree than had been the case throughout the Middle Ages. However, it was still Italian merchants, predominantly from Genoa and to a lesser degree from Florence, who dominated the multi-faceted business transactions among the merchants and in several cases the transactions of the merchants with the governments of that time. These Italian merchants made Seville and Lisbon two of the most important financial markets in Europe, and together with the Castilian fairs – the *feria de pagos* in Medina del Campo, Medina del Rioseco and Villalón – they were integrated into the cashless payments network[299] around the middle of the 16th century. This fact becomes evident when looking at the quotation of exchange rates at large international fairs (Lyons fairs, the Genoese fairs in Bisenzone) and at the important financial markets in Northwestern Europe (particularly in Antwerp), and in Italy on Seville and Lisbon (*type 5*).

In this century, however, the most conducive instrument for the integrative process within Europe was probably the establishment of a European system of ex-

---

295 SPUFFORD, *Handbook*, pp. 159–161.

296 PAGNINI DELLA VENTURA, *Della decima, vol. IV: La Pratica della Mercatura scritta de ... Uzzano ...*, cap. XXVII, pp. 133–135; BORLANDI (ed.), El libro, pp. 7, 11–13.

297 E.g. HEERS, *Le Livre de comptes de Giovanni Piccamiglio*, p. 346; DENZEL, *"Practica"*, p. 83.

298 Cf. Renate PIEPER, Informationszentren im Vergleich. Die Stellung Venedigs und Antwerpens im 16. Jahrhundert, in NORTH (ed.), *Kommunikationsrevolutionen*, pp. 45–60; Woodruff D. SMITH, The Function of Commercial Centers in the Modernization of European Capitalism: Amsterdam as an Information Exchange in the Seventeenth Century, *Journal of Economic History* 44 (1984), pp. 985–1005.

change fairs,[300] which connected the economically most potent regions. Specialized exchange fairs, at which the money trade almost completely superseded the goods trade, formed the basic network for the whole of Southern and Western Europe as far as cashless payments were concerned. A developing tendency from the goods fair into a specialization in exchange business can be seen at the Geneva fairs (see above), and this trend continued at the succeeding Lyons fairs from the 1460s onwards.[301] Last of all, the Brabant fairs in Antwerp and Bergen-op-Zoom began to replace the former financial centre of Northwestern Europe, Bruges, since the second half of the 15th century.[302] At that point, Antwerp became the main market for all financial transactions in Northwestern Europe. Here, a 'permanent market' was established by 1465/66, which made the fairs superfluous.[303] As mentioned above, the Castilian fairs were also integrated into the international fair system, as the Iberian Peninsula gradually gained in economic worth in the wake of the early European expansion.[304] Finally, in the second quarter of the 16th century, the Genoese Bisenzone fairs were founded with the clear intention to become exchange fairs[305] in competition with the Lyons fairs, which were controlled by the French crown and dominated by Florentine merchant bankers.[306] The Bisenzone fairs were dominated by the Genoese and served to finance state and military expenditures, especially those of the Spanish crown and the Habsburgs.[307] At the Bisenzone fairs,[308] the techniques of

---

299 Cf. LAPEYRE, *Les Ruiz*; Felipe RUIZ MARTÍN, *Lettres marchandes échangés entre Florence et Medina del Campo*, Paris 1965; idem, La banca en España hasta 1782, in *El Banco de España. Una historia económica*, Madrid 1970, pp. 1–196, esp. pp. 13–57; José Gentil DA SILVA, *Stratégie des affaires à Lisbonne entre 1595 et 1607. Lettres marchandes des Rodrigues d'Evora et Veiga*, Paris 1956; idem, *Marchandises et finances. Lettres de Lisbonne 1563–1578*, vol. II, Paris 1959, passim; vol. III, Paris 1961, passim; cf. *WdW IX*, pp. 58–67, 138–143. Cf. the recent short summary by Carmen SANZ AYÁN, Los procedimientos financieros: métodos y estrategias, in *El oro y la plata de las Indias en la época de los Austrias*, Madrid 1999, pp. 577–592; Enrique OTTE, Las Ferias Castellanas y Sevilla en el sistema bancario europeo del siglo XVI, in BERNAL (ed.), *Dinero, moneda y crédito*, pp. 31–42; Ricardo RODRÍGUEZ GONZÁLEZ, La negociación cambiaria en la banca de Simón Ruiz, in ibid., pp. 679–694. The Canaries were connected to the international system of cashless payment as well; Antonio M. MACÍAS HERNÁNDEZ, Génesis de una economía de base monetaria: Canarias, 1300–1500, in ibid., pp. 43–58, esp. pp. 53–55.

300 For a survey see Michael NORTH, Von den Warenmessen zu den Wechselmessen. Grundlagen des europäischen Zahlungsverkehrs in Spätmittelalter und Früher Neuzeit, in Peter JOHANEK / Heinz STOOB (eds.), *Europäische Messen und Märktesysteme in Mittelalter und Neuzeit*, Köln – Weimar – Wien 1996, pp. 223–238; DENZEL, *"Practica"*, chapter 5.

301 Jürgen SCHNEIDER / Nils BRÜBACH, Frankreichs Messeplätze und das europäische Messesystem in der frühen Neuzeit, in POHL (ed.), *Frankfurt*, pp. 171–190.

302 DE ROOVER, *Money, Banking and Credit*; idem, *The Bruges Money Market*.

303 VAN DER WEE, *Antwerp Market*.

304 Valentín VÁZQUEZ DE PRADA, Die kastilischen Messen im 16. Jahrhundert, in POHL (ed.), *Frankfurt*, pp. 113–131.

305 DA SILVA, *Banque et crédit*.

306 Marie-Thérèse BOYER-XAMBEU / Ghislain DELEPLACE / Lucien GILLARD, *Monnaie privé et pouvoir des princes. L'économie des relations monétaires à la Renaissance*, Paris 1986; idem, Goldstandard, Währung und Finanz im 16. Jahrhundert, in NORTH (ed.), *Geldumlauf*, pp. 167–181.

307 Cf. Herman VAN DER WEE / Ian BLANCHARD, The Habsburgs and the Antwerp Money Market: the Exchange Crises of 1521 and 1522–3, in BLANCHARD / GOODMAN / NEWMANN (eds.), *Industry and Finance*, pp. 27–57.

308 The Bisenzone fairs were held in several towns: from 1575 especially in Piacenza and from 1641 in Novi.

cashless payments were perfected to such an extent that they are considered as "foire[s] de change par excellence".[309] Therefore the consequences for the payment system can be seen in the closer connections among the financial markets of Medina del Campo, Seville, Lisbon, Lyons, Antwerp and the Italian markets of around 1580. At that time, the Bisenzone-centred system of the Genoese, which was based on the influx of precious metals from the New World and on the business with *asientos*, increasingly replaced the Lyons-centred system of the Florentine. The triangle formed by the Netherlands, the Iberian Peninsula and Italy constituted the backbone of the European cashless payment system, with which other economic regions, especially England (London, *type 5*), the Hanseatic area (Hamburg, *type 2* or *3*, and Danzig, *type 1* or *3*) and quite possibly Upper Germany (Frankfurt am Main, Nuremberg, Augsburg, all *type 2* or *3*), maintained increasingly close and regular exchange relations. The Mediterranean or rather the Italian-centred geographical structure of the European cashless payment system was broken up and all important exchange markets in Southern and Western Europe were integrated into this system.

Apart from this fair system, Antwerp – the destination port for Portuguese spices (since 1499) and Upper German metals – became not only the financial centre of Northwestern Europe, but also a financial market of pan-European relevance. Antwerp's 'permanent market' was the foundation for the establishment of the Antwerp new stock exchange (*nouvelle bourse*; 1531),[310] which succeeded and superseded the stock market in Bruges and was where exchange rates for nearly all important financial markets dealing in bills were quoted in exchange rate currents.[311] Here the endorsement, which had been developed in Italy and which was perfected at the Antwerp stock exchange, made bills of exchange negotiable to an extent that had never been existed before; the merchant bankers no longer needed brokers for their exchange business, and it was no longer necessary to draw a new bill for each new transaction.[312] The Antwerp stock exchange was also the market where the discount was practised by English merchants for the first time in 1536, and then (also at the Lyons fairs) more intensely from the middle of the 16th century on. With the spreading of the stock exchange as an institution in Northwestern Europe (Amsterdam 1530, London 1554, Hamburg 1558, Cologne 1566 etc.[313]), these new techniques won wider acceptance in this region of economic modernity.

Therefore the 16th century was the epoch in which the former Mediterranean-centred cashless payment system became an Atlantic-oriented one. The "model Italy" retained its dominance during the "Genoese age" (Braudel). A northwest European rise was made possible by means of the increased orientation towards the At-

---

309 GENTIL DA SILVA, *Banque et crédit*, p. 12. Cf. RACINE, Messen in Italien; José Ignacio MARTÍNEZ RUIZ, Mercato creditizio e profitti del cambio per lettera. Le operazioni di cambio con patto di ricorsa tra Siviglia e le fiere internazionali di 'Bisenzone' (1589–1621), *Storia economica. Rivista quadrimestrale diretta da Luigi de Rosa* 5/1 (2002), pp. 107–132.

310 Cf. Émile COORNAERT, *Les Français et le commerce international à Anvers (fin du XVe et XVIe siècle)*, 2 vols., Paris 1961, vol. II, pp. 148–150.

311 Cf. McCUSKER / GRAVESTEIJN, *The Beginnings of Commercial and Financial Journalism.*

312 SCHNEIDER, Messen, Banken und Börsen, pp. 148–154; idem, Indossament.

313 For the Holy Roman Empire in detail, see Karl Heinrich KAUFHOLD, Der Übergang zu Fonds- und Wechselbörsen vom ausgehenden 17. Jahrhundert bis zum ausgehenden 18. Jahrhundert, in Hans POHL (ed.), *Deutsche Börsengeschichte*, Frankfurt/Main 1992, pp. 77–132.

lantic region, which subsequently allowed Northwestern Europe to supersede Italy in its traditional leading role in the payment system during the 17th century.

Stage 3: The Northwest-European-dominated cashless payment system of the 17th and 18th centuries with Amsterdam as the world financial centre. After the 1620s, Northwestern Europe replaced the Mediterranean area as the central region of European trade as well as of the cashless payments system. There, the greatest significance for the European exchange trade was attached to the (Northern) Netherlands with its commercial and financial centre Amsterdam as the crucial point. The city of Amsterdam made a profit from various new types of institutions equally: on the one hand from the stock market, where endorsed and discounted bills were negotiated, and on the other hand the city benefited from the Wisselbank, set up after the Venetian model and having a stable currency, i.e. the bank money, which had to be used in all exchange transactions with an amount exceeding 600 guilders (300 guilders since 1643).[314] Thus Amsterdam was not only the most attractive but also the safest exchange market all over the world, having exchange connections with Venice, Seville, Lisbon, Paris, Rouen, London, Antwerp, Lille, Middelburg, with the fairs of Frankfurt am Main, Nuremberg, Hamburg and even with Danzig around 1630.[315] The other three important exchange markets of Northwestern Europe – London for the British Isles, Hamburg for Northern Germany and Paris for France – had a much more limited circle of exchange partners.[316] The range of Amsterdam's exchange partners shows that the process of integration within Europe gained momentum during the second quarter of the 17th century. From now on, a stronger linking to German exchange markets began. During the 16th century, they had been linked to the system particularly by means of Italian places, especially Venice, and they were now increasingly quoted at Northwestern European cities. In accordance with the above-mentioned typology, different German exchange markets, which can be considered as such at the beginning of the 17th century (Nuremberg, Frankfurt am Main, Augsburg, Hamburg, Cologne), developed from *type 3* to *type 5*. Hamburg can be regarded as a perfect example of this development since it was completely integrated into the system (*type 5*) by the end of the 17th century, last but not least because of the Dutch and Portuguese immigrants – the Sephardic Jews – to Hamburg, who brought with them not only their capital, but also their close commercial and financial relationships to Amsterdam and Lisbon. The whole northern German region was being connected to the system because of the Hamburg area. Moreover, various 'new' exchange markets were added in Central Europe during the 17th and 18th centuries. Their integrative process did not begin until then, for example especially at the exchange markets of Vienna (*type 3* since the turn of the 18th century), of the Leipzig fairs (*type 3* since the 1670s), of Breslau (*type 3* since the turn of the 18th century) and finally of Berlin (*type 1* or *2* since the 1720s)[317] as well as – in Switzer-

---

314 Johannes G. VAN DILLEN, The Bank of Amsterdam, in idem (ed.), *History of the Principal Public Banks*, The Hague 1934, pp. 79–100; DEHING / 'T HART, Linking the Fortunes, pp. 40, 43–51; Larry NEAL, How it All Began: The Monetary and Financial Architecture of Europe during the First Global Capital Markets, 1648–1815, *Financial History Review* 7 (2000), pp. 117–140.

315 *WdW III*, pp. 39–95; DENZEL, *"Practica"*, p. 402.

316 Ibid., pp. 418, 476, 422.

317 Idem, Integration Deutschlands, passim.

land – of Saint Gall (*type 3* or *4* during the 17th and early 18th century, *type 2* or *3* after c. 1720), of Basle (*type 3* in the 18th century, since the 1790s *type 4* or *5*), of Geneva (*type 3* since the 18th century), of Zurich (*type 2* during the 18th century) and of some smaller places.[318] While the exchange markets of Vienna, Leipzig and Breslau were already completely integrated in the 18th century, Berlin did not become a permanent partner in the system until 1815.[319] Consequently, the cashless payment system was clearly extended in Central Europe during the 17th and 18th centuries, whereas new exchange markets that had only just been linked to the system had an important role in the beginnings of the links with regions further east, such as the Leipzig fairs for Russia and Poland or Vienna's importance for the Ottoman Empire.[320]

Furthermore, the integrative process within the Netherlands, especially Amsterdam, extended to the Baltic Sea area and to the Russian Empire. As a result of Dutch commercial interests, an increased linking of the main trading centres of the eastern Baltic Sea area and also of Archangel to the cashless payment system started when the Dutch, who settled there, increasingly began to establish financial transactions with the mother country on the basis of bills of exchange. First exchange transactions between the Baltic Sea area and Northwestern Europe can be proven since the second half of the 16th century;[321] however, connections did not become stronger until the 17th century. As a rule, coastal cities of the Baltic Sea area (as well as Archangel) quoted at first exclusively on Amsterdam (*type 1*); when Hamburg gained in importance, it was quoted as well. It was only with the growing involvement of British merchants in the 18th century that a further quotation at London was added (*type 2*). Only Stockholm recorded a more numerous circle of exchange partners in the 18th century (with Paris and Danzig from 1740, with Copenhagen from 1760).[322] A continuation of the integrative process reaching far into the 18th century took place only in the case of the city of Danzig; however, only up to *type 3*. Amsterdam was the only completely integrated exchange market that quoted on Danzig in the 18th century (until the 1770s). Afterwards, Danzig suffered disintegration and was not able to move further than *type 2*.[323] Up to the 1870s, Saint Petersburg was the only place in the Northeastern part of Europe to be completely and permanently integrated into the cashless payment system. Although the exchange rate quotation (*type 1*) on Amsterdam was irregular from 1704, it became regular from the 1740s onwards. When the number of English merchants in the Russian trade and payment transactions increased, London (from the 1760s), Hamburg (especially since the end of the 18th century) and Stockholm (somewhat irregularly) became exchange partners of

---

318 Idem, Integration der Schweizer Finanzplätze, pp. 182–228.

319 Cf. Ilja MIECK, Berlins Aufstieg zum ersten preußischen Finanzplatz bis zur Industrialisierung, in Hans POHL (ed.), *Geschichte des Finanzplatzes Berlin*, Frankfurt/Main 2002, pp. 1–52.

320 DENZEL, *"Practica"*, pp. 464–476; idem, Integration Deutschlands, passim; idem, Zahlungsverkehr auf den Leipziger Messen vom 17. bis zum 19. Jahrhundert, in Hartmut ZWAHR / Thomas TOPFSTEDT / Günter BENTELE (eds.), *Leipzigs Messen 1497–1997. Gestaltwandel. Umbrüche. Neubeginn, vol. 1: 1497–1914*, Köln – Weimar – Wien 1999, pp. 149–165; *WdW VI*, passim; *HStD XII*, passim.

321 Gunter MICKWITZ, *Aus Revaler Handelsbüchern. Zur Technik des Ostseehandels in der ersten Hälfte des 16. Jahrhunderts*, Helsingfors 1938, pp. 84–86, 91–95; NORTH, *Geldumlauf*, pp. 149f.

322 *HStD XII*, pp. 289–361.

323 Ibid., pp. 257–275; DENZEL, Integration Deutschlands, pp. 70f.

Saint Petersburg apart from Amsterdam (*type 2*).[324] It was not until 1781 that Saint Petersburg was quoted by Leghorn (*type 3*), from 1807/10 by Stockholm (somewhat irregularly), from 1814 by Paris (also irregularly), from 1820 by Amsterdam and Berlin, and from 1821 by Hamburg and London.[325] All in all, integration of Saint Petersburg into the international cashless payment system can be assumed by the 1820s (*type 5*), whereas the transition to integration (*type 4)* was reached probably by the end of the 18th century but not later than the early 19th century. The Baltic Sea region was connected to the cashless payment system with less intensity than, for example, the Holy Roman Empire. In the Baltic Sea region a regional subsystem was only in a very rudimentary stage while in Central Europe a much more developed and comparatively interlinked type existed.

The Ottoman Empire and, thus, also South-Eastern Europe were bound even less intensively to the European cashless payment system. Since the end of the 17th century isolated exchange rate quotations are recorded for various cities of this area, in particular for Smyrna, Constantinople and Salonica, at places of the western Mediterranean Sea region (Marseille, Leghorn, Genoa), of Northwestern Europe (Amsterdam, London) as well as of Central Europe (Vienna), yet only the integrative process in Constantinople developed further than *type 2*.[326] The linking of the Ottoman exchange markets started from the direction of Southern and Central Europe from the 1780s. Vienna's exchange rate quotations on Constantinople (until 1858), Salonica (1780/81), and Smyrna (up to 1803) as well as the quotation of Leghorn, Genoa (only between 1802 and 1805) and Marseille on Constantinople and Smyrna around the turn of the 19th century[327] provide evidence for this course of events. At the end of the 18th century, Saloniki and Smyrna can be attributed to *type 3*, Constantinople even to *type 4*, i.e. it can therefore be equated with the transition to integration. The above-mentioned Southern and Central European exchange places held the key position in conveying European payment techniques to the Levant area. These first signs of the transition to integration were not strengthened in the further course of the 19th century, and even broke off in the 1850s and 1860s when Leghorn, Vienna and Trieste stopped their ultimately only sporadic quotations at Constantinople (also those from Leghorn at Smyrna).[328] Similar to the Baltic Sea region, evidence for the development of a subsystem of exchange connections within the Ottoman Empire can also be provided only in a rudimentary form.[329]

---

324 NEWMAN, 'A Very Delicate Experiment'; Hermann KELLENBENZ, Marchands en Russie aux XVIIe et XVIIIe siècles, in idem, *Europa, Raum wirtschaftlicher Begegnung. Kleine Schriften I*, Stuttgart 1991, pp. 205ff.; DENZEL, Integration ostmittel-, ost- und südosteuropäischer Städte, pp. 49–51; Klaus HELLER, *Die Geld- und Kreditpolitik des russischen Reiches in der Zeit der Assignaten (1768–1839/43)*, Wiesbaden 1983.

325 *Archives de la Chambre de Commerce et d'Industrie Marseille–Provence*, L.IX 1035; *HStD XII*, pp. 354–357; *WdW I/II*, pp. 106–109, 193–196, 370–377; *WdW I/III*, pp. 220f., 335–374.

326 Edhem ELDEM, La circulation de la lettre de change entre la France et Constantinople au XVIIIe siècle, in Hâmit BATU / Jean Louis BACQUÉ-GRAMMONT (eds.), *L'Empire Ottoman, la République Turquie et la France*, Istanbul – Paris 1986, p. 88; Nikos G. SVORONOS, *Le commerce de Salonique au XVIIIe siècle*, Paris 1956, p. 121; Ferréol REBUFFAT / Marcel COURDURIÉ, *Marseille et le négoce monétaire international (1785–1790)*, Marseille 1966, p. 124.

327 *WdW VI*, pp. 251–253; *WdW I/III*, pp. 223–225, 410f., 446d.; DENZEL, Die währungspolitische Einigung Italiens, p. 101 with note 61.

328 *WdW I/III*, pp. 224f., 410f., 446.

The integration of some 'new' exchange markets had also occurred in the Western and Southern European area, but their number was quite small in comparison to the expanding regions of Central and Eastern Europe. It is worth mentioning, among others, Cadiz, which replaced Seville as the most important Spanish port of trans-shipment,[330] Bilbao and Oporto, then Bordeaux and Marseilles – both were the most important ports of transshipment for the French Atlantic and Mediterranean trade during the 18th century – and Copenhagen at the border between the Atlantic and Baltic Sea-oriented trade. Leghorn in Italy, which as a free port became the centre of the English Mediterranean trade and also a central intermediary for transacting payments between Western Europe and the Levant in the 18th century, belongs to this group as well. While these places were recognized at the international level and can be regarded as being completely integrated as early as the mid-18th century (*type 5*), other 'new' exchange places were only of regional relevance and never got beyond the early stages of the integrative process, usually varying between *type 2* to *type 4*. Nevertheless, such regional exchange markets were quite important for the development of regional subsystems as they were established in the Netherlands (with Ghent, Brussels, Middleburg, Rotterdam), France (with Montpellier), Italy (among others with Ancona, Bari, Lecce, Messina, Palermo) or in the British Isles (with Dublin, Cork).

Stage 4: The Northwest-European-dominated cashless payment system of the 19th century with London as the world financial centre. Amsterdam's decline as commercial metropolis of Northwestern Europe began as late as during the 18th century, with London gradually taking over its position. Although Amsterdam was able to maintain its position as the most important exchange market in this region and in Europe until the French occupation (1795), London had increasingly become a significant competitor by the second half of the 18th century. Important factors of this development were not only Great Britain's modern banking system, its gradual transition to the currency tied to the gold standard and the successive extension of London's network of cashless payment relationships, but also and above all the enormous growth of English trade within Europe and also overseas, and last but not least the beginning of the Industrial Revolution. However, London almost exclusively admitted seaports as 'new' exchange markets to its exchange rate current. At the same time, London still used Amsterdam's exchange market as intermediary for cashless payments on exchange markets in the interior of the continent during the entire 18th century, which was a typical feature of the position of both exchange places in the cashless payment system. This 'division of tasks' came to an end with the decline of Amsterdam, whose position as the most important Northwest European exchange market was taken over by Hamburg for a short time. All the same, Hamburg's financial strength suffered heavily from the French occupation. That is why London was the unchallenged and most important exchange market in Northwestern Europe after 1815, strictly speaking throughout Europe: as in the 18th century all Eu-

329 Elena FRANGAKIS-SYRETT, *The Commerce of Smyrna in the Eighteenth Century (1700–1820)*, Athens 1992, p. 143.

330 Cf. John G. EVERAERT, Crédit, argent et lettres de change. La financement du commerce Flandres-Andalousie-Amérique, in BERNAL (ed.), *Dinero, moneda y crédito*, pp. 511–523.

ropean exchange markets quoted on Amsterdam, now they quoted on London, and almost all non-European exchange markets did this as well (see below). Thus London as the financial centre of the most important economic and trading power of the world had become, so to speak, the 'born' world financial centre and therefore also the most important exchange market of the world.[331]

During the post-Napoleonic era, continental Europe west of an imaginary line Stockholm/Danzig–Venice/Trieste can be considered as integrated into the international cashless payment system to a large extent. The Russian Empire was linked to this system via Saint Petersburg, which was integrated from c. 1820, and also via Odessa, which was just being integrated (*type 3*, via Leghorn).[332] It was similar in the case of the Ottoman Empire, although no exchange place succeeded in being completely integrated into the European cashless payment system (see above). In Europe, only a few 'new' exchange places were still passing through the integrative process. These were, as in the past, to be found rather at the periphery of the already integrated region: especially Trieste, which had been a free port in the 18th century and became a central intermediary of the Habsburg monarchy to the Levant in the 19th century,[333] and also Warsaw, which replaced Danzig as the most important Polish exchange market.[334] Close to the border between the Habsburg and the Russian Empires, the Galician Brody became an exchange place of regional importance (*type 2*) from the beginning of the 19th century.[335] Furthermore, Patras and Athens have to be mentioned; they became linked to the European system (*type 2*) from the independence of Greece, as well as the British-occupied Ionian Islands (Corfu, Zante and Cephalonia, from about 1815) and Malta (from 1809).[336] In the future Romania the contemporary merchant manuals mentioned Bucharest, the Walachian free port of Braila, the Moldavian free port of Galatz and the Moldavian Jassy fairs as exchange markets (*type 2*); only Vienna quoted one of them – Bucharest – relatively regularly around the middle of the 19th century (*type 3*).[337] And above all, Berlin's final international 'acknowledgement' by the world financial centre London and, thus, its complete integration (*type 5*) into the cashless payment system reached its conclusion by the second half of the 1860s.[338] It were especially Spanish places – beside Madrid, Cadiz and Bilbao, above all Seville, Barcelona, Santander, Malaga and Valencia (up to the 1880s) as well as Gibraltar (1809–1833) – that appeared in the London exchange rate currents as new exchange markets, but only for a few years. As a

---

331 Cf. Jürgen SCHNEIDER / Oskar SCHWARZER, International Rates of Exchange: Structures and Trends of Payments Mechanism in Europe, 17th to 19th Century, in FISCHER / MCINNIS / SCHNEIDER (eds.), *The Emergence of a World Economy, part I*, pp. 143–170, esp. pp. 155f.

332 Cf. DENZEL, Integration ostmittel-, ost- und südosteuropäischer Städte, passim.

333 *WdW I/III*, pp. 413–451; DENZEL, Integration ostmittel-, ost- und südosteuropäischer Städte, passim.

334 Ibid., pp. 54–56.

335 Ibid., pp. 62f., 72f.

336 NOBACK / NOBACK [1851], 1. Abth., pp. 67, 376; 2. Abth., pp. 1504ff., 1784; NOBACK [1877], pp. 407, 584, 703, 1126, 1163; *WdW I/II*, p. 110; DENZEL, Integration ostmittel-, ost- und südosteuropäischer Städte, p. 63.

337 *WdW I/III*, p. 412; DENZEL, Integration ostmittel-, ost- und südosteuropäischer Städte, pp. 64–66.

338 *WdW I/II*, p. 95. Cf. Hartmut BERGHOFF, Der Berliner Kapitalmarkt im Aufbruch (1830–1870), in POHL (ed.), *Geschichte des Finanzplatzes Berlin*, pp. 53–102, esp. pp. 53–57.

rule, however, they did not go beyond *type 3* of the integrative process.[339] The only exception is Barcelona – the developing centre of Catalonia – that became, as the most important Spanish Mediterranean port and industrial site, an internationally acknowledged and integrated exchange market quoted by different European financial places (*type 5*).[340]

Another characteristic of those decades is the declining importance and thus the resulting discontinuation of some exchange markets of the cashless payment system. Different reasons explain their becoming obsolete: the standardization or the take-over of currencies as in Ireland in 1826 led as much to the discontinuation of exchange markets – in this case of Dublin and Cork – as did the moving of trade currents,[341] for instance in France between Bordeaux and Le Havre or in Poland between Danzig and Warsaw. Danzig, for example, lost all its strategic trading advantages near the Prussian–Russian border due to its new geopolitic situation in 1826 and, therefore, also its importance in cashless payment transactions.[342] Owing to the gradual standardization of currencies in the area of the Zollverein, smaller exchange places in Central Europe lost in value, such as Augsburg in favour of Frankfurt am Main, and Leipzig in favour of Berlin. After the standardization of currencies in 1850, similar developments can also be observed in Switzerland, where Basle, Geneva and Zurich became the decisive exchange markets while Saint Gall, Lausanne or Winterthur retained their local importance at best.[343]

Essentially, the 19th century until around 1870 can be considered as an epoch of stagnation from the perspective of cashless payment transactions. Yet this should not be regarded as a negative element, but as a sign of high stability due to a highly efficient system, which was maintained over decades. One decisive element in this situation was the fact that significant financial and exchange markets worked together well, in particular London, the world financial centre and the only exchange market of international relevance in Great Britain, Paris (as well as Marseille) for France, Amsterdam for the Netherlands, Antwerp (and later also Brussels) for Belgium, Madrid for Spain, and Lisbon for Portugal. Genoa, Milan, Leghorn and Naples for the Italian states, Vienna (as well as Trieste) for the Habsburg monarchy, Hamburg, Frankfurt am Main and increasingly Berlin for the German states, and finally Saint Petersburg for the Russian Empire also belong to this group of important exchange markets.

5.3 The Development in the Non-European Regions of the World from the European Expansion up to c. 1870

The cashless payment transactions developed very differently in the non-European regions of the world, depending on the commercial need for them. Overseas companies and European merchants had brought these cashless payment transactions the-

---

339 *WdW I/II*, pp. 47–60.
340 Ibid., pp. 252–255, 393–395; *WdW I/III*, pp. 31–34, 193.
341 *WdW I/II*, pp. 6f.
342 Schwarzer / Denzel / Schnelzer, Geld- und Wechselkurse, p. 43.
343 Denzel, Integration der Schweizer Finanzplätze, pp. 228–233.

re since the European expansion. According to model 2, the integrative process can also be divided into five stages, which, however, differ from the development in Europe. The relatively close linking to one or more European exchange markets is a typical feature of the integrative process in the non-European countries. With these European exchange markets functioning as intermediaries, those non-European countries could conduct cashless payment transactions with other European places. Another characteristic element is the development of subsystems consisting of non-European exchange markets of a continent or subcontinent having links among themselves in order to do cashless business without an intermediating place in Europe.

Latin America[344]. In the development process of the worldwide cashless payment system, Latin America played a special role because most of the payments from the New World to the Old were made by precious metals in the form of mints and bars until the end of the colonial era, i.e. from the 16th to the 18th century, so that no regular transatlantic exchange business was established between the companies in the American trading centres and their European partners. As a rule, bills of exchange and *préstamos marítimos* served only to finance the colonial trade.[345] Therefore the financial centres of Spanish America (above all Mexico City, Lima, Havana, later Buenos Aires) and Brazil (Bahia and Pernambuco, and later on Rio de Janeiro) achieved no position of international importance as exchange markets, and only local or regional exchange markets developed in the colonial era.[346]

During the Latin American independence wars of the early 19th century, when the British began to finance and to dominate foreign trade,[347] former financial centres became foreign exchange markets for the first time. London was the most important and also the first, in multiple cases even the only, exchange partner of Latin-American exchange markets, since the pound sterling became a kind of 'barometer for exchange rate quotations' for the currency in most of the Latin American countries (most important exception: Venezuela); in part it became a 'key currency', which raised again the importance of the exchange rate quotation on London. The earliest exchange rate quotations existed from 1808 in Rio de Janeiro, followed by Buenos Aires (1824) and Valparaiso (by 1830). The Latin American exchange markets were not completely integrated into the international cashless payment system during the period of investigation; this was achieved only after World War I. Nevertheless, the exchange markets reached different stages of development: while places of the South American west coast (above all Valparaiso, Lima,[348] La Paz) mostly quoted

---

344 Cf. idem, Bargeldloser Zahlungsverkehr im europäischen Überseehandel, pp. 80–82, 96f.

345 BERNAL, Crédito, financiación y beneficio; OTTE, Letras de cambio; idem, Träger und Formen der wirtschaftlichen Erschließung Lateinamerikas, pp. 245f. In this way, a Spanish merchant banker could draw upon a merchant in America who paid the promised sum to the local factor or agent of the European supplier. The rates of the premium in these transactions were exorbitantly high; SAYOUS, Les changes de l'Espagne sur l'Amérique.

346 POHL, *Wirtschaft Hispanoamerikas*, pp. 205f.; MACLEOD, Aspects of the Internal Economy of Colonial Spanish America, pp. 262–264. For example, in Mexico in the late colonial era: BRADING, *Miners and Merchants*, pp. 100–102.

347 Desmond C.M. PLATT, *Latin America and British Trade 1806–1914*, London 1972; H.S. FERNS, Beginnings of British Investment in Argentina, *Economic History Review* sec. ser. 4 (1952), pp. 341–352.

regularly on London (*type 1*), the network of exchange rate quotations at the east coast extended to other European exchange markets (Paris, Hamburg, Lisbon, Spain, and Italy) and to New York as well. Rio de Janeiro and Buenos Aires have therefore been ascribed to *type 2* since the 1820s. Moreover, a regional subsystem with Rio de Janeiro as its dominating centre existed on the east coast until 1914, which apart from various Brazilian places (above all Bahia, Pernambuco), could be attributed to Buenos Aires and Montevideo (*type 3a/b*). In general, Brazilian exchange places – especially Rio de Janeiro – stood out in the Latin American payment transactions. From 1809 – after the resettlement of the Portuguese court in Brazil – London quoted Rio de Janeiro (since 1820 also on Bahia) as another European exchange market. Thus both exchange places succeeded quite early in getting to the stage between transition and integration (*type 4*). However, London abandoned this quotation in 1833 (Bahia) or in 1853 (Rio de Janeiro). Therefore this should be considered a special case rather than a transition to integration.[349]

In Central America, Ciudad de México became the most important exchange market during the 19th century and was linked to Europe, especially to London, to the North American subsystem as well as to the Caribbean (Havana) (*type 3a*). As a result of the very few available sources, the Caribbean connection can only be proved definitively for the beginning of the 20th century. All the other Central American exchange markets – such as Guatemala or San José in Costa Rica – were only of local relevance.[350]

North America and the Caribbean[351]. On the North American continent the payment system developed quite differently, because of the lack of precious metals. Therefore exchange transactions with Britain, in particular with London, started to be common practice in order to finance the transatlantic trade from the second half of the 17th century.[352] "In negotiating bills on the mother country, colonists followed the forms and procedures common to European Exchange. Bills were drawn, presented, and protested in much the same way between Philadelphia and London as between Amsterdam – or, better, Dublin – and London."[353] But – and here is a fundamental difference in comparison to Europe – the exchange business was, as a rule, transacted in a one-sided fashion, which means that bills were drawn from the Am-

---

348 In 1865 Lima quoted London (60 to 90 days' sight) with 37¼ pence per peso, Paris (60 to 90 days' sight) with 3.90 francs per peso and Valparaiso (30 days sight) with 20% premium; Karl VON SCHERZER, *Statistisch-commerzielle Ergebnisse einer Reise um die Erde, unternommen an Bord der österreichischen Fregatte Novara in den Jahren 1857–1859*, Leipzig – Wien ²1867, p. 591.

349 DENZEL, Finanzplätze, Wechselkurse und Währungsverhältnisse in Lateinamerika, pp. 9–55.

350 Ibid., pp. 55–65.

351 Cf. idem, Bargeldloser Zahlungsverkehr im europäischen Überseehandel, pp. 82–84, 90–92, 97; idem, The Transatlantic Cashless Payment System in the Northern Atlantic Zone from the 17th Century to c. 1840, in Horst PIETSCHMANN (ed.), *Atlantic History. History of the Atlantic System 1580–1830. Papers presented at an International Conference, held 28 August – 1 September, 1999 (Hamburg)*, Göttingen 2002, S. 263–277.

352 The following according to MCCUSKER, *Money and Exchange*, passim.

353 Ibid., p. 120. As an example see Jacob PRICE, Joshua Johnson in London, 1771–1775: Credit and Commercial Organization in the British Chesapeake Trade, in Anne WHITEMAN et al. (eds.), *Statesmen, Scholars and Merchants: Essays in Eighteenth-Century History Presented to Dame Lucy Sutherland*, Oxford 1973, pp. 153–180, especially p. 165.

erican colonies and were payable in London (*type 1*), but seldom vice versa. So the trade of the colonists was financed and mainly credited by the merchant bankers in the mother country, at least in the early decades of colonization. From around 1650 Boston (populated since 1630) became the first North American exchange market, followed by New York and Philadelphia (founded 1682) containing (still irregular) quotations from the 1680s, and finally Baltimore (founded 1745) as "Philadelphia's satellite city",[354] partially also New Orleans and Charleston.[355] In the southern colonies a kind of exchange fair in Williamsburg (Va.) substituted for the lack of an exchange place. In the exchange business of the Thirteen Colonies London was obviously the main partner, but Bristol, Ireland, Scotland and partially Amsterdam participated in transatlantic cashless payments as well. Furthermore, the exchange business was established inside the Thirteen Colonies as well as with their Canadian neighbours by means of *Inland Bills* (later *Domestic Exchange*), and with the Caribbean (especially with Jamaica and Barbados) by means of *West Indian Bills*. As a rule, however, these relations were irregular and supported only by some merchant bankers.[356] Among the North American exchange markets, Boston, on which even London merchant bankers partially drew bills,[357] played the role of the *primus inter pares* until this position was taken over by Philadelphia, presumably in the 1730s. In the course of the 18th century, "the Philadelphians had become the near-bankers of their corner of the world".[358] Relatively stable exchange rates on London as a consequence of its expansion in trade as well as the resulting income and the opportunities for arbitrage business made Philadelphia "the Amsterdam of the New World"[359] at the end of the colonial era.[360]

From all non-European countries taken into account, the linking to the international cashless payment system was best developed within the independent USA in around 1800. Until about 1840, the transcontinental exchange transactions of the Atlantic coast, which had still been distributed over different exchange places during the 18th and the early 19th centuries (see above), were increasingly concentrated on the New York exchange market, which became the most important exchange market on the American continent. In the USA, only New Orleans could survive until the end of the American Civil War due to its outstanding position in foreign trade. Furthermore, the developing San Francisco became the financial capital of the American West since the gold rush in California. All remaining US – and also most Canadian[361] – cities were integrated into the intra-American system, and because of New

---

354 McCusker, *Money and Exchange*, p. 175.

355 *The Pennsylvania Packet and Daily Advertiser*, 1785–1786.

356 Of course, the exchange rates between the North American markets and the West Indies were not quoted in official journals.

357 Their rates were not quoted in the official exchange rate current of London.

358 McCusker, *Money and Exchange*, p. 175.

359 M.G. Myers, Origins and Development, in B.H. Beckhart (ed.), *The New York Money Market, vol. I*, New York 1931, p. 6.

360 For the USA, Markus A. Denzel, Der Aufstieg und die Einbindung der Vereinigten Staaten von Amerika in die Weltwirtschaft: Transatlantische Wechselkurse von 1783 bis 1914, in *WdW I/I*, pp. 146–179.

361 Noback [1851], 2. Abth., p. 984, 1828; Noback / Noback [1858], p. 610; Noback [1877], p. 621; Nelkenbrecher [1871], p. 439; Swoboda [1889], pp. 379f.; Swoboda [1913], p. 702.

York's position they had a share in the international system.[362] These intra-American exchange rate quotations – the so-called *Domestic Exchange* – also give information about the extension of cashless payment transactions in North America: the mutual linking of those three or four financial markets in the North American colonies is only recorded from the turn of the 19th century – for example for Boston from 1797, New Orleans from 1804, and in the case of New York from 1813 (*type 3b*). In the early years of the United States, this subsystem of integrating or of already integrated financial markets was undoubtedly based upon older relationships. Therefore a development of such a subsystem can be assumed towards the end of the colonial era. By the mid-19th century, this subsystem covered only the Atlantic coast and the adjoining states of the Midwest, with St Louis as the most easterly outpost and Detroit as the most northerly one. During the closing years of the 19th century and the early 20th century, New Orleans, Boston, Chicago, St Louis, Charleston, Savannah and San Francisco, and for some years also Cincinnati and Montreal, were the most important exchange markets in North America apart from New York.[363] At the same time, the linking to European payment transactions became closer: aside from London, the United States' Atlantic exchange markets quoted mostly on Amsterdam, Paris, and/or Hamburg (New York since the 1830s also on Bremen) in around 1800. In this way, New York's regular transatlantic exchange rate quotations were extended to Antwerp, Switzerland, Frankfurt am Main and Berlin.[364]

In the West Indian colonies exchange transactions were common, especially with the European mother countries, and increasingly with North America throughout the 18th century (*type 1 or 2*). Among the British colonies in this region, Jamaica (Kingston) and Barbados (Bridgetown) became important exchange markets during the last decades of the 17th century (exceptionally even with bills drawn from London on Jamaica or Barbados) because of their economic resources. Also the French sugar and coffee producers St Domingue, Guadeloupe and Martinique had direct, though mostly irregular, exchange relations with their mother country (*type 1*). During the 19th century, most European colonies in the Caribbean possessed exchange relationships with their European mother countries, which, however, did not reach more than an exclusively local significance (*type 1*). From 1850 Jamaica or its central exchange market Kingston were mentioned in the London exchange rate current as the central British exchange market, which – apart from Havana on Cuba – was considered the only important exchange market of the Caribbean area with national significance. Jamaica's comparatively close linking to London was at least partly augmented by the regional linking to the North American exchange network (by New York), and maybe also by the linking to the Caribbean subsystem (*type 1/3a*). In the middle of the 19th century, Barbados and its central exchange rate on London and also partially on New York, on the West Indies as well as that on Danish St

---

362 Lawrence H. OFFICER, Integration in the American Foreign-Exchange Market, 1791–1900, *Journal of Economic History* 45 (1985), pp. 557–585; Charles P. KINDLEBERGER, The Formation of Financial Centers: A Study in Comparative Economic History, Princeton (N.J.) 1974, pp. 52–56. Cf. also Kenneth D. GARBADE / William L. SILBER, Technology, Communication and the Performance of Financial Markets: 1840–1975, *Journal of Finance* 33 (1978), pp. 819–832.

363 *WdW I/I*, pp. 369–387, 458–473.

364 Cf. ibid., pp. 320–368.

Thomas had only regional significance, especially since the turnover of the exchange transactions do not appear to have been very substantial.[365]

South and East Asia[366]. The Portuguese expansion during the 16th century[367] provides evidence for cashless payments in the Indian Ocean area. At this time, Italian-
style exchange business was not yet possible in this area because there were not
enough Europeans living there who traded in bills, and the Asian merchants did not
participate in the confidence-based European network of cashless payments until the
19th century. As a rule, the Asian merchants only seldom accepted various kinds of
promissory notes or credit papers from the Europeans. As the East India companies
established their trade and payments in this area, cashless payment transactions
between the companies' branches in Asia and the headquarters in Europe began to
become more common.[368] From the early 17th century on, the first intercontinental
cashless payment transactions between Asia and Europe served the companies'
agents to transfer their assets home; therefore, the Dutch Verenigde Oostindische
Compagnie issued assignatiës in Batavia, a kind of bill of exchange payable in the
Netherlands, especially in Amsterdam. During the late 17th and the 18th centuries
these assignatiës played an important role in arbitrage business with precious metals.[369] The English East India Company used bills of exchange and letters of credit
in Bengal and from Bengal to Europe not before the mid-17th century, and between
Surat and Bengal or Europe in the 1670s as well. In the following decades, Calcutta
as well as Madras and Bombay became the central British exchange markets in India. On these markets, exchange business of other companies and increasingly of
private agency houses was transacted with Europe or in India in the 18th century. As
the East India Company began to use bills of exchange for their transactions with
Europe and India in Canton starting in 1761,[370] a regional intra-Asiatic exchange network of Europeans was established in addition to the direct relations to Europe and
the transactions in India. Calcutta and Canton became the nuclei of the European exchange system in Asia reaching from the Cape of Good Hope to Japan and then to
Australia/New Zealand in the 19th century.[371] Calcutta rose to become by far the most
important exchange market within the (European) cashless payment system in the
Indian Ocean area of the late 18th and early 19th centuries, and maintained close relationships with Canton.[372] This not only applied to the East India Company's transactions but also to the increasingly larger exchange businesses of private businessmen
and trading houses. During the late 18th century various kinds of intercontinental ex-

---

365 DENZEL, Lateinamerika, pp. 63–75, 90–102.
366 Cf. idem, Bargeldloser Zahlungsverkehr im europäischen Überseehandel, pp. 84–89, 92–95;
    idem, Kolonialstädte, pp. 239–249; idem, Zur Finanzierung des europäischen Asienhandels.
367 MAGALHÃES-GODINHO, L'économie de l'empire portugais, p. 649.
368 PRICE, Transaction Costs, p. 288: "Bills of exchange were known in Asia, but were not as com-
    monly used in European–Asian trade as in European–American trade".
369 PRAKASH, Financing the European Trade with Asia; GAASTRA, Private Money for Company
    Trade; idem, De Verenigde Oost-Indische Compagnie, pp. 256–260.
370 MORSE, The Chronicles of the East India Company, vol. V, p. 102; DERMIGNY, La Chine et
    l'Occident, vol. II, p. 762.
371 DENZEL, Kolonialstädte, passim.
372 NELKENBRECHER [1828], p. 90; NELKENBRECHER [1832], p. 117.

change transactions existed, just like in Europe but, as a rule, they were one-sided. For example, the bills were drawn from a merchant or factor in Asia on a partner or a company in London or Amsterdam (and only very seldom vice versa). The European headquarters and companies were financing the trade to and from Asia by accepting the bills drawn from their factors or partners in Asia. This was the ultimate consequence of the negative European trade balance with Asia.

So, for the Indian Ocean area one can act on the assumption that the developing European exchange places in Asia became increasingly linked to the European system in early modern times. This connection became stronger during the 18th century. At first, there was probably only the linking to the mother country (*type 1*). However, in the case of the East India Company's exchange business, an intra-Asian exchange network expanded the linking very quickly from the second part of the 18th century; it was at first regionally still relatively limited. In contrast, the connections of the Verenigde Oostindische Compagnie with Batavia as its most important exchange market in Asia to the mother country remained dominant and the exchange business between various foreign trading posts did not succeed in achieving significance comparable to the East India Company. Thus, an Asian subsystem was essentially established in the international exchange system by the East India Company until around 1820, but it was used by all other European participants in the Asian trade. Within this system, an extensive linking of the Chinese side (Canton) to the Indian one (Calcutta) can be assumed. However, the question of mutual integration of these two exchange markets remains unanswered since Calcutta's exchange rate quotations on Canton have not yet been proven (therefore *type 3a*).[373] From the early 19th century, Manila was probably linked to this subsystem as well via exchange transactions with British India,[374] whereas such (regular) exchange relationships to exchange markets of the Asian system have not yet been recorded for Batavia for these decades. In comparison to the cashless payment transactions in Europe, the structures in the intra-Asian payment system were, of course, of a rudimentary kind, and the extent of intercontinental transactions was also comparatively small.

During the 19th century, exchange markets of South and East Asia succeeded in being linked very extensively to the international cashless payment system. However, both regions were only completely integrated after World War I. South and East Asia were characterized by a large number of exchange markets possessing exchange relationships to Europe that were of varying intensity, and they were increasingly integrated into their own Asian subsystem. A first stage of such an intra-Asian integration (*type 3b*) had already been reached in the 1820s/1830s, when Calcutta, Madras, Bombay and Canton mutually quoted each other; Calcutta as *primus inter pares* of this subsystem did not need an exchange rate quotation on Canton, which for its part was dependent on the cashless payment system. In addition, Mauritius, Manila, Batavia, Colombo and, probably shortly after 1830, also Singapore were linked to this Asian subsystem as well as to Europe by one or two exchange markets

373 In this way, *The Government Gazette, Calcutta* quoted on December 30th 1816 an exchange rate at London (*exchequer bills*), but none at Canton.

374 Weng E. CHEONG, *Mandarins and Merchants. Jardine Matheson & Co. A China Agency in the Early Nineteenth Century*, London – Malmö 1979, p. 39 and passim; MORSE, Chronicles, vol. II–V, passim; NELKENBRECHER [1828], p. 238; NELKENBRECHER [1832], p. 315.

(London as well as Madrid, Amsterdam or Paris). Around 1840, the first stage of the exchange network's development in the Indian Ocean area, i.e. the forming stage, was probably concluded. India with its three integrated exchange markets had obviously a greater significance in international payment transactions than East and South East Asia, which possessed only one integrated exchange market and, in addition, several only linked exchange markets.

The following development was introduced by the opening of the Chinese and Japanese contract ports. These entrepôts succeeded in linking Central China and Japan to the international system within only a few years. As a result of this, they were integrated into the Asian subsystem as well. Since the middle of the century, Shanghai became the centre of the new trade with Japan and gained in international significance in cashless payment transactions, followed by Yokohama from the 1860s.[375] Meanwhile, Canton in Southern China was replaced by Hong Kong; smaller exchange places kept their regional relevance, such as Amoy, Foutschou and Hiogo/Kobe, which were both only linked to the international system and to the Asian subsystem. In the broader sense, connections to other exchange markets were established within the Indian Ocean area during these years, as for example Cape Town with India,[376] Mauritius with Australia and in some cases with New Zealand as well. The establishment of trans-Pacific exchange relationships with the USA, first by Yokohama (with San Francisco from 1869/73, with New York from 1873), was of particular importance.[377] The transition to integration was achieved in the British Empire's financial centres in Asia, Calcutta, Bombay and Madras, from 1862 also in Hong Kong, Mauritius and Colombo, and also in Shanghai from 1874, when London started direct exchange rate quotations on these exchange markets (*type 4*) within the context of the India Exchange. Mauritius and Colombo were probably integrated into the Asian subsystem from the mid-1870s. This stage was characterized by the Asian exchange network's enormous expansion within a few decades by means of linking and integrating various 'new' exchange markets; this stage can be regarded as being completed during the first years of the 1880s. This stage also demonstrates a clear intensification of the exchange relationships with Europe, and above all the geographical far-reaching integration within the Asian subsystem.

Australia and Oceania[378]. From the 19th century, Australia and New Zealand participated in international cashless payment transactions. In this respect, New South Wales/Sydney started to quote exchange rates on London as early as 1822, Adelaide/South Australia in 1838, Victoria/Melbourne in 1851, and New Zealand from the 1840s.[379] At the same time, an Australian subsystem emerged with single quotations of different banks on neighbouring colonies or quotations of New Zealand on Australia. This system, however, did not go beyond the rudimentary stage. The

---

375 BASTER, British Exchange Banks in China, p. 145.

376 *WdW VIII*, pp. 94f.; Cf. Markus A. DENZEL, Finanzplätze in der Levante und Nordafrika im 19. und 20. Jahrhundert, in ibid., pp. 30–70, esp. pp. 19–28.

377 *WdW IV*, pp. 189, 191.

378 Cf. DENZEL, Bargeldloser Zahlungsverkehr im europäischen Überseehandel, p. 98.

379 Cf. idem, Neuseeländisch-europäischer Zahlungsverkehr: Neuseeländische Wechselkurse vor 1914, in *WdW V*, pp. 28–46. Some quotations of Perth and Tasmania (Hobart) may be found in BUTLIN, *Australian Monetary System*, pp. 346–349.

increasingly closer linking of Australia and New Zealand with the help of the Asian subsystem was of a much higher importance. From the 1860s the linking took place by means of the central traffic junction Mauritius, and from the beginning of the 20th century by Hong Kong and Yokohama.[380] In the context of the India Exchange, Sydney and Mauritius were directly quoted by London between 1862 and 1874. Similar to Asian exchange markets (see below), this transition to integration was broken off. All in all, the linking of Australia's and New Zealand's exchange markets to the international payment system during the first half of the century probably resembled *type 1*; in later decades the linking was increasingly similar to *type 3b*.[381] Moreover, Tahiti must be mentioned for the Pacific area; it had exchange relationships with Paris and London in the 1870s. It probably had exchange relationships with the USA (*type 2*), since it was the stopover of American whalers in the first half of the 19th century.[382]

Africa south of the Sahara[383]. Only one exchange place could be found in Africa south of the Sahara that gained international significance in the period under investigation: Cape Town. Quotations on London can be proved from 1811, as well as quotations on Amsterdam, France and the Indian exchange markets from the turn of the century (probably because of the sources). With regard to the model introduced above, Cape Town basically followed *type 1*, partly *type 3a*, and became linked to Europe as well as to the Asian subsystem. However, the linking of Cape Town to London – similar to that of the Australian exchange markets – was close and had been completed by 1908 with a regular exchange rate quotation from London on South Africa. Thus an integration into the international system could already be assumed for this point in time. Before World War I, however, the linking of Cape Town to Europe was established solely via London; therefore it should be described as an advanced transition to integration (*type 4a*), which could be followed by an integration immediately in the interwar period because of beginning exchange rate quotations on parts of other European and North American exchange markets. As investigations have discovered so far, all the other African exchange markets and countries south of the Sahara (Port Elizabeth, Sierra Leone, Gold Coast, Lagos, Nigeria and Kenya) achieved only local relevance in the system of cashless payment transactions. These places quoted London, partly without any fluctuation in their exchange rates over several years (*type 1*). Provided that they were not part of the British possessions, they also quoted now and then other financial centres of their mother countries or in East Africa and occasionally Indian exchange markets as well.[384] Their exchange transactions often served only to pay the troops; their turnover was correspondingly small. Incidentally, no subsystem emerged within the Black African area

---

380 Further investigation will be necessary to decide to what extent the integration of Australian exchange markets into the Asian subsystem had already taken place.

381 Individual banks in Australia, however, quoted above all Asian financial markets.

382 NOBACK [1877], pp. 866f.

383 DENZEL, Bargeldloser Zahlungsverkehr im europäischen Überseehandel, pp. 98f.; idem, Zahlungsverkehr, Wechselkurse und Währungsverhältnisse von Britischen Besitzungen in Afrika.

384 So not only Cape Town, but also Zanzibar (around 1900); Rudolf SONNDORFER, Die Währungsreformen in Ostasien und Ostafrika, *Zeitschrift für Handelswissenschaft und Handelspraxis* 2/10 (1910), pp. 337–343, esp. p. 338.

in the time investigated.

The Levant, Northern Africa and Central Asia[385]. This part of the world economy was located between the Atlantic economic zone on the one side and the economic zone of the Indian Ocean on the other. It is considered especially important because it borders directly on Europe and is connected to Europe not only by sea but
overland as well. Therefore the structures of cashless payment transactions could
expand in two different ways. The Ottoman Empire and its neighbour in the east,
Persia, made up the heart of this part of the world economy.

As already shown above, cashless payments became more intense between
Europe and the Ottoman Empire as well as inside the Ottoman Empire itself due to
the expansion of Dutch, French and English trade in the Levant from the second half
of the 17th century. From the 19th century, evidence for cashless payment can be
found not only on the central financial markets of the Ottoman Empire, Constantinople, Smyrna and Salonica, but also on only regionally important markets such as
Adrianople (Edirne),[386] Candia (Crete),[387] Bursa, Trapezunt,[388] Damascus, Alexan-
dretta and Aleppo (latest from the mid-18th century),[389] Janina (Albania) and at the
fairs in Usundschowa (Bulgaria), although only in single cases and in different time
periods so far. Here, contemporary merchant manuals show the small significance of
these exchange markets for international payments compared to Constantinople.
Constantinople's outstanding position in the field of cashless payment relations of
the Ottoman Empire with Europe can be explained by the central political and economic role that capital played for the whole region of the Eastern Mediterranean. On
all exchange markets of the Ottoman Empire cashless payments were mainly directed towards European financial centres, which themselves, however, quoted markets
of the Ottoman Empire only in special circumstances. Odessa, as the central exchange market in the Black Sea region and intermediary into the Russian Empire,
became the most important exchange partner outside West and Central Europe in the
19th century that was quoted by Ottoman markets. So Constantinople can be considered the exchange market in the Ottoman Empire that had been most integrated into
the international cashless payment system. Even Constantinople, however, could not
get beyond the integration phase (*type 4*), because quotations from Central Europe
were made only by markets of the Habsburg Monarchy and Italy. The remaining Ottoman markets reached only lower levels in the integration process (*type 1* or *2*) or
fell back to even lower levels, like Smyrna and Salonica from *type 3* to *type 2*. It was
mainly from the 1870s that markets in the Ottoman provinces normally used Constantinople as intermediary for their foreign transactions.

---

385 Cf. DENZEL, Bargeldloser Zahlungsverkehr im europäischen Überseehandel, p. 99.

386 NOBACK [1877], p. 460.

387 NOBACK [1851], 1. Abth., p. 190.

388 Ibid., 2. Abth., p. 868.

389 Gwilyn AMBROSE, English Traders at Aleppo (1658–1756), *Economic History Review* 3 (1931),
pp. 246–267, esp. p. 257: "Bills were ... drawn from Aleppo on Constantinople, where they were
payable to native merchants or their representatives." Cf. J. SPERLING, The International Payments Mechanism in the Seventeenth and Eighteenth Centuries, *Economic History Review* sec.
ser. 14 (1962), pp. 446–468, esp. pp. 461f.; NOBACK [1851], 1. Abth., p. 6; NOBACK [1877], p.
10.

In the Syrian–Mesopotamian region, Aleppo was the easternmost market, which made its exchange operations according to the customs of Constantinople (*type 1*).[390] Beirut, the main trading and financial market in Syria for trade with Europe, established as a relatively independent, regionally important exchange market (*type 2*)[391] in this region, at least from the first half of the 19th century, to which, for example, also Larnaca on Cyprus (*type 2*) was orientated. In Syria's Tripoli and in Baghdad the branches of the European houses at least drew bills on London (*type 1*), whilst exchange transactions in Basra were very rare.[392]

Alexandria and Cairo were Egypt's central financial markets in the 19th and early 20th centuries. The cashless payments made in Alexandria were mainly directed towards Europe and only in the early 20th century also towards Constantinople (*type 2*). Since quotations from inside Egypt are totally lacking so far, we can assume that the quotations documented here are mainly related to those of the European traders, but not to the cashless payments of the Levantine or domestic traders. No evidence has so far been found for exchange trade from or to the Arabian peninsula – apart from the British possessions (e.g. Aden).[393]

In Maghreb, European traders were able to establish exchange rate relations only in the 19th century, whilst this had simply not been possible before in the politically unstable Berber countries. The most important regional exchange markets became Algiers (after the French conquest in 1830) (*type 1*)[394] and Tunis. There, however, quotations were fluctuating heavily according to contemporary merchant manuals – a clear indication for a still little developed money and exchange market (*type 2*). In Morocco bills of exchange were common among the European traders trading in Fez, later also in Mogador (Essaouira), the centre of Moroccan foreign trade, and in Mazagan (El-Jadida), and from at least 1897 in Tangier[395] (*type 2*). The creditworthiness of those bills was often doubtful, however.[396]

In Central Asia, exchange rate quotations were recorded only in some particular cases, above all the quotation of Persian cities at London (*type 1*).[397] Exchange business on Central Asia's big markets, as for example in Buckara, seems to have existed occasionally because of frequent legal uncertainties. Therefore a linking of Central Asia to the cashless payment system cannot be assumed.[398]

---

390 NOBACK [1877], p. 10.
391 NOBACK [1851], 2. Abth., p. 1864; NOBACK / NOBACK [1858], p. 79; NELKENBRECHER [1871], p. 54; NOBACK [1877], p. 120. Cf. DENZEL, Levante, pp. 45f. Cf. J. MCGREGOR, *Commercial Statistics*, London 1847, vol. II, pp. 140–150; cited in ISSAWI (ed.), *Economic History of the Middle East*, pp. 221–225, esp. p. 225.
392 NOBACK [1877], pp. 86, 110, 245f., 879.
393 For Mocca, cf. NOBACK / NOBACK [1858], p. 679.
394 NOBACK [1851], 1. Abth., p. 12; 2. Abth., p. 1540; NOBACK [1877], p. 19.
395 *WdW VIII*, pp. 169-175.
396 NOBACK [1877], p. 1145.
397 ISSAWI (ed.), *Economic History of Iran*, pp. 339–356, esp. pp. 343–345.
398 NOBACK / NOBACK [1858], p. 106.

5.4 The World-Wide Cashless Payment System in the Age of the Gold Standard (from c. 1870 up to 1914)

With regard to monetary policies, this last stage of the integrative process before World War I can be described as the age of the gold standard. It is characterized by the fusion of European and non-European developments: the emergence of the world economy became very clear in the sphere of cashless payment transactions. Although Europe remained the nucleus of the entire worldwide system, North America with New York as the financial centre was integrated into this system. The European-dominated system became now a bi-polar Atlantic one. When European exchange markets (among others Paris in 1871, Bremen in 1873, Berlin in 1887, Zurich in 1890/98, Copenhagen in 1899, Trieste in 1900, Stockholm in 1907) started to quote New York from the 1870s,[399] the transition from linking to integration into the international payment system was completed: by around the turn of the century, New York had become the first equal partner in the cashless payment system outside Europe.

After 1870, the system's geographical structure on the European continent changed following the introduction of national currencies (for example in Italy or in the German Reich[400]) and national central banks.[401] Therefore several exchange markets in Europe became unnecessary. Because of these two new introductions into the financial system, branches of the national banks could offer financial services throughout the entire country. As a result, the official exchange rate currents quoted the exchange rates of the financial centres of the respective countries. Often, the national or central banks were located there, usually in the capitals (only partially supplied by the main seaport of the respective country, so, e.g., Berlin by Hamburg, Vienna by Trieste and Madrid by Barcelona). Thus the number of West, South and Central European exchange markets decreased, starting in the late 19th century. However, the mechanism of the gold standard,[402] the introduction of the telegraphic transfer[403] as well as that of the cheque led to an intensification of payment transactions between these national financial centres. Apart from London, Paris remained and Berlin became the most important exchange markets on the Continent: "For exchange-purposes, France, Belgium and Switzerland may be regarded as a unity, represented by Paris, while the Dutch, Scandinavian, Russian, and perhaps Austrian, exchanges may be considered as controlled from Berlin – that is to say, if bills on London become proportionately cheaper in Amsterdam or Stockholm than in Berlin, Berlin buys them, and if they become dearer, Berlin sells them."[404]

In addition, 'new' exchange markets were also integrated or linked in Europe:

399 Cf. *WdW I/II*, pp. 378f.; *WdW I/III*, pp. 300, 378f., 451; *WdW XI*, pp. 69, 155–157; *HStD XII*, p. 359.

400 Bernd SPRENGER, *Währungswesen und Währungspolitik in Deutschland von 1834 bis 1875*, Köln 1981.

401 Lee A. CRAIG / Douglas FISHER, *The Integration of the European Economy, 1850–1913*, Houndmills 1997, pp. 99–118.

402 Ibid., pp. 118–129; Oskar SCHWARZER, Goldwährungssysteme und internationaler Zahlungsverkehr zwischen 1870 und 1914, in SCHREMMER (ed.), *Geld- und Währung*, pp. 191–228.

403 Cf. AHVENAINEN, The Role of Telegraphs; BOYCE, Submarine Cables.

404 CLARE, Foreign Exchanges, p. 353.

the Swiss exchange markets in Basle, Geneva and Zurich were, for example, integrated in the international system from the 1870s (*type 5*).[405] The Scandinavian exchange markets (Stockholm, Copenhagen, later also Christiania/Oslo) were in 'transition to integration' (*type 3* or *type 4*) from the 1880s. Even Moscow belonged to this group of exchange markets from 1893, in particular because of Berlin's role as intermediary, when London – as the first Western European exchange market – started to quote the central Russian industrial capital in its exchange rate currents (*type 3*).[406] Moreover, the exchange markets of recently formed states in the Southeast European area (Belgrade in Serbia, Bucharest in Romania, Sofia or Rustschuk in Bulgaria) were linked more closely to European exchange markets (*type 2*) from the 1880s, without being quoted regularly by them before World War I. One exception is Bucharest (see above), which was quoted irregularly for only some years (1842–1863) by Vienna (during this period *type 3*).[407]

The other economic areas – the Indian Ocean area with East Asia and Australia, Latin America, Africa, and the Levant with Middle Asia – were, as a rule, not integrated into this emerging bi-polar system before World War I, but they became more closely connected with the nucleus.[408] The regularity and the density of exchange quotations of the non-European financial markets grew, as did the number of financial markets with exchange relations. Not only the capitals and the main seaports of the non-European countries (for example Rio de Janeiro, Buenos Aires, Valparaiso, Yokohama, Calcutta, Bombay, Singapore, Shanghai, Canton/Hong Kong, Sydney, Melbourne, Cape Town, Constantinople, Alexandria) transacted exchange business with Europe (*type 2*), but also regional and local centres such as Port Louis (Mauritius), Tientsin, Saigon, Kobe, Adelaide or Freetown (Sierra Leone) (*type 1* or *2*). Above all, financial markets with branches of European overseas banks and exchange banks establishing during the second half of the 19th century[409] quoted exchange rates on London, partially on New York, Paris and Hamburg. Apart from these intercontinental connections to the European centres of finance – from East Asia and Latin America also even to New York – the economically potent non-European areas grew together on the basis of 'regional' cashless payment systems; for example, North America with its so-called domestic exchange,[410] the Indian Ocean area including East Asia and Australia by means of very intense exchange transactions in the triangle between Bombay, Yokohama and Sydney, to some ex-

---

405 DENZEL, Integration der Schweizer Finanzplätze, pp. 228–233.
406 *WdW II*, p. 66; DENZEL, Integration ostmittel-, ost- und südosteuropäischer Städte, pp. 59f.
407 Idem, Integration ostmittel-, ost- und südosteuropäischer Städte, pp. 66–68.
408 For the following see Oskar SCHWARZER / Markus A. DENZEL / Friedrich ZELLFELDER, Ostasiatische, indische und australische Wechselkurse (1800–1914), in *WdW IV*, pp. 1–65; DENZEL, Zahlungsverkehr, Wechselkurse und Währungsverhältnisse von Britischen Besitzungen, passim; idem, Finanzplätze in der Levante und Nordafrika, passim; idem, Neuseeländisch-europäischer Zahlungsverkehr, passim; idem, Finanzplätze, Wechselkurse und Währungsverhältnisse in Lateinamerika, passim.
409 HAUSER, *Überseebanken*; Volker VINNAI, *Die Entstehung der Überseebanken und die Technik des Zahlungsverkehrs im Asienhandel von 1850 bis 1875*, Frankfurt/Main 1971; Stuart MUIRHEAD, *Crisis Banking in the East. The History of the Chartered Mercantile Bank of India, London and China, 1853–1893*, Aldershot – Brookfield 1996; Compton MACKENZIE, *Realms of Silver. One Hundred Years of Banking in the East*, London 1954.
410 OFFICER, Integration in the American Foreign-Exchange Market.

tent the Atlantic coast of Latin America (Rio de Janeiro, Buenos Aires, Montevideo), and finally the Levant.

The South and the East Asian regions exemplify how far this linking during the
closing years of the 19th and the beginning of the 20th centuries could extend. The
'transition to integration' of these centres was abruptly ended because London stopped its exchange rate quotations at those Asian financial centres. A stage of consolidation began with a falling number of Asian financial places quoting London and
with the exchange rate quotations concentrated at only few but central exchange
markets similarly to Europe. In India, Calcutta had the function of the central exchange market without any central bank being set up; besides, Bombay as the most
prominent port of exportation remained an internationally relevant exchange place,
even though its importance was clearly diminished in comparison to Calcutta. The
smaller entrepôt ports (for example Port Louis on Mauritius) became increasingly
superfluous for cashless payment transactions since direct connections grew in significance. In contrast to this, 'new' cities succeeded in becoming linked to the Asian
exchange network in case their hinterland obtained more economic value due to
their 'colonial rulers'. This process affected, for example, Saigon, Tientsin or
Wuhan (Hankow). Around the turn of the 20th century, a peak was achieved with the
linking of Singapore, Manila, Yokohama, Batavia, Saigon, Bangkok and Wuhan,
i.e. of all important exchange places of the East and Southeast Asian region, to the
Asian exchange network and with the linking of Sydney and Melbourne, especially
because the linking to Europe (start of exchange rate quotations on France and on
the German Reich) and to the United States was clearly strengthened at the end of
the 19th century. However, a complete integration of the Asian exchange markets into the international payment system had still not taken place; the start of exchange
rate quotations of Europe or of the USA at these financial centres would only happen after World War I. Nevertheless, the increasing significance of East Asian exchange markets (above all Hong Kong and Yokohama) compared to that of the Indian exchange markets could be noticed before 1914. Calcutta had lost its function as
primus inter pares within the Asian system; Hong Kong had gained at least an equal
value. This fact becomes obvious when Calcutta started to quote Hong Kong by the
end of the 1880s. In addition, the integration of the 'new' exchange places was conducted exclusively by East Asian centres, first of all by Hong Kong, increasingly by
Yokohama since World War I. Thus the main focus within the Asian exchange network had finally shifted from India to East Asia, i.e. to Southern China and Japan.

SOURCES AND BIBLIOGRAPHY

1. Unprinted Sources, Exchange Rate Currents and Price Currents in Archives and Libraries

Amsterdam

Internationaal Instituut voor Sociale Geschiedenis, Amsterdam: Nederlandsch Economisch-Historisch Archief / Economisch-Historisch Biblioteek [IISG]: Collectie *Commerciële couranten*, 15e–19e eeuw

- *Corsi di cambi* [Venice] (1609–1774)
- *Corsi di cambi* [Vienna] (1750–1771)
- *Corso delli Cambiati in Amsterdam* (1700–1711)
- *Cours der Koopmannschappen* [Amsterdam] (1732–1789)
- *Cours des Marchandises* [Amsterdam] (1731–1748)
- *Cours van Koopmannschappen tot Amsterdam* (1701–1731)
- *Le Memorial Des Marchands*, Londres (1681–1683, 1685)
- *Prix Courant des Marchandises a Londres* (1668, 1671–1675, 1679/80, 1682, 1684/85)
- *PrysCorant van de Coopmannschap* [Danzig] (1608, 1632)
- *Prys-Courant*, Hamburg (1672)
- *The Merchants Remembrancer*, London (1680)
- *The Prices of Merchandise in London* (1667)

Århus

Erhvervsarkivet Århus

- [Københavns] Fondsbørs, *Protokol for vekselkurser og diskonto*, 1789, 11. dec.–1802
- [Københavns] Fondsbørs, *Protokol for vekselkurser og diskonto*, 1803–1809
- [Københavns] Fondsbørs, *Protokol for vekselkurser og diskonto*, 1811–1872
- [Københavns] Fondsbørs, *Protokol for vekselkurser og diskonto*, 1872, 1. marts–1880 (*Cours-Note-rings-Protocol*)
- [Københavns] Fondsbørs, *Protokol for vekselkurser og diskonto*, 1881–1891, 3. mar.
- [Københavns] Fondsbørs, *Protokol for vekselkurser og diskonto*, 1891, 6. mar.– 1899, 1. aug.
- [Københavns] Fondsbørs, *Protokol for vekselkurser og diskonto*, 1899, 4. aug.–1906, 11. dec.

- [Københavns] Fondsbørs, *Protokol for vekselkurser og diskonto*, 1906, 14. dec.–1915, 24. dec.
- Købmandsfirmaet J.P. Suhr & Søn, København, *Børskurser* 1799–1805

Basel

Schweizerisches Wirtschaftsarchiv (SWA) Basel
- Handschriften 28, 415 diverse Kurszettel, 28. H) *3 Kurszettel der Venediger Devisenbörse*, fol. 1 (1759)
- Handschriften 28, 415 diverse Kurszettel, 28.k *Fotokopien diverser Kurszettel ausländischer Herkunft: Corsi di cambi*, Genova (1777)
- Segerhof Handschriften 420, F 38, 1796, *Belege, Cours de diverses places* 1796

Historisches Museum Basel
- HG Handelswesen 1988.270.1–26, here 2: *Corso di Cambi. Livorno* (1804)

Clausthal-Zellerfeld

Oberbergamt Clausthal (OBA Clausthal)
- Lüneburg – Salz Sachen, Saltz-Preiß 1, *Prys-Courant*, Hamburg (1689–1693)

Gdańsk

Wojewodzkie Archiwum Państowe w Gdańsku – Biblioteka Gdańska Polskíej Akademii Nauk
- *Anzeigen und Erläuterungen der Specie & Wechsel-Course* (1707–1774)
- *Acta der Ältesten der Kaufmannschaft zu Danzig betreffend die Coursberichte* (1829–1855)

Frankfurt am Main

Institut für Stadtgeschichte Frankfurt am Main
- Handel Ugb. Nr. 406: *Corsi di cambi, Genova* (1777)

Genoa

Biblioteca della Camera di Commercio, Industria e Agricultura di Genova
- "Corso dei cambi", anni 1822–1855, n. 6 vols.
- "Corso legale accertato del Sindacato dei Mediatori", anni 1856–1896, n. 41 vols. (1822–1859)

Göttingen

Niedersächsische Staats- und Universitätsbibliothek Göttingen (SUB)
- *Ot Gosudarstvennoj Kommerz-Kollegii Prejskurant, ili sostojanie cen pri Sanktpeterburgskom Porte Inostrannym i Rossijskim tovaram 1800 goda Ijunja 26 dnja* (June 26th 1800), in: Varia Russica (Privato studio collecta), Sign. 4° H RUSS 540/3

Hamburg

Staatsarchiv der Freien und Hansestadt Hamburg (StA Hamburg):
- Akten Senat: *Geld-Cours in Hamburg, Wechsel-Cours in Hamburg* (= Z 301/1)
- 111–1, Cl. VII Lit. Cb Nr. 4, vol. 9, Fasc. 28 (1687–1730)
- 621–1, C. Zeller, B 10, vol. 1 (1796–1799) and vol. 2 (1800–1802): *Exchange rate currents of Leg-*

horn (1797–1799) *and St Petersburg* (1796)

Commerzbibliothek, Handelskammer (CB HH):
- 456/1: *Preis Courant der Wahren in Partheÿen*, Hamburg, 1736–1780
- S/916, Bd. 2: *Geld- und Wechsel-Course*, 1721–1737
- S/653: *Wechsel-Cours in Hamburg* (*Amtliche Geld- und Wechselkurse* T. 1, 2, Hamburg 1710–
     1913, T. 1: *Amtliche Kurse für Wechsel*, 1710–1724, 1781–1814)

Leipzig
Stadtarchiv Leipzig (StadtA Leipzig)
- Tit. XLV G, Nr. 118/1-5: *Anzeigebuch derer wöchentlichen Cours-zettel von E.E. und Hochweisen
     Rath der Stadt Leipzig verpflichteten Sensalen* (1766–1815)

London
Public Record Office (PRO; now: The National Archives), Kew, Richmond, Surrey: War and Colo-
nial Department and Colonial Office (CO)
- CO 17: *Blue Books of the Colony of South Australia*, vols. 13–24 (1841–1851)
- CO 53: *Blue Books of the Colony of the Cape of Good Hope*, vols. 60–63, 75, 93–144 (1822–1825,
     1838, 1856–1907)
- CO 133: *Blue Books of the Colony of Hong Kong*, vols. 2–4 (1844–1846)
- CO 147: *Blue Books. Island of Jamaica*, Kingston, vols. 35–128 (1822–1914)
- CO 172: *Blue Books of the Colony of Mauritius*, vols. 44–72, 79–90 (1823–1846, 1853–1864)
- CO 206: *Blue Books of the Colony of New South Wales*, vols. 63–67, 69–77, 79–86 (1822–1845)
- CO 213: *Blue Book of the Colony of the Province of New Munster*, vols. 27–40 (1841–1854)
- CO 277: *Blue Books of the Straits Settlements*, vols. 1–46 (1868–1914)
- CO 313: *Blue Books of the Colony of Victoria*, vols. 31–34, 40–43 (1851–1854, 1860–1863)
- XP 1211 C 104/128 Pt 2: *Price currents* [Danzig] (1696–1698); *Prys-Courant*, Hamburg (1696–
     1698)

Madrid
Banco de España, Biblioteca
- *Cotizacíon de la Bolsa de Madrid resp. Cotización oficial del Colegio de agentes de cambios, Bolsa
     de Madrid* (1837–1870)
- *Bolitín de Cotización oficial* (1891–1910)

Hemeroteca Municipal
- *Cotización oficial del Colegio de agentes de cambios, Bolsa de Madrid* (1871–1885)
- *Bolitín de Cotización oficial* (1886–1890, 1911–1914)

Marseilles
Archives de la Chambre de Commerce et d'Industrie Marseille-Provence (ACCM)
- L. IX 1034, 1035: *Cours des Changes*

Stockholm

Riksarkivet Stockholm

- Strödda kamerala handlingar, vol. 23: *PrysCorant van de Coopmannschap* [Danzig] (1631, 1635, 1646)
- Strödda kamerala handlingar, vol. 24: *Pris-Courant i St. Petersburg* (1813)

Vienna

Archiv der Wiener Börse AG (AWB; former: Archiv der Wiener Börsekammer)
- *Corsi di Cambi in Vienna (dalla Borsa pubblica in Vienna)* (1771–1785)
- *Wechsel-Cours in Wien. Aus der K.K. öffentlichen Börse* (1786–1817)
- *Tabellarisches Compendium aller Course der Staatspapiere, Wechselbriefe und Münzen* (1811–1818)
- *Tabellarische Übersichten sämmtlicher Wechsel-, Münz- und Obligations-Course vom Jahre ...* (1823–1859)
- *Coursblatt der Wiener Börsekammer* (1840–1859)
- *Coursblatt des Gremiums der K.K. Börse-Sensale* (1860–1874)
- *Amtliches Kursblatt der Wiener Börse* (1881)

Hofkammerarchiv Wien
- Kommerz, 4. Litorale, Abteilung 64: Münzkurs, red number 561 (3), *Corsi di cambi* [Venice] (1756)

2. Commercial, Financial and Other Newspapers

Alta California. Steamer Edition [San Francisco] (1850–1852)

American Minerva [New York] (1794–1797)

American Prices Courant [Boston] (1789)

Amsterdamsch Effectenblad (1843–1913)

Avvisi di Genova (1778–1782, 1802–1804)

Bankers' Magazine (1846–1848, 1853–1859)

Bankers' Weekly Circular (1845–1847)

Berlinische Nachrichten von Staats- und Gelehrten Sachen (1815–1856, 1866–1872)

Boletín Financiero y Minero de México. Diario Consagrado a los Asuntos Financieros y Mineros del País (1900–1914)

Bombay Courier (1822–1843)

Bombay Gazette (1843–1869)

Bombay Times (1847–1848; 1870–1872)

British Packet and Argentine News, Buenos Aires (1827–1858)

Bulletin Commercial du Carnéen, Port Louis (1888–1892)

Calcutta Courier (1832–1839)

Calcutta Courier and Civil, Military and Naval Gazette (1842)

Calcutta Gazette or Oriental Advertiser (1791)

Calcutta Weekly Gazette or Civil, Military and Commercial Register (1840–1843)

Canton General Price Current (1827–1839)

Cape of Good Hope and Port Natal Shipping and Mercantile Gazette (1844–1855)

Carey's United States Recorder, Philadelphia (1798)

Chas. W. Brooks & Co's Circular [San Francisco] (1865–1866)

China Mail, Hong Kong (1848–1858, 1863–1888, 1901–1904)

China Overland Trade Report, Hong Kong (1861, 1863)

China Overland Trade Reporter, Hong Kong (1858–1871, 1878–1888)

Commercial Price Current, Canton (1835–1836)

Commercial Review [New Orleans] (1843–1846)

Corriere di Livorno (1847–1850)

Daily Alta California [San Francisco] (1849–1852)

Daily Shipping and Commercial News, Shanghai (1862)

Danziger Nachrichten, Danziger Erfahrungen, Wöchentliche Danziger Anzeigen und Dienstliche Nachrichten ... (1739–1807)

De Nederlandsche Financier – Dagelijksche Beurscourant (1914)

Egyptian Gazette, Alexandria & Cairo (1884, 1893–1914)

El Mercurio de Valparaiso (1827)

Financial Review [New York] (1865–1914)

Frankfurter Journal (1815)

Frankfurter Ober-Postamts-Zeitung (1817–1851)

Frankfurter Postzeitung (1852–1866)

Frankfurter Zeitung (1866–1874)

Gaceta de Madrid (1820–1837)

Gazette de France (1844–1856)

Gazette nationale [Paris] (1815, 1859–1860, 1863–1866)

Gazette nationale ou le moniteur industriel (1800–1814)

Gazette of the United States, Philadelphia (1789–1802)

General Advertiser, Philadelphia (1790–1793)

General Shipping and Commercial List, New York (1815)

Giornale delle Due Sicilie (1840–1876)

Giornale di commercio del porto-franco di Livorno (1822–1850)

Göteborgs Handels- och Sjöfartstidning (1832–1914)

Grotjan's Philadelphia Public Sale Report, and General Price Current (1814–1821)

Hamburger Correspondent (1834–1838)

Hamburger Privilegierte Liste der Börsenhalle / Börsenhalle. Hamburgische Abendzeitung für Handel, Schiffahrt und Politik (1815–1874)

Hong Kong Daily Press (1889–1896, 1908–1912)

Hong Kong Telegraph (1897–1908, 1912–1914)

Hope's Philadelphia Price-Current and Commercial Record (1796–1816)

Hunt's Merchants' Magazine (1840–1865)

Il Corriere Mercantile [Genoa] (1856–1896)

Il Monitore [Genoa] (1798–1812)

Indian Daily News / The Overland Summary of the Indian Daily News, Bengal Hurkarn and Indian Gazette (1875–1885, 1897–1901)

J. Russel's Gazette (1799–1800)

Jornal de Commercio, Rio de Janeiro (1821–1897)

Journal de Francfort (1816–1823)

Journal de Paris (1780–1783)

Journal des débats (1857–1859, 1861/62, 1867–1914)

Journal des débats politiques et littéraires, Paris (1894–1910)

Journal du commerce (feuille commercial) [Paris] (1763–1783, 1795–1800, 1810–1843)

Journal du commerce, Bruxelles (1760/61)

Journal Général de France (1784–1792)

Königlich privilegierte Berlinische Zeitung / Vossische Zeitung (1857/58)

La Gazzetta di Genova (1804–1821)

Le Memorial Des Marchands, Londres (1681–1683, 1685)

Le Temps, Paris (1892–1893, 1896–1913)

Levant Herald (*Constantinople Messenger – Eastern Express*) (1874–1914)

Levant Times & Shipping Gazette (1868–1873)

Listino della Borsa [Genoa] (1897–1914)

Louisiana Gazette (1804–1812)

Mauritius Price Current and Shipping List (1847–1853)

Mensagero Argentino, Buenos Aires (1824–1826)

Mercantile Gazette and Prices Courant [San Francisco] (1858–1868)

Mercantile Record Overland Edition, Port Louis (1877–1887)

Money Market (1864)

Neue Frankfurter Zeitung (1865/66)

Neue Zürcher Zeitung (1842–1914)

New Orleans Commercial Bulletin (1860–1862)

New Orleans Price Courant (1823–1829, 1836–1841)

New Orleans Times (1865–1872)

New Orleans Weekly Times (1865–1867)

New York American (1822–1829)

New York Commercial Advertiser (1830–1854)

New York Daily Advertiser (1817–1818)

New York Shipping and Commercial List (1815–1834)

New York Stock and Exchange Board (1818–1839)

New York Times (1853–1856)

New Zealand Trade Review and Wellington Price Current (1892–1914)

North China Daily News, Shanghai (1869–1879, 1889–1893)

Oram's New York Price Courant and Marine Register (1797–1803)

Oriental Observer, Calcutta (1828–1833)

Osservatore Triestino (1818–1825, 1861–1914)

Overland Commercial Gazette, Port Louis (1864–1878)

Overland Register and Price Current, Hong Kong (1846–1861)

Pennsylvania Mercury (1785–1786)

Porcupine's Gazette [Philadelphia] (1797–1799)

Post- och Inrikes Tidningar (1790–1824, 1844–1889)

Prijscourant der Effecten (1796–1842)

Prix Courant des Marchandises a Londres (1668, 1671–1675, 1679/80, 1682, 1684/85)

Rigische Anzeigen von allerhand Sachen (1763–1765)

San Francisco Herald (1851–1857, 1866).

San Francisco Shipping List (1852–1856)

Singapore Chronicle and Commercial Register (1834–1837)

Smyrna Mail (1862–1864)

Spenersche Zeitung [Berlin] (1872–1874)

Stockholms Handels Mercurius (1732 –1737)

Stockholms Stads Priscourant (1740–1755, 1757–1767)

Sydney Herald (*Sydney Morning Herald*) (1846–1849)

The American Naval and Commercial Register [Philadelphia] (1795–1797)

The American Sentinel (1837–1838)

The Bengal Weekly Messenger, Calcutta (1825)

The Boston Commercial Gazette (1817–1834)

The Boston Gazette (1795–1816)

The Boston Price Courant (1795–1820)

The China Mail, Hong Kong (1864)

The Commercial and Financial Chronicle [New York] (1865–1914)

The Commercial Gazette, Port Louis (1864–1869, 1893–1897)

The Constitutional Diary, Philadelphia (1799–1800)

The Courier [New Orleans] (1824, 1836–1843, 1854–1860)

The Course of the Exchange, and Other Things [London] (1698–1850)

The Daily Examiner [San Francisco] (1866)

The Daily Japan Herald, Yokohama (1866–1867)

The Economist, London (1844–1914)

The Financial Register [New York] (1837–1838)

The Herald, New York (1794–1796)

The Independent Gazetteer [Philadelphia] (1785–1786, 1796)

The Japan Herald, Yokohama (1861–1865)

The Japan Times, Yokohama (1865–1866)

The Japan Times' Overland Mail, Yokohama (1868–1869)

The Japan Weekly Chronicle, Commercial Supplement, Kobe (1897–1900, 1904–1910)

The Japan Weekly Mail, Yokohama (1870–1914)

The Level of Europe and North America [Philadelphia] (1795)

The Merchants and Planters Gazette (*Overland Mail Edition*), Port Louis (1897–1914).

The Merchants Remembrancer, London (1680)

The Nagasaki Shipping List and Advertiser (1861/62)

The National Gazette (Democratic Press, Philadelphia) (1820–1838)

The New York Herald (1849–1850)

The New York Price Current (1800)

The North American [New Orleans] (1839–1840)

The Philadelphia Price Current (1783–1784)

The Prices of Merchandise in London (1667)

The Shipping Gazette and Sydney General Trade List (1847–1853)

The Standard & River Plate News, Buenos Aires (1870–1914)

The Sydney Trade Review and Prices Current (1894–1911)

The Universal Gazette, Philadelphia (1798–1799)

Vossische Zeitung (1859–1865, 1874–1914)

Washington Gazette (1796)

Weekly Standard, Buenos Aires (1870–1874)

Weser-Zeitung [Bremen] (1843–1886)

Wiener Zeitung (1801–1810, 1872–1914)

Wm. T. Coleman & Co's Circular [San Francisco] (1857)

3. Merchant Manuals

BOCK, J[ohann] H[einrich] D[aniel] (ed.), *J.C. Nelkenbrechers allgemeines Taschenbuch der Münz-Maaß- und Gewichtskunde für Banquiers und Kaufleute*, Berlin [15]1832.

BOCK, J[ohann] H[einrich] D[aniel] / CRÜGER, Carl (eds.), *J.C. Nelkenbrechers allgemeines Taschenbuch der Münz-, Maaß- und Gewichtskunde für Banquiers und Kaufleute. Auf's neue herausgegeben und mit vielen Handelsplätzen Amerika's und Asien's, desgl. mit den Usancen der Staatspapiere vermehrt*, Berlin [14]1828.

DuPUYS DE LA SERRA, Jacques, *L'art des lettres de change suivant les plus célèbres places d'Europe*, Paris 1693.

G[ERHARDT], [Marcus Rudolf Balthasar] (ed.), *Johann Christian Nelkenbrechers Taschenbuch eines Banquiers und Kaufmanns ...*, Berlin [2]1769.

—— (ed.), *Johann Christian Nelkenbrechers Taschenbuch eines Banquiers und Kaufmanns ...*, Berlin [4]1775.

GERHARDT sen., M[arcus] R[udolf] B[althasar] (ed.), *Nelkenbrechers Taschenbuch der Münz- Maaß- und Gewichtskunde für Kaufleute*, Berlin [7]1793.

—— (ed.), *Nelkenbrechers Taschenbuch der Münz- Maaß- und Gewichtskunde für Kaufleute*, Berlin [8]1798.

HERBACH, Johann Christian, *Einleitung zum Gründlichen Verstand der Wechsel-Handlung ...*, Nürnberg 1716.

——, *Verbesserte und Viel-vermehrte Wechsel-Handlung ...*, Nürnberg 1726.

——, *Europäische Wechselhandlung ...*, Nürnberg 1756/57.

JERUSALEM, Ernst (ed.), *J.C. Nelkenbrecher's Taschenbuch für Kaufleute. I. Abth.: Taschenbuch der Münz-, Maass- und Gewichtskunde, der Wechsel-, Geld- und Fonds-curse u.s.w. für Kaufleute*, Berlin [20]1890.

KELLY, P[atrick], *The Universal Cambist and Commercial Instructor ...*, 2 vols., London [2]1821, repr. 1835.

KELLY, Patrick, *The Universal Cambist and Commercial Instructor; Being a General Treatise on Exchange ...*, 2 vols., London 1811.

KRUSE, Jürgen Elert, *Allgemeiner und besonders Hamburgischer Contorist*, Hamburg [4]1782.

LE MOINE DE L'ESPINE, Jacques, *Le Negoce [sic!] d'Amsterdam, ou Traité de sa Banque ...*, Amsterdam 1710.

NEUBAUER, C. (ed.), *J.C. Nelkenbrecher's Taschenbuch für Kaufleute, II part: Münz-Tabelle*, Berlin [20]1877.

NOBACK, Christian, *Vollständiges Handbuch der Münz-, Bank- und Wechsel-Verhältnisse aller Länder und Handelsplätze der Erde*, Rudolstadt 1833.

NOBACK, Christian / NOBACK, Friedrich, *Vollständiges Taschenbuch der Münz-, Maass- und Gewichts-Verhältnisse, der Staatspapiere, des Wechsel- und Bankwesens und der Usanzen aller Länder und Handelsplätze*, 2 parts, Leipzig 1851.

——, *Münz-, Maass- und Gewichtsbuch. Das Geld-, Maass- und Wechselwesen, die Kurse, Staatspapiere, Banken, Handelsanstalten und Usanzen aller Staaten und wichtigern Orte*, Leipzig 1858.

NOBACK, Friedrich, *Münz-, Maass- und Gewichtsbuch. Das Geld-, Maass- und Gewichtswesen, die Wechsel- und Geldkurse, das Wechselrecht und die Usanzen*, Leipzig [2]1877.

ODDY, John Jepson, *European Commerce ...*, London 1805.

OTTO, J.S.G. (ed.), *J.C. Nelkenbrechers allgemeines Taschenbuch der Münz-, Maaß- und Gewichtskunde für Banquiers und Kaufleute*, Berlin [11]1815.

—— (ed.), *J.C. Nelkenbrechers allgemeines Taschenbuch der Münz-, Maaß- und Gewichtskunde für Banquiers und Kaufleute*, Berlin [12]1817.

PAGNINI DELLA VENTURA, Giovanni-Francesco, *Della decima e di varie altre gravezze imposte dal commune di Firenze, Della moneta e della mercatura de' Fiorentini fino al secolo XVI*, 4 vols., Lisbona – Lucca 1765/66, *vol. IV: La Pratica della Mercatura scritta de Giovanni di Antonio da Uzzano nel 1442*.

PEGOLOTTI, Francesco Balducci, *La pratica della mercatura*, ed. Allan EVANS, Cambridge (Mass.) 1936 (repr. New York 1970).

SAVARY, Ja[c]ques, *Le parfait négociant ou instruction générale pour ce qui regarde le Commerce de toute sorte de Marchandises, tant de France, que des Pays Étrangers*, Genève 1676.

SCHELLENBERG, Johann Philipp, (ed.), *J.C. Nelkenbrechers allgemeines Taschenbuch der Münz-, Maaß- und Gewichtskunde für Banquiers und Kaufleute*, Berlin [13]1820.

SCHWABE, H. (ed.), *J.C. Nelkenbrecher's allgemeines Taschenbuch der Münz-, Maaß- und Gewichtskunde, der Wechsel-, Geld- und Fonds-Curse u.s.w.*, Berlin [19]1871.

SONNDORFER, Rudolf, *Die Technik des Welthandels. Ein Handbuch der internationalen Handelskunde*, Wien – Leipzig [2]1900.

SWOBODA, Otto, *Die kaufmännische Arbitrage. Eine Sammlung von Notizen und Usancen sämmtlicher Börsenplätze für den praktischen Gebrauch*, Berlin [7]1889.

——, *Die kaufmännische Arbitrage. Eine Sammlung von Notizen und Usancen sämtlicher Börsenplätze der Welt*, ed. by Adolf SANDHEIM, Berlin [11]1902.

——, *Die Arbitrage in Wertpapieren, Wechseln, Münzen und Edelmetallen. Handbuch des Börsen-, Münz- und Geldwesens sämtlicher Handelsplätze der Welt*, ed. Max FÜRST, Berlin [12]1905.

——, *Die Arbitrage in Wertpapieren, Wechseln, Münzen und Edelmetallen. Handbuch des Börsen-, Münz- und Geldwesens sämtlicher Handelsplätze der Welt*, ed. Max FÜRST, Berlin [13]1909.

——, *Die Arbitrage in Wertpapieren, Wechseln, Münzen und Edelmetallen. Handbuch des Börsen-, Münz- und Geldwesens sämtlicher Handelsplätze der Welt*, ed. Max FÜRST, Berlin [14]1913.

——, *Die Arbitrage in Wertpapieren, Wechseln, Münzen und Edelmetallen. Handbuch des Börsen-, Münz- und Geldwesens sämtlicher Handelsplätze der Welt*, ed. Max FÜRST, Berlin [16]1924/25.

——, *Die Arbitrage in Wertpapieren, Wechseln, Münzen und Edelmetallen. Handbuch des Börsen-, Münz- und Geldwesens sämtlicher Handelsplätze der Welt*, ed. Eduard WAGON, Berlin [17]1928.

VELDEN, M[artin] v[an], *Fondament van de Wisselhandeling: Onderrichtingh ghevende van alle voornaemste Wisselen van Christenrijck, so van Trates, Remessen, vergelijcking van prysen, verscheyden comissien, te vormen, voegen ende calcula van baet of schade te maecken naer den cours, die te oordeelen, ende naer gelegentheyd van tijdt of plaets te konnen scheyden*, Amsterdam 1629; [2]1647 (in German: *Underricht der Wechsel-Handlung*, Frankfurt 1669).

WOLFF, F. (ed.), *J.C. Nelkenbrecher's allgemeines Taschenbuch der Maaß-, Gewichts- und Münzkunde, der Wechsel- Geld- und Fondscourse u.s.w. für Banquiers und Kaufleute*, Berlin [16]1842.

4. Other Printed Sources

Administration des monnaies et des médailles, *Rapport au Ministre des Finances*, Paris 1916, pp. 138–145 (1888–1914).

Camara Syndical dos Corretores de Fundos Públicos da Capital Federal (ed.), *Relatorio da Camara Syndical dos Corretores de Fundos Públicos da Capital Federal (administração de 1 de abril de 1897 a 31 de março de 1898)*, annexo ao apresentado pelo Ministro de Estado dos Negocios da Facenda por Thomaz RABELLO, Rio de Janeiro 1898.

Camara Syndical dos Corretores de Fundos Públicos da Capital Federal (ed.), *Relatorio da Camara Syndical dos Corretores de Fundos Públicos da Capital Federal (administração de 1 de abril de 1898 a 31 de março de 1899)*, annexo ao apresentado pelo Ministro de Estado dos Negocios da Facenda por José Claudio DA SILVA, Rio de Janeiro 1899.

Camara Syndical dos Corretores de Fundos Públicos da Capital Federal (ed.), *Relatorio da Camara Syndical dos Corretores de Fundos Públicos da Capital Federal (administração de 1 de abril de 1899 a 31 de março de 1900)*, apresentado ao Ministro de Estado dos Negocios da Facenda por José Claudio DA SILVA, Rio de Janeiro 1900.

Camara Syndical dos Corretores de Fundos Públicos da Capital Federal (ed.), *Relatorio da Camara Syndical dos Corretores de Fundos Públicos da Capital Federal (administração de 1 de abril de 1900 a 31 de março de 1901)*, apresentado ao Ministro de Estado dos Negocios da Facenda por José Claudio DA SILVA, Rio de Janeiro 1901.

Camara Syndical dos Corretores de Fundos Públicos da Capital Federal (ed.), *Relatorio da Camara*

Syndical dos Corretores de Fundos Públicos da Capital Federal (administração de 1 de abril de 1901 a 31 de março de 1902), apresentado ao Ministro de Estado dos Negocios da Facenda por José Claudio DA SILVA, Rio de Janeiro 1902.

Camara Syndical dos Corretores de Fundos Públicos da Capital Federal (ed.), *Relatorio da Camara Syndical dos Corretores de Fundos Públicos da Capital Federal (administração de 1 de abril de 1902 a 31 de março de 1903)*, apresentado ao Ministro de Estado dos Negocios da Facenda por José Claudio DA SILVA, Rio de Janeiro 1903.

Camara Syndical dos Corretores de Fundos Públicos da Capital Federal (ed.), *Relatorio da Camara Syndical dos Corretores de Fundos Públicos da Capital Federal (administração de 1 de abril de 1903 a 31 de março de 1904)*, apresentado ao Ministro de Estado dos Negocios da Facenda por José Claudio DA SILVA, Rio de Janeiro 1904.

Camara Syndical dos Corretores de Fundos Públicos da Capital Federal (ed.), *Relatorio da Camara Syndical dos Corretores de Fundos Públicos da Capital Federal (administração de 1 de abril de 1904 a 31 de março de 1905)*, apresentado ao Ministro de Estado dos Negocios da Facenda por José Claudio DA SILVA, Rio de Janeiro 1905.

Camara Syndical dos Corretores de Fundos Públicos da Capital Federal (ed.), *Relatorio da Camara Syndical dos Corretores de Fundos Públicos da Capital Federal (administração de 1 de abril de 1905 a 31 de março de 1906)*, apresentado ao Ministro de Estado dos Negocios da Facenda por José Claudio DA SILVA, Rio de Janeiro 1906.

Camara Syndical dos Corretores de Fundos Públicos da Capital Federal (ed.), *Relatorio da Camara Syndical dos Corretores de Fundos Públicos da Capital Federal (administração de 1 de abril de 1906 a 31 de março de 1907)*, apresentado ao Ministro de Estado dos Negocios da Facenda por José Claudio DA SILVA, Rio de Janeiro 1907.

Camara Syndical dos Corretores de Fundos Públicos da Capital Federal (ed.), *Relatorio da Camara Syndical dos Corretores de Fundos Públicos da Capital Federal (administração de 1 de abril de 1907 a 31 de março de 1908)*, apresentado ao Ministro de Estado dos Negocios da Facenda por José Claudio DA SILVA, Rio de Janeiro 1908.

Camara Syndical dos Corretores de Fundos Públicos da Capital Federal (ed.), *Relatorio da Camara Syndical dos Corretores de Fundos Públicos da Capital Federal (administração de 1 de abril de 1908 a 31 de março de 1909)*, apresentado ao Ministro de Estado dos Negocios da Facenda por José Claudio DA SILVA, Rio de Janeiro 1909.

Camara Syndical dos Corretores de Fundos Públicos da Capital Federal (ed.), *Relatorio da Camara Syndical dos Corretores de Fundos Públicos da Capital Federal (administração de 1 de abril de 1909 a 31 de março de 1910)*, apresentado ao Ministro de Estado dos Negocios da Facenda por José Claudio DA SILVA, Rio de Janeiro 1910.

Camara Syndical dos Corretores de Fundos Públicos da Capital Federal (ed.), *Relatorio da Camara Syndical dos Corretores de Fundos Públicos da Capital Federal (administração de 1 de abril de 1910 a 31 de março de 1911)*, apresentado ao Ministro de Estado dos Negocios da Facenda por Adolpho SIMONSEN, Rio de Janeiro 1911.

Camara Syndical dos Corretores de Fundos Públicos da Capital Federal (ed.), *Relatorio da Camara Syndical dos Corretores de Fundos Públicos da Capital Federal (administração de 1 de abril de 1911 a 31 de março de 1912)*, apresentado ao Ministro de Estado dos Negocios da Facenda por Adolpho SIMONSEN, Rio de Janeiro 1913 (!).

Camara Syndical dos Corretores de Fundos Públicos da Capital Federal (ed.), *Relatorio da Camara Syndical dos Corretores de Fundos Públicos da Capital Federal (administração de 1 de abril de 1912 a 31 de março de 1913)*, apresentado ao Ministro de Estado dos Negocios da Facenda por Adolpho SIMONSEN, Rio de Janeiro 1913.

Camara Syndical dos Corretores de Fundos Públicos da Capital Federal (ed.), *Relatorio da Camara Syndical dos Corretores de Fundos Públicos da Capital Federal (administração de 1 de abril de 1913 a 31 de março de 1914)*, apresentado ao Ministro de Estado dos Negocios da Facenda por Adolpho SIMONSEN, Rio de Janeiro 1914.

Camara Syndical dos Corretores de Fundos Públicos da Capital Federal (ed.), *Relatorio da Camara Syndical dos Corretores de Fundos Públicos da Capital Federal (administração de 1 de abril de 1914 a 31 de março de 1915)*, apresentado ao Ministro de Estado dos Negocios da Facenda por Adolpho SIMONSEN, Rio de Janeiro 1915.

Departement van economische zaken (ed.), *Prijzen, indexcijfers en wisselkoersen op Java 1913–1937* (= *Mededeelingen van het centraal kantoor voor de statistiek*, No. 146), Batavia 1938.

Estadística Minera de Chile en 1910, Santiago 1911.

Staat van de wisselkoers van Java op Nederland en Engeland. Handelingen van de Tweed Kamer der Staaten General 1851/52 II, Annex VIII, B6, The Hague 1852.

Statistical Register of New South Wales for the Year 1871, Sydney 1872.

Statistics of the Colony of Victoria for the Year 1872. Compiled from the Official Records in the Registrar-General's Office, Melbourne 1873.

5. Bibliography

ADAMS, John / WEST, Robert Craig, Money, Prices, and Economic Development in India, 1861–1895, *Journal of Economic History* 39 (1979), pp. 55–68.

AGHASSIAN, Michel / KÉVONIAN, Kéram, The Armenian Merchant Network: Overall Autonomy and Local Integration, in Sushil CHAUDHURI / Michel MORINEAU (eds.), *Merchants, Companies and Trade. Europe and Asia in the Early Modern Era*, Cambridge 1999, pp. 74–94.

AHVENAINEN, Jorma, Telegraphs, Trade and Policy. The Role of the International Telegraphs in the Years 1870–1914, in Wolfram FISCHER / R. Marvin MCINNIS / Jürgen SCHNEIDER (eds.), *The Emergence of a World Economy 1500–1914. Papers of the IX International Congress of Economic History*, 2 parts, Stuttgart 1986, part II, pp. 505–518.

——, *The Far Eastern Telegraphs. The History of Telegraphic Communications between the Far East, Europe and America before the First World War*, Helsinki 1981.

——, The Role of Telegraphs in the 19th Century Revolution of Communications, in Michael NORTH (ed.), *Kommunikationsrevolutionen. Die neuen Medien des 16. und 19. Jahrhunderts*, Köln – Weimar – Wien 1995, pp. 73–80.

ALEMANN, Roberto T., *Goldunze, Silberpeso und Papiergeld. 150 Jahre argentinische Währungen* (= *Sonderdruck aus der Beilage vom 9. Juli 1966 des 'Argentinischen Tageblattes' zum 150. Jahrestag der argentinischen Unabhängigkeitserklärung*), Buenos Aires 1966.

ALVAREZ, Juan, *Temas de historia económica argentina*, Buenos Aires 1929.

ÅMARK, Karl, *Spannmålshandel och spannmålspolitik i Sverige 1719–1830*, Ph.D. thesis Stockholm 1915.

AMBROSE, Gwilyn, English Traders at Aleppo (1658–1756), *Economic History Review* 3 (1931), pp. 246–267.

ANDERSSON, Bertil, Early History of Banking in Gothenburg Discount House Operations 1783–1818, *Scandinavian Economic History Review* 31 (1983), pp. 50–67.

ARNDT, Ernst H.D., *Banking and Currency Development in South Africa, 1652–1927*, Cape Town et al. 1928.

ARNOLD, Anton, *Das indische Geldwesen unter besonderer Berücksichtigung seiner Reformen seit 1893*, Jena 1906.

ASHTON, T.S., The Bill of Exchange and Private Banks in Lancashire 1790–1830, *Economic History*

Review 15/1 (1945), pp. 25–35.

ASHTOR, Eliahu, Banking Instruments between the Muslim East and the Christian West, *Journal of European Economic History* 1 (1972), pp. 553–573.

ÅSTRÖM, Sven-Erik, From Cloth to Iron. The Anglo-Baltic Trade in the Seventeenth Century, *Commentationes Humanarum Literarum* 33 (1963), pp. 1–260; ibid., 37 (1965), pp. 1–85.

——, *From Stockholm to St. Petersburg. Commercial Factors in the Political Relations between England and Sweden, 1675–1700*, Helsinki 1962.

AUTIO, Jaakko, *Valuuttakurssit Suomessa 1864–1911. Katsaus ja tilastosarjat*, Helsinki 1992 (= *Suomen Pankin Keskustelualoitteita* 1/92).

BAAS, Norbert W.J., *Die Doppelwährungspolitik Frankreichs 1850–1885*, Firenze 1984.

BAASCH, Ernst (ed.), *Quellen zur Geschichte von Hamburgs Handel und Schiffahrt im 17., 18. und 19. Jahrhundert*, Hamburg 1910.

——, Aus der Entwicklungsgeschichte des Hamburger Kurszettels, *Bank-Archiv* 5 (1905/06), pp. 8–11.

BACHMAYER, Othmar, *Die Geschichte der österreichischen Währungspolitik*, Wien 1960.

BAGCHI, Amiya Kumar, Anglo-Indian Banking in British India: From the Paper Pound to the Gold Standard, *Journal of Imperial and Commonwealth History* 13 (1985), pp. 93–108.

——, Money and Credit as areas of Conflict in Colonial India, in B. CHANDRA (Organizer), *Typology of Colonial Economic Development* (= *Eighth International Economic History Congress, Budapest 1982*, B6), Budapest 1982, pp. 28–35.

BAILYN, Bernard, *The New England Merchants in the Seventeenth Century*, Cambridge (Mass.) – London 1955.

BALTZAREK, Franz, *Die Geschichte der Wiener Börse. Öffentliche Finanzen und privates Kapital im Spiegel einer österreichischen Wirtschaftsinstitution*, Wien 1973.

Banchi pubblici, banchi privati e monti di pietà nell'Europa preindustriale. Amministrazione, tecniche operative e ruoli economici, Genova 1991, 2 vols.

Bank of Japan (ed.), *The Recent Economic Development of Japan*, Tokyo 1915.

BARBANCE, Marthe, *Vie commerciale de la route du Cap Horn au XIXe siècle. L'armement A.-D. Bordes et fils*, Paris 1969.

BASTER, A.S.J., The Origins of the British Exchange Banks in China, *Economic History* (1934/1), pp. 140–151.

BATU, Hâmit / BACQUÉ-GRAMMONT, Jean Louis (eds.), *L'Empire Ottoman, la République Turquie et la France*, Istanbul – Paris 1986.

BAUER, Hans, Bank- und Finanzplatz Basel, in Louis H. MOTTET (ed.), *Geschichte der Schweizer Banken. Bankier-Persönlichkeiten aus fünf Jahrhunderten*, Zürich 1987 (Neuchâtel – Paris 1986), pp. 139–174.

BECK, Thomas / DOS SANTOS LOPES, Marília / RÖDEL, Christian (eds.), *Barrieren und Zugänge. Die Geschichte der europäischen Expansion. Festschrift für Eberhard Schmitt zum 65. Geburtstag*, Wiesbaden 2004.

BECK, Thomas et al. (eds.), *Überseegeschichte – Beiträge der jüngeren Forschung. Festschrift anläßlich der Gründung der Forschungsstiftung für vergleichende europäische Überseegeschichte 1999 in Bamberg*, Stuttgart 1999.

BECKHART, Benjamin H. (ed.), *The New York Money Market*, vol. I, New York 1931.

BERGHOFF, Hartmut, Der Berliner Kapitalmarkt im Aufbruch (1830–1870), in Hans POHL (ed.), *Geschichte des Finanzplatzes Berlin*, Frankfurt/Main 2002, pp. 53–102.

BERGIER, Jean-François, *Genève et l'économie européenne de la Renaissance*, Paris 1963.

——, *Wirtschaftsgeschichte der Schweiz. Von den Anfängen bis zur Gegenwart*, Zürich ²1990.

BERMAN, Harold J., *Recht und Revolution. Die Bildung der westlichen Rechtstradition*, Frankfurt/

Main 1991 (Engl. 1983).

BERNAL, Antonio M. (ed.), *Dinero, moneda y crédito en la Monarquía Hispánica. Actas del Simposio Internacional "Dinero, moneda y crédito. De la Monarquía Hispánica a la Integración Monetaria Europea", Madrid, 4–7 de mayo de 1999*, Madrid 2000.

——, Crédito, financiación y beneficio en el comercio colonial español a través de los cambios y préstamos marítimos (ss XVI–XVII), in José CASAS PARDO (ed.), *Economic Effects of the European Expansion, 1492–1824*, Stuttgart 1992, pp. 39–76.

——, *La financiación de la Carrera de Indias (1492–1824). Dinero y crédito en el comercio colonial español con América*, Sevilla – Madrid 1992.

BETHELL, Leslie (ed.), *The Cambridge History of Latin America, vol. II: Colonial Latin America*, Cambridge et al. 1984.

BLANCHARD, Ian / GOODMAN, Anthony / NEWMANN, Jennifer (eds.), *Industry and Finance in Early Modern History. Essays Presented to George Hammersley on the Occasion of his 74th Birthday*, Stuttgart 1992.

BLAUM, Kurt, *Das Geldwesen der Schweiz seit 1798*, Strassburg 1908.

BOGUCKA, Maria, La lettre de change et le crédit dans les échanges entre Gdansk et Amsterdam dans la premier moitié du XVIIe siècle, in Herman VAN DER WEE / Vladimir A. VINOGRADOV / Grigorii G. KOTOVSKY (eds.), *Fifth International Conference of Economic History, Leningrad 1970, vol. IV*, The Hague – Paris – New York 1976, pp. 31–41.

BORDO Michael D. / MACDONALD, Ronald, Violations of the "Rules of the Game" and the Credibility of the Classical Gold Standard, 1880–1914, in National Bureau of Economic Research (ed.), *Working Paper 6115*, Cambridge (Mass.) 1997.

BORDO, Michael D. / CAPIE, Forrest (eds.), *Monetary Regimes in Transition*, Cambridge 1993.

BORLANDI, Franco (ed.), *El Libro di Mercatantie et Usanze de' Paesi*, Torino 1936.

BOUBAKER, Sadok, Le transfert des capiteaux entre l'Empire Ottoman et l'Europe. L'utilisation de la lettre de change: L'éxemple de la société Garavaque et Cusson à Smyrne (1760–1772), *Revue d'histoire maghrébine (époque moderne et contemporaine)* 21 (n°. 75/76) (1994), pp. 199–218.

BOUCHARY, Jean, *Le marché des changes de Paris à la fin du XVIIIe siècle (1778–1800) avec des graphiques et le relevé des cours*, Paris 1937.

BOYCE, Robert, Submarine Cables as a Factor in Britain's Ascendency as a World Power, 1850–1914, in Michael NORTH (ed.), *Kommunikationsrevolutionen. Die neuen Medien des 16. und 19. Jahrhunderts*, Köln – Weimar – Wien 1995, pp. 81–99.

BOYER-XAMBEU, Marie-Thérèse / DELEPLACE, Ghislain / GILLARD, Lucien, A la recherche d'un âge d'or des marchés financiers: Intégration et efficience au XVIIIe siècle, *Cahiers d'économie politique* 20/21 (1992), pp. 33–65.

—— / —— / ——, Goldstandard, Währung und Finanz im 16. Jahrhundert, in Michael NORTH (ed.), *Geldumlauf, Währungssysteme und Zahlungsverkehr in Nordwesteuropa 1300–1800. Beiträge zur Geldgeschichte der späten Hansezeit*, Köln – Wien 1989, pp. 167–181.

—— / —— / ——, *Monnaie privé et pouvoir des princes. L'économie des relations monétaires à la Renaissance*, Paris 1986.

BRADING, D.A., *Miners and Merchants in Bourbon Mexico 1763–1810*, Cambridge 1971.

BRANDT, Walter, Kurs- und Kreditsicherung der Überseebanken, *Zeitschrift für Handelswissenschaft und Handelspraxis* (1913/12), pp. 362–367.

BRAUDEL, Fernand / SPOONER, Frank C., Prices in Europe from 1450 to 1750, in E.E. RICH / C.H. WILSON (eds.), *The Economy of Expanding Europe in the Sixteenth and Seventeenth Centuries* (= *The Cambridge Economic History of Europe*, vol. IV), Cambridge et al. 1967, pp. 378–486.

BRÉSSARD, Marc, *Les foires de Lyon au XVe et XVIe siècles*, Paris 1914.

BRÖTEL, Dieter, Die europäische und die asiatische Seidenindustrie 1860–1930. Modernisierung und Weltmarkteinbindung der Rohseideproduzenten China und Japan im Vergleich, *Geschichte und*

Gesellschaft 28/1 (2002), pp. 109–144.

BUESCU, Mircea, *300 anos de inflação*, Rio de Janeiro 1973.

BURON, E., Statistics on Franco-American Trade (1778–1806), *Journal of Economic and Business History* 1932/4, pp. 571–580.

BUSS, Georg, *Berliner Börse von 1685–1913. Zum 50. Gedenktage der ersten Versammlung im neuen Hause*, Berlin 1913.

BUTLIN, Noel G. / GINSWICK, J. / STATHAM, P., Colonial Statistics before 1850, in Australian National University, *Source Papers in Economic History* No. 12, June 1986.

BUTLIN, Noel G. , *Forming a Colonial Economy, Australia 1810–1850*, Cambridge 1994.

BUTLIN, Sydney J., *Australia and New Zealand Bank. The Bank of Australasia and the Union Bank of Australia Limited, 1828–1951*, London 1961.

——, *Foundations of the Australian Monetary System 1788–1851*, Melbourne 1953 (Sydney ²1968).

——, *The Australian Monetary System 1851 to 1914*, [Sydney] 1986.

CAFARO, P., *La borsa valori di Milano: origini e sviluppo*, Milano 1988.

CANZLER, Johann Georg, *Nachrichten zur genauern Kenntniß der Geschichte, Staatsverwaltung und ökonomischen Verfassung des Königreichs Schweden. Aus dem Französischen übersetzt und beträchtlich vermehrt*, Erster Theil, Dresden 1778.

CARDOSO DE MELLO, Manoel / DA CONCEIÇÃO TAVARES, Maria, The Capitalist Export Economy in Brazil, 1884–1930, in Roberto CORTÉS CONDE / Shane J. HUNT (eds.), *The Latin American Economies. Growth and Export Sector 1880–1930*, New York – London 1985, pp. 82–136.

CARIOLA, Carmen / SUNKEL, Osvaldo, The Growth of the Nitrate Industry and Socioeconomic Change in Chile, 1880–1930, in Roberto CORTÉS CONDE / Shane J. HUNT (eds.), *The Latin American Economies. Growth and Export Sector 1880–1930*, New York – London 1985, pp. 137–254.

CASAS PARDO, José (ed.), *Economic Effects of the European Expansion, 1492–1824*, Stuttgart 1992.

CASSANDRO, G., Art. "Cambiale", in *Enciclopedia del Diritto V*, Varese 1959, p. 836.

——, Vicende storiche della lettera di cambio, *Bolletino storico del Banco di Napoli* IX–XII/1, 1955/56.

CAVACIOCCHI, Simonetta (ed.), *Fiere e mercati nella integrazione delle economie europee, secc. XIII–XVIII. Atti della "Trentaduesima Settimana die Studi" 8–12 maggio 2000 sotto l'Alto Patronato del Parlamento Europeo con il patrozinio del prof. Romano Prodi, Presidente della Commissione Europea*, Prato 2001.

—— (ed.), *Produzione e commercio della carta e del libro, secc. XIII–XVIII*, Prato 1992.

CÉSPEDES DEL CASTILLO, Guillermo, *América Hispánica (1492–1898)*, Barcelona 1983.

CHABLANI, Hashmat-Rai Lekharaja, *Indian Currency, Banking and Exchange*, London 1932.

CHALMERS, Robert, *History of Currency in the British Colonies*, London 1893 [repr. Colchester 1972].

CHANDRA, B. (Organizer), *Typology of Colonial Economic Development* (= Eighth International Economic History Congress, Budapest 1982, B6), Budapest 1982.

CHAPMAN, S.D., The Evolution of Merchant Roles in Eighteenth-Century Finance, in Ranald C. MICHIE (ed.), *The Development of London as a Financial Centre*, London – New York 2000, vol. 1: 1700–1850, pp. 38–52.

CHAPMAN, Stanley C., *The Rise of Merchant Banking*, London – Boston – Sydney 1984, ¹1985.

CHAUDHURI, K[irti] N. (ed.), *The Economic Development of India under the East India Company 1814–58. A Selection of Contemporary Writings*, Cambridge 1971.

——, *The Trading World of Asia and the English East India Company 1660–1760*, Cambridge et al. 1978.

CHAUDHURI, Sus[h]il, *Trade and Commercial Organization in Bengal 1650–1720. With Special Ref-

nce to the English East India Company, Calcutta 1975.

ᴀUDHURI, Sushil, No Ready Money? No Problem! The Role of Hundis (Bills of Exchange) in Early Modern India, c. 1600–1800, in idem / Markus A. DENZEL (eds.), *Cashless Payments and Transactions from the Antiquity to 1914*, Stuttgart 2008, pp. 139–151.

—— / DENZEL, Markus A. (eds.), *Cashless Payments and Transactions from the Antiquity to 1914*, Stuttgart 2008.

—— / MORINEAU, Michel (eds.), *Merchants, Companies and Trade. Europe and Asia in the Early Modern Era*, Cambridge 1999.

CHEONG, Weng E., China Houses and the Bank of England Crisis of 1825, *Business History* 15 (1973), pp. 56–73.

——, *Mandarins and Merchants. Jardine Matheson & Co. A China Agency in the Early Nineteenth Century*, London – Malmö 1979.

——, Trade and Finance in China: 1784–1834. A Reappraisal, *Business History* 7/1 (1965), pp. 34–56.

[CHIAPPELLI, Fredi (ed.),] *The Dawn of Modern Banking*, New Haven – London 1979.

CIESLAK, Edmund, Amsterdam als Bankier von Danzig im 18. Jahrhundert, in *The Interactions of Amsterdam and Antwerp with the Baltic Region, 1400–1800. De Nederlanden en het Oostzeegebied, 1400–1800. Papers presented at the 3rd International Conference of the Association Internationale d'Histoire des Mers Nordiques de l'Europe (Utrecht 1982)*, Leiden 1983, pp. 123–132.

CIPOLLA, Carlo M., *Le avventure della lira*, Milano 1958.

CLARE, George, The A.B.C. of the Foreign Exchanges, *The Institute of Bankers* 13/II (1892), pp. 73–84, 121–149.

CLARK, John G., *New Orleans 1718–1812. An Economic History*, Baton Rouge 1970.

COLE, Arthur H., Seasonal Variation in Sterling Exchange, *Journal of Economic and Business History* 2 (1929), pp. 203–218.

——, Statistical Background of the Crisis Period 1837–42, *Review of Economic Statistics* 10 (1928), pp. 182–195.

——, The New York Money Market of 1843 to 1862, *Review of Economic Statistics* 11 (1929), pp. 164–170.

COLLINS, Michael, *Money and Banking in the UK*, London 1988.

——, Sterling Exchange Rates, 1847–80, *Journal of European Economic History* 15 (1986), pp. 511–533.

COORNAERT, Émile, *Les Français et le commerce international à Anvers (fin du XV͏ᵉ et XVI͏ᵉ siècle)*, 2 vols., Paris 1961.

CORTÉS CONDE, Roberto, Regímenes, experiencias monetarias y fluctuationes económicas. De la organización nacional al patrón oro (1862–1899), *Económica* (La Plata) 45/4 (1998), pp. 269–293.

——, The Export Economy of Argentina, 1880–1920, in idem / Shane J. HUNT (eds.), *The Latin American Economies. Growth and Export Sector 1880–1930*, New York – London 1985, pp. 319–381.

——, The Origins of Banking in Argentina, in Richard SYLLA / Richard TILLY / Gabriel TORTELLA (eds.), *The State, the Financial System and Economic Modernization*, Cambridge 1999, pp. 224–248.

CORTÉS CONDE, Roberto / HUNT, Shane J. (eds.), *The Latin American Economies. Growth and Export Sector 1880–1930*, New York – London 1985.

CRAIG, Lee A. / FISHER, Douglas, *The Integration of the European Economy, 1850–1913*, Basingstoke 1997.

CRAWFURD, John, A Sketch of the Commercial Resources and Monetary and Mercantile System of British India, with Suggestions for their Improvement, by Means of Banking Establishments (1837), in K[irti] N. CHAUDHURI (ed.), *The Economic Development of India under the East India*

Company 1814–58. A Selection of Contemporary Writings, Cambridge 1971, pp. 217–316.

CUNO, Kenneth M., *The Pasha's Peasants. Land, Society, and Economy in Lower Egypt, 1740–1858*, Cambridge 1992.

CUNZ, Reiner (ed.), *Währungsunionen. Beiträge zur Geschichte überregionaler Münz- und Geldpolitik*, Hamburg 2002.

DA POZZO, Mario / FELLONI, Giuseppe, La borsa valori di Genova nel secolo XIX, *Archivio economico dell' unificazione italiana* II 10 (1964), pp. 69–72, 81–89.

DAVIS, L.E. / HUGHES, J.R.T., A Dollar–Sterling Exchange, 1803–1895, *Economic History Review* sec. ser. 13 (1960/61), pp. 52–78.

DAY, John (ed.), *Études d'histoire monétaire, XII*ᵉ*–XIX*ᵉ *siècles*, Lille 1984.

DE CECCO, Marcello (ed.), *L'Italia e il sistema finanziario internazionale 1861–1914*, Roma 1990.

—, *Money and Empire. The International Gold Standard, 1890–1914*, Oxford 1974.

DE MADDALENA, Aldo, Affaires et gens d'affaires lombards sur les foires de Bisenzone. L'exemple des Lucini (1579–1619), *Annales. Économies – Sociétés – Civilisations* 22 (1967), pp. 939–990.

DE MALYNES, G., *Consuetudo vel lex mercatoria, or The Ancient Law-Merchant*, London 1622 (repr. Amsterdam 1979).

DE MATTIA, R., *L'unificazione monetaria italiana*, Torino 1959.

DE MERCADO, Thomás, *Summa de tratos, y contrados*, Sevilla 1571.

DE ROOVER, Raymond, Cambium ad Venetias. Contribution to the History of Foreign Exchange, in Julius KIRSHNER (ed.), *Business, Banking and Economic Thought in Late Medieval and Early Modern Europe. Selected Studies of Raymond de Roover*, Chicago – London 1974, pp. 239–259.

—, Il trattato di fra Santi Rucellai sul cambio, il monte comune e il monte delle doti, *Archivio Storico Italiano* 111 (1953), pp. 3–41.

—, *L'évolution de la lettre de change, XIV*ᵉ*–XVIII*ᵉ *siècles*, Paris 1953.

—, Le contrat de change depuis la fin du treizième siècle jusqu'au début du dix-septième, *Revue belge de philologie et d'histoire* 25/1–2 (1946/47), pp. 111–128.

—, Le marché monétaire au moyen âge et au début des temps modernes, *Revue historique* 94 (1970), pp. 34f.

—, Les doctrines économiques des scholastiques: à propos du traité sur l'usure d'Alexandre Lombard, *Revue d'histoire ecclésiastique* 59 (1964), pp. 854–866.

—, *Money, Banking and Credit in Medieval Bruges. Italian Merchant-Bankers, Lombards and Money-Changers. A Study in the Origins of Banking*, Cambridge (Mass.) 1948.

—, New Interpretations of the History of Banking, in Julius KIRSHNER (ed.), *Business, Banking and Economic Thought in Late Medieval and Early Modern Europe. Selected Studies of Raymond de Roover*, Chicago – London 1974, pp. 200–238.

—, Précisions sur l'histoire de la lettre et du contrat de change (d'après des documents inédits des Archivs Datini à Prato), *La vie économique et sociale* 23 (1952), pp. 44–67.

—, *The Bruges Money Market around 1400*, Brussels 1968.

—, The *cambium maritimum* Contract According to the Genoese Notarial Records of the Twelfth and Thirteenth Centuries, in David HERLIHY / Robert S. LOPEZ / Vsevolod SLESSAREV (eds.), *Economy, Society, and Government in Medieval Italy. Essays in Memory of Robert L. Reynolds*, Kent (Ohio) 1969, pp. 15–33.

—, *The Rise and Decline of the Medici Bank (1397–1494)*, Cambridge (Mass.) 1963.

—, The Scholastics, Usury, and Foreign Exchange, *Business History Review* 41 (1967), pp. 257–271.

—, What is Dry Exchange? A Contribution to the Study of English Mercantilism, in Julius KIRSHNER (ed.), *Business, Banking and Economic Thought in Late Medieval and Early Modern Europe. Selected Studies of Raymond de Roover*, Chicago – London 1974, pp. 183–199.

⸜, Luigi, *I cambi esteri del Regno di Napoli dal 1591 al 1707*, Napoli 1955.

⸜e origini della Borsa di Napoli, *Rivista orizzonti economici* 43, 1962, pp. 1–6.

–, The Beginnings of Paper-Money Circulation: the Neapolitan Public Banks (1540–1650), *Journal of European Economic History* 30 (2001), pp. 497–532.

DEHING, Pit / 'T HART, Marjolein, Linking the Fortunes: Currency and Banking, 1550–1800, in Marjolein 'T HART / Joost JONKER / Jan Luiten VAN ZANDEN (eds.), *A Financial History of The Netherlands*, Cambridge 1997, pp. 37–63.

DELSALLE, Paul / FERRER, André (eds.), *Les enclaves territoriales aux Temps Modernes (XVIe– XVIIIe siècles). Actes du Colloque de Besançon*, Besançon 2000.

DENZEL, Markus A. (ed.), *From Commercial Communication to Commercial Integration. Middle Ages to 19th Century*, Stuttgart 2004.

—— (ed.), *Gewürze in der Frühen Neuzeit: Produktion, Handel und Konsum. Beiträge zum 2. Ernährungshistorischen Kolloquium im Landkreis Kulmbach 1999*, St Katharinen 1999.

—— (ed.), *Währungen der Welt IX: Europäische Wechselkurse vor 1620*, Stuttgart 1995.

—— (ed.), *Währungen der Welt X: Geld- und Wechselkurse der deutschen Messeplätze Leipzig und Braunschweig (18. Jahrhundert bis 1823)*, Stuttgart 1994.

—— (ed.), *Währungen der Welt XI: Nordwestdeutsche und dänische Wechselkurse vom ausgehenden 17. Jahrhundert bis 1914*, Stuttgart 1999.

—— / HOCQUET, Jean Claude / WITTHÖFT, Harald (eds.), *Kaufmannsbücher und Handelspraktiken vom Spätmittelalter bis zum beginnenden 20. Jahrhundert / Merchant's Books and Mercantile Pratiche from the Late Middle Ages to the Beginning of the 20th Century*, Stuttgart 2002.

—— / SCHWARZER, Oskar, Art. "Wechsel", in Michael NORTH (ed.), *Von Aktie bis Zoll. Ein historisches Lexikon des Geldes*, München 1995, pp. 416f.

——, *"La Practica della Cambiatura". Europäischer Zahlungsverkehr vom 14. bis zum 17. Jahrhundert*, Stuttgart 1994.

——, "Zeit ist Geld". Usancen-'Systeme' im bargeldlosen Zahlungsverkehr nach italienischen Kaufmannsnotiz- und -handbüchern des 14. und 15. Jahrhunderts, *Scripta Mercaturae* 29/2 (1995), pp. 96–111.

——, Altona als Bank- und Wechselplatz im ausgehenden 18. und beginnenden 19. Jahrhundert, *Bankhistorisches Archiv* 24 (1998) [here: 1998a], pp. 13–37.

——, Art. "Indossament", in Michael NORTH (ed.), *Von Aktie bis Zoll. Ein historisches Lexikon des Geldes*, München 1995, pp. 165f.

——, Art. "Wechsel, Wechsler, Wechselbrief", in *Lexikon des Mittelalters*, vol. VIII, Zürich et al. 1997, pp. 2086–2089.

——, Art. "Dollar", in Michael NORTH (ed.), *Von Aktie bis Zoll. Ein historisches Lexikon des Geldes*, München 1995, pp. 87f.

——, Art. "Währungssystem", in ibid., pp. 409–411.

——, Bargeldloser Zahlungsverkehr im europäischen Überseehandel von der Europäischen Expansion bis zum Ersten Weltkrieg, *Jahrbuch für europäische Überseegeschichte* 2 (2002), pp. 71–103.

——, *Das System des bargeldlosen Zahlungsverkehrs europäischer Prägung vom Mittelalter bis 1914*, Stuttgart 2008.

——, Der Aufstieg und die Einbindung der Vereinigten Staaten von Amerika in die Weltwirtschaft: Transatlantische Wechselkurse von 1783 bis 1914, in Jürgen SCHNEIDER / Oskar SCHWARZER / Friedrich ZELLFELDER (eds.), *Währungen der Welt I: Europäische und nordamerikanische Devisenkurse 1777–1914*, 3 vols., Stuttgart 1991, vol. I, pp. 146–179.

——, Der Beitrag von Messen und Märkten zum Integrationsprozeß des internationalen bargeldlosen Zahlungsverkehrssystems in Europa (13.–18. Jahrhundert), in Simonetta CAVACIOCCHI (ed.), *Fiere e mercati nella integrazione delle economie europee, secc. XIII–XVIII. Atti della "Trenta-*

duesima Settimana die Studi" 8–12 *maggio 2000 sotto l'Alto Patronato del Parlamento Europeo con il patrozinio del prof. Romano Prodi, Presidente della Commissione Europea*, Prato 2001, pp. 819–835.

——, Der Nürnberger Wechselmarkt im ausgehenden 18. Jahrhundert, in Rainer GÖMMEL / Markus A. DENZEL (eds.), *Weltwirtschaft und Wirtschaftsordnung. Festschrift für Jürgen Schneider zum 65. Geburtstag*, Stuttgart 2002, pp. 169–192.

——, *Der Preiskurant des Handelshauses Pelloutier & Cᵢ aus Nantes (1763–1793)*, Stuttgart 1997.

——, Die Adaption 'europäischer Währungssysteme' in China und Japan im 19. und beginnenden 20. Jahrhundert. Zur Durchsetzung des Dollar-Systems im ostasiatischen Raum, in Harald WITTHÖFT with Karl Jürgen ROTH, *Acta Metrologiae Historicae V: 7. Internationaler Kongreß des Internationalen Komitees für Historische Metrologie (CIMH) 25.–27. September 1997 in Siegen)*, St Katharinen 1999, pp. 227–254

——, *Die Bozner Messen und ihr Zahlungsverkehr (1633–1850)*, Bozen 2005.

——, Die Braunschweiger Messen als regionaler und überregionaler Markt im norddeutschen Raum in der zweiten Hälfte des 18. und im beginnenden 19. Jahrhundert, *Vierteljahrschrift für Sozial- und Wirtschaftsgeschichte* 85 (1998) [here: 1998b], pp. 40–93.

——, Die Geschäftsbeziehungen des Schaffhauser Handels- und Bankhauses Amman 1748–1779. Ein mikroökonomisches Fallbeispiel, *Vierteljahrschrift für Sozial- und Wirtschaftsgeschichte* 89 (2002), pp. 1–40.

——, Die Integration der Schweizer Finanzplätze in das internationale Zahlungsverkehrssystem vom 17. Jahrhundert bis 1914, *Schweizerische Zeitschrift für Geschichte* 48 (1998), pp. 177–235.

——, Die Integration Deutschlands in das internationale Zahlungsverkehrssystem im 17. und 18. Jahrhundert, in Eckart SCHREMMER (ed.), *Wirtschaftliche und soziale Integration in historischer Sicht. Arbeitstagung der Gesellschaft für Sozial- und Wirtschaftsgeschichte in Marburg 1995*, Stuttgart 1996 [here: 1996a], pp. 58–109.

——, Die Integration ostmittel-, ost- und südosteuropäischer Städte in die internationalen Zahlungsverkehrsverbindungen im 19. und beginnenden 20. Jahrhundert, *Südost-Forschungen* 55 (1996) [here: 1996b], pp. 45–73.

——, Die währungspolitische Einigung Italiens: Italienische Wechselplätze zwischen 1815 und 1861, in Jürgen SCHNEIDER / Oskar SCHWARZER / Friedrich ZELLFELDER (eds.), *Währungen der Welt I: Europäische und nordamerikanische Devisenkurse 1777–1914*, 3 vols., Stuttgart 1991, vol. I, pp. 82–104.

——, Finanzplätze in der Levante und Nordafrika im 19. und 20. Jahrhundert, in Jürgen SCHNEIDER / Oskar SCHWARZER / Markus A. DENZEL (eds.), *Währungen der Welt VIII: Afrikanische und levantinische Devisenkurse im 19. und 20. Jahrhundert*, Stuttgart 1994, pp. 30–70.

——, Finanzplätze, Wechselkurse und Währungsverhältnisse in Lateinamerika (1808–1914), in Jürgen SCHNEIDER / Oskar SCHWARZER / Markus A. DENZEL (eds.), *Währungen der Welt VII: Lateinamerikanische Devisenkurse im 19. und 20. Jahrhundert*, Stuttgart 1997, pp. 1–106.

——, Geldwesen und Zahlungsverkehr in den deutschen Schutzgebieten (bis 1914). Eine währungshistorische Skizze mit Problemaufriß für künftige Forschungen, in Thomas BECK / Marília DOS SANTOS LOPES / Christian RÖDEL (eds.), *Barrieren und Zugänge. Die Geschichte der europäischen Expansion. Festschrift für Eberhard Schmitt zum 65. Geburtstag*, Wiesbaden 2004, pp. 322–342.

——, Geldwesen und Zahlungsverkehr in regionalen und internationalen Zusammenhängen in der Alten Schweiz. Das Fallbeispiel des Schaffhauser Kaufmann-Bankiers Amman (um 1750–1781), in Pascal LADNER / Gabriel IMBODEN (eds.), *Alpenländischer Kapitalismus in vorindustrieller Zeit. Vorträge des siebenten internationalen Symposiums zur Geschichte des Alpenraums*, Brig 2004, pp. 55–99.

——, Handelspraktiken als wirtschaftshistorische Quellengattung vom Mittelalter bis in das frühe 20. Jahrhundert. Eine Einführung, in idem / Jean Claude HOCQUET / Harald WITTHÖFT (eds.), *Kauf-*

.nsbücher und Handelspraktiken vom Spätmittelalter bis zum beginnenden 20. Jahrhundert / .erchant's Books and Mercantile Pratiche from the Late Middle Ages to the Beginning of the 20th Century, Stuttgart 2002, pp. 11–45.

——, Kaufmannshandbücher als Quellengattung zur europäischen Überseegeschichte im 19. und frühen 20. Jahrhundert, in Thomas BECK et al. (eds.), *Überseegeschichte – Beiträge der jüngeren Forschung. Festschrift anläßlich der Gründung der Forschungsstiftung für vergleichende europäische Überseegeschichte 1999 in Bamberg*, Stuttgart 1999, pp. 120–136.

——, Kleriker und Kaufleute. Polen im kurialen Zahlungsverkehrssystem des 14. Jahrhunderts, *Vierteljahrschrift für Sozial- und Wirtschaftsgeschichte* 82 (1995), pp. 305–331.

——, Kolonialstädte als Finanzplätze vom 18. Jahrhundert bis 1914. Das asiatische Wechselnetz und seine Anbindung an das europäisch-internationale Zahlungsverkehrssystem, in Horst GRÜNDER / Peter JOHANEK (eds.), *Kolonialstädte – Europäische Enklaven oder Schmelztigel der Kulturen?*, Münster 2001, pp. 225–259.

——, *Kurialer Zahlungsverkehr im 13. und 14. Jahrhundert. Servitien- und Annatenzahlungen aus dem Bistum Bamberg*, Stuttgart 1991.

——, Neuseeländisch-europäischer Zahlungsverkehr: Neuseeländische Wechselkurse vor 1914, in Jürgen SCHNEIDER / Oskar SCHWARZER / Markus A. DENZEL (eds.), *Währungen der Welt V: Asiatische und australische Devisenkurse im 20. Jahrhundert*, Stuttgart 1994, pp. 28–46.

——, Spanische Währungsreformen und Wechselkurse im 19. Jahrhundert, in Jürgen SCHNEIDER / Oskar SCHWARZER / Friedrich ZELLFELDER (eds.), *Währungen der Welt I: Europäische und nordamerikanische Devisenkurse 1777–1914*, 3 vols., Stuttgart 1991, vol. I, pp. 47–71.

——, The European Bill of Exchange. Its Development from the Middle Ages to 1914, in Sushil CHAUDHURI / Markus A. DENZEL (eds.), *Cashless Payments and Transactions from the Antiquity to 1914*, Stuttgart 2008, pp. 153–194.

——, The System of Cashless Payment as a Basis for the Commercial Integration of Europe and the World, in idem (ed.), *From Commercial Communication to Commercial Integration, Middle Ages to 19th Century*, Stuttgart 2004, pp. 199–248.

——, The Transatlantic Cashless Payment System in the Northern Atlantic Zone from the 17th Century to c. 1840, in Horst PIETSCHMANN (ed.), *Atlantic History. History of the Atlantic System 1580–1830. Papers presented at an International Conference, held 28 August – 1 September, 1999 (Hamburg)*, Göttingen 2002, pp. 263–277.

——, Vom "Schweizerfranken" zum "schweizer Franken" (1798–1860), in Jürgen SCHNEIDER / Oskar SCHWARZER / Friedrich ZELLFELDER (eds.), *Währungen der Welt I: Europäische und nordamerikanische Devisenkurse 1777–1914*, 3 vols., Stuttgart 1991, vol. I, pp. 72–81.

——, Wechselkurse und ihre Notierungen im 17. Jahrhundert, in Jürgen SCHNEIDER / Oskar SCHWARZER / Markus A. DENZEL (eds.), *Währungen der Welt III: Geld und Währungen in Europa im 17. Jahrhundert*, Stuttgart 1994, pp. 1–34.

——, Wechselplätze als territoriale Enklaven an der europäischen Peripherie: Von der Anbindung zur Integration von Finanzmärkten im System des bargeldlosen Zahlungsverkehrs (Spätmittelalter bis beginnendes 20. Jahrhundert), in Hartmut ZWAHR / Uwe SCHIRMER / Henning STEINFÜHRER (eds.), *Leipzig, Mitteldeutschland und Europa. Festgabe für Manfred Straube und Manfred Unger zum 70. Geburtstag*, Beucha 2000, pp. 545–560, or in French: Les places de change de la périphérie européenne considérées comme des enclaves territoriales: de l'association à l'intégration des marchés financiers dans le système de paiement par virements (bas Moyen Age – début du 20e siècle), in Paul DELSALLE / André FERRER (eds.), *Les enclaves territoriales aux Temps Modernes (XVI–XVIII siècles). Actes du Colloque de Besançon*, Besançon 2000, pp. 209–232.

——, Zahlungsverkehr auf den Leipziger Messen vom 17. bis zum 19. Jahrhundert, in Hartmut ZWAHR / Thomas TOPFSTEDT / Günter BENTELE (eds.), *Leipzigs Messen 1497–1997. Gestaltwandel. Umbrüche. Neubeginn, vol. 1: 1497–1914*, Köln – Weimar – Wien 1999, pp. 149–165.

——, Zahlungsverkehr, Wechselkurse und Währungsverhältnisse von Britischen Besitzungen in

Afrika (1822–1931), in Jürgen SCHNEIDER / Oskar SCHWARZER / Markus A. DENZEL (eds.), *Währungen der Welt VIII: Afrikanische und levantinische Devisenkurse im 19. und 20. Jahrhundert*, Stuttgart 1994, pp. 1–29.

——, Zur Finanzierung des europäischen Asienhandels in der Frühen Neuzeit: Vom Zahlungsausgleich im Gewürzhandel zum bargeldlosen Zahlungsverkehr, in idem (ed.), *Gewürze in der Frühen Neuzeit: Produktion, Handel und Konsum. Beiträge zum 2. Ernährungshistorischen Kolloquium im Landkreis Kulmbach 1999*, St Katharinen 1999, pp. 37–69.

DERMIGNY, Louis, *La Chine et l'Occident. Le commerce à Canton au XVIIIᵉ siècle 1719–1833*, Paris 1964.

DETTMANN, Eduard, *Das moderne Brasilien in seiner neuesten wirtschaftlichen Entwicklung*, Berlin 1912.

Dictionnaire universel théorique et pratique du commerce et de la navigation, tome I: A–G, Paris 1859.

DIESEN, Emil, *Exchange Rates of the World / Cours de changes du monde / Devisen-Kurse der Welt / Verdens Valutakurser, January 1ˢᵗ 1914 – December 31ˢᵗ 1921*, 2 vols., Christiania 1923.

DI VITTORIO, Antonio, *Gli Austriaci e il Regno di Napoli 1707–1734. Ideologia e politica di sviluppo*, Napoli 1973.

DOROŠENKO, Vasilij V. / HARDER-GERSDORFF, Elisabeth, Ost-Westhandel und Wechselgeschäfte zwi-schen Riga und westlichen Handelsplätzen: Lübeck, Hamburg, Bremen und Amsterdam (1758/59), *Zeitschrift des Vereins für Lübeckische Geschichte und Altertumskunde* 62 (1982), pp. 120–147.

DRUMMOND, Ian M., *The Gold Standard and the International Monetary System 1900–1939*, Basingstoke 1987.

EDLER, Florence, *Glossary of Medieval Terms of Business. Italian Series 1200–1600*, Cambridge (Mass.) 1934 (repr. New York 1970).

EHRENBERG, Richard, Ein Hamburgischer Waaren- und Wechsel-Preiscourant aus dem XVI. Jahrhundert, *Hansische Geschichtsblätter* 1883, Leipzig 1884, pp. 165–170.

EICHENGREEN, Barry (ed.), *The Gold Standard in Theory and History*, New York 1983.

——, *Vom Goldstandard zum Euro. Die Geschichte des internationalen Währungssystems*, Berlin 2000.

EKHOLM, Lars, Kontributioner och krediter. Svensk krigsfinansiering 1630–1631, in Hans LANDBERG / Lars EKHOLM / Roland NORDLUND (eds.), *Det kontinentala krigets ekonomi. Studier i krigsfinansiering under svensk stormaktstid*, Kristianstad 1971, pp. 143–270.

El Banco de España. Una historia económica, Madrid 1970.

El oro y la plata de las Indias en la época de los Austrias, Madrid 1999.

ELDEM, Edhem, La circulation de la lettre de change entre la France et Constantinople au XVIIIᵉ siècle, in Hâmit BATU / Jean Louis BACQUÉ-GRAMMONT (eds.), *L'Empire Ottoman, la République Turquie et la France*, Istanbul – Paris 1986.

——, Structure et acteures du commerce international d'Istanbul au XVIIIᵉ siècle, in Daniel PANZAC (ed.), *Les villes dans l'empire ottoman: Activité et sociétés*, Marseille 1990, pp. 243–272.

ELLSTÄTTER, Karl, *Indiens Silberwährung. Eine wirtschaftsgeschichtliche Studie*, Stuttgart 1894.

ELSTER, Karl, *Vom Rubel zum Tscherwonjez. Zur Geschichte der Sowjet-Währung*, Jena 1930.

EMMANUELLI, François-Xavier, *La crise marseillaise de 1774 et la chute des courtiers. Contribution à l'histoire du commerce du Levant et de la banque*, Paris 1979.

ESCH, Arnold, Bankiers der Kirche im Großen Schisma, *Quellen und Forschungen aus italienischen Archiven und Bibliotheken* 46 (1966), pp. 277–398.

Europäische Finanzplätze im Wettbewerb. 27. Symposium des Instituts für bankhistorische Forschung e.V. am 16. Juni 2004 im Hause der Deutschen Bundesbank, Hauptverwaltung Frankfurt am Main (= *Bankhistorisches Archiv. Zeitschrift zur Banken und Finanzgeschichte*, Beiheft 45), Stuttgart 2006.

EVERAERT, John G., Crédit, argent et lettres de change. La financement du commerce Flandres-Andalousie-Amérique, in Antonio M. BERNAL (ed.), *Dinero, moneda y crédito en la Monarquía Hispánica. Actas del Simposio Internacional "Dinero, moneda y crédito. De la Monarquía Hispánica a la Integración Monetaria Europea", Madrid, 4–7 de mayo de 1999*, Madrid 2000, pp. 511–523.

FACE, R.D., Techniques of Business in Trade between the Fairs of Champagne and the South of Europe in the 12th and 13th Centuries, *Economic History Review* 2nd ser. 10 (1957/58), pp. 427–438.

FASSL, Peter, *Konfession, Wirtschaft und Politik. Von der Reichsstadt zur Industriestadt, Augsburg 1750–1850*, Sigmaringen 1988.

FELLONI, Giuseppe, All'apogeo dell fiere genovesi: Banchieri ed affari di cambio a Piacenza nel 1600, in *Studi in onore di Gino Barbieri. Problemi e metodi di Storia ed Economica*, vol. II, Pisa 1983, pp. 883–901.

——, *Il mercato monetario in Piemonte nel secolo XVIII*, Milano 1968.

——, Kredit und Banken in Italien, 15.–17. Jahrhundert, in Michael NORTH (ed.), *Kredit im spätmittelalterlichen und frühneuzeitlichen Europa*, Köln – Wien 1991, pp. 9–23.

——, Monete e zecche negli Stati Sabaudi dal 1816 al 1860, *Archivio economico dell'unificazione italiana* II 2 (1956).

——, Un système monétaire atypique. La monnaie de marc dans les foires de change génois, XVIe–XVIIIe siècle, in John DAY (ed.), *Études d'histoire monétaire, XIIe–XIXe siècles*, Lille 1984, pp. 249–262.

FERNÁNDEZ, M.A., Merchants and Bankers: British Direct and Portfolio Investment in Chile During the Nineteenth Century, *Iberoamerikanisches Archiv* NF 9 (1983), pp. 349–379.

FERNS, H.S., Beginnings of British Investment in Argentina, *Economic History Review* sec. ser. 4 (1952), pp. 341–352.

FERRARA, Francesco, *La girata della cambiale*, Roma 1935.

FETTER, Frank Wh., *Monetary Inflation in Chile*, Princeton 1931.

FISCHER, Wolfram (ed.), *Europäische Wirtschafts- und Sozialgeschichte von der Mitte des 19. Jahrhunderts bis zum Ersten Weltkrieg* (= idem et al. [eds.], *Handbuch der europäischen Wirtschafts- und Sozialgeschichte*, vol. 5), Stuttgart 1985.

—— / KUNZ, Andreas (eds.), *Grundlagen der historischen Statistik von Deutschland. Quellen, Methoden, Forschungsziele*, Opladen 1991.

—— / McINNIS, R. Marvin / SCHNEIDER, Jürgen (eds.), *The Emergence of a World Economy 1500–1914. Papers of the IX International Congress of Economic History*, 2 parts, Stuttgart 1986.

FLANDREAU, Marc / KOMLOS, John, Core or Periphery? The Credibility of the Austro-Hungarian Currency 1867–1913, *Journal of European Economic History* 31 (2002), pp. 293–320.

FLOUD, R. / McCLOSKEY, D. (eds.), *The Economic History of Britain since 1700, vol. I: 1700–1860*, Cambridge ²1994.

FLYNN, Dennis O. / GIRALDEZ, Arturo, Silver and Ottoman Monetary History in Global Perspective, *Journal of European Economic History* 31 (2002), pp. 9–43.

FORD, A.G., *The Gold Standard 1880–1914. Britain and Argentina*, Oxford 1962.

FRANGAKIS-SYRETT, Elena, *The Commerce of Smyrna in the Eighteenth Century (1700–1820)*, Athens 1992.

FRATIANNI, Michele / SPINELLI, Franco, *A Monetary History of Italy*, Cambridge 1997.

FRAUZ, Emil, *Die Verfassung der staatlichen Zahlungsmittel Italiens seit 1861*, Straßburg 1911.

FRIED, Johannes (ed.), *Schulen und Studien im sozialen Wandel des hohen und späten Mittelalters*, Sigmaringen 1986.

FRIEDMAN, Milton / SCHWARTZ, Anna Jacobsen, *A Monetary History of the United States, 1867–1960*, Princeton 1963 (⁸1993).

FRIIS, Astrid / GLAMANN, Kristof, *A History of Prices and Wages in Denmark 1660–1800*, vol. I, London – New York – Toronto 1958.

FURRER, Norbert, *Das Münzgeld der Alten Schweiz. Grundriss*, Zürich 1995.

FURTAK, Tadeusz, *Ceny w Gdansku w latach 1701–1815*, Lwów 1935.

GAASTRA, Femme S., De Vereenigde Oost-Indische Compagnie in de zeventiende en achttiende eeuw: de groei van een bedrijf. Geld tegen goederen. Een structurele verandering in het Nederlands-Aziatisch handelsverkeer, *Bijdragen en mededelingen betreffende de geschiedenis der Nederlanden* 91 (1976), pp. 249–272.

——, Die Vereinigte Ostindische Compagnie der Niederlande – Ein Abriß ihrer Geschichte, in Eberhard SCHMITT / Thomas SCHLEICH / Thomas BECK (eds.), *Kaufleute als Kolonialherren: Die Handelswelt der Niederländer vom Kap der Guten Hoffnung bis Nagasaki 1600–1800*, Bamberg 1988, pp. 1–89.

——, Private Money for Company Trade. The Role of the Bills of Exchange in Financing the Return Cargoes of the VOC, *Itinerario. European Journal of Overseas History* 18, 1994, pp. 65–76.

——, The Exports of Precious Metal from Europe to Asia by the Dutch East India Company, 1602–1795, in John F. RICHARDS (ed.), *Precious Metals in the Later Medieval and Early Modern Worlds*, Durham (NC) 1983, pp. 447–475.

GAETTENS, Richard, *Geschichte der Inflationen. Vom Altertum bis zur Gegenwart*, München ²1957, pp. 59–72.

GALLAROTTI, Guilio M., The Scramble for Gold: Monetary Regime Transformation in the 1870s, in Michael D. BORDO / Forrest CAPIE (eds.), *Monetary Regimes in Transition*, Cambridge 1993, pp. 15–67.

GARBADE, Kenneth D. / SILBER, William L., Technology, Communication and the Performance of Financial Markets: 1840–1975, *Journal of Finance* 33 (1978), pp. 819–832.

GARCÍA-IGLESIAS, Concepción / KIPONEN, Juha, Monetary Aspects of a Changing Economy, in Jari OJALA / Jari ELORANTA / Juka JALAVA (eds.), *The Road to Prosperity. An Economic History of Finland*, Helsinki 2006, pp. 187–215.

GENTIL DA SILVA, José, *Banque et crédit en Italie au XVIIᵉ siècle*, Paris 1969.

——, *Marchandises et finances. Lettres de Lisbonne 1563–1578*, vol. II, Paris 1959; vol. III, Paris 1961.

——, *Stratégie des affaires à Lisbonne entre 1595 et 1607. Lettres marchandes des Rodrigues d'Evora et Veiga*, Paris 1956.

GERHARD, Hans-Jürgen, Ursachen und Folgen der Wandlungen im Währungssystem des Deutschen Reiches 1500–1625. Eine Studie zu den Hintergründen der sogenannten Preisrevolution, in Eckart SCHREMMER (ed.), *Geld und Währung vom 16. Jahrhundert bis zur Gegenwart. Referate der 14. Arbeitstagung der Gesellschaft für Sozial- und Wirtschaftsgeschichte vom 9. bis 13. April 1991 in Dortmund*, Stuttgart 1993, pp. 69–84.

——, Vom Leipziger Fuß zur Reichsgoldwährung. Der lange Weg zur „deutschen Währungsunion" von 1871/76, in Reiner CUNZ (ed.), *Währungsunionen. Beiträge zur Geschichte überregionaler Münz- und Geldpolitik*, Hamburg 2002, pp. 249–290.

GIL FARRÉS, Octavio, *Historia de la moneda española*, Madrid 1959.

GIUSTI, R., Corso delle monete e dei cambi sui mercati di Milano et di Venezia dal 1825 al 1866, *Archivio economico dell' unificazione italiana* VI 4 (1957), pp. 41–73.

GOLDSCHMIDT, L., Die Geschäftsoperationen auf den Messen der Champagne (Les divisions des foires de Champagne), *Zeitschrift für das Gesammte Handelsrecht* 40 (N.F. 25) (1892), pp. 1–32.

GÖMMEL, Rainer, Entstehung und Entwicklung der Effektenbörsen im 19. Jahrhundert bis 1914, in Hans POHL (ed.), *Deutsche Börsengeschichte*, Frankfurt/Main 1992, pp. 133–207.

GÖMMEL, Rainer / DENZEL, Markus A. (eds.), *Weltwirtschaft und Wirtschaftsordnung. Festschrift für Jürgen Schneider zum 65. Geburtstag*, Stuttgart 2002.

GORDON, G., Clearinghouses and the Origin of Central Banking in the United States, *Journal of Economic History* 45/2 (1985), pp. 277–283.

GREENBERG, Michael, *British Trade and the Opening of China 1800–1842*, New York – London 1951.

GRUBER, Ignaz, *Statistische Beiträge zur Frage der Währung der österreichisch-ungarischen Monarchie*, I. Heft, Jena 1890.

GRÜNDER, Horst / JOHANEK, Peter (eds.), *Kolonialstädte – Europäische Enklaven oder Schmelztigel der Kulturen?*, Münster 2001.

GRÜNHUT, Carl Samuel, *Wechselrecht*, vol. 1, Leipzig 1897.

GUMOWSKI, Marian, *Handbuch der polnischen Numismatik*, Graz 1960.

HABIB, Irfan, Merchant Communities in Precolonial India, in James D. TRACY (ed.), *The Rise of Merchant Empires. Long-Distance Trade in the Early Modern World, 1350–1750*, Cambridge 1990 (1993), pp. 371–399.

——, The Monetary System and Prices, in Tapan RAYCHAUDHURI / Irfan HABIB (eds.), *The Cambridge Economic History of India, vol. 1: c. 1200–c. 1750*, Cambridge 1982, pp. 360-381.

HAMELIN, Alonzo M., *Un traité de morale économique au XIV*ᵉ *siècle: Le tractatus de Usuris de Maître Alexandre d'Alexandrie*, Louvain 1962.

HAMILTON, Earl J., *War and Prices in Spain, 1651–1800*, Cambridge (Mass.) 1947.

HAMILTON, Henry, *An Economic History of Scotland in the Eighteenth Century*, Oxford 1963.

HARDER-GERSDORFF, Elisabeth, "Bullion Flow" and Rates of Exchange between Amsterdam and Riga (1783–1785), in Jacques Ph.S. LEMMINK et al. (eds.), *Baltic Affairs. Relations between the Netherlands and North-Eastern Europe 1500–1800*, Nijmegen 1990, pp. 97–119.

——, Aus Rigaer Handlungsbüchern (1783–1785): Geld, Währung und Wechseltechnik im Ost-West-Geschäft der frühen Neuzeit, in Eckart SCHREMMER (ed.), *Geld- und Währung vom 16. Jahrhundert bis zur Gegenwart. Referate der 14. Arbeitstagung der Gesellschaft für Sozial- und Wirtschaftsgeschichte vom 9. bis 13. April 1991 in Dortmund*, Stuttgart 1993, pp. 105–120.

——, Exportgeschäfte und Finanzverkehr zwischen Riga und Amsterdam 1783–1785, in Franz MATHIS / Josef RIEDMANN (eds.), *Exportgewerbe und Außenhandel vor der Industriellen Revolution [Festschrift für Georg Zwanowetz]*, Innsbruck 1984, pp. 167–184.

——, The Baltic Provinces – "Bridge" or "Barrier" to Russian Engagement in Western Trade? A Study of "Russians at Reval" During the Reign of Catherine II, *Jahrbücher für Geschichte Osteuropas* 45 (1997), pp. 561–576.

——, Zwischen Riga und Amsterdam: die Geschäfte des Herman Fromhold mit Frederik Beltgens & Comp., 1783–1785, in *The Interactions of Amsterdam and Antwerp with the Baltic Region, 1400–1800. De Nederlanden en het Oostzeegebied, 1400–1800. Papers presented at the 3*ʳᵈ *International Conference of the Association Internationale d'Histoire des Mers Nordiques de l'Europe (Utrecht 1982)*, Leiden 1983, pp. 171–180.

——, Zwischen Rubel und Reichstaler. Soziales Bezugsfeld und geographische Reichweite des Revaler Wechselmarktes (1762–1800), Lüneburg 2000.

HAUSER, Richard, *Die deutschen Überseebanken*, Jena 1906.

HECKSCHER, Eli F., *An Economic History of Sweden*, Cambridge (Mass.) 1954.

——, Sveriges Ekonomiska Historia. Första delen före frihetstiden. Andra boken hushållningen under internationell påverkan 1600–1720, Stockholm 1935.

——, The Bank of Sweden in its connection with the Bank of Amsterdam, in Johannes G. VAN DILLEN (ed.), *History of the Principal Public Banks accompanied by Extensive Bibliographies of the History of Banking and Credit in Eleven European Countries*, The Hague 1934, pp. 161–199.

HEERS, Jacques, *Gênes au XVᵉ siècle. Activité économique et problèmes sociaux*, Paris 1961.

——, *Le livre de comptes de Giovanni Piccamiglio homme d'affairs génois, 1456–1459*, Paris 1959.

HEFFER, Jean, *Le port de New York et le commerce extérieur américain 1860–1900*, Paris 1986.

HELLAUER, Erwin, *Internationale Finanzplätze. Ihr Wesen und ihre Entstehung unter besonderer Berücksichtigung Amsterdams*, Berlin 1936.

HELLER, Klaus, *Die Geld- und Kreditpolitik des russischen Reiches in der Zeit der Assignaten (1768–1839/43)*, Wiesbaden 1983.

HENNICKE, Alfred, *Die Entwicklung der spanischen Währung von 1868–1906*, Stuttgart – Berlin 1907.

HERLIHY, David / LOPEZ, Robert S. / SLESSAREV, Vsevolod (eds.), *Economy, Society, and Government in Medieval Italy. Essays in Memory of Robert L. Reynolds*, Kent (Ohio) 1969.

HERTNER, Peter, Italien, 1850–1914, in Wolfram FISCHER, *Europäische Wirtschafts- und Sozialgeschichte von der Mitte des 19. Jahrhunderts bis zum Ersten Weltkrieg* (= idem et al. [eds.], *Handbuch der europäischen Wirtschafts- und Sozialgeschichte*, vol. 5), Stuttgart 1985, pp. 705–776.

HEß, Wolfgang / KLOSE, Dietrich (Bearb.), *Vom Taler zum Dollar 1486–1986*, München 1986.

HIESTAND, Rudolf, Bologna als Vermittlerin im kurialen Zahlungsverkehr zu Beginn des 13. Jahrhunderts. Eine übersehene Rolle der frühen Universitäten, *Vierteljahrschrift für Sozial- und Wirtschaftsgeschichte* 82 (1995), pp. 332–349.

HO, F.L., An Index of Foreign Exchange Rates, 1898–1926, *Chinese Economic Journal* (1928), pp. 1–40.

HOLTFRERICH, Carl-Ludwig, Der Finanzplatz Frankfurt im Wettbewerb mit Berlin und anderen Städten seit dem 19. Jahrhundert, in *Europäische Finanzplätze im Wettbewerb. 27. Symposium des Instituts für bankhistorische Forschung e.V. am 16. Juni 2004 im Hause der Deutschen Bundesbank, Hauptverwaltung Frankfurt am Main* (= *Bankhistorisches Archiv. Zeitschrift zur Banken und Finanzgeschichte*, Beiheft 45), Stuttgart 2006, pp. 29–49.

—— *Finanzplatz Frankfurt. Von der mittelalterlichen Messestadt zum europäischen Bankenzentrum*, München 1999.

HOUTMAN-DE SMEDT, Helma, Art. "Akzeptkredit", in Michael NORTH (ed.), *Von Aktie bis Zoll. Ein historisches Lexikon des Geldes*, München 1995, pp. 20f.

HOUTMAN-DE SMEDT, Helma / VAN DER WEE, Herman, Die Entstehung des modernen Geld- und Finanzwesens Europas in der Neuzeit, in Hans POHL (ed.), *Europäische Bankengeschichte*, Frankfurt/Main 1993, pp. 73–173.

ILLIG, Hermann, *Das Geldwesen Frankreichs zur Zeit der ersten Revolution bis zum Ende der Papiergeldwährung*, Straßburg 1914.

INOUYE, Junnosuke, *Problems of the Japanese Exchange 1914–1926*, London 1931.

ISSAWI, Charles (ed.), *The Economic History of Iran 1800–1914*, Chicago – London 1971.

—— (ed.), *The Economic History of the Middle East, 1800–1914. A Book of Readings*, Chicago 1966.

——, Egypt since 1800: A Study in Lopsided Development, *Journal of Economic History* 21 (1961), pp. 1–25.

——, *The Economic History of Turkey 1800–1914*, Chicago 1981.

JAIN, L.C., *Indigenous Banking in India*, London 1929.

JAKOB, G., Die ältesten Spuren des Wechsels, *Westasiatische Studien* (1925), pp. 280f.

JOHANEK, Peter / STOOB, Heinz (eds.), *Europäische Messen und Märktesysteme in Mittelalter und Neuzeit*, Köln – Weimar – Wien 1996.

JONES, Geoffrey (ed.), *Banks as Multinationals*, London 1990.

JONKER, Joost, The Alternative Road to Modernity: Banking and Currency, 1814–1914, in Marjolein 'T HART / Joost JONKER / Jan Luiten VAN ZANDEN (eds.), *A Financial History of The Netherlands*, Cambridge 1997, pp. 94–123.

JÖRBERG, Lennart, *A History of Prices in Sweden 1732–1914*, vol. I, Lund 1972.

KALKMANN, Philipp, Hollands Geldwesen im 19. Jahrhundert, *Jahrbuch für Gesetzgebung, Verwaltung und Volkswirtschaft im Deutschen Reich* 25 (1901), pp. 1223–1256.

KANN, Eduard, *The Currencies of China. An Investigation of Silver & Gold Transactions Affecting China. With a Section on Copper*, Shanghai 1928.

KAUFHOLD, Karl Heinrich, Der Übergang zu Fonds- und Wechselbörsen vom ausgehenden 17. Jahrhundert bis zum ausgehenden 18. Jahrhundert, in Hans POHL (ed.), *Deutsche Börsengeschichte*, Frankfurt/Main 1992, pp. 77–132.

KEENE, Charles A., American Shipping and Trade, 1798–1820: The Evidence from Leghorn, *Journal of Economic History* 38/3 (1978), pp. 681–700.

KELLENBENZ, Hermann (ed.), *Weltwirtschaftliche und währungspolitische Probleme seit dem Ausgang des Mittelalters*, Stuttgart – New York 1981.

——, *Europa, Raum wirtschaftlicher Begegnung. Kleine Schriften I*, Stuttgart 1991.

——, Marchands en Russie aux XVIIᵉ et XVIIIᵉ siècles, in ibid., pp. 205ff.

KHOUW, Keng Liem, *De wisselkoers tusschen Indië en Nederland 1854–1925*, The Hague 1929.

KINDLEBERGER, Charles P., *The Formation of Financial Centers: A Study in Comparative Economic History*, Princeton (N.J.) 1974.

KING, David S.J., The Hamburg Branch: The German Period, 1889–1920, in Frank H.H. KING (ed.), *Eastern Banking. Essays in the History of The Hong Kong and Shanghai Banking Corporation*, London 1983, pp. 517–544.

KING, Frank H.H. (ed.), *Eastern Banking. Essays in the History of The Hong Kong and Shanghai Banking Corporation*, London 1983.

—— et al., *The History of the Hong Kong and Shanghai Banking Corporation, vol. I: The Hong Kong Bank in Late Imperial China, 1864–1902. On an Even Keel. Wayfoong, the Focus of Wealth*, Cambridge 1987; *vol. II: The Hong Kong Bank in the Period of Imperialism and War, 1895–1918. Wayfoong, the Focus of Wealth*, Cambridge 1988.

——, *Money and Monetary Policy in China 1845–1895*, Cambridge (Mass.) 1965.

KIRCHGÄSSNER, Bernhard, Zur Geschichte und Bedeutung der Order-Klausel am südwestdeutschen Kapitalmarkt im 14. und 15. Jahrhundert, in Jürgen SCHNEIDER (ed.), *Wirtschaftskräfte und Wirtschaftswege. Festschrift für Hermann Kellenbenz, vol. I: Mittelmeer und Kontinent*, Stuttgart 1978, pp. 373–386.

KIRSHNER, Julius (ed.), *Business, Banking and Economic Thought in Late Medieval and Early Modern Europe. Selected Studies of Raymond de Roover*, Chicago – London 1974.

KLEIN, Peter W., Dutch Monetary Policy in the East Indies. 1602–1942: A Case of Changing Continuity, in Eddy H.G. VAN CAUWENBERGHE (ed.), *Money, Coins, and Commerce: Essays in the Monetary History of Asia and Europe (From Antiquity to Modern Times)*, Leuven 1991, pp. 419–453.

KLOSE, Dietrich, Albertus-Taler in Deutschland und im Ostseegebiet, in Wolfgang HEß / Dietrich KLOSE (Bearb.), *Vom Taler zum Dollar 1486–1986*, München 1986, pp. 129f.

——, Der amerikanische Dollar, in ibid., pp. 202f.

——, Der Maria-Theresien-Taler, in ibid., pp. 195–199.

——, Der spanische Piaster als Welthandelsmünze und die von ihm abgeleiteten Großsilbermünzen, in ibid., pp. 187–190.

——, Der spanische Taler (Peso), in ibid., pp. 93f.

——, Die Crown in Großbritannien, in ibid., pp. 103f.

——, Frankreich: Écu blanc und Laubtaler, in ibid., pp. 133f.

——, Italienische Taler (Tallero, Scudo, Ducatone, Piastra), in ibid., pp. 88f.

——, Jefimok und Rubel, in ibid., pp. 136f.

——, Niederländische Taler, in ibid., pp. 97–100.

KÖRNER, Martin, Schweiz, in Hans POHL (ed.), *Europäische Bankengeschichte*, Frankfurt am Main 1993, pp. 279–285.

——, Zum Problem der Währungsvielfalt in der Schweiz, in Eddy VAN CAUWENBERGHE / Franz IRSIGLER (eds.), *Münzprägung, Geldumlauf und Wechselkurse / Minting, Monetary Circulation and Exchange Rates. Akten des 8th International Economic History Congress, Section C 7 (Budapest 1982)*, Trier 1984, pp. 219–236.

—— / FURRER, Norbert / BARTLOME, Niklaus with assistance of Thomas MEIER / Erika FLÜCKIGER, *Währungen und Sortenkurse in der Schweiz / Systèmes monétaires et cours des espèces en Suisse / Sistemi monetari e corsi delle specie in Svizzera 1600–1799*, Lausanne 2001.

KÖVER, György, Die Entwicklung des Banksystems in der österreichisch-ungarischen Monarchie, *Jahrbuch für Wirtschaftsgeschichte* 3 (1988), pp. 47–67.

KRIEGER, Martin, *Kaufleute, Seeräuber und Diplomaten. Der dänische Handel auf dem Indischen Ozean (1620–1868)*, Köln – Weimar – Wien 1998.

KU, Sui-lu, *Die Form bankmäßiger Transaktionen im inneren chinesischen Verkehr mit besonderer Rücksicht des Notengeschäfts*, Hamburg 1926.

La ville et la transmission des valeurs culturelles au bas Moyen Âge et aux Temps Modernes / Die Städte und die Übertragung von kulturellen Werten im Spätmittelalter und in die Neuzeit / Cities and the Transmission of Cultural Values in the Late Middle Ages and Early Modern Period. Actes / Abhandlungen / Records, Bruxelles 1996.

LADNER, Pascal / IMBODEN, Gabriel (eds.), *Alpenländischer Kapitalismus in vorindustrieller Zeit. Vorträge des siebenten internationalen Symposiums zur Geschichte des Alpenraums*, Brig 2004.

LANDES, David S., *Bankers and Pashas. International Finance and Economic Imperialism in Egypt*, London 1958.

LAPEYRE, Henri, Las origins del endorso de lettras de cambio en España, *Moneda y credito: Revista de economica* 52 (1952).

——, *Une famille de marchands: les Ruiz*, Paris 1953.

——, Une lettre de change endossée en 1430, *Annales. Économies, sociétés, civilisations* 13, 1958, pp. 260–264.

LE GOFF, Jacques, *Kaufleute und Bankiers im Mittelalter*, Frankfurt/Main – New York 1993 (Paris 1956).

——, *Wucherzins und Höllenqualen. Ökonomie und Religion im Mittelalter*, Stuttgart 1988.

LEBKÜCHNER, I.F., *De valore cambii in Imperio*, Diss. Erlangae 1765.

LEMMINK, Jacques Ph.S. et al. (eds.), *Baltic Affairs. Relations between the Netherlands and North-Eastern Europe 1500–1800*, Nijmegen 1990.

LEONE, Alfonso, Some Preliminary Remarks on the Study of Foreign Currency Exchange in the Medieval Period, *Journal of European Economic History* 12 (1983), pp. 619–629.

LEVY, Maria Bárbara et al., Arrolamento das fontes primárias do arquivo histórico da bolsa de valores do Rio de Janeiro (GB), in *Anais do VII Simpósio Nacional da ANPUH*, São Paolo 1974, pp. 1873–1916.

——, *História da bolsa de valores do Rio de Janeiro*, Rio de Janeiro 1977.

LÉVY-LEBOYER, Maurice, *Les banques européennes et l'industrialisation internationale dans la première moitié du XIXe siècle*, Paris 1964.

LIEBER, Alfred E., Eastern Business Practices and Medieval European Commerce, *Economic History Review* 21 (1968), pp. 230–243.

LINDGREN, T., The First Swedish Bank Notes, *Revue international d'histoire de la banque* (1968), pp. 402–408.

LOPEZ, R.S., Back to Gold, 1252, *Economic History Review* 9 (1956/57), pp. 219–240.

LoRomer, D.G., *Merchants and Reform in Livorno (1814–1868)*, Berkeley – Los Angeles – London 1987.

Lüthy, Herbert, *La banque protestante en France de la révocation de l'édit de Nantes à la révolution, t. II: De la banque aux finances (1730–1794)*, Paris 1961.

Macías Hernández, Antonio M., Génesis de una economía de base monetaria: Canarias, 1300–1500, in Antonio M. Bernal (ed.), *Dinero, moneda y crédito en la Monarquía Hispánica. Actas del Simposio Internacional "Dinero, moneda y crédito. De la Monarquía Hispánica a la Integración Monetaria Europea", Madrid, 4–7 de mayo de 1999*, Madrid 2000, pp. 43–58.

Mackenzie, Compton, *Realms of Silver. One Hundred Years of Banking in the East*, London 1954.

Macleod, Murdo J., Aspects of the Internal Economy of Colonial Spanish America: Labour; Taxation; Distribution and Exchange, in Leslie Bethell (ed.), *The Cambridge History of Latin America, vol. II: Colonial Latin America*, Cambridge et al. 1984, pp. 219–264.

Magalhães-Godinho, Vitorino, *L'économie de l'empire portugais au XVe et XVIe siècles*, Paris 1969.

Mahlberg, Walter, *Über asiatische Wechselkurse*, Leipzig ²1920.

Mandich, Giulio, Delle fiere genovesi di cambi particolarmente studiate come mercati periodici de credito, *Revista di storia economica* 4 (1939), pp. 257–276.

Manners, Robert A. (ed.), *Process and Pattern in Culture: Essays in Honor of Julian H. Steward*, Chicago 1964.

Marperger, Paul Jacob, *Beschreibung der Banquen ...*, Halle – Leipzig 1717 (repr. Frankfurt/Main 1969).

Marsilio, Claudio, *Dovè il denaro fa denaro. Gli operatori finanziari genovesi nelle fiere di cambio del XVII secolo*, Novi Ligure 2008.

Martin, Joseph G., *One Hundred Years. [Martin's] History of the Boston Stock and Money Market*, Boston 1898.

Martínez Ruiz, José Ignacio, Mercato creditizio e profitti del cambio per lettera. Le operazioni di cambio con patto di ricorsa tra Siviglia e le fiere internazionali di 'Bisenzone' (1589–1621), *Storia economica. Rivista quadrimestrale diretta da Luigi de Rosa* 5/1 (2002), pp. 107–132.

Mathis, Franz / Riedmann, Josef (eds.), *Exportgewerbe und Außenhandel vor der Industriellen Revolution [Festschrift für Georg Zwanowetz]*, Innsbruck 1984.

McCullough, Alan Bruce, *Money and Exchange in Canada to 1900*, Toronto – Charlottetown 1984.

McCusker, John J. (ed.), Essays in the Economic History of the Atlantic World, London – New York 1997.

—— / Gravesteijn, Cora, *The Beginnings of Commercial and Financial Journalism. The Commodity Price Currents, Exchange Rate Currents, and Money Currents of Early Modern Europe*, Amsterdam 1991.

—— / Hart, S., The Rate of Exchange on Amsterdam in London: 1590–1660, *Journal of European Economic History* 8 (1979), pp. 689–705.

—— / Riley, James C., Money Supply, Economic Growth, and the Quantity Theory of Money: France 1650–1788, in Eddy van Cauwenberghe / Franz Irsigler (eds.), *Münzprägung, Geldumlauf und Wechselkurse / Minting, Monetary Circulation and Exchange Rates. Akten des 8th International Economic History Congress, Section C 7 (Budapest 1982)*, Trier 1984, pp. 265–289.

——, Colonial Paper Money, in Eric P. Newman / Richard G. Doty (eds.), *Studies on Money in Early America*, New York 1976, pp. 94–104.

——, Information and Transaction Costs in Early Modern Europe, in Rainer Gömmel / Markus A. Denzel (eds.), *Weltwirtschaft und Wirtschaftsordnung. Festschrift für Jürgen Schneider zum 65. Geburtstag*, Stuttgart 2002, pp. 69–83.

——, *Money and Exchange in Europe and America, 1600–1775. A Handbook*, London – Basingstoke 1978.

——, The Business Press in England before 1775, *The Library: Transactions of the Bibliographical Society*, 6th ser., VIII (1986), pp. 205–231.

——, The Italian Business Press in Early Modern Europe, in Simonetta CAVACIOCCHI (ed.), *Produzione e commercio della carta e del libro, secc. XIII–XVIII*, Prato 1992, pp. 797–841.

——, The Role of Antwerp in the Emergence of Commercial and Financial Newspapers in Early Modern Europe, in *La ville et la transmission des valeurs culturelles au bas Moyen Âge et aux Temps Modernes / Die Städte und die Übertragung von kulturellen Werten im Spätmittelalter und in die Neuzeit / Cities and the Transmission of Cultural Values in the Late Middle Ages and Early Modern Period. Actes / Abhandlungen / Records*, Bruxelles 1996, pp. 303–332.

McGREGOR, J., *Commercial Statistics*, London 1847.

McMASTER, J., Aventuras asiáticas del peso mexicano, *Historia Mexicana* 8.3 (31) (1959), pp. 372–399.

MEINHARDT, Günther, *Die Geldgeschichte der ehemaligen deutschen Schutzgebiete 2: Togo*, Dortmund 1956.

MELIS, Federigo, Una girata cambiaria del 1410 nell'Archivio Datini di Prato, *Economia e storia* 5 (1958), pp. 412–421.

METZ, Rainer, Art. "Rechengeldsystem", in Michael NORTH (ed.), *Von Aktie bis Zoll. Ein historisches Lexikon des Geldes*, München 1995, pp. 330–333.

MICHIE, Ranald C. (ed.), General Introduction: The Rise of a Global Financial Centre – the City of London since 1700, in R.C. MICHIE (ed.), *The Development of London as a Financial Centre, vol. I: 1700–1850*, London – New York 2000.

——, *The Development of London as a Financial Centre, vol. 2: 1850–1914*, London – New York 2000.

——, The Invisible Stabliser: Asset Arbitrage and the International Monetary System since 1700, *Financial History Review* 15 (1998), pp. 5–26.

——, *The London and New York Stock Exchanges 1850–1914*, London et al. 1987.

——, *The London Stock Exchange. A History*, Oxford 1999.

MICKWITZ, Gunter, *Aus Revaler Handelsbüchern. Zur Technik des Ostseehandels in der ersten Hälfte des 16. Jahrhunderts*, Helsingfors 1938.

MIECK, Ilja, Berlins Aufstieg zum ersten preußischen Finanzplatz bis zur Industrialisierung, in Hans POHL (ed.), *Geschichte des Finanzplatzes Berlin*, Frankfurt/Main 2002, pp. 1–52.

MINTZ, Sydney W., Currency Problems in Eighteenth Century Jamaica and Gresham's Law, in Robert A. MANNERS (ed.), *Process and Pattern in Culture: Essays in Honor of Julian H. Steward*, Chicago 1964, pp. 248–265.

MOLLAT, Michel, *Der königliche Kaufmann. Jacques Cœur oder der Geist des Unternehmertums*, München 1991 (French edition: 1988).

MOSER, Heinz / RIZZOLLI, Helmut / TURSKY, Heinz (eds.), *Tiroler Münzbuch. Die Geschichte des Geldes aus den Prägestätten des alttirolischen Raumes*, Innsbruck 1984.

—— / TURSKY, Heinz, *Corpus Nummorum Tirolensium. Die Münzen Kaiser Rudolfs II. aus der Münzstätte Hall in Tirol 1602–1612*, Rum bei Innsbruck 1986.

—— / ——, Die Münzstätte Hall in Tirol [1984], in Heinz MOSER / Helmut RIZZOLLI / Heinz TURSKY (Hrsg.), *Tiroler Münzbuch. Die Geschichte des Geldes aus den Prägestätten des alttirolischen Raumes*, Innsbruck 1984, pp. 61–194.

MOTTET, Louis H. (ed.), *Geschichte der Schweizer Banken. Bankier-Persönlichkeiten aus fünf Jahrhunderten*, Zürich 1987 (Neuchâtel – Paris 1986).

MUELLER, Reinhold C., Art. "Ricorsa", in Michael NORTH (ed.), *Von Aktie bis Zoll. Ein historisches Lexikon des Geldes*, München 1995, pp. 344f.

——, Art. "Trockenwechsel", in ibid., pp. 398f.

——, Art. "Usance", in ibid., p. 403.

——, *The Venetian Money Market. Banks, Panics, and the Public Debt, 1200–1500* (= *Money and Banking in Medieval and Renaissance Venice*, vol. I), Baltimore – London 1997.

——, The Spufford Thesis on Foreign Exchange: The Evidence of Exchange Rates, *Journal of European Economic History* 24 (1995), pp. 121–129.

MUIRHEAD, Stuart, *Crisis Banking in the East. The History of the Chartered Mercantile Bank of India, London and China, 1853–1893*, Aldershot – Brookfield 1996.

MUNRO, John H., Art. "Diskont", in Michael NORTH (ed.), *Von Aktie bis Zoll. Ein historisches Lexikon des Geldes*, München 1995, pp. 85–87.

——, Art. "Inhaber-Klausel", in ibid., pp. 171f.

——, Art. "Inhaberschuldschein", in ibid., pp. 172–174.

——, Art. "Instrumentum Ex Causa Cambii", in ibid., pp. 174f.

——, Art. "Wechsel", in ibid., pp. 413–416.

——, Bullionism and the Bill of Exchange in England, 1272–1663: A Study in Monetary Management and Popular Prejudice, in [Fredi CHIAPPELLI (ed.),] *The Dawn of Modern Banking*, New Haven – London 1979, pp. 169–239.

——, Die Anfänge der Übertragbarkeit: Einige Kreditinnovationen im englisch-flämischen Handel des Spätmittelalters (1360–1540), in Michael NORTH (ed.), *Kredit im spätmittelalterlichen und frühneuzeitlichen Europa*, Köln – Wien 1991, pp. 39–69.

MYERS, M.G., Origins and Development, in Benjamin H. BECKHART (ed.), *The New York Money Market*, vol. I, New York 1931.

NARAIN, Brij, Exchange and Prices in India 1873–1924, *Weltwirtschaftliches Archiv (Chronik und Archivalien)* 23 (1926), pp. 247*–272*.

NASSE, Erwin, Die Münzreform und die Wechselcourse, *Annalen des Deutschen Reichs für Gesetzgebung, Verwaltung und Statistik. Staatsrechtliches, volkswirthschaftliches und statistisches Jahrbuch. Materialiensammlung und Reform-Zeitschrift* (1875), pp. 595–619.

NEAL, Larry, How it All Began: The Monetary and Financial Architecture of Europe during the First Global Capital Markets, 1648–1815, *Financial History Review* 7 (2000), pp. 117–140.

——, Integration of International Capital Markets: Quantitative Evidence from the Eighteenth to Twentieth Centuries, *Journal of Economic History* 45 (1985), pp. 219–226.

——, The Finance of Business During the Industrial Revolution, in R. FLOUD / D. MCCLOSKEY (eds.), *The Economic History of Britain since 1700, vol. I: 1700–1860*, Cambridge ²1994, pp. 151–181.

——, The Integration and Efficiency of the London and Amsterdam Stock Markets in the Eighteenth Century, *Journal of Economic History* 47 (1987), pp. 97–115.

NEGRIOLLI, Guido A., Monete venete nel Trentino e nell'Alto Adige, *Archivio per l'Alto Adige* 33 (parte prima) (1938), pp. 653–668.

NELSON, W. Evan, The Gold Standard in Mauritius and the Straits Settlements between 1850 and 1914, *Journal of Imperial and Commonwealth History* 16 (1987), pp. 48–76.

NEWMAN, Eric P. / DOTY, Richard G. (eds.), *Studies on Money in Early America*, New York 1976.

NEWMAN, Jennifer, 'A Very Delicate Experiment'. British Mercantile Strategies for Financing Trade in Russia, 1680–1780, in Ian BLANCHARD / Anthony GOODMAN / Jennifer NEWMAN (eds.), *Industry and Finance in Early Modern History. Essays Presented to George Hammersley on the Occasion of his 74th Birthday*, Stuttgart 1992, pp. 116–141.

NISHIMURA, Shizuya, *The Decline of Inland Bills of Exchange in the London Money Market 1855–1913*, Cambridge 1971.

NOGARO, Bertrand, Le problème du change español, *Revue économique internationale* 10 (1910), pp. 60–75.

NORTH, Michael (ed.), *Geldumlauf, Währungssysteme und Zahlungsverkehr in Nordwesteuropa*

1300–1800. Beiträge zur Geldgeschichte der späten Hansezeit, Köln – Wien 1989.

—— (ed.), *Kommunikationsrevolutionen. Die neuen Medien des 16. und 19. Jahrhunderts*, Köln – Weimar – Wien 1995.

—— (ed.), *Kredit im spätmittelalterlichen und frühneuzeitlichen Europa*, Köln – Wien 1991.

—— (ed.), *Nordwesteuropa in der Weltwirtschaft 1750–1950 / Northwestern Europe in the World Economy 1750–1950*, Stuttgart 1993.

—— (ed.), *Von Aktie bis Zoll. Ein historisches Lexikon des Geldes*, München 1995.

——, Art. "Dukat", in idem (ed.), *Von Aktie bis Zoll. Ein historisches Lexikon des Geldes*, München 1995, p. 95.

——, Art. "Währung", in *Lexikon des Mittelalters*, vol. VIII, München 2002, columns 1924f.

——, Banking and Credit in Northern Germany in the Fifteenth and Sixteenth Centuries, in *Banchi pubblici, banchi privati e monti di pietà nell'Europa preindustriale. Amministrazione, tecniche operative e ruoli economici*, Genova 1991, vol. II, pp. 809–826.

——, *Das Geld und seine Geschichte. Vom Mittelalter bis zur Gegenwart*, München 1994.

——, Von den Warenmessen zu den Wechselmessen. Grundlagen des europäischen Zahlungsverkehrs in Spätmittelalter und Früher Neuzeit, in Peter JOHANEK / Heinz STOOB (eds.), *Europäische Messen und Märktesysteme in Mittelalter und Neuzeit*, Köln – Weimar – Wien 1996, pp. 223–238.

OFFICER, Lawrence H., Dollar–Sterling Mint Parity and Exchange Rates (1791–1834), *Journal of Economic History* 43 (1983), pp. 579–616.

——, Integration in the American Foreign-Exchange Market, 1791–1900, *Journal of Economic History* 45 (1985), pp. 557–585.

——, The Remarkable Efficiency of the Dollar–Sterling Gold Standard, 1890–1906, *Journal of Economic History* 49 (1989), pp. 1–41.

OJALA, Jari / ELORANTA, Jari / JALAVA, Juka (eds.), *The Road to Prosperity. An Economic History of Finland*, Helsinki 2006.

ONODY, Oliver, *A inflação brasiliera, 1820–1958*, Rio de Janeiro 1960.

OPITZ, Peter, *Der Funktionswandel des Wechselindossaments*, Berlin 1967.

ORIGO, Iris, *"Im Namen Gottes und des Geschäfts". Lebensbild eines toskanischen Kaufmanns der Frührenaissance. Francesco di Marco Datini 1335–1410*, München 1985 (English edition 1957, repr. 1963).

OTRUBA, Gustav, Die Einführung des Goldstandards in Österreich-Ungarn und seine Auswirkungen auf die Preis- und Lohnentwicklung, in Hermann KELLENBENZ (ed.), *Weltwirtschaftliche und währungspolitische Probleme seit dem Ausgang des Mittelalters*, Stuttgart – New York 1981, pp. 123–162.

OTTE, Enrique, Las Ferias Castellanas y Sevilla en el sistema bancario europeo del siglo XVI, in Antonio M. BERNAL (ed.), *Dinero, moneda y crédito en la Monarquía Hispánica. Actas del Simposio Internacional "Dinero, moneda y crédito. De la Monarquía Hispánica a la Integración Monetaria Europea", Madrid, 4–7 de mayo de 1999*, Madrid 2000, pp. 31–42.

——, Letras de cambio de América, *Moneda y credito* 145, 1978, pp. 57–66.

——, Träger und Formen der wirtschaftlichen Erschließung Lateinamerikas im 16. Jahrhundert, *Jahrbuch für Geschichte von Staat, Wirtschaft und Gesellschaft Lateinamerikas* 4 (1967), pp. 226–266.

OWEN, Eduard R.J., *Cotton and the Egyptian Economy 1820–1914. A Study in Trade and Development*, Oxford 1969.

PAGANO DE DEVITIIS, Gigliola, *English Merchants in Seventeenth-Century Italy*, Cambridge 1997 [Ital. Venezia 1990].

PAMUK, Şevket, *A Monetary History of the Ottoman Empire*, Cambridge 2000.

——, *The Ottoman Empire and European Capitalism, 1820–1913. Trade, Investment and Production*,

Cambridge 1987.

PANZAC, Daniel (ed.), *Les villes dans l'empire ottoman: Activité et sociétés*, Marseille 1990.

PAOLERA Gerardo della / TAYLOR, Alan M., *Straining at the Anchor. The Argentine Currency Board and the Search for Macroeconomic Stability, 1880–1935*, Chicago – London 2001.

PARENTI, G., Monete e cambi nel Granducato di Toscana dal 1825 al 1859, *Archivio economico dell' unificazione italiana* II 1 (1956), pp. 1–11.

PATRICK, Hugh T., External Equilibrium and Internal Convertibility: Financial Policy in Meiji Japan, *Journal of Economic History* 25 (1965), pp. 187–213.

PELÁEZ, Carlos Manuel / SUZIGAN, Wilson, *Historía monetária do Brasil*, Brasilia ²1981.

PENNINGTON, James, *The Currency in the British Colonies*, London 1848 (repr. New York 1967).

PERKINS, Edwin J., Managing a Dollar-Sterling Exchange Account: Brown, Shipley and Co. in the 1850's, *Business History* 16 (1974), pp. 48–64.

PIATT ANDREW, A., The End of the Mexican Dollar, *Quarterly Journal of Economics* 18/3 (1904), pp. 321–356.

PIEPER, Renate, *Die Preisrevolution in Spanien (1500–1640). Neuere Forschungsergebnisse*, Stuttgart 1985.

——, Informationszentren im Vergleich. Die Stellung Venedigs und Antwerpens im 16. Jahrhundert, in Michael NORTH (ed.), *Kommunikationsrevolutionen. Die neuen Medien des 16. und 19. Jahrhunderts*, Köln – Weimar – Wien 1995, pp. 45–60.

PIETSCHMANN, Horst (ed.), *Atlantic History. History of the Atlantic System 1580–1830. Papers presented at an International Conference, held 28 August – 1 September, 1999 (Hamburg)*, Göttingen 2002.

PILLADO, Jorge, *El papel moneda argentino*, Buenos Aires 1901.

PINCHERA, S., Monete e zecche nello Stato Pontificio dalla restaurazione al 1870, *Archivio economico dell' unificazione italiana* V 5 (1957), pp. 1–20.

PINTO, Celsa, *Trade and Finance in Portuguese India. A Study of the Portuguese Country Trade 1770–1840*, New Delhi 1994.

PLATT, Desmond C.M., *Latin America and British Trade 1806–1914*, London 1972.

POHL, Hans (ed.), *Deutsche Börsengeschichte*, Frankfurt/Main 1992.

—— (ed.), *Die Bedeutung der Kommunikation für Wirtschaft und Gesellschaft. Referate der 12. Arbeitstagung der Gesellschaft für Sozial- und Wirtschaftsgeschichte vom 22.–25.4.1987 in Siegen*, Stuttgart 1989.

—— (ed.), *Europäische Bankengeschichte*, Frankfurt/Main 1993.

—— (ed.), *Frankfurt im Messenetz Europas – Erträge der Forschung* (= Rainer KOCH, *Brücke zwischen den Völkern – Zur Geschichte der Frankfurter Messe*, vol. I), Frankfurt/Main 1991.

—— (ed.), *Geschichte des Finanzplatzes Berlin*, Frankfurt/Main 2002.

—— (ed.), *Innovationen und Wandel der Beschäftigtenstruktur im Kreditgewerbe. Erstes wissenschaftliches Kolloquium des Instituts für bankhistorische Forschung e.V. am 20. Juni 1986 in München*, Frankfurt/Main 1988.

——, *Aufbruch der Weltwirtschaft. Geschichte der Weltwirtschaft von der Mitte des 19. Jahrhunderts bis zum Ersten Weltkrieg*, Stuttgart 1989.

——, *Die Portugiesen in Antwerpen (1567–1648). Zur Geschichte einer Minderheit*, Wiesbaden 1977.

——, *Die Wirtschaft Hispanoamerikas in der Kolonialzeit (1500–1800)*, Stuttgart 1996.

POL, Arent, Tot gerieff van India. Geldexport door de VOC en de muntproduktie in Nederland, 1720–1740, *Jaarboek voor munt- en penningkunde* 72 (1985), pp. 65–195.

POSTAN, M.M., Private Financial Instruments in Medieval England, *Vierteljahresschrift für Sozial- und Wirtschaftsgeschichte* 23 (1930), pp. 26–75.

POSTHUMUS, Nicolas W., *Inquiry in the History of Prices in Holland*, vol. I, Leiden 1946.

PRAKASH, Om, Financing the European Trade with Asia in the Early Modern Period: Dutch Initiatives and Innovations, *Journal of European Economic History* 27 (1998), pp. 331–356.

——, The Cashless Payment Mechanism in Mughal India: The Working of the Hundi Network, in Sushil CHAUDHURI / Markus A. DENZEL (eds.), *Cashless Payments and Transactions from the Antiquity to 1914*, Stuttgart 2008, pp. 131–137.

——, *The Dutch East India Company and the Economy of Bengal, 1630–1720*, Princeton (NJ) 1985.

PRIBRAM (ed.), A.F., *Materialien zur Geschichte der Preise und Löhne in Österreich*, vol. 1, Wien 1938.

PRICE, Jacob M., Multilateralism and/or Bilateralism: the Settlement of British Trade Balances with 'The North', c. 1700, *Economic History Review* sec. ser. 14 (1961/62), pp. 254–274.

——, Notes on Some London Price-Currents, 1667–1715, *Economic History Review*, sec. ser. 7 (1954/55), pp. 240–250.

——, Transaction Costs: A Note on Merchant Credit and the Organization of Private Trade, in James D. TRACY (ed.), *The Political Economy of Merchant Empires*, Cambridge 1991, pp. 276–297.

——, Joshua Johnson in London, 1771–1775: Credit and Commercial Organization in the British Chesapeake Trade, in Anne WHITEMAN et al. (eds.), *Statesmen, Scholars and Merchants: Essays in Eighteenth-Century History Presented to Dame Lucy Sutherland*, Oxford 1973, pp. 153–180.

PROBSZT, Günther, *Österreichische Münz- und Geldgeschiche*, Wien 1973.

QUINN, Stephen, Gold, Silver, and the Glorious Revolution: Arbitrage between Bills of Exchange and Bullion, *Economic History Review* 49/3, 1996, pp. 473–490.

RABINO, Joseph, Banking in Persia, *Journal of the Institute of Bankers* 13 (1892), pp. 1–54.

RABINO DI BORGOMALE, H.L., *Coins, Medals, and Seals of the Shâhs of Îrân, 1500–1941*, [Tehran] 1971.

RACINE, Pierre, Messen in Italien im 16. Jahrhundert: Die Wechselmessen von Piacenza, in Hans POHL (ed.), *Frankfurt im Messenetz Europas – Erträge der Forschung* (= Rainer KOCH, *Brücke zwischen den Völkern – Zur Geschichte der Frankfurter Messe*, vol. I), Frankfurt/Main 1991, pp. 155–170.

RASCH, Aage A., American Trade in the Baltic, 1783–1807, *Scandinavian Economic History Review* 13/1 (1965), pp. 31–64.

RAYCHAUDHURI, Tapan, Inland Trade, in idem / Irfan HABIB (eds.), *The Cambridge Economic History of India, vol. 1: c. 1200–c. 1750*, Cambridge 1982, pp. 325–359.

RAYCHAUDHURI, Tapan / HABIB, Irfan (eds.), *The Cambridge Economic History of India, vol. 1: c. 1200–c. 1750*, Cambridge 1982.

REBUFFAT, Ferréol / COURDURIÉ, Marcel, *Marseille et le négoce monétaire international (1785–1790)*, Marseille 1966.

REDLICH, Fritz, *Die deutsche Inflation des frühen Siebzehnten Jahrhunderts in der zeitgenössischen Literatur: Die Kipper und Wipper*, Köln – Wien 1972.

REISS, Winfried, Historical Exchange Rates, in Wolfram FISCHER / R. Marvin McINNIS / Jürgen SCHNEIDER (eds.), *The Emergence of a World Economy 1500–1914. Papers of the IX International Congress of Economic History*, 2 parts, Stuttgart 1986, part I, vol. I, pp. 171–189.

REISS, Winfried, Historische Wechselkurse, *Bankhistorisches Archiv* 11/2, 1985, pp. 3–41.

REMER, Charles F., *The Foreign Trade of China*, Shanghai 1926 (repr. Taipei 1967).

RENOUARD, Yves, *Les relations des papes d'Avignon et des compagnies commerciales et bancaires de 1316 à 1378*, Paris 1941.

Report on the Conditions and Prospects of British Trade in Oman, Bahrain and Arab Ports in the Persian Gulf, *Great Britain. Accounts and Papers* (1905), 85, pp. 2–4.

RESCH, Andreas, Wien – die wechselvolle Entwicklung eines Finanzplatzes in Zentraleuropa, in

Europäische Finanzplätze im Wettbewerb. 27. Symposium des Instituts für bankhistorische For-schung e.V. am 16. Juni 2004 im Hause der Deutschen Bundesbank, Hauptverwaltung Frankfurt am Main (= Bankhistorisches Archiv. Zeitschrift zur Banken- und Finanzgeschichte, Beiheft 45), Stuttgart 2006, pp. 93–138.

RICH, Edwin E. / WILSON, Charles H. (eds.), *The Economy of Expanding Europe in the Sixteenth and Seventeenth Centuries (= The Cambridge Economic History of Europe*, vol. IV), Cambridge et al. 1967.

—— / —— (eds.), *The Economic Organization of Early Modern Europe (= The Cambridge Economic History of Europe*, vol. V), Cambridge et al. 1977.

RICHARDS, David S. (ed.), *Islam and the Trade of Asia. A Colloquium*, London – Colchester 1970.

RICHARDS, John F. (ed.), *Precious Metals in the Later Medieval and Early Modern Worlds*, Durham (NC) 1983.

RITTMANN, Herbert, *Deutsche Geldgeschichte 1494–1914*, München 1975.

RODRÍGUEZ GONZÁLEZ, Ricardo, La negociación cambiaria en la banca de Simón Ruiz, in Antonio M. BERNAL (ed.), *Dinero, moneda y crédito en la Monarquía Hispánica. Actas del Simposio Internacional "Dinero, moneda y crédito. De la Monarquía Hispánica a la Integración Mone-taria Europea", Madrid, 4–7 de mayo de 1999*, Madrid 2000, pp. 679–694.

ROGERS, James Steven, *The Early History of the Law of Bills and Notes. A Study of the Origins of Anglo-American Commercial Law*, Cambridge 1995.

ROSENDORFF, Richard, Die deutschen Banken im überseeischen Verkehr, *Schmollers Jahrbuch für Gesetzgebung, Verwaltung und Volkswirtschaft* 28 (1904), pp. 93–134.

——, Le développement des banques allemands à l'étranger, *Revue économique internationale* 1 (1906), pp. 45–105.

ROSEVEARE, Henry (ed.), *Markets and Merchants of the Late Seventeenth Century. The Marescoe–David Letters 1668–1680*, New York 1987.

ROTH, Paul W., Die Kipper- und Wipperzeit in den Habsburgischen Ländern, 1620 bis 1623, in Eck-art SCHREMMER (ed.), *Geld- und Währung vom 16. Jahrhundert bis zur Gegenwart. Referate der 14. Arbeitstagung der Gesellschaft für Sozial- und Wirtschaftsgeschichte vom 9. bis 13. April 1991 in Dortmund*, Stuttgart 1993, pp. 85–103.

ROTHERMUND, Dietmar, *Indiens wirtschaftliche Entwicklung. Von der Kolonialherrschaft bis zur Gegenwart*, Paderborn et al. 1985.

——, The Monetary Policy of British Imperialism, *Indian Economic and Social History Review* 7 (1963), pp. 91–107.

RÜHE, Fritz, *Das Geldwesen Spaniens seit dem Jahre 1772*, Straßburg 1912.

RUIZ MARTÍN, Felipe, *La banca en España hasta 1782, in El Banco de España. Una historia económica*, Madrid 1970, pp. 1-196.

——, *Lettres marchandes échangés entre Florence et Medina del Campo*, Paris 1965.

SALVUCCI, R. J., The Real Exchange Rate of the Mexican Peso, 1762–1812: A Research Note and Estimates, *Journal of European Economic History* 23 (1994), pp. 131–140.

SAMUELSSON, Kurt, International Payments and Credit Movements by the Swedish Merchant-Houses, 1730–1815, *Scandinavian Economic History Review* 3 (1955), pp. 163–202.

SANZ AYÁN, Carmen, Los procedimientos financieros: métodos y estrategias, in *El oro y la plata de las Indias en la época de los Austrias*, Madrid 1999, pp. 577–592.

SAVILLE, Richard, *Bank of Scotland. A History, 1695–1995*, Edinburgh 1996.

SAY, Horace E., *Histoire des relations commerciales entre la France et le Brésil*, Paris 1839.

SAYOUS, André.-E., Les changes de l'Espagne sur l'Amérique au XVIe siècle, *Revue d'économie politique* 41 (1927), pp. 1417–1443.

SCAMMEL, W.M., The London Discount Market: The Later 19th Century, in Ranald C. MICHIE (ed.),

The Development of London as a Financial Centre, vol. 2: 1850–1914, London – New York 2000, pp. 151–177.

SCAMMELL, W., The Working of the Gold Standard, in Barry EICHENGREEN (ed.), *The Gold Standard in Theory and History*, New York 1983, pp. 103–120.

SCHAPS, Georg, *Zur Geschichte des Wechselindossaments*, Stuttgart 1892.

SCHMALENBACH, Eugen, Der Kurs des Pfund-Sterling-Wechsels, *Zeitschrift für handelswissenschaftliche Forschung* 1 (1906), pp. 241–256.

SCHMIDT, F., Die Wechselkurse Argentiniens, *Zeitschrift für Handelswissenschaft und Handelspraxis* 2 (1909), p. 54–56, 92–96, 147–151.

SCHMIDT, Reinhard H. / GROTE, Michael H., Was ist und was braucht ein "bedeutender Finanzplatz"?, in *Europäische Finanzplätze im Wettbewerb. 27. Symposium des Instituts für bankhistorische Forschung e.V. am 16. Juni 2004 im Hause der Deutschen Bundesbank, Hauptverwaltung Frankfurt am Main* (= *Bankhistorisches Archiv. Zeitschrift zur Banken und Finanzgeschichte*, Beiheft 45), Stuttgart 2006, pp. 11–27.

SCHMITT, Eberhard / SCHLEICH, Thomas / BECK, Thomas (eds.), *Kaufleute als Kolonialherren: Die Handelswelt der Niederländer vom Kap der Guten Hoffnung bis Nagasaki 1600–1800*, Bamberg 1988.

SCHNEIDER, Jürgen (ed.), *Wirtschaftskräfte und Wirtschaftswege. Festschrift für Hermann Kellenbenz, vol. I: Mittelmeer und Kontinent*, Stuttgart 1978.

—— / BRÜBACH, Nils, Frankreichs Messeplätze und das europäische Messesystem in der frühen Neuzeit, in Hans POHL (ed.), *Frankfurt im Messenetz Europas – Erträge der Forschung* (= Rainer KOCH, *Brücke zwischen den Völkern – Zur Geschichte der Frankfurter Messe*, vol. I), Frankfurt/Main 1991, pp. 171–190.

—— / SCHWARZER, Oskar (eds.), *Statistik der Geld- und Wechselkurse in Deutschland (1815–1913)* (= *Historische Statistik von Deutschland*, vol. XI), St Katharinen 1990.

—— / —— / DENZEL, Markus A. (eds.), *Währungen der Welt II: Europäische und nordamerikanische Devisenkurse 1914–1951*, Stuttgart 1997.

—— / —— / —— (eds.), *Währungen der Welt III: Geld und Währungen in Europa im 17. Jahrhundert*, Stuttgart 1994.

—— / —— / —— (eds.), *Währungen der Welt V: Asiatische und australische Devisenkurse im 20. Jahrhundert*, Stuttgart 1994.

—— / —— / —— (eds.), *Währungen der Welt VII: Lateinamerikanische Devisenkurse im 19. und 20. Jahrhundert*, Stuttgart 1997.

—— / —— / —— (eds.), *Währungen der Welt VIII: Afrikanische und levantinische Devisenkurse im 19. und 20. Jahrhundert*, Stuttgart 1994.

—— / —— / Petra SCHNELZER (eds.), *Statistik der Geld- und Wechselkurse in Deutschland und im Ostseeraum (18. und 19. Jahrhundert)* (= *Historische Statistik von Deutschland*, vol. XII), St Katharinen 1993.

—— / —— / ZELLFELDER, Friedrich (eds.), *Währungen der Welt I: Europäische und nordamerikanische Devisenkurse 1777–1914*, 3 vols., Stuttgart 1991.

—— / —— / —— / DENZEL, Markus A. (eds.), *Währungen der Welt IV: Asiatische und australische Devisenkurse im 19. Jahrhundert*, Stuttgart 1992.

—— / —— / —— / —— (eds.), *Währungen der Welt VI: Geld und Währungen in Europa im 18. Jahrhundert*, Stuttgart 1992.

—— / SCHWARZER, Oskar, International Rates of Exchange: Structures and Trends of Payments Mechanism in Europe, 17th to 19th Century, in Wolfram FISCHER / R. Marvin MCINNIS / Jürgen SCHNEIDER (eds.), *The Emergence of a World Economy 1500–1914. Papers of the IX International Congress of Economic History*, 2 parts, Stuttgart 1986, part I, pp. 143–170.

—— / ——, Währungsparitäten in Europa um 1850/1913, in Wolfram FISCHER (ed.), *Europäische*

Wirtschafts- und Sozialgeschichte von der Mitte des 19. Jahrhunderts bis zum Ersten Weltkrieg (= idem et al. [eds.], *Handbuch der europäischen Wirtschafts- und Sozialgeschichte*, vol. 5), Stuttgart 1985, pp. 778f.

——, Die Bedeutung von Kontoren, Faktoreien, Stützpunkten (von Kompanien), Märkten, Messen und Börsen im Mittelalter und Früher Neuzeit, in Hans POHL (ed.), *Die Bedeutung der Kommunikation für Wirtschaft und Gesellschaft. Referate der 12. Arbeitstagung der Gesellschaft für Sozial- und Wirtschaftsgeschichte vom 22.–25.4.1987 in Siegen*, Stuttgart 1989, pp. 37–63.

——, *Handel und Unternehmer im französischen Brasiliengeschäft 1815–1848. Versuch einer quantitativen Strukturanalyse*, Köln – Wien 1975.

——, Hat das Indossament zum Niedergang der Wechselmessen im 17. und 18. Jahrhundert beigetragen?, in Michael NORTH (ed.), *Geldumlauf, Währungssysteme und Zahlungsverkehr in Nordwesteuropa 1300–1800. Beiträge zur Geldgeschichte der späten Hansezeit*, Köln – Wien 1989, pp. 183–193.

——, Innovationen und Wandel der Beschäftigtenstruktur im Kreditgewerbe vom Spätmittelalter bis zur Mitte des 19. Jahrhunderts, in Hans POHL (ed.), *Innovationen und Wandel der Beschäftigtenstruktur im Kreditgewerbe. Erstes wissenschaftliches Kolloquium des Instituts für bankhistorische Forschung e.V. am 20. Juni 1986 in München*, Frankfurt/Main 1988, pp. 21–39.

——, Les relations commerciales de la France avec le Brésil et les capiteaux français au Brésil 1815–1865, *Lateinamerika-Studien* 3 (1977), pp. 183–202.

——, Messen, Banken und Börsen (15.–18. Jahrhundert), in *Banchi pubblici, banchi privati e monti di pietà nell'Europa preindustriale. Amministrazione, tecniche operative e ruoli economici*, Genova 1991, vol. I, pp. 133–169.

——, Zur deutschen Außenhandelsfinanzierung im 19. Jahrhundert: Der Zahlungsverkehr des Unternehmens Johann Bernhard Hasenclever & Söhne, Remscheid-Ehringhausen, im Brasiliengeschäft (1830–1863), in Hermann KELLENBENZ (ed.), *Weltwirtschaftliche und währungspolitische Probleme seit dem Ausgang des Mittelalters*, Stuttgart – New York 1981, pp. 77–92.

SCHNEIDER, Konrad, *"Banco, Species und Courant". Untersuchungen zur Hamburgischen Währung im 17. und 18. Jahrhundert*, Koblenz 1986.

——, Art. "Taler", in Michael NORTH (ed.), *Von Aktie bis Zoll. Ein historisches Lexikon des Geldes*, München 1995, pp. 389–391.

——, *Hamburgs Münz- und Geldgeschichte im 19. Jahrhundert bis zur Einführung der Reichswährung*, Koblenz 1983.

SCHREMMER, Eckart (ed.), *Geld- und Währung vom 16. Jahrhundert bis zur Gegenwart. Referate der 14. Arbeitstagung der Gesellschaft für Sozial- und Wirtschaftsgeschichte vom 9. bis 13. April 1991 in Dortmund*, Stuttgart 1993.

—— (ed.), *Wirtschaftliche und soziale Integration in historischer Sicht. Arbeitstagung der Gesellschaft für Sozial- und Wirtschaftsgeschichte in Marburg 1995*, Stuttgart 1996.

SCHUBERT, Eric S., Arbitrage in the Foreign Exchange Markets of London and Amsterdam during the 18th Century, *Explorations in Economic History* 26 (1989), pp. 1–20.

——, Innovations, Debts, and Bubbles: International Integration of Financial Markets in Western Europe, 1688–1720, *Journal of Economic History* 48 (1988), pp. 299–306.

SCHULZ, Günther (ed.), *Von der Landwirtschaft zur Industrie. Wirtschaftlicher und gesellschaftlicher Wandel im 19. und 20. Jahrhundert. Festschrift für Friedrich-Wilhelm Henning zum 65. Geburtstag*, Paderborn et al. 1996.

SCHUMACHER, Hermann, Die Organisation des Fremdhandels in China, *Jahrbuch für Gesetzgebung, Verwaltung und Volkswirtschaft im Deutschen Reich* 23 (1899), pp. 259–293.

SCHWARZER, Oskar / DENZEL, Markus A. / SCHNELZER, Petra, Geld- und Wechselkurse in Deutschland und im Ostseeraum (18. und 19. Jahrhundert), in Jürgen SCHNEIDER / Oskar SCHWARZER / Petra SCHNELZER (eds.), *Statistik der Geld- und Wechselkurse in Deutschland und im Ostseeraum (18. und 19. Jahrhundert)* (= *Historische Statistik von Deutschland*, vol. XII), St Katharinen 1993, pp. 2–43.

—— / —— / ZELLFELDER, Friedrich, Ostasiatische, indische und australische Wechselkurse (1800–1914), in Jürgen SCHNEIDER / Oskar SCHWARZER / Markus A. DENZEL (eds.), *Währungen der Welt IV: Asiatische und australische Devisenkurse im 19. Jahrhundert*, Stuttgart 1992, pp. 1–65.

—— / DENZEL, Markus A., Internationaler Zahlungsverkehr im 18. Jahrhundert: Amsterdam, London und Paris, in Jürgen SCHNEIDER / Oskar SCHWARZER / Friedrich ZELLFELDER / Markus A. DENZEL (eds.), *Währungen der Welt VI: Geld und Währungen in Europa im 18. Jahrhundert*, Stuttgart 1992, pp. 1–32.

—— / SCHNELZER, Petra, Quellen zur Statistik der Geld- und Wechselkurse in Deutschland, Nordwesteuropa und dem Ostseeraum im 18. und 19. Jahrhundert, in Wolfram FISCHER / Andreas KUNZ (eds.), *Grundlagen der historischen Statistik von Deutschland. Quellen, Methoden, Forschungsziele*, Opladen 1991, pp. 175–191.

—— with DENZEL, Markus A. / ZELLFELDER, Friedrich, Das System des internationalen Zahlungsverkehrs, in Jürgen SCHNEIDER / Oskar SCHWARZER / Friedrich ZELLFELDER (eds.), *Währungen der Welt I: Europäische und nordamerikanische Devisenkurse 1777–1914*, 3 vols., Stuttgart 1991, vol. I, pp. 1–34.

——, Eine EDV-gestützte Forschungskonzeption zur Bearbeitung historischer Geld- und Wechselkurse, in ibid., pp. 180–196.

——, Goldwährungssysteme und internationaler Zahlungsverkehr zwischen 1870 und 1914, in Eckart SCHREMMER (ed.), *Geld- und Währung vom 16. Jahrhundert bis zur Gegenwart. Referate der 14. Arbeitstagung der Gesellschaft für Sozial- und Wirtschaftsgeschichte vom 9. bis 13. April 1991 in Dortmund*, Stuttgart 1993, pp. 191–228.

SÉDILLOT, René, *Histoire du Franc*, Paris 1979.

——, *Le franc. Histoire d'une monnaie des origins à nos jours*, Paris 1953.

SEIDEL, Karl-Dieter, *Die deutsche Gesetzgebung seit 1871. Münzen – Papiergeld und Notenbanken mit den Münzverträgen der deutschen Staaten im 19. Jahrhundert*, München 1973.

SERRANO MANGAS, Fernando, El papel del vellón, in Antonio M. BERNAL (ed.), *Dinero, moneda y crédito en la Monarquía Hispánica. Actas del Simposio Internacional "Dinero, moneda y crédito. De la Monarquía Hispánica a la Integración Monetaria Europea", Madrid, 4–7 de mayo de 1999*, Madrid 2000, pp. 567–573.

SEYD, Ernst, *Das London Bank-, Check- und Clearinghouse-System nebst Winken für seine Einführung in Deutschland*, translated into German from the 3rd English edition by Otto SJÖSTRÖM, Leipzig 1874.

SHINJO, Hiroshi, *History of the Yen – 100 Years of Japanese Money-Economy*, Tokyo 1962.

SIEVEKING, Heinrich, Das Bankwesen in Genua und die Bank von S. Giorgo, in Johannes G. VAN DILLEN (ed.), *History of the Principal Public Banks Accompanied by Extensive Bibliographies of the History of Banking and Credit in Eleven European Countries*, The Hague 1934, pp. 15–38.

——, *Die Hamburger Bank*, in ibid., pp. 125–160.

SMITH, Walter B. / COLE, Arthur H., *Fluctuations in American Business 1790–1860*, New York 1935.

SMITH, Woodruff D., The Function of Commercial Centers in the Modernization of European Capitalism: Amsterdam as an Information Exchange in the Seventeenth Century, *Journal of Economic History* 44 (1984), pp. 985–1005.

SOETBEER, Adolf, Die Hamburger Bank, 1619–1866. Eine geschichtliche Skizze, *Vierteljahresschrift für Volkswirtschaft* 3 (1866), pp. 21–54.

SONNDORFER, Rudolf, Die Währungsreformen in Ostasien und Ostafrika, *Zeitschrift für Handelswissenschaft und Handelspraxis* 2/10 (1910), pp. 337–343.

SPALDING, William F., *Eastern Exchange, Currency and Finance*, London ²1918.

SPALLANZANI, Marco, A Note on Florentine Banking in the Renaissance: Orders of Payment and Cheques, *Journal of European Economic History* 7 (1978), pp. 145–168.

SPASSKIJ, Ivan Georgevic, *Das russische Münzsystem*, Berlin 1983.

SPERLING, J., The International Payments Mechanism in the Seventeenth and Eighteenth Centuries, *Economic History Review* sec. ser. 14 (1962), pp. 446–468.

SPOONER, Frank C., *The International Economy and Monetary Movements in France, 1493–1725*, Cambridge (Mass.) 1972.

SPRENGER, Bernd, *Das Geld der Deutschen. Geldgeschichte Deutschlands von den Anfängen bis zur Gegenwart*, Paderborn et al. ³2002.

——, Die Währungsunion des Deutschen Reichs 1871/76. Vorbild für die Europäische Währungsunion?, in Günther SCHULZ (ed.), *Von der Landwirtschaft zur Industrie. Wirtschaftlicher und gesellschaftlicher Wandel im 19. und 20. Jahrhundert. Festschrift für Friedrich-Wilhelm Henning zum 65. Geburtstag*, Paderborn et al. 1996, pp. 133–148.

——, Harmonisierungsbestrebungen im Geldwesen der deutschen Staaten zwischen Wiener Kongreß und Reichsgründung, in Eckart SCHREMMER (ed.), *Geld- und Währung vom 16. Jahrhundert bis zur Gegenwart. Referate der 14. Arbeitstagung der Gesellschaft für Sozial- und Wirtschaftsgeschichte vom 9. bis 13. April 1991 in Dortmund*, Stuttgart 1993, pp. 121–142.

——, *Währungswesen und Währungspolitik in Deutschland von 1834 bis 1875*, Köln 1981.

SPUFFORD, Peter, Financial Markets and Money Movements in the Medieval Occident, in *Viajeros, peregrinos, mercaderes en el Occidente Medieval. XVIII semana de estudios medievales*, Navarra 1991, pp. 201–216.

——, *Handbook of Medieval Exchange*, London 1986.

——, *Monetary Problems and Policies in the Burgundian Netherlands 1433–1496*, Leiden 1970.

——, *Money and its Use in Medieval Europe*, Cambridge 1988.

Studi in onore di Gino Barbieri. Problemi e metodi di Storia ed Economica, vol. II, Pisa 1983.

Sveriges Riksbank 1668–1924. Bankens Tillkomst och Verksamhet, Stockholm 1931.

SVORONOS, Nikos G., *Le commerce de Salonique au XVIIIᵉ siècle*, Paris 1956.

SYLLA, Richard / TILLY, Richard / TORTELLA, Gabriel (eds.), *The State, the Financial System and Economic Modernization*, Cambridge 1999.

SYLLA, Richard, Monetary Innovation in America, *Journal of Economic History* 42 (1982), pp. 21–30.

TALLADA, José Maria, El problema monetaria español en el siglo XIX, *Moneda y Credito* 58 (1956), pp. 53–64.

TAMAKI, Norio, The Yokohama Specie Bank: A Multinational in the Japanese Interest 1879–1931, in Geoffrey JONES (ed.), *Banks as Multinationals*, London 1990, pp. 191–216.

TEDDE DE LORCA, Pedro, *El Banco de San Carlos (1782–1829)*, Madrid 1988.

TEPASKE, John J., New World Silver, Castile and the Philippines 1590–1800, in John F. RICHARDS (ed.), *Precious Metals in the Later Medieval and Early Modern Worlds*, Durham (N.C.) 1983, pp. 425–445.

'T HART, Marjolein / JONKER, Joost / VAN ZANDEN, Jan Luiten (eds.), *A Financial History of The Netherlands*, Cambridge 1997.

The Interactions of Amsterdam and Antwerp with the Baltic Region, 1400–1800. De Nederlanden en het Oostzeegebied, 1400–1800. Papers presented at the 3rd International Conference of the Association Internationale d'Histoire des Mers Nordiques de l'Europe (Utrecht 1982), Leiden 1983.

THÉRY, E., *Le problème du change en Espagne*, Paris 1901.

THUILLIER, Guy, *La monnaie en France au début de XIXᵉ siècle*, Paris 1983.

TOM, C.F. Joseph, *Monetary Problems of an Entrepot: The Hong Kong Experience*, New York et al. 1989.

TONIOLO, Giani, *An Economic History of Liberal Italy 1850–1918*, London – New York 1990.

TOUSSAINT, Auguste, *History of Mauritius*, London – Basingstoke 1977 (1971).

TRACY, James D. (ed.), *The Rise of Merchant Empires. Long-Distance Trade in the Early Modern World, 1350–1750*, Cambridge 1990 (1993).

—— (ed.), *The Political Economy of Merchant Empires*, Cambridge 1991.

TUCCI, Ugo, Il banco pubblico a Venezia, in *Banchi pubblici, banchi privati e monti di pietà nell' Europa preindustriale. Amministrazione, tecniche operative e ruoli economici*, Genova 1991, vol. I, pp. 309–325.

——, Le monete del Regno Lombardo–Veneto dal 1815 al 1866, *Archivio economico dell'unificazione italiana* II 3 (1956), pp. 1–41.

——, Monete e riforme monetarie nell'Italia del settecento, *Rivista storica italiana* 98 (1986), pp. 78–119.

UDOVITCH, Abraham L., Bankers without Banks: The Islamic World, in [CHIAPPELLI, Fredi (ed.),] *The Dawn of Modern Banking*, New Haven – London 1979, pp. 255–273.

——, Commercial Techniques in Early Medieval Islamic Trade, in David S. RICHARDS (ed.), *Islam and the Trade of Asia. A Colloquium*, London – Colchester 1970, pp. 37–62.

ULLMANN, Hans-Peter, Der Frankfurter Kapitalmarkt um 1800: Entstehung, Struktur und Wirken einer modernen Finanzierungsinstitution, *Vierteljahrschrift für Sozial- und Wirtschaftsgeschichte* 77 (1990), pp. 75–92.

VAN CAUWENBERGHE, Eddy H.G. / IRSIGLER, Franz (eds.), *Münzprägung, Geldumlauf und Wechselkurse / Minting, Monetary Circulation and Exchange Rates. Akten des 8th International Economic History Congress, Section C 7 (Budapest 1982)*, Trier 1984.

—— (ed.), *Money, Coins, and Commerce: Essays in the Monetary History of Asia and Europe (From Antiquity to Modern Times)*, Leuven 1991.

VAN DER STRATEN-PONTHOZ, Gabriel-Auguste, *Le budget du Brésil ou recherches sur les resources de cet Empire dans leurs rapports avec les intérêts européens du commerce et de l'émigration*, 3 vols., Bruxelles 1854.

VAN DER WEE, Herman / BLANCHARD, Ian, The Habsburgs and the Antwerp Money Market: the Exchange Crises of 1521 and 1522–3, in Ian BLANCHARD / Anthony GOODMAN / Jennifer NEWMAN (eds.), *Industry and Finance in Early Modern History. Essays Presented to George Hammersley to the Occasion of His 74th Birthday*, Stuttgart 1992, pp. 27–57.

—— / VINOGRADOV, Vladimir A. / KOTOVSKY, Grigorii G. (eds.), *Fifth International Conference of Economic History, Leningrad 1970*, vol. IV, The Hague – Paris – New York 1976.

——, Monetary, Credit and Banking Systems, in Edwin E. RICH / Charles H. WILSON (eds.), *The Economic Organization of Early Modern Europe* (= *The Cambridge Economic History of Europe*, vol. V), Cambridge et al. 1977, pp. 290–392.

——, *The Growth of the Antwerp Market and the European Economy (14th–16th Centuries)*, The Hague 1963.

VAN DILLEN, Johannes G. (ed.), *History of the Principal Public Banks*, The Hague 1934.

——, The Bank of Amsterdam, in idem (ed.), *History of the Principal Public Banks*, The Hague 1934, pp. 79–100.

VAN LAANEN, J.T.M., *Money and Banking 1816–1940* (= P. CREUTZBERG / J.T.M. VAN LAANEN (eds.), *Changing Economy in Indonesia. A Selection of Statistical Source Material from the Early 19th Century up to 1940*, vol. 6), The Hague 1980.

VAN TIELHOF, Milja, *The 'Mother of All Trades'. The Baltic Grain Trade in Amsterdam from the Late 16th to the Early 19th Century*, Leiden – Boston – Köln 2002.

VAN WERVEKE, H., Monnaie de compte et monnaie réelle, *Revue belge de philologie et d'histoire* 13 (1934), pp. 123–152.

VÁZQUEZ DE PRADA, Valentín, Die kastilischen Messen im 16. Jahrhundert, in Hans POHL (ed.), *Frankfurt im Messenetz Europas – Erträge der Forschung* (= Rainer KOCH, *Brücke zwischen den*

Völkern – Zur Geschichte der Frankfurter Messe, vol. I), Frankfurt/Main 1991, pp. 113–131.

——, *Lettres marchandes d'Anvers*, 4 vols., Paris 1960/61.

Verwaltungsbericht der Reichsbank für das Jahr 1876, Berlin 1877.

Viajeros, peregrinos, mercaderes en el Occidente Medieval. XVIII semana de estudios medievales, Navarra 1991.

VIDAL, Emmanuel, *The History and Methods of the Paris Bourse*, Washington 1910.

VILLAR, Pierre, *Gold und Geld in der Geschichte. Vom Ausgang des Mittelalters bis zur Gegenwart*, München 1984 (French edition: *Or et monnaie dans l'histoire, 1450–1920*, Paris 1972).

VINNAI, Volker, *Die Entstehung der Überseebanken und die Technik des Zahlungsverkehrs im Asienhandel von 1850 bis 1875*, Frankfurt/Main 1971.

VON CANSTEIN, Raban, *Lehrbuch des Wechselrechts*, Berlin 1890.

VON EICHBORN, Kurt, *Das Soll und Haben von Eichborn & Co. in 200 Jahren. Schicksal und Gestaltung eines Bankhauses im Wandel der Zeiten*, München – Leipzig 1928.

VON SCHERZER, Karl, *Statistisch-commerzielle Ergebnisse einer Reise um die Erde, unternommen an Bord der österreichischen Fregatte Novara in den Jahren 1857–1859*, Leipzig – Wien ²1867.

VON SCHRÖTTER, Friedrich, *Das preußische Münzwesen im 18. Jahrhundert (= Acta Borussica. Denkmäler der Preußischen Staatsverwaltung im 18. Jahrhundert. Die einzelnen Gebiete der Verwaltung. Münzwesen. Münzgeschichtlicher Teil)*, vol. 4: *Die letzten vierzig Jahre. 1765–1806*, Berlin 1913.

WAGEMANN, Ernst, *Die Wirtschaftsverfassung der Republik Chile. Zur Entwicklungsgeschichte der Geldwirtschaft und der Papierwährung*, München – Leipzig 1913.

WAGNER-BRAUN, Margarete, Commercial Integration during the Era of the Classic Gold Standard, in Markus A. DENZEL (ed.), *From Commercial Communication to Commercial Integration. Middle Ages to 19ᵗʰ Century*, Stuttgart 2004, pp. 249–271.

WALDER, Franz, *Das Wechselrecht der Reichsstadt Augsburg*, Erlangen 1922.

WALTER, Rolf, Die nordwesteuropäische Wirtschaft in mikroökonomischer Perspektive: Das Beispiel Hasenclever, in Michael NORTH (ed.), *Nordwesteuropa in der Weltwirtschaft 1750–1950 / Northwestern Europe in the World Economy 1750–1950*, Stuttgart 1993, pp. 291–307.

——, Wechsel, Pari, Kurs und ihre Bedeutung für das Überseegeschäft des 19. Jahrhunderts, *Scripta mercaturae* 16/1 (1982), pp. 55–78.

WENDEHORST, Alfred, Wer konnte im Mittelalter lesen und schreiben?, in Johannes FRIED (ed.), *Schulen und Studien im sozialen Wandel des hohen und späten Mittelalter*, Sigmaringen 1986, pp. 9–33.

WHITE, David L., *Competition and Collaboration. Parsi Merchants and the English East India Company in 18ᵗʰ Century India*, New Delhi 1995.

WHITEMAN, Anne et al. (eds.), *Statesmen, Scholars and Merchants: Essays in Eighteenth-Century History Presented to Dame Lucy Sutherland*, Oxford 1973.

WILKINSON, Gardner, *Modern Egypt and Thebes: Being a Description of Egypt; Including the Information Required for Travellers in that Country*, vol. I, London 1843.

WILEMAN, J.P., *Brazilian Exchange. The Study of an Inconvertible Currency*, Buenos Aires 1896.

WILLIAMS, John H., *Argentine International Trade under Inconvertible Paper Money 1880–1900*, Cambridge (Mass.) 1920.

WITSCHI, Beat, *Schweizer auf imperialistischen Pfaden. Die schweizerischen Handelsbeziehungen mit der Levante 1848–1914*, Stuttgart 1987.

WITTHÖFT, Harald with ROTH, Karl Jürgen, *Acta Metrologiae Historicae V: 7. Internationaler Kongreß des Internationalen Komitees für Historische Metrologie (CIMH) 25.–27. September 1997 in Siegen*, St Katharinen 1999.

——, *Münzfuß, Kleingewichte, pondus Caroli und die Grundlegung des nordwesteuropäischen Maß-*

und Gewichtswesens in fränkischer Zeit, Ostfildern 1984.

WYSOCKI, Josef, Die österreichisch/ungarische Krone im Goldwährungsmechanismus, in Eckart SCHREMMER (ed.), *Geld und Währung vom 16. Jahrhundert bis zur Gegenwart. Referate der 14. Arbeitstagung der Gesellschaft für Sozial- und Wirtschaftsgeschichte vom 9. bis 13. April 1991 in Dortmund*, Stuttgart 1993, pp. 143–156.

ZELLFELDER, Friedrich, Art. "Skandinavische Münzunion", in Michael NORTH (ed.), *Von Aktie bis Zoll. Ein historisches Lexikon des Geldes*, München 1995, pp. 367f.

——, Der Lateinische Münzbund: Grundlagen, Entstehung und Scheitern, in Jürgen SCHNEIDER / Oskar SCHWARZER / Friedrich ZELLFELDER (eds.), *Währungen der Welt I: Europäische und nordamerikanische Devisenkurse 1777–1914*, 3 vols., Stuttgart 1991, vol. I, pp. 105–121.

——, Die Niederlande zwischen Silber- und Goldstandard 1816–1914, in ibid., pp. 35-46.

——, Die Währungsprobleme der Donaumonarchie, in ibid., pp. 122-135.

——, Glossar, in ibid., pp. 197-207.

ZERRES, Michael Peter, *Die Wechselplätze. Eine Untersuchung der Organisation und Technik des interregionalen und internationalen Zahlungsverkehrs Deutschlands in der ersten Hälfte des 19. Jahrhunderts*, Zürich – Frankfurt/Main – Thun 1977.

ZIEGLER, Dieter, Art. "Scheck", in Michael NORTH (ed.), *Von Aktie bis Zoll. Ein historisches Lexikon des Geldes*, München 1995, pp. 354f.

ZWAHR, Hartmut / SCHIRMER, Uwe / STEINFÜHRER, Henning (eds.), *Leipzig, Mitteldeutschland und Europa. Festgabe für Manfred Straube und Manfred Unger zum 70. Geburtstag*, Beucha 2000.

—— / TOPFSTEDT, Thomas / BENTELE, Günter (eds.), *Leipzigs Messen 1497–1997. Gestaltwandel. Umbrüche. Neubeginn, vol. 1: 1497–1914*, Köln – Weimar – Wien 1999.

EUROPE

1
England/Great Britain (1590–1914)

Exchange market: London (1590–1914)

Sources: MCCUSKER / HART [1979], pp. 697–700 (1590–1660); MCCUSKER [1978], pp. 37f., 56f., 75f., 93f., 103, 110 (1660–1697); IISG Amsterdam, *The Prices of Merchandise in London* (1667); ibid., *Prix Courant des Marchandises a Londres* (1668, 1671–1675, 1679/80, 1682, 1684/85); ibid., *The Merchants Remembrancer, London* (1680); ibid., *Le Memorial Des Marchands*, Londres (1681–1683, 1685); *The Course of the Exchange, and Other Things* (1698–1850); *The Economist*, London (1850–1914). For the India Exchange: *The Oriental Observer*, Calcutta (1830–1832); *The Economist*, London (1858–1882); *Indian Daily News / The Overland Summary of the Indian Daily News, Bengal Hurkarn and Indian Gazette* (1883–1885, 1897–1901); GRUBER [1890], pp. 37–40 (1885–1889).

Concordance: WdW III, pp. 113–122; WdW I/II, pp. 3–110; WdW VII, pp. 361–364; WdW IV, pp. 337–371; WdW II, pp. 66, 107–115

Currency: Since the Middle Ages the pound sterling at 20 shillings of 12 pence had been the currency unit of England, gold and silver being equally accepted as currency metals since 1423. Although a gold coin with a value of 1 pound, the so-called 'sovereign', had already been minted for the first time in 1489 and had gained greater importance for payment transactions after 1544, the shilling remained the most important money of account until late into the 17th century – especially within the exchange transactions – and silver did so as the most important currency metal. However, the silver money lost so much of its value at the end of the 17th century, above all after 1690, as a consequence of the Third Anglo-Dutch War (1672–1674) and the Nine Years' War (War of the League of Augsburg, 1689–1697) that on average only 48% of its expected weight was left in 1696 (cf. QUINN [1996], passim). Therefore, on the one hand, the premium on unminted silver money and the export of English silver was generally forbidden in 1695 (in 1696 this regulation was extended to gold coins) and, on the other hand, the withdrawal and the reminting of the English silver money was ordered. Thus the old silver money disappeared from circulation but since a new one could not be minted very quickly, gold coins became more and more important as means of payment, although bills of exchange and the notes of the Bank of England, founded in 1694, should normally have been paid with silver. It was not until the reminting was finished in 1699 that the English monetary system regained its position at the time before 1672, and in November 1696 the rate on Amsterdam once again exceeded the parity, since exchanges on the Netherlands could then be paid again with full weighted silver coins. It was also possible to force the premium for gold coins – to be more precise, for the 'guineas' minted since 1663 (officially at 20 shillings) – which had risen up to 30 shillings in 1695, in various steps down to 21½ shillings until 1699. This tariffing was immediately accepted in trade as well. Thus gold money circulated again in payment transactions after it had become a trade coin since the end of the 1660s, supplied with a premium, and had been withdrawn from internal English payment transactions; that was the temporary end of the bimetallism. But when the exploitation of the Brazilian gold mines started in 1698, the gold import to England was considerably intensified by trade relations with Portugal in the following years, while trade relations for example with France were constantly pushing forward the export of silver at the same time. Silver was the obligatory means of payment in trade, although the state had to accept gold as well. When the value of the guinea was again reduced to 21 shillings in 1717 and in 1728 respectively (according to KRUSE [1782], p. 264), the guinea with a fixed legal rate became the obligatory means of payment for trade as well, so that Britain (again) officially held bimetallism even though it was actually already proceeding to gold currency. In the course of the 18th century this gold currency became steadily more stable: the inclusion of the old, well-worn gold coins from 1732, the further inflow of gold in connection with an outflow of silver and the minting of smaller denominations of the guinea as compensation for the lack of silver money in the retail trade were responsible for that development. When at the end of the 18th century the amount of minted silver was drastically reincreasing as a consequence of the considerably raised silver prices, the free minting of silver was cancelled, the silver coins were reminted into token coins and, at last, England's gradual transition to a gold currency, starting in 1717/28, was settled. Therefore "the English monetary history of the 18th century is characterized by the change from a pure silver standard to a double standard and then to a pure gold standard" (REISS [1986], p. 177).

However, the complete implementation of the gold currency in Britain was delayed until 1816 by the paper money period of the Napoleonic Wars. There was no governmental paper money in the exact sense of the word, but the notes of the Bank of England, founded in 1694 as a private company of bankers with the right to issue banknotes, fulfilled this function. The notes of the Bank of England were based on the older goldsmiths' notes and, as money of a private payment community – the bank and its customers – they were at first something between money and a credit paper. Until about 1730 they had become established in trade and public finance in their main circulation area of London and Lancashire (cf. ASHTON [1945]), in particular since the bank was obliged to cash the notes into gold or silver. So, in London, bills of exchange were primarily paid with notes of the Bank of England. As in the whole of the 18th century – when the Bank of England survived the runs of 1707 and 1745 without greater loss – bills of exchange were the main financial supporters of the government during the Revolutionary Wars with France, because the state had always renewed the right to issue banknotes when it depended on credits of the bank. When more coins had to be raised on the continent to pay the troops, the reserves of the bank disappeared, so that issuing of metallic money in the amount of more than 1 pound sterling was forbidden by the bank by means of the Bank-Restriction Act of 1797 (extended several times). Thus the notes of the Bank of England were acknowledged as governmental means of payment even if they were privately issued, and now they could be used for all governmental payments within the country. Since the notes of the Bank of England could not be used to pay for imports from foreign countries, gold increasingly flowed out of Britain, the holdings of the public funds were deposited at the Bank of England in 1806, and payments of all governmental institutions were settled by transfers to this bank from then onwards. This actually meant the transition to paper currency, because the bank had already paid in notes since 1799 and the currency was nothing but paper money since 1806, although neither law on currency reform was enacted nor an acceptance obligation imposed. Until 1809 the notes had become England's only means of payment. In order to redress the lack of small coins, the silver minting was resumed in 1816 and, so, the reform of the British monetary system began. On July 1st 1817 a new gold coin, the sovereign at 20 shillings, was proclaimed, so that the unit of account coincided with the actual monetary unit. The reform was completed when, after the passing of Peel's Currency Bill of May 5th 1819, the Bank of England partially resumed cash payments on February 1st 1820 and to the full amount of the cashing sum on May 1st 1823. There were no essential changes in the currency up to 1914.

As a result of this currency reform of 1816–1823, Britain was the first state in the world to adopt the gold standard. Since the beginning of the 19th century the British currency was constantly replacing the Dutch guilder banco as the 'world trade currency' (together with the Spanish peso), and in the course of the 19th century it became the most stable, most reliable and, because of this, also the most important currency of the world, which was taken as a model for other currencies not only within the parts of the British Empire scattered all over the world but also far beyond them. This development was fostered by two facts: first, the British currency system was gradually spreading over large parts of the Empire – for example, to Australia, New Zealand, the Cape Colony and most of the other colonies and British territories in Africa – and, furthermore, traditional foreign currencies of imperial areas were linked to sterling, like those of Egypt, British India or the Straits Settlements, as it had been happening since the end of the 19th century; second, because of the great importance of the British economy and its worldwide trade relations in the era of the Industrial Revolution, many states in

Europe (especially the Ottoman Empire) and Latin America with close relations to Britain regarded dependence on the British gold standard as resonable and necessary, especially because the decline in silver prices taking place from the 1860/70s demanded a turning away from silver in favour of gold as currency metal for reasons of economic and monetary policy. On account of its international economic power and because it was the first state to introduce the gold standard, Britain became the driving power and the most important factor for the development of the international payment system in the era of the gold standard from the 1870s up to World War I.

Original quotations at London: Although the shilling was the most important unit of account until late into the 17th century, in the tables presented here all quotations have been converted into pounds sterling per 100 or 1,000 units of foreign currency in order to keep the continuity of the data series over the whole period of investigation.

on:	in:	per:
Amsterdam	shillings Flemish or Flemish banco resp.	1 pound sterling
from 1816 (10)	Dutch guilders	1 pound sterling
Antwerp	shillings Brabant exchange money	1 pound sterling
from 1816 (10)	Dutch guilders	1 pound sterling
from 1844	Belgian francs	1 pound sterling
Bahia	pence sterling	1 Brazil milrée
Barcelona	pence sterling	1 peso duro
from 1898 (12)	pesetas	1 pound sterling
Berlin	mark	1 pound sterling
Bombay	shillings and pence sterling	1 Company's rupee
from 1862	shillings and pence sterling	1 Government rupee
Cadiz	pence sterling	1 peso de plata antigua
Calcutta	shillings and pence sterling	1 Company's rupee
from 1862	shillings and pence sterling	1 Government rupee
Colombo	per cent premium or discount	1 pound sterling
from 1872 (5)	shillings and pence sterling	1 Government rupee
Copenhagen	rixdollar rigsmønt	1 pound sterling
from 1875 (2)	Danish crowns	1 pound sterling
Dublin	per cent premium on 100 pound Irish	100 pound sterling
Genoa	pence sterling	1 pezza fuori banco of 5¾ lire fuori banco
from 1827 (4)	Piedmontese lire nuove	1 pound sterling
from 1861 (8)	Italian lire	1 pound sterling
Gibraltar	pence sterling	1 current piaster of 8 reales
from 1826 (7)	pence sterling	1 current dollar of 12 reales
Hamburg	shillings Flemish or	1 pound sterling
	mark banco	1 pound sterling
from 1872 (12)	mark	1 pound sterling
Hong Kong	shillings and pence sterling	1 Mexican dollar
Leghorn	pence sterling	1 pezza da otto reali of 5¾ lire moneta buona
from 1837 (8)	Tuscan lire moneta buona	1 pound sterling
from 1860 (9)	Piedmontese lire nuove	1 pound sterling
from 1861 (8)	Italian lire	1 pound sterling
Lisbon and Porto	pence sterling	1 Portuguese milrée
Madras	shillings and pence sterling	1 Company's rupee
from 1862	shillings and pence sterling	1 Government rupee
Madrid	pence sterling	1 peso de plata antigua
from 1847 (5)	pence sterling	1 peso duro
from 1898 (12)	pesetas	1 pound sterling

on:	in:	per:
Malta	pence sterling	1 oncia
Mauritius	per cent premium or discount	1 pound sterling
since 1877 (6)	shillings and pence sterling	1 Government rupee
Melbourne	per cent premium or discount	1 pound sterling
Naples	pence sterling	1 ducato del regno
from 1862 (2)	Italian lire	1 pound sterling
Paris	pence sterling	1 écu of 3 livres tournois
from 1802	francs and centimes	1 pound sterling
Rio de Janeiro	pence sterling	1 Brazil milrée
Saint Petersburg	banco rouble	1 pound sterling
from 1841	pence sterling	1 silver rouble
from 1899	pence sterling	1 gold rouble
Shanghai	shillings and pence sterling	1 Shanghai tael
Singapore	shillings and pence sterling	1 Mexican dollar
South Africa	per cent premium or discount	1 pound sterling
Switzerland	franken	1 pound sterling
Sydney	per cent premium or discount	1 pound sterling
Venice	pence sterling	1 ducato di banco
from 1815	lire italiane	1 pound sterling
Vienna and Trieste	guilders Konventionskurant	1 pound sterling
from 1858 (11)	guilders Österreichische Währung	1 pound sterling
from 1900	Austrian crowns	1 pound sterling

Other data available: Amsterdam, 1m/d (1721–1796); 2½m/d (1735–1771); 2m/d (1802–1817); 3m/d (1814–1914) – Barcelona, 3m/d (1815–1914) – Bilbao, 3m/d (1714–1797, 1802–1837, 1873–1876) – Bombay, 60d/s (1850–1861, bank & commercial bills; 1858–1882, until 1861 Government bills; 1874–1882, agency & private bills); 30d/s (1858–1861, bank & commercial bills; 1874–1882, agency & private bills) – Bordeaux, Uso (1714–1722); s (1722–1731); 14d/s (1731–1741); 2m/d (1741–1850) – Brussels, 3m/d (1850–1876) – Calcutta, 60d/s (1850–1861, bank & commercial bills; 1858–1882, until 1861 Government bills; 1874–1882, agency & private bills); 30d/s (1858–1861, bank & commercial bills; 1874–1882, agency & private bills) – Colombo, 60d/s (1862–1882; 1874–1882, agency & private bills); 30d/s (1874–1882, agency and private bills) – Cork (1805–1826) – Hamburg, uso (1735–1757) – Hong Kong, 60d/s (1862–1879, since 1874 bank bills; 1874–1882, agency & private bills); 30d/s (1874–1879, agency & private bills) – Lyons (1698–1702, 1713–1715) – Madras, 60d/s (1850–1861, bank & commercial bills; 1858–1882, until 1861 Government bills); 30d/s (1858–1861, bank & commercial bills) – Malaga, 3m/d (1826, 1870–1887) – Marseilles, 3m/d (1835–1887, 1893–1914) – Mauritius, 60d/s (1862–1879; 1876–1881, agency & private bills); 30d/s (1876–1879, agency & private bills) – Melbourne (60d/s, 1862–1874) – Messina, 3m/d (1837–1867) – Milan, 3m/d (1860–1867) – Naples (1753–1755) – Palermo, 3m/d (1810–1867) – Paris, 2m/d (1733–1793, 1802–1817); 3m/d (1834–1914) – Oporto, 90d/s (1698–1873, 1877–1891); 30d/s (1851/52, 1870–1876) – Rotterdam, 1m/d (1698–1776); 2m/d (1735–1759); 2½m/d (1735 –1776); 3m/d (1777–1793, 1804–1876) – Santander, 3m/d (1870–1876) – Seville, 3m/d (1816–1833, 1873–1887) – Shanghai, 60d/s (1874–1879, bank bills; 1874–1882, agency & private bills); 30d/s (1874–1879, agency & private bills) – Singapore, 60d/s (1862–1879, since 1874 bank bills; 1874–1882, agency & private bills); 30d/s (1874–1879, agency & private bills) – South Africa, 120d/s (1908–1914); 90d/s (1908–1914); 60d/s (1908–1914); 30d/s (1908–1914) – Sydney, 60d/s (1862–1874) – Valencia, 3m/d (1877–1887) – Trieste, 2m/d (1820–1833); 3m/d (1834–1914).

As the only exchange place of the British Isles, London had been integrated into the international system of cashless payment transactions since the 14th century and maintained a close contact with the Italian and the Northwest European exchange places (cf. *WdW IX*, pp. 28–30, 130–133). Whereas Antwerp had been London's most important exchange partner on the continent in the 16th century, it was succeeded after its decline by Amsterdam as the most important financial market in Northwestern Europe and remained the only exchange place with relatively regular quotations of London until about 1660 that are now available. Price currents and exchange rate currents passed down from the 1660s (cf. MᶜCUSKER [1978], p. 29) recording Paris, Rouen, Antwerp, Lille, Amsterdam, Middelburg, Rotterdam, Dordrecht, Hamburg, Leghorn, Venice and Dublin, which are – apart from the two Italian exchange markets – exclusively Northwest European places, most of them Dutch. These early exchange rate currents list Venice as England's traditional exchange partner in Italy and Leghorn as definitely the most important trade and exchange place for English merchants and their trade in the Mediterranean region as far as the Levant. From the 1680s this geographically still quite limited network was expanding to the Iberian Peninsula where, henceforth, Cadiz, Lisbon, Madrid and Seville were quoted, but the latter two only rarely. Thus "Cadiz was the first and for a long time the only Spanish city quoted on the London Exchange" (ibid., p. 98). Whereas Cadiz was undoubtedly London's most important exchange partner in Spain during the early 1600s, Madrid became very important from the end of the 17th century onwards. So the data series documented here changed from Cadiz to Madrid in this time. "Lisbon as the capital and major commercial city of Portugal and its empire was the locus of most English–Portuguese exchange transactions" (ibid., p. 107). By the end of the 1690s Genoa and Oporto also joined the group, as documented in the single-paged, semi-weekly financial newspaper *The Course of the Exchange, and Other Things*, which was founded in 1697. At the same time, the payment transactions with the Netherlands were gradually concentrated on Amsterdam, Rotterdam and Antwerp, while the quotations on Lille and Rouen as well as those on the Lyons fairs – available for only a short period (1698–1702, 1713–1715) – were discontinued in the following decades. With its regular quotations on Ireland, on the Netherlands, on Northern Germany, France, Portugal and Spain, London kept close relationships with all important exchange markets on the European Atlantic Coast or in their hinterlands (Paris, Madrid), being able to conclude its financial transactions in the Mediterranean area via the Italian seaports and especially via Leghorn and the whole Levant.

In the British Isles only Dublin as the most important Irish exchange market was quoted, although "at the beginning of the eighteenth century, both Scotland and Ireland were still foreign countries for exchange purposes. The Act of Union in 1707 ended this condition for Scotland and altered its exchange relationship with London from a foreign to an inland basis" (ibid., p. 31). Some years before, in 1695/96, the London exchange rate on Scotland had fluctuated between par and 5% premium (SAVILLE [1996], p. 32). After 1707, London gradually became Scotland's central exchange market for foreign exchange relations, which had previously been kept with France, Spain, the Netherlands, Poland (Danzig) and Sweden. This development was decisively supported by Scotland's integration into the English currency system in 1707, because the Act of Union also terminated the era of the Scottish currency as also based on pounds, shillings and pence and having, however, 130 pounds Scottish corresponding to 100 pounds sterling. From that time on, "Scotland's real money and money of account were by law uniform with those of England" (MᶜCUSKER [1978], pp. 32f.). Bills of exchange from and on Scottish exchange places – like those on other English markets – were regarded as inland bills of exchange for which "there was no course of exchange at London ... despite their importance for the internal trade of the nation; nor do we have any quotations of the inland rates of exchange. We would expect these rates to be small, given the integrated economy of the nation and the comparative ease of arbitrage transactions", usually about 1% to 2% in favour of London (ibid., p. 31; cf. KELLY [1811], pp. 383f.). The usance varied from 40 to 60 days, "and small bills are mostly drawn at a longer term than larger ones" (ibid.). After 1707 there existed exchange relationships of Scottish merchant bankers not only with London, but also with the Netherlands, France, Italy, Spain and Portugal, especially from Edinburgh (HAMILTON [1963], p. 302), because "Glasgow was very awkwardly situated for bill transactions" (PRICE [1961/62], p. 266).

Until 1826 Ireland stood outside the standard national currency, which is why Irish bills of exchange were not regarded as inland bills. Therefore Ireland and its most important exchange market, Dublin, were quoted in the London exchange rate currents. Thus "Dublin was an early centre for foreign exchange and seems to have maintained a certain prominence into the nineteenth century", but outside of Ireland "London was certainly the centre for Irish exchange with foreign countries" (MCCUSKER [1978], p. 35). No exchange market on the Continent quoted an Irish place, because exchange transactions from continental places with Ireland were exclusively concluded via London.

Britain (and Great Britain by the second half of the 18th century) was foremost among the grat European powers in being focused on a metropolis with regard to economy and especially to payment transactions (cf. KINDLEBERGER [1974], p. 16), and almost all bills on England or Great Britain respectively were still payable in London at the turn of the 20th century (e.g. SWOBODA [1889], pp. 575f.; SWOBODA [1902], p. 361). When London was starting to extend its trade relations above all for overseas goods by means of its own distribution network, independent of continental depots after the Peace of Utrecht in 1713, it gained significantly in importance as an entrepôt for overseas imports from the second half of the 17th century, in parallel with the trade in the Baltic area and the Levant in the 18th century. Therefore London was the only exchange market of international relevance in Britain with the appropriate preconditions. "The City of London was already emerging as the payments centre for international trade because of its commercial importance" (MICHIE [2000], p. xxii). On the one hand, the network of London's exchange contacts was roughly speaking as branched and far-reaching as that of the world's trade centre at that time: Amsterdam. On the other hand, concerning the payment transactions with those exchange places with which London maintained no direct exchange contact, especially those of Central Europe as far as Sweden and Russia, it could carry on using the payment transaction structure of the continental places, especially that of Amsterdam but also that of Hamburg (cf. MCCUSKER [1978], pp. 42, 61). The close contact between the exchange markets of London and Amsterdam can also be shown by the fact that the stabilizing of the pound sterling in the 1690s considerably helped British merchant bankers in becoming almost as influential as the Dutch, not only on the capital market of London but also on that of Amsterdam. So, despite the constantly growing English involvement in trade with Russia, Amsterdam governed all capital transactions with the Baltic area until late into the 18th century, thus financing London's trade with Denmark, Sweden, the Baltic States and Russia. Bills from London, for example on Copenhagen, "were usually negotiated indirectly via Amsterdam" (MCCUSKER [1978], p. 80). "By the 1750s it was still common for bills to be drawn on Amsterdam to finance the expanding English export trade from Russia and for such bills, after acceptance by British merchants, to be met there" (ROSEVEARE [1987], p. 102).

Even after 1713 London continued concentrating on ports on the Atlantic Coast when expanding its network of directly quoted exchange partners and admitting Bordeaux and Bilbao to its exchange rate current in 1714. During the rest of the 18th century only two further places were added: Altona near to Hamburg in 1777 and Naples in 1796. Until well into the Napoleonic era, London payment transactions continued to be geared primarily to Continental coasts, in clear contrast to Amsterdam, whereas regularily quoted exchange partners were still missing in Central Europe. As far as trade policy was concerned this London structure of cashless payment transactions had its roots primarily in the negotiating of British and overseas goods on the Continent because the resulting payment transactions required only close exchange contacts with continental entrepôts. The same held in the 18th century for the growing British trade with the Levant, effected via the British main trade and exchange partner in Italy, Leghorn. So London required no direct quotations on Levantine places.

Fundamental expansions and even reorientations of the London exchange rate current took place during the Napoleanic era, i.e. in the years of the Continental System (from November 28th 1806), when Britain was officially excluded from the continental markets and most such markets ceased their quotations on London for lack of demand at least for some years. Because of the wool and food imports from southern Ireland to the capital, Cork had become the second most important Irish port next to Dublin to be newly established, after having supported direct exchange with London since the 1670s (MCCUSKER [1978], p. 35). After the Portuguese royal family had fled to Brazil and the Brazil ports had been opened for non-Portuguese trade, the quoting on Rio de Janeiro began in March 1809 (a further one on Bahia was added in 1820); this quotation was done in the same manner as that on Lisbon, so that in London Rio de Janeiro – as well as Bahia later on – was accepted as a 'European' exchange partner (up to 1853). This can be judged as a significant indication of Britain's new strong economic and financial involvement in Latin America, above all, on its most important market of that time, Brazil, after the (temporary) loss of European markets in 1808. However, the setting up of the trade and the direct payment transactions with South America could hardly support the exchange rate, which fell after 1795 and did so significantly after the Continental System had been announced. In 1809 the strategically important British possessions in the Mediterranean area, Gibraltar and Malta, were also given a quotation, and Palermo was quoted from 1810, being the political and economic centre as well as the most important exchange market of Sicily, which was independent since 1806 and did not belong to the Napoleonic sphere of control. In the post-Napoleonic era there was again a wave of expansion of the London exchange rate current. Apart from Antwerp (no quotation after 1758) and Barcelona (since 1815) as well as Seville (since 1816), continental exchange markets like Frankfurt am Main (since 1815), Vienna (since 1819), Saint Petersburg (since 1821) and for a short time Berlin (1822–1826) were also included for the first time.

The quotation on Vienna was added to the quotation list at Nathan M. Rothschild's instigation on September 24th 1819. Also the Mediterranean region, represented by Trieste (since 1820), Marseille (since 1835) and Messina (since 1837), was paid more attention than before. Thus Trieste took the place of Venice as most important exchange market in the Adriatic Sea in the 1820s because the quotation on Venice was stopped in 1826.

The 1820s and the 1830s brought about the end of even more existing quotations: when the English currency system was introduced on Malta in 1825 and in Ireland on January 5th 1826, the quotations on Malta, Dublin and Cork became obsolete. With the restructuring of the London exchange rate current in September 1833, which from then on also included fixed and regular usances, the rates on Altona, Bahia, Gibraltar, Seville and Barcelona were the first to be discontinued, as were, some years later, those on Bilbao (1837), which had already been stopped for the first time in 1833. During the early 1840s the *Course of Exchange* renewed the quotations on these places, but only up to January or September of 1844 respectively. As a consequence, those places were no longer quoted directly in the London exchange transaction network that were either of short-time interest or had a special function resumed by larger exchange markets in the same country, like Altona by Hamburg, Bahia by Rio de Janeiro or Bilbao by Madrid. However, those places no longer quoted often continued to appear in merchant manuals of later decades and, in addition to this, other places not mentioned before were listed as occasional exchange partners of London, for example Bremen, Constantinople, Smyrna, Copenhagen, Leipzig and Rome.

The next substantial restructuring of the London exchange rate current did not take place until the 1860s and the 1870s. 1860 saw the start of quoting on Milan and – after some occasional quotings – that on Berlin in 1865. Copenhagen followed in 1868, Leipzig, Barcelona, Malaga and Santander in 1870, Bilbao, Seville and – with a common quotation – Zurich and Basle in 1873, and, finally, Valencia in 1877. This indicates London's intensified orientation, on the one hand, towards Central Europe (Denmark, Northern Germany, Switzerland, Northern Italy) and, on the other hand, towards Spain, reflecting a quite remarkable involvement of British capital in transactions on the Iberian Peninsula. In 1868, after Italy's unification in national and monetary policy, the Italian exchange places Genoa, Milan, Naples, Leghorn, Messina and Palermo were assigned a common quotation under which Venice was subsumed from 1870 – after its occupation by Italy – as well.

However, this 'expansion' of the London exchange rate current did not last long. In 1876 another restucturing took place omitting Copenhagen, Bordeaux, Rotterdam, Santander, Bilbao, Zurich and Basle – partly after only some years of quoting. From that time on, the quotations within Italy were concentrated on the two most important ports, Genoa and Naples, which appeared under the category "Genoa, Naples, etc." in the *Economist* from 1881. The quotations on the Netherlands were concentrated on the financial centre of Amsterdam. From 1876 on, after the formation of the German Empire and its monetary unification, the quotations on the German places of Hamburg, Berlin and Frankfurt am Main differed only very seldom from one another, and if they did so, then only marginally; Leipzig, however, was no longer mentioned separately after 1876. That is why the three remaining series on German exchange places could have been combined in the documentation. Whereas different quotations on the various exchange markets seemed to have become obsolete owing to the introduction of standardized currencies in Italy (Italian lira) and Germany (mark Reichswährung), the Habsburg Monarchy, Portugal and Spain kept this differentiation up to the 1880s; in 1889 the quotations on Vienna and Trieste became identical, those on Lisbon and Oporto did so in 1884, and those on Madrid and Barcelona followed suit at the the the end of 1887 after Barcelona had risen to be Spain's most important port and business centre during the late 19th century. Nevertheless, these identical quotations were always listed separately as well. Since then the quotations on Cadiz, Seville and the striving Mediterranean ports of the second half of the 19th century, Malaga and Valencia, which had been independent until that time, even though they hardly differed, were dropped. This concentration of quotations on the Spanish exchange markets was probably brought about by the conversion of the foreign exchange rate quotations from the old currency unit peso duro to the new peseta (introduced in 1869) (see p. 307), although London did not make this step until the end of 1898.

In the late 19th and early 20th centuries the network of London's European exchange rate quotations was one of the most extensive in the whole of Europe: all Western and Central European exchange markets of international relevance were quoted directly from London, as a rule, with one quotation per quoted country, e.g. the Netherlands (Amsterdam), Belgium (Antwerp), Germany (Hamburg, Berlin and Frankfurt am Main), the Habsburg Monarchy (Vienna and Trieste), Italy (Genoa and Naples), Spain (Madrid and Barcelona), Portugal (Lisbon and Oporto) and finally, Switzerland from 1893, where Geneva had been quoted in 1888 and 1889. Only the various French and Russian exchange markets were quoted independently until 1914, although those quotations on Paris and Marseilles and on Saint Petersburg and Moscow hardly differed now, so that it is remarkable that in 1893 the world's financial centre, London – as the only foreign place – included Moscow, now Russia's industrial metropolis, on its exchange rate current and quoted it regularly. So, from the British point of view, Moscow was recognized as a Russian financial market of equal relevance to that of Saint Petersburg before World War I. In contrast to Berlin (see pp. 204f.), London kept direct contact neither to the Scandinavian exchange places nor with Poland. But London did "not quote Constantinople or Bucharest or Valparaiso, for instance, because there are no dealings in paper on these places. You can, of course, buy a draft in London on almost every town of importance in the world, but business of this exceptional nature would be negotiated in the drawer's office, and not, as a rule, on 'Change [exchange]" (CLARE [1892], p. 131).

Until 1914 the London quotations on the European places mentioned above were mainly effected for bills of exchange with a usance of three months' dato. Additionally, quotations for short sight bills (cheques from 1906) were quoted on Amsterdam. The same goes for Paris from 1834, even though these quotations were replaced by a quotation on cheques in 1877. By this means, "the 'short' quotation is understood to include all bills having up to about a week to run, a draft payable at sight would of course be worth more than one payable seven or ten days hence" (ibid., p. 129). The exchange markets of Lisbon (60 days' sight up to 1850; 30 days' sight in 1871) and of the Brazilian ports (60 days' sight), of Vienna and Trieste (two months' dato up to 1833) as well as of Hamburg (two and a half months' dato up to 1833) represent further exceptions concerning the usances. For Gibraltar, Malta and Dublin no usances are listed in the documented sources.

During the whole 19th and the early 20th centuries London was the most important centre for exchange business not only within Europe but also in the entire world. The 'bill on London' became an internationally accepted medium of payment (SCAMMEL [2000], p. 155). As "the dominant financial centre in the world" (MICHIE [2000], p. vii), taking the place of Amsterdam from the second half of the 18th century, London was the first European exchange market to have multiple exchange contacts to non-European financial markets. As early as 1832, when a parliamentary committee consulted Nathan M. Rothschild about trade and finances, he declared that "England in general is the Bank of the whole world … all transactions in India, in China, in Germany, in the whole world are guided here and settled through this country" (SPERLING [1962], p. 446). But "the major breakthrough internationally for the City of London was the laying of the submarine cables to Paris in 1851 and New York in 1866, after the first one had failed. By the late 1870s a worldwide web of telegraph lines was in existence connecting London with all other major financial and commercial centres, even as far distant as Buenos Aires in Argentina, Bombay in India, and Melbourne in Australia" (MICHIE [2000], p. xiv). Concerning the cashless payment transactions, those contacts to the Brazilian places Rio de Janeiro and Bahia which were regarded as 'European' exchange markets from the London point of view have already been mentioned (whereas British exports to the Pacific coast of South America were paid by six months' inland bills, so that there were not any quotations on such places as Valparaiso [NISHIMURA [1971], p. 35]). According to contemporary merchant manuals, single quotations on New York and Philadelphia as well as on Buenos Aires and Ciudad de Mexico are supposed to have existed by the 1840s (e.g. NELKENBRECHER [1828], p. 210; NOBACK [1851], pp. 532f.; NOBACK [1858], pp. 394f.; NOBACK [1877], p. 522), although only a few quotations can be found in the sources documented here: e.g. the *Course of Exchange* quoted New York (at 21 days' sight) at 19.38 pounds sterling per 100 US dollars between January 1840 and January 1844, Philadelphia (at 21 days' sight) at 19.17 pounds sterling per 100 US dollars during the same period – and both without any deviation; therefore these rates seem to be fixed rates, not market rates. Only between December 1847 and March 1850 could a few quotations on New York (at 60 days' dato) be found (1847: 19.79; 1848: 19.90; 1849: 20.41; 1850: 20.63 pounds sterling per 100 US dollars). The quotations on New York are supposed to be completely available up to the 20th century, although proof of this assumption can only be furnished for the time after the outbreak of World War I, when the quotations were published in the *Economist* from September 1914 (*WdW II*, p. 69). Exchange contacts from London to North American places had already existed during the colonial era, in particular to Massachusetts since 1669, which can be proved until 1774, even though only at irregular intervals, but nevertheless far more often than for London's cashless payment transactions on other colonies within this area, such as on Jamaica in the early 18th century (MCCUSKER [1978], pp. 122, 131–150, 248f.). "Bills drawn in London on the colonies were negotiated only occasionally, mostly during wartime when the army or the navy needed money in North America or the West Indies to purchase provisions or to pay troops. Even for this limited use of bills, we find little evidence. One reason is that there seems to have been a difficulty locating anyone in London with sufficient credits in the colonies to draw against.

London merchants preferred to bring such credits home in the form of colonial produce and in bullion. ... Perhaps the most important reason why bills were not used
more frequently was the existence of a convenient and profitable alternative. The government simply shipped specie" (ibid., p. 36). Furthermore, the British exports to the
United States were chiefly financed by drawing four months' inland bills, which were
drawn by the manufacturers on the merchants shipping the goods, whereas the British
imports from North America were paid by two months' bills drawn from there on Britain (NISHIMURA [1971], pp. 34f.). For these reasons, the exchange transactions of
London on North American or the West Indian colonies were too unimportant and,
all in all, of minor interest for the London merchants to be mentioned in the quotations
of the exchange rate currents.

   Moreover, London had been in exchange contact with its possessions in the Asiatic
region during the 18th century, although these relationships were primarily limited to
transactions of the East India Company. As the references for the 1830s show, a large
part of the territorial revenues of the East India Company was transferred to England
by bills of exchange drawn in England on the Indian treasuries, especially on the treasury in Calcutta. In contrast to this, commercial transactions from London to India covered only a minor volume since they were based on immense grantings of credit to
business partners in India who served to finance the trade with India via London
banks (DENZEL [2001], pp. 242–244). By the early 19th century contemporary
merchant manuals listed quotations on Calcutta, Bombay and Madras (as well as on
Buenos Aires and Mexico) (KELLY [1811], p. 136; cf. NELKENBRECHER [1828], p.
210; cf. KELLY [1835] II, p. 103), partially on Canton around the mid-19th century
(NOBACK [1851], p. 533; NOBACK [1858], p. 395), and, finally, on Hong Kong and
Shanghai in the 1870s (NOBACK [1877], p. 522). From the 1830s on, London's quotations on the three most important Indian exchange markets – Calcutta, Bombay and
Madras – could also be found in Indian commercial journals written in English. From
1850 the London *Economist* listed rates on Indian, South and East Asian as well as
Australian places in a section entitled *India Exchange*, although exports to India were
regularly paid by six months' inland bills, later on by four months' inland bills on
London or by two or three months' bills directly on the importers (NISHIMURA [1971],
pp. 36, 39). The oldest and most important quotations (references available since
1850) were those on Indian exchange places, which is why this section was entitled
India Exchange. From 1862 on, the *Economist* also listed quotations on Hong Kong,
Singapore, Colombo, Mauritius, Sydney and Melbourne, representing exclusively
places of the British Empire within the Asian–Australian region, and, finally, added
the semi-colonial metropolis of Shanghai in 1874. When the quotations of the *India
Exchange* in the *Economist* were stopped in 1882 – those on Australia as early as 1874
– this did not mean the end of the London quotations on non-European places. It was
again in Indian newspapers that London rates 'on India', i.e. on Calcutta, Bombay and
Madras, continued to be published. Calcutta, Bombay and Madras, Singapore, Hong
Kong and Shanghai were even quoted in London's Royal Exchange (SWOBODA
[1913], p. 394; SONNDORFER [1900], p. 207), although without being published in the
semi-official exchange rate currents of the *Economist*. But the official stock exchange
quotations of the Royal Exchange were of very little importance, because official exchange rate quotations were not carried out at all in London, there were no official

lists of exchange quotations (NOBACK [1877], p. 522), and the money and exchange trade in the City of London did not take place at the stock exchange but at the banks or via the brokers' agencies (SWOBODA [1913], p. 392; MAHLBERG [1920], p. 5). The existence of exchange transactions can be proved, but they were on a smaller scale than those of the Asiatic exchange markets on London. Often the European–Indian cashless payment transactions were concluded on the basis of the so-called 'Council bills', which were remittances sold in London by the India Council (Secretary of State for India) via the Bank of England "for the dual purpose of financing India's Home Charges, and enabling London merchants and bankers to make payments in India" (SPALDING [1918], p. 23), and payable in rupees (telegraphic transfers were possible as well) and drawn on the Treasuries in Calcutta, Bombay or Madras (SWOBODA [1913], p. 395; cf. SWOBODA [1889], p. 665; SWOBODA [1902], pp. 439f.). Finally, quotations of London on South Africa were listed in a separate table from 1908.

References: Ignaz GRUBER, *Statistische Beiträge zur Frage der Währung der österreichisch-ungarischen Monarchie*, I. Heft, Jena 1890, pp. 32–40; George CLARE, The A.B.C. of the Foreign Exchanges, *The Institute of Bankers* 13/III (1892), pp. 121–149; Eugen SCHMALENBACH, Der Kurs des Pfund-Sterling-Wechsels, *Zeitschrift für handelswissenschaftliche Forschung* 1 (1906), pp. 241–256; Walter MAHLBERG, *Über asiatische Wechselkurse*, Leipzig ²1920; William F. SPALDING, *Eastern Exchange, Currency and Finance*, London ²1918; T.S. ASHTON, The Bill of Exchange and Private Banks in Lancashire 1790–1830, *Economic History Review* 15/1 (1945), pp. 25–35; Jacob M. PRICE, Notes on Some London Price-Currents, 1667–1715, *Economic History Review* sec. ser. 7 (1954/55), pp. 240–250; idem, Multilateralism and/or Bilateralism: the Settlement of British Trade Balances with 'The North', c. 1700, *Economic History Review* sec. ser. 14 (1961/62), pp. 254–274; J. SPERLING, The International Payments Mechanism in the Seventeenth and Eighteenth Centuries, *Economic History Review* sec. ser. 14 (1961/62), pp. 446–468; Henry HAMILTON, *An Economic History of Scotland in the Eighteenth Century*, Oxford 1963; Shizuya NISHIMURA, *The Decline of Inland Bills of Exchange in the London Money Market 1855–1913*, Cambridge 1971; Charles P. KINDLEBERGER, *The Formation of Financial Centers: A Study in Comparative Economic History*, Princeton (N.J.) 1974, pp. 12–18; John J. MCCUSKER, *Money and Exchange in Europe and America, 1600–1775. A Handbook*, London – Basingstoke 1978, pp. 31–41; idem / S. HART, The Rate of Exchange on Amsterdam in London: 1590–1660, *Journal of European Economic History* 8 (1979), pp. 689–705; Barry EICHENGREEN (ed.), *The Gold Standard in Theory and History*, New York – London 1985; Michael COLLINS, Sterling Exchange Rates, 1847–80, *Journal of European Economic History* 15 (1986), pp. 511–533; Winfried REISS, Historical Exchange Rates, in Wolfram FISCHER / R. Marvin MCINNIS / Jürgen SCHNEIDER (eds.), *The Emergence of a World Economy 1500–1914, Part I: 1500–1850*, Wiesbaden 1986, pp. 171–190; Ranald C. MICHIE, *The London and New York Stock Exchanges 1850–1914*, London et al. 1987, ch. 5; Larry NEAL, The Finance of Business during the Industrial Revolution, in R. FLOUD / D. MCCLOSKEY (eds.), *The Economic History of Britain since 1700, vol. I*, Cambridge ²1994, pp. 151–181; Stephen QUINN, Gold, Silver, and the Glorious Revolution: Arbitrage between Bills of Exchange and Bullion, *Economic History Review* 49/3 (1996), pp. 473–490; Richard SAVILLE, *Bank of Scotland. A History, 1695–1995*, Edinburgh 1996; Ranald C. MICHIE, *The London Stock Exchange. A History*, Oxford 1999, pp. 15–142; idem, General Introduction. The Rise and Rise of a Global Financial Centre: The City of London since 1700, in idem (ed.), *The Development of London as a Financial Centre*, London – New York 2000, vol. 1, pp. vii–xxxii; W.M. SCAMMELL, The London Discount Market: The Later 19th Century, in ibid., vol. 2, pp. 151–177; Markus A. DENZEL, Kolonialstädte als Finanzplätze vom 18. Jahrhundert bis 1914. Das asiatische Wechselnetz und seine Anbindung an das europäisch-internationale Zahlungsverkehrssystem, in Horst GRÜNDER / Peter JOHANEK (eds.), *Kolonialstädte. Europäische Enklaven oder Schmelztigel der Kulturen?*, Münster 2001, pp. 225–259; idem, Bargeldloser Zahlungsverkehr im europäischen Überseehandel von der Europäischen Expansion bis zum Ersten Weltkrieg, *Jahrbuch für europäische Überseegeschichte* 2 (2002), pp. 71–103.

1.1 London foreign exchange rates

1.1.1 On Amsterdam, Antwerp and Paris

	LONDON on:				**LONDON on:**		
	Amsterdam				**Amsterdam**		
	per 1,000 guilders Flemish [a]				per 1,000 guilders Flemish or Flemish banco resp. [a]		
	in pounds sterling				**in pounds sterling**		
1590	98.24	[b]	(1)	1623	91.60	[b]	(6)
1591	97.10	[b]	(1)	1624	91.11	[b]	(5)
1592	95.24	[b]	(1)	1625	90.96	[b]	(6)
1593	91.45	[b]	(5)	1626	90.86	[b]	(6)
1594	92.04	[b]	(6)	1627	91.29	[b]	(6)
1595	98.74	[b]	(4)	1628	91.63	[b]	(12)
1596	95.94	[b]	(8)	1629	91.10	[b]	(12)
1597	97.15	[b]	(5)	1630	89.21	[b]	(8)
1598	99.15	[b]	(1)	1631	89.98	[b]	(12)
1599	97.65	[b]	(3)	1632	89.12	[b]	(12)
1600	96.13	[b]	(7)	1633	88.34	[b]	(12)
1601	93.48	[b]	(4)	1634	88.14	[b]	(12)
1602	91.08	[b]	(3)	1635	90.60	[b]	(12)
1603	90.19	[b]	(7)	1636	91.25	[b]	(12)
1604	89.99	[b]	(5)	1637	89.18	[b]	(5)
1605	93.48	[b]	(7)	1638	90.93	[b]	(6)
1606	94.50	[b]	(5)	1639	90.04	[b]	(7)
1607	91.65	[b]	(7)	1640	88.01	[b]	(5)
1608	93.43	[b]	(6)	1641	84.75	[b]	(6)
1609	95.48	[b]	(5)	1642	86.34	[b]	(5)
1610	95.72	[b]	(5)	1643	84.20	[b]	(6)
1611	93.77	[b]	(6)	1644	82.93	[b]	(6)
1612	93.16	[b]	(5)	1645	85.54	[b]	(7)
1613	94.36	[b]	(5)	1646	89.40	[b]	(7)
1614	95.23	[b]	(5)	1647	94.43	[b]	(6)
1615	95.17	[b]	(4)	1648	98.29	[b]	(7)
1616	95.19	[b]	(12)	1649	99.66	[b]	(6)
1617	94.42	[b]	(6)	1650	93.29	[b]	(8)
1618	93.78	[b]	(7)	1651	89.34	[b]	(6)
1619	94.28	[b]	(12)	1652	90.50	[b]	(7)
1620	96.97	[b]	(4)	1653	92.63	[b]	(5)
1621	97.12	[b]	(5)	1654	90.40	[b]	(5)
1622	95.61	[b]	(6)	1655	89.97	[b]	(5)

	LONDON on:		
	Amsterdam	**Antwerp**	**Paris**
	per 1,000 guilders Flemish banco [a]	per 1,000 guilders Brabant exchange money ('permißgeld') [c]	per 1,000 livres tournois [d]
	in pounds sterling		
1656	93.11 [b] (12)		
1657	95.76 [b] (12)		
1658	95.89 [b] (12)		
1659	93.78 [b] (12)		
1660	87.44 [b] (12)		
1661			
1662	95.12 2½m (1)		
1663	92.64 2½m (3)		69.24 2m (1)
1664			
1665			
1666			
1667	95.45 2½m (1)	96.85 2½m (1)	71.58 2m (1)
1668	93.06 2½m (4)	96.85 2½m (1)	70.80 2m (4)
1669	92.90 2½m (12)		70.17 2m (10)
1670			
1671	91.85 2½m (1)	92.70 2½m (1)	65.49 2m (1)
1672	94.40 2½m (7)	91.95 2½m (1)	67.86 2m (7)
1673	97.82 2½m (4)	97.32 2½m (1)	69.15 2m (12)
1674	96.81 2½m (5)	98.04 2½m (1)	70.53 2m (12)
1675	93.22 2½m (7)	95.92 2½m (1)	71.55 2m (12)
1676			68.70 2m (12)
1677	92.10 2½m (3)		68.55 2m (3)
1678			
1679	93.23 2½m (1)	93.02 2½m (1)	67.05 2m (1)
1680	92.43 2½m (4)	92.17 2½m (2)	68.07 2m (1)
1681	91.98 2½m (3)	92.38 2½m (1)	68.76 2m (9)
1682	93.47 2½m (5)	93.46 2½m (2)	68.94 2m (12)
1683	91.41 2½m (5)	93.46 2½m (1)	68.01 2m (12)
1684	92.49 2½m (2)	92.59 2½m (1)	68.58 2m (12)
1685	91.63 2½m (3)	91.64 2½m (1)	68.07 2m (12)
1686	92.59 2½m (1)	91.32 2½m (1)	67.95 2m (12)
1687	93.23 2½m (1)		67.23 2m (6)
1688	95.65 2½m (2)		66.63 2m (10)
1689	94.46 2½m (2)		69.93 2m (1)
1690			
1691	96.59 2½m (4)		

	LONDON on:		
	Amsterdam	**Antwerp**	**Paris**
	per 1,000 guilders Flemish banco [a]	per 1,000 guilders Brabant exchange money ('permißgeld') [c]	per 1,000 livres tournois [d]
	in pounds sterling		
1692	95.33　2½m　(2)		
1693	96.30　2½m　(2)		
1694	101.65　2½m　(2)		
1695	112.23　2½m　(12)		74.85　2m　(4)
1696	104.08　2½m　(12)		71.37　2m　(8)
1697	92.85　2½m　(12)	75.16　2½m　(12)	
1698	93.87　2½m　(12)	92.30　2½m　(12)	63.42　2m　(12)
1699	94.36　2½m　(12)	93.20　2½m　(12)	64.38　2m　(12)
1700	93.75　2½m　(12)	92.80　2½m　(12)	64.28　2m　(12)
1701	91.61　2½m　(12)	91.00　2½m　(12)	62.17　2m　(12)
1702	93.97　2½m　(12)	94.10　2½m　(5)	60.68　2m　(5)
1703	97.15　2½m　(12)		[e]
1704	97.21　2½m　(12)		[e]
1705	96.34　2½m　(12)		[e]
1706	96.40　2½m　(12)	96.60　2½m　(6)	[e]
1707	96.08　2½m　(12)	96.70　2½m　(12)	[e]
1708	96.61　2½m　(12)	97.70　2½m　(12)	[e]
1709	98.37　2½m　(12)	98.00　2½m　(12)	[e]
1710	98.19　2½m　(12)	98.20　2½m　(12)	[e]
1711	96.88　2½m　(12)	98.00　2½m　(12)	[e]
1712	98.20　2½m　(12)	98.40　2½m　(11)	[e]
1713	93.37　2½m　(12)	92.30　2½m　(12)	51.54　2m　(7)
1714	92.00　2½m　(12)	89.40　2½m　(12)	54.66　2m　(12)
1715	91.82　2½m　(12)	88.60　2½m　(12)	65.67　2m　(12)
1716	94.01　2½m　(12)	91.00　2½m　(12)	62.94　2m　(12)
1717	96.01　2½m　(12)	95.10　2½m　(12)	65.87　2m　(12)
1718	96.56　2½m　(12)	95.80　2½m　(12)	51.82　2m　(12)
1719	94.19　2½m　(12)	92.80　2½m　(12)	39.51　2m　(12)
1720	95.60　2½m　(12)	93.60　2½m　(12)	22.38　2m　(8)
1721	97.40　ss　(10)	93.90　2½m　(11)	33.55　ss　(10)
1722	94.33　ss　(12)	92.30　2½m　(12)	32.20　ss　(12)
1723	95.20　ss　(12)	93.30　2½m　(12)	31.25　ss　(12)
1724	95.39　ss　(12)	94.50　2½m　(12)	41.91　ss　(12)
1725	95.65　ss　(12)	94.20　2½m　(12)	52.66　ss　(12)
1726	94.65　ss　(12)	91.90　2½m　(12)	50.68　ss　(12)
1727	95.97　ss　(12)	93.10　2½m　(12)	45.90　ss　(12)
1728	97.48　ss　(11)	95.10　2½m　(11)	45.57　ss　(11)

	LONDON on:		
	Amsterdam	**Antwerp**	**Paris**
	per 1,000 guilders Flemish banco [a]	per 1,000 guilders Brabant exchange money ('permißgeld') [c]	per 1,000 livres tournois [d]
	in pounds sterling		
1729	97.70 ss (12)	94.40 2½m (12)	45.39 ss (12)
1730	97.18 ss (12)	94.70 2½m (12)	45.22 ss (12)
1731	96.03 ss (12)	92.90 2½m (12)	44.05 ss (12)
1732	95.48 ss (12)	92.90 2½m (12)	44.78 ss (12)
1733	95.38 ss (12)	93.70 2½m (12)	44.06 2m (12)
1734	93.43 ss (12)	91.60 2½m (12)	43.39 2m (12)
1735	93.40 ss (12)	92.00 2½m (12)	43.41 2m (12)
1736	94.64 ss (12)	92.80 2½m (12)	43.47 2m (12)
1737	95.72 ss (12)	94.60 2½m (12)	44.85 2m (12)
1738	95.24 ss (12)	93.60 2½m (11)	44.41 2m (12)
1739	94.29 ss (12)	91.60 2½m (10)	43.35 2m (12)
1740	95.25 ss (12)	92.50 2½m (12)	44.72 ss (12)
1741	96.58 ss (12)	94.40 2½m (11)	44.98 ss (12)
1742	95.86 ss (12)	94.20 2½m (12)	43.83 ss (12)
1743	96.47 ss (10)	94.50 2½m (10)	44.76 ss (10)
1744	96.65 ss (12)	94.80 2½m (12)	45.38 ss (12)
1745	95.57 ss (12)	93.60 2½m (11)	44.17 ss (12)
1746	93.01 ss (10)	89.90 2½m (10)	42.76 ss (10)
1747	94.75 ss (12)	91.50 2½m (12)	43.89 ss (12)
1748	93.89 ss (12)	90.50 2½m (7)	42.73 ss (11)
1749	93.85 ss (12)	90.20 2½m (10)	43.44 ss (11)
1750	95.64 ss (12)	92.40 2½m (10)	43.82 ss (12)
1751	94.46 ss (12)	91.60 2½m (9)	43.24 ss (12)
1752	95.02 ss (12)	92.00 2½m (11)	43.95 ss (12)
1753	95.45 ss (12)	93.30 2½m (12)	44.68 ss (12)
1754	93.78 ss (12)	92.20 2½m (11)	43.69 ss (12)
1755	92.24 ss (12)	91.40 2½m (4)	42.97 ss (12)
1756	92.58 ss (12)		42.27 ss (12)
1757	93.99 ss (12)		42.15 ss (12)
1758	96.23 ss (12)	93.40 2½m (2)	43.31 ss (12)
1759	94.24 ss (12)		42.47 ss (12)
1760	95.30 ss (12)		42.55 ss (12)
1761	98.36 ss (12)		43.38 ss (12)
1762	95.35 ss (9)		42.82 ss (9)
1763	96.05 ss (12)		43.99 ss (12)
1764	91.69 ss (12)		42.42 ss (12)
1765	92.83 ss (12)		43.14 ss (12)

	LONDON on:		
	Amsterdam	**Antwerp**	**Paris**
	per 1,000 guilders Flemish banco [a]	per 1,000 guilders Brabant exchange money ('permißgeld') [c]	per 1,000 livres tournois, from 1802 per 1,000 francs [d]
	in pounds sterling		
1766	96.24 ss (12)		44.12 ss (12)
1767	96.48 ss (12)		43.92 ss (12)
1768	96.17 ss (12)		43.59 ss (12)
1769	97.50 ss (12)		44.00 ss (12)
1770	97.87 ss (12)		43.94 ss (12)
1771	97.17 ss (12)		43.94 ss (12)
1772	96.02 ss (12)		43.90 ss (12)
1773	93.71 ss (12)		41.55 ss (12)
1774	92.75 ss (12)		41.96 ss (12)
1775	94.20 ss (12)		42.69 ss (12)
1776	96.00 ss (12)		42.51 ss (12)
1777	97.63 ss (12)		43.33 ss (12)
1778	94.05 ss (12)		41.49 ss (12)
1779	92.35 ss (12)		40.48 ss (12)
1780	93.31 ss (12)		41.20 ss (12)
1781	98.63 ss (11)		42.63 ss (11)
1782	97.64 ss (12)		43.68 ss (12)
1783	96.42 ss (12)		43.35 ss (12)
1784	91.89 ss (12)		41.22 ss (12)
1785	89.10 ss (12)		39.66 ss (12)
1786	91.23 ss (12)		40.33 ss (12)
1787	90.87 ss (12)		40.43 ss (12)
1788	88.75 ss (12)		40.00 ss (12)
1789	87.94 ss (12)		38.69 ss (12)
1790	86.35 ss (12)		36.51 ss (12)
1791	86.65 ss (12)		32.91 ss (12)
1792	90.89 ss (12)		25.02 ss (12)
1793	85.57 ss (12)		15.26 ss (9)
1794	84.54 ss (10)		
1795			
1796			
1797			
1798			
1799			
1800			
1801			
1802	91.54 2m (9)		42.13 ss (7)

	LONDON on:		
	Amsterdam	**Antwerp**	**Paris**
	per 1,000 guilders Flemish banco, from 1816 (10) per 1,000 Dutch guilders [a]	per 1,000 guilders Brabant exchange money ('permißgeld'), from 1816 (10) per 1,000 Dutch guilders [c]	per 1,000 francs [d]
	in pounds sterling		
1803	93.04 ss (12)		40.93 ss (12)
1804	89.65 ss (12)		39.75 ss (12)
1805	90.25 ss (12)		39.13 ss (12)
1806	93.25 ss (12)		40.88 ss (12)
1807	93.78 ss (12)		41.08 ss (12)
1808	96.09 ss (12)		42.84 ss (12)
1809	106.15 ss (12)		48.75 ss (12)
1810	105.16 ss (12)		48.35 ss (12)
1811	118.61 ss (12)		55.35 ss (11)
1812	112.79 ss (12)		52.27 ss (12)
1813	111.37 ss (12)		51.59 ss (12)
1814	104.21 ss (12)		46.95 ss (12)
1815	99.23 ss (12)	97.22 3m/d (11)	46.59 ss (12)
1816	84.50 ss (12)	83.06 3m/d (12)	39.59 ss (12)
1817	84.57 ss (7)	83.41 3m/d (7)	39.94 ss (7)
1818	89.09 ss (10)	86.88 3m/d (12)	41.25 ss (12)
1819	87.17 ss (12)	85.08 3m/d (12)	40.77 ss (12)
1820	83.15 ss (12)	81.43 3m/d (12)	39.13 ss (12)
1821	79.97 ss (12)	80.14 3m/d (12)	38.88 ss (12)
1822	81.95 ss (12)	81.73 3m/d (12)	39.27 ss (12)
1823	81.51 ss (12)	80.57 3m/d (12)	38.78 ss (12)
1824	83.66 ss (12)	81.92 3m/d (12)	39.36 ss (12)
1825	83.51 ss (12)	82.17 3m/d (12)	39.66 ss (12)
1826	81.56 ss (12)	80.20 3m/d (12)	38.97 ss (12)
1827	83.05 ss (12)	81.69 3m/d (12)	39.24 ss (12)
1828	83.15 ss (12)	82.32 3m/d (12)	39.43 ss (12)
1829	82.49 ss (12)	81.68 3m/d (12)	39.04 ss (12)
1830	81.87 ss (12)	81.16 3m/d (11)	39.03 ss (12)
1831	83.73 ss (12)	82.47 3m/d (9)	39.62 ss (12)
1832	81.96 ss (12)	81.18 3m/d (12)	38.82 ss (12)
1833	82.55 ss (12)	80.75 3m/d (8)	38.69 ss (9)
1834	82.99 ss (9)	81.95 3m/d (12)	39.39 ss (12)
1835	82.01 ss (12)	81.70 3m/d (12)	39.19 ss (12)
1836	81.42 ss (11)	81.92 3m/d (12)	39.26 ss (12)
1837	82.90 ss (12)	81.92 3m/d (12)	39.20 ss (12)
1838	82.44 ss (12)	81.88 3m/d (12)	39.21 ss (12)

	LONDON on:							
	Amsterdam [f]			**Antwerp**			**Paris**		
	per 1,000 Dutch guilders [a]			per 1,000 Dutch guilders, from 1844 per 1,000 Belgian francs [c]			per 1,000 francs [d]		
	in pounds sterling								
1839	83.66	ss	(12)	82.52	3m/d	(12)	39.56	ss	(12)
1840	83.85	ss	(11)	82.68	3m/d	(11)	39.56	ss	(11)
1841	82.80	ss	(12)	82.24	3m/d	(12)	39.34	ss	(12)
1842	82.19	ss	(12)	81.69	3m/d	(12)	39.15	ss	(12)
1843	82.12	ss	(12)	81.60	3m/d	(12)	39.00	ss	(12)
1844	82.46	ss	(12)	38.73	3m/d	(12)	39.14	ss	(12)
1845	81.49	ss	(12)	38.26	3m/d	(12)	38.90	ss	(12)
1846	81.83	ss	(12)	38.09	3m/d	(12)	38.94	ss	(12)
1847	82.53	ss	(12)	38.62	3m/d	(12)	39.19	ss	(12)
1848	83.08	ss	(9)	38.53	3m/d	(10)	39.20	ss	(12)
1849	83.06	ss	(12)	38.89	3m/d	(12)	39.38	ss	(12)
1850	83.13	ss	(12)	39.05	3m/d	(12)	39.36	ss	(12)
1851	84.54	ss	(12)	39.55	3m/d	(12)	39.90	ss	(12)
1852	83.68	ss	(12)	39.27	3m/d	(12)	39.60	ss	(12)
1853	89.87	ss	(12)	39.59	3m/d	(12)	39.94	ss	(12)
1854	85.22	ss	(12)	39.63	3m/d	(12)	39.99	ss	(12)
1855	84.32	ss	(12)	39.39	3m/d	(12)	39.73	ss	(12)
1856	84.38	ss	(12)	39.21	3m/d	(12)	39.50	ss	(12)
1857	84.60	ss	(12)	39.27	3m/d	(12)	39.59	ss	(12)
1858	83.27	ss	(12)	39.44	3m/d	(12)	39.83	ss	(12)
1859	85.50	ss	(12)	39.66	3m/d	(12)	39.85	ss	(12)
1860	85.42	ss	(12)	39.55	3m/d	(12)	39.80	ss	(12)
1861	84.01	ss	(12)	39.06	3m/d	(12)	39.48	ss	(12)
1862	84.82	ss	(12)	39.27	3m/d	(12)	39.73	ss	(12)
1863	84.69	ss	(12)	39.20	3m/d	(12)	39.63	ss	(12)
1864	84.41	ss	(12)	38.97	3m/d	(12)	39.58	ss	(12)
1865	84.26	ss	(12)	39.22	3m/d	(12)	39.69	ss	(12)
1866	84.30	ss	(11)	39.21	3m/d	(11)	39.70	ss	(11)
1867	84.14	ss	(12)	39.38	3m/d	(12)	39.71	ss	(12)
1868	83.85	ss	(12)	39.40	3m/d	(12)	39.70	ss	(12)
1869	83.20	ss	(12)	39.35	3m/d	(12)	39.70	ss	(12)
1870	83.91	ss	(12)	39.21	3m/d	(12)	39.70	ss	(9)
1871	83.81	ss	(11)	38.96	3m/d	(11)	39.12	ss	(8)
1872	83.07	ss	(12)	38.95	3m/d	(12)	39.19	ss	(12)
1873	83.01	ss	(12)	38.79	3m/d	(11)	39.30	ss	(12)
1874	84.02	ss	(12)	39.17	3m/d	(12)	39.64	ss	(12)

	LONDON on:							
	Amsterdam [f]			**Antwerp**			**Paris** [g]	
	per 1,000 Dutch guilders [a]			per 1,000 Belgian francs [c]			per 1,000 francs [d]	
	in pounds sterling							
1875	84.04	ss	(12)	39.23	3m/d	(12)	39.65	ss	(12)
1876	82.68	ss	(12)	39.33	3m/d	(12)	39.64	ss	(12)
1877	82.80	ss	(12)	39.43	3m/d	(12)	39.77	ch	(12)
1878	82.56	ss	(12)	39.34	3m/d	(12)	39.72	ch	(12)
1879	82.72	ss	(12)	39.26	3m/d	(12)	39.60	ch	(12)
1880	82.61	ss	(12)	39.18	3m/d	(12)	39.55	ch	(12)
1881	82.42	ss	(12)	39.07	3m/d	(12)	39.55	ch	(12)
1882	82.50	ss	(12)	39.12	3m/d	(12)	39.66	ch	(12)
1883	82.37	ss	(12)	39.22	3m/d	(12)	39.60	ch	(12)
1884	82.51	ss	(12)	39.34	3m/d	(12)	39.69	ch	(12)
1885	82.69	ss	(12)	39.19	3m/d	(12)	39.57	ch	(12)
1886	82.70	ss	(12)	39.29	3m/d	(12)	39.61	ch	(12)
1887	82.61	ss	(12)	39.13	3m/d	(12)	39.50	ch	(12)
1888	82.75	ss	(12)	39.13	3m/d	(12)	39.51	ch	(12)
1889	82.66	ss	(12)	39.22	3m/d	(12)	39.60	ch	(12)
1890	82.62	ss	(12)	39.23	3m/d	(12)	39.60	ch	(12)
1891	81.97	ss	(12)	39.22	3m/d	(12)	39.60	ch	(12)
1892	82.68	ss	(12)	39.43	3m/d	(12)	39.70	ch	(12)
1893	82.66	ss	(12)	39.36	3m/d	(12)	39.67	ch	(12)
1894	82.54	ss	(12)	39.48	3m/d	(12)	39.71	ch	(12)
1895	82.47	ss	(12)	39.41	3m/d	(12)	39.62	ch	(12)
1896	82.47	ss	(12)	39.42	3m/d	(12)	39.67	ch	(12)
1897	82.69	ss	(12)	39.47	3m/d	(12)	39.73	ch	(12)
1898	82.72	ss	(12)	39.17	3m/d	(12)	39.56	ch	(12)
1899	82.44	ss	(12)	39.19	3m/d	(12)	39.61	ch	(12)
1900	82.56	ss	(12)	39.38	3m/d	(12)	39.72	ch	(12)
1901	82.63	ss	(12)	39.39	3m/d	(12)	39.64	ch	(12)
1902	82.34	ss	(12)	39.43	3m/d	(12)	39.71	ch	(12)
1903	82.59	ss	(12)	39.36	3m/d	(12)	39.72	ch	(12)
1904	82.78	ss	(12)	39.39	3m/d	(12)	39.71	ch	(12)
1905	82.67	ss	(12)	39.38	3m/d	(12)	39.73	ch	(12)
1906	82.49	ch	(12)	39.24	3m/d	(12)	39.73	ch	(12)
1907	82.66	ch	(12)	39.11	3m/d	(12)	39.69	ch	(12)
1908	82.72	ch	(12)	39.36	3m/d	(12)	39.78	ch	(12)
1909	82.66	ch	(12)	39.35	3m/d	(12)	39.72	ch	(12)
1910	82.66	ch	(12)	39.14	3m/d	(12)	39.64	ch	(12)
1911	82.70	ch	(12)	39.11	3m/d	(12)	39.59	ch	(12)
1912	82.73	ch	(12)	39.03	3m/d	(12)	39.62	ch	(12)

	LONDON on:		
	Amsterdam [f]	**Antwerp**	**Paris** [g]
	per 1,000 Dutch guilders [a]	per 1,000 Belgian francs [c]	per 1,000 francs [d]
	in pounds sterling		
1913	82.50 ch (12)	38.87 3m/d (12)	39.61 ch (12)
1914	82.66 ch (7)	39.06 3m/d (7)	39.70 ch (7)

[a] Concerning the Dutch currency, see pp. 57–59. Although quotations and calculations in Amsterdam were predominantly done in livres (pounds) of 20 shillings Flemish until well into the 17th century, the data series has been completely converted into guilders (= 3 2/3 shillings), the main unit of account at the latest from the beginning of the 18th century, in order to guarantee the comparability of the quotations over a long period of time.

[b] No data concerning the usance available.

[c] Until 1816 the bills of exchange were paid in Brabant exchange money ('permißgeld'), which was invariably 16 2/3% better than current money, so that 6 guilders exchange money equal 7 guilders Brabant current, where 1 guilder = 3 2/3 shillings. The Belgian franc was introduced in 1832 and it was equal to the French franc, whereby 189 Dutch guilders = 400 Belgian francs (see p. 280).

[d] Concerning the French currency, see pp. 279f.

[e] Because of the War of the Spanish Succession (1701–1713/14), no quotation between June 1702 and May 1713 (Treaty of Utrecht, April 11th 1713).

[f] From the second half of 19th century the usance 'short sight' meant: 3 days after sight; NOBACK [1877], p. 521.

[g] Bills on England recorded in French francs were cashed in at Paris sight rate (SWOBODA [1889], pp. 575f.).

1.1.2 On Germany and the Habsburg Monarchy

	LONDON on:				LONDON on:		
	Hamburg				**Hamburg**		
	per 1,000 mark banco [a]				per 1,000 mark banco [a]		
	in pounds sterling				in pounds sterling		
1667	78.45	2½m/d	(1)	1704	81.58	2½m/d	(12)
1668	75.31	2½m/d	(4)	1705	81.42	2½m/d	(12)
1669	75.33	2½m/d	(9)	1706	79.80	2½m/d	(12)
1670				1707	79.11	2½m/d	(12)
1671	75.47	2½m/d	(1)	1708	79.66	2½m/d	(12)
1672	76.90	2½m/d	(7)	1709	81.33	2½m/d	(12)
1673	80.90	2½m/d	(4)	1710	81.65	2½m/d	(12)
1674	82.33	2½m/d	(5)	1711	80.15	2½m/d	(12)
1675	80.43	2½m/d	(7)	1712	80.38	2½m/d	(11)
1676				1713	77.45	2½m/d	(12)
1677				1714	76.56	2½m/d	(12)
1678				1715	76.19	2½m/d	(12)
1679	81.44	2½m/d	(1)	1716	77.30	2½m/d	(12)
1680	76.02	2½m/d	(2)	1717	78.75	2½m/d	(12)
1681	75.49	2½m/d	(4)	1718	78.97	2½m/d	(12)
1682	76.45	2½m/d	(3)	1719	77.31	2½m/d	(12)
1683	77.16	2½m/d	(5)	1720	77.84	2½m/d	(12)
1684	77.49	2½m/d	(1)	1721	78.05	2½m/d	(11)
1685	76.35	2½m/d	(3)	1722	76.14	2½m/d	(12)
1686				1723	77.14	2½m/d	(12)
1687				1724	78.33	2½m/d	(12)
1688				1725	78.56	2½m/d	(12)
1689	79.62	2½m/d	(1)	1726	76.79	2½m/d	(12)
1690				1727	76.53	2½m/d	(12)
1691	81.01	2½m/d	(2)	1728	78.36	2½m/d	(12)
1692	80.02	2½m/d	(1)	1729	79.84	2½m/d	(12)
1693	83.35	2½m/d	(1)	1730	80.38	2½m/d	(12)
1694	85.81	2½m/d	(2)	1731	78.80	2½m/d	(12)
1695	93.06	2½m/d	(12)	1732	77.98	2½m/d	(12)
1696	87.25	2½m/d	(12)	1733	77.75	2½m/d	(12)
1697	79.01	2½m/d	(4)	1734	74.83	2½m/d	(12)
1698	77.39	2½m/d	(12)	1735	75.47	2½m/d	(12)
1699	78.71	2½m/d	(12)	1736	76.86	2½m/d	(11)
1700	77.65	2½m/d	(12)	1737	78.17	2½m/d	(12)
1701	75.61	2½m/d	(12)	1738	78.47	2½m/d	(12)
1702	78.17	2½m/d	(12)	1739	77.64	2½m/d	(12)
1703	81.89	2½m/d	(12)	1740	78.04	2½m/d	(12)

	LONDON on:		
	Hamburg		
	per 1,000 mark banco [a]		
	in pounds sterling		
1741	79.15	2½m/d	(12)
1742	79.29	2½m/d	(12)
1743	79.27	2½m/d	(12)
1744	79.41	2½m/d	(12)
1745	78.13	2½m/d	(12)
1746	74.82	2½m/d	(12)
1747	76.08	2½m/d	(12)
1748	76.67	2½m/d	(12)
1749	77.53	2½m/d	(12)
1750	79.39	2½m/d	(12)
1751	79.43	2½m/d	(12)
1752	79.79	2½m/d	(12)
1753	80.10	2½m/d	(12)
1754	79.53	2½m/d	(12)
1755	77.41	2½m/d	(12)
1756	74.69	2½m/d	(12)
1757	73.59	2½m/d	(12)
1758	74.82	2½m/d	(8)
1759	72.00	2½m/d	(8)
1760	79.99	2½m/d	(6)
1761	82.27	2½m/d	(9)
1762	77.26	2½m/d	(8)
1763	77.94	2½m/d	(8)
1764	76.12	2½m/d	(10)
1765	76.89	2½m/d	(12)
1766	76.10	2½m/d	(12)
1767	74.85	2½m/d	(12)
1768	77.90	2½m/d	(10)
1769	79.85	2½m/d	(10)
1770	80.26	2½m/d	(12)
1771	80.28	2½m/d	(12)
1772	80.42	2½m/d	(11)
1773	76.97	2½m/d	(10)
1774	76.78	2½m/d	(11)
1775	77.78	2½m/d	(11)
1776	79.58	2½m/d	(11)
1777	81.84	2½m/d	(12)

	LONDON on:		
	Hamburg		
	per 1,000 mark banco [a]		
	in pounds sterling		
1778	78.46	2½m/d	(12)
1779	75.83	2½m/d	(12)
1780	77.22	2½m/d	(12)
1781	80.66	2½m/d	(12)
1782	82.45	2½m/d	(12)
1783	82.95	2½m/d	(12)
1784	77.91	2½m/d	(12)
1785	75.66	2½m/d	(12)
1786	77.08	2½m/d	(12)
1787	76.81	2½m/d	(12)
1788	76.09	2½m/d	(12)
1789	75.64	2½m/d	(12)
1790	75.39	2½m/d	(12)
1791	74.87	2½m/d	(12)
1792	77.43	2½m/d	(12)
1793	73.65	2½m/d	(12)
1794	74.86	2½m/d	(12)
1795	78.99	2½m/d	(12)
1796	78.83	2½m/d	(12)
1797	72.89	2½m/d	(12)
1798	70.76	2½m/d	(12)
1799	76.53	2½m/d	(12)
1800	83.90	2½m/d	(12)
1801	84.90	2½m/d	(12)
1802	81.08	2½m/d	(12)
1803	77.90	2½m/d	(12)
1804	75.21	2½m/d	(11)
1805	76.41	2½m/d	(12)
1806	78.11	2½m/d	(11)
1807	77.16	2½m/d	(12)
1808	78.05	2½m/d	(12)
1809	89.41	2½m/d	(12)
1810	88.71	2½m/d	(12)
1811	107.00	2½m/d	(12)
1812	96.33	2½m/d	(12)
1813	96.50	2½m/d	(12)
1814	88.66	2½m/d	(12)

	LONDON on:			
	Hamburg	**Frankfurt**	**Berlin**	**Vienna**
	per 1,000 mark banco [a]	per 1,000 guilders Frankfurt exchange money, from 1843 per 1,000 guilders South German current [b]	per 1,000 thaler Prussian current [c]	per 1,000 guilders Konventionskurant [d]
	in pounds sterling			
1815	84.53 2½m/d (12)	116.62 3m/d (10)		
1816	74.24 2½m/d (12)	102.30 3m/d (12)		
1817	75.19 2½m/d (12)	101.87 3m/d (12)		
1818	77.82 2½m/d (12)	105.54 3m/d (12)		
1819	75.93 2½m/d (12)	103.27 3m/d (12)		99.59 2m/d (4)
1820	72.10 2½m/d (12)	97.64 3m/d (12)		98.38 2m/d (12)
1821	69.83 2½m/d (11)	95.92 3m/d (12)		96.66 2m/d (12)
1822	70.87 2½m/d (12)	96.62 3m/d (12)	136.99 3m/d (5)	97.29 2m/d (12)
1823	70.08 2½m/d (12)	95.01 3m/d (12)	135.50 3m/d (11)	95.50 2m/d (12)
1824	71.48 2½m/d (12)	97.32 3m/d (12)	134.77 3m/d (12)	98.88 2m/d (12)
1825	72.25 2½m/d (12)	99.59 3m/d (12)	141.64 3m/d (12)	100.16 2m/d (12)
1826	70.77 2½m/d (12)	96.93 3m/d (12)	142.86 3m/d (6)	96.27 2m/d (12)
1827	71.84 2½m/d (12)	98.28 3m/d (12)		98.37 2m/d (12)
1828	72.46 2½m/d (12)	99.75 3m/d (12)		99.56 2m/d (12)
1829	71.94 2½m/d (12)	98.93 3m/d (12)		98.83 2m/d (12)
1830	71.33 2½m/d (12)	97.88 3m/d (12)		97.70 2m/d (12)
1831	72.73 2½m/d (12)	99.83 3m/d (12)		99.54 2m/d (12)
1832	71.68 2½m/d (12)	97.64 3m/d (12)		98.33 2m/d (12)
1833	72.10 2½m/d (12)	98.45 3m/d (12)		99.78 2m/d (12)
1834	72.99 3m/d (12)	99.50 3m/d (12)		100.50 3m/d (12)
1835	72.67 3m/d (12)	98.77 3m/d (12)		99.26 3m/d (12)
1836	72.41 3m/d (12)	98.44 3m/d (12)		98.26 3m/d (12)
1837	72.41 3m/d (12)	98.44 3m/d (12)		97.64 3m/d (12)
1838	72.89 3m/d (12)	98.36 3m/d (12)		98.15 3m/d (12)
1839	73.42 3m/d (12)	99.83 3m/d (12)		99.43 3m/d (12)
1840	73.91 3m/d (11)	100.67 3m/d (12)		100.12 3m/d (11)
1841	73.53 3m/d (12)	100.67 3m/d (12)		100.72 3m/d (12)
1842	72.89 3m/d (12)	99.59 3m/d (12)		100.99 3m/d (12)
1843	72.41 3m/d (12)	82.30 3m/d (12)		100.12 3m/d (12)
1844	72.73 3m/d (12)	82.64 3m/d (12)		101.40 3m/d (12)
1845	72.15 3m/d (12)	82.03 3m/d (12)		99.89 3m/d (12)
1846	72.25 3m/d (12)	81.97 3m/d (12)		97.45 3m/d (12)
1847	72.46 3m/d (12)	82.03 3m/d (12)		98.81 3m/d (12)
1848	72.41 3m/d (12)	81.77 3m/d (12)		90.66 3m/d (9)
1849	72.52 3m/d (12)	82.17 3m/d (12)		87.63 3m/d (11)

	LONDON on:			
	Hamburg	**Frankfurt**	**Berlin**	**Vienna**
	per 1,000 mark banco, from 1872 (12) per 1,000 mark [a]	per 1,000 guilders South German current, from 1874 (11) per 1,000 mark [b]	per 1,000 thaler Prussian current, from 1874 (10) per 1,000 mark [c]	per 1,000 guilders Konventionskurant from 1859 per 1,000 guilders Österreichische Währung [d]
	in pounds sterling			
1850	72.94 3m/d (12)	82.71 3m/d (12)	144.09 3m/d (1)	82.93 3m/d (12)
1851	74.02 3m/d (12)	83.89 3m/d (12)		78.96 3m/d (11)
1852	73.42 3m/d (12)	82.51 3m/d (12)		82.11 3m/d (12)
1853	74.40 3m/d (12)	83.47 3m/d (12)		89.86 3m/d (12)
1854	74.91 3m/d (12)	84.32 3m/d (12)		79.64 3m/d (11)
1855	74.13 3m/d (12)	84.18 3m/d (12)		82.12 3m/d (12)
1856	73.58 3m/d (12)	83.19 3m/d (12)		94.62 3m/d (12)
1857	73.86 3m/d (12)	83.61 3m/d (12)		94.35 3m/d (12)
1858	74.40 3m/d (12)	84.18 3m/d (12)		95.80 3m/d (12)
1859	74.96 3m/d (12)	85.18 3m/d (12)		81.49 3m/d (12)
1860	74.85 3m/d (12)	85.18 3m/d (12)	148.59 3m/d (1)	74.89 3m/d (11)
1861	73.64 3m/d (12)	84.03 3m/d (12)		68.24 3m/d (12)
1862	74.07 3m/d (12)	83.96 3m/d (12)		75.31 3m/d (12)
1863	74.07 3m/d (12)	83.82 3m/d (12)		85.94 3m/d (12)
1864	73.75 3m/d (12)	83.19 3m/d (12)		82.69 3m/d (12)
1865	73.64 3m/d (12)	82.85 3m/d (12)	144.30 3m/d (1)	88.30 3m/d (12)
1866	73.53 3m/d (11)	83.26 3m/d (12)	144.30 3m/d (11)	83.91 3m/d (10)
1867	73.58 3m/d (12)	83.19 3m/d (12)	145.35 3m/d (12)	77.21 3m/d (12)
1868	73.31 3m/d (12)	83.13 3m/d (12)	144.92 3m/d (12)	83.93 3m/d (12)
1869	72.99 3m/d (12)	82.78 3m/d (12)	144.51 3m/d (12)	79.41 3m/d (12)
1870	73.15 3m/d (12)	82.92 3m/d (12)	144.72 3m/d (12)	78.48 3m/d (12)
1871	73.26 3m/d (11)	83.54 3m/d (12)	145.99 3m/d (12)	80.03 3m/d (11)
1872	73.15/48.26 3m/d (11+1)	83.54 3m/d (12)	146.20 3m/d (12)	
1873	48.73 3m/d (12)	83.54 3m/d (12)	146.20 3m/d (12)	
1874	48.52 3m/d (12)	83.18/48.19 3m/d (10+1)	145.84/48.36 3m/d (9+3)	87.80 3m/d (12)
1875	48.26 3m/d (12)	48.26 3m/d (12)	48.24 3m/d (12)	87.49 3m/d (12)
	Hamburg, Frankfurt & Berlin			
	per 1,000 mark [e]			
1876	48.44 3m/d (12)			81.26 3m/d (12)
1877	48.45 3m/d (12)			80.23 3m/d (12)
1878	48.48 3m/d (12)			82.14 3m/d (12)
1879	48.52 3m/d (12)			84.05 3m/d (12)
1880	48.47 3m/d (12)			83.37 3m/d (12)
1881	48.36 3m/d (12)			83.80 3m/d (12)
1882	48.35 3m/d (12)			82.60 3m/d (12)

	LONDON on:	
	Hamburg, Frank-furt & Berlin	**Vienna, from 1889** also **Trieste**
	per 1,000 mark [e]	per 1,000 guilders Österreichische Wäh-rung, from 1900 per 1,000 Austrian crowns [d]
	in pounds sterling	
1883	48.42 3m/d (12)	82.39 3m/d (12)
1884	48.49 3m/d (12)	81.12 3m/d (12)
1885	48.53 3m/d (12)	79.31 3m/d (12)
1886	48.65 3m/d (12)	78.38 3m/d (12)
1887	48.63 3m/d (12)	77.99 3m/d (12)
1888	48.65 3m/d (12)	79.16 3m/d (12)
1889	48.50 3m/d (12)	82.40 3m/d (12)
1890	48.44 3m/d (12)	84.64 3m/d (12)
1891	48.60 3m/d (12)	84.57 3m/d (12)
1892	48.71 3m/d (12)	82.90 3m/d (12)
1893	48.53 3m/d (12)	80.02 3m/d (12)
1894	48.69 3m/d (12)	79.27 3m/d (12)
1895	48.59 3m/d (12)	81.03 3m/d (12)
1896	48.53 3m/d (12)	82.07 3m/d (12)
1897	48.61 3m/d (12)	82.51 3m/d (12)
1898	48.43 3m/d (12)	82.11 3m/d (12)
1899	48.31 3m/d (12)	81.74 3m/d (12)
1900	48.21 3m/d (12)	40.70 3m/d (12)
1901	48.46 3m/d (12)	41.13 3m/d (12)
1902	48.50 3m/d (12)	41.23 3m/d (12)
1903	48.45 3m/d (12)	41.26 3m/d (12)
1904	48.49 3m/d (12)	41.28 3m/d (12)
1905	48.46 3m/d (12)	41.21 3m/d (12)
1906	48.27 3m/d (12)	41.05 3m/d (12)
1907	48.09 3m/d (12)	40.90 3m/d (12)
1908	48.41 3m/d (12)	41.14 3m/d (12)
1909	48.48 3m/d (12)	41.19 3m/d (12)
1910	48.31 3m/d (12)	41.03 3m/d (12)
1911	48.35 3m/d (12)	41.04 3m/d (12)
1912	48.24 3m/d (12)	40.86 3m/d (12)
1913	48.17 3m/d (12)	40.75 3m/d (12)
1914	48.38 3m/d (7)	41.06 3m/d (7)

[a] Concerning the Hamburg currency, see pp. 191–193.

[b] Concerning the Frankfurt currency, see pp. 195f.

[c] Concerning the Prussian currency, see p. 197.

[d] Concerning the Austrian currency, see pp. 255f. From June 3rd 1848 the guilder Konventionskurant and from November 1858 the guilder Österreichische Währung were paper money in notes of the Wiener Nationalbank and government notes ('Wiener Banknoten').

[e] Concerning the German currency, see p. 197.

1.1.3 On Spain, Portugal and Brazil

	LONDON on:				
	Cadiz, from 1698 Madrid			Lisbon	
	per 100 pesos de plata antigua ('new money') [a]			per 100 milréis [b]	
	in pounds sterling				
1680	20.52	3m/d	(1)	34.27 25d/s	(1)
1681	20.52	3m/d	(3)	32.57 60d/s	(3)
1682	21.13	3m/d	(3)	32.78 60d/s	(3)
1683	21.31	3m/d	(5)	32.36 60d/s	(5)
1684	20.88	3m/d	(1)	31.29 60d/s	(3)
1685	20.90	3m/d	(3)	31.15 60d/s	(1)
1686	20.73	3m/d	(1)	31.46 60d/s	(1)
1687					
1688					
1689	20.63	3m/d	(1)	31.03 60d/s	(1)
1690					
1691	20.44	3m/d	(2)	30.21 60d/s	(2)
1692	20.11	3m/d	(1)	29.59 60d/s	(1)
1693				31.67 60d/s	(1)
1694	18.08	3m/d	(2)	33.86 60d/s	(2)
1695	19.88	3m/d	(12)	33.32 60d/s	(12)
1696	20.02	3m/d	(12)	31.96 60d/s	(12)
1697	20.19	3m/d	(12)	28.51 60d/s	(12)
1698	21.51	3m/d	(12)	27.83 60d/s	(12)
1699	22.36	3m/d	(12)	29.87 60d/s	(12)
1700	21.92	3m/d	(12)	30.41 60d/s	(12)
1701	21.08	3m/d	(12)	29.20 60d/s	(12)
1702	20.96	3m/d	(5)	29.01 60d/s	(12)
1703	[c]			29.08 60d/s	(12)
1704	[c]			30.23 60d/s	(12)
1705	[c]			28.98 60d/s	(12)
1706	[c]			29.01 60d/s	(12)
1707	[c]			28.14 60d/s	(12)
1708	[c]			25.93 60d/s	(12)
1709	[c]			27.10 60d/s	(12)
1710	[c]			27.64 60d/s	(12)
1711	[c]			25.61 60d/s	(12)
1712	[c]			26.32 60d/s	(11)
1713	20.40	3m/d	(7)	26.56 60d/s	(12)
1714	20.81	3m/d	(12)	27.18 60d/s	(12)

	LONDON on:	
	Madrid	**Lisbon**
	per 100 pesos de plata antigua [a]	per 100 milréis effective [b]
	in pounds sterling	
1715	20.40 3m/d (12)	27.16 60d/s (12)
1716	20.50 3m/d (12)	27.46 60d/s (12)
1717	21.28 3m/d (12)	27.71 60d/s (12)
1718	20.75 3m/d (12)	27.28 60d/s (12)
1719	20.02 3m/d (12)	26.85 60d/s (12)
1720	19.79 3m/d (12)	26.63 60d/s (12)
1721	19.67 3m/d (11)	26.81 60d/s (11)
1722	19.88 3m/d (12)	26.74 60d/s (12)
1723	20.40 3m/d (12)	27.08 60d/s (12)
1724	20.90 3m/d (12)	27.23 60d/s (12)
1725	20.44 3m/d (12)	27.30 60d/s (12)
1726	18.35 3m/d (12)	26.84 60d/s (12)
1727	18.06 3m/d (12)	27.10 60d/s (12)
1728	18.31 3m/d (11)	27.48 60d/s (11)
1729	18.14 3m/d (12)	27.53 60d/s (12)
1730	17.79 3m/d (12)	27.59 60d/s (12)
1731	17.41 3m/d (12)	27.36 60d/s (12)
1732	17.64 3m/d (12)	27.40 60d/s (12)
1733	17.51 3m/d (12)	27.27 60d/s (12)
1734	16.71 3m/d (12)	27.15 60d/s (12)
1735	16.76 3m/d (12)	27.50 60d/s (12)
1736	17.08 3m/d (12)	27.44 60d/s (12)
1737	17.09 3m/d (11)	27.38 60d/s (12)
1738	16.60 3m/d (12)	27.32 60d/s (12)
1739	16.54 3m/d (12)	27.22 60d/s (12)
1740	17.27 3m/d (11)	27.02 60d/s (12)
1741	17.25 3m/d (12)	27.17 60d/s (12)
1742	16.26 3m/d (12)	27.28 60d/s (12)
1743	16.91 3m/d (10)	27.55 60d/s (10)
1744	17.41 3m/d (12)	27.09 60d/s (12)
1745	16.70 3m/d (9)	26.92 60d/s (12)
1746	15.82 3m/d (9)	26.80 60d/s (10)
1747	16.72 3m/d (12)	27.15 60d/s (12)
1748	16.41 3m/d (8)	27.00 60d/s (12)
1749	16.34 3m/d (12)	27.32 60d/s (12)
1750	16.35 3m/d (12)	27.38 60d/s (12)
1751	16.39 3m/d (12)	27.35 60d/s (12)
1752	16.70 3m/d (12)	27.49 60d/s (12)

	LONDON on:	
	Madrid	**Lisbon**
	per 100 pesos de plata antigua [a]	per 100 milréis effective [b]
	in pounds sterling	
1753	16.79 3m/d (12)	27.53 60d/s (12)
1754	16.48 3m/d (12)	27.37 60d/s (12)
1755	16.19 3m/d (12)	27.12 60d/s (11)
1756	15.80 3m/d (12)	26.97 60d/s (12)
1757	15.95 3m/d (12)	26.91 60d/s (12)
1758	16.46 3m/d (12)	27.23 60d/s (12)
1759	16.48 3m/d (12)	27.33 60d/s (12)
1760	16.31 3m/d (12)	27.41 60d/s (12)
1761	16.50 3m/d (12)	27.44 60d/s (12)
1762	16.55 3m/d (9)	27.70 60d/s (9)
1763	16.49 3m/d (12)	27.78 60d/s (12)
1764	15.94 3m/d (12)	27.27 60d/s (12)
1765	16.36 3m/d (12)	27.47 60d/s (12)
1766	16.65 3m/d (12)	27.72 60d/s (12)
1767	16.57 3m/d (12)	27.83 60d/s (12)
1768	16.40 3m/d (12)	27.75 60d/s (12)
1769	16.51 3m/d (12)	27.90 60d/s (12)
1770	16.52 3m/d (12)	27.84 60d/s (12)
1771	16.57 3m/d (12)	28.04 60d/s (12)
1772	16.49 3m/d (12)	27.92 60d/s (12)
1773	15.76 3m/d (12)	27.35 60d/s (12)
1774	15.68 3m/d (12)	27.35 60d/s (12)
1775	16.02 3m/d (12)	27.15 60d/s (12)
1776	16.06 3m/d (12)	27.29 60d/s (12)
1777	16.32 3m/d (12)	27.28 60d/s (12)
1778	15.63 3m/d (12)	26.78 60d/s (12)
1779	15.12 3m/d (12)	26.00 60d/s (12)
1780	15.51 3m/d (12)	26.58 60d/s (12)
1781	15.06 3m/d (11)	27.51 60d/s (11)
1782	15.69 3m/d (12)	28.16 60d/s (12)
1783	14.79 3m/d (12)	28.40 60d/s (12)
1784	14.62 3m/d (12)	27.44 60d/s (12)
1785	14.34 3m/d (12)	26.54 60d/s (12)
1786	14.66 3m/d (12)	27.56 60d/s (12)
1787	15.07 3m/d (12)	27.56 60d/s (12)
1788	14.84 3m/d (12)	27.29 60d/s (12)
1789	14.59 3m/d (12)	27.41 60d/s (12)
1790	14.48 3m/d (12)	27.64 60d/s (12)

	LONDON on:			
	Madrid [d]	**Lisbon**	**Rio de Janeiro**	**Bahia**
	per 100 pesos de plata antigua [a]	per 100 milréis effective [b]	per 100 Brazilian milréis in notes [e]	
		in pounds sterling		
1791	14.92 3m/d (12)	28.07 60d/s (12)		
1792	15.43 3m/d (12)	29.71 60d/s (12)		
1793	14.25 3m/d (12)	28.22 60d/s (12)		
1794	12.67 3m/d (12)	26.83 60d/s (12)		
1795	12.27 3m/d (12)	28.28 60d/s (12)		
1796	12.05 3m/d (12)	29.13 60d/s (12)		
1797	10.42 3m/d (1)	28.50 60d/s (12)		
1798		27.57 60d/s (12)		
1799		28.28 60d/s (12)		
1800		25.82 60d/s (12)		
1801	16.36 3m/d (2)	25.87 60d/s (12)		
1802	15.60 3m/d (12)	28.25 60d/s (12)		
1803	15.14 3m/d (12)	26.67 60d/s (12)		
1804	14.52 3m/d (12)	25.46 60d/s (12)		
1805	13.74 3m/d (12)	25.33 60d/s (12)		
1806	14.92 3m/d (12)	25.39 60d/s (12)		
1807	16.24 3m/d (12)	26.24 60d/s (12)		
1808	17.40 3m/d (12)	25.87 60d/s (12)		
1809	17.98 3m/d (11)	27.23 60d/s (12)	28.71 60d/s (10)	
1810	18.34 3m/d (8)	27.61 60d/s (12)	30.07 60d/s (12)	
1811	*19.16* 3m/d (12)	28.15 60d/s (12)	28.79 60d/s (12)	
1812	*17.99* 3m/d (12)	28.67 60d/s (12)	28.91 60d/s (12)	
1813	21.46 3m/d (1)	31.74 60d/s (12)	31.77 60d/s (12)	
1814	19.26 3m/d (12)	28.88 60d/s (12)	32.31 60d/s (12)	
1815	16.83 3m/d (12)	27.78 60d/s (12)	29.51 60d/s (12)	
1816	14.45 3m/d (12)	23.73 60d/s (12)	25.38 60d/s (12)	
1817	14.74 3m/d (7)	23.81 60d/s (7)	24.38 60d/s (7)	
1818	16.88 3m/d (1)	24.45 60d/s (12)	27.76 60d/s (12)	
1819	15.64 3m/d (12)	23.03 60d/s (12)	25.24 60d/s (12)	
1820	14.48 3m/d (12)	21.02 60d/s (12)	22.90 60d/s (12)	24.11 60d/s (11)
1821	15.00 3m/d (12)	20.70 60d/s (12)	20.26 60d/s (12)	23.58 60d/s (12)
1822	15.27 3m/d (12)	21.42 60d/s (12)	18.99 60d/s (12)	21.25 60d/s (12)
1823	15.57 3m/d (12)	21.64 60d/s (12)	19.41 60d/s (12)	19.90 60d/s (12)
1824	15.18 3m/d (12)	21.24 60d/s (12)	20.06 60d/s (12)	20.78 60d/s (12)
1825	15.24 3m/d (12)	21.31 60d/s (12)	20.04 60d/s (12)	21.22 60d/s (12)
1826	14.64 3m/d (12)	20.81 60d/s (12)	18.25 60d/s (12)	19.15 60d/s (12)
1827	14.28 3m/d (12)	20.48 60d/s (12)	15.08 60d/s (11)	17.57 60d/s (12)
1828	14.98 3m/d (12)	19.21 60d/s (12)	13.06 60d/s (12)	14.58 60d/s (12)

	LONDON on:			
	Madrid	**Lisbon**	**Rio de Janeiro**	**Bahia**
	per 100 pesos de plata antigua, from 1847 (5) per 100 pesos duros [a]	per 100 milréis effective [b]	per 100 Brazilian milréis in notes [e]	
	in pounds sterling			
1829	15.20 3m/d (12)	18.83 60d/s (12)	10.64 60d/s (11)	12.90 60d/s (12)
1830	14.99 3m/d (12)	18.42 60d/s (12)	9.06 60d/s (12)	11.08 60d/s (12)
1831	15.40 3m/d (12)	19.41 60d/s (12)	8.35 60d/s (12)	10.87 60d/s (11)
1832	14.97 3m/d (12)	19.78 60d/s (12)	13.37 60d/s (12)	12.82 60d/s (11)
1833	15.47 3m/d (9)	19.91 60d/s (9)	15.48 60d/s (12)	13.15 60d/s (9)
1834	15.55 3m/d (10)	22.21 60d/s (12)		
1835	15.56 3m/d (12)	23.83 60d/s (11)	16.56 60d/s (10)	
1836	15.40 3m/d (12)	23.26 60d/s (12)	15.33 60d/s (5)	
1837	14.47 3m/d (12)	21.88 60d/s (12)	21.04 60d/s (2)	
1838	15.16 3m/d (12)	22.38 60d/s (12)	11.77 60d/s (1)	
1839	15.52 3m/d (12)	22.68 60d/s (12)	11.82 60d/s (4)	
1840	15.43 3m/d (11)	22.48 60d/s (11)	11.74 60d/s (12)	11.16 60d/s (12)
1841	15.13 3m/d (12)	21.84 60d/s (12)	11.82 60d/s (12)	10.97 60d/s (12)
1842	15.28 3m/d (12)	21.94 60d/s (12)	10.73 60d/s (12)	10.66 60d/s (12)
1843	15.43 3m/d (12)	22.10 60d/s (12)	10.37 60d/s (12)	10.14 60d/s (12)
1844	15.47 3m/d (12)	22.72 60d/s (12)	10.37 60d/s (12)	9.58 60d/s (9)
1845	15.33 3m/d (12)	22.28 60d/s (12)	9.98 60d/s (5)	
1846	15.08 3m/d (12)	22.05 60d/s (12)	10.44 60d/s (2)	
1847	15.07/19.61 3m/d (4+8)	22.05 60d/s (12)	10.52 60d/s (1)	
1848	19.25 3m/d (11)	21.53 60d/s (12)	9.92 60d/s (8)	
1849	20.51 3m/d (12)	22.03 60d/s (12)	10.86 60d/s (5)	
1850	20.62 3m/d (12)	22.23 60d/s (12)	11.30 60d/s (4)	
1851	20.75 3m/d (12)	22.18 3m/d (12)	11.98 60d/s (1)	
1852	20.72 3m/d (12)	21.91 3m/d (12)	11.15 60d/s (1)	
1853	20.87 3m/d (12)	22.17 3m/d (12)	11.30 60d/s (2)	
1854	20.80 3m/d (12)	22.09 3m/d (12)		
1855	20.77 3m/d (12)	22.14 3m/d (12)		
1856	20.59 3m/d (12)	21.98 3m/d (12)		
1857	20.33 3m/d (12)	21.68 3m/d (12)		
1858	20.36 3m/d (12)	21.60 3m/d (12)		
1859	20.62 3m/d (12)	21.70 3m/d (12)		
1860	20.64 3m/d (12)	21.96 3m/d (11)		
1861	20.23 3m/d (12)	21.88 3m/d (12)		
1862	20.45 3m/d (12)	21.89 3m/d (12)		
1863	20.39 3m/d (12)	21.98 3m/d (12)		
1864	19.86 3m/d (12)	21.59 3m/d (12)		
1865	19.74 3m/d (12)	21.46 3m/d (12)		

	LONDON on:	
	Madrid, from 1888 also **Barcelona** [f]	**Lisbon, 1884–1891** also **Oporto** [g]
	per 100 pesos duros, from 1898 (12) per 1,000 pesetas [a]	per 100 milréis effective [b]
	in pounds sterling	
1866	19.35 3m/d (11)	21.45 3m/d (10)
1867	20.23 3m/d (12)	21.63 3m/d (12)
1868	20.15 3m/d (12)	21.56 3m/d (12)
1869	20.16 3m/d (12)	21.67 3m/d (12)
1870	20.29 3m/d (12)	21.68 3m/d (12)
1871	20.35 3m/d (12)	22.01 30d/s (12)
1872	19.91 3m/d (12)	21.94 3m/d (12)
1873	19.79 3m/d (12)	22.00 3m/d (12)
1874	19.88 3m/d (12)	21.98 3m/d (12)
1875	19.70 3m/d (12)	21.91 3m/d (12)
1876	19.71 3m/d (12)	21.73 3m/d (12)
1877	19.52 3m/d (12)	21.64 3m/d (12)
1878	19.62 3m/d (12)	21.60 3m/d (12)
1879	19.49 3m/d (12)	21.68 3m/d (12)
1880	19.77 3m/d (12)	21.93 3m/d (12)
1881	19.66 3m/d (12)	21.73 3m/d (12)
1882	19.20 3m/d (12)	21.49 3m/d (12)
1883	19.25 3m/d (12)	21.63 3m/d (12)
1884	19.34 3m/d (12)	21.67 3m/d (12)
1885	19.15 3m/d (12)	21.59 3m/d (12)
1886	19.16 3m/d (12)	21.87 3m/d (12)
1887	19.32 3m/d (12)	21.95 3m/d (12)
1888	19.24 3m/d (12)	21.95 3m/d (12)
1889	19.02 3m/d (12)	21.96 3m/d (12)
1890	18.74 3m/d (12)	21.79 3m/d (12)
1891	18.42 3m/d (12)	19.68 3m/d (12)
1892	17.02 3m/d (12)	16.85 3m/d (12)
1893	16.45 3m/d (12)	17.43 3m/d (12)
1894	16.36 3m/d (12)	16.96 3m/d (12)
1895	17.14 3m/d (12)	17.26 3m/d (12)
1896	16.26 3m/d (12)	16.82 3m/d (12)
1897	15.20 3m/d (11)	14.90 3m/d (12)
1898	12.58/29.42 3m/d (11+1)	13.65 3m/d (12)
1899	26.48 3m/d (12)	15.21 3m/d (12)
1900	27.45 3m/d (12)	15.37 3m/d (12)
1901	29.37 3m/d (12)	15.47 3m/d (12)

	LONDON on:	
	Madrid & Barcelona [f]	**Lisbon**
	per 1,000 pesetas [a]	per 100 milréis effective [b]
	in pounds sterling	
1902	28.86 3m/d (12)	17.01 3m/d (12)
1903	28.75 3m/d (12)	17.51 3m/d (12)
1904	29.37 3m/d (12)	17.99 3m/d (12)
1905	27.93 3m/d (12)	20.33 3m/d (12)
1906	24.37 3m/d (12)	21.27 3m/d (12)
1907	23.76 3m/d (12)	21.07 3m/d (12)
1908	24.05 3m/d (12)	19.08 3m/d (12)
1909	23.47 3m/d (12)	18.96 3m/d (12)
1910	23.06 3m/d (12)	20.23 3m/d (12)
1911	23.14 3m/d (12)	20.22 3m/d (12)
1912	22.79 3m/d (12)	19.84 3m/d (12)
1913	22.99 3m/d (12)	18.80 3m/d (12)
1914	22.52 3m/d (7)	18.64 3m/d (7)

[a]   Concerning the Spanish currency, see p. 307. Until around the end of the 17th century the exchange quotations on Madrid were partly done for 'new money', partly for 'old money', 1 ducado 'old money' corresponding to 1¼ ducado 'new money' (cf. HERBACH [1716], p. 136). All documented rates are given in 'new money'; rates for 'old money' have been converted.

[b]   In the Portuguese currency system one reckoned in réis and in milréis (= 1,000 réis) respectively, but up to the 19th century the exchange rate quotations of and on Portuguese places were often effected in or for crusados (velhos or do cambio) as a unit of account of 400 réis. Therefore, the addendum 'effective' means 'payable in hard currency', i.e. in full-weighted silver or gold coins. The Portuguese silver standard with the milréis at 27.15 grammes of pure silver, which existed since July 1st 1835 according to the Coin Act of April 24th 1835, was succeeded by the gold standard – following the model of Great Britain – with the milréis at 1.6257 grammes of pure gold since the Coin Act of July 29th 1854. Portugal had the paper standard from July 1891 with a premium for gold coins up to 53% (in May 1897). The milréis was succeeded by the escudo of 100 centavos (1 escudo = 1 milréis) in 1912. It had to be officially reckoned in this new currency from the beginning of 1913, but for all commercial transactions the term 'milréis' continued to be usual (cf. NELKENBRECHER [1775], p. 131; NOBACK [1877], p. 507; SWOBODA [1913], pp. 518f.).

[c]   Because of the War of Spanish Succession (1701–1713/14) no quotation between June 1702 and May 1713 (Treaty of Utrecht, April 11th 1713).

[d]   1811/12: quotation on Cadiz.

[e]   Concerning the Brazilian currency, see pp. 437f.

[f]   The quotations of London on Barcelona have been equal to those on Madrid since 1888. Bills on Spanish places had expressly to be payable in silver, otherwise they would not have been accepted in London (NOBACK [1877], p. 523; SWOBODA [1889], pp. 575f.). This position persisted until the end of the 19th century (SWOBODA [1902], p. 363).

[g]   The quotations of London on Oporto were equal to those on Lisbon between 1884 and May 1891. Bills on Portuguese places had expressly to be payable in gold, otherwise they would not have been accepted in London (NOBACK [1877], p. 523; SWOBODA [1889], pp. 575f.). This position persisted until the end of the 19th century (SWOBODA [1902], p. 363).

1.1.4 On Italy

	LONDON on:		
	Venice	**Genoa**	**Leghorn**
	per 100 ducati di banco [a]	per 100 pezze of 5¾ lire fuori banco [b]	per 100 pezze da otto reali [c]
	in pounds sterling		
1667	22.08 3m/d (1)		22.50 3m/d (1)
1668	22.08 3m/d (1)		22.50 3m/d (1)
1669			
1670			
1671	20.99 3m/d (1)		21.77 3m/d (1)
1672	20.52 3m/d (1)		21.04 3m/d (1)
1673	21.25 3m/d (1)		21.67 3m/d (1)
1674	21.56 3m/d (1)		22.08 3m/d (1)
1675	22.60 3m/d (1)		23.02 3m/d (1)
1676			
1677			
1678			
1679	21.09 3m/d (1)		21.56 3m/d (1)
1680	21.20 3m/d (2)		22.08 3m/d (2)
1681	21.15 3m/d (1)		22.08 3m/d (1)
1682	21.28 3m/d (2)		22.17 3m/d (2)
1683	21.46 3m/d (1)		22.19 3m/d (1)
1684	20.94 3m/d (1)		22.24 3m/d (1)
1685	20.73 3m/d (1)		21.98 3m/d (1)
1686	19.95 3m/d (1)		21.56 3m/d (1)
1687			
1688			
1689			
1690			
1691			
1692			
1693			
1694			
1695			
1696			
1697			
1698	20.12 3m/d (12)	21.61 3m/d (12)	22.02 3m/d (12)
1699	20.92 3m/d (12)	22.89 3m/d (12)	23.09 3m/d (12)
1700	20.19 3m/d (12)	22.29 3m/d (12)	22.45 3m/d (12)
1701	20.33 3m/d (12)	21.95 3m/d (12)	22.07 3m/d (12)
1702	21.24 3m/d (12)	23.35 3m/d (12)	23.44 3m/d (12)

	LONDON on:		
	Venice	**Genoa**	**Leghorn**
	per 100 ducati di banco [a]	per 100 pezze of 5¾ lire fuori banco [b]	per 100 pezze da otto reali [c]
	in pounds sterling		
1703	20.57 3m/d (12)	22.71 3m/d (12)	22.82 3m/d (12)
1704	21.60 3m/d (12)	23.74 3m/d (12)	23.59 3m/d (12)
1705	21.46 3m/d (12)	23.67 3m/d (12)	23.53 3m/d (12)
1706	21.93 3m/d (12)	23.84 3m/d (12)	23.73 3m/d (12)
1707	21.20 3m/d (12)	23.41 3m/d (12)	23.33 3m/d (12)
1708	21.54 3m/d (12)	23.84 3m/d (12)	23.73 3m/d (12)
1709	21.82 3m/d (12)	23.88 3m/d (12)	23.80 3m/d (12)
1710	21.44 3m/d (12)	23.59 3m/d (12)	23.52 3m/d (12)
1711	21.11 3m/d (12)	23.30 3m/d (12)	22.91 3m/d (12)
1712	21.11 3m/d (11)	23.34 3m/d (11)	23.21 3m/d (11)
1713	20.06 3m/d (12)	21.97 3m/d (12)	21.82 3m/d (12)
1714	19.78 3m/d (12)	21.83 3m/d (12)	21.68 3m/d (12)
1715	18.96 3m/d (12)	21.61 3m/d (12)	21.59 3m/d (12)
1716	18.12 3m/d (12)	21.93 3m/d (12)	21.74 3m/d (12)
1717	17.76 3m/d (12)	22.84 3m/d (12)	22.60 3m/d (12)
1718	17.81 3m/d (12)	22.66 3m/d (12)	22.41 3m/d (12)
1719	18.44 3m/d (12)	22.32 3m/d (12)	21.88 3m/d (12)
1720	18.64 3m/d (12)	22.10 3m/d (12)	21.38 3m/d (12)
1721	18.66 3m/d (11)	22.25 3m/d (11)	21.75 3m/d (11)
1722	18.50 3m/d (12)	21.74 3m/d (12)	21.29 3m/d (12)
1723	18.67 3m/d (12)	22.10 3m/d (12)	21.33 3m/d (12)
1724	19.34 3m/d (12)	22.71 3m/d (12)	21.89 3m/d (12)
1725	19.38 3m/d (12)	22.49 3m/d (12)	21.56 3m/d (12)
1726	18.80 3m/d (12)	21.83 3m/d (12)	20.82 3m/d (12)
1727	18.92 3m/d (12)	22.27 3m/d (12)	20.92 3m/d (12)
1728	19.49 3m/d (11)	22.85 3m/d (11)	21.45 3m/d (11)
1729	19.50 3m/d (12)	22.78 3m/d (12)	21.44 3m/d (12)
1730	19.56 3m/d (12)	22.70 3m/d (12)	21.44 3m/d (12)
1731	19.35 3m/d (12)	22.30 3m/d (12)	21.05 3m/d (12)
1732	19.47 3m/d (12)	22.32 3m/d (12)	21.05 3m/d (12)
1733	19.60 3m/d (12)	22.52 3m/d (12)	21.02 3m/d (12)
1734	19.74 3m/d (12)	21.84 3m/d (12)	20.83 3m/d (12)
1735	20.64 3m/d (12)	22.20 3m/d (12)	21.36 3m/d (12)
1736	20.28 3m/d (12)	21.86 3m/d (12)	20.86 3m/d (12)
1737	20.16 3m/d (12)	21.99 3m/d (12)	20.75 3m/d (12)
1738	20.15 3m/d (12)	21.88 3m/d (12)	20.68 3m/d (12)
1739	20.13 3m/d (12)	21.78 3m/d (12)	20.58 3m/d (12)
1740	20.31 3m/d (12)	22.37 3m/d (12)	20.86 3m/d (12)

	LONDON on:		
	Venice	**Genoa**	**Leghorn**
	per 100 ducati di banco [a]	per 100 pezze of 5¾ lire fuori banco [b]	per 100 pezze da otto reali [c]
	in pounds sterling		
1741	20.45 3m/d (12)	22.53 3m/d (12)	20.89 3m/d (12)
1742	20.36 3m/d (12)	22.34 3m/d (12)	20.79 3m/d (12)
1743	20.70 3m/d (10)	22.69 3m/d (10)	21.22 3m/d (10)
1744	20.67 3m/d (12)	22.82 3m/d (12)	21.23 3m/d (12)
1745	20.23 3m/d (11)	22.11 3m/d (11)	20.76 3m/d (12)
1746	19.52 3m/d (10)	21.10 3m/d (8)	20.11 3m/d (10)
1747	20.27 3m/d (12)		20.65 3m/d (12)
1748	20.23 3m/d (12)		20.63 3m/d (12)
1749	20.24 3m/d (12)		20.61 3m/d (12)
1750	21.14 3m/d (12)		20.35 3m/d (12)
1751	20.91 3m/d (12)	20.01 3m/d (11)	20.14 3m/d (12)
1752	21.69 3m/d (12)	20.88 3m/d (12)	21.09 3m/d (11)
1753	21.48 3m/d (12)	20.61 3m/d (8)	20.91 3m/d (12)
1754	21.00 3m/d (12)	19.86 3m/d (12)	20.22 3m/d (12)
1755	20.67 3m/d (12)	19.66 3m/d (11)	19.81 3m/d (12)
1756	20.32 3m/d (12)	19.33 3m/d (12)	19.56 3m/d (12)
1757	20.56 3m/d (11)	19.57 3m/d (12)	19.90 3m/d (12)
1758	21.31 3m/d (12)	20.23 3m/d (12)	20.63 3m/d (12)
1759	21.03 3m/d (12)	20.07 3m/d (12)	20.48 3m/d (12)
1760	20.99 3m/d (12)	20.01 3m/d (12)	20.35 3m/d (12)
1761	21.80 3m/d (12)	20.87 3m/d (12)	21.20 3m/d (12)
1762	21.23 3m/d (9)	20.44 3m/d (9)	20.77 3m/d (9)
1763	21.94 3m/d (12)	21.00 3m/d (12)	21.33 3m/d (12)
1764	20.91 3m/d (12)	19.77 3m/d (12)	20.12 3m/d (12)
1765	21.27 3m/d (12)	20.33 3m/d (12)	20.79 3m/d (12)
1766	21.52 3m/d (12)	20.49 3m/d (12)	20.93 3m/d (12)
1767	21.10 3m/d (12)	20.30 3m/d (12)	20.61 3m/d (12)
1768	21.17 3m/d (12)	20.27 3m/d (12)	20.71 3m/d (12)
1769	21.53 3m/d (12)	20.61 3m/d (12)	21.06 3m/d (12)
1770	21.57 3m/d (12)	20.61 3m/d (12)	21.05 3m/d (12)
1771	21.60 3m/d (12)	20.60 3m/d (12)	21.03 3m/d (12)
1772	21.59 3m/d (12)	20.45 3m/d (12)	20.88 3m/d (12)
1773	20.37 3m/d (12)	19.49 3m/d (12)	19.91 3m/d (12)
1774	20.54 3m/d (12)	19.49 3m/d (12)	19.88 3m/d (12)
1775	20.90 3m/d (12)	19.97 3m/d (12)	20.32 3m/d (12)
1776	21.18 3m/d (12)	20.28 3m/d (12)	20.68 3m/d (12)
1777	19.38 3m/d (12)	20.40 3m/d (12)	20.88 3m/d (12)
1778	20.24 3m/d (12)	19.52 3m/d (12)	19.98 3m/d (12)

	LONDON on:			
	Venice	**Genoa**	**Leghorn**	**Naples**
	per 100 ducati di banco, from 1815 per 1,000 lire italiane [a]	per 100 pezze of 5¾ lire fuori banco [b]	per 100 pezze da otto reali [c]	per 100 ducati del regno [d]
	in pounds sterling			
1779	20.72 3m/d (12)	18.81 3m/d (12)	19.52 3m/d (12)	
1780	20.43 3m/d (12)	19.15 3m/d (12)	20.03 3m/d (12)	
1781	19.84 3m/d (11)	19.66 3m/d (11)	20.60 3m/d (11)	
1782	18.90 3m/d (12)	20.27 3m/d (12)	21.26 3m/d (12)	
1783	19.17 3m/d (12)	19.94 3m/d (12)	21.08 3m/d (12)	
1784	20.00 3m/d (12)	19.14 3m/d (12)	20.43 3m/d (12)	
1785	20.73 3m/d (12)	18.64 3m/d (12)	19.61 3m/d (12)	
1786	20.03 3m/d (12)	19.06 3m/d (12)	20.34 3m/d (12)	
1787	20.24 3m/d (12)	19.08 3m/d (12)	20.30 3m/d (12)	
1788	20.73 3m/d (12)	18.83 3m/d (12)	19.86 3m/d (12)	
1789	21.04 3m/d (12)	18.48 3m/d (12)	19.88 3m/d (1)	
1790	21.01 3m/d (12)	18.37 3m/d (12)	19.87 3m/d (12)	
1791	21.07 3m/d (12)	18.39 3m/d (12)	19.87 3m/d (12)	
1792	20.14 3m/d (12)	19.31 3m/d (12)	20.86 3m/d (12)	
1793	21.86 3m/d (12)	18.08 3m/d (12)	19.45 3m/d (12)	
1794	21.49 3m/d (12)	17.92 3m/d (12)	19.44 3m/d (12)	
1795	20.11 3m/d (12)	19.19 3m/d (12)	21.06 3m/d (12)	
1796	19.80 3m/d (12)	19.40 3m/d (12)	21.44 3m/d (7)	15.32 3m/d (4)
1797	22.39 3m/d (12)	17.60 3m/d (12)	19.00 3m/d (6)	14.61 3m/d (12)
1798	24.64 3m/d (12)	17.56 3m/d (12)	19.09 3m/d (12)	12.88 3m/d (12)
1799	23.97 3m/d (12)	18.37 3m/d (12)	20.18 3m/d (12)	11.25 3m/d (1)
1800	21.16 3m/d (12)	19.08 3m/d (12)	21.62 3m/d (12)	15.92 3m/d (12)
1801	23.16 3m/d (12)	19.95 3m/d (12)	22.41 3m/d (12)	17.02 3m/d (12)
1802	20.23 3m/d (12)	19.83 3m/d (12)	21.55 3m/d (12)	18.38 3m/d (12)
1803	18.02 3m/d (12)	19.14 3m/d (12)	20.76 3m/d (12)	16.96 3m/d (5)
1804	17.03 3m/d (12)	18.85 3m/d (12)	20.48 3m/d (12)	15.77 3m/d (12)
1805	16.81 3m/d (12)	19.10 3m/d (12)	21.07 3m/d (12)	16.93 3m/d (12)
1806	16.75 3m/d (12)	19.46 3m/d (12)	21.37 3m/d (12)	18.37 3m/d (12)
1807	19.23 3m/d (12)	19.45 3m/d (12)	20.75 3m/d (12)	17.37 3m/d (12)
1808	19.23 3m/d (12)	19.26 3m/d (12)	20.89/23.75 3m/d (11+1)	17.50 3m/d (12)
1809	19.23 3m/d (12)	21.25 3m/d (12)	24.17 3m/d (12)	17.50 3m/d (12)
1810	19.23 3m/d (12)	22.87 3m/d (12)	24.66 3m/d (2)	17.50 3m/d (12)
1811	19.23 3m/d (12)	22.50 3m/d (12)	24.17 3m/d (12)	17.50 3m/d (12)
1812	19.23 3m/d (12)	22.50 3m/d (12)	23.99 3m/d (12)	17.50 3m/d (12)
1813	19.23 3m/d (12)	22.50 3m/d (12)	25.07 3m/d (12)	17.50 3m/d (12)
1814	19.23 3m/d (6)	21.25 3m/d (12)	24.39 3m/d (12)	18.39 3m/d (12)
1815	40.00 3m/d (2)	21.05 3m/d (12)	22.33 3m/d (12)	18.68 3m/d (12)

	LONDON on:			
	Venice	**Genoa**	**Leghorn**	**Naples**
	per 1,000 lire italiane [a]	per 100 pezze of 5¾ lire fuori banco, from 1827 (4) per 1,000 Piedmontese lire nuove [b]	per 100 pezze da otto reali, from 1837 (8) per 1,000 Tuscan lire moneta buona [c]	per 100 ducati del regno [c]
	in pounds sterling			
1816	38.38 3m/d (12)	18.61 3m/d (12)	19.72 3m/d (12)	17.14 3m/d (12)
1817	37.04 3m/d (7)	18.49 3m/d (7)	19.73 3m/d (7)	16.39 3m/d (7)
1818	40.17 3m/d (12)	19.68 3m/d (12)	21.35 3m/d (12)	18.15 3m/d (12)
1819	38.64 3m/d (12)	19.09 3m/d (12)	20.89 3m/d (12)	16.91 3m/d (12)
1820	36.34 3m/d (12)	17.78 3m/d (12)	19.50 3m/d (12)	16.13 3m/d (12)
1821	36.30 3m/d (12)	18.25 3m/d (12)	19.57 3m/d (12)	16.35 3m/d (12)
1822	36.35 3m/d (12)	18.20 3m/d (12)	19.72 3m/d (12)	16.56 3m/d (12)
1823	35.90 3m/d (12)	17.97 3m/d (12)	19.34 3m/d (12)	16.14 3m/d (12)
1824	37.01 3m/d (12)	18.29 3m/d (12)	19.65 3m/d (12)	15.97 3m/d (12)
1825	37.04 3m/d (12)	18.75 3m/d (12)	20.63 3m/d (12)	16.85 3m/d (12)
1826	38.98 3m/d (3)	18.00 3m/d (12)	19.76 3m/d (12)	16.05 3m/d (12)
1827		18.12/38.88 3m/d (3+9)	19.87 3m/d (12)	15.95 3m/d (12)
1828		39.29 3m/d (12)	20.12 3m/d (12)	16.40 3m/d (12)
1829		38.93 3m/d (12)	19.85 3m/d (12)	16.52 3m/d (12)
1830		38.63 3m/d (12)	19.89 3m/d (12)	16.49 3m/d (12)
1831		39.13 3m/d (12)	19.96 3m/d (12)	16.38 3m/d (12)
1832		38.53 3m/d (12)	19.79 3m/d (12)	16.73 3m/d (12)
1833		38.22 3m/d (9)	19.62 3m/d (9)	16.53 3m/d (9)
1834		39.03 3m/d (12)	20.23 3m/d (12)	17.01 3m/d (12)
1835		38.75 3m/d (12)	19.92 3m/d (12)	16.90 3m/d (12)
1836		38.77 3m/d (12)	20.07 3m/d (12)	16.91 3m/d (12)
1837		38.00 3m/d (11)	19.79/32.05 3m/d (7+5)	16.45 3m/d (12)
1838		38.35 3m/d (12)	31.87 3m/d (12)	16.37 3m/d (12)
1839		38.96 3m/d (12)	32.97 3m/d (12)	16.86 3m/d (12)
1840		38.99 3m/d (11)	32.92 3m/d (11)	17.11 3m/d (11)
1841		38.92 3m/d (12)	32.69 3m/d (12)	16.63 3m/d (12)
1842		38.70 3m/d (12)	33.05 3m/d (12)	16.86 3m/d (12)
1843		38.51 3m/d (12)	32.58 3m/d (12)	16.63 3m/d (12)
1844		38.75 3m/d (12)	32.81 3m/d (12)	16.47 3m/d (12)
1845		38.27 3m/d (12)	32.61 3m/d (12)	16.70 3m/d (12)
1846		38.10 3m/d (12)	32.76 3m/d (12)	16.67 3m/d (12)
1847		38.36 3m/d (12)	32.62 3m/d (12)	16.82 3m/d (12)
1848		38.26 3m/d (11)	31.62 3m/d (11)	15.86 3m/d (11)
1849		37.83 3m/d (12)	31.67 3m/d (12)	16.80 3m/d (12)
1850		38.40 3m/d (12)	32.57 3m/d (12)	16.99 3m/d (12)
1851		39.25 3m/d (12)	32.71 3m/d (12)	17.10 3m/d (12)

	LONDON on:		
	Genoa	**Leghorn**	**Naples**
	per 1,000 Piedmontese lire nuove, from 1861 (8) per 1,000 Italian lire [b]	per 1,000 Tuscan lire moneta buona, from 1860 (9) per 1,000 Piedmontese lire nuove, from 1861 (8) per 1,000 Italian lire [c]	per 100 ducati del regno, from 1863 (2) per 1,000 Italian lire [d]
	in pounds sterling		
1852	39.06 3m/d (12)	32.57 3m/d (12)	17.02 3m/d (12)
1853	39.38 3m/d (12)	33.32 3m/d (12)	17.37 3m/d (12)
1854	39.28 3m/d (12)	32.82 3m/d (12)	17.77 3m/d (12)
1855	39.15 3m/d (12)	33.10 3m/d (12)	18.30 3m/d (12)
1856	38.75 3m/d (12)	33.40 3m/d (12)	18.28 3m/d (12)
1857	38.76 3m/d (12)	33.57 3m/d (12)	17.73 3m/d (12)
1858	39.13 3m/d (12)	33.52 3m/d (12)	17.15 3m/d (12)
1859	39.14 3m/d (12)	33.19 3m/d (12)	16.85 3m/d (12)
1860	39.31 3m/d (12)	32.93/39.08 3m/d (8+4)	16.68 3m/d (12)
1861	38.82 3m/d (12)	38.71 3m/d (12)	16.45 3m/d (12)
1862	39.12 3m/d (12)	39.11 3m/d (12)	16.61 3m/d (12)
1863	39.02 3m/d (12)	39.03 3m/d (12)	16.59/39.00 3m/d (1+11)
1864	38.74 3m/d (12)	38.75 3m/d (12)	38.72 3m/d (12)
1865	39.06 3m/d (12)	39.06 3m/d (12)	39.05 3m/d (12)
1866	37.46 3m/d (11)	37.39 3m/d (12)	37.38 3m/d (12)
1867	36.51 3m/d (12)	36.52 3m/d (12)	36.52 3m/d (12)
	Genoa & Naples [e]		
	per 1,000 Italian lire [f]		
1868	35.66 3m/d (12)		
1869	37.54 3m/d (12)		
1870	37.37 3m/d (12)		
1871	36.95 3m/d (12)		
1872	35.96 3m/d (12)		
1873	34.12 3m/d (12)		
1874	34.84 3m/d (12)		
1875	36.20 3m/d (12)		
1876	36.13 3m/d (12)		
1877	36.06 3m/d (12)		
1878	35.92 3m/d (12)		
1879	35.40 3m/d (12)		
1880	35.49 3m/d (6)		
1881	38.47 3m/d (8)		
1882	38.17 3m/d (12)		
1883	39.10 3m/d (12)		
1884	39.22 3m/d (12)		

	LONDON on:				LONDON on:		
	Genoa & Naples				**Genoa & Naples**		
	per 1,000 Italian lire [e]				per 1,000 Italian lire [e]		
	in pounds sterling				**in pounds sterling**		
1885	39.77	3m/d	(12)	1900	36.78	3m/d	(12)
1886	39.11	3m/d	(12)	1901	37.46	3m/d	(12)
1887	38.68	3m/d	(12)	1902	38.73	3m/d	(12)
1888	38.63	3m/d	(12)	1903	39.23	3m/d	(12)
1889	38.75	3m/d	(12)	1904	39.20	3m/d	(12)
1890	38.62	3m/d	(12)	1905	39.32	3m/d	(12)
1891	38.48	3m/d	(12)	1906	39.23	3m/d	(12)
1892	38.08	3m/d	(12)	1907	39.12	3m/d	(12)
1893	36.50	3m/d	(12)	1908	39.32	3m/d	(12)
1894	35.32	3m/d	(12)	1909	39.16	3m/d	(12)
1895	37.20	3m/d	(12)	1910	38.90	3m/d	(12)
1896	36.32	3m/d	(12)	1911	38.89	3m/d	(12)
1897	37.36	3m/d	(12)	1912	38.71	3m/d	(12)
1898	36.65	3m/d	(12)	1913	38.37	3m/d	(12)
1899	35.78	3m/d	(12)	1914	39.00	3m/d	(7)

[a] Concerning the Venetian currency, see pp. 104f.

[b] Concerning the Genoese currency, see pp. 107f. The banco valuta di San Giorgio fell into disuse and was no longer paid off after 1746; NELKENBRECHER [1775], p. 101.

[c] Concerning the Tuscan currency, see p. 106. Between December 1808 and July 1837 including 7% premium for payment in gold.

[d] The system of accounting in ducati (called 'ducati del regno' or 'ducati di regno' from the 18th century) of 10 carlini at 10 grani or of 5 tari at 20 grani had been common practice in the Kingdom of Naples for centuries and was continued during the Restoration era (after the Act of August 18th 1814). The Act of April 20th 1818 fixed the fineness of the ducato at 19.12 grammes of pure silver as it had already been when it was officially introduced in 1794 and confirmed in 1804 (from 1784 18.96 grammes of pure silver; cf. NOBACK [1851], pp. 710s.). This new silver ducato – later generally called 'ducato del regno' or 'ducato di regno' – should have been divided into 100 centesimi or grani. Simultaneously, it became the unit of account of the whole Kingdom of the Two Sicilies.

[e] Also on Leghorn, Milan, Messina, Palermo up to 1876 and on Venice from 1870; on "Genoa, Naples, etc." since 1881.

[f] Concerning the Italian currency after 1861, see pp. 108f.

1.1.5 On Saint Petersburg, Switzerland and Copenhagen

	LONDON on:
	Saint Petersburg
	per 1,000 banco roubles, from 1841 per 1,000 silver roubles in credit notes [a]
	in pounds sterling
1821	110.23 3m/d (11)
1822	109.10 3m/d (12)
1823	112.52 3m/d (12)
1824	111.12 3m/d (12)
1825	106.32 3m/d (12)
1826	114.05 3m/d (12)
1827	104.54 3m/d (12)
1828	100.00 3m/d (12)
1829	100.00 3m/d (12)
1830	99.76 3m/d (10)
1831	100.00 3m/d (12)
1832	100.00 3m/d (12)
1833	100.00 3m/d (9)
1834	
1835	
1836	
1837	
1838	90.91 3m/d (2)
1839	88.21 3m/d (2)
1840	
1841	157.56 3m/d (1)
1842	
1843	
1844	
1845	
1846	
1847	
1848	151.63 3m/d (4)
1849	151.26 3m/d (12)
1850	155.65 3m/d (12)
1851	154.19 3m/d (11)
1852	156.14 3m/d (11)
1853	157.77 3m/d (12)
1854	146.85 3m/d (10)
1855	146.22 3m/d (11)

	LONDON on:		
	Saint Petersburg	**Zurich & Basle**	**Copenhagen**
	per 1,000 silver roubles in credit notes [a]	per 1,000 franken [b]	per 1,000 rixdollar rigsmønt, from 1875 (2) per 1,000 Danish crowns [c]
		in pounds sterling	
1856	153.45 3m/d (12)		
1857	151.74 3m/d (12)		
1858	145.38 3m/d (12)		
1859	142.80 3m/d (12)		
1860	144.77 3m/d (12)		
1861	138.72 3m/d (12)		
1862	140.69 3m/d (12)		
1863	147.90 3m/d (12)		
1864	132.21 3m/d (12)		
1865	126.96 3m/d (12)		
1866	120.27 3m/d (11)		
1867	130.78 3m/d (12)		
1868	133.60 3m/d (12)		108.69 3m/d (5)
1869	125.35 3m/d (12)		108.37 3m/d (12)
1870	119.75 3m/d (12)		108.36 3m/d (12)
1871	129.10 3m/d (11)		108.75 3m/d (12)
1872	132.78 3m/d (12)		108.71 3m/d (12)
1873	131.19 3m/d (12)	38.80 3m/d (11)	108.45 3m/d (11)
1874	134.86 3m/d (12)	39.10 3m/d (12)	108.05 3m/d (12)
1875	133.78 3m/d (12)	39.21 3m/d (12)	107.24/53.75 3m/d (1+11)
1876	125.99 3m/d (12)	39.29 3m/d (12)	53.84 3m/d (12)
1877	108.21 3m/d (12)		
1878	99.79 3m/d (12)		
1879	98.72 3m/d (12)		
1880	102.32 3m/d (12)		
1881	102.64 3m/d (12)		
1882	98.65 3m/d (12)		
1883	96.52 3m/d (12)		
1884	98.58 3m/d (12)		
1885	99.08 3m/d (12)		
1886	95.97 3m/d (12)		
1887	88.02 3m/d (12)	**Geneva**	
1888	90.49 3m/d (12)	38.67 3m/d (11)	
1889	102.67 3m/d (12)	38.75 3m/d (12)	
1890	113.06 3m/d (12)		
1891	109.03 3m/d (12)		

	LONDON on:	
	Saint Petersburg	**Switzerland**
	per 1,000 silver roubles, from 1899 per 1,000 gold roubles [a]	per 1,000 franken [b]
	in pounds sterling	
1892	98.92 3m/d (12)	38.24 3m/d (1)
1893	102.20 3m/d (12)	39.21 3m/d (1)
1894	105.49 3m/d (12)	39.40 3m/d (12)
1895	105.82 3m/d (12)	39.28 3m/d (12)
1896	104.32 3m/d (12)	39.20 3m/d (12)
1897	104.52 3m/d (12)	39.22 3m/d (12)
1898	104.19 3m/d (12)	39.02 3m/d (12)
1899	103.76 3m/d (12)	38.96 3m/d (12)
1900	103.32 3m/d (12)	38.96 3m/d (12)
1901	104.21 3m/d (12)	39.27 3m/d (12)
1902	103.91 3m/d (12)	39.25 3m/d (12)
1903	103.95 3m/d (12)	39.32 3m/d (12)
1904	103.39 3m/d (12)	39.28 3m/d (12)
1905	103.39 3m/d (11)	39.30 3m/d (12)
1906	101.70 3m/d (12)	39.25 3m/d (12)
1907	101.89 3m/d (12)	39.22 3m/d (12)
1908	102.65 3m/d (12)	39.34 3m/d (12)
1909	103.98 3m/d (12)	39.38 3m/d (12)
1910	103.54 3m/d (12)	39.20 3m/d (12)
1911	104.11 3m/d (12)	39.17 3m/d (12)
1912	104.00 3m/d (12)	39.17 3m/d (12)
1913	103.30 3m/d (12)	39.01 3m/d (12)
1914	103.17 3m/d (7)	39.26 3m/d (7)

[a] Concerning the Russian currency, see pp. 359f.

[b] Concerning the Swiss currency, see p. 313.

[c] Concerning the Danish currency, see pp. 327f.

1.2 London exchange rates on British possessions

1.2.1 On Massachusetts

	LONDON on:				LONDON on:		
	Massachusetts				**Massachusetts**		
	per 100 pounds Massachusetts currency [a]				per 100 pounds Massachusetts currency, after 1712 payable in 'Old Tenor' [a]		
	in pounds sterling				**in pounds sterling**		
1660	80.00	[b]	(1)	1693			
1661				1694	77.42	[b]	(2)
1662				1695	76.92	[b]	(4)
1663	85.11	[b]	(1)	1696	76.92	[b]	(2)
1664	83.33	[b]	(1)	1697	74.07	[b]	(5)
1665	83.33	[b]	(1)	1698			
1666				1699	75.19	[b]	(2)
1667				1700	74.07	[b]	(2)
1668				1701	74.27	[b]	(2)
1669	80.00	[b]	(3)	1702	75.19	[b]	(1)
1670	80.00	[b]	(2)	1703	73.96	[b]	(3)
1671	80.00	[b]	(5)	1704	71.43	[b]	(2)
1672	80.00	[b]	(2)	1705	68.97	[b]	(2)
1673	80.00	[b]	(2)	1706			
1674	80.00	[b]	(1)	1707	68.03	[b]	(1)
1675	80.00	[b]	(2)	1708			
1676	80.00	[b]	(3)	1709			
1677	78.13	[b]	(1)	1710	71.43	[b]	(1)
1678	78.13	[b]	(2)	1711	71.43	[b]	(2)
1679	79.37	[b]	(3)	1712	80.00	[b]	(1)
1680	80.00	[b]	(1)	1713			
1681	80.08	[b]	(2)	1714			
1682	78.13	[b]	(2)	1715			
1683	78.13	[b]	(1)	1716			
1684	76.92	[b]	(2)	1717			
1685	75.76	[b]	(2)	1718			
1686				1719	47.62	[b]	(1)
1687	78.13	[b]	(2)	1720			
1688	78.13	[b]	(2)	1721			
1689				1722	40.00	[b]	(1)
1690	77.92	[b]	(5)	1723	38.46	[b]	(1)
1691	77.52	[b]	(2)	1724			
1692	77.07	[b]	(5)	1725	33.33	[b]	(1)

	LONDON on:				LONDON on:		
	Massachusetts				**Massachusetts**		
	per 100 pounds Massachusetts currency payable in 'Old Tenor', from 1750 in 'Lawful Money'				per 100 pounds Massachusetts currency payable in 'Lawful Money'		
	in pounds sterling				**in pounds sterling**		
1726	32.26	[b]	(2)	1751	79.47	[b]	(2)
1727	33.26	[b]	(2)	1752	78.95	[b]	(1)
1728	33.33	[b]	(1)	1753	75.00	[b]	(1)
1729	33.26	[b]	(1)	1754	75.00	[b]	(1)
1730	29.41	[b]	(1)	1755	76.92	[b]	(2)
1731	28.57	[b]	(2)	1756	76.92	[b]	(1)
1732	28.57	[b]	(1)	1757	75.00	[b]	(1)
1733	28.57	[b]	(2)	1758	75.00	[b]	(2)
1734	26.32	[b]	(1)	1759	77.52	[b]	(2)
1735	23.26	[b]	(1)	1760	77.52	[b]	(1)
1736	20.00	[b]	(2)	1761	77.52	[b]	(2)
1737	19.05	[b]	(3)	1762	75.00	[b]	(2)
1738	20.00	[b]	(1)	1763	74.07	[b]	(2)
1739	20.00	[b]	(1)	1764	74.07	[b]	(1)
1740	19.05	[b]	(1)	1765	74.07	[b]	(2)
1741	19.05	[b]	(1)	1766	74.07	[b]	(1)
1742	18.18	[b]	(1)	1767	74.07	[b]	(1)
1743	18.18	[b]	(1)	1768	74.07	[b]	(1)
1744	17.86	[b]	(1)	1769	74.07	[b]	(1)
1745	16.67	[b]	(1)	1770	80.00	[b]	(1)
1746	13.33	[b]	(1)	1771	75.00	[b]	(1)
1747	10.00	[b]	(1)	1772	74.07	[b]	(1)
1748	9.52	[b]	(1)	1773	74.07	[b]	(1)
1749	9.52	[b]	(1)	1774	75.38	[b]	(2)
1750							

[a] Concerning the Massachusetts currency, see pp. 399f.

[b] No data available concerning the usances.

1.2.2 On Dublin, Malta and Gibraltar

	LONDON on:				**LONDON on:**	
	Dublin [a]				**Dublin** [a]	
	per 100 pounds Irish currency [b]				per 100 pounds Irish currency [b]	
	in pounds sterling				**in pounds sterling**	
1662	97.10	21d/s	(3)	1698	85.67 21d/s	(12)
1663				1699	84.15 21d/s	(12)
1664				1700	82.69 21d/s	(12)
1665				1701	87.05 21d/s	(11)
1666	94.79	21d/s	(3)	1702	91.33 21d/s	(12)
1667				1703	92.86 21d/s	(12)
1668				1704	93.30 21d/s	(12)
1669				1705	92.48 21d/s	(12)
1670				1706	92.50 21d/s	(12)
1671	86.96	21d/s	(1)	1707	92.93 21d/s	(12)
1672	88.94	21d/s	(2)	1708	91.93 21d/s	(12)
1673				1709	90.99 21d/s	(12)
1674				1710	92.15 21d/s	(12)
1675				1711	92.60 21d/s	(12)
1676				1712	92.20 21d/s	(11)
1677				1713	93.33 21d/s	(12)
1678				1714	93.16 21d/s	(12)
1679	97.09	21d/s	(1)	1715	91.57 21d/s	(12)
1680	92.39	21d/s	(2)	1716	90.79 21d/s	(12)
1681	92.60	21d/s	(2)	1717	90.75 21d/s	(12)
1682	92.54	21d/s	(6)	1718	90.09 21d/s	(12)
1683	91.52	21d/s	(5)	1719	89.47 21d/s	(12)
1684				1720	88.34 21d/s	(12)
1685	92.17	21d/s	(2)	1721	90.37 21d/s	(11)
1686				1722	90.56 21d/s	(12)
1687				1723	90.23 21d/s	(12)
1688				1724	89.42 21d/s	(12)
1689				1725	90.62 21d/s	(12)
1690				1726	88.90 21d/s	(12)
1691				1727	88.96 21d/s	(12)
1692				1728	89.76 21d/s	(11)
1693				1729	89.75 21d/s	(12)
1694				1730	89.84 21d/s	(12)
1695				1731	90.04 21d/s	(12)
1696				1732	90.19 21d/s	(12)
1697				1733	89.80 21d/s	(12)

	LONDON on:		LONDON on:
	Dublin [a]		**Dublin** [a]
	per 100 pounds Irish currency [b]		per 100 pounds Irish currency [b]
	in pounds sterling		**in pounds sterling**
1734	89.79 21d/s (12)	1772	91.64 21d/s (12)
1735	89.42 21d/s (12)	1773	91.10 21d/s (12)
1736	89.89 21d/s (12)	1774	92.58 21d/s (12)
1737	91.06 21d/s (12)	1775	92.52 21d/s (12)
1738	92.43 21d/s (12)	1776	92.56 21d/s (12)
1739	91.89 21d/s (12)	1777	91.60 21d/s (12)
1740	92.49 21d/s (12)	1778	90.95 21d/s (12)
1741	91.59 21d/s (12)	1779	92.86 21d/s (12)
1742	90.86 21d/s (12)	1780	92.35 21d/s (12)
1743	91.99 21d/s (10)	1781	92.19 21d/s (11)
1744	92.56 21d/s (12)	1782	90.98 21d/s (12)
1745	91.07 21d/s (12)	1783	91.63 21d/s (12)
1746	92.88 21d/s (10)	1784	91.26 21d/s (12)
1747	92.85 21d/s (12)	1785	91.59 21d/s (12)
1748	91.98 21d/s (12)	1786	92.21 21d/s (12)
1749	92.39 21d/s (12)	1787	92.30 21d/s (12)
1750	91.66 21d/s (12)	1788	91.79 21d/s (12)
1751	91.88 21d/s (12)	1789	92.20 21d/s (12)
1752	92.50 21d/s (12)	1790	92.21 21d/s (12)
1753	91.16 21d/s (12)	1791	92.24 21d/s (12)
1754	91.15 21d/s (12)	1792	92.16 21d/s (12)
1755	92.16 21d/s (12)	1793	91.41 21d/s (12)
1756	92.28 21d/s (12)	1794	92.20 21d/s (12)
1757	92.86 21d/s (12)	1795	92.20 21d/s (12)
1758	92.46 21d/s (12)	1796	91.18 21d/s (12)
1759	91.22 21d/s (12)	1797	92.64 21d/s (12)
1760	92.41 21d/s (12)	1798	91.74 21d/s (12)
1761	93.01 21d/s (12)	1799	89.93 21d/s (12)
1762	92.59 21d/s (9)	1800	89.75 21d/s (12)
1763	92.43 21d/s (12)	1801	88.44 21d/s (12)
1764	91.69 21d/s (12)	1802	89.15 21d/s (12)
1765	91.80 21d/s (12)	1803	86.84 21d/s (12)
1766	92.02 21d/s (12)	1804	86.80 21d/s (12)
1767	91.48 21d/s (12)	1805	89.26 21d/s (12)
1768	92.14 21d/s (12)	1806	89.04 21d/s (12)
1769	91.69 21d/s (12)	1807	90.16 21d/s (12)
1770	91.01 21d/s (12)	1808	90.62 21d/s (12)
1771	91.76 21d/s (12)		

	LONDON on:		
	Dublin [a]	**Malta** [c]	**Gibraltar** [e]
	per 100 pounds Irish currency [b]	per 100 oncie [d]	per 100 current dollars, from 1826 (7) per 100 hard dollars ('cobs') [f]
	in pounds sterling		
1809	91.30 21d/s (12)	22.55 3m/d (10)	15.05 2m/d (10)
1810	91.21 21d/s (12)	23.51 3m/d (12)	15.72 2m/d (12)
1811	90.78 21d/s (12)	26.08 3m/d (12)	16.62 2m/d (12)
1812	91.49 21d/s (12)	25.90 3m/d (12)	17.26 2m/d (12)
1813	94.16 21d/s (12)	27.28 3m/d (12)	18.58 2m/d (12)
1814	93.76 21d/s (12)	24.62 3m/d (12)	16.25 2m/d (12)
1815	91.87 21d/s (12)	21.74 3m/d (12)	14.97 2m/d (12)
1816	87.90 21d/s (12)	19.60 3m/d (12)	13.09 2m/d (12)
1817	89.21 21d/s (7)	19.35 3m/d (7)	13.10 2m/d (7)
1818	91.23 21d/s (12)	21.01 3m/d (12)	14.31 2m/d (12)
1819	89.06 21d/s (12)	20.35 3m/d (12)	13.54 2m/d (12)
1820	92.19 21d/s (12)	18.96 3m/d (12)	13.16 2m/d (12)
1821	92.08 21d/s (12)	18.75 3m/d (12)	12.71 2m/d (12)
1822	91.28 21d/s (12)	18.75 3m/d (11)	12.71 2m/d (12)
1823	91.33 21d/s (12)	18.75 3m/d (11)	12.71 2m/d (12)
1824	91.33 21d/s (12)	19.03 3m/d (9)	12.76 2m/d (12)
1825	91.33 21d/s (12)		12.92 2m/d (12)
1826	91.33 21d/s (1)		12.92/18.79 2m/d (6+6)
1827			18.86 2m/d (12)
1828			19.17 2m/d (12)
1829			20.04 2m/d (11)
1830			19.75 2m/d (12)
1831			19.70 2m/d (12)
1832			19.70 2m/d (12)
1833			19.73 2m/d (9)

[a] "Bills on Dublin are mostly drawn on at 21 days' sight, or, what is considered equivalent, at 31 days' date, and such are called *Bills in Course*. If the term is longer, an advance is accordingly made in the price of exchange. Thus bills at 41 days' date are charged 1/8 per cent. more; but, beyond this term, the advance is in a higher proportion, being at the rate of ½ per cent. per month" (KELLY [1811], p. 221).

[b] When Dublin was quoted at the London exchange market, "Ireland had no mint, therefore, no coin of its own. Its real money was English with a considerable admixture of foreign coin, amongst which Spanish silver and Portuguese gold played a major role. Ireland's money of account was English too – the usual pounds, shillings and pence" (MCCUSKER [1978], p. 34). The difference between sterling currency and Irish currency resulted from the different valuation of the guinea: 1 guinea = 21 shillings sterling = 22¾ shillings Irish. The par of exchange between Irish currency and sterling was 105.56 pounds Irish per 100 pounds sterling from January 20th 1660/61 (confirmed on June 6th 1683), 108.33 pounds Irish from March 25th 1689, 116.67 pounds Irish from May

29th 1695, and again 108.33 pounds Irish for 100 pounds sterling from June 2nd 1701. This ratio was in force until January 5th 1826, "when, subsequent to the union of Ireland and Great Britain, a separate Irish money ceased to exist" (ibid.), so that further quotations on Dublin (as on Cork) were no longer necessary.

[c]   As there is no information about the usances for Malta in the documented sources, usances according to NELKENBRECHER [1828], p. 210 are presented here.

[d]   In Malta reckoning was done in scudi of 12 tari at 20 grani, and 2½ scudi were equal to 1 oncia (KELLY [1821, repr. 1835], p. 236; NELKENBRECHER [1832], p. 312). In 1825 the pound sterling was introduced in Malta, which is why further quotations on Malta were not necessary any longer.

[e]   As there is no information about the usances for Gibraltar in the documented sources, usances according to NELKENBRECHER [1828], p. 210 are presented here. In the *Course of Exchange* one can find some further quotations on Gibraltar in the 1840s: 20.00 pounds sterling per 100 hard dollars in 1840, 19.07 pounds sterling per 100 hard dollars – without any deviation – from January of 1841 to January of 1844; therefore, these rates seem to be fixed rates, not market rates.

[f]   At Gibraltar accounts were kept in the imaginary current dollar of 8 reales or in the effective hard dollar, the so-called 'cob', of 12 reales. Therefore the hard dollar was equal to 1½ current dollars having the estimated parity of 4 shillings 6 pence sterling (KELLY [1821, repr. 1835], p. 164).

1.3 London's India exchange

1.3.1 On India and Ceylon

	LONDON on:			
	Calcutta	**Bombay**	**Madras**	**Colombo**
	per 1,000 Sicca rupees, from 1850 per 1,000 Company's rupees, from 1862 per 100 Government rupees [a]	per 1,000 Bombay rupees, from 1850 per 1,000 Company's rupees, from 1862 per 100 Government rupees [a]	per 1,000 Madras rupees, from 1850 per 1,000 Company's rupees, from 1862 per 100 Government rupees [a]	per 100 pounds sterling, from 1872 (5) per 1,000 Government rupees [b]
	in pounds sterling			
1830	85.25 60d/s (3)	78.48 60d/s (3)	78.48 60d/s (3)	
1831	85.21 60d/s (11)	78.27 60d/s (11)	78.27 60d/s (11)	
1832	84.38 60d/s (1)	78.13 60d/s (1)	78.13 60d/s (1)	
...				
1850	99.66 60d/s (12)	101.57 60d/s (12)	99.66 60d/s (12)	
1851	102.95 60d/s (12)	104.86 60d/s (12)	102.95 60d/s (12)	
1852	101.05 60d/s (12)	103.13 60d/s (12)	101.05 60d/s (12)	
1853	102.43 60d/s (12)	104.60 60d/s (12)	102.52 60d/s (12)	
1854	98.09 60d/s (12)	100.18 60d/s (12)	98.09 60d/s (12)	
1855	105.13 60d/s (12)	106.95 60d/s (12)	105.04 60d/s (12)	
1856	100.87 60d/s (12)	102.96 60d/s (12)	100.87 60d/s (12)	
1857	104.17 60d/s (11)	106.25 60d/s (11)	104.17 60d/s (11)	
1858	108.99 60d/s (12)	110.28 60d/s (12)	108.54 60d/s (12)	
1859	110.04 60d/s (12)	111.10 60d/s (12)	109.54 60d/s (12)	
1860	109.67 60d/s (12)	110.32 60d/s (12)	109.32 60d/s (12)	
1861	108.58 60d/s (11)	109.01 60d/s (11)	107.12 60d/s (11)	
1862	100.12 30d/s (11)	100.74 30d/s (11)	99.93 30d/s (11)	102.32 30d/s (11)
1863	99.63 30d/s (12)	100.24 30d/s (12)	99.85 30d/s (12)	102.50 30d/s (12)
1864	99.98 30d/s (11)	100.57 30d/s (11)	99.77 30d/s (11)	101.62 30d/s (12)
1865	99.12 30d/s (12)	98.26 30d/s (12)	98.03 30d/s (12)	100.20 30d/s (12)
1866	96.92 30d/s (12)	97.57 30d/s (12)	96.97 30d/s (12)	100.50 30d/s (12)
1867	97.25 30d/s (12)	97.25 30d/s (12)	97.18 30d/s (12)	99.36 30d/s (12)
1868	96.62 30d/s (11)	96.88 30d/s (11)	96.62 30d/s (11)	98.91 30d/s (11)
1869	97.60 30d/s (9)	97.83 30d/s (9)	97.95 30d/s (9)	99.38 30d/s (12)
1870	95.24 30d/s (11)	95.34 30d/s (11)	95.24 30d/s (10)	98.66 30d/s (12)
1871	95.11 30d/s (12)	95.16 30d/s (12)	95.14 30d/s (12)	97.34 30d/s (12)
1872	96.07 30d/s (11)	96.07 30d/s (11)	96.07 30d/s (11)	99.50/95.76 30d/s (2+7)
1873	93.42 30d/s (7)	93.36 30d/s (7)	93.49 30d/s (7)	93.79 30d/s (7)
1874	93.35 30d/s (12)	93.35 30d/s (12)	93.41 30d/s (12)	94.17 30d/s (10)
1875	90.64 30d/s (12)	90.76 30d/s (12)	90.93 30d/s (12)	91.54 30d/s (12)
1876	85.17 30d/s (12)	85.06 30d/s (12)	85.21 30d/s (12)	85.34 30d/s (12)

	LONDON on:			
	Calcutta	**Bombay**	**Madras**	**Colombo**
	per 1,000 Government rupees [a, b]			
	in pounds sterling			
1877	87.89 30d/s (12)	87.89 30d/s (12)	87.90 30d/s (12)	87.99 30d/s (12)
1878	83.81 30d/s (11)	83.81 30d/s (11)	83.80 30d/s (11)	83.97 30d/s (11)
1879	82.06 30d/s (12)	82.07 30d/s (12)	82.11 30d/s (12)	82.21 30d/s (12)
1880	83.75 30d/s (12)	83.75 30d/s (12)	83.75 30d/s (12)	83.82 30d/s (12)
1881	82.69 30d/s (11)	82.69 30d/s (11)	82.69 30d/s (11)	82.70 30d/s (11)
1882	83.27 30d/s (10)	83.27 30d/s (10)	83.27 30d/s (10)	83.23 30d/s (9)
1883	81.11 60d/s (9)	81.10 60d/s (8)	81.04 60d/s (6)	
1884	81.49 60d/s (10)	81.47 60d/s (9)	81.55 60d/s (7)	
1885	77.68 2–6m/s (12)	79.62 60d/s (1)	79.69 60d/s (1)	
1886	72.90 2–6m/s (12)			
1887	71.32 2–6m/s (12)			
1888	68.19 2–6m/s (12)			
1889	67.83 2–6m/s (6)			

[a] Concerning the Indian currencies, see pp. 481f.

[b] From 1825 the currency on Ceylon was the British one, whereby the former unit of accont, the Dutch rixdollar, was valued at 1 shilling 6 pence sterling. Because one reckoned in the commodity trade with Ceylon very often in rupees (the same as in British India), the London quotation on Colombo was effected for rupees from May 1872; cf. NOBACK [1851], p. 201; SONNDORFER [1900], p. 247.

1.3.2 On Mauritius, Hong Kong, Singapore and Shanghai

	LONDON on:			
	Mauritius [a]	**Hong Kong** [b]	**Singapore** [c]	**Shanghai** [b]
	per 100 pounds sterling, from June 1877 per 1,000 Government rupees [d]	per 1,000 Mexican dollars [e]	per 1,000 Mexican dollars [f]	per 1,000 Shanghai taels [g]
	in pounds sterling			
1862	102.18 30d/s (10)	232.58 30d/s (11)	232.58 30d/s (11)	
1863	102.42 30d/s (12)	237.76 30d/s (12)	237.76 30d/s (12)	
1864	101.00 30d/s (11)	237.67 30d/s (12)	237.67 30d/s (12)	
1865	100.22 30d/s (12)	225.00 30d/s (12)	225.00 30d/s (12)	
1866	100.42 30d/s (12)	224.48 30d/s (12)	224.48 30d/s (12)	
1867	99.34 30d/s (12)	222.23 30d/s (12)	222.23 30d/s (12)	
1868	98.91 30d/s (11)	221.62 30d/s (12)	221.62 30d/s (12)	
1869	99.38 30d/s (12)	219.68 30d/s (9)	219.68 30d/s (9)	
1870	98.84 30d/s (11)	223.27 30d/s (11)	223.64 30d/s (12)	
1871	97.34 30d/s (12)	222.92 30d/s (12)	222.92 30d/s (12)	
1872	99.50 30d/s (12)	222.92 30d/s (12)	222.92 30d/s (12)	
1873	99.50 30d/s (12)	222.92 30d/s (12)	222.92 30d/s (12)	
1874	97.06 30d/s (12)	211.81 30d/s (12)	211.81 30d/s (12)	284.64 30d/s (8)
1875	95.84 30d/s (12)	200.48 30d/s (12)	200.48 30d/s (12)	280.04 30d/s (12)
1876	88.42 30d/s (12)	191.84 30d/s (12)	191.84 30d/s (12)	256.73 30d/s (12)
1877	84.50/87.05 30d/s (2+7)	197.24 30d/s (12)	197.24 30d/s (12)	261.18 30d/s (12)
1878	83.96 30d/s (11)	186.98 30d/s (11)	186.98 30d/s (11)	257.99 30d/s (11)
1879	82.56 30d/s (12)	177.35 30d/s (12)	175.26 30d/s (12)	242.93 30d/s (12)
1880	80.78 30d/s (6)	182.88 30d/s (12)	182.97 30d/s (12)	250.68 30d/s (12)
1881	82.03 30d/s (2)	182.01 30d/s (11)	182.14 30d/s (11)	248.92 30d/s (11)
1882		182.96 30d/s (10)	183.34 30d/s (10)	250.05 30d/s (9)

[a]   Private bills and documents.
[b]   1879–1882: private bills and documents.
[c]   1874–1878: bank bills; 1879–1882: private bills and documents.
[d]   Concerning the currency on Mauritius, see p. 541.
[e]   Concerning the Hong Kong currency, see p. 494.
[f]   Concerning the currency in the Straits Settlements, see p. 523.
[g]   Concerning the Shanghai currency, see pp. 495f.

1.3.3 On Australia

	LONDON on:		
	Sydney & Melbourne		
	per 100 pounds sterling [a]		
	in pounds sterling		
1862	99.50	30d/s	(11)
1863	99.46	30d/s	(12)
1864	99.25	30d/s	(12)
1865	99.05	30d/s	(12)
1866	98.59	30d/s	(12)
1867	99.00	30d/s	(12)
1868	99.22	30d/s	(12)
1869	99.50	30d/s	(12)
1870	99.50	30d/s	(12)
1871	99.50	30d/s	(12)
1872	99.50	30d/s	(12)
1873	99.50	30d/s	(12)
1874	99.50	30d/s	(4)

[a] Concerning the Australian currency, see pp. 567f.

1.4 London exchange rates on South Africa

	LONDON on:		
	South Africa		
	per 100 pounds sterling [a]		
	in pounds sterling		
1908	100.49	s	(8)
1909	100.61	s	(12)
1910	100.57	s	(12)
1911	100.39	s	(12)
1912	100.39	s	(12)
1913	100.52	s	(12)
1914	100.48	s	(7)

[a] Concerning the South African currency, see pp. 593f.

2
The Netherlands (1593–1914)

Exchange market: Amsterdam (1593–1914)

Sources: MCCUSKER / HART [1979], pp. 701f. (1593–1622); POSTHUMUS [1946], vol. I, pp. 590–595 (1609–1699); IISG Amsterdam, *Corso delli Cambiati in Amsterdam* (1700–1711); ibid., *Cours van Koopmannschappen tot Amsterdam* (1701–1731); ibid., *Cours des Marchandises* (1731–1748); ibid., *Cours der Koopmannschappen* (1732–1789); *Prijscourant der Effecten* (1796–1842); *Amsterdamsch Effectenblad* (1843–1913); *De Nederlandsche Financier – Dagelijksche Beurscourant* (1914).

Concordance: *WdW III*, pp. 39–94; *WdW VI*, pp. 57–124; *HStD XII*, pp. 65–102; *WdW I/II*, pp. 111–196; *HStD XI*, pp. 563–581.

Currency: The high stability of the currency in Holland and in the whole United Netherlands from the end of the 17th century was one of the most important factors in the pre-eminence of Amsterdam as an international exchange market and financial centre in the 17th and 18th centuries. While there was quite a large number of different coexisting coins, "the money of account at Amsterdam was expressed in two interconnected sets of moneys reflecting in their origin something of the divergent political and economic background of the area" (MCCUSKER [1978], pp. 42f.), the pound system and the guilder system:

- 1 pound Flemish (pond-Vlaamsch) = 20 shillings Flemish (schelling-Vlaamsch) = 240 groot
- 1 guilder (gulden, florijn) = 20 stivers (stuiver) = 320 penning

Therefore, one can reckon as follows:

1 pound Flemish =	6 guilders =	20 shillings =	120 stivers =	240 groot =	1,920 penning
	1 guilder =	3 2/3 shillings =	20 stivers =	40 groot =	320 penning
		1 shilling =	6 stivers =	12 groot =	96 penning
			1 stiver =	2 groot =	16 penning
				1 groot =	8 penning

Until well into the 17th century the way of quoting and accounting in pounds (pond) and shillings Flemish remained dominant. Nevertheless, the data series has been completely converted for the records into guilders, the main unit of account by the beginning of the 18th century (cf. LE MOINE DE L'ESPINE [1710], p. 13; HERBACH [1716], p. 66) in order to ensure the comparability of the quotations over a long period. Principally, the Wisselbank at Amsterdam, founded in 1609, calculated in guilders and, as a consequence, the wholesale trade followed suit. This guilder of the Wisselbank – the so-called 'guilder banco' or 'bank guilder' – became not only "a money of account, whose value was determined fundamentally by the combined silver content of the rijksdaalers, leeuwendaalers, pata-cons and ducatons" (VAN DER WEE [1977], pp. 338f.), but also one of the most important and most stable exchange monies throughout Europe: "In 1638 the city council settled its silver currency, in particular the ratio of the current guilder *vis-à-vis* the guilder of account. As a result, the bank guilder was officially disentangled from its current counterpart. In 1659 the States General followed suit. A major consequence was extreme stability in the value of the guilder" (DEHING / 'T HART [1997], p. 40). The basis of the guilder banco was the rixdollar, issued according to the standard of coinage of the Holy Roman Empire during the 16th century (rijksdaaler; 25.99 grammes of pure silver, from 1616

25.69 grammes of pure silver) for the first time in 1586. The rixdollar attained a value of 50 stivers (= 2½ guilders or 100 groot) during the 17th century. When the slightly lighter patagon from the Southern Netherlands ousted the rixdollar from the money circulation, the latter was officially accepted and minted as zilveren dukaat (24.66 grammes of pure silver) at 50 stivers current and at 48 stivers banco only in the United Netherlands after a change of the standard of coinage in 1659. Therefore a nominal relation of 48 guilders banco = 50 guilders current was established from 1659. From 1648, the guilder banco was quoted in the price currents of the Amsterdam stock exchange:

Annual average premium, 1794–1802 and 1810 discount of Flemish banco against Flemish current

1651	3.25	...		1744	4.96	1781	4.74
...		1708	4.82	1745	4.96	1782	4.85
1653	2.00	1709	4.81	1746	4.87	...	
1654	1.97	1710	4.71	1747	4.56	1784	3.74
...		1711	4.29	1748	4.77	1785	2.93
1661	3.30	1712	3.79	1749	4.65	1786	2.56
1662	3.32	1713	4.44	1750	4.60	1787	3.31
1663	3.19	1714	4.44	1751	4.90	1788	2.77
1664	3.25	1715	5.00	1752	4.50	1789	2.56
1665	3.25	1716	5.17	1753	4.62	1790	0.62
...		1717	4.69	1754	4.54	1791	0.21
1674	4.30	1718	4.70	1755	4.15	1792	0.59
1675	3.57	1719	4.85	1756	4.19	1793	1.56
...		1720	4.47	1757	3.75	1794	*–3.01*
1679	4.10	1721	5.50	1758	3.35	1795	*–9.33*
...		1722	5.21	1759	2.27	1796	*–0.56*
1682	4.25	1723	4.97	1760	3.03	1797	*–3.20*
...		1724	4.58	1761	4.51	1798	*–4.51*
1686	5.19	1725	4.43	1762	3.02	1799	*–7.53*
...		1726	4.86	1763	2.32	1800	*–7.69*
1688	4.99	1727	4.98	1764	3.08	1801	*–7.57*
1689	4.07	1728	4.79	1765	3.73	1802	*–0.67*
1690	4.25	1729	4.79	1766	4.75	1803	4.88
...		...		1767	4.81	1804	4.39
1692	5.07	1731	4.48	1768	4.59	1805	4.78
1693	6.13	1732	4.13	1769	4.87	1806	3.91
1694	4.63	1733	3.91	1770	4.91	1807	3.58
...		1734	4.27	1771	4.84	1808	3.00
1698	5.13	1735	4.00	1772	4.67	1809	2.69
1699	5.44	1736	3.86	1773	4.64	1810	*–0.08*
1700	5.00	1737	4.05	1774	4.69	1811	1.74
1701	4.62	1738	4.41	1775	4.63	1812	3.71
1702	4.50	1739	5.15	1776	4.71	1813	2.34
1703	2.94	1740	5.22	1777	4.88	1814	2.75
1704	3.19	1741	4.61	1778	4.64		
1705	3.44	1742	4.46	1779	4.60		
1706	5.61	1743	4.82	1780	4.52		

Source: *WdW III*, p. 95; *HStD XII*, pp. 103-107

Thus bank money became the dominant element of Dutch currency by the second half of the 17th century, since it symbolized, as clearing unit of the Wisselbank, the stability of the Dutch currency on the international financial markets. That is why the data in the price currents of the Amsterdam stock exchange are quoted consistently in bank money from 1683 on. From 1681, the guilder (1 zilveren dukaat = 2½ guilders current) was the basic silver coin of Amsterdam and Holland, henceforth issued at 9.59 grammes of pure silver; other provinces followed in 1686. In 1694, the currency system of the province of Holland was formally taken over by the whole United Netherlands giving their currency system a standardized structure consistently in force until 1806.

Changes in the currency system of the Netherlands did not occur until the eras of the Batavian Republic (1795–1806), the Kingdom of Holland (1806–1810) and the occupation by the French Empire – intensified by the Napoleonic Wars and the Continental System – but these periods remained without influence on the way of quoting exchange rates. By the Coin Act of September 28th 1816, the Dutch guilder at 100 cents with a weight of 9.613 grammes of fine silver (by the act of March 22nd 1839 reduced to 9.45 grammes of fine silver) or 0.6056 grammes of fine gold was declared national currency in the new Kingdom of the Netherlands. As a consequence of the Coin Acts of November 26th 1847 and June 9th 1850, this officially bimetallistic, but at most times *de facto*, gold standard was superseded by a pure silver standard with remarkable issues of notes of the Nederlandsche Bank (founded in 1814).

Following the example of the neighbouring European states, the gold standard was introduced by the Coin Acts of June 6th 1875 and May 10th 1876 (1 guilder equal to 0.6048 grammes of fine gold). Owing to the extremely small gold reserves of the Nederlandsche Bank, however, the silver coins and banknotes (legal tender by the Coin Act of July 18th 1904) determined the internal money circulation of the Netherlands up to World War I.

Original quotations at Amsterdam until 1874

on:	in:	per:
Antwerp	pounds Brabant exchange money	100 pounds Flemish banco
from 1874	Dutch guilders	100 Belgian francs
Augsburg	guilders Flemish banco	30 guilders Augsburg current
from 1816 (10)	Dutch guilders	30 guilders Augsburg current
from 1859	Dutch guilders	100 guilders South German current
Breslau	stivers Flemish banco	1 rixdollar in Kaisergeld
from 1764 (4)	stivers Flemish banco	1 rixdollar in 'new money'
from 1765	stivers Flemish banco	1 livre Prussian banco
Frankfurt	groot Flemish current	1 rixdollar current
from c. 1700	rixdollars current in Frankfurt	100 rixdollars Flemish current
from 1815	guilders Flemish banco	30 guilders Frankfurt exchange money
from 1816 (10)	Dutch guilders	30 guilders Frankfurt exchange money
from 1843	Dutch guilders	100 guilders South German current
Danzig	groszy Polish current	1 pound Flemish banco
Genoa	groot Flemish banco	1 pezza of 5 lire banco or of 5¾ lire fuori banco (since 1741)
from 1816 (10)	Dutch guilders	40 pezze of 5¾ lire fuori banco
from 1827 (4)	Dutch guilders	100 Piedmontese lire nuove
from 1861 (8)	Dutch guilders	100 Italian lire
Hamburg	stivers Flemish banco	1 exchange dollar or 2 mark banco
from 1816 (10)	Dutch guilders	40 mark banco
from 1873 (3)	Dutch guilders	100 mark
Leghorn	groot Flemish banco	1 pezza da otto reali of 5¾ lire moneta buona
from 1816 (10)	Dutch guilders	40 pezze da otto reali of 5¾ lire mon. buona
from 1837 (7)	Dutch guilders	100 Tuscan lire moneta buona
from 1860 (9)	Dutch guilders	100 Piedmontese lire nuove
from 1861 (8)	Dutch guilders	100 Italian lire
Leipzig	stivers Flemish current	1 rixdollar current
from 1764	stivers Flemish current	1 rixdollar Konventions-Wechselzahlung
Lisbon	groot Flemish banco	1 crusado of 400 réis
from 1816 (10)	Dutch guilders	40 crusados of 400 réis

on:	in:	per:
London	shillings Flemish banco	1 pound sterling
from 1816 (10)	Dutch guilders	1 pound sterling
Madrid	groot Flemish banco	1 ducado de cambio of 375 maravedis
from 1816 (10)	Dutch guilders	40 ducados de cambio of 375 maravedis
from 1847 (6)	Dutch guilders	1 peso duro or 100 pesos duros
Naples	groot Flemish banco	1 ducato del regno
from 1816 (10)	Dutch guilders	40 ducati del regno
from 1863	Dutch guilders	100 Italian lire
Paris	groot Flemish banco	1 écu of 3 livres tournois or of 3 francs
from 1816 (10)	Dutch guilders	40 écus or 120 francs
Saint Petersburg	Dutch guilders	20 banco roubles
from 1839 (9)	Dutch guilders	100 silver roubles
Venice	groot Flemish banco	1 ducato di banco
Vienna	stivers Flemish banco	1 guilder Konventionskurant
from 1816 (10)	Dutch guilders	30 guilders Konventionskurant effective
from 1858 (11)	Dutch guilders	100 guilders Österreichische Währung [a]

[a]   Payable in *Wiener Banknoten*

From 1875, price quotations were given for 1 (on London, New York and Saint Petersburg) or 100 units of foreign currency.

Other data available: Altona, ss (1777–1789); 2 m/d (1777–1789) – Belgian places, 3 m/d (1875–1914) – Berlin, 6 w/d (1821–1824) – Bilbao, 2 m/d (1698–1804); 3 m/d (1804–1874) – Bordeaux, 2 m/d (1678–1874); 1 m/d (1777–1814); 15 d/d (1815–1874) – Brussels (1733–1797) – Cadiz, 2 m/d (1678–1804); 3m/d (1804–1874) – Cologne, 8 d/s (1609–1688); ss (1619–1645); 14 d/s (1661–1686) – Frankfurt am Main, 14 d/s (1711–1731) – Ghent, s (1700–1797) – Hamburg, 2 m/d (1766–1872); 3 m/d (1872–1875); 1 m/d (1796–1812) – Königsberg, 41 d/d (1719–1750) – Lille/Ryssel, s (1624–1719) – London, 2 m/d (1634–1914); ss (1683–1698) – Lyons, fairs (1678–1719/36); 2 m/d (1700–1711) – Middelburg (1624–1682) – Nantes, 2 m/d (1683–1698) – Nuremberg, 14 d/s (1609–1633) – Paris, 2 m/d (1634–1909) – Oporto, 3 m/d (1796–1874) – Prussian places, 3 m/d (1875–1914) – La Rochelle, 2 m/d (1683–1698, 1736, 1750) – Rotterdam, s (1686–1782) – Rouen, 1 m/d (1609–1679); 2 m/d (1634–1764) – Seville, 2 m/d (1619, 1661–1804); 3 m/d (1804–1874) – South German places, 3 m/d (1875) – Stockholm, 20–25w/s (1664–1672) – Swiss places, 3 m/d (1875–1914) – Vienna and Trieste, ss (1875–1894) – Zeeland, sight (1698–1804).

From the end of the 16th century, Amsterdam had become the central financial market of Northwestern Europe, succeeding Antwerp and obtaining the dominant position in European exchange operations after 1620: "The exchange at Amsterdam functioned as a clearinghouse for commercial transactions linking the Atlantic and the Mediterranean with the North Sea, the Baltic, and beyond" (MCCUSKER [1978], p. 42). The outstanding position of the Amsterdam exchange market in the 17th century was based on three facts: modern technologies for transferring bills of exchange (the endorsement and the discount) taken over from Antwerp; the security of the Wisselbank – founded on the model of the Venetian Banco della Piazza di Rialto in 1609 – where all exchanges amounting to more than 600 guilders (and to more than 300 guilders since 1643; DEHING / 'T HART [1997], p. 46) had to be paid in; its stable exchange money, the gulden banco, which symbolized, as the clearing unit of the Wisselbank, the stability of the currency on international financial markets and which functioned as the international key currency. Therefore the prices of the Amsterdam stock market price list were quoted uniformly in bank money from 1683. Furthermore, two other facts were of great importance for Amsterdam's position as world financial centre: the unrestricted trade with precious metal, providing the bank with the world's largest reserves of precious metal for that time; and the omnipresence of the Dutch trade interests, combined with the intermediary role of Holland and its political as well as economic centre Amsterdam with regard to the trade between the Baltic area and the Northwest European and German commercial enterprises on the one hand and Spain with its Atlantic empire on the other hand. With their acceptance credit, Amsterdam merchant bankers succeeded in financing not only the trade of Amsterdam and the Netherlands but also increasingly and in large measure the international trade of London, Hamburg, Danzig and other towns (SCHNEIDER / SCHWARZER [1986], p. 152).

The extensive trade relations in Amsterdam are reflected in the exchange rate currents of the 16th, 17th and 18th centuries: according to the few exchange rate currents handed down, Amsterdam was still of mainly regional importance in the Northwest European area at the end of the 16th century. Only the quotation for Danzig exceeded this regional dimension, for Danzig was the place where the trade with Poland and the Baltic area was settled up – Danzig had been an important source of wealth for Amsterdam since the late Middle Ages (ibid., p. 145). Around 1620 Amsterdam quoted Danzig, Hamburg, Rouen (up to 1679), Frankfurt am Main and Cologne (up to 1688) as well as London, Paris, Antwerp, Ryssel/Lille, Middelburg, Nuremberg (up to 1633), Venice and occasionally even Lisbon. The quotation on Lisbon resulted from the exchange business of the Sephardic Jews, who had emigrated from Lisbon to Amsterdam. At the end of the 17th century – approximately three decades after the end of the Netherlands' fight for independence and the Eighty Years War – the quotations on Iberian places became more regular (apart from Lisbon, on Madrid, Seville and Cadiz, as well as on Bilbao since 1698), which can be regarded as an expression of intensified payment relations, above all with Spain. "With the quotation on Madrid, Amsterdam had obviously entered the business of government stocks" (ibid., p. 146). In addition to this, the quotations on two further Italian Mediterranean ports, Genoa and Leghorn, started at the end of the 1670s, and there were also quotations on the Lyons fairs – as intermediaries in this region – for a short time. Only occasionally, one may find quotations on the entrepôt ports on the French Atlantic coast (Bordeaux, Nantes, La Rochelle). Additionally, Stockholm (1664–1672) and Königsberg (1719–1750) were quoted for a short time as representatives of the Baltic area, but Danzig remained the only long-term partner of Amsterdam in this region, because the commercial conditions in Königsberg became too unfavourable for the Dutch from the early 18th century (cf. VAN TIELHOF [2002], p. 178). The inclusion of the Leipzig fairs (1676) and later on of Breslau (1700) in the exchange rate current of Amsterdam shows the increasing importance of Central Europe for the exchange transactions of Amsterdam. Moreover, there were several connections with places within the Netherlands themselves (above all with Antwerp, Rotterdam, Brussels, Middelburg/Zeeland and Ghent). Apart from these 'official' quotations, contemporary merchant manuals of the early 18th century also note exchange relations with Copenhagen, Stockholm and Archangel, Florence, Milan, Geneva and Saint Gall (e.g. HERBACH [1716], p. 66), although no (regular) quotations are available. After all, Amsterdam was also the most important clearing centre for the assignatiës transactions between the overseas possessions of the VOC and the mother country (see p. 533; DENZEL [1999], pp. 53–

58). Consequently, the geographic extension of the direct exchange net of Amsterdam reached its climax in the decades between 1670 and 1740. Around the turn of the 18th century "Amsterdam was the city where almost all bills of exchange made payable within the confines of Europe, were drafted, remitted, discounted or otherwise transacted. Amsterdam was then the centre of the international exchange trade, which was made possible by the free import and export of precious metal" (POSTHUMUS [1946], vol. I, p. 579). During most of the 18th century "the actual buying and selling of bills of exchange ... was ... centred on Amsterdam ... It was largely conducted by the city's colony of Sephardic Jews, who connected it with the precious metals trade between London and Amsterdam" (CHAPMAN [2000], p. 39).

Otherwise, the rest of the 18th century seems to have been mainly a period of stagnation: the only important new exchange contact was the one with Vienna from 1758/60, the one with Oporto following much later in 1796. This development was accompanied by the gradual decline of Amsterdam as an international trading and financial centre and the simultaneous rise of London. The foreign trade and the transport business of the Netherlands fell off remarkably, above all in the Baltic area between 1740 and 1780 – partly in the wake of the financial crises of 1763 and 1772/73. It may be regarded as an indication of this diminishing importance that the quotation on Danzig ceased in the 1770s – probably because of the declining grain exports from the Baltic (VAN TIELHOF [2002], pp. 338f.). Nevertheless, Amsterdam continued to direct all capital movements towards this region. It financed significant parts of the British trade there, and remained not only an important entrepôt between the Baltic Sea, the Atlantic area and Southern Europe, but also a financial centre in Europe with one of the most stable currencies. It was not until the French invasion and the internal tension at the time of the Batavian Republic (1795–1806) that Amsterdam finally lost its outstanding position in the international cashless payment system once and for all.

In the era of the kingdom of the Netherlands (i.e. from 1815 on), Amsterdam was the state's national financial and exchange centre. Its international importance was no longer based on payment transactions or trades with precious metals, but on transactions with debenture bonds of European and overseas states and on stock dealing from the middle of the century. During the first two decades of the 19th century the Amsterdam exchange rate current shows only a few changes: Venice was dropped as well as Breslau in 1806, representing a significant indication of the retreat of the Dutch merchant bankers from Central Europe, which became evident for the first time when the quotation on Leipzig was given up in 1742/65. The following places were newly included on the exchange rate currents: namely Naples in 1811, Frankfurt am Main (once again) in 1815, Augsburg one year later and Saint Petersburg in 1820, as well as Berlin for a short time (1821–1824). During the last decades of the 19th century this network changed in such a way that, first, Berlin joined the group in 1875, second, the quotations on the South German places were given up in November 1875 and those on Hamburg in 1884; third, the quotations on Vienna were supplemented by identical ones on Trieste (until 1894). The quotations on the Portuguese places were given up in 1891/98 and those on the Spanish ones in 1909. It was not until that year that not only the earliest quotation on an overseas place – New York – but also those on exchange markets of the Scandinavian Monetary Union (Copenhagen, Stockholm and Christiania [Oslo]) were initiated.

At the end of the 19ᵗʰ century the Amsterdam exchange rate current was so bound by tradition that Berlin and the other German bank places were still quoted under the section 'Prussian places' from 1875 to 1909, and that the quotation on Spain was not given in the new currency (peseta) but in the old one (pesos duros) even after the Spanish currency reform in 1887 (see p. 307). Quotations on London were made only on Tuesdays and Fridays, those for continental places only on Mondays and Thursdays, which is exactly the same way of quoting as was used at the time when the ship or the stagecoach arrived on only those days (HELLAUER [1936], p. 134). By the way, the weekly exchange quotations were often nominal. In the case of the less important exchange partners they were often only revised at infrequent intervals (ibid.). All in all, exchange transactions at the Amsterdam stock exchange were relatively unimportant around the turn of the 20ᵗʰ century (excluding those on London, Paris and Germany) (SWOBODA [1912], p. 44).

References: Paul Jacob MARPERGER, *Beschreibung der Banquen* ..., Halle – Leipzig 1717 (repr. Frankfurt/Main 1969), chapter VII; Philipp KALKMANN, Hollands Geldwesen im 19. Jahrhundert, *Jahrbuch für Gesetzgebung, Verwaltung und Volkswirtschaft im Deutschen Reich* 25 (1901), pp. 1223–1256; Erwin HELLAUER, *Internationale Finanzplätze. Ihr Wesen und ihre Entstehung unter besonderer Berücksichtigung Amsterdams*, Berlin 1936; Nicolas W. POSTHUMUS, *Inquiry in the History of Prices in Holland, vol. I*, Leiden 1946; Herman VAN DER WEE, Monetary, Credit, and Banking System, in *The Cambridge Economic History of Europe, vol. V: The Economic Organization of Early Modern Europe*, ed. by E.E. RICH / C. WILSON, Cambridge 1977, pp. 290–392; John J. MCCUSKER, *Money and Exchange in Europe and America, 1600–1775. A Handbook*, London – Basingstoke 1978, pp. 42–61; idem / S. HART, The Exchange on Amsterdam in London: 1590–1660, *Journal of European Economic History* 8 (1979), pp. 689–705; Jürgen SCHNEIDER / Oskar SCHWARZER, International Rates of Exchange: Structures and Trends of Payments Mechanism in Europe, 17ᵗʰ to 19ᵗʰ Century, in Wolfram FISCHER / R. Marvin MCINNIS / Jürgen SCHNEIDER (eds.), *The Emergence of a World Economy 1500–1914, Part I: 1500–1800*, Wiesbaden 1986, pp. 143–170; Friedrich ZELLFELDER, Die Niederlande zwischen Silber- und Goldstandard 1816–1914, in *WdW I/I*, pp. 35–46; Oskar SCHWARZER / Markus A. DENZEL, Internationaler Zahlungsverkehr im 18. Jahrhundert: Amsterdam, London und Paris, in *WdW VI*, pp. 1–32; Markus A. DENZEL, Wechselkurse und ihre Notierungen im 17. Jahrhundert, in *WdW III*, pp. 1–34; Pit DEHING / Marjolein 'T HART, Linking the Fortunes: Currency and Banking, 1550–1800, in Marjolein 'T HART / Joost JONKER / Jan Luiten VAN ZANDEN (eds.), *A Financial History of The Netherlands*, Cambridge 1997, pp. 37–63; Joost JONKER, The Alternative Road to Modernity: Banking and Currency, 1814–1914, in ibid., pp. 94–123; Markus A. DENZEL, Zur Finanzierung des europäischen Asienhandels in der Frühen Neuzeit: Vom Zahlungsausgleich im Gewürzhandel zum bargeldlosen Zahlungsverkehr, in idem (ed.), *Gewürze in der Frühen Neuzeit: Produktion, Handel und Konsum*, St. Katharinen 1999, pp. 37–69; Stanley D. CHAPMAN, The Evolution of Merchant Roles in Eighteenth-Century Finance, in Ranald C. MICHIE (ed.), *The Development of London as a Financial Centre*, London – New York 2000, *vol. 1: 1700–1850*, pp. 38–52; Milja VAN TIELHOF, *The 'Mother of All Trades'. The Baltic Grain Trade in Amsterdam from the Late 16ᵗʰ to the Early 19ᵗʰ Century*, Leiden – Boston – Köln 2002.

2.1 Amsterdam exchange rates

2.1.1. On London, Paris, Hamburg/Berlin and Antwerp/Belgium

	AMSTERDAM on:			
	London	**Paris**	**Hamburg**	**Antwerp**
	per 10 pounds sterling [a]	per 100 livres tournois [b]	per 100 mark banco [c]	per 100 guilders Brabant exchange money ('permißgeld') [d]
	in guilders Flemish			
1593	107.43 1m/d (2)			
1594				
1595	98.09 1m/d (3)			
1596				
1597	100.74 1m/d (1)			
1598				
1599	100.26 1m/d (1)			
1600	102.04 1m/d (3)			
1601				
1602				
1603	107.49 1m/d (1)			
1604	108.75 1m/d (1)			
1605	103.81 1m/d (3)			
1606	104.18 1m/d (3)			
1607	106.50 1m/d (2)			
1608	105.00 1m/d (2)			
1609	102.32 1m/d (4)		103.75 ss (1)	98.53 ss (1)
1610	102.99 1m/d (1)			
1611				
1612				
1613				
1614	102.00 1m/d (1)			
1615	102.24 1m/d (1)			
1616				
1617				
1618	105.00 1m/d (1)			
1619	104.52 1m/d (3)	104.17 2m/d (1)	92.50 ss (1)	97.56 ss (1)
1620	100.50 1m/d (1)			
1621				
1622	102.99 1m/d (2)			
1623				
1624	107.58 1m/d (7)	103.84 2m/d (7)	81.05 ss (7)	96.68 ss (7)
1625	108.02 1m/d (8)	103.00 2m/d (8)	81.20 ss (8)	95.99 ss (8)

	AMSTERDAM on:			
	London	**Paris**	**Hamburg**	**Antwerp**
	per 10 pounds sterling [a]	per 100 livres tournois [b]	per 100 mark banco [c]	per 100 guilders Brabant exchange money ('permißgeld') [d]
	in guilders Flemish or Flemish banco resp.			
1626	107.41 1m/d (8)	100.93 2m/d (8)	82.56 ss (8)	97.11 ss (7)
1627	107.13 1m/d (1)	104.38 2m/d (1)	81.72 ss (1)	96.16 ss (1)
1628	105.60 1m/d (2)	101.67 2m/d (2)	81.25 ss (1)	97.45 ss (2)
1629				
1630	107.80 1m/d (3)	101.36 2m/d (3)	81.54 ss (3)	98.09 ss (3)
1631	107.38 1m/d (6)	95.83 2m/d (6)	83.18 ss (6)	97.33 ss (6)
1632	109.71 1m/d (3)	96.39 2m/d (3)	82.01 ss (3)	96.20 ss (3)
1633	107.29 1m/d (4)	97.27 2m/d (4)	82.33 ss (4)	95.66 ss (4)
1634	111.38 1m/d (1)	98.86 2m/d (1)	82.50 ss (1)	96.74 ss (1)
1635	107.77 1m/d (3)	93.92 2m/d (3)	81.62 ss (3)	96.86 ss (3)
1636	105.85 1m/d (4)	87.78 2m/d (3)	81.28 ss (4)	98.48 ss (4)
1637	109.50 1m/d (2)	85.83 2m/d (2)	82.43 ss (2)	97.48 ss (2)
1638	107.75 1m/d (3)	80.35 2m/d (3)	82.66 ss (3)	97.89 ss (3)
1639				
1640	111.88 1m/d (1)	80.52 2m/d (1)	82.74 ss (1)	99.38 ss (1)
1641	116.57 1m/d (2)	84.17 2m/d (2)	83.52 ss (2)	99.02 ss (2)
1642	114.75 1m/d (4)	84.19 2m/d (4)	82.74 ss (4)	99.63 ss (1)
1643	116.21 1m/d (3)	84.20 2m/d (3)	83.63 ss (3)	95.76 ss (2)
1644				
1645	114.80 1m/d (5)	82.72 2m/d (5)	82.61 ss (5)	99.26 ss (5)
1646	111.07 1m/d (10)	82.16 2m/d (10)	81.21 ss (10)	98.66 ss (10)
1647				
1648	101.38 1m/d (4)	86.13 2m/d (3)	84.15 ss (4)	98.71 ss (4)
1649	98.25 1m/d (8)	87.03 2m/d (4)	83.72 ss (8)	99.41 ss (8)
1650	100.55 1m/d (5)	81.67 2m/d (1)	84.29 ss (5)	98.94 ss (5)
1651	110.75 1m/d (1)	81.93 2m/d (2)	82.35 ss (1)	99.51 ss (1)
1652	104.13 1m/d (2)	79.52 2m/d (3)	81.64 ss (2)	98.35 ss (2)
1653	107.09 1m/d (3)	77.31 2m/d (5)	81.93 ss (3)	97.64 ss (3)
1654	107.42 1m/d (5)		82.41 ss (5)	97.61 ss (5)
1655				
1656				
1657				
1658				
1659				
1660				
1661	109.60 1m/d (5)	81.58 2m/d (5)	81.45 ss (6)	99.05 ss (6)
1662	105.50 1m/d (2)	81.46 2m/d (2)	83.08 ss (2)	98.71 ss (2)

	AMSTERDAM on:			
	London	**Paris**	**Hamburg**	**Antwerp**
	per 10 pounds sterling [a]	per 100 livres tournois [b]	per 100 mark banco [c]	per 100 guilders Brabant exchange money ('permißgeld') [d]
	in guilders Flemish or Flemish banco resp.			
1663	108.75 1m/d (1)	82.08 2m/d (1)	80.63 ss (1)	98.65 ss (1)
1664	105.13 1m/d (1)	82.08 2m/d (1)	82.43 ss (1)	98.65 ss (1)
1665	100.63 1m/d (1)	77.50 2m/d (1)	82.27 ss (1)	99.08 ss (1)
1666				
1667				
1668	105.59 1m/d (11)	83.94 2m/d (10)	82.13 ss (10)	98.02 ss (10)
1669	106.31 1m/d (6)	82.57 2m/d (6)	80.73 ss (6)	98.70 ss (6)
1670	103.69 1m/d (2)	79.38 2m/d (2)	79.22 ss (2)	99.81 ss (2)
1671	106.69 1m/d (2)	81.30 2m/d (2)	81.25 ss (2)	99.63 ss (2)
1672	104.88 1m/d (3)	80.07 2m/d (3)	81.46 ss (3)	99.47 ss (3)
1673	102.30 1m/d (5)	78.78 2m/d (3)	81.66 ss (5)	99.38 ss (4)
1674	102.36 1m/d (6)	81.25 2m/d (6)	85.82 ss (6)	98.75 ss (6)
1675	105.75 1m/d (1)	83.75 2m/d (1)	85.00 ss (1)	99.20 ss (1)
1676	108.57 1m/d (2)	82.81 2m/d (2)	84.77 ss (2)	99.01 ss (2)
1677	108.68 1m/d (5)	82.80 2m/d (5)	83.44 ss (5)	98.62 ss (5)
1678	104.19 1m/d (2)	79.38 2m/d (1)	82.82 ss (2)	99.29 ss (2)
1679	106.94 1m/d (2)	80.57 2m/d (2)	82.89 ss (2)	99.35 ss (2)
1680	107.75 1m/d (2)	82.80 2m/d (3)	82.87 ss (3)	99.20 ss (2)
1681	106.25 1m/d (1)	81.46 2m/d (1)	81.88 ss (1)	99.51 ss (1)
1682	106.07 1m/d (2)	81.54 2m/d (2)	81.72 ss (2)	99.79 ss (2)
1683	108.50 1m/d (1)	81.88 2m/d (1)	85.79 ss (1)	99.14 ss (1)
1684				
1685	105.25 1m/d (1)	81.36 2m/d (1)	81.72 ss (1)	99.26 ss (1)
1686	108.69 1m/d (2)	81.49 2m/d (2)	83.95 ss (2)	99.88 ss (2)
1687	109.50 1m/d (1)	81.67 2m/d (1)	84.22 ss (1)	100.33 ss (1)
1688	106.75 1m/d (1)	78.54 2m/d (1)	82.89 ss (5)	100.98 ss (5)
1689	100.75 2m/d (1)	72.29 2m/d (1)	82.66 ss (1)	100.51 ss (1)
1690	101.38 2m/d (2)	74.17 2m/d (2)	82.93 ss (2)	100.48 ss (2)
1691	104.00 1m/d (1)	76.04 2m/d (1)	85.00 ss (1)	99.75 ss (1)
1692	103.25 1m/d (1)	75.11 2m/d (1)	84.14 ss (2)	99.88 ss (2)
1693	100.22 1m/d (6)	74.62 2m/d (6)	84.60 ss (7)	100.00 ss (6)
1694	97.00 1m/d (7)	76.61 2m/d (7)	84.38 ss (7)	100.00 ss (7)
1695	90.08 1m/d (10)	74.44 2m/d (10)	83.28 ss (10)	100.00 ss (10)
1696	86.63 1m/d (1)	71.88 2m/d (1)	82.97 ss (1)	100.00 ss (1)
1697				
1698	105.19 2m/d (2)	68.44 2m/d (2)	82.35 ss (2)	101.93 ss (2)
1699	105.46 1m/d (2)	76.56 2m/d (2)	83.48 ss (4)	99.83 ss (4)

	AMSTERDAM on:			
	London	**Paris**	**Hamburg**	**Antwerp**
	per 10 pounds sterling [a]	per 100 livres tournois [b]	per 100 mark banco [c]	per 100 guilders Brabant exchange money ('permißgeld') [d]
	in guilders Flemish banco			
1700	105.00 ss (4)	67.57 2m/d (3)	83.16 ss (3)	98.98 ss (4)
1701	105.69 ss (1)	67.62 2m/d (6)	82.58 ss (1)	99.30 ss (6)
1702	106.13 2m/d (1)	65.94 2m/d (1)	82.35 ss (1)	96.86 ss (1)
1703	101.75 ss (3)		84.56 ss (3)	
1704	101.66 2m/d (2)	65.42 2m/d (1)	84.14 ss (2)	99.51 ss (1)
1705	102.00 ss (2)	63.23 2m/d (1)	84.11 ss (2)	97.42 ss (2)
1706	102.39 ss (4)	66.00 2m/d (2)	81.96 ss (4)	99.57 ss (4)
1707				
1708	101.55 ss (2)	66.83 2m/d (2)	82.56 ss (3)	98.51 ss (3)
1709	99.79 ss (9)	67.19 2m/d (7)	82.74 ss (8)	98.26 ss (8)
1710	99.84 ss (9)	65.33 2m/d (6)	83.74 ss (9)	99.08 ss (9)
1711	101.96 ss (4)	58.04 2m/d (5)	82.48 ss (4)	98.65 ss (5)
1712	101.65 ss (6)	57.23 2m/d (6)	81.97 ss (5)	98.83 ss (6)
1713	106.27 ss (8)	55.52 2m/d (6)	83.03 ss (7)	98.71 ss (7)
1714	107.44 ss (11)	58.52 2m/d (9)	83.36 ss (10)	97.15 ss (9)
1715	109.00 ss (1)		82.50 ss (1)	
1716	105.66 ss (10)	66.97 2m/d (10)	82.26 ss (11)	96.96 ss (7)
1717	103.23 ss (9)	68.66 2m/d (7)	82.13 ss (9)	98.84 ss (6)
1718	103.07 ss (8)	53.93 2m/d (9)	82.00 ss (9)	98.95 ss (9)
1719	106.38 ss (1)	43.08 2m/d (1)	82.27 ss (1)	98.65 ss (1)
1720	107.25 ss (2)		82.23 ss (2)	98.35 ss (2)
1721	103.07 ss (1)	34.69 ss (1)	80.63 ss (1)	
1722	106.22 ss (2)	34.38 ss (1)	81.02 ss (2)	98.16 ss (2)
1723	104.57 ss (1)		80.94 ss (1)	98.89 ss (1)
1724	104.94 ss (1)	43.60 ss (1)	82.74 ss (1)	99.38 ss (1)
1725				
1726	106.57 ss (1)	49.01 ss (1)	81.33 ss (1)	96.86 ss (1)
1727	104.94 ss (1)	48.08 ss (1)	79.93 ss (1)	97.68 ss (1)
1728	102.41 ss (2)	47.09 ss (2)	80.90 ss (2)	99.08 ss (2)
1729	102.30 ss (3)	47.82 ss (2)	82.24 ss (3)	97.55 ss (3)
1730	102.75 ss (1)	46.36 ss (1)		
1731	103.47 ss (2)	45.63 ss (2)	81.06 ss (2)	96.97 ss (2)
1732	103.44 ss (2)	46.85 ss (2)	82.19 ss (2)	97.21 ss (1)
1733	105.03 ss (4)	45.96 ss (4)	81.35 ss (4)	98.04 ss (3)
1734	106.44 ss (9)	46.45 ss (5)	80.66 ss (8)	98.57 ss (8)
1735	106.85 ss (4)	46.87 ss (4)	81.41 ss (4)	99.69 ss (8)
1736	105.45 ss (11)	45.93 ss (10)	81.93 ss (11)	98.34 ss (10)

	London			Paris			Hamburg			Antwerp		
	AMSTERDAM on:											
	London			**Paris**			**Hamburg**			**Antwerp**		
	per 10 pounds sterling [a]			per 100 livres tournois [b]			per 100 mark banco [c]			per 100 guilders Brabant exchange money ('permißgeld') [d]		
	in guilders Flemish banco											
1737	104.17	ss	(8)	46.80	ss	(8)	82.36	ss	(8)	99.12	ss	(8)
1738	105.07	ss	(3)	46.62	ss	(3)	83.21	ss	(3)	98.25	ss	(2)
1739	105.89	ss	(9)	45.75	ss	(9)	82.87	ss	(9)	97.42	ss	(9)
1740	104.27	ss	(2)	47.02	ss	(2)	82.89	ss	(2)	97.21	ss	(2)
1741	103.55	ss	(8)	46.81	ss	(8)	82.46	ss	(8)	98.46	ss	(8)
1742	104.60	ss	(6)	45.77	ss	(6)	83.40	ss	(6)	98.68	ss	(6)
1743	103.10	ss	(2)	45.75	ss	(2)	82.86	ss	(2)	98.04	ss	(2)
1744	103.44	ss	(5)	47.00	ss	(5)	82.94	ss	(5)	98.75	ss	(5)
1745	103.57	ss	(1)	46.17	ss	(2)	82.27	ss	(2)	98.07	ss	(2)
1746	105.14	ss	(4)	45.81	ss	(4)	81.04	ss	(4)	97.25	ss	(4)
1747	105.72	ss	(2)	46.41	ss	(2)	81.02	ss	(2)	97.17	ss	(2)
1748	106.52	ss	(9)	45.72	ss	(7)	82.62	ss	(9)	96.48	ss	(8)
1749												
1750	104.45	ss	(8)	45.58	ss	(8)	83.75	ss	(8)	96.89	ss	(8)
1751	106.14	ss	(5)	45.76	ss	(5)	84.63	ss	(5)	97.20	ss	(5)
1752	105.00	ss	(4)	46.28	ss	(4)	84.42	ss	(4)	97.40	ss	(4)
1753	104.44	ss	(4)	45.69	ss	(4)	84.40	ss	(4)	97.96	ss	(3)
1754	106.96	ss	(8)	46.55	ss	(8)	85.47	ss	(8)	98.30	ss	(8)
1755	108.18	ss	(12)	46.49	ss	(12)	84.14	ss	(12)	98.69	ss	(12)
1756	107.84	ss	(10)	45.53	ss	(10)	81.61	ss	(10)	98.07	ss	(10)
1757	104.92	ss	(3)	44.67	ss	(3)	78.49	ss	(3)	96.27	ss	(3)
1758	103.42	ss	(6)	44.80	ss	(1)	78.31	ss	(6)	97.01	ss	(6)
1759												
1760	104.15	ss	(8)	44.38	ss	(7)	85.83	ss	(7)	95.96	ss	(7)
1761	103.00	ss	(3)	44.37	ss	(3)	84.85	ss	(2)	96.04	ss	(2)
1762	104.86	ss	(4)	44.85	ss	(4)	83.50	ss	(4)	95.93	ss	(4)
1763	104.90	ss	(6)	45.81	ss	(6)	83.04	ss	(6)	97.00	ss	(5)
1764	108.85	ss	(10)	46.00	ss	(10)	84.00	ss	(10)	98.02	ss	(9)
1765	108.23	ss	(6)	46.25	ss	(6)	83.53	ss	(6)	97.90	ss	(5)
1766	103.85	ss	(11)	45.75	ss	(12)	79.88	ss	(12)	97.42	ss	(12)
1767	103.54	ss	(12)	45.45	ss	(12)	78.66	ss	(12)	97.03	ss	(12)
1768	103.79	ss	(11)	45.33	ss	(11)	82.44	ss	(11)	96.39	ss	(11)
1769	102.52	ss	(11)	44.99	ss	(9)	82.76	ss	(11)	95.74	ss	(11)
1770	101.88	ss	(5)	44.83	ss	(5)	82.75	ss	(4)	95.20	ss	(5)
1771	103.12	ss	(12)	45.03	ss	(11)	83.56	ss	(12)	95.87	ss	(12)
1772	104.25	ss	(11)	45.50	ss	(10)	84.83	ss	(11)	96.69	ss	(11)
1773	106.95	ss	(12)	44.47	ss	(12)	83.30	ss	(12)	95.96	ss	(11)

	AMSTERDAM on:			
	London	**Paris**	**Hamburg**	**Antwerp**
	per 10 pounds sterling [a, e]	per 100 livres tournois, from 1796 per 100 francs [b]	per 100 mark banco [c]	per 100 guilders Brabant exchange money ('permißgeld') [d]
	in guilders Flemish banco			
1774	107.80 ss (12)	45.18 ss (12)	83.90 ss (12)	96.45 ss (12)
1775	106.10 ss (12)	45.30 ss (12)	83.45 ss (12)	96.90 ss (12)
1776	102.62 ss (11)	44.63 ss (8)	84.65 ss (11)	95.63 ss (10)
1777	102.55 ss (12)	44.51 ss (12)	84.94 ss (12)	95.28 ss (12)
1778	106.56 ss (12)	44.25 ss (12)	84.66 ss (12)	95.47 ss (12)
1779	108.31 ss (12)	43.94 ss (12)	83.53 ss (12)	95.28 ss (12)
1780	107.01 ss (10)	43.91 ss (4)	83.80 ss (10)	94.99 ss (9)
1781	101.60 ss (12)	43.56 ss (11)	83.83 ss (12)	93.74 ss (12)
1782	101.19 ss (4)	44.33 ss (3)	84.95 ss (3)	94.34 ss (3)
1783	101.63 ss (1)			
1784	109.79 ss (9)	45.00 ss (9)	85.70 ss (9)	96.76 ss (9)
1785	112.33 ss (12)	44.54 ss (12)	85.77 ss (12)	96.07 ss (12)
1786	109.89 ss (12)	44.41 ss (10)	85.33 ss (12)	95.86 ss (12)
1787	110.29 ss (12)	44.80 ss (12)	85.47 ss (12)	95.30 ss (12)
1788	113.00 ss (12)	45.34 ss (11)	87.24 ss (12)	96.47 ss (12)
1789	113.98 ss (11)	44.21 ss (12)	87.13 ss (12)	95.76 ss (12)
1790	116.12 ss (11)		88.13 ss (11)	
1791	115.46 ss (11)		87.37 ss (11)	
1792	110.55 ss (10)		86.68 ss (12)	
1793	116.14 ss (12)		87.11 ss (12)	
1794	119.80 ss (12)		90.35 ss (12)	
1795	121.50 ss (1)		95.01 ss (9)	
1796		49.35 ss (4)	93.37 ss (12)	98.04 ss (4)
1797		48.57 ss (12)	94.52 ss (12)	98.04 ss (7)
1798		48.69 ss (12)	94.76 ss (12)	
1799		50.98 ss (12)	99.72 ss (12)	
1800	*113,28* ss (8)	50.42 ss (12)	97.21 ss (12)	
1801	*112,51* ss (12)	50.95 ss (12)	98.53 ss (12)	
1802	*109,66* ss (12)	46.31 ss (12)	88.36 ss (12)	
1803	107.02 ss (12)	44.58 ss (12)	85.45 ss (12)	
1804	111.32 ss (12)	45.00 ss (11)	85.63 ss (12)	
1805	110.57 ss (12)	43.94 ss (11)	86.59 ss (12)	
1806	107.19 ss (12)	45.16 ss (12)	85.48 ss (12)	
1807	107.57 ss (8)	44.62 ss (12)	83.70 ss (12)	
1808		46.21 ss (12)	83.53 ss (12)	
1809		47.76 ss (12)	86.98 ss (12)	
1810		47.47 ss (12)	86.98 ss (12)	

	AMSTERDAM on:							
	London [f]			Paris			Hamburg		
	per 10 pounds sterling [a]			per 100 francs [b]			per 100 mark banco [c]		
	in guilders Flemish banco, from 1816 (10) in Dutch guilders								
1811				47.18	ss	(11)	87.07	ss	(11)
1812				46.48	ss	(12)	85.11	ss	(12)
1813	88.25	ss	(2)	47.71	ss	(2)	88.00	ss	(12)
1814	94.48	ss	(12)	46.17	ss	(12)	87.62	ss	(12)
1815	99.07	ss	(12)	46.17	ss	(12)	85.99	ss	(12)
1816	115.59	ss	(12)	46.51	ss	(12)	88.17	ss	(12)
1817	113.36	ss	(12)	46.36	ss	(12)	87.63	ss	(12)
1818	109.50	ss	(12)	45.58	ss	(12)	87.04	ss	(12)
1819	111.99	ss	(12)	45.99	ss	(12)	86.39	ss	(12)
1820	119.79	ss	(12)	47.16	ss	(12)	87.52	ss	(12)
1821	124.48	ss	(12)	48.68	ss	(12)	88.75	ss	(12)
1822	121.33	ss	(12)	47.83	ss	(12)	87.28	ss	(12)
1823	122.12	ss	(12)	47.40	ss	(12)	87.11	ss	(12)
1824	117.97	ss	(12)	47.00	ss	(12)	86.32	ss	(12)
1825	119.13	ss	(12)	47.57	ss	(12)	87.65	ss	(12)
1826	121.59	ss	(12)	47.43	ss	(12)	87.62	ss	(12)
1827	119.88	ss	(12)	47.33	ss	(12)	87.77	ss	(12)
1828	119.91	ss	(12)	47.38	ss	(12)	88.01	ss	(12)
1829	120.95	ss	(12)	47.35	ss	(12)	88.41	ss	(12)
1830	121.64	ss	(12)	47.56	ss	(12)	88.22	ss	(12)
1831	118.92	ss	(12)	47.32	ss	(12)	87.86	ss	(12)
1832	120.51	ss	(12)	46.86	ss	(12)	87.73	ss	(12)
1833	120.25	ss	(12)	46.79	ss	(12)	87.82	ss	(12)
1834	121.12	ss	(12)	47.72	ss	(12)	89.31	ss	(12)
1835	121.68	ss	(12)	47.62	ss	(12)	88.92	ss	(12)
1836	121.24	ss	(12)	47.57	ss	(12)	88.71	ss	(12)
1837	120.34	ss	(12)	47.24	ss	(12)	88.19	ss	(12)
1838	121.32	ss	(12)	47.50	ss	(12)	88.69	ss	(12)
1839	120.06	ss	(12)	47.56	ss	(12)	89.29	ss	(12)
1840	119.69	ss	(12)	47.37	ss	(12)	89.17	ss	(12)
1841	120.54	ss	(12)	47.48	ss	(12)	89.55	ss	(11)
1842	121.46	ss	(12)	47.52	ss	(12)	89.35	ss	(12)
1843	121.63	ss	(12)	47.42	ss	(12)	88.60	ss	(12)
1844	121.04	ss	(12)	47.37	ss	(12)	88.77	ss	(12)
1845	122.57	ss	(12)	47.69	ss	(12)	89.55	ss	(12)
1846	122.09	ss	(12)	47.45	ss	(11)	89.26	ss	(12)
1847	120.61	ss	(12)	47.29	ss	(12)	88.98	ss	(12)
1848	119.73	ss	(12)	47.04	ss	(12)	87.21	ss	(11)

	AMSTERDAM on:			
	London [f]	**Paris** [g]	**Hamburg, since 1875 Berlin**	**Belgium** [h]
	per 10 pounds sterling [a]	per 100 francs [b]	per 100 mark banco, from 1873 (3) per 100 mark [c]	per 100 Belgian francs [i]
	in Dutch guilders			
1849	120.25 ss (12)	47.39 ss (12)	87.45 ss (12)	
1850	119.80 ss (12)	47.17 ss (12)	88.08 ss (12)	
1851	118.13 ss (12)	47.09 ss (12)	88.12 ss (12)	
1852	119.27 ss (10)	47.14 ss (10)	88.54 ss (10)	
1853	117.96 ss (12)	47.16 ss (12)	88.79 ss (12)	
1854	117.07 ss (11)	46.83 ss (11)	88.40 ss (11)	
1855	118.11 ss (12)	47.00 ss (12)	88.53 ss (12)	
1856	118.12 ss (12)	46.68 ss (12)	88.47 ss (12)	
1857	117.55 ss (12)	46.64 ss (12)	88.62 ss (12)	
1858	117.21 ss (12)	46.77 ss (12)	87.97 ss (12)	
1859	116.84 ss (12)	46.56 ss (12)	88.44 ss (12)	
1860	116.94 ss (12)	46.54 ss (12)	88.18 ss (12)	
1861	118.75 ss (12)	46.93 ss (11)	88.31 ss (12)	
1862	117.63 ss (12)	46.73 ss (12)	87.99 ss (12)	
1863	117.85 ss (12)	46.77 ss (12)	88.23 ss (12)	
1864	118.22 ss (12)	46.85 ss (12)	88.43 ss (12)	
1865	118.41 ss (12)	47.14 ss (12)	88.25 ss (12)	
1866	118.15 ss (12)	46.92 ss (12)	88.13 ss (12)	
1867	118.69 ss (12)	46.97 ss (12)	88.01 ss (12)	
1868	119.01 ss (12)	47.32 ss (12)	87.92 ss (12)	
1869	119.92 ss (12)	47.67 ss (12)	88.44 ss (12)	
1870	118.73 ss (12)	47.13 ss (9)	87.78 ss (12)	
1871	119.03 ss (12)	46.65 ss (8)	87.91 ss (12)	
1872	120.19 ss (12)	47.13 ss (12)	88.36 ss (12)	
1873	120.14 ss (12)	47.21 ss (12)	88.05/59.31 ss (2+10)	
1874	118.78 ss (11)	47.14 ss (11)	58.14 ss (11)	
1875	118.67 ss (12)	47.11 ss (12)	57.88 ss (12)	47.05 ss (12)
1876	120.69 ss (12)	47.90 ss (12)	58.89 ss (12)	47.76 ss (12)
1877	120.99 ss (12)	47.97 ss (12)	58.88 ss (12)	47.85 ss (12)
1878	120.92 ss (12)	48.02 ss (12)	59.09 ss (12)	47.90 ss (12)
1879	120.70 ss (12)	47.76 ss (12)	58.98 ss (12)	47.67 ss (12)
1880	120.84 ss (12)	47.80 ss (12)	59.02 ss (12)	47.66 ss (12)
1881	121.00 ss (12)	47.88 ss (12)	59.03 ss (12)	47.73 ss (12)
1882	121.01 ss (11)	48.02 ss (11)	59.12 ss (11)	47.88 ss (11)
1883	120.93 ss (12)	47.90 ss (12)	59.06 ss (12)	47.76 ss (12)
1884	121.00 ss (12)	48.01 ss (12)	59.12 ss (12)	47.87 ss (12)

	AMSTERDAM on:										
	London [f]			**Paris** [g]			**Berlin**			**Belgium** [j]		
	per 10 pounds sterling [a]			per 100 francs [b]			per 100 mark [c]			per 100 Belgian francs [i]		
						in Dutch guilders					
1885	120.68	ss	(12)	47.78	ss	(12)	59.02	ss	(12)	47.65	ss	(12)
1886	120.69	ss	(12)	47.82	ss	(12)	59.09	ss	(12)	47.72	ss	(12)
1887	120.82	ss	(12)	47.74	ss	(12)	59.17	ss	(12)	47.61	ss	(12)
1888	121.07	ss	(12)	47.66	ss	(12)	59.01	ss	(12)	47.55	ss	(12)
1889	120.80	ss	(12)	47.85	ss	(12)	59.06	ss	(12)	47.76	ss	(12)
1890	120.83	ss	(12)	47.88	ss	(12)	59.08	ss	(12)	47.82	ss	(12)
1891	120.67	ss	(12)	47.80	ss	(12)	59.16	ss	(12)	47.69	ss	(12)
1892	120.82	ss	(12)	47.98	ss	(12)	59.14	ss	(12)	47.88	ss	(12)
1893	120.80	ss	(12)	47.94	ss	(12)	59.09	ss	(12)	47.81	ss	(12)
1894	120.70	ss	(12)	47.93	ss	(12)	59.06	ss	(12)	47.88	ss	(12)
1895	121.06	ss	(12)	47.98	ss	(12)	59.14	ss	(12)	47.92	ss	(12)
1896	121.05	ss	(12)	48.06	ss	(12)	59.24	ss	(12)	47.99	ss	(12)
1897	120.75	ss	(12)	47.98	ss	(12)	59.16	ss	(12)	47.92	ss	(12)
1898	120.67	ss	(12)	47.76	ss	(12)	58.95	ss	(12)	47.66	ss	(12)
1899	121.07	ss	(12)	47.99	ss	(12)	59.17	ss	(12)	47.89	ss	(12)
1900	120.90	ss	(12)	48.05	ss	(12)	58.99	ss	(12)	47.97	ss	(12)
1901	120.84	ss	(12)	48.00	ss	(12)	59.10	ss	(12)	47.94	ss	(12)
1902	121.25	ss	(12)	48.19	ss	(12)	59.24	ss	(12)	48.13	ss	(12)
1903	120.90	ss	(12)	48.07	ss	(12)	59.15	ss	(12)	47.99	ss	(12)
1904	120.66	ss	(12)	47.96	ss	(12)	58.99	ss	(12)	47.91	ss	(12)
1905	120.86	ss	(12)	48.05	ss	(12)	59.07	ss	(12)	47.97	ss	(12)
1906	121.12	ss	(12)	48.14	ss	(12)	59.06	ss	(12)	48.02	ss	(12)
1907	120.87	ss	(12)	47.98	ss	(12)	58.98	ss	(12)	47.86	ss	(12)
1908	120.79	ss	(12)	48.06	ss	(12)	59.11	ss	(12)	48.00	ss	(12)
1909	120.89	ss	(12)	48.00	ss	(11)	59.07	ss	(11)	47.88	ss	(11)
1910	120.75	ss	(6)	47.53	2m/d	(6)	59.02	ss	(6)	47.67	ss	(6)
1911	120.82	ss	(12)	47.52	2m/d	(12)	59.03	ss	(12)	47.67	ss	(12)
1912	120.78	ss	(12)	47.55	2m/d	(12)	58.97	ss	(12)	47.65	ss	(12)
1913	121.21	ss	(12)	47.65	2m/d	(12)	59.21	ss	(12)	47.73	ss	(12)
1914	120.96	ss	(7)	47.65	2m/d	(7)	59.06	ss	(7)	47.72	ss	(7)

[a] Concerning the English or the British currency resepctively, see pp. 3–5.

[b] Concerning the French currency, see pp. 279f.

[c] Concerning the Hamburg and the German currencies, see pp. 171–173, 179.

[d] Until 1816 the bills of exchange were paid in Brabant exchange money ('permißgeld'), which was invariably 16 2/3% better than current money (6 guilders exchange money = 7 guilders Brabant current).

[e] From 1800 to October 1802 the original quotations were made in Flemish currency and are, therefore, converted into banco on the basis of the annual average discount for bank money with regard

to current.

[f]   In the case of quotations on London, the usance 'short sight' means eight days' dato or paying out after eleven days (SWOBODA [1912], p. 46).

[g]   In the case of quotations on Paris, the usance 'short sight' means six to eight days' dato or paying out between four and eight days (ibid., p. 46).

[h]   "The internal border with Belgium presented the most formidable barrier. Until at least 1824, exchange rates between Brussels and Amsterdam fluctuated so much that the cost of specie settlements outweighed the risk of drawing bills" (JONKER [1997], p. 96).

[i]   The Belgian franc was introduced in 1832 and it was equal to the French franc, whereby 189 Dutch guilders = 400 Belgian francs (see *France*).

[j]   Identical quotations on Antwerp and Brussels since 1909.

2.1.2 On Frankfurt am Main, Leipzig, Breslau, Augsburg and Vienna/Austria

	AMSTERDAM on:				AMSTERDAM on:		
	Frankfurt				**Frankfurt**		
	per 100 rixdollars current [a]				per 100 rixdollars current [a]		
	in guilders Flemish or Flemish banco resp.				**in guilders Flemish or Flemish banco resp.**		
1609	202.50	fair	(1)	1643	213.29	fair	(3)
1610				1644			
1611				1645	211.06	fair	(4)
1612				1646	208.58	fair	(10)
1613				1647			
1614				1648	208.60	fair	(4)
1615				1649	209.79	fair	(8)
1616				1650	211.72	fair	(4)
1617				1651	202.18	fair	(1)
1618				1652	209.69	fair	(2)
1619	214.07	fair	(1)	1653	204.76	fair	(3)
1620				1654	205.94	fair	(5)
1621				1655			
1622				1656			
1623				1657			
1624	204.94	fair	(7)	1658			
1625	210.16	fair	(8)	1659			
1626	210.08	fair	(8)	1660			
1627	217.50	fair	(1)	1661	204.87	fair	(5)
1628	210.32	fair	(2)	1662	207.79	fair	(2)
1629				1663	206.70	fair	(1)
1630	209.22	fair	(3)	1664	204.91	fair	(1)
1631	210.26	fair	(6)	1665	200.67	fair	(1)
1632	212.35	fair	(3)	1666			
1633	212.50	fair	(4)	1667			
1634	213.75	fair	(1)	1668			
1635	209.74	fair	(3)	1669	205.72	fair	(6)
1636	201.10	fair	(4)	1670			
1637	204.54	fair	(2)	1671	203.21	fair	(2)
1638	209.90	fair	(3)	1672	201.69	fair	(3)
1639				1673			
1640				1674	201.47	fair	(6)
1641	206.88	fair	(2)	1675	199.14	fair	(1)
1642	208.05	fair	(4)				

	AMSTERDAM on:		
	Frankfurt	**Leipzig**	**Breslau**
	per 100 rixdollars current [a]	per 100 rixdollars current [b]	per 100 rixdollars in Kaisergeld [c]
	in guilders Flemish or guilders Flemish banco resp.		
1676	197.93 fair (1)	233.82 fair (1)	
1677	205.70 fair (4)	232.64 fair (4)	
1678	198.13 fair (2)	231.15 fair (1)	
1679	202.04 fair (2)		
1680	205.73 fair (3)	233.36 fair (3)	
1681	201.14 fair (1)		
1682	202.64 fair (2)	234.42 fair (1)	
1683	202.64 fair (1)		
1684			
1685	198.16 fair (1)		
1686	199.57 fair (2)	209.74 fair (2)	
1687	198.64 fair (1)		
1688	198.16 fair (4)	207.92 fair (4)	
1689	202.39 fair (1)	201.79 fair (1)	
1690	202.34 fair (2)	203.84 fair (1)	
1691			
1692	200.02 fair (2)	199.28 fair (1)	
1693	204.06 fair (1)	194.34 fair (1)	
1694	202.05 fair (2)	194.73 fair (2)	
1695			
1696		192.32 fair (1)	
1697		190.87 fair (1)	
1698	198.64 fair (2)	188.70 fair (1)	
1699	197.84 fair (2)	189.38 fair (3)	
1700	187.01 fair (3)		183.44 6w/d (3)
1701	188.75 fair (6)	192.88 fair (3)	182.30 6w/d (6)
1702	188.37 fair (1)	192.01 fair (1)	185.00 6w/d (1)
1703	196.59 fair (3)		186.05 6w/d (3)
1704	192.88 fair (2)	187.16 fair (2)	187.82 6w/d (2)
1705	194.52 fair (1)		187.82 6w/d (1)
1706	189.97 fair (4)	186.19 fair (2)	186.49 6w/d (4)
1707			
1708	191.20 fair (2)	188.94 fair (7)	185.08 6w/d (2)
1709	188.46 fair (7)	191.29 fair (8)	183.60 6w/d (8)
1710	192.13 fair (6)	187.29 fair (4)	184.04 6w/d (6)
1711	189.53 fair (4)	187.40 fair (5)	182.82 6w/d (5)
1712	187.02 fair (2)	189.51 fair (3)	182.39 6w/d (7)

	AMSTERDAM on:		
	Frankfurt	**Leipzig**	**Breslau**
	per 100 rixdollars current [a]	per 100 rixdollars current [b]	per 100 rixdollars in Kaisergeld [c]
	in guilders Flemish banco		
1713	186.02 fair (5)	188.55 fair (8)	186.31 6w/d (6)
1714	186.50 fair (9)	187.50 fair (1)	187.09 6w/d (8)
1715	186.75 fair (1)	185.20 fair (8)	
1716	187.11 fair (8)	186.67 fair (9)	184.34 6w/d (8)
1717	186.89 fair (7)	186.07 fair (5)	185.66 6w/d (9)
1718	188.10 fair (7)	184.20 fair (1)	183.86 6w/d (9)
1719	185.68 fair (1)	*185.77* fair (1)	
1720	186.05 fair (2)	*183.65* fair (1)	181.64 6w/d (2)
1721			178.13 6w/d (1)
1722	186.37 fair (1)		182.43 6w/d (2)
1723	186.07 fair (1)		180.63 6w/d (1)
1724			185.47 6w/d (1)
1725			
1726	187.85 fair (2)		182.50 6w/d (1)
1727	187.31 fair (2)		178.60 6w/d (1)
1728	189.04 fair (1)	185.49 fair (1)	182.43 6w/d (2)
1729	185.14 fair (1)	184.30 fair (1)	182.40 6w/d (3)
1730	184.68 fair (1)		182.19 6w/d (1)
1731	187.08 fair (3)		180.00 6w/d (1)
1732		186.37 fair (1)	184.61 6w/d (2)
1733		185.33 fair (2)	184.11 6w/d (4)
1734		183.72 fair (5)	180.46 6w/d (9)
1735		185.95 fair (3)	184.81 6w/d (4)
1736		187.53 fair (4)	183.61 6w/d (10)
1737		185.61 fair (2)	182.88 6w/d (8)
1738		185.27 fair (5)	183.39 6w/d (3)
1739		184.90 fair (4)	183.58 6w/d (9)
1740		185.92 fair (1)	183.60 6w/d (2)
1741		187.09 fair (4)	184.18 6w/d (8)
1742		187.17 fair (3)	184.95 6w/d (5)
1743			183.21 6w/d (2)
1744			181.57 6w/d (5)
1745			181.88 6w/d (1)
1746			181.62 6w/d (3)
1747			183.60 6w/d (2)
1748			182.50 6w/d (8)
1749			
1750			180.38 6w/d (8)

	AMSTERDAM on:		
	Leipzig	**Breslau**	**Vienna**
	per 100 rixdollars current, from 1764 per 100 rixdollars Konventions-Wechselzahlung [b]	per 100 rixdollars in Kaisergeld, from 1764 (4) in 'new money', from 1765 (12) per 100 livres Prussian banco [c]	per 100 guilders Konventionskurant [d]
	in guilders Flemish banco		
1751		177.07 6w/d (5)	
1752		176.14 6w/d (4)	
1753		174.30 6w/d (4)	
1754		172.91 6w/d (7)	
1755		170.60 6w/d (12)	
1756		167.47 6w/d (10)	
1757		168.44 6w/d (3)	
1758		164.48 6w/d (6)	119.17 6w/d (1)
1759			
1760		116.41 6w/d (8)	117.38 6w/d (7)
1761		110.21 6w/d (3)	117.37 6w/d (3)
1762		110.00 6w/d (4)	118.75 6w/d (3)
1763		113.02 6w/d (6)	118.72 6w/d (5)
1764	172.81 6w/d (6)	108.75/169.77 6w/d (3+4)	118.49 6w/d (8)
1765	172.93 6w/d (5)	167.19/206.25 6w/d (4+1)	119.57 6w/d (6)
1766		208.34 6w/d (12)	118.32 6w/d (12)
1767		209.07 6w/d (10)	117.09 6w/d (12)
1768		215.60 6w/d (11)	117.98 6w/d (11)
1769		216.03 6w/d (11)	116.80 6w/d (9)
1770		213.44 6w/d (4)	117.50 6w/d (5)
1771		217.89 6w/d (12)	117.22 6w/d (12)
1772		218.54 6w/d (10)	117.62 6w/d (11)
1773		215.03 6w/d (12)	115.61 6w/d (12)
1774		216.57 6w/d (12)	115.78 6w/d (12)
1775		218.72 6w/d (10)	116.57 6w/d (10)
1776		217.80 6w/d (8)	115.91 6w/d (7)
1777		218.13 6w/d (12)	115.74 6w/d (12)
1778		218.65 6w/d (12)	115.87 6w/d (12)
1779		215.91 6w/d (11)	115.72 6w/d (9)
1780		214.69 6w/d (4)	114.74 6w/d (4)
1781		215.20 6w/d (12)	113.86 6w/d (11)
1782		217.50 6w/d (3)	115.98 6w/d (3)
1783			
1784		224.83 6w/d (7)	118.34 6w/d (9)
1785		225.79 6w/d (4)	118.41 6w/d (11)

	AMSTERDAM on:			
	Frankfurt	**Breslau**	**Augsburg**	**Vienna**
	per 100 guilders Frankfurt exchange money [e]	per 100 livres Prussian banco [c]	per 100 guilders Augsburg current, from 1859 per 100 guilders South German current [f]	per 100 guilders Konventionskurant, from 1800 per 100 guilders Wiener Währung, from 1815 per 100 guilders Konventionskurant effective [d]
	in guilders Flemish, since 1816 (10) in Dutch guilders			
1786		223.75 6w/d (7)		117.56 6w/d (12)
1787		218.44 6w/d (6)		116.22 6w/d (11)
1788		222.66 6w/d (6)		118.32 6w/d (11)
1789		221.67 6w/d (3)		117.82 6w/d (10)
1790				117.58 6w/d (11)
1791				116.37 6w/d (11)
1792				117.30 6w/d (12)
1793				116.47 6w/d (12)
1794				121.99 6w/d (12)
1795				132.63 6w/d (10)
1796		242.50 6w/d (4)		127.92 6w/d (12)
1797		240.42 6w/d (12)		123.34 6w/d (12)
1798		242.50 6w/d (4)		124.87 6w/d (12)
1799				120.63 6w/d (12)
1800				113.18 6w/d (12)
1801				111.57 6w/d (12)
1802				95.33 6w/d (12)
1803		220.00 6w/d (1)		86.05 6w/d (11)
1804				84.88 6w/d (11)
1805		225.00 6w/d (2)		85.20 6w/d (11)
1806		225.00 6w/d (5)		67.71 6w/d (11)
1807				53.63 6w/d (12)
1808				50.91 6w/d (12)
1809				43.82 6w/d (12)
1810				28.84 6w/d (12)
1811				11.03 6w/d (11)
1812				11.52 6w/d (12)
1813				75.00 6w/d (2)
1814				57.54 6w/d (12)
1815	118.36 6w/d (2)		118.87 6w/d (12)	
1816	119.84 6w/d (12)		119.59 6w/d (11)	119.80 6w/d (11)
1817	117.74 6w/d (12)		117.46 6w/d (12)	118.20 6w/d (12)
1818	117.36 6w/d (12)		117.40 6w/d (12)	119.21 6w/d (12)
1819	117.08 6w/d (12)		117.46 6w/d (12)	118.09 6w/d (12)

	AMSTERDAM on:		
	Frankfurt	**Augsburg**	**Vienna**
	per 100 guilders Frankfurt exchange money, from 1843 per 100 guilders South German current [e]	per 100 guilders Augsburg current [f]	per 100 guilders Konventionskurant effective [d]
	in Dutch guilders		
1820	118.45 6w/d (12)	118.12 6w/d (12)	118.81 6w/d (12)
1821	121.25 6w/d (12)	121.24 6w/d (12)	122.23 6w/d (12)
1822	118.26 6w/d (12)	118.32 6w/d (12)	118.84 6w/d (12)
1823	117.00 6w/d (12)	116.80 6w/d (12)	117.92 6w/d (12)
1824	117.11 6w/d (12)	116.95 6w/d (12)	118.64 6w/d (12)
1825	120.22 6w/d (12)	120.13 6w/d (12)	120.72 6w/d (12)
1826	119.02 6w/d (12)	118.74 6w/d (12)	118.62 6w/d (12)
1827	119.26 6w/d (12)	118.91 6w/d (12)	119.30 6w/d (12)
1828	120.48 6w/d (12)	120.13 6w/d (12)	120.50 6w/d (12)
1829	120.73 6w/d (12)	120.23 6w/d (12)	120.54 6w/d (12)
1830	120.32 6w/d (12)	119.63 6w/d (12)	119.62 6w/d (12)
1831	120.23 6w/d (12)	119.64 6w/d (12)	119.62 6w/d (12)
1832	118.85 6w/d (12)	118.56 6w/d (12)	119.48 6w/d (12)
1833	119.38 6w/d (12)	119.28 6w/d (12)	120.44 6w/d (12)
1834	121.51 6w/d (12)	121.21 6w/d (12)	122.59 6w/d (12)
1835	120.89 6w/d (12)	120.70 6w/d (12)	121.32 6w/d (12)
1836	120.14 6w/d (12)	119.71 6w/d (12)	119.99 6w/d (12)
1837	119.28 6w/d (12)	118.84 6w/d (12)	118.41 6w/d (12)
1838	119.84 6w/d (12)	119.28 6w/d (12)	119.50 6w/d (12)
1839	120.19 6w/d (12)	119.78 6w/d (12)	119.90 6w/d (12)
1840	121.10 6w/d (12)	120.19 6w/d (12)	120.07 6w/d (12)
1841	122.04 6w/d (11)	121.10 6w/d (11)	122.39 6w/d (11)
1842	121.52 6w/d (12)	121.32 6w/d (12)	123.22 6w/d (12)
1843	100.46 6w/d (12)	120.14 6w/d (12)	122.19 6w/d (12)
1844	100.51 6w/d (12)	120.25 6w/d (12)	123.08 6w/d (12)
1845	101.00 6w/d (12)	120.54 6w/d (12)	123.02 6w/d (12)
1846	100.58 6w/d (12)	120.22 6w/d (12)	120.72 6w/d (12)
1847	99.48 6w/d (12)	118.87 6w/d (12)	119.67 6w/d (12)
1848	98.25 6w/d (12)	116.08 6w/d (12)	108.89 6w/d (12)
1849	98.97 6w/d (12)	117.68 6w/d (12)	104.69 6w/d (12)
1850	99.40 6w/d (12)	118.24 6w/d (12)	99.24 6w/d (12)
1851	99.16 6w/d (12)	117.50 6w/d (12)	93.48 6w/d (12)
1852	98.69 6w/d (10)	117.55 6w/d (10)	98.61 6w/d (11)
1853	98.90 6w/d (12)	117.85 6w/d (12)	106.05 6w/d (12)
1854	98.99 6w/d (11)	117.62 6w/d (11)	91.90 6w/d (11)
1855	99.84 6w/d (12)	118.72 6w/d (12)	96.81 6w/d (12)

	AMSTERDAM on:		
	Frankfurt	**Augsburg**	**Vienna, from 1875 Austria** [g]
	per 100 guilders South German current [e]	per 100 guilders Augsburg current, from 1859 per 100 guilders South German current [f]	per 100 guilders Konventionskurant effective, from 1859 per 100 guilders Österreichische Währung [d]
	in Dutch guilders		
1856	98.68 6w/d (12)	118.28 6w/d (12)	111.77 6w/d (12)
1857	99.12 6w/d (12)	117.85 6w/d (12)	111.06 6w/d (12)
1858	99.07 6w/d (12)	117.59 6w/d (12)	111.36 6w/d (12)
1859	99.69 6w/d (12)	98.97 6w/d (12)	96.10 6w/d (11)
1860	99.67 6w/d (12)	99.13 6w/d (12)	86.46 6w/d (12)
1861	99.88 6w/d (11)	99.54 6w/d (11)	81.19 6w/d (11)
1862	98.96 6w/d (12)	98.93 6w/d (12)	88.38 6w/d (12)
1863	98.82 6w/d (12)	98.50 6w/d (12)	100.90 6w/d (12)
1864	98.77 6w/d (12)	98.63 6w/d (12)	97.63 6w/d (12)
1865	98.34 6w/d (12)	98.27 6w/d (12)	104.50 6w/d (12)
1866	98.57 6w/d (12)	98.55 6w/d (12)	95.67 6w/d (12)
1867	98.64 6w/d (12)	98.64 6w/d (12)	91.34 6w/d (12)
1868	98.85 6w/d (12)	98.85 6w/d (12)	99.94 6w/d (12)
1869	99.25 6w/d (12)	99.25 6w/d (12)	95.00 6w/d (12)
1870	98.46 6w/d (11)	98.46 6w/d (11)	93.48 6w/d (11)
1871	99.30 6w/d (12)	99.13 6w/d (12)	94.57 6w/d (12)
1872	100.27 6w/d (12)	100.17 6w/d (12)	104.69 6w/d (12)
1873	100.34 6w/d (12)	100.34 6w/d (12)	104.71 6w/d (12)
1874	98.95 6w/d (10)	98.84 6w/d (11)	104.07 6w/d (11)
1875	98.46 ss (11)	98.46 ss (11)	103.71 3m/d (12)
1876			97.59 3m/d (12)
1877			95.38 3m/d (12)
1878			99.52 3m/d (12)
1879			101.05 3m/d (12)
1880			100.55 3m/d (12)
1881			100.98 3m/d (12)
1882			99.16 3m/d (11)
1883			99.17 3m/d (12)
1884			97.94 3m/d (12)
1885			95.17 3m/d (12)
1886			94.00 3m/d (12)
1887			93.75 3m/d (12)
1888			94.63 3m/d (12)
1889			97.98 3m/d (12)
1890			101.32 3m/d (12)

	AMSTERDAM on:
	Austria [g]
	per 100 guilders Öster-reichische Währung, from 1900 per 100 Austrian crowns [d]
	in Dutch guilders
1891	100.92 3m/d (12)
1892	98.98 3m/d (12)
1893	96.00 3m/d (12)
1894	95.17 3m/d (12)
1895	97.75 3m/d (12)
1896	99.17 3m/d (12)
1897	99.30 3m/d (12)
1898	98.34 3m/d (12)
1899	98.50 3m/d (12)
1900	48.92 3m/d (12)
1901	49.44 3m/d (12)
1902	50.00 3m/d (12)
1903	49.86 3m/d (12)
1904	49.82 3m/d (12)
1905	49.76 3m/d (12)
1906	49.71 3m/d (12)
1907	49.39 3m/d (12)
1908	49.59 3m/d (12)
1909	49.77 3m/d (12)
1910	49.58 3m/d (6)
1911	49.58 3m/d (12)
1912	49.35 3m/d (12)
1913	49.34 3m/d (12)
1914	49.56 3m/d (7)

[a] In Frankfurt up to 1766, cashless payment was effected in the imaginary rixdollar current of 90 kreuzer. The bills had to be paid half in the so-called 'edict money', i.e. in full speciesthaler (at 25.98 grammes of fine silver), the other half in the so-called 'münze', i.e. in small silver coins (e.g. in 12-kreuzer pieces, batzen, albus), whereby there was a premium (a fixed premium of 4% in the 18th century) of the imaginary rixdollar current against the rixdollar payable in edict money and in münze: 100 rixdollars current = 104 rixdollars payable in edict money and in münze (HER-BACH [1716], p. 173). The quotations in Flemish current from 1651 onwards are converted into banco on the basis of the annual average premium for bank money against current money.

[b] In Leipzig one reckoned in rixdollar of 24 good groschen at 12 pfennige, whereby in exchange transactions the rixdollar current was payable above all in two-thirds pieces (of the rixdollar, the so-called 'zweidrittel'; equal to the guilder) of Saxony or Brunswick-Lüneburg and their divisions (ibid., p. 177). The quotations in Flemish current from 1651 onwards are converted into banco on the basis of the annual average premium for bank money against current money.

[c] Up to the Prussian conquest of Silesia the Amsterdam quotations on Breslau were effected for rix-dollars 'in Kaisergeld', especially in the so-called 'Kaisergroschen', a term meaning silver groschen, but also in rixdollars specie and pieces of 17 and 7 kreuzer. Thus 1 rixdollar current was equal to 30 Kaisergroschen or silver groschen at 12 pfennige current or 90 kreuzer, 1 rixdollar specie to 40 Kaisergroschen or silver groschen or 120 kreuzer. By an edict of the Prussian king of 1751 all bills had to be paid in Prussian currency. "If the bill be payable in any other money, the payment must nevertheless be made in the said currency, allowance being made for the agio on the particular money expressed in the bill" (KELLY [1811], p. 77). The Prussian currency was the livre or pound banco of 24 groschen banco at 12 denars.

[d] Concerning the Austrian currency see pp. 255f. 'Effective' means here 'payable in hard currency', i.e. in pieces of 10 and 20 kreuzer. Since November 1858 the guilder Österreichische Währung were notes of the Wiener Nationalbank and governmental notes ('Wiener Banknoten').

[e] Concerning the Frankfurt currency since 1815, see pp. 195f.

[f] 'Augsburg current' meant – in modification of Konventionskurant, which became common especially from 1764 (NOBACK [1851], 1. Abth., p. 70) – a standard of coinage of 20 5/12 guilders per mark of Cologne. So the guilder Augsburg current of 60 kreuzer was equal to 11.45 grammes of fine silver. The guilder South German current (standard of coinage: 24½ guilders per 233.855 grammes of fine silver or 52½ guilders per pound of 500 grammes of fine silver) of 60 kreuzer became legal tender in Augsburg at the beginning of the year 1859 as a consequence of the Vienna coin treaty of 1857.

[g] Continuation of the prevailing exchange rate series on Vienna and Trieste.

2.1.3 On Italian places

	AMSTERDAM on:				AMSTERDAM on:		
	Venice				Venice		
	per 100 ducati di banco [a]				per 100 ducati di banco [a]		
	in guilders Flemish				in guilders Flemish or Flemish banco resp.		
1609	265.00	2m/d	(2)	1644			
1610				1645	229.14	2m/d	(4)
1611				1646	226.93	2m/d	(10)
1612				1647			
1613				1648	193.13	2m/d	(4)
1614				1649	192.33	2m/d	(8)
1615				1650	200.07	2m/d	(5)
1616				1651	232.50	2m/d	(1)
1617				1652	236.88	2m/d	(2)
1618				1653	232.92	2m/d	(3)
1619	239.38	2m/d	(1)	1654	233.88	2m/d	(5)
1620				1655			
1621				1656			
1622				1657			
1623				1658			
1624	254.42	2m/d	(7)	1659			
1625	259.22	2m/d	(8)	1660			
1626	252.93	2m/d	(8)	1661	234.54	2m/d	(6)
1627	252.82	2m/d	(1)	1662	236.10	2m/d	(2)
1628	241.41	2m/d	(2)	1663	243.13	2m/d	(1)
1629				1664	239.07	2m/d	(1)
1630	238.91	2m/d	(2)	1665	228.44	2m/d	(1)
1631	223.88	2m/d	(5)	1666			
1632	221.88	2m/d	(3)	1667			
1633	218.75	2m/d	(4)	1668	233.91	2m/d	(4)
1634	218.13	2m/d	(1)	1669	237.50	2m/d	(6)
1635	221.25	2m/d	(2)	1670	231.56	2m/d	(2)
1636	220.79	2m/d	(4)	1671	233.67	2m/d	(2)
1637	233.13	2m/d	(1)	1672	222.09	2m/d	(3)
1638	233.13	2m/d	(1)	1673	220.42	2m/d	(3)
1639				1674	228.70	2m/d	(6)
1640	230.00	2m/d	(1)	1675	235.00	2m/d	(1)
1641	237.50	2m/d	(1)	1676	233.37	2m/d	(1)
1642	239.27	2m/d	(3)	1677	233.82	2m/d	(5)
1643	242.04	2m/d	(2)				

	AMSTERDAM on:		
	Venice	**Leghorn**	**Genoa**
	per 100 ducati di banco [a]	per 100 pezze da otto reali [b]	per 100 pezza of 5 lire banco [c]
	in guilders Flemish or Flemish banco resp.		
1678	228.44 2m/d (2)	232.50 2m/d (1)	227.50 2m/d (1)
1679	228.44 2m/d (2)		
1680	229.38 2m/d (3)	239.80 2m/d (3)	
1681	230.00 2m/d (1)	239.38 2m/d (1)	
1682	228.44 2m/d (2)	238.75 2m/d (1)	
1683	230.32 2m/d (1)	239.69 2m/d (1)	235.63 2m/d (1)
1684			
1685	228.75 2m/d (1)	238.13 2m/d (1)	
1686	220.32 2m/d (2)	235.63 2m/d (2)	232.19 2m/d (2)
1687	223.75 2m/d (1)	233.75 2m/d (1)	
1688	223.57 2m/d (5)	232.07 2m/d (5)	231.00 2m/d (5)
1689	225.32 2m/d (1)	230.00 2m/d (1)	227.50 2m/d (1)
1690	222.89 2m/d (2)	227.97 2m/d (2)	226.25 2m/d (2)
1691	233.75 2m/d (1)	243.75 2m/d (1)	
1692	232.04 2m/d (2)	240.32 2m/d (2)	235.94 2m/d (2)
1693	233.64 2m/d (7)	241.52 2m/d (7)	240.94 2m/d (1)
1694	232.12 2m/d (7)	244.25 2m/d (7)	241.25 2m/d (1)
1695	231.63 2m/d (10)	242.10 2m/d (10)	
1696	233.13 2m/d (1)	242.50 2m/d (1)	
1697			
1698	224.46 2m/d (2)	232.97 2m/d (2)	231.25 2m/d (2)
1699	230.94 2m/d (4)	239.46 2m/d (4)	233.44 2m/d (1)
1700	232.98 2m/d (3)	237.71 2m/d (3)	236.98 2m/d (3)
1701	244.48 2m/d (6)	241.54 2m/d (6)	241.62 2m/d (6)
1702	251.31 2m/d (1)	256.88 2m/d (1)	258.13 2m/d (1)
1703	226.14 2m/d (3)	232.76 2m/d (3)	230.26 2m/d (3)
1704	243.17 2m/d (2)	250.00 2m/d (2)	251.56 2m/d (2)
1705	243.02 2m/d (1)	242.82 2m/d (1)	242.82 2m/d (1)
1706	247.00 2m/d (4)	245.74 2m/d (4)	245.98 2m/d (4)
1707			
1708	245.62 2m/d (2)	244.69 2m/d (2)	245.63 2m/d (2)
1709	239.53 2m/d (5)	240.22 2m/d (7)	239.64 2m/d (6)
1710	237.64 2m/d (6)	240.21 2m/d (6)	240.78 2m/d (6)
1711	235.27 2m/d (5)	238.07 2m/d (5)	238.66 2m/d (5)
1712	235.44 2m/d (6)	238.07 2m/d (6)	238.44 2m/d (6)
1713	234.68 2m/d (7)	235.09 2m/d (7)	237.06 2m/d (7)
1714	232.61 2m/d (10)	234.35 2m/d (10)	236.19 2m/d (10)

	AMSTERDAM on:		
	Venice	**Leghorn**	**Genoa**
	per 100 ducati di banco [a]	per 100 pezze da otto reali [b]	per 100 pezza of 5 lire banco or of 5¾ lire fuori banco (from 1741) [c]
	in guilders Flemish banco		
1715	222.02 2m/d (1)	234.38 2m/d (1)	232.82 2m/d (1)
1716	205.98 2m/d (11)	230.99 2m/d (11)	233.44 2m/d (11)
1717	198.85 2m/d (9)	236.53 2m/d (9)	238.18 2m/d (9)
1718	200.84 2m/d (9)	232.59 2m/d (9)	234.76 2m/d (9)
1719	216.15 2m/d (1)	232.50 2m/d (1)	238.75 2m/d (1)
1720	219.58 2m/d (2)	228.75 2m/d (2)	236.72 2m/d (2)
1721	212.25 2m/d (1)	229.69 2m/d (1)	234.69 2m/d (1)
1722	212.41 2m/d (2)	225.16 2m/d (2)	231.41 2m/d (2)
1723	213.23 2m/d (1)	223.13 2m/d (1)	232.50 2m/d (1)
1724	222.66 2m/d (1)	230.94 2m/d (1)	240.63 2m/d (1)
1725			
1726	217.30 2m/d (1)	221.25 2m/d (1)	232.35 2m/d (1)
1727	214.85 2m/d (1)	217.19 2m/d (1)	231.41 2m/d (1)
1728	218.52 2m/d (2)	221.09 2m/d (2)	235.08 2m/d (2)
1729	217.45 2m/d (3)	220.83 2m/d (3)	233.70 2m/d (3)
1730	220.06 2m/d (1)	222.35 2m/d (1)	235.94 2m/d (1)
1731	220.72 2m/d (2)	220.08 2m/d (2)	234.15 2m/d (2)
1732	223.32 2m/d (2)	221.65 2m/d (2)	234.38 2m/d (2)
1733	229.47 2m/d (4)	223.36 2m/d (4)	236.22 2m/d (4)
1734	229.41 2m/d (9)	222.69 2m/d (9)	233.77 2m/d (9)
1735	246.92 2m/d (4)	233.05 2m/d (4)	241.99 2m/d (4)
1736	234.29 2m/d (10)	221.22 2m/d (10)	231.97 2m/d (10)
1737	229.49 2m/d (8)	217.56 2m/d (8)	230.55 2m/d (8)
1738	231.40 2m/d (3)	218.91 2m/d (3)	230.52 2m/d (3)
1739	233.42 2m/d (9)	219.47 2m/d (9)	231.34 2m/d (9)
1740	233.90 2m/d (2)	221.25 2m/d (2)	237.81 2m/d (2)
1741	230.94 2m/d (8)	218.70 2m/d (8)	235.06 2m/d (8)
1742	233.28 2m/d (6)	219.12 2m/d (6)	235.13 2m/d (6)
1743	233.41 2m/d (2)	220.32 2m/d (2)	235.24 2m/d (2)
1744	232.56 2m/d (5)	219.41 2m/d (5)	235.57 2m/d (5)
1745	231.05 2m/d (2)	217.03 2m/d (2)	231.41 2m/d (2)
1746	231.09 2m/d (4)	216.88 2m/d (4)	223.65 2m/d (3)
1747	234.38 2m/d (2)	219.06 2m/d (2)	
1748	236.59 2m/d (9)	221.66 2m/d (8)	
1749			
1750	240.34 2m/d (8)	213.05 2m/d (8)	

	AMSTERDAM on:		
	Venice	Leghorn	Genoa
	per 100 ducati di banco [a]	per 100 pezze da otto reali [b]	per 100 pezze of 5¾ lire fuori banco [c]
	in guilders Flemish banco		
1751	245.75 2m/d (5)	217.16 2m/d (5)	216.25 2m/d (5)
1752	246.70 2m/d (4)	222.15 2m/d (4)	221.72 2m/d (4)
1753	244.36 2m/d (4)	220.71 2m/d (4)	226.25 2m/d (2)
1754	245.51 2m/d (8)	216.76 2m/d (8)	214.77 2m/d (8)
1755	244.76 2m/d (12)	215.67 2m/d (12)	213.83 2m/d (12)
1756	239.62 2m/d (10)	211.70 2m/d (10)	209.28 2m/d (10)
1757	240.08 2m/d (3)	211.77 2m/d (9)	209.37 2m/d (3)
1758	239.40 2m/d (1)	213.13 2m/d (1)	210.00 2m/d (1)
1759			
1760	240.37 2m/d (7)	214.66 2m/d (7)	211.85 2m/d (7)
1761	244.95 2m/d (3)	218.28 2m/d (3)	216.04 2m/d (3)
1762	245.67 2m/d (4)	219.89 2m/d (4)	216.60 2m/d (4)
1763	247.60 2m/d (6)	221.43 2m/d (6)	219.14 2m/d (6)
1764	248.10 2m/d (10)	220.35 2m/d (10)	217.63 2m/d (10)
1765	249.21 2m/d (6)	222.84 2m/d (6)	219.74 2m/d (6)
1766	243.49 2m/d (12)	218.11 2m/d (12)	214.99 2m/d (11)
1767	239.42 2m/d (12)	214.52 2m/d (12)	212.15 2m/d (12)
1768	240.97 2m/d (11)	217.01 2m/d (11)	212.65 2m/d (11)
1769	240.80 2m/d (9)	216.98 2m/d (9)	213.08 2m/d (9)
1770	242.49 2m/d (5)	216.72 2m/d (5)	213.25 2m/d (5)
1771	243.55 2m/d (12)	218.72 2m/d (12)	214.14 2m/d (12)
1772	246.12 2m/d (11)	219.78 2m/d (11)	215.57 2m/d (11)
1773	239.07 2m/d (12)	214.26 2m/d (12)	211.04 2m/d (12)
1774	243.11 2m/d (12)	215.99 2m/d (12)	212.66 2m/d (12)
1775	242.86 2m/d (12)	217.15 2m/d (12)	214.04 2m/d (11)
1776	246.86 2m/d (1)	220.63 2m/d (1)	212.81 2m/d (8)
1777	246.88 2m/d (12)	215.51 2m/d (12)	210.45 2m/d (12)
1778	245.42 2m/d (12)	214.53 2m/d (12)	208.90 2m/d (12)
1779	243.97 2m/d (12)	213.50 2m/d (12)	216.32 2m/d (10)
1780	243.03 2m/d (4)	214.53 2m/d (3)	205.05 2m/d (4)
1781	241.05 2m/d (12)	211.83 2m/d (11)	202.46 2m/d (12)
1782	248.55 2m/d (3)	217.01 2m/d (3)	207.12 2m/d (3)
1783			
1784	255.32 2m/d (9)	224.54 2m/d (9)	210.62 2m/d (9)
1785	252.61 2m/d (12)	221.09 2m/d (12)	210.39 2m/d (10)
1786	254.49 2m/d (12)	224.83 2m/d (12)	209.13 2m/d (12)
1787	253.45 2m/d (12)	225.63 2m/d (12)	210.97 2m/d (11)
1788	253.76 2m/d (12)	226.55 2m/d (12)	212.64 2m/d (11)

	AMSTERDAM on:			
	Venice	**Leghorn**	**Genoa**	**Naples**
	per 100 ducati di banco [a]	per 100 pezze da otto reali [b]	per 100 pezze of 5¾ lire fuori banco [c]	per 100 ducati del regno [d]
	in guilders Flemish banco, from 1816 (10) in Dutch guilders			
1789	252.72 2m/d (12)	227.76 2m/d (12)	211.77 2m/d (11)	
1790				
1791				
1792				
1793				
1794				
1795				
1796	277.93 2m/d (4)	250.18 2m/d (4)	228.91 2m/d (4)	
1797	266.57 2m/d (12)	249.32 2m/d (12)	227.64 2m/d (12)	
1798	251.05 2m/d (12)	254.09 2m/d (12)	234.20 2m/d (12)	
1799	253.86 2m/d (12)	265.54 2m/d (12)	244.09 2m/d (12)	
1800	254.28 2m/d (12)	252.08 2m/d (12)	228.05 2m/d (8)	
1801	229.49 2m/d (12)	259.27 2m/d (12)	234.49 2m/d (12)	
1802	189.80 2m/d (3)	233.22 2m/d (12)	213.67 2m/d (12)	
1803		226.44 2m/d (12)	208.09 2m/d (12)	
1804		231.96 2m/d (11)	212.12 2m/d (11)	
1805	29.79 2m/d (2)	237.13 2m/d (11)	216.26 2m/d (11)	
1806	29.26 2m/d (2)	233.51 2m/d (12)	214.94 2m/d (12)	
1807		226.49 2m/d (12)	209.36 2m/d (12)	
1808		234.20 2m/d (11)	219.59 2m/d (11)	
1809		245.12 2m/d (12)	227.36 2m/d (12)	
1810		245.12 2m/d (12)	226.55 2m/d (12)	
1811		235.87 2m/d (11)	218.67 2m/d (11)	201.25 2m/d (2)
1812		233.62 2m/d (12)	219.88 2m/d (12)	199.85 2m/d (12)
1813		238.17 2m/d (2)	225.34 2m/d (2)	202.50 2m/d (2)
1814		232.24 2m/d (12)	219.88 2m/d (12)	197.19 2m/d (12)
1815		225.34 2m/d (12)	212.06 3m/d (12)	190.32 2m/d (12)
1816		230.58 2m/d (12)	215.57 3m/d (12)	191.72 2m/d (12)
1817		230.75 2m/d (12)	216.32 3m/d (12)	192.63 2m/d (12)
1818		236.84 2m/d (12)	218.56 3m/d (12)	200.73 2m/d (12)
1819		236.21 2m/d (12)	215.40 3m/d (12)	191.15 2m/d (12)
1820		237.59 2m/d (12)	222.12 3m/d (12)	195.26 2m/d (12)
1821		246.16 2m/d (12)	229.25 3m/d (12)	207.24 2m/d (12)
1822		242.36 2m/d (12)	224.08 3m/d (12)	204.82 2m/d (12)
1823		238.57 2m/d (12)	222.18 3m/d (12)	198.55 2m/d (12)
1824		236.50 2m/d (12)	219.71 3m/d (12)	192.14 2m/d (12)
1825		247.02 2m/d (12)	226.32 3m/d (12)	202.61 2m/d (12)
1826		242.88 2m/d (12)	222.18 3m/d (12)	198.49 2m/d (12)

	AMSTERDAM on:		
	Leghorn	**Genoa**	**Naples**
	per 100 pezze da otto reali, from 1837 (7) per 100 Tuscan lire moneta buona, from 1860 (9) per 100 Piedmontese lire nuove [b]	per 100 pezze of 5¾ lire fuori banco, from 1827 (4) per 100 Piedmontese lire nuove [c]	per 100 ducati del regno [d]
		in Dutch guilders	
1827	239.83 2m/d (12)	220.51/46.77 3m/d (3+9)	193.34 2m/d (12)
1828	242.13 2m/d (12)	47.30 3m/d (12)	197.82 2m/d (12)
1829	241.21 2m/d (12)	47.24 3m/d (12)	201.38 2m/d (12)
1830	242.31 2m/d (12)	47.09 3m/d (12)	201.07 2m/d (12)
1831	238.68 2m/d (12)	46.72 3m/d (12)	197.61 2m/d (12)
1832	239.55 2m/d (12)	46.74 3m/d (12)	202.71 2m/d (12)
1833	238.22 2m/d (12)	46.64 3m/d (12)	201.59 2m/d (12)
1834	246.33 2m/d (12)	47.50 3m/d (12)	206.49 2m/d (12)
1835	243.17 2m/d (12)	47.29 3m/d (12)	205.71 2m/d (12)
1836	244.15 2m/d (12)	47.11 3m/d (12)	205.29 2m/d (12)
1837	239.32/38.73 2m/d (6+6)	46.31 3m/d (12)	198.31 2m/d (12)
1838	38.74 2m/d (12)	46.75 3m/d (12)	198.49 2m/d (12)
1839	39.65 2m/d (12)	46.76 3m/d (12)	200.00 2m/d (12)
1840	39.64 2m/d (12)	46.74 3m/d (12)	201.67 2m/d (12)
1841	39.97 2m/d (12)	46.98 3m/d (12)	200.06 2m/d (12)
1842	40.31 2m/d (12)	47.05 3m/d (12)	203.21 2m/d (12)
1843	39.61 2m/d (12)	46.82 3m/d (12)	202.45 2m/d (12)
1844	39.73 2m/d (12)	46.85 3m/d (12)	199.80 2m/d (12)
1845	39.89 2m/d (12)	47.06 3m/d (12)	204.12 2m/d (12)
1846	39.88 2m/d (12)	46.79 3m/d (12)	203.70 2m/d (11)
1847	39.44 2m/d (12)	46.40 3m/d (12)	201.88 2m/d (12)
1848	37.50 2m/d (12)	45.21 3m/d (12)	188.13 2m/d (12)
1849	37.50 2m/d (12)	44.75 3m/d (12)	197.30 2m/d (12)
1850	38.81 2m/d (12)	45.71 3m/d (12)	202.35 2m/d (12)
1851	38.40 2m/d (12)	46.05 3m/d (12)	201.20 2m/d (12)
1852	38.62 2m/d (10)	46.47 3m/d (10)	201.97 2m/d (10)
1853	39.09 2m/d (12)	46.34 3m/d (12)	204.09 2m/d (12)
1854	38.17 2m/d (11)	45.56 3m/d (11)	206.08 2m/d (11)
1855	38.83 2m/d (12)	45.96 3m/d (12)	214.64 2m/d (12)
1856	39.12 2m/d (12)	45.56 3m/d (12)	214.90 2m/d (12)
1857	39.17 2m/d (12)	45.46 3m/d (12)	206.83 2m/d (12)
1858	39.02 2m/d (12)	45.50 3m/d (12)	200.42 2m/d (12)
1859	38.58 2m/d (11)	45.32 3m/d (12)	196.59 2m/d (11)
1860	38.36/45.66 2m/d (8+4)	45.81 3m/d (12)	193.18 2m/d (12)

	AMSTERDAM on:		
	Leghorn	**Genoa**	**Naples**
	per 100 Piedmontese lire nuove, from 1861 (8) per 100 Italian lire [e]		per 100 ducati del regno, from 1863 per 100 Italian lire [d]
	in Dutch guilders		
1861	45.75 2m/d (12)	45.89 3m/d (11)	192.96 2m/d (11)
1862	45.90 2m/d (12)	45.90 3m/d (12)	194.93 2m/d (12)
1863	45.77 2m/d (12)	45.77 3m/d (12)	45.75 2m/d (12)
1864	45.60 2m/d (12)	45.60 3m/d (12)	45.60 2m/d (12)
1865	46.06 2m/d (12)	46.06 3m/d (12)	46.06 2m/d (12)
1866	43.38 2m/d (12)	43.10 3m/d (12)	43.10 2m/d (12)
1867	43.08 2m/d (12)	43.08 3m/d (12)	42.86 2m/d (12)
1868	42.11 2m/d (12)	42.11 3m/d (12)	42.11 2m/d (12)
1869	44.85 2m/d (12)	44.85 3m/d (12)	44.85 2m/d (12)
1870	44.42 2m/d (12)	44.42 3m/d (10)	44.42 2m/d (12)
1871	43.81 2m/d (12)	43.81 3m/d (12)	43.81 2m/d (12)
1872	42.86 2m/d (12)	42.86 3m/d (12)	42.86 2m/d (12)
1873	40.77 2m/d (12)	40.77 3m/d (12)	40.77 2m/d (12)
1874	41.25 2m/d (12)	41.25 3m/d (11)	41.25 2m/d (12)
	Italy [f]		
	per 100 Italian lire [e]		
	in Dutch guilders		
1875		42.73 3m/d (12)	
1876		43.40 3m/d (12)	
1877		42.83 3m/d (12)	
1878		43.15 3m/d (12)	
1879		42.41 3m/d (12)	
1880		42.82 3m/d (12)	
1881		46.13 3m/d (12)	
1882		45.71 3m/d (11)	
1883		46.99 3m/d (12)	
1884		47.29 3m/d (12)	
1885		46.72 3m/d (12)	
1886		47.02 3m/d (12)	
1887		46.29 3m/d (12)	
1888		46.14 3m/d (12)	
1889		46.63 3m/d (12)	
1890		46.20 3m/d (12)	
1891		45.76 3m/d (12)	
1892		44.94 3m/d (12)	
1893		43.07 3m/d (12)	
1894		41.44 3m/d (12)	

	AMSTERDAM on:
	Italy [f]
	per 100 Italian lire [e]
	in Dutch guilders
1895	44.05 3m/d (12)
1896	42.92 3m/d (12)
1897	44.25 3m/d (12)
1898	43.77 3m/d (12)
1899	43.42 3m/d (12)
1900	43.67 3m/d (12)
1901	44.48 3m/d (12)
1902	46.73 3m/d (12)
1903	47.50 3m/d (12)
1904	47.09 3m/d (12)
1905	47.36 3m/d (12)
1906	47.46 3m/d (12)
1907	47.30 3m/d (12)
1908	47.37 3m/d (12)
1909	47.18 3m/d (12)
1910	46.89 3m/d (6)
1911	46.81 3m/d (12)
1912	46.73 3m/d (12)
1913	46.39 3m/d (12)
1914	47.06 3m/d (7)

[a]   Concerning the Venetian currency, see pp. 104f.

[b]   Concerning the Tuscan currency, see p. 106. From 1796 to June 1837 including 7% premium for lire d'oro: 107 lire moneta buona = 100 lire d'oro.

[c]   Concerning the Genoese currency, see pp. 107f.

[d]   The system of accounting in ducati (called 'ducati del regno' or 'ducati di regno' from the 18th century) of 10 carlini at 10 grani or of 5 tari at 20 grani had been common practice in the kingdom of Naples for centuries and was continued during the Restoration era (after the Act of August 18th 1814). The Act of April 20th 1818 fixed the fineness of the ducato at 19.12 grammes of fine silver as it had already been when it was officially introduced in 1794 and confirmed in 1804 (from 1784 18.96 grammes of fine silver; cf. NOBACK [1851], pp. 710f.). This new silver ducato – later generally called 'ducato del regno' or 'ducato di regno' – should have been divided into 100 centesimi or grani. Simultaneously, it became the unit of account of the whole Kingdom of the Two Sicilies which means that the hitherto independent Sicilian system based on the oncia (56.896 gr. fine silver) of 30 tari (or carlini; 1 oncia = 3 ducati) at 20 grani was removed by this act. With the integration of the Kingdom of the Two Sicilies into the new Kingdom of Italy in 1862 the Italian lira of 100 centesimi became the currency and accounting unit in Naples.

[e]   Concerning the Italian currency, see p. 108.

[f]   Continuation of the prevailing exchange rate series on Genoa, Naples and Leghorn.

2.1.4 On Madrid/Spain, Lisbon/Portugal, Danzig and Saint Petersburg

	AMSTERDAM on:
	Danzig
	per 100 guilders Polish current [a]
	in guilders Flemish
1609	169.02 1m/s (2)
1610	
1611	
1612	
1613	
1614	
1615	
1616	
1617	
1618	
1619	145.75 1m/s (1)
1620	
1621	
1622	
1623	
1624	94.53 1m/s (7)
1625	91.52 1m/s (8)
1626	89.67 1m/s (8)
1627	77.42 1m/s (1)
1628	75.80 1m/s (2)
1629	
1630	81.30 1m/s (3)
1631	81.43 1m/s (6)
1632	80.30 1m/s (3)
1633	81.04 1m/s (4)
1634	82.76 1m/s (1)
1635	82.01 1m/s (3)
1636	82.46 1m/s (4)
1637	81.64 1m/s (2)
1638	80.45 1m/s (3)
1639	
1640	81.27 1m/s (1)
1641	80.87 1m/s (2)
1642	81.03 1m/s (4)
1643	81.02 1m/s (3)

	AMSTERDAM on:		
	Madrid	**Lisbon**	**Danzig**
	per 100 ducados de cambio ('new money') [b]	per 100 crusados [c]	per 100 guilders Polish current [a]
	in guilders Flemish or Flemish banco resp.		
1644			
1645			79.73 1m/s (5)
1646			79.28 1m/s (10)
1647			
1648			80.81 1m/s (4)
1649			81.33 1m/s (8)
1650			81.95 1m/s (7)
1651			80.90 1m/s (1)
1652			80.99 1m/s (2)
1653			79.69 1m/s (3)
1654			79.72 1m/s (5)
1655			
1656			
1657			
1658			
1659			
1660			
1661	244.00 2m/d (1)	175.00 2m/d (1)	80.61 1m/s (6)
1662			82.57 1m/s (2)
1663			81.64 1m/s (1)
1664			76.68 1m/s (1)
1665			75.95 1m/s (1)
1666			
1667			
1668			
1669			74.89 1m/s (6)
1670			
1671			70.80 1m/s (2)
1672			70.46 1m/s (3)
1673			
1674			77.66 1m/s (6)
1675			79.47 1m/s (1)
1676	241.50 2m/d (1)	149.38 2m/d (1)	77.60 1m/s (2)
1677	244.00 2m/d (4)	148.29 2m/d (3)	73.58 1m/s (5)
1678	226.00 2m/d (1)	140.94 2m/d (2)	73.63 1m/s (2)
1679			70.87 1m/s (2)
1680	244.84 2m/d (3)	149.48 2m/d (3)	65.50 1m/s (3)

	AMSTERDAM on:		
	Madrid	**Lisbon**	**Danzig**
	per 100 ducados de cambio ('new money') [b]	per 100 crusados [c]	per 100 guilders Polish current [a]
	in guilders Flemish banco		
1681	250.00 2m/d (1)	140.63 2m/d (1)	
1682	245.75 2m/d (2)	139.69 2m/d (2)	69.91 1m/s (2)
1683	253.00 2m/d (1)	138.75 2m/d (1)	70.04 1m/s (1)
1684			
1685	248.00 2m/d (1)	141.25 2m/d (1)	69.37 1m/s (1)
1686	252.00 2m/d (2)	135.63 2m/d (2)	69.70 1m/s (2)
1687	247.00 2m/d (1)	131.88 2m/d (1)	66.67 1m/s (1)
1688	247.94 2m/d (5)	137.88 2m/d (5)	66.12 1m/s (1)
1689	237.50 2m/d (1)	126.25 2m/d (1)	66.30 1m/s (1)
1690	238.75 2m/d (2)	127.19 2m/d (2)	66.46 1m/s (2)
1691	239.00 2m/d (1)	123.75 2m/d (1)	
1692	248.75 2m/d (1)	125.00 2m/d (1)	67.29 1m/s (1)
1693	244.51 2m/d (7)	128.55 2m/d (7)	70.87 1m/s (1)
1694	242.59 2m/d (7)	128.62 2m/d (7)	69.66 1m/s (2)
1695	244.33 2m/d (10)	119.80 2m/d (10)	
1696	253.75 2m/d (1)	119.22 2m/d (1)	
1697			
1698	251.25 2m/d (2)	119.07 2m/d (2)	69.50 1m/s (1)
1699	251.64 2m/d (4)	126.25 2m/d (4)	71.01 1m/s (1)
1700	254.70 2m/d (3)	129.38 2m/d (3)	65.94 40d/s (4)
1701	253.70 2m/d (6)	128.20 2m/d (6)	64.27 40d/s (6)
1702	240.32 2m/d (1)	119.38 2m/d (1)	64.40 40d/s (1)
1703		118.02 2m/d (3)	67.00 40d/s (3)
1704	240.00 2m/d (1)	122.82 2m/d (2)	65.70 40d/s (2)
1705	241.25 2m/d (1)	118.13 2m/d (1)	65.52 40d/s (2)
1706	251.18 2m/d (4)	118.48 2m/d (4)	64.21 40d/s (4)
1707			
1708	256.72 2m/d (2)	107.50 2m/d (2)	65.20 40d/s (3)
1709	245.76 2m/d (7)	107.30 2m/d (7)	68.08 40d/s (6)
1710	248.81 2m/d (6)	110.65 2m/d (6)	66.32 40d/s (6)
1711	245.13 2m/d (5)	104.47 2m/d (5)	63.52 40d/s (5)
1712	245.06 2m/d (6)	109.47 2m/d (5)	63.17 40d/s (6)
1713	240.10 2m/d (7)	112.92 2m/d (7)	65.55 40d/s (7)
1714	246.58 2m/d (10)	116.78 2m/d (10)	68.13 40d/s (11)
1715	245.94 2m/d (1)	116.25 2m/d (1)	64.06 40d/s (1)
1716	238.92 2m/d (11)	115.57 2m/d (11)	64.03 40d/s (11)
1717	244.07 2m/d (9)	114.48 2m/d (9)	62.36 40d/s (8)

	AMSTERDAM on:		
	Madrid	**Lisbon**	**Danzig**
	per 100 ducados de cambio [b]	per 100 crusados [c]	per 100 guilders Polish current [a]
	in guilders Flemish banco		
1718	235.97 2m/d (9)	111.95 2m/d (9)	62.36 40d/s (9)
1719	232.50 2m/d (1)	113.13 2m/d (1)	63.61 40d/s (1)
1720	230.94 2m/d (2)	112.19 2m/d (2)	64.46 40d/s (2)
1721	221.88 2m/d (1)	111.56 2m/d (1)	62.29 40d/s (1)
1722	233.75 2m/d (2)	112.89 2m/d (2)	61.54 40d/s (2)
1723	230.94 2m/d (1)	113.13 2m/d (1)	63.83 40d/s (1)
1724	242.19 2m/d (1)	114.38 2m/d (1)	64.29 40d/s (1)
1725			
1726	251.26 2m/d (1)	112.50 2m/d (1)	63.83 40d/s (1)
1727	255.00 2m/d (1)	112.50 2m/d (1)	61.44 40d/s (1)
1728	256.88 2m/d (2)	112.82 2m/d (2)	62.94 40d/s (2)
1729	253.86 2m/d (3)	112.76 2m/d (3)	63.05 40d/s (3)
1730	251.88 2m/d (1)	113.60 2m/d (1)	61.44 40d/s (1)
1731	247.67 2m/d (2)	113.20 2m/d (2)	61.35 40d/s (2)
1732	254.61 2m/d (2)	114.46 2m/d (2)	61.44 40d/s (2)
1733	244.49 2m/d (4)	114.73 2m/d (4)	62.70 40d/s (4)
1734	246.56 2m/d (9)	115.43 2m/d (9)	63.70 40d/s (5)
1735	248.99 2m/d (4)	117.23 2m/d (4)	63.78 40d/s (4)
1736	249.91 2m/d (10)	115.61 2m/d (10)	61.80 40d/s (10)
1737	245.61 2m/d (8)	113.92 2m/d (8)	61.83 40d/s (7)
1738	241.72 2m/d (3)	115.13 2m/d (3)	61.72 40d/s (3)
1739	241.81 2m/d (9)	115.34 2m/d (9)	62.22 40d/s (9)
1740	253.76 2m/d (2)	112.89 2m/d (2)	64.07 40d/s (2)
1741	247.36 2m/d (8)	112.15 2m/d (8)	62.43 40d/s (8)
1742	233.89 2m/d (6)	114.02 2m/d (6)	61.88 40d/s (6)
1743	239.46 2m/d (2)	114.61 2m/d (2)	61.75 40d/s (2)
1744	250.75 2m/d (5)	110.97 2m/d (5)	61.38 40d/s (5)
1745	238.21 2m/d (2)	110.47 2m/d (2)	61.23 40d/s (2)
1746	237.39 2m/d (4)	114.98 2m/d (4)	61.41 40d/s (4)
1747	243.68 2m/d (2)	114.38 2m/d (2)	61.75 40d/s (2)
1748	239.20 2m/d (9)	114.97 2m/d (9)	61.98 40d/s (9)
1749			
1750	236.76 2m/d (8)	113.92 2m/d (8)	60.61 40d/s (8)
1751	242.07 2m/d (5)	116.22 2m/d (5)	59.27 40d/s (5)
1752	243.52 2m/d (2)	115.28 2m/d (4)	58.50 40d/s (4)
1753	243.52 2m/d (4)	115.00 2m/d (4)	58.26 40d/s (4)
1754	244.34 2m/d (8)	117.13 2m/d (8)	56.86 40d/s (8)
1755	243.14 2m/d (12)	117.25 2m/d (11)	56.77 40d/s (10)

	AMSTERDAM on:		
	Madrid	**Lisbon**	**Danzig**
	per 100 ducados de cambio [b]	per 100 crusados [c]	per 100 guilders Polish current [a]
	in guilders Flemish banco		
1756	236.24 2m/d (10)	116.09 2m/d (9)	55.89 40d/s (9)
1757	233.96 2m/d (3)	112.29 2m/d (3)	56.49 40d/s (3)
1758	235.31 2m/d (1)	111.56 2m/d (1)	56.37 40d/s (6)
1759			
1760	237.97 2m/d (7)	114.69 2m/d (7)	45.13 40d/s (4)
1761	236.36 2m/d (3)	113.39 2m/d (3)	44.05 40d/s (3)
1762	238.76 2m/d (4)	114.42 2m/d (4)	45.14 40d/s (4)
1763	240.52 2m/d (6)	115.55 2m/d (6)	47.11 40d/s (6)
1764	240.26 2m/d (9)	118.34 2m/d (10)	46.73 40d/s (11)
1765	244.45 2m/d (6)	118.57 2m/d (6)	44.78 40d/s (6)
1766	240.21 2m/d (12)	114.82 2m/d (12)	43.42 40d/s (8)
1767	237.86 2m/d (12)	115.04 2m/d (11)	
1768	237.10 2m/d (11)	114.90 2m/d (10)	42.56 40d/s (8)
1769	232.95 2m/d (8)	114.25 2m/d (8)	42.38 40d/s (5)
1770	234.03 2m/d (5)	113.84 2m/d (5)	42.89 40d/s (4)
1771	237.01 2m/d (12)	115.45 2m/d (12)	43.08 40d/s (8)
1772	239.16 2m/d (11)	116.10 2m/d (11)	42.26 40d/s (3)
1773	235.44 2m/d (12)	116.85 2m/d (11)	
1774	235.23 2m/d (12)	118.24 2m/d (12)	
1775	236.46 2m/d (12)	115.37 3m/d (12)	
1776	240.00 2m/d (1)	115.94 3m/d (1)	43.69 40d/s (1)
1777	232.71 2m/d (12)	111.71 3m/d (12)	
1778	230.86 2m/d (12)	113.83 3m/d (12)	
1779	227.88 2m/d (11)	112.86 3m/d (11)	
1780	227.81 2m/d (4)	113.36 3m/d (4)	
1781	211.70 2m/d (12)	112.43 3m/d (11)	
1782	222.50 2m/d (3)	114.06 3m/d (3)	
1783			
1784	223.97 2m/d (9)	119.58 3m/d (9)	
1785	223.13 2m/d (12)	118.82 3m/d (12)	
1786	222.09 2m/d (12)	120.71 3m/d (12)	
1787	229.41 2m/d (12)	121.75 3m/d (12)	
1788	231.76 2m/d (12)	123.75 3m/d (12)	
1789	230.09 2m/d (12)	124.79 3m/d (12)	
1790			
1791			
1792			
1793			

	AMSTERDAM on:		
	Madrid	**Lisbon**	**Saint Petersburg**
	per 100 ducados de cambio [b]	per 100 crusados [c]	per 100 banco roubles [d]
	in guilders Flemish banco, from 1816 (10) in Dutch guilders		
1794			
1795			
1796	*189.84* 2m/d (4)	135.43 3m/d (4)	
1797	*204.93* 2m/d (12)	143.28 3m/d (12)	
1798	*206.28* 2m/d (12)	144.04 3m/d (12)	
1799	*163.39* 2m/d (10)	142.69 3m/d (10)	
1800	256.36 2m/d (6)	116.98 3m/d (12)	
1801	267.38 2m/d (12)	119.27 3m/d (12)	
1802	232.50 2m/d (12)	120.44 3m/d (12)	
1803	224.79 2m/d (12)	113.32 3m/d (12)	
1804	224.21 3m/d (11)	113.21 3m/d (11)	
1805	213.47 3m/d (11)	111.15 3m/d (11)	
1806	223.13 3m/d (12)	110.18 3m/d (12)	
1807	236.24 3m/d (12)	113.35 3m/d (12)	
1808	250.95 3m/d (8)	120.78 3m/d (8)	
1809	262.25 3m/d (10)		
1810	259.19 3m/d (10)		
1811	249.15 3m/d (11)		
1812	239.79 3m/d (12)		
1813	240.63 3m/d (2)		
1814	245.06 3m/d (12)	109.69 3m/d (8)	
1815	229.04 3m/d (12)	109.03 3m/d (12)	
1816	232.22 3m/d (12)	110.29 3m/d (12)	
1817	236.46 3m/d (12)	110.20 3m/d (12)	
1818	248.82 3m/d (12)	107.37 3m/d (12)	
1819	243.43 3m/d (12)	103.14 3m/d (12)	
1820	241.67 3m/d (12)	101.38 3m/d (12)	49.95 2m/d (3)
1821	260.94 3m/d (12)	103.81 3m/d (12)	48.25 2m/d (12)
1822	256.76 3m/d (12)	104.05 3m/d (12)	47.99 2m/d (12)
1823	256.05 3m/d (12)	105.42 3m/d (12)	47.61 2m/d (12)
1824	249.04 3m/d (12)	100.75 3m/d (12)	45.97 2m/d (12)
1825	250.55 3m/d (12)	101.19 3m/d (12)	49.07 2m/d (12)
1826	245.50 3m/d (12)	100.50 3m/d (12)	46.93 2m/d (12)
1827	237.27 3m/d (12)	98.26 3m/d (12)	49.98 2m/d (12)
1828	248.18 3m/d (12)	91.98 3m/d (12)	50.79 2m/d (12)
1829	254.74 3m/d (12)	90.95 3m/d (12)	52.76 2m/d (12)
1830	252.19 3m/d (12)	89.01 3m/d (12)	52.74 2m/d (12)
1831	253.57 3m/d (12)	92.19 3m/d (12)	51.59 2m/d (12)

	AMSTERDAM on:		
	Madrid	**Lisbon**	**Saint Petersburg**
	per 100 ducados de cambio, from 1847 (6) per 100 pesos duros [b]	per 100 crusados [c]	per 100 banco roubles, from 1839 (9) per 100 silver roubles, from 1843 (11) payable in credit notes [d]
	in Dutch guilders		
1832	248.70 3m/d (12)	95.17 3m/d (12)	51.46 2m/d (12)
1833	256.31 3m/d (12)	95.96 3m/d (12)	52.03 2m/d (12)
1834	257.81 3m/d (12)	108.67 3m/d (12)	52.69 2m/d (12)
1835	259.36 3m/d (12)	115.29 3m/d (12)	52.32 2m/d (12)
1836	255.79 3m/d (12)	110.81 3m/d (12)	52.09 2m/d (12)
1837	238.47 3m/d (12)	103.88 3m/d (12)	51.85 2m/d (12)
1838	250.78 3m/d (12)	108.26 3m/d (12)	52.89 2m/d (12)
1839	254.35 3m/d (12)	107.96 3m/d (12)	55.20/192.13 2m/d (8+4)
1840	252.89 3m/d (12)	108.00 3m/d (12)	190.67 2m/d (12)
1841	249.54 3m/d (12)	105.16 3m/d (12)	191.00 2m/d (12)
1842	253.29 3m/d (12)	106.34 3m/d (12)	188.42 2m/d (12)
1843	256.78 3m/d (12)	107.01 3m/d (12)	187.34 2m/d (12)
1844	256.41 3m/d (12)	109.14 3m/d (12)	189.13 2m/d (12)
1845	258.39 3m/d (12)	108.65 3m/d (12)	189.96 2m/d (12)
1846	253.03 3m/d (12)	106.62 3m/d (12)	188.46 2m/d (12)
1847	247.89/235.50 3m/d (5+7)	105.10 3m/d (12)	189.21 2m/d (12)
1848	220.42 3m/d (12)	101.41 3m/d (12)	178.92 2m/d (12)
1849	244.34 3m/d (12)	104.27 3m/d (12)	181.92 2m/d (12)
1850	245.59 3m/d (12)	105.47 3m/d (12)	186.42 2m/d (12)
1851	242.46 3m/d (12)	103.54 3m/d (12)	182.09 2m/d (12)
1852	244.80 3m/d (12)	104.32 3m/d (12)	184.70 2m/d (10)
1853	244.50 3m/d (12)	103.39 3m/d (12)	186.38 2m/d (12)
1854	240.50 3m/d (12)	102.19 3m/d (12)	172.14 2m/d (11)
1855	243.00 3m/d (12)	103.65 3m/d (12)	172.30 2m/d (12)
1856	240.50 3m/d (12)	102.71 3m/d (12)	179.80 2m/d (12)
1857	237.17 3m/d (12)	100.86 3m/d (12)	178.17 2m/d (12)
1858	235.75 3m/d (12)	100.60 3m/d (12)	170.00 2m/d (12)
1859	237.67 3m/d (12)	100.78 3m/d (12)	167.37 2m/d (11)
1860	240.50 3m/d (12)	102.14 3m/d (12)	168.67 2m/d (12)
1861	237.75 3m/d (12)	103.15 3m/d (12)	164.78 2m/d (11)
1862	238.17 3m/d (12)	102.79 3m/d (12)	164.55 2m/d (12)
1863	238.42 3m/d (12)	102.94 3m/d (12)	173.25 2m/d (12)
1864	231.50 3m/d (12)	101.80 3m/d (12)	154.88 2m/d (12)
1865	230.92 3m/d (12)	100.63 3m/d (12)	149.67 2m/d (12)
1866	224.40 3m/d (10)	100.78 3m/d (12)	139.42 2m/d (12)
1867	236.00 3m/d (12)	101.56 3m/d (12)	154.17 2m/d (12)

	AMSTERDAM on:		
	Madrid, from 1876 **Spain** [e]	**Lisbon**, from 1876 **Portugal** [f]	**Saint Petersburg**
	per 100 pesos duros [b]	per 100 crusados, from 1875 per 100 milréis [c]	per 100 silver roubles payable in credit notes, from 1899 per 100 gold roubles [d]
	in Dutch guilders		
1868	238.00 3m/d (12)	102.08 3m/d (12)	158.38 2m/d (12)
1869	241.17 3m/d (12)	103.54 3m/d (12)	149.63 2m/d (12)
1870	238.82 3m/d (11)	102.08 3m/d (12)	141.21 2m/d (12)
1871	240.67 3m/d (12)	103.52 3m/d (12)	151.92 2m/d (12)
1872	237.17 3m/d (12)	104.66 3m/d (12)	158.75 2m/d (12)
1873	234.63 3m/d (8)	104.79 3m/d (12)	157.67 2m/d (12)
1874	232.09 3m/d (12)	103.75 3m/d (12)	159.87 2m/d (11)
1875	230.67 3m/d (12)	257.55 3m/d (12)	158.80 2m/d (12)
1876	235.92 3m/d (12)	259.42 3m/d (12)	151.42 2m/d (12)
1877	233.92 3m/d (12)	259.84 3m/d (12)	129.14 2m/d (11)
1878	234.67 3m/d (12)	260.00 3m/d (12)	118.92 2m/d (12)
1879	232.50 3m/d (12)	257.84 3m/d (12)	117.80 2m/d (12)
1880	236.84 3m/d (12)	262.17 3m/d (12)	123.00 2m/d (12)
1881	235.75 3m/d (12)	260.84 3m/d (12)	122.80 2m/d (12)
1882	230.09 3m/d (11)	256.91 3m/d (11)	118.28 2m/d (11)
1883	230.17 3m/d (12)	259.00 3m/d (12)	116.00 2m/d (12)
1884	230.50 3m/d (12)	259.84 3m/d (12)	118.17 2m/d (12)
1885	229.17 3m/d (12)	258.50 3m/d (12)	118.00 2m/d (12)
1886	226.59 3m/d (12)	260.67 3m/d (12)	115.09 2m/d (12)
1887	227.00 3m/d (12)	264.00 3m/d (12)	105.55 2m/d (12)
1888	227.50 3m/d (12)	263.34 3m/d (12)	108.58 2m/d (12)
1889	226.67 3m/d (12)	264.00 3m/d (12)	122.59 2m/d (12)
1890	220.00 3m/d (12)	261.25 3m/d (12)	135.25 2m/d (12)
1891	215.42 3m/d (12)	260.00 3m/d (5)	129.25 2m/d (12)
1892	198.09 3m/d (12)		117.50 2m/d (12)
1893	192.00 3m/d (12)		122.34 2m/d (12)
1894	188.59 3m/d (12)		125.63 2m/d (12)
1895	198.25 3m/d (12)		126.34 2m/d (12)
1896	192.09 3m/d (12)	201.73 3m/d (11)	125.25 2m/d (12)
1897	178.50 3m/d (12)	177.67 3m/d (12)	125.00 2m/d (12)
1898	160.34 3m/d (9)	173.75 3m/d (4)	125.00 2m/d (12)
1899	183.50 3m/d (12)		124.96 2m/d (12)
1900	180.34 3m/d (12)		124.88 2m/d (12)
1901	167.59 3m/d (12)		125.13 2m/d (12)
1902	171.84 3m/d (12)		126.09 2m/d (12)

	AMSTERDAM on:	
	Spain [e]	**Saint Petersburg**
	per 100 pesos duros [b]	per 100 gold roubles [d]
	in Dutch guilders	
1903	170.67 3m/d (12)	126.00 2m/d (12)
1904	167.84 3m/d (12)	125.61 2m/d (12)
1905	178.34 3m/d (12)	124.63 2m/d (12)
1906	202.34 3m/d (12)	123.75 2m/d (12)
1907	210.59 3m/d (12)	123.94 2m/d (12)
1908	207.00 3m/d (12)	124.04 2m/d (12)
1909	209.91 3m/d (11)	125.55 2m/d (12)
1910		125.82 2m/d (6)
1911		125.89 2m/d (12)
1912		125.62 2m/d (12)
1913		125.37 2m/d (12)
1914		124.90 2m/d (7)

[a] Concerning the Danzig currency, see p. 379.

[b] Concerning the Spanish currency, see p. 307. Up to the mid-19th century the ducado de cambio was the Spanish imaginary unit of account in cashless payment. Thus until the end of the 17th century, the quotations on Madrid were effected partially for 'new money', partially for 'old money', whereby 1 ducado 'old money' = 1¼ ducado 'new money' (cf. HERBACH [1716], p. 136). All documented exchange rates are given for 'new money'; original data for 'old money' were converted into 'new money'. The quotations on Madrid from 1796 to 1799 were given per ducados de cambio payable in 'vales reales', the Spanish paper money of those years.

[c] In the Portuguese currency system one reckoned in réis and milréis (= 1,000 réis) respectively, but the exchange rate quotations of and on Portuguese places were often effected in or for crusados (velhos or do cambio) as a unit of account of 400 réis up to the 19th century. Since the Coin Act of July 29th 1854, the Portuguese silver standard with the milréis at 27.15 grammes of fine silver (since July 1st 1835 according to the Coin Act of April 24th 1835) was succeeded by the gold standard with the milréis at 1.6257 grammes of fine gold following the British pattern. So, in the case of the Amsterdam quotation on Lisbon, the term 'crusado' meant a unit of account of 400 reís gold valuta after 1854. Since July 1891, Portugal had the paper standard with a premium for gold coins up to 53% (in May 1897). In 1912 the milréis was succeded by the escudo of 100 centavos (1 escudo = 1 milréis); it had officially to be reckoned in this new currency from the beginning of 1913, but for all commercial transactions the term 'milréis' was still in use (cf. NELKENBRECHER [1771], p. 131; NOBACK [1877], pp. 507f.; SWOBODA [1913], pp. 518f.).

[d] Concerning the Russian currency, see pp. 359f.

[e] Continuation of the prevailing exchange rate series on Madrid, Bilbao, Cadiz and Seville.

[f] Continuation of the prevailing exchange rate series on Lisbon and Oporto.

2.1.5 On Switzerland, Scandinavian places and New York

	AMSTERDAM on:		
	Switzerland [a]	**Scandinavian places**	**New York**
	per 100 franken [b]	per 100 Swedish, Danish or Norwegian crowns [c]	per 100 US dollars [d]
	in Dutch guilders		
1875	46.89　ss　(12)		
1876	47.68　ss　(12)		
1877	47.72　ss　(12)		
1878	47.75　ss　(12)		
1879	47.60　ss　(12)		
1880	47.60　ss　(12)		
1881	47.60　ss　(12)		
1882	47.76　ss　(11)		
1883	47.72　ss　(12)		
1884	47.79　ss　(12)		
1885	47.55　ss　(12)		
1886	47.62　ss　(12)		
1887	47.52　ss　(12)		
1888	47.47　ss　(12)		
1889	47.54　ss　(12)		
1890	47.65　ss　(12)		
1891	47.48　ss　(12)		
1892	47.66　ss　(12)		
1893	47.71　ss　(12)		
1894	47.75　ss　(12)		
1895	47.75　ss　(12)		
1896	47.73　ss　(12)		
1897	47.74　ss　(12)		
1898	47.55　ss　(12)		
1899	47.77　ss　(12)		
1900	47.79　ss　(12)		
1901	47.92　ss　(12)		
1902	48.00　ss　(12)		
1903	48.01　ss　(12)		
1904	47.85　ss　(12)		
1905	47.99　ss　(12)		
1906	48.12　ss　(12)		
1907	47.92　ss　(12)		
1908	48.00　ss　(12)		
1909	48.00　ss　(12)	66.60　ch　(2)	248.57　s　(2)

	AMSTERDAM on:		
	Switzerland [a]	**Scandinavian places**	**New York**
	per 100 franken [b]	per 100 Swedish, Danish or Norwegian crowns [c]	per 100 US dollars [d]
		in Dutch guilders	
1910	47.77 ss (6)	66.34 ch (6)	248.00 s (6)
1911	47.78 ss (12)	66.39 ch (12)	248.08 s (12)
1912	47.73 ss (12)	66.27 ch (12)	247.73 s (12)
1913	47.89 ss (12)	66.42 ch (12)	248.63 s (12)
1914	47.96 ss (7)	66.50 ch (7)	248.50 s (7)

[a]   Identical quotations on Zurich, Basle and Geneva since 1909.

[b]   Concerning the Swiss currency, see p. 313.

[c]   Concerning the Scandinavian currencies, see pp. 327f., 339f.

[d]   Concerning the US currency, see p. 404.

3
Italy (1590–1914)

Exchange market: The Bisenzone fairs (1590–1650)

Sources: GENTIL DA SILVA [1969], vol. II, pp. 102–148 (1593–1650). Cf. MCCUSKER/GRAVESTEIJN [1991], pp. 379–392.
Concordance: *WdW IX*, pp. 68–103; *WdW III*, pp. 255–331

Currency: At the Genoese exchange fairs, the most important fairs in the late 16th century, the quoting was done in units of foreign currency for scudi (d'oro) di marche. This was an accounting unit that have been introduced by merchants following the example of the Lyons fairs (at the Lyons fairs the écu de marc d'or at 3.08 grammes of fine gold was used as clearing unit). From 1594/95 the value of the scudi (d'oro) di marche derived from the average weight of the seven internationally circulating gold coins of Antwerp, Spain, Genoa, Venice, Florence, Piacenza and Naples and, therefore, it was independent of single national currencies. Before 1594/95, all scudi d'oro (in oro), which had been minted in Spain, Antwerp and the most important Italian trading cities, as well as the French écu d'or au soleil, served as official tender. Whenever payments in cash were necessary to settle a balance, they were expressed in scudi di marche but done in scudi d'oro (in oro); the ratio of the unit of account scudo di marche to the average troy weight of the scudi d'oro remaining unchanged from 1552 to 1763 (100:101) (HOUTMAN-DE SMEDT / VAN DER WEE [1993], p. 110; DENZEL [1994], pp. 315f.; NORTH [1996], p. 230; FELLONI [1983]).

Original quotations at 'Bisenzone'

on:	in:	per:
Amsterdam	groot Flemish	1 scudo di marche
Antwerp	groot Flemish	1 scudo di marche
Barcelona	sueldos	1 scudo di marche
Cologne	groot Flemish	1 scudo di marche
Florence	scudi d'oro	100 scudi di marche
Frankfurt	kreuzer	1 scudo di marche
Genoa	soldi	1 scudo di marche
from 1631	scudi d'argento	100 scudi di marche
Lisbon	réis	1 scudo di marche
Lucca	scudi d'oro (ducatoni)	100 scudi di marche
Lyons	scudi di marche	100 écus d'or (au soleil)
Milan	scudi imperiale	100 scudi di marche
Naples	ducati moneta corrente	100 scudi di marche
Nuremberg	kreuzer	1 scudo di marche
Palermo	carlini	1 scudo di marche
Rome	scudi d'oro di stampa	100 scudi di marche
Saragossa	sueldos	1 scudo di marche
Seville	maravédis	1 scudo di marche
Valencia	sueldos	1 scudo di marche

on:	in:	per:
Venice	ducati correnti	100 scudi di marche
Vienna	rixdollars	100 scudi di marche

Cf. GENTIL DA SILVA [1969], vol. I, p. 291

Other data available (1590–1650): Ancona (1606–1650) – Bari (1594–1650) – Bergamo (1592–1650) – Bologna (1591–1650) – Lecce (1594–1650) – Mantua (1614–1628) – Medina del Campo (1590–1650) – Messina (1590–1650) – Palermo (1591–1650).

Exchange market: Venice (1623–1797)

Sources: IISG Amsterdam, *Corsi di cambi* [Venice] (1609–1774); Hofkammerarchiv Wien, Kommerz, 4. Litorale, Abteilung 64: Münzkurs, red number 561 (3), *Corsi di cambi* [Venice] (1756); SWA Basel, Handschriften 28, 415 diverse Kurszettel, 28. H: 3 *Kurszettel der Venediger Devisenbörse*, fol. 1 (1759); ACCM Marseille, L. IX 1035, *Exchange rate currents* (1772–1789); VON EICHBORN [1928], picture XVI after p. 224: *Exchange rate current* (1793); SWA Basel, Segerhof Handschriften 420, F 38, 1796, Belege, *Cours de diverses places 1796* (1796). Cf. MCCUSKER/GRAVESTEIJN [1991], pp. 399–420.
It is remarkable that the Venetian exchange rate current "was one of a very few completely printed exchange rate currents published in Europe in the seventeenth century", but "sometime between 1719 and 1740, for reasons we can only guess at, the publishers stopped issuing a fully printed newspaper, reverted to the less sophisticated mode of presentation, and began publishing their newspaper as a pre-printed form filled in by hand using pen and ink. ... It seems fair to assume that Venetian businessmen and their overseas customers constituted a far smaller market for the city's exchange rate current in the early eighteenth century than they had in the early seventeenth" (ibid., p. 399).
Concordance: *WdW III*, pp. 123–202; *WdW VI*, pp. 255–282.

Currency in Venice (until 1797/1823): In Venice the quoting was done in or for ducati of 24 grossi at 12 denari or grossetti, although the lire of 20 soldi or marchetti at 12 denari (di lira) could be used as well, 1 ducato being equal to 6 1/5 lire or 124 soldi. The ducato, which had been minted since 1284, was the oldest Venetian gold coin. Until the end of the republic in 1797 it was only slightly changed just once in 1526 (from 3.54 grammes to 3.49 grammes; NORTH [1995], p. 95). From 1593 the legal means of payment for exchange transactions was the valuta di banco (bank money), an imaginary currency in which the accounts of the Banco della Piazza di Rialto and later on those of the Banco (del) Giro were kept (in lire grossi of 10 ducati or 62 lire di banco), and payments were settled through the bank (KRUSE [1781], p. 380). So, from that time on the quotations in Venice were to be understood in or for ducati di banco or its subdivisions. In contrast to this, the valuta corrente (current money), i.e. the coins of the Republic of Venice which had been tariffed by the Signoria in 1686 and which disposed of a fixed premium of 20% against the bank money (100 ducati di banco = 120 ducati correnti or 5 ducati di banco = 6 ducati correnti), was of no importance within the cashless payment transactions. It was only towards the end of the 18th and during the early 19th century, i.e. around the closure of the Banco Giro, that the quotations on Venice could partly also be done for moneta piccola corrente, being the current money used for commodity trade at that time. From 1750 the ducato di banco was fixed at 9 lire 12 soldi (= 9.6 lire) piccoli correnti so that the moneta piccola corrente had a fixed premium of 54 26/31% (actually calculated at 54 5/6%) in comparison to the bank money and quoted a premium (here the so-called 'sopra-agio') of 29 1/3% in comparison to the older valuta corrente (cf. ibid., p. 379). Around 1820, merchants and bankers still used to make out their bills in ducati, but the payments were generally done in moneta piccola corrente (also called 'moneta di

Piazza'), because the bank money had drastically decreased in value in comparison to this current money since the 1790s, Therefore, payments in bank money were no longer accepted (NELKENBRE-CHER [1820], p. 341). That is why bills of exchange were henceforth mostly charged against lire (at 2.35 grammes of fine silver) and soldi piccoli corrente. After the so-called 'münzpatent' of 1823, by which the lira austriaca (at 3.897 grammes of fine silver) was introduced in Lombardo–Venetia, this system was still in use until 1834.

Original quotations at Venice

on:	in:	per:
Amsterdam	groot Flemish	1 ducato di banco
Antwerp	groot Flemish	1 ducato di banco
Augsburg	rixdollars giro	100 ducati di banco
Bisenzone fairs	ducati di banco	100 scudi di marche
Bolzano	soldi di banco	1 scudo di cambio
Cologne	groot Flemish	1 ducato di banco
Constantinople	para	1 ducato di banco
Florence	scudi d'oro	100 ducati di banco
Frankfurt	rixdollars Münze	100 ducati di banco
Genoa	soldi di banco	1 scudo di cambio
Hamburg	groot Flemish	1 ducato di banco
Leghorn	pezze da otto reali	100 ducati di banco
London	pence sterling	1 ducato di banco
Lucca	scudi d'oro	100 ducati di banco
Lyons	ducati di banco	100 écus d'or of 3 livres tournois
Milan	soldi di banco	1 scudo imperiale
Naples	ducati moneta corrente / del regno	100 ducati di banco
Nuremberg	guilders current	100 ducati di banco
Rome	scudi d'oro di stampe	100 ducati di banco
Saint Gall	guilders exchange money	100 ducati di banco
Vienna	rixdollar	100 ducati di banco
from 1665	guilders current	100 ducati di banco
	guilders Konventionskurant	100 ducati di banco

Other data available: Ancona (1623–1756) – Bari (1623–1755) – Bergamo (1623–1697) – Bologna (1627–1684/94) – Lecce (1623–1754) – Lisbon (1627) – Madrid (1627/28) – Messina (1626/27) – Paris (1768–1773) – Piacenza (1623–1630, 1686) – Seville (1627) – Verona (1631–1650).

Exchange market: Leghorn (1776–1850)

Sources: ACCM Marseille, L. IX 1035 *Corsi dei cambi* (1776–1790, 1809, 1812, 1817); SWA Basel, Segerhof Handschriften 420, F38, 1796, Belege, *Cours de diverses places 1796: exchange rate currents of Leghorn* (1796); StA Hamburg, 621-1, C. Zeller, B 10, vol. 1 (1796–1799) and vol. 2 (1800–1802): *Exchange rate currents of Leghorn* (1797–1799); Erhvervsarkivet Århus, Købmandsfirmaet J.P. Suhr & Søn, København, *Børskurser 1799–1805* (1801–1804); Historisches Museum Basel, HG Handelswesen 1988.270.1–26, here 2: *Corso di Cambi. Livorno* (1804); KELLY [1811], vol. II, p. 52 (1806); KELLY [1835], vol. II, p. 69 (1820); *Giornale di commercio del porto-franco di Livorno* (1822–1850); *Corriere di Livorno* (1847–1850). For the period up to 1775, cf. McCUSKER/GRAVE-STEIJN [1991], pp. 253–263.

Concordance: *WdW I/III*, pp. 183–227.

Currency: In Leghorn, the *porto franco* of the Grand Duchy of Tuscany from 1593, exchange rate quotations were done in or for pezze da otto reali of 20 soldi or 240 denari di pezza, the pezza being equal to 6 lire moneta lunga or 5¾ lire moneta buona (23 lire moneta buona = 24 lire moneta lunga), each lira of 20 soldi or 240 denari. As the exchange prices were to be understood in gold (that is in Florence zecchini or rusponi) and the ratio fluctuating between lire d'oro and lire moneta buona had often been the cause of disputes among merchants, the ratio was fixed at 100 lire d'oro = 107 lire moneta buona (3.87 grammes of fine silver) by the Camera di comercio in Leghorn in 1809. So, lire in gold were traded with a fixed agio of 7%, so that 100 lire d'oro invariably amounted to 107 lire moneta buona. In order to remove the great variety of coins within the Grand Duchy of Tuscany, the minting of a fiorino (6.304 grammes of fine silver) at 100 quattrini, as the new and only basis of the Tuscan currency, was ordered on July 10th 1826, although this coin could not gain any acceptance in trade. For this reason it was fixed on December 26th 1836 and published in Leghorn on January 17th 1837 that, henceforth, all price and exchange rate quotations were to be done in Tuscan lire moneta buona (3.78 grammes of fine silver) of 20 soldi at 12 denari or of 100 centesimi. The fixed agio of 7% was already included in the quotation in order to ease the charging of the current gold coins. After the Grand Duchy of Tuscany had been incorporated into the Kingdom of Piedmont–Sardinia and the Kingdom of Italy, by decree of September 29th 1859 the settlement of accounts in Piedmontese and Italian currency respectively was ordered for the time from November 11th 1859 and January 1st 1860 and 84 Piedmontese or Italian centesimi = 1 Tuscan lira moneta buona were fixed as parity.

Original quotations at Leghorn (until 1836):

on:	in:	per:
Amsterdam	groot Flemish banco	1 pezza da otto reali
Augsburg	guilders Augsburg current	100 pezze da otto reali
Constantinople	paras	1 pezza da otto reali
Florence	soldi moneta buona (in Florence)	1 pezza da otto reali
Geneva	écus of 3 livres Geneva current	100 pezze da otto reali
Genoa	soldi fuori banco	1 pezza da otto reali
Hamburg	groot Flemish banco	1 pezza da otto reali
Lisbon	réis	1 pezza da otto reali
London	pence sterling	1 pezza da otto reali
Madrid	pesos de plata antigua	100 pezze da otto reali
Malta	tari	1 pezza da otto reali
Milan	soldi correnti	1 pezza da otto reali
Naples	ducati del regno	100 pezze da otto reali
Palermo (& Messina)	tari	1 pezza da otto reali
Paris	sous tournois	1 pezza da otto reali
Rome	soldi moneta buona	1 scudo romano or moneta
Saint Petersburg	roubles banco	100 pezze da otto reali
Turin	Piedmontese soldi	1 pezza da otto reali
Venice	ducati di banco	100 pezze da otto reali
	from 1803 lire piccole correnti	1 or 50 pezze da otto reali
Vienna	soldi moneta buona	1 guilder Konventionskurant
	from 1800 soldi moneta buona	1 guilder Wiener Währung
	from 1816 soldi moneta buona	1 guilder Konventionskurant

From 1837 all quotations were effected in Tuscan lire moneta buona per 1 (on London) or 100 units of foreign currency.

Other data available: Ancona, 30d/s (1771–1850) – Bologna, 30d/s (1771–1850) – Cadiz, 2m/d (1771–1825); 90d/d (1825–1850) – Lyons, fairs (1771–1790); 1m/d (1796–1825); 90d/d (1825–1850); 30d/d (1825–1850) – Marseille, 1m/d (1771–1825); 90d/d (1825–1850); 30d/d (1825–1850) – Messina, 60d/s (1771–1850) – Novi, fairs (1771–1790).

Exchange market: Genoa (1778–1914)

Sources: Institut für Stadtgeschichte Frankfurt am Main, Handel Ugb. Nr. 406: *Corsi di cambi*, Genova (1777); SWA Basel, Handschriften 28, 415 diverse Kurszettel, 28.k *Fotokopien diverser Kurszettel ausländischer Herkunft: Corsi di cambi, Genova* (1777); Avvisi di Genova (1778–1782, 1802–1804); REBUFFAT / COURDURIÉ [1966], pp. 122f., tableaux XXII (1787–1790); SWA Basel, Segerhof Handschriften 420, F 38, 1796, Belege, *Cours de diverses places 1796* (1796/97); *Il Monitore* (1798–1812); *La Gazzetta di Genova* (1804–1821); Biblioteca della Camera di Commercio, Industria e Agricultura di Genova, "Corso dei cambi", anni 1822–1855, n. 6 vols., and "Corso legale accertato del Sindacato dei Mediatori", anni 1856–1896, n. 41 vols. (1822–1859); *Il Corriere Mercantile* (1856–1896); *Listino della Borsa* (1897–1914); cf. DA POZZO / FELLONI [1964], pp. 515–527 (quotations on Paris, London and Hamburg/Berlin, 1856–1896). <u>Naples:</u> *Giornale delle Due Sicilie* (1840–1876).
Concordance: WdW I/III, pp. 3–76, 180f.

Currency: In Genoa payments in trade were settled in lire moneta corrente of 20 soldi, each soldo of 12 denari. In the late 16th and the early 17th centuries this current money suffered from devaluation last but not least because of the inflow of foreign money which could not even be changed by the decree of 1637 acknowledging the moneta corrente as the basis for all payment transactions. However, the scudo d'argento was fixed as the actual standard unit of currency, at the same time determining the value of the moneta corrente. Since different fixings brought about no stabilization of the moneta corrente the Banco di moneta corrente was opened on April 1st 1675, authorized to conclude all payments of more than 100 lire moneta corrente. The fedi di credito or biglietti di credito issued by this bank circulated as a means of payment in Genoa and at the Genoese exchange fairs at Novi in particular, because they were denominated in the more stable bank money (lira di banco) that had a rising premium since 1710 in comparison to the moneta corrente, the so-called 'lira fuori banco'. In 1741 this premium was fixed at 15% and the fixed lira di banco was called 'lira di permesso' and was supposed to be used henceforth for exchange transactions. When in autumn 1746 the Banco di moneta corrente had to cease payments owing to a Genoese war contribution payment to Austria, the rate of bank money dropped to 68% in 1751 in comparison to the moneta corrente (SIEVEKING [1934], pp. 30–35). Then people went over to doing exchange payments in lire fuori banco. In the following years the premium on bank money rose up to about 8 2/3% in comparison to the lira di permesso, but according to the Coin Edict of January 3rd 1755 the lire fuori banco moneta buona (3.75 grammes of fine silver) had to be used for trade and payment transactions. The additional 'moneta buona' helped to differentiate this currency from the valuable valuta fuori banco moneta abusiva, generally used in commodity trade (cf. NELKENBRECHER [1775], pp. 101s.; NELKENBRECHER [1798], pp. 99s.). However, fictitious pezze and, in addition to them, scudi d'oro (of the former old doppia), scudi di cambio or scudi d'oro marche, each subdivided into 20 soldi at 12 denari, were used for quoting in order to avoid monetary fluctuations in exchange transactions throughout the entire 17th and 18th centuries. In 1755, these coins were fixed in value as follows:

– 1 pezza	= 5 lire di permesso	= 5.75 lire fuori banco or 115 soldi
– 1 scudo d'oro	= 9.4 lire di permesso	= 10.81 lire fuori banco
– 1 scudo di cambio	= 4 lire di permesso	= 4.6 lire fuori banco
– 1 scudo d'oro marche	= 9.3 lire di permesso	= 10.7 lire fuori banco

After the French occupation of Genoa on July 5th 1802, the French franc (1 lira fuori banco = 0.825 francs) was declared legal tender in the new Ligurian Republic, but the French currency was not accepted as unit of account. With the annexation of Genoa to the Kingdom of Piedmont–Sardinia in May 1814, the seaport became part of the Piedmontese currency area (for the time being still without Sardinia) in which the French currency system, well established since the period of occupation (see p. 280), was officially introduced on August 6th 1816 in order to support trade with France. The Piedmontese lira nuova of 100 centesimi was equal to the French franc of 1803 (4.50 grammes of fine silver). However, in the porto franco and in the exchange business of Genoa the traditional Genoese unit continued to be used until the lira nuova became the only valid money of account on the Piedmontese mainland on October 26th 1826. That is why the exchange rate quotations at Genoa were changed over to lire nuove at the turn of the year 1827. At the beginning of 1843 the new Piedmontese currency system was introduced on Sardinia as well.

Currency in the Kingdom of Italy since 1861: The predominance of Piedmont–Sardinia in the united Kingdom of Italy led to the takeover of the Piedmontese lira nuova under its new name 'Italian lira' (lira italiana) at 100 centesimi (as proclaimed on July 17th 1861). Its coins in gold (lira at 0.2903 grammes of fine gold) and silver (lira at 4.50 grammes of fine silver) were exactly equal to those of the Piedmontese lira nuova and, therefore, the Italian system was subject to the rules of the French currency system and its bimetallism (decree of December 12th 1861). With the annexation of the Habsburg territories and the Kingdom of the Two Sicilies the silver standard of their currencies was removed. Since the old valuations continued to be used in everyday transactions, a coin standardization act was enacted on August 24th 1862 (also applying to Mantua and Venice from September 3rd 1868 and to Rome from October 13th 1870) and the coins of the former Italian states were gradually withdrawn from circulation between 1864 and 1871. As a founding member of the Latin Monetary Union of 1865 (see p. 280), which acknowledged the bimetallistic currency system, Italy officially belonged to the currency area of the franc dominated by France throughout the whole further period of documentation, although it played a special role: the balance of payments, being negative since the formation of the Kingdom and, above all, the costs of the war of Venetia against the Habsburg Monarchy, resulted in a compulsory rate for the Italian banknotes of the Banca Nazionale nel Regno d'Italia, the greatest bank of the country, since May 1st 1866 and in the stopping of cash redemptions, so that finally all debenture bonds had to be treated as nominal debts, and metal money was no longer allowed in payment. So the Italian exchange rates on foreign countries which were then payable in notes or in 'valuta legale' deviated more and more from the coin parity (the so-called 'corso forzoso'). In the following years the most important quotation, i.e. the one on Paris, was actually subject to the same fluctuations as the premium on gold, which reached its highest level with 18.75% after the defeat of Italy near Custozza (1866) (BAAS [1984], pp. 80ff.).

Italian lire in notes per 100 lire gold

1866, from July 10th	106.81	1871	105.49	1876	108.62	1881	101.89
1867	107.44	1872	108.76	1877	109.85	1882	102.78
1868	109.70	1873	114.50	1878	109.62	1883, up to April 25th	100.84
1869	104.06	1874	112.48	1879	111.25		
1870	104.75	1875	108.35	1880	109.45		

Source: DA POZZO / FELLONI [1964], pp. 512–514

In several waves Italian silver token coins flew into the adjoining countries of the Latin Monetary Union which had given up the minting of silver coins and had gone over to the limping gold standard after 1873/74. In 1881 a law allowed return to the complete convertibility of the lira, and even circulating paper money could gradually be cashed in from 1883, so that Italy actually followed the gold standard (in contrast to the regulations of the Latin Monetary Union). As early as in the middle of the 1880s the circulating notes had again reached the limit of cover, which is why the lira was traded with discount again from 1887. In 1893, at the peak of the crisis, the central banking was reformed with the foundation of the Banca d'Italia as one of three central banks, but the discount of the lira went up to nearly 16% at the beginning of 1894, so that the compulsory rate was officially reintroduced on February 21st 1894 (HERTNER [1985], p. 766). Additionally, Italian token coins had been withdrawn from the money rate at the request of Italy in 1893, which meant the end of Italy's membership in the Latin Monetary Union, although this was not officially enforced. When the discount was decreasing more and more after 1896 as a result of sound budgetary policy and significant economic growth, it was possible to keep the rates largely stable and close to parity from 1902 by offering a part of the Italian government's custom revenue for sale to the central banks in order to buy foreign exchanges, treasury notes and balances on current accounts payable in gold. This meant, though not officially, the adjustment of the Italian currency to the gold standard (ibid.).

Original quotations at Genoa until 1826

on:	in:	per:
Amsterdam	groot Flemish banco	1 pezza of 5¾ lire fuori banco
Augsburg	soldi fuori banco	1 guilder Augsburg current
Constantinople	soldi fuori banco	1 piastre
Hamburg	soldi fuori banco	1 mark banco
Leghorn and Florence	soldi fuori banco	1 pezza da otto reali
Lisbon	réis	1 pezza of 5¾ lire fuori banco
London	pence sterling	1 pezza of 5¾ lire fuori banco
Madrid	maravédis	1 scudo d'oro marche
Milan	soldi correnti	1 scudo di cambio of 4 3/5 lire fuori banco
Naples	soldi fuori banco	1 ducato del regno
Palermo	carlini	1 scudo d'oro marche
from 1815	grani	1 lira fuori banco
Paris	sous	1 pezza of 5¾ lire fuori banco
Rome	soldi fuori banco	1 scudo romano or scudo moneta
Venice	soldi (marchetti) di banco	1 scudo di cambio of 4 3/5 lire fuori banco
from 1805	lire or soldi fuori banco	soldi piccoli correnti
Vienna	soldi fuori banco	1 guilder Konventionskurant
from 1799 (4)	soldi fuori banco	1 guilder Wiener Währung
from 1816	soldi fuori banco	1 guilder Konventionskurant

From 1827 all quotations were effected in Piedmontese lire nuove and centesimi per unit of foreign currency; **from 1861 (8)** in Italian lire per unit of foreign currency.

Other data available: Ancona, 1m/d (1860–1869) – Berlin, 3 m/d (1873–1877); s (1879–1889) – Bologna, 1m/d (1840–1869) – Cadiz, 60d/d (1802–1806) – Florence, 1m/d (1860–1869) – Hamburg, s (1879–1889) – Leghorn, 1m/d (1860–1869) – London, 3m/d (1861–1882, 1890–1909) – Lyons, 30d/d (1798–1869); s (1870–1889) – Marseilles, 30d/d (1860–1869); s (1870–1889) – Messina, 2m/d (1815–1817, 1860–1869) – Milan, 1m/d (1860–1869) – Naples, 1m/d (1863–1869) – Palermo, 1m/d (1840–1869) – Smyrna, 31d/s (1802–1805) – Trieste, 3m/d (1860–1870) – Turin, 1m/d (1827–1869).

Since the Middle Ages a multitude of internationally more or less important exchange markets had existed in Italy, the mother country of the bill of exchange and the cashless payment system in Europe. The great seaports and economic centres, above all Venice, Genoa, Milan, Florence, Rome, Naples, and also Leghorn from the 17th century, characterized the image of the Italian cashless payment system from the international perspective with their alternating importance. In the 19th century, four places remained that increasingly seized Italy's inward and outward exchange transactions: Genoa and Milan were dominant in Upper Italy, and Leghorn was the most important port and financial market in Tuscany and Central Italy. Naples was the commercial and financial centre of the Kingdom of the Two Sicilies, so that the whole South of Italy was its hinterland. "Its importance is indicated by the fact that the Rothschilds established a branch of their house there after the Napoleonic Wars" (KINDLEBERGER [1974], p. 32). Rome as the centre of the Papal States played only a secondary role within the Italian cashless payment system, and Trieste, which belonged to the Habsburg Monarchy, had taken over from Venice as the most important exchange market in the Adriatic region. Although Turin was the banking centre of Italy during and after the unification of Italy (from 1860 up to c.1890), which had started in Piedmont–Sardinia (ibid., pp. 32, 34), it had no internationally relevant position as exchange market. Apart from this, several other cities occupied the positions of regionally and nationally important exchange markets within Italy, such as Bologna, Ancona, Palermo, Messina, Bari and Lecce.

In the late 16th and early 17th centuries – i.e. during the "age of the Genoese" – the Genoese exchange fairs, the so-called Bisenzone fairs, the "foire[s] des changes par définition" (GENTIL DA SILVA [1969], vol. I, p. 12) were of outstanding importance for the entire European payment system. In contrast to the medieval fairs, where commodity trade was the basis of the payment transactions, the financial transactions of a small group of about 50 to 60 highly specialized bankers (in around 1600) became the exclusive and highly efficiently handled field of activity. Since 1579 the Genoese exchange fairs, named after their original meeting place, Besançon (in Italian: Bisenzone), were primarily held in Piacenza and after the severe financial crisis of 1619–1622 mostly in Novi (from 1621). The Bisenzone fairs had been founded to compete with the older Lyons fairs on which they were modelled and they were dominated by Genoese bankers under the political supervision of the republic of Genoa. The Lyons as well as the Bisenzone fairs were held four times a year synchronized with each other with an interval of a few days. The fairs always started towards the beginning of February (*fiera d'apparizione* with the payment period at the beginning of April), May (*fiera di pasqua* with the payment period at the beginning of July), August (*fiera d'agosto* with the payment period at the end of September) and November (*fiera de tutti-santi* with the payment period at the end of December) and used to take one week. On the third day of each fair the *banchieri di conto* from Genoa, Venice, Milan and Florence fixed the official rates – the so-called 'conto' – of the bills of exchange that were freshly concluded by taking the quotations of the other exchange places on the Bisenzone fairs as a basis. For this reason and because of the stable fair currency, no price losses were to be feared for the exchanges on the Bisenzone fairs, making them highly attractive. When concluding their exchange transactions the bankers largely aligned with these quotations officially fixed by the *banchieri di conto*, although the contracts were concluded on the basis of independent exchange rates ('cambio libero') (HOUTMAN-DE SMEDT / VAN DER WEE [1993], p. 111; NORTH [1996], p. 230; RACINE [1991], pp. 157–159). They are the basis of the data already presented by GENTIL DA SILVA, whose rates of the Genoese exchange fairs on other European exchange markets are documented here; the quotations of some exchange places on the Bisenzone fairs will not be presented here since they cannot be dated exactly – only the respective fairs as 'payees' came down to us. Nor will the quotations for the period after 1650 be documented here, because the Genoese exchange fairs lost their outstanding importance as international exchange markets during the second quarter of the 17th century. Since c.1650 they were at best of regional relevance, finding their official end in 1763 (HOUTMAN-DE SMEDT / VAN DER WEE [1993], p. 110; for the exchange rates of the Bisenzone fairs from 1651 to 1722, see *WdW III*, pp. 255–331).

The Bisenzone fairs played such a central role within Europe's cashless payment system during the age of the Genoese because of the close involvement of the Genoese *banchieri* (which largely dominated them) in the Spanish public finance through the system of the *asientos* permitting Genoa to control and regulate the circulation of money and precious metals – especially those from Spanish America – between all important financial markets of Western Europe and, at the same time, making considerable speculative profit with the help of *ricorsa* bills. The official conto was the binding exchange rate for *ricorsa* transactions, i.e. concealed loans at interest. After the third Spanish national bankruptcy in 1607, the following withdrawal of the Genoese from the transactions with the Spanish crown and, above all, after the crisis between 1619 and 1622 speculative transactions clearly became the centre of Genoese attention at the Bisenzone fairs (FELLONI [1991], p. 21; NORTH [1996], p. 231; RACINE [1991], pp. 160–167). The international relevance of the Bisenzone exchange fairs within the entire European cashless payment system is represented by the multitude of exchange rate quotations effected there by the *banchieri di conto*: although these fairs were meant to serve Italian *banchieri* as an opportunity to settle their claims, almost the whole of Western and Southern Europe and increasingly Central Europe as well became part of this network of fairs. So the Lyons fairs, Lisbon (up to 1601), Antwerp and, from the late 1620s, Amsterdam as well, the Spanish markets (Seville, Barcelona, Valencia and Saragossa as well as the fairs of Medina del Campo and from 1694/1712 Cadiz) and the places of the Holy Roman Empire (the Frankfurt fairs, Cologne up to 1601, then Nuremberg, and Vienna from 1636) also appear on the conti of Bisenzone in addition to the most important Italian exchange markets of that time – Venice, Genoa, Milan, Florence, Lucca, Rome, Naples – and the quite regionally important Italian places – Palermo, Messina, Bergamo, Bologna, Ancona, Bari and Lecce (from 1625), later on Turin as well (from 1677) and Leghorn (from 1693/ 1712). So the quotations of Bisenzone (cf. VAN VELDEN [1629], pp. 298f.; DENZEL [1994], pp. 438–440) covered the whole area that was to an extremely high degree of interest to the Italian brokers and bankers. Only England and the North of France as well as the Baltic region were left out. On the whole, the exchange rates of the Bisenzone fairs reflected the traditional cashless payment system, still centred in Italy and dominated by Italian – especially Genoese – bankers and how it had grown since the Middle Ages.

Venice was not of the same outstanding international importance as the Bisenzone exchange fairs had been in the past but it was undoubtedly of great importance within the entire European cashless payment system in the 17th and also still in parts of the 18th century. Quotations of its exchange market are available on a large scale and with comparatively high regularity between the 1620s and the 1770s, even though there are two large gaps (1698–1710, 1720–1739). From the end of the 16th century the Venetian exchange transactions were mostly effected through the public Banco della Piazza di Rialto, which had been established in 1587 in order to ensure greater safety and currency stability for the cashless payment transactions with the help of municipal supervision. After 1593 all exchanges expressed in bank money (valuta di banco; see above) had to be honoured in banco. Since the 1620s/1630s the functions of the Banco della Piazza di Rialto were passing on to a new public bank, the Banco (del) Giro (established in 1619), so that the older banco was closed in 1637. Until it was finally liquidated in 1806, credits could be cashed in Banco (del) Giro with hardly any exception; this was only not possible between 1650 and 1666 and between 1714 and 1739 although cashless payment transactions and money transfers were effected by means of a clearing system via the bank even at that time (TUCCI [1991], pp. 320–324). However, it seems to be rather chance than the result of the fact that credits could be cashed again in the Banco (del) Giro that the Venetian quotations restarted with high regularity in 1740. Bills of exchange expressed in bank money to be cashed in banco remained common practice within the Venetian cashless payment transactions until the end of the 18th century. Bills of exchange expressed in current money without any obligation to redeem them were used mostly by foreigners and private persons who needed cash on the spot or wanted to transfer it from Venice to another place (KRUSE [1781], p. 381).

The comparison of the network of exchange partners quoted here with that of other Italian financial places shows that Venice was a central financial market within Italy in the 17th and partly also in the 18th centuries: during the 17th century Naples, for example, the most important South Italian financial centre, was oriented only towards Spanish places, i.e. Madrid, Barcelona and Cadiz for a few years at the end of the century, and other Italian exchange markets. The reason for the close relationship between Naples and the Spanish places was that the Kingdom of Naples and the Kingdom of Spain were connected in personal union (DE ROSA [1955], pp. 253–307; DI VITTORIO [1973], pp. 350f.; *WdW III*, pp. 21–26, 203–253). In contrast to this, Venice quoted almost all important exchange places north of the Alps in the 17th century: Amsterdam, Antwerp, London, the Lyons fairs, Cologne, Hamburg (since 1626), Frankfurt am Main, Nuremberg, Augsburg, Vienna, and even Saint Gall (since 1637) together with numerous Italian places such as Milan, Genoa, the Bisenzone fairs, Leghorn (since 1624/57), Florence, Lucca (since 1632), Rome and Naples, but also Ancona, Bari, Lecce, Bergamo, Piacenza (1623–1630), Bologna (since 1627/30) and Messina (1626/27) (cf. VAN VELDEN [1629], pp. 262f.; DENZEL [1994], pp. 429–431). The Iberian places do not seem to have played a central role in the direct Venetian exchange transactions, for Seville, Madrid and Lisbon are listed only in the Venetian exchange rate currents of 1627(/28), even though these exchange places do partly appear as exchange partners of Venice in merchant manuals of the 18th century (e.g. HERBACH [1716], p. 91; HERBACH [1756/57], p. 78). Traditionally, the Upper German region was of central importance to Venice, since Venice had both the most frequent and the closest contact of all (Upper) Italian towns with the Upper German region. As intermediary for this region, the Bolzano fairs and, for a short time, also the Verona fairs were quoted; the Veronese fairs had been founded by Venice in order to compete with the Genoese Bisenzone fairs, which had been transferred to Novi in 1621/22 (SIEVEKING [1934], p. 26; DENZEL [2006]).

Whereas only a few exchange rate currents have been found for the period between the end of the 1680s and 1740 until now, relatively regular quotations can be presented for the following decades until around the mid-1770s. The network of quotation partners had been downsized by three German places, because Cologne and Nuremberg had lost their international importance and the Frankfurt fairs became increasingly irrelevant to Italy. So the Venetian exchange transactions with Upper Germany concentrated gradually on Augsburg, even though contemporary merchant manuals still list Nuremberg, Frankfurt am Main and even Leipzig as exchange partners of Venice during the late 18th century (e.g. NELKENBRECHER [1775], pp. 240f.; KRUSE [1781], p. 384). The contact with Saint Gall, which is still mentioned in merchant manuals around the mid-18th century (e.g. HERBACH [1716], p. 91; HERBACH [1756/57], p. 78), seems to have stopped during the early 18th century. In 1768 the quoting on Paris started, and this began to replace the Lyons fairs as the most important French exchange market from the Venetian point of view, and the quotation on Constantinople was introduced by the late 1780s. The comparison with other Italian exchange places of that time – for example Florence (cf. *WdW VI*, pp. 283–293) – shows that Venice still had one of the most extensive quotation networks, although numerous quotations within Italy had also been stopped meanwhile for lack of relevance – or for lack of sources – like the quotations on Lucca, Bergamo, the Bisenzone fairs (1745), Bari and Lecce (in the 1750s).

So the development of the international Mediterranean trade at that time supported the rise of other Italian exchange markets which surpassed Venice in importance within international payment transactions at the latest from the middle of the century, although Venice had unmistakably been suffering certain loss of relevance within the international cashless payment system since the 18th century, of which the different kind of publication of the exchange rate currents (see above) is also an indicator. Especially the two porti franci Leghorn (with this status from 1593, renewed in 1737) and Genoa (from 1751) competed for pre-eminence within the payment transaction system on the Apennines Peninsula. From the second half of the 17th century, Leghorn "played a crucially important part in England's Levant trade as a centre where English exports or re-exports could be converted into valuable currency" (PAGANO DE DE-VITIIS [1997], p. 123). As central English entrepôt in the Mediterranean region (cf. KEENE [1978], p. 684) and Western outpost of the most important Levantine trading 'nations' – i.e. the Jews, Greeks and Armenians – Leghorn seems to comply with the requirements to become Italy's central market for international cashless payment transactions by 1737. This can clearly be demonstrated by the fact that Leghorn listed the majority of exchange partners among all Italian exchange markets from the 1770s, when exchange rate currents were available for the first time on a larger scale. Leghorn quoted Amsterdam, London, Paris, Lyons and Marseilles in Western Europe, Hamburg, Augsburg and Vienna in the Holy Roman Empire, Madrid, Cadiz and Lisbon on the Iberian Peninsula, additionally Geneva in Switzerland and even Saint Petersburg in Russia (from 1781). The contact with the latter is the earliest regular quotation of an internationally important exchange market on an Russian exchange place. It probably resulted from the imports of South Russian grain to Italy which were settled via Saint Petersburg. In addition to this, all internationally important Italian exchange markets (Milan, Genoa, Venice, Florence, Rome, Naples) were quoted in Leghorn, but also some only regionally relevant markets such as Turin, Novi (at least until 1812) – the place of the old Bisenzone fairs – Bologna, Ancona, Palermo and Messina.

Even though only a few quotations of Leghorn could be found for the period from 1805 to 1821 to date, Leghorn remained the preferred Italian trading and exchange place for English merchants throughout the first half of the 19th century; above all, it did so for their trade to the Levant and from the Mediterranean region to overseas. Various contemporary merchant manuals emphasized that Leghorn turned from being a rather insignificant place into Italy's most important trading centre in less than one century, and exchange transactions played an outstanding part here not being subject to much change until the middle of the century (cf. NELKENBRECHER [1828], p. 204; NOBACK [1851], p. 514). At the beginning of Leghorn's golden age, in about 1820, the quoted places outside Italy were London, Amsterdam, Lisbon, Saint Petersburg,

Vienna, Geneva, Paris, Lyons, Marseilles, Frankfurt am Main, Augsburg, Hamburg, Madrid, Cadiz, Barcelona (from 1829) and Berlin (from 1846); additionally Constantinople, Smyrna, Odessa and Malta and even Corfu (from 1842). Because of the great number of Jews, Greeks and Armenians among the merchants trading here, Leghorn was the exchange market with the closest contact to the Levant and even to the Black Sea region in the Western Mediterranean and even in the whole of Europe. Genoa, Milan, Venice, Rome, Naples, Palermo and Messina, Bologna and Turin as well as Trieste, continued to be quoted within Italy. However, not all of the quoted towns were of the same importance for Leghorn's cashless payment transactions, which becomes evident after the way of quoting changed at the end of 1837: while the 'normal' exchange partners of Leghorn continued to be quoted with only one usance, the more important ones were listed with two usances (30 and 90 days' dato), such as London, the French and the Austrian places as well as Augsburg (and Berlin from 1846) and also Genoa, Milan and Venice in Italy. Since the mid-19th century Leghorn began to lose its importance within the cashless payment system. London, by far the most important exchange partner outside the Mediterranean region, quoted Leghorn together with Genoa and Naples after 1867, and after 1881 Leghorn no longer appeared on the London quotation lists (see p. 10).

In the meantime, Leghorn's fiercest competitor had risen to Italy's most important maritime trading place and to the second-most important one within the Western Mediterranean region (after Marseilles). As early as the second half of the 18th century Genoa had undergone considerable expansion of its trade and had an extensive network of exchange rate quotations at its disposal as a result of the reforms concerning its *porto franco* and primarily based on exchange with Spain. Since the end of the 18th century London, Amsterdam, Hamburg, Madrid, Cadiz and Lisbon, Paris, Lyons, Marseilles, Vienna and Augsburg as well as several Italian places (Milan, Rome, Naples, Leghorn, Venice and Palermo, to some extent also Messina and Turin) were quoted in Genoa. At the beginning of the 19th century even rates on Constantinople and Smyrna were given for a short time (1802–1805). However, the obstruction of free navigation during the Napoleonic era rapidly diminished Genoa's importance, especially as the Ligurian metropole was oriented towards the Western Mediterranean region and the trading centres of Northwestern Europe. After the Congress of Vienna, Genoese trade continued to stagnate, but the integration of Genoa into the Kingdom of Piedmont–Sardinia and the resulting expansion of its hinterland after 1814/15 enabled the town to rise again slowly but steadily in comparison to Leghorn from the 1830s, and even more so when the relaxation of the *porto franco* was expanded in 1834. There were four main reasons for Genoa's rise to supreme Italian port and the second-most important port of the Mediterranean after Marseilles from the middle of the 19th century: first, the general increase in world trade; second, Genoa's position as the main port of the rising Kingdom of Piedmont–Sardinia; third, the Turin government's turning away from protectionism; and, fourth, Leghorn's decline, starting in 1845. In comparison with the early 19th century, the circle of Genoese exchange partners changed only slightly since then: in 1833, Barcelona was added to the exchange rate current as a further Spanish exchange market. By quoting the Catalan capital, the most important Italian–Spanish transfer axis in the Western Mediterranean entered the records. In 1821, quoting on Leghorn was stopped and Turin was quoted instead. References for regular quotations on Turin are available for the time after the currency reform in Genoa in 1827. In addition to this, the following places were recorded (again) as Genoese exchange partners: Messina during 1815 and 1817 and after 1860; Bologna from 1840; Ancona, Trieste, Leghorn and Marseilles from 1860. Although they were listed in contemporary merchant manuals (e.g. NOBACK [1851], pp. 282f.), quotations on Iberian (Madrid, Cadiz, Gibraltar and Lisbon) and South German places (Frankfurt am Main and Augsburg) cannot be found in the sources documented here.

As English merchants continued to be interested in Genoa as a Mediterranean seaport, Genoa retained its importance as an exchange market even after Italy's unification, and even became more so, because the Piedmontese currency, valid in Genoa as well, rose to be the standard Italian currency after 1861. According to contemporary merchant manuals, Genoa was Italy's most important trading centre at the end of the 1870s, all Italian places except Leghorn following Genoa's way of quoting exchange rates (except the usances). From the 1870s, the exchange contacts of the other official Italian stock exchanges – Milan, Florence, Naples, Rome and Turin – also corresponded to those of Genoa, with slight deviations (cf. NOBACK [1877], p. 412). From the 1870s Genoa quoted almost all important European exchange markets, namely London, Amsterdam as well as Paris, Lyons and Marseilles, with the same quotations and partially under 'France' (from 1869), Belgium (from 1871), Switzerland (from 1872), Germany, where the quotations on Hamburg and Berlin (quoted from 1873) were combined since the end of 1877, Vienna – quoted quite irregularly owing to the conflict with Austria between 1866 and 1874 – and Barcelona, which appeared together with Madrid under the category 'Spain' from 1898 (before either Madrid or Lisbon did so, according to the sources documented here; cf. NOBACK [1877], pp. 314f.). Only the quotations on Augsburg (1869), Trieste (1870) and on the Italian places were suspended, because the internal Italian quotations had increasingly become obsolete when the Piedmontese lira nuova or the lira italiana respectively were introduced as standard currency to the new Kingdom of Italy. When no significant price movement had taken place over a period of several years, the quoting was stopped at various Italian exchange places during the 1860s and in the early 1870s. In Genoa most of the internal Italian quotations ended in September 1869, those on Venice did so as early as in May 1866 and, finally, those on Rome stopped after the Italian occupation of the Papal States in September 1870.

The only special case pointing beyond the Genoese exchange network of the second half of the 19th century is the quotation of Naples on Saint Petersburg, which is available for the period from 1840 until 1876 and which is documented here as well. The most important South Italian financial market was – probably because of its corn trade with Southern Russia – the only Italian exchange place having quoted a Russian exchange partner in the second half of the 19th century.

At the Italian stock exchanges 'a-vista' payments (cheques) and 'vista meno sconto' (long-sight bills) were predominantly traded at the end of the 19th and early 20th centuries (SWOBODA [1902], p. 303f).

In order to document the exchange rate quotations of Italian places, the following data have been chosen:

 – 1590 to 1650: the rates of the Bisenzone fairs;

- 1623 to 1797 (i.e. the end of the Republic): the rates of Venice;
- 1771 to 1850: the rates of Leghorn;
- from 1778: the rates of Genoa, supplemented by quotations of Naples on Saint Petersburg for the years 1840 to 1876.

When possible, I document here those places that may be regarded as having been Italy's most important centres for international exchange transactions during their respective period of prosperity. It may be surprising to learn that Genoa as an exchange market was seen as more important at the end of the 19th and early 20th centuries than, for example, Milan (and, therefore, Genoa was documented here). It is true that Milan has been "the undisputed financial center *in* Italy" since the crisis of 1907 (KINDLE-BERGER [1974], p. 35), but nonetheless Genoa was still of more relevance to cashless payment transactions from the international and intercontinental point of view. This estimation strongly emphasizes that London, the world financial centre, quoted the two seaports Genoa and Naples (but not Milan!) with the same quotation until World War I and that the only intercontinental quotation on an Italian place before World War I was that of Buenos Aires on Genoa from 1872 onwards (see pp. 452f.), whereas Milan was the most important exchange partner in Italy only for Swiss, Austrian and South German places. Regarding bank history, KINDLEBERGER bases his statements on the fact that "from 1860 to 1885, Italy, even Central and Northern Italy was not an integrated financial market" (ibid., p. 36), so from the perspective of the international system of cashless payments this seems to be the case until World War I.

References: Paul Jacob MARPERGER, *Beschreibung der Banquen* ..., Halle – Leipzig 1717 (repr. Frankfurt/Main 1969), chapters X, XI; Emil FRAUZ, *Die Verfassung der staatlichen Zahlungsmittel Italiens seit 1861*, Straßburg 1911; Heinrich SIEVEKING, Das Bankwesen in Genua und die Bank von S. Giorgo, in Johannes G. VAN DILLEN (ed.), *History of the Principal Public Banks Accompanied by Extensive Bibliographies of the History of Banking and Credit in Eleven European Countries*, The Hague 1934, pp. 15–38; Luigi DE ROSA, *I cambi esteri del Regno di Napoli dal 1591 al 1707*, Napoli 1955; G. PARENTI, Monete e cambi nel Granducato di Toscana dal 1825 al 1859, *Archivio economico dell'unificazione italiana* II 1 (1956), pp. 1–11; Ugo TUCCI, Le monete del Regno Lombardo–Veneto dal 1815 al 1866, *Archivio economico dell' unificazione italiana* II 3 (1956), pp. 1–41; R. GIUSTI, Corso delle monete e dei cambi sui mercati di Milano et di Venezia dal 1825 al 1866, *Archivio economico dell' unificazione italiana* VI 4 (1957), pp. 41–73; S. PINCHERA, Monete e zecche nello Stato Pontificio dalla restaurazione al 1870, *Archivio economico dell' unificazione italiana* V 5 (1957), pp. 1–20; Kurt VON EICHBORN, *Das Soll und Haben von Eichborn & Co. in 200 Jahren. Schicksal und Gestaltung eines Bankhauses im Wandel der Zeiten*, München – Leipzig 1928; Luigi DE ROSA, Le origini della Borsa di Napoli, *Rivista orizzonti economici* 43, 1962, pp. 1–6; Mario DA POZZO / Giuseppe FELLONI, La borsa valori di Genova nel secolo XIX, *Archivio economico dell' unificazione italiana* II 10, Torino 1964; Ferréol REBUFFAT / Marcel COURDURIÉ, *Marseille et le négoce monétaire international (1785–1790)*, Marseille 1966; José GENTIL DA SILVA, *Banque et crédit en Italie au XVIIe siècle*, Paris 1969; Antonio DI VITTORIO, *Gli Austriaci e il Regno di Napoli 1707–1734. Ideologia e politica di sviluppo*, Napoli 1973; Charles P. KINDLEBERGER, *The Formation of Financial Centers: A Study in Comparative Economic History*, Princeton (N.J.) 1974, pp. 32–36; Charles A. KEENE, American Shipping and Trade, 1798–1820: The Evidence from Leghorn, *Journal of Economic History* 38/3 (1978), pp. 681–700; Giuseppe FELLONI, All'apogeo delle fiere genovesi: Banchieri ed affari di cambio a Piacenza nel 1600, in *Studi in onore di Gino Barbieri. Problemi e metodi di Storia ed Economica, vol. II*, Pisa 1983, pp. 883–901; N.W.J. BAAS, *Die Doppel-währungspolitik Frankreichs 1850–1885*, Firenze 1984; Ira A. GLAZIER, Tradition et innovation monétaires en Italie de 1815 à 1848: la Lombardie–Vénétie et le Munzpatent de 1823, in John DAY (ed.), *Études d'histoire monétaire*, Lille 1984, pp. 423–448; Peter HERTNER, Italien, 1850–1914, in

Wolfram FISCHER et al. (eds.), *Handbuch der europäischen Wirtschafts- und Sozialgeschichte, vol. 5: Europäische Wirtschafts- und Sozialgeschichte von der Mitte des 19. Jahrhunderts bis zum Ersten Weltkrieg*, ed. Wolfram FISCHER, Stuttgart 1985, pp. 705–776; D.G. LOROMER, *Merchants and Reform in Livorno (1814–1868)*, Berkeley – Los Angeles – London 1987; P. CAFARO, *La borsa valori di Milano: origini e sviluppo*, Milano 1988; Marcello DE CECCO (ed.), *L'Italia e il sistema finanziario internazionale 1861–1914*, Roma 1990; Giuseppe FELLONI, Kredit und Banken in Italien, 15.–17. Jahrhundert, in Michael NORTH (ed.), *Kredit im spätmittelalterlichen und frühneuzeitlichen Europa*, Köln – Wien 1991, pp. 9–23; John J. MCCUSKER / Cora GRAVESTEIJN, *The Beginnings of Commercial and Financial Journalism. The Commodity Price Currents, Exchange Rate Currents, and Money Currents of Early Modern Europe*, Amsterdam 1991; Pierre RACINE, Messen in Italien im 16. Jahrhundert. Die Wechselmessen von Piacenza, in Hans POHL (ed.) unter Mitarb. v. Monika POHLE, *Frankfurt im Messenetz Europas – Erträge der Forschung (= Brücke zwischen den Völkern – Zur Geschichte der Frankfurter Messe*, ed. Rainer KOCH, vol. I), Frankfurt/Main 1991, pp. 155–169; Ugo TUCCI, Il banco pubblico a Venezia, in *Banchi pubblici, banchi privati e monti di pietà nell' Europa preindustriale. Amministrazione, tecniche operative e ruoli economici*, Genova 1991, vol. I, pp. 309–325; Helma HOUTMAN-DE SMEDT / Herman VAN DER WEE, Die Entstehung des modernen Geld- und Finanzwesens Europas in der Neuzeit, in Hans POHL (ed.), *Europäische Bankengeschichte*, Frankfurt/Main 1993, pp. 73–173; Markus A. DENZEL, *"La Practica della Cambiatura". Europäischer Zahlungsverkehr vom 14. bis zum 17. Jahrhundert*, Stuttgart 1994; Michael NORTH, Art. "Dukat", in idem (ed.), *Von Aktie bis Zoll. Ein historisches Lexikon des Geldes*, München 1995, p. 95; idem, Von den Warenmessen zu den Wechselmessen. Grundlagen des europäischen Zahlungsverkehrs in Spätmittelalter und Früher Neuzeit, in Peter JOHANEK / Heinz STOOB (ed.), *Europäische Messen und Märktesysteme in Mittelalter und Neuzeit*, Köln – Weimar – Wien 1996, pp. 223–238; Michele FRATIANNI / Franco SPINELLI, *A Monetary History of Italy*, Cambridge 1997; Gigliola PAGANO DE DEVITIIS, *English Merchants in Seventeenth-Century Italy*, Cambridge 1997 [Ital. Venezia 1990]; Luigi DE ROSA, The Beginnings of Paper-Money Circulation: the Neapolitan Public Banks (1540–1650), *Journal of European Economic History* 30 (2001), pp. 497–532; Markus A. DENZEL, *Der bargeldlose Zahlungsverkehr auf den Bozner Messen (1618 bis 1850)*, Bozen 2005; Claudio MARSILIO, *Dovè il denaro fa denaro. Gli operatori finanziari genovesi nelle fiere di cambio del XVII secolo*, Novi Ligure 2008.

3.1 Exchange rates of the Genoese exchange fairs (Bisenzone fairs)

Usances: No information is available concerning the usances.

3.1.1 On Antwerp, Amsterdam, Lyons and Lisbon

	BISENZONE FAIRS on:					
	Antwerp		Lyons		Lisbon	
	per 10,000 groot Flemish [a]		per 100 écus d'or au soleil [b]		per 100 crusados [c]	
	in scudi di marche					
1590			93.21	(4)		
1591	86.25	(4)	94.90	(4)	84.85	(3)
1592	83.48	(3)	93.99	(4)	82.99	(3)
1593	79.89	(4)	95.32	(4)	79.70	(3)
1594	79.90	(4)	96.97	(4)	83.14	(4)
1595	80.03	(4)	93.30	(4)	76.92	(4)
1596	80.89	(4)	94.06	(4)	79.57	(4)
1597	79.58	(3)	93.65	(4)	80.00	(3)
1598	78.44	(4)	91.86	(4)	80.00	(3)
1599	77.42	(4)	91.20	(4)	80.00	(4)
1600	82.51	(4)	95.86	(4)	80.00	(4)
1601	81.25	(4)	98.72	(4)	80.41	(2)
1602	79.06	(4)	99.56	(4)		
1603	80.15	(4)	97.61	(4)		
1604	79.19	(4)	93.71	(4)		
1605	78.41	(4)	92.43	(4)		
1606	80.01	(3)	91.51	(4)		
1607	77.61	(4)	92.16	(4)		
1608	74.08	(3)	91.01	(4)		
1609	71.01	(4)	87.46	(4)		
1610	70.81	(4)	85.58	(4)		
1611	70.74	(4)	86.26	(4)		
1612	70.21	(4)	86.12	(4)		
1613	68.28	(4)	84.12	(4)		
1614	71.19	(4)	82.77	(4)		
1615	69.70	(4)	83.24	(4)		
1616	67.46	(4)	83.86	(4)		
1617	68.09	(4)	83.08	(4)		
1618	68.33	(4)	83.47	(4)		
1619	69.91	(4)	84.10	(4)		
1620	69.45	(4)	83.34	(4)		
1621	69.34	(4)	80.13	(4)		

	BISENZONE FAIRS on:		
	Antwerp	**Amsterdam**	**Lyons**
	per 10,000 groot Flemish [a]	per 10,000 groot Flemish [d]	per 100 écus d'or au soleil [b]
		in scudi di marche	
1622	72.37 (4)		83.69 (4)
1623	68.97 (4)		82.00 (4)
1624	68.36 (4)		80.50 (4)
1625	69.03 (4)		81.50 (4)
1626	69.87 (4)		80.00 (4)
1627	69.53 (4)		80.63 (4)
1628	70.24 (4)	68.03 (1)	81.13 (4)
1629	73.59 (4)		85.75 (4)
1630	73.22 (4)		84.75 (4)
1631	70.01 (4)		77.00 (4)
1632	68.73 (4)	66.45 (2)	73.50 (4)
1633	67.80 (4)	65.22 (3)	73.25 (4)
1634	64.63 (4)	62.50 (1)	73.50 (4)
1635	64.74 (4)		70.72 (4)
1636	66.23 (4)	65.36 (1)	67.16 (4)
1637	63.30 (4)	61.73 (1)	60.31 (4)
1638	61.97 (4)		57.38 (4)
1639	61.45 (4)	60.65 (4)	57.33 (4)
1640	61.07 (4)	60.25 (4)	56.63 (4)
1641	59.36 (4)	58.57 (4)	57.69 (4)
1642	58.10 (4)	57.75 (4)	57.35 (4)
1643	56.06 (4)	55.85 (4)	58.63 (4)
1644	57.75 (4)	57.58 (4)	58.19 (4)
1645	59.13 (4)	58.23 (4)	58.31 (4)
1646	59.36 (4)	58.06 (4)	57.75 (4)
1647	59.49 (4)	58.49 (4)	57.50 (4)
1648	59.75 (4)	58.69 (4)	59.25 (4)
1649	60.22 (4)	59.12 (4)	60.00 (4)
1650	54.21 (4)	53.56 (4)	57.31 (4)

[a] The Antwerp currency system was equal to that of the Northern Netherlands (Amsterdam) (see pp. 57–59).

[b] Since September 1577 the écu d'or au soleil (of 20 sous d'or or 240 deniers d'or), the unit of account and payment at the Lyons fairs, was officially fixed with 60 sous tournois of 12 deniers tournois, which was equal to 3 livres tournois (DENZEL [1994], p. 304).

[c] In the Portuguese currency system one reckoned in réis and milréis (= 1,000 réis), but the exchange rate quotations of and on Portuguese places were effected in or for crusados (velhos or do cambio) as a unit of account of 400 réis.

[d] Concerning the Dutch currency, see pp. 57–59.

3.1.2 On Spanish places

	BISENZONE FAIRS on:						
	Seville		**Barcelona**		**Valencia**		**Saragossa**
	per 100 ducados de cambio [a]		per 100 libras of Catalonia [b]		per 100 libras of Valencia [c]		per 100 libras of Aragon [d]
	in scudi di marche						
1591	86.36	(4)	82.39	(3)	82.91	(4)	81.98	(4)
1592	86.88	(3)	81.63	(3)	81.91	(3)	81.45	(3)
1593	85.74	(4)	81.00	(4)	81.77	(4)	80.82	(4)
1594	87.06	(4)	81.60	(4)	83.05	(4)	81.88	(4)
1595	82.48	(4)	80.46	(4)	82.28	(4)	80.08	(4)
1596	84.97	(4)	80.21	(4)	81.63	(4)	80.20	(4)
1597	84.97	(3)	83.05	(3)	83.53	(3)	82.67	(3)
1598	85.00	(4)	80.81	(3)	82.20	(3)	80.81	(3)
1599	84.66	(4)	81.16	(4)	81.63	(4)	81.16	(4)
1600	83.57	(4)	80.54	(4)	81.63	(4)	81.17	(4)
1601	85.29	(4)	80.69	(4)	81.91	(4)	80.89	(4)
1602	83.34	(4)	79.47	(4)	81.36	(4)	79.47	(4)
1603	85.55	(4)	79.74	(4)	82.05	(4)	80.00	(4)
1604	83.71	(4)	79.54	(4)	81.63	(4)	79.47	(4)
1605	84.29	(4)	79.61	(4)	81.43	(4)	79.61	(4)
1606	82.42	(3)	76.94	(3)	78.45	(3)	76.94	(3)
1607	81.97	(4)	75.12	(4)	76.20	(4)	75.12	(4)
1608	82.36	(3)	75.32	(3)	76.44	(3)	75.80	(3)
1609	83.57	(4)	78.07	(4)	78.77	(4)	78.07	(4)
1610	84.19	(4)	79.25	(4)	79.25	(4)	79.25	(4)
1611	83.29	(4)	75.84	(4)	75.59	(4)	76.20	(4)
1612	83.95	(4)	76.56	(4)	76.07	(4)	76.56	(4)
1613	82.97	(4)	76.74	(4)	76.20	(4)	76.74	(4)
1614	82.20	(4)	74.11	(4)	73.99	(4)	75.12	(4)
1615	81.00	(4)	75.47	(4)	74.19	(2)	75.84	(4)
1616	79.37	(4)	72.74	(4)	72.74	(4)	73.40	(4)
1617	79.01	(4)	72.08	(4)	72.62	(4)	72.08	(4)
1618	79.21	(4)	71.79	(4)	72.19	(4)	73.81	(4)
1619	80.08	(4)	72.57	(4)	72.62	(4)	73.62	(4)
1620	81.12	(4)	73.51	(4)	73.74	(4)	74.31	(4)
1621	80.71	(4)	71.44	(4)	72.40	(4)	73.07	(4)
1622	79.83	(4)	71.73	(4)	73.02	(4)	72.95	(4)
1623	79.37	(4)	72.68	(4)	73.18	(4)	74.25	(4)
1624	78.83	(4)	70.49	(4)	72.73	(4)	73.65	(4)
1625	78.13	(4)	71.22	(4)	72.73	(4)	72.84	(4)
1626	78.14	(4)	72.68	(4)	72.73	(4)	73.34	(4)

	BISENZONE FAIRS on:			
	Seville	**Barcelona**	**Valencia**	**Saragossa**
	per 100 ducados de cambio [a]	per 100 libras of Catalonia [b]	per 100 libras of Valencia [c]	per 100 libras of Aragon [d]
	in scudi di marche			
1627	78.95 (4)	72.84 (4)	72.84 (4)	73.32 (4)
1628	78.70 (4)	72.62 (4)	72.73 (4)	73.29 (4)
1629	84.99 (4)	78.04 (4)	77.75 (4)	79.36 (4)
1630	83.37 (4)	81.02 (4)	79.31 (4)	81.02 (4)
1631	76.63 (4)	72.85 (4)	72.74 (4)	72.74 (4)
1632	75.08 (4)	71.97 (4)	71.76 (4)	71.97 (4)
1633	74.27 (4)	70.18 (4)	69.89 (4)	70.18 (4)
1634	73.25 (4)	70.18 (4)	70.18 (4)	70.18 (4)
1635	72.64 (4)	70.18 (4)	70.18 (4)	70.18 (4)
1636	72.19 (4)	69.37 (4)	68.83 (4)	69.57 (4)
1637	71.81 (4)	68.09 (4)	67.80 (4)	68.09 (4)
1638	71.50 (4)	66.77 (4)	65.58 (4)	66.77 (4)
1639	71.26 (4)	65.45 (4)	64.66 (4)	65.45 (4)
1640	70.10 (4)	65.32 (4)	63.75 (4)	65.32 (4)
1641	69.94 (4)	65.06 (4)	62.88 (4)	64.54 (4)
1642	69.29 (4)	60.16 (4)	61.43 (4)	60.48 (4)
1643	73.90 (4)	58.43 (4)	64.26 (4)	59.29 (4)
1644	69.73 (4)	55.56 (4)	64.27 (4)	55.56 (4)
1645	68.97 (4)	55.37 (4)	63.76 (4)	55.37 (4)
1646	69.94 (4)	56.15 (4)	62.14 (4)	56.15 (4)
1647	69.74 (4)	56.15 (4)	61.55 (4)	56.15 (4)
1648	69.58 (4)	56.65 (4)	62.22 (4)	56.65 (4)
1649	69.19 (4)	57.15 (4)	62.14 (4)	57.15 (4)
1650	68.59 (4)	55.18 (4)	61.66 (4)	55.18 (4)

[a] 1 ducado de cambio = 375 maravédis, whereby 34 maravédis = 1 real. See also p. 308.

[b] 1 libra of Catalonia = 20 sueldos = 240 dineros, whereby 1 sueldo = 1/24 ducado; the libra was equal to 31.00 grammes of fine silver or 27.60 grammes of fine silver respectively from 1617 (DENZEL [1994], pp. 455f.).

[c] 1 libra of (the kingdom of) Valencia = 20 sueldos = 240 dineros, whereby 1 sueldo = 1/21 ducado (ibid.).

[d] 1 libra of Aragon = 20 sueldos = 240 dineros, whereby 1 sueldo = 1/22 ducado (ibid.).

3.1.3 On Italian places (I)

	BISENZONE FAIRS on:			
	Venice	**Genoa**	**Milan**	**Florence**
	per 100 ducati d'oro, from 1593 per 100 ducati di banco [a]	per 100 lire moneta corrente [b]	per 100 scudi imperiali [c]	per 100 scudi d'oro [d]
	in scudi di marche			
1590	77.23 (2)	29.70 (4)	90.42 (4)	95.39 (3)
1591	77.36 (4)	29.85 (4)	90.44 (4)	93.54 (4)
1592	75.54 (4)	29.93 (4)	89.63 (4)	91.83 (4)
1593	74.45 (4)	29.77 (4)	88.29 (4)	91.46 (4)
1594	75.91 (4)	29.82 (4)	88.88 (4)	91.33 (4)
1595	75.26 (4)	29.98 (4)	89.54 (4)	92.76 (4)
1596	73.98 (4)	29.86 (4)	88.44 (4)	91.06 (4)
1597	74.38 (3)	29.86 (4)	88.79 (4)	93.60 (4)
1598	74.47 (4)	29.66 (4)	87.74 (4)	91.76 (4)
1599	74.34 (4)	29.76 (4)	88.26 (4)	91.43 (4)
1600	75.20 (4)	29.73 (4)	88.19 (4)	90.86 (4)
1601	75.16 (4)	29.80 (4)	88.64 (4)	91.78 (4)
1602	74.02 (4)	29.97 (4)	88.52 (4)	91.63 (4)
1603	74.01 (4)	29.72 (4)	86.92 (4)	90.59 (4)
1604	72.91 (4)	29.70 (4)	86.83 (4)	91.13 (4)
1605	73.30 (4)	29.65 (4)	86.77 (4)	90.28 (4)
1606	75.00 (4)	30.12 (4)	87.49 (4)	91.06 (4)
1607	73.53 (4)	29.81 (4)	86.95 (4)	90.67 (4)
1608	71.01 (4)	29.56 (3)	85.95 (4)	89.94 (4)
1609	72.34 (4)	29.60 (4)	84.80 (4)	89.12 (4)
1610	72.76 (4)	29.32 (4)	83.02 (4)	89.51 (4)
1611	70.98 (4)	29.24 (4)	84.66 (4)	89.44 (4)
1612	71.61 (4)	29.31 (4)	84.87 (4)	90.56 (4)
1613	69.37 (4)	28.61 (4)	82.37 (4)	87.67 (4)
1614	70.56 (4)	28.28 (4)	82.75 (4)	86.59 (4)
1615	70.05 (4)	28.51 (4)	82.92 (4)	86.70 (4)
1616	69.03 (4)	29.30 (4)	80.89 (4)	84.97 (4)
1617	68.31 (4)	29.79 (4)	81.27 (4)	85.13 (4)
1618	66.99 (4)	29.81 (4)	80.00 (4)	83.91 (4)
1619	66.20 (4)	29.82 (4)	79.29 (4)	83.84 (4)
1620	66.24 (4)	29.75 (4)	78.88 (4)	82.82 (4)
1621	67.50 (4)	29.84 (4)	67.32 (4)	83.84 (4)
1622	68.62 (4)	30.19 (4)	68.12 (4)	82.61 (4)
1623	68.40 (4)	29.98 (4)	67.86 (4)	84.70 (4)
1624	68.48 (4)	29.23 (4)	67.44 (4)	84.93 (4)

	BISENZONE FAIRS on:			
	Venice	**Genoa**	**Milan**	**Florence**
	per 100 ducati di banco [a]	per 100 lire moneta corrente, from 1631 per 100 scudi d'argento [b]	per 100 scudi imperiali [c]	per 100 scudi d'oro [d]
	in scudi di marche			
1625	69.02 (4)	29.52 (4)	68.12 (4)	85.76 (4)
1626	68.61 (4)	29.79 (4)	67.86 (4)	85.53 (4)
1627	67.38 (4)	30.16 (4)	66.78 (4)	84.98 (4)
1628	66.90 (4)	30.22 (4)	68.17 (4)	85.77 (4)
1629	72.11 (4)	33.03 (4)	74.35 (4)	85.58 (4)
1630	71.35 (4)	33.20 (4)	76.18 (4)	82.97 (4)
1631	62.25 (4)	90.21 (4)	66.24 (4)	83.29 (4)
1632	58.31 (4)	90.62 (4)	63.61 (4)	81.66 (4)
1633	56.41 (4)	86.31 (4)	62.82 (4)	80.62 (4)
1634	55.60 (4)	86.84 (4)	61.93 (4)	78.85 (4)
1635	56.69 (4)	85.70 (4)	61.07 (4)	78.34 (4)
1636	57.56 (4)	84.41 (4)	60.82 (4)	78.26 (4)
1637	57.18 (4)	83.29 (4)	61.00 (4)	76.47 (4)
1638	56.46 (4)	83.00 (4)	60.75 (4)	75.94 (4)
1639	56.19 (4)	82.96 (4)	60.31 (4)	75.23 (4)
1640	55.10 (4)	82.32 (4)	59.59 (4)	74.95 (4)
1641	55.79 (4)	82.22 (4)	58.17 (4)	75.20 (4)
1642	55.97 (4)	82.38 (4)	58.06 (4)	76.05 (4)
1643	55.30 (4)	83.28 (4)	58.24 (4)	75.28 (4)
1644	54.58 (4)	82.34 (4)	58.02 (4)	74.50 (4)
1645	53.90 (4)	82.40 (4)	57.82 (4)	73.56 (4)
1646	52.88 (4)	84.11 (4)	57.56 (4)	74.05 (4)
1647	52.83 (4)	84.94 (4)	57.56 (4)	74.51 (4)
1648	48.91 (4)	84.40 (4)	58.32 (4)	73.66 (4)
1649	45.84 (4)	84.92 (4)	58.02 (4)	72.48 (4)
1650	42.98 (4)	84.49 (4)	57.23 (4)	74.53 (4)

[a] Concerning the Venetian currency, see pp. 104f.

[b] Concerning the Genoese currency, see pp. 107f.

[c] The scudo imperiale or scudo di cambio was the Milanese imaginary unit of account in cashless payment and equal to 5 lire imperiale or 5 lire 17 soldi correnti.

[d] The scudo d'oro (of 20 soldi at 12 denari d'oro) was the Florentine imaginary unit of account in cashless payment and equal to 7½ lire moneta buona or 1 7/23 pezze da otto reali (1 pezza = 184 denari d'oro) (NELKENBRECHER [1775], pp. 87f.).

3.1.3 On Italian places (II)

	BISENZONE FAIRS on:						
	Lucca		**Rome**		**Naples**		**Palermo**
	per 100 scudi d'oro [a]		per 100 scudi d'oro di stampe [b]		per 100 ducati moneta corrente [c]		per 100 oncie [d]
	in scudi di marche						
1591	86.38	(4)	99.86	(4)	77.65	(4)	204.97	(4)
1592	85.48	(3)	98.30	(3)	77.76	(4)	203.15	(3)
1593	85.39	(3)	101.06	(4)	77.10	(4)	204.35	(4)
1594	85.66	(4)	100.88	(4)	76.73	(4)	200.82	(4)
1595	86.04	(4)	103.25	(4)	73.51	(4)	198.00	(4)
1596	85.66	(4)	100.68	(3)	72.28	(4)	198.85	(4)
1597	85.84	(3)	100.68	(3)	71.56	(3)	190.52	(3)
1598	85.20	(3)	101.55	(4)	74.02	(4)	208.45	(4)
1599	85.07	(4)	101.98	(4)	76.01	(4)	207.78	(4)
1600	84.93	(4)	100.17	(3)	75.33	(4)	203.88	(4)
1601	84.87	(3)	100.82	(4)	75.80	(4)	202.71	(4)
1602	84.71	(4)	101.45	(4)	74.15	(4)	204.65	(4)
1603	84.37	(4)	100.85	(4)	72.84	(4)	192.97	(4)
1604	84.17	(4)	102.07	(4)	72.73	(4)	196.27	(4)
1605	83.95	(4)	100.90	(4)	72.88	(4)	197.17	(4)
1606	84.04	(3)	100.87	(4)	69.63	(3)	192.60	(3)
1607	84.13	(4)	103.09	(4)	68.33	(4)	172.34	(4)
1608	83.57	(3)	104.32	(4)	67.60	(3)	163.32	(3)
1609	81.70	(4)	102.45	(4)	69.99	(4)	177.25	(4)
1610	81.42	(4)	100.66	(4)	69.52	(4)	173.19	(4)
1611	82.35	(4)	98.45	(4)	70.68	(4)	171.39	(4)
1612	82.86	(4)	102.06	(4)	69.99	(4)	175.92	(4)
1613	80.66	(4)	99.75	(4)	68.55	(4)	180.51	(4)
1614	80.45	(4)	98.59	(4)	66.38	(4)	176.17	(4)
1615	80.53	(4)	99.50	(4)	65.49	(4)	178.32	(4)
1616	78.59	(4)	99.54	(4)	63.98	(4)	185.75	(4)
1617	78.67	(4)	99.93	(4)	62.76	(4)	181.87	(4)
1618	76.74	(4)	99.00	(4)	59.35	(3)	182.17	(4)
1619	76.50	(4)	99.19	(4)	59.71	(4)	185.40	(4)
1620	75.77	(4)	100.36	(4)	57.66	(4)	183.23	(4)
1621	75.12	(4)	100.69	(4)	44.44	(1)	175.08	(4)
1622	75.69	(4)	100.17	(4)			171.48	(4)
1623	75.69	(4)	102.24	(4)	64.85	(4)	174.36	(4)
1624	76.06	(4)	102.06	(4)	68.43	(4)	182.52	(4)
1625	77.30	(4)	103.67	(4)	70.07	(4)	180.48	(4)
1626	77.53	(4)	103.21	(4)	70.82	(4)	177.84	(4)

	BISENZONE FAIRS on:			
	Lucca	**Rome**	**Naples**	**Palermo**
	per 100 scudi d'oro [a]	per 100 scudi d'oro di stampe [b]	per 100 ducati moneta corrente [c]	per 100 oncie [d]
	in scudi di marche			
1627	77.37 (4)	102.14 (4)	69.97 (4)	176.52 (4)
1628	77.49 (4)	102.78 (4)	71.91 (4)	176.52 (4)
1629	87.87 (4)	102.78 (4)	77.56 (4)	184.86 (4)
1630	87.27 (4)	111.75 (4)	80.11 (4)	192.24 (4)
1631	75.78 (4)	101.94 (4)	70.64 (4)	178.50 (4)
1632	74.08 (4)	99.63 (4)	69.35 (4)	179.40 (4)
1633	72.53 (4)	97.83 (4)	68.13 (4)	167.88 (4)
1634	71.19 (4)	98.64 (4)	64.64 (4)	162.48 (4)
1635	70.49 (4)	100.94 (4)	64.73 (4)	159.24 (4)
1636	69.81 (4)	100.70 (4)	64.87 (4)	160.62 (4)
1637	69.21 (4)	100.07 (4)	63.18 (4)	157.92 (4)
1638	68.85 (4)	99.40 (4)	62.32 (4)	157.50 (4)
1639	67.72 (4)	99.51 (4)	60.21 (4)	154.92 (4)
1640	67.46 (4)	98.29 (4)	59.93 (4)	138.18 (4)
1641	67.92 (4)	98.77 (4)	59.30 (4)	141.60 (4)
1642	68.64 (4)	100.76 (4)	61.45 (4)	155.34 (4)
1643	68.26 (4)	100.32 (4)	60.88 (4)	160.98 (4)
1644	67.89 (4)	99.45 (4)	60.75 (4)	165.06 (4)
1645	67.46 (4)	98.53 (4)	60.81 (4)	167.88 (4)
1646	67.58 (4)	99.02 (4)	61.71 (4)	168.78 (4)
1647	68.15 (4)	100.89 (4)	60.78 (4)	167.28 (4)
1648	67.12 (4)	99.11 (4)	62.14 (4)	170.22 (4)
1649	65.15 (4)	94.61 (4)	60.10 (4)	169.98 (4)
1650	66.51 (4)	100.08 (4)	63.14 (4)	169.08 (4)

[a]   The scudo d'oro (of 20 soldi at 12 denari d'oro) was the Lucchese imaginary unit of account.

[b]   In Rome the scudo d'oro di stampe of 20 soldi at 12 denari d'oro was the imaginary unit of account in cashless payment, equal to 1,500 mezzi quattrini. Concerning exchange business, there was a fixed premium of 23 or 25 mezzi quattrini: if one bought a bill of exchange at Rome, one had to pay 1,523 mezzi quattrini per each scudo di stampa d'oro. If a foreign bill of exchange, however, had to be paid at Rome, one had to pay 1,525 mezzi quattrini per each scudo di stampa d'oro (NELKENBRECHER [1775], p. 207). So the ratio of the scudo di stampa d'oro to the scudo moneta or scudo romano of 10 paoli or giuli at 10 baiocchi of 10 mezzi quattrini, which was the current money in the Papal States, was 2:3 without the premium (2 scudi di stampa d'oro = 3 scudi romani). Therefore 40 scudi di stampa d'oro of 1,525 mezzi quattrini = 61 scudi moneta.

[c]   The system of accounting in ducati ('moneta corrente') of 10 carlini at 10 grani or of 5 tari at 20 grani had been common practice in the kingdom of Naples for centuries. Especially in the second decade of the 17th century the Neapolitan currency was marked by strong devaluations (1611: 8.4%, 1617: 15.9%, 1618: 20.3%, 1620: 33.1%); these appeared in the quotations only with some delay (DE ROSA [1955], pp. 33f.).

[d]   The oncia of 30 tari or 60 carlini was the Sicilian imaginary unit of account.

3.1.4 On places of the Holy Roman Empire

	BISENZONE FAIRS on:					
	Cologne		**Frankfurt**		**Nuremberg**	
	per 10,000 groot Flemish [a]		per 100 rixdollars current [b]		per 100 rixdollars current [c]	
	in scudi di marche					
1591	84.68	(4)	86.22	(4)		
1592	82.05	(3)	87.26	(3)		
1593	78.58	(4)	85.57	(4)		
1594	78.77	(4)	86.25	(4)		
1595	79.08	(4)	85.93	(4)		
1596	79.43	(4)	85.79	(4)		
1597	78.64	(3)	84.66	(3)		
1598	77.68	(3)	82.93	(3)		
1599	76.83	(4)	83.30	(4)		
1600	81.40	(4)	84.58	(4)		
1601	81.22	(2)	84.56	(4)		
1602			83.16	(4)	85.52	(2)
1603			83.36	(4)	85.56	(4)
1604			81.95	(4)	83.15	(4)
1605			81.93	(4)	82.39	(4)
1606			82.09	(3)	83.48	(3)
1607			81.81	(4)	80.28	(4)
1608			78.31	(3)	76.30	(3)
1609			76.29	(4)	71.59	(4)
1610			77.69	(4)	71.94	(4)
1611			80.02	(4)	72.97	(4)
1612			78.75	(4)	71.30	(4)
1613			76.03	(4)	69.18	(4)
1614			77.43	(4)	69.17	(4)
1615			76.69	(4)	67.46	(4)
1616			74.88	(4)	64.12	(4)
1617			76.42	(4)	64.58	(4)
1618			76.53	(4)	62.61	(4)
1619			78.63	(4)	61.91	(4)
1620			79.24	(4)	48.36	(4)
1621			72.59	(4)	42.06	(4)
1622			72.05	(4)		
1623			70.11	(4)		
1624			68.08	(4)	61.82	(3)
1625			68.65	(4)	63.20	(4)
1626			69.03	(4)	62.88	(4)

	BISENZONE FAIRS on:					
	Frankfurt		**Nuremberg**		**Vienna**	
	per 100 rixdollars current [b]		per 100 rixdollars current [c]		per 100 rixdollars current [d]	
	in scudi di marche					
1627	69.03	(4)	62.72	(4)		
1628	69.48	(3)	62.95	(3)		
1629	71.39	(4)	65.24	(4)		
1630	70.51	(4)	63.04	(4)		
1631	67.24	(4)	60.00	(4)		
1632	67.51	(4)	59.21	(4)		
1633	67.93	(4)	58.45	(4)		
1634	66.97	(4)	57.51	(4)		
1635	66.41	(4)	57.42	(4)		
1636	66.88	(4)	57.82	(4)	59.90	(2)
1637	64.19	(4)	56.00	(4)	58.24	(4)
1638	62.21	(4)	56.38	(4)	56.35	(4)
1639	62.61	(4)	57.38	(4)	57.40	(4)
1640	61.84	(4)	58.59	(4)	57.57	(4)
1641	60.32	(4)	55.83	(4)	55.33	(4)
1642	60.70	(4)	55.57	(4)	55.99	(4)
1643	59.31	(4)	55.57	(4)	55.03	(4)
1644	59.82	(4)	56.03	(4)	55.81	(4)
1645	57.86	(4)	56.43	(4)	55.79	(4)
1646	58.08	(4)	56.34	(4)	55.25	(4)
1647	57.05	(4)	55.99	(4)	55.45	(4)
1648	57.05	(4)	55.39	(4)	54.73	(4)
1649	55.51	(4)	53.96	(4)	54.22	(4)
1650	52.87	(4)	52.07	(4)	51.99	(4)

[a]   In Cologne, cashless payment was effected in the Flemish system of account, as was also common in Amsterdam and Antwerp (see pp. 57–59).

[b]   Frankfurt am Main was quoted per rixdollars of 1566 (at 25.98 grammes of fine silver), nominally of 68 kreuzer (until the 1580s). During the following years, especially in the Kipper-and-Wipper era (1619–1623), one had to pay more and more kreuzer for 1 rixdollar: from 72 kreuzer in September 1596 up to 195 kreuzer in July 1621, because of the decreasing value of the small coins. This inflation of current money is visible in the data presented here (RITTMANN [1975], pp. 1020f.). After 1623, 1 rixdollar was equal to 90 kreuzer.

[c]   Nuremberg was quoted per rixdollars of 1566 (at 25.98 grammes of fine silver), nominally of 68 kreuzer (until the 1580s). During the following years, especially in the Kipper-and-Wipper era (1619–1623), one had to pay more and more kreuzer for 1 rixdollar because of the decreasing value of the small coins:

1596, October:	72 kreuzer
1610, November:	84 kreuzer
1615, March:	88 kreuzer
1617, October:	90 kreuzer

1618, May:	92 kreuzer
1619, October:	108 kreuzer
1619, December:	124 kreuzer
1620, November:	140 kreuzer
1621, May:	195 kreuzer
1622, June:	195 kreuzer
since 1623, August:	90 kreuzer

Source: Ibid.

The inflation of the exchange rates presented here was the reason why Nuremberg was not quoted at the Bisenzone fairs from 1622 to spring 1624.

[d] Vienna was quoted per rixdollars of 1566 (at 25.98 grammes of fine silver), which was equal to 90 kreuzer in the period documented here.

3.2 Venice exchange rates

Usances: Since there is no information about the usances in the documented exchange rate currents, the following usances are given according to KRUSE [1781], p. 385. They differ in some details from the information given by NELKENBRECHER [1775], p. 241. Here, the usance on Augsburg, Nuremberg and Vienna is 14 days after sight, on Leghorn and Florence 15 days after sight and on Bolzano on the fairs.

3.2.1 On Amsterdam, Antwerp, London and Lyons

	VENICE on:			
	Amsterdam	**Antwerp**	**London**	**Lyons**
	per 100 guilders Flemish or Flemish banco resp. [a]	per 100 guilders Flemish or Brabant exchange money ('permißgeld') resp. [b]	per 10 pounds sterling [c]	per 100 écus d'or au soleil [d]
	in ducati di banco			
1623	38.50 2m/d (3)	40.12 2m/d (3)	41.75 3m/d (3)	119.25 fairs (3)
1624	37.90 2m/d (10)	39.80 2m/d (10)	41.59 3m/d (10)	117.50 fairs (9)
1625				
1626	38.98 2m/d (2)	41.14 2m/d (3)	42.02 3m/d (2)	120.00 fairs (2)
1627	38.72 2m/d (12)	41.04 2m/d (12)	41.38 3m/d (12)	121.55 fairs (12)
1628	39.45 2m/d (8)	40.61 2m/d (8)	42.06 3m/d (8)	121.18 fairs (8)
1629	39.19 2m/d (5)	40.17 2m/d (5)	41.72 3m/d (5)	123.07 fairs (4)
1630	42.06 2m/d (9)	43.15 2m/d (9)	45.77 3m/d (9)	127.31 fairs (9)
1631	43.49 2m/d (11)	44.92 2m/d (11)	47.16 3m/d (11)	123.98 fairs (11)
1632	44.47 2m/d (12)	46.51 2m/d (12)	48.62 3m/d (12)	128.73 fairs (10)
1633	44.39 2m/d (12)	46.87 2m/d (12)	49.04 3m/d (12)	129.47 fairs (9)
1634	43.51 2m/d (8)	45.28 2m/d (8)	48.75 3m/d (8)	130.96 fairs (7)
1635	43.92 2m/d (9)	45.70 2m/d (9)	47.80 3m/d (8)	122.97 fairs (7)
1636	42.97 2m/d (10)	44.06 2m/d (10)	45.75 3m/d (10)	112.42 fairs (5)
1637	41.27 2m/d (10)	42.98 2m/d (10)	45.80 3m/d (10)	103.39 fairs (9)
1638	41.92 2m/d (12)	43.13 2m/d (12)	45.45 3m/d (12)	101.90 fairs (10)
1639	42.78 2m/d (9)	43.35 2m/d (9)	46.34 3m/d (9)	101.69 fairs (8)
1640	42.22 2m/d (11)	42.89 2m/d (11)	47.25 3m/d (11)	102.89 fairs (9)
1641	40.29 2m/d (6)	40.85 2m/d (6)	46.61 3m/d (6)	101.13 fairs (6)
1642	40.67 2m/d (12)	40.70 2m/d (12)	46.89 3m/d (12)	102.70 fairs (10)
1643	40.73 2m/d (5)	39.01 2m/d (5)	48.71 3m/d (5)	104.28 fairs (3)
1644	43.27 2m/d (10)	43.09 2m/d (10)	50.65 3m/d (10)	106.97 fairs (8)
1645	42.67 2m/d (11)	43.11 2m/d (11)	49.05 3m/d (11)	106.40 fairs (11)
1646	43.24 2m/d (8)	43.92 2m/d (8)	48.17 3m/d (8)	107.32 fairs (8)
1647	43.14 2m/d (11)	44.11 2m/d (11)	44.58 3m/d (11)	109.59 fairs (9)
1648	48.16 2m/d (6)	48.64 2m/d (6)	47.17 3m/d (6)	121.67 fairs (6)
1649	50.32 2m/d (10)	50.97 2m/d (10)	49.40 3m/d (10)	130.42 fairs (9)
1650	48.60 2m/d (4)	48.93 2m/d (4)	51.55 3m/d (4)	129.25 fairs (4)

	VENICE on:			
	Amsterdam	**Antwerp**	**London**	**Lyons**
	per 100 guilders Flemish or Flemish banco resp. [a]	per 100 guilders Flemish or Brabant exchange money ('permißgeld') resp. [b]	per 10 pounds sterling [c]	per 100 écus d'or au soleil [d]
	in ducati di banco			
1651	43.50 2m/d (9)	43.97 2m/d (9)	47.91 3m/d (9)	112.17 fairs (9)
1652	41.14 2m/d (4)	41.73 2m/d (4)	43.12 3m/d (4)	99.50 fairs (3)
1653	40.93 2m/d (4)	41.80 2m/d (4)	43.21 3m/d (4)	94.50 fairs (3)
1654	40.83 2m/d (2)	42.01 2m/d (2)	44.14 3m/d (2)	102.25 fairs (2)
1655	41.14 2m/d (3)	42.15 2m/d (3)	44.72 3m/d (3)	103.38 fairs (2)
1656	41.95 2m/d (4)	43.14 2m/d (4)	44.30 3m/d (4)	100.34 fairs (3)
1657	41.78 2m/d (5)	42.24 2m/d (5)	42.74 3m/d (5)	97.20 fairs (5)
1658	41.84 2m/d (9)	42.45 2m/d (9)	42.95 3m/d (9)	101.65 fairs (7)
1659	41.83 2m/d (8)	42.81 2m/d (8)	44.88 3m/d (8)	101.17 fairs (6)
1660	41.89 2m/d (8)	42.88 2m/d (8)	46.98 3m/d (8)	102.29 fairs (8)
1661	41.43 2m/d (9)	42.14 2m/d (9)	44.38 3m/d (9)	101.25 fairs (8)
1662	40.96 2m/d (12)	41.76 2m/d (12)	43.20 3m/d (12)	100.23 fairs (11)
1663	40.21 2m/d (10)	40.79 2m/d (10)	43.15 3m/d (10)	99.45 fairs (9)
1664	40.71 2m/d (8)	41.07 2m/d (8)	42.86 3m/d (8)	100.32 fairs (8)
1665	42.61 2m/d (9)	43.12 2m/d (9)	42.73 3m/d (9)	101.91 fairs (9)
1666	42.63 2m/d (8)	43.12 2m/d (8)	42.47 3m/d (8)	102.57 fairs (6)
1667	41.77 2m/d (8)	42.59 2m/d (8)	43.18 3m/d (8)	103.29 fairs (7)
1668	41.34 2m/d (11)	42.21 2m/d (11)	43.56 3m/d (11)	104.60 fairs (10)
1669	41.38 2m/d (10)	42.08 2m/d (10)	43.72 3m/d (10)	102.22 fairs (9)
1670	42.41 2m/d (11)	42.74 2m/d (11)	44.25 3m/d (11)	102.33 fairs (11)
1671	42.99 2m/d (9)	43.15 2m/d (9)	45.47 3m/d (9)	104.28 fairs (7)
1672	44.52 2m/d (8)	45.21 2m/d (10)	45.50 3m/d (10)	105.41 fairs (7)
1673	44.03 2m/d (7)	44.54 2m/d (7)	44.76 3m/d (7)	104.62 fairs (7)
1674	43.20 2m/d (4)	43.46 2m/d (4)	44.17 3m/d (4)	104.38 fairs (4)
1675	41.46 2m/d (2)	42.11 2m/d (2)	43.82 3m/d (2)	104.88 fairs (2)
1676	42.91 2m/d (4)	43.29 2m/d (4)	45.30 3m/d (4)	105.17 fairs (3)
1677	42.05 2m/d (6)	42.58 2m/d (6)	45.28 3m/d (6)	104.18 fairs (6)
1679				
1680	42.91 2m/d (8)	43.15 2m/d (8)	45.00 3m/d (8)	103.69 fairs (8)
1681	42.48 2m/d (6)	43.17 2m/d (6)	45.49 3m/d (6)	105.75 fairs (6)
1682	42.45 2m/d (6)	42.88 2m/d (6)	45.20 3m/d (6)	105.13 fairs (6)
1683	42.59 2m/d (4)	42.93 2m/d (4)	45.77 3m/d (4)	105.07 fairs (4)
1684	42.33 2m/d (1)	42.90 2m/d (1)	46.04 3m/d (1)	103.25 fairs (1)
1685				
1686	44.95 2m/d (1)	45.07 2m/d (1)	48.24 3m/d (1)	110.00 fairs (1)
1687				

	VENICE on:			
	Amsterdam	**Antwerp**	**London**	**Lyons**
	per 100 guilders Flemish banco [a]	per 100 guilders Brabant exchange money ('permißgeld') [b]	per 10 pounds sterling [c]	per 100 écus d'or au soleil, from 1740 per 100 livres tournois
	in ducati di banco			
1688				
1689				
1690				
1691				
1692				
1693				
1694	41.89 2m/d (1)	42.22 2m/d (1)	43.05 3m/d (1)	104.50 fairs (1)
1695				
1696	42.63 2m/d (3)	42.63 2m/d (3)	45.41 3m/d (3)	91.25 fairs (3)
1697	43.01 2m/d (1)	43.01 2m/d (1)	45.50 3m/d (1)	91.75 fairs (1)
1698				
1699				
1700				
1701				
1702				
1703				
1704				
1705				
1706				
1707				
1708				
1709				
1710				
1711	43.16 2m/d (2)	43.81 2m/d (2)	43.54 3m/d (2)	
1712				
1713				
1714				
1715	47.06 2m/d (1)		50.00 3m/d (1)	
1716				
1717				
1718				
1719	46.79 2m/d (1)	46.16 2m/d (1)	48.98 3m/d (1)	
...				
1740	43.82 2m/d (9)	42.99 2m/d (9)	45.80 3m/d (9)	20.60 fairs (9)
1741	44.40 2m/d (9)	43.63 2m/d (9)	45.76 3m/d (9)	20.59 fairs (8)
1742	44.29 2m/d (11)	43.66 2m/d (11)	46.02 3m/d (11)	20.22 fairs (8)
1743	43.92 2m/d (11)	43.10 2m/d (11)	45.30 3m/d (11)	20.11 fairs (11)

	VENICE on:			
	Amsterdam	**Antwerp**	**London**	**Lyons**
	per 100 guilders Flemish banco [a]	per 100 guilders Brabant exchange money ('permißgeld') [b]	per 10 pounds sterling [c]	per 100 livres tournois [d]
	in ducati di banco			
1744	43.88 2m/d (9)	43.46 2m/d (9)	45.35 3m/d (9)	20.63 fairs (9)
1745	44.48 2m/d (3)	43.56 2m/d (3)	46.57 3m/d (3)	20.46 fairs (2)
1746	44.21 2m/d (9)	43.34 2m/d (8)	47.52 3m/d (9)	20.40 fairs (8)
1747				
1748	44.70 2m/d (1)	43.72 2m/d (1)	45.93 3m/d (1)	20.75 fairs (1)
1749	44.95 2m/d (1)	44.29 2m/d (1)	46.76 3m/d (1)	20.67 fairs (1)
1750	44.17 2m/d (5)	42.70 2m/d (5)	46.14 3m/d (5)	20.24 fairs (5)
1751	44.05 2m/d (7)	42.77 2m/d (7)	46.62 3m/d (7)	20.11 fairs (7)
1752	43.57 2m/d (2)	42.11 2m/d (2)	45.81 3m/d (2)	19.96 fairs (2)
1753	43.56 2m/d (5)	42.58 2m/d (5)	45.98 3m/d (5)	20.25 fairs (7)
1754	43.74 2m/d (11)	42.74 2m/d (11)	46.35 3m/d (11)	20.33 fairs (11)
1755	43.77 2m/d (10)	42.84 2m/d (10)	46.97 3m/d (10)	20.30 fairs (10)
1756	44.22 2m/d (5)	43.14 2m/d (5)	47.88 3m/d (5)	20.25 fairs (5)
1757	44.37 2m/d (11)	42.85 2m/d (11)	47.26 3m/d (11)	20.10 fairs (11)
1758				
1759	43.96 2m/d (1)		46.15 3m/d (1)	19.92 fairs (1)
1760				
1761				
1762				
1763				
1764	43.42 2m/d (2)	42.16 2m/d (2)	47.29 3m/d (2)	19.80 fairs (2)
1765				
1766	43.57 2m/d (6)	42.26 2m/d (3)	45.32 3m/d (6)	20.08 fairs (6)
1767	44.42 2m/d (2)	43.13 2m/d (1)	45.99 3m/d (2)	20.80 fairs (2)
1768	44.49 2m/d (3)	43.21 2m/d (3)	46.34 3m/d (3)	20.27 fairs (2)
1769	43.96 2m/d (8)	42.28 2m/d (7)	44.99 3m/d (8)	20.03 fairs (8)
1770	44.12 2m/d (6)	42.39 2m/d (4)	44.78 3m/d (6)	19.92 fairs (6)
1771	43.84 2m/d (1)	42.22 2m/d (1)	44.45 3m/d (1)	20.00 fairs (1)
1772	43.18 2m/d (2)	41.56 2m/d (1)	44.76 3m/d (2)	19.94 fairs (2)
1773	44.70 2m/d (3)	42.67 2m/d (3)	48.49 3m/d (3)	20.00 fairs (3)
1774	43.96 2m/d (1)	42.44 2m/d (1)	47.64 3m/d (1)	19.96 fairs (1)
1775	44.32 2m/d (2)		46.60 3m/d (2)	19.94 fairs (2)
1776	43.71 2m/d (4)	42.22 2m/d (3)	45.91 3m/d (4)	19.47 fairs (4)
1777	44.57 2m/d (1)	42.44 2m/d (1)	46.72 3m/d (1)	20.06 fairs (1)
1778	44.48 2m/d (3)	42.67 2m/d (1)	46.65 3m/d (3)	19.64 fairs (4)
1779	44.94 2m/d (3)	42.78 2m/d (1)	49.22 3m/d (3)	19.71 fairs (2)
1780	45.39 2m/d (1)	42.44 2m/d (1)	47.88 3m/d (1)	19.92 fairs (1)

	VENICE on:			
	Amsterdam	**Antwerp**	**London**	**Lyons**
	per 100 guilders Flemish banco [a]	per 100 guilders Brabant exchange money ('permißgeld') [b]	per 10 pounds sterling [c]	per 100 livres tournois [d]
			in ducati di banco	
1781	44.90 2m/d (2)	41.67 2m/d (1)	46.10 3m/d (2)	19.69 fairs (2)
1782	42.34 2m/d (4)	40.61 2m/d (1)	43.61 3m/d (4)	19.36 fairs (3)
1783	42.90 2m/d (1)	40.65 2m/d (1)	45.07 3m/d (1)	
1784	43.01 2m/d (1)		47.06 3m/d (1)	19.13 fairs (1)
1785	43.16 2m/d (2)		48.24 3m/d (2)	19.38 fairs (2)
1786	42.33 2m/d (1)		45.71 3m/d (1)	18.92 fairs (1)
1787	43.72 2m/d (1)		47.43 3m/d (1)	19.21 fairs (1)
1788				
1789	43.01 2m/d (1)		49.48 3m/d (1)	19.46 fairs (1)
1790				
1791				
1792				
1793	43.01 2m/d (1)		49.10 3m/d (1)	
1794				
1795				
1796	38.74 2m/d (2)		44.44 3m/d (2)	
1797				

[a] Concerning the Dutch currency, see pp. 57–59.

[b] The Antwerp currency system was equal to that of the Northern Netherlands (Amsterdam) (see pp. 57–59). Until far into the 17ᵗʰ century the way of quoting and accounting by pound (pond) and shillings Flemish remained dominant. Nevertheless, the data series has been completely converted for the records into guilders, the main unit of account by the beginning of the 18ᵗʰ century (cf. LE MOINE DE L'ESPINE [1710], p. 13; HERBACH [1716], p. 66), in order to ensure the comparability of the quotations over a long period. The term 'exchange money' (or contemporarily: 'permißgeld') meant payable in patagons, or later in kreuzthaler or albertthaler (HERBACH [1716], p. 167; HERBACH [1756/57, p. 231). According to HERBACH, 100 guilders exchange money were equal to 108 1/3 guilders current. According to NELKENBRECHER [1775], p. 17, a fixed premium of 16 2/3% between the exchange money and the current money existed in Antwerp.

[c] Concerning the English currency, see pp. 3–5.

[d] Concerning the French currency, see pp. 279f.

3.2.2 On places of the Holy Roman Empire (I)

	VENICE on:			
	Hamburg	**Frankfurt**	**Cologne**	**Nuremberg**
	per 100 mark banco [a]	per 100 rixdollar Münze [b]	per 100 pounds Flemish [c]	per 100 guilders current [d]
	in ducati di banco			
1623		74.59 15d/s (3)	234.00 2m/d (3)	62.02 15d/s (3)
1624		73.15 15d/s (9)	230.46 2m/d (10)	60.14 15d/s (10)
1625				
1626	32.41 2m/d (2)	76.78 15d/s (2)	242.76 2m/d (2)	63.60 15d/s (2)
1627	32.09 2m/d (12)	75.92 15d/s (11)	239.64 2m/d (12)	63.60 15d/s (12)
1628	32.11 2m/d (8)	76.36 15d/s (6)	240.36 2m/d (8)	63.25 15d/s (8)
1629	31.66 2m/d (5)	75.99 15d/s (4)	236.16 2m/d (5)	63.26 15d/s (5)
1630	34.02 2m/d (9)	79.98 15d/s (8)	256.32 2m/d (9)	68.93 15d/s (9)
1631	35.32 2m/d (11)	80.98 15d/s (9)	264.54 2m/d (11)	68.67 15d/s (11)
1632	36.57 2m/d (12)	87.73 15d/s (8)	274.98 2m/d (12)	73.68 15d/s (10)
1633	36.78 2m/d (12)	87.54 15d/s (10)	279.42 2m/d (12)	75.31 15d/s (12)
1634	36.13 2m/d (8)	86.52 15d/s (7)	270.96 2m/d (8)	73.83 15d/s (5)
1635	36.10 2m/d (8)	84.74 15d/s (7)	273.66 2m/d (8)	69.69 15d/s (6)
1636	35.34 2m/d (10)	82.02 15d/s (9)	264.42 2m/d (10)	68.81 15d/s (10)
1637	34.21 2m/d (10)	80.05 15d/s (10)	258.60 2m/d (10)	65.48 15d/s (10)
1638	34.91 2m/d (12)	82.61 15d/s (12)	259.92 2m/d (12)	67.16 15d/s (12)
1639	35.47 2m/d (9)	83.33 15d/s (7)	264.12 2m/d (9)	69.38 15d/s (9)
1640	34.97 2m/d (11)	82.57 15d/s (10)	261.12 2m/d (11)	69.15 15d/s (11)
1641	33.62 2m/d (6)	79.69 15d/s (6)	247.80 2m/d (6)	66.28 15d/s (6)
1642	33.70 2m/d (12)	79.25 15d/s (10)	248.10 2m/d (12)	66.32 15d/s (12)
1643	33.89 2m/d (5)	80.12 15d/s (5)	247.68 2m/d (5)	67.17 15d/s (5)
1644	36.31 2m/d (10)	84.15 15d/s (10)	261.18 2m/d (10)	69.40 15d/s (10)
1645	35.30 2m/d (11)	83.77 15d/s (11)	261.48 2m/d (11)	69.41 15d/s (11)
1646	35.01 2m/d (8)	83.94 15d/s (7)	262.68 2m/d (8)	69.84 15d/s (8)
1647	35.12 2m/d (11)	84.06 15d/s (11)	265.56 2m/d (11)	70.53 15d/s (11)
1648	40.33 2m/d (6)	92.50 15d/s (5)	296.88 2m/d (6)	78.16 15d/s (6)
1649	42.05 2m/d (10)	97.90 15d/s (10)	308.22 2m/d (10)	82.35 15d/s (10)
1650	40.36 2m/d (4)	96.13 15d/s (4)	296.52 2m/d (4)	81.65 15d/s (4)
1651	35.85 2m/d (9)	86.46 15d/s (9)	267.00 2m/d (9)	71.37 15d/s (9)
1652	33.36 2m/d (3)	81.09 15d/s (3)	247.62 2m/d (4)	67.06 15d/s (4)
1653	33.58 2m/d (4)	79.69 15d/s (4)	249.54 2m/d (4)	67.20 15d/s (4)
1654	33.56 2m/d (2)	80.99 15d/s (2)	250.08 2m/d (2)	67.12 15d/s (2)
1655	34.02 2m/d (3)	80.12 15d/s (3)	252.90 2m/d (3)	67.99 15d/s (3)
1656	34.74 2m/d (4)	83.08 15d/s (4)	256.20 2m/d (4)	69.21 15d/s (4)
1657	34.79 2m/d (5)	81.71 15d/s (5)	254.28 2m/d (5)	68.33 15d/s (5)
1658	34.76 2m/d (9)	81.67 15d/s (8)	252.66 2m/d (9)	68.68 15d/s (9)

	VENICE on:			
	Hamburg	**Frankfurt**	**Cologne**	**Nuremberg**
	per 100 mark banco [a]	per 100 rixdollar Münze [b]	per 100 pounds Flemish [c]	per 100 guilders current [d]
	in ducati di banco			
1659	34.35 2m/d (8)	81.87 15d/s (8)	254.52 2m/d (8)	68.57 15d/s (8)
1660	34.25 2m/d (8)	82.83 15d/s (8)	255.96 2m/d (8)	68.97 15d/s (8)
1661	33.79 2m/d (9)	81.98 15d/s (9)	251.34 2m/d (9)	68.73 15d/s (9)
1662	33.65 2m/d (12)	81.27 15d/s (12)	249.78 2m/d (12)	67.97 15d/s (12)
1663	33.00 2m/d (10)	80.14 15d/s (9)	243.96 2m/d (10)	66.90 15d/s (10)
1664	33.24 2m/d (8)	80.11 15d/s (7)	247.14 2m/d (8)	67.25 15d/s (8)
1665	34.77 2m/d (9)	81.54 15d/s (9)	257.22 2m/d (9)	68.08 15d/s (9)
1666	35.04 2m/d (8)	82.14 15d/s (8)	258.12 2m/d (8)	68.13 15d/s (8)
1667	34.49 2m/d (8)	82.10 15d/s (8)	254.82 2m/d (8)	67.90 15d/s (8)
1668	34.11 2m/d (11)	81.61 15d/s (11)	250.92 2m/d (11)	67.99 15d/s (11)
1669	33.63 2m/d (10)	80.98 15d/s (10)	251.58 2m/d (10)	67.45 15d/s (10)
1670	34.57 2m/d (11)	81.77 15d/s (11)	255.84 2m/d (11)	67.67 15d/s (11)
1671	34.97 2m/d (9)	82.17 15d/s (9)	256.74 2m/d (9)	68.91 15d/s (9)
1672	36.23 2m/d (10)	85.38 15d/s (10)	267.84 2m/d (10)	70.58 15d/s (10)
1673	36.26 2m/d (7)	84.81 15d/s (6)	263.58 2m/d (7)	70.57 15d/s (7)
1674	36.59 2m/d (4)	83.18 15d/s (3)	259.92 2m/d (4)	69.83 15d/s (4)
1675	35.91 2m/d (2)	83.34 15d/s (2)	250.02 2m/d (2)	67.92 15d/s (2)
1676	36.04 2m/d (4)	84.17 15d/s (3)	257.88 2m/d (3)	67.45 15d/s (4)
1677	34.91 2m/d (6)	83.29 15d/s (6)	252.12 2m/d (6)	65.72 15d/s (6)
1679				
1680	35.60 2m/d (8)	84.07 15d/s (8)	257.46 2m/d (8)	64.79 15d/s (8)
1681	34.91 2m/d (6)	83.37 15d/s (6)	254.88 2m/d (6)	63.85 15d/s (6)
1682	35.16 2m/d (6)	83.50 15d/s (6)	254.82 2m/d (6)	67.34 15d/s (6)
1683	35.78 2m/d (4)	84.22 15d/s (4)	255.18 2m/d (4)	69.33 15d/s (4)
1684	35.96 2m/d (1)		253.98 2m/d (1)	68.73 15d/s (1)
1685				
1686	37.65 2m/d (1)	84.93 15d/s (1)	269.70 2m/d (1)	70.93 15d/s (1)
1687				
1688				
1689				
1690				
1691				
1692				
1693				
1694	36.16 2m/d (1)	82.14 15d/s (1)	249.36 2m/d (1)	68.50 15d/s (1)
1695				
1696	35.23 2m/d (3)	81.53 15d/s (3)		
1697	35.36 2m/d (1)	82.65 15d/s (1)		

	VENICE on:					VENICE on:		
	Hamburg					**Hamburg**		
	per 100 mark banco [a]					per 100 mark banco [a]		
	in ducati di banco					**in ducati di banco**		
...					1763			
1710					1764	36.58	2m/d	(2)
1711	35.76	2m/d	(1)		1765			
1712					1766	35.02	2m/d	(6)
1713					1767	34.65	2m/d	(2)
1714					1768	36.21	2m/d	(3)
1715					1769	36.27	2m/d	(8)
1716					1770	36.32	2m/d	(6)
1717					1771	36.68	2m/d	(1)
1718					1772	36.81	2m/d	(2)
1719	38.10	2m/d	(1)		1773	37.54	2m/d	(3)
...					1774	36.73	2m/d	(1)
1740	36.27	2m/d	(9)		1775	36.87	2m/d	(1)
1741	36.73	2m/d	(9)		1776	36.74	2m/d	(5)
1742	36.99	2m/d	(11)		1777	38.21	2m/d	(1)
1743	36.38	2m/d	(11)		1778	37.61	2m/d	(3)
1744	36.30	2m/d	(9)		1779	37.51	2m/d	(3)
1745	36.63	2m/d	(3)		1780	37.54	2m/d	(1)
1746	36.03	2m/d	(9)		1781	37.10	2m/d	(2)
1747					1782	36.21	2m/d	(2)
1748	36.73	2m/d	(1)		1783			
1749	37.43	2m/d	(1)		1784			
1750	36.69	2m/d	(5)		1785			
1751	37.37	2m/d	(7)		1786			
1752	37.00	2m/d	(2)		1787	36.89	2m/d	(1)
1753	36.81	2m/d	(5)		1788			
1754	37.23	2m/d	(11)		1789			
1755	37.09	2m/d	(10)		1790			
1756	35.45	2m/d	(5)		1791			
1757	35.26	2m/d	(11)		1792			
1758					1793			
1759	33.51	2m/d	(1)		1794			
1760					1795			
1761					1796	36.52	2m/d	(2)
1762					1797			

[a]   Concerning the Hamburg currency, see pp. 191–193.

[b]   In Frankfurt am Main up to 1766, cashless payment was effected in the imaginary rixdollar current of 90 kreuzer. The bills had to be paid half in the so-called 'edict money', i.e. in full or half speciesthaler (at 25.98 grammes of fine silver), the other half in the so-called 'münze', i.e. in small silver coins (among others in 12-kreuzer pieces, batzen, albus), whereby there was a premium (a fixed premium of 4% in the 18th century) of the imaginary rixdollar current against the rixdollar payable in edict money and in münze: 100 rixdollars current = 104 rixdollars payable in edict money and in münze. Venetian bills on Frankfurt, however, had to be paid in münze only. Therefore one had to pay the 'normal' premium of 4% plus the variable premium of edict money against münze for the second half of the sum of the bill (HERBACH [1716], p. 173). Concerning the Frankfurt currency after 1766, see pp. 195f.

[c]   In Cologne, cashless payment was effected in the Flemish system of account, as was also common in Amsterdam and Antwerp (see pp. 57–59).

[d]   In Nuremberg, one reckoned in guilders current of 60 kreuzer, whereby the 'current' money functioned as bank money as well. In this context, 'current' meant payable in full and half speciesthaler, i.e. the full-weighted rixdollar of 1566 at 25.98 grammes of fine silver (equal to 2 or 1 guilder of 60 kreuzer respectively). All bills with a sum of more than 200 guilders had to be effected via the Banco publico, founded in 1621.

3.2.2 On places of the Holy Roman Empire (II), Saint Gall and Constantinople

	VENICE on:			
	Augsburg	**Vienna**	**Saint Gall**	**Bolzano** [a]
	per 100 rixdollars giro [b]	per 100 rixdollars current [c]	per 100 guilders Saint Gall exchange money [d]	per 100 scudi di cambio [e]
	in ducati di banco			
1623	93.54 15d/s (3)	90.50 15d/s (1)		93.65 15d/s (2)
1624	90.96 15d/s (10)	87.57 15d/s (6)		93.10 15d/s (9)
1625				
1626	96.04 15d/s (2)	94.57 15d/s (2)		98.19 15d/s (2)
1627	95.92 15d/s (12)	93.36 15d/s (12)		98.33 15d/s (11)
1628	95.74 15d/s (8)	93.09 15d/s (8)		98.16 15d/s (7)
1629	95.34 15d/s (5)	92.90 15d/s (5)		99.10 15d/s (4)
1630	103.78 15d/s (9)	101.28 15d/s (9)		105.36 15d/s (7)
1631	103.41 15d/s (11)	101.86 15d/s (11)		105.45 15d/s (11)
1632	108.07 15d/s (11)	104.35 15d/s (12)		107.04 15d/s (10)
1633	111.08 15d/s (12)	102.24 15d/s (12)		109.09 15d/s (11)
1634	110.21 15d/s (5)	106.99 15d/s (8)		110.91 15d/s (7)
1635	104.91 15d/s (8)	102.16 15d/s (8)		103.70 15d/s (9)
1636	102.49 15d/s (10)	103.79 15d/s (10)		104.79 15d/s (8)
1637	97.51 15d/s (10)	99.02 15d/s (10)	59.64 15d/s (6)	100.41 15d/s (9)
1638	99.36 15d/s (12)	99.46 15d/s (12)	62.75 15d/s (12)	101.71 15d/s (11)
1639	102.98 15d/s (9)	103.20 15d/s (9)	64.21 15d/s (9)	104.94 15d/s (8)
1640	102.87 15d/s (10)	103.65 15d/s (11)	62.33 15d/s (10)	105.17 15d/s (10)
1641	99.00 15d/s (6)	99.51 15d/s (6)	59.26 15d/s (6)	101.75 15d/s (6)
1642	99.59 15d/s (12)	99.69 15d/s (12)	59.16 15d/s (12)	103.18 15d/s (12)
1643	100.24 15d/s (5)	99.32 15d/s (5)	60.26 15d/s (5)	103.71 15d/s (5)
1644	103.71 15d/s (10)	102.31 15d/s (10)	60.68 15d/s (10)	106.07 15d/s
1645	103.76 15d/s (11)	101.91 15d/s (11)	61.01 15d/s (11)	105.74 15d/s (11)
1646	104.24 15d/s (8)	103.61 15d/s (8)	61.33 15d/s (8)	106.43 15d/s (7)
1647	105.34 15d/s (11)	104.55 15d/s (11)	63.00 15d/s (11)	108.89 15d/s (9)
1648	116.49 15d/s (6)	118.36 15d/s (6)	69.20 15d/s (6)	118.96 15d/s (5)
1649	122.84 15d/s (10)	123.33 15d/s (10)	73.15 15d/s (10)	124.71 15d/s (9)
1650	122.98 15d/s (4)	122.92 15d/s (4)	73.48 15d/s (4)	126.16 15d/s (4)
1651	106.90 15d/s (9)	106.63 15d/s (9)	64.00 15d/s (9)	108.85 15d/s (8)
1652	100.57 15d/s (4)	100.45 15d/s (4)	59.42 15d/s (4)	104.10 15d/s (3)
1653	100.45 15d/s (4)	100.01 15d/s (4)	59.13 15d/s (4)	103.43 15d/s (4)
1654	100.38 15d/s (2)	100.01 15d/s (2)	59.53 15d/s (2)	104.24 15d/s (2)
1655	101.96 15d/s (3)	101.28 15d/s (3)	60.25 15d/s (3)	105.51 15d/s (3)
1656	103.51 15d/s (4)	103.50 15d/s (4)	61.03 15d/s (4)	107.11 15d/s (4)
1657	102.41 15d/s (5)	102.41 15d/s (5)	60.08 15d/s (5)	105.29 15d/s (5)

	VENICE on:			
	Augsburg	**Vienna**	**Saint Gall**	**Bolzano** [a]
	per 100 rixdollars giro [b]	per 100 rixdollars current, from 1665 per 100 guilders current [c]	per 100 guilders Saint Gall exchange money [d]	per 100 scudi di cambio [e]
	in ducati di banco			
1658	102.92 15d/s (9)	102.60 15d/s (9)	60.74 15d/s (9)	106.32 15d/s (9)
1659	103.00 15d/s (8)	102.73 15d/s (8)	60.85 15d/s (8)	106.66 15d/s (7)
1660	103.80 15d/s (8)	103.59 15d/s (8)	61.37 15d/s (8)	107.06 15d/s (6)
1661	102.87 15d/s (9)	103.02 15d/s (9)	60.80 15d/s (9)	106.46 15d/s (8)
1662	101.65 15d/s (12)	101.06 15d/s (12)	60.06 15d/s (12)	105.59 15d/s (10)
1663	100.30 15d/s (10)	100.40 15d/s (10)	59.24 15d/s (10)	103.99 15d/s (9)
1664	100.67 15d/s (8)	100.72 15d/s (8)	59.86 15d/s (8)	104.04 15d/s (6)
1665	101.96 15d/s (9)	63.08 15d/s (9)	60.45 15d/s (9)	104.79 15d/s (9)
1666	102.53 15d/s (7)	64.56 15d/s (8)	60.77 15d/s (8)	106.25 15d/s (6)
1667	101.87 15d/s (8)	63.91 15d/s (8)	60.87 15d/s (8)	104.97 15d/s (8)
1668	102.12 15d/s (11)	64.54 15d/s (11)	60.65 15d/s (11)	105.43 15d/s (9)
1669	101.28 15d/s (10)	64.99 15d/s (10)	59.96 15d/s (10)	104.97 15d/s (7)
1670	102.40 15d/s (11)	64.81 15d/s (11)	60.43 15d/s (11)	105.77 15d/s (11)
1671	103.65 15d/s (9)	66.28 15d/s (9)	61.29 15d/s (9)	106.90 15d/s (8)
1672	106.33 15d/s (10)	67.80 15d/s (10)	62.69 15d/s (10)	108.89 15d/s (8)
1673	106.20 15d/s (7)	67.88 15d/s (7)	62.62 15d/s (7)	108.44 15d/s (7)
1674	104.53 15d/s (4)	67.33 15d/s (4)	62.00 15d/s (4)	108.14 15d/s (3)
1675	104.44 15d/s (2)	64.73 15d/s (2)	61.83 15d/s (2)	108.47 15d/s (2)
1676	105.28 15d/s (4)	64.59 15d/s (4)	62.29 15d/s (4)	108.42 15d/s (4)
1677	103.71 15d/s (6)	62.04 15d/s (6)	61.24 15d/s (6)	107.13 15d/s (6)
1679				
1680	105.07 15d/s (8)	62.19 15d/s (8)	61.58 15d/s (8)	108.46 15d/s (8)
1681	104.16 15d/s (6)	60.35 15d/s (6)	61.53 15d/s (6)	107.60 15d/s (6)
1682	104.40 15d/s (6)	61.18 15d/s (6)	61.52 15d/s (6)	108.03 15d/s (6)
1683	105.14 15d/s (4)	63.82 15d/s (4)	61.91 15d/s (4)	109.35 15d/s (3)
1684	104.17 15d/s (1)	63.30 15d/s (1)	61.17 15d/s (1)	107.67 15d/s (1)
1685				
1686	106.67 15d/s (1)	62.21 15d/s (1)	63.70 15d/s (1)	111.90 15d/s (1)
1687				
1688				
1689				
1690				
1691				
1692				
1693				
1694	104.99 15d/s (1)	65.90 15d/s (1)	61.73 15d/s (1)	107.87 15d/s (1)
1695				

	VENICE on:			
	Augsburg	**Vienna**	**Saint Gall**	**Bolzano** [a]
	per 100 rixdollars giro [b]	per 100 guilders current [c]	per 100 guilders Saint Gall exchange money [d]	per 100 scudi di cambio [e]
	in ducati di banco			
1696	100.68 15d/s (3)	50.85 15d/s (3)	60.67 15d/s (3)	109.08 15d/s (2)
1697	100.76 15d/s (1)	50.89 15d/s (1)	60.61 15d/s (1)	109.68 15d/s (1)
1698				
1699				
1700				
1701				
1702				
1703				
1704				
1705				
1706				
1707				
1708				
1709				
1710				
1711	98.60 15d/s (2)	53.23 15d/s (2)		109.88 15d/s (2)
1712				
1713				
1714				
1715	105.84 15d/s (1)			115.33 15d/s (1)
1716				
1717				
1718				
1719	102.79 15d/s (1)	55.87 15d/s (1)		115.73 15d/s (1)
...				
1740	99.38 15d/s (9)	53.40 15d/s (9)		109.30 15d/s (9)
1741	99.94 15d/s (9)	53.81 15d/s (8)		109.19 15d/s (7)
1742	100.20 15d/s (11)	54.60 15d/s (11)		110.23 15d/s (10)
1743	98.47 15d/s (11)	53.27 15d/s (11)		109.32 15d/s (10)
1744	98.79 15d/s (9)	53.09 15d/s (9)		109.69 15d/s (8)
1745	99.75 15d/s (3)	53.32 15d/s (3)		109.01 15d/s (3)
1746	97.99 15d/s (9)	53.01 15d/s (9)		108.87 15d/s (7)
1747				
1748	100.15 15d/s (1)	53.62 15d/s (1)		109.28 15d/s (1)
1749	101.35 15d/s (1)	55.25 15d/s (1)		111.09 15d/s (1)
1750	100.18 15d/s (5)	54.08 15d/s (5)		109.00 15d/s (5)
1751	97.71 15d/s (7)	53.24 15d/s (7)		107.13 15d/s (6)

	VENICE on:			
	Augsburg	**Vienna**	**Bolzano** [a]	**Constantinople**
	per 100 rixdollars giro [b]	per 100 guilders Konventionskurant [c]	per 100 scudi di cambio [e]	per 100 piastres [f]
	in ducati di banco			
1752	96.68 15d/s (2)	52.36 15d/s (2)		106.35 15d/s (2)
1753	96.89 15d/s (5)	52.79 15d/s (5)	107.26 15d/s (5)	
1754	97.54 15d/s (11)	53.42 15d/s (11)	107.06 15d/s (9)	
1755	97.99 15d/s (10)	53.07 15d/s (10)	107.53 15d/s (9)	
1756	98.30 15d/s (5)	53.88 15d/s (5)	107.76 15d/s (5)	
1757	98.93 15d/s (11)	53.46 15d/s (11)	107.62 15d/s (9)	
1758				
1759	97.63 15d/s (1)	52.70 15d/s (1)	107.86 15d/s (1)	
1760				
1761				
1762				
1763				
1764	96.02 15d/s (2)	52.22 15d/s (2)		
1765				
1766	100.08 15d/s (6)	52.23 15d/s (6)	108.23 15d/s (5)	
1767	100.52 15d/s (2)	52.22 15d/s (2)		
1768	100.64 15d/s (3)	52.75 15d/s (3)	107.26 15d/s (1)	
1769	98.88 15d/s (8)	51.99 15d/s (8)		
1770	98.86 15d/s (6)	52.16 15d/s (6)		
1771	99.02 15d/s (1)	51.75 15d/s (1)		
1772	98.77 15d/s (2)	51.91 15d/s (2)		
1773	99.38 15d/s (3)	51.15 15d/s (3)		
1774	98.04 15d/s (1)	51.29 15d/s (1)		
1775	98.89 15d/s (1)	51.68 15d/s (1)		
1776	98.33 15d/s (5)	51.16 15d/s (5)		
1777	99.01 15d/s (1)	51.51 15d/s (1)		
1778	99.05 15d/s (3)	51.88 15d/s (3)		
1779	99.50 15d/s (3)	52.54 15d/s (3)		
1780	98.89 15d/s (1)	51.55 15d/s (1)		
1781	98.77 15d/s (2)	51.45 15d/s (2)		
1782	96.96 15d/s (4)	51.02 15d/s (4)		
1783	98.40 15d/s (1)	51.68 15d/s (1)		
1784	96.85 15d/s (1)	50.96 15d/s (1)		
1785	97.92 15d/s (2)	51.55 15d/s (2)		
1786	97.56 15d/s (1)	51.15 15d/s (1)		
1787	97.32 15d/s (1)	50.63 15d/s (4)		46.51 [g] (1)
1788				
1789	97.32 15d/s (1)	50.70 15d/s (1)		50.00 [g] (1)

	VENICE on:		
	Augsburg	**Vienna**	**Constantinople**
	per 100 rixdollars giro [b]	per 100 guilders Konventionskurant [c]	per 100 piastres [f]
	in ducati di banco		
1790			
1791			
1792			
1793	98.52 15d/s (1)	50.76 15d/s (1)	51.28 [g] (1)
1794			
1795			
1796	97.44 15d/s (2)	50.63 15d/s (2)	
1797			

[a] Although bills drawn on Bolzano were mostly payable at the fairs, Venice quoted for 15 days after sight. Concerning the Bolzano fairs, see DENZEL [2005].

[b] 100 rixdollars giro or exchange money (of 90 kreuzer) = 150 guilders giro (of 60 kreuzer) = 127 rixdollars current or – from the second half of the 18th century – Augsburg current respectively = 190½ guilders Augsburg current. 'Augsburg current' meant a standard of coinage of 20 5/12 guilders per mark of Cologne in modification of Konventionskurant, which became common in Augsburg especially from 1764 (NOBACK [1851], 1. Abth., p. 70). So the guilder Augsburg current of 60 kreuzer was equal to 11.45 grammes of fine silver.

[c] Vienna was quoted per rixdollars current, i.e. nominally the rixdollar of 1566 (not at 25.98, but at 25.78 grammes of fine silver), which rose up to 270 kreuzer in the Kipper-and-Wipper era (in January 1622; RITTMANN [1975], p. 1020), but was valued with 90 kreuzer by the end of 1623. Because of the fact that the accounting in guilders was more common than that in rixdollars in the Habsburg Monarchy, there was a change in the manner of quotation, whereby 3 guilders current (of 60 kreuzer) were equal to 2 rixdollars current. Concerning the Austrian currency, see pp. 255f.

[d] The guilder Saint Gall exchange money of 60 kreuzer was payable in speciesthaler or Burgundian thaler (= c. 102 kreuzer) and louisblancs (= c. 105 kreuzer) (cf. HERBACH [1716], p. 151). In the 18th century the relation was 1,190 guilders exchange money (or the so-called 'species') = 1,383 guilders current (cf. NELKENBRECHER [1775], pp. 214f.).

[e] The scudo di cambio of 93 kreuzer giro or exchange money (therefore 20 scudi di cambio = 31 guilders giro of 60 kreuzer giro) was a special imaginary monetary unit of Bolzano only for exchange between Venice (i.e. its Banco del Giro) and Bolzano. Between the giro or exchange money, which consisted of Spanish doubloons and old French louis d'ors, and the so-called Meß-valuta we have the following ratio: 5 guilders 34 kreuzer giro = 7½ guilders Meßvaluta (cf. NELKENBRECHER [1775], p. 56; see also p. 269).

[f] Concerning the Turkish currency, see pp. 387f.

[g] No information concerning the usance is available.

3.2.3 On Italian places (I)

	VENICE on:			
	Milan	**Genoa**	**Bisenzone fairs**	**Leghorn**
	per 100 scudi di cambio [a]	per 100 scudi di cambio [b]	per 100 scudi di marche [c]	per 100 pezze da otto reali [d]
	in ducati di banco			
1623	115.53 20d/d (1)		147.00 fairs (3)	
1624	115.56 20d/d (6)		145.27 fairs (10)	
1625				
1626	115.73 20d/d (2)	99.80 15d/s (2)	147.84 fairs (2)	
1627	116.43 20d/d (12)	99.99 15d/s (11)	147.68 fairs (12)	
1628	119.26 20d/d (8)	100.00 15d/s (7)	148.38 fairs (6)	
1629	123.19 20d/d (5)	100.16 15d/s (4)	137.75 fairs (2)	
1630	133.09 20d/d (8)	107.75 15d/s (9)	143.31 fairs (8)	
1631	126.27 20d/d (11)	102.20 15d/s (11)	163.90 fairs (10)	
1632	126.97 20d/d (12)	103.78 15d/s (12)	170.87 fairs (11)	
1633	130.36 20d/d (12)	104.42 15d/s (12)	175.22 fairs (11)	
1634	129.64 20d/d (8)	104.39 15d/s (8)	178.24 fairs (8)	
1635	124.82 20d/d (9)	100.34 15d/s (9)	173.32 fairs (7)	
1636	123.59 20d/d (10)	97.83 15d/s (10)	171.70 fairs (9)	
1637	124.38 20d/d (10)	97.75 15d/s (10)	175.23 fairs (10)	
1638	123.81 20d/d (12)	96.91 15d/s (12)	175.01 fairs (10)	
1639	124.74 20d/d (9)	96.96 15d/s (9)	176.72 fairs (9)	
1640	124.84 20d/d (11)	98.04 15d/s (11)	179.80 fairs (10)	
1641	120.03 20d/d (6)	95.90 15d/s (6)	176.46 fairs (6)	
1642	121.09 20d/d (12)	96.06 15d/s (12)	176.49 fairs (12)	
1643	122.83 20d/d (5)	97.83 15d/s (5)	180.40 fairs (5)	
1644	124.70 20d/d (10)	98.05 15d/s (10)	182.98 fairs (10)	
1645	124.25 20d/d (11)	97.99 15d/s (11)	183.55 fairs (11)	
1646	126.62 20d/d (8)	97.79 15d/s (8)	187.04 fairs (7)	
1647	127.79 20d/d (11)	98.59 15d/s (11)	189.19 fairs (11)	
1648	139.18 20d/d (6)	105.58 15d/s (6)	202.92 fairs (6)	
1649	146.98 20d/d (10)	111.46 15d/s (10)	215.05 fairs (10)	
1650	152.73 20d/d (4)	115.28 15d/s (4)	226.75 fairs (4)	
1651	132.80 20d/d (9)	98.75 15d/s (9)	199.29 fairs (7)	
1652	125.61 20d/d (4)	93.05 15d/s (4)	189.38 fairs (4)	
1653	123.64 20d/d (4)	89.52 15d/s (4)	183.84 fairs (3)	
1654	123.29 20d/d (2)	87.91 15d/s (2)	183.25 fairs (2)	
1655	125.34 20d/d (3)	87.77 15d/s (3)	184.17 fairs (3)	
1656	124.65 20d/d (4)	87.45 15d/s (4)	181.42 fairs (3)	
1657	123.71 20d/d (5)	89.60 15d/s (5)	185.85 fairs (5)	103.36 5d/s (1)
1658	125.72 20d/d (9)	88.29 15d/s (9)	186.82 fairs (8)	102.89 5d/s (8)

	VENICE on:			
	Milan	**Genoa**	**Bisenzone fairs**	**Leghorn**
	per 100 scudi di cambio [a]	per 100 scudi di cambio [b]	per 100 scudi di marche [c]	per 100 pezze da otto reali [d]
	in ducati di banco			
1659	125.43 20d/d (8)	86.57 15d/s (8)	186.54 fairs (8)	104.21 5d/s (8)
1660	125.94 20d/d (8)	86.19 15d/s (8)	187.35 fairs (8)	104.51 5d/s (8)
1661	125.41 20d/d (9)	85.85 15d/s (9)	186.13 fairs (6)	103.14 5d/s (9)
1662	123.79 20d/d (12)	84.63 15d/s (12)	184.66 fairs (11)	101.92 5d/s (12)
1663	123.25 20d/d (10)	83.81 15d/s (10)	184.00 fairs (9)	101.24 5d/s (10)
1664	123.09 20d/d (8)	83.47 15d/s (8)	183.85 fairs (8)	100.82 5d/s (8)
1665	121.25 20d/d (9)	82.70 15d/s (9)	181.57 fairs (8)	100.05 5d/s (9)
1666	123.19 20d/d (8)	83.71 15d/s (8)	184.66 fairs (8)	101.34 5d/s (8)
1667	121.53 20d/d (8)	83.24 15d/s (8)	183.19 fairs (8)	101.31 5d/s (8)
1668	123.39 20d/d (11)	84.27 15d/s (11)	186.93 fairs (10)	103.05 5d/s (11)
1669	123.27 20d/d (10)	83.63 15d/s (10)	187.64 fairs (10)	103.63 5d/s (10)
1670	121.61 20d/d (11)	81.48 15d/s (11)	187.06 fairs (9)	101.93 5d/s (11)
1671	121.73 20d/d (9)	82.61 15d/s (9)	188.06 fairs (9)	102.83 5d/s (9)
1672	122.00 20d/d (10)	82.69 15d/s (10)	187.78 fairs (9)	102.45 5d/s (10)
1673	121.72 20d/d (7)	81.76 15d/s (7)	186.50 fairs (5)	101.77 5d/s (7)
1674	124.00 20d/d (4)	82.16 15d/s (4)	188.13 fairs (4)	102.53 5d/s (4)
1675	123.19 20d/d (2)	80.45 15d/s (2)	187.75 fairs (2)	103.77 5d/s (2)
1676	123.34 20d/d (4)	81.71 15d/s (4)	189.13 fairs (4)	103.24 5d/s (4)
1677	123.91 20d/d (6)	80.82 15d/s (6)	190.00 fairs (6)	102.87 5d/s (6)
1679				
1680	124.20 20d/d (8)	80.90 15d/s (8)	189.04 fairs (7)	102.03 5d/s (8)
1681	126.99 20d/d (6)	83.20 15d/s (6)	194.25 fairs (6)	104.13 5d/s (6)
1682	124.67 20d/d (6)	81.49 15d/s (6)	190.38 fairs (6)	103.37 5d/s (6)
1683	124.65 20d/d (4)	80.90 15d/s (4)	188.44 fairs (4)	103.83 5d/s (4)
1684	123.59 20d/d (1)	81.05 15d/s (1)	188.50 fairs (1)	104.17 5d/s (1)
1685				
1686	124.00 20d/d (1)	83.07 15d/s (1)	192.00 fairs (1)	104.44 5d/s (1)
1687				
1688				
1689				
1690				
1691				
1692				
1693				
1694	124.20 20d/d (1)	81.86 15d/s (1)	189.00 fairs (1)	102.83 5d/s (1)
1695				
1696	122.04 20d/d (1)	83.30 15d/s (3)	194.25 fairs (3)	105.41 5d/s (3)
1697		83.47 15d/s (1)	193.75 fairs (1)	105.27 5d/s (1)

	VENICE on:			
	Milan	**Genoa**	**Bisenzone fairs**	**Leghorn**
	per 100 scudi di cambio [a]	per 100 scudi di cambio [b]	per 100 scudi di marche [c]	per 100 pezze da otto reali [d]
	in ducati di banco			
1698				
...				
1710				
1711	128.64 20d/d (2)	82.96 15d/s (2)	196.63 fairs (2)	105.02 5d/s (2)
1712				
1713				
1714				
1715	132.27 20d/d (1)	87.92 15d/s (1)	205.50 fairs (1)	109.29 5d/s (1)
1716				
1717				
1718				
1719	134.08 20d/d (2)	90.76 15d/s (1)	212.00 fairs (1)	109.59 5d/s (1)
...				
1740	125.13 20d/d (9)	84.08 15d/s (9)	192.94 fairs (6)	97.96 5d/s (9)
1741	124.61 20d/d (7)	84.36 15d/s (7)	194.80 fairs (6)	97.82 5d/s (9)
1742	124.96 20d/d (10)	83.76 15d/s (11)	193.68 fairs (10)	97.53 5d/s (9)
1743	124.84 20d/d (11)	83.60 15d/s (11)	193.09 fairs (11)	97.69 5d/s (11)
1744	125.48 20d/d (9)	84.20 15d/s (9)	194.88 fairs (8)	98.27 5d/s (9)
1745	124.78 20d/d (3)	82.40 15d/s (3)	193.00 fairs (1)	97.73 5d/s (3)
1746	123.84 20d/d (8)	80.16 15d/s (8)		97.69 5d/s (9)
1747				
1748	124.84 20d/d (1)	82.28 15d/s (1)		97.09 5d/s (1)
1749	123.79 20d/d (1)	83.08 15d/s (1)		96.62 5d/s (1)
1750	127.18 20d/d (5)	76.88 15d/s (5)		96.03 5d/s (5)
1751	125.19 20d/d (7)	76.44 15d/s (7)		95.54 5d/s (7)
1752	126.36 20d/d (2)	77.24 15d/s (2)		97.56 5d/s (2)
1753	124.96 20d/d (5)	76.04 15d/s (5)		96.32 5d/s (5)
1754	124.96 20d/d (11)	75.76 15d/s (11)		95.39 5d/s (11)
1755	125.19 20d/d (10)	75.96 15d/s (10)		95.69 5d/s (10)
1756	125.25 20d/d (5)	75.80 15d/s (5)		95.86 5d/s (5)
1757	125.48 20d/d (11)	76.04 15d/s (11)		95.90 5d/s (11)
1758				
1759	126.21 20d/d (1)	77.22 15d/s (1)		97.32 5d/s (1)
1760				
1761				
1762				
1763				
1764	127.24 20d/d (2)	76.48 15d/s (2)		96.27 5d/s (2)

	VENICE on:		
	Milan	**Genoa**	**Leghorn**
	per 100 scudi di cambio [a]	per 100 scudi di cambio [b]	per 100 pezze da otto reali [d]
		in ducati di banco	
1765			
1766	126.54 20d/d (6)	75.92 15d/s (6)	97.32 5d/s (6)
1767	126.42 20d/d (2)	76.64 15d/s (2)	97.09 5d/s (2)
1768	127.00 20d/d (3)	76.76 15d/s (3)	97.68 5d/s (3)
1769	127.30 20d/d (8)	76.48 15d/s (8)	97.37 5d/s (8)
1770	127.12 20d/d (6)	76.08 15d/s (6)	96.98 5d/s (6)
1771	126.24 20d/d (1)	75.64 15d/s (1)	95.93 5d/s (1)
1772	124.60 20d/d (2)	75.91 15d/s (2)	96.62 5d/s (2)
1773	126.42 20d/d (3)	76.04 15d/s (3)	97.09 5d/s (3)
1774	126.24 20d/d (1)	76.24 15d/s (1)	96.39 5d/s (1)
1775	126.21 20d/d (1)	75.81 15d/s (1)	96.85 5d/s (1)
1776	125.40 20d/d (5)	75.85 15d/s (5)	96.83 5d/s (5)
1777	125.81 20d/d (1)	75.66 15d/s (1)	96.74 5d/s (1)
1778	125.54 20d/d (3)	75.08 15d/s (3)	96.42 5d/s (3)
1779	128.49 20d/d (3)	74.70 15d/s (3)	97.24 5d/s (3)
1780	129.03 20d/d (1)	74.70 15d/s (1)	97.80 5d/s (1)
1781	127.42 20d/d (1)	74.29 15d/s (2)	97.21 5d/s (2)
1782	126.06 20d/d (4)	73.19 15d/s (4)	96.15 5d/s (4)
1783	125.81 20d/d (1)	73.59 15d/s (1)	95.92 5d/s (1)
1784	125.00 20d/d (1)	72.58 15d/s (1)	96.15 5d/s (1)
1785	125.40 20d/d (2)	72.17 15d/s (2)	96.10 5d/s (2)
1786	123.79 20d/d (1)	71.77 15d/s (1)	97.56 5d/s (2)
1787	123.79 20d/d (1)	74.19 15d/s (1)	98.04 5d/s (1)
1788			
1789	125.40 20d/d (1)	73.79 15d/s (1)	100.25 5d/s (1)
1790			
1791			
1792			
1793	125.00 20d/d (1)	75.20 15d/s (1)	101.52 5d/s (1)
1794			
1795			
1796	125.81 20d/d (1)	73.89 15d/s (2)	100.38 5d/s (2)
1797			

[a] The scudo di cambio or scudo imperiale was the Milanese imaginary unit of account for cashless payment and was equal to 5 lire imperiale or 5 lire 17 soldi correnti.

[b] For the Genoese currency, see pp. 107f. 1 scudo di cambio = 4 lire banco or 4 3/5 lire fuori banco.

[c] Concerning the currency at the Bisenzone fairs, see p. 103.

[d] Concerning the Tuscan currency, see p. 106.

3.2.3 On Italian places (II)

	VENICE on:			
	Florence	**Lucca**	**Rome** [a]	**Naples**
	per 100 scudi d'oro [b]	per 100 scudi d'oro [c]	per 100 scudi d'oro di stampe [d]	per 100 ducati moneta corrente [e]
	in ducati di banco			
1623	123.46 5d/s (1)		148.15 10d/s (1)	102.57 15d/s (1)
1624	124.00 5d/s (6)		148.17 10d/s (6)	100.75 15d/s (6)
1625				
1626	125.79 5d/s (2)		150.10 10d/s (2)	104.44 15d/s (2)
1627	126.48 5d/s (12)		151.45 10d/s (12)	104.99 15d/s (12)
1628	128.42 5d/s (8)		153.98 10d/s (8)	105.72 15d/s (8)
1629	134.80 5d/s (5)		161.81 10d/s (5)	110.17 15d/s (5)
1630	130.38 5d/s (9)		168.97 10d/s (9)	116.76 15d/s (9)
1631	136.71 5d/s (11)		*165.43* 10d/s (11)	114.66 15d/s (11)
1632	139.82 5d/s (12)	126.50 5d/s (12)	*168.28* 10d/s (12)	118.82 15d/s (12)
1633	141.41 5d/s (12)	129.52 5d/s (12)	*167.70* 10d/s (12)	116.58 15d/s (12)
1634	140.74 5d/s (8)	127.81 5d/s (8)	*176.54* 10d/s (8)	114.75 15d/s (8)
1635	135.45 5d/s (9)	122.83 5d/s (9)	*175.08* 10d/s (9)	111.62 15d/s (9)
1636	134.25 5d/s (10)	120.86 5d/s (10)	*174.48* 10d/s (10)	109.96 15d/s (9)
1637	133.44 5d/s (10)	121.00 5d/s (10)	*173.88* 10d/s (10)	108.94 15d/s (10)
1638	133.47 5d/s (12)	120.34 5d/s (12)	175.44 10d/s (5)	108.20 15d/s (12)
1639	132.66 5d/s (9)	119.13 5d/s (9)	174.20 10d/s (8)	103.84 15d/s (9)
1640	134.94 5d/s (11)	120.02 5d/s (11)	177.45 10d/s (11)	106.84 15d/s (11)
1641	133.10 5d/s (6)	120.08 5d/s (6)	176.63 10d/s (6)	105.52 15d/s (5)
1642	134.38 5d/s (12)	120.59 5d/s (12)	178.46 10d/s (12)	107.81 15d/s (12)
1643	134.87 5d/s (5)	120.56 5d/s (5)	181.30 10d/s (5)	105.94 15d/s (5)
1644	135.74 5d/s (10)	121.02 5d/s (10)	182.72 10d/s (10)	112.09 15d/s (10)
1645	134.48 5d/s (11)	121.22 5d/s (11)	181.25 10d/s (11)	111.83 15d/s (11)
1646	143.54 5d/s (8)	123.11 5d/s (7)	185.17 10d/s (8)	114.12 15d/s (8)
1647	140.66 5d/s (11)	127.04 5d/s (11)	190.81 10d/s (10)	111.52 15d/s (7)
1648	149.80 5d/s (6)	137.62 5d/s (6)	200.84 10d/s (6)	127.46 15d/s (3)
1649	154.50 5d/s (10)	141.66 5d/s (10)	204.62 10d/s (10)	127.99 15d/s (10)
1650	166.09 5d/s (4)	149.11 5d/s (4)	223.66 10d/s (4)	136.45 15d/s (4)
1651	144.68 5d/s (9)	132.97 5d/s (9)	195.31 10d/s (9)	117.21 15d/s (9)
1652	138.20 5d/s (4)	125.00 5d/s (3)	185.84 10d/s (4)	112.85 15d/s (4)
1653	134.80 5d/s (4)	119.95 5d/s (4)	180.80 10d/s (4)	111.51 15d/s (4)
1654	136.53 5d/s (2)	120.49 5d/s (2)	183.92 10d/s (2)	114.46 15d/s (2)
1655	136.68 5d/s (3)	120.61 5d/s (3)	180.47 10d/s (3)	113.05 15d/s (3)
1656	136.30 5d/s (4)	119.86 5d/s (4)	182.27 10d/s (4)	109.75 15d/s (4)
1657	137.19 5d/s (5)	121.45 5d/s (5)	184.01 10d/s (5)	110.40 15d/s (5)
1658	135.50 5d/s (9)	119.57 5d/s (9)	180.59 10d/s (9)	105.87 15d/s (9)

	VENICE on:							
	Florence		Lucca		Rome		Naples	
	per 100 scudi d'oro [b]		per 100 scudi d'oro [c]		per 100 scudi d'oro di stampe [d]		per 100 ducati moneta corrente [e]	
	in ducati di banco							
1659	137.58 5d/s	(8)	120.72 5d/s	(8)	184.40 10d/s	(8)	110.75 15d/s	(8)
1660	138.33 5d/s	(8)	123.43 5d/s	(8)	187.15 10d/s	(8)	111.08 15d/s	(8)
1661	138.79 5d/s	(9)	125.00 5d/s	(9)	187.32 10d/s	(9)	112.52 15d/s	(9)
1662	134.98 5d/s	(12)	122.68 5d/s	(12)	183.53 10d/s	(12)	111.40 15d/s	(12)
1663	136.06 5d/s	(10)	121.51 5d/s	(10)	182.78 10d/s	(10)	111.97 15d/s	(10)
1664	135.65 5d/s	(8)	121.86 5d/s	(8)	183.15 10d/s	(8)	112.69 15d/s	(8)
1665	135.02 5d/s	(9)	122.29 5d/s	(9)	182.94 10d/s	(9)	111.57 15d/s	(9)
1666	137.53 5d/s	(8)	124.24 5d/s	(8)	186.66 10d/s	(8)	113.69 15d/s	(8)
1667	136.39 5d/s	(8)	123.78 5d/s	(6)	185.03 10d/s	(8)	111.15 15d/s	(8)
1668	136.94 5d/s	(11)	125.00 5d/s	(10)	183.02 10d/s	(11)	111.08 15d/s	(11)
1669	137.17 5d/s	(10)	124.70 5d/s	(10)	185.07 10d/s	(10)	111.96 15d/s	(10)
1670	136.86 5d/s	(11)	124.86 5d/s	(11)	185.12 10d/s	(11)	111.59 15d/s	(11)
1671	137.95 5d/s	(9)	125.00 5d/s	(9)	186.59 10d/s	(9)	112.37 15d/s	(9)
1672	136.43 5d/s	(10)	125.00 5d/s	(10)	183.91 10d/s	(10)	108.69 15d/s	(10)
1673	136.51 5d/s	(6)	125.00 5d/s	(7)	184.20 10d/s	(7)	107.87 15d/s	(7)
1674	135.95 5d/s	(4)	125.00 5d/s	(4)	183.60 10d/s	(4)	109.53 15d/s	(4)
1675	138.26 5d/s	(2)	125.00 5d/s	(2)	178.58 10d/s	(2)	110.05 15d/s	(2)
1676	138.18 5d/s	(4)	125.00 5d/s	(4)	187.18 10d/s	(4)	110.39 15d/s	(4)
1677	139.40 5d/s	(6)	125.00 5d/s	(6)	188.27 10d/s	(6)	109.79 15d/s	(6)
1679								
1680	138.13 5d/s	(8)	124.81 5d/s	(8)	186.23 10d/s	(8)	111.89 15d/s	(8)
1681	139.82 5d/s	(6)	124.23 5d/s	(6)	189.02 10d/s	(6)	108.30 15d/s	(6)
1682	136.96 5d/s	(6)	124.23 5d/s	(6)	185.82 10d/s	(6)	102.61 15d/s	(6)
1683	136.88 5d/s	(4)	124.23 5d/s	(4)	186.38 10d/s	(4)	101.16 15d/s	(4)
1684	137.70 5d/s	(1)	124.23 5d/s	(1)	188.68 10d/s	(1)	103.63 15d/s	(1)
1685								
1686	137.46 5d/s	(1)			186.05 10d/s	(1)	100.25 15d/s	(1)
1687								
1688								
1689								
1690								
1691								
1692								
1693								
1694	138.41 5d/s	(1)	125.00 5d/s	(1)	187.80 10d/s	(1)	91.50 15d/s	(1)
1695								
1696	138.49 5d/s	(3)			184.90 10d/s	(3)	88.43 15d/s	(3)
1697	138.65 5d/s	(1)			185.19 10d/s	(1)	88.30 15d/s	(1)

	VENICE on:		
	Florence	**Rome**	**Naples**
	per 100 scudi d'oro [b]	per 100 scudi d'oro di stampe [d]	per 100 ducati moneta corrente/del regno [e]
	in ducati di banco		
1698			
...			
1710			
1711	137.10 5d/s (2)	183.92 10d/s (2)	87.34 15d/s (2)
1712			
1713			
1714			
1715	143.63 5d/s (1)	191.11 10d/s (1)	92.38 15d/s (1)
1716			
1717			
1718			
1719	145.20 5d/s (1)	197.37 10d/s (1)	96.39 15d/s (1)
...			
1740	128.40 5d/s (9)	165.14 10d/s (9)	86.76 15d/s (9)
1741	128.10 5d/s (9)	165.84 10d/s (9)	87.12 15d/s (9)
1742	127.95 5d/s (10)	162.60 10d/s (11)	85.26 15d/s (11)
1743	128.03 5d/s (11)	163.42 10d/s (11)	84.07 15d/s (11)
1744	128.70 5d/s (9)	163.14 10d/s (9)	85.54 15d/s (9)
1745	127.80 5d/s (3)	160.87 10d/s (3)	84.64 15d/s (3)
1746	127.88 5d/s (9)	160.05 10d/s (9)	84.37 15d/s (9)
1747			
1748	126.98 5d/s (1)	160.01 10d/s (1)	84.21 15d/s (1)
1749	126.38 5d/s (1)	160.45 10d/s (1)	85.47 15d/s (1)
1750	125.48 5d/s (5)	159.26 10d/s (5)	86.40 15d/s (5)
1751	124.28 5d/s (7)	160.84 10d/s (7)	86.56 15d/s (7)
1752	124.73 5d/s (2)	162.44 10d/s (2)	88.01 15d/s (2)
1753	125.70 5d/s (5)	160.97 10d/s (5)	84.45 15d/s (5)
1754	125.25 5d/s (10)	159.76 10d/s (11)	83.27 15d/s (11)
1755	125.25 5d/s (10)	160.36 10d/s (10)	82.49 15d/s (10)
1756	124.50 5d/s (5)	159.17 10d/s (5)	83.49 15d/s (5)
1757	125.03 5d/s (11)	160.52 10d/s (11)	83.29 15d/s (11)
1758			
1759	127.39 5d/s (1)	161.00 10d/s (1)	86.77 15d/s (1)
1760			
1761			
1762			
1763			
1764	125.18 5d/s (2)	158.42 10d/s (2)	80.73 15d/s (2)

	VENICE on:		
	Florence	**Rome**	**Naples**
	per 100 scudi d'oro [b]	per 100 scudi d'oro di stampe [d]	per 100 ducati del regno [e]
	in ducati di banco		
1765			
1766	125.18 5d/s (6)	159.34 10d/s (6)	86.68 15d/s (6)
1767	125.78 5d/s (2)	158.12 10d/s (2)	86.49 15d/s (2)
1768	127.50 5d/s (3)	161.30 10d/s (3)	86.37 15d/s (3)
1769	126.90 5d/s (4)	159.21 10d/s (8)	84.66 15d/s (8)
1770	127.05 5d/s (6)	159.64 10d/s (6)	84.09 15d/s (6)
1771	125.40 5d/s (1)	156.56 10d/s (1)	84.57 15d/s (1)
1772	125.89 5d/s (2)	160.22 10d/s (2)	83.59 15d/s (2)
1773	126.15 5d/s (3)	158.10 10d/s (3)	83.86 15d/s (3)
1774	125.40 5d/s (1)	160.33 10d/s (1)	84.39 15d/s (1)
1775	126.06 5d/s (1)	156.86 10d/s (1)	84.39 15d/s (1)
1776	126.14 5d/s (5)	160.34 10d/s (5)	84.91 15d/s (5)
1777	125.79 5d/s (1)	159.77 10d/s (1)	84.75 15d/s (1)
1778	126.32 5d/s (3)	160.47 10d/s (3)	83.51 15d/s (3)
1779	126.92 5d/s (3)	159.36 10d/s (3)	83.51 15d/s (3)
1780	127.80 5d/s (1)	158.73 10d/s (1)	84.03 15d/s (1)
1781	127.39 5d/s (1)	158.73 10d/s (2)	83.59 15d/s (2)
1782	125.20 5d/s (4)	153.92 10d/s (4)	84.30 15d/s (4)
1783	124.22 5d/s (1)	154.44 10d/s (1)	84.39 15d/s (1)
1784		156.56 10d/s (1)	84.39 15d/s (1)
1785		157.64 10d/s (2)	85.33 15d/s (2)
1786		154.14 10d/s (1)	85.84 15d/s (2)
1787		158.73 10d/s (1)	84.75 15d/s (1)
1788			
1789		158.73 10d/s (1)	85.29 15d/s (1)
1790			
1791			
1792			
1793		153.85 10d/s (1)	78.43 15d/s (1)
1794			
1795			
1796			84.38 15d/s (2)
1797			

[a] 1631–1637: exchange rates on Ancona, originally quoted per 100 scudi moneta, are here converted into quotations per 100 scudi d'oro di stampe (see [d]).

[b] The scudo d'oro (of 20 soldi at 12 denari d'oro) was the Florentine imaginary unit of account in cashless payment and equal to 7½ lire moneta buona or to 1 7/23 pezze da otto reali (1 pezza = 184 denari d'oro) (NELKENBRECHER [1775], pp. 87f.).

[c] The scudo d'oro (of 20 soldi at 12 denari d'oro) was the Lucchese imaginary unit of account (NEL-
     KENBRECHER [1793], p. 129).

[d] In Rome the scudo d'oro di stampe of 20 soldi at 12 denari d'oro was the imaginary unit of ac-
     count in cashless payment and equal to 1,500 mezzi quattrini. Concerning exchange business,
     there was a fixed premium of 23 or 25 mezzi quattrini: if one bought a bill of exchange at Rome,
     one had to pay 1,523 mezzi quattrini per each scudo di stampa d'oro. If a foreign bill of exchange,
     however, had to be paid at Rome, one had to pay 1,525 mezzi quattrini per each scudo di stampa
     d'oro (NELKENBRECHER [1775], p. 207). So the ratio of the scudo di stampa d'oro to the scudo
     moneta or scudo romano of 10 paoli or giuli at 10 baiocchi of 10 mezzi quattrini, which was the
     current money in the Papal States, was 2:3 without the premium, i.e. 2 scudi di stampa d'oro were
     equal to 3 scudi romani. Therefore 40 scudi di stampa d'oro of 1,525 mezzi quattrini were equal
     to 61 scudi moneta.

[e] The system of accounting in ducati ('moneta corrente' in the 17th century, but called 'ducati del
     regno' or 'ducati di regno' since the 18th century) of 10 carlini at 10 grani or 5 tari at 20 grani had
     been common practice in the Kingdom of Naples for centuries. Especially in the second decade
     of the 17th century the Neapolitan currency was marked by strong devaluations (1611: 8.4%, 1617:
     15.9%, 1618: 20.3%, 1620: 33.1%), only appearing in quotations with some delay (DE ROSA
     [1955], pp. 33f.).

3.3 Leghorn exchange rates

Usances: According to the sources documented here, the changing of the usances in Leghorn started in August 1826.

3.3.1 On London, Amsterdam, Paris and Hamburg

	LEGHORN on:			
	London	**Amsterdam**	**Paris**	**Hamburg**
	per 10 pounds sterling [a]	per 100 guilders Flemish banco [b]	per 100 livres tournois, from 1796 per 100 francs [c]	per 100 mark banco [d]
	in pezze da otto reali			
1771	46.51　3m/d　(6)	44.82　2m/d　(6)	20.24　1m/d　(6)	37.50　2m/d　(6)
1772	45.39　3m/d　(1)	45.27　2m/d　(1)	20.46　1m/d　(1)	37.87　2m/d　(1)
1773				
1774				
1775				
1776	45.88　3m/d　(1)	44.14　2m/d　(1)	19.76　1m/d　(1)	37.32　2m/d　(1)
1777	46.85　3m/d　(4)	45.64　2m/d　(4)	20.36　1m/d　(4)	38.59　2m/d　(4)
1778	48.13　3m/d　(1)	45.27　2m/d　(1)	19.90　1m/d　(1)	38.10　2m/d　(1)
1779	48.94　3m/d　(3)	46.01　2m/d　(3)	20.22　1m/d　(3)	38.05　2m/d　(3)
1780	48.13　3m/d　(2)	45.46　2m/d　(2)	20.31　1m/d　(2)	38.10　2m/d　(2)
1781	46.87　3m/d　(11)	46.22　2m/d　(11)	20.13　1m/d　(11)	38.44　2m/d　(11)
1782	45.52　3m/d　(9)	44.63　2m/d　(9)	20.04　1m/d　(9)	37.95　2m/d　(9)
1783	47.06　3m/d　(1)	44.45　2m/d　(1)	20.21　1m/d　(1)	37.87　2m/d　(1)
1784	47.74　3m/d　(9)	44.06　2m/d　(9)	19.73　1m/d　(9)	37.71　2m/d　(9)
1785	49.82　3m/d　(9)	44.51　2m/d　(9)	19.86　1m/d　(9)	38.16　2m/d　(9)
1786	48.16　3m/d　(6)	43.80　2m/d　(6)	19.40　1m/d　(6)	37.24　2m/d　(6)
1787	48.05　3m/d　(12)	43.68　2m/d　(12)	19.49　1m/d　(12)	37.26　2m/d　(12)
1788	48.80　3m/d　(6)	43.46　2m/d　(6)	19.59　1m/d　(6)	37.45　2m/d　(6)
1789	49.21　3m/d　(5)	42.98　2m/d　(5)	19.10　1m/d　(5)	37.22　2m/d　(5)
1790	49.29　3m/d　(5)	42.66　2m/d　(5)	18.19　1m/d　(5)	37.45　2m/d　(5)
1791				
1792				
1793				
1794				
1795				
1796	44.04　3m/d　(4)	34.78　2m/d　(4)	19.05　1m/d　(4)	36.37　2m/d　(4)
1797	48.90　3m/d　(3)	38.87　2m/d　(2)	19.02　1m/d　(3)	36.73　2m/d　(3)
1798	50.39　3m/d　(9)	36.95　2m/d　(9)	18.51　1m/d　(9)	36.62　2m/d　(9)
1799	49.27　3m/d　(3)	36.92　2m/d　(3)	18.43　1m/d　(3)	36.12　2m/d　(3)
1800				
1801	44.24　3m/d　(1)	38.10　2m/d　(1)	18.96　1m/d　(1)	36.89　2m/d　(1)

	LEGHORN on:			
	London	**Amsterdam**	**Paris**	**Hamburg**
	per 10 pounds sterling [a]	per 100 guilders Flemish banco, from 1816 (10) per 100 Dutch guilders [b]	per 100 francs [c]	per 100 mark banco [d]
	in pezze da otto reali			
1802	45.28 3m/d (1)	40.10 2m/d (1)	19.32 1m/d (1)	36.89 2m/d (1)
1803	47.06 3m/d (1)	43.24 2m/d (1)	19.42 1m/d (1)	37.43 2m/d (1)
1804	46.83 3m/d (2)	42.55 2m/d (2)	19.00 1m/d (2)	36.26 2m/d (2)
1805				
1806	44.86 3m/d (1)	41.99 2m/d (1)	19.23 1m/d (1)	35.85 2m/d (1)
1807				
1808				
1809		39.60 2m/d (1)	21.20 1m/d (1)	33.95 2m/d (1)
1810				
1811				
1812		40.82 2m/d (10)	20.60 1m/d (10)	34.78 2m/d (10)
1813				
1814				
1815				
1816				
1817	50.63 3m/d (1)	38.20 2m/d (1)	20.50 1m/d (1)	34.80 2m/d (1)
1818				
1819				
1820	49.23 3m/d (1)	41.67 2m/d (1)	19.61 1m/d (1)	36.68 2m/d (1)
1821				
1822	52.36 3m/d (5)	43.06 2m/d (5)	20.54 1m/d (5)	37.67 2m/d (5)
1823	53.20 3m/d (12)	43.68 2m/d (12)	20.71 1m/d (12)	38.09 2m/d (12)
1824	52.09 3m/d (12)	43.73 2m/d (12)	20.62 1m/d (12)	37.87 2m/d (12)
1825	49.69 3m/d (12)	42.00 2m/d (12)	19.95 1m/d (12)	36.81 2m/d (12)
1826	52.06 90d/d (12)	42.79 90d/d (12)	20.43 90d/d (12)	37.61 90d/d (12)
1827	52.17 90d/d (12)	43.48 90d/d (12)	20.60 90d/d (12)	38.05 90d/d (12)
1828	51.61 90d/d (12)	43.14 90d/d (12)	20.49 90d/d (12)	37.99 90d/d (12)
1829	52.15 90d/d (12)	43.21 90d/d (12)	20.51 90d/d (12)	38.03 90d/d (12)
1830	52.12 90d/d (12)	42.68 90d/d (12)	20.39 90d/d (12)	37.49 90d/d (12)
1831	51.78 90d/d (12)	43.31 90d/d (12)	20.66 90d/d (12)	38.03 90d/d (12)
1832	52.48 90d/d (12)	43.43 90d/d (12)	20.46 90d/d (12)	37.92 90d/d (12)
1833	52.43 90d/d (12)	43.57 90d/d (12)	20.47 90d/d (12)	37.99 90d/d (12)
1834	51.25 90d/d (12)	42.31 90d/d (12)	20.25 90d/d (12)	37.64 90d/d (12)
1835	51.80 90d/d (12)	42.62 90d/d (12)	20.37 90d/d (12)	38.00 90d/d (12)
1836	51.40 90d/d (12)	42.41 90d/d (12)	20.19 90d/d (12)	37.44 90d/d (12)

	LEGHORN on:			
	London	**Amsterdam**	**Paris**	**Hamburg**
	per 10 pounds sterling [a]	per 100 Dutch guilders [b]	per 100 francs [c]	per 100 mark banco [d]
	in Tuscan lire moneta buona			
1837	303.45 30d/d (12)	248.67 90d/d (12)	118.65 30d/d (12)	219.67 90d/d (12)
1838	304.71 30d/d (12)	250.80 90d/d (12)	119.30 30d/d (12)	222.30 90d/d (12)
1839	294.59 30d/d (12)	244.19 90d/d (12)	116.84 30d/d (12)	218.02 90d/d (12)
1840	295.38 30d/d (12)	245.45 90d/d (12)	116.96 30d/d (12)	218.18 90d/d (12)
1841	294.67 30d/d (12)	243.71 90d/d (12)	116.29 30d/d (12)	217.66 90d/d (12)
1842	295.71 30d/d (12)	242.02 90d/d (12)	115.90 30d/d (12)	216.09 90d/d (12)
1843				
1844				
1845				
1846	298.00 30d/d (1)	246.00 90d/d (1)	116.75 30d/d (1)	218.00 90d/d (1)
1847	299.13 30d/d (12)	245.50 90d/d (12)	117.30 30d/d (12)	217.75 90d/d (12)
1848	307.43 30d/d (12)	251.25 90d/d (12)	119.32 30d/d (12)	220.30 90d/d (12)
1849	309.00 30d/d (12)	253.25 90d/d (12)	121.21 30d/d (12)	222.34 90d/d (12)
1850	301.41 30d/d (11)	249.41 90d/d (11)	118.37 30d/d (11)	219.12 90d/d (11)

[a]   Concerning the British currency, see pp. 3–5.
[b]   Concerning the Dutch currency, see pp. 57–59.
[c]   Concerning the French currency, see pp. 279f.
[d]   Concerning the Hamburg currency, see pp. 191–193.

3.3.2 On Augsburg, Frankfurt, Vienna and Geneva

	LEGHORN on:			
	Augsburg	**Frankfurt**	**Vienna**	**Geneva**
	per 100 guilders Augsburg current [a]	per 100 guilders Frankfurt exchange money [b]	per 100 guilders Konventionskurant, from 1800 per 100 guilders Wiener Währung [c]	per 100 livres Geneva current [d]
	in pezze da otto reali			
1771	53.03 15d/s (6)			
1772	54.06 15d/s (1)			
1773				
1774				
1775				
1776	52.57 15d/s (1)	60.63 15d/s (1)		33.76 1m/d (1)
1777	53.44 15d/s (4)	61.10 15d/s (4)		34.15 1m/d (4)
1778	53.13 15d/s (1)	60.82 15d/s (1)		34.01 1m/d (1)
1779	53.67 15d/s (3)	61.67 15d/s (3)		34.19 1m/d (3)
1780	53.05 15d/s (2)	59.94 15d/s (2)		33.84 1m/d (2)
1781	52.92 15d/s (11)	60.42 15d/s (11)		33.84 1m/d (11)
1782	53.04 15d/s (9)	60.99 15d/s (9)		33.92 1m/d (9)
1783	53.20 15d/s (1)	60.50 15d/s (1)		33.76 1m/d (1)
1784	52.31 15d/s (9)	60.07 15d/s (9)		33.62 1m/d (9)
1785	52.78 15d/s (9)	60.93 15d/s (9)		33.43 1m/d (9)
1786	52.07 15d/s (6)		59.69 15d/s (6)	32.82 1m/d (6)
1787	51.56 15d/s (12)		58.76 15d/s (12)	32.52 1m/d (12)
1788	51.78 15d/s (6)		59.40 15d/s (6)	33.00 1m/d (6)
1789	50.95 15d/s (5)		58.20 15d/s (5)	32.88 1m/d (5)
1790	50.88 15d/s (5)		58.20 15d/s (5)	32.15 1m/d (5)
1791				
1792				
1793				
1794				
1795				
1796	50.22 15d/s (4)		50.03 15d/s (4)	31.30 1m/d (4)
1797	49.96 15d/s (3)		48.77 15d/s (3)	31.60 1m/d (3)
1798	49.02 15d/s (9)		48.26 15d/s (9)	30.58 1m/d (8)
1799	49.14 15d/s (3)		47.14 15d/s (3)	30.58 1m/d (3)
1800				
1801	49.50 15d/s (1)		41.30 15d/s (1)	30.58 1m/d (1)
1802	49.75 15d/s (1)		41.30 15d/s (1)	30.58 1m/d (1)
1803	50.00 15d/s (1)		37.61 15d/s (1)	30.58 1m/d (1)
1804	49.32 15d/s (2)		35.92 15d/s (2)	30.58 1m/d (2)

	LEGHORN on:			
	Augsburg	**Frankfurt**	**Vienna**	**Geneva**
	per 100 guilders Augsburg current [a]	per 100 guilders Frankfurt exchange money [b]	per 100 guilders Wiener Währung, from 1816 per 100 guilders Konventionskurant [c]	per 100 livres Geneva current, from 1837 per 100 (French) francs [d]
	in pezze da otto reali			
1805				
1806	49.02 15d/s (1)		25.43 15d/s (1)	30.58 1m/d (1)
1807				
1808				
1809	48.54 15d/s (1)		34.78 15d/s (1)	30.58 1m/d (1)
1810				
1811				
1812	49.50 15d/s (10)		10.14 15d/s (10)	30.58 1m/d (10)
1813				
1814				
1815				
1816				
1817	50.00 15d/s (1)		50.13 15d/s (1)	30.58 1m/d (1)
1818				
1819				
1820	49.63 15d/s (1)		49.63 15d/s (1)	30.58 1m/d (1)
1821				
1822	51.57 15d/s (5)	51.69 15d/s (5)	51.59 15d/s (5)	32.72 1m/d (5)
1823	51.94 15d/s (12)	51.78 15d/s (12)	52.20 15d/s (12)	33.08 1m/d (12)
1824	52.13 15d/s (12)	52.20 15d/s (12)	52.58 15d/s (12)	33.33 1m/d (12)
1825	51.09 15d/s (12)	51.24 15d/s (12)	51.24 15d/s (12)	32.65 1m/d (12)
1826	51.80 90d/d (12)	51.65 90d/d (12)	51.59 90d/d (12)	32.47 90d/d (12)
1827	52.27 90d/d (12)	51.95 90d/d (12)	52.27 90d/d (12)	33.13 90d/d (12)
1828	52.34 90d/d (12)	52.26 90d/d (12)	52.35 90d/d (12)	33.65 90d/d (12)
1829	52.54 90d/d (12)	52.20 90d/d (6)	52.43 90d/d (12)	33.67 90d/d (12)
1830	52.00 90d/d (12)		51.83 90d/d (12)	33.55 90d/d (12)
1831	52.64 90d/d (12)		52.26 90d/d (12)	33.33 90d/d (12)
1832	52.21 90d/d (12)		52.13 90d/d (12)	33.33 90d/d (12)
1833	52.53 90d/d (12)		52.65 90d/d (12)	33.49 90d/d (12)
1834	51.93 90d/d (12)		52.12 90d/d (12)	33.22 90d/d (12)
1835	52.23 90d/d (12)		52.27 90d/d (12)	33.06 90d/d (12)
1836	51.53 90d/d (12)		51.31 90d/d (12)	33.48 90d/d (12)
	in Tuscan lire moneta buona			
1837	302.35 30d/d (12)		300.42 30d/d (12)	116.67 30d/d (12)
1838	303.46 30d/d (12)		302.30 30d/d (12)	117.94 30d/d (12)
1839	298.71 30d/d (12)		297.61 30d/d (12)	116.40 30d/d (12)

	LEGHORN on:			
	Augsburg	**Frankfurt**	**Vienna**	**Geneva**
	per 100 guilders Augsburg current [a]	per 100 guilders exchange money, from 1847 per 100 guilders South German current [b]	per 100 guilders Konventionskurant [c]	per 100 (French) francs [d]
	in Tuscan lire moneta buona			
1840	298.69 30d/d (12)		297.96 30d/d (12)	116.00 30d/d (12)
1841	300.77 30d/d (12)		300.19 30d/d (12)	115.77 30d/d (12)
1842	298.65 30d/d (12)		301.30 30d/d (12)	115.11 30d/d (12)
1843				
1844				
1845				
1846	298.00 30d/d (1)		299.50 30d/d (1)	115.00 30d/d (1)
1847	297.73 30d/d (12)	248.00 90d/d (3)	299.63 30d/d (12)	115.38 30d/d (12)
1848	300.25 30d/d (12)	248.59 90d/d (12)	282.84 30d/d (12)	117.09 30d/d (12)
1849	305.19 30d/d (12)	251.67 90d/d (12)	268.34 30d/d (12)	118.67 30d/d (12)
1850	299.82 30d/d (11)	247.46 90d/d (11)	253.82 30d/d (11)	117.19 30d/d (11)

[a]   100 rixdollars giro or exchange money (of 90 kreuzer) = 150 guilders giro (of 60 kreuzer) = 127 rixdollars current or – from the second half of the 18th century – Augsburg current respectively = 190½ guilders Augsburg current. 'Augsburg current' meant a standard of coinage of 20 5/12 guilders per mark of Cologne in modification of Konventionskurant, which became common especially from 1764 (NOBACK [1851], 1. Abth., p. 70). So the guilder Augsburg current of 60 kreuzer was equal to 11.45 grammes of fine silver.

[b]   Concerning the Austrian currency, see pp. 255f. Payable in 20-kreuzer pieces from 1817. The guilder Konventionskurant was paper money in notes of the Wiener Nationalbank and governmental notes from June 3rd 1848.

[c]   The imaginary livre argent courant (of 20 sols argent courant) was equal to 3½ florins or guilders petite monnaie – a real coin of 20 sols petite monnaie – so that 1 livre argent courant = 42 sols petite monnaie of Geneva. The French franc (see pp. 279f.) did not become legal tender in Geneva until January 1st 1839, but had been used as a unit of account for many years (cf. NELKENBRECHER [1832], p. 196).

[d]   Concerning the Frankfurt currency, see pp. 195f.

3.3.3 On Iberian places

	LEGHORN on:		
	Madrid	**Lisbon**	
	per 100 pesos de plata antigua, from 1801 effective [a]	per 100 crusados [b]	
	in pezze da otto reali		
1771	77.27	2m/d	(6)	52.00	3m/d	(6)
1772	77.64	2m/d	(1)	52.22	3m/d	(1)
1773			
1774			
1775			
1776	75.69	2m/d	(1)	51.29	3m/d	(1)
1777	77.41	2m/d	(4)	51.77	3m/d	(4)
1778	76.05	2m/d	(1)	52.43	3m/d	(1)
1779	75.52	2m/d	(3)	52.66	3m/d	(3)
1780	74.91	2m/d	(2)	52.43	3m/d	(2)
1781	71.40	2m/d	(11)	52.84	3m/d	(11)
1782	73.32	2m/d	(9)	52.19	3m/d	(9)
1783	68.50	2m/d	(1)	52.50	3m/d	(1)
1784	70.56	2m/d	(9)	52.42	3m/d	(9)
1785	71.76	2m/d	(9)	52.75	3m/d	(9)
1786	71.05	2m/d	(6)	53.05	3m/d	(6)
1787	72.51	2m/d	(12)	53.06	3m/d	(12)
1788	72.67	2m/d	(6)	53.66	3m/d	(6)
1789	71.98	2m/d	(5)	53.54	3m/d	(5)
1790	72.05	2m/d	(5)	54.38	3m/d	(5)
1791			
1792			
1793			
1794			
1795			
1796	54.79	2m/d	(4)	52.25	3m/d	(4)
1797	57.92	2m/d	(3)	55.94	3m/d	(3)
1798	54.35	2m/d	(9)	55.40	3m/d	(9)
1799	51.28	2m/d	(3)	55.04	3m/d	(3)
1800			
1801	73.26	2m/d	(1)	49.08	3m/d	(1)
1802	73.00	2m/d	(1)	50.00	3m/d	(1)
1803	71.43	2m/d	(1)	48.19	3m/d	(1)
1804	68.97	2m/d	(2)	48.19	3m/d	(2)
1805			

	LEGHORN on:		
	Madrid	**Barcelone**	**Lisbon**
	per 100 pesos de plata antigua effective [a]	per 100 libras of Catalonia [c]	per 100 crusados, from 1837 per 100 milréis [b]
	in pezze da otto reali		
1806	71.43 2m/d (1)		46.78 3m/d (1)
1807			
1808			
1809	71.43 2m/d (1)		48.48 3m/d (1)
1810			
1811			
1812	71.43 2m/d (10)		48.48 3m/d (10)
1813			
1814			
1815			
1816			
1817	73.80 2m/d (1)		46.51 3m/d (1)
1818			
1819			
1820	73.53 2m/d (1)		43.01 3m/d (1)
1821			
1822	79.26 2m/d (5)		45.05 3m/d (5)
1823	79.26 2m/d (12)		46.19 3m/d (12)
1824	78.97 2m/d (12)		45.00 3m/d (12)
1825	76.38 2m/d (12)		42.80 3m/d (12)
1826	76.92 90d/d (12)		43.63 90d/d (12)
1827	76.71 90d/d (12)		43.24 90d/d (12)
1828	77.21 90d/d (12)		39.91 90d/d (12)
1829	79.56 90d/d (12)	78.68 90d/d (6)	39.91 90d/d (12)
1830	79.26 90d/d (12)	78.68 90d/d (12)	37.84 90d/d (12)
1831	80.15 90d/d (12)	79.85 90d/d (12)	39.29 90d/d (12)
1832	79.54 90d/d (12)	79.39 90d/d (12)	41.06 90d/d (12)
1833	81.46 90d/d (12)	81.09 90d/d (12)	41.86 90d/d (12)
1834	79.36 90d/d (12)	79.36 90d/d (12)	43.89 90d/d (12)
1835	80.26 90d/d (12)	80.22 90d/d (12)	47.44 90d/d (12)
1836	79.83 90d/d (12)	79.90 90d/d (12)	47.56 90d/d (12)
1834	79.36 90d/d (12)	79.36 90d/d (12)	43.89 90d/d (12)
1835	80.26 90d/d (12)	80.22 90d/d (12)	47.44 90d/d (12)
1836	79.83 90d/d (12)	79.90 90d/d (12)	47.56 90d/d (12)
	in Tuscan lire moneta buona		
1837	447.26 90d/d (12)	321.55 90d/d (12)	653.02 90d/d (12)
1838	446.00 90d/d (12)	322.42 90d/d (12)	654.17 90d/d (12)

	LEGHORN on:		
	Madrid	**Barcelone**	**Lisbon**
	per 100 pesos de plata antigua effective [a]	per 100 libras of Catalonia [c]	per 100 milréis [b]
	in Tuscan lire moneta buona		
1839	442.34 90d/d (12)	320.25 90d/d (12)	650.84 90d/d (12)
1840	442.00 90d/d (12)	320.00 90d/d (12)	652.50 90d/d (12)
1841	442.00 90d/d (12)	320.00 90d/d (12)	639.59 90d/d (12)
1842	440.50 90d/d (12)	320.17 90d/d (12)	637.42 90d/d (12)
1843			
1844			
1845			
1846	440.00 90d/d (1)	325.00 90d/d (1)	635.00 90d/d (1)
1847	440.00 90d/d (12)	321.42 90d/d (12)	635.00 90d/d (12)
1848	440.00 90d/d (12)	322.00 90d/d (12)	635.00 90d/d (12)
1849	440.00 90d/d (12)	330.42 90d/d (12)	635.00 90d/d (12)
1850	440.00 90d/d (11)	335.00 90d/d (11)	635.00 90d/d (11)

[a]   Concerning the Spanish currency, see p. 307.

[b]   In the Portuguese currency system, one reckoned in réis and in milréis (= 1,000 réis), but the exchange rate quotations of and on Portuguese places were often effected in or for crusados ('velhos' or 'do cambio') as a unit of account of 400 réis up to the 19th century (cf. NELKENBRECHER [1771], p. 131).

[c]   1 libra of Catalonia = 10 reales Ardites = 20 sueldos = 240 dineros. 1 doblón de cambio = 5 libras 12 sueldos cataluños; 1 peso de plata antigua = 28 sueldos cataluños; 1 ducado de cambio = 38 sueldos 7 4/17 dineros cataluños; 1,000 pesos duros = 1,875 libras of Catalonia or libras de Ardites (cf. KELLY [1811], p. 41).

3.3.4 On Saint Petersburg, Constantinople, Malta and Corfu

	LEGHORN on:	
	Saint Petersburg [a]	**Constantinople**
	per 100 roubles banco [b]	per 100 piastres [c]
	in pezze da otto reali	
1781	78.85 3m/d (7)	
1782	78.56 3m/d (7)	
1783	76.93 3m/d (1)	
1784	73.16 3m/d (8)	
1785	73.00 3m/d (8)	
1786	73.00 3m/d (4)	
1787	73.90 3m/d (12)	
1788	71.52 3m/d (6)	
1789	63.44 3m/d (5)	
1790	57.37 3m/d (5)	
1791		
1792		
1793		
1794		
1795		
1796	41.67 3m/d (4)	
1797	41.67 3m/d (3)	
1798	41.67 3m/d (5)	
1799	42.86 3m/d (3)	
1800		
1801	41.67 3m/d (1)	
1802	41.67 3m/d (1)	
1803	62.50 3m/d (1)	
1804	58.82 3m/d (2)	
1805		
1806	52.63 3m/d (1)	
1807		
1808		
1809	40.00 3m/d (1)	
1810		
1811		
1812	28.99 3m/d (6)	13.79 31d/s (1)
1813		
1814		
1815		

	Saint Petersburg [a]	Constantinople	Malta	Corfu
	LEGHORN on:			
	per 100 roubles banco, from 1839 (10) per 100 silver roubles (from 1843 [11] in credit notes) [b]	per 100 piastres [c]	per 100 scudi [d]	per 100 colonnati [e]
	in pezze da otto reali			
1816				
1817		13.79 31d/s (1)	39.34 31d/s (1)	
1818				
1819				
1820	20.41 90d/d (1)	13.51 31d/s (1)	39.34 31d/s (1)	
1821				
1822	19.82 90d/d (5)	14.03 31d/s (5)	41.76 31d/s (5)	
1823	20.16 90d/d (12)	12.96 31d/s (12)	41.76 31d/s (12)	
1824	20.30 90d/d (12)	11.75 31d/s (12)	41.76 31d/s (12)	
1825	20.02 90d/d (12)	10.27 31d/s (12)	41.76 31d/s (12)	
1826	20.00 90d/d (12)	8.74 31d/s (12)	41.37 31d/s (12)	
1827	20.63 90d/d (12)	8.59 31d/s (12)	41.29 31d/s (12)	
1828	20.92 90d/d (12)	8.44 31d/s (12)	42.19 31d/s (12)	
1829	21.40 90d/d (12)	7.54 31d/s (12)	41.48 31d/s (12)	
1830	21.40 90d/d (12)	6.74 31d/s (12)	41.42 31d/s (12)	
1831	21.47 90d/d (12)	6.41 31d/s (12)	41.98 31d/s (12)	
1832	22.29 90d/d (12)	5.87 31d/s (12)	41.99 31d/s (12)	
1833	22.51 90d/d (12)	5.30 31d/s (12)	42.80 31d/s (12)	
1834	21.97 90d/d (12)	5.11 31d/s (12)	42.57 31d/s (12)	
1835	21.90 90d/d (12)	5.18 31d/s (12)	42.34 31d/s (12)	
1836	21.63 90d/d (12)	5.07 31d/s (12)	41.87 31d/s (12)	
	in Tuscan lire moneta buona			
1837	125.11 90d/d (12)	26.84 31d/s (12)	243.19 31d/s (12)	
1838	129.63 90d/d (12)	27.00 31d/s (12)	243.46 31d/s (12)	
1839	130.99/459.00 90d/d (9+3)	26.63 31d/s (12)	240.67 31d/s (12)	
1840	462.75 90d/d (12)	26.50 31d/s (12)	241.34 31d/s (12)	
1841	468.67 90d/d (12)	26.38 31d/s (12)	238.25 31d/s (12)	
1842	454.09 90d/d (12)	22.67 31d/s (12)	236.50 31d/s (12)	617.34 31d/s (12)
1843				
1844				
1845				
1846	466.00 90d/d (1)	24.50 31d/s (1)	243.00 31d/s (1)	620.00 31d/s (1)
1847	466.75 90d/d (12)	25.42 31d/s (12)	244.17 31d/s (12)	620.92 31d/s (12)
1848	455.00 90d/d (12)	25.17 31d/s (12)	241.42 31d/s (12)	617.50 31d/s (12)
1849	467.67 90d/d (12)	25.84 31d/s (12)	246.67 31d/s (12)	600.00 31d/s (12)

	LEGHORN on:			
	Saint Petersburg [a]	**Constantinople**	**Malta**	**Corfu**
	per 100 silver roubles in credit notes [b]	per 100 piastres [c]	per 100 scudi [d]	per 100 colonnati [e]
	in pezze da otto reali			
1850	466.55 90d/d (11)	25.69 31d/s (11)	247.09 31d/s (11)	601.82 31d/s (11)

[a] From 1822 the quotation on Odessa is generally equal to that on Saint Petersburg although the usances differ from one another (Odessa until 1841: 30 days' dato, from 1837 additionally 90 days' dato).

[b] Concerning the Russian currency, see pp. 359f.

[c] Concerning the Turkish currency, see pp. 387f.

[d] In Malta one reckoned in scudi of 12 tari at 20 grani, and 2½ scudi were equal to 1 oncia (NEL-KENBRECHER [1832], p. 312). Although sterling currency was introduced as legal tender and unit of account in Malta in 1825, the quotations of Leghorn on Malta were made for tari up to the end of the period of documentation.

[e] Corfu officially used the pound sterling or the pound Ionian currency respectively based on the valuation of the Spanish piece of eight (peso de ocho reales) at 52 pence sterling. According to the Coin Act of May 29th 1772 the colonnato or 'dollar' at 100 oboli or cents was equal to the Spanish peso.

3.3.5 On Italian places (I)

	LEGHORN on:			
	Milan	**Genoa**	**Florence**	**Venice**
	per 100 lire corrente [a]	per 100 lire fuori banco [b]	per 100 Tuscan lire moneta buona [c]	per 100 ducati di banco, from 1803 per 100 lire piccoli corrente [d]
	in pezze da otto reali			
1771	15.70 15d/s (6)	16.99 8d/s (6)	17.20 3d/s (6)	101.96 5d/s (6)
1772	15.82 15d/s (1)	16.99 8d/s (1)	17.28 3d/s (1)	102.63 5d/s (1)
1773				
1774				
1775				
1776	15.57 15d/s (1)	16.88 8d/s (1)	17.28 3d/s (1)	102.04 5d/s (1)
1777	15.70 15d/s (4)	16.98 8d/s (4)	17.30 3d/s (4)	103.36 5d/s (4)
1778	15.73 15d/s (1)	16.92 8d/s (1)	17.32 3d/s (1)	103.36 5d/s (1)
1779	15.97 15d/s (3)	16.60 8d/s (3)	17.29 3d/s (3)	102.66 5d/s (3)
1780	15.87 15d/s (2)	16.59 8d/s (2)	17.30 3d/s (2)	101.59 5d/s (2)
1781	15.77 15d/s (11)	16.52 8d/s (11)	17.30 3d/s (11)	101.98 5d/s (11)
1782	15.85 15d/s (9)	16.57 8d/s (9)	17.26 3d/s (9)	103.57 5d/s (9)
1783	15.75 15d/s (1)	16.45 8d/s (1)	17.06 3d/s (1)	101.53 5d/s (1)
1784	15.60 15d/s (9)	16.34 8d/s (9)	17.15 3d/s (9)	102.21 5d/s (9)
1785	15.67 15d/s (9)	16.50 8d/s (9)	17.16 3d/s (9)	102.60 5d/s (9)
1786	15.33 15d/s (6)	16.22 8d/s (6)	16.94 3d/s (6)	101.75 5d/s (6)
1787	15.22 15d/s (12)	16.30 8d/s (12)	16.88 3d/s (12)	101.41 5d/s (12)
1788	15.23 15d/s (6)	16.31 8d/s (6)	16.78 3d/s (6)	100.06 5d/s (6)
1789	15.16 15d/s (5)	16.07 8d/s (5)	16.70 3d/s (5)	99.58 5d/s (5)
1790	15.18 15d/s (5)	16.01 8d/s (5)	16.73 3d/s (5)	100.02 5d/s (5)
1791				
1792				
1793				
1794				
1795				
1796	14.71 15d/s (4)	15.68 8d/s (4)	15.87 3d/s (4)	96.91 5d/s (4)
1797	14.84 15d/s (3)	15.84 8d/s (3)	16.06 3d/s (3)	91.39 5d/s (3)
1798	14.55 15d/s (9)	15.72 8d/s (9)	16.06 3d/s (9)	90.91 5d/s (9)
1799	14.61 15d/s (3)	15.89 8d/s (3)	16.06 3d/s (3)	87.72 5d/s (3)
1800				
1801	14.60 15d/s (1)	15.75 8d/s (1)	16.06 3d/s (1)	67.11 5d/s (1)
1802	14.63 15d/s (1)	15.87 8d/s (1)	16.06 3d/s (1)	
1803	14.65 15d/s (1)	16.03 8d/s (1)	16.06 3d/s (1)	9.09 5d/s (1)
1804	14.52 15d/s (2)	15.83 8d/s (2)	16.06 3d/s (2)	9.09 5d/s (1)
1805				

	LEGHORN on:			
	Milan	**Genoa**	**Florence**	**Venice**
	per 100 lire corrente, from 1824 per 100 lire austriache [a]	per 100 lire fuori banco, from 1827 (3) per 100 Piedmontese lire nuove [b]	per 100 Tuscan lire moneta buona [c]	per 100 lire piccoli corrente, from 1824 per 100 lire austriache [d]
	in pezze da otto reali			
1806	14.60 15d/s (1)	16.00 8d/s (1)	16.46 3d/s (1)	9.52 5d/s (1)
1807				
1808				
1809	14.76 15d/s (1)	16.10 8d/s (1)	16.10 3d/s (1)	9.38 5d/s (1)
1810				
1811				
1812	14.93 15d/s (10)	16.19 8d/s (10)	16.19 3d/s (10)	9.62 5d/s (10)
1813				
1814				
1815				
1816				
1817	15.09 15d/s (1)	16.32 8d/s (1)	16.19 3d/s (1)	9.36 5d/s (1)
1818				
1819				
1820	14.93 15d/s (1)	16.26 8d/s (1)	16.26 3d/s (1)	9.52 5d/s (1)
1821				
1822	15.60 15d/s (5)	17.06 8d/s (5)		9.25 5d/s (5)
1823	15.67 15d/s (12)	17.16 8d/s (12)		9.75 5d/s (12)
1824	17.62 15d/s (12)	17.07 8d/s (12)		17.66 5d/s (12)
1825	17.22 15d/s (12)	16.77 8d/s (12)		17.18 5d/s (12)
1826	17.32 30d/d (12)	16.89 30d/d (12)		17.24 30d/d (12)
1827	17.54 30d/d (12)	17.02/20.75 30d/d (2+10)		17.49 30d/d (12)
1828	17.49 30d/d (12)	20.71 30d/d (12)		17.49 30d/d (12)
1829	17.61 30d/d (12)	20.74 30d/d (12)		17.61 30d/d (12)
1830	17.42 30d/d (12)	20.54 30d/d (12)		17.41 30d/d (12)
1831	17.61 30d/d (12)	20.67 30d/d (12)		17.55 30d/d (12)
1832	17.55 30d/d (12)	20.55 30d/d (12)		17.52 30d/d (12)
1833	17.70 30d/d (12)	20.64 30d/d (12)		17.69 30d/d (12)
1834	17.52 30d/d (12)	20.32 30d/d (12)		17.47 30d/d (12)
1835	17.61 30d/d (12)	20.48 30d/d (12)		17.56 30d/d (12)
1836	17.31 30d/d (12)	20.32 30d/d (12)		17.26 30d/d (12)
	in Tuscan lire moneta buona			
1837	100.25 30d/d (12)	117.91 30d/d (12)		99.55 30d/d (12)
1838	101.30 30d/d (12)	118.90 30d/d (12)		100.84 30d/d (12)
1839	99.48 30d/d (12)	116.69 30d/d (12)		98.98 30d/d (12)
1840	99.86 30d/d (12)	116.69 30d/d (12)		99.19 30d/d (12)

	LEGHORN on:		
	Milan	**Genoa**	**Venice**
	per 100 lire austriache [a]	per 100 Piedmontesian lire nuove [b]	per 100 lire austriache [d]
	in Tuscan lire moneta buona		
1841	100.52 30d/d (12)	116.05 30d/d (12)	99.84 30d/d (12)
1842	100.80 30d/d (12)	115.61 30d/d (12)	100.17 30d/d (12)
1843			
1844			
1845			
1846	99.75 30d/d (1)	116.00 30d/d (1)	99.75 30d/d (1)
1847	100.24 30d/d (12)	116.90 30d/d (12)	99.68 30d/d (12)
1848	100.52 30d/d (12)	118.82 30d/d (12)	97.65 30d/d (12)
1849	99.73 30d/d (12)	117.40 30d/d (12)	77.46 30d/d (12)
1850	99.41 30d/d (11)	116.62 30d/d (11)	99.09 30d/d (11)

[a]   The Leghorn quotations on Milan were given per lire corrente of 20 soldi at 12 denari corrente, whereby 150 lire corrente = 106 lire imperiale (1 scudo imperiale = 117 soldi imperiali) from 1750. On November 1st 1823 the Austrian lira (lira austriaca) of 100 centesimi with 3.897 grammes of fine silver was introduced in Lombardo–Venetia by the so-called Münzpatent and became legal tender just as the guilder Konventionskurant did (see pp. 255f.). This lira was equal to the 20-kreuzer piece (or the third part of the guilder) of the Habsburg Monarchy and therefore used to be called 'la svanzica' or the 'zwanziger'.

[b]   Concerning the Genoese currency, see pp. 107f.

[c]   Concerning the Tuscan currency, see pp. 106.

[d]   Concerning the Venetian currency, see pp. 104f. For the time after 1823 see note [a] above.

3.3.5 On Italian places (II)

	LEGHORN on:			
	Rome	**Naples**	**Palermo**	**Turin**
	per 100 scudi romani [a]	per 100 ducati del regno [b]	per 10 oncie (moneta buona) [c]	per 100 Piedmontese lire [d]
	in pezze da otto reali			
1771	107.63 21d/s (6)	88.82 34d/d (6)	26.45 45d/d (6)	24.09 15d/s (6)
1772	106.77 21d/s (1)	84.48 34d/d (1)	24.79 45d/d (1)	24.17 15d/s (1)
1773				
1774				
1775				
1776	108.07 21d/s (1)	87.15 34d/d (1)	26.55 45d/d (1)	24.10 15d/s (1)
1777	108.13 21d/s (4)	86.75 34d/d (4)	26.09 45d/d (4)	24.24 15d/s (4)
1778	108.18 21d/s (1)	86.40 34d/d (1)	25.97 45d/d (1)	24.25 15d/s (1)
1779	106.57 21d/s (3)	86.15 34d/d (3)	25.94 45d/d (3)	24.14 15d/s (3)
1780	106.24 21d/s (2)	85.84 34d/d (2)	26.03 45d/d (2)	22.94 15d/s (2)
1781	105.96 21d/s (11)	85.72 34d/d (11)	25.71 45d/d (11)	24.04 15d/s (11)
1782	106.03 21d/s (9)	87.36 34d/d (9)	26.45 45d/d (9)	23.95 15d/s (9)
1783	103.76 21d/s (1)	87.34 34d/d (1)	25.97 45d/d (1)	23.88 15d/s (1)
1784	103.66 21d/s (9)	87.50 34d/d (9)	25.98 45d/d (9)	23.70 15d/s (9)
1785	104.12 21d/s (9)	87.32 34d/d (9)	26.10 45d/d (9)	23.72 15d/s (9)
1786	104.57 21d/s (6)	87.46 34d/d (6)	26.05 45d/d (6)	23.19 15d/s (6)
1787	105.26 21d/s (12)	86.40 34d/d (12)	25.89 45d/d (12)	23.51 15d/s (12)
1788	104.52 21d/s (6)	84.93 34d/d (6)	25.54 45d/d (6)	23.19 15d/s (6)
1789	104.50 21d/s (5)	86.21 34d/d (5)	25.89 45d/d (5)	23.07 15d/s (5)
1790	103.66 21d/s (5)	86.48 34d/d (5)	25.94 45d/d (5)	22.99 15d/s (5)
1791				
1792				
1793				
1794				
1795				
1796	164.24 21d/s (4)	74.63 34d/d (4)	25.00 45d/d (4)	14.55 15d/s (4)
1797	204.06 21d/s (3)	76.53 34d/d (3)	25.00 45d/d (3)	14.25 15d/s (3)
1798	292.17 21d/s (9)	61.45 34d/d (9)	24.60 45d/d (9)	8.11 15d/s (9)
1799	114.64 21d/s (3)	46.44 34d/d (3)	27.07 45d/d (3)	8.33 15d/s (3)
1800				
1801	111.30 21d/s (1)	86.02 34d/d (1)	23.30 45d/d (1)	21.51 15d/s (1)
1802	111.52 21d/s (1)	85.84 34d/d (1)	23.50 45d/d (1)	21.51 15d/s (1)
1803	111.30 21d/s (1)	85.47 34d/d (1)	25.10 45d/d (1)	21.51 15d/s (1)
1804	110.76 21d/s (2)	84.03 34d/d (2)	24.40 45d/d (2)	21.51 15d/s (2)
1805				
1806	118.95 21d/s (1)	84.75 34d/d (1)	25.64 45d/d (1)	21.51 15d/s (1)

	LEGHORN on:			
	Rome	**Naples**	**Palermo, from 1817 also Messina**	**Turin**
	per 100 scudi romani [a]	per 100 ducati del regno [b]	per 10 oncie (moneta buona up to 1815), from 1820 per 100 ducati del regno [c]	per 100 Piedmontese lire, since 1826 (4) per 100 Piedmontese lire nuove [d]
	in pezze da otto reali			
1807				
1808				
1809	112.61 21d/s (1)	82.99 34d/d (1)	20.00 45d/d (1)	21.51 15d/s (1)
1810				
1811				
1812	110.65 21d/s (10)	86.96 34d/d (10)	20.00 45d/d (1)	21.51 15d/s (1)
1813				
1814				
1815				
1816				
1817	110.00 21d/s (1)	84.39 34d/d (1)	25.86 45d/d (1)	21.63 15d/s (1)
1818				
1819				
1820	111.30 21d/s (1)	81.14 34d/d (1)	81.63 45d/d (1)	22.10 15d/s (1)
1821				
1822	110.40 21d/s (5)	88.87 34d/d (5)	87.85 45d/d (5)	23.75 15d/s (5)
1823	110.34 21d/s (12)	88.53 34d/d (12)	87.68 45d/d (12)	23.78 15d/s (12)
1824	111.48 21d/s (12)	85.51 34d/d (12)	85.41 45d/d (12)	23.78 15d/s (12)
1825	112.11 21d/s (12)	86.70 34d/d (12)	86.07 45d/d (12)	23.78 15d/s (12)
1826	112.29 30d/d (12)	86.33 30d/d (12)	85.69 60d/d (12)	23.78/20.33 30d/d (3+9)
1827	111.72 30d/d (12)	85.64 30d/d (12)	85.27 60d/d (12)	20.53 30d/d (12)
1828	111.32 30d/d (12)	86.69 30d/d (12)	86.59 60d/d (12)	20.53 30d/d (12)
1829	110.02 30d/d (12)	88.53 30d/d (12)	88.16 60d/d (12)	20.58 30d/d (12)
1830	110.85 30d/d (12)	87.95 30d/d (12)	87.50 60d/d (12)	20.45 30d/d (12)
1831	111.01 30d/d (12)	87.43 30d/d (12)	87.20 60d/d (12)	20.62 30d/d (12)
1832	109.35 30d/d (12)	89.82 30d/d (12)	88.62 60d/d (12)	20.54 30d/d (12)
1833	108.56 30d/d (12)	89.46 30d/d (12)	89.11 60d/d (12)	20.47 30d/d (12)
1834	110.08 30d/d (12)	88.87 30d/d (12)	88.16 60d/d (12)	20.29 30d/d (12)
1835	109.47 30d/d (12)	89.41 30d/d (12)	88.50 60d/d (12)	20.44 30d/d (12)
1836	109.81 30d/d (12)	88.71 30d/d (12)	88.01 60d/d (12)	20.23 30d/d (12)
	in Tuscan lire moneta buona			
1837	636.46 30d/d (12)	505.35 30d/d (12)	500.02 60d/d (12)	117.04 30d/d (12)
1838	638.75 30d/d (12)	502.75 30d/d (12)	496.53 60d/d (12)	118.63 30d/d (12)
1839	633.42 30d/d (12)	504.00 30d/d (12)	496.02 60d/d (12)	116.46 30d/d (12)
1840	636.00 30d/d (12)	509.42 30d/d (12)	506.21 60d/d (12)	116.27 30d/d (12)

	LEGHORN on:			
	Rome	**Naples**	**Palermo & Messina**	**Turin**
	per 100 scudi romani [a]	per 100 ducati del regno [b]	per 100 ducati del regno [c]	per 100 Piedmontese lire nuove [d]
	in Tuscan lire moneta buona			
1841	629.59 30d/d (12)	496.92 30d/d (12)	492.64 60d/d (12)	115.59 30d/d (12)
1842	629.67 30d/d (12)	502.67 30d/d (12)	499.95 60d/d (12)	115.05 30d/d (12)
1843				
1844				
1845				
1846	632.00 30d/d (1)	507.00 30d/d (1)	503.34 60d/d (1)	115.50 30d/d (1)
1847	630.75 30d/d (12)	509.75 30d/d (12)	505.98 60d/d (12)	116.13 30d/d (12)
1848	625.09 30d/d (12)	495.34 30d/d (12)	498.62 60d/d (12)	117.34 30d/d (12)
1849	560.25 30d/d (12)	522.17 30d/d (12)	509.59 60d/d (12)	116.84 30d/d (12)
1850	562.73 30d/d (11)	516.64 30d/d (11)	514.09 60d/d (11)	116.30 30d/d (11)

[a]   The Roman unit of account was the scudo moneta or scudo romano of 10 paoli or 100 baiocchi or 1,000 mezzi quattrini. This scudo was equivalent to 24.23 grammes of fine silver up to 1834 and – after the currency reform of Pope Gregory XVI – to 24.21 grammes of fine silver between 1835 and 1866 (PINCHERA [1957], pp. 1, 4).

[b]   The system of accounting in ducati (called 'ducati del regno' or 'ducati di regno' since the 18th century) of 10 carlini at 10 grani or 5 tari at 20 grani had been common practice in the Kingdom of Naples for centuries and was continued during the Restoration era (after the Act of August 18th 1814). The Act of April 20th 1818 fixed the fineness of the ducato at 19.12 grammes of fine silver, as it had been when it was officially introduced in 1794 and confirmed in 1804 (from 1784 18.96 grammes of fine silver; cf. NOBACK [1851], pp. 710f.). This new silver ducato – later generally called 'ducato del regno' or 'ducato di regno' – should have been divided into 100 centesimi or grani. Simultaneously, it became the unit of account of the whole Kingdom of the Two Sicilies.

[c]   The old Sicilian unit of account was the oncia of 30 tari (at 20 grani) or 60 carlini (at 10 grani), which was equal to 3 ducati del regno since 1815. When selling Sicilian bills at Leghorn up to 1815 one usually reckoned 61 Sicilian carlini for 60 carlini moneta buona (= 1 oncia = 3 ducati del regno), i.e. the buyer of the bill was refunded 1 carlino per oncia 'a titolo di moneta buona' (cf. NELKENBRECHER [1798], p. 103). By the means of the Act of April 20th 1818 (see [b]), the new (Neapolitan) silver ducato – later generally called 'ducato del regno' or 'ducato di regno' – became the unit of account of the whole Kingdom of the Two Sicilies which means that the hitherto independent Sicilian system based on the oncia at 56.896 grammes of fine silver was removed by this Act.

[d]   Up to 1826, the (old) Piedmontese lira of 20 soldi at 12 denari functioned as unit of account. From 1770, this lira was equal to 5.28 grammes of fine silver. For the new Piedmontese currency of the post-Napoleonic era, see p. 108.

3.4 Genoa exchange rates

3.4.1 On London, Amsterdam, Paris and Hamburg

	GENOA on:			
	London	**Amsterdam**	**Paris**	**Hamburg**
	per 10 pounds sterling [a]	per 100 guilders Flemish banco [b]	per 100 livres tournois, from 1796 per 100 francs [c]	per 100 mark banco [d]
	in pezze of 5¾ lire fuori banco			
1777	48.08 90d/d (4)	46.67 90d/d (4)	20.82 30d/d (4)	
1778	49.49 90d/d (12)	46.95 90d/d (12)	20.87 30d/d (12)	
1779	51.54 90d/d (12)	47.97 90d/d (12)	21.14 30d/d (12)	
1780	50.43 90d/d (12)	47.56 90d/d (12)	21.09 30d/d (12)	
1781	49.16 90d/d (12)	48.62 90d/d (12)	21.18 30d/d (12)	
1782	48.06 90d/d (1)	47.76 90d/d (1)	20.94 30d/d (1)	
1783				
1784				
1785				
1786				
1787	51.01 90d/d (7)	46.48 90d/d (8)	20.87 30d/d (7)	
1788	52.31 90d/d (4)	46.33 90d/d (6)	21.04 30d/d (4)	
1789	53.02 90d/d (9)	46.49 90d/d (12)	22.58 30d/d (12)	
1790	53.50 90d/d (12)	46.27 90d/d (12)	19.61 30d/d (12)	
1791				
1792				
1793				
1794				
1795				
1796	48.65 90d/d (8)	43.22 90d/d (7)	21.41 30d/d (3)	42.06 60d/d (8)
1797	47.17 90d/d (6)	43.36 90d/d (6)	21.62 30d/d (6)	41.74 60d/d (6)
1798	54.70 90d/d (4)	41.32 90d/d (4)	20.33 30d/d (4)	39.86 60d/d (4)
1799	53.30 90d/d (7)	39.87 90d/d (5)	20.11 30d/d (7)	38.91 60d/d (7)
1800				
1801	48.39 90d/d (6)	42.27 90d/d (6)	21.43 30d/d (6)	41.06 60d/d (6)
1802	48.80 90d/d (12)	45.05 90d/d (12)	21.14 30d/d (12)	40.33 60d/d (12)
1803	50.16 90d/d (12)	46.86 90d/d (12)	21.08 30d/d (12)	40.11 60d/d (12)
1804	51.42 90d/d (12)	46.41 90d/d (11)	20.95 30d/d (12)	39.67 60d/d (11)
1805	50.39 90d/d (12)	45.12 90d/d (12)	20.28 30d/d (10)	39.15 60d/d (12)
1806	49.50 90d/d (10)	46.06 90d/d (10)	20.92 30d/d (10)	39.31 60d/d (10)
1807		47.13 90d/d (12)	21.18 30d/d (12)	39.69 60d/d (11)
1808		44.62 90d/d (12)	20.72 30d/d (12)	37.26 60d/d (11)
1809		43.26 90d/d (12)	20.75 30d/d (12)	37.51 60d/d (12)

	GENOA on:			
	London	**Amsterdam**	**Paris**	**Hamburg**
	per 10 pounds sterling [a]	per 100 guilders Flemish banco, from 1816 (10) per 100 Dutch guilders [b]	per 100 francs [c]	per 100 mark banco [d]
	in pezze of 5¾ lire fuori banco			
1810	41.74 90d/d (1)	43.36 90d/d (9)	20.81 30d/d (12)	37.89 60d/d (12)
1811			21.27 30d/d (12)	39.05 60d/d (12)
1812			21.03 30d/d (11)	38.38 60d/d (11)
1813			20.98 30d/d (12)	38.23 60d/d (5)
1814	45.40 90d/d (6)		21.27 30d/d (9)	39.68 60d/d (4)
1815	45.95 90d/d (12)	46.22 90d/d (7)	21.41 30d/d (12)	39.77 60d/d (12)
1816	52.77 90d/d (12)	45.14 90d/d (10)	21.21 30d/d (12)	40.20 60d/d (12)
1817	51.41 90d/d (12)	44.30 90d/d (11)	21.02 30d/d (12)	39.48 60d/d (12)
1818	49.20 90d/d (12)	44.15 90d/d (12)	20.65 30d/d (12)	39.13 60d/d (12)
1819	50.66 90d/d (12)	44.52 90d/d (12)	20.89 30d/d (12)	39.33 60d/d (12)
1820	52.97 90d/d (12)	44.34 90d/d (12)	20.94 30d/d (12)	38.92 60d/d (12)
1821	53.30 90d/d (12)	42.96 90d/d (12)	20.88 30d/d (12)	37.96 60d/d (12)
1822	53.53 90d/d (4)	44.43 90d/d (4)	21.06 30d/d (4)	38.48 60d/d (4)
1823	54.14 90d/d (11)	44.44 90d/d (12)	21.11 30d/d (12)	38.64 60d/d (12)
1824	53.15 90d/d (12)	44.74 90d/d (12)	21.05 30d/d (12)	38.66 60d/d (12)
1825	51.64 90d/d (12)	43.55 90d/d (12)	20.76 30d/d (12)	38.17 60d/d (12)
1826	53.90 90d/d (12)	44.18 90d/d (12)	21.11 30d/d (12)	38.83 60d/d (12)
	in Piedmontese lire nuove			
1827	252.50 3m/d (12)	210.75 2m/d (12)	121.90/99.70 1m/d (2+10)	184.27 2m/d (12)
1828	249.65 3m/d (12)	208.32 2m/d (12)	99.26 1m/d (12)	183.67 2m/d (12)
1829	252.13 3m/d (12)	208.73 2m/d (12)	99.15 1m/d (12)	184.34 2m/d (12)
1830	253.55 3m/d (12)	207.86 2m/d (12)	99.45 1m/d (12)	183.49 2m/d (12)
1831	250.75 3m/d (12)	210.17 2m/d (12)	99.93 1m/d (10)	185.02 2m/d (12)
1832	255.35 3m/d (11)	210.91 2m/d (11)	99.45 1m/d (11)	185.09 2m/d (11)
1833	253.97 3m/d (12)	210.92 2m/d (12)	99.21 1m/d (12)	185.29 2m/d (12)
1834	251.97 3m/d (12)	208.23 2m/d (12)	99.54 1m/d (12)	185.45 2m/d (12)
1835	253.10 3m/d (12)	208.21 2m/d (12)	99.53 1m/d (12)	185.61 2m/d (12)
1836	252.39 3m/d (12)	208.52 2m/d (12)	99.42 1m/d (9)	184.77 2m/d (12)
1837	254.86 3m/d (12)	211.40 2m/d (12)	100.24 1m/d (12)	186.34 2m/d (12)
1838	254.20 3m/d (12)	210.25 2m/d (12)	100.02 1m/d (9)	186.34 2m/d (12)
1839	250.41 3m/d (12)	208.77 2m/d (12)	99.76 1m/d (10)	186.30 2m/d (12)
1840	250.73 3m/d (12)	209.71 2m/d (12)	99.82 1m/d (12)	186.86 2m/d (12)
1841	251.70 3m/d (12)	209.46 2m/d (12)	99.85 1m/d (12)	187.32 2m/d (12)
1842	253.35 3m/d (12)	208.94 2m/d (12)	99.70 1m/d (12)	186.61 2m/d (12)
1843	255.35 3m/d (12)	209.50 2m/d (12)	99.75 1m/d (12)	186.18 2m/d (12)
1844	253.90 3m/d (12)	209.69 2m/d (12)	99.59 1m/d (12)	186.05 2m/d (12)

	GENOA on:			
	London	**Amsterdam**	**Paris** [e]	**Hamburg**, since 1877 (11) **Germany** [f]
	per 10 pounds sterling [a]	per 100 Dutch guilders [b]	per 100 francs [c]	per 100 mark banco, from 1872/73 per 100 mark [d]
	in Piedmontese lire nuove, from 1861 (8) in Italian lire			
1845	255.10 3m/d (12)	208.40 2m/d (12)	99.68 1m/d (12)	185.87 2m/d (12)
1846	255.60 3m/d (12)	208.67 2m/d (12)	99.93 1m/d (12)	186.80 2m/d (12)
1847	252.65 3m/d (12)	209.96 2m/d (12)	99.94 1m/d (12)	186.63 2m/d (12)
1848	256.05 3m/d (10)	211.37 2m/d (9)	100.15 1m/d (10)	185.73 2m/d (9)
1849	261.18 3m/d (12)	216.50 2m/d (11)	102.45 1m/d (12)	189.64 2m/d (11)
1850	256.45 3m/d (12)	213.61 2m/d (12)	101.15 1m/d (12)	188.13 2m/d (12)
1851	250.40 3m/d (12)	212.57 2m/d (12)	100.35 1m/d (12)	187.38 2m/d (12)
1852	252.01 3m/d (12)	211.42 2m/d (12)	99.81 1m/d (12)	186.36 2m/d (12)
1853	248.84 3m/d (12)	211.23 2m/d (12)	99.86 1m/d (12)	186.88 2m/d (12)
1854	248.59 3m/d (11)	212.98 2m/d (11)	100.00 1m/d (11)	188.28 2m/d (11)
1855	249.34 3m/d (12)	212.61 2m/d (12)	99.87 1m/d (12)	187.52 2m/d (12)
1856	250.77 3m/d (12)	212.96 2m/d (12)	99.80 1m/d (12)	187.73 2m/d (12)
1857	249.47 3m/d (12)	212.91 2m/d (12)	99.78 1m/d (12)	188.06 2m/d (12)
1858	249.93 3m/d (12)	213.32 2m/d (12)	99.95 1m/d (12)	187.72 2m/d (12)
1859	251.03 3m/d (12)	215.05 2m/d (12)	100.27 1m/d (12)	189.78 2m/d (12)
1860	251.55 s (12)	213.66 2m/d (12)	99.67 1m/d (12)	188.66 2m/d (12)
1861	253.94 s (12)	212.21 2m/d (11)	99.75 1m/d (12)	187.52 2m/d (12)
1862	252.73 s (12)	212.49 2m/d (12)	99.78 1m/d (12)	187.72 2m/d (12)
1863	252.67 s (12)	213.10 2m/d (12)	99.83 1m/d (12)	187.80 2m/d (12)
1864	253.49 s (12)	211.70 2m/d (12)	99.74 1m/d (12)	187.46 2m/d (12)
1865	252.56 s (12)	211.31 2m/d (12)	99.75 1m/d (11)	186.57 2m/d (12)
1866	264.71 s (12)	219.29 2m/d (12)	104.64 1m/d (12)	195.13 2m/d (11)
1867	269.92 s (12)	224.59 2m/d (11)	106.48 1m/d (12)	199.31 2m/d (12)
1868	276.38 s (12)	230.08 2m/d (12)	109.89 1m/d (11)	203.23 2m/d (12)
1869	262.21 s (12)	216.61 2m/d (12)	103.90 1m/d (11)	191.56 2m/d (12)
1870	262.52 s (12)	215.61 2m/d (7)	104.23 s (12)	189.95 3m/d (7)
1871	266.42 s (12)	222.50 2m/d (8)	104.40 s (12)	195.40 3m/d (9)
1872	274.23 s (12)	226.64 2m/d (9)	107.89 s (12)	200.35/133.50 3m/d (11+1)
1873	288.45 s (12)	234.22 2m/d (7)	113.72 s (12)	205.31/141.83 3m/d (4+3)
1874	284.10 s (12)	232.35 2m/d (5)	112.33 s (12)	137.74 3m/d (11)
1875	272.66 s (12)	224.50 2m/d (2)	108.19 s (12)	131.54 3m/d (12)
1876	273.87 s (12)	224.23 2m/d (12)	108.71 ch (12)	132.23 3m/d (12)
1877	276.12 s (12)	226.13 2m/d (8)	109.81 ch (12)	133.92 3m/d (9)
1878	276.08 s (12)	225.60 2m/d (11)	109.64 ch (12)	134.02 3m/d (12)
1879	280.35 s (12)	229.55 2m/d (11)	110.99 ch (12)	136.07 3m/d (11)

	GENOA on:										
	London			**Amsterdam**			**Paris** [e]			**Germany** [f]		
	per 10 pounds sterling [a]			per 100 Dutch guilders [b]			per 100 francs [c]			per 100 mark [d]		
	in Italian lire											
1880	277.22	s	(12)	228.58	s	(12)	109.66	ch	(12)	135.21	3m/d	(11)
1881	256.62	s	(12)	210.61	s	(12)	101.49	ch	(12)	123.48	3m/d	(10)
1882	258.29	s	(12)	212.80	s	(10)	102.44	ch	(12)	125.43	3m/d	(12)
1883	252.44	s	(12)	208.33	s	(11)	100.06	ch	(12)	122.15	3m/d	(12)
1884	252.11	s	(12)	207.74	s	(12)	100.04	ch	(12)	122.23	3m/d	(12)
1885	253.67	s	(12)	209.42	s	(12)	100.41	ch	(12)	123.04	3m/d	(10)
1886	253.00	s	(12)	209.02	s	(12)	100.25	ch	(12)	123.03	3m/d	(12)
1887	255.20	s	(12)	210.40	s	(12)	100.81	ch	(12)	123.98	3m/d	(10)
1888	255.75	s	(12)	211.64	s	(11)	101.05	ch	(12)	125.27	3m/d	(7)
1889	254.10	s	(12)	210.17	s	(12)	101.94	ch	(12)	*123.19*	3m/d	(11)
1890	255.24	ch	(12)	210.59	s	(12)	101.10	ch	(12)	125.12	3m/d	(12)
1891	256.38	ch	(12)	211.88	s	(12)	101.55	ch	(12)	125.89	3m/d	(12)
1892	260.79	ch	(12)	215.34	s	(12)	103.57	ch	(12)	127.86	3m/d	(12)
1893	271.30	ch	(12)	222.37	s	(11)	107.22	ch	(12)	132.88	3m/d	(12)
1894	*280.13*	ch	(12)	231.34	s	(12)	110.90	ch	(12)	137.35	3m/d	(12)
1895	*265.80*	ch	(12)	219.13	s	(12)	105.40	ch	(12)	130.00	3m/d	(12)
1896	*271.76*	ch	(12)	224.34	s	(12)	107.86	ch	(12)	133.13	3m/d	(12)
1897	264.18	ch	(9)	218.87	s	(11)	105.03	ch	(11)	129.66	3m/d	(11)
1898	270.18	ch	(12)	223.53	s	(12)	106.88	ch	(12)	132.15	ch	(12)
1899	270.89	ch	(12)	223.25	s	(12)	107.39	ch	(12)	132.48	ch	(12)
1900	267.95	ch	(12)	221.39	s	(12)	106.47	ch	(12)	130.84	ch	(12)
1901	263.00	ch	(12)	217.24	s	(12)	104.47	ch	(12)	128.69	ch	(12)
1902	254.71	ch	(12)	209.98	s	(12)	101.24	ch	(12)	124.49	ch	(12)
1903	251.50	ch	(12)	207.58	s	(12)	99.97	ch	(12)	122.98	ch	(12)
1904	251.95	ch	(12)	208.70	s	(12)	100.13	ch	(12)	123.32	ch	(12)
1905	251.47	ch	(12)	207.94	s	(12)	100.37	ch	(12)	122.92	ch	(12)
1906	251.55	ch	(12)	207.30	s	(12)	99.96	ch	(12)	123.21	ch	(12)
1907	251.82	ch	(12)	208.12	s	(12)	99.95	ch	(12)	122.85	ch	(12)
1908	251.38	ch	(12)	207.79	s	(12)	100.01	ch	(12)	122.98	ch	(12)
1909	252.83	ch	(12)	208.96	s	(12)	100.43	ch	(12)	123.58	ch	(12)
1910	253.64	ch	(12)				100.55	ch	(12)	123.94	ch	(12)
1911	253.98	ch	(12)	210.12	s	(12)	100.56	ch	(12)	124.11	ch	(12)
1912	254.77	ch	(12)	210.79	s	(12)	100.95	ch	(12)	124.41	ch	(12)
1913	257.04	ch	(12)	212.02	s	(12)	101.90	ch	(12)	125.58	ch	(12)
1914	252.04	ch	(5)	209.06	s	(5)	100.40	ch	(5)	123.52	ch	(5)

[a]   Concerning the British currency, see pp. 3–5.

[b]   Concerning the Dutch currency, see pp. 57–59.

[c]   Concerning the French currency, see pp. 279f.

[d]   Concerning the Hamburg and the German currencies, see pp. 191–193, 197.

[e]   From November 1869 Lyons and Marseilles were listed with the same quotation as Paris (partly called 'French bank places').

[f]   Quotation on Hamburg and Berlin.

3.4.2 On Augsburg, Vienna, Switzerland and Belgium

	GENOA on:	
	Augsburg	**Vienna**
	per 100 guilders Augsburg current [a]	per 100 guilders Konventionskurant, from 1799 (4) per 100 guilders Wiener Währung [b]
	in pezze of 5¾ lire fuori banco	
1777	55.00 14d/s (4)	54.46 14d/s (4)
1778	55.23 14d/s (11)	55.06 14d/s (11)
1779	55.89 14d/s (12)	56.02 14d/s (12)
1780	55.17 14d/s (11)	54.54 14d/s (12)
1781	55.77 14d/s (11)	55.24 14d/s (10)
1782	55.76 14d/s (1)	55.65 14d/s (1)
1783		
1784		
1785		
1786		
1787		54.76 14d/s (5)
1788		55.02 14d/s (6)
1789		54.83 14d/s (12)
1790		54.95 14d/s (12)
1791		
1792		
1793		
1794		
1795		
1796	55.05 14d/s (9)	54.71 14d/s (9)
1797	55.65 14d/s (6)	55.43 14d/s (6)
1798	53.90 14d/s (4)	53.59 14d/s (4)
1799	53.23 14d/s (6)	51.74/45.98 14d/s (3+4)
1800		
1801	55.12 14d/s (6)	46.68 14d/s (6)
1802	54.57 14d/s (12)	44.07 14d/s (12)
1803	54.28 14d/s (12)	41.09 14d/s (12)
1804	54.11 14d/s (12)	39.82 14d/s (11)
1805	53.60 14d/s (12)	40.17 14d/s (10)
1806	53.99 14d/s (10)	31.24 14d/s (7)
1807	53.65 14d/s (12)	25.28 14d/s (11)
1808	52.72 14d/s (12)	22.90 14d/s (11)
1809	53.06 14d/s (12)	21.77 14d/s (4)
1810	52.31 14d/s (12)	14.13 14d/s (5)

	GENOA on:	
	Augsburg [c]	**Vienna**
	per 100 guilders Augsburg current [a]	per 100 guilders Wiener Währung, from 1816 per 100 guilders Konventionskurant [b]
	in pezze of 5¾ lire fuori banco	
1811	52.61 14d/s (12)	
1812	53.78 14d/s (11)	
1813	53.86 14d/s (12)	
1814	54.13 14d/s (9)	
1815	54.68 14d/s (11)	
1816	54.92 14d/s (12)	54.92 14d/s (6)
1817	53.65 14d/s (12)	54.25 14d/s (12)
1818	53.40 14d/s (12)	54.19 14d/s (12)
1819	53.89 14d/s (12)	54.21 14d/s (12)
1820	52.94 14d/s (12)	53.22 14d/s (12)
1821	52.57 14d/s (12)	52.76 14d/s (12)
1822	52.87 14d/s (12)	52.76 14d/s (4)
1823	52.65 14d/s (10)	52.85 14d/s (12)
1824	53.22 14d/s (12)	53.61 14d/s (12)
1825	53.15 14d/s (12)	53.10 14d/s (12)
1826	53.29 14d/s (9)	53.11 14d/s (12)
	in Piedmontese lire nuove	
1827	253.12 1m/d (12)	253.59 1m/d (12)
1828	253.36 1m/d (12)	253.30 1m/d (12)
1829	254.25 1m/d (12)	253.90 1m/d (12)
1830	252.92 1m/d (12)	252.40 1m/d (12)
1831	255.04 1m/d (12)	254.11 1m/d (12)
1832	254.06 1m/d (12)	254.91 1m/d (11)
1833	254.48 1m/d (12)	256.46 1m/d (12)
1834	254.95 1m/d (12)	257.17 1m/d (12)
1835	254.91 1m/d (12)	255.52 1m/d (12)
1836	253.61 1m/d (12)	253.11 1m/d (12)
1837	252.56 1m/d (12)	253.47 1m/d (12)
1838	254.78 1m/d (12)	253.50 1m/d (12)
1839	255.55 1m/d (12)	254.04 1m/d (12)
1840	256.35 1m/d (12)	254.34 1m/d (12)
1841	258.16 1m/d (12)	258.44 1m/d (12)
1842	258.21 1m/d (12)	260.07 1m/d (12)
1843	256.58 1m/d (12)	258.77 1m/d (12)
1844	256.16 1m/d (12)	260.40 1m/d (12)
1845	255.58 1m/d (12)	259.10 1m/d (12)

	GENOA on:			
	Augsburg [c]	**Vienna**	**Switzerland**	**Belgium** [d]
	per 100 guilders Augsburg current, from 1858 (12) per 100 guilders South German current [a]	per 100 guilders Konventionskurant, from 1858 (11) per 100 guilders Österreichische Währung [b]	per 100 franken [e]	per 100 Belgian francs [e]
	in Piedmontese lire nuove			
1846	*256.61* 1m/d (12)	256.42 1m/d (12)		
1847	*255.71* 1m/d (12)	255.34 1m/d (12)		
1848	*253.23* 1m/d (7)	243.25 1m/d (5)		
1849	*258.70* 1m/d (11)	230.90 1m/d (10)		
1850	*256.94* 1m/d (12)	217.13 1m/d (4)		
1851	*255.73* 1m/d (12)	203.88 1m/d (8)		
1852	*252.99* 1m/d (12)	209.13 1m/d (12)		
1853	*240.55* 1m/d (12)	228.85 1m/d (10)		
1854	*255.66* 1m/d (12)	207.00 1m/d (3)		
1855	*256.51* 1m/d (9)	211.72 1m/d (7)		
1856	*257.13* 1m/d (12)	244.69 1m/d (11)		
1857	*257.12* 1m/d (12)	241.84 1m/d (12)		
1858	*257.25/212.09* 1m/d (10+1)	242.42 1m/d (12)		
1859	*214.60* 1m/d (12)	216.97 1m/d (8)		
1860	214.73 1m/d (12)	189.23 1m/d (9)		
	in Piedmontese lire nuove, from 1861 (8) in Italian lire			
1861	214.05 1m/d (12)	177.38 1m/d (8)		
1862	212.97 1m/d (12)	189.94 1m/d (12)		
1863	212.94 1m/d (12)	218.09 1m/d (12)		
1864	212.44 1m/d (12)	211.50 1m/d (12)		
1865	211.05 1m/d (11)	223.09 1m/d (12)		
1866	220.73 1m/d (11)	234.13 1m/d (4)		
1867	224.64 1m/d (11)	219.00 1m/d (2)		
1868	230.08 1m/d (12)	231.57 1m/d (4)		
1869	216.33 1m/d (10)	211.50 1m/d (2)		
1870		210.00 1m/d (1)		
1871		213.43 1m/d (7)	105.37 s (6)	*104.85* s (10)
1872		250.00 1m/d (1)	109.04 s (6)	108.16 s (12)
1873		253.34 1m/d (3)	113.58 s (12)	113.82 s (12)
1874		248.60 1m/d (5)	112.30 s (11)	112.15 s (12)
1875		242.29 1m/d (12)	108.50 s (12)	108.15 s (12)
1876		226.42 1m/d (12)	108.55 s (12)	108.51 s (12)
1877		222.11 1m/d (12)	109.64 s (12)	109.61 s (12)
1878		231.32 1m/d (11)	109.44 s (12)	109.38 s (12)
1879		238.30 1m/d (12)	110.84 s (12)	110.80 s (12)
1880		237.69 1m/d (12)	109.53 s (12)	109.56 s (12)

	GENOA on:		
	Vienna	**Switzerland**	**Belgium**
	per 100 guilders Öster-reichische Währung, from 1900 per 100 Austrian crowns [b]	per 100 franken [e]	per 100 Belgian francs [f]
	in Italian lire		
1881	217.11 1m/d (12)	101.33 s (12)	101.32 s (12)
1882	215.68 1m/d (11)	102.28 s (12)	102.28 s (11)
1883	210.92 1m/d (12)	99.96 s (12)	99.94 s (12)
1884	207.37 1m/d (12)	99.90 s (12)	99.89 s (12)
1885	203.87 1m/d (12)	100.19 s (12)	100.26 s (12)
1886	200.49 1m/d (12)	100.05 s (12)	100.14 s (12)
1887	201.55 1m/d (12)	100.67 s (12)	100.67 s (1)
1888	204.55 1m/d (11)	100.90 s (11)	100.95 s (11)
1889	212.19 1m/d (12)	100.52 s (12)	100.57 s (12)
1890	219.17 1m/d (12)	100.90 ch (11)	101.02 ch (12)
1891	219.21 1m/d (12)	101.27 ch (12)	101.40 ch (12)
1892	218.09 1m/d (12)	103.35 ch (11)	103.46 ch (12)
1893	217.96 1m/d (11)	107.36 ch (12)	107.39 ch (12)
1894	224.30 1m/d (12)	111.21 ch (12)	111.21 ch (12)
1895	217.71 1m/d (12)	105.15 ch (12)	105.23 ch (12)
1896	225.84 1m/d (12)	107.58 ch (12)	107.75 ch (12)
1897	220.54 1m/d (11)	104.65 ch (11)	104.90 ch (11)
1898	224.52 1m/d (12)	106.48 ch (12)	106.73 ch (12)
1899	224.81 1m/d (11)	106.87 ch (12)	107.23 ch (12)
1900	110.55 ch (12)	105.70 ch (12)	106.28 ch (12)
1901	109.46 ch (11)	104.12 ch (12)	104.33 ch (12)
1902	106.28 ch (12)	100.89 ch (12)	101.12 ch (12)
1903	104.95 ch (12)	99.90 ch (12)	99.76 ch (12)
1904	105.12 ch (12)	99.93 ch (12)	99.96 ch (12)
1905	104.70 ch (12)	99.83 ch (12)	99.74 ch (12)
1906	103.60 ch (3)	99.88 ch (12)	99.63 ch (12)
1907	104.46 ch (2)	99.82 ch (12)	99.60 ch (12)
1908	104.71 ch (12)	99.91 ch (12)	99.70 ch (12)
1909	105.32 ch (12)	100.37 ch (12)	100.09 ch (11)
1910		100.39 ch (12)	
1911	105.63 ch (12)	100.46 ch (12)	100.18 ch (12)
1912	105.56 ch (12)	100.72 ch (12)	100.52 ch (12)
1913	106.45 ch (12)	101.57 ch (12)	101.23 ch (12)
1914	105.11 ch (5)	100.29 ch (5)	99.77 ch (5)

[a] 'Augsburg current' meant – in modification of Konventionskurant, which became common espe-cially from 1764 (NOBACK [1851], 1. Abth., p. 70) – a standard of coinage of 20 5/12 guilders per

mark of Cologne. So the guilder Augsburg current of 60 kreuzer was equal to 11.45 grammes of fine silver. As a consequence of the Vienna Coin Treaty of 1857 the guilder South German current (standard of coinage: 24½ guilders per 233.855 grammes of fine silver or 52½ guilders per pound of 500 grammes of fine silver) of 60 kreuzer became legal tender in Augsburg from the beginning of 1859.

[b]   Concerning the Austrian currency, see pp. 255f. From June 3rd 1848 the guilder Konventionsku-rant and from November 1858 the guilder Österreichische Währung was paper money in notes of the Wiener Nationalbank and governmental notes ('Wiener Banknoten').

[c]   Between 1822 and 1859 there are quotations only of Milan on Augsburg, which were converted into Genoese and Piedmontese currency respectively. Owing to a lack of sources, Genoa did not quote Augsburg during this time. Its special function as a connector to South Germany, finding its expression in the quotations on Augsburg and Frankfurt (since 1821), had become obsolete for Milan. This process had already started after the defeat of the South Germans near Königgrätz in 1866 and was driven forward by the extinction of families of Italian origin.

[d]   1871 quotation only for Antwerp.

[e]   Concerning the Swiss currency, see p. 313.

[f]   The Belgian franc was introduced in 1832 and it was equal to the French franc (see pp. 279f.).

3.4.3 On Lisbon, Spain and Constantinople

	GENOA on:		
	Lisbon	**Madrid**	**Constantinople**
	per 100 crusados [a]	per 100 ducados de cambio [b]	per 100 piastres [c]
	in pezze of 5¾ lire fuori banco		
1777	52.75 90d/d (4)		
1778	54.16 90d/d (12)		
1779	54.87 90d/d (12)		
1780	54.87 90d/d (12)		
1781	55.60 90d/d (12)		
1782	55.10 90d/d (1)		
1783			
1784			
1785			
1786			
1787			
1788			
1789			
1790			
1791			
1792			
1793			
1794			
1795			
1796	58.32 90d/d (9)	*535.83* 90d/d (9)	
1797	60.61 90d/d (1)	*520.97* 90d/d (1)	
1798	61.40 90d/d (4)		
1799	60.05 90d/d (6)		
1800			
1801	51.56 90d/d (6)		
1802	55.67 90d/d (12)	656.00 90d/d (7)	32.46 31d/s (6)
1803	55.33 90d/d (12)	673.00 90d/d (12)	31.53 31d/s (9)
1804	52.81 90d/d (11)	653.12 90d/d (11)	28.65 31d/s (11)
1805	51.42 90d/d (12)	632.87 90d/d (10)	28.26 31d/s (3)
1806	51.38 90d/d (10)	677.73 90d/d (5)	
1807	54.17 90d/d (12)		
1808	54.77 90d/d (6)		
1809			
1810			
1811			
1812			

	GENOA on:	
	Lisbon	**Barcelona**
	per 100 crusados [a]	per 100 libras of Catalonia [d]
	in pezze of 5¾ lire fuori banco	
1813		
1814	53.51 90d/d (4)	
1815	52.34 90d/d (12)	
1816	51.18 90d/d (12)	
1817	50.84 90d/d (7)	
1818		
1819		
1820		
1821		
1822		
1823		
1824		
1825		
1826		
	in Piedmontese lire nuove	
1827		
1828		
1829		
1830		
1831		
1832		
1833		282.59 1m/d (11)
1834		281.09 1m/d (12)
1835		280.92 1m/d (12)
1836		281.46 1m/d (12)
1837		278.90 1m/d (5)
1838		278.90 1m/d (10)
1839		280.17 1m/d (12)
1840		278.92 1m/d (12)
1841		276.21 1m/d (12)
1842		279.50 1m/d (11)
1843		279.57 1m/d (8)
1844		279.38 1m/d (12)
1845		279.50 1m/d (12)
1846		279.90 1m/d (12)
1847		279.00 1m/d (12)
1848		277.18 1m/d (7)
1849		286.25 1m/d (12)

	GENOA on:		
	Barcelona		
	per 100 libras of Catalonia, from 1863 (11) per 100 pesos duros [d]		
	in Piedmontese lire nuove, from 1861 (8) in Italian lire		
1850	284.67	1m/d	(12)
1851	281.98	1m/d	(12)
1852	281.32	1m/d	(12)
1853	278.48	1m/d	(12)
1854	281.37	1m/d	(11)
1855	281.34	1m/d	(12)
1856	280.67	1m/d	(12)
1857	278.67	1m/d	(12)
1858	277.96	1m/d	(12)
1859	281.07	1m/d	(12)
1860	279.50	1m/d	(12)
1861	278.48	1m/d	(12)
1862	278.75	1m/d	(12)
1863	279.01/520.75	1m/d	(10+2)
1864	517.05	1m/d	(12)
1865	513.21	1m/d	(12)
1866	529.97	1m/d	(10)
1867	553.30	1m/d	(12)
1868	564.82	1m/d	(12)
1869	537.58	1m/d	(12)
1870	539.79	1m/d	(8)
1871	552.06	s	(10)
1872	561.32	s	(12)
1873	583.39	s	(9)
1874	578.61	s	(9)
1875	553.25	s	(11)
1876	553.88	s	(12)
1877	558.69	s	(12)
1878	553.68	s	(12)
1879	552.67	s	(12)
1880	557.17	s	(12)
1881	511.96	s	(12)
1882	503.85	s	(10)
1883	497.00	s	(1)
1884			
1885			

	GENOA on:		
	Barcelona, from 1898 also Madrid		
	per 100 pesos duros [d]		
	in Italian lire		
1886			
1887			
1888	494.83	ch	(7)
1889	489.46	ch	(12)
1890	483.55	ch	(12)
1891	479.55	ch	(12)
1892	450.80	ch	(12)
1893	451.05	ch	(11)
1894	461.25	ch	(12)
1895	462.80	ch	(12)
1896	449.13	ch	(12)
1897	421.50	ch	(2)
1898	364.25	ch	(10)
1899	434.75	ch	(12)
1900	415.59	ch	(12)
1901	382.75	ch	(12)
1902	376.13	ch	(12)
1903	373.34	ch	(12)
1904	365.75	ch	(12)
1905	381.86	ch	(12)
1906	442.02	ch	(12)
1907	452.09	ch	(12)
1908	443.88	ch	(12)
1909	456.21	ch	(12)
1910			
1911	465.50	ch	(12)
1912	474.05	ch	(12)
1913	473.96	ch	(12)
1914	476.85	ch	(5)

[a] In the Portuguese currency system one reckoned in réis and in milréis (= 1,000 réis), but exchange rate quotations of and on Portuguese places often were effected in or for crusados (velhos or do cambio) as a unit of account of 400 réis up to the 19th century (NELKENBRECHER [1771], p. 131).

[b] Concerning the Spanish currency, see p. 313. 1796/97 quotation for ducados de cambio payable in 'vales reales' (paper money).

[c] Concerning the Turkish currency, see pp. 387f.

[d] 1 libra of Catalonia = 10 reales Ardites = 20 sueldos = 240 dineros. 1 doblón de cambio = 5 libras 12 sueldos cataluños; 1 peso de plata antigua = 28 sueldos cataluños; 1 ducado de cambio = 38 sueldos 7 4/17 dineros cataluños; 1,000 pesos duros = 1,875 libras of Catalonia or libras de Ardites (KELLY [1811], p. 41). Concerning the Spanish currency, see p. 313. 1 peso duro = 5 pesetas.

3.4.4 On Italian places (I)

	GENOA on:			
	Milan [a]	**Venice**	**Leghorn**	**Rome**
	per 100 lire corrente, from 1823 per 100 lire austriache [b]	per 100 lire piccole correnti [c]	per 100 pezze da otto reali, from 1822 per 100 Tuscan lire moneta buona [d]	per 100 scudi romani [e]
	in pezze of 5¾ lire fuori banco			
1777		106.67 30d/s (4)	102.58 30d/s (4)	111.01 30d/s (4)
1778	16.65 8d/s (12)	109.28 30d/s (12)		111.83 30d/s (12)
1779	16.47 8d/s (12)	108.77 30d/s (12)		111.92 30d/s (12)
1780	16.50 8d/s (12)	108.82 30d/s (12)		111.38 30d/s (12)
1781	16.41 8d/s (12)	108.03 30d/s (12)		111.44 30d/s (12)
1782	16.54 8d/s (1)	107.64 30d/s (1)		110.87 30d/s (1)
...				
1796		112.16 30d/s (9)	109.81 8d/s (9)	110.18 30d/s (9)
1797		112.37 30d/s (1)	110.65 8d/s (1)	109.50 30d/s (1)
1798	17.09 8d/s (4)	115.09 30d/s (4)		111.36 30d/s (4)
1799	17.17 8d/s (7)	122.07 30d/s (3)		111.23 30d/s (3)
1800				
1801	16.19 8d/s (6)	118.93 30d/s (3)	110.13 30d/s (6)	115.43 30d/s (6)
1802	16.42 8d/s (12)		108.90 30d/s (12)	113.68 30d/s (12)
1803	16.45 8d/s (12)		108.69 30d/s (12)	111.42 30d/s (12)
1804	16.58 8d/s (12)	95.36 30d/s (4)	109.54 30d/s (11)	114.86 30d/s (11)
1805	17.01 8d/s (12)	94.22 30d/s (2)	109.87 30d/s (12)	113.37 30d/s (12)
1806	16.51 8d/s (10)		108.61 30d/s (10)	114.15 30d/s (10)
1807	16.41 8d/s (12)	108.61 30d/s (6)	108.26 30d/s (12)	111.99 30d/s (12)
1808	16.68 8d/s (12)	108.75 30d/s (12)	107.47 30d/s (12)	112.54 30d/s (12)
1809	16.71 8d/s (12)	108.75 30d/s (12)	107.60 30d/s (12)	111.66 30d/s (12)
1810	16.70 8d/s (12)	107.57 30d/s (12)	108.42 30d/s (12)	114.61 30d/s (12)
1811	16.37 8d/s (12)	106.94 30d/s (12)	107.23 30d/s (12)	112.55 30d/s (12)
1812	16.52 8d/s (11)	109.87 30d/s (11)	106.55 30d/s (11)	112.79 30d/s (11)
1813	16.48 8d/s (12)	110.56 30d/s (10)	106.04 30d/s (12)	110.46 30d/s (12)
1814	16.21 8d/s (9)	109.87 30d/s (6)	106.68 30d/s (9)	111.62 30d/s (9)
1815	16.19 8d/s (12)	109.84 30d/s (12)	105.89 30d/s (12)	112.43 30d/s (12)
1816	16.42 8d/s (12)	109.78 30d/s (12)	106.82 30d/s (12)	112.42 30d/s (12)
1817	16.51 8d/s (5)	107.59 30d/s (12)	105.97 30d/s (12)	112.83 30d/s (12)
1818		109.38 30d/s (12)	108.88 30d/s (12)	114.00 30d/s (12)
1819		107.55 30d/s (12)	108.74 30d/s (12)	112.01 30d/s (12)
1820		106.47 30d/s (12)	106.55 30d/s (12)	111.31 30d/s (12)
1821		106.47 30d/s (12)	107.09 30d/s (12)	112.27 30d/s (12)
1822			17.26 30d/s (4)	111.59 30d/s (4)
1823	*18.12* 8d/d (2)		17.33 30d/s (12)	111.35 30d/s (12)

	GENOA on:			
	Milan [a]	**Venice**	**Leghorn**	**Rome**
	per 100 lire austriache [b]	per 100 lire austriache [c]	per 100 Tuscan lire moneta buona [d]	per 100 scudi romani [e]
	in pezze of 5¾ lire fuori banco			
1824	*18.04* 8d/d (12)		17.29 30d/s (12)	110.93 30d/s (12)
1825	*17.94* 8d/d (12)		16.95 30d/s (12)	112.31 30d/s (12)
1826	*17.90* 8d/d (12)		17.03 30d/s (12)	111.48 30d/s (12)
1827	*17.88* 8d/d (2)		17.10 30d/s (2)	
	in Piedmontese lire nuove			
1827	*84.89* 8d/d (10)		83.13 1m/d (10)	524.75 1m/d (12)
1828	*84.68* 8d/d (12)		83.24 1m/d (12)	526.80 1m/d (12)
1829	*85.27* 8d/d (12)		83.16 1m/d (12)	531.71 1m/d (12)
1830	*85.11* 8d/d (12)		83.66 1m/d (12)	531.40 1m/d (12)
1831	*85.43* 8d/d (12)		83.25 1m/d (12)	528.05 1m/d (12)
1832	*85.54* 8d/d (12)		83.71 1m/d (11)	538.87 1m/d (11)
1833	*86.19* 8d/d (12)		83.25 1m/d (12)	540.05 1m/d (12)
1834	*86.36* 8d/d (12)		84.50 1m/d (12)	540.38 1m/d (12)
1835	*86.15* 8d/d (12)		83.66 1m/d (12)	539.25 1m/d (12)
1836	*85.56* 8d/d (12)		84.29 1m/d (12)	541.92 1m/d (12)
1837	*85.46* 8d/d (12)		83.77 1m/d (12)	538.92 1m/d (12)
1838	*85.59* 8d/d (12)		82.91 1m/d (12)	535.13 1m/d (12)
1839	*85.72* 8d/d (12)		84.69 1m/d (12)	541.21 1m/d (12)
1840	85.15 1m/d (12)	84.74 1m/d (12)	84.59 1m/d (12)	543.00 1m/d (12)
1841	86.29 1m/d (12)	85.95 1m/d (12)	85.01 1m/d (12)	539.92 1m/d (12)
1842	87.10 1m/d (12)	86.81 1m/d (12)	85.39 1m/d (12)	542.13 1m/d (12)
1843	86.67 1m/d (12)	86.35 1m/d (12)	84.22 1m/d (12)	538.44 1m/d (12)
1844	86.35 1m/d (12)	86.60 1m/d (12)	84.26 1m/d (12)	537.55 1m/d (12)
1845	86.58 1m/d (12)	86.50 1m/d (12)	84.70 1m/d (12)	539.21 1m/d (12)
1846	85.95 1m/d (12)	85.70 1m/d (12)	85.30 1m/d (12)	539.88 1m/d (12)
1847	85.50 1m/d (12)	85.25 1m/d (12)	84.44 1m/d (12)	537.67 1m/d (12)
1848	84.81 1m/d (8)	84.44 1m/d (3)	82.78 1m/d (10)	528.50 1m/d (6)
1849	85.59 1m/d (11)	85.75 1m/d (1)	83.84 1m/d (12)	497.92 1m/d (6)
1850	85.04 1m/d (12)	84.80 1m/d (2)	84.64 1m/d (12)	486.00 1m/d (7)
1851	85.26 1m/d (12)	85.17 1m/d (3)	83.18 1m/d (12)	516.50 1m/d (12)
1852	84.63 1m/d (12)	84.46 1m/d (11)	83.02 1m/d (12)	506.34 1m/d (12)
1853	84.47 1m/d (12)	84.32 1m/d (12)	84.35 1m/d (12)	518.98 1m/d (12)
1854	84.14 1m/d (12)	84.07 1m/d (12)	83.04 1m/d (12)	501.13 1m/d (12)
1855	85.06 1m/d (12)	84.92 1m/d (12)	84.16 1m/d (12)	527.96 1m/d (12)
1856	85.56 1m/d (12)	85.26 1m/d (12)	85.60 1m/d (12)	528.48 1m/d (12)
1857	85.01 1m/d (12)	84.82 1m/d (12)	85.72 1m/d (12)	527.09 1m/d (12)

	GENOA on:			
	Milan [a]	**Venice**	**Leghorn**	**Rome**
	per 100 lire austriache, from 1858 (11) per 100 Guilders Österreichische Währung [b]	per 100 lire austriache, from 1858 (11) per 100 guilders Österreichische Währung [c]	per 100 Tuscan lire moneta buona [d]	per 100 scudi romani, from 1868 (6) per 100 lire pontificie [e]
	in Piedmontese lire nuove, from 1861 (8) in Italian lire			
1858	85.05/245.50 1m/d (8+2)	84.84/245.50 1m/d (8+2)	85.27 1m/d (12)	531.21 1m/d (12)
1859	247.18 1m/d (9)	246.59 1m/d (6)	84.50 1m/d (12)	530.25 1m/d (12)
1860		246.43 1m/d (12)	83.40 1m/d (7)	526.48 1m/d (12)
1861		246.89 1m/d (8)		529.80 1m/d (12)
1862		246.44 1m/d (12)		527.23 1m/d (12)
1863		246.50 1m/d (12)		526.88 1m/d (12)
1864		246.34 1m/d (12)		522.26 1m/d (12)
1865		245.49 1m/d (12)		506.73 1m/d (12)
1866		245.23 1m/d (5)		482.39 1m/d (11)
1867				522.50 1m/d (10)
1868				562.2/104.21 1m/d (5+7)
1869				100.55 1m/d (12)
1870				101.30 1m/d (8)

[a]   1823–1839: converted exchange rate of Milan on Genoa, because no quotation of Genoa on Milan could be found for these years.

[b]   The Genoese quotations on Milan were given per lire corrente of 20 soldi at 12 denari corrente, whereby 150 lire corrente = 106 lire imperiale (1 scudo imperiale = 117 soldi imperiali) from 1750. On November 1st 1823 the Austrian lira (lira austriaca) of 100 centesimi with 3.897 grammes of fine silver was introduced in Lombardo–Venetia by the so-called 'Münzpatent' and became legal tender just as the guilder Konventionskurant did (see pp. 255f.). This lira was equal to the 20-kreuzer piece (or the third part of the guilder) of the Habsburg Monarchy and therefore used to be called 'la svanzica' or the 'zwanziger'. With the introduction of the new guilder Österreichische Währung in the Habsburg Monarchy, the exceptional monetary position of Lombardo–Venetia was abolished in 1858/59. After the integration of Lombardy into the new Kingdom of Italy, the Piedmontese and the Italian currency system respectively were put in use here (see pp. 108f.).

[c]   Concerning the Venetian currency, see p. 104. On November 1st 1823 the Austrian lira (lira austriaca) of 100 centesimi with 3.897 grammes of fine silver was introduced in Lombardo–Venetia by the so-called 'Münzpatent' and became legal tender just as the guilder Konventionskurant did (see pp. 255f.). This lira was equal to the 20-kreuzer piece (or the third part of the guilder) of the Habsburg Monarchy and therefore used to be called 'la svanzica' or the 'zwanziger'. With the introduction of the new guilder Österreichische Währung in the Habsburg Monarchy the exceptional monetary position of Lombardo–Venetia was abolished in 1858/59. After the integration of the Veneto into the new Kingdom of Italy, the Piedmontese and the Italian currency system respectively were put in use here (see pp. 108f.).

[d]   Concerning the Tuscan currency, see p. 106. Until 1821 including 7% premium for payment in gold.

[e]   The Roman unit of account was the scudo moneta or scudo romano of 10 paoli or 100 baiocchi or 1,000 mezzi quattrini. This scudo was equivalent to 24.23 grammes of fine silver up to 1834 and – after the currency reform of Pope Gregory XVI – to 24.21 grammes of fine silver between 1835

and 1866 (PINCHERA [1957], pp. 1, 4). From 1867 the currency of the Papal States (from 1849 protected by French troops) was the lira pontificia of 20 soldi at 5 centesimi, which was introduced by a papal edict from June 18th 1866 and minted (from August 1866) in agreement with the terms of the treaty of the Latin Monetary Union. Therefore the lira pontificia was equal to the French franc and the Italian lira but the quotations given here are for paper money. After the occupation of the Papal States by the Kingdom of Italy (in September 1870) the division of the lira into 100 centesimi was introduced in 1871 (NOBACK [1877], p. 771; see pp. 108f., 279f.).

3.4.4 On Italian places (II)

	GENOA on:	
	Naples	**Palermo**
	per 100 ducati del regno [a]	per 100 oncie (moneta buona up to 1815) [b]
	in pezze of 5¾ lire fuori banco	
1777	88.59 22d/s (4)	248.76 15d/s (4)
1778	88.93 22d/s (12)	239.18 15d/s (12)
1779	89.57 22d/s (12)	241.70 15d/s (12)
1780	89.95 22d/s (12)	243.90 15d/s (12)
1781	90.26 22d/s (12)	245.72 15d/s (12)
1782	90.65 22d/s (1)	245.79 15d/s (1)
...		
1796	87.44 22d/s (9)	277.90 60d/d (9)
1797	86.09 22d/s (1)	279.10 60d/d (1)
1798		257.53 60d/d (3)
1799		238.83 60d/d (4)
1800		
1801	96.74 22d/s (6)	277.29 60d/d (6)
1802	92.73 22d/s (12)	268.16 60d/d (12)
1803	86.22 22d/s (12)	247.79 60d/d (12)
1804	91.02 22d/s (11)	253.32 60d/d (11)
1805	92.06 22d/s (12)	258.83 60d/d (12)
1806	92.49 22d/s (10)	269.36 60d/d (7)
1807	89.64 22d/s (12)	267.20 60d/d (7)
1808	92.49 22d/s (12)	
1809	89.37 22d/s (11)	
1810	94.54 22d/s (12)	
1811	91.31 22d/s (12)	
1812	90.94 22d/s (11)	
1813	90.96 22d/s (12)	
1814	89.85 22d/s (9)	
1815	89.38 22d/s (12)	258.63 30d/d (12)
1816	89.13 22d/s (12)	262.97 30d/d (12)

	GENOA on:		
	Naples	**Palermo**	**Turin**
	per 100 ducati del regno [a]	per 100 oncie (moneta buona up to 1815), from 1841 per 100 ducati del regno [b]	per 100 Piedmontese lire nuove (from 1827) [c]
	in pezze of 5¾ lire fuori banco		
1817	89.30 22d/s (12)	268.12 30d/d (5)	
1818	92.38 22d/s (12)		
1819	87.75 22d/s (12)		
1820	87.60 22d/s (12)		
1821	90.22 22d/s (12)		
1822	90.72 22d/s (4)		
1823	89.80 22d/s (12)		
1824	87.26 22d/s (12)		
1825	90.28 22d/s (12)		
1826	88.92 22d/s (12)		
	in Piedmontese lire nuove		
1827	412.74 1m/d (12)		99.40 1m/d (12)
1828	419.69 1m/d (12)		99.35 1m/d (12)
1829	427.40 1m/d (12)		99.49 1m/d (12)
1830	427.11 1m/d (12)		99.64 1m/d (12)
1831	422.88 1m/d (12)		99.63 1m/d (10)
1832	436.50 1m/d (11)		99.64 1m/d (11)
1833	432.42 1m/d (12)		99.45 1m/d (12)
1834	435.48 1m/d (12)		99.58 1m/d (11)
1835	435.71 1m/d (12)		99.51 1m/d (12)
1836	435.55 1m/d (12)		99.40 1m/d (12)
1837	429.13 1m/d (12)		99.52 1m/d (12)
1838	423.46 1m/d (12)		99.50 1m/d (12)
1839	431.75 1m/d (12)		99.48 1m/d (12)
1840	435.05 1m/d (12)		99.50 1m/d (12)
1841	427.17 1m/d (12)	434.67 1m/d (12)	99.48 1m/d (12)
1842	434.15 1m/d (12)	424.81 1m/d (12)	99.48 1m/d (12)
1843	429.92 1m/d (12)	431.89 1m/d (12)	99.61 1m/d (12)
1844	424.13 1m/d (12)	428.98 1m/d (12)	99.50 1m/d (12)
1845	433.13 1m/d (12)	423.59 1m/d (12)	99.51 1m/d (12)
1846	433.30 1m/d (12)	431.53 1m/d (12)	99.52 1m/d (12)
1847	435.00 1m/d (12)	432.25 1m/d (12)	99.46 1m/d (12)
1848	424.75 1m/d (6)	432.42 1m/d (5)	99.49 1m/d (9)
1849	443.88 1m/d (12)	427.07 1m/d (9)	99.52 1m/d (12)
1850	441.73 1m/d (12)	440.08 1m/d (12)	99.58 1m/d (12)
1851	435.48 1m/d (12)	441.34 1m/d (12)	99.56 1m/d (12)

	GENOA on:		
	Naples	**Palermo**	**Turin**
	per 100 ducati del regno [a]		per 100 Piedmontese lire nuove [c]
	in Piedmontese lire nuove, from 1861 (8) in Italian lire		
1852	435.25 1m/d (12)	433.98 1m/d (12)	99.58 1m/d (12)
1853	439.25 1m/d (12)	438.12 1m/d (12)	99.53 1m/d (12)
1854	449.42 1m/d (12)	446.20 1m/d (12)	99.50 1m/d (12)
1855	465.36 1m/d (12)	463.89 1m/d (12)	99.50 1m/d (12)
1856	470.02 1m/d (12)	469.42 1m/d (12)	99.49 1m/d (12)
1857	452.69 1m/d (12)	452.20 1m/d (12)	99.37 1m/d (12)
1858	437.46 1m/d (12)	435.75 1m/d (12)	99.52 1m/d (12)
1859	429.17 1m/d (12)	427.66 1m/d (11)	99.60 1m/d (12)
1860	426.23 1m/d (9)	423.23 1m/d (8)	99.55 1m/d (12)
1861	422.34 1m/d (11)	419.00 1m/d (12)	99.43 1m/d (7)
1862	423.80 1m/d (12)	421.14 1m/d (12)	
1863	423.50 1m/d (1)	420,67 1m/d (1)	

[a] The system of accounting in ducati (called 'ducati del regno' or 'ducati di regno' from the 18th century) of 10 carlini at 10 grani or 5 tari at 20 grani had been common practice in the Kingdom of Naples for centuries and was continued during the Restoration era (after the Act of August 18th 1814). The Act of April 20th 1818 fixed the fineness of the ducato at 19.12 grammes of fine silver as it had been when it was officially introduced in 1794 and confirmed in 1804 (from 1784 18.96 grammes of fine silver; cf. NOBACK [1851], pp. 710f.). This new silver ducato – later generally called 'ducato del regno' or 'ducato di regno' – should have been divided into 100 centesimi or grani. Simultaneously, it became the unit of account of the whole Kingdom of the Two Sicilies which means that the hitherto independent Sicilian system basing on the oncia (56.896 grammes fine silver) of 30 tari (or carlini; 1 oncia = 3 ducati) at 20 grani was removed by this Act. With the integration of the Kingdom of the Two Sicilies into the new Kingdom of Italy in 1862, the Italian lira of 100 centesimi became the currency and accounting unit in Naples.

[b] The old Sicilian unit of account was the oncia of 30 tari (at 20 grani) or 60 carlini (at 10 grani), which was equal to 3 ducati del regno from 1815. When selling Sicilian bills at Genoa up to 1815 one usually reckoned 61 Sicilian carlini for 60 carlini moneta buona (= 1 oncia = 3 ducati del regno), i.e. the buyer of the bill was refunded 1 carlino per oncia 'a titolo di moneta buona' (cf. NEL-KENBRECHER [1798], p. 103). By the means of the Act of April 20th 1818 (see [a]) the new (Neapolitan) silver ducato – later generally called 'ducato del regno' or 'ducato di regno' – became the unit of account of the whole Kingdom of the Two Sicilies which means that the hitherto independent Sicilian system basing on the oncia at 56.896 grammes of fine silver was removed by this Act.

[c] Concerning the Piedmontese currency, see p. 108.

3.5 Naples exchange rates

3.5.1 On Saint Petersburg

	NAPLES on:				**NAPLES on:**		
	Saint Petersburg				**Saint Petersburg**		
	per 100 silver roubles, from 1843 (11) in credit notes [a]				per 100 silver roubles in credit notes [a]		
	in ducati del regno [b]				**in ducati del regno, from 1862 in Italian lire** [b]		
1840	90.77	80d/d	(6)	1859	85.77	80d/d	(12)
1841	92.06	80d/d	(12)	1860	87.09	80d/d	(12)
1842	90.35	80d/d	(12)	1861	87.50	80d/d	(12)
1843	90.27	80d/d	(12)	1862	351.25	80d/d	(12)
1844	90.99	80d/d	(12)	1863	370.00	80d/d	(9)
1845	91.04	80d/d	(12)	1864	370.00	80d/d	(12)
1846	90.34	80d/d	(12)	1865	336.67	80d/d	(12)
1847	90.30	80d/d	(12)	1866	330.00	80d/d	(12)
1848	90.72	80d/d	(12)	1867	330.00	80d/d	(12)
1849	88.25	80d/d	(12)	1868	339.17	80d/d	(12)
1850	89.92	80d/d	(12)	1869	327.50	80d/d	(12)
1851	88.25	80d/d	(12)	1870	315.34	80d/d	(12)
1852	88.00	80d/d	(12)	1871	307.17	80d/d	(12)
1853	87.84	80d/d	(12)	1872	360.67	80d/d	(12)
1854	85.42	80d/d	(12)	1873	374.34	80d/d	(12)
1855	82.46	80d/d	(12)	1874	375.00	80d/d	(12)
1856	76.67	80d/d	(12)	1875	375.00	80d/d	(11)
1857	86.50	80d/d	(12)	1876	358.00	80d/d	(12)
1858	83.50	80d/d	(12)				

[a]   Concerning the Russian currency, see pp. 359f.

[b]   The system of accounting in ducati (called 'ducati del regno' or 'ducati di regno' since the 18th century) of 10 carlini at 10 grani or 5 tari at 20 grani had been common practice in the Kingdom of Naples for centuries and was continued during the Restoration era (after the Act of August 18th 1814). The Act of April 20th 1818 fixed the fineness of the ducato at 19.12 grammes of fine silver, as it had been when it was officially introduced in 1794 and confirmed in 1804 (from 1784 18.96 grammes of fine silver; cf. NOBACK [1851], pp. 710f.). This new silver ducato – later generally called 'ducato del regno' or 'ducato di regno' – should have been divided into 100 centesimi or grani. Simultaneously, it became the unit of account of the whole Kingdom of the Two Sicilies which means that the hitherto independent Sicilian system basing on the oncia (56.896 grammes fine silver) of 30 tari (or carlini; 1 oncia = 3 ducati) at 20 grani was removed by this Act. With the integration of the Kingdom of the Two Sicilies into the new Kingdom of Italy in 1862, the Italian lira of 100 centesimi became the currency and accounting unit in Naples.

4
Germany (1657–1914)

Exchange market: Hamburg (1657–1873)

Sources: McCusker [1978], pp. 73f. (1657–1697); Roseveare (ed.) [1987], pp. 596–607 (1668–1680); IISG Amsterdam, *Prys-Courant*, Hamburg (1672); StA Hamburg, 111–1 Cl. VII Lit. Cb Nr. 4, vol. 9, Fasc. 28 (1687–1730); OBA Clausthal, *Lüneburg – Salz Sachen, Saltz-Preiß 1, Prys-Courant*, Hamburg (1689–1693); PRO London, XP 1211 C 104/128 Pt 2, *Prys-Courant*, Hamburg (1696–1698); CB Hamburg, S/653: *Wechsel-Cours in Hamburg (Amtliche Geld- und Wechselkurse* T. 1,2, Hamburg 1710–1913, T. 1: *Amtliche Kurse für Wechsel*, 1710–1724, 1781–1814); ibid., S/916, Bd. 2: *Geld- und Wechsel-Course.* 1721–1737 (1726–1735); ibid., 456/1 *Preiscourant der Wahren in Partheyen* (1737–1780); *Hamburger Privilegierte Liste der Börsenhalle* (1815–1874); *Hamburger Correspondent* (1834–1838).

Concordance: *WdW VI*, pp. 193–222; *HStD XII*, pp. 147–191, 279f.; *WdW I/III*, pp. 301–337; *HStD XI*, pp. 137–191

Currency: Until February 1873, when the mark 'Reichswährung' as new standard currency of the German Empire became the basis of the Hamburg exchange rate quotations, the exchange rates in Hamburg were fixed in or for mark banco, rixdollars (in the 19th century 'dollars' or 'thaler') banco, exchange dollars (the so-called 'Wechseltaler') or their sub-units. In particular, the different Hamburg units of account, among which the mark banco was by far the most important (so that as a basic unit it is used for documenting the rate series), were connected in the following way:

The Hamburg currency system between the 17th and the 19th centuries:

1 rixdollar = 1½ exchange dollars = 3 mark (banco) =	8 sh. Flem. =	48 sh. Lub. =	96 d. Flem.
1 exchange dollar = 2 mark (banco) =	5 1/3 sh. Flem. =	32 sh. Lub. =	64 d. Flem.
1 mark (banco) =	2 2/3 sh. Flem. =	16 sh. Lub. =	32 d. Flem.
	1 sh. Flem. =	6 sh. Lub. =	12 d. Flem.
		1 sh. Lub. =	2 d. Flem.

sh. = shilling   d. = pence or groot   Flem. = Flemish   Lub. = Lubish

The Hamburg bank money was the never-minted currency of account of the Hamburg banco, which was established in 1619 under the influence of Dutch merchants to stabilize the Hamburg currency and exchange. This bank money was based on the rixdollar or speciesthaler of 1566 at 25.98 grammes of fine silver: therefore the standard of coinage was *de jure* 9 rixdollar or – in Hamburg – 27 mark banco per mark of Cologne, but *de facto* 9 5/24 rixdollars or 27 5/8 mark banco per mark of Cologne (Rittmann [1975], pp. 428f.). When Hamburg began to mint new coins according to the new Zinna standard of coinage (of 1667; 10½ rixdollars per mark of Cologne) in 1669, the city now had two different currencies: the 'banco', based on the speciesthaler, and the 'courant' as the city's real means of payment, which was quoted with a significant discount against the banco. In the following decades this current money levelled off at a standard of coinage of 34 mark or 11 1/3 rixdollars per mark of Cologne (therefore 1 mark current was equival to 8.43 grammes of fine silver), and Lübeck, Holstein,

Annual average discount of the Hamburg current money against bank money (in per cent)

1710	16.75	1758	7.67	1796	18.02	1836	19.96
1711	16.71	1759	7.97	1797	19.49	1837	19.89
1712	16.57	1760	17.62	1798	20.74	1838	19.64
1713	17.23	1761	24.72	1799	22.58	1839	19.17
1714	18.23	1762	22.43	1800	20.98	1840	18.89
1715	19.62	1763	23.70	1801	21.09	1841	19.37
1716	20.89	1764	26.13	1802	22.87	1842	20.02
1717	24.84	1765	21.85	1803	23.13	1843	20.36
1718	27.61	1766	20.06	1804	22.94	1844	19.69
1719	29.45	1767	17.76	1805	23.27	1845	19.46
1720	27.71	1768	22.18	1806	23.64	1846	19.44
1721	28.79	1769	24.77	1807	23.14	1847	19.55
1722	19.42	1770	24.28	1808	21.88	1848	19.95
1723	30.33	1771	24.69	1809	23.50	1849	20.27
1724	31.49	1772	25.07	1810	22.86	1850	20.60
1725	33.01	1773	24.69	1811	24.00	1851	20.46
1726	-----	1774	23.92	1812–1814	[a]	1852	20.98
1727–1737	16.00	1775	22.75	1815	20.18	1853	20.70
1738	16.30	1776	22.38	1816	20.14	1854	19.64
1739	17.46	1777	22.20	1817	18.66	1855	19.59
1740	17.93	1778	20.50	1818	19.53	1856	21.26
1741	17.50	1779	21.35	1819	19.19	1857	20.83
1742	17.76	1780	21.71	1820	19.86	1858	20.42
1743	18.77	1781	21.99	1821	20.22	1859	20.21
1744	19.35	1782	22.42	1822	19.90	1860	20.07
1745	19.97	1783	23.05	1823	20.11	1861	20.15
1746	18.66	1784	22.86	1824	19.96	1862	20.72
1747	16.65	1785	23.43	1825	18.87	1863	20.66
1748	16.18	1786	24.29	1826	19.81	1864	20.60
1749	17.06	1787	24.76	1827	19.48	1865	20.85
1750	17.46	1788	22.13	1828	19.54	1866	20.65
1751	17.74	1789	20.94	1829	19.50	1867	20.57
1752	16.42	1790	22.29	1830	20.41	1868	20.56
1753	17.31	1791	22.71	1831	20.74	1869	20.46
1754	17.30	1792	22.01	1832	20.60	1870	20.33
1755	17.54	1793	22.00	1833	20.32	1871	19.89
1756	17.44	1794	20.81	1834	20.20	1872	19.55
1757	11.89	1795	19.54	1835	20.18	1873 [b]	18.94

[a]   No data available

[b]   Quotations only for January and February

Source: *HStD XII*, pp. 192–195; *HStD XI*, pp. 99–101

Mecklenburg and Denmark followed this standard of coinage as well in 1693. So the difference between the two currencies and the two standards of coinage represented 16 2/3%. From 1695, Hamburg renounced the minting of its own current money, using the coins of its neighbours circulating in the town as current money. But when in 1710 Denmark put in circulation small coins of less than their own value in a standard of coinage of 40 mark per mark of Cologne, from 1717 at the latest the ratio of Hamburg bank to Hamburg current money was severely disturbed. During the following Hamburg–Danish currency conflict (1717–1736), Hamburg tried to establish its own stable current money at a – now official – standard of coinage of 34 mark per mark of Cologne with a fixed relation of 116 rixdollars current = 100 rixdollars banco (the so-called 'species-banco') from 1725/26. When Denmark reacted with a trade and currency embargo against Hamburg, Hamburg's economy was so severely affected that according to a settlement of April 28th 1736 the city had to remove all legal provisions that were an obstacle to the free circulation of Danish current money – especially the fixed premium of current money against species-banco (1737) – whereas Denmark committed itself to keeping the standard of coinage of 34 mark per mark of Cologne. Nevertheless, the Hamburg bank currency was from then on regarded as one of the most stable currencies on the European continent, in particular when in 1771 – last but not least as a reaction to the financial crises of 1755 and 1763 – the banco also accepted silver bars (from 1770; from July 8th 1790 exclusively) and the exclusive silver standard was introduced. Stabilized this way, the Hamburg Bank money survived the crises of the Napoleonic era. It was not until July 1st 1856 that Hamburg superseded the standard of coinage of 34 mark per mark of Cologne for its current money with the (Prussian and North German) standard of coinage of 14 thaler per mark of Cologne (see p. 197). This was the result of the increasing quantity of Prussian thaler in the Hamburg coin circulation after 1815 (1 thaler = 2½ mark current = 40 shillings Lubish current), which led to a *de facto* standard of coinage of 35 mark per mark of Cologne, and this standard of coinage was officially accepted in 1856. Nevertheless, the bank money furthermore served as the basis for the Hamburg payment transactions until the *de facto* introduction of the mark Reichswährung (see p. 197) on February 15th/16th 1873, whereby 100 mark banco were equal to 150 mark Reichswährung. Officially the Reichswährung was introduced by a decree of the Senate of July 25th 1874 with effect from January 1st 1875, whereby 100 mark current were equal to 120 mark Reichswährung. In consequence, the Hamburg Bank was closed on December 31st 1875.

Original quotations at Hamburg

on:	in:	per:
Amsterdam	stivers Flemish banco	1 exchange dollar
from 1816 (10)	Dutch guilders	40 mark banco
Antwerp	Dutch rixdollars	100 rixdollars or 300 mark banco
from 1828	stivers Flemish banco	1 exchange dollar
from 1852	Belgian francs	100 mark banco
Augsburg	guilders Augsburg current	200 mark banco
from 1859	guilders South German current	100 mark banco
Basle	shillings Lubish banco	1 écu of 3 livres tournois or 3 francs
Berlin	thaler Prussian current	300 mark banco
Breslau	rixdollars in Kaisergeld	100 rixdollars or 300 mark banco
from 1776	shillings Lubish banco	1 livre Prussian banco
from 1826	thaler Prussian current	300 mark banco
Cadiz	pence (groot) Flemish banco	1 ducado de cambio of 375 maravédis
Copenhagen	per cent premium on rixdollars Danish current	100 rixdollars or 300 mark banco
from 1813	rigsbankdaler	100 rixdollars or 300 mark banco
from 1854 (3)	rixdollar rigsmønt	100 rixdollars or 300 mark banco
Danzig	(per cent premium on) rixdollars (Polish) current	100 rixdollars or 300 mark banco
Frankfurt	guilders Frankfurt exchange money	200 mark banco
from 1843	guilders South German current	100 mark banco
Genoa	pence (groot) Flemish banco	1 pezza of 5¾ lire fuori di banco
from 1827 (5)	Piedmontese lire nuove	100 mark banco
from 1861 (8)	Italian lire	100 mark banco
Leghorn	pence (groot) Flemish banco	1 pezza da otto reali
from 1839	Tuscan lire moneta buona	100 mark banco
from 1861 (1)	Piedmontese lire nuove	100 mark banco
from 1861 (8)	Italian lire	100 mark banco
Leipzig	(% premium on) rixdollars Leipzig exchange money	100 rixdollars or 300 mark banco
from 1841	thaler Saxon current	100 mark banco

on:	in:	per:
Lisbon	pence (groot) Flemish banco	1 crusado of 400 réis
from 1829	shillings Lubish banco	1 milrée
London	shillings and pence Flemish banco	1 pound sterling
or	mark banco	1 pound sterling
Madrid	pence (groot) Flemish banco	1 ducado de cambio of 375 maravédis
from 1847	shillings Lubish banco	1 peso duro
Nuremberg	(% premium on) rixdollars current	100 rixdollars or 300 mark banco
Paris	shillings Lubish banco	1 écu of 3 livres tournois or 3 francs
or	francs	100 mark banco
Saint Petersburg	shillings Lubish banco	1 banco rouble
from 1839 (9)	shillings Lubish banco	1 silver rouble
Vienna	rixdollars current	100 rixdollars or 300 mark banco
from 1754	rixdollars Konventionskurant	100 rixdollars or 300 mark banco
or	guilders Konventionskurant	200 mark banco
from 1800	guilders Wiener Währung	200 mark banco
from 1816	rixdollars Konventionskurant	100 rixdollars or 300 mark banco
or	guilders Konventionskurant	200 mark banco
from 1858 (11)	guilders Österreichische Währung	100 mark banco
Venice	pence (groot) Flemish banco	1 ducato di banco

Other data available: Amsterdam, ss (in current money, 1710–1814), 2m/d (in bank money, 1764–1813; in current money 1764–1865); 3m/d (1866–1873) – Antwerp, 3m/d (1866–1873) – Augsburg, 33d/d (1712–1714, 1737–1755) – Austrian bank places, 3m/d (1869–1873) – Basle, ss (1796–1800, 1810/12) – Bilbao, 3m/d (1776/77, 1781/82, 1814/15, 1820, 1825–1868) – Bordeaux, 2m/d (1724/39–1848); 3m/d (1849–1873); 1m/d (1737/38) – Bremen, 2m/d (1859–1868); 3m/d (1869–1873) – Breslau, 6w/d (1836–1842); 2m/d (1843–1868) – Cadiz, 2m/d (1737–1775); 3m/d (1776–1806, 1814–1873) – Copenhagen, ss (1768–1802, 1810–1814); 2m/d (1764–1767) – Danzig (1717) – French bank places (1869–1873) – Leipzig, fairs (1827–1839/41) – London, ss (1801–1806/13); 2m/d (1817–1849); 3m/d (1850–1873) – Naumburg, fair (1710–1723) – Paris, 1m/d (1721–1724/26, 1737–1748); 2m/d (1832–1849); 3m/d (1850–1873) – Oporto, 3m/d (1799–1808, 1814–1873) – Prague, 4w/d (1721, 1741/45–1766); 6w/d (1767–1842); 2m/d (1843–1868) – Prussian bank places, 3m/d (1869–1873) – Saxon bank places, 3m/d (1869–1873) – Trieste, 6w/d (1828–1842); 2m/d (1843–1868).

Exchange market: Leipzig (1766–1815)

Sources: StadtA Leipzig, Tit. XLV G, Nr. 118/1-5: *Anzeigebuch derer wöchentlichen Cours-zettel von E.E. und Hochweisen Rath der Stadt Leipzig verpflichteten Sensalen* (1766–1815).
Concordance: *WdW X*, pp. 27–55, 99

Currency: At Leipzig thehange rate quotations were effected in rixdollars (reichstaler) Leipzig exchange money or – meaning the same – in rixdollars 'Konventions-Wechselzahlung' of 24 (good) groschen. This term indicates that since May 14th 1763 the Saxon currency was minted according to the standard of coinage of the Bavarian–Austrian Münzkonvention of 1753 (see p. 255), the so-called 'Konventionsfuß', which was a standard of coinage of 13 1/3 rixdollars per mark of Cologne (RITT-MANN [1975], pp. 344–347). According to the Dresden Münzkonvention of July 30th 1838, this currency was superseded by the thaler Saxon current of 30 groschen (neugroschen; standard of coinage of 14 thaler per mark of Cologne), which was introduced from the beginning of 1841 and which was *de facto* equal to the thaler Prussian current (see p. 197). Finally, from the beginning of 1875 the exchange rates were quoted in or for mark Reichswährung.

Original quotations at Leipzig

on:	in:	per:
Amsterdam	rixdollars Leipzig exchange money	100 rixdollars Flemish current
Augsburg	rixdollars Leipzig exchange money	100 rixdollars Augsburg current
Hamburg	rixdollars Leipzig exchange money	100 rixdollars banco
London	rixdollars and groschen Leipzig exchange money	1 pound sterling
Paris	rixdollars Leipzig exchange money	100 écus of 3 livres tournois or 3 francs
Vienna	rixdollars Leipzig exchange money	100 rixdollars Konventionskurant

Other data available: Amsterdam, 14d/d in banco (1766–1794); 14d/d in current (1818–1823) – Lyons, fairs (1766–1801); 2m/d (1801–1815) – Prague, 14d/d (1766–1815).

Exchange market: Frankfurt am Main (1814–1874)

Sources: NELKENBRECHER [1820], p. 104 (1814); *Hamburger Privilegierte Liste der Börsenhalle* (1815–1825); *Frankfurter Journal* (1815); *Journal de Francfort* (1816–1823); *Frankfurter Ober-Postamts-Zeitung* (1817–1851); *Frankfurter Postzeitung* (1852–1866); *Neue Frankfurter Zeitung* (1865/66); *Frankfurter Zeitung* (1866–1874).

Concordance: *HStD XI*, pp. 237–290

Currency: Until 1842 the fixing of rates was done in guilders exchange money (= 2/3 rixdollar) of 15 batzen or 60 kreuzer. Exchanges in Frankfurt already had to be made with exactly fixed money (thalers and ducats), the so-called 'Wechselzahlung', for which the carolin – a gold coin established in 1732 – was the basis from 1736. In order to maintain close contact with the South German territories and the Habsburg Monarchy with regard to monetary policy, the 'Konventionsfuß' (standard of coinage of 20 guilders per mark of Cologne; see p. 255) was introduced in Frankfurt in 1766 as a currency of account obligatory for all official and exchange transfers, i.e. as exchange money, whereas the standard of coinage of 24 guilders per mark of Cologne was permitted for the trade in goods. In addition – on the basis of the valuation of the carolin – there was from 1766 until 1842 the fixed relation of 11 guilders in the standard of coinage of 24 guilders (later on actually 24½ guilders) per mark of Cologne (the so-called 'Warenzahlung' or 'Münze') = 9 1/5 guilders exchange money in the standard of coinage of 20 guilders per mark of Cologne (the so-called 'Wechselzahlung' or 'Wechselgeld') or 46 guilders exchange money = 55 guilders in the standard of 24 guilders per mark of Cologne. However, from the end of the 18th century the Cologne mark fine silver was calculated at 20 27/55 guilders exchange money (RITTMANN [1975], pp. 344f.).

With the beginning of the currency standardization in the German Zollverein (Munich Coin Treaty of August 15th 1837, Dresden Coin Treaty of July 30th 1838), the exchange money was abolished in Frankfurt at the end of 1842 and the guilder South German current of 60 kreuzer became the only currency used for all exchange rate quotations from the beginning of 1843. The standard of coinage of this guilder South German current was 24½ guilders per mark of Cologne of 233.855 grammes of fine silver or – in terms of the Vienna Treaty of 24th January 1857 – 52½ guilders per pound of 500 grammes of fine silver. Despite being able to uphold its guilder currency until the end of 1874, Frankfurt had already been dominated by the Prussian thaler currency for a long time before the town was annexed by Prussia in 1866 (cf. HOLTFRERICH [1999], p. 142). With the beginning of the year 1875 it was introduced to quote at Frankfurt in the new mark Reichswährung (see p. 197).

Original quotations at Frankfurt am Main

on:	in:	per:
Amsterdam	rixdollars exchange money	250 Dutch guilders
from 1843	guilders South German current	100 Dutch guilders
Augsburg	rixdollars exchange money	150 guilders Augsburg current
from 1843	guilders South German current	100 guilders Augsburg current
from 1859	guilders South German current	100 guilders South German current in Augsburg
Berlin	thaler Prussian current	100 rixdollars exchange money
from 1843	guilders South German current	60 thaler Prussian current
Hamburg	rixdollars exchange money	300 mark banco
from 1843	guilders South German current	100 mark banco
from 1873 (3)	guilders South German current	100 mark
London	batzen exchange money	1 pound sterling
from 1843	guilders South German current	10 pounds sterling
Milan	rixdollars exchange money	300 lire austriache
from 1843	guilders South German current	250 lire austriache
from 1858 (11)	guilders South German current	100 guilders Österreichische Währung
from 1860	guilders South German current	100 Piedmontese lire nuove
from 1861 (8)	guilders South German current	100 Italian lire
Paris	rixdollars exchange money	300 francs
from 1843	guilders South German current	200 francs
Vienna	rixdollars exchange money	150 guilders Konventionskurant
from 1843	guilders South German current	100 guilders Konventionskurant
from 1858 (11)	guilders South German current	100 guilders Österreichische Währung

Other data available: – Amsterdam, 2m/d (1815–1851); ls (1865–1874) Augsburg, 2m/d (1816–1818) – Bremen, ls (1866–1872) – Cologne, ss (1853–1874) – Hamburg, 2m/d (1815–1851); ls (1865–1872) – Leipzig, fair (1815–1847) – London, 2m/d (1836–1845); 3m/d (1846–1853); ls (1865–1874) – Munich, ss (1860–1874) – Nuremberg, ss (1817–1822) – Paris, 2m/d (1815–1840/47); 3m/d (1841–1848); ls (1865–1874) – Vienna, 2m/d (1815–1822, 1833–1835, 1866–1874); 3m/d (1836–1874).

Exchange market: Berlin (1813–1914)

Sources: *Berlinische Nachrichten von Staats- und Gelehrten Sachen* (1813–1856, 1866–1872); *Königlich privilegierte Berlinische Zeitung / Vossische Zeitung* (1857/58); *Vossische Zeitung* (1859–1865, 1874–1914); *Spenersche Zeitung* [Berlin] (1872–1874). Danzig: Wojewodzkie Archiwum Państowe w Gdańsku – Biblioteka Gdańska Polskíej Akademii Nauk, *Acta der Ältesten der Kaufmannschaft zu Danzig betreffend die Coursberichte* (1829–1855). Bremen: *Weser-Zeitung* [Bremen] (1843–1886).

Concordance: *WdW I/III*, pp. 339–379; *HStD XI*, pp. 310–351, 631–651; *HStD XI*, pp. 279f.; *WdW XI*, pp. 126f., 155

Currency: In Prussia the exchange rates were quoted in or for thaler Prussian current of 24 (good) groschen or 288 pfennig, whereby a standard of coinage of 14 thalers per Prussian mark of fine silver

– the so-called 'Graumannsche Münzfuß' (named after the Prussian general director of the mint Johann Philipp Graumann) – came *de facto* into force in 1750 and *de jure* on March 29th 1764. The currency of Prussia was in fact a bimetallic one, with the thaler as standard unit of currency in silver (16.67 grammes of fine silver) and the friedrichsd'or as standard unit of currency in gold (6.032 grammes of fine gold), whereby the ratio of both standard units fluctuated (cf. *HStD XI*, pp. 301–303). From 1826 on it was common practice to divide the thaler Prussian current into 30 silver-groschen or 360 pfennige (Coin Act of September 30th 1821 and Royal Cabinet Order of October 25th 1825). From 1830/31 the friedrichsd'or was fixed, with 5 2/3 thaler current for all public payments, whose rate became generally accepted for private transactions as well – this was the first step towards the silver standard.

From the 1830s the Prussian currency turned increasingly into a silver currency, although the bimetallic standard was officially introduced in 1842. The reason for this was that from the 1840s the value of gold had dropped, so that the friedrichsd'ors went out of circulation and were hoarded only by the treasury, which stabilized its rate by diminishing its circulation. From the mid-19th century the circulation of gold coins was so unimportant that the Prussian currency became a real silver currency (SPRENGER [1981], pp. 20–22). From the 1830s, but above all after the Dresden Coin Treaty of July 30th 1838, the Prussian standard of coinage was gradually adopted by the states of Northern Germany (with the exception of the city states Hamburg, Bremen and Lübeck as well as the Danish Schleswig–Holstein), so that it is actually a North German currency we are dealing with. Thereby, the thaler Prussian or North German current corresponded to 1.75 guilders South German current. By means of the Vienna Coin Treaty of January 24th 1857, which enacted the predominance of the Prussian/North German thaler currency over the South German states with the guilder currency within the area of the German Zollverein, this standard of coinage was changed only slightly (henceforth 30 so-called 'vereinsthaler' per pound of 500 grammes of fine silver; introduction in Prussia by means of the Coin Act of May 4th 1857).

Currency of the German Empire after 1871: After the foundation of the German Empire in 1871, a reform of the German monetary system started that lasted several years and that meant – following the example of Great Britain – the transition of the German states from the silver to the gold standard. First there was the Act concerning the minting of imperial gold coins from December 4th 1871, which fixed the mark 'Reichswährung' at 100 pfennige with 0.3584 grammes of fine gold. The term 'mark' for the new monetary unit was chosen out of respect for Hamburg and Lübeck and their mark standard, which had existed for centuries and had been stable for more than one and a half centuries (RITTMANN [1975], p. 767). The Act of July 9th 1873 garanteed the legal basis for the gold currency and annulled the old national currencies in favour of the new Reichswährung, which was officially introduced at the beginning of 1876 (Imperial Order of September 22th 1875), defining 1 thaler Prussian/North German current as equal to 3 mark Reichswährung and 1 guilder South German current equal to 1.71 mark Reichswährung. In Prussia the quoting of the exchange rates in thaler Prussian current was replaced by that in mark Reichswährung at the beginning of 1875. Since the old thalers (at the standard of the Vienna Coin Treaty, by which old thalers of the 14-thaler standard were declared to coins of the new 30-thaler standard) continued to circulate for some more decades, Germany had a limping gold standard until all thalers were withdrawn from circulation on October 1st 1907.

Note: The term 'Reichsmark' must be avoided during this time. It became the official name of the German currency in 1924, after the great inflation in the early 1920s.

Original quotations at Berlin (until 1874)

on:	in:	per:
Amsterdam	thaler Prussian current	250 Dutch guilders
Augsburg	thaler Prussian current	150 guilders Augsburg current
	from 1843 thaler Prussian current	100 guilders South German current
Frankfurt	thaler Prussian current	150 rixdollars Frankfurt exchange money
	from 1843 thaler Prussian current	100 guilders South German current
Hamburg	thaler Prussian current	300 mark banco

on:	in:	per:
Leipzig	thaler Prussian current	100 rixdollars Leipzig exchange money
	from 1841 thaler Prussian current	100 thaler Saxon current
London	thaler Prussian current	1 pound sterling
Paris	thaler Prussian current	300 francs
Saint Petersburg	thaler Prussian current	1 silver rouble
Vienna	thaler Prussian current	150 guilders Wiener Währung
	from 1820 thaler Prussian current	150 guilders Konventionskurant
	from 1859 thaler Prussian current	100 guilders Österreichische Währung
Warsaw	thaler Prussian current	600 guilders Polish current
	from 1860 thaler Prussian current	1 silver rouble

From 1875 all exchange rates were effected in mark Reichswährung per 1 (on London) or 100 units of foreign currency.

Other data available: Amsterdam, 2m/d (1813–1909/13) – Bremen, ss (1858–1872); 3m/d (1870–1872) – Breslau, 2m/d (1820–1855); ss (1830–1845) – Brussels and Antwerp, 2m/d (1875–1914) – Hamburg, 2m/d (1813–1872) – Leipzig, fair (1826/27); 14d/d (1828–1832); 2m/d (1843–1870) – London, 3m/d (1813–1914); 8d/d (1874/75) – Madrid, 60d/d (1886–1899) – Paris, 2m/d (1813–1914); 10d/d (1870–1874); 8d/d (1875) – Saint Petersburg, 3m/d (1875–1913) – Vienna, 2m/d (1859–1875).

In Germany, i.e. in the area of the Holy Roman Empire, of the future Deutschen Bund and, from 1871, of the German Empire respectively, there were relatively many exchange places of very varying international importance. There were great international financial markets like Hamburg in the North, Frankfurt am Main with its fairs and Augsburg in the South of Germany. According to the quotations in contemporary merchant manuals, Augsburg was the most important place for contacts of Southern Germany to Italy and Switzerland, whereas Frankfurt was much more geared to Northwestern Europe (FASSL [1988], p. 125; KAUFHOLD [1992], p. 108; DENZEL [1996], pp. 80–88). Vienna as the financial centre of Austria–Hungary can also be included within the German area up to 1866, but from the 18th century it was increasingly geared to South East Europe (see Chapter 5). Leipzig with its fairs and, finally, Breslau were of international importance as well, even though Breslau was significant for the Eastern part of Central Europe until it was replaced by Berlin from the beginning of the 19th century. Cologne in the Rhineland, with its traditionally close contact to Northwestern Europe, Bremen as the central cotton market and emigrant port in the 19th century, and Danzig and Königsberg within the Baltic area were still of some national relevance, whereas Nuremberg (by the middle of the 18th century; DENZEL [2002]), the fairs of Brunswick (DENZEL [1998b], pp. 87f.) and Naumburg, Altona (DENZEL [1998a]), Stuttgart, Emden, Stettin, Rostock, Stralsund, Lübeck and other towns were only of regional or local relevance. In the 19th century, also, new industrial towns became locally important exchange places – for example Barmen and Elberfeld – and Munich took the place of the traditionally much more important Augsburg in around 1870 (cf. GÖMMEL [1992], p. 188). Nevertheless, all these later developments had no far-reaching consequences, because together with the foundation of the German Empire, the official introduction of the mark at 100 pfennige as currency of the whole German Empire and the establishing of the Reichsbank as the central bank (on

January 1st 1876), the structures of finance and payment transactions concentrated on Berlin as the political and economic centre of the Empire.

During early modern times as well as for large parts of the 19th century, Hamburg as the most important German exchange place and seaport had also been the central money and exchange market, and also kept the greatest number of international quotations among all German exchange markets (cf. KAUFHOLD [1992], pp. 112f.). The data series available for Hamburg is the most back-reaching in German history: whereas some few exchange rate currents are at most available for Augsburg, Frankfurt am Main, Berlin or Breslau and regular quotations for Leipzig only from 1766, relatively regular data series for quotations of Hamburg began as early as in the second half of the 17th century; some single exchange rate currents even date from the 16th century (cf. EHRENBERG [1884]). For the period between 1668 and 1680, quotations from the *Marescoe–David Letters* are available, namely those on Amsterdam, London, Paris and Venice, occasionally even on Antwerp and Rouen (ROSEVEARE [ed.] [1987], pp. 596–607). The quotations 'officially' start with handwritten or printed exchange rate currents respectively of privileged brokers or publishers in 1710, and with the *Preis Courant der Wahren in Partheÿen*, the official publication of the Hamburg Kommerzdeputation from February 10th/24th 1735. This price current was published twice a week, namely on the ordinary post-days and, from 1781, on Tuesdays and Fridays. From 1790 it was decided to quote the minimum and the maximum rate of a certain foreign exchange market if the transactions were maintained at different rates (BAASCH [1905/06], pp. 8f.). With the exception of the Napoleonic era (1806–1814), the quotations of Hamburg can be documented in full from that time.

The rise of Hamburg as an international centre of exchange business began in the late 16th century, as Dutch merchants as well as Sephardic Jews from Portugal immigrated to Hamburg and brought not only their financial capital, but also their knowledge about financial innovations, to Hamburg. Then, Hamburg owed its great importance within the international cashless payment system in the 18th century first, to the Girobank, founded in 1619 following the model of the Wisselbank of Amsterdam, via which all exchange transactions amounting to more than 400 mark Lubish current had to be conducted; second, to its bank money stable from 1726/36 (cf. REISS [1986], pp. 171–173); and – as a result of this – to its increasing capability to grant long-term credits. Therefore "Hamburg occupied a place in European finance similar to that of Amsterdam, in that merchants and brokers in the city served as the intermediaries in exchange transactions between the Mediterranean, the Atlantic, and the Baltic" (MCCUSKER [1978], p. 61). The increase of the trade, above all with the Iberian Peninsula but also with the French Atlantic coast, and the fact that only some financial crises (1755, 1763, 1799) unsettled the town, were very conducive to the development of the Hamburg exchange market (SOETBEER [1866], pp. 27, 35–38, 48). During the 1790s when Amsterdam, because of the French invasion, and Paris, because of the interruption of exchange operations owing to the political confusion, were unable to maintain their positions as central Northwest European financial markets, Hamburg even succeeded for a short time in becoming the most important financial centre of Northern Continental Europe, but this period of success ended rapidly with the French occupation of Hamburg and the subsequent suspension of the quotation on London on November 28th 1806 due to the Continental System (REISS [1986], pp. 182f.;

SCHWARZER / DENZEL / SCHNELZER [1993], pp. 9–15).

Hamburg had many of the most important financial markets and trading places of Europe among its exchange partners: according to the small number of exchange rate currents available, Hamburg quoted Venice, Antwerp, Amsterdam, London, Paris, Rouen, Nuremberg, Frankfurt am Main, Leipzig and Naumburg, Breslau and Danzig in the 17th century, and after 1672 Seville, Cadiz, Copenhagen and Lubeck as well (cf. BAASCH [1905/06], p. 10). For the 18th century there are quotations on Amsterdam and London in Northwest Europe, on Paris and Bordeaux (from 1724/37) in France, on Venice, on Genoa and Leghorn (the latter not before 1796) in Italy and on Cadiz and Lisbon, on Madrid (since 1776) and on Oporto (since 1799) on the Iberian Peninsula; the Biscayan places Bilbao and San Sebastian, however, were quoted only for short periods. Hamburg's direct exchange rate quotations on Iberian markets were the only regularly effected German ones on Spain or Portugal. Their special importance for the Hamburg exchange market is reflected, above all, in the fact that at the beginning of 1776 the exchange period for these places was raised from two to three months in order to extend the time of crediting, whereas this arrangement did not apply to the Northwest European places. Similar measures were taken only in the case of Breslau, which was an important exchange partner of Hamburg because of the Silesian linen trade, as well as in the case of Vienna (quoted from 1718), for which the exchange period was raised from four to six weeks in 1755/57 (BAASCH [1905/06], p. 10). Apart from this, within Central Europe the Leipzig and Naumburg fairs (until 1723), Nuremberg and Augsburg – quoted more irregularly – (both until 1755) and Prague (from the 1740s) were quoted. The quotation on Basle (from 1796 to 1812) and on the Frankfurt fairs (not until 1812) arose comparatively late, but both markets became exchange partners of Hamburg and were quoted relatively regularly. Thus Basle 'replaced' the financial market of Paris in a certain sense in this time; Paris was no longer attractive for foreign merchants because of its inflationary assignat currency. And this also explains why Hamburg quoted Basle for the traditional French currency, but not for the Basle currency itself. In the Baltic area, Hamburg quoted only Copenhagen for a longer period (from 1715), whereas Danzig was mentioned only for some months in 1717. Rouen, Lübeck, Danzig, Naumburg and Nuremberg were deleted from the official exchange rate currents, because the commercial basis for the necessity of quoting no longer existed, whereas attempts at adding Berlin (in 1765) or Saint Petersburg – in the wake of the Fourth Anglo-Dutch War (1780–1784) – to these quotation lists failed in the 18th century (ibid.).

In the 1820s and 1830s a great number of exchange partners was added to the exchange rate current of Hamburg: Saint Petersburg in 1812, Antwerp and (regularly) Bilbao in 1825, Trieste in 1828 and Berlin in 1836. In order to include the quotation on Antwerp as a quite important Hamburg exchange partner on the exchange rate current, the Hamburg Kommerzdeputation had to negotiate with the Hamburg Senate for seven years (1817–1824). The plan to introduce an exchange rate on Brazil according to the model of London (see p. 9) in 1827 was not taken into consideration at all by the persons responsible. The application of Swedish merchants for a quotation on Stockholm in 1863 was rejected as well (not introduced until 1881). Bremen was not recorded until 1859 because this neighbouring port was not accepted as an equal exchange partner until then (ibid.). At the end of 1868, the quotation on Madrid ended, but Cadiz as the more important partner for Hamburg's exchange business was quoted for some more years.

After the Seven Years' War, at the latest, Leipzig, the most important German fair at that time, achieved enormous international importance as an exchange place. Three annual fairs, namely the *Neujahrsmesse* (opening on January 1st), the *Oster-* or *Jubilate-Messe* (opening on Jubilate Sunday) and the *Michaelis-Messe* (opening on the Sunday after September 29th, St Michael's Day) were held at Leipzig, whereas a fourth fair – the *Peter-und-Pauls-Messe* (opening on June 29th, Saints Peter and Paul Day), which was less important – took place at Naumburg, 60 kilometres away from Leipzig. During the 15th and 16th centuries Leipzig had already been a regionally important exchange market for money and bills of exchange in Saxony and Thuringia. Having revived its fairs after the Thirty Years' War, and thus having shortly become the most important place for fairs all over Central Europe, Leipzig also rose to become one of the leading exchange markets within the whole Holy Roman Empire at least during the fair's opening time. The exchange market in Leipzig benefited immensely from the increasing trade in goods and remained dependent on it for a long time, until the end of the 18th century. The Leipzig Stock Exchange was founded in 1678, and the Leipzig Wechselordnung was introduced in 1682. In 1690, one of the most important monetary conferences in the history of the Holy Roman Empire took place in Leipzig and gave its name to the 'Leipzig standard of coinage'. At the end of the 17th and during the first half of the 18th century very few exchange rate currents were available. In the following years Leipzig quoted the most important exchange markets of the Empire and North Western Europe, the fairs of Frankfurt am Main, Breslau, Lyons and Bolzano, then Amsterdam, Hamburg, Augsburg, Vienna, Nuremberg, Paris, Prague and London, sometimes Danzig as well. The available exchange rate quotations starting in 1766 verify that the Leipzig cashless payment focused on these important exchange markets even during the late 18th and the early 19th centuries. But, over the years, rather insignificant exchange partners like Bolzano and Nuremberg were left out. Leipzig's standing as an international exchange market after the Seven Years War was based mainly on the importance of its fairs, which could be seen as a turntable for the circulation of goods and money between Western and Eastern Europe. After 1763, the importance of the exchange payments for the fair business rapidly increased. The bills of exchange on Amsterdam, London, Hamburg and Vienna were the most popular and, consequently, the most important papers for the Leipzig exchange market. Leipzig's success was influenced by two main factors: first, the successful transactions with the exchange markets at Amsterdam, London, Hamburg and Vienna; and, second, the function of Amsterdam, London and Hamburg as intermediate institutions. These three Northwest European centres acted as intermediaries for payments to the Iberian Peninsula whereas transactions into Switzerland were carried out via Paris and Augsburg. After the Seven Years War the increasing number of merchants from Russia, Poland and the Ottoman Empire (the so-called 'Greeks') became extremely important to the Leipzig fairs. From the 1770s they diversified means of making payments by using both current money and bills of exchange. The Greeks mainly used bills that they had bought on credit from merchant bankers in Vienna (mostly Jews) on their journey to Leipzig and repaid them on their way back home. The Russian and Polish merchants paid with bills on Amsterdam which they had received in return for selling raw materials and grain to the Netherlands. Then, the Leipzig merchant bankers sent these bills of exchange back to Amsterdam to get them honoured. Starting in the 1790s, the bills on Amsterdam were replaced by bills on London or Hamburg. Therefore, one can occasionally observe money rates for the rouble in Flemish currency from the 1770s because the Russian merchants had to know in their own currency which value was assigned to the bills of exchange denominated in Flemish currency. However, direct exchange rate quotations from the Leipzig fairs on Russia occurred infrequently (DENZEL [1999], pp. 152–156]).

The circulation of bills of exchange via fairs had its greatest success at the Leipzig fairs during the last third of the 18th century. But in the 1820s it experienced a clear decrease, although the fair business in general flourished continuously. One important reason for this was that bills on Leipzig had to be accepted only 14 days before their expiry date. Consequently, the acceptor did not immediately have the required liquidity. Because of that, one can find only very few exchange rate quotations on Leipzig during the 18th and 19th centuries made by financial markets outside Germany or Switzerland. Besides, Berlin also became an important exchange market and competitor of Leipzig. The exchange rate quotations of Leipzig and Berlin became very similar and nearly equal from 1841. Therefore the Leipzig exchange rate quotations have been suspended and only Berlin exchange rate quotations have been documented in the following tables for the period after 1815. Although the circulation of bills of exchange at the fairs had already lost influence around 1830, Leipzig maintained its status as a year-round acting financial market within Germany. In addition, Leipzig also became very attractive for Central European and Southeast European exchange places, which needed Leipzig to become connected to the international system of cashless payment in the 19th century (ibid., pp. 159–163).

Hamburg remained the most important exchange market of Northern Germany for large parts of the 19th century, as did Frankfurt am Main for Southern Germany. Since the late Middle Ages the Frankfurt fairs had been one centre of international cashless payment in Germany. In the second half of the 16th century the exchange business began to become independent of the fair trade, for which French and Dutch immigrants with their new techniques in cashless payment transactions were responsible (ULLMANN [1990], p. 77). In the 17th and 18th centuries the town had developed into one of the most important domains of German private bankers by means of innovative laws relating to bills – especially the authorization of the multiple endorsement (1666), carried out for the first time in the Holy Roman Empire – and the resulting stimulation of the stock exchange trade. This development was reinforced by the increasing importance of trade with government bonds in the last third of the 18th century, which was still the 'speciality' of the Frankfurt financial market even in the 19th century (HOLTFRERICH [1999], pp. 104–118, 148ff.). But unfortunately for the time before 1800 only a few exchange rate currents are available to give some information about the places quoted in Frankfurt. An official fixing of rates had already existed from 1625 (in printed exchange rate currents from 1642), but these ceased again in the 18th century when private exchange rate currents (with quite a few quoted places) took over this function; such exchange rate currents were published by brokers under municipal supervision from 1687. In 1748 a Frankfurt exchange rate current was published for the first time, for just a few years printed in a newspaper, whereas an official price current of the Frankfurt stock exchange was not available until 1851 (ibid., pp. 107, 110, 167). Therefore it is impossible to state which places were quoted at exactly what time. Nevertheless, the Frankfurt exchange operations reveal a tendency to be geared primarily to German (Hamburg, Augsburg, Nuremberg, Leipzig as well as Vienna, and also Breslau, Cologne and others) and West European markets (Amsterdam, Antwerp, Paris, Lyons, London, and also Geneva, Basle, Strasbourg, Rotterdam, Dordrecht and Lille) as early as at the end of the 17th century, whereas the traditionally high importance of Italy (especially Venice) declined considerably. A concentration on the most important Northwest European and German exchange markets (including Vienna) is evident by the 1770s. Frankfurt continued these quotations in the 19th century (DENZEL [1996], pp. 80–82; cf. HOLTFRERICH [1999], p. 155), proved by the documentation available for some decades after 1814. Henceforth, Frankfurt regularly quoted London, Amsterdam, Paris and Lyons, Hamburg, Augsburg, Leipzig, Bremen as well as Vienna and Trieste, and also Berlin from 1815, Nuremberg (again) from 1817, but only up to 1822, Cologne from 1853 and Munich from 1860. In addition, Frankfurt maintained one important contact of South Germany with Italy by means of the quotation on Milan following the quotation on Venice from 1824, whereas Augsburg quoted four Italian markets, namely Milan, Genoa, Leghorn and Venice (cf. *WdW VI*, pp. 304–309). Even though some contemporary merchant manuals supplement references of single quotations on New York from the middle of the 19th century as a consequence of the trade with American loans (e.g. NOBACK [1851], p. 201), the rate series documented here gives no proof of this connection. Thus the circle of the Frankfurt exchange partners did not change much until after the foundation of the German Empire. Up to the 1870s Frankfurt dominated the exchange operations of the South German guilder countries, to some extent even the neighbouring Swiss exchange markets – a position that Frankfurt had been holding since the 17th century – although its importance as a financial market was fading significantly in favour of the ambitious Berlin at that time. For this reason is seems to be justified to end the Frankfurt quotations with the transition to the new Reichswährung at the turn of the year 1875.

Like Frankfurt and Leipzig, Hamburg also had to accept a considerable weakening of its position as a Central European exchange market in the 19th century, although it remained the most important German seaport and trading centre. Consequently, international and – towards the end of the 19th century – even intercontinental quotations for bills of exchange on Germany were no longer primarily given on Hamburg but increasingly on Berlin or on 'German bank places' and on 'Germany' respectively, i.e. Hamburg, Berlin and to some extent several other places (especially Frankfurt am Main). The reason for this development rests with the fact that after Prussia had gained hegemony in Germany and, above all, after the Empire had been founded in 1871, Berlin became the most important financial centre of Germany. Since about 1725 Berlin had been an exchange place of relevance only for the Brandenburg–Prussian state, but during the early 19th century it remained still in the shadow of the Silesian exchange market of Breslau. The few exchange rate currents available from the 18th century indicate that Berlin exclusively quoted Central and Northwest European places, among them quite often towns or areas of the Brandenburg–Prussian state. Apart from Breslau, there were Kleve and Westfalen, Königsberg, Stettin, Magdeburg and Halberstadt, and the principality of Neuchâtel. These were places where branches of the Königliche Giro- and Leihbank (founded in 1765; head office Berlin) had been established (BUSS [1913], p. 68). However, Berlin did not gain regional and international recognition as an exchange place until the post-Napoleonic era (DENZEL [1996], pp. 100–102). Whereas references are available for some quotations of other German places on Berlin, such as those of Frankfurt am Main from 1815, of Leipzig from 1818, of Hamburg from 1836 and of Augsburg from 1846, international (regular) quoting was effected for the first time by Paris in 1820; Amsterdam and London quoted Berlin only for a short period in the 1820s (1821–1824 and 1822–1826 respectively), and regularly much later (from 1875 and from 1865 respectively), whereas for example Leghorn started quoting on Berlin in 1846, then Zurich and Saint Petersburg in 1859 (very irregularly) and Genoa by 1873 (*HStD XI*, pp. 570, 589; *WdW X*, p. 48; *WdW VI*, p. 311; *WdW I/II*, pp. 95, 186, 339; *WdW I/III*, pp. 69, 213, 281, 473). Until the 1860s the Berlin exchange operations were geared to German places and to Northwestern Europe as well as to Saint Petersburg, and from 1860 to Warsaw. By 1865 – when regular quotations from the world financial centre of London set in – Berlin could be regarded as an internationally accepted exchange market. In only a few years the Prussian and later German metropolis superseded all other exchange markets of the German Empire. Frankfurt am Main remained the leading German place for the Swiss markets (SWOBODA [1902], p. 124). Therefore the Berlin quotations are given as the relevant data of the German Empire for the time from the introduction of the Reichswährung in the Kingdom of Prussia on January 1st 1875 until 1914, whereas the documented Hamburg rate series end with the transition from the Hamburg bank currency to the new Reichswährung on February $15^{th}/16^{th}$ 1873.

The changes in exchange rate currents in the 1870s and 1880s mirror the international status that the Berlin exchange market had reached: even though Berlin principally quoted German and Northwest European partners (London, Amsterdam and Paris; and both Antwerp and Brussels from 1850) before the foundation of the Empire, all these German places ceased to be quoted in the course of the currency standardization in the German Empire. When the mark Reichswährung had become the official means of payment at the various German exchange markets, the internal German quotations became obsolete, because the newly founded Reichsbank in Berlin discounted the bills of exchange by clearing them via the network of the so-called 'Reichsbankplätze' (German bank places with a branch of the Reichsbank) branching out into all directions (SWOBODA [1902], pp. 118–126). However, numerous foreign financial markets were newly added to the exchange rate currents of Berlin: 'Italian bank places' were added in 1882 (i.e. Florence, Genoa, Leghorn, Milan, Naples, Rome, Turin and Venice) as well as 'Swiss bank places' (namely Basle, Berne, Geneva, Saint Gall, Winterthur and Zurich) (SWOBODA [1902], pp. 136f.). Copenhagen and 'Scandinavian bank places' (namely Stockholm, Göteborg and Christiania [Oslo]) were included in 1884, then Madrid in 1886 and, finally, New York in 1887. Even if there had been references to Rotterdam, Barcelona, Lisbon and Oporto in contemporary merchant manuals, they were not quoted in the official exchange rate currents of Berlin. Budapest was listed in the exchange rate currents as well, but no quotations were given (ibid., pp. 135–137). In comparison with other European financial centres the network of Berlin's quotations shows two significant features: first, there was a particularly close contact with the Russian Empire, quoting not only Saint Petersburg (from 1820), but also Warsaw (from 1860). The exchange business not only with Saint Petersburg and Warsaw, but also with Vienna, was much more important than the exchange trade with all other financial places quoted. This fact can be demonstrated by the exchange trading frequency; those bills drawn on these three Eastern partners were traded daily at the Berlin stock exchange, whereas those on other places were traded only every other day (ibid., p. 135). Second, Berlin was the only European exchange market that quoted Copenhagen and the Scandinavian places regularly and over the long term. Thus Berlin was the unchallenged financial centre of the German Empire before World War I, whereas Hamburg was responsible for supplementary tasks within the field of overseas trades and payment transactions.

The documented rate series of Hamburg (until 1874), Leipzig (until 1815), Frankfurt (until 1874) and Berlin are complemented by:

- the quotations of Danzig on Warsaw (1828–1855): in these decades the rates of Danzig were the only regular quotations on Warsaw available to date. Belonging to the Kingdom of Prussia since 1793 Danzig therefore quoted in thaler Prussian current in the decades relevant here. The exchange rate quotations in Danzig end in the documented sources in 1855.

- the quotation of Bremen on New York (1873–1886): Bremen, the most significant trading centre for cotton and the most important emigrant port of the German Empire, was the first German (followed by Hamburg) and one of the first European financial places to quote New York which had already been recorded in the exchange rate currents of Bremen since the 1840s, although it appears without quotations (*WdW XI*, p. 108). Noback's merchant manual reports that the quotation on 'North America' could also mean that on New York or on New Orleans, sometimes even that on Baltimore or other important markets of the United States (NOBACK [1851], 2. Abth., p. 1606).

One can find the Danzig quotations on Warsaw and the Bremen quotations on New York in the following tables for the Berlin exchange rates.

References: Paul Jacob MARPERGER, *Beschreibung der Banquen* ..., Halle – Leipzig 1717 (repr. Frankfurt/Main 1969), chapters VII, VIII, XII; Adolf SOETBEER, Die Hamburger Bank, 1619–1866. Eine geschichtliche Skizze, *Vierteljahresschrift für Volkswirtschaft* 3 (1866), pp. 21–54; Erwin NASSE, Die Münzreform und die Wechselcourse, *Annalen des Deutschen Reichs für Gesetzgebung, Verwaltung und Statistik. Staatsrechtliches, volkswirthschaftliches und statistisches Jahrbuch. Materialiensammlung und Reform-Zeitschrift* 1875, pp. 595–619; Richard EHRENBERG, Ein Hamburgischer Waaren- und Wechsel-Preiscourant aus dem XVI. Jahrhundert, *Hansische Geschichtsblätter* 1883, Leipzig 1884, pp. 165–170; Ernst BAASCH, Aus der Entwicklungsgeschichte des Hamburger Kurszettels, *Bank-Archiv* 5 (1905/06), pp. 8–11; Georg BUSS, *Berliner Börse von 1685–1913. Zum 50. Gedenktage der ersten Versammlung im neuen Hause*, Berlin 1913; Kurt VON EICHBORN, *Das Soll und Haben von Eichborn & Co in 200 Jahren. Schicksal und Gestaltung eines Bankhauses im Wandel der Zeiten*, München – Leipzig 1928; Heinrich SIEVEKING, Die Hamburger Bank, in Johannes G. VAN DILLEN, *History of the Principal Public Banks accompanied by Extensive Bibliographies of the History of Banking and Credit in Eleven European Countries*, The Hague 1934, pp. 125–160; Herbert RITTMANN, *Deutsche Geldgeschichte 1484–1914*, München 1975; John J. MCCUSKER, *Money and Exchange in Europe and America, 1600–1775. A Handbook*, London – Basingstoke 1978, pp. 73f.; Bernd SPRENGER, *Währungswesen und Währungspolitik in Deutschland von 1834 bis 1875*,

Köln 1981; Konrad SCHNEIDER, *Hamburgs Münz- und Geldgeschichte im 19. Jahrhundert bis zur Einführung der Reichswährung*, Koblenz 1983; Winfried REISS, Historische Wechselkurse, in *Bankhistorisches Archiv* 11/2 (1985), pp. 3–41; idem., Historical Exchange Rates, in Wolfram FISCHER / R. Marvin MCINNIS / Jürgen SCHNEIDER (eds.), *The Emergence of a World Economy 1500–1914. Papers of the IX International Congress of Economic History, 2 parts*, Stuttgart 1986, *part I: 1500–1850*, Wiesbaden 1986, pp. 171–189; Konrad SCHNEIDER, *"Banco, Species und Courant". Untersuchungen zur Hamburgischen Währung im 17. und 18. Jahrhundert*, Koblenz 1986; Henry ROSEVEARE (ed.), *Markets and Merchants of the Late Seventeenth Century. The Marescoe–David Letters 1668–1680*, New York 1987; Peter FASSL, *Konfession, Wirtschaft und Politik. Von der Reichsstadt zur Industriestadt, Augsburg 1750–1850*, Sigmaringen 1988; Hans-Peter ULLMANN, Der Frankfurter Kapitalmarkt um 1800: Entstehung, Struktur und Wirken einer modernen Finanzierungsinstitution, *Vierteljahrschrift für Sozial- und Wirtschaftsgeschichte* 77 (1990), pp. 75–92; Karl Heinrich KAUFHOLD, Der Übergang zu Fonds- und Wechselbörsen vom ausgehenden 17. Jahrhundert bis zum ausgehenden 18. Jahrhundert, in Hans POHL (ed.), *Deutsche Börsengeschichte*, Frankfurt/Main 1992, pp. 77–132; Rainer GÖMMEL, Entstehung und Entwicklung der Effektenbörsen im 19. Jahrhundert bis 1914, in ibid., pp. 133–207; Oskar SCHWARZER / Markus A. DENZEL / Petra SCHNELZER, Geld- und Wechselkurse in Deutschland und im Ostseeraum (18. und 19. Jahrhundert), in *HStD XII*, pp. 2–43; Bernd SPRENGER, Harmonisierungsbestrebungen im Geldwesen der deutschen Staaten zwischen Wiener Kongreß und Reichsgründung, in Eckart SCHREMMER (ed.), *Geld und Währung vom 16. Jahrhundert bis zur Gegenwart*, Stuttgart 1993, pp. 121–142; Markus A. DENZEL, Die Integration Deutschlands in das internationale Zahlungsverkehrssystem im 17. und 18. Jahrhundert, in Eckart SCHREMMER (ed.), *Wirtschaftliche und soziale Integration in historischer Sicht*, Stuttgart 1996, pp. 58–109; Bernd SPRENGER, Die Währungsunion des Deutschen Reichs 1871/76. Vorbild für die Europäische Währungsunion?, in Günther SCHULZ (ed.), *Von der Landwirtschaft zur Industrie. Wirtschaftlicher und gesellschaftlicher Wandel im 19. und 20. Jahrhundert. Festschrift für Friedrich-Wilhelm Henning zum 65. Geburtstag*, Paderborn et al. 1996, pp. 133–148; Markus A. DENZEL, Altona als Bank- und Wechselplatz im ausgehenden 18. und beginnenden 19. Jahrhundert, *Bankhistorisches Archiv* 24 (1998) [here: 1998a], pp. 13–37; idem, Die Braunschweiger Messen als regionaler und überregionaler Markt im norddeutschen Raum in der zweiten Hälfte des 18. und im beginnenden 19. Jahrhundert, *Vierteljahrschrift für Sozial- und Wirtschaftsgeschichte* 85 (1998) [here: 1998b], pp. 40–93; idem, Zahlungsverkehr auf den Leipziger Messen vom 17. bis zum 19. Jahrhundert, in Hartmut ZWAHR / Thomas TOPFSTEDT / Günter BENTELE (eds.), *Leipzigs Messen 1497–1997. Gestaltwandel. Umbrüche. Neubeginn, vol. 1: 1497–1914*, Köln – Weimar – Wien 1999, pp. 149–165; Carl-Ludwig HOLTFRERICH, *Finanzplatz Frankfurt. Von der mittelalterlichen Messestadt zum europäischen Bankenzentrum*, München 1999; Markus A. DENZEL, Der Nürnberger Wechselmarkt im ausgehenden 18. Jahrhundert, in Rainer GÖMMEL / Markus A. DENZEL (eds.), *Weltwirtschaft und Wirtschaftsordnung. Festschrift für Jürgen Schneider zum 65. Geburtstag*, Stuttgart 2002, pp. 169–192; Hans POHL (ed.), *Geschichte des Finanzplatzes Berlin*, Frankfurt/Main 2002; Bernd SPRENGER, *Das Geld der Deutschen. Geldgeschichte Deutschlands von den Anfängen bis zur Gegenwart*, Paderborn – München – Wien – Zürich ³2002, chapters 7 to 10; Carl-Ludwig HOLTFRERICH, Der Finanzplatz Frankfurt im Wettbewerb mit Berlin und anderen Städten seit dem 19. Jahrhundert, in *Europäische Finanzplätze im Wettbewerb. 27. Symposium des Instituts für bankhistorische Forschung e.V. am 16. Juni 2004 im Hause der Deutschen Bundesbank, Hauptverwaltung Frankfurt am Main* (= Bankhistorisches Archiv. Zeitschrift zur Banken- und Finanzgeschichte, Beiheft 45), Stuttgart 2006, pp. 29–49.

4.1 Hamburg exchange rates

4.1.1 On London, Amsterdam, Paris and Copenhagen

	HAMBURG on:			
	London	**Amsterdam**	**Paris**	**Copenhagen**
	per 10 pounds sterling [a]	per 100 guilders Flemish banco [b]	per 100 livres tournois [c]	per 100 rixdollars Danish current [d]
	in mark banco			
1657	121.87 2m/d (1)			
1658	122.47 2m/d (2)			
1659	127.42 2m/d (12)			
1660	137.02 2m/d (7)			
1661	137.81 2m/d (1)			
1662				
1663	133.87 2m/d (6)			
1664	130.80 2m/d (12)			
1665	125.66 2m/d (6)			
1666	120.11 2m/d (8)			
1667	127.05 2m/d (6)			
1668	127.92 2m/d (11)	121.32 ss (11)	71.07 2m/d (10)	
1669	129.87 2m/d (12)	123.02 ss (12)	72.15 2m/d (11)	
1670	128.96 2m/d (3)	121.67 ss (3)	71.64 2m/d (3)	
1671	128.78 2m/d (9)	120.86 ss (9)	71.55 2m/d (9)	
1672	125.05 2m/d (12)	121.69 ss (12)	69.47 2m/d (12)	278.42 ss (1)
1673	125.62 2m/d (3)	123.71 ss (3)	69.79 2m/d (3)	
1674	118.12 2m/d (1)	115.94 ss (1)	65.63 2m/d (1)	
1675	120.81 2m/d (12)	115.77 ss (12)	67.12 2m/d (12)	
1676	126.51 2m/d (12)	117.52 ss (12)	70.28 2m/d (11)	
1677	129.79 2m/d (12)	120.26 ss (12)	72.11 2m/d (12)	
1678	125.21 2m/d (12)	120.64 ss (12)	69.56 2m/d (12)	
1679	129.40 2m/d (12)	121.33 ss (12)	71.89 2m/d (12)	
1680	129.48 2m/d (3)	119.83 ss (3)	71.93 2m/d (3)	
1681				
1682				
1683				
1684				
1685				
1686				
1687	126.56 2m/d (3)	119.04 ss (3)		
1688	125.63 2m/d (2)	118.96 ss (2)		
1689	123.82 2m/d (6)	119.70 ss (2)	96.61 2m/d (1)	270.27 ss (1)
1690	121.87 2m/d (2)	120.19 ss (2)	89.32 2m/d (1)	271.49 ss (1)

	London	Amsterdam	Paris	Copenhagen
	HAMBURG on:			
	per 10 pounds sterling [a]	per 100 guilders Flemish banco [b]	per 100 livres tournois [c]	per 100 rixdollars Danish current [d]
	in mark banco			
1691	121.91 2m/d (3)	117.65 ss (2)		
1692	118.91 2m/d (2)	117.02 ss (2)	89.58 2m/d (2)	275.23 ss (2)
1693	118.59 2m/d (2)	118.08 ss (2)	88.28 2m/d (2)	
1694	114.84 2m/d (1)	118.19 ss (2)		
1695	104.38 2m/d (2)	120.01 ss (2)		
1696	111.26 2m/d (5)	120.83 ss (2)	86.46 2m/d (6)	267.86 ss (6)
1697	129.07 2m/d (2)	122.72 ss (2)	87.24 2m/d (2)	
1698	127.35 2m/d (1)	120.55 ss (2)	81.77 2m/d (1)	
1699	124.84 2m/d (2)	119.63 ss (2)		
1700	126.56 2m/d (2)	120.34 ss (2)		
1701	129.84 2m/d (2)	120.72 ss (2)		
1702	123.75 2m/d (2)	118.56 ss (2)		
1703	119.53 2m/d (2)	118.19 ss (2)		
1704	119.22 2m/d (2)	118.30 ss (2)		
1705	121.09 2m/d (2)	118.74 ss (2)		
1706	123.91 2m/d (2)	121.21 ss (2)		
1707	121.72 2m/d (2)	120.19 ss (2)		
1708	122.34 2m/d (2)	121.21 ss (2)		
1709	118.91 2m/d (2)	119.85 ss (2)		
1710	118.81 2m/d (12)	119.31 ss (12)		
1711	122.13 2m/d (12)	120.48 ss (12)		
1712	122.52 2m/d (12)	121.63 ss (12)	69.01 2m/d (1)	
1713	126.57 2m/d (12)	120.21 ss (12)	66.62 2m/d (12)	
1714	127.71 2m/d (12)	119.65 ss (12)	70.15 2m/d (12)	
1715	128.66 2m/d (12)	120.13 ss (12)	85.43 2m/d (12)	249.37 ss (7)
1716	127.89 2m/d (12)	121.16 ss (12)	82.21 2m/d (9)	248.11 ss (12)
1717	125.13 2m/d (12)	121.53 ss (12)	83.29 2m/d (12)	238.00 ss (12)
1718	124.21 2m/d (12)	121.61 ss (12)	66.74 2m/d (11)	233.34 ss (12)
1719	126.89 2m/d (12)	121.30 ss (12)	51.88 2m/d (12)	230.33 ss (12)
1720	124.62 2m/d (12)	121.65 ss (12)	29.63 2m/d (9)	230.43 ss (11)
1721	125.34 2m/d (12)	123.07 ss (12)	43.75 2m/d (1)	230.86 ss (11)
1722	129.59 2m/d (12)	122.87 ss (12)	41.93 2m/d (2)	230.45 ss (12)
1723	128.02 2m/d (12)	122.62 ss (12)		228.03 ss (11)
1724	125.79 2m/d (12)	120.67 ss (12)		226.77 ss (12)
1725	124.69 2m/d (2)	120.53 ss (2)		
1726	127.20 2m/d (12)	*121.75* ss (12)	52.50 2m/d (1)	233.43 ss (11)
1727	125.86 2m/d (2)	123.67 ss (2)	51.56 2m/d (1)	
1728	124.22 2m/d (2)	121.90 ss (2)		

	London			Amsterdam			Paris [e]			Copenhagen		
	HAMBURG on:											
	London			**Amsterdam**			**Paris** [e]			**Copenhagen**		
	per 10 pounds sterling [a]			per 100 guilders Flemish banco [b]			per 100 livres tournois [c]			per 100 rixdollars Danish current [d]		
	in mark banco											
1729	122.19	2m/d	(2)	120.41	ss	(2)						
1730	122.66	2m/d	(2)	119.40	ss	(2)						
1731	125.86	2m/d	(3)	121.21	ss	(3)	50.16	2m/d	(3)			
1732	126.56	2m/d	(3)	121.67	ss	(3)	50.86	2m/d	(3)			
1733	126.98	2m/d	(3)	122.14	ss	(3)	50.86	2m/d	(3)			
1734	131.25	2m/d	(9)	123.08	ss	(9)	52.03	2m/d	(9)			
1735	130.63	2m/d	(5)	122.89	ss	(5)	51.33	2m/d	(5)			
1736	128.23	2m/d	(11)	121.82	ss	(11)	*55.54*	2m/d	(11)			
1737	125.36	2m/d	(12)	120.78	ss	(12)	*54.04*	2m/d	(9)			
1738	125.32	2m/d	(12)	120.09	ss	(12)	*53.47*	2m/d	(7)			
1739	126.53	2m/d	(12)	120.38	ss	(12)	55.26	2m/d	(10)			
1740	125.99	2m/d	(12)	120.56	ss	(12)	56.37	2m/d	(9)			
1741	123.66	2m/d	(12)	120.44	ss	(12)	56.23	2m/d	(10)			
1742	124.27	2m/d	(12)	119.64	ss	(12)	54.48	2m/d	(11)			
1743	124.60	2m/d	(12)	120.48	ss	(12)	55.78	2m/d	(11)			
1744	123.71	2m/d	(12)	120.30	ss	(12)	56.06	2m/d	(12)			
1745	125.54	2m/d	(12)	121.20	ss	(12)	55.72	2m/d	(12)			
1746	131.44	2m/d	(12)	122.65	ss	(12)	56.15	2m/d	(12)			
1747	129.01	2m/d	(12)	123.09	ss	(12)	56.69	2m/d	(12)			
1748	128.06	2m/d	(12)	121.31	ss	(12)	54.96	2m/d	(11)			
1749	127.18	2m/d	(12)	119.86	ss	(12)	55.15	2m/d	(12)			
1750	124.15	2m/d	(12)	119.39	ss	(12)	54.46	2m/d	(12)			
1751	124.28	2m/d	(12)	118.03	ss	(12)	53.76	2m/d	(12)	253.45	ss	(11)
1752	123.58	2m/d	(12)	118.17	ss	(12)	54.19	2m/d	(12)	254.46	ss	(12)
1753	122.98	2m/d	(12)	118.24	ss	(12)	54.95	2m/d	(12)	252.43	ss	(12)
1754	124.31	2m/d	(12)	117.18	ss	(12)	54.19	2m/d	(12)	251.47	ss	(12)
1755	127.41	2m/d	(12)	118.61	ss	(12)	54.85	2m/d	(12)	252.93	ss	(11)
1756	132.05	2m/d	(12)	123.16	ss	(12)	55.85	2m/d	(12)	251.35	ss	(12)
1757	133.57	2m/d	(12)	126.56	ss	(12)	56.18	2m/d	(12)	261.01	ss	(12)
1758	131.74	2m/d	(12)	127.49	ss	(12)	56.89	2m/d	(12)	266.54	ss	(12)
1759	135.49	2m/d	(12)	129.33	ss	(12)	57.72	2m/d	(12)	268.36	ss	(12)
1760	124.79	2m/d	(12)	119.80	ss	(12)	52.93	2m/d	(11)	248.32	ss	(12)
1761	118.77	2m/d	(12)	117.15	ss	(12)	51.82	2m/d	(12)	229.52	ss	(12)
1762	126.16	2m/d	(12)	120.85	ss	(12)	53.91	2m/d	(12)	229.40	ss	(12)
1763	125.32	2m/d	(12)	120.55	ss	(12)	55.35	2m/d	(11)	237.22	ss	(12)
1764	128.77	2m/d	(12)	118.82	ss	(12)	54.77	2m/d	(12)	229.26	ss	(12)
1765	127.91	2m/d	(12)	119.57	ss	(12)	55.14	2m/d	(12)	246.44	ss	(12)
1766	129.08	2m/d	(12)	125.04	ss	(12)	56.94	2m/d	(12)	247.29	ss	(11)

	HAMBURG on:			
	London	**Amsterdam**	**Paris**	**Copenhagen**
	per 10 pounds sterling [a]	per 100 guilders Flemish banco [b]	per 100 livres tournois, from 1796 (10) per 100 francs [c]	per 100 rixdollars Danish current [d]
	in mark banco			
1767	130.98 2m/d (12)	127.09 ss (12)	57.70 2m/d (12)	246.68 ss (6)
1768	125.99 2m/d (12)	121.89 ss (12)	55.05 2m/d (12)	242.92 2m/d (8)
1769	122.76 2m/d (12)	120.50 ss (12)	54.20 2m/d (12)	235.80 2m/d (9)
1770	122.09 2m/d (12)	120.26 ss (12)	53.71 2m/d (12)	235.19 2m/d (10)
1771	122.15 2m/d (12)	119.26 ss (12)	53.75 2m/d (12)	232.23 2m/d (11)
1772	122.46 2m/d (12)	117.96 ss (12)	53.71 2m/d (12)	228.93 2m/d (11)
1773	127.56 2m/d (12)	119.91 ss (12)	53.35 2m/d (12)	225.40 2m/d (10)
1774	127.91 2m/d (12)	119.08 ss (12)	53.60 2m/d (12)	232.75 2m/d (12)
1775	126.03 2m/d (12)	119.44 ss (12)	53.98 2m/d (12)	240.93 2m/d (12)
1776	122.84 2m/d (12)	118.81 ss (12)	52.60 2m/d (12)	241.29 2m/d (12)
1777	119.51 2m/d (12)	117.64 ss (12)	52.08 2m/d (12)	241.08 2m/d (9)
1778	124.39 2m/d (12)	118.28 ss (12)	52.01 2m/d (12)	240.89 2m/d (10)
1779	128.96 2m/d (12)	120.02 ss (12)	52.38 2m/d (11)	233.90 2m/d (12)
1780	126.79 2m/d (12)	119.24 ss (12)	52.45 2m/d (12)	234.86 2m/d (12)
1781	120.06 2m/d (12)	119.08 ss (12)	51.56 2m/d (12)	228.22 2m/d (12)
1782	117.96 2m/d (12)	116.43 ss (12)	51.77 2m/d (12)	222.00 2m/d (12)
1783	117.96 2m/d (12)	114.22 ss (12)	51.24 2m/d (12)	214.40 2m/d (12)
1784	125.49 2m/d (12)	116.48 ss (12)	52.24 2m/d (12)	215.88 2m/d (12)
1785	130.02 2m/d (12)	116.72 ss (12)	51.74 2m/d (12)	219.67 2m/d (12)
1786	127.53 2m/d (12)	117.08 ss (12)	51.45 2m/d (12)	217.63 2m/d (11)
1787	127.82 2m/d (12)	116.92 ss (12)	51.83 2m/d (12)	210.17 2m/d (12)
1788	128.83 2m/d (12)	114.95 ss (12)	51.59 2m/d (12)	203.83 2m/d (12)
1789	129.48 2m/d (12)	114.41 ss (12)	50.33 2m/d (12)	190.67 2m/d (12)
1790	130.39 2m/d (12)	113.55 ss (12)	48.34 2m/d (12)	199.33 2m/d (12)
1791	131.46 2m/d (12)	114.25 ss (12)	43.17 2m/d (12)	216.87 2m/d (11)
1792	126.50 2m/d (12)	115.32 ss (12)	31.86 2m/d (11)	217.99 2m/d (12)
1793	133.35 2m/d (12)	114.89 ss (12)	21.89 2m/d (12)	218.19 2m/d (11)
1794	130.13 2m/d (12)	110.57 ss (12)	21.21 2m/d (12)	235.57 2m/d (12)
1795	121.07 2m/d (12)	115.39 ss (6)	4.44 2m/d (11)	243.95 2m/d (12)
1796	122.43 2m/d (12)	105.36 ss (4)	0.21/50.00 2m/d (6+3)	243.91 2m/d (11)
1797	133.02 2m/d (12)	105.92 ss (12)	50.57 2m/d (12)	242.27 2m/d (12)
1798	137.22 2m/d (12)	105.48 ss (12)	50.39 2m/d (12)	239.81 2m/d (12)
1799	125.08 2m/d (12)	100.03 ss (12)	49.98 2m/d (12)	233.07 2m/d (11)
1800	115.76 2m/d (12)	103.24 ss (12)	51.63 2m/d (12)	227.70 2m/d (12)
1801	115.06 2m/d (12)	101.78 ss (12)	51.34 2m/d (12)	216.17 2m/d (12)
1802	120.72 2m/d (12)	112.74 ss (12)	51.70 2m/d (12)	211.56 2m/d (12)
1803	123.83 2m/d (12)	116.36 ss (12)	51.51 2m/d (12)	211.39 2m/d (12)

	HAMBURG on:			
	London	**Amsterdam**	**Paris**	**Copenhagen**
	per 10 pounds sterling [a]	per 100 guilders Flemish banco, from 1816 (10) per 100 Dutch guilders [b]	per 100 francs [c]	per 100 rixdollars Danish current, from 1813 per 100 rigsbankdaler [d]
	in mark banco			
1804	129.27 2m/d (12)	116.47 ss (12)	52.00 2m/d (12)	205.61 2m/d (12)
1805	126.62 2m/d (12)	115.02 ss (12)	50.24 2m/d (12)	211.44 2m/d (12)
1806	124.69 2m/d (11)	116.72 ss (12)	52.47 2m/d (12)	211.50 2m/d (11)
1807	[f]	119.08 ss (12)	53.17 2m/d (12)	203.63 2m/d (9)
1808	[f]	119.82 ss (12)	55.06 2m/d (12)	187.02 2m/d (11)
1809	[f]	114.99 ss (12)	54.46 2m/d (12)	109.41 2m/d (12)
1810	[f]	114.32 ss (12)	54.08 2m/d (12)	68.60 2m/d (10)
1811	[f]	113.52 ss (12)	54.01 2m/d (12)	38.31 ss (11)
1812	[f]	116.36 ss (12)	54.44 2m/d (12)	35.09 ss (9)
1813	103.75 2m/d (2)	117.58 ss (3)	52.82 2m/d (11)	16.34 ss (6)
1814	112.64 2m/d (7)	115.63 ss (7)	51.77 2m/d (7)	9.68 ss (1)
1815	114.40 2m/d (12)	113.44 ss (12)	53.32 2m/d (12)	
1816	133.80 2m/d (12)	110.96 ss (12)	52.23 2m/d (12)	43.38 ss (4)
1817	129.20 ss (12)	111.07 ss (12)	52.51 2m/d (12)	58.13 ss (7)
1818	125.00 ss (12)	112.04 ss (12)	51.76 2m/d (12)	104.99 ss (7)
1819	129.50 ss (12)	112.90 ss (12)	52.55 2m/d (12)	125.89 ss (9)
1820	136.90 ss (12)	113.83 ss (12)	53.46 2m/d (12)	115.43 ss (3)
1821	140.00 ss (12)	112.21 ss (12)	54.38 2m/d (12)	114.04 ss (10)
1822	138.80 ss (12)	114.06 ss (12)	54.31 2m/d (12)	119.36 ss (11)
1823	139.70 ss (12)	114.33 ss (12)	54.07 2m/d (12)	120.67 ss (12)
1824	137.00 ss (12)	115.48 ss (12)	53.85 2m/d (12)	125.09 ss (10)
1825	135.10 ss (12)	113.54 ss (12)	53.69 2m/d (12)	141.39 ss (11)
1826	138.20 ss (12)	113.52 ss (12)	53.55 2m/d (12)	131.91 ss (12)
1827	136.80 ss (12)	113.73 ss (12)	53.62 2m/d (12)	134.52 ss (12)
1828	136.10 ss (12)	113.24 ss (12)	53.44 2m/d (12)	140.10 ss (12)
1829	136.40 ss (12)	112.70 ss (12)	53.11 2m/d (12)	144.32 ss (12)
1830	137.40 ss (12)	112.75 ss (12)	53.41 2m/d (12)	143.26 ss (12)
1831	135.00 ss (12)	113.37 ss (12)	53.45 2m/d (12)	142.03 ss (12)
1832	137.50 ss (12)	113.44 ss (12)	53.39 ss (12)	141.05 ss (12)
1833	137.00 ss (12)	113.53 ss (12)	53.30 ss (12)	141.90 ss (12)
1834	135.50 ss (12)	111.36 ss (12)	53.30 ss (12)	145.29 ss (12)
1835	136.50 ss (12)	111.83 ss (12)	53.32 ss (12)	145.76 ss (12)
1836	135.80 ss (12)	111.91 ss (12)	53.27 ss (12)	148.57 ss (12)
1837	136.20 ss (12)	112.88 ss (12)	53.46 ss (12)	149.63 ss (12)
1838	135.90 ss (12)	112.04 ss (12)	53.36 ss (12)	149.63 ss (12)
1839	133.60 ss (12)	111.31 ss (12)	53.00 ss (12)	152.04 ss (12)

	HAMBURG on:			
	London	**Amsterdam**	**Paris**	**Copenhagen** [g]
	per 10 pounds sterling [a]	per 100 Dutch guilders [b]	per 100 francs [c]	per 100 rigsbankdaler, from 1854 (3) per 100 rixdollars rigsmønt [d]
			in mark banco	
1840	133.50 ss (12)	111.42 ss (12)	52.92 ss (12)	152.07 ss (12)
1841	133.90 ss (12)	110.83 ss (12)	52.85 ss (12)	150.70 ss (12)
1842	135.60 ss (12)	111.19 ss (12)	53.02 ss (12)	150.77 ss (12)
1843	137.10 ss (12)	112.09 ss (12)	53.27 ss (12)	149.70 ss (12)
1844	135.80 ss (12)	111.82 ss (12)	53.08 ss (12)	150.96 ss (12)
1845	136.30 ss (12)	110.83 ss (12)	53.03 ss (12)	152.29 ss (12)
1846	136.00 ss (12)	110.81 ss (12)	52.93 ss (12)	150.95 ss (12)
1847	134.90 ss (12)	111.13 ss (12)	52.84 ss (12)	152.19 ss (12)
1848	135.90 ss (12)	112.72 ss (12)	53.59 ss (12)	152.29 ss (10)
1849	136.70 ss (12)	113.37 ss (12)	53.86 ss (12)	
1850	135.50 ss (12)	112.46 ss (12)	53.31 ss (12)	
1851	133.40 ss (12)	112.40 ss (12)	53.21 ss (12)	
1852	134.20 ss (12)	112.04 ss (12)	52.98 ss (12)	
1853	132.20 ss (12)	111.48 ss (12)	52.78 ss (12)	
1854	131.60 ss (12)	111.93 ss (12)	52.62 ss (12)	
1855	132.70 ss (12)	111.75 ss (12)	52.75 ss (12)	
1856	132.70 ss (12)	111.63 ss (12)	52.40 ss (12)	
1857	132.00 ss (12)	111.42 ss (12)	52.22 ss (12)	
1858	132.50 ss (12)	112.68 ss (12)	52.82 ss (12)	147.79 ss (1)
1859	131.50 ss (12)	112.27 ss (12)	52.43 ss (12)	
1860	131.80 ss (12)	112.51 ss (12)	52.47 ss (12)	
1861	133.60 ss (12)	112.19 ss (12)	52.77 ss (12)	
1862	132.90 ss (12)	112.63 ss (12)	52.73 ss (12)	148.89 ss (4)
1863	132.90 ss (12)	112.43 ss (12)	52.65 ss (12)	
1864	132.80 ss (12)	111.75 ss (12)	52.59 ss (12)	
1865	133.30 ss (12)	112.35 ss (12)	52.96 ss (12)	
1866	133.50 ss (12)	112.74 ss (12)	52.99 ss (12)	
1867	134.70 ss (12)	113.35 ss (12)	53.53 ss (12)	
1868	135.20 ss (12)	113.38 ss (12)	53.70 ss (12)	
1869	135.50 ss (12)	112.80 ss (12)	53.80 ss (12)	
1870	134.90 ss (12)	113.49 ss (12)	53.37 ss (12)	
1871	135.20 ss (12)	113.42 ss (12)	53.01 ss (12)	
1872	135.40 ss (12)	112.50 ss (12)	53.05 ss (12)	
1873	136.20 ss (2)	113.21 ss (2)	53.41 ss (2)	

[a]   Concerning the British currency, see pp. 3–5.

[b]   Concerning the Dutch currency, see pp. 57–59.

[c]   Concerning the French currency, see pp. 279f.

[d]   Concerning the Danish currency, see pp. 327f.

[e]   1736–1738 quotation on Bordeaux.

[f]   Because of the Continental System, no quotations were given from December 1806 up to March 1813.

[g]   Even in 1844 the editor of the exchange rate current recommended leaving out the quotation on Copenhagen, as the Kommerzdeputation did in November 1862, because from a business point of view this category was no longer in demand within the exchange rate currents, so that it remained empty for most of the time. However, in recognition of this fact the Hamburg senate declared itself to be in favour of keeping this category (BAASCH [1905/06], p. 10).

4.1.2 On Iberian and Italian places

	HAMBURG on:	
	Cadiz [a]	**Venice**
	per 100 ducados de cambio [b]	per 100 ducati di banco [c]
	in mark banco	
1668		285.47 2m/d (10)
1669		291.60 2m/d (10)
1670		288.28 2m/d (2)
1671		280.66 2m/d (6)
1672	*328.13* 2m/d (1)	272.07 2m/d (10)
1673		270.31 2m/d (1)
1674		275.00 2m/d (1)
1675		272.09 2m/d (12)
1676		271.00 2m/d (12)
1677		279.62 2m/d (12)
1678		274.61 2m/d (11)
1679		275.39 2m/d (12)
1680		276.61 2m/d (3)
1681		
1682		
1683		
1684		
1685		
1686		
1687		
1688		
1689	351.56 2m/d (1)	266.80 2m/d (1)
1690	357.03 2m/d (1)	271.28 2m/d (1)
1691		
1692	358.59 2m/d (2)	269.92 2m/d (2)
1693	355.47 2m/d (2)	272.66 2m/d (2)
1694		
1695		
1696	364.06 2m/d (6)	279.69 2m/d (6)
1697	354.69 2m/d (1)	275.00 2m/d (2)
1698		273.44 2m/d (1)
1699		
1700		
1701		
1702		
1703		

	HAMBURG on:		
	Cadiz	**Lisbon**	**Venice**
	per 100 ducados de cambio [b]	per 100 crusados [d]	per 100 ducati di banco [c]
		in mark banco	
1704			
1705			
1706			
1707			
1708			
1709			
1710		284.52 2m/d (11)	
1711		284.48 2m/d (12)	
1712		135.16 2m/d (1)	287.51 2m/d (12)
1713		136.15 2m/d (12)	283.72 2m/d (12)
1714		140.19 2m/d (8)	280.30 2m/d (11)
1715		140.43 2m/d (7)	272.99 2m/d (10)
1716		140.27 2m/d (12)	251.64 2m/d (10)
1717		138.64 2m/d (10)	244.91 2m/d (8)
1718		135.63 2m/d (12)	246.34 2m/d (10)
1719		136.22 2m/d (12)	261.29 2m/d (10)
1720		134.63 2m/d (7)	266.83 2m/d (8)
1721		133.57 2m/d (9)	266.69 2m/d (10)
1722		138.75 2m/d (8)	269.89 2m/d (11)
1723		138.60 2m/d (10)	267.11 2m/d (9)
1724		138.03 2m/d (10)	269.15 2m/d (11)
1725			
1726		136.72 2m/d (11)	265.60 2m/d (11)
1727		136.72 2m/d (1)	257.03 2m/d (1)
1728			
1729			
1730			
1731		137.50 2m/d (3)	257.81 2m/d (3)
1732		138.67 2m/d (3)	258.33 2m/d (3)
1733		138.28 2m/d (3)	260.16 2m/d (3)
1734		142.58 2m/d (9)	275.00 2m/d (9)
1735		143.75 2m/d (5)	285.94 2m/d (3)
1736	304.47 2m/d (11)	140.87 2m/d (11)	276.42 2m/d (11)
1737	295.82 2m/d (10)	137.60 2m/d (12)	267.90 2m/d (11)
1738	286.43 2m/d (11)	136.78 2m/d (12)	267.05 2m/d (11)
1739	290.76 2m/d (12)	138.61 2m/d (12)	270.04 2m/d (10)
1740	297.66 2m/d (6)	136.10 2m/d (12)	269.39 2m/d (11)
1741	302.12 2m/d (7)	135.37 2m/d (12)	269.08 2m/d (11)

	HAMBURG on:		
	Cadiz, from 1776 **Madrid** [e]	**Lisbon** [e]	**Venice**
	per 100 ducados de cambio [b]	per 100 crusados [d]	per 100 ducati di banco [c]
	in mark banco		
1742	284.38 2m/d (7)	136.44 2m/d (12)	266.32 2m/d (9)
1743	290.05 2m/d (12)	137.60 2m/d (12)	269.57 2m/d (10)
1744	294.89 2m/d (9)	135.41 2m/d (11)	270.67 2m/d (11)
1745	283.36 2m/d (10)	136.23 2m/d (12)	269.21 2m/d (12)
1746	286.10 2m/d (10)	141.73 2m/d (12)	273.07 2m/d (12)
1747	295.80 2m/d (9)	140.43 2m/d (12)	277.56 2m/d (12)
1748	287.51 2m/d (9)	138.87 2m/d (12)	277.35 2m/d (10)
1749	286.64 2m/d (10)	139.35 2m/d (11)	270.96 2m/d (11)
1750	280.00 2m/d (9)	136.25 2m/d (12)	276.95 2m/d (12)
1751	281.14 2m/d (12)	136.41 2m/d (12)	271.66 2m/d (9)
1752	284.08 2m/d (12)	136.38 2m/d (12)	280.66 2m/d (10)
1753	286.48 2m/d (11)	135.68 2m/d (12)	279.04 2m/d (11)
1754	284.99 2m/d (11)	136.04 2m/d (11)	274.88 2m/d (10)
1755	286.78 2m/d (7)	138.56 2m/d (10)	277.60 2m/d (10)
1756	290.20 2m/d (10)	143.45 2m/d (9)	283.03 2m/d (12)
1757	295.67 2m/d (10)	143.95 2m/d (12)	291.19 2m/d (11)
1758	301.03 2m/d (11)	144.01 2m/d (12)	296.38 2m/d (9)
1759	311.33 2m/d (11)	148.47 2m/d (12)	301.87 2m/d (12)
1760	283.81 2m/d (11)	137.08 2m/d (11)	280.57 2m/d (11)
1761	273.14 2m/d (12)	131.22 2m/d (12)	274.09 2m/d (11)
1762	285.55 2m/d (12)	140.53 2m/d (12)	282.83 2m/d (12)
1763	287.43 2m/d (10)	139.46 2m/d (11)	289.07 2m/d (10)
1764	284.19 2m/d (12)	140.97 2m/d (12)	283.30 2m/d (12)
1765	287.92 2m/d (12)	140.86 2m/d (12)	285.02 2m/d (12)
1766	297.46 2m/d (12)	143.48 2m/d (12)	290.57 2m/d (9)
1767	300.85 2m/d (11)	146.43 2m/d (11)	292.49 2m/d (7)
1768	286.61 2m/d (11)	139.75 2m/d (12)	280.24 2m/d (5)
1769	280.31 2m/d (12)	137.37 2m/d (12)	278.42 2m/d (8)
1770	279.11 2m/d (12)	136.59 2m/d (12)	278.84 2m/d (12)
1771	280.02 2m/d (12)	137.60 2m/d (12)	278.36 2m/d (9)
1772	278.18 2m/d (10)	136.61 2m/d (11)	277.20 2m/d (9)
1773	278.75 2m/d (12)	139.73 2m/d (12)	277.76 2m/d (4)
1774	276.87 2m/d (12)	140.84 2m/d (12)	276.62 2m/d (10)
1775	278.95 3m/d (12)	137.44 3m/d (12)	276.95 2m/d (8)
1776	275.82 3m/d (7)	134.77 3m/d (12)	277.40 3m/d (5)
1777	272.69 3m/d (10)	131.73 3m/d (9)	275.20 3m/d (5)
1778	272.63 3m/d (9)	134.02 3m/d (11)	271.40 3m/d (1)

	HAMBURG on:			
	Madrid [f]	**Lisbon**	**Venice**	**Leghorn**
	per 100 ducados de cambio [b]	per 100 crusados [d]	per 100 ducati di banco [c]	per 100 pezze da otto reali [g]
	in mark banco			
1779	272.34 3m/d (11)	134.98 3m/d (11)	274.50 3m/d (2)	
1780	274.51 3m/d (7)	136.04 3m/d (11)	254.50 3m/d (7)	
1781	250.01 3m/d (1)	133.14 3m/d (12)	268.60 3m/d (5)	
1782	263.75 3m/d (5)	133.44 3m/d (12)	275.10 3m/d (2)	
1783	241.41 3m/d (6)	133.92 3m/d (11)	271.80 3m/d (1)	
1784	255.69 3m/d (9)	138.18 3m/d (12)		
1785	259.32 3m/d (12)	138.41 3m/d (12)		
1786	259.05 3m/d (12)	141.31 3m/d (12)		
1787	267.02 3m/d (11)	142.11 3m/d (12)		
1788	265.11 3m/d (10)	141.33 3m/d (12)		
1789	262.20 3m/d (10)	143.22 3m/d (11)		
1790	263.15 3m/d (11)	145.32 3m/d (11)		
1791	272.03 3m/d (12)	149.04 3m/d (12)		
1792	270.39 3m/d (11)	150.85 3m/d (11)		
1793	265.86 3m/d (12)	153.32 3m/d (12)	**Genoa**	
1794	227.21 3m/d (11)	141.54 3m/d (12)	per 100 pezze of 5¾	
1795	207.04 3m/d (8)	139.06 3m/d (11)	lire fuori banco [h]	
1796	209.71 3m/d (12)	144.27 3m/d (12)	244.43 3m/d (12)	266.51 3m/d (12)
1797	218.82 3m/d (12)	152.83 3m/d (12)	240.24 3m/d (12)	263.35 3m/d (12)
1798	215.56 3m/d (11)	152.15 3m/d (12)	244.89 3m/d (12)	267.26 3m/d (12)
1799	157.24 3m/d (12)	141.02 3m/d (12)	247.42 3m/d (11)	264.67 3m/d (12)
1800	107.95 3m/d (12)	120.70 3m/d (12)	236.33 3m/d (11)	259.61 3m/d (12)
1801	123.45 3m/d (12)	121.48 3m/d (12)	239.72 3m/d (12)	265.13 3m/d (12)
1802	*263.55* 3m/d (12)	137.34 3m/d (12)	242.02 3m/d (12)	263.35 3m/d (12)
1803	*262.83* 3m/d (12)	133.14 3m/d (12)	242.89 3m/d (12)	264.04 3m/d (12)
1804	*261.47* 3m/d (12)	132.49 3m/d (12)	247.19 3m/d (11)	269.85 3m/d (11)
1805	*247.93* 3m/d (12)	128.97 3m/d (12)	248.86 3m/d (12)	272.90 3m/d (12)
1806	*258.34* 3m/d (9)	128.45 3m/d (12)	248.75 3m/d (12)	272.61 3m/d (12)
1807	*282.88* 3m/d (12)	134.77 3m/d (12)	249.73 3m/d (12)	269.96 3m/d (12)
1808	*302.74* 3m/d (8)	145.12 3m/d (8)	265.59 3m/d (12)	283.30 3m/d (12)
1809			262.03 3m/d (12)	282.33 3m/d (12)
1810			259.56 3m/d (12)	280.31 3m/d (12)
1811			253.46 3m/d (12)	271.86 3m/d (12)
1812			255.53 3m/d (12)	272.67 3m/d (12)
1813			248.57 3m/d (9)	269.39 3m/d (11)
1814	276.82 3m/d (3)	131.25 3m/d (5)	247.31 3m/d (4)	264.85 3m/d (6)
1815	263.81 3m/d (12)	127.74 3m/d (12)	245.53 3m/d (12)	261.57 3m/d (12)
1816	263.02 3m/d (12)	125.72 3m/d (12)	246.04 3m/d (12)	261.57 3m/d (12)

	HAMBURG on:			
	Madrid	**Lisbon**	**Genoa**	**Leghorn**
	per 100 ducados de cambio, from 1847 (7) per 100 pesos duros [b]	per 100 crusados, from 1829 per 100 milréis [d]	per 100 pezze of $5\frac{3}{4}$ lire fuori banco, from 1827 (5) per 100 Piedmontese lire nuove [h]	per 100 pezze da otto reali, from 1839 per 100 Tuscan lire moneta buona [g]
			in mark banco		
1817	270.58 3m/d (12)	125.72 3m/d (12)	246.79 3m/d (12)	263.12 3m/d (12)
1818	285.98 3m/d (12)	123.70 3m/d (12)	250.13 3m/d (12)	271.98 3m/d (12)
1819	281.00 3m/d (12)	119.92 3m/d (12)	250.24 3m/d (11)	273.47 3m/d (12)
1820	280.12 3m/d (10)	116.08 3m/d (12)	254.55 3m/d (12)	272.72 3m/d (12)
1821	293.59 3m/d (12)	116.67 3m/d (12)	260.65 3m/d (12)	278.65 3m/d (12)
1822	294.09 3m/d (12)	119.79 3m/d (12)	257.03 3m/d (12)	277.38 3m/d (12)
1823	297.37 3m/d (12)	121.88 3m/d (12)	255.53 3m/d (12)	274.68 3m/d (12)
1824	288.64 3m/d (12)	116.83 3m/d (12)	254.15 3m/d (12)	274.10 3m/d (12)
1825	287.01 3m/d (12)	115.32 3m/d (12)	258.18 3m/d (12)	282.04 3m/d (12)
1826	280.80 3m/d (12)	114.80 3m/d (12)	254.78 3m/d (12)	277.38 3m/d (12)
1827	271.49 3m/d (12)	112.63 3m/d (12)	253.92/53.73 3m/d (4+8)	273.76 3m/d (12)
1828	282.49 3m/d (12)	104.59 3m/d (12)	53.87 3m/d (12)	275.31 3m/d (12)
1829	288.16 3m/d (12)	259.25 3m/d (12)	53.42 3m/d (12)	273.07 3m/d (12)
1830	284.77 3m/d (12)	253.39 3m/d (12)	53.42 3m/d (12)	274.45 3m/d (12)
1831	286.72 3m/d (12)	262.83 3m/d (12)	53.27 3m/d (12)	270.71 3m/d (12)
1832	284.57 3m/d (12)	273.25 3m/d (12)	53.23 3m/d (12)	273.47 3m/d (12)
1833	291.15 3m/d (12)	274.03 3m/d (12)	53.16 3m/d (12)	271.63 3m/d (12)
1834	286.53 3m/d (12)	301.63 3m/d (12)	53.07 3m/d (12)	273.87 3m/d (12)
1835	288.16 3m/d (12)	323.90 3m/d (12)	52.81 3m/d (12)	271.75 3m/d (12)
1836	287.18 3m/d (12)	313.48 3m/d (12)	52.86 3m/d (12)	271.11 3m/d (12)
1837	272.92 3m/d (12)	293.62 3m/d (12)	52.40 3m/d (12)	268.76 3m/d (12)
1838	279.69 3m/d (12)	301.31 3m/d (12)	52.47 3m/d (12)	265.65 3m/d (12)
1839	283.47 3m/d (12)	300.07 3m/d (12)	52.28 3m/d (12)	43.93 3m/d (12)
1840	281.51 3m/d (12)	300.00 3m/d (12)	52.18 3m/d (12)	43.94 3m/d (12)
1841	275.39 3m/d (12)	291.02 3m/d (12)	52.04 3m/d (12)	44.14 3m/d (12)
1842	281.91 3m/d (12)	295.25 3m/d (12)	52.11 3m/d (12)	44.72 3m/d (12)
1843	285.69 3m/d (12)	299.42 3m/d (12)	52.63 3m/d (12)	44.55 3m/d (12)
1844	286.86 3m/d (12)	304.95 3m/d (12)	52.58 3m/d (12)	44.42 3m/d (12)
1845	284.12 3m/d (12)	302.35 3m/d (12)	52.50 3m/d (12)	44.35 3m/d (12)
1846	280.74 3m/d (12)	296.94 3m/d (12)	52.16 3m/d (12)	44.35 3m/d (12)
1847	276.56/264.85 3m/d (6+6)	291.41 3m/d (12)	52.01 3m/d (12)	44.25 3m/d (12)
1848	248.05 3m/d (12)	287.50 3m/d (12)	52.47 3m/d (12)	43.50 3m/d (12)
1849	271.62 3m/d (12)	295.97 3m/d (12)	51.88 3m/d (12)	42.59 3m/d (12)
1850	275.13 3m/d (12)	298.18 3m/d (12)	52.00 3m/d (12)	43.85 3m/d (12)
1851	272.40 3m/d (12)	292.71 3m/d (12)	51.24 3m/d (12)	43.05 3m/d (12)
1852	273.96 3m/d (12)	293.49 3m/d (12)	51.82 3m/d (12)	43.29 3m/d (12)

	HAMBURG on:			
Madrid, from 1869 Cadiz	**Lisbon**	**Genoa**	**Leghorn**
per 100 pesos duros [b]	per 100 milréis [d]	per 100 Piedmontese lire nuove, from 1861 (8) per 100 Italian lire [h]	per 100 Tuscan lire moneta buona, from 1861 (1) per 100 Piedmontese lire nuove, from 1861 (8) per 100 Italian lire [g]
		in mark banco		
1853	271.68 3m/d (12)	291.15 3m/d (12)	52.05 3m/d (12)	43.58 3m/d (12)
1854	269.54 3m/d (12)	288.81 3m/d (12)	51.55 3m/d (12)	43.26 3m/d (12)
1855	269.54 3m/d (12)	290.63 3m/d (12)	52.08 3m/d (12)	43.61 3m/d (12)
1856	269.99 3m/d (12)	289.39 3m/d (12)	51.51 3m/d (12)	43.33 3m/d (12)
1857	267.45 3m/d (12)	283.86 3m/d (12)	50.96 3m/d (12)	43.97 3m/d (12)
1858	262.63 3m/d (12)	281.64 3m/d (12)	51.38 3m/d (12)	44.08 3m/d (12)
1859	263.55 3m/d (12)	281.91 3m/d (12)	50.80 3m/d (12)	43.48 3m/d (12)
1860	267.06 3m/d (12)	285.94 3m/d (12)	51.55 3m/d (12)	43.14 3m/d (12)
1861	264.91 3m/d (12)	285.88 3m/d (12)	51.66 3m/d (12)	51.53 3m/d (12)
1862	266.35 3m/d (12)	288.68 3m/d (12)	52.02 3m/d (12)	51.89 3m/d (12)
1863	264.59 3m/d (12)	288.22 3m/d (12)	51.93 3m/d (12)	51.84 3m/d (12)
1864	260.36 3m/d (12)	285.29 3m/d (12)	51.47 3m/d (12)	51.47 3m/d (12)
1865	259.25 3m/d (12)	283.86 3m/d (12)	52.10 3m/d (12)	52.10 3m/d (12)
1866	253.65 3m/d (12)	282.95 3m/d (12)	50.79 3m/d (9)	50.79 3m/d (9)
1867	268.56 3m/d (12)	289.72 3m/d (12)	49.17 3m/d (12)	49.17 3m/d (12)
1868	270.71 3m/d (12)	290.56 3m/d (12)	48.04 3m/d (12)	48.04 3m/d (12)
1869	270.71 3m/d (12)	292.84 3m/d (12)	50.70 3m/d (12)	
1870	265.50 3m/d (12)	290.43 3m/d (12)	49.85 3m/d (12)	
1871	269.67 3m/d (12)	295.51 3m/d (12)	49.55 3m/d (12)	
1872	271.36 3m/d (12)	295.19 3m/d (12)	48.38 3m/d (12)	
1873	269.01 3m/d (2)	296.88 3m/d (2)	47.29 3m/d (2)	

[a]   1672: quotation on Seville.

[b]   Concerning the Spanish currency, see p. 307.

[c]   Concerning the Venetian currency, see pp. 104f.

[d]   In the Portuguese currency system one reckoned in réis, respectively in milréis (= 1,000 réis), but up to the 19th century the exchange rate quotations of and on Portuguese places were often effected in or for crusados ('velhos' or 'do cambio') as a unit of account of 400 réis. Since the Coin Act of July 29th 1854, the Portuguese silver standard with the milréis at 27.15 grammes of fine silver (from July 1st 1835 according to the Coin Act of April 24th 1835) was succeeded by the gold standard – following the model of Great Britain – with the milréis at 1.6257 grammes of fine gold. From July 1891 Portugal had the paper standard with a premium for gold coins up to 53% (in May 1897). In 1912 the milréis was succeded by the escudo of 100 centavos (1 escudo = 1 milréis); from the beginning of 1913 it had to be officially reckoned in this new currency, but for all commercial transactions the term 'milréis' continued to be common (cf. NELKENBRECHER [1771], p. 131; NOBACK [1877], p. 507; SWOBODA [1913], pp. 518f.).

[e]   In 1755 the usance for the Iberian places was extended to 3 months (BAASCH [1905/06], p. 10).

[f]   From 1802 to 1808 'zahlbar in Effectiv', i.e. payable in hard currrency (not in paper money).

[g]   Concerning the Tuscan and the Italian currencies, see p. 106. Until 1838 inclusive of 7% premium for payment in gold: 107 lire moneta buona = 100 lire d'oro.

[h]   Concerning the Genoese and the Italian currencies, see pp. 107–109.

4.1.3 On Danzig, German and Austrian places

	HAMBURG on:			
	Danzig	**Nuremberg**	**Leipzig**	**Breslau**
	per 100 guilders Polish current [a]	per 100 guilders current [b]	per 100 rixdollars current [c]	per 100 rixdollars in Kaisergeld [d]
	in mark banco			
1672	196.56 4w/d (1)	161.87 4w/d (1)	*287.08* fair (1)	*277.78* 4w/d (1)
1673				
1674				
1675				
1676				
1677				
1678				
1679				
1680				
1681				
1682				
1683				
1684				
1685				
1686				
1687				
1688				
1689	198.83 4w/d (1)	167.01 4w/d (1)	252.10 fair (1)	250.00 4w/d (1)
1690	197.04 4w/d (1)	164.10 4w/d (1)	243.65 fair (1)	247.42 4w/d (1)
1691				
1692		155.95 4w/d (2)	231.88 fair (2)	237.62 4w/d (2)
1693		150.52 4w/d (2)	230.99 fair (2)	243.90 4w/d (2)
1694				
1695				
1696		148.70 4w/d (6)	221.81 fair (4)	214.29 4w/d (6)
1697	168.07 4w/d (1)	148.98 4w/d (1)	227.70 fair (2)	223.46 4w/d (1)
1698		150.09 4w/d (1)	236.22 fair (1)	*273.97* 4w/d (1)
1699				
1700				
1701				
1702				
1703				
1704				
1705				
1706				
1707				

	HAMBURG on:			
	Vienna	**Nuremberg**	**Leipzig**	**Breslau**
	per 100 guilders current [e]	per 100 guilders current [b]	per 100 rixdollars current [c]	per 100 rixdollars in Kaisergeld [d]
	in mark banco			
1708				
1709				
1710		147.28 4w/d (11)	227.46 fair (11)	230.31 4w/d (12)
1711		147.78 4w/d (12)	227.62 fair (11)	217.43 4w/d (10)
1712		147.72 4w/d (11)	227.22 fair (10)	217.29 4w/d (12)
1713		147.96 4w/d (12)	226.50 fair (11)	211.23 4w/d (12)
1714		148.59 4w/d (11)	226.27 fair (10)	206.03 4w/d (12)
1715		149.04 4w/d (10)	225.27 fair (11)	205.51 4w/d (12)
1716		148.18 4w/d (10)	224.74 fair (11)	213.25 4w/d (12)
1717		149.86 4w/d (11)	225.45 fair (12)	204.82 4w/d (12)
1718	148.95 4w/d (6)	148.48 4w/d (8)	225.06 fair (11)	210.69 4w/d (11)
1719	146.88 4w/d (5)	146.56 4w/d (10)	222.99 fair (12)	225.79 4w/d (11)
1720	145.82 4w/d (3)	145.87 4w/d (10)	223.08 fair (10)	228.87 4w/d (10)
1721	145.81 4w/d (11)	146.36 4w/d (8)	224.48 fair (11)	228.49 4w/d (12)
1722	148.59 4w/d (7)	148.48 33d/d (11)	226.96 fair (12)	211.98 4w/d (9)
1723	148.73 4w/d (9)	148.45 33d/d (12)	226.59 fair (11)	211.38 4w/d (9)
1724	148.79 4w/d (10)	148.40 33d/d (11)	225.79 fair (11)	212.08 4w/d (11)
1725				
1726	138.89 4w/d (1)	147.73 33d/d (11)	224.65 fair (11)	218.88 4w/d (12)
1727	141.84 4w/d (1)	147.06 33d/d (1)	238.10 fair (1)	212.01 4w/d (1)
1728				
1729				
1730				
1731	132.45 4w/d (3)	135.14 33d/d (3)	218.98 fair (2)	202.70 4w/d (3)
1732	140.19 4w/d (3)	139.60 33d/d (3)	230.77 fair (1)	209.79 4w/d (1)
1733	145.63 4w/d (3)	146.12 33d/d (3)	236.22 fair (1)	222.22 4w/d (3)
1734	144.93 4w/d (8)	149.25 33d/d (8)	237.53 fair (5)	220.59 4w/d (8)
1735	144.40 4w/d (3)	147.06 33d/d (3)	240.00 fair (2)	225.56 4w/d (3)
1736	148.29 4w/d (11)	148.35 33d/d (11)	224.79 fair (6)	223.88 4w/d (11)
1737	147.35 4w/d (10)	148.32 33d/d (12)	221.14 fair (9)	220.25 4w/d (11)
1738	146.33 4w/d (11)	146.93 33d/d (12)	219.03 fair (10)	226.85 4w/d (11)
1739	146.19 4w/d (9)	146.91 33d/d (12)	219.63 fair (10)	226.07 4w/d (11)
1740	145.96 4w/d (10)	147.69 33d/d (12)	221.05 fair (10)	223.73 4w/d (11)
1741	144.69 4w/d (10)	148.01 33d/d (12)	221.45 fair (9)	217.04 4w/d (10)
1742	145.94 4w/d (12)	147.43 33d/d (12)	220.75 fair (8)	223.96 4w/d (12)
1743	145.15 4w/d (11)	147.53 33d/d (12)	219.83 fair (10)	229.69 4w/d (12)
1744	144.54 4w/d (10)	147.77 33d/d (12)	219.63 fair (10)	232.36 4w/d (12)
1745	144.15 4w/d (12)	148.04 33d/d (12)	217.49 fair (8)	231.11 4w/d (11)

	HAMBURG on:			
	Vienna	**Nuremberg**	**Leipzig**	**Breslau** [f]
	per 100 guilders current, from 1754 per 100 guilders Konventionskurant [e]	per 100 guilders current [b]	per 100 rixdollars current, from 1764 per 100 rixdollars Leipzig exchange money [c]	per 100 rixdollars in Kaisergeld, from 1776 per 100 livres Prussian banco [d]
	in mark banco			
1746	145.47 4w/d (12)	148.05 33d/d (12)	218.53 fair (7)	226.03 4w/d (11)
1747	148.36 4w/d (12)	149.53 33d/d (10)	220.81 fair (8)	212.47 4w/d (12)
1748	145.64 4w/d (10)	148.59 33d/d (9)	218.00 fair (10)	225.33 4w/d (12)
1749	144.87 4w/d (12)	145.86 33d/d (9)	214.89 fair (9)	233.24 4w/d (12)
1750	143.16 4w/d (12)	143.94 33d/d (11)	210.99 fair (9)	246.98 4w/d (12)
1751	141.01 4w/d (11)	141.93 33d/d (12)	205.37 fair (8)	261.46 4w/d (6)
1752	141.91 4w/d (11)	142.79 33d/d (10)	204.73 fair (6)	270.84 4w/d (12)
1753	142.77 4w/d (12)	144.12 33d/d (8)	203.29 fair (9)	291.51 4w/d (12)
1754	141.78 4w/d (11)	142.46 33d/d (7)	201.69 fair (11)	302.61 4w/d (12)
1755	142.15 4w/d (12)	143.26 33d/d (4)	204.14 fair (7)	303.56 6w/d (11)
1756	146.76 4w/d (11)		212.87 fair (8)	288.68 6w/d (12)
1757	150.48 6w/d (12)		217.50 fair (2)	
1758	152.50 6w/d (11)		221.11 fair (4)	
1759	153.34 6w/d (11)			
1760	140.78 6w/d (11)			
1761	139.16 6w/d (12)			
1762	143.73 6w/d (11)			
1763	144.83 6w/d (12)			
1764	141.39 6w/d (12)		212.77 fair (1)	
1765	142.96 6w/d (11)			
1766	147.66 6w/d (12)			
1767	148.39 6w/d (12)			
1768	144.34 6w/d (11)			
1769	140.69 6w/d (11)		209.35 fair (4)	
1770	140.60 6w/d (12)		209.79 fair (1)	
1771	139.43 6w/d (12)			
1772	139.35 6w/d (11)		206.54 fair (2)	
1773	137.51 6w/d (11)		207.38 fair (3)	
1774	137.81 6w/d (12)		208.34 fair (5)	
1775	139.30 6w/d (12)		209.43 fair (2)	
1776	138.04 6w/d (8)		207.99 fair (6)	258.33 6w/d (11)
1777	136.61 6w/d (10)		206.10 fair (7)	257.23 6w/d (12)
1778	136.21 6w/d (5)		207.57 fair (7)	259.10 6w/d (7)
1779	138.90 6w/d (12)		207.69 fair (8)	258.99 6w/d (10)
1780	135.64 6w/d (12)		206.20 fair (7)	279.39 6w/d (12)
1781	134.93 6w/d (12)		205.79 fair (6)	257.30 6w/d (12)

	HAMBURG on:			
	Vienna	**Augsburg**	**Leipzig**	**Breslau**
	per 100 guilders Konventionskurant, from 1800 per 100 guilders Wiener Währung, from 1816 per 100 guilders Konventionskurant [e]	per 100 guilders Augsburg current [g]	per 100 rixdollars Leipzig exchange money [c]	per 100 livres Prussian banco [d]
			in mark banco	
1782	136.37 6w/d (12)		205.08 fair (7)	255.91 6w/d (12)
1783	136.57 6w/d (11)		205.52 fair (6)	258.67 6w/d (11)
1784	137.98 6w/d (12)		206.73 fair (7)	261.12 6w/d (12)
1785	138.27 6w/d (12)		209.62 fair (6)	262.85 6w/d (12)
1786	137.63 6w/d (12)		209.64 fair (4)	260.76 6w/d (12)
1787	135.76 6w/d (12)		207.08 fair (6)	257.28 6w/d (12)
1788	136.19 6w/d (12)		207.59 fair (5)	255.02 6w/d (12)
1789	134.40 6w/d (11)		207.72 fair (4)	256.22 6w/d (11)
1790	133.74 6w/d (12)		209.67 fair (3)	257.28 6w/d (11)
1791	133.34 6w/d (12)		211.50 fair (5)	257.72 6w/d (12)
1792	135.21 6w/d (12)		210.61 fair (6)	253.13 6w/d (12)
1793	133.63 6w/d (12)		209.79 fair (1)	251.07 6w/d (12)
1794	134.15 6w/d (11)			253.29 6w/d (12)
1795	134.94 6w/d (12)			256.47 6w/d (12)
1796	135.69 6w/d (12)			257.95 6w/d (12)
1797	131.25 6w/d (12)			254.17 6w/d (12)
1798	131.58 6w/d (12)			255.31 6w/d (12)
1799	122.52 6w/d (12)			252.97 6w/d (12)
1800	114.58 6w/d (12)			256.45 6w/d (12)
1801	113.44 6w/d (12)			257.78 6w/d (12)
1802	108.12 6w/d (11)	133.32 6w/d (12)		260.13 6w/d (12)
1803	100.62 6w/d (12)	132.96 6w/d (12)		256.77 6w/d (12)
1804	99.35 6w/d (12)	133.95 6w/d (12)		253.98 6w/d (12)
1805	98.05 6w/d (12)	134.48 6w/d (12)		256.12 6w/d (12)
1806	78.36 6w/d (12)	134.14 6w/d (12)		251.10 6w/d (10)
1807	64.01 6w/d (12)	134.21 6w/d (12)		243.88 6w/d (12)
1808	61.11 6w/d (12)	140.04 6w/d (12)		250.59 6w/d (12)
1809	53.58 6w/d (8)	139.59 6w/d (12)		247.46 6w/d (12)
1810	32.90 6w/d (11)	135.59 6w/d (12)		254.11 6w/d (12)
1811	15.45/55.90 6w/d (3+9)	133.73 6w/d (12)		248.70 6w/d (12)
1812	66.86 6w/d (11)	139.27 6w/d (12)		264.42 6w/d (12)
1813	88.46 6w/d (7)	137.56 6w/d (11)		267.06 6w/d (6)
1814	61.09 6w/d (4)	135.21 6w/d (7)		261.40 6w/d (6)
1815	40.91 6w/d (5)	135.73 6w/d (12)		259.35 6w/d (12)

	HAMBURG on:			
	Vienna	**Augsburg**	**Leipzig**	**Breslau, from 1836 Berlin**
	per 100 guilders Konventionskurant [e]	per 100 guilders Augsburg current [g]	per 100 rixdollars Leipzig exchange money, from 1841 per 100 thaler Saxon current [c]	per 100 livres Prussian banco [d], from 1826 per 100 thaler Prussian current [h]
			in mark banco	
1816	135.17 6w/d (9)	135.14 6w/d (12)		259.68 6w/d (12)
1817	134.16 6w/d (12)	133.27 6w/d (12)	200.20 fair (5)	257.20 6w/d (12)
1818	136.07 6w/d (12)	134.56 6w/d (12)	201.38 fair (5)	259.06 6w/d (12)
1819	136.03 6w/d (12)	135.31 6w/d (12)	202.58 fair (5)	256.16 6w/d (12)
1820	135.54 6w/d (11)	135.10 6w/d (12)	202.72 fair (6)	254.97 6w/d (12)
1821	137.12 6w/d (12)	136.66 6w/d (12)	204.79 fair (6)	255.75 6w/d (12)
1822	136.10 6w/d (12)	135.58 6w/d (12)	202.86 fair (7)	254.42 6w/d (12)
1823	134.95 6w/d (12)	134.32 6w/d (12)	201.42 fair (5)	252.83 6w/d (12)
1824	136.89 6w/d (12)	135.59 6w/d (12)	202.62 fair (7)	256.58 6w/d (12)
1825	136.86 6w/d (12)	136.61 6w/d (12)	204.92 fair (4)	259.22 6w/d (12)
1826	134.62 6w/d (12)	135.05 6w/d (12)	202.94 fair (3)	194.19 6w/d (12)
1827	135.82 6w/d (12)	135.84 6w/d (12)	202.99 6w/d (12)	196.38 6w/d (12)
1828	136.76 6w/d (12)	136.42 6w/d (12)	203.73 6w/d (12)	197.11 6w/d (12)
1829	135.85 6w/d (12)	135.86 6w/d (12)	203.56 6w/d (12)	197.54 6w/d (12)
1830	135.23 6w/d (12)	135.58 6w/d (12)	202.04 6w/d (12)	197.16 6w/d (12)
1831	135.77 6w/d (12)	136.03 6w/d (12)	202.62 6w/d (12)	197.87 6w/d (12)
1832	135.63 6w/d (12)	135.12 6w/d (12)	200.31 6w/d (12)	194.09 6w/d (12)
1833	136.83 6w/d (12)	135.72 6w/d (12)	201.69 6w/d (12)	195.90 6w/d (12)
1834	136.63 6w/d (12)	135.48 6w/d (12)	201.37 6w/d (12)	195.09 6w/d (12)
1835	135.94 6w/d (12)	135.58 6w/d (12)	201.42 6w/d (12)	195.45 6w/d (12)
1836	134.47 6w/d (12)	134.75 6w/d (12)	201.07 6w/d (12)	195.81 2m/d (12)
1837	133.85 6w/d (12)	134.58 6w/d (12)	199.52 6w/d (12)	196.35 2m/d (12)
1838	133.91 6w/d (12)	134.39 6w/d (12)	200.22 6w/d (12)	196.53 2m/d (12)
1839	133.74 6w/d (12)	134.26 6w/d (12)	200.80 6w/d (12)	196.47 2m/d (12)
1840	133.94 6w/d (12)	134.83 6w/d (12)	202.21 6w/d (12)	197.93 2m/d (12)
1841	135.90 6w/d (12)	135.30 6w/d (12)	198.93 6w/d (12)	199.09 2m/d (12)
1842	137.30 6w/d (12)	135.73 6w/d (12)	197.96 6w/d (12)	197.81 2m/d (12)
1843	137.11 2m/d (12)	135.52 2m/d (12)	197.17 2m/d (12)	197.07 2m/d (12)
1844	137.77 2m/d (12)	135.38 2m/d (12)	197.37 2m/d (12)	197.29 2m/d (12)
1845	136.70 2m/d (12)	134.95 2m/d (12)	196.85 2m/d (12)	196.72 2m/d (12)
1846	134.58 2m/d (12)	134.42 2m/d (12)	196.57 2m/d (12)	196.40 2m/d (12)
1847	133.97 2m/d (12)	133.75 2m/d (12)	195.50 2m/d (12)	195.53 2m/d (12)
1848	124.89 2m/d (10)	133.80 2m/d (12)	195.24 2m/d (12)	195.34 2m/d (12)
1849	118.78 2m/d (11)	134.33 2m/d (12)	197.29 2m/d (12)	197.43 2m/d (12)
1850	113.21 2m/d (12)	134.63 2m/d (12)	196.43 2m/d (12)	196.66 2m/d (12)

	HAMBURG on:			
	Vienna	**Augsburg**	**Leipzig**	**Berlin**
	per 100 guilders Konventionskurant, from 1858 (11) per 100 guilders Österreichische Währung [e]	per 100 guilders Augsburg current, from 1859 per 100 guilders South German current [g]	per 100 thaler Saxon current [c]	per 100 thaler Prussian current [h]
	in mark banco			
1851	105.62 2m/d (12)	134.17 2m/d (12)	196.73 2m/d (12)	196.83 2m/d (12)
1852	110.50 2m/d (12)	133.58 2m/d (12)	195.05 2m/d (12)	195.31 2m/d (12)
1853	119.86 2m/d (12)	133.07 2m/d (12)	194.81 2m/d (12)	194.89 2m/d (12)
1854	104.66 2m/d (12)	132.91 2m/d (12)	197.24 2m/d (12)	197.59 2m/d (12)
1855	110.01 2m/d (12)	134.00 2m/d (12)	197.49 2m/d (12)	197.91 2m/d (12)
1856	126.70 2m/d (12)	132.97 2m/d (12)	193.21 2m/d (12)	193.57 2m/d (12)
1857	125.40 2m/d (12)	132.86 2m/d (12)	193.57 2m/d (12)	193.96 2m/d (12)
1858	127.02/126.60 2m/d (10+2)	133.18 2m/d (12)	195.18 2m/d (12)	195.81 2m/d (12)
1859	107.74 2m/d (12)	112.29 2m/d (12)	195.81 2m/d (12)	196.48 2m/d (12)
1860	98.70 2m/d (12)	112.44 2m/d (12)	196.67 2m/d (12)	197.10 2m/d (12)
1861	91.75 2m/d (12)	112.43 2m/d (12)	196.83 2m/d (12)	197.13 2m/d (12)
1862	100.62 2m/d (12)	111.72 2m/d (12)	195.53 2m/d (12)	195.67 2m/d (12)
1863	115.20 2m/d (12)	111.39 2m/d (12)	195.14 2m/d (12)	195.27 2m/d (12)
1864	110.55 2m/d (12)	110.71 2m/d (12)	193.69 2m/d (12)	193.94 2m/d (12)
1865	118.52 2m/d (12)	110.66 2m/d (12)	193.45 2m/d (12)	193.78 2m/d (12)
1866	110.24 2m/d (12)	111.42 2m/d (12)	193.72 2m/d (12)	193.85 2m/d (12)
1867	104.47 2m/d (12)	112.02 2m/d (12)	196.08 2m/d (12)	196.31 2m/d (12)
1868	114.03 2m/d (12)	112.17 2m/d (12)	196.32 2m/d (12)	196.47 2m/d (12)
1869	107.57 3m/d (12)	111.74 3m/d (12)	195.78 3m/d (12)	196.01 3m/d (12)
1870	106.34 3m/d (12)	111.30 3m/d (12)	195.57 3m/d (12)	195.90 3m/d (12)
1871	108.26 3m/d (12)	112.47 3m/d (12)	197.32 3m/d (12)	197.53 3m/d (12)
1872	118.63 3m/d (12)	112.77 3m/d (12)	197.97 3m/d (12)	198.18 3m/d (12)
1873	121.77 3m/d (2)	113.48 3m/d (2)	199.26 ss (2)	199.59 3m/d (2)

[a]   Concerning the Danzig currency, see p. 379.

[b]   In Nuremberg one reckoned in guilders current of 60 kreuzer, whereby the 'current' money functioned as bank money as well. In this function, 'current' meant payable in full and half speciesthaler, i.e. the full-weighted rixdollars of 1566 at 25.98 grammes of fine silver (equal to 2 or 1 guilder of 60 kreuzer respectively). All bills with a sum of more than 200 guilders had to be effected via the Banco publico, founded in 1621.

[c]   In Leipzig one reckoned in rixdollars of 24 good groschen at 12 pfennige, whereby in exchange transactions the rixdollar current was payable above all in two-thirds pieces (of the rixdollar, the so-called 'zweidrittel'; equal to the guilder) of Saxony and Brunswick–Lüneburg and their divisions (HERBACH [1716], p. 177). In 1672 the rate was per 100 rixdollars specie or speciesthaler, i.e. the full-weighted rixdollars of 1566 at 25.98 grammes of fine silver. Concerning the Saxon currency since the introduction of the Konventionskurant in 1763, see pp. 194f.

[d]   Up to the Prussian conquest of Silesia the Hamburg quotations on Breslau were effected for rixdollars in Kaisergeld, imperial coins, especially the so-called 'Kaisergroschen', meaning silver

groschen, but also rixdollars specie or speciesthaler (i.e. the full-weighted rixdollars of 1566 at 25.98 grammes of fine silver). Thus the rixdollar current was equal to 30 Kaisergroschen or silver groschen at 12 pfennige current or 90 kreuzer, 1 rixdollar specie to 40 Kaisergroschen or silver groschen or 120 kreuzer. In 1672 and in 1698 the rate was per 100 rixdollars specie or speciesthaler. Due to an edict of the Prussian king from 1751, all bills had to be paid in Prussian currency: "If the bill be payable in any other money, the payment must nevertheless be made in the said currency, allowance being made for the agio on the particular money expressed in the bill" (KELLY [1811], p. 77). The livre or pound banco of 24 groschen banco at 12 denars was the Prussian currency in Breslau up to 1825, whereby 16 livres banco were equal to 21 thaler Prussian current.

[e] Concerning the Austrian currency from 1748/50, see pp. 255f. From June 3rd 1848 the guilder Konventionskurant and from November 1858 the guilder Österreichische Währung were paper money issued in notes by the Wiener Nationalbank and in government notes.

[f] In 1755 the usance was extended to 6 weeks (BAASCH [1905/06], p. 10).

[g] Augsburg current meant – in modification of Konventionskurant, which became common especially since 1764 (NOBACK [1851], 1. Abth., p. 70) – a standard of coinage of 20 5/12 guilders per mark of Cologne. So the guilder Augsburg current of 60 kreuzer was equal to 11.45 grammes of fine silver. As a consequence of the Vienna Coin Treaty of 1857, the guilder South German current (standard of coinage: 24½ guilders per 233.855 grammes of fine silver or 52½ guilders per pound of 500 grammes of fine silver) of 60 kreuzer became legal tender in Augsburg from the beginning of the year 1859.

4.1.4 On Frankfurt, Basle, Antwerp and Saint Petersburg

	HAMBURG on:			
	Frankfurt	**Basle**	**Antwerp**	**Saint Petersburg**
	per 100 guilders Frankfurt exchange money [a]	per 100 livres tournois, from 1796 (10) per 100 French francs [b]	per 100 Dutch guilders [c]	per 100 banco roubles [d]
	in mark banco			
1796		52.50 2m/d (12)		
1797		51.22 2m/d (12)		
1798		51.03 2m/d (12)		
1799		51.30 2m/d (12)		
1800		51.51 2m/d (12)		
1801		51.00 2m/d (12)		
1802		51.40 2m/d (12)		
1803		51.45 2m/d (12)		
1804		51.78 2m/d (12)		
1805		51.22 2m/d (12)		
1806		51.68 2m/d (12)		
1807		52.16 2m/d (12)		
1808		54.54 2m/d (12)		
1809		54.22 2m/d (12)		
1810		52.96 2m/d (12)		
1811		52.69 2m/d (12)		
1812	140.91 fair (3)	52.48 2m/d (4)		
1813				
1814	135.18 fair (5)			
1815	136.30 fair (12)			
1816	135.71 fair (12)			
1817	133.78 fair (12)			
1818	134.42 fair (12)			
1819	135.14 fair (12)			
1820	135.31 fair (12)			
1821	136.45 fair (12)			54.22 2m/d (12)
1822	135.55 fair (12)			54.92 2m/d (12)
1823	134.35 fair (12)			54.16 2m/d (12)
1824	135.47 fair (12)			53.57 2m/d (12)
1825	136.63 fair (12)		113.42 ss (12)	56.39 2m/d (11)
1826	135.65 fair (12)		113.50 ss (12)	54.05 2m/d (10)
1827	136.14 6w/d (12)		113.69 ss (12)	57.00 2m/d (12)
1828	136.68 6w/d (12)		113.13 ss (12)	57.93 2m/d (12)
1829	136.26 6w/d (12)		112.50 ss (12)	59.61 2m/d (12)
1830	135.88 6w/d (12)		112.95 ss (11)	59.57 2m/d (12)

	HAMBURG on:		
	Frankfurt	**Antwerp**	**Saint Petersburg**
	per 100 guilders Frankfurt exchange money, from 1843 per 100 guilders South German current [a]	per 100 Dutch guilders, from 1852 per 100 Belgian francs [c]	per 100 banco roubles, from 1839 (9) per 100 silver roubles, from 1843 (11) payable in credit notes [d]
		in mark banco	
1831	136.39 6w/d (12)	113.37 ss (12)	58.73 2m/d (12)
1832	135.24 6w/d (12)	112.63 ss (12)	58.80 2m/d (12)
1833	135.83 6w/d (12)	112.35 ss (12)	59.17 2m/d (12)
1834	135.59 6w/d (12)	112.15 ss (12)	58.88 2m/d (12)
1835	135.58 6w/d (12)	112.44 ss (12)	58.70 2m/d (12)
1836	134.89 6w/d (12)	112.40 ss (12)	58.70 2m/d (12)
1837	135.07 6w/d (12)	112.66 ss (12)	58.79 2m/d (12)
1838	134.74 6w/d (12)	112.26 ss (12)	59.43 2m/d (12)
1839	134.64 6w/d (12)	111.66 ss (12)	61.58/214.27 2m/d (8+4)
1840	135.25 6w/d (12)	111.47 ss (12)	213.74 2m/d (12)
1841	135.58 6w/d (12)	111.13 ss (12)	212.54 2m/d (12)
1842	135.68 6w/d (12)	111.46 ss (12)	210.13 2m/d (12)
1843	113.03 2m/d (12)	112.27 ss (12)	210.68 2m/d (12)
1844	112.80 2m/d (12)	111.88 ss (12)	212.28 2m/d (12)
1845	112.43 2m/d (12)	111.54 ss (12)	212.21 2m/d (12)
1846	112.09 2m/d (12)	111.13 ss (12)	210.32 2m/d (12)
1847	111.50 2m/d (12)	110.96 ss (12)	213.02 2m/d (12)
1848	112.34 2m/d (12)	112.21 ss (12)	204.24 2m/d (12)
1849	112.83 2m/d (12)	112.83 ss (12)	206.94 2m/d (12)
1850	112.52 2m/d (12)	112.43 ss (12)	211.72 3m/d (12)
1851	112.31 2m/d (12)	112.06 ss (12)	206.25 3m/d (12)
1852	111.24 2m/d (12)	52.96 ss (12)	209.05 3m/d (12)
1853	111.12 2m/d (12)	52.69 ss (12)	209.44 3m/d (12)
1854	111.54 2m/d (12)	52.45 ss (12)	194.60 3m/d (12)
1855	112.30 2m/d (12)	52.63 ss (12)	194.86 3m/d (12)
1856	110.87 2m/d (12)	52.37 ss (12)	203.85 3m/d (12)
1857	111.04 2m/d (12)	52.34 ss (12)	200.33 3m/d (12)
1858	112.01 2m/d (12)	52.84 ss (12)	193.43 3m/d (12)
1859	112.37 2m/d (12)	52.55 ss (12)	189.33 3m/d (12)
1860	112.60 2m/d (12)	52.57 ss (12)	191.74 3m/d (12)
1861	112.59 2m/d (12)	52.70 ss (12)	186.59 3m/d (12)
1862	111.92 2m/d (12)	52.65 ss (12)	187.50 3m/d (12)
1863	111.54 2m/d (12)	52.56 ss (12)	196.81 3m/d (12)
1864	110.86 2m/d (12)	52.51 ss (12)	175.26 3m/d (12)
1865	110.81 2m/d (12)	52.92 ss (12)	169.80 3m/d (12)
1866	111.51 2m/d (12)	52.92 ss (12)	159.83 3m/d (12)

	HAMBURG on:		
	Frankfurt	**Antwerp**	**Saint Petersburg**
	per 100 guilders South German current [a]	per 100 Belgian francs [c]	per 100 silver roubles payable in credit notes [d]
	in mark banco		
1868	112.43 2m/d (12)	53.64 ss (12)	181.16 3m/d (12)
1869	112.04 3m/d (12)	53.68 ss (12)	170.25 3m/d (12)
1870	112.14 3m/d (12)	53.53 ss (12)	162.31 3m/d (12)
1871	112.87 3m/d (12)	53.33 ss (12)	174.16 3m/d (12)
1872	113.17 3m/d (12)	53.34 ss (12)	179.89 3m/d (12)
1873	113.96 3m/d (2)	53.70 ss (2)	180.08 3m/d (2)

[a]   Concerning the Frankfurt currency, see pp. 195f.

[b]   Concerning the French currency at Basle, see pp. 279f.

[c]   Concerning the Dutch and French currencies at Antwerp, see pp. 57–59, 279f. In 1832 the Belgian franc was introduced and it was equal to the French franc, whereby 189 Dutch guilders = 400 Belgian francs.

[d]   Concerning the Russian currency, see pp. 359f.

4.2 Leipzig exchange rates

4.2.1 On Amsterdam, London, Hamburg and Paris

	LEIPZIG on:			
	Amsterdam	**London**	**Hamburg**	**Paris** [a]
	per 100 guilders Flemish current [b]	per 10 pounds sterling [c]	per 100 mark banco [d]	per 100 livres tournois, from 1797 per 100 francs [e]
	in rixdollars Leipzig exchange money			
1766	53.27 14d/d (9)	57.80 1m/d (9)	44.45 14d/d (12)	*25.54* (2)
1767	53.78 14d/d (12)	58.32 1m/d (12)	44.48 14d/d (12)	*25.75* (3)
1768	53.30 14d/d (12)	57.92 1m/d (12)	45.69 14d/d (12)	25.25 14d/d (1)
1769	53.71 14d/d (12)	57.65 1m/d (12)	46.92 14d/d (12)	25.54 14d/d (7)
1770	53.87 14d/d (12)	57.46 1m/d (12)	46.91 14d/d (12)	25.41 14d/d (11)
1771	53.71 14d/d (12)	57.85 1m/d (12)	47.19 14d/d (12)	25.39 14d/d (9)
1772	53.91 14d/d (12)	58.51 1m/d (12)	47.88 14d/d (12)	25.72 14d/d (9)
1773	54.74 14d/d (12)	61.06 1m/d (12)	47.86 14d/d (12)	25.67 14d/d (12)
1774	54.41 14d/d (12)	61.28 1m/d (12)	47.79 14d/d (12)	25.67 14d/d (8)
1775	53.93 14d/d (12)	60.31 1m/d (12)	47.21 14d/d (12)	25.72 14d/d (11)
1776	54.34 14d/d (12)	59.23 1m/d (12)	47.91 14d/d (12)	25.40 14d/d (12)
1777	54.19 14d/d (12)	58.09 1m/d (12)	48.15 14d/d (12)	25.34 14d/d (12)
1778	54.17 14d/d (12)	60.07 1m/d (12)	47.94 14d/d (12)	25.08 14d/d (12)
1779	54.58 14d/d (12)	61.85 1m/d (12)	47.65 14d/d (11)	25.14 14d/d (12)
1780	55.01 14d/d (12)	61.27 1m/d (12)	48.20 14d/d (12)	25.41 14d/d (12)
1781	55.30 14d/d (12)	58.81 1m/d (12)	48.52 14d/d (12)	25.27 14d/d (12)
1782	54.00 14d/d (12)	57.49 1m/d (12)	48.67 14d/d (12)	25.37 14d/d (12)
1783	53.73 14d/d (12)	57.49 1m/d (12)	48.54 14d/d (12)	25.11 14d/d (12)
1784	53.88 14d/d (12)	60.36 1m/d (12)	48.06 14d/d (12)	25.18 14d/d (12)
1785	53.97 14d/d (12)	61.92 1m/d (12)	47.67 14d/d (12)	24.79 14d/d (12)
1786	54.63 14d/d (12)	61.14 1m/d (12)	47.87 14d/d (12)	24.76 14d/d (11)
1787	54.84 14d/d (12)	61.92 2m/d (12)	48.42 14d/d (12)	25.20 2m/d (12)
1788	54.26 14d/d (12)	62.67 2m/d (11)	48.47 14d/d (12)	25.15 2m/d (12)
1789	54.74 14d/d (12)	63.72 2m/d (12)	49.02 14d/d (12)	24.93 2m/d (12)
1790	54.92 14d/d (12)	63.93 2m/d (12)	48.89 14d/d (12)	23.77 2m/d (12)
1791	55.72 14d/d (12)	64.53 2m/d (12)	49.02 14d/d (12)	21.75 2m/d (11)
1792	55.60 14d/d (12)	61.45 2m/d (12)	48.48 14d/d (11)	15.32 2m/d (8)
1793	55.20 14d/d (12)	65.27 2m/d (12)	48.90 14d/d (12)	14.75 2m/d (2)
1794	54.39 14d/d (12)	63.92 2m/d (12)	48.64 14d/d (12)	
1795	53.54 14d/d (9)	58.66 2m/d (11)	48.21 14d/d (11)	
1796	51.16 14d/d (12)	59.36 2m/d (12)	48.22 14d/d (6+3)	
1797	53.46 14d/d (12)	65.50 2m/d (12)	49.06 14d/d (12)	25.28 2m/d (6)
1798	54.31 14d/d (12)	68.09 2m/d (12)	49.09 14d/d (12)	25.06 2m/d (11)

	Amsterdam	London	Hamburg	Paris
	LEIPZIG on:			
	per 100 guilders Flemish current [b]	per 10 pounds sterling [c]	per 100 mark banco [d]	per 100 francs [e]
	in rixdollars Leipzig exchange money			
1799	53.28 14d/d (12)	61.85 2m/d (12)	49.49 14d/d (12)	25.07 2m/d (9)
1800	54.65 14d/d (12)	57.26 2m/d (12)	49.16 14d/d (12)	25.49 2m/d (9)
1801	54.18 14d/d (12)	57.08 2m/d (12)	49.26 14d/d (12)	25.21 2m/d (12)
1802	55.32 14d/d (12)	59.66 2m/d (12)	49.23 14d/d (12)	25.31 2m/d (12)
1803	55.08 14d/d (12)	61.98 2m/d (12)	49.40 14d/d (12)	25.32 2m/d (12)
1804	55.11 14d/d (12)	63.86 2m/d (12)	49.27 14d/d (12)	25.43 2m/d (12)
1805	54.05 14d/d (12)	62.38 2m/d (12)	49.07 14d/d (12)	24.66 2m/d (12)
1806	56.23 14d/d (12)	62.52 2m/d (10)	49.93 14d/d (12)	25.92 2m/d (12)
1807	57.25 14d/d (12)	[f]	49.80 14d/d (12)	26.16 2m/d (12)
1808	55.10 14d/d (12)	[f]	47.31 14d/d (12)	25.81 2m/d (12)
1809	53.45 14d/d (10)	[f]	47.79 14d/d (12)	25.82 2m/d (10)
1810	55.64 14d/d (12)	[f]	48.73 14d/d (12)	26.09 2m/d (12)
1811	55.89 14d/d (12)	[f]	49.67 14d/d (12)	26.59 2m/d (12)
1812	53.98 14d/d (12)	[f]	47.70 14d/d (12)	25.68 2m/d (12)
1813	53.45 14d/d (12)	45.00 2m/d (3)	47.92 14d/d (11)	25.37 2m/d (12)
1814	54.29 14d/d (12)	52.90 2m/d (12)	49.25 14d/d (12)	25.84 2m/d (10)
1815	55.68 14d/d (10)	55.40 2m/d (3)	49.06 14d/d (11)	26.23 2m/d (8)

[a]   1766/67: quotations of the Leipzig fairs on Paris. No usance available.

[b]   Concerning the Dutch currency, see pp. 57f.

[c]   Concerning the British currency, see pp. 3–5.

[d]   Concerning the Hamburg currency, see pp. 191–193.

[e]   Concerning the French currency, see pp. 279f.

[f]   No quotation because of the Continental System.

4.2.2 On Augsburg and Vienna

	LEIPZIG on:	
	Augsburg	**Vienna**
	per 100 guilders Augsburg current [a]	per 100 guilders Konventionskurant, from 1800 per 100 guilders Wiener Währung [b]
	in rixdollars Leipzig exchange money	
1766	66.27 15d/d (9)	66.27 14d/d (9)
1767	66.58 15d/d (12)	66.00 14d/d (12)
1768	66.15 15d/d (12)	66.21 14d/d (12)
1769	66.25 15d/d (12)	66.42 14d/d (12)
1770	66.10 15d/d (12)	66.41 14d/d (12)
1771	66.31 15d/d (12)	66.06 14d/d (12)
1772	66.82 15d/d (12)	66.83 14d/d (11)
1773	66.71 15d/d (12)	66.13 14d/d (12)
1774	66.74 15d/d (12)	66.10 14d/d (12)
1775	66.68 15d/d (12)	66.11 14d/d (12)
1776	66.71 15d/d (12)	66.38 14d/d (12)
1777	66.63 15d/d (12)	66.20 14d/d (12)
1778	66.28 15d/d (12)	66.06 14d/d (12)
1779	66.43 15d/d (12)	66.53 14d/d (12)
1780	66.31 15d/d (12)	65.71 14d/d (12)
1781	66.35 15d/d (12)	65.97 14d/d (12)
1782	66.64 15d/d (12)	66.70 14d/d (12)
1783	66.43 15d/d (12)	66.46 14d/d (12)
1784	66.50 15d/d (12)	66.46 14d/d (12)
1785	66.17 15d/d (12)	66.13 14d/d (12)
1786	66.27 15d/d (12)	66.23 14d/d (12)
1787	66.50 15d/d (12)	66.07 14d/d (12)
1788	66.05 15d/d (11)	66.29 14d/d (11)
1789	66.32 15d/d (12)	66.12 14d/d (12)
1790	66.11 15d/d (12)	65.72 14d/d (12)
1791	66.00 15d/d (12)	65.59 14d/d (12)
1792	66.24 15d/d (12)	66.03 14d/d (12)
1793	66.32 15d/d (12)	65.63 14d/d (12)
1794	65.93 15d/d (12)	65.53 14d/d (12)
1795	65.87 15d/d (12)	65.63 14d/d (12)
1796	65.70 15d/d (12)	65.81 14d/d (12)
1797	66.09 15d/d (12)	64.78 14d/d (12)
1798	65.87 15d/d (12)	65.01 14d/d (12)
1799	66.03 15d/d (12)	61.71 14d/d (12)
1800	66.09 15d/d (12)	56.64 14d/d (12)

	LEIPZIG on:	
	Augsburg	**Vienna** [c]
	per 100 guilders Augsburg current [a]	per 100 guilders Wiener Währung [b]
	in rixdollars Leipzig exchange money	
1801	65.79 15d/d (12)	56.37 14d/d (12)
1802	65.98 15d/d (12)	53.43 14d/d (12)
1803	66.25 15d/d (12)	50.27 14d/d (12)
1804	66.23 15d/d (12)	49.32 14d/d (12)
1805	66.42 15d/d (12)	48.70 14d/d (12)
1806	67.21 15d/d (12)	39.77 14d/d (12)
1807	66.89 15d/d (12)	32.15 14d/d (12)
1808	66.67 15d/d (12)	29.56 14d/d (12)
1809	66.95 15d/d (10)	24.36 14d/d (8)
1810	66.56 15d/d (12)	16.06 14d/d (11)
1811	66.79 15d/d (12)	6.39 14d/d (12)
1812	66.43 15d/d (12)	6.50/34.48 14d/d (1+10)
1813	66.49 15d/d (12)	46.00 14d/d (5)
1814	66.87 15d/d (12)	29.73 14d/d (11)
1815	66.95 15d/d (10)	19.69 14d/d (10)

[a] Augsburg current meant – in modification of Konventionskurant, which became common especially since 1764 (NOBACK [1851], 1. Abth., p. 70) – a standard of coinage of 20 5/12 guilders per mark of Cologne. So the guilder Augsburg current (1 rixdollar = 1½ guilders) of 60 kreuzer was equal to 11.45 grammes of fine silver.

[b] Concerning the Austrian currency, see pp. 57–59.

[c] There was no quotation on Vienna during the Austrian rebellion against Napoleon from May to July 1809.

4.3 Frankfurt exchange rates

4.3.1 On London, Amsterdam, Paris and Milan

	FRANKFURT on:			
	London	**Amsterdam**	**Paris**	**Milan**
	per 10 pounds sterling [a]	per 100 guilders Flemish banco, from 1816 (10) per 100 Dutch guilders [b]	per 100 francs [c]	per 100 lire austriache [d]
	in guilders Frankfurt exchange money			
1814	80.00 ss (1)	82.80 ss (1)	39.06 ss (1)	
1815	87.69 ss (6)	82.83 ss (6)	39.22 ss (6)	
1816	99.32 2m/d (1)	82.36 ss (1)	39.25 ss (1)	
1817	96.37 2m/d (12)	82.93 ss (12)	39.30 ss (12)	
1818	92.50 2m/d (12)	83.27 ss (12)	38.77 ss (12)	
1819	95.29 2m/d (12)	83.54 ss (12)	39.07 ss (12)	
1820	100.71 2m/d (12)	84.18 ss (12)	39.72 ss (12)	
1821	102.22 2m/d (12)	82.41 ss (12)	39.99 ss (12)	
1822	101.80 2m/d (12)	84.13 ss (12)	40.20 ss (12)	
1823	103.29 2m/d (8)	85.25 ss (8)	40.33 ss (8)	
1824	100.88 2m/d (12)	85.32 ss (12)	39.99 ss (12)	34.08 ss (12)
1825	98.05 2m/d (12)	82.81 ss (12)	39.32 ss (12)	33.97 ss (9)
1826	101.46 2m/d (12)	83.72 ss (12)	39.72 ss (12)	33.68 ss (12)
1827	100.15 2m/d (12)	83.70 ss (12)	39.58 ss (12)	33.67 ss (12)
1828	99.16 2m/d (12)	82.93 ss (12)	39.29 ss (12)	33.56 ss (12)
1829	99.53 2m/d (12)	82.63 ss (12)	39.12 ss (12)	33.67 ss (12)
1830	100.63 2m/d (12)	83.05 ss (12)	39.48 ss (12)	33.77 ss (12)
1831	98.79 2m/d (12)	83.18 ss (12)	39.35 ss (12)	33.31 ss (12)
1832	100.99 2m/d (12)	83.96 ss (12)	39.39 ss (12)	33.90 ss (12)
1833	100.56 2m/d (12)	83.76 ss (12)	39.18 ss (12)	34.08 ss (12)
1834	99.42 2m/d (12)	82.36 ss (12)	39.33 ss (12)	34.11 ss (12)
1835	100.00 2m/d (12)	82.54 ss (12)	39.33 ss (12)	34.01 ss (12)
1836	100.36 ss (12)	82.74 ss (12)	39.44 ss (12)	33.90 ss (12)
1837	100.68 ss (12)	83.54 ss (12)	39.50 ss (12)	33.61 ss (12)
1838	100.78 ss (11)	83.13 ss (12)	39.46 ss (12)	33.78 ss (12)
1839	99.11 ss (12)	82.62 ss (12)	39.30 ss (12)	33.71 ss (12)
1840	98.59 ss (12)	82.32 ss (12)	39.12 ss (12)	33.59 ss (12)
1841	98.59 ss (12)	81.87 ss (12)	38.92 ss (12)	34.07 ss (12)
1842	99.69 ss (12)	82.06 ss (12)	39.05 ss (12)	34.29 ss (12)
	in guilders South German current			
1843	120.38 ss (12)	98.85 ss (12)	46.89 ss (12)	41.02 ss (12)
1844	119.88 ss (12)	98.84 ss (12)	46.80 ss (12)	40.91 ss (12)
1845	120.56 ss (12)	98.20 ss (12)	46.88 ss (12)	41.04 ss (12)

	FRANKFURT on:			
	London	**Amsterdam**	**Paris**	**Milan**
	per 10 pounds sterling [a]	per 100 Dutch guilders [b]	per 100 francs [c]	per 100 lire austriache, from 1858 (11) per 100 guilders Konventions-kurant, from 1860 per 100 Piedmontese lire nuove, from 1861 (8) per 100 Italian lire [d]
	in guilders South German current			
1843	120.38 ss (12)	98.85 ss (12)	46.89 ss (12)	41.02 ss (12)
1844	119.88 ss (12)	98.84 ss (12)	46.80 ss (12)	40.91 ss (12)
1845	120.56 ss (12)	98.20 ss (12)	46.88 ss (12)	41.04 ss (12)
1846	120.50 ss (12)	98.61 ss (12)	46.87 ss (12)	40.64 ss (12)
1847	120.19 ss (12)	99.52 ss (12)	47.08 ss (12)	40.66 ss (12)
1848	120.88 ss (12)	100.85 ss (12)	47.34 ss (12)	40.45 ss (7)
1849	121.00 ss (12)	100.56 ss (12)	47.60 ss (12)	39.60 ss (12)
1850	120.08 ss (12)	99.98 ss (12)	47.29 ss (12)	40.03 ss (12)
1851	118.50 ss (12)	100.16 ss (12)	47.17 ss (12)	40.42 ss (12)
1852	120.33 ss (12)	100.67 ss (12)	47.48 ss (12)	40.57 ss (12)
1853	118.50 ss (12)	100.25 ss (12)	47.29 ss (12)	40.41 ss (12)
1854	117.33 ss (12)	100.05 ss (12)	46.91 ss (12)	39.95 ss (12)
1855	117.38 ss (12)	99.15 ss (12)	46.68 ss (12)	40.30 ss (12)
1856	118.67 ss (12)	100.22 ss (12)	46.83 ss (12)	40.57 ss (12)
1857	117.88 ss (12)	99.95 ss (12)	46.58 ss (12)	40.14 ss (12)
1858	117.50 ss (12)	100.06 ss (12)	46.71 ss (12)	40.07/115.98 ss (10+2)
1859	116.25 ss (12)	99.46 ss (12)	46.38 ss (12)	116.04 ss (12)
1860	116.75 ss (12)	99.79 ss (12)	46.44 ss (12)	46.69 ss (12)
1861	118.19 ss (12)	99.50 ss (12)	46.63 ss (12)	46.86 ss (12)
1862	118.33 ss (12)	100.32 ss (12)	46.85 ss (12)	47.02 ss (12)
1863	118.33 ss (12)	10.29 ss (12)	46.83 ss (12)	47.06 ss (12)
1864	118.56 ss (12)	100.11 ss (12)	46.91 ss (12)	47.19 ss (12)
1865	119.33 ss (12)	100.49 ss (12)	47.32 ss (12)	47.56 ss (12)
1866	118.09 ss (12)	99.95 ss (12)	46.88 ss (12)	45.66 ss (10)
1867	119.33 ss (11)	100.39 ss (12)	47.39 ss (12)	45.44 ss (5)
1868	119.38 ss (12)	100.23 ss (12)	47.42 ss (12)	43.06 ss (6)
1869	119.67 ss (12)	99.66 ss (12)	47.53 ss (12)	46.18 ss (4)
1870	119.09 ss (12)	100.16 ss (12)	47.26 ss (9)	46.06 ss (5)
1871	118.56 ss (12)	99.55 ss (12)	46.69 ss (9)	45.11 ss (11)
1872	118.38 ss (12)	98.39 ss (12)	46.39 ss (12)	43.50 ss (9)
1873	118.09 ss (12)	98.18 ss (12)	46.43 ss (12)	41.32 ss (8)
1874	118.88 ss (12)	100.02 ss (12)	47.22 ss (12)	42.24 ss (10)

[a]   Concerning the British currency, see pp. 3–5.

[b]   Concerning the Dutch currency, see pp. 57–59.

[c] Concerning the French currency, see pp. 279f.

[d] On November 1ˢᵗ 1823 the Austrian lira (lira austriaca) of 100 centesimi with 3.897 grammes of fine silver was introduced in Lombardy–Veneto by the so-called 'Münzpatent' and became legal tender just like the guilder Konventionskurant did (see pp. 255f.). This lira was equal to the 20-kreuzer piece (or the third part of the guilder) of the Habsburg Monarchy and therefore used to be called 'la svanzica' or the 'zwanziger'. From 1843 bills of Frankfurt on Milan were payable in silver money, i.e. in these zwanziger. With the introduction of the new guilder Österreichische Währung in the Habsburg Monarchy, the exceptional monetary position of Lombardy–Veneto was abolished in 1858/59. After the integration of Lombardy in the new Kingdom of Italy the Piedmontese and the Italian currency system respectively were in force here.

4.3.2 On Vienna, Hamburg, Berlin and Augsburg

	FRANKFURT on:										
	Vienna			**Hamburg**			**Berlin**			**Augsburg**		
	per 100 guilders Wiener Währung, from 1817 per 100 guilders Konventionskurant [a]			per 100 mark banco [b]			per 100 thaler Prussian current [c]			per 100 guilders Augsburg current [d]		
	in guilders Frankfurt exchange money											
1814	47.25	ss	(1)	74.45	ss	(1)				100.75	ss	(1)
1815	28.88	ss	(6)	72.67	ss	(6)	146.57	ss	(5)	99.75	ss	(6)
1816	31.00	2m/d	(1)	73.36	ss	(1)	146.02	ss	(1)	99.64	ss	(1)
1817	100.41	ss	(5)	74.01	ss	(12)	146.65	ss	(5)	99.62	ss	(11)
1818	101.29	ss	(9)	73.58	ss	(12)	147.30	ss	(9)	99.94	ss	(12)
1819	101.14	ss	(12)	73.44	ss	(12)	146.40	ss	(12)	99.95	ss	(12)
1820	100.51	ss	(12)	73.53	ss	(12)	144.82	ss	(12)	99.82	ss	(12)
1821	100.77	ss	(12)	72.63	ss	(12)	144.07	ss	(12)	99.86	ss	(12)
1822	100.82	ss	(12)	73.33	ss	(12)	144.03	ss	(12)	99.95	ss	(12)
1823	100.66	ss	(8)	73.80	ss	(9)	144.01	ss	(8)	99.78	ss	(8)
1824	101.20	ss	(12)	73.15	ss	(12)	143.93	ss	(12)	99.92	ss	(12)
1825	100.37	ss	(12)	72.44	ss	(12)	144.31	ss	(12)	99.87	ss	(12)
1826	99.85	ss	(12)	73.18	ss	(12)	143.90	ss	(12)	99.78	ss	(12)
1827	100.33	ss	(12)	72.96	ss	(12)	144.13	ss	(12)	99.83	ss	(12)
1828	100.34	ss	(12)	72.81	ss	(12)	144.76	ss	(12)	99.81	ss	(12)
1829	100.19	ss	(12)	72.76	ss	(12)	145.47	ss	(12)	99.74	ss	(12)
1830	99.92	ss	(12)	72.84	ss	(12)	145.13	ss	(12)	99.76	ss	(12)
1831	100.12	ss	(12)	72.88	ss	(12)	145.70	ss	(12)	99.77	ss	(12)
1832	100.85	ss	(12)	73.38	ss	(12)	144.67	ss	(12)	99.95	ss	(12)
1833	101.12	ss	(10)	73.18	ss	(12)	144.90	ss	(12)	99.93	ss	(12)
1834	101.43	ss	(12)	73.24	ss	(12)	145.02	ss	(12)	99.95	ss	(12)
1835	100.86	ss	(12)	73.28	ss	(12)	145.06	ss	(12)	99.95	ss	(12)
1836	100.27	ss	(12)	73.33	ss	(12)	145.57	ss	(12)	99.81	ss	(12)
1837	99.61	ss	(12)	73.43	ss	(12)	146.16	ss	(12)	99.76	ss	(12)
1838	99.92	ss	(12)	73.53	ss	(12)	145.85	ss	(12)	99.83	ss	(12)
1839	99.82	ss	(12)	73.46	ss	(12)	146.34	ss	(12)	99.68	ss	(12)
1840	99.59	ss	(12)	73.18	ss	(12)	146.44	ss	(12)	99.59	ss	(12)
1841	100.69	ss	(12)	73.02	ss	(12)	147.33	ss	(12)	99.72	ss	(12)
1842	101.68	ss	(12)	72.98	ss	(12)	146.57	ss	(12)	99.86	ss	(12)
	in guilders South German current											
1843	121.48	ss	(12)	87.62	ss	(12)	174.69	ss	(12)	119.78	ss	(12)
1844	122.39	ss	(12)	87.72	ss	(12)	174.89	ss	(12)	119.76	ss	(12)
1845	121.70	ss	(12)	87.84	ss	(12)	174.99	ss	(12)	119.77	ss	(12)
1846	120.01	ss	(12)	87.91	ss	(12)	175.02	ss	(12)	119.75	ss	(12)
1847	120.22	ss	(12)	88.58	ss	(12)	175.14	ss	(12)	119.75	ss	(12)

	FRANKFURT on:			
	Vienna	**Hamburg**	**Berlin**	**Augsburg**
	per 100 guilders Konventionskurant, from 1858 (11) per 100 guilders Österreichische Währung [a]	per 100 mark banco, from 1873 (3) per 100 mark [b]	per 100 thaler Prussian current [c]	per 100 guilders Augsburg current, from 1859 per 100 guilders South German current [d]
	in guilders South German current			
1848	110.22 ss (12)	87.97 ss (12)	174.19 ss (12)	119.52 ss (12)
1849	106.23 ss (12)	88.07 ss (12)	175.49 ss (12)	119.86 ss (12)
1850	110.89 ss (12)	88.12 ss (10)	175.37 ss (12)	119.95 ss (12)
1851	94.79 ss (12)	88.35 ss (12)	175.65 ss (12)	119.84 ss (12)
1852	100.06 ss (12)	89.07 ss (12)	175.80 ss (12)	120.00 ss (12)
1853	108.25 ss (12)	89.00 ss (12)	175.38 ss (12)	119.87 ss (12)
1854	94.53 ss (12)	88.58 ss (12)	177.78 ss (12)	119.78 ss (12)
1855	98.15 ss (12)	88.04 ss (12)	176.43 ss (12)	119.84 ss (12)
1856	114.64 ss (12)	88.82 ss (12)	174.90 ss (12)	119.90 ss (12)
1857	113.23 ss (12)	88.67 ss (12)	175.06 ss (12)	119.76 ss (12)
1858	114.80 ss (12)	87.56 ss (12)	175.04 ss (12)	119.84 ss (12)
1859	96.46 ss (12)	87.98 ss (12)	174.92 ss (12)	99.85 ss (12)
1860	88.36 ss (12)	88.09 ss (12)	175.39 ss (12)	99.77 ss (12)
1861	82.26 ss (12)	87.87 ss (12)	175.26 ss (12)	99.83 ss (12)
1862	90.30 ss (12)	88.32 ss (12)	174.93 ss (12)	99.81 ss (12)
1863	103.12 ss (12)	88.30 ss (12)	174.93 ss (12)	99.84 ss (12)
1864	99.88 ss (12)	88.66 ss (12)	175.09 ss (12)	99.86 ss (12)
1865	107.12 ss (12)	88.83 ss (12)	174.90 ss (12)	99.88 ss (12)
1866	98.73 ss (12)	88.18 ss (12)	174.40 ss (12)	99.85 ss (12)
1867	93.38 ss (12)	88.30 ss (12)	175.03 ss (12)	99.96 ss (12)
1868	101.81 ss (12)	88.26 ss (12)	175.00 ss (12)	99.87 ss (12)
1869	96.21 ss (12)	88.23 ss (12)	174.96 ss (12)	99.91 ss (12)
1870	95.29 ss (12)	88.11 ss (12)	174.79 ss (12)	99.83 ss (12)
1871	96.60 ss (12)	87.59 ss (12)	175.05 ss (12)	99.74 ss (12)
1872	105.21 ss (12)	87.59 ss (12)	174.59 ss (12)	99.82 ss (12)
1873	105.59 ss (11)	86.69/58.40 ss (2+10)	174.73 ss (12)	99.99 ss (12)
1874	105.93 ss (12)	58.41 ss (12)	174.69 ss (12)	100.00 ss (12)

[a] Concerning the Austrian currency, see pp. 255f. From June 3rd 1848 the guilder Konventionskurant and from November 1858 the guilder Österreichische Währung was paper money issued in notes by the Wiener Nationalbank and in government notes ('Wiener Banknoten').

[b] For the Hamburg currency, see pp. 191–193.   [c] For the Prussian currency, see pp. 196f.

[d] 'Augsburg current' meant – in modification of Konventionskurant, which became common especially since 1764 – a standard of coinage of 20 5/12 guilders per mark of Cologne. So the guilder Augsburg current of 60 kreuzer was equal to 11.45 grammes of fine silver. As a consequence of the Vienna Coin Treaty of 1857, the guilder South German current (standard of coinage: 24½ guilders per 233.855 grammes of fine silver or 52½ guilders per pound of 500 grammes of fine silver) of 60 kreuzer became legal tender in Augsburg from the beginning of 1859.

4.3.3 On Leipzig and Bremen

	FRANKFURT on:					
	Leipzig			**Bremen**		
	per 100 rixdollars Leipzig exchange money, from 1841 (2) per 100 thaler Saxon current [a]			per 100 rixdollars gold [b]		
	in guilders exchange money					
1814	150.75	ss	(1)	163.50	ss	(1)
1815	149.55	ss	(5)	159.88	ss	(6)
1816	149.63	ss	(1)	161.63	ss	(1)
1817	149.37	ss	(3)	162.76	ss	(12)
1818	150.27	ss	(7)	162.55	ss	(12)
1819	149.91	ss	(8)	162.05	ss	(12)
1820	150.16	ss	(11)	162.55	ss	(12)
1821	149.93	ss	(8)	164.66	ss	(12)
1822	149.96	ss	(12)	165.75	ss	(12)
1823	149.89	ss	(7)	166.34	ss	(8)
1824	149.40	ss	(10)	166.60	ss	(12)
1825	149.39	ss	(9)	164.88	ss	(12)
1826	149.53	ss	(11)	163.44	ss	(12)
1827	149.65	ss	(10)	165.05	ss	(12)
1828	149.61	ss	(11)	163.94	ss	(12)
1829	149.82	ss	(11)	164.43	ss	(12)
1830	149.26	ss	(11)	164.60	ss	(12)
1831	149.68	ss	(12)	164.52	ss	(12)
1832	149.07	ss	(12)	164.52	ss	(12)
1833	149.39	ss	(12)	164.74	ss	(12)
1834	149.52	ss	(12)	164.55	ss	(12)
1835	149.36	ss	(11)	164.58	ss	(12)
1836	149.73	ss	(12)	164.80	ss	(12)
1837	149.01	ss	(12)	165.47	ss	(12)
1838	149.30	ss	(12)	165.16	ss	(12)
1839	149.99	ss	(11)	164.44	ss	(12)
1840	149.55	ss	(12)	159.91	ss	(12)
1841	149.82/147.22	ss	(1+11)	159.00	ss	(12)
1842	146.52	ss	(9)	160.80	ss	(12)
	in guilders South German current					
1843	174.67	ss	(12)	194.75	ss	(12)
1844	174.78	ss	(12)	196.02	ss	(12)
1845	174.89	ss	(9)	195.65	ss	(12)
1846	174.95	ss	(12)	195.92	ss	(12)

	FRANKFURT on:				
	Leipzig		Bremen		
	per 100 thaler Saxon current [a]		per 100 rixdollars gold, from 1872 (8) per 100 mark [b]		
	in guilders South German current				
1847	175.13	ss	(12)	196.56	ss	(12)
1848	174.48	ss	(12)	196.96	ss	(12)
1849	175.47	ss	(12)	197.86	ss	(12)
1850	175.26	ss	(12)	196.67	ss	(12)
1851	175.52	ss	(12)	191.32	ss	(12)
1852	175.65	ss	(12)	194.50	ss	(12)
1853	175.26	ss	(12)	194.71	ss	(12)
1854	177.14	ss	(12)	191.86	ss	(12)
1855	176.20	ss	(12)	191.02	ss	(12)
1856	174.73	ss	(12)	192.94	ss	(12)
1857	174.99	ss	(12)	192.63	ss	(12)
1858	174.97	ss	(12)	191.57	ss	(12)
1859	174.74	ss	(12)	190.17	ss	(12)
1860	175.28	ss	(12)	190.27	ss	(12)
1861	175.28	ss	(12)	192.34	ss	(12)
1862	175.06	ss	(12)	192.63	ss	(12)
1863	175.02	ss	(12)	193.07	ss	(12)
1864	174.92	ss	(12)	193.30	ss	(12)
1865	174.92	ss	(12)	194.36	ss	(12)
1866	174.33	ss	(12)	193.17	ss	(12)
1867	174.99	ss	(12)	194.44	ss	(12)
1868	174.95	ss	(12)	195.50	ss	(12)
1869	174.81	ss	(10)	194.61	ss	(11)
1870	174.86	ss	(12)	194.37	ss	(12)
1871	174.95	ss	(12)	193.01	ss	(12)
1872	174.93	ss	(12)	192.17/58.37	ss	(6+5)
1873	175.00	ss	(12)	58.41	ss	(12)
1874	175.00	ss	(12)	58.41	ss	(12)

[a] Concerning the Saxon currency, see pp. 194f.

[b] The quotations on Bremen were effected for rixdollars or thaler gold of 72 grote at 5 schwaren. This thaler gold was equal to one-fifth of the 'louis d'or', meaning the different pistoles of the North German territories and of Denmark (from 1828). In Bremen the new mark Reichswährung was introduced on July 1st 1872 (by the Act of April 30th 1872), whereby 28 thaler gold were equal to 93 mark (cf. *WdW XI*, pp. 108f.).

4.4 Berlin exchange rates

4.4.1 On London, Amsterdam, Paris and Vienna

	BERLIN on:			
	London	**Amsterdam**	**Paris**	**Vienna**
	per 10 pounds sterling [a]	per 100 guilders Flemish banco, from 1816 (10) per 100 Dutch guilders [b]	per 100 francs [c]	per 100 guilders Wiener Währung, from 1820 per 100 guilders Konventionskurant [d]
	in thaler Prussian current			
1813	45.55 3m/d (8)	54.38 2m/d (8)	26.57 2m/d (5)	43.60 2m/d (9)
1814	52.00 3m/d (12)	54.97 2m/d (12)	26.44 2m/d (8)	31.89 2m/d (12)
1815	56.67 3m/d (12)	56.34 2m/d (12)	26.78 2m/d (9)	19.08 2m/d (12)
1816	64.50 3m/d (12)	55.44 2m/d (12)	26.34 2m/d (12)	21.10 2m/d (12)
1817	63.93 3m/d (12)	55.48 2m/d (12)	26.41 2m/d (12)	20.30 2m/d (12)
1818	61.78 3m/d (12)	56.40 2m/d (3)	26.08 2m/d (12)	23.20 2m/d (3)
1819	64.00 3m/d (12)	56.94 2m/d (12)	26.68 2m/d (12)	27.67 2m/d (12)
1820	67.77 3m/d (12)	57.76 2m/d (12)	27.30 2m/d (12)	69.07 2m/d (6)
1821	70.50 3m/d (12)	56.92 2m/d (12)	27.70 2m/d (12)	69.79 2m/d (12)
1822	69.98 3m/d (12)	58.09 2m/d (12)	27.80 2m/d (12)	69.47 2m/d (11)
1823	71.32 3m/d (12)	58.78 2m/d (12)	28.00 2m/d (12)	69.66 2m/d (12)
1824	68.10 3m/d (12)	58.40 ss (9)	27.54 2m/d (12)	69.66 2m/d (12)
1825	67.50 3m/d (12)	57.29 ss (12)	27.15 2m/d (12)	69.14 2m/d (12)
1826	70.30 3m/d (12)	57.90 ss (12)	27.48 2m/d (12)	69.22 2m/d (12)
1827	68.93 3m/d (12)	57.74 ss (12)	27.29 2m/d (12)	69.10 2m/d (12)
1828	68.10 3m/d (12)	57.04 ss (12)	27.01 2m/d (12)	68.96 2m/d (12)
1829	68.24 3m/d (12)	56.67 ss (12)	26.77 2m/d (12)	68.51 2m/d (12)
1830	68.89 3m/d (12)	56.64 ss (12)	26.99 2m/d (12)	68.37 2m/d (12)
1831	67.50 3m/d (12)	57.06 ss (12)	26.92 2m/d (12)	68.55 2m/d (12)
1832	69.50 3m/d (12)	57.90 ss (12)	27.10 2m/d (12)	69.20 2m/d (12)
1833	69.00 3m/d (12)	57.68 ss (12)	26.89 2m/d (12)	69.43 2m/d (12)
1834	68.40 3m/d (12)	56.72 ss (12)	26.96 2m/d (12)	69.52 2m/d (12)
1835	68.87 3m/d (12)	56.85 ss (12)	27.01 2m/d (12)	69.29 2m/d (12)
1836	68.40 3m/d (12)	56.73 ss (11)	26.91 2m/d (12)	68.32 2m/d (11)
1837	68.24 3m/d (12)	56.95 ss (12)	26.87 2m/d (12)	67.71 2m/d (12)
1838	68.32 3m/d (11)	56.69 ss (12)	26.81 2m/d (12)	67.86 2m/d (12)
1839	66.95 3m/d (12)	56.22 ss (12)	26.67 2m/d (12)	67.69 2m/d (12)
1840	66.43 3m/d (12)	55.96 ss (12)	26.43 2m/d (12)	67.39 2m/d (12)
1841	66.23 3m/d (12)	55.37 ss (12)	26.22 2m/d (12)	67.85 2m/d (12)
1842	67.50 3m/d (12)	55.92 ss (12)	26.50 2m/d (12)	69.05 2m/d (12)
1843	68.55 3m/d (12)	56.55 ss (12)	26.71 2m/d (12)	69.24 2m/d (12)
1844	67.88 3m/d (12)	56.35 ss (12)	26.56 2m/d (12)	69.51 2m/d (12)
1845	68.25 3m/d (12)	56.05 ss (12)	26.64 2m/d (12)	69.09 2m/d (12)

	BERLIN on:			
	London	**Amsterdam**	**Paris**	**Vienna**
	per 10 pounds sterling [a]	per 100 Dutch guilders [b]	per 100 francs [c]	per 100 guilders Konventionskurant, from 1859 per 100 guilders Österreichische Währung [d]
	in thaler Prussian current			
1846	68.12 3m/d (12)	56.20 ss (12)	26.56 2m/d (12)	68.07 2m/d (12)
1847	67.75 3m/d (12)	56.71 ss (12)	26.66 2m/d (12)	68.07 2m/d (12)
1848	68.50 3m/d (12)	57.61 ss (12)	27.12 2m/d (10)	64.14 2m/d (9)
1849	68.50 3m/d (12)	57.20 ss (12)	27.03 2m/d (12)	59.90 2m/d (12)
1850	68.00 3m/d (12)	56.91 ss (12)	26.82 2m/d (12)	57.22 2m/d (12)
1851	66.93 3m/d (12)	56.88 ss (12)	26.71 2m/d (12)	53.43 2m/d (12)
1852	67.93 3m/d (12)	57.20 ss (12)	26.86 2m/d (12)	56.44 2m/d (12)
1853	66.66 3m/d (12)	56.99 ss (12)	26.75 2m/d (12)	61.25 2m/d (12)
1854	65.24 3m/d (12)	56.24 ss (12)	26.20 2m/d (12)	52.45 2m/d (12)
1855	65.80 3m/d (12)	56.15 ss (12)	26.26 2m/d (12)	55.28 2m/d (12)
1856	67.00 3m/d (12)	57.25 ss (12)	26.56 2m/d (12)	64.89 2m/d (12)
1857	66.12 3m/d (12)	56.97 ss (12)	26.35 2m/d (12)	63.98 2m/d (12)
1858	66.67 3m/d (12)	57.05 ss (12)	26.53 2m/d (12)	64.48 2m/d (12)
1859	66.00 3m/d (12)	56.72 ss (12)	26.30 2m/d (12)	53.01 8d/d (10)
1860	65.93 3m/d (12)	56.80 ss (12)	26.31 2m/d (12)	50.17 8d/d (12)
1861	66.67 3m/d (12)	56.64 ss (12)	26.41 2m/d (12)	46.73 8d/d (12)
1862	67.25 3m/d (12)	57.33 ss (12)	26.65 2m/d (12)	51.69 8d/d (12)
1863	66.75 3m/d (12)	57.17 ss (12)	26.59 2m/d (12)	58.99 8d/d (12)
1864	66.66 3m/d (12)	57.17 ss (12)	26.59 2m/d (12)	57.05 8d/d (12)
1865	67.50 3m/d (12)	57.49 ss (12)	26.92 2m/d (12)	61.27 8d/d (12)
1866	67.00 3m/d (12)	57.32 ss (12)	26.77 2m/d (12)	56.47 8d/d (12)
1867	67.67 3m/d (12)	57.25 ss (12)	26.94 2m/d (12)	53.48 8d/d (12)
1868	68.00 3m/d (12)	57.30 ss (12)	27.04 2m/d (12)	58.29 8d/d (12)
1869	68.00 3m/d (12)	57.00 ss (12)	27.08 2m/d (12)	55.02 8d/d (12)
1870	67.67 3m/d (12)	57.24 ss (12)	26.91 2m/d (12)	54.60 8d/d (12)
1871	67.25 3m/d (12)	56.80 ss (12)	26.53 10d/d (10)	55.23 8d/d (12)
1872	67.12 3m/d (12)	56.24 ss (12)	26.51 10d/d (12)	60.35 8d/d (12)
1873	66.75 3m/d (11)	56.10 ss (11)	26.49 10d/d (12)	60.25 8d/d (12)
1874	67.50 3m/d (9)	57.24 ss (9)	27.02 10d/d (12)	60.56 8d/d (12)
	in mark			
1875	204.63 8d/d (12)	172.18 8d/d (12)	81.21 8d/d (12)	181.75 8d/d (12)
1876	204.34 8d/d (12)	169.20 8d/d (12)	81.11 8d/d (12)	168.72 8d/d (12)
1877	204.39 8d/d (12)	169.32 8d/d (12)	81.30 8d/d (12)	165.75 8d/d (12)
1878	204.23 8d/d (12)	168.77 8d/d (12)	81.11 8d/d (12)	171.12 8d/d (12)
1879	204.33 8d/d (12)	169.13 8d/d (12)	80.90 8d/d (12)	174.10 8d/d (12)
1880	204.30 8d/d (12)	168.95 8d/d (12)	80.89 8d/d (12)	172.18 8d/d (12)

	BERLIN on:			
	London	**Amsterdam**	**Paris**	**Vienna**
	per 10 pounds sterling [a]	per 100 Dutch guilders [b]	per 100 francs [c]	per 100 guilders Öster-reichische Währung, from 1900 per 100 Austrian crowns [d]
		in mark		
1881	204.33 8d/d (12)	168.91 8d/d (12)	80.94 8d/d (12)	173.58 8d/d (12)
1882	204.70 8d/d (12)	168.71 8d/d (12)	81.06 8d/d (12)	170.61 8d/d (12)
1883	204.35 8d/d (12)	168.87 8d/d (12)	80.90 8d/d (12)	170.41 8d/d (12)
1884	204.27 8d/d (12)	168.71 8d/d (12)	81.04 8d/d (12)	167.82 8d/d (12)
1885	204.06 8d/d (12)	168.90 8d/d (12)	80.80 8d/d (12)	163.46 8d/d (12)
1886	203.92 8d/d (12)	168.86 8d/d (12)	80.82 8d/d (12)	161.63 8d/d (12)
1887	203.82 8d/d (12)	168.60 8d/d (12)	80.52 8d/d (12)	160.88 8d/d (12)
1888	203.96 8d/d (12)	168.93 8d/d (12)	80.62 8d/d (12)	163.43 8d/d (12)
1889	204.37 8d/d (12)	169.05 8d/d (12)	81.00 8d/d (12)	170.60 8d/d (12)
1890	203.86 8d/d (12)	168.65 8d/d (12)	80.78 8d/d (12)	175.09 8d/d (12)
1891	203.55 8d/d (12)	168.37 8d/d (12)	80.64 8d/d (12)	174.58 8d/d (12)
1892	203.82 8d/d (12)	168.64 8d/d (12)	81.00 8d/d (12)	170.99 8d/d (12)
1893	203.94 8d/d (12)	168.72 8d/d (12)	80.99 8d/d (12)	164.92 8d/d (12)
1894	203.94 8d/d (12)	168.86 8d/d (12)	81.05 8d/d (12)	163.43 8d/d (12)
1895	204.40 8d/d (12)	168.74 8d/d (12)	81.06 8d/d (12)	167.61 8d/d (12)
1896	204.10 8d/d (12)	168.47 8d/d (12)	81.03 8d/d (12)	169.78 8d/d (12)
1897	203.72 8d/d (12)	168.62 8d/d (12)	81.00 8d/d (12)	170.12 8d/d (12)
1898	204.23 8d/d (12)	169.11 8d/d (12)	80.86 8d/d (12)	169.81 8d/d (12)
1899	204.31 8d/d (12)	168.73 8d/d (12)	81.02 8d/d (12)	169.34 8d/d (12)
1900	204.55 8d/d (11)	169.22 8d/d (11)	81.34 8d/d (11)	84.47 8d/d (11)
1901	204.14 8d/d (12)	169.00 8d/d (12)	81.14 8d/d (12)	85.11 8d/d (12)
1902	204.79 8d/d (12)	168.56 8d/d (12)	81.30 8d/d (12)	85.14 8d/d (12)
1903	204.20 8d/d (12)	168.89 8d/d (12)	81.23 8d/d (12)	85.25 8d/d (12)
1904	204.07 8d/d (12)	169.12 8d/d (12)	81.14 8d/d (12)	85.15 8d/d (12)
1905	204.34 8d/d (12)	169.11 8d/d (12)	81.34 8d/d (12)	85.11 8d/d (12)
1906	204.40 8d/d (12)	168.90 8d/d (12)	81.44 8d/d (12)	85.08 8d/d (12)
1907	204.67 8d/d (12)	169.24 8d/d (12)	81.33 8d/d (12)	85.00 8d/d (12)
1908	203.81 8d/d (12)	168.99 8d/d (12)	81.27 8d/d (12)	85.05 8d/d (12)
1909	204.41 8d/d (12)	169.07 8d/d (12)	81.25 8d/d (12)	85.12 8d/d (12)
1910	204.26 8d/d (12)	169.05 8d/d (12)	81.12 8d/d (12)	85.00 8d/d (12)
1911	204.34 8d/d (12)	169.31 8d/d (12)	81.03 s (12)	85.01 8d/d (12)
1912	204.48 8d/d (12)	169.42 8d/d (12)	81.13 s (12)	84.71 8d/d (12)
1913	204.33 8d/d (12)	168.77 8d/d (12)	81.08 s (12)	84.69 8d/d (12)
1914	204.53 8d/d (7)	169.19 8d/d (7)	81.45 s (7)	84.99 8d/d (7)

[a] Concerning the British currency, see pp. 3–5.

[b] Concerning the Dutch currency, see pp. 57–59.

[c]   Concerning the French currency, see pp. 279f.

[d]   Concerning the Austrian currency, see pp. 225f. From June 3rd 1848 the guilder Konventionsku-
       rant and from November 1858 the guilder Österreichische Währung were paper money issued in
       notes by the Wiener Nationalbank and in government notes ('Wiener Banknoten').

4.4.2 On Belgium, Switzerland, Italy and Madrid

	BERLIN on:		
	Belgium [a]	**Switzerland**	**Italy**
	per 100 Belgian francs [b]	per 100 franken [c]	
	in thaler Prussian current		
1850	26.81 2m/d (12)		
1851	26.82 2m/d (12)		
1852	26.82 2m/d (12)		
1853	26.80 2m/d (12)		
1854	26.81 2m/d (12)		
1855	26.82 2m/d (12)		
1856			
1857			
1858			
1859			
1860			
1861			
1862			
1863			
1864			
1865			
1866			
1867			
1868			
1869			
1870			
1871	26.65 8d/d (10)		
1872	26.63 8d/d (12)		
1873	26.85 8d/d (11)		
1874	26.98 8d/d (9)		
	in mark		
1875	81.17 8d/d (12)		
1876	81.03 8d/d (12)		
1877	81.21 8d/d (12)		
1878	81.03 8d/d (12)		
1879	80.82 8d/d (12)		
1880	80.70 8d/d (12)		
1881	80.71 8d/d (5)		per 100 Italian lire [d]
1882	80.97 8d/d (12)	80.50 10d/d (3)	80.25 10d/d (3)
1883	80.88 8d/d (12)	80.98 10d/d (10)	81.02 10d/d (10)
1884	80.96 8d/d (12)	80.93 10d/d (9)	80.86 10d/d (9)

	BERLIN on:			
	Belgium [a]	**Switzerland**	**Italy**	**Madrid**
	per 100 Belgian francs [b]	per 100 franken [c]	per 100 Italian lire [d]	per 100 pesetas [e]
	in mark			
1885	80.69 8d/d (12)	80.54 10d/d (11)	80.35 10d/d (11)	
1886	80.76 8d/d (12)	80.70 10d/d (12)	80.57 10d/d (12)	79.80 14d/d (2)
1887	80.45 8d/d (12)	80.41 10d/d (12)	79.76 10d/d (12)	79.46 14d/d (11)
1888	80.52 8d/d (12)	80.43 10d/d (12)	79.67 10d/d (12)	79.05 14d/d (12)
1889	80.96 8d/d (11)	80.85 10d/d (11)	80.44 10d/d (11)	78.58 14d/d (11)
1890	80.76 8d/d (12)	80.60 10d/d (12)	79.76 10d/d (12)	77.19 14d/d (12)
1891	80.54 8d/d (12)	80.36 10d/d (12)	78.85 10d/d (12)	75.87 14d/d (12)
1892	80.93 8d/d (12)	80.82 10d/d (12)	78.07 10d/d (12)	70.09 14d/d (11)
1893	80.82 8d/d (12)	80.80 10d/d (12)	75.17 10d/d (12)	68.27 14d/d (11)
1894	80.99 8d/d (12)	80.94 10d/d (12)	72.75 10d/d (12)	67.21 14d/d (12)
1895	80.91 8d/d (12)	80.90 8d/d (12)	76.82 10d/d (11)	70.78 14d/d (12)
1896	80.94 8d/d (12)	80.74 8d/d (11)	75.47 10d/d (12)	67.13 14d/d (11)
1897	80.89 8d/d (12)	80.65 8d/d (12)	76.93 10d/d (12)	62.83 14d/d (12)
1898	80.70 8d/d (12)	80.51 8d/d (12)	75.62 10d/d (12)	55.58 14d/d (7)
1899	80.85 8d/d (12)	80.58 8d/d (12)	75.38 10d/d (12)	65.47 14d/d (9)
1900	81.19 8d/d (11)	80.85 8d/d (10)	76.44 10d/d (10)	62.98 14d/d (9)
1901	81.06 8d/d (12)	80.97 8d/d (12)	77.61 10d/d (12)	59.03 14d/d (10)
1902	81.19 8d/d (12)	80.99 8d/d (12)	80.23 10d/d (12)	54.43 14d/d (10)
1903	81.11 8d/d (12)	81.17 8d/d (12)	81.22 10d/d (12)	60.26 14d/d (11)
1904	81.07 8d/d (12)	80.98 8d/d (12)	81.02 10d/d (12)	54.67 14d/d (11)
1905	81.13 8d/d (12)	81.19 8d/d (12)	81.33 10d/d (12)	61.99 14d/d (11)
1906	81.16 8d/d (12)	81.28 8d/d (12)	81.36 10d/d (12)	70.50 14d/d (11)
1907	81.06 8d/d (11)	81.23 8d/d (11)	81.29 10d/d (11)	73.77 14d/d (9)
1908	81.05 8d/d (12)	81.18 8d/d (12)	81.21 10d/d (12)	72.03 14d/d (11)
1909	80.99 8d/d (12)	81.21 8d/d (12)	80.82 10d/d (12)	73.69 14d/d (9)
1910	80.76 8d/d (12)	80.90 8d/d (12)	80.59 10d/d (12)	75.75 14d/d (8)
1911	80.66 8d/d (12)	80.90 8d/d (12)	80.46 10d/d (12)	74.67 14d/d (7)
1912	80.72 8d/d (12)	80.89 8d/d (12)	80.24 10d/d (11)	76.03 14d/d (8)
1913	80.53 8d/d (12)	80.76 8d/d (11)	79.55 10d/d (12)	75.19 14d/d (8)
1914	80.74 8d/d (7)	81.15 8d/d (7)	80.86 10d/d (7)	77.11 14d/d (7)

[a] Identical quotations on Brussels and Antwerp.

[b] In 1832 the Belgian franc was introduced, equal to the French franc (see p. 279).

[c] Concerning the Swiss currency, see p. 313.

[d] Concerning the Italian currency, see pp. 108f.

[e] Concerning the Spanish currency, see p. 307.

4.4.3 On Saint Petersburg, Warsaw and New York

	BERLIN on:	DANZIG [a] on:
	Saint Petersburg	**Warsaw**
	per 100 roubles banco, from 1840 per 100 silver roubles, from 1843 (11) in credit notes [b]	per 100 guilders Polish current [c], from 1860 per 100 silver roubles payable in credit notes [b]
	in thaler Prussian current	
1823	28.38 3w/d (12)	
1824	27.54 3w/d (12)	
1825	28.54 3w/d (12)	
1826	28.15 3w/d (12)	
1827	29.18 3w/d (10)	
1828	29.35 3w/d (12)	16.55 8d/d (12)
1829	30.16 3w/d (12)	16.65 8d/d (11)
1830	30.38 3w/d (12)	16.69 8d/d (11)
1831	29.88 3w/d (12)	16.50 8d/d (2)
1832	30.32 3w/d (12)	16.65 8d/d (12)
1833	30.29 3w/d (12)	16.58 8d/d (12)
1834	30.25 3w/d (12)	16.43 8d/d (12)
1835	30.09 3w/d (8)	16.32 8d/d (12)
1836	30.06 3w/d (11)	16.32 8d/d (12)
1837	29.90 3w/d (12)	16.19 8d/d (12)
1838	30.25 3w/d (8)	16.28 8d/d (11)
1839	31.43 3w/d (12)	16.59 8d/d (5)
1840	113.20 3w/d (12)	16.39 8d/d (10)
1841	110.63 3w/d (12)	16.09 8d/d (6)
1842	109.55 3w/d (12)	16.05 8d/d (12)
1843	106.93 3w/d (12)	16.22 8d/d (12)
1844	107.51 3w/d (12)	16.30 8d/d (12)
1845	107.59 3w/d (12)	16.14 8d/d (12)
1846	106.72 3w/d (12)	16.03 8d/d (12)
1847	108.62 3w/d (12)	16.43 8d/d (10)
1848	105.65 3w/d (10)	15.86 8d/d (11)
1849	105.11 3w/d (12)	15.80 8d/d (11)
1850	107.44 3w/d (12)	16.12 8d/d (12)
1851	104.84 3w/d (12)	
1852	107.33 3w/d (12)	16.11 8d/d (10)
1853	107.73 3w/d (12)	16.35 8d/d (11)
1854	100.00 3w/d (12)	15.26 8d/d (11)
1855	99.01 3w/d (12)	15.04 8d/d (5)
1856	105.36 3w/d (12)	

	BERLIN on:		BREMEN [d], from 1887 BERLIN on:
	Saint Petersburg	**Warsaw**	**New York**
	per 100 silver roubles payable in credit notes [b]		per 100 US dollars [e]
	in thaler Prussian current		
1857	102.85 3w/d (12)		
1858	99.72 3w/d (12)		
1859	96.24 3w/d (12)		
1860	97.39 3w/d (12)	88.23 8d/d (6)	
1861	94.94 3w/d (12)	86.01 8d/d (12)	
1862	96.05 3w/d (12)	86.42 8d/d (12)	
1863	101.21 3w/d (12)	91.60 8d/d (12)	
1864	91.00 3w/d (12)	81.80 8d/d (12)	
1865	87.96 3w/d (12)	79.36 8d/d (12)	
1866	82.16 3w/d (12)	74.74 8d/d (12)	
1867	90.90 3w/d (12)	82.90 8d/d (12)	
1868	92.69 3w/d (12)	83.48 8d/d (12)	
1869	87.07 3w/d (12)	78.42 8d/d (12)	
1870	83.11 3w/d (12)	74.85 8d/d (12)	
1871	88.79 3w/d (12)	80.06 8d/d (12)	
1872	91.19 3w/d (12)	82.24 8d/d (12)	**in mark**
1873	89.94 3w/d (12)	81.16 8d/d (12)	416.88 ss (12)
1874	92.91 3w/d (12)	93.10 8d/d (12)	415.88 ss (12)
	in mark		
1875	277.25 3w/d (12)	278.00 8d/d (12)	418.63 ss (12)
1876	261.86 3w/d (12)	262.22 8d/d (12)	418.08 ss (12)
1877	224.03 3w/d (12)	224.70 8d/d (12)	419.50 ss (12)
1878	206.33 3w/d (12)	206.60 8d/d (12)	419.13 ss (12)
1879	203.72 3w/d (12)	203.86 8d/d (12)	420.00 ss (12)
1880	211.83 3w/d (12)	211.99 8d/d (12)	421.08 ss (12)
1881	207.44 3w/d (5)	207.81 8d/d (5)	422.34 ss (12)
1882	204.12 3w/d (12)	204.78 8d/d (12)	419.00 ss (12)
1883	200.09 3w/d (12)	200.57 8d/d (12)	420.38 ss (12)
1884	204.14 3w/d (12)	204.69 8d/d (12)	420.06 ss (12)
1885	204.10 3w/d (12)	204.56 8d/d (12)	419.62 ss (12)
1886	197.47 3w/d (12)	197.79 8d/d (12)	418.50 ss (12)
1887	181.05 3w/d (12)	181.46 8d/d (12)	419.57 8d/d (8)
1888	186.64 3w/d (12)	188.52 8d/d (11)	417.85 8d/d (10)
1889	212.54 3w/d (11)	213.37 8d/d (11)	418.62 8d/d (11)
1890	233.87 3w/d (12)	234.41 8d/d (12)	418.19 8d/d (11)
1891	225.24 3w/d (12)	225.81 8d/d (12)	418.50 8d/d (8)

	BERLIN on:		
	Saint Petersburg	**Warsaw**	**New York**
	per 100 silver roubles payable in credit notes, from 1899 per 100 gold roubles [b]		per 100 US dollars [e]
	in mark		
1892	204.17 3w/d (12)	204.50 8d/d (12)	417.90 8d/d (7)
1893	210.80 3w/d (12)	211.18 8d/d (12)	419.25 8d/d (9)
1894	217.88 3w/d (12)	218.38 8d/d (12)	418.08 8d/d (11)
1895	219.19 8d/d (12)	219.19 8d/d (12)	417.50 8d/d (12)
1896	216.24 8d/d (12)	216.32 8d/d (12)	417.96 8d/d (11)
1897	216.07 8d/d (12)	216.10 8d/d (12)	418.45 8d/d (12)
1898	216.11 8d/d (12)	216.20 8d/d (12)	421.19 8d/d (11)
1899	215.75 8d/d (11)	215.78 8d/d (11)	419.64 8d/d (12)
1900	215.62 8d/d (6)	215.68 8d/d (6)	420.30 8d/d (10)
1901	215.59 8d/d (7)	215.84 8d/d (11)	418.70 8d/d (10)
1902	214.75 8d/d (2)	215.73 8d/d (9)	419.30 8d/d (12)
1903	215.75 8d/d (6)	215.90 8d/d (7)	419.59 8d/d (12)
1904	215.67 8d/d (4)	215.65 8d/d (7)	419.27 8d/d (12)
1905			419.83 8d/d (12)
1906	212.65 8d/d (2)	214.35 8d/d (3)	421.09 8d/d (12)
1907			421.66 8d/d (11)
1908	213.78 8d/d (9)	213.83 8d/d (6)	419.48 8d/d (12)
1909	214.94 8d/d (3)	213.85 8d/d (2)	419.32 8d/d (12)
1910	213.00 3m/d (1)		419.94 8d/d (12)
1911			420.38 8d/d (12)
1912			420.25 8d/d (11)
1913	215.00 8d/d (1)	215.00 8d/d (1)	419.99 8d/d (11)
1914	214.90 8d/d (1)		420.06 8d/d (7)

[a] From 1828 to 1855, quotations from Danzig on Warsaw. Berlin quoted Warsaw only in 1830 (16.65 thaler Prussian current per 100 guilders Polish current, at short sight).

[b] Concerning the Russian currency, see pp. 359f.

[c] Guilders Polish current according to the Ukaz of the Russian government of November 19th/ December 1st 1815. According to the Ukaz of February 2nd/September 15th 1841, the Russian currency was meant to be in force within the whole Kingdom of Poland, but it gained acceptance only very slowly. Until the 1850s the exchange rates were quoted for guilders (zloty) Polish current.

[d] From 1873 to 1886 quotations from Bremen on New York. In Bremen the mark Reichswährung was introduced on July 1st 1872, whereby 1 (rix)dollar gold was equal to 3.32 mark Reichswährung (cf. *WdW XI*, pp. 108f.; SPRENGER [1996], p. 141).

[e] Concerning the US currency, see p. 404.

4.4.4 On Scandinavian places

	BERLIN on:		
	Stockholm & Gothenborg	**Copenhagen**	**Christiana (Oslo)**
	per 100 Swedish crowns [a]	per 100 Danish crowns [b]	per 100 Norwegian crowns [c]
	in mark		
1884	112.18 10d/d (12)	112.15 10d/d (12)	
1885	112.01 10d/d (12)	111.98 10d/d (12)	
1886	112.20 10d/d (12)	112.22 10d/d (12)	
1887	112.13 10d/d (12)	112.12 10d/d (12)	
1888	112.26 10d/d (12)	112.28 10d/d (12)	
1889	112.33 10d/d (11)	112.32 10d/d (11)	
1890	112.08 10d/d (12)	112.06 10d/d (12)	
1891	112.05 10d/d (12)	112.06 10d/d (12)	
1892	112.28 10d/d (12)	112.29 10d/d (12)	
1893	112.27 10d/d (12)	112.23 10d/d (12)	
1894	112.35 10d/d (12)	112.34 10d/d (12)	
1895	112.45 10d/d (12)	112.46 8d/d (12)	
1896	112.32 10d/d (12)	112.30 8d/d (12)	
1897	112.25 10d/d (12)	112.24 8d/d (12)	
1898	112.23 10d/d (12)	112.29 8d/d (9)	
1899	112.07 10d/d (12)	112.09 8d/d (7)	112.14 10d/d (7)
1900	112.08 10d/d (11)	112.10 8d/d (11)	112.08 10d/d (11)
1901	112.31 10d/d (11)	112.29 8d/d (11)	112.31 10d/d (11)
1902	112.40 10d/d (11)	112.37 8d/d (9)	112.40 10d/d (11)
1903	112.22 10d/d (11)	112.23 8d/d (11)	112.22 10d/d (11)
1904	112.20 10d/d (11)	112.23 8d/d (11)	112.20 10d/d (11)
1905	112.46 10d/d (12)	112.41 8d/d (11)	112.46 10d/d (6)
1906	112.35 10d/d (11)	112.36 8d/d (11)	112.30 10d/d (2)
1907	112.06 10d/d (10)	112.14 8d/d (10)	112.10 10d/d (8)
1908	112.14 10d/d (11)	112.14 8d/d (12)	112.14 10d/d (12)
1909	112.32 10d/d (10)	112.34 8d/d (12)	112.32 10d/d (9)
1910	112.30 10d/d (11)	112.32 8d/d (7)	112.27 10d/d (6)
1911	112.39 10d/d (11)	112.36 8d/d (8)	112.39 10d/d (8)
1912	112.34 10d/d (12)	112.29 8d/d (11)	112.30 10d/d (8)
1913	112.10 10d/d (10)	112.09 8d/d (6)	112.10 10d/d (4)
1914	112.31 10d/d (6)	112.29 8d/d (4)	112.34 10d/d (4)

[a]   For the Swedish currency, see pp. 339f.   [b]   For the Danish currency, see pp. 327f.

[c]   According to the treaty of the Scandinavian Monetary Union (see [a] and [b]), the crown (0.4032 grammes of fine gold) of 100 öre was the currency of Norway from 1877, exactly equal to the Swedish and Danish crowns (cf. SWOBODA [1902], p. 238).

4.4.5 On German places

	BERLIN on:			
	Hamburg	**Frankfurt**	**Augsburg**	**Leipzig**
	per 100 mark banco [a]	per 100 guilders Frankfurt exchange money, from 1843 per 100 guilders South German current [b]	per 100 guilders Augsburg current [c]	per 100 rixdollars Leipzig exchange money, from 1841 per 100 thaler Saxon current [d]
	in thaler Prussian current			
1813	48.47 s (10)	68.20 2m/d (6)	66.89 2m/d (6)	
1814	50.00 s (8)	66.77 2m/d (12)	67.64 2m/d (12)	
1815	49.84 s (12)	67.18 2m/d (12)	68.04 2m/d (12)	
1816	50.22 s (12)	68.00 2m/d (12)	68.12 2m/d (12)	
1817	50.21 s (12)	67.06 2m/d (12)	67.40 2m/d (12)	
1818	50.17 s (12)	66.86 2m/d (12)	67.64 2m/d (12)	
1819	50.71 s (12)	68.06 2m/d (12)	67.56 2m/d (12)	
1820	51.06 ss (12)	68.39 2m/d (12)	69.07 2m/d (12)	103.98 ss (12)
1821	50.87 ss (12)	69.18 2m/d (12)	69.65 2m/d (12)	104.50 ss (11)
1822	50.92 ss (12)	69.01 2m/d (10)	69.46 2m/d (10)	104.14 ss (11)
1823	51.32 ss (12)	69.28 2m/d (11)	69.46 2m/d (11)	103.95 ss (12)
1824	50.88 ss (12)	68.68 2m/d (12)	69.30 2m/d (12)	103.63 ss (12)
1825	50.39 ss (12)	68.79 2m/d (12)	69.04 2m/d (12)	103.40 ss (12)
1826	51.26 ss (12)	69.16 2m/d (12)	69.42 2m/d (12)	103.71 fair/ss (12)
1827	50.75 ss (12)	80.89 2m/d (12)	69.13 2m/d (12)	103.66 fair/ss (12)
1828	50.43 ss (12)	68.74 2m/d (12)	68.96 2m/d (12)	103.30 14d/d (12)
1829	50.26 ss (12)	68.37 2m/d (12)	68.48 2m/d (12)	102.86 14d/d (12)
1830	50.34 ss (12)	68.32 2m/d (12)	68.45 2m/d (12)	102.65 14d/d (12)
1831	50.27 ss (12)	68.44 2m/d (12)	68.57 2m/d (12)	102.79 14d/d (10)
1832	51.01 ss (12)	68.74 2m/d (12)	69.05 2m/d (12)	102.94 14d/d (12)
1833	50.65 ss (12)	68.64 2m/d (12)	68.88 2m/d (12)	102.99 ss (12)
1834	50.77 ss (12)	68.68 2m/d (12)	69.00 2m/d (12)	103.01 ss (12)
1835	50.77 ss (12)	68.63 2m/d (12)	68.94 2m/d (12)	102.89 ss (12)
1836	50.58 ss (12)	68.20 2m/d (11)	68.36 2m/d (11)	102.55 ss (11)
1837	50.43 ss (12)	67.90 2m/d (12)	67.92 2m/d (12)	101.51 ss (12)
1838	50.43 ss (12)	67.89 2m/d (12)	68.02 2m/d (12)	101.93 ss (12)
1839	50.42 ss (12)	67.70 2m/d (12)	67.73 2m/d (12)	102.13 ss (12)
1840	50.00 ss (12)	67.66 2m/d (12)	67.69 2m/d (12)	102.07 ss (12)
1841	49.73 ss (12)	67.40 2m/d (12)	67.61 2m/d (12)	99.76 ss (12)
1842	50.04 ss (12)	67.88 2m/d (12)	68.23 2m/d (12)	99.88 ss (12)
1843	50.22 ss (12)	56.88 2m/d (12)	68.32 2m/d (12)	99.56 ss (11)
1844	50.09 ss (12)	56.63 2m/d (12)	68.09 2m/d (12)	99.87 ss (12)
1845	50.26 ss (12)	56.66 2m/d (12)	68.00 2m/d (12)	99.87 ss (12)
1846	50.22 ss (12)	56.59 2m/d (12)	67.91 2m/d (12)	99.75 ss (12)

	BERLIN on:			
	Hamburg	**Frankfurt**	**Augsburg**	**Leipzig**
	per 100 mark banco [a]	per 100 guilders South German current [b]	per 100 guilders Augsburg current, from 1859 per 100 guilders South German current [c]	per 100 thaler Saxon current [d]
	in thaler Prussian current			
1847	50.53 ss (12)	56.58 2m/d (12)	67.91 2m/d (12)	99.74 ss (12)
1848	50.42 ss (12)	56.93 2m/d (12)	67.91 2m/d (11)	99.73 ss (7)
1849	50.16 ss (12)	56.73 2m/d (12)	67.91 2m/d (12)	99.70 ss (12)
1850	50.26 ss (12)	56.70 2m/d (12)	68.06 2m/d (12)	99.69 ss (12)
1851	50.22 ss (12)	56.59 2m/d (12)	67.82 2m/d (12)	99.70 ss (12)
1852	50.66 ss (12)	56.55 2m/d (12)	67.85 2m/d (12)	99.74 ss (12)
1853	50.65 ss (12)	56.54 2m/d (12)	67.72 2m/d (12)	99.75 ss (12)
1854	49.83 ss (12)	55.92 2m/d (12)	66.91 2m/d (12)	99.74 ss (12)
1855	49.86 ss (12)	56.17 2m/d (12)	67.31 2m/d (12)	99.82 ss (12)
1856	50.84 ss (12)	56.76 2m/d (12)	68.11 2m/d (12)	99.80 ss (12)
1857	50.58 ss (12)	56.54 2m/d (12)	67.79 2m/d (12)	99.75 ss (12)
1858	50.23 ss (12)	56.70 2m/d (12)	67.98 2m/d (12)	99.74 ss (12)
1859	50.21 ss (12)	56.82 2m/d (12)	56.72 2m/d (12)	99.77 ss (12)
1860	50.13 ss (12)	56.70 2m/d (12)	56.65 2m/d (12)	99.82 ss (12)
1861	50.12 ss (12)	56.72 2m/d (12)	56.71 2m/d (12)	99.82 ss (12)
1862	50.49 ss (12)	56.90 2m/d (12)	56.84 2m/d (12)	99.55 ss (12)
1863	50.67 ss (12)	56.77 2m/d (12)	56.74 2m/d (12)	99.72 ss (12)
1864	50.70 ss (12)	56.73 2m/d (12)	56.70 2m/d (12)	99.75 ss (11)
1865	50.83 ss (12)	56.83 2m/d (12)	56.77 2m/d (12)	99.80 ss (12)
1866	50.66 ss (12)	56.90 2m/d (12)	56.83 2m/d (12)	99.83 ss (12)
1867	50.47 ss (12)	56.83 2m/d (12)	56.78 2m/d (12)	99.80 ss (12)
1868	50.40 ss (12)	56.92 2m/d (12)	56.85 2m/d (12)	99.84 ss (12)
1869	50.46 ss (12)	56.84 2m/d (12)	56.80 2m/d (12)	99.80 ss (12)
1870	50.41 ss (12)	56.82 2m/d (12)	56.73 2m/d (12)	99.75 ss (12)
1871	50.02 ss (12)	56.76 2m/d (12)	56.70 2m/d (12)	99.71 ss (12)
1872	49.88 ss (12)	56.74 2m/d (6)	56.68 2m/d (12)	99.75 ss (12)
1873	49.67 ss (2)		56.56 2m/d (11)	99.75 ss (11)
1874			56.67 2m/d (9)	99.75 ss (9)

[a] Concerning the Hamburg currency, see pp. 191–193.

[b] Concerning the Frankfurt currency, see pp. 195f.

[c] 'Augsburg current' meant – in modification of Konventionskurant, which became common especially from 1764 – a standard of coinage of 20 5/12 guilders per mark of Cologne. So the guilder Augsburg current of 60 kreuzer was equal to 11.45 grammes of fine silver. As a consequence of the Vienna Coin Treaty of 1857, the guilder South German current (standard of coinage: 24½ guilders per 233.855 grammes of fine silver or 52½ guilders per pound of 500 grammes of fine silver) of 60 kreuzer became legal tender in Augsburg from the beginning of 1859.

[d]   Concerning the Saxon currency, see pp. 194f.

5
Habsburg Monarchy (1754–1914)

Exchange markets: Vienna (1754–1914) and Trieste (1819–1914)

Sources: <u>Vienna</u>: IISG Amsterdam, *Corsi di cambi* [Vienna] (1750–1771); AWB Wien, *Corsi di Cambi in Vienna (dalla Borsa pubblica in Vienna)* (1771–1785); ibid., *Wechsel-Cours in Wien. Aus der K.K. öffentlichen Börse* (1786–1817); *Wiener Zeitung* (1801–1810, 1872–1914); AWB Wien, *Tabellarisches Compendium aller Course der Staatspapiere, Wechselbriefe und Münzen* (1811–1818); KELLY [1811] II, p. 125 (1807); *Hamburger Börsenhalle* (1815–1822); AWB Wien, *Tabellarische Übersichten sämmtlicher Wechsel-, Münz- und Obligations-Course vom Jahre ...* (1823–1859); ibid., *Coursblatt der Wiener Börsekammer* (1840–1859); ibid., *Coursblatt des Gremiums der K.K. Börse-Sensale* (1860–1874); ibid., *Amtliches Kursblatt der Wiener Börse* (1881). <u>Trieste</u>: *Osservatore Triestino* (1818–1825, 1861–1914).

Concordance: *WdW VI*, pp. 239–254; *HStD XII*, pp. 235–253; *WdW I/III*, pp. 381–451; *HStD XI*, pp. 487–519

Currency: From 1748/50 the Habsburg Monarchy issued its guilder (gulden = 2/3 rixdollar) of 60 kreuzer at 11.69 grammes of fine silver (standard of coinage: 20 guilders per mark of Cologne), which was termed 'Konventionskurant' after the so-called 'Münzkonvention' with the Electorate of Bavaria had been concluded in 1753. Near the end of the Seven Years' War (1762), the issuing of paper money by the Wiener Stadtbanco started, so that this paper money was called 'Bancozettel' or, later on, 'Wiener Währung'. Above all, towards the end of the 18th century in the wake of the Napoleonic Wars, the volume of circulating paper money increased drastically up to a sum of 44 million guilders in 1796 and clearly weakened the value of the currency. So a compulsory rate was imposed on the Bancozettel or the Wiener Währung respectively in 1797, and in 1800 the convertibility of the Wiener Währung was suspended. Therefore all exchange rate quotations of or on the Austrian exchange markets are made in or for Wiener Währung from then on. In the wake of the military defeats of 1805 and 1809, the circulation of paper money rose up to more than 1 billion guilders. By means of the 'Bankrottpatent' from February 20th 1811, the Bancozettel were converted into the so-called 'Einlösungsscheine', which stabilized the Wiener Währung on a low level for the following years: whereas one paid only c. 8 guilders Konventionskurant for 100 guilders Wiener Währung in December 1810 and c. 12 until March 1811, there was an average of about 42 guilders Konventionskurant for 100 guilders Wiener Währung for the rest of 1811, i.e. after the establishment of the Einlösungsscheine. From February 1st 1812, the Wiener Währung was the only current money in the Habsburg Monarchy. Additionally, new 'Antizipationsscheine' were issued in 1813/14 to finance the Austrian military engagement in the years 1813 to 1815. In the exchange rate currents the Wiener Währung was quoted with a remarkable discount against Konventionskurant:

Guilders Konventionskurant for 100 guilders Wiener Währung (annual average)

1809	23.96	1813	39.23	1817	29.86	1821	40.02
1810	16.84	1814	29.98	1818	39.27	1822	40.02
1811	20.70	1815	28.82	1819	40.12	1823	40.02
1812	32.96	1816	30.56	1820	39.99	1824	40.02

Sources: *HStD XII*, p. 254; *HStD XI*, p. 464

After the definitive stabilization of the Wiener Währung at a rate of 250 guilders Wiener Währung for 100 guilders Konventionskurant, the Vienna exchange rate quotations were reconverted into guilders Konventionskurant in June 1818. From 1820 there was no more fluctuation of the Wiener Währung aginst the Konventionskurant and most of the paper money was cashed in by the Österreichische Nationalbank. Owing to the revolution of 1848, a compulsory rate was again imposed on the notes of the Österreichische Nationalbank on May 21st 1848, which is why the quotations of and on Vienna and Trieste are to be understood – if not indicated differently – in or for guilders Konventionskurant payable in bank and newly issued government notes – the so-called 'Wiener Banknoten' – from June 3rd 1848. The conclusion of the Wiener Münzvertrag on January 24th 1857 meant the monetary affiliation of the Austrian currency system with the Zollverein system until the Treaty of Berlin 1867, which resolved this affiliation (see p. 197). The Wiener Münzvertrag also laid the foundations for the introduction of the new guilder Österreichische Währung (11.11 grammes of fine silver) of 100 neu-kreuzer (standard of coinage: 45 guilders per pound of 500 grammes) by the Imperial patent of September 19th 1857 which became legal tender of the monarchy on November 1st 1858. However, in the quotations on Vienna the transition to the new currency was for the most part not effected until the following weeks and months, in Vienna itself not until the beginning of 1859. From 1848 the guilder Österreichische Währung was also payable in bank and government notes, like the guilder Konventionskurant, and fluctuated more or less in the wake of the various political and military crises of the 1850s and 1860s. The rapid drop-off in silver prices from 1873 resulted in the Habsburg Monarchy having an exclusive paper currency from 1879. Henceforth, only the value of the paper notes – the Wiener Banknoten – determined the value of the Austrian–Hungarian currency within the international payment system (PRIBRAM [1938], p. 68).

To stabilize the currency of the monarchy, the transition to the gold standard became inevitable. It was initiated by the Act of August 2nd 1892, which generally introduced the gold standard and fixed the ratio of the new crown (krone; in Hungary: korona; 0.3048 grammes of fine gold) to the guilder Österreichische Währung at 2:1. On this basis the Imperial decree of September 21st 1899 established *de facto* the crown of 100 heller (in Hungary: fillér) as the obligatory unit of account from January 1st 1900, introducing the gold standard at the same time, whereas a limping gold standard can be observed between 1892 and 1899 (OTRUBA [1981], pp. 131–146).

Original quotations at Vienna and Trieste up to October 1858

on:	in:	per:
Amsterdam	rixdollars Konventionskurant or Wiener Währung	100 rixdollars or 250 guilders Flemish banco
Augsburg	rixdollars Konventionskurant or Wiener Währung or	100 rixdollars Augsburg current
	guilders Konventionskurant or Wiener Währung	100 guilders Augsburg current
Bolzano	guilders Konventionskurant	100 guilders Meßvaluta
Bucharest	para or paralle	1 guilder Konventionskurant
Constantinople	para	1 guilder Konventionskurant
Frankfurt	guilders Konventionskurant or Wiener Währung	100 guilders Frankfurt exchange money
from 1843	guilders Konventionskurant	100 guilders South German current
Genoa	soldi fuori banco	1 guilder Konventionskurant or Wiener Währung
from 1827 (3)	guilders Konventionskurant	300 Piedmontese lire nuove
Hamburg	rixdollars Konventionskurant or Wiener Währung	100 rixdollars or 300 mark banco
London	guilders Konventionskurant or Wiener Währung	1 pound sterling
Leghorn	soldi moneta buona	1 guilder Konventionskurant or Wiener Währung
from 1837	guilders Konventionskurant	300 Tuscan lire moneta buona

on:	in:	per:
Milan	soldi correnti	1 guilder Konventionskurant or Wiener Währung
from 1824	guilders Konventionskurant	300 lire austriache
Paris	guilders Konventionskurant or Wiener Währung	100 écus or 300 francs
Venice	rixdollars Konventionskurant or Wiener Währung	100 ducati di banco

From 1859 all quotations were effected for 10 (on London) or 100 units foreign currency.

Other data available from Vienna: Amsterdam, 4w/d (1769–1777/79); 2m/d (1803–1812) – Augsburg, 2m/d (1815–1854) – Breslau, 14d/d (1752–1764) – Brussels, s (1900–1913) – Frankfurt, 2m/d (1765–1770, 1805–1812) – Germany, ls (1900–1907/12) – Hamburg, 4w/d (1769–1779); 2m/d (1803–1813) – London, 1m/d (1769–1772/75, 1814); 3m/d (1803–1808) – Munich, 3m/d (1870/71) – Nuremberg, 14d/d (1754–1769/73) – Prague, 14d/d (1754–1807); ss (1809–1814) – Salonica, 1m/d (1780/81) – Smyrna, 1m/d (1803–1811). **From Trieste:** Amsterdam, 2m/d (1819–1825); 3m/d (1852–1876); s (1877–1914) – Augsburg, 1m/d (1818–1825); 3m/d (1818–1825, 1852–1876) – Belgium, s (1900–1914) – France, 3m/d (1867–1876) – Frankfurt, 3m/d (1852–1874) – Genoa, 1m/d (1819–1825); 3m/d (1819–1825, 1852–1858) – Germany, s (1878–1914) – Hamburg, 2 m/d (1818–1825); 3m/d (1821–1825, 1852–1877) – Italy, s (1867–1914) – Lisbon, 3m/d (1819/20, 1852–1857) – London, 14d/s (1818–1825); 3m/d (1852–1865); ls (1866–1914); ss (1881–1914) – Marseilles, 2m/d (1819–1825); 3m/d (1852–1859) – Milan, 1m/d (1818–1825); 3m/d (1818–1825, 1852–1866) – Naples, 6w/d (1818–1825); 1m/d (1852–1862) – Paris, 2m/d (1818–1825); 3m/d (1819–1825); 3m/d (1857–1867); s (1877–1914) – Saint Petersburg, (1900–1914) – Switzerland, s (1900–1914) – Venice, 1m/d (1818–1825); 3m/d (1819–1825, 1852–1861).

In Vienna the official quotation of exchange rates started with the foundation of the stock exchange on September 1st 1771 and the publication of the *Börsekurszettel*. Twice a week, the post and bills of exchange were delivered, bringing along new orders, the exchange brokers ascertained the average prices, noted them down on the exchange rate currents in Italian until 1785 and published them on the following day (for the first time on September 4th 1771; BALTZAREK [1973], pp. 25–28). For the time between the Bavarian–Austrian Münzkonvention of 1753 and 1771 quotations are available quite irregularly. A matter of priority, Central European places (Augsburg, Nuremberg, Frankfurt am Main, Hamburg, Breslau, Prague) and Northwest European ones (Amsterdam, London) were quoted in Vienna. The same held for Venice in Italy and the Bolzano fairs, functioning as an intermediary for the Upper Italian and the Austrian economic areas. Despite this, the quotations on Frankfurt am Main, Breslau, Nuremberg and Bolzano, which were often made irregularly, ended as early as during the 1760s or in the early 1770s. From September 1771 on, the official exchange rate currents also listed columns for Paris, Leghorn, Milan, Frankfurt am Main, Nuremberg and Breslau, but (relatively) regular rate series for the first years can be provided only for Amsterdam, London, Hamburg, Augsburg and Venice, as well as for Prague, even though other places were mentioned, and Bolzano, Leipzig, Brussels, Graz and Linz were listed as exchange partners of Vienna in contemporary merchant manuals (e.g. NELKENBRECHER [1775], p. 252; NELKENBRECHER [1798], p. 290). There are relatively regular quotations on Constantinople from 1780 as well as on Salonica for a short time, on Genoa, Milan and Leghorn from 1786, then on Frankfurt am Main not again until 1805 – and up to 1819 quite irregularly – and quite irregularly on Paris since 1815 as well. So the special relevance of Vienna in the international cashless payment system was that its exchange market connected the Ottoman Empire to Central Europe from the end of the 18th century and, at the same time, it intensified its contact with Italy.

When in 1800 the convertibility of the Austrian paper money, the Bankozettel, into specie was suspended and the Vienna stock exchange started to quote in Wiener Währung, the stock exchange quotations were published in the *Wiener Zeitung* in order to avoid false speculations about stock exchange trends. Nonetheless, the quotations of the Napoleonic era became much less regular owing to the political and military conflicts and the economic and monetary complications that ensued. So, in the course of the Continental System, which Austria joined after the Peace of Tilsit in 1807, the quotation on London was suspended. The Italian markets were also, for the most part, not quoted for years, and in the case of Venice they were not quoted at all after 1802. Additionally, the rate fluctuations increased drastically because of political and military conflicts of the Napoleonic era and the resulting disturbances in monetary policy, as shown in the monetary history above (BALTZAREK [1973], pp. 33–44). When quoted again in Konventionskurant after a temporary stabilization of the Austrian currency system from May 20th 1818, the quotations at last became more regular once more.

Since the 18th century, Vienna had not only become a financial centre of Central Europe but also indisputably the most important, even dominant, exchange market of the Habsburg Monarchy. Most of the international transactions of the Habsburg Monarchy within the cashless payment system were completed and the other exchange places – Prague, later Budapest, but not Trieste – were connected to the international system via Vienna. After 1818, the quotations were still orientated primarily to Northwest European (intensified by the quotation on Paris), the German and the Italian area. Vienna was at the same time the only financial centre within Central Europe keeping regular exchange contact with the Levant (with Constantinople up to 1858 and with Smyrna from 1803 to 1811) and the Balkan area (with Bucharest from 1842 to 1863), for Viennese merchants had close personal and commercial relationships with these areas. So, in 1811, more than a quarter of the people admitted to the Vienna stock exchange were Ottoman subordinates and Ottoman Jews (ibid., p. 32). In particular, this special importance of the Levant for the period before the revolution of 1848 is reflected in the Viennese quotations (ibid., p. 50), whereas it seems that the Levant lost its significance after 1848, as the increasing irregularity of the quotations on Constantinople shows (cf. NOBACK [1851], pp. 1426f.). In the official exchange rate currents documented here, one cannot find quotations on Leipzig, Marseilles, Naples, Smyrna, Berlin and Breslau, or on Prague and Trieste, which are proved in contemporary merchant manuals (e.g. ibid.). As a result of the quarrels about Northern Italy in the 1850s, the quotations on the Italian partners became more irregular and were finally stopped little by little, for example the quotations on Genoa and Leghorn in 1858 (the latter occasionally continuing until 1865) and those on Milan in 1866/69.

It was not until the 1870s that the network of quoted places was enlarged once again: Brussels (though quite irregularly and with a break in the 1880s), Zurich and Basle were quoted from 1872 and Saint Petersburg from 1876. The quotations on the South German places (Frankfurt am Main, Augsburg and Munich) stopped after 1871. From 1875, after the introduction of the mark Reichswährung as the uniform

currency of the united German Empire, the quotations for the German exchange markets were consolidated in 'German bank places'. Because of that, the number of regular quotations on Vienna was relatively small in comparison with those on other
European markets and especially when the formerly close contact with Italy had
ceased completely (by 1888). Since Lombardy–Veneto's separation from the Habsburg Monarchy, exchange operations between Vienna and Milan had become extremely rare, particularly since both Austria-Hungary and Italy had rather instable
paper currencies, complicating direct exchange operations. Instead of this, gold coins
were sent to Italy or exchanges were remitted on London if required. There was a similar development in the exchanges with Russia, which had a paper currency as well.
Owing to the currency fluctuations in both countries, all payments to Saint Petersburg
were settled by means of bills of exchange on London, Hamburg and Berlin at least
until 1876 (NOBACK [1877], pp. 915f. with notes 1–4). Further changes of the Viennese exchange rate current with regard to the quoted exchange places were not carried
out before the First World War, although New York, Bucharest and Copenhagen were
nominally (i.e. without quotation) included in it, as an exchange rate current from
1912 shows (SWOBODA [1913], p. 503). From the beginning of 1881 all quotations on
the official exchange rate current of the Viennese stock market (as well as in Trieste)
were made at sight (cf. SWOBODA [1889], p. 887; SWOBODA [1902], pp. 624, 660).

Although the quotations of exchange rates of Vienna dominated most of the quotations of the only regionally important financial places of the Habsburg Monarchy,
i.e. Prague and Budapest, there was one exception: Trieste. Although it was the Monarchy's free and only important port, Trieste had not been an important exchange
place during most decades of the 18th century. Trieste quoted only Vienna and Venice
(cf. KELLY [1811], p. 410), and for other exchange transactions the port adopted the
quotations of the Viennese exchange rate current. From the end of the 18th century,
however, Trieste became one of the most important exchange markets of the Mediterranean region, with quotations on Amsterdam, Genoa, Hamburg, Leghorn, London, Lyons, Milan, Messina, Naples and Venice (so in 1805/10; NOBACK [1851], p.
1248), and on Paris, Marseilles, Augsburg, Lisbon (for a few months), Constantinople
and Smyrna in around 1820. Around the middle of the 19th century the network of the
quotations of Trieste principally stretched across Italian and German places as well as
across Amsterdam, London, Paris and Marseilles. Up to World War I, Trieste maintained its position as an exchange place relatively independent of Vienna, whose quotations hardly differed from those of Vienna, but which also listed places Vienna did
not quote (DENZEL [1996b], pp. 60f). Before the actual introduction of the gold standard in 1900, the currency fluctuations in Austria made it indispensable for exporters
to pay attention to the settling of bills when initiating transactions and, therefore, to
buy or sell currency as needed. The result of this was the great importance of (daily)
exchange transactions, in Trieste above all with London, France, Italy and Germany,
amounting to sums of various sizes with periods of validity not exceeding one year.
There were also exchange transactions with Switzerland, and with the Netherlands,
though not regularly, whereas bills of exchange on Saint Petersburg were drawn
rather infrequently (SWOBODA [1902], pp. 624–628). Because of the urgent need for
such direct transactions, bills on Italy (above all on Milan) were traded daily in Trieste
even in those years when these exchange markets were not quoted in Vienna (No-

BACK [1877], pp. 915f., note 3). In addition to this, there are quotations on New York and Belgium (here: Antwerp) as well as on the Turkish and the Greek paper money from 1900 onwards (only occasionally from the 1870s, regularly from 1900). Together with the important transactions in Marie Theresa thaler, which were effected with Egypt and from there with the whole of North and East Africa, Trieste was the European place that maintained the closest payment connections with the Levant after the decline of Leghorn (see pp. 114f.), although an official quotation on Malta given in contemporary merchant manuals cannot be proved (SWOBODA [1902], pp. 628–630). So the exchange market of Trieste as the gateway of the Monarchy to the world complemented the quotations of Vienna concerning the financial markets especially in Italy and in the Levant, as well as in the USA. Therefore it would be possible to complement the Viennese quotations with those of Trieste, because the Viennese quotations are not sufficiently representative of the Habsburg Monarchy as a whole in many respects. This will be done in the particular cases of:

– the quotations on the Italian places (1818–1825 and 1859–1887) as well as on German ones (1872–1875);
– the quotations on Constantinople (1819–1823), and on Turkish and Greek paper money from 1861/1900 onwards, which will replace the original exchange rate quotations on Constantinople and Athens;
– the quotations on New York as well as on Belgium (the latter because of their clearly higher regularity of quotation in comparison to those of Vienna).

References: Alfred F. PRIBRAM (ed.), *Materialien zur Geschichte der Preise und Löhne in Österreich, vol. 1*, Wien 1938; Othmar BACHMAYER, *Die Geschichte der österreichischen Währungspolitik*, Wien 1960, pp. 80–121; Franz BALTZAREK, *Die Geschichte der Wiener Börse. Öffentliche Finanzen und privates Kapital im Spiegel einer österreichischen Wirtschaftsinstitution*, Wien 1973; Günther PROBSZT, *Österreichische Münz- und Geldgeschiche*, Wien 1973; Gustav OTRUBA, Die Einführung des Goldstandards in Österreich-Ungarn und seine Auswirkungen auf die Preis- und Lohnentwicklung, in Hermann KELLENBENZ (ed.), *Weltwirtschaftliche und währungspolitische Probleme seit dem Ausgang des Mittelalters*, Stuttgart – New York 1981, pp. 123–162; Friedrich ZELLFELDER, Die Währungsprobleme der Donaumonarchie, in *WdW I/I*, pp. 122–135; Josef WYSOCKI, Die österreichisch/ungarische Krone im Goldwährungsmechanismus, in Eckart SCHREMMER (ed.), *Geld und Währung vom 16. Jahrhundert bis zur Gegenwart*, Stuttgart 1993, pp. 143–156; Markus A. DENZEL, Die Integration Deutschlands in das internationale Zahlungsverkehrssystem im 17. und 18. Jahrhundert, in Eckart SCHREMMER (ed.), *Wirtschaftliche und soziale Integration in historischer Sicht*, Stuttgart 1996 [here: 1996a], pp. 58–109, here pp. 92–94; idem, Die Integration ostmittel-, ost- und südosteuropäischer Städte in die internationalen Zahlungsverkehrsverbindungen im 19. und beginnenden 20. Jahrhundert, *Südost-Forschungen* 55 (1996) [here: 1996b], pp. 45–73; Marc FLANDREAU / John KOMLOS, Core or Periphery? The Credibility of the Austro-Hungarian Currency 1867–1913, *Journal of European Economic History* 31 (2002), pp. 293–320; Andreas RESCH, Wien – die wechselvolle Entwicklung eines Finanzplatzes in Zentraleuropa, in *Europäische Finanzplätze im Wettbewerb. 27. Symposium des Instituts für bankhistorische Forschung e.V. am 16. Juni 2004 im Hause der Deutschen Bundesbank, Hauptverwaltung Frankfurt am Main* (= *Bankhistorisches Archiv. Zeitschrift zur Banken- und Finanzgeschichte*, Beiheft 45), Stuttgart 2006, pp. 93–138.

5.1 Vienna and Trieste exchange rates

From June 3rd 1848 the guilder Konventionskurant and from November 1858 the guilder Österreichische Währung were paper money in notes of the Wiener Nationalbank and government notes.

5.1.1 On London, Amsterdam, Hamburg/Germany and Augsburg

	VIENNA on:			
	London [a]	**Amsterdam**	**Hamburg** [a]	**Augsburg** [a]
	per 10 pounds sterling [b]	per 100 guilders Flemish banco [c]	per 100 mark banco [d]	per 100 guilders (Augsburg) current [e]
	in guilders Konventionskurant			
1754	86.71 14d/s (6)	82.14 2m/d (6)	70.00 14d/s (6)	100.25 14d/s (6)
1755	89.53 14d/s (6)	82.85 2m/d (6)	69.88 14d/s (6)	101.70 14d/s (6)
1756	89.50 14d/s (1)	83.10 2m/d (1)	67.13 14d/s (1)	99.50 14d/s (1)
1757	88.51 14d/s (8)	82.96 2m/d (8)	66.52 14d/s (8)	101.32 14d/s (8)
1758	85.00 14d/s (1)	82.35 2m/d (1)	64.63 14d/s (1)	101.00 14d/s (1)
1759	88.34 14d/s (1)	83.40 2m/d (1)	63.13 14d/s (1)	101.25 14d/s (1)
1760				
1761	86.17 14d/s (2)	83.18 2m/d (2)	70.38 14d/s (2)	99.21 14d/s (2)
1762				
1763				
1764	89.67 14d/s (1)	82.65 2m/d (1)	69.27 14d/s (1)	99.25 14d/s (1)
1765	87.25 14d/s (2)	82.43 2m/d (2)	68.42 14d/s (2)	99.25 14d/s (2)
1766	86.89 14d/s (12)	83.59 2m/d (12)	67.20 14d/s (12)	99.62 14d/s (12)
1767	88.04 14d/s (11)	85.04 2m/d (12)	66.85 14d/s (12)	100.28 14d/s (12)
1768	87.29 14d/s (10)	83.96 2m/d (10)	68.45 14d/s (10)	99.42 14d/s (10)
1769	86.80 14d/s (8)	84.71 2m/d (7)	70.34 6w/d (10)	99.62 14d/s (11)
1770	86.56 2m/d (11)	84.84 2m/d (9)	70.52 6w/d (9)	99.43 14d/s (11)
1771	86.94 2m/d (9)	84.63 2m/d (10)	70.91 6w/d (9)	99.86 14d/s (12)
1772	86.80 2m/d (11)	84.14 2m/d (11)	71.04 6w/d (10)	99.77 14d/s (11)
1773	92.32 2m/d (12)	86.65 2m/d (12)	72.03 6w/d (10)	100.33 14d/s (12)
1774	92.57 2m/d (12)	85.77 2m/d (11)	71.87 6w/d (12)	100.35 14d/s (12)
1775	90.25 2m/d (10)	84.93 2m/d (12)	70.99 6w/d (12)	100.19 14d/s (11)
1776	88.23 2m/d (12)	85.64 2m/d (10)	71.59 6w/d (11)	99.85 14d/s (9)
1777	87.87 2m/d (12)	85.50 2m/d (7)	72.36 6w/d (9)	100.11 14d/s (10)
1778	89.96 2m/d (12)	85.56 2m/d (12)	72.25 6w/d (11)	99.82 14d/s (12)
1779	92.87 2m/d (12)	85.56 2m/d (11)	71.05 6w/d (10)	99.28 14d/s (11)
1780	93.37 2m/d (12)	87.26 2m/d (12)	72.87 6w/d (12)	100.20 14d/s (12)
1781	89.35 2m/d (12)	87.40 2m/d (12)	73.07 6w/d (12)	99.87 14d/s (12)
1782	86.23 2m/d (12)	84.41 2m/d (12)	72.28 6w/d (12)	99.46 14d/s (12)
1783	86.07 2m/d (12)	82.84 2m/d (12)	72.49 6w/d (12)	99.43 14d/s (12)
1784	90.28 2m/d (12)	83.82 2m/d (12)	71.89 6w/d (12)	99.75 14d/s (12)
1785	93.57 2m/d (12)	83.59 2m/d (12)	71.52 6w/d (12)	99.38 14d/s (12)

	VIENNA on:			
	London	**Amsterdam**	**Hamburg**	**Augsburg**
	per 10 pounds sterling [b]	per 100 guilders Flemish banco, from 1816 (10) per 100 Dutch guilders [c]	per 100 mark banco [d]	per 100 guilders Augsburg current [e]
	in guilders Konventionskurant			
1786	91.89 2m/d (12)	84.02 2m/d (12)	71.70 6w/d (12)	99.58 2m/d (12)
1787	93.56 2m/d (12)	85.22 2m/d (12)	72.74 6w/d (12)	100.24 2m/d (12)
1788	94.09 2m/d (12)	83.73 2m/d (12)	72.60 6w/d (12)	99.87 2m/d (12)
1789	96.00 2m/d (12)	84.61 2m/d (12)	73.69 6w/d (12)	99.89 2m/d (12)
1790	97.23 2m/d (12)	84.11 2m/d (12)	73.87 6w/d (12)	100.01 2m/d (12)
1791	98.21 2m/d (12)	84.97 2m/d (12)	74.19 6w/d (11)	100.12 2m/d (12)
1792	92.73 2m/d (12)	84.10 2m/d (12)	72.77 6w/d (12)	99.87 2m/d (12)
1793	99.14 2m/d (12)	85.29 2m/d (12)	74.06 6w/d (12)	100.50 2m/d (12)
1794	97.00 2m/d (12)	83.08 2m/d (11)	73.85 6w/d (12)	99.88 2m/d (12)
1795	89.40 2m/d (12)	87.00 2m/d (1)	72.99 6w/d (12)	99.79 2m/d (12)
1796	89.39 2m/d (12)		72.85 6w/d (12)	100.25 2m/d (11)
1797	99.70 2m/d (12)	83.10 2m/d (1)	75.85 6w/d (12)	101.51 2m/d (12)
1798	103.84 2m/d (12)	81.49 2m/d (6)	74.88 6w/d (12)	101.12 2m/d (12)
1799				
	in guilders Wiener Währung			
1800	100.77 2m/d (12)	95.44 6w/d (12)	86.38 6w/d (12)	114.62 2m/d (12)
1801	101.08 2m/d (12)	96.19 6w/d (12)	86.68 6w/d (12)	115.73 2m/d (12)
1802	110.93 2m/d (12)	102.88 6w/d (12)	91.43 6w/d (12)	121.81 2m/d (12)
1803	121.84 2m/d (12)	109.02 6w/d (8)	96.89 6w/d (8)	131.22 14d/s (11)
1804	128.24 2m/d (12)	110.99 6w/d (8)	98.97 6w/d (7)	134.45 14d/s (11)
1805	126.05 2m/d (11)	108.15 6w/d (7)	97.17 6w/d (5)	134.89 14d/s (12)
1806	157.02 2m/d (11)	144.52 6w/d (9)	126.65 6w/d (7)	171.09 14d/s (11)
1807	197.84 2m/d (7)	174.00 6w/d (4)	154.29 6w/d (8)	207.78 14d/s (11)
1808		182.99 6w/d (7)	157.40 6w/d (5)	225.57 14d/s (12)
1809		253.17 6w/d (8)	221.12 6w/d (9)	292.02 14d/s (12)
1810		377.75 6w/d (6)	381.40 6w/d (10)	498.96 14d/s (12)
1811		721.20/201.36 6w/d (2+7)	613.00/158.60 6w/d (2+9)	831.00/212.58 14d/s (3+9)
1812		156.40 6w/d (11)	141.50 6w/d (9)	197.85 14d/s (12)
1813	113.88 2m/d (4)	124.34 6w/d (12)	109.48 6w/d (9)	154.09 14d/s (12)
1814		182.05 6w/d (12)	181.34 6w/d (6)	232.62 14d/s (12)
1815	292.90 1m/d (12)	293.94 6w/d (11)	257.81 6w/d (12)	356.20 14d/s (12)
1816	307.50 2m/d (7)	261.26 6w/d (10)	238.92 6w/d (11)	327.79 14d/s (12)
1817	305.90 2m/d (4)	268.26 6w/d (7)	255.62 6w/d (5)	329.57 14d/s (10)
1818	255.74 2m/d (5)	231.96 6w/d (5)	205.35 6w/d (5)	268.01 14d/s (5)
	in guilders Konventionskurant			
1818	88.93 2m/d (7)	80.88 6w/d (7)	71.98 6w/d (7)	98.30 14d/s (7)

	VIENNA on:			
	London	**Amsterdam**	**Hamburg**	**Augsburg**
	per 10 pounds sterling [b]	per 100 Dutch guilders [c]	per 100 mark banco [d]	per 100 guilders Augsburg current [e]
	in guilders Konventionskurant			
1819	91.20 2m/d (12)	82.35 6w/d (9)	72.80 6w/d (8)	99.10 14d/s (12)
1820	97.80 2m/d (8)	83.12 6w/d (9)	72.82 6w/d (9)	99.30 14d/s (11)
1821	99.40 2m/d (5)	81.09 6w/d (8)	71.96 6w/d (9)	99.31 14d/s (12)
1822	100.50 2m/d (9)	83.13 6w/d (10)	72.79 6w/d (9)	99.35 14d/s (12)
1823	100.20 2m/d (5)	84.40 6w/d (10)	73.36 2m/d (8)	99.20 14d/s (12)
1824	95.20 2m/d (8)	83.29 6w/d (8)	72.01 2m/d (12)	98.81 14d/s (12)
1825	94.60 2m/d (6)	82.03 6w/d (8)	71.81 2m/d (10)	99.44 14d/s (12)
1826	104.20 2m/d (6)	83.42 6w/d (9)	73.05 2m/d (10)	100.02 14d/s (12)
1827	96.40 2m/d (6)	83.01 6w/d (9)	72.59 2m/d (9)	99.47 14d/s (12)
1828	95.10 2m/d (5)	82.28 6w/d (8)	72.44 2m/d (11)	99.50 14d/s (12)
1829	95.40 2m/d (6)	82.17 6w/d (9)	72.54 2m/d (9)	99.66 14d/s (12)
1830	99.80 3m/d (10)	82.53 6w/d (8)	72.57 2m/d (11)	99.65 14d/s (12)
1831	94.90 3m/d (11)	82.50 6w/d (10)	72.72 2m/d (10)	99.68 14d/s (12)
1832	97.20 3m/d (11)	82.98 6w/d (10)	72.56 2m/d (10)	98.83 14d/s (12)
1833	95.50 3m/d (7)	82.16 6w/d (9)	72.14 2m/d (7)	98.64 14d/s (12)
1834	94.60 3m/d (7)	80.91 6w/d (10)	72.09 2m/d (11)	98.57 14d/s (12)
1835	95.90 3m/d (9)	81.84 6w/d (8)	72.70 2m/d (10)	99.40 14d/s (12)
1836	95.70 3m/d (11)	82.26 6w/d (9)	73.00 2m/d (11)	99.50 14d/s (12)
1837	98.80 3m/d (12)	83.21 2m/d (7)	73.38 2m/d (11)	100.07 14d/s (12)
1838	98.20 3m/d (12)	82.69 2m/d (12)	73.43 2m/d (12)	99.83 14d/s (11)
1839	94.90 3m/d (12)	82.07 2m/d (12)	73.33 2m/d (12)	99.91 14d/s (11)
1840	94.80 3m/d (12)	82.23 2m/d (12)	73.37 2m/d (12)	99.97 14d/s (12)
1841	94.00 3m/d (12)	80.74 2m/d (12)	72.20 2m/d (12)	99.07 14d/s (12)
1842	94.30 3m/d (12)	80.10 2m/d (12)	71.70 2m/d (12)	98.36 14d/s (12)
1843	94.90 3m/d (12)	80.85 2m/d (12)	71.71 2m/d (12)	98.29 14d/s (12)
1844	94.20 3m/d (12)	80.08 2m/d (11)	71.19 2m/d (12)	97.52 14d/s (12)
1845	94.90 3m/d (12)	80.21 2m/d (12)	71.69 2m/d (12)	98.28 14d/s (12)
1846	96.00 3m/d (12)	81.29 2m/d (12)	72.70 2m/d (12)	99.40 14d/s (12)
1847	96.20 3m/d (12)	82.01 2m/d (11)	73.03 2m/d (12)	99.26 14d/s (12)
1848	109.10 3m/d (12)	89.22 2m/d (11)	79.93 2m/d (12)	107.36 14d/s (12)
1849	113.10 3m/d (12)	95.12 2m/d (12)	83.70 2m/d (12)	113.95 14d/s (12)
1850	115.50 3m/d (12)	97.31 2m/d (11)	87.18 2m/d (12)	118.21 14d/s (12)
1851	122.60 3m/d (12)	105.25 2m/d (12)	93.07 2m/d (12)	126.49 14d/s (12)
1852	117.60 3m/d (12)	100.69 2m/d (11)	88.73 2m/d (11)	119.92 14d/s (12)
1853	106.30 3m/d (12)	91.95 2m/d (9)	81.72 2m/d (12)	110.36 14d/s (12)
1854	122.70 3m/d (12)	107.00 2m/d (6)	93.57 2m/d (11)	126.73 14d/s (12)
1855	116.70 3m/d (12)	102.67 2m/d (6)	88.87 2m/d (12)	121.66 14d/s (12)
1856	102.50 3m/d (11)	86.84 2m/d (3)	76.62 2m/d (12)	104.58 14d/s (12)

	VIENNA and TRIESTE on: [f]			
	London	**Amsterdam**	**Hamburg, from 1875 Germany** [g]	**Augsburg**
	per 10 pounds sterling [b]	per 100 Dutch guilders [c]	per 100 mark banco, from 1873 per 100 mark [d]	per 100 guilders South German current, from 1876 per 100 mark [e]
	in guilders Konventionskurant			
1857	102.40 3m/d (12)	86.50 2m/d (4)	77.42 2m/d (11)	105.35 14d/s (12)
1858	108.87 3m/d (11)	87.88 2m/d (2)	76.82 2m/d (11)	104.88 14d/s (12)
	in guilders Österreichische Währung			
1859	120.60 3m/d (12)	104.63 3m/d (2)	89.73 3m/d (11)	103.65 3m/d (12)
1860	130.80 3m/d (12)	113.22 3m/d (5)	99.50 3m/d (11)	112.06 3m/d (12)
1861	142.20 3m/d (12)	119.57 3m/d (10)	106.35 3m/d (12)	120.66 3m/d (12)
1862	130.30 3m/d (12)	110.32 3m/d (8)	97.22 3m/d (12)	109.97 3m/d (12)
1863	113.20 3m/d (12)	96.09 3m/d (12)	84.85 3m/d (12)	95.76 3m/d (12)
1864	116.67 3m/d (12)	99.43 3m/d (9)	87.74 3m/d (12)	98.70 3m/d (12)
1865	110.00 3m/d (12)	92.01 3m/d (10)	82.10 3m/d (12)	92.14 3m/d (12)
1866	120.30 3m/d (12)	100.97 3m/d (9)	89.27 3m/d (11)	101.59 3m/d (12)
1867	126.80 3m/d (12)	107.70 3m/d (8)	93.92 3m/d (12)	105.90 3m/d (12)
1868	116.80 3m/d (12)	98.10 3m/d (10)	86.06 3m/d (12)	97.29 3m/d (12)
1869	123.10 3m/d (11)	102.88 3m/d (11)	90.83 3m/d (12)	102.83 3m/d (12)
1870	124.00 3m/d (12)	103.34 3m/d (9)	91.17 3m/d (11)	103.69 3m/d (12)
1871	121.90 3m/d (12)	101.87 3m/d (10)	90.00 3m/d (12)	102.33 3m/d (12)
1872	110.97 3m/d (12)	93.25 3m/d (8)	*81.75* 3m/d (12)	*93.17* 3m/d (12)
1873	110.83 3m/d (12)	92.21 3m/d (10)	*56.63* 3m/d (12)	*93.26* 3m/d (12)
1874	111.16 3m/d (12)	93.53 3m/d (11)	*54.42* 3m/d (12)	*93.20* 3m/d (12)
1875	111.73 3m/d (12)	94.03 3m/d (11)	54.97 3m/d (11)	*92.82* 3m/d (11)
1876	120.70 3m/d (12)	100.18 3m/d (9)	58.94 3m/d (12)	*59.46* 3m/d (3)
1877	122.48 3m/d (12)	102.34 3m/d (8)	59.77 3m/d (11)	
1878	118.47 3m/d (12)	98.21 3m/d (6)	57.91 3m/d (12)	
1879	116.81 3m/d (11)	96.31 3m/d (9)	56.96 3m/d (11)	
1880	117.93 3m/d (12)	97.36 3m/d (9)	57.47 3m/d (12)	
1881	118.04 s (12)	97.41 s (7)	57.63 s (12)	
1882	119.86 s (12)	98.96 s (9)	58.61 s (12)	
1883	120.03 s (12)	99.14 s (9)	58.70 s (12)	
1884	121.89 s (12)	100.71 s (10)	59.62 s (12)	
1885	124.99 s (12)	103.38 s (11)	61.22 s (12)	
1886	126.20 s (12)	104.34 s (10)	61.86 s (12)	
1887	126.74 s (12)	104.71 s (12)	62.13 s (12)	
1888	124.66 s (12)	103.25 s (12)	61.10 s (12)	
1889	119.94 s (12)	99.07 s (12)	58.62 s (12)	
1890	116.94 s (12)	96.67 s (12)	57.31 s (12)	
1891	116.71 s (12)	96.63 s (12)	57.29 s (12)	

	VIENNA on:							
	London			**Amsterdam**			**Germany**		
	per 10 pounds sterling [b]			per 100 Dutch guilders [c]			per 100 mark [d]		
	in guilders Österreichische Währung								
1892	119.45	s	(12)	98.73	s	(12)	58.54	s	(12)
1893	123.86	s	(12)	102.44	s	(12)	60.69	s	(12)
1894	124.87	s	(12)	103.35	s	(12)	61.20	s	(12)
1895	121.96	s	(12)	100.56	s	(12)	59.63	s	(12)
1896	120.38	s	(12)	99.29	s	(12)	58.94	s	(12)
1897	119.79	s	(12)	99.12	s	(12)	58.77	s	(12)
1898	120.33	s	(10)	99.62	s	(11)	58.90	s	(11)
1899	120.69	s	(12)	99.65	s	(12)	59.02	s	(12)
	in Austrian crowns								
1900	242.18	s	(12)	200.29	s	(12)	118.32	s	(12)
1901	239.94	s	(12)	198.50	s	(12)	117.47	s	(12)
1902	239.79	s	(12)	197.74	s	(12)	117.22	s	(12)
1903	239.68	s	(10)	198.25	s	(10)	117.24	s	(10)
1904	239.73	s	(11)	198.66	s	(11)	117.45	s	(11)
1905	240.09	s	(12)	198.67	s	(12)	117.46	s	(12)
1906	240.57	s	(12)	198.51	s	(12)	117.51	s	(12)
1907	241.18	s	(11)	199.43	s	(11)	117.69	s	(11)
1908	240.06	s	(12)	198.73	s	(12)	117.52	s	(12)
1909	240.09	s	(11)	198.48	s	(11)	117.41	s	(11)
1910	240.58	s	(12)	199.03	s	(12)	117.61	s	(12)
1911	240.43	s	(11)	199.13	s	(11)	117.58	s	(11)
1912	241.61	s	(11)	199.88	s	(12)	117.93	s	(12)
1913	241.56	s	(12)	199.33	s	(12)	118.02	s	(12)
1914	241.11	s	(7)	199.21	s	(7)	117.68	s	(7)

[a]   In Vienna the usance of 14 days corresponded to the 'uso' meaning 14 days after acceptance.

[b]   Concerning the British currency, see pp. 3–5.

[c]   Concerning the Dutch currency, see pp. 57–59.

[d]   Concerning the Hamburg and the German currencies, see pp. 191–193, 197.

[e]   Augsburg current meant – in modification of Konventionskurant, which became common especially after 1764 (NOBACK [1851], 1. Abth., p. 70) – a standard of coinage of 20 5/12 guilders per mark of Cologne. So the guilder Augsburg current of 60 kreuzer was equal to 11.45 grammes of pure silver. As a consequence of the Vienna Coin Treaty of 1857, the guilder South German current (standard of coinage: 24½ guilders per 233.855 grammes of pure silver or 52½ guilders per pound of 500 grammes of pure silver) of 60 kreuzer became legal tender in Augsburg at the beginning of the year 1859. Concerning the German currency in Augsburg, see pp. 197.

[f]   Data in *italics*: quotations of Trieste.

[g]   Common quotations on 'German bank places' (Hamburg, Frankfurt am Main and Augsburg).

5.1.2 On Italy

	VIENNA on:	
	Venice [a]	**Bolzano** [b]
	per 100 ducati di banco [c]	per 100 guilders Meßvaluta [d]
	in guilders Konventionskurant	
1754	179.53 14d/s (6)	95.49 fair (6)
1755	182.81 14d/s (6)	96.10 fair (5)
1756	178.67 14d/s (1)	94.25 fair (1)
1757	179.65 14d/s (4)	96.00 fair (1)
1758	181.59 14d/s (1)	
1759	185.24 14d/s (1)	97.50 fair (1)
1760		
1761	182.50 14d/s (2)	97.50 fair (1)
1762		
1763		
1764	184.15 14d/s (1)	97.50 fair (1)
1765	186.88 14d/s (1)	
1766	184.41 14d/s (11)	98.98 fair (7)
1767	183.72 14d/s (12)	98.35 fair (5)
1768	182.47 14d/s (10)	97.62 fair (7)
1769	184.39 14d/s (11)	97.50 fair (4)
1770	184.92 14d/s (11)	
1771	185.73 14d/s (12)	
1772	185.54 14d/s (12)	
1773	187.49 14d/s (12)	
1774	187.59 14d/s (12)	
1775	187.38 14d/s (12)	
1776	186.67 2m/d (12)	
1777	187.55 2m/d (12)	
1778	186.25 2m/d (12)	
1779	184.34 2m/d (12)	
1780	183.26 2m/d (12)	
1781	182.17 2m/d (12)	
1782	183.44 2m/d (12)	
1783	180.08 2m/d (12)	
1784	182.63 2m/d (12)	
1785	181.63 2m/d (12)	

	VENICE and TRIESTE on: [e]			
	Venice	**Milan**	**Leghorn**	**Genoa**
	per 100 ducati di banco [c]	per 100 lire corrente, from 1814 per 100 lire italiane [f]	per 100 pezze da otto reali [g]	per 100 lire fuori banco [h]
	in guilders Konventionskurant			
1786	183.08 2m/d (12)	29.20 2m/d (7)	188.66 2m/d (7)	30.52 2m/d (12)
1787	185.62 2m/d (12)	29.35 2m/d (12)	192.22 2m/d (11)	31.27 2m/d (12)
1788	182.99 2m/d (12)	29.20 2m/d (12)	191.13 2m/d (10)	31.04 2m/d (10)
1789	183.81 2m/d (12)	29.38 2m/d (12)	194.12 2m/d (12)	31.16 2m/d (12)
1790	184.80 2m/d (12)	29.49 2m/d (11)	194.52 2m/d (11)	31.02 2m/d (11)
1791	185.71 2m/d (12)	29.64 2m/d (12)	194.81 2m/d (12)	31.42 2m/d (12)
1792	184.08 2m/d (12)	29.56 2m/d (12)	195.16 2m/d (9)	31.32 2m/d (11)
1793	184.08 2m/d (12)	29.58 2m/d (12)	196.36 2m/d (11)	31.34 2m/d (12)
1794	183.35 2m/d (12)	29.45 2m/d (11)	195.62 2m/d (11)	31.33 2m/d (10)
1795	183.44 2m/d (12)	29.55 2m/d (9)	196.71 2m/d (11)	31.36 2m/d (12)
1796	184.99 2m/d (12)	29.96 2m/d (5)	196.77 2m/d (6)	31.46 2m/d (3)
1797	182.81 2m/d (12)		200.91 2m/d (5)	32.07 2m/d (5)
1798	169.92 2m/d (11)		201.42 2m/d (11)	32.13 2m/d (9)
1799				
	in guilders Wiener Währung			
1800	194.24 2m/d (12)		223.68 2m/d (12)	
1801	173.91 2m/d (11)		232.13 2m/d (10)	36.20 2m/d (7)
1802	133.88 2m/d (10)	36.65 2m/d (3)	246.96 2m/d (11)	39.09 2m/d (12)
1803			259.90 2m/d (8)	42.05 ss (5)
1804		39.53 ss (5)	268.76 2m/d (7)	42.85 ss (4)
1805		39.58 ss (7)	268.87 2m/d (4)	42.88 ss (6)
1806		53.36 ss (7)	337.18 2m/d (6)	56.71 ss (5)
1807		62.47 ss (8)	407.33 2m/d (3)	68.84 ss (4)
1808		68.15 ss (8)	445.40 2m/d (9)	73.13 ss (7)
1809		75.92 ss (5)	504.51 2m/d (4)	100.00 2m/d (1)
1810		182.87 ss (4)	975.83 2m/d (3)	
1811		253.97/63.21 ss (2+5)		
1812		58.30 ss (5)		
1813		45.26 ss (2)		
1814		74.25 ss (2)		
1815				
1816				
1817				
	in guilders Konventionskurant			
1818		*39.59* 1m/d (1)		
1819		*38.08* 1m/d (12)		*31.74* 1m/d (12)
1820		*38.46* 1m/d (12)		*32.25* 1m/d (12)

VIENNA and TRIESTE on: [e]		
Milan	**Leghorn**	**Genoa**
per 100 lire italiane, from 1823 (11) per 100 lire austriache [f]	per 100 pezze da otto reali, from 1837 (9) per 100 Tuscan lire moneta buona [g]	per 100 lire fuori banco, from 1827 (3) per 100 Piedmontese lire nuove [h]
in guilders Konventionskurant		
1821	38.76 1m/d (11)		32.54 1m/d (11)
1822	38.81 1m/d (12)		32.55 1m/d (12)
1823	38.71/33.11 1m/d (8+2)	196.94 2m/d (1)	32.43 1m/d (10)
1824	33.17 1m/d (12)	200.45 2m/d (3)	32.07 1m/d (12)
1825	33.28 1m/d (12)	202.98 2m/d (5)	32.34 2m/d (8)
1826	33.18 2m/d (4)	203.38 2m/d (4)	32.34 2m/d (7)
1827	33.06 2m/d (4)	199.81 2m/d (8)	32.13/39.06 2m/d (1+6)
1828	32.99 2m/d (9)	200.10 2m/d (7)	39.12 2m/d (10)
1829	33.03 2m/d (11)	199.30 2m/d (12)	39.04 2m/d (10)
1830	33.18 2m/d (10)	201.37 2m/d (12)	39.18 2m/d (12)
1831	33.12 2m/d (10)	199.01 2m/d (12)	38.97 2m/d (11)
1832	33.07 2m/d (12)	199.87 2m/d (12)	38.85 2m/d (11)
1833	33.05 2m/d (11)	197.51 2m/d (12)	38.57 2m/d (12)
1834	33.08 2m/d (9)	200.22 2m/d (12)	38.55 2m/d (12)
1835	33.23 2m/d (12)	199.93 2m/d (11)	38.82 2m/d (11)
1836	33.22 2m/d (9)	202.34 2m/d (12)	39.06 2m/d (12)
1837	33.18 2m/d (8)	201.56/32.47 2m/d (8+4)	38.98 2m/d (12)
1838	33.22 2m/d (12)	32.30 2m/d (12)	38.98 2m/d (12)
1839	33.12 2m/d (12)	32.87 2m/d (12)	38.85 2m/d (12)
1840	33.14 2m/d (11)	32.87 2m/d (12)	38.83 2m/d (12)
1841	33.02 2m/d (12)	32.45 2m/d (12)	38.15 2m/d (12)
1842	33.22 2m/d (12)	32.55 2m/d (12)	37.99 2m/d (12)
1843	33.23 2m/d (12)	32.21 2m/d (12)	38.14 2m/d (12)
1844	32.94 2m/d (12)	32.12 2m/d (12)	37.92 2m/d (12)
1845	33.16 2m/d (12)	32.46 2m/d (12)	38.16 2m/d (12)
1846	33.24 2m/d (12)	32.91 2m/d (12)	38.51 2m/d (12)
1847	33.20 2m/d (12)	32.78 2m/d (12)	38.63 2m/d (12)
1848	35.05 2m/d (12)	34.11 2m/d (10)	40.19 2m/d (6)
1849	36.65 2m/d (12)	36.60 2m/d (12)	43.08 2m/d (10)
1850	34.21 2m/d (4)	38.73 2m/d (12)	45.64 2m/d (12)
1851	40.99 2m/d (7)	41.13 2m/d (11)	49.60 2m/d (7)
1852	40.04 2m/d (11)	39.49 2m/d (8)	
1853	36.60 2m/d (12)	36.65 2m/d (8)	42.89 2m/d (4)
1854	41.88 2m/d (9)	41.68 2m/d (5)	
1855	40.12 2m/d (9)	38.37 2m/d (3)	43.50 2m/d (1)
1856	34.78 2m/d (9)	34.41 2m/d (5)	40.38 2m/d (3)

	VIENNA and TRIESTE on: [e]		
	Milan	**Leghorn**	**Genoa**
	per 100 lire austriache, from 1859 per 100 guilders Österreichische Währung, from 1860 per 100 Piedmontese lire nuove, from 1861 (8) per 100 Italian lire [f]	per 100 Tuscan lire moneta buona, from 1860 per 100 Piedmon-tese lire nuove, from 1861 (8) per 100 Italian lire [g]	per 100 lire fuori banco, from 1827 (3) per 100 Piedmontese lire nuove [h]
	in guilders Konventionskurant		
1857	34.59 2m/d (10)	34.94 2m/d (2)	40.15 2m/d (2)
1858	34.90 2m/d (5)	34.80 2m/d (4)	40.67 2m/d (1)
1859	116.98 3m/d (5)	*48.00* 3m/d (1)	
1860	52.75 3m/d (1)	42.20 3m/d (1)	
1861	55.97 3m/d (5)		
1862	50.41 3m/d (4)		
1863	44.82 3m/d (5)	43.95 3m/d (1)	
1864	45.93 3m/d (6)	45.48 3m/d (2)	
1865	43.32 3m/d (6)	42.87 3m/d (2)	
1866	43.63 3m/d (2)		

[a]   In Vienna the usance of 14 days corresponded to the 'uso' meaning: 14 days after acceptance.

[b]   At Bolzano four fairs of 15 days each were held, the first beginning on the first Monday in March, the second beginning on the first working day after Corpus Christi, the third on the first working day after September 8th and the last on December 1st (Saint Andrew's fair). "Bills payable at such fairs are accepted on the 12th day, and the payments begin on the 13th day, and end two days after the close of the fair. All bills drawn on this place must be payable to one person; all indorsed bills, or bills payable to more persons than one, are forbidden under a fine of 200 Rixdollars" (KELLY [1811], p. 69).

[c]   Concerning the Venetian currency, see pp. 104f.

[d]   The so-called 'Meßvaluta' (or just 'Valuta') was a kind of money at the Bolzano fairs that was more or less 4% worse than the current money or moneta lunga, i.e. the Konventionskurant from the 1750s, whereby the rixdollar specie was equal to 1½ guilders or 90 kreuzer moneta lunga. The guilder Meßvaluta was subdivided into the same units as the guilder moneta longa: 1 guilder Meß-valuta = 60 kreuzer of 4 pfennige Meßvaluta. Its ratio to the Bolzano exchange money or giro, which consisted of Spanish doublons and old French louis d'ors and which was 31% more or less better than the moneta lunga, was: 7½ guilders Meßvaluta = 5 guilders 34 kreuzer giro or ex-change money (cf. NELKENBRECHER [1775], p. 56).

[e]   Data in *italics*: quotations of Trieste.

[f]   Milan was traditionally quoted per lire corrente of 20 soldi at 12 denari, whereby the lira corrente was equal to 3.464 grammes of pure silver since the monetary reform of 1778. During the period of the Napoleonic Kingdom of Italy a new lira italiana (or better: lira of the Kingdom of Italy) of 100 centesimi was created and introduced, which was equal to the French franc (4.50 grammes of pure silver), but the Viennese exchange rates on Milan were not converted to the new currency until 1813/14. On November 1st 1823 the Austrian lira (lira austriaca) of 100 centesimi with 3.897 grammes of pure silver was introduced in Lombardy–Veneto by the so-called Münzpatent and be-came legal tender as well as the guilder Konventionskurant. This lira was equal to the 20-kreuzer piece (or the third part of the guilder) of the Habsburg Monarchy and, therefore, used to be called 'la svanzica' or the 'zwanziger'. With the introduction of the new guilder Österreichische Wäh-

rung in the Habsburg Monarchy the exceptional monetary position of Lombardy–Veneto was abolished in 1858/59. After the integration of Lombardy into the new Kingdom of Italy the Piedmontese or the Italian currency system respectively came into force here (see pp. 108f.).

[g]　Concerning the Tuscan currency, see pp. 106. Between the beginning of 1800 and August 1837 quotations include 7% premium for payment in gold.

[h]　Concerning the Genoese currency, see pp. 107f.

TRIESTE & VIENNA on: [a]				TRIESTE & VIENNA on: [a]			
Italy (Milan)				**Italy (Milan)**			
per 100 Italian lire [b]				per 100 Italian lire [b]			
in guilders Österreichische Währung				in guilders Österreichische Währung			
1867	*41.98*	3m/d	(2)	1892	45.76	s	(12)
1868	*42.30*	3m/d	(2)	1893	45.65	s	(12)
1869	*47.75*	3m/d	(1)	1894	44.69	s	(12)
1870	*46.98*	3m/d	(6)	1895	45.80	s	(12)
1871	*45.50*	3m/d	(12)	1896	44.29	s	(12)
1872	*40.29*	3m/d	(12)	1897	45.28	s	(12)
1873	*38.23*	3m/d	(12)	1898	44.77	s	(11)
1874	*39.11*	3m/d	(12)	1899	44.59	s	(12)
1875	*40.76*	3m/d	(12)	**in Austrian crowns**			
1876	*43.91*	3m/d	(12)	1900	90.44	s	(11)
1877	*44.07*	3m/d	(12)	1901	91.59	s	(12)
1878	*42.64*	3m/d	(12)	1902	95.09	s	(12)
1879	*41.42*	3m/d	(12)	1903	95.44	s	(10)
1880	*42.45*	3m/d	(12)	1904	95.22	s	(11)
1881	*45.90*	s	(12)	1905	95.55	s	(12)
1882	*46.26*	s	(12)	1906	95.60	s	(12)
1883	*47.40*	s	(12)	1907	95.75	s	(11)
1884	*48.21*	s	(12)	1908	95.50	s	(12)
1885	*49.08*	s	(12)	1909	94.94	s	(10)
1886	*49.77*	s	(12)	1910	94.89	s	(12)
1887	*49.49*	s	(12)	1911	94.71	s	(11)
1888	48.55	s	(10)	1912	94.77	s	(12)
1889	47.10	s	(12)	1913	94.08	s	(12)
1890	45.75	s	(12)	1914	95.33	s	(7)
1891	45.52	s	(12)				

[a]　Data in *italics*: quotations of Trieste.

[b]　Concerning the Italian currency, see pp. 108f. Underlined quotations 1867–1888: payable in Italian notes.

5.1.3 On Frankfurt on the Main, Paris, Switzerland and Belgium

	VIENNA on:	
	Frankfurt	**Paris**
	per 100 guilders Frankfurt exchange money [a]	per 100 francs [b]
	in guilders Wiener Währung	
1805	201.38 ss (2)	
1806		
1807		
1808	336.38 ss (2)	
1809		
1810	483.00 ss (1)	
1811	330.00 ss (3)	
1812	293.31 ss (3)	
1813		
1814	331.99 ss (2)	
1815		146.12 2m/d (1)
1816		116.12 2m/d (5)
1817		129.75 2m/d (3)
	in guilders Konventionskurant	
1818		37.67 2m/d (1)
1819	99.74 ss (2)	38.47 2m/d (4)
1820	99.86 ss (5)	39.18 2m/d (10)
1821	99.71 ss (4)	39.33 2m/d (10)
1822	99.86 ss (11)	39.61 2m/d (12)
1823	99.78 ss (12)	39.81 2m/d (11)
1824	99.14 ss (11)	39.06 2m/d (12)
1825	100.01 ss (8)	38.86 2m/d (8)
1826	100.60 ss (6)	39.53 2m/d (10)
1827	100.06 ss (8)	39.21 2m/d (11)
1828	100.16 ss (12)	38.97 2m/d (9)
1829	100.28 ss (12)	38.83 2m/d (11)
1830	100.46 ss (12)	39.18 2m/d (12)
1831	100.20 ss (12)	39.11 2m/d (8)
1832	99.65 ss (12)	38.86 2m/d (11)
1833	99.11 ss (12)	38.48 2m/d (10)
1834	99.06 ss (11)	38.51 2m/d (7)
1835	99.79 ss (12)	38.80 2m/d (8)
1836	100.00 ss (12)	39.08 2m/d (11)
1837	100.58 ss (10)	39.36 2m/d (12)
1838	100.26 ss (11)	39.24 2m/d (12)
1839	100.34 ss (12)	39.00 2m/d (12)

	VIENNA on:			
	Frankfurt	**Paris**	**Zurich & Basle**	**Brussels** [c]
	per 100 guilders Frankfurt exchange money, from 1843 per 100 guilders South German current [a]	per 100 francs [b]		
	in guilders Konventionskurant			
1840	100.27 3m/d (12)	39.05 2m/d (12)		
1841	98.66 3m/d (12)	38.29 2m/d (12)		
1842	97.94 3m/d (12)	38.14 2m/d (12)		
1843	81.34 3m/d (12)	38.32 2m/d (12)		
1844	80.70 3m/d (12)	37.97 2m/d (12)		
1845	81.19 3m/d (12)	38.29 2m/d (12)		
1846	82.26 3m/d (12)	38.73 2m/d (12)		
1847	82.11 3m/d (12)	38.87 2m/d (12)		
1848	89.52 3m/d (12)	42.53 2m/d (12)		
1849	94.81 3m/d (12)	45.22 2m/d (12)		
1850	98.11 3m/d (12)	46.47 2m/d (11)		
1851	104.80 3m/d (12)	49.67 2m/d (12)		
1852	99.42 3m/d (11)	47.06 2m/d (11)		
1853	91.34 3m/d (12)	43.38 2m/d (12)		
1854	104.61 3m/d (11)	49.88 2m/d (11)		
1855	100.31 3m/d (11)	47.18 2m/d (12)		
1856	86.18 3m/d (12)	40.51 2m/d (12)		
1857	87.01 3m/d (12)	40.68 2m/d (12)		
1858	86.88 3m/d (12)	40.75 2m/d (12)		
	in guilders Österreichische Währung			
1859	103.70 3m/d (12)	48.07 3m/d (12)		
1860	112.34 3m/d (12)	52.11 3m/d (12)		
1861	120.86 3m/d (12)	56.20 3m/d (12)		
1862	110.11 3m/d (12)	51.52 3m/d (12)		
1863	95.92 3m/d (12)	44.86 3m/d (12)		
1864	98.83 3m/d (12)	46.23 3m/d (12)		
1865	92.27 3m/d (12)	43.75 3m/d (12)		
1866	101.86 3m/d (12)	47.98 3m/d (12)		
1867	106.09 3m/d (12)	50.33 3m/d (12)		
1868	97.44 3m/d (12)	46.34 3m/d (12)		
1869	102.94 3m/d (12)	49.11 3m/d (12)		
1870	104.11 3m/d (12)	49.28 3m/d (9)	per 100 franken [d]	per 100 Belgian francs [e]
1871	102.42 3m/d (12)	46.79 3m/d (7)		
1872		43.45 3m/d (11)	44.27 3m/d (8)	43.88 30d/d (7)
1873	*93.57* 3m/d (2)	43.47 3m/d (11)	43.35 3m/d (8)	43.55 30d/d (7)
1874	*94.00* 3m/d (1)	44.05 3m/d (12)	44.06 3m/d (5)	

	VIENNA on:		VIENNA & TRIESTE on: [f]
	Paris	**Zurich & Basle**	**Brussels / Belgium** [c]
	per 100 francs [b]	per 100 franken [d]	per 100 Belgian francs [e]
in guilders Österreichische Währung			
1875	44.24　3m/d　(12)	44.22　3m/d　(6)	44.40　30d/d　(6)
1876	47.74　3m/d　(12)	47.88　3m/d　(5)	48.57　30d/d　(4)
1877	48.73　3m/d　(12)	47.98　3m/d　(4)	48.23　30d/d　(3)
1878	47.15　3m/d　(12)	46.69　3m/d　(4)	47.43　30d/d　(2)
1879	46.21　3m/d　(11)	46.17　3m/d　(6)	46.35　30d/d　(1)
1880	46.62　3m/d　(12)	46.56　3m/d　(8)	46.48　30d/d　(1)
1881	46.62　3m/d　(12)	46.55　3m/d　(8)	
1882	47.54　3m/d　(12)	47.51　3m/d　(7)	
1883	47.55　s　(12)	47.50　s　(7)	
1884	48.33　s　(12)	48.32　s　(9)	
1885	49.43　s　(12)	49.28　s　(6)	
1886	49.98　s　(12)	49.88　s　(10)	
1887	50.03　s　(12)	49.94　s　(12)	
1888	49.26　s　(12)	49.12　s　(12)	
1889	47.46　s　(12)	47.36　s　(12)	
1890	46.30　s　(12)	46.18　s　(12)	
1891	46.21　s　(12)	46.09　s　(12)	45.70　s　(3)
1892	47.84　s　(12)	47.35　s　(12)	
1893	49.15　s　(12)	49.09　s　(12)	
1894	49.58　s　(12)	49.54　s　(12)	
1895	48.39　s　(11)	48.24　s　(12)	47.88　s　(1)
1896	47.74　s　(12)	47.61　s　(12)	47.89　s　(2)
1897	47.59　s　(12)	47.41　s　(12)	
1898	47.61　s　(10)	47.42　s　(11)	
1899	47.83　s　(12)	47.58　s　(12)	
in Austrian crowns			
1900	96.31　s　(12)	95.76　s　(12)	*96.08*　s　(12)
1901	95.35　s　(12)	95.16　s　(12)	*95.16*　s　(12)
1902	95.34　s　(12)	95.09　s　(12)	*95.14*　s　(12)
1903	95.42　s　(10)	95.29　s　(10)	*95.19*　s　(12)
1904	95.27　s　(11)	95.16　s　(11)	*95.15*　s　(12)
1905	95.49　s　(12)	95.33　s　(12)	*95.41*　s　(12)
1906	95.58　s　(12)	95.51　s　(12)	*95.39*　s　(12)
1907	95.73　s　(11)	95.58　s　(11)	*95.46*　s　(12)
1908	95.55　s　(12)	95.44　s　(12)	*95.38*　s　(12)
1909	95.37　s　(11)	95.35　s　(11)	*95.22*　s　(12)

	VIENNA on:			TRIESTE on: [f]
	Paris		**Zurich & Basle**	**Belgium** [c]
	per 100 francs [b]		per 100 franken [d]	per 100 Belgian francs [e]
			in Austrian crowns	
1910	95.40	s	(12)	95.29	s	(12)	*95.39*	s	(12)
1911	95.22	s	(11)	95.13	s	(11)	*95.02*	s	(12)
1912	95.84	s	(12)	95.41	s	(12)	*95.23*	s	(12)
1913	95.63	s	(12)	95.42	s	(12)	*95.16*	s	(12)
1914	95.69	s	(7)	95.59	s	(7)	*95.06*	s	(7)

[a] Concerning the Frankfurt currency, see pp. 196f.

[b] Concerning the French currency, see pp. 279f.

[c] Vienna quoted Brussels whereas Trieste drew bills on Antwerp, because of its sea borne trade relations with Belgium, although the quotations have been made on 'Belgium' from 1900 (cf. No-BACK [1877], p. 874).

[d] Concerning the Swiss currency, see p. 313.

[e] In 1832 the Belgian franc was introduced, equal to the French franc (see pp. 279f.).

[f] Data in *italics*: quotations of Trieste.

5.1.4 On Constantinople, Bucharest, Saint Petersburg, Greece and New York

	VIENNA on:		VIENNA & TRIESTE on: [b]	VIENNA on:
	Constantinople		**Constantinople**	**Bucharest**
	per 100 piastres [a]		per 100 piastres [a]	per 100 lei [c]
	in guilders Konventionskurant		**in guilders Wiener Währung**	
1780	88.42 31d/s (12)	1814		
1781	90.38 31d/s (12)	1815		
1782	91.50 31d/s (12)	1816		
1783	86.40 31d/s (12)	1817		
1784	89.28 31d/s (11)		**in guilders Konventionskurant**	
1785	87.23 31d/s (11)	1818		
1786	85.46 31d/s (7)	1819	*26.66* 31d/s (8)	
1787	87.00 31d/s (3)	1820	*28.15* 31d/s (5)	
1788	89.05 31d/s (4)	1821	*17.88* 31d/s (1)	
1789	86.75 31d/s (6)	1822	*27.07* 31d/s (4)	
1790	84.44 31d/s (5)	1823	*23.57* 31d/s (1)	
1791	80.23 31d/s (9)	1824	22.01 31d/s (9)	
1792	79.67 31d/s (3)	1825	20.15 31d/s (11)	
1793	74.75 31d/s (4)	1826	17.48 31d/s (6)	
1794	68.75 31d/s (5)	1827	16.43 31d/s (9)	
1795	65.94 31d/s (4)	1828	16.41 31d/s (3)	
1796	63.92 31d/s (10)	1829	14.25 31d/s (8)	
1797	67.98 31d/s (10)	1830	12.85 31d/s (6)	
1798	67.64 31d/s (6)	1831	12.06 31d/s (6)	
1799		1832	11.11 31d/s (9)	
	in guilders Wiener Währung	1833	9.92 31d/s (8)	
1800	75.16 31d/s (11)	1834	9.80 31d/s (12)	
1801	75.20 31d/s (5)	1835	9.81 31d/s (12)	
1802	73.05 31d/s (6)	1836	9.78 31d/s (12)	
1803	75.13 31d/s (8)	1837	8.92 31d/s (12)	
1804	72.42 31d/s (10)	1838	9.34 31d/s (6)	
1805	74.20 31d/s (7)	1839	9.26 31d/s (4)	
1806	90.41 31d/s (7)	1840	8.99 31d/s (5)	
1807	108.33 31d/s (10)	1841	8.60 31d/s (6)	
1808	124.16 31d/s (8)	1842	8.17 31d/s (1)	14.40 1m/s (4)
1809	137.57 31d/s (4)	1843	8.34 31d/s (1)	
1810	182.40 31d/s (5)	1844	8.85 31d/s (3)	14.50 1m/s (2)
1811	310.00/83.93 31d/s (1+5)	1845	8.82 31d/s (7)	14.35 1m/s (2)
1812	97.25 31d/s (1)	1846	8.82 31d/s (3)	14.63 1m/s (2)
1813		1847		14.55 1m/s (7)

	VIENNA & Trieste on: [b]	VIENNA on:	VIENNA on:
	Constantinople	**Bucharest**	**Saint Petersburg**
	per 100 piastres [a]	per 100 lei [c]	per 100 silver roubles in credit notes [d]
	in guilders Konventionskurant		
1848	9.49 31d/s (10)	14.32 1m/s (4)	
1849	9.93 31d/s (6)	15.48 1m/s (6)	
1850	10.53 31d/s (11)	17.27 1m/s (11)	
1851	10.94 31d/s (12)	18.13 1m/s (12)	
1852	10.42 31d/s (5)	17.56 1m/s (9)	
1853	9.35 31d/s (2)	16.05 1m/s (3)	
1854	10.93 31d/s (1)	17.98 1m/s (7)	
1855	9.56 31d/s (5)	17.39 1m/s (9)	
1856	8.45 31d/s (4)	15.25 1m/s (12)	
1857	8.68 31d/s (5)	15.04 1m/s (12)	
1858	8.45 31d/s (5)	15.93 1m/s (12)	
	in guilders Österreichische Währung		
1859		17.27 1m/s (12)	
1860		19.19 1m/s (12)	
1861	*12.91* 31d/s (2)	20.00 1m/s (1)	
1862			
1863		15.75 1m/s (1)	
1864	*10.75* 31d/s (2)		
1865	*9.81* 31d/s (1)		
1866			
1867			
1868			
1869			
1870			
1871			
1872			
1873			
1874			
1875			
1876	*11.21* (3)		156.21 (11)
1877	*11.27* (7)		134.64 (12)
1878	*10.85* (3)		118.45 (9)
1879	*10.61* (4)		117.40 (11)
1880	*10.58* (4)		123.13 (12)
1881			123.42 (12)
1882	*10.72* (1)		119.96 (12)
1883			117.64 (12)

	TRIESTE on: [b]	VIENNA on:	TRIESTE on: [b]	
	Constantinople	**Saint Petersburg**	**Greece**	**New York**
	per 100 piastres, from 1900 in banknotes [a]	per 100 silver roubles in credit notes, from 1899 per 100 gold roubles [d]	per 100 drachma in banknotes [e]	per 100 US dollars [f]
			in guilders Österreichische Währung		
1884		122.14 (12)		
1885	*11.33* (1)	125.42 (12)		
1886	*11.30* (1)	122.13 (12)		
1887		112.47 (12)		
1888		115.37 (12)		
1889		125.07 (12)		
1890		134.50 (12)		
1891		129.85 (12)		
1892		118.99 (12)		
1896		127.71 (11)		
1897		127.19 (12)		
1898		127.45 (9)		
1899		127.58 (11)		
			in Austrian crowns		
1900	*21.84* (12)	255.68 (11)		*497.30* s (12)
1901	*21.78* (12)	253.74 (10)	*58.63* (12)	*491.05* s (12)
1902	*21.66* (12)	253.65 (12)	*58.71* (12)	*491.42* s (12)
1903	*21.63* (12)	253.51 (10)	*59.00* (12)	*491.71* s (12)
1904	*21.67* (12)	253.69 (10)	*67.80* (12)	*491.92* s (12)
1905	*21.75* (12)	253.56 (12)	*74.84* (12)	*492.04* s (12)
1906	*21.79* (12)	252.56 (10)	*86.25* (12)	*492.05* s (12)
1907	*21.75* (12)	253.16 (10)	*88.11* (12)	*492.84* s (12)
1908	*21.74* (12)	251.54 (11)	*88.63* (12)	*491.92* s (12)
1909	*21.68* (12)	253.25 (10)	*91.46* (12)	*491.25* s (12)
1910	*21.68* (12)	254.31 (11)	*95.65* (12)	*491.94* s (12)
1911	*21.71* (12)	254.18 (10)	*95.14* (12)	*493.08* s (12)
1912	*21.68* (12)	254.42 (12)	*95.50* (12)	*493.35* s (12)
1913	*21.74* (12)	254.05 (12)	*95.50* (12)	*493.96* s (12)
1914	*21.69* (7)	252.72 (7)	*95.50* (7)	*492.92* s (7)

[a]   Concerning the Turkish currency, see pp. 387f.

[b]   Data in *italics*: quotations of Trieste.

[c]   The leu of 40 paralle (or para) at 3 aspers was the Walachian unit of account, whereas the current money consisted of Austrian, Russian and – up to 1830 – also Turkish coins. The Walachian leu was at least 37.5% better than the Turkish piastre (NOBACK [1851], pp. 184f.). From January 1st 1868 the Walachian leu was succeeded by the leu nou (new leu) of 100 bani, which was equal to the French franc (4.50 grammes of fine silver or 0.2903 grammes of fine gold respectively) (cf. SWOBODA [1902], p. 218).

[d]   Concerning the Russian currency, see pp. 359f.

[e]   After Greece joined the Latin Monetary Union the drachma at 100 lepta was legally equal to the French franc (4.50 grammes of fine silver or 0.2903 grammes of fine gold respectively), but the relevant Act of April 10th 1867 was not in force until November 1st 1882. The notes of the Greek National Bank in Athens, the Ionian Bank, and the Epirothessalian Bank circulated as obligatory legal tender (with the exception of some months in 1885) (cf. SWOBODA [1902], pp. 69s.).

[f]   Concerning the US currency, see p. 404.

6
France (1760–1914)

Exchange market: Paris (1760–1914)

Sources: *Journal de commerce*, Bruxelles (1760/61); *Journal de commerce (feuille commercial)*, Paris (1763–1783, 1795–1800, 1810–1843); *Journal de Paris* (1780–1783); *Journal général de France* (1784–1792); BOUCHARY [1937], pp. 109–180 (1789–1795); *Gazette nationale ou le moniteur industriel* (1800–1814); *Gazette de France* (1844–1856); *Gazette nationale* (1815, 1859/60, 1863–1866); *Journal des débats* (1857–1859, 1861/62, 1867–1914); *Le Temps*, Paris (1897–1914).

Concordance: *WdW VI*, pp. 223–237; *HStD XII*, pp. 215–233; *WdW I/II*, pp. 197–381; *HStD XI*, pp. 599–627, 667–674

Currency: From 1602 the livres tournois of 20 sous or 240 deniers functioned as a means of payment within France, whereas for foreign exchange trade the écu or crown (écu de change) of 3 livres or 60 sous tournois was used (MCCUSKER [1978], pp. 87f.). After the Coin Acts of 1726, which were meant to stabilize the French currency after the financial experiments of John Law, the livre tournois was equal to 4.5052 grammes of fine silver. The most important circulating gold coin was the louis d'or (from 1726 nominally 7.48 grammes of fine gold) of 24 livres tournois, the most important silver coins in circulation were the double écu (écu neuf or louis blanc; from 1726 nominally 26.94 grammes of fine silver up to 1783) of 6 livres tournois and the écu (half écu neuf; from 1726 nominally 13.47 grammes of fine silver up to 1783) of 3 livres tournois. The gold–silver relation of 1:14.5, which had been unfavourable to France, was changed on October 30th 1785 to 1:15.5 (1 louis d'or being equal to 7.01 grammes of fine gold). Although the Scottish mercantilist John Law had already introduced paper money in France (1716–1720), and the Caisse d'escompte, founded on March 24th 1776, also issued paper money, the so-called 'billets', France had a paper currency in use only with the introduction of the 'assignats': created in December 1789 in the wake of the Revolution and its financial problems, the assignats became legal tender with an official rate that was accepted at all official banks in April 1790. From September 1790 the assignats were issued in such great quantities (and even in the smallest denominations) that in the following years – except for a few phases of stabilization – their rate dropped drastically. With sometimes hourly changes of rate, the peaks of the actual phase of inflation were reached in Thermidor (July/August) 1794 and under the government of the Directory (until June 1796). In early summer of 1793 the Paris stock exchange had been closed, public exchange rate quoting had been forbidden and the obligation to accept assignats had been introduced. As assignats were the only legal tender from December 1793, exchange rate quotations were henceforth made in them as well. "L'histoire du marché des changes de Paris se développe parallèlement à celle du papier-monnaie" (BOUCHARY [1937], p. 94). In order to consolidate the French currency system, the franc (4.50 grammes of fine silver) of 100 centimes, a renamed and slightly modified version of the livre tournois, was introduced. It was, however, based on the decimal classification, "le franc continue donc pratiquement la livre" (SÉDILLOT [1979], p. 69), 1 livre presumably being equal to 99 centimes or 1 sou being equal to 5 centimes (Act of August 15th 1795). Even the names 'livre' and 'franc' – the latter being introduced officially by the Act of May 6th 1799 – could be used synonymously until the old coins in circulation were finally reminted in 1829/30–1834. The resumption of the daily exchange rate quoting at the Paris stock exchange (December 1795) – henceforth in francs – the resumption of the minting and silver circulation, national bankruptcy (of two-thirds), reform of national financial policy, the repeal of the obligation to accept assignats (February 1797) and the resulting increasing disappearance of assignats from the money circulation brought about the stabilization of the currency conditions in France, even if various waves of speculation continued to cause rapid fluctuations of the assignat rates. After the founding of the Banque de France in 1800 and the gradual establishing of the franc the 'charter' of the so-called 'franc-germinal' was enacted on April 7th 1803 (Germinal 17th an [year] XI) according to which the franc in silver was meant to correspond to 4.50 grammes of fine silver, the franc in gold to 0.2903 grammes of fine gold. This bimetallistic system remained the basis of the French currency system for the whole 19th and the early 20th century, and was 'exported' to various European countries. So the French currency system was adopted by Piedmont–Sardinia in 1816, by Belgium in 1832, by Switzerland in 1850/60 and by Italy in 1861/62.

With the Latin Monetary Union between France, Belgium, Italy and Switzerland, founded on December 23rd 1865, the dominance of French monetary policy over several European countries reached its peak, following the French example of bimetallism. Greece entered into the Union in 1868. The Papal States (in 1866/67), Romania (in 1868), Spain and Finland (1866/77) adopted the Union's standard of coinage without becoming formal members. A further convention of the partners of the Latin Monetary Union of November 5th 1878 suspended the unlimited minting of 5-francs pieces as well as of the same nominals of the other countries, so that the countries of the Union had a limping gold standard from then on. From time to time the fine weight of some smaller coins was slightly reduced in some countries and the coins were given local names. Even if the following decades brought various more or less important 'cosmetic' corrections to the Acts of 1865 and 1878, no more fundamental changes of the French currency system were carried out until the First World War. Only in the wake of the German–French war of 1870/71 was the convertibility of French paper money suspended and the notes were declared obligatory legal tender (August 12th 1870 to January 1st 1878) (ZELLFELDER [1991], passim).

Original quotations at Paris until 1867:

on:	in:	per:
Amsterdam	stuivers Flemish banco	1 écu of 3 livres tournois
from 1816 (10)	groot Dutch current	3 francs
from 1840 (4)	francs	100 Dutch guilders
Antwerp	per cent discount or premium	100 francs
from 1826	groot Dutch current	3 francs
from 1840 (4)	per cent discount or premium	100 Belgian francs
Augsburg	francs	100 guilders Augsburg current
from 1859	francs	100 guilders South German current
Basle	francs	100 francs payable in carolins
Berlin	francs	100 thaler Prussian current
Frankfurt	per cent discount or francs	100 francs payable in carolins
from 1840 (4)	francs	100 guilders South German current
Geneva	francs	100 livres Geneva current
Genoa	sous tournois	1 pezza of 5¾ lire fuori banco
from 1801	francs	100 pezze of 5¾ lire fuori banco
from 1827 (3)	per cent discount or premium	100 Piedmontese lire nuove
from 1861 (8)	per cent discount or premium	100 Italian lire
Hamburg	livres tournois or	100 mark banco
	shillings Lubish banco or	1 écu of 3 livres tournois or 3 francs
(up to 1826)	écus of 3 livres tournois	100 rixdollars banco of 3 mark
Leghorn	sous tournois	1 pezza da otto reali of 5¾ lire moneta buona
from 1801	francs	100 pezze da otto reali
from 1837 (8)	francs	100 Tuscan lire moneta buona
Lisbon	réis	3 francs
from 1839	francs and centimes	1 milrée

on:	in:	per:
London	pence sterling	1 écu of 3 livres tournois
from 1814	francs and centimes	1 pound sterling
Madrid	livres and sous tournois	1 peso de plata antigua
or	francs and centimes	1 doblón de cambio of 4 pesos de plata antigua
from 1847 (4)	francs	100 pesos duros or 500 pesetas
Milan	lire and soldi correnti	6 francs
from 1813 (9)	francs	100 lire italiane
from 1824	francs	100 lire austriache
from 1859 (3)	francs	100 guilders Österreichische Währung
from 1860 (7)	per cent discount or premium	100 Piedmontese lire nuove
from 1861 (8)	per cent discount or premium	100 Italian lire
Naples	centimes or	1 ducato del regno
	francs	100 ducati del regno
from 1863 (5)	per cent discount or premium	100 Italian lire
Saint Petersburg	francs	100 banco roubles
from 1839 (9)	francs	100 silver roubles
Vienna	francs	100 guilders Konventionskurant
from 1858 (11)	francs	100 guilders Österreichische Währung

From 1867 all exchange rates were effected in francs (and centimes) per 1 (London) or 100 units of foreign currency. The only exceptions were the quotations on the financial markets or states of the Latin Monetary Union (Italy, Belgium, Switzerland), which were effected in % discount or premium per 100 units of foreign currency.

Other data available: Amsterdam, 90d/d–3m/d (1799–1914) – Antwerp, 90d/d (1815–1867) – Augsburg, 90d/d–3m/d (1801–1862) – Barcelona, 3m/d (1867–1902); s (1867–1902) – Basle, 90d/d (1797–1843) – Belgium, 3m/d (1867–1914) – Berlin, 90d/d–3m/d (1820–1876) – Bilbao, 90d/d (1811–1861); 30d/d (1811–1860) – Bordeaux, 90d/d (1805–1839); 30d/d (1796–1843) – Cadiz, 90d/d–3m/d (1801–1876); 30d/d–s (1763–1876) – Frankfurt, 90d/d–3m/d (1805–1876) – Geneva, 3m/d (1872–1874) – Genoa, 90d/d (1799–1866) – Germany, 3m/d (1876–1914) – Hamburg, 90d/d–3m/d (1799–1876) – Italy, 3m/d (1867–1914) – Leghorn, 90d/d (1799–1866) – Lisbon, 90d/d–3m/d (1804–1898) – London, 90d/d–3m/d (1801–1914); ch (1895–1907) – Lyons, 90d/d (1784–1839), 30d/d (1780–1843) – Madrid, 90d/d–3m/d (1801–1902) – Marseilles, 90d/d (1805–1839); 30d/d (1797–1843) – Milan, 90d/d (1802–1866) – Montpellier, 30d/d (1797–1843) – Naples, 90d/d (1802–1866) – New York, 3m/d (1871–1914) – Oporto, 90d/d–3m/d (1814–1876); 30d/d–s (1814–1823, 1854–1876) – Portugal, 3m/d (1907–1914) – Rome, 3m/d (1867–1878); s (1871–1878) – Saint Petersburg, 90d/d–3m/d (1853–1914) – Scandinavia, 3m/d (1910–1912) – Spain, 3m/d (1902–1914) – Stockholm, 3m/d (1892–1899) – Switzerland, 3m/d (1875–1914) – Trieste, 90d/d–3m/d (1821–1878); 30d/d–s (1821–1914) – Venice, 90d/d (1815–1866); 30d/d (1815–1866) – Vienna, 90d/d–3m/d (1803–1914).

Although France was one of the most important countries participating in the cashless payment system from the late Middle Ages, longer exchange rate series for the period to be documented here are available only from the second half of the 18th century. The rates of the Lyons fairs, available before then, end in 1596 and those of Rouen in 1589 (LAPEYRE [1953], pp. 464–474; cf. *WdW IX*, pp. 35–57, 135–137). For the 17th and the 18th century some single quotations of Rouen (1668–1680; ROSEVEARE [1987], pp. 619–628), Nantes (1764–1776; DENZEL [1997], p. 147), Marseilles and Lyons (1787–1790; REBUFFAT / COURDURIÉ [1966], pp. 118–121) can be found, as well as some quotations from Bordeaux and La Rochelle in a few price currents. Only for

Paris, by far the most important French exchange market since the 18th century, can almost complete series be presented for the period from 1760 to 1914, whereas for the 17th century only some Paris rates on Amsterdam and London (1671–1679) are available (ROSEVEARE [1987], pp. 621–627).

Despite the far-reaching connections of its bankers (cf. LÜTHY [1961], passim), and in comparison with other European exchange markets of similar importance, Paris was in charge of only a rather small network of quoted foreign exchange partners in the second half of the 18th century, limited to Northwestern Europe (Amsterdam, London, Hamburg), Spain (Madrid, Cadiz) and Italy (Leghorn, from 1770 also Genoa) (cf. HERBACH [1756/57], p. 252; NELKENBRECHER [1775], p. 196). Additionally, there were some internal French quotations like those on Lyons (available from 1780). Only during and after the Wars of Revolution was the Paris exchange rate current considerably expanded: Swiss places (Basle from 1794, Geneva from 1805) were quoted, just like South German ones (Augsburg from 1801, Frankfurt am Main from 1805), Vienna (from 1801), Lisbon (from 1804) and also Milan (from 1801) and Naples (from 1802/06) in Italy, and Bilbao (from 1811) in Spain and Bordeaux (from 1796), Marseilles and Montpellier (from 1797) within France. The general background was the politically and militarily, as well as economically, motivated expansion of French interests in the East and the South in the wake of the wars of revolution and Europe's reorganization in the Napoleonic era. But also the confusion relating to financial policy throughout the Revolution promoted the integration of new exchange partners into the Paris exchange rate current. Thus, during the years of the assignat inflation (1793–1796), exchange transactions were moved at least to some extent from Paris to Hamburg and Basle, which explains the relatively early quotation on Basle (1794) (cf. BOUCHARY [1937], p. 32). With the end of the Napoleonic era the quotations on Saint Petersburg, Antwerp, Berlin, Oporto (from 1814), Venice (from 1815) and finally Trieste (from 1821) began, so that from then on Paris quoted almost all important European exchange markets. Only the quotation on Geneva was terminated again in 1819; obviously due to a lack of sources the quotations on Basle and the French places came to an end in 1843.

According to all merchant manuals scrutinized (e.g. NOBACK [1851], pp. 819f.), Paris was one of the most important European exchange markets after 1815. Its outstanding relevance as a financial centre and exchange market resulted not only from its importance as France's commercial and industrial centre, but above all from the international financial dominance of the 'haute banque parisienne' (cf. LÉVY-LE-BOYER [1964], passim). This is reflected in the numerous exchange rate quotations on almost all important European exchange markets, and the decades of dominance of the French money and capital market, by which other European countries, which brought millions of francs into the country by public loans and private investments, became more and more decisive. With the foundation of the Latin Monetary Union between France, Belgium, Italy and Switzerland on December 23rd 1865, this dominance reached a peak and France could rigorously enforce its favoured bimetallism against its partners' ideas of a monetary policy (ZELLFELDER [1991], pp. 114f.). Thus Paris was the financial centre of the most important member state and, at the same time, the dominant partner in the exchange business of the financial markets of the other countries allied to the Latin Monetary Union.

In 1867 a new way of presenting the Paris exchange rate quotations was introduced. Until then it had been common to quote dato bills of different periods of validity (usually 30 or 90 days) for every exchange partner, but henceforth a distinction was made between places with usances of three months' dato and places that were quoted at sight. Whereas London and the financial markets of the Latin Monetary Union states were counted among the the latter, the former included all other exchange partners. At the same time, all quotations were classified according to long sight and short sight, long-sight bills having a duration of 75 to 90 days, short-sight bills up to 15 days. A three-months bill had to be charged at the given rate *plus* the interest for the number of days the bill still had to run. Regardless of the quoted place the rate of discount was always 4%, the difference between the imaginary rate of discount of 4% and the actual bank rate being reflected in the quotation. In contrast to this, sight bills were charged at the given rate *minus* the interest for the number of days the bill still had to run. Their rate of discount corresponded to the bank rate of the quoted partner. A special case was the quotation on New York, starting in November 1871 and being given for three months' dato bills until March 1884 and afterwards for sight bills, although in the case of the quotation on New York the fictitious rate of discount for three months' dato bills amounted to 5% (NOBACK [1877], pp. 686f.; SWOBODA [1889], pp. 695–699). According to the documented sources, from October 1895 all quotations were divided into 'papier à trois mois' ('long paper', which had more than one month to run) on the one hand and 'papier court' ('short paper', payable within one month) on the other, the latter usance mostly being on a par with 'chèque versement' (e.g. SWOBODA [1909], p. 451; SWOBODA [1913], p. 320). From May 1907 the exchange rate currents in *Le Temps* combined papier court and chèque versement since the marginal differences between these usances could be ignored. "The necessity for double quotation is caused by a real duality of markets for 'long paper' and 'short paper'" (VIDAL [1910], p. 80). The short paper was exclusively an instrument of payment and "solely regulated by local conditions" (ibid., p. 81). Therefore the rates for short paper are listed in the tables presented here. In contrast to this, long paper functioned as a medium of investment and comprised a speculative element (ibid.).

In the second half of the 19th century the network of the exchange partners quoted at the Paris stock exchange changed, like other important European financial markets: in 1867 the Italian and in 1879 the German exchange places were combined to produce a common quotation on 'Italy' and on 'Germany' respectively. The only exception was Rome, which was quoted separately from 1867 to 1878, because Rome, capital of the Papal States, was protected by French troops and became part of the new Kingdom of Italy by September 1870. While the quotation on Bilbao had already been abandoned in 1861, Barcelona as the most important Spanish Mediterranean port and striving industrial centre was quoted from 1867. The quotations on Cadiz and (for the time being) on Oporto ended in 1876. In 1902 the quotations on the two remaining Spanish places were combined into one, and from 1907 'Portugal' meant the rates for both Lisbon and Oporto. In addition to this, Paris already began to quote New York as one of the first European financial centres in 1871. Finally, Stockholm as the most important Scandinavian exchange market was the last to be included in the exchange rate currents in 1892, although this quotation ended once again in 1899 when exchanges of Paris on Scandinavian places mostly went via Berlin. From 1910 to 1912 'Scandinavia', i.e. a common quotation for the places and currencies of the Scandinavian Monetary Union (Sweden, Denmark and Norway) was again listed in the exchange rate currents. In addition to this, bills on Algiers, Bône and Constantine were traded in Paris as well (NOBACK [1877], p. 687), although this is not reflected in the quotation lists since these places were treated as internal French exchange partners.

References: Emmanuel VIDAL, *The History and Methods of the Paris Bourse*, Washington 1910, pp. 76–85; Hermann ILLIG, *Das Geldwesen Frankreichs zur Zeit der ersten Revolution bis zum Ende der Papiergeldwährung*, Straßburg 1914; Jean BOUCHARY, *Le marché des changes de Paris à la fin du XVIIIe siècle (1778–1800). Avec des graphiques et le relevé des cours*, Paris 1937; Henry LAPEYRE, *Une famille de marchands: Les Ruiz*, Paris 1953; René SÉDILLOT, *Le franc. Histoire d'une monnaie des origins à nos jours*, Paris 1953; Herbert LÜTHY, *La banque protestante en France de la révocation de l'édit de Nantes à la révolution, t. II: De la banque aux finances (1730–1794)*, Paris 1961; Maurice LÉVY-LEBOYER, *Les banques européennes et l'industrialisation internationale dans la première moitié du XIXe siècle*, Paris 1964; Ferréol REBUFFAT / Marcel COURDURIÉ, *Marseille et le négoce monétaire international (1785–1790)*, Marseille 1966; Frank C. SPOONER, *The International Economy and Monetary Movements in France, 1493–1725*, Cambridge (Mass.) 1972; René SÉDILLOT, *Histoire du Franc*, Paris 1979; Guy THUILLIER, *La monnaie en France au début de XIXe siècle*, Paris 1983; Norbert W.J. BAAS, *Die Doppelwährungspolitik Frankreichs 1850–1885*, Florenz 1984; John J. MCCUSKER, *Money and Exchange in Europe and America, 1600–1775. A Handbook*, London – Basingstoke 1978, p. 87; Henry ROSEVEARE (ed.), *Markets and Merchants of the Late Seventeenth Century. The Marescoe-David Letters 1668–1680*, New York 1987; Friedrich ZELLFELDER, Der Lateinische Münzbund: Grundlagen, Entstehung und Scheitern, in *WdW I/I*, pp. 105–121; Markus A. DENZEL / Oskar SCHWARZER, Internationaler Zahlungsverkehr im 18. Jahrhundert: Amsterdam, London und Paris, in *WdW VI*, pp. 1–32, here pp. 28–32; *WdW IX*, pp. 35–37, 135–137; Markus A. DENZEL, *Der Preiskurant des Handelshauses Pelloutier & Cie aus Nantes (1763–1793)*, Stuttgart 1997.

6.1 Paris exchange rates

Underlined quotations are given in assignats.

6.1.1 On London, Amsterdam, Spain and Portugal

	PARIS on:		
	London	**Amsterdam**	**Madrid**
	per 10 pounds sterling [a]	per 100 guilders Flemish banco [b]	per 100 pesos de plata antigua [c]
	in livres tournois		
1760	234.30 30d/d (11)	222.08 30d/d (11)	386.48 30d/d (11)
1761	228.31 30d/d (6)	223.65 30d/d (6)	383.75 30d/d (6)
1762			
1763	225.48 30d/d (12)	215.10 30d/d (12)	379.05 30d/d (12)
1764	232.40 30d/d (12)	214.50 30d/d (12)	382.23 30d/d (12)
1765	230.68 30d/d (11)	213.42 30d/d (11)	379.75 30d/d (11)
1766	225.05 30d/d (12)	215.48 30d/d (12)	379.00 30d/d (12)
1767	225.13 30d/d (12)	218.19 30d/d (12)	378.85 30d/d (12)
1768	226.82 30d/d (12)	216.72 30d/d (10)	378.33 30d/d (12)
1769	224.36 30d/d (12)	218.79 30d/d (12)	374.78 30d/d (12)
1770	225.72 30d/d (11)	220.70 30d/d (11)	377.73 30d/d (11)
1771	225.87 30d/d (12)	218.63 30d/d (12)	379.05 30d/d (12)
1772	226.34 30d/d (12)	216.90 30d/d (12)	378.18 30d/d (12)
1773	238.70 30d/d (11)	221.97 30d/d (11)	382.15 30d/d (11)
1774	236.25 30d/d (12)	219.51 30d/d (12)	376.20 30d/d (12)
1775	232.95 30d/d (12)	218.18 30d/d (12)	377.95 30d/d (12)
1776	233.25 30d/d (12)	222.75 30d/d (12)	379.38 30d/d (12)
1777	229.52 30d/d (12)	222.10 30d/d (12)	378.47 60d/d (12)
1778	238.42 30d/d (12)	224.18 30d/d (11)	378.88 60d/d (12)
1779	244.20 30d/d (10)	225.75 30d/d (9)	376.34 60d/d (7)
1780	239.62 30d/d (10)	224.53 30d/d (11)	377.30 60d/d (9)
1781	231.59 30d/d (10)	225.89 30d/d (10)	353.13 60d/d (4)
1782	225.47 30d/d (10)	220.08 30d/d (9)	354.12 60d/d (6)
1783	227.45 90d/d (10)	218.51 90d/d (10)	342.30 60d/d (9)
1784	240.54 90d/d (9)	220.66 90d/d (9)	359.59 60d/d (9)
1785	249.26 90d/d (12)	221.75 90d/d (12)	363.86 60d/d (12)
1786	246.06 90d/d (12)	223.14 90d/d (12)	363.91 60d/d (12)
1787	242.93 90d/d (12)	220.69 90d/d (12)	370.86 60d/d (11)
1788	247.08 90d/d (12)	218.59 90d/d (12)	372.07 60d/d (10)
1789	255.28 90d/d (10)	223.60 90d/d (10)	376.63 60d/d (10)
1790	270.82 90d/d (11)	233.71 90d/d (12)	396.73 60d/d (11)
1791	304.06 90d/d (11)	258.37 90d/d (10)	457.50 60d/d (12)
1792	404.01 30d/d (12)	363.12 30d/d (12)	623.96 60d/d (12)

	PARIS on:			
	London	**Amsterdam**	**Madrid** [d]	**Lisbon**
	per 10 pounds sterling [a]	per 100 guilders Flemish banco, from 1816 (10) per 100 Dutch guilders [b]	per 100 pesos de plata antigua [c]	per 100 milréis [e]
	in livres tournois			
1793	525.50 30d/d (8)	557.22 30d/d (9)	723.44 60d/d (4)	
1794		<u>11,842.23</u> 30d/d (11)		
	in francs			
1795		196.50 30d/d (5)	*285.23* 60d/d (6)	
1796	294.84 30d/d (1)	202.69 30d/d (3)	*278.63* 60d/d (5)	
1797	283.83 30d/d (12)	208.67 30d/d (10)	355.21 60d/d (12)	
1798		214.33 30d/d (7)	378.13 60d/d (7)	
1799		208.89 30d/d (8)	367.71 60d/d (3)	
1800		211.79 30d/d (10)	361.61 30d/d (7)	
1801	227.34 30d/d (3)	210.83 30d/d (7)	385.84 30d/d (6)	
1802	229.80 30d/d (12)	213.25 30d/d (12)	369.27 30d/d (12)	
1803	237.85 30d/d (11)	212.52 30d/d (11)	369.53 30d/d (11)	
1804	245.97 30d/d (11)	212.08 30d/d (11)	365.23 30d/d (12)	628.51 90d/d (9)
1805	250.34 30d/d (12)	213.98 30d/d (12)	362.15 30d/d (10)	632.36 90d/d (12)
1806	237.64 30d/d (11)	212.47 30d/d (12)	377.25 30d/d (10)	613.46 90d/d (12)
1807		216.07 30d/d (12)	385.73 30d/d (12)	633.48 90d/d (12)
1808		209.61 30d/d (12)	396.69 30d/d (8)	632.73 90d/d (8)
1809		203.66 30d/d (12)	391.88 30d/d (10)	
1810		210.16 30d/d (11)	402.30 30d/d (12)	
1811	228.25 30d/d (2)	208.97 30d/d (11)	370.75 30d/d (10)	
1812		206.64 30d/d (6)	381.25 30d/d (3)	
1813		206.73 30d/d (12)		
1814	211.97 30d/d (8)	210.17 30d/d (12)	374.78 30d/d (11)	625.00 90d/d (1)
1815	222.61 30d/d (7)	209.82 30d/d (7)	357.50 30d/d (1)	593.75 90d/d (7)
1816	248.40 30d/d (12)	211.15 30d/d (12)	365.11 30d/d (12)	596.00 90d/d (12)
1817	244.09 30d/d (12)	210.97 30d/d (12)	371.30 30d/d (12)	591.63 90d/d (11)
1818	238.77 30d/d (12)	213.48 30d/d (12)	397.40 30d/d (12)	589.81 90d/d (12)
1819	240.62 30d/d (9)	213.43 30d/d (8)	389.47 30d/d (7)	567.39 90d/d (9)
1820	253.73 30d/d (11)	211.59 30d/d (11)	376.71 30d/d (11)	536.85 90d/d (11)
1821	255.48 30d/d (12)	205.37 30d/d (12)	391.98 30d/d (12)	534.00 90d/d (12)
1822	252.34 30d/d (12)	208.93 30d/d (12)	391.25 30d/d (11)	543.94 90d/d (12)
1823	254.48 30d/d (11)	210.42 30d/d (12)	395.94 30d/d (12)	555.25 90d/d (11)
1824	252.23 30d/d (12)	212.57 30d/d (12)	390.21 30d/d (12)	538.76 90d/d (12)
1825	250.07 30d/d (12)	209.60 30d/d (12)	386.67 30d/d (12)	533.59 90d/d (12)
1826	254.53 30d/d (11)	210.01 30d/d (11)	378.58 30d/d (11)	532.92 90d/d (11)
1827	253.05 30d/d (10)	210.69 30d/d (10)	367.63 30d/d (10)	522.01 90d/d (10)

	PARIS on:			
	London	**Amsterdam**	**Madrid**	**Lisbon**
	per 10 pounds sterling [a]	per 100 Dutch guilders [b]	per 100 pesos de plata antigua, from 1847 (4) per 100 pesos duros [c]	per 100 milréis [e]
			in francs	
1828	252.22 30d/d (12)	210.32 30d/d (12)	383.96 30d/d (12)	485.74 90d/d (12)
1829	254.59 30d/d (12)	210.55 30d/d (12)	393.02 30d/d (12)	485.06 90d/d (12)
1830	254.73 30d/d (12)	209.61 30d/d (12)	388.44 30d/d (12)	471.11 90d/d (12)
1831	251.37 30d/d (11)	210.54 30d/d (11)	391.57 30d/d (8)	483.24 90d/d (10)
1832	256.15 30d/d (10)	212.97 30d/d (10)	389.00 30d/d (10)	506.81 90d/d (9)
1833	255.25 30d/d (7)	213.08 30d/d (7)	401.25 30d/d (7)	518.01 90d/d (7)
1834	253.08 30d/d (10)	209.11 30d/d (10)	393.63 30d/d (10)	565.83 90d/d (10)
1835	254.19 30d/d (12)	209.10 30d/d (12)	398.70 30d/d (12)	608.18 90d/d (12)
1836	253.79 30d/d (12)	209.38 30d/d (12)	393.49 30d/d (12)	590.62 90d/d (11)
1837	254.17 30d/d (11)	210.92 30d/d (11)	391.39 30d/d (11)	555.22 90d/d (11)
1838	254.17 30d/d (11)	209.98 30d/d (11)	388.98 30d/d (11)	567.15 90d/d (10)
1839	251.46 30d/d (12)	209.55 30d/d (12)	394.69 30d/d (12)	570.43 90d/d (12)
1840	251.51 30d/d (12)	210.31 30d/d (11)	393.16 30d/d (12)	559.40 90d/d (12)
1841	252.61 30d/d (11)	209.65 30d/d (11)	386.20 30d/d (11)	555.00 90d/d (11)
1842	254.60 30d/d (12)	209.65 30d/d (12)	391.41 30d/d (12)	559.59 90d/d (12)
1843	255.71 30d/d (9)	210.11 30d/d (8)	393.75 30d/d (2)	560.63 90d/d (2)
1844	254.97 30d/d (12)	210.62 30d/d (10)	408.50 30d/d (12)	572.50 90d/d (1)
1845	256.12 30d/d (11)	208.72 30d/d (11)	406.34 30d/d (12)	
1846	256.03 30d/d (9)	209.02 30d/d (9)	400.16 30d/d (12)	
1847	254.11 30d/d (11)	210.34 30d/d (11)	396.83/519.75 30d/d (3+9)	
1848	254.63 30d/d (12)	211.82 30d/d (11)	486.38 30d/d (12)	
1849	253.35 30d/d (12)	210.38 30d/d (12)	527.15 30d/d (12)	
1850	253.06 30d/d (12)	211.27 30d/d (12)	530.22 30d/d (12)	
1851	250.39 30d/d (11)	211.98 30d/d (11)	513.00 30d/d (1)	
1852	252.63 30d/d (12)	212.12 30d/d (12)	525.84 30d/d (6)	537.50 90d/d (1)
1853	251.15 30d/d (12)	211.48 30d/d (11)	526.23 30d/d (12)	547.92 90d/d (6)
1854	250.11 30d/d (12)	212.91 30d/d (10)	526.81 30d/d (9)	549.87 90d/d (12)
1855	251.95 30d/d (12)	212.42 30d/d (12)	527.00 30d/d (10)	544.25 90d/d (2)
1856	253.00 30d/d (11)	213.45 30d/d (11)	518.34 30d/d (11)	552.78 90d/d (9)
1857	252.27 30d/d (11)	213.67 30d/d (11)	519.25 30d/d (7)	544.09 90d/d (11)
1858	251.22 30d/d (8)	213.19 30d/d (8)	524.15 30d/d (12)	538.72 90d/d (7)
1859	251.19 30d/d (12)	215.25 30d/d (12)	524.49 30d/d (10)	543.45 90d/d (10)
1860	251.33 30d/d (10)	214.84 30d/d (10)	520.91 30d/d (5)	544.34 90d/d (9)
1861	253.25 30d/d (12)	213.14 30d/d (9)	523.00 30d/d (12)	528.34 90d/d (3)
1862	252.24 30d/d (12)	213.63 30d/d (10)	522.38 30d/d (12)	
1863	252.46 30d/d (12)	214.06 30d/d (12)	513.13 30d/d (12)	
1864	252.47 30d/d (12)	212.94 30d/d (12)	507.50 30d/d (12)	

	PARIS on:			
	London [f]	**Amsterdam**	**Madrid** [f]	**Lisbon, from 1895 Portugal**
	per 10 pounds sterling [a]	per 100 Dutch guilders [b]	per 100 pesos duros [c]	per 100 milréis [e]
	in francs			
1865	251.93 30d/d (12)	212.41 30d/d (12)	497.05 30d/d (11)	
1866	251.88 30d/d (12)	212.86 30d/d (12)	490.73 30d/d (12)	
1867	251.47 s (12)	209.97 3m/d (12)	508.94 s (11)	545.19 3m/d (11)
1868	251.72 s (12)	209.43 3m/d (12)	510.86 s (12)	543.67 3m/d (12)
1869	251.70 s (12)	207.66 3m/d (12)	514.37 s (9)	548.00 3m/d (12)
1870	251.97 s (9)	209.93 3m/d (9)	522.15 s (7)	548.45 3m/d (9)
1871	255.33 s (7)	213.01 3m/d (7)	509.57 s (12)	555.58 3m/d (7)
1872	254.94 s (12)	210.36 3m/d (12)	507.00 s (9)	557.64 3m/d (12)
1873	254.17 s (12)	209.83 3m/d (12)	508.44 s (12)	558.88 3m/d (12)
1874	251.87 s (12)	210.16 3m/d (12)	499.38 s (12)	554.35 3m/d (12)
1875	251.81 s (12)	209.80 3m/d (12)	498.65 s (12)	553.09 3m/d (12)
1876	251.98 s (12)	206.45 3m/d (12)	492.00 s (12)	545.80 3m/d (12)
1877	251.47 s (12)	206.19 3m/d (12)	495.14 s (11)	543.92 3m/d (12)
1878	251.66 s (11)	205.84 3m/d (11)	492.19 s (12)	544.14 3m/d (11)
1879	252.49 s (12)	207.13 3m/d (12)	499.75 s (12)	548.23 3m/d (12)
1880	252.76 s (12)	206.96 3m/d (12)	497.57 s (12)	555.19 3m/d (12)
1881	252.63 s (12)	206.55 3m/d (12)	485.02 s (12)	551.15 3m/d (12)
1882	251.96 s (12)	205.91 3m/d (12)	486.76 s (12)	543.05 3m/d (12)
1883	252.31 s (12)	206.53 3m/d (12)	488.82 s (12)	546.88 3m/d (12)
1884	251.92 s (12)	206.05 3m/d (12)	485.00 s (12)	546.34 3m/d (12)
1885	252.45 s (12)	206.93 3m/d (12)	482.92 s (12)	546.71 3m/d (12)
1886	252.23 s (12)	206.86 3m/d (12)	488.38 s (12)	552.17 3m/d (12)
1887	252.97 s (12)	207.24 3m/d (12)	485.38 s (12)	555.88 3m/d (12)
1888	253.05 s (12)	207.54 3m/d (12)	479.00 s (12)	555.57 3m/d (12)
1889	252.30 s (12)	206.72 3m/d (12)	472.88 s (12)	553.75 3m/d (12)
1890	252.25 s (12)	206.54 3m/d (12)	466.13 s (12)	551.13 3m/d (12)
1891	252.32 s (12)	206.90 3m/d (12)	430.13 s (12)	545.06 3m/d (6)
1892	251.65 s (12)	206.18 3m/d (12)	415.96 s (12)	
1893	251.72 s (12)	206.22 3m/d (12)	411.97 s (12)	
1894	251.55 s (12)	206.28 3m/d (12)	432.98 s (12)	
1895	252.37 s (12)	205.54 3m/d (12)	410.67 s (12)	437.50 3m/d (3)
1896	251.81 p.c. (12)	205.95 p.c. (12)	382.46 p.c. (12)	425.88 p.c. (12)
1897	251.41 p.c. (12)	206.12 p.c. (12)	337.35 p.c. (10)	375.42 p.c. (12)
1898	252.51 p.c. (12)	207.07 p.c. (12)	401.71 p.c. (12)	348.75 p.c. (6)
1899	252.05 p.c. (12)	206.10 p.c. (12)	387.59 p.c. (12)	
1900	251.43 p.c. (12)	205.79 p.c. (12)	361.84 p.c. (12)	
1901	251.50 p.c. (12)	206.12 p.c. (12)	401.40 p.c. (12)	

	PARIS on:			
	London	**Amsterdam** [g]	**Madrid, from** 1902 (4) **Spain** [h]	**Portugal** [i]
	per 10 pounds sterling [a]	per 100 Dutch guilders [b]	per 100 pesos duros [c]	per 100 milreís [e]
	in francs			
1902	251.38 p.c. (12)	205.25 p.c. (12)	364.28 p.c. (12)	
1903	251.43 p.c. (12)	205.85 p.c. (12)	368.36 p.c. (12)	
1904	251.52 p.c. (12)	206.31 p.c. (12)	359.50 p.c. (12)	
1905	251.36 p.c. (12)	205.97 p.c. (12)	381.21 p.c. (12)	
1906	251.48 p.c. (12)	205.59 p.c. (12)	440.73 p.c. (12)	
1907	251.94 p.c. (12)	207.47 p.c. (12)	450.25 p.c. (12)	535.00 p.c. (8)
1908	251.49 p.c. (12)	208.18 p.c. (12)	445.75 p.c. (12)	490.92 p.c. (12)
1909	251.98 p.c. (12)	208.29 p.c. (12)	456.42 p.c. (12)	487.00 p.c. (12)
1910	252.30 p.c. (12)	208.48 p.c. (12)	467.11 p.c. (12)	511.25 p.c. (12)
1911	252.59 p.c. (12)	208.98 p.c. (12)	461.94 p.c. (12)	515.88 p.c. (12)
1912	252.41 p.c. (12)	209.05 p.c. (12)	469.23 p.c. (12)	510.34 p.c. (12)
1913	252.45 p.c. (12)	208.24 p.c. (12)	464.85 p.c. (12)	483.42 p.c. (12)
1914	251.75 p.c. (7)	208.31 p.c. (7)	474.23 p.c. (7)	477.00 p.c. (7)

[a]   Concerning the British currency, see pp. 3–5.

[b]   Concerning the Dutch currency, see pp. 57–59.

[c]   Concerning the Spanish currency, see p. 307.

[d]   1795/96: quotation for pesos de plata antigua payable in Spanish paper money, the so-called 'vales reales'.

[e]   In the Portuguese currency system one reckoned in réis or in milréis (= 1,000 réis) respectively. Since the Coin Act from July 29th 1854 the Portuguese silver standard with the milréis at 27.15 grammes of pure silver (from July 1st 1835 according to the Coin Act of April 24th 1835) was succeeded by the gold standard – following the model of Great Britain – with the milréis at 1.6257 grammes of pure gold. From July 1891 Portugal had the paper standard with a premium for gold coins up to 53% (in May 1897). In 1912 the milréis was succeeded by the escudo of 100 centavos (1 escudo = 1 milréis); from the beginning of 1913 it had to be officially reckoned in this new currency, but for all commercial transactions the term 'milréis' continued to be used (cf. NOBACK [1877], pp. 507f.; SWOBODA [1913], pp. 518f.).

[f]   1867–1895 (8): quotation for short sight bills.

[g]   From August 1907 'Holland' was quoted instead of Amsterdam.

[h]   From April 1902 common quotation on Madrid and Barcelona.

[i]   From 1907 common quotation on Lisbon and Oporto.

6.1.2 On Italian places

	PARIS on:	
	Genoa	**Leghorn**
	per 100 pezze of 5¾ lire fuori banco [a]	per 100 pezze da otto reali [b]
	in livres tournois	
1760		516.35 30d/d (11)
1761		519.28 30d/d (6)
1762		
1763		486.97 30d/d (12)
1764		476.27 30d/d (12)
1765		481.56 30d/d (11)
1766		476.16 30d/d (12)
1767		471.27 30d/d (11)
1768		475.41 30d/d (12)
1769		479.90 30d/d (12)
1770	473.05 30d/d (7)	481.22 30d/d (11)
1771	472.31 30d/d (12)	482.31 30d/d (12)
1772	470.00 30d/d (12)	479.26 30d/d (12)
1773	472.48 30d/d (11)	482.43 30d/d (11)
1774	469.37 30d/d (12)	476.96 30d/d (12)
1775	470.12 30d/d (12)	478.98 30d/d (12)
1776	478.34 30d/d (12)	488.00 30d/d (12)
1777	473.46 30d/d (12)	483.92 30d/d (12)
1778	473.97 30d/d (12)	484.84 30d/d (12)
1779	468.00 30d/d (9)	484.90 30d/d (8)
1780	467.19 30d/d (10)	488.58 30d/d (10)
1781	467.53 30d/d (9)	483.75 30d/d (9)
1782	465.87 30d/d (9)	487.77 30d/d (9)
1783	463.68 30d/d (8)	488.06 90d/d (7)
1784	470.41 30d/d (9)	497.84 90d/d (9)
1785	472.08 30d/d (12)	495.48 90d/d (12)
1786	472.02 30d/d (12)	506.06 90d/d (12)
1787	472.65 30d/d (11)	503.30 90d/d (12)
1788	470.64 30d/d (10)	500.25 90d/d (12)
1789	480.47 30d/d (10)	510.20 90d/d (10)
1790	502.67 30d/d (11)	542.46 90d/d (12)
1791	561.66 30d/d (10)	607.49 90d/d (10)
1792	787.92 30d/d (12)	840.02 30d/d (12)
1793	1,040.00 30d/d (6)	1,008.78 30d/d (4)
1794	19,738.96 30d/d (4)	20,999.63 30d/d (1)
1795	20,325.74 30d/d (2)	20,299.69 30d/d (1)

	PARIS on:			
	Genoa	**Leghorn**	**Milan**	**Naples**
	per 100 lire fuori banco, from 1827 (3) per 100 Piedmontese lire nuove [a]	per 100 pezze da otto reali [b]	per 100 lire corrente, from 1813 (9) per 100 lire italiane, from 1824 per 100 lire austriache [c]	per 100 ducati del regno [d]
			in francs	
1795	77.78 30d/d (4)	475.01 30d/d (1)		
1796	80.09 30d/d (4)	510.83 30d/d (3)		
1797	80.55 30d/d (12)	509.34 30d/d (12)		
1798	83.36 30d/d (7)	520.72 30d/d (7)		
1799	83.84 30d/d (6)	531.76 30d/d (5)		
1800	78.63 30d/d (10)	499.39 30d/d (8)		
1801	80.35 30d/d (7)	512.15 30d/d (7)	74.31 30d/d (2)	
1802	80.83 30d/d (12)	506.29 30d/d (12)	74.25 30d/d (9)	465.00 30d/d (1)
1803	81.40 30d/d (11)	508.99 30d/d (11)	75.39 30d/d (11)	
1804	82.18 30d/d (12)	517.04 30d/d (12)	75.16 30d/d (12)	
1805	85.57 30d/d (7)	538.95 30d/d (12)	78.16 30d/d (12)	
1806	82.79 30d/d (8)	520.61 30d/d (12)	76.60 30d/d (12)	410.00 30d/d (1)
1807	81.35 30d/d (12)	506.92 30d/d (12)	75.78 30d/d (12)	421.25 30d/d (4)
1808	83.08 30d/d (12)	511.35 30d/d (12)	76.80 30d/d (12)	449.29 30d/d (7)
1809	83.29 30d/d (12)	516.12 30d/d (12)	77.13 30d/d (12)	427.00 30d/d (12)
1810	82.99 30d/d (12)	517.67 30d/d (12)	76.77 30d/d (12)	451.59 30d/d (12)
1811	80.98 30d/d (8)	493.24 30d/d (11)	74.10 30d/d (9)	446.37 30d/d (11)
1812	82.38 30d/d (6)	505.83 30d/d (6)	76.76 30d/d (6)	436.00 30d/d (6)
1813	82.08 30d/d (12)	502.03 30d/d (12)	76.50/98.94 30d/d (8+4)	430.17 30d/d (12)
1814	81.38 30d/d (12)	500.54 30d/d (12)	98.77 30d/d (12)	410.50 30d/d (12)
1815	81.12 30d/d (7)	489.67 30d/d (7)	98.36 30d/d (7)	414.00 30d/d (7)
1816	81.34 30d/d (12)	500.02 30d/d (12)	98.55 30d/d (12)	417.50 30d/d (12)
1817	81.86 30d/d (12)	501.17 30d/d (12)	98.63 30d/d (12)	420.67 30d/d (12)
1818	83.61 30d/d (12)	522.04 30d/d (12)	100.51 30d/d (12)	445.34 30d/d (12)
1819	82.98 30d/d (9)	519.80 30d/d (9)	99.55 30d/d (9)	421.23 30d/d (9)
1820	82.69 30d/d (11)	507.21 30d/d (11)	98.75 30d/d (11)	419.00 30d/d (11)
1821	82.97 30d/d (12)	510.20 30d/d (12)	98.76 30d/d (12)	431.75 30d/d (12)
1822	82.18 30d/d (12)	510.66 30d/d (12)	98.16 30d/d (12)	431.25 30d/d (12)
1823	81.87 30d/d (11)	506.75 30d/d (11)	96.98 30d/d (11)	421.91 30d/d (11)
1824	81.90 30d/d (12)	507.44 30d/d (12)	84.03 30d/d (12)	412.34 30d/d (12)
1825	83.19 30d/d (12)	524.00 30d/d (12)	85.69 30d/d (12)	431.42 30d/d (12)
1826	81.67 30d/d (11)	514.28 30d/d (11)	84.08 30d/d (11)	419.23 30d/d (11)
1827	81.49/99.65 30d/d (2+7)	509.97 30d/d (10)	84.24 30d/d (10)	410.70 30d/d (10)
1828	99.69 30d/d (11)	513.99 30d/d (12)	84.77 30d/d (12)	420.63 30d/d (12)
1829	100.03 30d/d (12)	512.96 30d/d (12)	85.30 30d/d (12)	428.75 30d/d (12)
1830	99.85 30d/d (12)	514.86 30d/d (12)	84.87 30d/d (12)	427.59 30d/d (12)

	PARIS on:			
	Genoa	**Leghorn**	**Milan**	**Naples**
	per 100 Piedmontese lire nuove, from 1861 (8) per 100 Italian lire [a], [f]	per 100 pezze da otto reali [a], from 1837 (8) per 100 Tuscan lire moneta buona, from 1860 (12) per 100 Piedmontese lire nuove, from 1861 (8) per 100 Italian lire [b], [f]	per 100 lire austriache, from 1859 (8) 100 guilders Österreichische Währung, from 1860 per 100 Piedmontese lire nuove, from 1861 (8) per 100 Italian lire [c], [f]	per 100 ducati del regno, from 1863 (5) per 100 Italian lire [e], [f]
			in francs	
1831	98.84 30d/d (11)	511.41 30d/d (11)	85.08 30d/d (11)	419.00 30d/d (10)
1832	99.83 30d/d (10)	516.01 30d/d (9)	85.29 30d/d (10)	436.35 30d/d (10)
1833	99.90 30d/d (6)	513.99 30d/d (7)	85.91 30d/d (7)	433.36 30d/d (7)
1834	99.95 30d/d (10)	518.88 30d/d (10)	86.24 30d/d (10)	435.20 30d/d (10)
1835	99.73 30d/d (12)	514.22 30d/d (12)	85.91 30d/d (12)	436.25 30d/d (12)
1836	99.72 30d/d (12)	516.87 30d/d (12)	85.00 30d/d (12)	435.17 30d/d (12)
1837	98.87 30d/d (11)	511.23/82.6 30d/d (6+5)	84.34 30d/d (11)	423.69 30d/d (11)
1838	99.19 30d/d (11)	82.44 30d/d (11)	84.74 30d/d (11)	421.32 30d/d (11)
1839	99.17 30d/d (12)	84.33 30d/d (12)	85.01 30d/d (12)	429.90 30d/d (12)
1840	99.37 30d/d (12)	84.19 30d/d (12)	85.08 30d/d (12)	434.48 30d/d (12)
1841	99.43 30d/d (11)	84.84 30d/d (11)	86.22 30d/d (11)	425.84 30d/d (11)
1842	99.60 30d/d (12)	85.34 30d/d (11)	87.29 30d/d (12)	433.75 30d/d (12)
1843	99.35 30d/d (2)	83.97 30d/d (2)	86.75 30d/d (2)	434.00 30d/d (2)
1844	99.63 30d/d (1)	84.88 30d/d (1)	87.18 30d/d (12)	430.29 30d/d (12)
1845			87.30 30d/d (12)	439.17 30d/d (12)
1846		85.65 30d/d (1)	86.57 30d/d (12)	438.21 30d/d (12)
1847		85.25 30d/d (12)	86.09 30d/d (7)	440.14 30d/d (12)
1848		83.81 30d/d (12)	85.00 30d/d (11)	417.89 30d/d (12)
1849		82.50 30d/d (12)	83.08 30d/d (12)	430.63 30d/d (12)
1850		84.48 30d/d (11)	84.53 30d/d (12)	434.80 30d/d (12)
1851			85.54 30d/d (12)	433.13 30d/d (12)
1852	99.57 30d/d (1)	84.25 90d/d (1)	85.50 30d/d (12)	434.98 30d/d (12)
1853	99.73 30d/d (6)	84.00 30d/d (1)	84.44 30d/d (4)	437.67 30d/d (3)
1854	99.49 30d/d (10)	83.18 30d/d (8)	84.39 30d/d (12)	449.00 30d/d (7)
1855	99.59 30d/d (3)	84.71 30d/d (9)	85.19 30d/d (2)	463.98 30d/d (11)
1856	99.63 30d/d (9)	85.59 30d/d (10)	85.71 30d/d (9)	467.85 30d/d (5)
1857	99.58 30d/d (11)	86.17 30d/d (10)	85.38 30d/d (11)	447.05 30d/d (11)
1858	99.61 30d/d (7)	84.25 90d/d (10)	85.02 30d/d (8)	437.00 30d/d (4)
1859	99.09 30d/d (11)	83.41 90d/d (12)	86.75/249.25 30d/d (2+5)	429.75 30d/d (4)
1860	99.32 30d/d (9)	83.23/98.38 90d/d (9+1)	[d] 99.99 30d/d (5)	426.84 30d/d (6)
1861	99.84 30d/d (9)	99.32 30d/d (12)	99.81 30d/d (12)	422.53 30d/d (9)
1862	99.87 30d/d (12)	99.71 30d/d (12)	99.86 30d/d (12)	424.25 30d/d (12)
1863	99.93 30d/d (12)	99.70 30d/d (12)	99.97 30d/d (12)	423/99.75 30d/d (4+8)

	PARIS on:			
	Genoa	**Leghorn**	**Milan**	**Naples**
	per 100 Italian lire [f]			
	in francs			
1864	99.82 30d/d (12)	99.81 30d/d (12)	99.89 30d/d (12)	99.73 30d/d (12)
1865	99.87 30d/d (12)	99.87 30d/d (12)	99.88 30d/d (12)	99.83 30d/d (12)
1866	95.90 30d/d (10)	95.85 30d/d (10)	99.73 30d/d (5)	95.82 30d/d (10)

[a] Concerning the Genoese currency, see pp. 107f.

[b] Concerning the Leghorn currency, see p. 106. 1796–1837 (8) inclusive of 7% premium for payment in gold.

[c] Milan traditionally reckoned in lire corrente of 20 soldi at 12 denari, so that from the lira corrente was equal to 3.464 grammes of pure silver the monetary reform of 1778. In the Napoleonic Kingdom of Italy a new lira italiana (or lira of the Kingdom of Italy) of 100 centesimi was created and introduced, which was equal to the French franc (4.50 grammes of pure silver), but the Paris exchange rates on Milan were converted into the new currency not before September 1813. Thus the relation between old and new currency was: 27 lire corrente = 20.723 lire italiane. On November 1st 1823 the Austrian lira (lira austriaca) of 100 centesimi with 3.897 grammes of pure silver was introduced in Lombardy–Veneto by the so-called 'Münzpatent' and became legal tender like the guilder Konventionskurant (see Habsburg Monarchy). This lira was equal to the 20-kreutzer piece (or one-third part of the guilder) of the Habsburg Monarchy and, therefore, used to be called 'la svanzica' or the 'zwanziger'. With the introduction of the new guilder Österreichische Währung in the Habsburg Monarchy, the exceptional monetary position of Lombardy–Veneto was abolished in 1858/59. After the integration of Lombardy into the new Kingdom of Italy (1860), the Piedmontese and the Italian currency system respectively came into force here.

[d] There was no quotation during the French occupation in 1859/60.

[e] The system of accounting in ducati (called 'ducati del regno' or 'ducati di regno' since the 18th century) of 10 carlini at 10 grani or 5 tari at 20 grani had been common practice in the Kingdom of Naples for centuries and was continued during the Restoration era (after the Act of August 18th 1814). The Act of April 20th 1818 fixed the fineness of the ducato at 19.12 grammes of fine silver as it had been when it was officially introduced in 1794 and confirmed in 1804 (from 1784 18.96 grammes of fine silver; cf. NOBACK [1851], pp. 710s.). This new silver ducato – later generally called 'ducato del regno' or 'ducato di regno' – should have been divided into 100 centesimi or grani. Simultaneously, it became the unit of account of the whole Kingdom of the Two Sicilies, which means that the hitherto independent Sicilian system based on the oncia (56.896 gr. fine silver) of 30 tari (or carlini; 1 oncia = 3 ducati) at 20 grani was removed by this Act. With the integration of the Kingdom of the Two Sicilies into the new Kingdom of Italy in 1862, the Italian lira of 100 centesimi became the currency and accounting unit in Naples.

[f] Concerning the Italian currency system since 1861, see pp. 108f.

	PARIS on:				PARIS on:
	Italy [a]	**Rome**			**Italy** [a]
	per 100 Italian lire [b]	per 100 lire pontificie [c], from 1871 per 100 Italian lire [b]			per 100 Italian lire [b]
	in francs				in francs
1867	94.02 s (11)	98.59 ss (3)		1891	98.40 s (12)
1868	90.52 s (9)	93.58 ss (11)		1892	96.61 s (12)
1869	96.08 s (12)	98.32 ss (12)		1893	92.84 s (12)
1870	95.60 s (9)	97.28 ss (9)		1894	89.82 s (12)
1871	95.56 s (7)	94.82 ss (6)		1895	95.11 s (12)
1872	92.56 s (12)	92.60 ss (12)		1896	92.65 p.c. (12)
1873	87.72 s (12)	87.78 ss (12)		1897	94.99 p.c. (12)
1874	88.80 s (12)	88.13 ss (12)		1898	93.43 p.c. (12)
1875	92.44 s (12)	92.38 ss (12)		1899	93.06 p.c. (12)
1876	92.09 s (12)	92.08 ss (12)		1900	93.82 p.c. (12)
1877	91.04 s (12)	91.00 ss (12)		1901	95.69 p.c. (12)
1878	91.22 s (11)	90.73 ss (9)		1902	98.79 p.c. (12)
1879	90.13 s (12)			1903	99.93 p.c. (12)
1880	90.99 s (12)			1904	99.86 p.c. (12)
1881	98.37 s (12)			1905	100.03 p.c. (12)
1882	97.89 s (12)			1906	99.97 p.c. (12)
1883	99.76 s (12)			1907	100.02 p.c. (12)
1884	99.94 s (12)			1908	100.07 p.c. (12)
1885	99.64 s (12)			1909	99.65 p.c. (12)
1886	99.60 s (12)			1910	99.43 p.c. (12)
1887	99.26 s (12)			1911	99.46 p.c. (12)
1888	98.92 s (12)			1912	99.06 p.c. (12)
1889	99.21 s (12)			1913	98.19 p.c. (12)
1890	98.72 s (12)			1914	99.63 p.c. (7)

[a] Common quotation on Genoa, Milan, Leghorn, Naples and Venice.

[b] Concerning the Italian currency system, see pp. 108f. Concerning the problem of the different quotations per lire in notes and per lire in gold, see ibid.

[c] Since 1867 the currency of the Papal States (from 1849 protected by French troops) was the lira pontificia of 20 soldi at 5 centesimi, introduced by a papal edict from June 18th 1866 and minted (from August 1866) in agreement with the terms of the treaty of the Latin Monetary Union. Therefore the lira pontificia was equal to the French franc and the Italian lira but the quotations given here are for paper money. After the occupation of the Papal States by the Kingdom of Italy (in September 1870), the division of the lira into 100 centesimi was introduced in 1871 (NOBACK [1877], p. 771; see pp. 108f.).

6.1.3 On Belgium, Switzerland and Vienna

	PARIS on:			
	Antwerp	**Basle**	**Geneva**	**Vienna**
	per 100 French francs, from 1826 per 100 Dutch guilders [a]	per 100 francs payable in carolins [b]	per 100 livres Geneva current [c]	per 100 guilders Wiener Währung (from 1800), from 1816 per 100 guilders Konventionskurant [d]
			in francs	
1794		95.00 30d/d (11)		
1795		98.41 30d/d (8)		
1796		98.19 30d/d (4)		
1797		99.11 30d/d (10)		
1798		100.05 30d/d (6)		
1799		100.14 30d/d (9)		
1800		99.48 30d/d (9)		
1801		99.50 30d/d (6)		214.23 30d/d (3)
1802		99.36 30d/d (12)		212.00 30d/d (4)
1803		99.63 30d/d (8)		196.00 30d/d (4)
1804		99.58 30d/d (7)		201.38 30d/d (8)
1805		101.66 30d/d (11)	159.38 90d/d (6)	195.34 30d/d (12)
1806		100.31 30d/d (10)	161.25 90d/d (2)	149.50 30d/d (8)
1807		99.25 30d/d (12)		120.50 30d/d (8)
1808		99.53 30d/d (11)	161.00 90d/d (4)	114.23 30d/d (9)
1809		99.65 30d/d (7)	160.64 90d/d (12)	111.50 30d/d (2)
1810		99.16 30d/d (8)	160.30 90d/d (5)	59.78 30d/d (9)
1811		97.23 30d/d (10)	159.50 90d/d (1)	25.00 30d/d (1)
1812		99.38 30d/d (4)	159.25 90d/d (6)	
1813		100.24 30d/d (8)	159.25 90d/d (12)	
1814		100.10 30d/d (9)	158.32 90d/d (12)	
1815	99.50 30d/d (5)	99.57 30d/d (4)	158.20 90d/d (5)	
1816		99.37 30d/d (10)		257.38 30d/d (12)
1817	99.17 30d/d (6)	99.73 30d/d (6)	159.00 90d/d (4)	255.88 30d/d (12)
1818	99.63 30d/d (11)	99.25 30d/d (12)	159.00 90d/d (12)	260.80 30d/d (12)
1819	99.49 30d/d (9)	99.75 30d/d (3)	159.00 90d/d (9)	260.12 30d/d (9)
1820	99.16 30d/d (11)	99.07 30d/d (11)		252.99 30d/d (11)
1821	99.11 30d/d (12)	99.22 30d/d (12)		251.88 30d/d (12)
1822	99.36 30d/d (12)	98.54 30d/d (12)		250.30 30d/d (12)
1823	99.51 30d/d (12)	97.96 30d/d (12)		249.25 30d/d (12)
1824	99.52 30d/d (12)	98.15 30d/d (12)		251.64 30d/d (12)
1825	99.32 30d/d (12)	98.71 30d/d (12)		254.38 30d/d (12)
1826	209.95 30d/d (11)	99.00 30d/d (11)		250.59 30d/d (11)
1827	210.21 30d/d (10)	99.00 30d/d (10)		252.50 30d/d (10)

	PARIS on:		
	Antwerp	**Basle**	**Vienna**
	per 100 Dutch guilders, from 1840 (4) per 100 Belgian francs [a]	per 100 francs payable in carolins [b]	per 100 guilders Konventionskurant, from 1858 (11) per 100 guilders Österreichi-sche Währung [d]
	in francs		
1828	210.00 30d/d (12)	99.00 30d/d (12)	254.52 30d/d (12)
1829	210.26 30d/d (12)	99.21 30d/d (12)	255.24 30d/d (12)
1830	209.72 30d/d (12)	99.50 30d/d (12)	252.61 30d/d (12)
1831	210.45 30d/d (11)	99.32 30d/d (11)	252.78 30d/d (11)
1832	210.91 30d/d (10)	99.00 30d/d (8)	254.92 30d/d (9)
1833	210.60 30d/d (7)	99.00 30d/d (7)	257.31 30d/d (7)
1834	209.66 30d/d (10)	99.00 30d/d (10)	257.35 30d/d (10)
1835	209.88 30d/d (12)	99.00 30d/d (12)	255.73 30d/d (12)
1836	210.07 30d/d (12)	99.38 30d/d (12)	252.69 30d/d (12)
1837	210.34 30d/d (11)	99.49 30d/d (11)	251.38 30d/d (11)
1838	210.32 30d/d (11)	99.41 30d/d (11)	252.25 30d/d (11)
1839	210.30 30d/d (12)	99.25 30d/d (12)	253.26 30d/d (12)
1840	210.45/99.45 30d/d (3+9)	99.00 30d/d (12)	253.70 30d/d (12)
1841	99.44 30d/d (11)	99.00 30d/d (11)	258.07 30d/d (11)
1842	99.48 30d/d (12)	99.00 30d/d (12)	259.98 30d/d (12)
1843	99.50 30d/d (2)	99.00 30d/d (2)	258.50 30d/d (2)
1844	99.59 30d/d (9)		259.81 30d/d (9)
1845	99.39 30d/d (11)		258.53 30d/d (11)
1846	99.46 30d/d (9)		255.37 30d/d (9)
1847	99.23 30d/d (11)		254.05 30d/d (11)
1848	99.35 30d/d (4)		238.10 30d/d (10)
1849			224.68 30d/d (10)
1850	99.75 30d/d (3)		214.37 30d/d (11)
1851	99.25 90d/d (10)		197.00 30d/d (2)
1852	99.25 90d/d (7)		216.82 30d/d (4)
1853	99.25 90d/d (6)		229.62 30d/d (9)
1854	99.21 90d/d (12)		208.59 90d/d (6)
1855	99.25 90d/d (2)		215.84 30d/d (3)
1856	99.38 90d/d (9)		245.32 30d/d (8)
1857	99.67 30d/d (3)		242.06 30d/d (9)
1858	99.86 30d/d (7)		233.00/246.50 30d/d (1+2)
1859	99.54 30d/d (12)		226.75 30d/d (9)
1860	99.75 30d/d (10)		209.34 30d/d (6)
1861	99.92 30d/d (10)		177.55 90d/d (12)
1862	99.94 30d/d (7)		183.25 30d/d (4)
1863	99.98 30d/d (12)		217.80 90d/d (12)

	PARIS on:		
	Antwerp, from 1867 **Belgium**	**Geneva, from 1875** **Switzerland**	**Vienna**
	per 100 Belgian francs [a]	per 100 franken [e]	per 100 guilders Öster-reichische Währung [d]
	in francs		
1864	100.05 30d/d (10)		212.46 30d/d (12)
1865	100.00 30d/d (11)		226.35 30d/d (12)
1866	100.15 30d/d (12)		215.25 30d/d (10)
1867	99.94 s (12)		195.50 3m/d (12)
1868	99.93 s (12)		212.46 3m/d (12)
1869	99.88 s (12)		200.69 3m/d (12)
1870	99.92 s (9)		200.06 3m/d (9)
1871	100.53 s (7)		207.20 3m/d (7)
1872	100.22 s (12)	100.36 s (6)	223.59 3m/d (12)
1873	100.18 s (12)	100.24 s (12)	224.50 3m/d (12)
1874	99.92 s (12)	99.82 s (12)	221.74 3m/d (12)
1875	99.99 s (12)	99.99 s (12)	221.31 3m/d (12)
1876	99.92 s (12)	99.95 s (12)	204.84 3m/d (12)
1877	99.89 s (12)	99.88 s (12)	200.59 3m/d (12)
1878	99.91 s (11)	99.81 s (11)	209.28 3m/d (11)
1879	99.91 s (12)	99.92 s (12)	212.68 3m/d (12)
1880	99.91 s (12)	99.93 s (12)	210.82 3m/d (12)
1881	99.87 s (12)	99.89 s (12)	212.40 3m/d (12)
1882	99.89 s (12)	99.96 s (11)	209.27 3m/d (12)
1883	99.90 s (12)	100.00 s (12)	208.32 3m/d (12)
1884	99.90 s (12)	99.90 s (12)	205.09 3m/d (12)
1885	99.84 s (12)	99.82 s (12)	200.38 3m/d (12)
1886	99.93 s (12)	99.75 s (12)	198.36 3m/d (12)
1887	99.89 s (12)	99.88 s (12)	197.75 3m/d (12)
1888	99.90 s (12)	99.75 s (12)	201.09 3m/d (12)
1889	99.90 s (11)	99.52 s (12)	208.07 3m/d (12)
1890	99.93 s (12)	99.74 s (12)	214.32 3m/d (12)
1891	99.85 s (12)	99.71 s (12)	214.34 3m/d (12)
1892	99.90 s (12)	99.80 s (12)	209.06 3m/d (12)
1893	99.82 s (12)	99.77 s (12)	201.88 3m/d (12)
1894	99.91 s (12)	99.84 s (12)	199.67 3m/d (12)
1895	99.85 s (12)	99.79 s (12)	204.80 3m/d (12)
1896	99.89 p.c. (12)	99.71 p.c. (12)	207.58 p.c. (12)
1897	99.85 p.c. (12)	99.51 p.c. (12)	208.03 p.c. (12)
1898	99.84 p.c. (12)	99.57 p.c. (12)	207.88 p.c. (12)
1899	100.22 p.c. (12)	99.46 p.c. (12)	206.95 p.c. (12)

	PARIS on:		
	Belgium	**Switzerland**	**Vienna**
	per 100 Belgian francs [a]	per 100 franken [e]	per 100 Austrian crowns [d]
	in francs		
1900	100.19 p.c. (12)	99.42 p.c. (12)	102.78 p.c. (12)
1901	99.86 p.c. (12)	99.79 p.c. (12)	103.82 p.c. (12)
1902	99.85 p.c. (12)	99.64 p.c. (12)	103.82 p.c. (12)
1903	99.82 p.c. (12)	99.95 p.c. (12)	103.88 p.c. (12)
1904	99.84 p.c. (12)	99.77 p.c. (12)	103.99 p.c. (12)
1905	99.80 p.c. (12)	99.87 p.c. (12)	103.65 p.c. (12)
1906	99.73 p.c. (12)	99.89 p.c. (12)	103.55 p.c. (12)
1907	99.73 p.c. (12)	99.87 p.c. (12)	104.10 p.c. (12)
1908	99.77 p.c. (12)	99.93 p.c. (12)	104.77 p.c. (12)
1909	99.76 p.c. (12)	99.95 p.c. (12)	104.96 p.c. (12)
1910	99.61 p.c. (12)	99.80 p.c. (12)	104.78 p.c. (12)
1911	99.61 p.c. (12)	99.89 p.c. (12)	104.98 p.c. (12)
1912	99.55 p.c. (12)	99.71 p.c. (12)	104.52 p.c. (12)
1913	99.39 p.c. (12)	99.70 p.c. (12)	104.56 p.c. (12)
1914	99.41 p.c. (7)	99.89 p.c. (7)	104.65 p.c. (7)

[a]   Concerning the Dutch and French currency in Antwerp, see pp. 57–59, 279f. The Belgian franc was introduced in 1832 and was equal to the French franc, so that 189 Dutch guilders = 400 Belgian francs.

[b]   1 carolin or new louis d'or = 24 livres tournois = 16 Swiss francs ('schweizerfranken') = 11 guilders at the standard of coinage of 24 guilders per mark of Cologne, whereby 81 livres = 80 francs; therefore commonly 40 francs = 27 schweizerfranken (cf. NELKENBRECHER [1832], pp. 47f., 179f.).

[c]   The imaginary livre argent courant (of 20 sols argent courant) was equal to 3½ florins or guilders petite monnaie – a real coin of 20 sols petite monnaie – so that 1 livre argent courant = 42 sols petite monnaie of Geneva (cf. ibid., p. 196). 14.525 livres Geneva current = 1 new louis d'or.

[d]   Concerning the Austrian currency, see pp. 255f. From 1827 to 1836 the quotation on Vienna was made explicitly for 100 guilders Konventionskurant in silver coins. From June 3rd 1848 the guilder Konventionskurant and from November 1858 the guilder Österreichische Währung were paper money in notes of the Wiener Nationalbank and government notes.

[e]   Concerning the Swiss currency since 1852, see p. 313.

6.1.4 On German places

	PARIS on:
	Hamburg
	per 100 mark banco [a]
	in livres tournois
1760	182.56 30d/d (11)
1761	190.45 30d/d (5)
1762	
1763	176.65 30d/d (12)
1764	179.12 30d/d (12)
1765	177.55 30d/d (11)
1766	172.25 30d/d (12)
1767	169.56 30d/d (12)
1768	177.72 30d/d (12)
1769	180.88 30d/d (12)
1770	182.17 30d/d (11)
1771	182.16 30d/d (12)
1772	182.61 30d/d (12)
1773	185.02 30d/d (11)
1774	184.08 30d/d (12)
1775	182.05 30d/d (12)
1776	186.60 30d/d (12)
1777	187.35 30d/d (12)
1778	188.83 30d/d (12)
1779	187.38 30d/d (10)
1780	187.65 30d/d (11)
1781	188.73 30d/d (12)
1782	188.02 30d/d (10)
1783	190.57 90d/d (10)
1784	
1785	190.52 90d/d (12)
1786	190.63 90d/d (12)
1787	188.91 90d/d (12)
1788	189.68 90d/d (12)
1789	194.43 90d/d (10)
1790	205.19 90d/d (12)
1791	226.63 90d/d (12)
1792	312.34 30d/d (12)
1793	408.17 30d/d (6)
1794	11.156.37 30d/d (11)

	Hamburg	Augsburg	Frankfurt	Berlin
	PARIS on:			
	per 100 mark banco [a]	per 100 guilders Augsburg current [b]	per 100 francs payable in carolins [c]	per 100 thaler Prussian current [d]
	in francs			
1795	182.65 30d/d (6)			
1796	193.25 30d/d (3)			
1797	190.63 30d/d (12)			
1798	190.88 30d/d (7)			
1799	191.33 30d/d (10)			
1800	189.53 30d/d (10)			
1801	190.75 30d/d (7)	249.00 30d/d (3)		
1802	189.57 30d/d (12)	254.50 30d/d (8)		
1803	190.04 30d/d (11)	255.00 30d/d (11)		
1804	188.75 30d/d (11)	254.70 30d/d (10)		
1805	193.70 30d/d (12)	260.42 30d/d (12)	99.50 30d/d (3)	
1806	187.68 30d/d (12)	255.20 30d/d (10)	99.67 30d/d (1)	
1807	186.58 30d/d (12)	251.59 30d/d (11)		
1808	179.57 30d/d (12)	251.00 30d/d (5)		
1809	180.90 30d/d (12)	254.50 30d/d (12)	99.02 30d/d (9)	
1810	182.02 30d/d (12)	249.75 30d/d (12)	97.57 30d/d (12)	
1811	182.53 30d/d (11)	244.90 30d/d (10)	95.05 30d/d (10)	
1812	181.34 30d/d (6)	256.00 30d/d (6)	98.88 30d/d (6)	
1813	184.42 30d/d (12)	256.00 30d/d (12)	98.84 30d/d (12)	
1814	186.45 30d/d (10)	257.75 30d/d (12)	99.17 30d/d (9)	
1815	184.04 30d/d (7)	254.75 30d/d (5)	98.65 30d/d (7)	379.00 30d/d (1)
1816	188.91 30d/d (12)			376.67 30d/d (12)
1817	187.85 30d/d (12)	254.46 30d/d (6)	98.31 30d/d (12)	366.59 30d/d (12)
1818	189.77 30d/d (12)	257.82 30d/d (12)	99.24 30d/d (9)	378.34 30d/d (12)
1819	188.05 30d/d (9)	258.75 30d/d (9)	99.62 30d/d (9)	378.78 30d/d (9)
1820	185.14 30d/d (11)	252.67 30d/d (11)	97.56 30d/d (11)	359.55 30d/d (11)
1821	181.46 30d/d (12)	251.00 30d/d (12)	96.63 30d/d (12)	358.17 30d/d (12)
1822	182.43 30d/d (12)	249.84 30d/d (12)	96.28 30d/d (12)	354.17 30d/d (12)
1823	182.82 30d/d (12)	248.00 30d/d (12)	95.96 30d/d (12)	353.63 30d/d (12)
1824	183.19 30d/d (12)	250.55 30d/d (12)	96.65 30d/d (12)	355.63 30d/d (12)
1825	183.82 30d/d (12)	253.90 30d/d (12)	98.15 30d/d (12)	362.34 30d/d (12)
1826	183.94 30d/d (11)	251.09 30d/d (11)	97.32 30d/d (11)	359.09 30d/d (11)
1827	184.28 30d/d (10)	252.20 30d/d (10)	97.55 30d/d (10)	360.40 30d/d (10)
1828	185.04 30d/d (12)	254.52 30d/d (12)	98.41 30d/d (12)	364.34 30d/d (12)
1829	186.02 30d/d (12)	255.00 30d/d (12)	98.84 30d/d (12)	367.84 30d/d (12)
1830	184.42 30d/d (12)	252.55 30d/d (12)	97.90 30d/d (12)	362.42 30d/d (12)
1831	184.95 30d/d (11)	253.59 30d/d (11)	98.41 30d/d (11)	370.00 30d/d (11)
1832	186.24 30d/d (9)	253.73 30d/d (9)	97.93 30d/d (7)	365.30 30d/d (10)

	PARIS on:			
	Hamburg	**Augsburg**	**Frankfurt**	**Berlin**
	per 100 mark banco [a]	per 100 guilders Augsburg current, from 1859 per 100 guilders South German current [b]	per 100 francs payable in carolins, from 1840 (4) per 100 guilders South German current [c]	per 100 thaler Prussian current [d]
	in francs			
1833	186.88 30d/d (7)	255.13 30d/d (7)	98.77 30d/d (7)	370.00 30d/d (7)
1834	186.45 30d/d (10)	254.80 30d/d (10)	98.23 30d/d (10)	367.80 30d/d (10)
1835	186.27 30d/d (12)	254.59 30d/d (12)	98.47 30d/d (12)	367.59 30d/d (12)
1836	185.79 30d/d (12)	252.90 30d/d (12)	97.88 30d/d (12)	366.00 30d/d (12)
1837	185.80 30d/d (11)	252.34 30d/d (11)	97.96 30d/d (11)	367.46 30d/d (11)
1838	186.32 30d/d (11)	252.89 30d/d (11)	97.92 30d/d (11)	367.78 30d/d (11)
1839	186.68 30d/d (12)	254.08 30d/d (12)	98.36 30d/d (12)	369.88 30d/d (12)
1840	187.35 30d/d (12)	254.65 30d/d (12)	98.81/213.31 30d/d (3+9)	372.05 30d/d (12)
1841	187.86 30d/d (11)	256.77 30d/d (11)	214.15 30d/d (11)	376.37 30d/d (11)
1842	187.18 30d/d (12)	257.05 30d/d (12)	213.40 30d/d (12)	374.75 30d/d (12)
1843	186.68 30d/d (9)	256.38 30d/d (2)	213.13 30d/d (2)	373.88 30d/d (2)
1844	186.85 30d/d (9)	256.48 30d/d (11)	213.67 30d/d (12)	376.51 30d/d (12)
1845	186.50 30d/d (11)		213.31 30d/d (12)	375.38 30d/d (12)
1846	186.67 30d/d (9)	256.41 30d/d (10)	213.36 30d/d (12)	376.50 30d/d (12)
1847	186.91 30d/d (11)	255.36 30d/d (12)	212.40 30d/d (12)	375.09 30d/d (12)
1848	184.96 30d/d (11)	252.78 30d/d (10)	211.24 30d/d (12)	368.73 30d/d (12)
1849	184.44 30d/d (12)	252.33 30d/d (9)	210.08 30d/d (12)	369.96 30d/d (12)
1850	185.88 30d/d (12)	254.00 30d/d (12)	211.46 30d/d (12)	372.86 30d/d (12)
1851	186.88 30d/d (11)	254.39 30d/d (9)	212.00 30d/d (12)	374.39 30d/d (12)
1852	187.56 30d/d (12)	253.23 30d/d (12)	211.12 30d/d (6)	371.67 30d/d (3)
1853	188.07 30d/d (12)	254.45 30d/d (1)	211.07 30d/d (11)	369.67 30d/d (6)
1854	188.89 30d/d (12)	255.00 30d/d (2)	212.80 30d/d (12)	377.88 30d/d (2)
1855	188.45 30d/d (12)	255.75 30d/d (2)	213.73 30d/d (12)	379.03 30d/d (9)
1856	189.06 30d/d (11)	254.50 30d/d (9)	212.82 30d/d (10)	370.32 30d/d (8)
1857	189.33 30d/d (10)	256.50 30d/d (5)	213.62 30d/d (11)	374.73 30d/d (11)
1858	187.88 30d/d (8)	252.88 90d/d (8)	213.25 30d/d (6)	374.53 30d/d (4)
1859	189.02 30d/d (12)	215.96 30d/d (8)	214.89 30d/d (12)	376.84 30d/d (12)
1860	189.19 30d/d (10)	215.34 30d/d (10)	215.18 30d/d (10)	374.83 90d/d (10)
1861	188.40 30d/d (12)	215.25 30d/d (3)	214.71 30d/d (6)	372.73 90d/d (11)
1862	188.42 30d/d (11)	212.25 90d/d (4)	213.66 30d/d (8)	370.46 90d/d (12)
1863	188.79 30d/d (12)		211.98 90d/d (12)	370.09 90d/d (12)
1864	188.90 30d/d (12)		213.14 30d/d (12)	371.25 30d/d (7)
1865	187.97 30d/d (12)		211.16 30d/d (12)	369.42 30d/d (12)
1866	188.12 30d/d (12)		212.38 30d/d (11)	370.79 30d/d (11)
1867	108.18 3m/d (12)		209.22 30d/d (12)	365.85 30d/d (12)
1868	184.34 3m/d (12)		208.62 3m/d (12)	364.46 30d/d (12)

	PARIS on:		
	Hamburg	**Frankfurt**	**Berlin**
	per 100 mark banco, from 1873 (3) per 100 mark [a]	per 100 guilders South German current, from 1875 per 100 mark [c]	per 100 thaler Prussian current, from 1875 per 100 mark [d]
	in francs		
1869	183.91 3m/d (12)	208.30 3m/d (12)	364.31 3m/d (12)
1870	184.76 3m/d (9)	209.56 3m/d (9)	365.81 3m/d (9)
1871	187.69 3m/d (7)	213.92 3m/d (7)	375.40 3m/d (7)
1872	186.63 3m/d (12)	213.03 3m/d (12)	373.18 3m/d (12)
1873	185.58/124.16 3m/d (2+10)	212.79 3m/d (12)	373.00 3m/d (12)
1874	122.25 3m/d (12)	209.68 3m/d (12)	366.87 3m/d (12)
1875	121.56 3m/d (12)	121.56 3m/d (12)	121.57 3m/d (12)
1876	121.86 3m/d (3)	121.86 3m/d (3)	121.54 3m/d (3)

[a]   Concerning the Hamburg currency and the German mark Reichswährung, see pp. 191–193, 197.

[b]   'Augsburg current' meant – in modification of Konventionskurant, which became common especially from 1764 (NOBACK [1851], 1. Abth., p. 70) – a standard of coinage of 20 5/12 guilders per mark of Cologne. So the guilder Augsburg current of 60 kreuzer was equal to 11.45 grammes of pure silver. As a consequence of the Vienna Coin Treaty of 1857, the guilder South German current (standard of coinage: 24½ guilders per 233.855 grammes of pure silver or 52½ guilders per pound of 500 grammes of pure silver) of 60 kreuzer became legal tender in Augsburg from the beginning of 1859.

[c]   Concerning the Frankfurt currency and the German mark Reichswährung, see pp. 195, 197. 1 carolin or new louis d'or = 24 livres tournois = 9 1/5 guilders Frankfurt exchange money = 11 guilders at the standard of coinage of 24 guilders per mark of Cologne, whereby 81 livres = 80 francs; therefore 297 guilders (in the standard of coinage of 24 guilders per mark of Cologne) = 640 francs (cf. NELKENBRECHER [1832], p. 180).

[d]   Concerning the Prussian currency and the German mark Reichswährung, see pp. 196f.

	PARIS on:		
	Germany [a]		
	per 100 mark [b]		
	in francs		
1877	121.72	3m/d	(12)
1878	121.91	3m/d	(11)
1879	122.37	3m/d	(12)
1880	122.45	3m/d	(12)
1881	122.22	3m/d	(12)
1882	122.04	3m/d	(12)
1883	122.25	3m/d	(12)
1884	122.12	3m/d	(12)
1885	122.50	3m/d	(12)
1886	122.48	3m/d	(12)
1887	122.98	3m/d	(12)
1888	122.83	3m/d	(12)
1889	122.24	3m/d	(12)
1890	122.43	3m/d	(12)
1891	122.72	3m/d	(12)
1892	122.21	3m/d	(12)
1893	122.19	3m/d	(12)
1894	122.04	3m/d	(12)
1895	122.22	3m/d	(12)

	PARIS on:		
	Germany [a]		
	per 100 mark [b]		
	in francs		
1896	122.11	p.c.	(12)
1897	122.16	p.c.	(12)
1898	122.41	p.c.	(12)
1899	122.13	p.c.	(12)
1900	121.63	p.c.	(12)
1901	121.94	p.c.	(12)
1902	121.71	p.c.	(12)
1903	121.87	p.c.	(12)
1904	121.94	p.c.	(12)
1905	121.75	p.c.	(12)
1906	121.64	p.c.	(12)
1907	122.46	p.c.	(12)
1908	123.12	p.c.	(12)
1909	123.12	p.c.	(12)
1910	123.25	p.c.	(12)
1911	123.41	p.c.	(12)
1912	123.21	p.c.	(12)
1913	123.35	p.c.	(12)
1914	123.00	p.c.	(7)

[a]   Common quotation on Hamburg, Frankfurt and Berlin.

[b]   Concerning the German currency, see p. 197.

6.1.5 On Saint Petersburg, Scandinavian places and New York

	PARIS on:
	Saint Petersburg
	per 100 banco roubles, from 1839 (9) per 100 silver roubles, from 1843 (11) payable in credit notes [a]
	in francs
1817	111.30 90d/d (10)
1818	115.48 90d/d (12)
1819	112.23 90d/d (9)
1820	105.69 90d/d (11)
1821	99.50 90d/d (12)
1822	99.46 90d/d (12)
1823	99.22 90d/d (12)
1824	97.71 90d/d (12)
1825	102.38 90d/d (12)
1826	99.30 90d/d (11)
1827	104.68 90d/d (10)
1828	106.80 90d/d (12)
1829	111.13 90d/d (12)
1830	110.96 90d/d (12)
1831	109.39 90d/d (11)
1832	109.95 90d/d (9)
1833	110.61 90d/d (7)
1834	109.08 90d/d (10)
1835	110.07 90d/d (12)
1836	109.64 90d/d (12)
1837	109.78 90d/d (11)
1838	111.55 90d/d (10)
1839	115.94/407.50 90d/d (8+4)
1840	402.52 90d/d (12)
1841	402.14 90d/d (11)
1842	396.02 90d/d (12)
1843	394.92 90d/d (6)
1844	398.00 90d/d (1)
1845	
1846	
1847	
1848	
1849	385.55 90d/d (12)
1850	395.67 90d/d (12)

	PARIS on:	
	Saint Petersburg	**New York**
	per 100 silver roubles payable in credit notes [a]	per 100 US dollars [b]
	in francs	
1851	387.75 90d/d (12)	
1852	394.67 90d/d (12)	
1853	402.50 30d/d (1)	
1854	384.95 30d/d (9)	
1855	371.84 30d/d (6)	
1856	391.63 30d/d (8)	
1857	393.45 30d/d (9)	
1858	367.50 30d/d (1)	
1859	348.00 30d/d (3)	
1860	374.00 30d/d (1)	
1861	359.92 30d/d (12)	
1862	354.67 30d/d (3)	
1863	388.21 30d/d (3)	
1864	338.48 30d/d (12)	
1865	325.34 30d/d (12)	
1866	311.23 30d/d (11)	
1867	333.75 3m/d (11)	
1868	338.21 3m/d (12)	
1869	318.27 3m/d (12)	
1870	302.62 3m/d (9)	
1871	333.68 3m/d (7)	467.50 3m/d (2)
1872	340.09 3m/d (12)	467.50 3m/d (12)
1873	336.00 3m/d (12)	467.50 3m/d (12)
1874	341.34 3m/d (12)	467.50 3m/d (12)
1875	339.50 3m/d (12)	460.21 3m/d (12)
1876	321.00 3m/d (11)	450.00 3m/d (10)
1877	277.41 3m/d (11)	510.75 3m/d (1)
1878	255.37 3m/d (11)	522.50 3m/d (2)
1879	250.98 3m/d (12)	522.50 3m/d (12)
1880	259.96 3m/d (12)	522.50 3m/d (2)
1881	260.48 3m/d (12)	
1882	250.65 3m/d (12)	516.50 3m/d (8)
1883	245.50 3m/d (12)	517.40 3m/d (12)
1884	249.17 3m/d (12)	516.71 3m/d, s (12)
1885	251.75 3m/d (12)	518.05 s (12)
1886	242.55 3m/d (12)	514.88 s (12)
1887	224.05 3m/d (12)	518.59 s (12)

	PARIS on:		
	Saint Petersburg	**Stockholm, from** 1910 **Scandinavian places**	**New York**
	per 100 silver roubles payable in credit notes, from 1899 per 100 gold roubles [a]	per 100 Swedish crowns, from 1910 per 100 Swedish, Danish or Norwegian crowns [c]	per 100 US dollars [b]
	in francs		
1888	231.32 3m/d (12)		518.75 s (12)
1889	260.21 3m/d (12)		516.46 s (12)
1890	285.13 3m/d (12)		516.88 s (12)
1891	275.38 3m/d (12)		517.13 s (12)
1892	248.21 3m/d (12)	138.50 3m/d (11)	515.80 s (12)
1893	256.71 3m/d (12)	138.50 3m/d (12)	515.67 s (12)
1894	267.30 3m/d (12)	138.50 3m/d (12)	515.48 s (12)
1895	267.25 3m/d (12)	138.50 3m/d (12)	514.36 s (12)
1896	264.30 ss (12)	138.50 ss (12)	514.84 ss (12)
1897	264.47 ss (12)	138.19 ss (12)	515.88 ss (12)
1898	266.19 ss (12)	138.13 ss (12)	519.92 ss (12)
1899	266.81 ss (12)	138.00 ss (12)	517.58 ss (12)
1900	265.57 ss (12)		516.02 ss (12)
1901	266.04 ss (12)		515.09 ss (11)
1902	265.79 ss (12)		514.71 ss (12)
1903	265.92 ss (12)		516.25 ss (12)
1904	266.11 ss (12)		516.13 ss (12)
1905	265.32 ss (12)		516.30 ss (12)
1906	263.58 ss (12)		517.57 ss (12)
1907	264.49 ss (12)		517.98 ss (12)
1908	264.35 ss (12)		517.28 ss (12)
1909	266.64 ss (12)		517.46 ss (12)
1910	266.88 ss (12)	139.07 ss (4)	517.63 ss (12)
1911	267.05 ss (12)	139.23 ss (12)	518.66 ss (12)
1912	266.25 ss (12)	138.50 ss (10)	517.76 ss (12)
1913	265.86 ss (12)		518.05 ss (12)
1914	264.54 ss (7)		516.54 ss (7)

[a] Concerning the Russian currency, see pp. 359f.

[b] Concerning the US currency, see p. 404. 1871–1876 quotation for 100 US dollars in notes (the so-called 'greenbacks').

[c] According to the treaty of the Scandinavian Monetary Union (see pp. 328, 340), from 1877 the currency of Norway was the crown (0.4032 grammes of pure gold) of 100 öre, which was exactly equal to the Swedish and Danish crowns (cf. SWOBODA [1902], p. 238).

7

Spain (1820–1914)

Exchange market: Madrid (1820–1914)

Sources: *Gaceta de Madrid* (1820–1837); Banco de España, Biblioteca, and Hemeroteca Municipal, both Madrid, *Cotización de la Bolsa de Madrid / Cotización oficial del Colegio de agentes de cambios, Bolsa de Madrid* (1837–1885); ibid., *Bolitín de Cotización oficial* (1886–1914).
Concordance: *WdW I/II*, pp. 383-421

Currency: In the first half of the 19th century the legal basis of the Spanish currency system was the law of May 29th 1772 which fixed the peso duro at 24.43 grammes of fine silver. 64 pesos duros came to 85 pesos de plata antigua or pesos de cambio of 8 reales de plata antigua or 272 maravédis, whereas 4 pesos de plata antigua came to 1 doblón de plata antigua or doblón de cambio. Until the middle of the 19th century peso and doblón de plata antigua were used as the basis for the fixing of the exchange rates on and from Spanish exchange places. Beyond that the ducado de cambio of 375 maravédis was a further Spanish imaginary unit of account in cashless payment up to the mid-19th century. The monetary history of Spain in the 19th century was essentially determined by the French monetary policy, because after the French occupation of Spain in the Napoleonic era a compulsory rate was imposed on the French and silver money circulating in Spain (especially the 5 francs piece, in Spain called 'napoleon'), whereas Spanish silver coins went out of the country. Due to the lack of Spanish coins Portuguese and British coins were declared obligatory on November 11th 1835, especially since no more silver coins were brought into Spain from the former overseas possessions in Latin America after their independence. Up to 1841 even the small silver coins disappeared from circulation. So, a currency reform became unalterably necessary. In the wake of the currency reform in 1847/48 (Royal Decree of February 18th 1847) the peso duro of 20 reales de vellon became the national unit of account, in which all quotations had to be done. At first, this peso duro corresponded to 23.66 grammes of fine silver (Currency Law of April 15th 1848), from 1850 to 23.49 grammes of fine silver (Currency Law of 1850) and from 1854 it corresponded to 23.36 grammes of fine silver (Currency Law of February 3rd 1854). But this peso duro was only a unit of exchange, whereas all payments had to be done in napoleons (5 francs pieces) due to the lack of silver pesos. On April 15th 1848 the real (of 1.17 grammes of fine silver) was established as the new unit of silver money, whereby 1 doblón was equal to 10 escudos or 100 reales and the new real was declared equal to the former real de vellon, although they had different fine weights. But the most important coin in the Spanish circulation remained the napoleon, and there was no remarkable change in the exchange rate quotations. As a result, Spain had a bimetallistic standard with the doblón as the only minted gold coin, which was suspended between 1851 and 1854 because of the decreasing gold price after the gold rushes in California and Australia. After 1854 a creeping transition to the gold standard began, since no more silver coins were minted, but instead of them small gold coins (since 1861). A new currency reform was initiated by the coin act of June 26th 1864 with the escudo (of 11.68 grammes of fine silver) of 100 centimos as the new unit of account, whereby the doblón was equal to 10 escudos and the peso to 2 escudos. But only the state reckoned in escudos, the merchants in reales. After the September revolution in 1868 the Spanish currency was reorganized in accordance with the official requirements of the Latin Monetary Union of December 23rd 1865 without formally entering into that union. By decree of October 19th 1868 the peseta was treated as an equivalent to 4 reales de vellon or 1 franc and was officially introduced as currency unit in the beginning of the year 1871 following the model of the French franc (see pp. 279f.). Furthermore, the peso duro was minted at 22.50 grammes of fine silver having the value of the French 5 francs piece. By decree of March 23rd 1869 the previous peso duro came to 5.19 pesetas, whereas the new one was fixed at 5 pesetas with a corresponding devaluation of 3.84%. On August 20th 1876 a government decree ordered the transition to the gold standard and the minting of a new gold coin, the alfonso d'or, of 25 pesetas. In the following years partially gold coins, partially silver coins dominated the Spanish circulation. Since 1883 silver coins and notes of the Banco de España became definitely the most important means of payment in the Spanish circulation and remained so up to World War I. Like the escudo, currency of the time from 1864 to 1870, did not play any part in the exchange rate quotations, the peseta (0.2903 grammes of fine gold) of 100 centimos was of no importance for the cashless payment system. The peseta did not become the basis of the exchange rate quotations until the end of the year 1887 even though not all foreign financial markets which quoted Spanish places followed that reform but carried on quoting for pesos duros.

Original quotations at Madrid:

on:	in:	per:
London	pence sterling	1 peso de plata antigua (peso de cambio)
from 1847 (4)	pesos duros	1 pound sterling
from 1887	pesetas	1 pound sterling
Paris	francs	1 doblón de cambio or 4 pesos de plata antigua
from 1847 (4)	francs	1 peso duro
from 1887	pesetas	100 francs

Other data available: Barcelona, 8d/s (1820–1902) – Bilbao, 8d/s (1821–1902) – Cadiz, 8d/s (1821–1902) – Granada, 8d/s (1821–1902) – Malaga, 8d/s (1821–1902) – San Sebastian, 8d/s (1855–1902) – Santander, 8d/s (1821–1823, 1829–1902) – Seville, 8d/s (1821–1902) – Valencia, 8d/s (1820–1850, 1858–1902) – Saragossa, 8d/s (1821–1902).

Spanish exchange markets were integrated into the international system of cashless payment partly since the end of the Middle Ages, partly since the 16th century. Due to a lack of sources longer exchange rate series can only be presented from the 19th century onwards, with the exceptions of the fairs of Medina del Campo, of which data are available for the time from 1578 to 1605 (cf. WdW IX, pp. 58–67), or of Seville with its quotations on the Bisenzone fairs from 1589 to 1613 (MARTINEZ RUIZ [2002], pp. 130–132). Single exchange rate currents are not sufficiently complete to document longer data series, for instance those from Cadiz in the 18th century with quotations on Paris, Amsterdam, London, Madrid and partly on Genoa and Leghorn in the 1740s and 1750s (e.g. A.C.C.M., L. IX 1034, Cours des Changes).

Taking a look at the sources concerning the financial place of Madrid, the most important exchange market of Spain in the 19th century (cf. NOBACK [1877], p. 569), which are available from 1820 onwards, one will recognize that among foreign places only London and Paris are quoted. One exception is the *Gaceta de Madrid* of the year 1820, listing also quotations on Amsterdam and Hamburg for some months. In addition to this, Bordeaux, Marseilles, Bayonne, Hamburg, Genoa and Lisbon are listed in different combinations on the official current lists of the Madrid stock exchange, though always without quotations. Contemporary merchant manuals refer to the fact that quotations on these and other places (e.g. on Rome, Naples or Leghorn) were only made from time to time and only in private exchange rate currents (NOBACK [1858], p. 602; NOBACK [1877], p. 569). Around the turn of the 20th century, Lyons,

Le Havre, Brussels, Milan, Berne, Geneva, Liverpool, Berlin, Stockholm, Bergen, Ålesund and Christiansand were listed in general without quotations in addition to the places mentioned above. Only in very few cases quotations on Lisbon or Berlin can be found. Apart from its foreign exchanges during the whole 19th century Madrid quoted numerous Spanish exchange places ('plazas de la Península') from important Atlantic and Mediterranean ports like Cadiz, Barcelona, Bilbao, Seville and Valencia to smaller provincial towns with only local importance. When from 1902 onwards these data were not given any longer, 62 places were put on the list, each place with quotations with a rate up to ½% premium or discount. Finally, even a table for the three places of the remaining Spanish colonial empire ('plazas ultramar'), that is Havana, Puerto Rico and Manila, was set up in the last decades of the 19th century, although quotations were not given for those places either.

Only two foreign quotations seemed to be enough for the official exchange market of Madrid because foreign payment transfers within Europe (except those to London) and to overseas were regularly effected via Paris at the latest since 1850, so that Paris became the most important foreign financial market for Spain. Last but not least, this was the result of the Spanish monetary dependency on France since the Napoleonic occupation. This monetary dependency again resulted from the silver inflow from France, which was necessary for the Spanish economy since the independence of the Latin American continental colonies, the French involvement in Spanish loans and bonds, the French credits for the building of the railroad system and the late industrialization in comparison with other European countries. However, London did not gain the same importance as exchange partner of Madrid as Paris, because in Spain bills of exchange on London were generally less useful than bills of exchange on Paris. This was caused by two facts: firstly, there were fewer British capital investments in Spain and, secondly, payment balancing on the basis of precious metals was rather limited, because Spain had been a country of silver currency for large parts of the 19th century (officially up to 1868, from 1873 to 1876 and since 1882/83 again). Having a negative balance of trade and payments in Spain, the exchange rates could be regulated by remittances of silver coins and so it was done with France, but not with Great Britain, because the balance had the advantage of no greater long-term deviations from the parity. Those deviations started vehemently during the external and internal crisis of the Spanish state in the 1890s reaching their climax during the Spanish American War after the sea battle of Manila in May 1898 and not softening noticeably until 1906. As the relevant listings in the *Bolitín de Cotización oficial* have proven for the time from 1902 onwards, the turnover of bills of exchange on Paris and London was quite low at the stock market of Madrid until 1914, because most part of the transactions were not effected there, but in the banks (SWOBODA [1913], p. 627).

References: Fritz RÜHE, *Das Geldwesen Spaniens seit dem Jahre 1772*, Straßburg 1912; José Maria TALLADA, El problema monetaria español en el siglo XIX, *Moneda y Credito* 58 (1956), pp. 53–64; Octavio GIL FARRÉS, *Historia de la moneda española*, Madrid 1959; Markus A. DENZEL, Spanische Währungsreformen und Wechselkurse im 19. Jahrhundert, in *WdW I/I*, pp. 47–71; Antonio M. BERNAL (ed.), *Dinero, moneda y crédito en la Monarquía Hispánica*, Madrid 2000; José Ignacio MARTÍNEZ RUIZ, Mercato creditizio e profitti del cambio per lettera. Le operazioni di cambio con patto di ricorsa tra Siviglia e le fiere internazionali di 'Bisenzone' (1589–1621), *Storia economica. Rivista quadrimestrale diretta da Luigi de Rosa* 5/1 (2002), pp. 107–132.

7.1 Madrid exchange rates

7.1.1 On London and Paris

	MADRID on:		
	London		**Paris**
	per 10 pounds sterling [a]		per 100 francs [b]
	in pesos de plata antigua		
1820	65.19 90d/s	(4)	25.51 8d/s (4)
1821	64.37 90d/s	(9)	24.88 8d/s (9)
1822	63.28 90d/s	(10)	24.76 8d/s (10)
1823	62.54 90d/s	(2)	24.73 8d/s (2)
1824	64.22 90d/s	(4)	25.30 8d/s (4)
1825	63.84 90d/s	(11)	25.31 8d/s (11)
1826	66.89 90d/s	(12)	25.82 8d/s (12)
1827	68.04 90d/s	(12)	26.48 8d/s (12)
1828	64.93 90d/s	(10)	25.73 8d/s (10)
1829	63.93 90d/s	(12)	24.87 8d/s (12)
1830	64.99 90d/s	(12)	25.16 8d/s (12)
1831	63.05 90d/s	(12)	24.98 8d/s (12)
1832	65.30 90d/s	(12)	25.21 8d/s (12)
1833	62.93 90d/s	(12)	25.26 8d/s (12)
1834	63.35 90d/s	(12)	24.85 8d/s (12)
1835	63.74 90d/s	(12)	24.53 8d/s (12)
1836	63.64 90d/s	(12)	24.86 8d/s (12)
1837	67.47 90d/s	(12)	26.22 8d/s (12)
1838	64.45 90d/s	(12)	25.09 8d/s (12)
1839	62.63 90d/s	(12)	24.60 8d/s (12)
1840	63.22 90d/s	(12)	25.84 8d/s (12)
1841	64.54 90d/s	(11)	25.14 8d/s (11)
1842	63.81 90d/s	(12)	24.69 8d/s (12)
1843	63.54 90d/s	(12)	24.44 8d/s (12)
1844	63.65 90d/s	(12)	24.48 8d/s (12)
1845	64.02 90d/s	(12)	24.61 8d/s (12)
1846	65.11 90d/s	(12)	24.99 8d/s (12)
1847	64.44 90d/s	(3)	25.20 8d/s (3)
	in pesos duros		
1847	48.86 90d/s	(9)	19.24 8d/s (9)
1848	52.44 90d/s	(12)	20.56 8d/s (12)
1849	47.87 90d/s	(12)	18.97 8d/s (12)
1850	47.69 90d/s	(12)	18.86 8d/s (12)
1851	47.21 90d/s	(12)	18.98 8d/s (12)

	MADRID on:		
	London		**Paris** [c]
	per 10 pounds sterling [a]		per 100 francs [b]
	in pesos duros		
1852	47.45	90d/s	(12)	18.83	8d/s	(12)
1853	46.94	90d/s	(12)	18.92	8d/s	(12)
1854	46.76	90d/s	(12)	18.96	8d/s	(12)
1855	46.99	90d/s	(12)	18.93	8d/s	(12)
1856	47.26	90d/s	(12)	18.91	8d/s	(12)
1857	47.62	90d/s	(12)	19.13	8d/s	(12)
1858	47.89	90d/s	(12)	19.23	8d/s	(12)
1859	47.49	90d/s	(12)	19.03	8d/s	(12)
1860	47.48	90d/s	(12)	19.06	8d/s	(12)
1861	48.13	90d/s	(12)	19.21	8d/s	(12)
1862	47.93	90d/s	(12)	19.10	8d/s	(12)
1863	47.92	90d/s	(12)	19.17	8d/s	(12)
1864	48.30	90d/s	(12)	*19.47*	8d/s	(12)
1865	49.11	90d/s	(12)	*19.73*	8d/s	(12)
1866	49.59	90d/s	(12)	*20.04*	8d/s	(12)
1867	48.28	90d/s	(12)	19.36	8d/s	(12)
1868	48.76	90d/s	(12)	19.48	8d/s	(12)
1869	48.38	90d/s	(12)	19.37	8d/s	(12)
1870	48.12	90d/s	(12)	19.31	8d/s	(9)
1871						
1872						
1873	48.99	90d/s	(12)	19.50	8d/s	(12)
1874	48.66	90d/s	(12)	19.48	8d/s	(12)
1875	49.51	90d/s	(12)	19.80	8d/s	(11)
1876	49.66	90d/s	(12)	19.83	8d/s	(12)
1877						
1878						
1879	50.42	90d/s	(12)	20.09	8d/s	(12)
1880	49.68	90d/s	(12)	19.80	8d/s	(12)
1881	49.85	90d/s	(12)	19.91	8d/s	(12)
1882	50.82	90d/s	(12)	20.37	8d/s	(12)
1883	50.80	90d/s	(12)	20.33	8d/s	(12)
1884	50.59	90d/s	(12)	20.25	8d/s	(12)
1885	51.27	90d/s	(12)	20.41	8d/s	(12)
1886	51.46	90d/s	(12)	20.44	8d/s	(12)
1887	51.01	90d/s	(11)	20.21	8d/s	(9)
	in pesetas		
1887	254.10	s	(1)	100.83	s	(2)

	MADRID on:				
	London [d]		**Paris** [d]		
	per 10 pounds sterling [a]		per 100 francs [b]		
	in pesetas				
1888	256.02	s	(12)	101.62	s	(11)
1889	259.57	s	(12)	103.10	s	(12)
1890	261.59	s	(12)			
1891	265.62	s	(12)	105.99	s	(12)
1893	298.65	s	(12)	118.48	s	(11)
1894	302.80	s	(12)	120.66	s	(11)
1895	288.62	s	(12)	114.65	s	(12)
1896	303.83	s	(12)	120.66	s	(11)
1897	326.04	s	(12)	129.45	s	(12)
1898	395.08	s	(12)	152.42	s	(11)
1899	314.80	s	(12)	124.40	s	(12)
1900	325.51	s	(12)	129.55	s	(10)
1901	347.93	s	(12)	138.62	s	(11)
1902	340.08	s	(12)	135.75	s	(12)
1903	340.08	s	(12)	134.99	s	(9)
1904	347.03	s	(12)	137.77	s	(12)
1905	330.00	s	(12)	131.02	s	(11)
1906	287.00	s	(12)	114.41	s	(11)
1907	280.51	s	(12)	111.37	s	(12)
1908	283.85	s	(12)	112.98	s	(12)
1909	277.58	s	(12)	110.28	s	(12)
1910	270.44	s	(12)	107.16	s	(12)
1911	274.08	s	(12)	108.33	s	(11)
1912	269.14	s	(12)	106.66	s	(12)
1913	270.78	s	(12)	107.60	s	(12)
1914	265.94	s	(7)	105.70	s	(7)

[a] Concerning the British currency, see pp. 3–5.

[b] Concerning the French currency, see pp. 279f.

[c] The rates hardly dropped during the banking crisis between 1864 and 1866 because there was an extensive capital transfer from France to Spain, above all for the building of the railways. In fact, Spain was very much in debt to France.

[d] From 1903 to 1914 the *cambio medio* is given, which was the average daily rate listed in the sources and which resulted from the various daily turnovers on Paris or London.

8
Switzerland (1842–1914)

Exchange market: Zurich (1842–1914)

Source: *Neue Zürcher Zeitung* (1842–1914)
Concordance: *WdW I/III*, pp. 229–300

Currency: Up to the foundation of the Schweizerische Eidgenossenschaft/Confédération Suisse in 1848, control of currencies was in the hands of the single Swiss cantons. Therefore there was a great variety of currencies and coins for centuries (cf. KÖRNER / FURRER / BARTLOME [2001]), and some attempts at reform, which began in the Helvetic Republic (1798–1803), brought no practical results. So, up to 1852 the Zurich exchange rate quotations were given in guilders Zurich exchange money (of 10.51 grammes of fine silver; the so-called 'Zürchergulden') of 16 Zürcher batzen or 60 kreuzer, whereby in the first half of the 19th century 34 Zürcher batzen were equal to 5 French francs. The guilder Zurich exchange money was equal to 1/10 new louis d'or corresponded to 1 guilder at the standard of coinage of 22½ guilders per mark of Cologne.

After the foundation of the Schweizerische Eidgenossenschaft/Confédération Suisse, the Swiss franken/franc at 100 rappen or centimes was introduced by the Bundesgesetz über das eidgenössische Münzwesen of May 7th 1850. The new franken followed the French model, i.e. the French franc, because of the Swiss commercial interests that were focused on France at this time. The Swiss franken corresponded exactly to the French franc, with 4.50 grammes of fine silver. The currency reform was completed at the end of 1852, so that the manner of quoting in Zurich changed to the new Swiss standard currency from April 1852. Since the introduction of the franken/franc currency in Switzerland, the country was more or less dependent on the French mint and currency policy up to World War I. In the 1850s the Swiss means of payment in circulation – above all foreign coins – changed: more and more gold coins came into Switzerland, whereas silver money disappeared. French gold coins in particular functioned as a kind of 'bank money' for the exchange business. From 1860 the gold coins of France and Piedmont–Sardinia were accepted as legal tender. On December 23rd 1865 Switzerland became one of the founder members of the Latin Monetary Union (see pp. 279f.), and from then on the Swiss franken corresponded not only to the French franc in silver, but also to the gold franc of 0.2903 grammes of fine gold.

Original quotations at Zurich up to 1852 (3)

on:	in:	per:
Amsterdam	kreuzer Zurich exchange money	1 Dutch guilder
Augsburg	guilders Zurich exchange money	100 guilders Augsburg current
Frankfurt	guilders Zurich exchange money	110 guilders South German current
Genoa	guilders Zurich exchange money	240 Piedmontese lire nuove
Hamburg	guilders Zurich exchange money	300 mark banco
Leghorn	guilders Zurich exchange money	300 Tuscan lire moneta buona
London	guilders and kreuzer Zurich exchange money	1 pound sterling
Milan	guilders Zurich exchange money	300 lire austriache
Paris	guilders Zurich exchange money	240 francs

on:	in:	per:
Vienna	guilders Zurich exchange money	100 guilders Konventionskurant

From April 1852 all rates are quoted in franken per 1 (on London) or 100 units of foreign currency.

Other data available: Amsterdam, 3m/d (1842–1914); 60d/d (1886–1888, 1914) – Antwerp, 3m/d (1859–1872) – Augsburg, 3m/d (1842–1872) – Basle, 3m/d (1859–1871); ss (1842–1871) – Belgian bank places, 3m/d (1878–1914); 60d/d (1886–1888, 1914) – Berlin, 3m/d (1859–1872) – Bremen, ss (1864–1876); 5d/d (1871/82) – Brussels, 3m/d (1864–1872) – Frankfurt am Main, 3m/d (1842–1872) – Geneva, 3m/d (1859–1872); ss (1859–1872) – Genoa, ss (1871/72) – German bank places, 3m/d (1878–1914); 60d/d (1886–1888, 1914) – Hamburg, 3m/d (1842–1872) – Leghorn and Florence, 3m/ d (1861–1864); ss (1865/66) – Leipzig, 3m/d (1859–1872); ss (1854–1876) – London, 3m/d (1842–1914); 60d/d (1886–1888, 1914); ss (1884–1914) – Lyons, 3m/d (1843–1911); 2m/d (1906); ss (1842–1911); ch (1884/85) – Milan, 3m/d (1842–1914) – New York, t.t. (1911–1914); bank gold (1902–1907) – Paris, 3m/d (1842–1914); 60d/d (1886–1888, 1914) – Saint Gall, 3m/d (1859–1871); ss (1852–1871) – Trieste, 3m/d (1859–1869); ss (1842–1869) – Turin, 3m/d (1859–1872); ss (1859–1872) – Vienna, 3m/d (1843–1914); 60d/d (1886–1888, 1914).

Similar to the Holy Roman Empire or Germany respectively, Switzerland had various exchange markets in early modern times, as well as in the the 19th century. Since the 18th century Zurich had been a Swiss exchange place of primarily local importance. In this respect it was only second to the financial markets of Basle and Geneva, which were of comparatively more importance for the European cashless payment system even though the Zurich exchange rate quotations extended as far as the centres of Northern Italy, Northwestern Europe, Southern Germany and Vienna, as well as the fairs of Frankfurt am Main, Lyons and Leipzig. Generally speaking, these results are also valid for the first half of the 19th century. Because the sources comprise all Zurich exchange rates from 1842 onwards, the exchange rate quotations for Zurich as one of the various Swiss exchange markets can be documented here. In addition to this, the exchange rate current of the Schweizerische Kreditanstalt, i.e. the earliest official list of exchange rate quotations available from Switzerland, was published independently in Zurich from 1867 (BERGIER [1990], p. 333).

First and foremost, private bankers were still dealing with regional and international exchange operations of Swiss foreign trade around 1850, as they had done for centuries, whereas the few cantonal state institutes and some local banks operated only on a comparatively small scale in exchange business (KÖRNER [1993], p. 279). It was not until the Confederation had been founded in 1848 and the coinage had been standardized that capital transfer among the different financial markets in Switzerland became possible and there was no longer any need to change the different cantonal currencies. Before this, the different financial markets of Switzerland had mostly effected their quotations in their respective cantonal currency or the so-called 'schweizerfranken' of 1819 (= 1.5 livres tournois). After the introduction of the Swiss franken in 1850, based on the model of the French franc and completed at the end of 1852, and as a result of the commercial relationships with France and overseas, which also had to be conducted via France and which became increasingly important for the Swiss economy, Switzerland took the appropriate step and oriented itself very strongly towards France and its monetary policy. This culminated in the Swiss membership of the Latin Monetary Union in 1865.

For the exchange transactions of the Swiss financial places this meant that the relationships with the West European partners then became more important than those
with the markets in the South German region. Around 1850 the Zurich quotations still
corroborated that Swiss towns maintained exchange transactions mainly with markets
in Western and Central Europe: apart from London and Amsterdam, German places
(Augsburg, Frankfurt, Hamburg), Vienna, French places (Paris, Lyons, Marseilles)
and Milan were quoted in particular. During the 1850s and 1860s, the orientation towards the North and the West was intensified. In 1854 the quotation on Leipzig was
set up, that on Brussels and Antwerp followed in 1859, and that on Bremen in 1864.
In comparison with Milan, the most important Zurich exchange partner in Italy, Genoa, Leghorn, Florence and Trieste remained rather second-rate, as is verified by the
usances quoted in Zurich from the mid-19th century on. While the French and German
places, Vienna, Amsterdam, London and Milan were generally quoted at short sight
(here: at sight) as well as at long sight (here: 3 months' dato), the other Italian partners
were quoted only for one usance (short sight; here: at sight).

From the mid-19th century Zurich began "its meteoric rise" (KINDLEBERGER
[1974], p. 38) to take the place of Basle and Geneva and become the most important
exchange place of Switzerland, though for the time being no other financial place in
Switzerland could claim the role as *primus inter pares*. This can be demonstrated
above all by those results showing that foreign exchange partners did not usually quote individual Swiss exchange markets but summarized 'Swiss bank places', which
included primarily Zurich, Basle and Geneva, but sometimes only two of them. This
was above all the consequence of the standardization of coins and currencies in
Switzerland since 1850, and of the resulting process of integration among the Swiss
exchange markets. Thus exchange rate fluctuations among the Swiss financial places
because of different cantonal currencies became unnecessary. Since the 1870s, exchange rates among the Swiss financial markets were no longer quoted on the exchange rate currents. So the quotations of Zurich on Saint Gall came to an end in 1871
and those on Geneva in 1872. The Zurich rates on Berne and Winterthur only were
quoted from 1869 to 1872, those on Lausanne only for some months in 1871/72.

After the standardization of coins and currencies of the Swiss cantons in 1850, the
exchange rates among the different Swiss financial places had come closer to parity,
so that the par of exchange was quoted almost exclusively in around 1870. Finally,
these consistent quotations of the par of exchange were no longer necessary; there
were no longer any differences between the quotations of the Swiss exchange places
and therefore exchange profits resulted only from the discount rate. Thus different
quotations at the different Swiss financial markets on foreign places became obsolete
as well, which is why one place after another now did without an independent quotation and oriented itself towards the quotation of some neighbouring financial market
playing a more important role in the international cashless payment system. So,
among the Swiss bank places Zurich and Basle became the most influential exchange
markets of the country, with Zurich playing a special role, because it was home to the
central headquarters of the administration and the directorate of the Schweizerische
Nationalbank (founded in 1905), with its legal and administrative seat in Berne (SWO-
BODA [1913], p. 589). Furthermore, Zurich had benefited from a peculiarity of the
Basle financial market, which did not give up the exchange stamp until 1899, repre-

senting a fiscal instrument at Basle that had been turning exchange business away from Basle to Zurich for many years (BAUER [1987], p. 164). Therefore the exchange market of Zurich can be regarded as the most important financial centre of Switzerland by the turn of the 20th century, especially when the importance of Geneva seems to have declined. So "Zurich emerged as the financial center at the end of the nineteenth century, despite the connections and traditions of Geneva and Basle and the fact that the government seat was at Bern after the confederation in 1848. Zurich's success can be ascribed to its focal location in the railroad age, especially after the building of the Gotthard tunnel, and to the pushiness of its bankers" (KINDLEBERGER [1974], p. 37).

References: Charles P. KINDLEBERGER, *The Formation of Financial Centers: A Study in Comparative Economic History*, Princeton (N.J.) 1974, pp. 37–39; Hans BAUER, Bank- und Finanzplatz Basel, in Louis H. MOTTET (ed.), *Geschichte der Schweizer Banken. Bankier-Persönlichkeiten aus fünf Jahrhunderten*, Zürich 1987, pp. 139–174; Jean-François BERGIER, *Wirtschaftsgeschichte der Schweiz. Von den Anfängen bis zur Gegenwart*, Zürich ²1990; Markus A. DENZEL, Vom 'Schweizerfranken' zum 'schweizer Franken' (1798–1860), in *WdW I/I*, pp. 72–81; Martin KÖRNER, Schweiz, in Hans POHL (ed.), *Europäische Bankengeschichte*, Frankfurt am Main 1993, pp. 279–285; Markus A. DENZEL, Die Integration der Schweizer Finanzplätze in das internationale Zahlungsverkehrssystem vom 17. Jahrhundert bis 1914, *Schweizerische Zeitschrift für Geschichte* 48 (1998), pp. 177–235; Martin KÖRNER / Norbert FURRER / Niklaus BARTLOME with contribution of Thomas MEIER / Erika FLÜCKIGER, *Währungen und Sortenkurse in der Schweiz / Systèmes monétaires et cours des espèces en Suisse / Sistemi monetari e corsi delle specie in Svizzera 1600–1799*, Lausanne 2001.

8.1 Zurich exchange rates

Usances: In Zurich, 'short sight' always means 'at sight'.

8.1.1 On London, Amsterdam, Paris and Belgium

	ZURICH on:			
	London	**Amsterdam**	**Paris**	**Brussels**
	per 10 pounds sterling [a]	per 100 Dutch guilders [b]	per 100 francs [c]	per 100 Belgian francs [d]
	in guilders Zurich exchange money			
1842	108.67 ss (1)	88.96 ss (1)	42.35 ss (1)	
1843	109.07 ss (10)	89.76 ss (10)	42.49 ss (10)	
1844	108.48 ss (12)	89.79 ss (12)	42.44 ss (12)	
1845	109.21 ss (12)	89.33 ss (12)	42.50 ss (12)	
1846	109.34 ss (12)	89.53 ss (12)	42.50 ss (12)	
1847	108.67 ss (12)	90.16 ss (12)	42.58 ss (12)	
1848	109.15 ss (11)	90.92 ss (12)	42.75 ss (12)	
1849	109.34 ss (11)	91.09 ss (11)	42.95 ss (11)	
1850	109.14 ss (12)	90.62 ss (12)	42.84 ss (12)	
1851	107.21 ss (12)	90.75 ss (12)	42.76 ss (12)	
1852	108.78 ss (3)	91.67 ss (3)	43.04 ss (3)	
	in franken			
1852	253.06 ss (9)	211.64 ss (9)	99.93 ss (9)	
1853	250.25 ss (10)	211.13 ss (10)	99.69 ss (10)	
1854	249.17 ss (12)	213.25 ss (12)	99.72 ss (12)	
1855	250.94 ss (12)	212.31 ss (12)	99.70 ss (12)	
1856	252.93 ss (10)	213.63 ss (10)	99.75 ss (11)	
1857	252.71 ss (12)	214.07 ss (11)	99.82 ss (12)	
1858	251.91 ss (11)	213.70 ss (12)	99.89 ss (12)	
1859	252.34 ss (12)	214.12 ss (12)	99.84 ss (12)	100.00 3m/d (1)
1860	251.28 ss (11)	214.39 ss (11)	100.00 ss (12)	100.13 3m/d (12)
1861	253.32 ss (12)	213.28 ss (10)	100.00 ss (12)	99.94 3m/d (12)
1862	252.43 ss (10)	214.05 ss (10)	100.00 ss (10)	99.97 3m/d (10)
1863	252.50 ss (12)	214.15 ss (12)	100.00 ss (12)	99.97 3m/d (12)
1864	253.17 ss (12)	213.32 ss (12)	100.00 ss (11)	99.99 ss (12)
1865	252.21 ss (12)	212.73 ss (12)	100.00 ss (12)	99.98 ss (12)
1866	252.17 ss (11)	209.09 ss (12)	100.00 ss (12)	99.96 ss (11)
1867	251.80 ss (12)	212.13 ss (12)	100.02 ss (11)	100.00 ss (6)
1868	251.78 ss (12)	211.23 ss (12)	99.95 ss (12)	100.00 ss (2)
1869	251.79 ss (12)	209.77 ss (12)	99.97 ss (12)	99.79 ss (4)
1870	251.31 ss (12)	211.05 ss (12)	99.73 ss (9)	99.66 ss (12)
1871	252.45 ss (12)	211.90 ss (12)	98.45 ss (5)	99.65 ss (12)

	ZURICH on:										
	London			**Amsterdam**			**Paris**			**Belgium**		
	per 10 pounds sterling [a]			per 100 Dutch guilders [b]			per 100 francs [c]			per 100 Belgian francs [d]		
	in franken											
1872	253.24	ss	(11)	210.95	ss	(11)	99.48	ss	(11)	99.80	ss	(11)
1873	253.51	ss	(11)	210.79	ss	(11)	99.68	ss	(11)	99.83	ss	(11)
1874	252.21	ss	(12)	212.00	ss	(12)	100.09	ss	(12)	99.97	ss	(12)
1875	251.94	ss	(12)	211.93	ss	(12)	100.06	ss	(12)	99.94	ss	(12)
1876	252.10	ss	(12)	208.80	ss	(12)	100.07	ss	(12)	99.87	ss	(12)
1877	251.64	ss	(12)	208.57	ss	(12)	100.05	ss	(12)	99.86	ss	(12)
1878	252.27	ss	(11)	208.46	ss	(11)	100.08	ss	(11)	99.97	ss	(11)
1879	252.56	ss	(12)	209.25	ss	(12)	100.01	ss	(12)	99.90	ss	(12)
1880	252.76	ss	(12)	208.91	ss	(12)	100.01	ss	(12)	99.95	ss	(12)
1881	252.89	ss	(12)	208.88	ss	(12)	100.07	ss	(12)	99.94	ss	(12)
1882	252.09	ss	(12)	208.21	ss	(12)	100.00	ss	(12)	99.87	ss	(12)
1883	252.26	ss	(12)	208.53	ss	(12)	99.99	ss	(12)	99.89	ss	(12)
1884	252.26	ch	(11)	208.33	ss	(12)	100.10	ss	(12)	99.98	ss	(12)
1885	253.13	ch	(12)	209.59	ss	(12)	100.21	ss	(12)	100.08	ss	(12)
1886	252.72	ch	(12)	209.18	ss	(12)	100.14	ss	(12)	100.07	ss	(12)
1887	253.33	ch	(11)	209.56	ss	(11)	100.12	ss	(11)	100.03	ss	(11)
1888	253.56	ch	(12)	209.98	ss	(12)	100.21	ss	(12)	100.11	ss	(12)
1889	252.92	ch	(12)	209.15	ss	(12)	100.20	ss	(12)	100.11	ss	(12)
1890	252.81	ch	(12)	209.13	ss	(12)	100.22	ss	(12)	100.18	ss	(12)
1891	253.21	ch	(11)	209.57	ss	(11)	100.30	ss	(11)	100.18	ss	(11)
1892	252.15	ch	(11)	208.54	ss	(11)	100.20	ss	(11)	100.09	ss	(11)
1893	252.42	ch	(12)	208.80	ss	(12)	100.20	ss	(12)	100.07	ss	112
1894	252.00	ch	(12)	208.63	ss	(12)	100.10	ss	(12)	100.05	ss	(12)
1895	252.67	ch	(12)	208.59	ss	(12)	100.18	ss	(12)	100.09	ss	(12)
1896	252.69	ch	(12)	208.60	ss	(12)	100.29	ss	(12)	100.19	ss	(12)
1897	252.61	ch	(12)	209.12	ss	(12)	100.42	ss	(12)	100.29	ss	(12)
1898	253.87	ch	(11)	210.01	ss	(11)	100.43	ss	(11)	100.24	ss	(11)
1899	253.60	ch	(10)	209.40	ss	(10)	100.54	ss	(10)	100.35	ss	(10)
1900	252.97	ch	(9)	209.10	ss	(9)	100.58	ss	(9)	100.41	ss	(9)
1901	252.25	ch	(12)	208.62	ss	(12)	100.18	ss	(12)	100.10	ss	(12)
1902	252.57	ch	(12)	208.18	ss	(12)	100.38	ss	(12)	100.26	ss	(12)
1903	251.82	ch	(12)	208.18	ss	(12)	100.11	ss	(12)	99.96	ss	(12)
1904	252.20	ch	(11)	208.89	ss	(11)	100.21	ss	(11)	100.08	ss	(11)
1905	251.90	ch	(12)	208.34	ss	(12)	100.14	ss	(12)	99.96	ss	(12)
1906	251.89	ch	(12)	207.79	ss	(12)	100.08	ss	(12)	99.83	ss	(12)
1907	252.22	ch	(12)	208.50	ss	(12)	100.14	ss	(12)	99.88	ss	(12)
1908	251.59	ch	(12)	208.19	ss	(12)	100.11	ss	(12)	99.88	ss	(12)
1909	251.86	ch	(12)	208.20	ss	(12)	100.04	ss	(12)	99.76	ss	(12)

	London	Amsterdam [e]	Paris	Belgium
	ZURICH on:			
	per 10 pounds sterling [a]	per 100 Dutch guilders [b]	per 100 francs [c]	per 100 Belgian francs [d]
	in franken			
1910	252.62 ch (11)	208.77 ss (12)	100.14 ss (12)	99.77 ss (11)
1911	252.73 ch (11)	209.14 ss (11)	100.07 ss (11)	99.72 ss (11)
1912	253.01 ch (12)	209.47 ss (12)	100.25 ss (12)	99.81 ss (12)
1913	253.06 ch (11)	208.78 ss (11)	100.27 ss (11)	99.68 ss (11)
1914	252.20 ch (7)	208.49 ch (7)	100.10 ch (7)	99.50 ch (7)

[a] Concerning the British currency, see pp. 3–5.

[b] Concerning the Dutch currency, see pp. 57–59.

[c] Concerning the French currency, see pp. 279f.

[d] In 1832 the Belgian franc was introduced, equal to the French franc (see p. 279).

[e] In 1914 the quotation on Rotterdam was the same as that on Amsterdam.

8.1.2 On Italy and Vienna

	ZURICH on:										
	Milan			**Genoa**			**Leghorn** [a]			**Vienna** [b]		
	per 100 lire austriache, from 1858 (11) per 100 guilders Österreichische Währung, from 1860 per 100 Piedmontese lire nuove, from 1861 (8) per 100 Italian lire, from 1868 in notes [c]			per 100 Piedmontese lire nuove, from 1861 (8) per 100 Italian lire, from 1868 in notes [d]			per 100 Tuscan lire moneta buona, from 1861 per 100 Piedmontese lire nuove, from 1861 (8) per 100 Italian lire [e]			per 100 guilders Konventionskurant, from 1858 (11) per 100 guilders Österreichische Währung [f]		
in guilders Zurich exchange money												
1842	36.80	ss	(1)	42.19	ss	(1)	35.75	ss	(1)	109.94	ss	(1)
1843	37.02	ss	(10)	42.31	ss	(10)	35.80	ss	(10)	110.15	ss	(10)
1844	36.94	ss	(12)	42.42	ss	(12)	35.94	ss	(12)	110.91	ss	(12)
1845	37.03	ss	(12)	42.45	ss	(12)	35.94	ss	(12)	110.38	ss	(12)
1846	36.73	ss	(12)	42.45	ss	(12)	36.10	ss	(12)	109.01	ss	(12)
1847	36.63	ss	(12)	42.42	ss	(11)	35.95	ss	(12)	108.87	ss	(12)
1848	36.40	ss	(12)	42.60	ss	(12)	35.31	ss	(12)	101.97	ss	(11)
1849	36.15	ss	(11)	41.93	ss	(11)	35.04	ss	(11)	96.13	ss	(10)
1850	36.17	ss	(12)	42.30	ss	(12)	35.81	ss	(12)	93.34	ss	(10)
1851	36.48	ss	(12)	42.43	ss	(12)	35.34	ss	(12)	86.75	ss	(11)
1852	36.56	ss	(3)	42.87	ss	(3)	35.59	ss	(3)	89.33	ss	(3)
in franken												
1852	85.03	ss	(9)	99.88	ss	(9)	83.31	ss	(9)	212.61	ss	(9)
1853	84.89	ss	(9)	99.60	ss	(10)	84.25	ss	(6)	230.56	ss	(9)
1854	84.62	ss	(12)	99.57	ss	(9)				211.34	ss	(3)
1855	85.25	ss	(12)	99.47	ss	(8)				210.00	ss	(3)
1856	86.08	ss	(11)	99.52	ss	(10)				248.15	ss	(7)
1857	85.58	ss	(12)	99.62	ss	(12)				245.42	ss	(12)
1858	85.42/246.50	ss	(10+2)	99.57	ss	(12)				244.70/248.50	ss	(10+2)
1859	248.65	ss	(12)	99.55	ss	(12)	83.25	3m/d	(1)	220.50	ss	(12)
1860	100.14	ss	(11)	99.88	ss	(12)	83.00	3m/d	(4)	196.72	ss	(7)
1861	99.98	ss	(12)	99.86	ss	(12)	99.05	3m/d	(11)	182.59	ss	(12)
1862	99.97	ss	(10)	99.87	ss	(10)	99.43	3m/d	(10)	199.88	ss	(8)
1863	99.96	ss	(12)	99.82	ss	(12)	99.38	3m/d	(12)	226.25	ss	(12)
1864	99.97	ss	(12)	99.81	ss	(12)	99.59	3m/d	(12)	218.00	ss	(12)
1865	100.01	ss	(12)	99.91	ss	(12)	99.63	ss	(3)	226.60	ss	(5)
1866	98.37	ss	(9)	99.88	ss	(2)	99.75	ss	(1)	211.67	ss	(3)
1867	93.13	ss	(6)									
1868	91.13	ss	(10)							216.10	ss	(8)
1869	95.94	ss	(8)							203.18	ss	(8)
1870												

	ZURICH on:								
	Milan			**Genoa**			**Vienna**		
	per 100 Italian lire in notes [c]						per 100 guilders Öster-reichische Währung, from 1900 per 100 Austrain crowns [f]		
	in franken								
1871	94.59	ss	(6)	95.02	ss	(6)	208.67	ss	(6)
1872	92.09	ss	(11)	93.13	ss	(6)	221.67	ss	(6)
1873	88.29	ss	(11)				225.64	3m/d	(11)
1874	89.17	ss	(12)				224.45	3m/d	(12)
1875	92.63	ss	(12)				223.93	3m/d	(12)
1876	92.08	ss	(12)				209.23	3m/d	(10)
1877	91.09	ss	(12)				204.08	3m/d	(12)
1878	92.12	ss	(11)				211.32	ss	(11)
1879	89.69	ss	(12)				215.12	ss	(11)
1880	90.46	ss	(12)				213.32	ss	(12)
1881	98.06	ss	(12)				214.73	ss	(12)
1882	97.19	ss	(12)				211.02	ss	(12)
1883	99.89	ss	(12)				210.63	ss	(12)
1884	100.09	ss	(12)				207.36	ss	(12)
1885	99.88	ss	(12)				203.19	ss	(12)
1886	99.97	ss	(12)				200.55	ss	(12)
1887	99.40	ss	(11)				200.64	ss	(11)
1888	99.13	ss	(12)				203.37	ss	(12)
1889	99.51	ss	(12)				211.18	ss	(12)
1890	99.10	ss	(12)				217.32	ss	(12)
1891	98.75	ss	(11)				216.97	ss	(11)
1892	96.73	ss	(11)				211.73	ss	(11)
1893	93.28	ss	(12)				204.46	ss	(12)
1894	90.03	ss	(12)				201.96	ss	(12)
1895	95.03	ss	(12)				207.21	ss	(12)
1896	92.91	ss	(12)				210.16	ss	(12)
1897	95.50	ss	(12)				211.02	ss	(12)
1898	94.08	ss	(11)				210.90	ss	(11)
1899	93.70	ss	(10)				210.28	ss	(10)
1900	94.63	ss	(9)				104.46	ss	(9)
1901	95.92	ss	(12)				105.10	ss	(12)
1902	99.13	ss	(12)				105.33	ss	(12)
1903	100.12	ss	(12)				105.05	ss	(12)
1904	100.08	ss	(11)				105.17	ss	(11)
1905	100.16	ss	(12)				104.85	ss	(12)
1906	100.11	ss	(12)				104.68	ss	(12)

	ZURICH on:				
	Milan		**Vienna**		
	per 100 Italian lire in notes		per 100 Austrian crowns		
	in franken				
1907	100.16	ss	(12)	104.63	ss	(12)
1908	100.10	ss	(12)	104.75	ss	(12)
1909	99.63	ss	(12)	104.91	ss	(12)
1910	99.59	ss	(12)	104.96	ss	(12)
1911	99.51	ss	(11)	105.05	ss	(11)
1912	99.32	ss	(12)	104.81	ss	(12)
1913	98.50	ss	(11)	104.84	ss	(11)
1914	99.70	ch	(7)	104.74	ch	(7)

[a]　From 1859 to 1864 the quotation on Florence was the same as that on Leghorn.

[b]　From 1851 to 1869 the quotation on Trieste was the same as that on Vienna.

[c]　On November 1st 1823 the Austrian lira (lira austriaca) of 100 centesimi with 3.897 grammes of fine silver was introduced in Lombardy–Veneto by the so-called 'Münzpatent' and became legal tender just like the guilder Konventionskurant (see pp. 255f.). This lira was equal to the 20 kreuzer piece (or one-third part of a guilder) of the Habsburg Monarchy and therefore used to be called 'la svanzica' or the 'zwanziger'. With the introduction of the new guilder Österreichische Währung in the Habsburg Monarchy, the exceptional monetary position of Lombardy–Veneto was abolished in 1858/59. After the integration of Lombardy in the new Kingdom of Italy, the Piedmontese and the Italian currency system respectively came into force there. Concerning the Italian currency after 1861, see p. 197.

[d]　Concerning the Genoese currency before 1861, see pp. 196f.

[e]　Concerning the Tuscan currency, see p. 195.

[f]　Concerning the Austrian currency, see pp. 255f. The guilder Konventionskurrant was payable in notes from June 3rd 1848, and so was the guilder Österreichische Währung from November 1858 ('Wiener Banknoten').

8.1.3 On Germany

	ZURICH on:			
	Augsburg	**Frankfurt**	**Hamburg**	**Berlin**
	per 100 guilders Augsburg current, from 1859 (2) per 100 guilders South German current [a]	per 100 guilders South German current [b]	per 100 mark banco, from 1873 (3) per 100 mark [c]	per 100 thaler Prussian current [d]
	in guilders Zurich exchange money			
1842	108.75 ss (1)	90.52 ss (1)	79.34 ss (1)	
1843	108.69 ss (10)	90.63 ss (10)	79.24 ss (10)	
1844	108.70 ss (12)	90.60 ss (12)	80.23 ss (12)	
1845	108.62 ss (12)	90.57 ss (12)	79.33 ss (12)	
1846	108.62 ss (12)	90.59 ss (12)	79.37 ss (12)	
1847	108.62 ss (12)	90.56 ss (12)	79.48 ss (12)	
1848	108.42 ss (12)	90.35 ss (12)	79.27 ss (12)	
1849	108.42 ss (11)	90.36 ss (11)	79.43 ss (11)	
1850	108.58 ss (12)	90.55 ss (12)	79.54 ss (12)	
1851	108.62 ss (12)	90.57 ss (12)	79.74 ss (12)	
1852	108.75 ss (3)	90.57 ss (3)	80.00 ss (3)	
	in franken			
1852	251.83 ss (9)	209.88 ss (9)	186.75 ss (9)	
1853	252.63 ss (9)	210.61 ss (10)	186.94 ss (10)	
1854	254.76 ss (12)	212.94 ss (12)	188.15 ss (11)	372.00 ss (1)
1855	255.57 ss (12)	213.55 ss (12)	187.50 ss (12)	
1856	255.71 ss (11)	213.30 ss (11)	188.50 ss (11)	371.15 ss (7)
1857	256.62 ss (11)	214.05 ss (12)	189.21 ss (12)	374.59 ss (12)
1858	256.41 ss (12)	213.72 ss (12)	187.64 ss (11)	374.30 ss (10)
1859	256.25/214.39 ss (1+11)	214.63 ss (12)	188.71 ss (12)	374.42 ss (12)
1860	214.96 ss (12)	214.96 ss (12)	189.25 ss (1)	376.91 ss (11)
1861	214.36 ss (12)	214.38 ss (12)	188.18 ss (10)	375.67 ss (12)
1862	213.58 ss (10)	213.58 ss (10)	188.55 ss (10)	373.90 ss (10)
1863	213.46 ss (12)	213.48 ss (12)	188.94 ss (12)	373.84 ss (12)
1864	213.07 ss (12)	213.05 ss (12)	188.86 ss (12)	372.86 ss (12)
1865	211.69 ss (12)	211.60 ss (12)	188.02 ss (12)	370.00 ss (12)
1866	212.92 ss (12)	212.95 ss (12)	187.65 ss (12)	374.27 ss (12)
1867	211.46 ss (12)	211.39 ss (12)	186.71 ss (12)	370.13 ss (12)
1868	210.82 ss (12)	210.72 ss (12)	185.82 ss (12)	368.35 ss (12)
1869	210.32 ss (12)	210.32 ss (12)	185.61 ss (12)	367.87 ss (12)
1870	210.46 (12)	210.40 (12)	185.46 (12)	368.55 ss (12)
1871	212.46 ss (12)	212.57 ss (12)	186.30 ss (12)	371.94 ss (12)
1872	214.01 ss (11)	213.86 ss (11)	186.85 ss (11)	374.28 ss (11)
1873	214.28 ss (10)	214.42 ss (11)	186.00/125.06 ss (2+9)	375.12 ss (11)

	ZURICH on:			
	Augsburg	**Frankfurt**	**Hamburg**	**Berlin**
	per 100 guilders South German current, from 1876 per 100 mark [a]	per 100 guilders South German current, from 1874 (12) per 100 mark [b]	per 100 mark [c]	per 100 thaler Prussian current, from 1874 (12) per 100 mark [d]
			in franken	
1874	211.98 ss (12)	212.17/122.75 ss (11+1)	123.77 ss (12)	367.06/122.75 ss (1+11)
1875	210.60 ss (12)	123.16 ss (12)	123.19 ss (12)	123.16 ss (12)
1876	123.59 ss (8)	123.60 ss (8)	123.60 ss (8)	123.60 ss (8)

	ZURICH on:
	Germany [e]
	per 100 mark [f]
	in franken
1876	123.47 ss (4)
1877	123.39 ss (12)
1878	123.50 ss (11)
1879	127.37 ss (12)
1880	123.73 ss (12)
1881	123.73 ss (12)
1882	123.41 ss (12)
1883	123.53 ss (12)
1884	123.55 ss (12)
1885	124.09 ss (12)
1886	123.94 ss (12)
1887	124.27 ss (11)
1888	124.29 ss (12)
1889	123.70 ss (12)
1890	123.99 ss (12)
1891	124.30 ss (11)
1892	123.69 ss (11)
1893	123.75 ss (12)
1894	123.50 ss (12)
1895	123.60 ss (12)
1896	123.77 ss (12)
1897	123.97 ss (12)
1898	124.18 ss (9)
1899	124.02 ss (10)
1900	123.56 ss (9)
1901	123.42 ss (12)
1902	123.42 ss (12)

	ZURICH on:		
	Germany [e]		
	per 100 mark [f]		
	in franken		
1903	123.17	ss	(12)
1904	123.43	ss	(11)
1905	123.11	ss	(12)
1906	122.97	ss	(12)
1907	123.06	ss	(12)
1908	123.12	ss	(12)
1909	123.09	ss	(12)
1910	123.42	ss	(12)
1911	123.47	ss	(11)
1912	123.53	ss	(12)
1913	123.63	ss	(11)
1914	123.14	ch	(7)

[a] In modification of the Konventionskurant 'Augsburg current', which became common especially from 1764 (NOBACK [1851], 1. Abth., p. 70), meant a standard of coinage of 20 5/12 guilders per mark of Cologne. So the guilder Augsburg current of 60 kreuzer was equal to 11.45 grammes of fine silver. The guilder South German current (standard of coinage: 24½ guilders per 233.855 grammes of fine silver or 52½ guilders per pound of 500 grammes of fine silver) of 60 kreuzer became legal tender in Augsburg from the beginning of 1859 as a consequence of the Vienna Coin Treaty of 1857.

[b] Concerning the Frankfurt currency, see pp. 195f. In Zurich the South German currency was called 'Reichsgeld'.

[c] Concerning the Hamburg currency, see pp. 191–193.

[d] Concerning the Prussian currency, see pp. 196f.

[e] Combines the series on Hamburg, Frankfurt am Main, Berlin, Augsburg and Leipzig, which had been listed separately on the exchange rate current until 1876.

[f] Concerning the German currency, see pp. 197.

8.1.4 On New York

	ZURICH on:		
	New York		
	per 100 US dollars [a]		
	in franken		
1890	521.50	ss	(1)
1891			
1892			
1893			
1894			
1895			
1896			
1897			
1898	522.67	ss	(9)
1899	520.37	ss	(10)
1900	519.20	ss	(9)
1901	516.78	ss	(12)
1902	517.57	ss	(12)
1903	516.98	ss	(12)
1904	517.75	ss	(11)
1905	516.84	ss	(12)
1906	517.65	ss	(12)
1907	518.02	ss	(12)
1908	516.52	ss	(12)
1909	516.35	ss	(12)
1910	518.42	ss	(12)
1911	519.21	ss	(11)
1912	519.19	ss	(12)
1913	519.47	ss	(11)
1914	517.34	ss	(7)

[a]   Concerning the US currency, see p. 404.

9
Denmark (1696–1914)

Exchange market: Copenhagen (1696–1914)

Sources: FRIIS/GLAMANN [1958], vol. I, pp. 66–103 (1696–1789); Erhvervsarkivet Århus, [København] Fondsbørs, *Protokol for vekselkurser og diskonto*, 1789, 11. Dec.–1802; ibid., 1803–1809; ibid., 1811–1872; ibid., 1872, 1. Marts–1880 (*Cours-Noterings-Protocol*); ibid., 1881–1891, 3. Mar.; ibid., 1891, 6. Mar.–1899, 1. Aug.; ibid., 1899, 4. Aug.–1906, 11. Dec.; ibid., 1906, 14. Dec.–1915, 24. Dec. (1789–1914); KELLY [1811] II, p. 90 (1806).
Concordance: *WdW XI*, pp. 19–69. Concerning the quotations on London up to 1775 see also McCUSKER [1978], pp. 32–86

Currency: Although the official currency of the Kingdom of Denmark was the rixdollar specie (speciedaler; 25.28 grammes of pure silver) of 6 mark or 96 shillings from 1625, the actual standard monetary unit was the rixdollar Danish current (rigsdaler kurantmønt; 20.57 grammes of pure silver) of 96 shillings (skilling) from the end of the 17th century. It was fixed that 48 rixdollars specie = 59 rixdollars current or 1 rixdollar specie = 118 shillings current but in everyday business the rixdollar species had a value of 120 shillings Danish current or 1¼ rixdollars current, which resulted in the common relation of 4 rixdollars specie = 5 rixdollars current. From 1737 the kurantbanken issued notes on a large scale but they were only convertible into current money for a few years (from 1737 until October 16th 1745 and from March 1747 until 1757). As the quotation of Copenhagen on Hamburg from the second half of the 18th century explicitly proves, the increasing amount of paper money caused a remarkable stock market loss of the Danish currency on the Hamburg money market which was of central importance for the Kingdom. First attempts at stabilizing the Danish currency against the Hamburg monetary system were initiated during the late 1780s, but owing to constantly new issues of paper money, especially during the Napoleonic era, they remained unsuccessful.

Rixdollar Danish current in notes per 100 rixdollar specie

1800	131.00	1803	140.66	1806	139.08	1809	282.50	1812	757.17
1801	139.25	1804	146.20	1807	146.65	1810	---		
1802	140.07	1805	140.59	1808	161.38	1811	793.13		

Source: *WdW XI*, p. 72

When the Danish currency was at its low at the turn of 1812 to 1813, it had just 1/12 of its former value in comparison with the Hamburg currency. Only the Currency and Bank Law of January 5th 1813, which introduced the rigsbankdaler (12.64 grammes of pure silver; = ½ rixdollar specie) of 6 mark or 96 shillings, took remedial action. With regard to the rigsbankdaler in silver, the previous paper money had been based on a fixed rate from February 26th 1813 until April 6th 1818, which from that time on was refixed every quarter of a year (which is why it is called 'kwartaalskurser', i.e. quarterly rate) although in practice it was significantly exceeded in the following years. When in spring 1818 the rate for rixdollar species dropped under 375 rigsbankdaler in notes, the fixed rate was suspended by means of the Currency Law of April 6th 1818. Until the end of the 1820s this quotation largely came closer to parity, which was finally reached in autumn 1838.

Rigsbankdaler in notes per 100 rixdollar specie

1813	1035.00	1820	264.84	1827	224.84	1834	206.84
1814	550.00	1821	260.59	1828	216.67	1835	205.75
1815	631.67	1822	252.17	1829	208.59	1836	201.88
1816	693.75	1823	249.84	1830	209.55	1837	202.00
1817	514.17	1824	242.50	1831	210.92	1838	201.59
1818	303.59	1825	215.59	1832	210.75	1839–1845	200.00
1819	243.59	1826	227.75	1833	209.88		

Source: *WdW XI*, pp. 72–74

In 1845 silver and paper money were legally treated as equal. By means of the coin patent of February 10th 1854 the present rigsbankdaler 'rixdollar (rigsdaler) rigsmønt' (12.64 grammes of pure silver) of 96 shillings was renamed. The Scandinavian Monetary Union between Denmark, Sweden and Norway from December 17th/18th 1872 was finally followed by the introduction of the gold currency on January 1st 1875 with the crown (kroner; 0.4032 grammes of pure gold) at 100 øre as monetary unit and legal tender of payment and account. The value of the crown corresponded to 0.4718 rixdollar or 45.288 shillings of the previous Danish currency and it remained the Danish monetary unit without any changes for the remaining period of documentation.

Original quotations at Copenhagen (until 1874)

on:	in:	per:
Amsterdam	per cent premium	100 rixdollars Flemish current
	from 1796 (8) rixdollars Danish current	100 rixdollars Flemish current
	from 1813 rigsbankdaler	100 rixdollars Flemish current
	from 1816 (10) rigsbankdaler	100 Dutch guilders
Hamburg	per cent premium	100 rixdollars banco of 3 mark banco
	from 1796 (8) rixdollars Danish current	100 rixdollars banco of 3 mark banco
	from 1813 rigsbankdaler	100 rixdollars banco of 3 mark banco
	from 1854 rixdollars rigsmønt	100 rixdollars banco of 3 mark banco
London	shillings Danish current	1 pound sterling
	from 1807 (8) rixdollars Danish current	1 pound sterling
	from 1813 rigsbankdaler	1 pound sterling
	from 1818 (12) shillings Danish current	1 pound sterling
Paris	shillings Danish current	1 livre tournois
	from 1802 shillings Danish current	1 franc

From 1875 all places are quoted in crowns per 1 (London) or 100 units of foreign currency.

Other data available: Hamburg, 2m/d (1789–1825); 3m/d (1873–1914); 10d/d (1881–1914) – Amsterdam, 2m/d (1789–1820) – London, 2m/d (1789–1818); 3m/d (1848–1914); 10d/d (1881–1914) – Paris, ss (1789–1819).

Exchange quotations from Denmark, or its most important exchange market Copenhagen, respectively, are available from the end of the 17th century onwards. For large parts of the 18th century, Amsterdam, Hamburg and London were the only exchange partners quoted more or less regularly, but "bills from London were usually negotiated indirectly via Amsterdam" (MCCUSKER [1978], p. 80). Lubeck, Paris, Danzig, Königsberg and Stockholm were listed only occasionally or in private price currents (FRIIS/GLAMANN [1958], vol. I, p. 61). For the period from December 1789 onwards the official quotations of the Copenhagen stock market are presented here, as ordered by the Danish government on February 27th 1787, having taken Hamburg as a model, but these were not carried out until December 1789 and were then given twice a week by the stock market committee of the *Grosserersocietetet*, i.e. the committee of the merchant bankers. These official stock market quotations were published regularly, whereas the publication of other exchange rate currents was forbidden (ibid., p. 64), although on the private currents of various brokers or merchant bankers we can find quotations deviating from this instruction.

Hamburg was by far the most important exchange partner of Copenhagen. Being territorially adjoining, the Kingdom of Denmark, with its duchies Schleswig and Holstein, was forced to orientate towards Hamburg in questions of monetary policy. At the same time, it was in many cases dependent on the Hamburg exchange market as the most important one within the North German area in order to maintain its cashless payment transactions. Because Danish foreign exchange rates were regulated by those of Hamburg and exchange operations from Copenhagen were almost always completed via Hamburg (KELLY [1811], p. 106; NOBACK [1858], p. 344; NOBACK [1877], p. 472) the exchange rate quotation on Hamburg was of central importance for the Danish exchange rates for large parts of the 19th century. According to the sources documented here, the Hamburg currency was the only one being officially quoted at the Copenhagen stock market between 1823 and 1848 (except for 1836). The quotation on London, which had temporarily been given up in 1823, was taken up again for two months in 1836 and then from 1848 onwards. Amsterdam, which had just as rarely been quoted from 1823, resumed its official exchange rate quotations by 1881. The same holds for Paris, which had been quoted irregularly between 1789 and 1821, and Antwerp. In 1899, Saint Petersburg, Helsinki and New York followed, and Vienna finally joined the group in 1906. For further places, such as Rome, which was listed in a contemporary private exchange rate current, no quotations could be found. In particular, in the late 19th and the early 20th centuries a quotation on the neighbouring places Stockholm and Christiania (Oslo) (cf. SWOBODA [1889], p. 419) was not necessary since there was parity between the currencies of Denmark, Sweden and Norway, based on the crown, owing to the Scandinavian Monetary Union from 1872. Hamburg and London remained the most important exchange partners for Copenhagen even during the late 19th and the early 20th centuries which is shown by the usances of the quotations: Hamburg and London were the only markets quoted with three usances (three months' dato, ten days' dato and avista), Paris, Amsterdam and Antwerp were quoted with only two usances (eight or ten days' dato and avista), all the other towns are quoted with only one usance (avista). The usance 'avista' has to be regarded as a particular case at the Copenhagen stock market, because these rates were used for cheques and payouts instead of sight bills in order to save the stamp tax of ½‰ (SWOBODA [1913], p. 275).

References: Astrid FRIIS / Kristof GLAMANN, *A History of Prices and Wages in Denmark 1660–1800, vol. I,* London – New York – Toronto 1958; Herbert RITTMANN, *Deutsche Geldgeschichte 1494–1914,* München 1975, pp. 456–460; John J. MCCUSKER, *Money and Exchange in Europe and America, 1600–1775. A Handbook,* London – Basingstoke 1978, pp. 80–86; Markus A. DENZEL, Altona als Bank- und Wechselplatz im ausgehenden 18. und beginnenden 19. Jahrhundert, *Bankhistorisches Archiv* 24 (1998), pp. 13–37; *WdW XI,* pp. 14–18.

9.1 Copenhagen exchange rates

9.1.1 On Hamburg, Amsterdam, London and Paris

	COPENHAGEN on:		
	Hamburg	**Amsterdam**	**London**
	per 100 mark banco [a]	per 100 guilders Flemish current [b]	per 10 pounds sterling [c]
	in rixdollars Danish current		
1696		42.25 14d/d (4)	
1697		44.30 14d/d (1)	
1698		42.77 14d/d (9)	
1699		41.91 14d/d (9)	
1700		42.78 14d/d (8)	
1701	37.17 14d/d (1)	43.05 14d/d (4)	
1702		42.70 14d/d (1)	
1703		43.47 14d/d (3)	
1704		44.17 14d/d (6)	
1705		44.34 14d/d (5)	
1706		44.50 14d/d (6)	
1707		44.30 14d/d (2)	
1708		43.94 14d/d (6)	
1709			
1710		44.00 14d/d (2)	
1711		44.00 14d/d (2)	
1712		45.16 14d/d (5)	
1713	38.17 14d/d (1)	44.64 14d/d (6)	
1714	37.90 14d/d (4)	43.58 14d/d (2)	47.50 60d/s (1)
1715	38.17 14d/d (1)	47.60 14d/d (1)	
1716	38.39 14d/d (3)	46.10 14d/d (2)	50.32 60d/s (1)
1717	38.72 14d/d (3)	48.00 14d/d (4)	50.00 60d/s (2)
1718	38.67 14d/d (1)	48.00 14d/d (2)	50.00 60d/s (3)
1719	38.50 14d/d (1)	50.20 14d/d (6)	
1720		50.20 14d/d (2)	
1721		50.70 14d/d (4)	
1722	43.38 14d/d (2)	50.66 14d/d (7)	56.05 60d/s (1)
1723	43.52 14d/d (8)	50.78 14d/d (10)	54.80 60d/s (4)
1724	43.91 14d/d (8)	50.58 14d/d (9)	54.52 60d/s (9)
1725	44.63 14d/d (8)	51.38 14d/d (9)	56.07 60d/s (8)
1726	42.12 14d/d (8)	47.88 14d/d (8)	52.03 60d/s (7)
1727	40.31 14d/d (1)	48.15 14d/d (8)	51.88 60d/s (7)
1728	39.42 14d/d (2)	47.08 14d/d (5)	51.05 60d/s (1)
1729		46.60 14d/d (7)	

	COPENHAGEN on:		
	Hamburg	**Amsterdam**	**London**
	per 100 mark banco [a]	per 100 guilders Flemish current [b]	per 10 pounds sterling [c]
	in rixdollars Danish current		
1730	39.79 14d/d (3)	45.93 14d/d (4)	48.75 60d/s (1)
1731	39.53 14d/d (11)	45.68 14d/d (11)	49.28 60d/s (11)
1732	39.33 14d/d (11)	45.79 14d/d (10)	49.69 60d/s (9)
1733	39.52 14d/d (9)	46.28 14d/d (11)	49.65 60d/s (9)
1734	39.80 14d/d (12)	47.24 14d/d (11)	51.53 60d/s (11)
1735	39.90 14d/d (11)	47.00 14d/d (9)	51.92 60d/s (8)
1736	39.86 14d/d (9)	46.83 14d/d (11)	51.44 60d/s (8)
1737		44.59 14d/d (5)	48.02 60d/s (2)
1738	39.17 14d/d (1)	45.30 14d/d (7)	49.02 60d/s (6)
1739	39.54 14d/d (6)	45.28 14d/d (8)	50.05 60d/s (7)
1740	39.82 14d/d (5)	45.61 14d/d (7)	49.90 60d/s (4)
1741	39.70 14d/d (3)	45.46 14d/d (11)	49.77 60d/s (4)
1742	39.33 14d/d (2)	45.38 14d/d 10	48.83 60d/s (4)
1743	39.97 14d/d (3)	46.23 14d/d (7)	50.33 60d/s (5)
1744	40.33 14d/d (2)	46.60 14d/d (11)	50.84 60d/s (2)
1745	40.92 14d/d (2)	47.06 14d/d (7)	51.15 60d/s (4)
1746	39.90 14d/d (5)	46.62 14d/d (8)	52.23 60d/s (3)
1747	39.00 14d/d (1)	46.28 14d/d (6)	50.84 60d/s (2)
1748	38.99 14d/d (12)	45.22 14d/d (12)	49.82 60d/s (12)
1749	39.24 14d/d (12)	44.92 14d/d (11)	49.85 60d/s (11)
1750	39.10 14d/d (12)	44.66 14d/d (12)	48.41 60d/s (12)
1751	39.42 14d/d (12)	44.35 14d/d (12)	48.74 60d/s (12)
1752	39.29 14d/d (12)	44.32 14d/d (12)	48.41 60d/s (12)
1753	39.47 14d/d (12)	44.58 14d/d (12)	48.52 60d/s (12)
1754	39.66 14d/d (12)	44.48 14d/d (12)	49.07 60d/s (12)
1755	39.50 14d/d (12)	44.86 14d/d (12)	50.26 60d/s (12)
1756	39.62 14d/d (12)	46.68 14d/d (12)	52.25 60d/s (12)
1757	38.17 14d/d (12)	46.31 14d/d (12)	50.92 60d/s (12)
1758	37.28 14d/d (12)	45.81 14d/d (12)	48.92 60d/s (12)
1759	37.11 14d/d (12)	46.56 14d/d (12)	49.99 60d/s (12)
1760	40.14 14d/d (12)	46.73 14d/d (12)	49.96 60d/s (12)
1761	43.28 14d/d (12)	48.54 14d/d (12)	51.39 60d/s (12)
1762	43.66 14d/d (12)	50.98 14d/d (12)	54.64 60d/s (12)
1763	42.23 14d/d (12)	49.83 14d/d (12)	52.81 60d/s (12)
1764	43.57 14d/d (12)	50.35 14d/d (12)	55.86 60d/s (12)
1765	40.74 14d/d (12)	47.02 14d/d (12)	52.06 60d/s (12)
1766	40.53 14d/d (12)	48.33 14d/d (12)	52.16 60d/s (12)
1767	40.58 14d/d (12)	49.29 14d/d (12)	53.15 60d/s (12)

	Hamburg [d]			Amsterdam [d]			London [d]			Paris		
	COPENHAGEN on:											
	per 100 mark banco [a]			per 100 guilders Flemish current [b]			per 10 pounds sterling [c]			per 100 livres tournois, from 1802 per 100 francs [e]		
	in rixdollars Danish current											
1768	41.46	14d/d	(12)	48.36	14d/d	(12)	52.31	60d/s	(12)			
1769	42.46	14d/d	(12)	48.90	14d/d	(12)	52.40	60d/s	(12)			
1770	42.29	14d/d	(12)	48.64	14d/d	(12)	51.68	60d/s	(12)			
1771	42.64	14d/d	(10)	48.68	14d/d	(12)	52.16	60d/s	(12)			
1772	43.33	14d/d	(12)	48.97	14d/d	(12)	52.63	60d/s	(12)			
1773	44.13	14d/d	(10)	50.64	14d/d	(12)	56.02	60d/s	(12)			
1774	42.70	14d/d	(12)	48.52	14d/d	(12)	54.52	60d/s	(12)			
1775	41.32	14d/d	(12)	47.16	14d/d	(12)	52.10	60d/s	(12)			
1776	41.33	14d/d	(12)	46.90	14d/d	(12)	50.90	60d/s	(12)			
1777	41.24	14d/d	(12)	46.33	14d/d	(12)	49.47	60d/s	(12)			
1778	41.24	14d/d	(12)	46.73	14d/d	(12)	51.47	60d/s	(12)			
1779	42.41	14d/d	(12)	48.74	14d/d	(12)	54.87	60d/s	(12)			
1780	42.32	14d/d	(11)	48.36	14d/d	(11)	53.93	60d/s	(11)			
1781	43.17	14d/d	(7)	49.16	14d/d	(7)	51.75	60d/s	(7)			
1782	44.33	14d/d	(7)	49.32	14d/d	(7)	52.44	60d/s	(7)			
1783	46.43	14d/d	(11)	51.37	14d/d	(12)	54.75	60d/s	(12)			
1784	45.88	14d/d	(12)	51.50	14d/d	(12)	57.58	60d/s	(12)			
1785	45.26	14d/d	(11)	51.39	14d/d	(11)	58.76	60d/s	(11)			
1786	45.62	14d/d	(12)	52.04	14d/d	(12)	58.19	60d/s	(12)			
1787	47.29	14d/d	(12)	53.63	14d/d	(12)	60.39	60d/s	(12)			
1788	48.59	14d/d	(12)	54.41	14d/d	(12)	62.76	60d/s	(12)			
1789	52.15	14d/d	(12)	58.24	14d/d	(12)	67.60	60d/s	(12)	25.52	60d/s	(1)
1790	49.97	ss	(12)	56.08	ss	(12)	65.47	ss	(12)	23.92	60d/s	(12)
1791	45.79	ss	(12)	52.19	ss	(12)	60.69	ss	(12)	20.21	60d/s	(9)
1792	45.65	ss	(12)	52.42	ss	(12)	58.02	ss	(12)	13.41	60d/s	(1)
1793	45.72	ss	(12)	51.95	ss	(12)	61.31	ss	(12)			
1794	42.07	ss	(12)	46.99	ss	(12)	55.44	ss	(12)			
1795	40.38	ss	(12)	45.76	ss	(12)	49.25	ss	(12)			
1796	40.56	ss	(12)	42.90	ss	(12)	50.00	ss	(12)			
1797	40.97	ss	(12)	44.72	ss	(12)	54.75	ss	(12)			
1798	41.40	ss	(12)	45.69	ss	(12)	57.23	ss	(12)			
1799	42.11	ss	(11)	45.26	ss	(12)	54.96	ss	(12)			
1800	43.63	ss	(12)	48.56	ss	(12)	50.90	ss	(12)			
1801	46.19	ss	(12)	50.86	ss	(12)	53.29	ss	(12)			
1802	46.93	ss	(12)	52.75	ss	(12)	56.97	ss	(12)	24.29	60d/s	(2)
1803	46.97	ss	(12)	52.38	ss	(12)	58.56	ss	(12)	23.24	60d/s	(7)
1804	48.06	ss	(12)	53.77	ss	(12)	62.54	ss	(12)			

	COPENHAGEN on:			
	Hamburg	**Amsterdam**	**London**	**Paris**
	per 100 mark banco [a]	per 100 guilders Flemish current, from 1816 (10) per 100 Dutch guilders [b]	per 10 pounds sterling [c]	per 100 francs [e]
	in rixdollars Danish current			
1805	46.59 ss (12)	51.28 ss (12)	59.55 ss (12)	
1806	46.62 ss (12)	52.27 ss (12)	58.35 ss (12)	
1807	48.86 ss (10)	56.31 ss (10)	61.27 ss (8)	26.04 60d/s (1)
1808	53.06 ss (12)	59.95 ss (8)	[f]	31.90 60d/s (4)
1809	96.12 ss (7)	137.50 ss (2)	[f]	
1810			[f]	
1811	267.75 ss (8)	303.12 ss (5)	[f]	146.88 60d/s (1)
1812	281.33 ss (10)	478.54 ss (3)	[f]	138.54 60d/s (1)
	in rigsbankdaler			
1813	222.93 ss (10)	298.00 ss (3)	[f]	
1814	170.86 ss (11)	192.80 ss (9)	197.19 ss (8)	130.38 60d/s (1)
1815	211.11 ss (12)	237.26 ss (10)	238.33 ss (8)	
1816	230.28 ss (12)	257.64 ss (10)	306.50 ss (5)	133.33 60d/s (2)
1817	169.17 ss (12)	181.52 ss (5)	267.50 ss (1)	91.67 60d/s (2)
1818	100.53 ss (12)	123.44 ss (5)	132.19 ss (2)	57.95 60d/s (2)
1819	80.78 ss (12)	83.20 ss (1)	99.90 ss (10)	38.55 60d/s (2)
1820	88.70 ss (12)	94.10 ss (1)	119.70 ss (7)	44.79 60d/s (1)
1821	87.08 ss (12)	95.00 ss (1)		41.67 60d/s (1)
1822	83.56 ss (12)	95.60 ss (3)	114.03 ss (3)	
1823	82.47 ss (12)	94.94 ss (3)	113.55 ss (3)	
1824	80.03 ss (12)			
1825	71.03 ss (12)			
1826	75.56 ss (12)			
1827	74.22 ss (12)			
1828	71.45 ss (12)			
1829	68.70 ss (12)			
1830	69.68 ss (12)			
1831	70.75 ss (12)			
1832	71.06 ss (12)			
1833	70.02 ss (12)			
1834	68.92 ss (12)			
1835	68.60 ss (12)			
1836	67.44 ss (12)		93.42 ss (2)	
1837	67.25 ss (12)			
1838	66.75 ss (12)			
1839	66.07 ss (12)			

	Hamburg			Amsterdam	London			Paris
	COPENHAGEN on:							
	per 100 mark banco, from 1873 (2) per 100 mark [a]			per 100 Dutch guilders [b]	per 10 pounds sterling [c]			per 100 francs [e]
	in rigsbankdaler, from 1854 (3) in rixdollars rigsmønt							
1840	65.82	ss	(12)					
1841	66.39	ss	(12)					
1842	66.72	ss	(12)					
1843	67.27	ss	(12)					
1844	66.28	ss	(12)					
1845	66.36	ss	(12)					
1846	66.12	ss	(12)					
1847	66.11	ss	(12)					
1848	66.38	ss	(12)		89.80	ss	(7)	
1849	66.47	ss	(12)		90.82	ss	(12)	
1850	66.68	ss	(12)		90.26	ss	(12)	
1851	67.29	ss	(12)		89.66	ss	(12)	
1852	67.33	ss	(12)		90.23	ss	(12)	
1853	66.52	ss	(12)		87.83	ss	(12)	
1854	65.42	ss	(12)		86.03	ss	(12)	
1855	65.39	ss	(12)		86.71	ss	(12)	
1856	66.92	ss	(12)		88.81	ss	(12)	
1857	67.03	ss	(12)		88.45	ss	(12)	
1858	66.78	ss	(12)		88.81	ss	(12)	
1859	66.82	ss	(12)		88.18	ss	(12)	
1860	66.81	ss	(12)		88.36	ss	(12)	
1861	66.84	ss	(12)		89.59	ss	(12)	
1862	66.99	ss	(12)		89.50	ss	(12)	
1863	66.87	ss	(12)		89.09	ss	(12)	
1864	66.83	ss	(12)		89.05	ss	(12)	
1865	66.94	ss	(12)		89.50	ss	(12)	
1866	66.89	ss	(12)		89.37	ss	(12)	
1867	66.72	ss	(12)		89.75	ss	(12)	
1868	66.83	ss	(12)		90.35	ss	(12)	
1869	66.93	ss	(12)		90.66	ss	(12)	
1870	66.78	ss	(12)		90.12	ss	(12)	
1871	66.53	ss	(10)		89.99	ss	(10)	
1872	66.37	ss	(12)		89.91	ss	(12)	
1873	66.40/44.64	ss	(1+11)		90.40	ss	(12)	
1874	44.49	ss	(12)		90.67	ss	(12)	
	in Danish crowns							
1875	88.88	ss	(12)		181.96	ss	(12)	

	COPENHAGEN on:			
	Hamburg	Amsterdam	London	Paris
	per 100 mark [a]	per 100 Dutch guilders [b]	per 10 pounds sterling [c]	per 100 francs [e]
	in Danish crowns			
1876	88.84 ss (12)		181.44 ss (12)	
1877	88.93 ss (12)		181.87 ss (12)	
1878	89.02 ss (12)		181.82 ss (12)	
1879	88.85 ss (12)		181.50 ss (12)	
1880	88.76 ss (12)		181.25 ss (12)	
1881	88.97 av (12)	150.38 av (12)	181.97 av (12)	72.00 60d/s (12)
1882	89.09 av (12)	150.57 av (12)	182.07 av (12)	72.30 60d/s (12)
1883	88.96 av (12)	150.50 av (12)	181.90 av (12)	72.16 60d/s (12)
1884	89.06 av (12)	150.39 av (12)	181.89 av (12)	72.31 60d/s (12)
1885	89.20 av (12)	150.92 av (12)	182.02 av (12)	72.15 60d/s (12)
1886	89.00 av (12)	150.47 av (12)	181.47 av (12)	72.03 60d/s (12)
1887	89.07 av (12)	150.41 av (12)	181.56 av (12)	71.83 60d/s (12)
1888	89.02 av (12)	150.55 av (12)	181.56 av (12)	71.80 60d/s (12)
1889	88.97 av (12)	150.60 av (12)	181.86 av (12)	72.10 60d/s (12)
1890	89.14 av (12)	150.60 av (12)	181.84 av (12)	72.16 60d/s (12)
1891	89.16 av (12)	150.52 av (12)	181.54 av (12)	72.02 60d/s (12)
1892	89.00 av (12)	150.35 av (12)	181.40 av (12)	72.19 60d/s (12)
1893	89.00 av (12)	150.34 av (12)	181.55 av (12)	72.17 60d/s (12)
1894	88.95 av (12)	150.25 av (12)	181.32 av (12)	72.13 60d/s (12)
1895	88.90 av (12)	150.14 av (12)	181.57 av (12)	72.01 60d/s (12)
1896	88.99 av (12)	150.10 av (12)	181.60 av (12)	72.18 60d/s (12)
1897	89.04 av (12)	150.30 av (12)	181.43 av (12)	72.19 60d/s (12)
1898	89.05 av (12)	150.80 av (12)	181.95 av (12)	72.10 60d/s (12)
1899	89.14 av (12)	150.61 av (12)	182.20 av (12)	72.35 60d/s (12)
1900	89.12 av (12)	150.87 av (12)	182.40 av (12)	72.57 60d/s (12)
1901	88.96 av (12)	150.49 av (12)	181.69 av (12)	72.27 60d/s (12)
1902	88.96 av (12)	150.17 av (12)	181.92 av (12)	72.40 60d/s (12)
1903	89.06 av (12)	150.57 av (12)	181.97 av (12)	72.44 60d/s (12)
1904	89.05 av (12)	150.80 av (12)	181.81 av (12)	72.39 60d/s (12)
1905	88.92 av (12)	150.56 av (12)	181.77 av (12)	72.38 60d/s (12)
1906	89.01 av (12)	150.47 av (12)	182.22 av (12)	72.47 60d/s (12)
1907	89.21 av (12)	151.27 av (12)	182.75 av (12)	72.62 60d/s (12)
1908	89.12 av (12)	150.80 av (12)	182.04 av (12)	72.51 60d/s (12)
1909	89.01 av (12)	150.61 av (12)	182.01 av (12)	72.36 60d/s (12)
1910	88.99 av (12)	150.59 av (12)	182.04 av (12)	72.21 60d/s (12)
1911	88.95 av (12)	150.70 av (12)	181.98 av (12)	72.10 60d/s (12)
1912	89.05 av (12)	150.93 av (12)	182.21 av (12)	72.24 60d/s (12)
1913	89.16 av (12)	150.62 av (12)	182.50 av (12)	72.35 60d/s (12)

	COPENHAGEN on:			
	Hamburg	**Amsterdam**	**London**	**Paris**
	per 100 mark [a]	per 100 Dutch guilders [b]	per 10 pounds sterling [c]	per 100 francs [e]
	in Danish crowns			
1914	88.99 av (7)	150.73 av (7)	182.23 av (7)	72.37 60d/s (7)

[a]   Concerning the Hamburg and the German currency, since 1873 see pp. 191–193, 197.

[b]   Concerning the Dutch currency, see pp. 57–59.

[c]   Concerning the British currency, see pp. 3–5.

[d]   Since December 1789 short sight.

[e]   Concerning the French currency, see pp. 279f.

[f]   In August 1807 Copenhagen was shot at by a British fleet after Denmark had joined the Continental System. Afterwards the quotation on London was suspended until 1814.

9.1.2 On Antwerp, Vienna, Saint Petersburg and Helsinki

	COPENHAGEN on:			
	Antwerp	**Vienna**	**Saint Petersburg**	**Helsinki**
	per 100 Belgian francs [a]	per 100 Austrian crowns (from 1900) [b]	per 100 gold roubles (from 1899 [7]) [c]	per 100 markkaa [d]
	in Danish crowns			
1881	72.00 av (12)			
1882	72.27 av (12)			
1883	72.12 av (12)			
1884	72.27 av (12)			
1885	72.09 av (12)			
1886	71.99 av (12)			
1887	71.73 av (12)			
1888	71.74 av (12)			
1889	72.05 av (12)			
1890	72.15 av (12)			
1891	71.96 av (12)			
1892	72.15 av (12)			
1893	72.08 av (12)			
1894	72.09 av (12)			
1895	72.01 av (12)			
1896	72.10 av (12)			
1897	72.08 av (12)			
1898	71.97 av (12)			
1899	72.20 av (12)		193.35 av (5)	71.92 av (5)
1900	72.44 av (12)		193.65 av (12)	72.01 av (12)
1901	72.20 av (12)		193.50 av (12)	72.00 av (12)
1902	72.32 av (12)		193.61 av (12)	72.03 av (12)
1903	72.34 av (12)		192.42 av (12)	72.10 av (12)
1904	72.27 av (12)		193.46 av (12)	72.02 av (12)
1905	72.22 av (12)		192.94 av (12)	71.99 av (12)
1906	72.27 av (12)	76.07 av (8)	192.38 av (12)	72.00 av (12)
1907	72.41 av (12)	76.03 av (12)	192.92 av (12)	72.00 av (12)
1908	72.36 av (12)	76.07 av (12)	191.86 av (12)	71.93 av (12)
1909	72.15 av (12)	75.91 av (12)	193.13 av (12)	71.86 av (12)
1910	71.97 av (12)	75.76 av (12)	193.84 av (12)	71.89 av (12)
1911	71.85 av (12)	75.76 av (12)	193.38 av (12)	71.88 av (12)
1912	71.92 av (12)	75.57 av (12)	192.77 av (12)	71.91 av (12)
1913	71.90 av (12)	75.60 av (12)	192.88 av (12)	71.90 av (12)
1914	71.94 av (7)	75.70 av (7)	191.84 av (7)	71.83 av (7)

[a]   The Belgian franc was equal to the French franc; see p. 280.

[b] Concerning the Austrian currency, see p. 256.

[c] Concerning the Russian currency, see p. 360.

[d] Concerning the Finnish currency, see p. 361.

9.1.3 On New York

	LONDON on:		
	New York		
	per 100 US dollars [a]		
	in Danish crowns		
1899	376.80	av	(5)
1900	378.00	av	(12)
1901	377.09	av	(12)
1902	377.34	av	(12)
1903	376.67	av	(12)
1904	377.67	av	(12)
1905	376.84	av	(12)
1906	377.92	av	(12)
1907	379.00	av	(12)
1908	376.67	av	(12)
1909	374.50	av	(12)
1910	376.05	av	(12)
1911	375.80	av	(12)
1912	375.46	av	(12)
1913	375.50	av	(12)
1914	375.36	av	(7)

[a] Concerning the US currency, see p. 402.

10
Sweden (1700–1914)

Exchange market: Stockholm (1700–1914)

Sources: PRICE [1961/62], p. 267 (table 3) (1700/01); HECKSCHER [1934], pp. 195f. (1703–1732, 1738/39); *Stockholms Handels Mercurius* (1733–1737); *Stockholms Stads Priscourant* (1740–1767); CANZLER [1778], table (unpaginated) "Stockholmer Wechselcours in den verschiedenen Monaten der Jahre 1743–1767. nach den Büchern des Mäckler-Comptoirs dieser Residenz" (1743–1767); *Sveriges Riksbank* [1931], pp. 146–149 (1768–1789); *Post- och Inrikes Tidningar* (1790–1824, 1844–1914); *Hamburger Privilegierte Liste der Börsenhalle* (1825–1831); *Göteborgs Handels- och Sjöfartstidning* (1832–1843). Concerning exchange rate quotations on Hamburg (1740–1775), cf. also ÅMARK [1915], p. 364.

Concordance: *HStD XII*, pp. 289–359

Currency: From 1625 Sweden had silver and copper currency and used dollars (daler) silver money of 4 mark silver money equal to 3 dollars (daler) copper money or 12 mark copper money. So, after the fixing of the standard of coinage on September 1st 1664, the dollar silver money as 1/3 rixdollar (riksdaler) corresponded to about 8.57 grammes of fine silver. Nevertheless, the monetary situation of Sweden in the 18th century was principally influenced by the issue of paper money: after banknotes had been issued for the first time in 1661, transport-sedlars, circulating since 1701, were accepted for all sorts of payment since 1726, so that the exchange rate quotations in or for daler silver money became payable in transport sedlar as well. When the transport sedlar could also be used for public loans from 1738/39, and when they were issued in constantly increasing amounts and ever-smaller denominations, their value dropped in comparison to the coinage (especially the rixdollar specie) as late as the 1760s. It could no longer be guaranteed that the transport sedlar could be cashed in. *De facto*, the paper currency prevailed in Sweden.

Dollars silver money in transport sedlar per rixdollar specie

1740	3.00	1747	3.72	1754	3.39	1761	5.96
1741	3.00	1748	3.86	1755	3.39	1762	7.03
1742	3.14	1749	3.88	1756	---	1763	7.42
1743	3.33	1750	3.81	1757	---	1764	7.63
1744	3.47	1751	3.46	1758	---	1765	7.35
1745	3.43	1752	3.48	1759	3.67	1766	6.40
1746	3.34	1753	3.37	1760	5.32	1767	5.12

Source: *HStD XII*, p. 361

On November 27th 1776 – after the insolvency of the Sveriges Riksbank after issuing the transport sedlar – the rixdollar specie of 25.70 (and 25.52 grammes of fine silver respectively from June 25th 1830) was declared as the monetary unit. So the silver standard was (re-)introduced. However, since new paper money was issued, i.e. the rixdollar banco (banko sedlar) and additionally the riksgäld sedlar since 1789, the silver currency "was more or less put out of operation" at the end of the 18th century (JÖRBERG [1972], vol. I, p. 81). An attempt at reintroducing the silver currency failed in 1809, and between 1818 and 1834 the notes could not be cashed in. From 1777 exchange rate quotations were done in or for rixdollars banco of 6 dollars silver money or 48 shillings (skillingar) payable in banko sedlar. The payment in riksgäld sedlar set down by the legislation of May 23rd 1845 (1 rixdollar banco = 1½ rixdollars riksgäld from 1803) is not recorded in the exchange rate quotations documented here (cf. NOBACK [1851], pp. 1155f.). The abolition of the paper currency succeeded by means of the legislation of February 3rd 1855 introducing the rixdollar riksmynt (= ¼ rixdollar species; equal to 6.38 grammes of fine silver) as the new currency unit at the beginning of the year 1856, which could be seen in the Swedish exchange rate quotations after 1858. After the introduction of the silver currency in 1855/56 and in the wake of the Scandinavian Monetary Union of December 17th/18th 1872, which oriented its monetary policy to that of the German Reich, the introduction of the gold standard followed with the crown (kronor; 0.4032 grammes of fine gold) of 100 öre as the standard unit of currency at the beginning of the year 1875 which was kept consistently until World War I.

Original quotations at Stockholm until 1874

on:	in:	per:
Amsterdam	mark copper money	1 rixdollar Flemish current of 2½ guilders
	from 1777 shillings banco	1 rixdollar Flemish current of 2½ guilders
	from 1816 (10) shillings banco	1 rixdollar of 2½ Dutch guilders
Berlin	shillings banco	1 thaler Prussian current
Copenhagen	mark copper money	1 rixdollar Danish current
	from 1777 shillings banco	1 rixdollar Danish current
	from 1814 (9) shillings banco	1 rigsbankdaler
Danzig	mark copper money	1 guilder Polish current
Hamburg	mark copper money	1 rixdollar banco of 3 mark banco
	from 1777 shillings banco	1 rixdollar banco of 3 mark banco
London	dollars copper money	1 pound sterling
	from 1777 rixdollars and shillings	1 pound sterling
Paris	mark copper money	1 livre tournois
	from 1777 shillings banco	1 livre tournois
	from 1798 shillings banco	1 franc
Pomerania	mark copper money	1 rixdollar Pomeranian current
Saint Petersburg	shillings banco	1 banco rouble
	from 1840 (5) shillings banco	1 silver rouble

From 1875 all quotations were effected for 1 (on London and New York) or 100 units of foreign currency.

Other data available: Altona, 2 to 3m/d (1810–1824) – Amsterdam, 1m/d (1760–1766); 3m/d (1861–1914) – Antwerp, 3m/d (1860–1887); ss (1869–1890) – Berlin, 3m/d (1880–1889) – Brussels, ss (1885–1914); 3m/d (1909–1914) – Christiania (Oslo), 3m/d (1909–1914); s (1909–1914) – German bank places, 3m/d (1909–1914) – Hamburg, 1m/d (1760–1766); 3m/d (1826–1895); ss (1875–1908) – Le Havre, 3m/d (1817–1824); ss (1862–1881) – London, 1m/d (1760–1766); 3m/d (1812–1914) – Lubeck, 2 to 3m/d (1803–1857); 3m/d (1876–1887) – Lyons, ss (1879–1883) – Marseilles, 3m/d (1818–1854) – Paris, 3m/d (1816–1914) – Reval, ss (1813–1817) – Riga, ss (1814–1816) – Rotterdam (1814–1824) – Saint Petersburg, 2m/d (1860–1862); 3m/d (1870–1875) – Stettin, ss (1874–1886); 3m/d (1875–1887) – Vienna, s (1911–1914)

Although exchange business – above all with Amsterdam, but also with Lubeck, Hamburg, Riga and other Central European places – played an important role within the Swedish war finance of the first half of the 17th century (HECKSCHER [1935], pp. 275f., 625; idem [1954], p. 86; EKHOLM [1971], p. 221), relatively regular exchange rate quotations of Stockholm, Sweden's most important exchange market, are unavailable until they were quoted in the local naval and commercial registers of the early

18th century. In particular, these were the quotations on the Northwest European financial centres, mostly financing Swedish external trade. Since the second half of the 17th century the Swedish export zone, i.e. Stockholm and its hinterland, was affiliated to the international network of the cashless payment system (ÅSTRÖM [1963], pp. 89–91, 116; PRICE [1961/62], passim). Relatively rarely the world financial centre, Amsterdam, even quoted Stockholm in the 1660s and 1670s. At that time, Amsterdam functioned as the most important financier of the Swedish export of raw material effected via Stockholm and carried out between the Swedish hinterland and Northwestern Europe, later on even with Finland and the Baltic areas. Concerning this trade, Stockholm had among other things the role of supplying advance cash for the Northwest European purchases of raw material and of passing on remittances on Amsterdam as well as transfering currency from the Netherlands (cf. SAMUELSSON [1955], pp. 190–195). From the foreign countries' point of view, bills of exchange on Amsterdam or on other places in Dutch currency represented, therefore, the means of payment necessary for transactions with Sweden. The same held for London as the most important financing money market from the first half of the 19th century. For large parts of the documented period Stockholm has not been quoted in the European financial centres, because "bills of exchange are seldom drawn from abroad on Sweden, as this country, like Russia, mostly settles her commercial debts by drawing and remitting foreign bills" (KELLY [1811], p. 406).

It can be shown for the period from 1700/33 that Stockholm itself quoted Amsterdam, Hamburg and London. Additionally it quoted Paris from 1740 as well as Copenhagen from 1760. Around the mid-18th century Stockholm also had exchange relations with Poland (Danzig) and Swedish West Pomerania (Stralsund). So, in the 18th century Stockholm was the financial place in the Baltic Sea area with the most diverse and most extensive quotations at its disposal, showing that it was clearly ahead of Saint Petersburg, Riga, Danzig, Gothenburg or other towns. At the beginning of the 19th century the quotation on Saint Petersburg began (1807). Further continuous enlargements of the exchange rate currents followed when Berlin was first listed in 1831/45, Antwerp in 1860, Brussels in 1885/90, New York in 1907, Christiania (Oslo) in 1909 and finally Helsinki and Vienna in 1911. Apart from this, a multitude of places on the coasts of the Baltic Sea (Lübeck, Stralsund, Stettin, Reval, Riga etc.), Denmark, England (above all Kingston-upon-Hull, payable in London), the Netherlands and France (Marseilles, Le Havre and others) as well as in the German interior were quoted irregularly from 1800 to 1890, and played no central role in international payment transactions (cf. SCHWARZER / DENZEL / SCHNELZER, pp. 38, 40). This may be put down to the exchange transactions of individual merchant houses whose exchange rate quotations were published in partly private exchange rate currents. However, proof cannot be furnished for Leghorn, Lisbon and Cadiz, which were mentioned in addition as temporary exchange partners of Stockholm in some merchant manuals of the 19th century.

Therefore it can be assumed that the Stockholm exchange market and its exchange rate currents have not been consolidated to the same extent as most of the other European financial places until well into the 19th century. The listed usances also varied comparatively frequently at up to 120 days' dato within different periods of sight, so that it was rare to find twelve quotations with the same usance in each year. Accordingly, the variation in turnover in the Stockholm exchange transactions was very high and its frequency extremely variable. These circumstances did not change until the end of the 19ᵗʰ century. Therefore the Swedish financial centre continued to play a rather secondary role in the European cashless payment system, even though Stockholm was the most important financial place within the Scandinavian Monetary Union between Sweden, Denmark and Norway, founded in 1872 and in force in 1875. Berlin was the first financial centre of international importance listing a regular quotation on Stockholm before World War I (from 1884), because Stockholm had kept close trading relations with the northern part of Germany since 1875/80 (cf. ibid., p. 43). Amsterdam's quotation on Stockholm followed much later, from 1907 on.

References: Paul Jacob MARPERGER, *Beschreibung der Banquen ...*, Halle – Leipzig 1717 (repr. Frankfurt am Main 1969), pp. 299-301; Johann Georg CANZLER, *Nachrichten zur genauern Kenntniß der Geschichte, Staatsverwaltung und ökonomischen Verfassung des Königreichs Schweden. Aus dem Französischen übersetzt und beträchtlich vermehrt, Erster Theil*, Dresden 1778; Karl ÅMARK, *Spannmålshandel och spannmålspolitik i Sverige 1719–1830*, Ph.D. thesis Stockholm 1915; *Sveriges Riksbank 1668–1924. Bankens Tillkomst och Verksamhet*, Stockholm 1931; Eli F. HECKSCHER, The Bank of Sweden in its Connection with the Bank of Amsterdam, in Johannes G. VAN DILLEN (ed.), *History of the Principal Public Banks accompanied by Extensive Bibliographies of the History of Banking and Credit in Eleven European Countries*, The Hague 1934, pp. 161–199; idem, *Sveriges Ekonomiska Historia. Första delen före frihetstiden. Andra boken hushållningen under internationell påverkan 1600–1720*, Stockholm 1935; idem, *An Economic History of Sweden*, Cambridge (Mass.) 1954; Kurt SAMUELSSON, International Payments and Credit Movements by the Swedish Merchant-Houses, 1730–1815, *Scandinavian Economic History Review* 3/2 (1955), pp. 163–202; Jacob M. PRICE, Multilateralism and/or Bilateralism: the Settlement of British Trade Balances with 'The North', c. 1700, *Economic History Review* sec. ser. 14 (1961/62), pp. 254–274; Sven-Erik ÅSTRÖM, From Cloth to Iron. The Anglo-Baltic Trade in the Seventeenth Century, *Commentationes Humanarum Literarum* 33 (1963), pp. 1–260; ibid., 37 (1965), pp. 1–85; Torgny LINDGREN, *Riksbankens sedelhistoria 1668–1968*, Stockholm 1968; Lars EKHOLM, Kontributioner och krediter. Svensk krigsfinansiering 1630–1631, in Hans LANDBERG / Lars EKHOLM / Roland NORDLUND (eds.), *Det kontinentala krigets ekonomi. Studier i krigsfinansiering under svensk stormaktstid*, Kristianstad 1971, pp. 143–270; Lennart JÖRBERG, *A History of Prices in Sweden 1732–1914, vol. I*, Lund 1972; Oskar SCHWARZER / Markus A. DENZEL / Petra SCHNELZER, Geld- und Wechselkurse in Deutschland und im Ostseeraum (18. und 19. Jahrhundert), in *HStD XII*, pp. 2–43, here pp. 21f., 38–42.

10.1 Stockholm exchange rates

10.1.1 On London, Amsterdam, Hamburg and Berlin

	STOCKHOLM on:								
	London			Amsterdam			Hamburg		
	per 10 pounds sterling [a]			per 100 guilders Flemish current [b]			per 100 mark banco [c]		
	in dollars silver money								
1700	83.27	[d]	(7)	76.04	[d]	(8)	66.30	[d]	(8)
1701	85.00	[d]	(5)	76.92	[d]	(5)	67.88	[d]	(4)
1702									
1703							73.94	2m/s	(y)
1704									
1705							75.36	2m/s	(y)
1706							75.36	2m/s	(y)
1707							74.67	2m/s	(y)
1708							74.03	2m/s	(y)
1709							78.58	2m/s	(y)
1710							76.67	2m/s	(y)
1711							73.25	2m/s	(y)
1712							76.67	2m/s	(y)
1713							76.39	2m/s	(y)
1714							71.53	2m/s	(y)
1715							70.50	2m/s	(y)
1716							72.92	2m/s	(y)
1717									
1718									
1719							109.72	2m/s	(y)
1720							100.00	2m/s	(y)
1721							101.39	2m/s	(y)
1722							102.78	2m/s	(y)
1723							99.50	2m/s	(y)
1724							98.28	2m/s	(y)
1725							93.06	2m/s	(y)
1726							93.75	2m/s	(y)
1727							96.89	2m/s	(y)
1728							98.61	2m/s	(y)
1729							96.89	2m/s	(y)
1730							97.22	2m/s	(y)
1731							97.22	2m/s	(y)
1732							97.92	2m/s	(y)
1733	125.16	2m/s	(12)	115.30	2m/s	(12)	97.98	2m/s	(12)

	STOCKHOLM on:							
	London			Amsterdam			Hamburg		
	per 10 pounds sterling [a]			per 100 guilders Flemish current [b]			per 100 mark banco [c]		
	in dollars silver money								
1734	130.17	2m/s	(11)	116.75	2m/s	(11)	98.27	2m/s	(11)
1735	131.27	2m/s	(10)	117.58	2m/s	(11)	99.20	2m/s	(11)
1736	128.72	2m/s	(11)	117.31	2m/s	(12)	99.48	2m/s	(12)
1737	127.09	2m/s	(3)	116.95	2m/s	(3)	99.95	2m/s	(3)
1738							100.00	2m/s	(y)
1739							100.36	2m/s	(y)
1740	129.57	2m/s	(10)	118.65	2m/s	(10)	103.02	2m/s	(10)
1741	131.43	2m/s	(12)	121.13	2m/s	(12)	104.88	2m/s	(12)
1742	137.97	2m/s	(12)	127.49	2m/s	(12)	110.71	2m/s	(12)
1743	140.25	2m/s	(12)	128.79	2m/s	(12)	111.61	2m/s	(12)
1744	151.22	2m/s	(12)	140.00	2m/s	(12)	121.78	2m/s	(12)
1745	150.26	2m/s	(8)	136.30	2m/s	(10)	117.78	2m/s	(11)
1746	138.34	2m/s	(9)	127.50	2m/s	(11)	111.12	2m/s	(11)
1747	155.21	2m/s	(10)	141.19	2m/s	(10)	121.09	2m/s	(11)
1748	160.73	2m/s	(12)	143.72	2m/s	(12)	123.98	2m/s	(12)
1749	156.41	2m/s	(10)	138.36	2m/s	(12)	120.84	2m/s	(12)
1750	144.83	2m/s	(12)	132.23	2m/s	(12)	116.06	2m/s	(12)
1751	140.46	2m/s	(12)	126.65	2m/s	(12)	112.04	2m/s	(12)
1752	132.30	2m/s	(12)	119.92	2m/s	(12)	105.81	2m/s	(12)
1753	129.97	2m/s	(12)	119.29	2m/s	(12)	105.69	2m/s	(12)
1754	133.46	2m/s	(12)	120.21	2m/s	(12)	107.59	2m/s	(12)
1755	136.46	2m/s	(12)	120.61	2m/s	(12)	107.08	2m/s	(12)
1756	147.50	2m/s	(11)	130.28	2m/s	(12)	111.66	2m/s	(12)
1757	165.68	2m/s	(11)	149.48	2m/s	(12)	124.17	2m/s	(12)
1758	187.58	2m/s	(11)	173.89	2m/s	(12)	141.09	2m/s	(12)
1759	189.17	2m/s	(10)	173.89	2m/s	(12)	138.19	2m/s	(12)
1760	218.75	2m/s	(12)	203.46	2m/s	(11)	174.51	2m/s	(12)
1761	238.86	2m/s	(12)	226.09	2m/s	(12)	201.36	2m/s	(12)
1762	296.46	2m/s	(12)	276.22	2m/s	(12)	235.45	2m/s	(12)
1763	284.17	2m/s	(11)	269.38	2m/s	(12)	228.71	2m/s	(12)
1764	306.05	2m/s	(12)	274.41	2m/s	(12)	239.91	2m/s	(12)
1765	304.42	2m/s	(10)	272.09	2m/s	(12)	236.81	2m/s	(11)
1766	258.62	2m/s	(10)	236.95	2m/s	(12)	200.24	2m/s	(12)
1767	207.71	2m/s	(12)	191.25	2m/s	(12)	157.59	2m/s	(12)
1768	153.00	2m/s	(y)	138.80	2m/s	(y)	116.67	2m/s	(y)
1769				138.64	2m/s	(y)	116.67	2m/s	(y)
1770	210.47	2m/s	(y)	190.50	2m/s	(y)	168.17	2m/s	(y)
1771	213.20	2m/s	(y)	198.04	2m/s	(y)	174.81	2m/s	(y)

	STOCKHOLM on:								
	London			Amsterdam			Hamburg		
	per 10 pounds sterling [a]			per 100 guilders Flemish current [b]			per 100 mark banco [c]		
	in dollars silver money								
1772	239.27	2m/s	(y)	220.27	2m/s	(y)	195.17	2m/s	(y)
1773	285.94	2m/s	(y)	256.27	2m/s	(y)	222.87	2m/s	(y)
1774	266.94	2m/s	(y)	239.70	2m/s	(y)	210.42	2m/s	(y)
1775	242.37	2m/s	(y)	219.07	2m/s	(y)	192.50	2m/s	(y)
1776	236.44	2m/s	(y)	216.34	2m/s	(y)	191.84	2m/s	(y)
	in rixdollars specie								
1777	38.35	2m/s	(y)	36.00	2m/s	(y)	32.06	2m/s	(y)
1778	39.48	2m/s	(y)	36.00	2m/s	(y)	31.93	2m/s	(y)
1779	41.06	2m/s	(y)	36.68	2m/s	(y)	31.96	2m/s	(y)
1780	40.90	2m/s	(y)	36.70	2m/s	(y)	32.12	2m/s	(y)
1781	37.58	2m/s	(y)	35.86	2m/s	(y)	31.47	2m/s	(y)
1782	37.13	2m/s	(y)	34.84	2m/s	(y)	31.55	2m/s	(y)
1783	38.30	2m/s	(y)	36.17	2m/s	(y)	32.53	2m/s	(y)
1784	43.82	2m/s	(y)	38.76	2m/s	(y)	34.27	2m/s	(y)
1785	44.74	2m/s	(y)	38.80	2m/s	(y)	34.42	2m/s	(y)
1786	42.39	2m/s	(y)	37.70	2m/s	(y)	33.18	2m/s	(y)
1787	41.22	2m/s	(y)	36.35	2m/s	(y)	32.27	2m/s	(y)
1788	41.79	2m/s	(y)	35.94	2m/s	(y)	32.36	2m/s	(y)
1789	46.35	2m/s	(y)	40.40	2m/s	(y)	35.80	2m/s	(y)
1790	50.32	60d/s	(6)	43.01	60d/s	(7)	37.82	60d/s	(6)
1791	49.03	60d/s	(9)	41.31	60d/s	(12)	36.14	60d/s	(12)
1792	44.69	60d/s	(10)	40.38	60d/s	(10)	35.11	60d/s	(10)
1793	50.30	60d/s	(10)	43.07	60d/s	(11)	37.16	60d/s	(11)
1794	46.44	60d/s	(12)	39.39	60d/s	(12)	35.41	60d/s	(12)
1795	40.03	60d/s	(12)	36.69	60d/s	(9)	32.90	60d/s	(12)
1796							36.25	60d/s	(y)
1797	46.28	60d/s	(12)	38.84	60d/s	(12)	34.83	60d/s	(12)
1798	53.35	60d/s	(11)	42.23	60d/s	(9)	36.93	60d/s	(11)
1799	64.23	60d/s	(11)	53.20	60d/s	(9)	38.12	60d/s	(11)
1800	49.93	60d/s	(9)	50.28	60d/s	(9)	36.98	60d/s	(9)
1801	59.36	60d/s	(9)	57.35	60d/s	(11)	38.42	60d/s	(12)
1802	57.90	60d/s	(12)	47.34	60d/s	(12)	36.64	60d/s	(12)
1803	56.78	60d/s	(12)	49.64	60d/s	(12)	35.28	60d/s	(12)
1804	45.98	60d/s	(12)	39.57	60d/s	(12)	35.21	60d/s	(12)
1805	44.96	60d/s	(12)	39.20	60d/s	(12)	35.36	60d/s	(12)
1806	44.19	60d/s	(12)	39.47	60d/s	(10)	35.36	60d/s	(12)
1807	46.89	60d/s	(11)	43.32	60d/s	(10)	37.79	60d/s	(11)
1808	45.31	60d/s	(11)	44.59	60d/s	(2)	37.43	60d/s	(10)

	STOCKHOLM on:			
	London	**Amsterdam**	**Hamburg**	**Berlin**
	per 10 pounds sterling [a]	per 100 guilders Flemish current, from 1816 (10) per 100 Dutch guilders [b]	per 100 mark banco [c]	per 100 thaler Prussian current [e]
	in rixdollars specie			
1809	45.84 60d/s (11)		42.56 60d/s (9)	
1810	58.22 60d/s (11)	63.02 60d/s (4)	53.46 60d/s (11)	
1811			71.07 60d/s (11)	
1812	64.07 60d/s (4)	74.59 60d/s (2)	62.59 60d/s (12)	
1813	69.88 60d/s (12)	74.17 60d/s (1)	64.76 60d/s (6)	
1814	74.33 60d/s (12)	74.59 60d/s (8)	65.93 60d/s (8)	
1815	84.17 60d/s (11)	82.92 60d/s (11)	72.64 60d/s (11)	
1816	106.64 60d/s (12)	91.29 60d/s (12)	79.94 60d/s (11)	
1817	98.01 60d/s (12)	85.79 60d/s (12)	76.39 3m/s (11)	
1818	94.62 60d/s (12)	85.77 60d/s (12)	76.45 3m/s (12)	
1819	110.02 60d/s (12)	97.35 60d/s (11)	85.41 3m/s (12)	
1820	123.96 60d/s (12)	104.42 60d/s (11)	91.61 3m/s (12)	
1821	118.68 60d/s (12)	95.77 60d/s (12)	84.81 3m/s (12)	
1822	118.34 60d/s (12)	97.87 60d/s (12)	86.04 3m/s (12)	
1823	120.14 60d/s (12)	99.12 60d/s (12)	86.52 3m/s (12)	
1824	122.08 60d/s (12)	103.16 60d/s (12)	89.12 3m/s (12)	
1825		97.50 60d/s (1)	85.77 60d/s (1)	
1826	126.93 60d/s (6)	102.38 60d/s (7)	90.42 60d/s (10)	
1827	128.39 60d/s (8)	107.85 60d/s (10)	94.93 60d/s (10)	
1828	118.55 60d/s (10)	99.00 60d/s (8)	87.61 60d/s (10)	
1829	117.84 60d/s (8)	96.88 60d/s (8)	86.53 60d/s (8)	
1830	124.17 60d/s (11)	102.31 60d/s (11)	90.94 60d/s (11)	
1831	130.33 60d/s (11)	109.59 60d/s (9)	97.05 60d/s (11)	197.92 ss (1)
1832	139.05 60d/s (11)	114.72 60d/s (10)	101.62 60d/s (12)	
1833	137.38 ss (12)	114.57 ss (12)	100.64 60d/s (12)	
1834	126.20 ss (12)	103.50 ss (11)	93.57 60d/s (12)	189.59 ss (4)
1835	121.98 ss (12)	100.35 ss (12)	89.96 60d/s (12)	187.50 ss (1)
1836	119.02 ss (12)	107.71 ss (2)	88.05 60d/s (12)	
1837	122.09 ss (12)	101.25 ss (5)	89.93 60d/s (12)	
1838	122.90 ss (11)	100.81 ss (8)	90.70 60d/s (12)	
1839	117.77 3m/s (12)	98.77 ss (5)	88.88 60d/s (12)	
1840	118.76 3m/s (12)	99.38 ss (6)	89.40 60d/s (12)	
1841	119.56 3m/s (12)	100.00 ss (2)	89.70 60d/s (12)	
1842	122.36 3m/s (12)	100.50 ss (5)	90.36 60d/s (12)	
1843	123.53 3m/s (12)	102.17 ss (5)	90.48 60d/s (12)	
1844	121.54 3m/s (12)	101.00 ss (9)	89.75 ss (12)	

	STOCKHOLM on:			
	London	**Amsterdam**	**Hamburg**	**Berlin**
	per 10 pounds sterling [a]	per 100 Dutch guilders [b]	per 100 mark banco, from 1873 (3) per 100 mark [c]	per 100 thaler Prussian current, from 1874 (12) per 100 mark [e]
	in rixdollars specie			
1845	121.48 ss (8)	97.99 ss (7)	88.40 ss (11)	184.03 ss (3)
1846	120.50 ss (12)	98.12 ss (7)	88.42 ss (10)	183.34 ss (2)
1847	119.19 ss (10)	98.08 ss (9)	88.38 ss (12)	182.30 ss (1)
1848	123.17 ss (11)	101.41 ss (8)	90.15 ss (12)	187.50 ss (2)
1849	123.55 ss (9)	101.88 ss (10)	90.05 ss (11)	185.42 ss (2)
1850	121.27 ss (10)	100.57 ss (9)	89.19 ss (12)	184.38 ss (5)
1851	119.21 ss (12)	100.52 ss (8)	89.29 ss (12)	183.34 ss (2)
1852	120.10 ss (11)	100.88 ss (9)	89.23 ss (12)	183.34 ss (4)
1853	117.14 ss (10)	99.35 ss (7)	88.87 ss (12)	179.17 ss (1)
1854	116.80 ss (12)	99.72 ss (9)	89.07 ss (12)	183.34 ss (3)
1855	118.66 ss (11)	99.44 ss (11)	89.28 ss (12)	183.34 ss (2)
1856	118.49 3m/s (12)	100.25 ss (11)	88.57 3m/s (12)	
1857	117.50 3m/s (12)	100.30 ss (10)	88.55 3m/s (12)	183.34 ss (3)
	in rixdollars rixmynt			
1858	177.75 3m/s (10)	151.15 3m/s (5)	134.46 ss (7)	275.00 ss (2)
1859	176.18 3m/s (10)	151.45 3m/s (10)	134.25 ss (3)	272.00 ss (1)
1860	176.74 ss (11)	150.58 3m/s (8)	134.00 ss (11)	271.72 ss (7)
1861	180.33 ss (12)	152.91 ss (6)	134.28 ss (12)	272.00 ss (2)
1862	179.21 ss (12)	152.22 ss (7)	134.16 ss (12)	271.00 ss (2)
1863	177.90 ss (12)	152.26 ss (8)	133.86 ss (12)	268.20 ss (5)
1864	177.24 ss (12)	151.24 ss (8)	133.86 ss (12)	268.00 ss (2)
1865	179.28 ss (12)	151.62 ss (9)	133.50 ss (12)	267.57 ss (4)
1866	178.84 ss (12)	152.49 ss (8)	134.03 ss (12)	266.88 ss (8)
1867	180.27 ss (11)	152.09 ss (7)	133.94 ss (11)	267.00 ss (4)
1868	181.05 ss (12)	152.30 ss (10)	133.91 ss (12)	267.38 ss (1)
1869	180.66 ss (12)	150.96 ss (8)	133.51 ss (12)	266.20 ss (5)
1870	179.28 ss (12)	151.85 ss (5)	133.30 ss (12)	267.13 ss (6)
1871	178.41 ss (12)	150.79 ss (10)	132.37 ss (12)	266.34 ss (7)
1872	178.11 ss (12)	148.96 ss (6)	131.70 ss (11)	265.39 ss (9)
1873	180.41 ss (12)	150.39 ss (10)	132.18/89.19 ss (2+10)	266.49 ss (10)
1874	182.25 ss (12)	149.33 ss (11)	89.10 ss (12)	267.13/89.25 ss (7+1)
	in Swedish crowns			
1875	182.54 ss (12)	153.30 ss (10)	89.03 ss (12)	88.74 ss (4)
1876	181.80 ss (12)	150.86 ss (11)	88.93 ss (12)	89.14 ss (4)
1877	182.11 ss (12)	151.09 ss (11)	89.02 ss (12)	88.94 ss (3)
1878	182.15 ss (12)	150.89 ss (10)	89.10 ss (12)	
1879	181.97 ss (12)	150.88 ss (12)	89.01 ss (12)	88.94 ss (4)

	STOCKHOLM on:			
	London	**Amsterdam**	**Hamburg**	**Berlin**
	per 10 pounds sterling [a]	per 100 Dutch guilders [b]	per 100 mark [c]	per 100 mark [e]
	in Swedish crowns			
1880	181.51 ss (12)	150.38 ss (10)	88.91 ss (12)	88.95 ss (1)
1881	181.87 ss (12)	150.14 ss (12)	88.93 ss (12)	88.90 ss (2)
1882	182.02 ss (12)	150.68 ss (12)	89.02 ss (12)	89.08 ss (2)
1883	181.84 ss (12)	150.41 ss (10)	88.95 ss (12)	89.03 ss (10)
1884	181.75 ss (12)	150.37 ss (12)	88.96 ss (12)	89.05 ss (12)
1885	181.85 ss (12)	150.78 ss (12)	89.06 ss (12)	89.18 ss (12)
1886	181.49 ss (12)	150.52 ss (12)	88.95 ss (12)	89.00 ss (12)
1887	181.45 ss (12)	150.35 ss (12)	88.99 ss (12)	89.04 ss (12)
1888	181.44 ss (12)	150.55 ss (12)	88.97 ss (12)	89.02 ss (12)
1889	181.54 ss (12)	150.44 ss (12)	88.91 ss (12)	88.98 ss (12)
1890	181.69 ss (12)	150.49 ss (12)	89.04 ss (12)	89.13 ss (12)
1891	181.48 ss (12)	150.49 ss (12)	89.10 ss (12)	89.12 ss (12)
			Germany [f]	
			per 100 mark [e]	
1892	181.55 ss (12)	150.38 ss (12)	88.97 ss (12)	
1893	181.66 ss (12)	150.37 ss (12)	89.00 ss (12)	
1894	181.39 ss (12)	150.40 ss (12)	88.90 ss (12)	
1895	181.70 ss (12)	150.15 ss (12)	88.87 ss (12)	
1896	181.65 ss (12)	149.96 ss (12)	88.95 ss (12)	
1897	181.47 ss (12)	150.26 ss (12)	89.02 ss (12)	
1898	182.02 ss (8)	150.58 ss (8)	89.02 ss (8)	
1899	182.27 ss (12)	150.46 ss (12)	89.12 ss (12)	
1900	182.48 ss (12)	150.84 ss (12)	89.08 ss (12)	
1901	181.73 ss (12)	150.35 ss (12)	88.94 ss (12)	
1902	181.97 ss (12)	150.02 ss (12)	88.93 ss (12)	
1903	182.04 ss (12)	150.44 ss (12)	89.05 ss (12)	
1904	181.88 ss (12)	150.68 ss (12)	89.05 ss (12)	
1905	181.85 ss (12)	150.09 ss (12)	88.90 ss (12)	
1906	182.22 ss (12)	150.35 ss (12)	88.97 ss (12)	
1907	182.79 ss (12)	151.14 ss (12)	89.17 ss (12)	
1908	182.10 ss (12)	150.69 ss (12)	89.11 ss (12)	
1909	182.07 ss (12)	150.51 ss (12)	88.97 ss (12)	
1910	182.12 ss (12)	149.95 ss (12)	88.99 ss (12)	
1911	182.01 ss (12)	150.33 ss (12)	88.94 ss (12)	
1912	182.18 ss (12)	150.87 ss (12)	88.93 ss (12)	
1913	182.40 ss (12)	150.54 ss (12)	89.12 ss (12)	
1914	182.18 ss (7)	150.65 ss (7)	88.97 ss (7)	

[a] Concerning the British currency, see pp. 3–5.

[b] Concerning the Dutch currency, see pp. 57–59.

[c] Concerning the Hamburg currency, see pp. 191–193.

[d] For the years 1700 and 1701 no usance is given.

[e] Concerning the Prussian and German currencies, see pp. 196f.

[f] From 1892 equal quotations on Hamburg and Berlin, officially combined under the title 'Germany' in 1909.

10.1.2 On places of the Baltic Sea area

	STOCKHOLM on:		
	Copenhagen	**Danzig**	**Pommerania**
	per 100 rixdollars Danish current [a]	per 100 guilders Polish current [b]	per 100 rixdollars Pomeranian current [c]
	in dollars silver money		
1740		79.69 (6)	228.34 (5)
1741		79.65 (12)	237.50 (12)
1742		81.95 (3)	258.34 (1)
1743		83.49 (7)	250.00 (1)
1744		89.59 (2)	266.67 (1)
1745		81.25 (1)	277.09 (2)
1746			
1747		87.09 (5)	256.25 (5)
1748		97.45 (11)	281.10 (9)
1749		94.27 (8)	278.48 (6)
1750		89.07 (12)	272.69 (9)
1751		83.34 (12)	250.00 (12)
1752		78.49 (10)	
1753		75.52 (8)	
1754		75.00 (4)	
1755		75.00 (2)	
1756			
1757			
1758			
1759			
1760	458.34 (4)	110.42 (8)	
1761	475.00 (2)	125.93 (9)	
1762		156.77 (4)	
1763	550.00 (2)	162.50 (2)	
1764	564.29 (7)	138.89 (3)	
1765	558.34 (2)	145.84 (2)	
1766	416.67 (1)	107.59 (7)	
1767	416.67 (3)	103.39 (8)	
1768			
1769			
1770			
1771			
1772			
1773			
1774			

	STOCKHOLM on:		
	Copenhagen	**Saint Petersburg**	
	per 100 rixdollars Danish current, from 1813 per 100 rigsbankdaler [a]	per 100 banco roubles [d]	
	in rixdollars specie		
...			
1790	78.13 ss (2)		
1791	79.52 ss (3)		
1792	77.61 ss (2)		
1793	87.50 ss (1)		
1794	85.42 ss (4)		
1795	82.09 ss (5)		
1796			
1797	86.06 ss (10)		
1798	91.24 ss (6)		
1799			
1800			
1801	77.09 ss (1)		
1802			
1803	73.45 ss (7)		
1804	72.66 ss (12)		
1805	75.47 ss (12)		
1806	75.59 ss (12)		
1807	77.56 ss (11)	54.17 ss (1)	
1808	77.09 ss (3)		
1809			
1810	36.34 ss (11)	33.34 ss (1)	
1811	29.23 ss (12)	35.17 ss (9)	
1812	19.90 ss (12)	44.83 ss (11)	
1813	37.02 ss (5)	47.08 ss (12)	
1814	7.49/39.33 ss (5+4)	38.11 ss (12)	
1815	36.94 ss (11)	37.65 ss (11)	
1816	37.55 ss (11)	44.84 ss (12)	
1817	39.74 ss (5)	45.97 ss (6)	
1818			
1819			
1820			
1821			
1822			
1823			
1824	116.15 ss (1)	49.05 ss (1)	

	STOCKHOLM on:		
	Copenhagen		**Saint Petersburg**
	per 100 rigsbankdaler, from 1854 (3) per 100 rixdollars rigsmønt [a]		per 100 banco roubles, from 1840 (5) per 100 silver roubles, from 1843 (11) in credit notes (kreditnye bilety) [d]
	in rixdollars specie		
1825	126.05	ss	(1)	50.52	ss	(1)
1826	124.69	ss	(10)	50.98	ss	(8)
1827	131.38	ss	(10)	55.00	ss	(9)
1828	126.02	ss	(9)	51.82	ss	(10)
1829	128.26	ss	(8)	52.63	ss	(4)
1830	133.19	ss	(9)	55.31	ss	(9)
1831	139.29	ss	(11)	59.15	ss	(11)
1832	145.65	ss	(11)	61.18	ss	(12)
1833	147.05	ss	(12)	60.22	ss	(12)
1834	137.98	ss	(12)	55.84	ss	(11)
1835	134.31	ss	(12)	53.77	ss	(12)
1836	134.03	ss	(3)	51.74	ss	(2)
1837	136.49	ss	(9)	53.65	ss	(7)
1838	139.67	ss	(9)	54.84	ss	(9)
1839	137.11	ss	(10)	56.38	ss	(10)
1840	139.70	ss	(9)	54.95/195.84	ss	(1+1)
1841	139.98	ss	(4)	192.37	ss	(3)
1842	137.30	ss	(5)	192.15	ss	(7)
1843	137.19	ss	(5)	192.39	ss	(6)
1844	137.45	ss	(9)	192.19	ss	(8)
1845	135.38	ss	(7)	190.98	ss	(7)
1846	136.93	ss	(9)	190.70	ss	(7)
1847	135.94	ss	(7)	193.49	ss	(8)
1848	139.22	ss	(7)	187.17	ss	(7)
1849	136.95	ss	(11)	189.07	ss	(10)
1850	135.02	ss	(9)	190.47	ss	(10)
1851	134.05	ss	(8)	187.57	ss	(8)
1852	134.66	ss	(11)	190.73	ss	(7)
1853	134.49	ss	(9)	190.17	ss	(8)
1854	135.57	ss	(7)	177.35	ss	(4)
1855	136.81	ss	(6)	177.48	ss	(8)
1856	135.77	ss	(9)	189.89	ss	(6)
1857	136.16	ss	(7)	185.50	ss	(7)

	STOCKHOLM on:				
	Copenhagen		Saint Petersburg		
	per 100 rixdollars rigsmønt, from 1875 per 100 Danish crowns [a]			per 100 silver roubles in credit notes (kredit-nye bilety) [b]	
	in rixdollars rixmynt				
1858	203.75	ss	(2)	266.88	ss	(7)
1859	201.17	ss	(6)	262.82	ss	(10)
1860	201.57	ss	(8)	262.50	ss	(10)
1861	200.00	ss	(4)	258.02	ss	(9)
1862	199.50	ss	(6)	256.91	ss	(11)
1863	199.94	ss	(8)	268.43	ss	(10)
1864	200.47	ss	(7)	239.60	ss	(8)
1865	198.57	ss	(4)	237.78	ss	(9)
1866	200.70	ss	(5)	222.86	ss	(7)
1867	200.50	ss	(4)	249.40	ss	(7)
1868	199.34	ss	(3)	248.88	ss	(10)
1869	199.57	ss	(4)	229.67	ss	(6)
1870	199.25	ss	(5)	222.90	ss	(7)
1871	198.59	ss	(4)	235.25	ss	(9)
1872	198.24	ss	(6)	242.32	ss	(8)
1873				239.75	ss	(1)
1874	199.20	ss	(9)	252.04	ss	(7)
	in Swedish crowns				
1875	99.74	ss	(8)	223.50	ss	(5)
1876	99.58	ss	(5)	237.88	ss	(4)
1877	98.45	3m/s	(5)	189.34	ss	(3)
1878	98.75	3m/s	(1)	183.71	ss	(6)
1879				179.00	ss	(3)
1880				185.84	ss	(3)
1881				194.17	ss	(3)
1882						
1884				189.25	ss	(3)
1885				181.00	ss	(1)
1886						
1887						
1888				183.50	ss	(1)
1889				190.50	ss	(3)
1890						
1891						
1892						
1893				193.00	ss	(1)

	STOCKHOLM on:		
	Copenhagen & Christiania (Oslo) (from 1909)	**Saint Petersburg**	**Helsinki**
	per 100 Danish [a] or (from 1909) Norwegian crowns [e]	per 100 silver roubles in credit notes (kreditnye bilety), from 1899 (7) per 100 gold roubles [d]	per 100 markkaa [f]
		in Swedish crowns	
1894		196.75 ss (1)	
1895			
1896		193.70 ss (1)	
1897			
1898			
1899			
1900			
1901			
1902			
1903			
1904			
1905			
1906			
1907			
1908			
1909	99.95 3m/s (5)		
1910	99.95 3m/s (12)		
1911	99.95 3m/s (12)	193.25 ss (4)	71.92 ss (10)
1912	99.87 3m/s (12)	192.76 ss (12)	71.98 ss (12)
1913	99.85 3m/s (12)	192.53 ss (12)	72.01 ss (12)
1914	99.85 3m/s (7)	191.97 ss (7)	71.88 ss (7)

[a] Concerning the Danish currency, see pp. 327f.

[b] Concerning the Polish currency, see p. 379.

[c] Pomeranian current meant Leipzig standard of coinage, i.e. 18 guilders per mark of Cologne. The Pomeranian current was payable in guilders (at 60 kreutzer) or pieces of two-thirds of the rixdollar (at 90 kreutzer, the so-called 'zweidrittel'), which were equal to 12.92 grammes of fine silver according to the Leipzig standard of coinage; CANZLER [1778] (unpaginated).

[d] Concerning the Russian currency, see pp. 359f.

[e] From 1877 the currency of Norway was the crown (0.4032 grammes of pure gold) of 100 öre according to the treaty of the Scandinavian Monetary Union, which was exactly equal to the Swedish and Danish crowns (cf. SWOBODA [1902], p. 238).

[f] Concerning the Finnish currency, see p. 361.

10.1.3 On Paris, Belgium and New York

	STOCKHOLM on:				STOCKHOLM on:		
	Paris				Paris		
	per 100 livres tournois [a]				per 100 livres tournois, from 1798 per 100 francs [a]		
	in dollars silver money				**in dollars silver money**		
1740	60.05	60d/s	(7)	1775	106.67	60d/s	(y)
1741	60.59	60d/s	(12)	1776	104.25	60d/s	(y)
1742	62.71	60d/s	(5)		**in rixdollars specie**		
1743	62.50	60d/s	(2)	1777	17.23	60d/s	(y)
1744	72.92	60d/s	(2)	1778	17.42	60d/s	(y)
1745	75.00	60d/s	(3)	1779	17.15	60d/s	(y)
1746				1780	17.40	60d/s	(y)
1747	63.55	60d/s	(4)	1781	17.00	60d/s	(y)
1748	74.59	60d/s	(10)	1782	16.69	60d/s	(y)
1749	70.84	60d/s	(8)	1783	17.11	60d/s	(y)
1750	69.54	60d/s	(12)	1784	19.05	60d/s	(y)
1751	66.15	60d/s	(12)	1785	18.00	60d/s	(y)
1752	61.81	60d/s	(3)	1786	17.48	60d/s	(y)
1753	62.30	60d/s	(5)	1787	17.07	60d/s	(y)
1754	61.46	60d/s	(3)	1788	17.07	60d/s	(y)
1755	62.50	60d/s	(3)	1789	17.80	60d/s	(y)
1756				1790	19.49	60d/s	(2)
1757				1791	17.54	60d/s	(4)
1758				1792	12.50	60d/s	(1)
1759	65.63	60d/s	(1)	1793			
1760	98.96	60d/s	(8)	1794			
1761	109.03	60d/s	(9)	1795			
1762	122.33	60d/s	(7)	1796			
1763	137.50	60d/s	(5)	1797			
1764	144.35	60d/s	(7)	1798	20.84	60d/s	(1)
1765	144.05	60d/s	(7)	1799			
1766	120.84	60d/s	(3)	1800	25.79	60d/s	(2)
1767	109.38	60d/s	(8)	1801	28.22	60d/s	(2)
1768				1802	27.00	60d/s	(3)
1769				1803	25.81	60d/s	(3)
1770	91.67	60d/s	(y)	1804	19.57	60d/s	(5)
1771				1805	19.36	60d/s	(4)
1772				1806	18.93	60d/s	(3)
1773	120.84	60d/s	(y)	1807			
1774	112.50	60d/s	(y)	1808	22.23	60d/s	(1)

	STOCKHOLM on:		
	Paris		
	per 100 francs [a]		
	in rixdollars specie		
1809			
1810	27.61	60d/s	(2)
1811	40.40	60d/s	(3)
1812	35.94	60d/s	(6)
1813	35.63	60d/s	(1)
1814	36.12	60d/s	(4)
1815	40.89	60d/s	(2)
1816	43.41	60d/s	(6)
1817	41.72	60d/s	(5)
1818	40.06	60d/s	(8)
1819	44.67	60d/s	(8)
1820	50.72	60d/s	(8)
1821	46.92	60d/s	(10)
1822	47.29	60d/s	(10)
1823	47.59	60d/s	(11)
1824	48.26	60d/s	(12)
1825	46.36	60d/s	(1)
1826	48.81	60d/s	(10)
1827	50.70	60d/s	(10)
1828	47.14	60d/s	(10)
1829	46.04	60d/s	(8)
1830	48.70	60d/s	(10)
1831	52.31	60d/s	(11)
1832	54.59	60d/s	(9)
1833	53.14	60d/s	(11)
1834	49.68	60d/s	(12)
1835	47.90	60d/s	(11)
1836	46.86	60d/s	(10)
1837	48.35	60d/s	(9)
1838	48.42	60d/s	(10)
1839	47.10	60d/s	(8)
1840	47.54	60d/s	(9)
1841	47.81	60d/s	(9)
1842	48.61	60d/s	(10)
1843	48.40	60d/s	(10)
1844	47.88	60d/s	(9)
1845	47.37	60d/s	(10)
1846	47.18	ss	(7)

	STOCKHOLM on:				
	Paris		**Antwerp**		
	per 100 francs [a]		per 100 Belgian francs [b]		
	in rixdollars specie				
1847	47.05	ss	(9)		
1848	48.96	ss	(5)		
1849	48.90	ss	(11)		
1850	48.17	ss	(10)		
1851	48.13	ss	(9)		
1852	47.93	ss	(10)		
1853	47.59	ss	(10)		
1854	47.14	ss	(8)		
1855	46.94	3m/s	(12)		
1856	46.98	3m/s	(12)		
1857	46.65	3m/s	(11)		
	in rixdollars rixmynt				
1858	71.67	3m/s	(6)		
1859	70.23	3m/s	(11)		
1860	70.95	ss	(11)	69.88	3m/s	(2)
1861	71.43	ss	(12)	69.94	3m/s	(3)
1862	71.06	ss	(12)		
1863	70.94	ss	(11)	69.75	3m/s	(2)
1864	70.80	ss	(11)	69.35	3m/s	(5)
1865	71.19	ss	(12)	70.05	3m/s	(6)
1866	71.27	ss	(12)	70.00	3m/s	(5)
1867	71.68	ss	(11)	70.80	3m/s	(4)
1868	71.93	ss	(12)	71.35	3m/s	(3)
1869	71.79	ss	(12)	71.25	3m/s	(5)
1870	71.30	ss	(9)	70.43	3m/s	(6)
1871	70.21	ss	(9)	69.82	3m/s	(9)
1872	69.89	ss	(12)	69.42	3m/s	(9)
1873	70.82	ss	(12)		
1874	72.04	ss	(12)	71.94	ss	(10)
	in Swedish crowns				
1875	72.44	ss	(12)	72.29	ss	(11)
1876	72.15	ss	(12)	72.14	ss	(10)
1877	72.41	ss	(12)	72.35	ss	(12)
1878	72.29	ss	(12)	72.19	ss	(12)
1879	71.93	ss	(12)	71.91	ss	(9)
1880	71.82	ss	(12)	71.76	ss	(9)
1881	71.92	ss	(12)	71.93	ss	(12)
1882	72.21	ss	(12)	72.21	ss	(12)

	STOCKHOLM on:								
	Paris			**Brussels**			**New York**		
	per 100 francs [a]			per 100 Belgian francs [b]			per 100 US dollars [c]		
	in Swedish crowns								
1883	72.02	ss	(10)	72.03	ss	(12)			
1884	72.07	ss	(12)	72.17	ss	(12)			
1885	72.03	ss	(12)	72.07	ss	(12)			
1886	71.96	ss	(12)	71.96	ss	(10)			
1887	71.70	ss	(12)	71.67	ss	(6)			
1888	71.76	ss	(12)	71.80	ss	(6)			
1889	71.97	ss	(12)	71.91	ss	(7)			
1890	72.07	ss	(12)	72.06	ss	(8)			
1891	71.97	ss	(12)	71.96	ss	(12)			
1892	72.10	ss	(12)	72.12	ss	(12)			
1893	72.10	ss	(12)	72.14	ss	(12)			
1894	72.08	ss	(12)	72.10	ss	(12)			
1895	72.04	ss	(12)	72.09	ss	(12)			
1896	72.06	ss	(12)	72.12	ss	(12)			
1897	72.09	ss	(12)	72.16	ss	(12)			
1898	71.89	ss	(7)	72.02	ss	(8)			
1899	72.13	ss	(12)	72.27	ss	(12)			
1900	72.41	ss	(12)	72.53	ss	(12)			
1901	72.14	ss	(12)	72.21	ss	(12)			
1902	72.24	ss	(12)	72.33	ss	(12)			
1903	72.27	ss	(12)	72.37	ss	(12)			
1904	72.20	ss	(12)	72.31	ss	(12)			
1905	72.18	ss	(12)	72.30	ss	(12)			
1906	72.23	ss	(12)	72.42	ss	(12)			
1907	72.38	ss	(12)	72.59	ss	(12)	377.29	ss	(7)
1908	72.30	ss	(12)	72.47	ss	(12)	377.00	ss	(12)
1909	72.27	ss	(12)	72.25	ss	(12)	375.25	ss	(12)
1910	72.22	ss	(12)	71.95	ss	(12)	375.00	ss	(12)
1911	72.07	ss	(12)	71.84	ss	(12)	375.00	ss	(12)
1912	72.22	ss	(12)	71.86	ss	(12)	374.62	ss	(12)
1913	72.27	ss	(12)	71.85	ss	(12)	375.25	ss	(12)
1914	72.33	ss	(7)	72.03	ss	(7)	375.15	ss	(7)

[a] Concerning the French currency, see pp. 279f.

[b] From 1832, the Belgian franc was equal to the French franc.

[c] Concerning the US currency, see pp. 403f.

11
Russian Empire (1695–1914)

Exchange market: Saint Petersburg (1695–1914)

Sources: NEWMAN [1992], pp. 136–141 (1695–1780); ODDY [1805], pp. 135, 197 (1695, 1710, 1763, 1788–1805); HELLER [1983], pp. 250f. (1769–1814); RASCH [1965], p. 61 (1784–1804); StA Hamburg, 621-1, C. Zeller, B 10, vol. 1 (1796–1799) and vol. 2 (1800–1802): *Exchange rate current of St Petersburg* (1796); SUB Göttingen: *Ot Gosudarstvennoj Kommerz-Kollegii Prejskurant, ili sostojanie cen pri Sanktpeterburgskom Porte Inostrannym i Rossijskim tovaram 1800 goda Ijunja 26 dnja* (June 26th 1800 old style); KELLY [1811] II, p. 112 (1807); v. EICHBORN [1928], table XIX after p. 288 (1810); Riksarkivet Stockholm, Strödda kamerala handlingar, vol. 24: *Pris-Courant i St. Petersburg* (1813); *Neue Hamburger Börsenhalle* (1815–1905); *The Economist*, London (1906–1914); SWOBODA [1913], p. 565 (1912).

Concordance: *HStD XII*, pp. 365–383; *WdW I/III*, pp. 455–474

Currency: After the currency reform of 1698/1704 the Russian currency system followed Western models: the silver rouble of 100 kopecks, which contained 24.20 grammes of fine silver, was accepted as a great silver coin in Western Europe, and the Russian Empire "became a hard currency area" (NEWMAN [1992], p. 127). In 1731 the fineness of the rouble was reduced to 20.75 grammes of fine silver and to 17.90 grammes in 1762, the latter being acknowledged by the ukaz of October 3rd 1790 after the attempt had failed to rase the fineness to 25.40 grammes of fine silver on the basis of the ukaz of January 20th/February 1st 1790. On June 20th/July 2nd 1810 the rouble was fixed at 17.996 grammes of fine silver. Moreover, the bank assignations (assignacii), the so-called banco rouble or assignat rouble, which had been issued by the government, were legal tender in Russia since the ukaz of December 29th 1768/January 10th 1769. From 1786 the paper money served as credit paper of the state. In cashless payments bills of exchanges might not be accepted if they were not payable in silver roubles but in banco roubles (ELSTER [1930], pp. 2f.). Nevertheless, at Saint Petersburg all transactions were done in banco roubles (ODDY [1805], p. 137), and, therefore, the quotations were effected in this paper money as well.

The money rate of the banco or assignat rouble in silver roubles at Saint Petersburg: silver roubles for 100 banco or assignat roubles (annual average)

1769	99.00	1790	87.00	1801	71.67	1812	25.20	1823	26.40
1770	99.00	1791	81.33	1802	80.00	1813	25.20	1824	26.50
1771	98.00	1792	79.33	1803	79.33	1814	20.00	1825	26.40
1772	97.00	1793	71.00	1804	77.00	1815	20.00	1826	26.67
1773	98.00	1794	68.50	1805	73.00	1816	25.33	1827	26.85
1774	100.00	1795	70.50	1806	67.50	1817	25.17	1828	26.85
1775–83	99.00	1796	79.00	1807	53.75	1818	25.25	1829	27.29
1784–86	98.00	1797	73.00	1808	44.67	1819	26.33	1830	26.33
1787	97.00	1798	62.50	1809	43.33	1820	26.33	1831	26.89
1788	92.75	1799	65.50	1810	25.67	1821	25.67	1832	27.17
1789	91.75	1800	66.25	1811	26.40	1822	26.25	1833–43	27.25

Source: HELLER [1983], pp. 248f.

Because of the high financial needs of the state resulting from the Napoleonic Wars, the banco rouble had to be accepted at a compulsory rate of 3:1 to the silver rouble since April 9th/21st 1812; the real ratio was about 4:1. In this time the banco rouble had officially been raised to the actual national currency of the Russian Empire. It was not until the ukaz of July 1st/13th 1839 that the silver rouble at 3.5 banco rouble became again the main means of payment representing the currency in or for which the exchange rate quotations were to be quoted. When on the basis of the ukaz of June 1st/13th 1843 a new paper money, the kreditnye bilety, was introduced on November 1st/13th 1843, this meant that all bills were payable in paper money as well, the paper money being for the first time of the same value as the silver money. Owing to its loss in value since the Crimean War, a compulsory rate was imposed on that non-convertible paper money in 1855. The fall in silver prices, especially from the 1870s, and the close trade relations with gold standard countries finally required the transition to the gold standard: from 1877, business transactions could be done in gold on the basis of the (older) imperial of 10 gold roubles or 10.30 silver roubles (until the end of 1885 at 11.997 grammes of fine gold) and its subdivisions. In 1886 the minting of the gold rouble at 0.7742 grammes of fine gold (according to the ukaz of 1885) initiated Russia's real transition to the gold standard, which was finally attained in 1895 when it was guaranteed that the paper money could be cashed in gold. The ukaz of June 7th/19th 1899 declared the gold rouble to be the unit of the Russian currency, and thus the gold standard was officially introduced, the (new) imperial at 11.6118 grammes of fine gold being reckoned at 15 gold roubles.

Original quotations at Saint Petersburg until 1885

on:	in:	per:
Amsterdam	stivers (= 1/20 guilder)	1 silver rouble
	from 1786 stivers (= 1/20 guilder)	1 banco rouble
	from 1826 Dutch cents	1 banco rouble
	from 1839 (8) Dutch cents	1 silver rouble
Hamburg	shillings banco (= 1/16 mark banco)	1 banco rouble
	from 1839 (8) shillings banco (= 1/16 mark banco)	1 silver rouble
London	pence sterling	1 silver rouble
	from 1786 pence sterling	1 banco rouble
	from 1839 (8) pence sterling	1 silver rouble
Paris	centimes	1 banco rouble
	from 1839 (8) centimes	1 silver rouble

From 1886 all quotations were made in roubles per 1 (on London) or 100 units of foreign currency.

Other data available: Amsterdam, 65d/d (1826–1835) – Berlin, 15d/d (1859–1878) – Brussels & Antwerp, 3m/d (1871–1881) – Hamburg, 65d/d (1826–1836) – Paris, 70d/d (1827–1831).

Exchange market: Riga (1757–1809)

Sources: DOROŠENKO / HARDER-GERSDORFF [1982], pp. 144, 147 (1757–1759); *Rigische Anzeigen von allerhand Sachen* (1762–1766); HARDER-GERSDORFF [1993], pp. 118-120 (1783–1786); Erhvervsarkivet Århus, J.P. Suhr & Søn, København, 1799–1875, *Priskuranter I* (1799–1809); ODDY [1805], p. 145 (1803); Riksarkivet Stockholm, Strödda kamerala handlingar, vol. 24: *Preis-Courant. Riga* (1808).

Currency: The exchange rate quotations at Riga were effected in Albertthaler (c. 24.65 grammes of fine silver) of 90 groschen. These Albertthaler were silver coins minted in the Netherlands only for export into the Baltic Sea area as compensating payment for the export surplus from there (DORO-ŠENKO / HARDER-GERSDORFF [1982], p. 143). From the end of the 17th century and especially in the 18th century the Albertthaler was the most popular trade coin in the whole of the Baltic Sea area.

Original quotations at Riga

on:	in:	per:
Amsterdam	rixdollars (= 2½ guilders) Flemish current	100 Albertthaler
Hamburg	Albertthaler	100 rixdollars (= 3 mark) banko
London	groschen	1 pound sterling

Exchange market: Helsinki (1865–1914)

Sources: AUTIO [1992] (1865–1914)

Concordance: *WdW II*, pp. 407–451

Currency: Although the grand principality of Finland was part of the Russian Empire and of the rouble currency area from 1809, Finland had its own currency system within the Russian Empire from the early 1860s, because the grand principality served as a kind of 'test model' for new strategies of Russian monetary policy. Since April 4th 1860 Finland's currency system consisted of the markka of 100 penniä. The markka of 4.499 grammes of fine silver was equal to 1/4 Russian silver rouble or approximately 1 French franc (minted before 1866). From 1863 all public accounts were effected in markkaa, and on November 8th 1865 the Finnish silver money and the Russian silver coins were declared the only legal tender of the grand principality. In Finland the gold standard was introduced on August 9th 1877, whereby the markka was equal to the franc in gold (at 0.2903 grammes of fine gold). At the same time the Russian currency lost its status as legal tender in the grand principality.

Original quotations at Helsinki: All quotations (of the Suomen Pankki, the Bank of Finland) were made in markkaa per 1 (on London) or 100 units of foreign currency (cf. NOBACK [1877], p. 7). The tables below present average rates between the highest and the lowest quotations of each month.

Other data available: Brussels, 3m/d (1887–1914)

Although the earliest quotation of the Russian currency against the Dutch currency is said to have been made in Moscow in 1540 and the next in 1633 (ODDY [1805], p. 196), exchange rate quotations from the Russian Empire are not available on a larger scale until the end of the 17th century. At the beginning, these quotations were money rates from the Russian heartland quoted unofficially in foreign currency, "as foreign bills could not circulate in Russia because they were not acceptable in internal trade and the financial networks did not exist to handle them" (NEWMAN [1992], p. 128). This was also why Saint Petersburg, founded in 1703 and capital of the Russian Empire from 1712, had not been quoted by foreign financial places for decades. A first quotation of Saint Petersburg on Amsterdam was carried out in 1704, but there is no certain regularity until the 1740s. Since the end of the Nordic War in 1721, Czar Peter the Great "made sure that his new capital became the financial centre of his empire. The exchange was opened there in the commercial quarter on Vasili Ostrov and the system which had evolved was acknowledged by officialdom" (ibid.). With that, the use of the bills of exchange as means of payment with the Russian Empire gradually "became the norm" (ibid.).

In Saint Petersburg this development was supported on the one hand by the relatively high legal certainty in all questions of cashless payment and on the other hand by the obviously better geographical location in comparison with Archangel, previously the only exportation port. This becomes obvious because of the shorter usance in the capital (65 days' dato) in comparison with Archangel (75 days' dato), reflecting the obviously shorter shipping route to Western Europe (ibid.). But the rise of Saint Petersburg to be the central Russian exchange market in the 18th century was above all the result of its quickly developing trade relations with Northwestern Europe, especially with the Netherlands and Great Britain. The intensive involvement of the Dutch merchants in the Russian Empire – originally via Archangel – also became noticeable in the cashless payment system when the quotation on Amsterdam remained the dominating and often even the only one quoted in Saint Petersburg, probably until the early 1760s. Even when the number of English merchants taking part in Russian trade and the number of payment transactions rose in the course of the 18th century, a large part of the exchange transactions continued to be carried out via Amsterdam, since the British trade with Russia had been financed by Dutch investors for large parts of the 18th century. While the Netherlands was increasingly ousted from trade in goods after the 1740s, "by the 1750s it was still common for bills to be drawn on Amsterdam to finance the expanding English export trade from Russia and for such bills, after acceptance by British merchants, to be met there" (ÅSTRÖM [1962], p. 102). It is not until 1763 that direct exchange rate quotations on London are available on a larger scale (cf. ODDY [1805], p. 197). So there is evidence of regular, direct exchange quotations from Saint Petersburg on London from that time on, although they were first probably limited to only a few companies.

Hamburg and Stockholm also began to play a role in the expanding exchange network of Saint Petersburg (NEWMAN [1992], p. 129), even though proof of Hamburg as direct exchange partner of Saint Petersburg cannot be furnished until the end of the 18th century, and for Stockholm there is no proof at all. According to contemporary merchant manuals, the importance of Hamburg for the cashless payment system of the Russian capital around the turn of the 19th century has its roots on the one hand in the growing instability of the Amsterdam Wisselbank and on the other in the increasing rate fluctuations for remittances on the Netherlands and England, which is why the payment transactions between Russia and England were frequently carried out via Hamburg (BAASCH [ed.] [1910], pp. 391, 396f., 403f.).

While there is only one single quotation from Moscow, but none from Saint Petersburg for the decade between 1805 and 1814 available until now, regular quotations from Saint Petersburg on London, Amsterdam, Paris and Hamburg were published regularly in the *Neue Hamburger Börsenhalle* – a clear indication of the high importance of the exchange market of Saint Petersburg for Hamburg and the whole of Central Europe. In the wake of London's rise to become the world's financial centre in the 19th century, Saint Petersburg, which was the most important trading city with the closest contact to English merchants in the Baltic area, had also risen to be the most important financial centre in that region (whereas the centres connected with Amsterdam largely lost their position). By around 1820 Saint Petersburg had become the most important exchange market of the whole Baltic area. Nevertheless there was no greater geographical expansion of Saint Petersburg's network of exchange quotations. At best, contemporary merchant manuals refer to the fact that Augsburg, Vienna and Trieste, Constantinople and Smyrna, Berlin, Breslau and Leipzig were occasionally quoted as well, apart from the four exchange partners mentioned above (cf. KELLY [1821, repr. 1835], vol. I., p. 304; vol. II, p. 84; NOBACK [1858], pp. 926f.). In particular, the official quoting on Vienna, which had still been done from time to time at the beginning of the century – for example in the price current of the Chamber of Commerce of Saint Petersburg in 1800 (see above) – was now rare (ibid., p. 925). Extensions of the exchange rate currents only happened when Berlin (1859/60, 1871–1878 and from 1899 instead of Hamburg) and Belgium (Antwerp, Brussels; 1871–1881) were added, and this is also evidenced in contemporary merchant manuals (e.g. NOBACK [1877], p. 719). This continued even during the years before World War I. Owing to a lack of sources, the quotations on Vienna and Copenhagen cannot be presented here, although some merchant manuals mentioned them as future close exchange partners of Saint Petersburg (SWOBODA [1902], pp. 535f.). So during the 19th century the foreign exchange relations of Saint Petersburg were mainly limited to the Northwest European area. The financial places there could function as intermediaries for all other important European exchange places and, at the same time, they functioned as the most important investors for Russia.

Exchange transactions of Saint Petersburg with other exchange places of the Russian Empire are not mentioned in the official quotations, although they no doubt exist and were even increasing over the period of documentation (cf. NOBACK [1858], p. 925). Above all, Archangel (cf. NEWMAN [1992], especially pp. 138f.) and Riga (cf. DOROŠENKO / HARDER-GERSDORFF [1982]; HARDER-GERSDORFF [1984]), and apart from this probably already Moscow, ranked as the most important members among the internal Russian exchange partners of Saint Petersburg in the 18th century. In the late 18th century "Riga grew ... into an international banking centre, linked especially to Amsterdam and Hamburg, as well as a centre for the Eastern rouble zone" (HARDER-GERSDORFF [1997], p. 564). In the 19th century Odessa, Warsaw and Helsinki joined the group. As a rule the exchange partners quoted there and the way of quoting them corresponded to the practices at Saint Petersburg. As exchange markets within the Russian Empire all these places were of only regional importance. So, in the 18th century, Archangel mostly maintained exchange relations with Amsterdam and Hamburg owing to its trade relations (cf. KELLENBENZ [1991], p. 221), whereas Riga functioned as the most important Baltic exchange market with similar close contact with Amsterdam and the Hanseatic towns, and had its own trading currency. Like the quotations of Saint Petersburg, those of Riga were published in the *Neue Hamburger Börsenhalle* until they were no longer of interest to the German merchants after 1882 (cf. *HDSt XII*, pp. 389–401).

In the 19th century Warsaw succeeded Danzig (see pp. 379f.) as the central Polish exchange market. From the 1840s on it maintained close exchange contact with Berlin. From 1865 there are regular quotations available from Helsinki, the regional financial centre of the grand principality of Finland, which at the end of the 19th century increasingly mentioned Scandinavian financial places (Stockholm; Copenhagen from

1882; Christiania [Oslo] from 1887) and even New York (from 1913) apart from North and Central European exchange partners (London, Amsterdam, Hamburg, Paris and Brussels from 1887) and Saint Petersburg (AUTIO [1992]; *WdW II*, pp. 407–451).

Only the free port of Odessa represented the financial centre for the Southern Russian area at least for some decades around the mid-19th century. Odessa had been relatively independent from the Saint Petersburg market and maintained exchange contact primarily with the Russian centres, Northwest European cities, Italy, the South of France, the Habsburg Monarchy and the Ottoman Empire, although London and Marseilles remained the only exchange partners quoted there around 1870 (*WdW VIII*, p. 66).

As an exchange place, Moscow stood completely in the shadow of Saint Petersburg until the second half of the 19th century. Contemporary merchant manuals report that the exchange operations of Moscow, which were quite marginal, were carried out for the most part via Saint Petersburg and, apart from this, via Odessa and Riga until 1866. There was no direct exchange relation with other countries and, therefore, there are no corresponding quotations available either – apart from some rare exceptions (see above). It was not until the setting up of the private Moscow merchants' bank in 1866, the increasing confidence in private banks since the end of 1868 and, above all, the opening of the Moscowische Disconto-Bank on January 2nd/14th that the exchange operations in Moscow developed to such a great extent that there was an official Moscow quotation from 1870 on. The exchanges on foreign countries were a little bit more expensive than in Saint Petersburg, but most of the remittance transactions could now be carried out directly (NOBACK [1877], pp. 623f.). It is remarkable that in 1893 the world's financial centre, London – as the only foreign place – included Moscow, now Russia's industrial metropolis, on its exchange rate current and quoted it regularly, though with only minimal differences in the exchange rates compared to Saint Petersburg. So, from the British point of view, Moscow was recognized as a Russian financial market of equal relevance to that of Saint Petersburg before World War I.

In Saint Petersburg there was a daily trade with foreign bills, but rates were officially fixed only on Tuesdays and Fridays, that is one day before the foreign mail arrived. The same holds for Odessa; in Moscow rates were always fixed one day later (NOBACK [1877], p. 719; SWOBODA [1902], p. 533). In Helsinki the usances were regularly three months' dato and at sight, on Saint Petersburg they were also at short sight and from there on the Scandinavian places only at sight (SWOBODA [1913], p. 577).

References: Ernst BAASCH (ed.), *Quellen zur Geschichte von Hamburgs Handel und Schiffahrt im 17., 18. und 19. Jahrhundert*, Hamburg 1910; Kurt VON EICHBORN, *Das Soll und Haben von Eichborn & Co. in 200 Jahren. Schicksal und Gestaltung eines Bankhauses im Wandel der Zeiten*, München – Leipzig 1928; Karl ELSTER, *Vom Rubel zum Tscherwonjez. Zur Geschichte der Sowjet-Währung*, Jena 1930, pp. 1–22; Sven-Erik ÅSTRÖM, *From Stockholm to St. Petersburg. Commercial Factors in the Political Relations between England and Sweden, 1675–1700*, Helsinki 1962; Aage A. RASCH, American Trade in the Baltic, 1783–1807, *Scandinavian Economic History Review* 13/1 (1965), pp. 31–64; Vasilii V. DOROŠENKO / Elisabeth HARDER-GERSDORFF, Ost-Westhandel und Wechselgeschäfte zwischen Riga und westlichen Handelsplätzen: Lübeck, Hamburg, Bremen und Amsterdam (1758/59), *Zeitschrift des Vereins für Lübeckische Geschichte und Altertumskunde* 62 (1982), pp. 120–147; Elisabeth HARDER-GERSDORFF, Zwischen Riga und Amsterdam: die Geschäfte des Herman Fromhold mit Frederik Beltgens & Comp., 1783–1785, in *The Interactions of Amsterdam and Antwerp with the Baltic Region 1400–1800 (NEHA 16)*, Leiden 1983, pp. 171–180; Klaus HELLER, *Die Geld- und Kreditpolitik des russischen Reiches in der Zeit der Assignaten (1768–1839/43)*, Wiesbaden 1983; Ivan Georgevic SPASSKIJ, *Das russische Münzsystem*, Berlin 1983; Elisabeth HARDER-GERSDORFF, Exportgeschäfte und Finanzverkehr zischen Riga und Amsterdam 1783–1785, in Franz MATHIS / Josef RIEDMANN (eds.), *Exportgewerbe und Außenhandel vor der Industriellen Revolution [Festschrift für Georg Zwanowetz]*, Innsbruck 1984, pp. 167–184; eadem, "Bullion Flow" and Rates of Exchange between Amsterdam and Riga (1783–1785), in Jacques Ph.S. LEMMINK et al. (eds.), *Baltic Affairs. Relations between the Netherlands and North-Eastern Europe 1500–1800 (Baltic Studies I)*, Nijmegen 1990, pp. 97–119; Hermann KELLENBENZ, Marchands en Russie aux XVIIᵉ et XVIIIᵉ siècles, in idem, *Europa, Raum wirtschaftlicher Begegnung. Kleine Schriften I*, Stuttgart 1991, pp. 205ff.; Jaakko AUTIO, *Valuuttakurssit Suomessa 1864–1911. Katsaus ja tilastosarjat*, Helsinki 1992 (= *Suomen Pankin Keskustelualoitteita* 1/92); Jennifer NEWMAN, 'A Very Delicate Experiment'. British Mercantile Strategies for Financing Trade in Russia, 1680–1780, in Ian BLANCHARD / Anthony GOODMAN / Jennifer NEWMAN (eds.), *Industry and Finance in Early Modern History. Essays Presented to George Hammersley on the Occasion of his 74ᵗʰ Birthday*, Stuttgart 1992, pp. 116–141; Elisabeth HARDER-GERSDORFF, Aus Rigaer Handlungsbüchern (1783–1785): Geld, Währung und Wechseltechnik im Ost-West-Geschäft der frühen Neuzeit, in Eckart SCHREMMER (ed.), *Geld- und Währung vom 16. Jahrhundert bis zur Gegenwart*, Stuttgart 1993, pp. 105–120; Markus A. DENZEL, Die Integration ostmittel-, ost- und südosteuropäischer Städte in die internationalen Zahlungsverkehrsverbindungen im 19. und beginnenden 20. Jahrhundert, *Südost-Forschungen* 55 (1996), pp. 45–73; Elisabeth HARDER-GERSDORFF, The Baltic Provinces – "Bridge" or "Barrier" to Russian Engagement in Western Trade? A Study of "Russians at Reval" During the Reign of Catherine II, *Jahrbücher für Geschichte Osteuropas* 45 (1997), pp. 561–576; Concepción GARCÍA-IGLESIAS / Juha KIPONEN, Monetary Aspects of a Changing Economy, in Jari OJALA / Jari ELORANTA / Juka JALAVA (eds.), *The Road to Prosperity. An Economic History of Finland*, Helsinki 2006, pp. 187–215.

11.1 Saint Petersburg exchange rates

11.1.1 On London, Amsterdam, Germany and Paris

	SAINT PETERSBURG on: [a]				
	London			Amsterdam	
	per 10 pounds sterling [b]			per 100 guilders Flemish banco [c]	
	in silver roubles				
1695	*20.00*	3m/d	(y)	*17.54*	65d/d	(y)
1696				*21.05*	65d/d	(y)
1697				*21.05*	65d/d	(y)
1698				*21.05*	65d/d	(y)
1699				*21.05*	65d/d	(y)
1700				*25.00*	65d/d	(y)
1701						
1702						
1703						
1704				22.35	65d/d	(1)
1705	32.88	3m/d	(y)	25.00	65d/d	(y)
1706						
1707						
1708						
1709						
1710	33.33	3m/d	(y)	30.77	65d/d	(2)
1711				29.41	65d/d	(1)
1712				28.57	65d/d	(1)
1713				31.50	65d/d	(3)
1714						
1715				31.25	65d/d	(1)
1716				36.48	65d/d	(3)
1717				35.71	65d/d	(1)
1718				30.71	65d/d	(4)
1719				34.19	65d/d	(y)
1720	40.00	3m/d	(y)	30.49	65d/d	(5)
1721	37.65	3m/d	(y)	35.71	65d/d	(y)
1722				38.10	65d/d	(y)
1723				38.46	65d/d	(3)
1724				37.04	65d/d	(y)
1725				36.36	65d/d	(2)
1726				35.71	65d/d	(1)
1727				40.40	65d/d	(1)
1728				37.91	65d/d	(y)

	SAINT PETERSBURG on:	
	London	**Amsterdam**
	per 10 pounds sterling [b]	per 100 guilders Flemish banco [c]
		in silver roubles
1729		37.98 65d/d (3)
1730		39.22 65d/d (y)
1731		34.48 65d/d (y)
1732		41.24 65d/d (y)
1733		40.00 65d/d (y)
1734		40.00 65d/d (y)
1735		41.03 65d/d (1)
1736		39.22 65d/d (1)
1737		38.55 65d/d (y)
1738		40.61 65d/d (1)
1739		41.24 65d/d (y)
1740		40.20 65d/d (1)
1741		40.00 65d/d (1)
1742		42.80 65d/d (6)
1743		43.78 65d/d (11)
1744		43.30 65d/d (10)
1745		43.26 65d/d (12)
1746		42.12 65d/d (12)
1747		41.28 65d/d (12)
1748		42.88 65d/d (12)
1749		44.74 65d/d (11)
1750		43.35 65d/d (10)
1751		43.22 65d/d (9)
1752		42.26 65d/d (9)
1753		39.66 65d/d (12)
1754		38.42 65d/d (4)
1755		41.22 65d/d (5)
1756		40.04 65d/d (5)
1757		43.48 65d/d (7)
1758		44.37 65d/d (9)
1759		49.18 65d/d (3)
1760		48.78 65d/d (1)
1761		47.62 65d/d (1)
1762		48.19 65d/d (2)
1763	43.64 3m/d (y)	42.33 65d/d (y)
1764	45.28 3m/d (y)	44.20 65d/d (y)
1765	50.00 3m/d (y)	41.24 65d/d (1)
1766	48.48 3m/d (y)	43.24 65d/d (y)

	London	Amsterdam	Hamburg	Paris
	SAINT PETERSBURG on:			
	per 10 pounds sterling [b, d]	per 100 guilders Flemish banco [c, d]	per 100 mark banco [e]	per 100 francs (from 1802) [f]
	in silver roubles			
1767	48.00 3m/d (y)	44.69 65d/d (y)		
1768	48.98 3m/d (y)	45.98 65d/d (y)		
1769	48.36 3m/d (y)	45.45 65d/d (y)		
1770	49.87 3m/d (y)	49.08 65d/d (y)		
1771	52.17 3m/d (y)	47.48 65d/d (y)		
1772	51.34 3m/d (y)	46.24 65d/d (y)		
1773	49.74 3m/d (y)	49.69 65d/d (y)		
1774	58.18 3m/d (y)	49.38 65d/d (y)		
1775	55.17 3m/d (y)	45.98 65d/d (y)		
1776	51.06 3m/d (y)	45.58 65d/d (y)		
1777	50.26 3m/d (y)	46.51 65d/d (y)		
1778	49.87 3m/d (y)	47.34 65d/d (y)		
1779	51.06 3m/d (y)	50.63 65d/d (y)		
1780	54.39 3m/d (y)	50.63 65d/d (y)		
1781	52.17 3m/d (y)	51.28 65d/d (y)	47.06 65d/d (y)	
1782	53.33 3m/d (y)	51.28 65d/d (y)	45.71 65d/d (y)	
1783	55.81 3m/d (y)	52.63 65d/d (y)	47.06 65d/d (y)	
1784	59.08 3m/d (y)	52.63 65d/d (y)	48.48 65d/d (y)	
1785	57.31 3m/d (y)	51.28 65d/d (y)		
	in banco roubles			
1786	57.14 3m/d (y)	51.28 65d/d (y)		
1787	58.54 3m/d (y)	51.28 65d/d (y)		
1788	69.00 3m/d (12)	58.82 65d/d (y)		
1789	77.10 3m/d (12)	66.67 65d/d (y)		
1790	77.94 3m/d (12)	66.67 65d/d (y)		
1791	82.49 3m/d (12)	71.43 65d/d (y)		
1792	83.21 3m/d (12)	74.07 65d/d (y)		
1793	95.01 3m/d (12)	80.00 65d/d (y)		
1794	88.37 3m/d (12)	74.07 65d/d (y)	66.67 65d/d (y)	
1795	80.20 3m/d (12)	71.43 65d/d (y)	64.65 65d/d (y)	
1796	77.07 3m/d (12)	67.23 65d/d (1)	61.54 65d/d (y)	
1797	81.31 3m/d (12)	66.67 65d/d (y)	61.54 65d/d (y)	
1798	92.66 3m/d (12)	74.07 65d/d (y)		
1799	89.48 3m/d (12)	80.00 65d/d (y)	72.73 65d/d (y)	
1800	83.57 3m/d (12)	82.47 65d/d (1)	73.56 65d/d (y)	
1801	80.22 3m/d (12)	80.00 65d/d (y)	69.57 65d/d (y)	
1802	79.37 3m/d (12)	71.43 65d/d (y)	70.33 65d/d (y)	169.49 3m/d (y)
1803	70.29 3m/d (12)	62.50 65d/d (y)	68.82 65d/d (y)	149.25 3m/d (y)

	SAINT PETERSBURG on:			
	London	**Amsterdam**	**Hamburg**	**Paris**
	per 10 pounds sterling [b]	per 100 guilders Flemish banco, from 1816 (10) per 100 Dutch guilders [c]	per 100 mark banco [e]	per 100 francs [f]
	in banco roubles			
1804	74.98 3m/d (12)	64.52 65d/d (y)	58.18 65d/d (y)	156.25 3m/d (y)
1805	77.07 3m/d (4)	64.52 65d/d (y)	59.26 65d/d (y)	69.93 3m/d (y)
1806	80.00 3m/d (y)	71.43 65d/d (y)	64.00 65d/d (y)	166.67 3m/d (y)
1807	88.07 3m/d (1)	79.21 65d/d (1)	68.82 65d/d (1)	37.04 3m/d (1)
1808	114.29 3m/d (y)	111.11 65d/d (y)	94.12 65d/d (y)	52.91 3m/d (y)
1809	120.00 3m/d (y)	125.00 65d/d (y)	114.29 65d/d (y)	61.73 3m/d (y)
1810	171.43 3m/d (y)	181.82 65d/d (y)	160.00 65d/d (y)	86.21 3m/d (y)
1811	171.43 3m/d (y)	222.22 65d/d (y)	200.00 65d/d (y)	105.26 3m/d (y)
1812	133.33 3m/d (y)	153.85 65d/d (y)	133.33 65d/d (y)	82.64 3m/d (y)
1813	150.00 3m/d (y)	235.29 65d/d (1)	200.00 65d/d (1)	80.65 3m/d (y)
1814	184.62 3m/d (y)	200.00 65d/d (y)	177.78 65d/d (y)	92.59 3m/d (y)
1815	221.02 3m/d (12)	219.57 3m/d (12)	193.62 3m/d (12)	97.65 3m/d (6)
1816	241.07 3m/d (12)	203.06 3m/d (12)	181.14 3m/d (12)	96.27 3m/d (11)
1817	214.89 3m/d (12)	183.05 3m/d (12)	164.63 3m/d (12)	88.05 3m/d (12)
1818	201.37 3m/d (12)	180.07 3m/d (12)	161.34 3m/d (12)	83.56 3m/d (6)
1819	219.78 3m/d (12)	191.46 3m/d (12)	170.29 3m/d (12)	90.02 3m/d (12)
1820	243.70 3m/d (12)	200.68 3m/d (12)	176.43 3m/d (12)	94.96 3m/d (12)
1821	252.45 3m/d (12)	203.68 3m/d (12)	180.12 3m/d (12)	99.44 3m/d (12)
1822	244.82 3m/d (12)	203.20 3m/d (12)	178.28 3m/d (12)	97.62 3m/d (12)
1823	250.01 3m/d (12)	207.78 3m/d (12)	180.56 3m/d (12)	98.64 3m/d (12)
1824	252.75 3m/d (12)	212.02 3m/d (12)	184.05 3m/d (12)	99.89 3m/d (11)
1825	233.86 3m/d (12)	197.77 3m/d (12)	174.62 3m/d (12)	94.45 3m/d (12)
1826	252.74 3m/d (12)	209.98 3m/d (11)	183.51 3m/d (12)	99.23 3m/d (11)
1827	235.41 3m/d (11)	197.92 3m/d (8)	172.13 3m/d (11)	93.68 3m/d (11)
1828	231.12 3m/d (12)	192.74 3m/d (12)	169.53 3m/d (12)	91.99 3m/d (12)
1829	225.21 3m/d (10)	187.20 3m/d (10)	165.22 3m/d (10)	88.58 3m/d (10)
1830	226.78 3m/d (12)	185.82 3m/d (12)	164.20 3m/d (12)	88.93 3m/d (12)
1831	223.31 3m/d (11)	189.83 3m/d (10)	165.10 3m/d (11)	90.42 3m/d (11)
1832	229.27 3m/d (12)	190.26 3m/d (11)	167.13 3m/d (12)	90.03 3m/d (12)
1833	226.24 3m/d (12)	189.38 3m/d (10)	165.61 3m/d (12)	88.97 3m/d (12)
1834	225.36 3m/d (12)	187.37 3m/d (9)	166.24 3m/d (12)	89.19 3m/d (12)
1835	228.33 3m/d (12)	188.72 3m/d (11)	167.66 3m/d (12)	89.83 3m/d (12)
1836	226.03 3m/d (12)	187.70 3m/d (11)	166.62 3m/d (12)	89.39 3m/d (12)
1837	226.97 3m/d (12)	189.30 3m/d (11)	167.00 3m/d (12)	89.92 3m/d (12)
1838	223.00 3m/d (12)	185.61 3m/d (12)	164.16 3m/d (12)	88.32 3m/d (12)
1839	209.15 3m/d (7)	176.26 3m/d (7)	156.88 3m/d (7)	84.80 3m/d (7)

	SAINT PETERSBURG on:			
	London	**Amsterdam**	**Hamburg**	**Paris**
	per 10 pounds sterling [b]	per 100 Dutch guilders [c]	per 100 mark banco, from 1873 per 100 mark [e]	per 100 francs [f]
	in silver roubles, from 1843 (11) payable in credit notes (kreditnye bilety)			
1839	60.77 3m/d (5)	51.10 3m/d (5)	45.66 3m/d (5)	24.27 3m/d (5)
1840	61.53 3m/d (11)	51.65 3m/d (11)	46.09 3m/d (11)	24.58 3m/d (11)
1841	61.69 3m/d (12)	51.36 3m/d (11)	46.15 3m/d (12)	24.55 3m/d (12)
1842	63.14 3m/d (12)	52.19 3m/d (12)	46.62 3m/d (12)	24.86 3m/d (12)
1843	63.87 3m/d (12)	52.33 3m/d (12)	46.56 3m/d (12)	24.90 3m/d (12)
1844	63.03 3m/d (12)	52.08 3m/d (12)	46.25 3m/d (12)	24.65 3m/d (12)
1845	63.31 3m/d (12)	51.66 3m/d (12)	46.17 3m/d (12)	24.66 3m/d (12)
1846	63.21 3m/d (12)	51.59 3m/d (12)	46.20 3m/d (12)	24.66 3m/d (12)
1847	63.38 3m/d (12)	51.62 3m/d (12)	45.24 3m/d (12)	24.48 3m/d (12)
1848	65.55 3m/d (12)	54.84 3m/d (12)	48.10 3m/d (12)	25.70 3m/d (4)
1849	65.32 3m/d (11)	53.97 3m/d (9)	47.60 3m/d (11)	25.63 3m/d (8)
1850	63.03 3m/d (10)	52.51 3m/d (10)	46.52 3m/d (10)	24.94 3m/d (10)
1851	63.53 3m/d (10)	53.62 3m/d (9)	47.34 3m/d (10)	25.54 3m/d (10)
1852	62.59 3m/d (4)	52.87 3m/d (4)	46.71 3m/d (4)	25.02 3m/d (4)
1853	62.11 3m/d (12)	52.57 3m/d (12)	46.59 3m/d (12)	24.83 3m/d (12)
1854	65.54 3m/d (12)	55.93 3m/d (12)	49.67 3m/d (12)	26.45 3m/d (12)
1855	66.42 3m/d (12)	56.46 3m/d (12)	50.11 3m/d (12)	26.67 3m/d (12)
1856	63.19 3m/d (12)	53.64 3m/d (12)	47.22 3m/d (12)	25.18 3m/d (12)
1857	64.20 3m/d (12)	54.56 3m/d (12)	48.27 3m/d (12)	25.52 3m/d (12)
1858	67.11 3m/d (12)	57.29 3m/d (12)	50.64 3m/d (12)	26.75 3m/d (12)
1859	68.50 3m/d (12)	58.63 3m/d (12)	51.92 3m/d (12)	27.40 3m/d (12)
1860	67.25 3m/d (12)	57.59 3m/d (12)	50.99 3m/d (12)	26.88 3m/d (12)
1861	69.70 3m/d (12)	58.87 3m/d (12)	52.06 3m/d (12)	27.56 3m/d (12)
1862	69.72 3m/d (12)	59.00 3m/d (12)	52.05 3m/d (12)	27.71 3m/d (12)
1863	65.72 3m/d (12)	55.82 3m/d (12)	49.32 3m/d (12)	26.17 3m/d (12)
1864	73.48 3m/d (12)	62.20 3m/d (12)	55.17 3m/d (12)	29.26 3m/d (12)
1865	76.27 3m/d (12)	64.30 3m/d (12)	56.90 3m/d (12)	30.39 3m/d (12)
1866	81.01 3m/d (12)	68.41 3m/d (12)	60.49 3m/d (12)	32.38 3m/d (12)
1867	73.88 3m/d (12)	62.08 3m/d (11)	54.79 3m/d (12)	29.44 3m/d (12)
1868	72.94 3m/d (11)	61.23 3m/d (11)	53.93 3m/d (11)	29.05 3m/d (11)
1869	78.13 3m/d (12)	64.99 3m/d (12)	57.57 3m/d (12)	31.04 3m/d (12)
1870	81.09 3m/d (12)	67.95 3m/d (12)	60.05 3m/d (12)	32.45 3m/d (9)
1871	75.52 3m/d (12)	63.23 3m/d (12)	55.73 3m/d (12)	28.65 3m/d (5)
1872	73.32 3m/d (12)	61.02 3m/d (12)	52.70 3m/d (12)	28.68 3m/d (12)
1873	73.94 3m/d (12)	61.33 3m/d (12)	36.48 3m/d (12)	29.01 3m/d (12)
1874	72.23 3m/d (12)	60.69 3m/d (12)	35.45 3m/d (12)	28.65 3m/d (12)
1875	73.00 3m/d (12)	61.44 3m/d (11)	35.61 3m/d (12)	28.93 3m/d (12)

	SAINT PETERSBURG on:			
	London	**Amsterdam**	**Hamburg, since 1899 Berlin**	**Paris**
	per 10 pounds sterling [b]	per 100 Dutch guilders [c]	per 100 mark [e]	per 100 francs [f]
	in silver roubles payable in credit notes (kreditnye bilety), from 1899 (7) in gold roubles			
1876	77.36 3m/d (12)	63.91 3m/d (12)	37.77 3m/d (12)	30.72 3m/d (12)
1877	91.15 3m/d (12)	75.33 3m/d (12)	44.48 3m/d (12)	36.14 3m/d (12)
1878	97.70 3m/d (6)	80.77 3m/d (6)	46.97 3m/d (6)	38.89 3m/d (6)
1879	103.22 3m/d (4)	85.10 3m/d (4)	50.47 3m/d (4)	40.89 3m/d (4)
1880	95.49 3m/d (12)	78.90 3m/d (12)	46.70 3m/d (12)	37.80 3m/d (12)
1881	95.02 3m/d (12)	77.96 3m/d (9)	46.41 3m/d (11)	37.49 3m/d (11)
1882	99.02 3m/d (12)	81.61 3m/d (12)	48.44 3m/d (12)	39.28 3m/d (12)
1883	100.31 3m/d (12)	83.37 3m/d (12)	49.40 3m/d (12)	40.13 3m/d (12)
1884	100.75 3m/d (12)	81.86 3m/d (12)	48.48 3m/d (12)	39.30 3m/d (12)
1885	99.06 3m/d (12)	81.94 3m/d (12)	48.46 3m/d (12)	39.17 3m/d (12)
1886	102.63 3m/d (12)	84.83 3m/d (12)	50.29 3m/d (12)	40.62 3m/d (12)
1887	111.74 3m/d (12)	92.32 3m/d (12)	54.83 3m/d (12)	44.10 3m/d (12)
1888	118.71 3m/d (6)	98.20 3m/d (6)	58.27 3m/d (6)	46.54 3m/d (6)
1889	95.37 3m/d (12)	78.62 3m/d (12)	46.46 3m/d (12)	37.63 3m/d (12)
1890	86.33 3m/d (12)	71.33 3m/d (12)	42.27 3m/d (12)	34.20 3m/d (12)
1891	90.39 3m/d (11)	74.71 3m/d (10)	44.37 3m/d (11)	35.88 3m/d (11)
1892	99.35 3m/d (12)	81.85 3m/d (11)	48.69 3m/d (12)	39.32 3m/d (12)
1893	95.90 3m/d (12)	79.34 3m/d (12)	46.91 3m/d (12)	37.61 3m/d (12)
1894	93.07 3m/d (12)	77.05 3m/d (9)	45.51 3m/d (12)	36.90 3m/d (12)
1895	92.99 3m/d (12)	76.43 3m/d (5)	45.20 3m/d (12)	36.81 3m/d (12)
1896	93.98 3m/d (12)	77.18 3m/d (12)	45.86 3m/d (12)	37.27 3m/d (12)
1897	93.77 3m/d (12)	77.34 3m/d (12)	45.87 3m/d (12)	37.27 3m/d (12)
1898	93.89 3m/d (12)	77.34 3m/d (12)	45.83 3m/d (12)	37.21 3m/d (12)
1899	93.83 3m/d (12)	77.37 3m/d (3)	45.77 3m/d (12)	36.88 3m/d (12)
1900	93.84 3m/d (11)	77.63 3m/d (2)	45.74 3m/d (11)	37.34 3m/d (11)
1901	93.75 3m/d (12)	77.26 3m/d (12)	45.93 3m/d (12)	37.34 3m/d (11)
1902	94.01 3m/d (11)	76.65 3m/d (12)	45.73 3m/d (6)	37.27 3m/d (12)
1903	93.65 3m/d (12)	76.71 3m/d (12)	45.83 3m/d (7)	37.14 3m/d (12)
1904	93.89 3m/d (8)	76.95 3m/d (12)	45.94 3m/d (6)	37.18 3m/d (12)
1905	94.17 3m/d (10)	77.58 3m/d (12)	46.02 3m/d (4)	37.35 3m/d (12)
1906	95.78 3m/d (12)	78.15 3m/d (6)	47.17 3m/d (1)	38.05 3m/d (12)
1907	95.60 3m/d (12)	78.02 3m/d (12)		37.27 3m/d (12)
1908	94.87 3m/d (12)	77.96 3m/d (12)	46.30 3m/d (4)	37.07 3m/d (12)
1909	93.62 3m/d (12)	76.99 3m/d (12)	46.37 3m/d (2)	36.75 3m/d (12)
1910	94.03 3m/d (12)	76.82 3m/d (12)	45.93 3m/d (1)	36.72 3m/d (12)
1911	93.50 3m/d (12)	76.77 3m/d (12)		36.71 3m/d (12)
1912	93.60 3m/d (12)	76.95 3m/d (12)	45.75 3m/d (1)	36.82 3m/d (12)

	SAINT PETERSBURG on:			
	London	**Amsterdam**	**Berlin**	**Paris**
	per 10 pounds sterling [b]	per 100 Dutch guilders [c]	per 100 mark [e]	per 100 francs [f]
	in gold roubles			
1913	94.26 3m/d (12)	77.10 3m/d (12)	46.15 3m/d (1)	36.88 3m/d (12)
1914	94.38 3m/d (7)	77.40 3m/d (7)		37.06 3m/d (7)

[a]   Up to 1700, internal Russian money rate for the mentioned foreign currencies.

[b]   Concerning the British currency, see pp. 3–5.

[c]   Concerning the Dutch currency, see pp. 57–59.

[d]   "The big jump in the rate of exchange from 1787 to 1788 was due to the fact, that a new bank which opened in 1787 immediately issued notes for 15 million roubles, while during the war the issue was heavily increased, which led to a further fall in the rate of exchange" (RASCH [1965], pp. 61f.). Further "the exchange rate in summer could on rare occasions rise to a fifth over that in winter" (SPOONER [1983], p. 121).

[e]   Concerning the Hamburg and the German currency respectively, see pp. 191–193, 197.

[f]   Concerning the French currency, see pp. 279f.

11.2 Riga exchange rates

11.2.1 On Amsterdam, Hamburg and London

	RIGA on:		
	Amsterdam [a]	**Hamburg**	**London**
	per 100 guilders Flemish current [b]	per 100 mark banco [c]	per 10 pounds sterling [d]
	in Albertthaler		
1757	37.04 65d/d (1)	36.00 65d/d (1)	
1758	38.62 65d/d (12)	35.03 65d/d (12)	
1759	39.28 65d/d (10)	35.20 65d/d (10)	
...			
1762	37.56 65d/d (1)	35.50 65d/d (1)	
1763	37.78 65d/d (12)	34.81 65d/d (12)	
1764	38.45 65d/d (12)	33.70 65d/d (12)	
1765	38.62 65d/d (12)	33.90 65d/d (12)	
1766	37.73 65d/d (1)	34.00 65d/d (1)	
...			
1777	38.74 65d/d (1)	32.33 65d/d (1)	
1778	38.30 65d/d (12)	32.68 65d/d (12)	
1779	38.52 65d/d (12)	32.78 65d/d (12)	
1780	39.22 65d/d (1)	32.33 65d/d (1)	
...			
1783	*36.99* [a] (7)		
1784	*37.30* [a] (11)		
1785	*37.65* [a] (7)		
1786	*38.28* [a] (1)		
...			
1799	34.83 36d/d (3)	33.50 36d/d (3)	42.04 3m/d (3)
1800	37.04 36d/d (2)	33.58 36d/d (2)	37.78 3m/d (1)
1801	36.90 36d/d (5)	33.27 36d/d (5)	38.22 3m/d (3)
1802	37.34 36d/d (4)	33.13 36d/d (4)	40.50 3m/d (4)
1803	38.65 65d/d (1)	34.33 65d/d (1)	43.11 65d/d (1)
1804	38.00 36d/d (4)	32.33 36d/d (4)	43.53 3m/d (4)
1805	37.76 36d/d (3)	33.89 36d/d (3)	43.63 3m/d (3)
1806	38.88 36d/d (4)	32.00 36d/d (4)	43.67 3m/d (4)
1807	38.84 36d/d (4)	31.29 36d/d (4)	44.58 3m/d (4)
1808	38.83 36d/d (1)	32.33 36d/d (1)	
1809	39.30 36d/d (1)	31.33 36d/d (1)	43.78 3m/d (1)

[a] 1783–1786: broker's quotation at Riga. No information is available concerning the usance: 36 or 65 days' dato are possible.

[b] Concerning the Dutch currency, see pp. 57f.

[c]   Concerning the Hamburg currency, see pp. 171–173.

[d]   Concerning the British currency, see pp. 3–5.

11.3 Helsinki exchange rates

The following quotations are average rates of the highest and the lowest quotations of each month given by the Bank of Finland (Suomen Pankki).

11.3.1 On London, Amsterdam, Germany and Paris

	HELSINKI on:			
	London	**Amsterdam**	**Hamburg**	**Paris**
	per 10 pounds sterling [a]	per 100 Dutch guilders [b]	per 100 mark banco, from 1873 per 100 mark [c]	per 100 francs [d]
	in markkaa			
1865	253.00 3m/d (1)	209.80 3m/d (1)	193.00 3m/d (1)	102.00 3m/d (1)
1866	253.55 3m/d (12)	210.15 3m/d (12)	189.67 3m/d (12)	100.96 3m/d (12)
1867	253.84 3m/d (12)	210.00 3m/d (12)	189.00 3m/d (12)	101.00 3m/d (12)
1868	254.09 3m/d (12)	212.25 3m/d (12)	189.00 3m/d (12)	101.00 3m/d (12)
1869	254.38 3m/d (12)	212.55 3m/d (12)	189.00 3m/d (12)	101.00 3m/d (12)
1870	253.59 3m/d (12)	211.57 3m/d (12)	188.50 3m/d (12)	100.68 3m/d (8)
1871	253.50 3m/d (12)	211.50 3m/d (12)	187.60 3m/d (12)	99.05 3m/d (6)
1872	251.94 3m/d (12)	209.90 3m/d (12)	186.46 3m/d (12)	99.02 3m/d (12)
1873	251.05 3m/d (12)	207.85 3m/d (12)	123.82 3m/d (12)	98.50 3m/d (12)
1874	251.66 3m/d (12)	210.43 3m/d (12)	123.35 3m/d (12)	99.47 3m/d (12)
1875	257.72 3m/d (12)	216.44 3m/d (12)	125.65 3m/d (12)	102.15 3m/d (12)
1876	281.72 3m/d (12)	232.30 3m/d (12)	137.53 3m/d (12)	111.72 3m/d (12)
1877	263.30 3m/d (12)	217.23 3m/d (12)	128.49 3m/d (12)	104.70 3m/d (12)
1878	253.62 3m/d (12)	209.13 3m/d (12)	124.32 3m/d (12)	100.95 3m/d (12)
1879	252.18 3m/d (12)	208.00 3m/d (12)	123.70 3m/d (12)	100.11 3m/d (12)
1880	252.89 3m/d (12)	207.69 3m/d (12)	124.07 3m/d (12)	100.01 3m/d (12)
1881	253.27 3m/d (12)	207.50 3m/d (12)	124.22 3m/d (12)	100.16 3m/d (12)
1882	253.77 3m/d (12)	207.19 3m/d (12)	124.34 3m/d (12)	100.40 3m/d (12)
1883	253.50 3m/d (12)	207.00 3m/d (12)	124.27 3m/d (12)	100.48 3m/d (12)
1884	253.50 3m/d (12)	207.37 3m/d (12)	124.20 3m/d (12)	100.38 3m/d (12)
1885	253.61 3m/d (12)	208.21 3m/d (12)	124.21 3m/d (12)	100.52 3m/d (12)
1886	253.57 3m/d (12)	208.35 3m/d (12)	124.25 3m/d (12)	100.30 3m/d (12)
1887	253.61 3m/d (12)	208.90 3m/d (12)	124.27 3m/d (12)	100.23 3m/d (12)
1888	253.61 3m/d (12)	209.50 3m/d (12)	124.34 3m/d (12)	100.25 3m/d (12)
1889	253.42 3m/d (12)	209.50 3m/d (12)	124.28 3m/d (12)	100.42 3m/d (12)
1890	253.80 3m/d (12)	209.23 3m/d (12)	124.38 3m/d (12)	100.30 3m/d (12)
1891	253.32 3m/d (12)	209.00 3m/d (12)	124.44 3m/d (12)	100.51 3m/d (12)
1892	253.24 3m/d (12)	209.21 3m/d (12)	124.45 3m/d (12)	100.55 3m/d (12)
1893	253.82 3m/d (12)	209.40 3m/d (12)	124.33 3m/d (12)	100.14 3m/d (12)
1894	252.49 3m/d (12)	209.19 3m/d (12)	123.81 3m/d (12)	100.45 3m/d (12)
1895	252.70 3m/d (12)	208.96 3m/d (12)	123.85 3m/d (12)	100.41 3m/d (12)

	HELSINKI on:			
	London	**Amsterdam**	**Hamburg**	**Paris**
	per 10 pounds sterling [a]	per 100 Dutch guilders [b]	per 100 mark [c]	per 100 francs [d]
	in markkaa			
1896	252.94 3m/d (12)	208.72 3m/d (12)	124.04 3m/d (12)	100.24 3m/d (12)
1897	252.96 3m/d (12)	208.79 3m/d (12)	123.81 3m/d (12)	100.12 3m/d (12)
1898	252.88 3m/d (12)	209.40 3m/d (12)	123.79 3m/d (12)	100.12 3m/d (12)
1899	253.62 3m/d (12)	209.13 3m/d (12)	123.97 3m/d (12)	100.53 3m/d (12)
1900	254.15 3m/d (12)	209.80 3m/d (12)	124.10 3m/d (12)	101.04 3m/d (12)
1901	253.61 3m/d (12)	209.90 3m/d (12)	124.05 3m/d (12)	100.90 3m/d (12)
1902	253.60 3m/d (12)	209.50 3m/d (12)	123.98 3m/d (12)	100.85 3m/d (12)
1903	253.55 3m/d (12)	209.66 3m/d (12)	124.00 3m/d (12)	100.82 3m/d (12)
1904	253.48 3m/d (12)	210.04 3m/d (12)	124.02 3m/d (12)	100.74 3m/d (12)
1905	253.67 3m/d (12)	209.91 3m/d (12)	123.95 3m/d (12)	100.82 3m/d (12)
1906	253.97 3m/d (12)	209.59 3m/d (12)	124.04 3m/d (12)	100.96 3m/d (12)
1907	254.55 3m/d (12)	210.51 3m/d (12)	124.26 3m/d (12)	101.06 3m/d (12)
1908	253.98 3m/d (12)	210.25 3m/d (12)	124.17 3m/d (12)	101.07 3m/d (12)
1909	253.76 3m/d (12)	209.84 3m/d (12)	124.03 3m/d (12)	100.79 3m/d (12)
1910	253.69 3m/d (12)	209.77 3m/d (12)	123.90 3m/d (12)	100.60 3m/d (12)
1911	253.58 3m/d (12)	209.96 3m/d (12)	123.90 3m/d (12)	100.48 3m/d (12)
1912	253.57 3m/d (12)	209.99 3m/d (12)	123.81 3m/d (12)	100.53 3m/d (12)
1913	253.88 3m/d (12)	209.55 3m/d (12)	124.07 3m/d (12)	100.62 3m/d (12)
1914	254.11 3m/d (7)	210.08 3m/d (7)	124.05 3m/d (7)	100.92 3m/d (7)

[a]   Concerning the British currency, see pp. 3–5.

[b]   Concerning the Dutch currency, see pp. 57–59.

[c]   Concerning the Hamburg and the German currency respectively, see pp. 171–173, 179.

[d]   Concerning the French currency, see pp. 279f.

11.3.2 On Saint Petersburg, Scandinavian places and New York

	HELSINKI on:		
	Saint Petersburg	**Stockholm**	**Copenhagen,** from 1887 (5) also **Christiania (Oslo)**
	per 100 silver roubles payable in credit notes (kreditnye bilety) [a]	per 100 rixdollar rixmynt, from 1875 per 100 Swedish crowns [b]	per 100 Danish crowns (from 1875), from 1887 (5) also per 100 Norwegian crowns [c]
	in markkaa		
1865	329.75 3m/d (2)	147.00 s (1)	
1866	312.67 3m/d (12)	143.59 s (12)	
1867	343.17 3m/d (12)	142.60 s (12)	
1868	348.21 3m/d (12)	141.54 s (12)	
1869	326.00 3m/d (12)	141.50 s (12)	
1870	314.32 3m/d (12)	141.97 s (12)	
1871	336.13 3m/d (12)	142.00 s (12)	
1872	343.80 3m/d (12)	141.63 s (12)	
1873	339.50 3m/d (12)	140.68 s (12)	
1874	348.92 3m/d (12)	139.72 s (12)	
1875	353.21 3m/d (12)	142.62 s (12)	
1876	363.92 3m/d (12)	156.05 s (12)	
1877	288.30 3m/d (12)	145.66 s (12)	
1878	261.21 3m/d (12)	140.33 s (12)	
1879	255.63 3m/d (12)	139.67 s (12)	
1880	263.75 3m/d (12)	139.35 s (12)	
1881	265.05 3m/d (12)	139.06 s (12)	
1882	254.67 3m/d (12)	139.23 s (12)	139.20 s (12)
1883	249.55 3m/d (12)	139.15 s (12)	139.20 s (12)
1884	255.59 3m/d (12)	139.15 s (12)	139.19 s (12)
1885	254.42 3m/d (12)	139.12 s (12)	139.16 s (12)
1886	245.67 3m/d (12)	139.11 s (12)	139.16 s (12)
1887	225.80 3m/d (12)	139.29 s (12)	139.34 s (12)
1888	235.84 3m/d (12)	139.33 s (12)	139.34 s (12)
1889	266.80 3m/d (12)	139.31 s (12)	139.31 s (12)
1890	292.92 3m/d (12)	139.35 s (12)	139.35 s (12)
1891	279.42 3m/d (12)	139.47 s (12)	139.47 s (12)
1892	254.67 3m/d (12)	139.39 s (12)	139.39 s (12)
1893	263.38 3m/d (12)	139.50 s (12)	139.50 s (12)
1894	269.27 3m/d (12)	139.30 s (12)	139.30 s (12)
1895	270.59 3m/d (12)	139.30 s (12)	139.30 s (12)
1896	268.00 3m/d (12)	139.28 s (12)	139.28 s (12)

	HELSINKI on:			
	Saint Petersburg	**Stockholm**	**Copenhagen & Christiania (Oslo)**	**New York**
	per 100 silver roubles payable in credit notes (kreditnye bilety), from 1899 (7) per 100 gold roubles [a]	per 100 Swedish crowns [b]	per 100 Danish or Norwegian crowns [c]	per 100 US dollars
	in markkaa			
1897	267.51 3m/d (12)	139.03 s (12)	139.03 s (12)	
1898	267.50 3m/d (12)	138.98 s (12)	138.98 s (12)	
1899	267.65 3m/d (12)	139.04 s (12)	139.04 s (12)	
1900	267.80 3m/d (12)	139.10 s (12)	139.10 s (12)	
1901	267.80 3m/d (12)	139.30 s (12)	139.30 s (12)	
1902	267.80 3m/d (12)	139.30 s (12)	139.30 s (12)	
1903	267.80 3m/d (12)	139.30 s (12)	139.30 s (12)	
1904	267.80 3m/d (12)	139.30 s (12)	139.30 s (12)	
1905	267.57 3m/d (12)	139.30 s (12)	139.30 s (12)	
1906	267.04 3m/d (12)	139.30 s (12)	139.30 s (12)	
1907	267.04 3m/d (12)	139.30 s (12)	139.30 s (12)	
1908	266.22 3m/d (12)	139.43 s (12)	139.43 s (12)	
1909	267.78 3m/d (12)	139.34 s (12)	139.34 s (12)	
1910	268.24 3m/d (12)	139.28 s (12)	139.28 s (12)	
1911	267.89 3m/d (12)	139.32 s (12)	139.32 s (12)	
1912	267.25 3m/d (12)	139.21 s (12)	139.21 s (12)	
1913	267.19 3m/d (12)	139.19 s (12)	139.19 s (12)	523.00 3m/d (12)
1914	266.96 3m/d (7)	139.40 s (7)	139.40 s (7)	523.00 3m/d (7)

[a] Concerning the Russian currency, see pp. 359f.

[b] Concerning the Swedish currency, see pp. 339f.

[c] Concerning the Danish currency, see pp. 327f. According to the treaty of the Scandinavian Monetary Union, the currency of Norway was from 1877 the crown (0.4032 grammes of pure gold) of 100 öre, which was exactly equal to the Swedish and Danish crowns (cf. SWOBODA [1902], p. 238).

[d] Concerning the US currency, see pp. 403f.

12

Poland (1696–1812)

Exchange market: Danzig (1696–1812)

Sources: PRO London, XP 1211 C 104/128 Pt 2: *Price currents* [Danzig] (1696–1698); Wojewodz-kie Archiwum Państowe w Gdańsku – Biblioteka Gdańska Polskiej Akademii Nauk, *Anzeigen und Erläuterungen der Specie & Wechsel-Course* [Danzig] (1707–1774); *Danziger Nachrichten, Danziger Erfahrungen, Wöchentliche Danziger Anzeigen und Dienliche Nachrichten* (1739–1812).
Concordance: *HStD XII*, pp. 257–280

Currency: The basis of the currency in Poland was the guilder (zlot) Polish current of 30 groszy at 18 pfennig. In the course of the 18th century the guilder, which was equal to 1/3 thaler, lost in value from about 6.75 (in c. 1705) to about 4.18 grammes of pure silver (from 1766 up to c. 1810). In 1812 the guilder contained only 3.78 grammes of pure silver (FURTAK [1935], pp. 76–78). Between 1766 and 1786 the guilder was minted at a standard of 80 guilders per mark of Cologne. This standard was oriented towards the standard of 20 guilders per mark of Cologne (the so-called Konventionsfuß), which was common usage in the Electorate of Saxony (at this time Poland and Saxony were united). So 4 guilders Polish current were equal to 1 guilder Konventionskurant. Thereafter, Poland had a standard of coinage of 13 11/12 thaler per mark of Cologne up to 1794 and of 14 1/12 thaler per mark of Cologne from 1794 (VON SCHRÖTTER [1913], p. 231). Since Danzig had lost its territorial connection to the Kingdom of Poland because of the First Polish Division in 1772, another name for the guilder Polish current in Danzig also gained acceptance in contemporary merchant manuals, namely the guilder Danzig current. Even after the occupation by Prussia in 1793, the previous currency system was maintained in Danzig until 1814, 4 guilders Danzig current being equal to 1 thaler Prussian current (see pp. 196f.).

Original quotations at Danzig

on:	in:	per:
Amsterdam	groszy Polish/Danzig current	1 pound of 6 guilders Flemish banco
Hamburg	groszy Polish/Danzig current	1 rixdollar species-banco [a]
London	guilders Polish/Danzig current	1 pound sterling

[a]   In Hamburg 999 rixdollars specie-banco were equal to 1,000 rixdollars banco = 3,000 mark banco.

Other data available: Amsterdam, 40d/d (1794–1803, 1812) – Hamburg, 6w/d (1793–1800).

Even after its golden age in the 17th century, Danzig was not only the most important trade centre and port of export between Poland and the rest of Europe, but also the central Polish exchange market. Although exchange rate quotations of Danzig are available in some price currents of the 17th century, longer data series cannot be compiled until the turn of the 18th century. In particular, the Dutch immigrants, whose number had been rising, especially in the 1640s, had introduced their forms of bills of exchange representing innovative forms in Poland. "They dominated the granting of credit as well as banking operations in the city" (VAN TIELHOF [2002], p. 175). Therefore and because of the trade relations of Danzig, Amsterdam and Hamburg were its central exchange partners, Amsterdam also being the most important foreign creditor of the city of Danzig (CIESLAK [1983], passim). For large parts of the 18ᵗʰ century both financial markets were quoted exclusively. In the case of Amsterdam the differences between both quoted usances (40 and 70 days' dato) amounted to 1 grosz, in the case of Hamburg (six and ten weeks' dato) they amounted to ½ grosz (ODDY [1805], p. 261). It was not until 1791 that London became an additional exchange partner. Quotations on Nuremberg, Leipzig or Frankfurt am Main can be proved only for some periods of the 17ᵗʰ century, whereas there is no evidence for them during the 18ᵗʰ century.

Belonging to Prussia since April 1793 because of the Second Polish Division, Danzig was under French occupation between 1807 and 1814. Owing to the resulting Continental System, the quotation on London was suspended during those years. In 1811 KELLY wrote that Danzig "does not generally exchange, in a direct way, with any other places than the above", i.e. with Amsterdam, Hamburg and London. "When, however, a direct transaction of the kind takes place with Leipsic, Breslau, Konigsberg, Berlin, Francfort on the Oder, &c., the exchange is done in monies of the same denomination, at 30 per cent. more or less; that is, 130 Rixdollars, Dantzic currency, are given for 100 Rixdollars of the above places" (KELLY [1811], p. 113).

After Danzig had been subsumed once again in the Kingdom of Prussia, and its economic decline had started, the city stood in the shadow of Berlin, which became the central Prussian exchange market in those years. After that the quotations of Danzig on Hamburg, Amsterdam, London and Paris (from 1829) corresponded approximately to those of Berlin on these financial markets, even though Danzig still had its particular way of quotation until September 1823. Therefore no rates are documented from 1814 onwards. Danzig was the only financial market in Prussia, perhaps in the whole of Europe that quoted Warsaw, the capital of the Kingdom of Poland, and this was the only unusual and remarkable feature of Danzig's quotations of the second quarter of the 19ᵗʰ century. This is why only these quotations of Danzig on Warsaw are documented here (see pp. 248 and 363).

As a result of the customs border between Prussia and the Russian Empire, Danzig lost most of its former hinterland. This fact, the competition between Danzig, Hamburg and Stettin for supremacy in the German and Polish trade in the Baltic Sea and the disregard shown for Danzig when the railway was built, meant that the former importance of Danzig as a financial place in the cashless payment system declined quickly and became obsolete after 1850. In 1855 the exchange rate quotations in the *Danziger Nachrichten* ceased.

References: Friedrich VON SCHRÖTTER, *Das preußische Münzwesen im 18. Jahrhundert (= Acta Borussica. Denkmäler der Preußischen Staatsverwaltung im 18. Jahrhundert. Die einzelnen Gebiete der Verwaltung. Münzwesen. Münzgeschichtlicher Teil), 4. Bd.: Die letzten vierzig Jahre. 1765–1806*, Berlin 1913; Tadeusz FURTAK, *Ceny w Gdansku w latach 1701–1815*, Lwów 1935, pp. 46–52; Marian GUMOWSKI, *Handbuch der polnischen Numismatik*, Graz 1960, pp. 67–77; Herbert RITTMANN, *Deutsche Geldgeschichte 1484–1914*, München 1975; Edmund CIESLAK, *Amsterdam als*

Bankier von Danzig im 18. Jahrhundert, in *The Interactions of Amsterdam and Antwerp with the Baltic Region, 1400–1800. De Nederlanden en het Oostzeegebied, 1400–1800. Papers presented at the 3rd International Conference of the Association Internationale d'Histoire des Mers Nordiques de l'Europe (Utrecht 1982)*, Leiden 1983, pp. 123–132; Oskar SCHWARZER / Markus A. DENZEL / Petra SCHNELZER, Geld- und Wechselkurse in Deutschland und im Ostseeraum (18. und 19. Jahrhundert), in *HStD XII*, pp. 2–43; Markus A. DENZEL, Die Integration Deutschlands in das internationale Zahlungsverkehrssystem im 17. und 18. Jahrhundert, in Eckart SCHREMMER (ed.), *Wirtschaftliche und soziale Integration in historischer Sicht*, Stuttgart 1996, pp. 58–109, here pp. 71f., 88f.; Milja VAN TIELHOF, *The 'Mother of All Trades'. The Baltic Grain Trade in Amsterdam from the Late 16th to the Early 19th Century*, Leiden – Boston – Köln 2002.

12.1 Danzig exchange rates

12.1.1 On Amsterdam, Hamburg and London

	DANZIG on: [a]	
	Amsterdam	**Hamburg**
	per 100 guilders Flemish banco [b]	per 100 mark specie-banco [c]
	in guilders Polish current	
1696	149.36 40d/d (4)	120.58 3w/d (4)
1697	142.83 40d/d (5)	117.33 3w/d (5)
1698	141.53 40d/d (4)	117.16 3w/d (4)
1699		
1700		
1701		
1702		
1703		
1704		
1705		
1706		
1707	155.00 40d/d (1)	128.52 3w/d (1)
1708	154.79 40d/d (12)	128.29 3w/d (12)
1709	144.36 40d/d (12)	121.24 3w/d (12)
1710	149.96 40d/d (12)	126.70 3w/d (12)
1711	155.42 40d/d (12)	129.40 3w/d (12)
1712	157.83 40d/d (12)	129.80 3w/d (12)
1713	151.65 40d/d (12)	127.19 3w/d (12)
1714	146.09 40d/d (12)	122.19 3w/d (12)
1715	150.07 40d/d (12)	125.31 3w/d (12)
1716	155.10 40d/d (12)	128.60 3w/d (12)
1717	158.89 40d/d (12)	130.47 3w/d (12)
1718	158.73 40d/d (12)	130.24 3w/d (12)
1719	155.70 40d/d (12)	128.23 3w/d (12)
1720	155.88 40d/d (12)	128.55 3w/d (12)
1721	160.47 40d/d (12)	130.51 3w/d (12)
1722	160.84 40d/d (12)	130.88 3w/d (12)
1723	155.44 40d/d (12)	127.12 3w/d (12)
1724	153.99 40d/d (12)	128.14 3w/d (12)
1725	153.80 40d/d (12)	127.97 3w/d (12)
1726	156.39 40d/d (12)	129.48 3w/d (12)
1727	158.87 40d/d (12)	128.46 3w/d (12)
1728	157.74 40d/d (12)	128.34 3w/d (12)
1729	156.81 40d/d (12)	128.65 3w/d (12)

	DANZIG on: [d]	
	Amsterdam	**Hamburg**
	per 100 guilders Flemish banco [b]	per 100 mark specie-banco [c]
	in guilders Polish current	
1730	160.79 40d/d (12)	132.72 3w/d (12)
1731	160.51 40d/d (12)	133.38 3w/d (12)
1732	160.81 40d/d (12)	132.09 3w/d (12)
1733	158.08 40d/d (12)	130.03 3w/d (12)
1734	157.04 40d/d (9)	127.64 3w/d (9)
1735	158.41 40d/d (12)	129.26 3w/d (12)
1736	161.97 40d/d (12)	132.77 3w/d (12)
1737	162.41 40d/d (12)	134.66 3w/d (12)
1738	162.25 40d/d (12)	134.99 3w/d (12)
1739	159.96 40d/d (12)	133.15 3w/d (12)
1740	157.64 40d/d (12)	131.33 3w/d (12)
1741	161.26 40d/d (12)	133.45 3w/d (12)
1742	162.92 40d/d (12)	135.76 3w/d (12)
1743	163.15 40d/d (12)	135.70 3w/d (12)
1744	162.69 40d/d (12)	135.14 3w/d (12)
1745	163.01 40d/d (12)	134.87 3w/d (12)
1746	163.06 40d/d (12)	133.55 3w/d (12)
1747	161.16 40d/d (12)	131.35 3w/d (12)
1748	160.14 40d/d (12)	132.10 3w/d (12)
1749	159.52 40d/d (12)	133.21 3w/d (12)
1750	162.64 40d/d (12)	136.38 3w/d (12)
1751	165.70 40d/d (12)	140.82 3w/d (12)
1752	167.60 40d/d (12)	142.43 3w/d (12)
1753	173.11 40d/d (12)	146.30 3w/d (12)
1754	173.70 40d/d (12)	148.60 3w/d (12)
1755	173.34 40d/d (12)	147.50 3w/d (12)
1756	175.93 40d/d (12)	143.89 3w/d (12)
1757	174.36 40d/d (12)	137.60 3w/d (12)
1758	176.07 40d/d (12)	138.32 3w/d (12)
1759	191.46 40d/d (12)	148.34 3w/d (12)
1760	214.10 40d/d (12)	179.99 3w/d (12)
1761	219.54 40d/d (12)	187.61 3w/d (12)
1762	211.97 40d/d (12)	175.28 3w/d (12)
1763	209.29 40d/d (12)	174.08 3w/d (12)
1764	212.48 40d/d (12)	179.11 3w/d (12)
1765	221.74 40d/d (12)	186.19 3w/d (12)
1766	227.87 40d/d (12)	184.12 3w/d (12)
1767	239.66 40d/d (12)	189.45 3w/d (12)

	DANZIG on:		
	Amsterdam	**Hamburg**	**London** [e]
	per 100 guilders Flemish banco [b]	per 100 mark specie-banco [c]	per 10 pounds sterling [f]
	in guilders Polish current or Danzig current resp.		
1768	233.01 40d/d (12)	191.67 3w/d (12)	
1769	229.75 40d/d (12)	193.01 3w/d (12)	
1770	230.10 40d/d (12)	192.49 3w/d (12)	
1771	230.81 40d/d (12)	194.40 3w/d (12)	
1772	237.80 40d/d (12)	202.57 3w/d (12)	
1773	241.30 40d/d (12)	203.38 3w/d (12)	
1774	238.75 40d/d (10)	200.85 3w/d (12)	
1775	235.99 40d/d (12)	198.23 3w/d (12)	
1776	238.39 40d/d (11)	201.14 3w/d (11)	
1777	236.31 40d/d (10)	201.30 10w/d (12)	
1778	235.75 40d/d (10)	199.87 10w/d (12)	
1779	237.66 40d/d (11)	198.57 10w/d (12)	
1780	236.91 40d/d (11)	199.75 10w/d (11)	
1781	236.90 40d/d (11)	199.01 10w/d (12)	
1782	234.83 40d/d (8)	202.04 10w/d (12)	
1783	230.63 40d/d (8)	200.86 10w/d (12)	
1784	231.12 40d/d (11)	198.80 10w/d (12)	
1785	229.63 40d/d (3)	196.95 10w/d (12)	
1786		195.84 10w/d (12)	
1787	230.16 40d/d (7)	196.72 10w/d (12)	
1788	226.56 40d/d (10)	195.42 10w/d (12)	
1789	224.00 40d/d (10)	195.28 10w/d (12)	
1790	221.67 40d/d (5)	194.59 10w/d (12)	
1791	225.48 40d/d (7)	195.05 10w/d (12)	256.62 3m (9)
1792	223.62 40d/d (12)	192.94 10w/d (12)	245.16 3m (12)
1793	225.15 40d/d (12)	195.15 10w/d (12)	259.64 3m (12)
1794	213.48 70d/d (12)	191.72 10w/d (12)	251.46 3m (12)
1795	203.89 70d/d (9)	186.60 10w/d (12)	227.13 3m (12)
1796	196.64 70d/d (10)	184.96 10w/d (12)	225.42 3m (12)
1797	207.45 70d/d (10)	190.00 10w/d (12)	252.75 3m (12)
1798	207.21 70d/d (12)	186.86 10w/d (12)	258.16 3m (12)
1799	197.51 70d/d (12)	183.91 10w/d (12)	229.92 3m (12)
1800	206.65 70d/d (12)	185.21 10w/d (12)	213.20 3m (12)
1801	207.53 70d/d (11)	188.23 10w/d (12)	217.70 3m (12)
1802	213.45 70d/d (12)	190.70 10w/d (12)	231.55 3m (12)
1803	209.74 70d/d (12)	188.20 10w/d (12)	235.41 3m (12)
1804	211.74 70d/d (12)	188.85 10w/d (12)	244.70 3m (12)
1805	203.01 70d/d (12)	183.64 10w/d (12)	234.00 3m (12)

	DANZIG on:		
	Amsterdam	**Hamburg**	**London** [e]
	per 100 guilders Flemish banco [b]	per 100 mark specie-banco [c]	per 10 pounds sterling [f]
	in guilders Polish current or Danzig current resp.		
1806	213.78 70d/d (12)	191.42 10w/d (12)	236.87 3m (12)
1807	217.34 70d/d (10)	192.18 10w/d (11)	233.25 3m (4)
1808	207.23 70d/d (12)	178.31 10w/d (12)	
1809	200.65 70d/d (12)	177.67 10w/d (12)	
1810	213.08 70d/d (11)	187.65 10w/d (12)	
1811		183.34 10w/d (11)	
1812	188.89 70d/d (4)	167.04 10w/d (12)	

[a] Price currents with exchange rate quotations from Danzig for the time before 1696 are only available for a few months: Internationaal Instituut voor Sociale Geschiedenis, Amsterdam: *PrysCorant van de Coopmannschap* [Danzig] (1608, 1632); Riksarkivet Stockholm, Strödda kamerala handlingar, vol. 23: *PrysCorant van de Coopmannschap* [Danzig] (1631, 1635, 1646).

[b] Concerning the Dutch currency, see pp. 57f.

[c] Concerning the Hamburg currency, see pp. 191–193.

[d] Because of the siege of the town by a Russian army no quotations were given between March 6th and July 9th 1734.

[e] There is neither a note in the sources nor in contemporary merchant manuals explaining whether the usance for bills of exchange on London is after dato or after sight.

[f] Concerning the British currency, see pp. 3–5.

13

Ottoman Empire (1760–1914)

Exchange markets: Smyrna (1760–1790) and Constantinople (1790–1914)

Sources: Smyrna: ACCM Marseille, L. IX 1034/1035: *Cours des Changes* (1760–1788); REBUFFAT / COUDURIÉ [1966], p. 124, tableau XXIII (1787–1790). Constantinople: ISSAWI [1981], pp. 329f. (1790–1844); PAMUK [2000], p. 168 (1798); NOBACK [1851], 2. Abth., pp. 1711–1714, 1852 (1849/50); NOBACK [1858], pp. 335, 666 (1853/55); *Smyrna Mail* (1862–1864); *Levant Times & Shipping Gazette* (1868–1873); *Levant Herald* (*Constantinople Messenger – Eastern Express*) (1874–1914); *The Economist*, London (1874–1892).

Concordance: *WdW VIII*, pp. 107–134

Currency: The monetary system in the Ottoman Empire was based upon the (new) silver piastre (kurus) of 40 paras at 3 aspers (akçes), which became the leading unit of account in the Ottoman Empire during the 18th century. So, at Smyrna and Constantinople the exchange rates were quoted in or for these piastres. After an era of relatively high stability, the debasement of the Turkish piastre started during the third quarter of the 18th century and continued over a long period of the 19th century:

The debasement of the piastre 1708–1844: fine silver content in grammes

1708	15.4	1766	11.5	1808	5.90	1829	0.72
1716	15.9	1774	10.9	1809	4.42	1831	0.53
1720	15.8	1780	10.0	1810	3.74	1832	0.94
1730	14.9	1788	9.40	1818	4.42	1839	0.94
1740	14.5	1789	6.90	1820	2.95	1844	1.00
1754	14.2	1794	5.90	1822	2.32		
1757	11.4	1800	5.90	1828	1.47		

Source: PAMUK [2000], pp. 163, 191

This development was a result of the war with Russia for predominance in the Black Sea area (1768–1774) and the following decline of trade with the Ottoman Empire. The attempts at stabilizing the currency always resulted in a loss in value of the silver coins against gold. The value of the piastre reached a low in 1831, subsequent to the fiscal difficulties caused by the wars against Persia (1820–1828) and Russia (1828/29, the latter being connected to the Greek Revolution and necessitating extensive reparations to the Russian Empire). "Closely paralleling the debasement of the currency was the sharp fall in its exchange rate" (PAMUK [2000], p. 193). The bimetallism and new standards for gold and silver coinage had not been introduced until the currency reform of 1844 was carried out in the Tanzimat era (i.e. during the politics of 'reorganization' between 1839 and 1876, urged by Western powers) following the model of the Egyptian currency reform of 1834 (see p. 585). The piastre or kurus (0.998 grammes of fine silver) and the new gold lira or Turkish pound (6.6147 grammes of fine gold) became standard units of currency and legal tender, being freely convertible at the fixed rate of 1 lira = 100 piastres (PAMUK [2000], pp. 208s.). In addition, a fixed ratio to sterling was established (1 lira = 18 shillings sterling). At the same time the matter of currency stability again became more severe because of the interest-bearing uncovered paper money in the area of Constantinople and its hinterland. This paper money was the so-called 'kaime-i muteber-i nakdiyye' (for short: 'kaime'), which was issued for the first time in 1839 to reduce the budget deficit. However, the issued paper money did not play a part in exchange rate quoting since these quotings were done in or for specie. Due to international trade agreements over low import duties, the pledging of revenues and the growing external debt of the Ottoman Empire, which was largely economically as well as financially exposed to the influences of the Western consulates in Constantinople since the Crimean war (1853–1856), led into national bankruptcy on October 6th 1875. The result was a crisis of the Turkish bankers in Galata, prompting the Sublime Porte to issue more kaime money so that in 1879/80 there was finally a total of 14 million liras in kaime in circulation. With the currency reform of January 1st 1881 the Ottoman Empire moved from the bimetallic standard to a limping gold standard with the gold lira (6.6134 grammes of fine gold) of 100 piastres gold (kurus sag) or 105.26 piastres silver as the standard unit of coinage (new notes payable in gold were only offered by the Imperial Ottoman Bank until World War I; cf. SWOBODA [1902], p. 243). Therefore "the premium for gold over silver usually increased with the distance from Istanbul" and "from the 1880s until World War I, the silver kurus steadily lost value against the gold lira and other foreign currencies. The exchange rate of the old lira rose from 114 kurus in 1886 to 137 kurus in 1914 but remained stable against foreign currencies" (PAMUK [2000], p. 219). So the government succeeded in its policy of consistent external stabilizing of the currency but it "did not have the reserves and financial strength to redeem the existing silver stock and move to a full-fledged gold standard" (ibid., p. 217).

Original quotations at Smyrna

on:	in:	per:
Amsterdam	paras	1 guilder Flemish current
Leghorn	paras	1 pezza da otto reali
Marseilles	per cent discount in piastres	100 livres tournois
Vienna	paras	1 guilder Konventionskurant

Original quotations at Constantinople

on:	in:	per:
Berlin	mark	100 piastres
London	piastres	1 pound sterling
Marseilles	paras	1 franc
Odessa	kopecks	1 piastre
	from 1870 piastres	1 imperial [a]
	from 1896 gold roubles	100 piastres
Paris	paras	1 franc
	from 1881 francs	100 piastres
Trieste	paras	1 guilder Österreichische Währung
Vienna	paras	1 Austrian ducat
	1888 paras	1 Marie Theresa thaler
	from 1889 guilders Österreichische Währung	100 piastres
	from 1900 Austrian crowns	100 piastres

[a]   Up to 1885 1 (old) imperial (11.9974 grammes of fine gold) = 10 gold roubles or – legally fixed – 10.30 silver roubles; from 1885 1 (new) imperial (11.6118 grammes of fine gold) = 10 gold roubles (from January 3rd/15th 1897 equal to 15 gold roubles); cf. SWOBODA [1902], pp. 508f. For the documentation the money rates for imperials have been calculated in roubles.

Other data available from Constantinople: Berlin, 3m/s (1894–1900) – London, 3m/s (bank bills, 1894–1914); 3m/s (commercial bills, 1869, 1881–1888, 1894–1909) – Marseilles, 3m/s (1868–1870) – Paris, 3m/s (bank bills, 1881–1914); 3m/s (commercial bills, 1869, 1881–1888, 1894–1909) – Vienna, 3m/s (1894–1901); 8d/s (1894–1905).

"With the growth of the European Trade, the Ottoman economy began to be incorporated, increasingly from the 1760s, into the European network of multilateral payments. Bills of exchange had been used as a means of payment in trade between the Ottoman Empire and Europe in the seventeenth century. Their volume increased substantially in the second half of the eighteenth century. In addition, suftajas and hawales continued to be used in payments flows within the Empire, especially in the transfer of tax revenues from the provinces to the capital city" (PAMUK [2000], p. 169). Constantinople "developed into an international exchange center during the last quarter of the century, joining the multilateral payments networks involving the leading European centers of commerce, London, Amsterdam, Trieste, Livorno, Venice, Vienna, and others. A busy market in bills of exchange and foreign exchange flourished in the capital city where all of the leading European currencies were quoted on a daily basis" (ibid., pp. 169s.; cf. BOUBAKER [1994], p. 200). So, by the end of the 18th century payment transactions between Constantinople and Marseilles were mostly effected without cash (REBUFFAT / COURDURIÉ [1966]; ELDEM [1986]; idem [1990], pp. 261–263). One reason for the incipient integration of Constantinople into the European system of cashless payment was its negative balance of trade. As European merchants were well stocked with goods to export from Constantinople to Europe, "they found it useful to join the payments networks between the capital city and the provinces. The tax revenues of the provinces being sent to the capital city by the tax collectors were thus exchanged with the funds European merchants wanted to send from Istanbul to their associates in the provinces so that the latter could pay for the goods they wanted to purchase and ship to Europe" (PAMUK [2000], p. 170). In that way other trade centres of the Ottoman Empire were simultaneously connected with the European system of cashless payment.

According to Pamuk, "it is thus possible to obtain detailed time series for the exchange rates of the Ottoman currency against the leading European currencies from European financial sources as well as the Ottoman sources beginning late in the eighteenth century" (ibid., p. 170 ann. 42), but this work has not been done so far. That is why exchange rates of several financial places from the Ottoman Empire are only available for relatively short periods during the 18th and 19th centuries. As merchant manuals and price currents prove, these data have already been quoted in past decades, but their records are too incomplete to be documented here. As the only exception a few exchange rate quotations of Smyrna could be compiled for the second half of the 18th century, when Smyrna was undoubtedly maintaining the closest cashless payment relations with Europe apart from Constantinople, just as it did during the 19th century. According to the sources documented here Smyrna regularly quoted Amsterdam, Leghorn and Marseilles, as well as Vienna (from the 1780s), while it was partly also quoting Constantinople and London. Thus "la situation privilégiée du change sur Amsterdam tenait au fait que le taux de change à Smyrne était lié en primeur lieu au commerce du coton. ... Amsterdam était pour Smyrne un pôle financier tout en étant une grande place du commerce de commission" (BOUBAKER [1994], p. 213).

Data series of Constantinople are available from the end of the 18th century until World War I and even though they are somewhat incomplete due to the sources so far available, only quotations on London can be presented here for the first decades. In contemporary merchant manuals, however, Amsterdam, Genoa, Hamburg, Leghorn,

London, Marseilles, Naples, Paris, Venice, Vienna and Trieste are listed as further foreign exchange partners of the early 19th century. Within the Ottoman Empire "the exchanges between Constantinople and other trading places, where Turkish money is used, are done at a premium of 10 per cent. more or less, in favour of Constantinople" (KELLY [1811] I, p. 100; cf. ibid., p. 388; II, p. 86). Oddy mentioned only London, Holland, Vienna and Leghorn as exchange partners of Constantinople, but he referred to the economic trend of the prices of the bills of exchange at that time: "The exchanges are observed to rise in the Spring, and continue to do so till the approach of Autumn, when they invariably fall. This latter being the season when all staple commodities of that country come to market, the returns being then made in goods, the number of remitters become of course diminished, and bills on Europe more plentiful" (ODDY [1805], p. 186).

In the 19th century the cashless payments at Constantinople were effected by private bankers, the so-called Galata bankers, who derived from the money changers (sarrafs) of the 18th century and who succeeded in the wake of the fiscal difficulties of the Ottoman Empire and the resulting state need for short- and long-term finance in becoming large financiers and "private bankers ... with connections in Europe" (PAMUK [1987], p. 56; cf. idem [2000], p. 200), because "in the aftermath of the French Revolution, these financiers were also able to replace the European merchants in Istanbul and assume control of important parts of the trade in bills of exchange" (ibid., p. 202). As the first bank of the whole Ottoman Empire, the Banque de Constantinople was founded by two of the leading Galata bankers (the bankers Alléon & Cie and Baltazzi) in 1847, who could be characterized as 'bankers without banks' (UDOVITCH [1979]) until then (PAMUK [2000], pp. 212s.). "The bank was to provide short-term loans to the government and stabilize the exchange rate of the Ottoman paper currency" (ibid., p. 212) as well as the rate on the most important foreign exchange partners (Great Britain, France and the Habsburg Monarchy). Therefore two exchange rates were quoted at Constantinople as long as the bank was in business. First, there was the "bank rate", i.e. the rate of the Banque de Constantinople, which was regularly quoted on London and Marseilles, only and which was a little bit lower than the "private rate". Second, the private rate reflected the quotations of the Galata bankers. Around the mid-19th century their exchange rate currents contained a much wider range of foreign places than those of the bank: regularly London, Marseilles, Leghorn, Odessa, Trieste and Vienna, sometimes also Amsterdam, Augsburg, Genoa, Madrid, Malta, Taganrog, Saint Petersburg, Smyrna and Salonica – but in various combinations (NOBACK [1851], 2. Abth., pp. 1709–1713; NOBACK [1858], pp. 334f.; cf. KELLY [1821, repr. 1835], vol. II, p. 40). "Because of the expansion in the volume of paper currency, however, the bank could not prevent the deterioration of the exchange rate for long. Due to the mounting losses and the inability of the state to continue to provide financial support for its activities, the bank was forced to close in 1852" (PAMUK [2000], p. 212), and the difference in the quotation between "private rates" and "bank rates" was suspended for some years.

Up to 1868 only quotations on London can be presented in reasonable quantity; beyond that a few rates on French, Austrian and Russian places can be found in contemporary merchant manuals. From 1868 exchange rates issued in newspapers are available on London and Paris, as well as, for some years, on Marseilles (and partly from Smyrna on Trieste). These documented exchange rates can mainly be regarded as relatively stable because of their fundamental basis in specie. Until 1909 a distinction was drawn between rates for bank bills and rates for commercial bills, whereby the commercial rates corresponded to those of the private Galata bankers and the bank rates to those of the banks, which were established by British and French financial groups or by Galata bankers in alliance with British, French and Austrian financial groups since the Crimean War. These banks "played the role of intermediaries between the purchasers of the Ottoman bonds and the Ottoman state" (PAMUK [2000], p. 213).

According to the sources documented here, the quotation on Vienna was resumed in 1888, the one on Odessa one year later, whereas the one on Berlin began in 1894. Because the entire quotation on Odessa is only available from 1889/94 to 1909, it has been completed with money rates for imperials. The same holds in particular for Vienna, where money rates for the Austrian ducat and the Marie Theresa thaler have been added to the series. According to the merchant manuals of the late 19th and early 20th centuries Belgium, Egypt, Greece, the Netherlands, Italy, New York, Romania and Switzerland might also have been quoted in Constantinople (e.g. SWOBODA [1902], pp. 250f.) but no proof has so far been found for this assumption. One reason could be that Constantinople constituted only a limited market with low turnover and only rare transactions for Dutch and Italian bills and Russian ones as well (SONNDORFER [1899], p. 260).

In Constantinople, three months' sight bills were usually quoted; in the case of London and Paris cheques were also quoted between 1894 and 1911. On Odessa only cheques were quoted. On Vienna we can also find quotations for eight days' sight bills. Regarding the quotations on Berlin and Vienna, the indication for cheques was replaced by the term 'at sight' in 1911 (cf. SWOBODA [1889], p. 406).

References: Ferréol REBUFFAT / Marcel COURDURIÉ, *Marseille et le négoce monétaire international (1785–1790)*, Marseille 1966; Abraham L. UDOVITCH, Bankers without Banks: Commerce, Banking, and Society in the Islamic World of the Middle Ages, in *The Dawn of Modern Banking*, New Haven – London 1979, pp. 255–273; Charles ISSAWI, *The Economic History of Turkey 1800–1914*, Chicago 1981; Edhem ELDEM, La circulation de la lettre de change entre la France et Constantinople au XVIIIᵉ siècle, in Hâmit BATU / Jean-Louis BACQUE-GRAMMONT (eds.), *L'empire ottoman, la république de Turquie et la France*, Istanbul 1986, pp. 87–97; Sevket PAMUK, *The Ottoman Empire and European Capitalism, 1820–1913. Trade, Investment and Production*, Cambridge 1987, pp. 55–81; Edhem ELDEM, Structure et acteurs du commerce international d'Istanbul au XVIIIᵉ siècle, in Daniel PANZAC (ed.), *Les villes dans l'empire ottoman: Activité et sociétés*, Marseille 1990, pp. 243–272; Sadok BOUBAKER, Le transfert des capiteaux entre l'Empire Ottoman et l'Europe. L'utilisation de la lettre de change: L'éxemple de la société Garavaque et Cusson à Smyrne (1760–1772), *Revue d'histoire maghrébine (époque moderne et contemporaine)* 21 (num. 75/76) (1994), pp. 199–218; Markus A. DENZEL, Finanzplätze in der Levante und Nordafrika im 19. und 20. Jahrhundert, in *WdW VIII*, pp. 30–70, here pp. 34–44; Sevket PAMUK, *A Monetary History of the Ottoman Empire*, Cambridge 2000; Dennis O. FLYNN / Arturo GIRALDEZ, Silver and Ottoman Monetary History in Global Perspective, *Journal of European Economic History* 31 (2002), pp. 9–43.

13.1 Smyrna exchange rates

13.1.1 On Amsterdam, Marseilles, Leghorn and Vienna

	SMYRNA on:										
	Amsterdam			**Marseilles**			**Leghorn**			**Vienna**		
	per 100 guilders Flemish current [a]			per 100 livres tournois [b]			per 100 pezze da otto reali [c]			per 100 guilders Konventionskurant [d]		
	in piastres											
1760	74.69	[e]	(3)	35.67	[e]	(3)	170.00	[e]	(3)			
1761	77.92	[e]	(1)	36.50	[e]	(1)	173.13	[e]	(1)			
1762												
1763												
1764												
1765												
1766												
1767												
1768												
1769												
1770												
1771	74.58	[e]	(1)				170.94	[e]	(1)			
1772	78.54	[e]	(2)	37.42	[e]	(1)	178.31	[e]	(2)			
1773	81.46	[e]	(4)	36.67	[e]	(4)	181.25	[e]	(4)			
1774												
1775												
1776												
1777												
1778												
1779												
1780												
1781												
1782												
1783												
1784												
1785	91.67	[e]	(1)	43.67	[e]	(1)	219.17	[e]	(1)	111.25	[e]	(1)
1786												
1787	92.34	[e]	(11)	42.79	[e]	(12)	216.74	[e]	(11)	111.56	[e]	(11)
1788	90.63	[e]	(8)	42.76	[e]	(12)	215.64	[e]	(8)	110.52	[e]	(8)
1789	95.23	[e]	(12)	44.19	[e]	(12)	223.31	[e]	(12)	113.74	[e]	(12)
1790	96.74	[e]	(12)	43.04	[e]	(12)	225.56	[e]	(12)	114.30	[e]	(12)

[a]   Concerning the Dutch currency, see pp. 57f.   [b]   Concerning the French currency, see p. 279.
[c]   Concerning the Tuscan currency, see p. 106.   [d]   Concerning the Austrian currency, see p. 255.
[e]   No usance given.

13.2 Constantinople exchange rates

13.2.1 On London, France, the Habsburg Monarchy and Odessa

	CONSTANT-INOPLE on:				CONSTANT-INOPLE on: [b]		
	London				London		
	per 1 pound sterling [a]				per 1 pound sterling [a]		
	in piastres				in piastres		
1790	11.10	3m/s	(y)	1820	32.00	3m/s	(y)
1791				1821			
1792				1822	40.00	3m/s	(y)
1793				1823			
1794	12.00	3m/s	(y)	1824			
1795	13.50	3m/s	(y)	1825	*53.50*	3m/s	(y)
1796	13.50	3m/s	(y)	1826	58.15	3m/s	(y)
1797				1827	60.80	3m/s	(y)
1798	*15.00*	[c]		1828	60.55	3m/s	(2)
1799	15.80	3m/s	(y)	1829	69.16	3m/s	(5)
1800	12.00	3m/s	(y)	1830	76.70	3m/s	(4)
1801				1831	81.28	3m/s	(4)
1802	14.10	3m/s	(y)	1832	88.95	3m/s	(4)
1803	15.00	3m/s	(y)	1833	95.93	3m/s	(4)
1804	15.00	3m/s	(y)	1834	*97.30*	3m/s	(y)
1805	16.70	3m/s	(y)	1835	99.45	3m/s	(4)
1806	15.00	3m/s	(y)	1836	100.44	3m/s	(5)
1807	14.90	3m/s	(y)	1837	106.90	3m/s	(2)
1808	19.00	3m/s	(y)	1838	104.00	3m/s	(1)
1809	20.50	3m/s	(y)	1839	104.03	3m/s	(4)
1810	19.60	3m/s	(y)	1840	108.85	3m/s	(4)
1811				1841	111.05	3m/s	(4)
1812				1842	116.73	3m/s	(4)
1813				1843	113.20	3m/s	(4)
1814	*23.00*	3m/s	(y)	1844	109.03	3m/s	(4)
1815				1845			
1816	19.00	3m/s	(y)	1846			
1817	32.00	3m/s	(y)	1847			
1818	32.00	3m/s	(y)	1848			
1819	32.00	3m/s	(y)				

	CONSTANTINOPLE on: [b]			
	London	**Marseilles, from 1873 Paris** [d]	**Trieste, from 1873 Vienna**	**Odessa**
	per 1 pound sterling [a]	per 100 francs [e]	per 100 guilders Österreichische Währung, from 1873 per 1 Austrian ducat [f]	per 100 silver roubles in credit notes (kreditnye bilety), from 1870 per 100 gold roubles [g]
			in piastres	
1849	112.00 3m/s (4)	438.75 3m/s (4)	1003.13 3m/s (4)	500.00 3m/s (1)
1850	110.75 3m/s (1)	433.75 3m/s (1)	935.00 3m/s (1)	
1851				
1852				
1853	117.50 3m/s (1)	464.69 3m/s (1)	1046.25 3m/s (1)	526.32 3m/s (1)
1854				
1855	115.50 3m/s (1)	455.00 3m/s (1)	1062.50 3m/s (1)	
1856				
1857				
1858				
1859				
1860				
1861				
1862	124.88 3m/s (4)	495.44 3m/s (4)	1015.00 3m/s (2)	
1863	125.66 3m/s (4)	497.50 3m/s (4)		
1864	128.50 3m/s (2)	498.13 3m/s (2)	1090.00 3m/s (2)	
1865				
1866				
1867				
1868	108.79 3m/s (2)	430.48 3m/s (1)		
1869	109.61 3m/s (11)	434.03 3m/s (5)		
1870	110.13 3m/s (2)	435.50 3m/s (2)		1122.59 [c] (2)
1871	109.81 3m/s (2)	434.38 3m/s (2)		
1872				
1873	110.37 3m/s (12)	431.95 3m/s (12)	51.00 [c] (3)	1121.69 [c] (7)
1874	110.37 3m/s (12)	435.95 3m/s (12)	51.00 [c] (12)	1120.17 [c] (12)
1875	110.74 3m/s (12)	438.17 3m/s (12)	51.00 [c] (12)	1120.09 [c] (12)
1876	110.07 3m/s (11)	437.14 3m/s (11)	51.23 [c] (11)	1126.04 [c] (11)
1877	109.21 3m/s (12)	433.76 3m/s (11)	50.82 [c] (11)	1129.72 [c] (11)
1878	108.86 3m/s (9)	432.00 3m/s (4)	50.30 [c] (10)	1127.45 [c] (10)
1879	109.35 3m/s (7)			
1880	109.83 3m/s (5)	431.27 3m/s (2)	51.20 [c] (2)	1110.54 [c] (3)
1881	109.31 3m/s (12)	432.04 3m/s (12)		1113.71 [c] (12)
1882	110.15 3m/s (12)	436.44 3m/s (12)		1109.95 [c] (12)
1883	109.81 3m/s (12)	436.37 3m/s (12)		1111.60 [c] (12)

	CONSTANTINOPLE on: [b]			
	London	**Paris** [d]	**Vienna**	**Odessa**
	per 1 pound sterling [a]	per 100 francs [e]	per 1 Austrian ducat, 1888 per 1 Marie The-resa thaler, from 1889 per 100 guilders Öster-reichische Währung, from 1900 per 100 Austrian crowns [f]	per 100 gold roubles [g]
	in piastres			
1884	110.12 3m/s (12)	436.37 3m/s (12)		*1110.44* (12)
1885	110.26 3m/s (12)	436.27 3m/s (10)		*1109.55* (10)
1886	110.58 3m/s (11)	437.83 3m/s (11)		*1108.75* (11)
1887	110.94 3m/s (12)	438.49 3m/s (12)	*51.00* [c] (1)	*1108.28* (12)
1888	110.85 3m/s (12)	438.15 3m/s (11)	*22.42* [c] (1)	*1100.85* (11)
1889	109.54 3m/s (12)	435.93 3m/s (12)	991.93 3m/s (11)	1119.92 (12)
1890	108.97 3m/s (12)	433.63 3m/s (12)	1000.00 3m/s (3)	*1108.56* (12)
1891	109.38 3m/s (12)	433.59 3m/s (12)	934.59 3m/s (3)	*1115.38* (12)
1892	110.01 3m/s (12)	435.90 3m/s (12)	927.04 3m/s (12)	*1118.95* (12)
1893	109.97 3m/s (12)	436.74 3m/s (12)	897.54 3m/s (12)	*1111.64* (12)
1894	110.77 ch (12)	439.31 ch (12)	875.73 ch (10)	1131.50 ch (2)
1895	110.89 ch (12)	439.84 ch (12)	942.78 ch (12)	1134.50 ch (2)
1896	110.02 ch (12)	438.72 ch (11)	964.92 ch (11)	1164.15 ch (1)
1897	109.79 ch (11)	436.55 ch (12)	963.87 ch (12)	1162.46 ch (4)
1898	110.24 ch (12)	436.23 ch (12)	955.26 ch (12)	1165.73 ch (6)
1899	110.24 ch (12)	437.05 ch (12)	948.04 ch (12)	1163.47 ch (2)
1900	110.10 ch (12)	437.72 ch (12)	454.77 ch (11)	1165.06 ch (6)
1901	110.19 ch (12)	438.05 ch (12)	459.42 ch (6)	1166.09 ch (7)
1902	110.06 ch (12)	437.56 ch (12)	459.27 ch (12)	1162.70 ch (12)
1903	109.79 ch (12)	436.12 ch (12)	457.80 ch (12)	1163.48 ch (10)
1904	109.99 ch (12)	436.87 ch (11)	458.74 ch (12)	1161.81 ch (11)
1905	109.80 ch (12)	436.35 ch (12)	457.50 ch (12)	1156.76 ch (10)
1906				
1907	109.24 ch (12)	436.24 ch (12)		1155.28 ch (5)
1908	109.93 ch (12)	437.07 ch (12)		1153.41 ch (4)
1909	109.88 ch (11)	436.97 ch (11)		1160.18 ch (6)
1910	109.26 ch (12)	436.26 ch (12)		*1161.22* [c] (12)
1911	109.00 ch (8)	436.30 ch (8)	441.05 s (4)	*1159.56* [c] (12)
1912	110.28 3m/s (12)	437.96 3m/s (12)	457.32 s (12)	*1156.71* [c] (12)
1913	110.22 3m/s (12)	437.44 3m/s (12)	450.06 s (12)	*1156.09* [c] (12)
1914	110.13 3m/s (7)	438.74 3m/s (7)	440.51 s (7)	*1154.12* [c] (7)

[a] Concerning the British currency, see pp. 3–5.

[b] 1825:   exchange rate of Smyrna.
       1834:   exchange rate of Trapezunt.

1849:	private rate. In comparison to these private rates, the following bank rates were quoted in 1849: on London, 4m/s: 110 piastres per 1 pound sterling; and on Marseilles, 4m/s: 432.50 piastres per 100 francs.
1850:	exchange rate of Smyrna (payable in besliks, i.e. the 5-piastres piece of about 5 grammes of fine silver).
1853:	private rate.
1855:	exchange rate of Smyrna (payable in besliks).
1862–1864:	quotations of Smyrna.
1871–1873:	quotations of Salonica.

[c] Money rate.

[d] From 1873 to 1893 bank bills.

[e] Concerning the French currency, see pp. 279f.

[f] Concerning the Austrian currency, see pp. 255f. From June 3rd 1848 the guilder Konventionskurant and from November 1858 the guilder Österreichische Währung were paper money in notes of the Wiener Nationalbank and government notes. The Austrian ducat (of 3.4424 grammes of fine gold) and the Marie Theresa thaler (of 23.39 grammes of fine silver) were the most important Austrian trade coins for the Levant in the period from the 18th to the 20th century.

[g] Concerning the Russian currency, see pp. 359f. Since the entire quotation on Odessa is only available from 1894 to 1909, it has been completed with money rates for imperials (in *italics*). Up to 1885 1 (old) imperial (11.9974 grammes of fine gold) = 10 gold roubles or – legally fixed – 10.30 silver roubles; from 1885, 1 (new) imperial (11.6118 grammes of fine gold) = 10 gold roubles (since January 3rd/15th 1897 equal to 15 gold roubles); cf. SWOBODA [1902], pp. 508f.

13.2.2 On Berlin

	CONSTANT-INOPLE on:		
	Berlin		
	per 100 mark [a]		
	in piastres		
1894	543.86	ch	(10)
1895	544.53	ch	(12)
1896	540.84	ch	(10)
1897	539.40	ch	(12)
1898	539.23	ch	(12)
1899	539.70	ch	(12)
1900	538.44	ch	(12)
1901	539.74	ch	(12)
1902	538.01	ch	(12)
1903	536.54	ch	(12)
1904	538.34	ch	(12)
1905	536.27	ch	(12)
1906			
1907	536.15	ch	(12)
1908	537.81	ch	(12)
1909	536.80	ch	(11)
1910	536.77	ch	(12)
1911	536.77	ch	(8)
1912	538.89	s	(12)
1913	538.77	s	(12)
1914	539.01	s	(12)

[a]   Concerning the German currency, see p. 197.

AMERICA

14

The British Colonies in North America and the USA (1660–1914)

Exchange markets in the British Colonies in North America: Boston (1660–1775), Philadelphia (1683–1775), New York (1680–1775) and Maryland/Baltimore (1702–1775)

Sources: Boston: MᴄCᴜsᴋᴇʀ [1978], pp. 138–142 (1660–1775). Philadelphia: Ibid., pp. 183–186 (1683–1775). New York: Ibid., pp. 162–165 (1680–1775). Maryland/Baltimore: Ibid., pp. 197–204 (1702–1775).

Currency of the colonial era: During the colonial era the pound of 20 shillings at 12 pence was the unit of account in all British colonies in North America, as in the mother country, whereas the main coin in circulation was the Spanish dollar, i.e. the peso de ocho reales or the piece of eight (at 24.43 grammes of fine silver). The variations between the currencies of the different colonies "were determined by the different legal valuation each colony gave to that coin" (MᴄCᴜsᴋᴇʀ [1978], p. 132).

So the Spanish dollar had been fixed in Massachusetts, with its capital and its economic centre Boston, at 5 shillings colonial currency since 1642, so that 100 pounds sterling corresponded to 111.11 pounds Massachusetts currency. This relation was changed in 1672 to 100:133.33, in 1692 to 100:136.60 and in 1705 to 100:154.78 to the disadvantage of the colonial currency, because colonial paper money was circulating in Massachusetts increasingly from 1690, when paper bills of credit were issued for the first time in Massachusetts on the occasion of the expedition against Quebec. The paper money – designed as legal tender – actually constituted the real money of the colony from 1710 to 1750 and was also used to pay bills of exchange. The value of this paper money, later called 'Old Tenor', dropped drastically in the following decades until 100 pounds sterling were worth more than 1,000 pounds Massachusetts currency at the end of the 1740s. On March 31ˢᵗ 1750 the silver standard was introduced again on the basis of the Spanish dollar, the parity to sterling being fixed at 133.33 pounds Massachusetts currency to 100 pounds sterling. As this rate reverted to that of the Royal Proclamation in 1704 and the subsequent Act of 1708, the new money was called the 'Lawful Money', 7.5 pounds Old Tenor being of equal value to 1 pound Lawful Money and consequently 1,000 pounds Old Tenor being equal to 100 pounds sterling. Since the Old Tenor paper money was cashed in at the same time, the currency conditions in Massachusetts remained stable until the end of the colonial era (MᴄCᴜsᴋᴇʀ [1978], pp. 132s.).

In New York, too, the rates of exchange were expressed in terms of the New York money of account during the British colonial era. As the Spanish dollar had been fixed there at 6 shillings colonial currency in 1672, 133.33 pounds New York currency corresponded to 100 pounds sterling from then on. With the reevaluation of the Spanish dollar in 1684, this ratio increased to 150 pounds New York currency to 100 pounds sterling and even to 154.83:100 in October 1708. After the introduction of paper bills of credit in 1709, "over the next thirty years the currency of New York inflated in value, just as did that of New England, but to nowhere near the same extent" (ibid., p. 158). From the 1740s until the end of the colonial era the par of exchange between the New York currency and sterling lay at 177.77:100, because the Spanish dollar had a market value of 8 shillings colonial currency then. In around 1770 the New York currency was important as a means of payment also for Connecticut, Rhode Island, New Jersey and Canada (ibid., pp. 156–158).

From 1683 the value of the Spanish dollar in Pennsylvania and its capital Philadelphia was fixed at 6 shillings, so that 133.33 pounds Pennsylvania currency corresponded to 100 pounds sterling. In 1693 this ratio altered to 137:100, to 174:100 in 1700 and later on even to 177.77:100. On May 1ˢᵗ 1709 Pennsylvania adopted the ratio of 133.33 pounds Pennsylvania currency to 100 pounds sterling, which had been fixed by the Act of 1708 – therefore this money was called 'Proclamation Money' (in New England: 'Lawful Money') – devaluing the Pennsylvania currency by a quarter. After the introduction of paper money in 1723 – which is relatively late in comparison to the other colonies – Pennsylvania "left Proclamation Money and the par of exchange intact – at least theoretically" (ibid., p. 176). So, until the end of the 1720s the exchange rates were given in premium on the official silver parity of 133.33 pounds Pennsylvania currency to 100 pounds sterling; this so-called 'silver exchange' fluctuated from 10% to 30%. Although there had not been any official, legally established value for silver or silver coins in the colony since then, "the market value itself began to stabilize and acquire the force of custom". In 1742 the value of the Spanish dollar of 7.5 shillings colonial currency and the resulting par of exchange of 166.67 pounds Pennsylvania currency to 100 pounds sterling was accepted publicly in a private agreement of 75 merchants, becoming 'official', so to speak. This situation remained unchanged until the revolution. New Jersey and Maryland adopted this ratio and parity within a decade as well (ibid., pp. 175–177).

Maryland was an exception among the colonies inasmuch as the Spanish dollar circulated there from 1634 to 1708 mostly at its official sterling value of 4 shillings 6 pence, so that 100 pounds Maryland currency corresponded to 100 pounds sterling. From April 1671 to June 1676, from November 1686 to November 1688 and from June 1692 to June 1694 the Spanish dollar circulated at 6 shillings and, therefore, the par of exchange was 133.33:100. In spring 1709, after the Royal Proclamation of 1704 and the subsequent Act of 1708, Maryland raised the legal value of the Spanish dollar to the level of the Proclamation Money (133.33 pounds Maryland currency to 100 pounds sterling); this ratio remained unchanged until autumn 1753. From 1733 onwards, bills of credit were issued in Maryland, but as they were not legal tender they were already cashed in by 1765. In contrast to this paper money, which was the "current money of Maryland" from the 1730s to the mid-1750s, McCusker called the "Maryland current silver" and the "Maryland current gold", which means the coins circulating on the basis of the parity of 1709, "hard currency". "An important effect of this dual currency was the extra-legal creation of a new par of exchange for hard currency" (ibid., p. 192), amounting to 166.67 pounds Maryland hard currency for 100 pounds sterling from 1752 (officially accepted and confirmed by law in 1753). "After as early as mid-1752 Maryland and Pennsylvania had the same par of exchange, used a common currency, and had bill rates that were almost always related in their fluctuations" (ibid.). This resulted from the fact that since the 1750s Pennsylvania's (paper) money was increasingly circulating as "hard currency" in Maryland. With the (second) redemption of Maryland paper currency (the so-called "Maryland currency" or "Maryland money") in 1764/65 a fixed relation of 100 pounds "Maryland currency" to 125 pounds Maryland hard currency was established, which ended the previous decades of more or less intense fluctuations between the two currencies. A paper money newly introduced in 1766 was valued as hard currency and denominated in "dollars" (ibid., pp. 189–194).

Original quotations in the colonial era

on:	in:	per:
London	pounds colonial currency or	100 pounds sterling
	per cent premium or discount [a]	1 pound sterling

[a] These terms frequently meant the percentage above or below the actual parity (cf. ibid., p. 133).

Exchange markets in the USA: Philadelphia (1783–1840), New York (1794–1914), Boston (1789–1834), Baltimore (1796–1828), New Orleans (1804–1872) and San Francisco (1849–1868)

Sources: Philadelphia: *The Philadelphia Price Current* (1783–1784); *Pennsylvania Mercury* (1785–1786); *The Independent Gazetteer* [Philadelphia] (1785–1786, 1796); *General Advertiser*, Philadelphia (1790–1793); *Gazette of the United States*, Philadelphia (1790–1802); *The Level of Europe and North America* [Philadelphia] (1795); *The American Naval and Commercial Register* [Philadelphia] (1795–1797); *Washington Gazette* (1796); *Porcupine's Gazette* [Philadelphia] (1797–1799); *Carey's United States Recorder*, Philadelphia (1798); *The Universal Gazette*, Philadelphia (1798–1799); *The Constitutional Diary*, Philadelphia (1799–1800); *The New York Price Current* (1800); *The Boston Gazette* (1803–1815); *The Boston Price Current* (1803–1815); *Hope's Philadelphia Price-Current and Commercial Record* (1811–1813); *Grotjan's Philadelphia Public Sale Report, and General Price Current* (1814–1821); *General Shipping and Commercial List*, New York (1815); *New York Shipping and Commercial List* (1816–1823); *The National Gazette* (*Democratic Press*, Philadelphia) (1820–1838); *The American Sentinel* (1837–1838); *The North American* (1839–1840). New York: *Gazette of the United States*, Philadelphia (1789); *The Herald*, New York (1794–1796); *American Minerva* [New York] (1794–1797); *The American Naval and Commercial Register* (1795–1797); *Porcupine's Gazette* (1797–1798); *Oram's New York Prices Courant and Marine Register* (1797–1803); *The Boston Price Current* (1803–1815); *The Boston Gazette* (1803–1815); *Hope's Philadelphia Price-Current and Commercial Record* (1811–1813); *Grotjan's Philadelphia Public Sale Report, and General Price Current* (1814–1815, 1819); *New York Shipping and Commercial List* (1815–1831); *New York Daily Advertiser* (1817–1818); *New York Stock and Exchange Board* (1818–1839); *New York American* (1822–1829); *New York Commercial Advertiser* (1830–1854); *The Financial Register* [New York] (1837–1838); *Hunt's Merchants' Magazine* (1840–1865); *Bankers' Weekly Circular* (1845–1847); *The New York Herald* (1849–1850); *Bankers' Magazine* (1853–1859); *New York Times* (1853–1856); *The Commercial and Financial Chronicle* [New York] (1865–1914); *Financial Review* [New York] (1865–1914). Boston: *American Prices Courant* [Boston] (1789); *The Boston Gazette* (1795–1816); *The Boston Price Courant* (1795–1820); *Oram's New York Price Courant and Marine Register* (1797–1802); *J. Russel's Gazette* (1799–1800); *Hope's Philadelphia Price-Current and Commercial Record* (1811–1813); *New York Shipping and Commercial List* (1816–1821); *The Boston Commercial Gazette* (1817–1834). Baltimore: *The Boston Gazette* (1796–1816); *Hope's Philadelphia Price-Current and Commercial Record* (1796–1816); *Oram's New York Price Courant and Marine Register* (1797–1802); *The Boston Price Courant* (1809–1815); *New York Shipping and Commercial List* (1815–1821); *The Boston Commercial Gazette* (1817–1829). New Orleans: *Louisiana Gazette* (1804–1812); *Hope's Philadelphia Price-Current and Commercial Record* (1811–1813); *New York Shipping and Commercial List* (1816–1822, 1829–1834); *Grotjan's Philadelphia Public Sale Report, and General Price Current* (1821); *New Orleans Price Courant* (1823–1829, 1836–1841); *The Courier* [New Orleans] (1824, 1836–1843, 1854–1860); *The North American* [New Orleans] (1839); *Commercial Review* [New Orleans] (1843–1846); *Bankers' Magazine* (1846–1848); *Bankers' Weekly Circular* (1846); *Hunt's Merchants' Magazine* (1848–1859); *New Orleans Commercial Bulletin* (1860–1862); *Money Market* (1864); *New Orleans Weekly Times* (1865–1867); *New Orleans Times* (1865–1872). San Francisco: *Daily Alta California* [San Francisco] (1849–1852); *Alta California. Steamer Edition* [San Francisco] (1850–1852); *San Francisco Herald* (1851–1857); *San Francisco Shipping List* (1852–1856); *Wm. T. Coleman & Co's Circular* [San Francisco] (1857); *Mercantile Gazette and Prices Courant* [San Francisco] (1858–1868); *Chas. W. Brooks & Co's Circular* [San Francisco] (1865–1866); *The Daily Examiner* [San Francisco] (1866); *San Francisco Herald* (1866).

Concordance: *WdW I/I*, pp. 309–387, 411–453

Currency in the USA: When reorganizing the monetary system in the newly constituted USA in 1785/86 – after the experiment with bills of credit (the so-called Continental money) for financing the

War of Independence – the currency with the widest circulation was followed, i.e. the Spanish dollar (peso) of Mexican strike (24.43 grammes of fine silver) at only 24.34 grammes of fine silver, the average value of the actual circulating coins subdividing into tenths (dimes), hundredths (cents) and thousandths (mills). When a national mint was established by the Mint Act of April 2nd 1792, the standard of coinage of the new US dollar was fixed at 24.05 grammes of fine silver. Officially the bimetallism prevailed from the 1790s (gold–silver ratio of 1:15; from 1794/95 1:15.127), but in fact it was a silver standard. However, as not enough silver dollars were minted and, additionally, because of their low fine weight, it was more profitable to export them to the West Indies than to have them circulating in the USA. For everyday circulation the Spanish and the Mexican dollar respectively – legal tender since February 9th 1793 – remained the principally used coinage until 1853/57. In 1834 the Mexican and the Patriot dollars of the South American Republics were legal tender and the gold–silver ratio was newly fixed in 1834 (1:16.002) and in 1837 (1:15.988; since then 1 US dollar was equal to 1.5050 grammes of fine gold) reintroducing bimetallism in fact. It was not until the end of the economic crisis of 1839 that the USA began to focus exclusively on the US dollar currency. As a result of the gold rush in California, from 1848 the silver coins disappeared from the payment transactions, having been devalued to 22.39 grammes of fine silver in 1853, so that the USA had the gold standard from then. Owing to the War of Succession and the resulting requirements to finance the war, this gold standard was replaced by a paper standard based on a new paper money, the 'greenbacks' (Greenback Act, February 25th 1862), with gold being used continually in foreign trade and on the west coast (San Francisco). However, since all money and exchange rates were quoted in greenbacks, the consequences were daily rate fluctuations and a considerable rise of the exchange rates. With the return to paying with coins and the standard of coinage on the pre-war parity of January 1st 1879 (Resumption Act, January 14th 1875), the reintroduction of a partial and official bimetallism followed as a result of the renewed minting of silver dollars (Bland–Allison Act, February 25th 1878). However, the falling price of silver brought about an actual gold standard that was finally legalized with the Gold Standard Act of March 14th 1900, the economic preconditions having been created by the gold rush in the 1890s.

Original quotations at Philadelphia after independence

on:	in:	per:
Amsterdam	shillings and pence Pennsylvania currency	1 guilder Flemish current
from 1792	US cents	1 guilder Flemish current
from 1816 (10)	US cents	1 Dutch guilder
Hamburg	US cents	1 mark banco
London	pounds Pennsylvania currency	100 pounds sterling
from 1808 (12)	per cent premium on the par of 1 pound sterling = 4.44 US dollars [a]	1 pound sterling
Paris	shillings and pence Pennsylvania currency	5 livres tournois
from 1815	francs	1 US dollar

Original quotations at New York after independence

on:	in:	per:
Amsterdam	US cents	1 Dutch guilder
Antwerp	US cents	1 Belgian franc
Berlin	US cents	1 thaler Prussian current
from 1874 (11)	US cents	1 mark
Bremen	US cents	1 rixdollar gold
from 1872 (7)	US cents	1 mark
Frankfurt	US cents	1 guilder South German current
from 1874 (11)	US cents	1 mark
Germany	US cents	1 mark

on:	in:	per:
Hamburg	US cents	1 mark banco
from 1872 (12)	US cents	1 mark
London	per cent premium on the par of 1 pound sterling = 4.44 US dollars [a]	1 pound sterling
from 1874	US dollars	1 pound sterling
Paris	US cents	1 franc
Zurich & Basle	US cents	1 franken

Original quotations at Boston, Baltimore and New Orleans after independence:

on:	in:	per:
London	per cent premium on the par of 1 pound sterling = 4.44 US dollars [a]	1 pound sterling
New York	per cent premium or discount	1 US dollar

Original quotations at San Francisco:

on:	in:	per:
London	pence sterling	1 US dollar
New York	per cent premium or discount	1 US dollar

[a]   With the introduction of the dollar as a counterpart to the Spanish or Mexican peso/dollar, the silver parity to the English currency was fixed at 4 shillings 6 pence ('nominal par'): 1 pound sterling
= 4.44 US dollars (Act to Establish the Value of Foreign Coin and Currency of July 31ˢᵗ 1789).
The nominal par was accepted by the merchants as a basis for the quotation until the end of 1873.
But as Britain had officially introduced the gold standard in 1816 and transatlantic exchanges had
to be paid in gold, the following 'technical' or 'customary par' resulted: 1 pound sterling = 4.867
US dollars. This difference of c. 9½% (true par: 9.45625%) necessitated the continual quoting of
the pound sterling in % premium, although actual discount values should be recorded. It was not
until the passing of the Act of March 3ʳᵈ 1873 that the quotation was fixed on the real price of the
pound in dollars and cents, from January 1ˢᵗ 1874 and the true mint par was fixed at 4.8665 dollars
per pound sterling. Furthermore, the Act of March 3ʳᵈ 1873 stipulated a more precise quotation, at
first by stating precisely right down to 1/32, later on to 1/64 dollar, in order to indicate even the
slightest rate fluctuation.

Other data from Boston available: Amsterdam, 60d/s (1796–1810) – Hamburg, 60d/s, via London
(1795–1803); via Amsterdam (1797–1802) – London, 90d/s (1795–1814); 30 days (1795–1820) –
Domestic exchange: Baltimore, 30d/s (1797–1813); s (1814–1834) – New York, 60d/s (1797–1814);
30d/s (1797–1813); s (1814–1834) – Philadelphia, 60d/s (1797–1814); 30d/s (1797–1813); s (1814–
1834) – **from Philadelphia:** Amsterdam, 60d/s (1783–1834/40) – Paris, 60d/s (1783–1794, 1815–
1834/40) – Hamburg (1794–1840) – **from New York:** Amsterdam, 60d/s (1796–1914); on demand
(1880–1908), cable transfer (1909–1914) – Antwerp, 60d/s (1871–1880) – Berlin, 60d/s (1871–
1901); s (1881–1901) – Bremen, 60d/s (1871–1901); s (1881–1901) – "Deutsches Reich" or "German
bankers' marks", 60d/s (1902–1914) – Frankfurt am Main, 60d/s (1871–1901); s (1881–1901) –
Hamburg, 60d/s (1871–1901); s (1881–1901) – London, 60d/s (1871–1880, good bankers' bills;
1881–1914, bankers' bills; 1867–1880, prime/best commercial bills and good commercial bills;
1881–1902, commercial bills; 1875–1902, documentary bills); s (1865/66; 1867–1880, prime/best
bankers' bills; 1874–1880, good bankers' bills; 1867–1880, prime/best commercial bills and good
commercial bills; 1875–1880, documentary bills); on demand (1881–1914, bankers' bills; 1881–
1883, documentary bills) – Paris, 60d/s (1865–1914); s (1848–1857) – Zurich & Basle, 60d/s (1871–
1880) – *Domestic exchange*: Baltimore, s (1815–1854) – Boston, s (1813–1854) – Charleston, s
(1816–1854) – Cincinnati, s (1838–1851) – Detroit, s (1838–1851) – Louisville, s (1838–1851) –
Mobile, s (1838–1851) – New Orleans, s (1824–1854) – North Carolina/Wilmington, s (1816–1851)
– Philadelphia, s (1814–1854) – Savannah, s (1817–1851) – St Louis, s (1838–1851) – Virginia/Rich-

mond, s (1824–1854) – **from New Orleans:** Havana, s (1839–1846) – Paris, 60d/s (1804–1874) – *Domestic exchange*: Baltimore, 60d/s (1804–1837) – Boston, 60d/s (1804–1842); s (1843 – 1784) – Philadelphia, 60d/s (1804–1838) – Richmond, s (1861/62) – St Louis, s (1831–1833, 1866–1869) – **from San Francisco:** Hamburg, 60d/s (1850–1865) – Paris, 60d/s (1850–1868).

From the 17th century exchange operations became increasingly popular in large parts of the British Colonies in the North American area. "In negotiating bills on the mother country, colonists followed the forms and procedures common to European Exchange. Bills were drawn, presented, and protested in much the same way between Philadelphia and London as between Amsterdam – or, better, Dublin – and London" (MCCUSKER [1978], p. 120). The special importance of the sterling exchange – the "barometer by which the banker sailed his bark" (MYERS [1931], p. 71) – had a long tradition in all North American exchange markets: until 1807, imports came mainly from Britain since only British merchants granted long-term credits of six up to 18 months. Apart from this, the British–American volume of trade as well as the long colonial tradition were decisive factors for London being and remaining the main partner for exchange transactions in Europe, so that exchange rate quotations on the financial centre of the mother country may be seen as of central importance for all the British colonies. Thus the bills of exchange drawn from North America on London were "only as good as the drawer's reliability and the drawer's credit in England. ... By 1650 good bills of exchange on England could be found only in the Boston Bay towns and in Salem" (BAILYN [1955], pp. 91, 98).

Until well into the 19th century, exchange transactions of the North American area were not dominated by one single financial centre, but merchants from many places competed in carrying out business transactions. First of all Boston, populated since 1630, adopted the role of a central exchange place in the New England Colonies. From 1660 on, the quotations of Massachusetts on London became increasingly regular. To a large extent these quotations were also used by Rhode Island, New Hampshire and Connecticut, as well as by the British parts of Nova Scotia from 1710/13, with the exception of the years after the Boston Tea Party when exchange rate crashes in Boston contrasted with stable rates in, for example, Portsmouth, New Hampshire. Because 'Boston money' served as a common currency in all New England Colonies, there was no need for exchange transactions between the colonies except for the period of the currency reform in Massachusetts between 1750 and 1765. Furthermore, there are references to exchange transactions by single merchants in the 18th century between Massachusetts on the one hand and Pennsylvania/Philadelphia, Maryland, New York and South Carolina as well as Amsterdam on the other.

New York appeared as a further exchange place in the 18th century; it had been British since 1664 and had expanded the sphere of influence of its currency and its exchange rate transactions over the whole Hudson valley, the Mohawk valley, eastern New Jersey, the Long Island Sound and after 1760 as far as Canada – the latter development enduring up to the early 20th century. There are references for the year 1768 proving that apart from transactions on New York, for which proof is furnished by occasional quotations from the end of the 17th century, there were also transactions with inland bills of the other North American colonies as early as the end of the colonial era. In single cases there are references to exchange rate transactions with the

British West Indies as early as in the 1720s and the 1730s, presumably with New Scotland in the 1760s as well. The former contact of the old New Amsterdam with Amsterdam and the Dutch colonies in the Atlantic area did not break off completely after 1664, so that there were single transactions with and via Amsterdam in the British colonial era even though a special market for exchanges on Amsterdam does not seem to have existed in New York (MCCUSKER [1978], pp. 122, 156–167).

The third exchange place of international relevance that could gain a fixed position on the British North American market was Philadelphia, whose connections extended via western New Jersey, Delaware and the Chesapeake in inland Virginia. The tobacco planters of that region used the merchant bankers from Philadelphia for their transactions: "The Philadelphians had become the near-bankers of their corner of the world" (ibid., p. 175). It can be shown that occasional quotations of Pennsylvania on London were effected as early as from 1683 onwards – which is one year after the colonization of Philadelphia. Transactions were also carried out with Bristol, Ireland, New York and the New England colonies (via New York). As there are only single sources available, no details can be given about the frequency or even the regularity of those transactions. The special importance of Philadelphia as an exchange place was based on the quotations on London, which were (relatively) stable from the middle of the 1730s until the War of Independence, and which were the effect of the London trade expansion, the resulting profits and the possibility of arbitrage transactions (ibid., pp. 122s., 175–188).

Apart from these three centres of transatlantic exchange transactions, Baltimore, which was not founded until 1745, also became an important exchange place, although in a much more modest way. At the end of the colonial era it was regarded as "Philadelphia's satellite city" of the payment system (ibid., p. 175). Although single exchange rates of the colony of Maryland on London can be found as early as the early 18th century, they do not turn up regularly until 1758/60. This shows the increasing importance of the striving Baltimore within the cashless payment system; from time to time it won over some exchange transactions of, for example, the tobacco planters of Chesapeake from Philadelphia for its own market. However, no centres of nationwide importance within the cashless payment system developed in the British colonies further to the south of North America during the colonial era, even though proof can be furnished in all colonies of exchange transactions with London and within North America. Only Charleston seems to have established itself as an important exchange place since its quotations on London and 'Holland' were published in 1785/86 in *The Pennsylvania Packet and Daily Advertiser*.

Consequently, Boston could be regarded as *primus inter pares* within the North American exchange markets of the 17th and the early 18th centuries, until Philadelphia gradually took over the leading role among the financial places of the North American colonies, probably from the 1730s: Philadelphia became "the Amsterdam of the New World" (MYERS [1931], p. 6). It gained even more in value in the early USA than in the colonial era because, as the provisional capital, its money market became the centre of financing the War of Independence. Philadelphia's position as the central trading place and export market for the whole North Atlantic coast had developed so far that its volume of trade became the largest in the whole USA. These circumstances were the basis for the successful foundation of the Bank of Pennsylvania by Robert

Morris (1781) which later became the Bank of the United States (from 1791) and Phil-adelphia became "the undisputed banking center of the country" (ibid., p. 4). This po-sition as the bank and trading centre of the USA made the exchange rate quotations of Philadelphia, especially those on London, so interesting and important for the merchant bankers throughout the whole country that they were also published in other financial places. In addition to this, Philadelphia regularly quoted Paris, Amsterdam and – as a result of the increasing direct trade between the USA and the German coast – Hamburg from 1794. Some quotations on Spain, Portugal, Sweden and Ostend via London, found for the years 1783 to 1785, seem to be strange exceptions among the normal exchange business of Philadelphia. During the first years of the French Revo-lution, Paris gained much more in value as a partner in Philadelphia's exchange busi-ness, because the trade relations between revolutionary France and the independent USA became stronger than ever before. However, Philadelphia's decline began just a few decades later, especially because of the tight relationship of Philadelphia's merchant bankers with the Bank of the United States. As the first charter of this bank expired in 1811, Philadelphia's importance in the transatlantic and the intra-American exchange business diminished. The opening of the Erie Canal in 1825 let the flow of commodities bypass Philadelphia. After 1834 the financial difficulties of the newly chartered bank (1816), which was highly involved in the transatlantic exchange busi-ness, led to a crisis in Philadelphia's goods and money market that culminated in a huge decline of trade and even in the failure of some merchant bankers. The general crisis of 1839/40 led to the end of Philadelphia's former position of strength in the transatlantic and intra-American exchange business (DAVIS/HUGHES [1960/61], pp. 57, 61).

In around 1800 the other financial markets of the colonial era were still inferior to Philadelphia, not only in terms of their significance in the international exchange business but in foreign trade as well. Soon after the independence of the USA, New York tried to copy all the financial institutions that had been established in Philadel-phia, which then strengthened its exceptional position in commerce, especially in the banking sector. Through its grain trade and the continuously increasing traffic with the (Mid)West after the opening of the Erie Canal in 1825, New York gained so much in economic value that it began to supersede Philadelphia not only as the financial but also as the general economic centre of the Atlantic coast of the USA. London was, of course, by far the most important partner for the New York exchange market in the transatlantic exchange business. From 1796 onwards Amsterdam was also quoted quite regularly, as was Hamburg, between 1803 and 1809 and after 1832. After 1815 Paris also became a partner of New York in its transatlantic exchange business, and so did Bremen in 1832/37.

Behind Philadelphia and New York, Baltimore ranked in third position as ex-change market in the USA in the late 18th and early 19th centuries. "Exchange rates in the three key ports, Baltimore, Philadelphia and New York, were normally about the same" (OFFICER [1985], p. 561). In particular, Baltimore's geographical location near Washington, the seat of government, turned it into the trading and financial centre not only of Maryland but also, and most importantly, of the capital. In this role Baltimore quoted London, then Amsterdam from 1809 and Paris from 1815. These quotations of Baltimore came to an end in the late 1820s when the capital of Maryland lost its relevance as regional financial centre and international exchange market as a result of the increasingly dominant role of New York in the transatlantic exchange business.

Boston, the capital of Massachusetts, ranked after Philadelphia, New York and Baltimore in the early USA as far as its volume of trade and its importance as a trading and financial centre are concerned. It was only after the War of 1812 (to 1814) that Boston could take a leading position among the financial markets. Hoping that the New England States would abandon the Union because of their discontent with the war, Great Britain treated them indulgently. Therefore Boston could largely keep its transatlantic trade and financial business, whereas the transactions of the other Atlantic ports were interrupted to such an extent that the Boston bills on New York, Philadelphia and Baltimore were quoted with a discount of up to 20% (from autumn 1814 to summer 1816). Boston was able to maintain this special position of major trade independence for the rest of the 19th century. London was an even more dominant exchange partner for Boston than for the other financial markets in the USA. After 1810 it was even the only partner in the transatlantic exchange business, because the quotations on Hamburg (via Amsterdam) ended in 1802 and those on Amsterdam in 1810. Therefore Boston had the most limited connections to the European exchange markets among all the financial markets on the Atlantic coast mentioned here, and its 'network' of exchange relations remained finally in traditional, i.e. colonial, structures. From 1820 on, most exchange transactions from Boston to London were made via New York, its most important partner in the domestic exchange. In 1834 the independent quotation of Boston on London was suspended (MARTIN [1898], pp. 10–28, 51aa; SMITH/COLE [1935], pp. 187–190).

Therefore the transatlantic exchange business of the Atlantic coast was mainly and increasingly concentrated in the New York exchange market from the 1820s/1830s. After around 1815 the other cities on the Atlantic coast were more frequently conducting their transatlantic exchange transactions via New York. The domestic exchange quotations of New York reflected the network of these intra-American (mutual) exchange relations becoming increasingly close from the 1830s and integrating not only the old financial markets on the Atlantic Coast and New Orleans but also the new exchange markets of the South and the (Mid)West (COLE [1929], p. 166). During the 1810s the network of the domestic exchange became closer than ever before: "The differences between prices of bills on London at Boston, New York, Philadelphia, and Baltimore showed a high correlation with the depreciation of domestic exchanges" (SMITH/COLE [1935], p. 26). In its *Course of Exchange*, New York's financial market listed rates on all important exchange markets of the USA, such as Philadelphia, Baltimore, Boston, New Orleans, Charleston, Richmond, Savannah and Wilmington. A further extension of this network can be observed in the late 1830s and in the 1840s, when the new cities of the former hinterland of the Atlantic coast also became exchange places of importance for nearer regions, for example Augusta, Cincinnati, Columbus, Detroit, Louisville, Mobile, Nashville, and St Louis, for some time even Annapolis, Michigan, Natchez, and the states of Indiana and Illinois as well. Therefore the new southern and western exchange markets were quoted in part with a discount of up to 10% whereas the traditional exchange partners at the Atlantic coast were usually quoted with a discount of only up to 2½%, sometimes with a small premium. This means that the bills on the new financial markets were not demanded to such an extent as the bills on the traditional ones on the Northern Atlantic coast. The parallel exchange quotations of Philadelphia and New Orleans on other financial markets also indicated this development. Vice versa, the new southern and western exchange markets quoted the Atlantic ports and the European exchange partners with a considerable premium. Therefore the quotations of Mobile on New York, London and Paris in the 1840s are a remarkable example: their premium reached 20% and more, in some cases even 30%, because the bills were paid in notes of the Bank of Alabama, which were quoted with a large discount against bullion (NOBACK [1851], 1st part, p. 675).

Apart from New York, which had become the financial centre for the USA from around 1840, only New Orleans could keep its position as an exchange market of international relevance until the War of Secession. The increasing economic relevance of the South for the USA as a whole meant that New Orleans gained in economic worth to a far greater extent than during the 18th century. Sufficient references proving the importance of New Orleans as an international exchange market – in contrast to the colonial period (CLARK [1970], pp. 107–125) – are not available until 1804, one year after the USA had acquired Louisiana (1803). As the main shipping port for cotton and tobacco, the most important exports, and as the gateway to the Caribbean, New Orleans held a strong position as a financial market, with quite regular quotations on London, Paris and other American places, and with single quotations on Amsterdam (1829–1833), Trieste (1836) and Havana (cf. WdW I/I, p. 175). New Orleans' most important link within the domestic exchange was that on New York because a major part of New Orleans' transatlantic exchange business was transacted via New York before the War of Secession (cf. COLE [1928/29], p. 394). The end of the independent position of New Orleans within the cashless payment system after 1864/65 was not only the result of the defeat of the Confederates and the economic decline of the South, but also of the economic and political reorientation of the Union towards the North after the Civil War. So the New Orleans' exchange rate quotations were resumed in the early 1870s.

San Francisco, the financial centre of the West, joined New York and New Orleans in the mid-19th century owing to the gold rush in California at the end of the 1840s. In quick succession the town was connected to the internal American as well as the transpacific and transatlantic trade. During the first years after the foundation of San Francisco (in around 1850), not only London, Paris and Hamburg but occasionally also Amsterdam, Frankfurt am Main, Bremen, Havana, Valparaiso, Lima, Mexico City, Shanghai and Hong Kong and, additionally, New York, Boston, New Orleans and Philadelphia were quoted. The rapid link-up to London and its precious metals market ensured the taking over of British customs, particularly because the sea route to Europe was easier to manage than the overland route to New York. This may be seen, for example, in the manner of fixing quotations on London; in San Francisco the rate was fixed in pence sterling per US dollar, whereas in all other American cities the exchange rate on London was quoted in % premium on a fixed parity. With the establishment of a mint in 1852, San Francisco, the trade centre for gold, also became the financial centre of the West and the North American Pacific coast. After the transcontinental cable had been laid in 1861, San Francisco merchants began to orientate themselves towards the New York financial market. Therefore most of the business transactions were carried out via New York after the Civil War. Nonetheless, San Francisco still kept a relatively independent position within the transpacific payment transactions for some decades, for example regarding the transactions from Japan to the USA until about 1910: eight Japanese banks were working for Japanese immigrants in San Francisco after 1903. From the 1880s on New York became increasingly dominant also for the western part of the USA and the Pacific trade, particularly when San Francisco's importance for gold export began to fade after the gold rush in Australia and even more after the one in Alaska during the 1890s.

So "the half century between 1863 and 1913 marked a growth in the status of New York to a world money market" (MYERS [1931], p. 350) – a position occupied by New York in the 20th century. The more the town had grown within the 19th century, the more the transactions and exchange operations of the Atlantic coast and, finally, of the whole USA had concentrated on the Hudson river: New York was the unchallenged financial centre within the currency area of the USA and of the whole of North America from c. 1870/80. From 1876 on, the most important North American trade and financial places – for example Boston, New Orleans, Charleston, Chicago, St Louis, Savannah (all from 1876), Milwaukee (1877/78), Cincinnati (1876–1878, from 1911), San Francisco (from 1899), Minneapolis, Montreal and St Paul (from 1909) – quoted only one single rate for sight bills on New York, linking them up to the network of the international cashless payment system. This rate was only some thousandths away from parity (*WdW I/I*, pp. 457–473).

But even the network of foreign exchange rate quotations of New York, which expanded once again in the mid-19th century, shows the town's outstanding position as the North American financial centre. From the 1850s on New York also quoted Antwerp, Zurich and Basle, Berlin and Frankfurt am Main as well as occasionally even Cologne and Leipzig (ibid., p. 360). In 1881 the exchange rate current was limited to the four most important exchange partners of the USA, i.e. London, Paris, Amsterdam and the German Empire. There were two reasons for this: on the one hand, the German currency had been standardized in 1872, so that only one quotation on "German bankers' marks" (as they were called in the documented sources) became necessary from 1880. On the other hand, there was no longer any need to quote each single financial market of the the states of the Latin Monetary Union because Paris became the dominating financial centre and the French franc the dominating currency after the foundation of the Latin Monetary Union in 1867. A further significant extension of the New York exchange rate current did not start until World War I.

Since the 17th century all exchange operations and payment transactions were handled by merchants, transatlantic exchange operations being carried out exclusively by merchant bankers at the ports on the Atlantic coast up to the 19th century. During the colonial era and the early days of the USA bills of exchange were needed mainly for credits and only occasionally for investments in foreign currencies. The volume and the importance of these transactions were still relatively small – above all in comparison with later decades – and the quoted rates were subject to relatively high fluctuations. From 1824 the private (second) Bank of the United States became increasingly involved in exchange operations on London. During the following years this market of dollar–sterling exchange was controlled above all by merchants from New York (COLE [1928/29]). Additionally, specialized exchange brokers emerged, and clearing via stock banks began to replace the traditional custom of drawing bills directly among the merchants.

Primarily, time bills were drawn for money transfers and the covering of export expenses in the transatlantic trade until the War of Secession, owing to the irregular transports of precious metals on sailing ships. These bills were always quoted at a usance of 60 days' sight. Bills with usances longer than 60 days' sight appeared only rarely then, whereas they had been quite common in the 18th century. When the packet lines started their business and sailing ships were later on substitued by steamships, transports could be carried out not only more regularly but also more cheaply and, above all – with regard to the insurance costs – much more quickly. Nevertheless, the 60 days' usance was kept up in order to have enough time for the distribution of the goods on the home market and for receiving the payments. At the same time exchange operations were increasingly scheduled around the fixed departure days of the ships. After the (third) Atlantic cable had been laid in 1866, the risks of transatlantic exchange operations were again reduced (OFFICER [1985], p. 559; HEFFER [1986], p. 215), even though cable transfer (on London) was not quoted until 1879 and became much more valuable in the early 20th century. Apart from this, three days' sight drafts on demand, which had been used before primarily for domestic exchange, were also used for transatlantic transactions during the War of Secession, giving the opportunity of "choosing between the two varieties then available the type which seemed most advantageous under the particuliar circumstances of the movement" (COLE [1928/29], p. 404). Finally, sight drafts became predominant from the early 1880s (NISHIMURA [1971], p. 39).

When the stock banks rose in importance, finance bills were used together with clean bills (COLE [1928/29], pp. 401–403). Among the clean bills were best or prime bankers' [bills], bills of exchange drawn from overseas on the Bank of England, good bankers' [bills], first-class credits or prime commercial [bills] and good commercial [bills]. The reliability of the companies on which the bills were drawn determined their classification according to the categories best/prime, good or those without any additional remark. In the New York quotations on London can be found the differentiation between bankers' and commercial bills for 60 days' sight bills as well as for sight bills after 1867. In the case of the bankers' bills the differentiation between prime/best and good is listed for the period from 1871 to 1880, and commercial bills are available for the period from 1867 to 1880. The separate quoting of 60 days' commercial bills ended in November 1902, that of commercial sight bills having already ended in 1880. Unlike clean and finance bills, documentary bills were always sent together with one copy of the shipping documents (bill of lading, sea insurance policy) for certification. These documentary bills made up the biggest part of bills from North America (SONNDORFER [1900], pp. 247, 282, 324), particularly because the real trade still predominated over the speculative transactions at that time, and the influence the banks had on exchange operations remained relatively low at the end of the 19th century (MYERS [1931], p. 348). Quotations for New York documentary bills on London are available for the period from 1875 to 1902 (at 60 days' sight) and from 1875 to 1883 (at sight). In the early 20th century a constantly increasing number of finance bills was used in relation to trade bills, which were continually used until the crisis in 1907 when finance bills were refused in London and Berlin (ibid., pp. 344s.).

The following rate series are documented:

- for the colonial era: the quotations of the four main exchange places of the North American Atlantic coast – Boston, New York, Philadelphia and Baltimore – and of their associated colonies, on London;
- for the period after independence: the foreign exchange rate quotations of New York, the main exchange market of the USA and – from the end of the 19th century – one of the most important financial places of the world;
- the quotations of the other important exchange places of the USA – Philadelphia, Baltimore, Boston, New Orleans and San Francisco – on London, the most important exchange partner for those periods, with independent quotations;
- the rates of Philadelphia on other European exchange markets until 1834;
- the available domestic exchange rates of Boston, New Orleans and San Francisco on New York (until 1870), in order to be able to calculate the exchange relations between the towns mentioned and the places quoted by New York on the basis of cross rates via New York.

References: Joseph G. MARTIN, *One Hundred Years. [Martin's] History of the Boston Stock and Money Market*, Boston 1898; Arthur H. COLE, Statistical Background of the Crisis Period 1837–42, *Review of Economic Statistics* 10 (1928), pp. 182–195; idem, Evolution of the Foreign Exchange Market of the United States, *Journal of Economic and Business History* 1 (1928/29), pp. 384–421; idem, The New York Money Market of 1843 to 1862, *Review of Economic Statistics* 11 (1929), pp. 164–170; idem, Seasonal Variation in Sterling Exchange, *Journal of Economic and Business History* 2 (1929), pp. 203–218; Margaret G. MYERS, *Origins and Development (The New York Money Market*, ed. Benjamin H. BECKHART, vol. I), New York 1931; Walter B. SMITH / Arthur H. COLE, *Fluctuations in American Business 1790–1860*, New York 1935; Bernard BAILYN, *The New England Merchants in the Seventeenth Century*, Cambridge (Mass.) – London 1955; L.E. DAVIS / J.R.T. HUGHES, A Dollar Sterling Exchange, 1803–1895, *Economic History Review* sec. ser. 13 (1960/61), pp. 52–78; Milton FRIEDMAN / Anna Jacobsen SCHWARTZ, *A Monetary History of the United States, 1867–1960*, Princeton 1963 (⁸1993); John G. CLARK, *New Orleans 1718–1812. An Economic History*, Baton Rouge 1970; Shizuya NISHIMURA, *The Decline of Inland Bills of Exchange in the London Money Market 1855–1913*, Cambridge 1971; Charles P. KINDLEBERGER, *The Formation of Financial Centers: A Study in Comparative Economic History*, Princeton (N.J.) 1974, pp. 52–56; Edwin J. PERKINS, Managing a Dollar–Sterling Exchange Account: Brown, Shipley and Co. in the 1850's, *Business History* 16 (1974), pp. 48–64; Kenneth D. GARBADE / William L. SILBER, Technology, Communication and the Performance of Financial Markets: 1840–1975, *Journal of Finance* 33 (1978), pp. 819–832; John J. MCCUSKER, *Money and Exchange in Europe and America, 1600–1775. A Handbook*, London – Basingstoke 1978; Lawrence H. OFFICER, Dollar–Sterling Mint Parity and Exchange Rates (1791–1834), *Journal of Economic History* 43 (1983), pp. 579–616; idem, Integration in the American Foreign-Exchange Market (1791–1900), *Journal of Economic History* 45 (1985), pp. 557–585; Jean HEFFER, *Le port de New York et le commerce extérieur américain 1860–1900*, Paris 1986; Lawrence H. OFFICER, The Remarkable Efficiency of the Dollar–Sterling Gold Standard, 1890–1906, *Journal of Economic History* 49 (1989), pp. 1–41; Markus A. DENZEL, Der Aufstieg und die Einbindung der Vereinigten Staaten von Amerika in die Weltwirtschaft: Transatlantische Wechselkurse von 1783 bis 1914, in *WdW I/I*, pp. 146–179; idem, The Transatlantic Cashless Payment System in the Northern Atlantic Zone from the 17th Century to c.1840, in Horst PIETSCHMANN (ed.), *Atlantic History. History of the Atlantic System 1580–1830*, Göttingen 2002, pp. 263–277.

14.1 Exchange on London

14.1.1 Of Boston, Philadelphia, New York and Maryland/Baltimore

	BOSTON on:		PHILADEL- PHIA on:		NEW YORK on:	
	London [a]		London [b]		London [c]	
	per 100 pounds sterling [d]					
	in pounds Massa- chussetts currency		in pounds Penn- sylvania currency		in pounds New York currency	
1660	112.00	(1)				
1661						
1662						
1663	112.00	(1)				
1664	113.30	(1)				
1665	115.33	(1)				
1666						
1667	116.00	(1)				
1668	115.75	(1)				
1669	116.00	(1)				
1670						
1671	125.00	(1)				
1672						
1673	125.00	(1)				
1674	123.89	(1)				
1675	129.17	(1)				
1676						
1677						
1678						
1679	122.00	(2)				
1680	120.25	(2)			125.00	(1)
1681						
1682						
1683			125.00	(1)		
1684	130.00	(1)	125.00	(1)		
1685	127.50	(2)				
1686	125.00	(3)				
1687	120.94	(3)				
1688	140.00	(1)			130.06	(1)
1689			130.00	(1)		
1690						
1691	131.25	(3)				
1692	130.50	(2)				

	BOSTON on:		PHILADEL- PHIA on:		NEW YORK on:		MARYLAND on:	
	London [a]		London [b]		London [c]		London [a]	
	per 100 pounds sterling [d]							
	in pounds Massa- chussatts currency, after 1710 in Old Tenor		in pounds Penn- sylvania currency, from 1709 (5) in Proclamation Money		in pounds New York currency		in pounds Maryland hard currency	
1693	130.00	(1)						
1694	133.66	(2)	135.86	(1)	129.16	(2)		
1695	139.86	(1)			130.00	(1)		
1696	129.17	(1)	150.00	(1)	130.00	(2)		
1697	136.00	(1)						
1698			150.00	(1)	130.00	(1)		
1699	140.48	(3)						
1700	139.43	(2)	155.00	(1)	134.96	(3)		
1701	136.50	(2)	147.92	(4)	132.50	(2)		
1702	130.00	(1)	150.72	(8)	133.33	(1)	111.11	(1)
1703	140.00	(1)	150.84	(12)	140.00	(1)		
1704			150.00	(12)				
1705	135.00	(1)	150.14	(12)			105.00	(1)
1706	150.00	(1)	150.58	(12)				
1707			152.58	(12)				
1708			153.96	(12)				
1709	151.06	(2)	120.05	(10)	150.00	(2)		
1710	155.00	(2)	128.16	(6)	145.05	(3)		
1711	146.67	(3)			151.12	(2)		
1712	150.00	(2)	128.93	(6)	155.62	(2)		
1713	150.00	(2)	130.36	(9)	153.75	(1)		
1714	153.33	(4)	132.50	(8)	154.90	(6)		
1715	160.33	(4)	130.36	(5)	153.20	(7)		
1716	162.50	(4)	133.52	(5)	157.78	(2)		
1717	170.00	(2)	134.72	(5)	160.00	(1)		
1718	200.00	(3)	132.22	(3)				
1719	216.88	(5)	135.42	(3)	154.17	(4)	113.33	(1)
1720	219.43	(12)	138.75	(3)	162.92	(5)	133.33	(1)
1721	225.98	(12)	137.50	(1)	163.33	(3)	114.36	(1)
1722	229.79	(6)	135.01	(5)			127.50	(1)
1723	241.81	(12)	140.37	(3)	165.22	(2)	128.78	(3)
1724	267.92	(12)	143.11	(4)	165.00	(3)		
1725	289.11	(12)	139.34	(2)	165.00	(2)	128.00	(1)
1726	290.19	(12)			165.00	(5)		
1727	291.98	(12)	149.58	(3)	165.00	(4)		

	BOSTON on:		PHILADEL- PHIA on:		NEW YORK on:		MARYLAND on:	
	London [a]		London [b]		London [c]		London [a]	
	per 100 pounds sterling [d]							
	in pounds Massa- chussatts currency in Old Tenor, from 1750 in Lawful Money		in pounds Penn- sylvania currency		in pounds New York currency		in pounds Maryland hard currency	
1728	298.82	(12)	150.62	(3)	165.00	(2)	136.25	(2)
1729	313.33	(12)	148.61	(5)	165.00	(4)	133.33	(1)
1730	337.71	(12)	152.03	(5)	166.88	(5)	133.33	(1)
1731	334.31	(6)	153.28	(7)	165.00	(2)	133.37	(3)
1732	339.51	(8)	160.90	(5)	165.00	(3)	133.33	(5)
1733	350.00	(2)	166.94	(3)	165.00	(4)		
1734	355.00	(2)	170.00	(1)	165.00	(2)	133.33	(4)
1735	360.00	(1)	166.11	(3)	165.00	(6)	133.33	(1)
1736	430.00	(2)	167.00	(5)	165.00	(4)	133.42	(4)
1737	516.67	(3)	170.25	(2)	165.00	(6)	140.00	(2)
1738	500.00	(1)	160.42	(3)	165.00	(5)	135.42	(2)
1739	500.00	(3)	169.69	(7)	166.67	(5)		
1740	525.00	(3)	165.65	(12)	166.25	(4)	139.17	(4)
1741	548.44	(7)	146.14	(12)	159.44	(5)	138.82	(8)
1742	550.28	(8)	159.38	(12)	170.97	(6)	138.64	(8)
1743	550.70	(12)	159.79	(12)	174.67	(4)	137.78	(6)
1744	588.61	(6)	166.67	(12)	175.42	(5)	139.44	(3)
1745	644.79	(12)	174.77	(12)	183.33	(3)	140.00	(1)
1746	642.50	(2)	179.86	(12)	185.83	(3)	137.78	(4)
1747	925.00	(3)	183.78	(12)	191.46	(4)	142.50	(2)
1748	912.50	(2)	174.12	(12)	183.39	(5)	140.97	(2)
1749	1033.33	(3)	171.39	(12)	176.46	(4)		
1750	137.33	(6)	170.60	(12)	179.33	(7)	131.66	(2)
1751	133.33	(1)	169.86	(12)	181.50	(6)	140.00	(1)
1752			166.85	(12)	175.92	(4)		
1753	130.00	(2)	167.49	(12)	179.39	(6)	150.00	(3)
1754	133.33	(1)	168.35	(12)	179.72	(5)	159.58	(3)
1755	133.33	(7)	168.79	(12)	180.13	(12)	165.00	(1)
1756	133.33	(12)	172.57	(12)	182.65	(12)	165.00	(4)
1757	133.33	(3)	166.07	(12)	178.40	(12)	164.53	(5)
1758	128.34	(4)	159.00	(12)	172.60	(12)	157.01	(12)
1759			153.52	(12)	168.39	(12)	153.75	(6)
1760	129.54	(4)	158.61	(12)	167.20	(12)	154.58	(12)
1761	140.10	(6)	172.71	(12)	181.41	(12)	168.58	(12)
1762	142.33	(5)	176.26	(12)	189.76	(12)	170.65	(12)

	BOSTON on:		PHILADEL- PHIA on:		NEW YORK on:		MARYLAND on:	
	London [a]		London [b]		London [c]		London [a]	
	per 100 pounds sterling [d]							
	in pounds Massa- chussatts currency in Lawful Money		in pounds Penn- sylvania currency		in pounds New York currency		in pounds Maryland hard currency	
1763	136.00	(6)	173.00	(12)	186.73	(12)	167.24	(12)
1764	133.75	(6)	172.86	(12)	184.85	(12)	166.77	(12)
1765	133.54	(12)	169.90	(12)	182.80	(12)	166.65	(12)
1766	133.03	(12)	162.96	(12)	177.18	(12)	163.99	(12)
1767	133.33	(6)	166.02	(12)	178.96	(12)	164.59	(12)
1768	133.33	(5)	166.62	(12)	179.87	(12)	164.92	(12)
1769	129.86	(5)	157.56	(12)	172.47	(12)	160.68	(12)
1770	126.31	(12)	153.92	(12)	165.90	(12)	151.03	(12)
1771	133.33	(2)	165.69	(12)	178.43	(12)	161.84	(12)
1772	131.00	(5)	160.83	(12)	173.27	(12)	158.63	(12)
1773	132.19	(12)	166.27	(12)	177.71	(12)	165.13	(12)
1774	135.30	(12)	169.46	(12)	180.62	(12)	167.10	(12)
1775	117.45	(5)	161.12	(12)	171.55	(11)	156.68	(12)
1776								
1777								
1778								
1779								
1780								
1781								
1782								
1783			172.00 60d/s	(5)				
1784			171.86 60d/s	(9)				
1785			177.00 60d/s	(12)				
1786			178.75 60d/s	(9)				
1787			175.00 60d/s	(1)				
1788	in US dollars		172.47 60d/s	(12)				
1789	466.20 60d/s	(1)	172.61 60d/s	(12)				
1790			166.11 60d/s	(12)				
1791			172.35 60d/s	(12)				
1792			165.12 60d/s	(12)	in US dollars			
1793			167.01 60d/s	(12)				
1794			173.35 60d/s	(12)	476.31 60d/s	(9)		
1795	443.45 60d/s	(4)	170.17 60d/s	(12)	454.96 60d/s	(8)		
1796	432.81 60d/s	(12)	162.05 60d/s	(12)	435.21 60d/s	(12)	427.58 60d/s	(12)
1797	440.30 60d/s	(12)	165.18 60d/s	(12)	439.38 60d/s	(12)	442.59 60d/s	(12)
1798	435.40 60d/s	(12)	161.36 60d/s	(12)	439.56 60d/s	(12)		

	BOSTON on:	PHILADEL-PHIA on:	NEW YORK on:	MARYLAND on:
	London	London	London	London
		per 100 pounds sterling [d]		
	in US dollars	in pounds Pennsylvan-ia currency, from 1808 (12) in US dollars	in US dollars	
1799	412.92 60d/s (12)	152.42 60d/s (12)	410.06 60d/s (12)	412.23 60d/s (12)
1800	445.48 60d/s (12)	168.69 60d/s (11)	447.24 60d/s (12)	453.71 60d/s (12)
1801	431.42 60d/s (12)	163.17 60d/s (3)	430.96 60d/s (12)	437.04 60d/s (12)
1802	436.97 60d/s (12)	168.38 60d/s (12)	438.73 60d/s (12)	447.41 60d/s (12)
1803	452.79 60d/s (12)	170.18 60d/s (12)	452.79 60d/s (12)	452.97 60d/s (12)
1804	450.57 60d/s (12)	171.06 60d/s (12)	456.21 60d/s (12)	454.08 60d/s (12)
1805	432.16 60d/s (12)	164.43 60d/s (11)	436.14 60d/s (12)	433.71 60d/s (12)
1806	438.64 60d/s (12)	166.13 60d/s (12)	440.95 60d/s (12)	441.48 60d/s (12)
1807	435.12 60d/s (12)	165.66 60d/s (12)	436.14 60d/s (12)	
1808	467.13 60d/s (12)	176.36/492.84 60d/s (11+1)	468.98 60d/s (12)	456.18 60d/s (12)
1809	455.02 60d/s (12)	460.29 60d/s (12)	457.23 60d/s (12)	424.39 60d/s (12)
1810	423.75 60d/s (12)	429.99 60d/s (8)	424.21 60d/s (12)	381.17 60d/s (12)
1811	388.97 60d/s (12)	403.67 60d/s (12)	383.88 60d/s (12)	361.89 60d/s (12)
1812	358.16 60d/s (12)	361.03 60d/s (12)	357.89 60d/s (12)	373.30 60d/s (12)
1813	374.91 60d/s (12)	370.00 60d/s (12)	374.63 60d/s (12)	416.33 60d/s (12)
1814	394.88 60d/s (12)	410.24 60d/s (12)	408.30 60d/s (12)	480.53 60d/s (12)
1815	410.65 60d/s (12)	471.57 60d/s (12)	453.81 60d/s (12)	521.11 60d/s (12)
1816	448.07 60d/s (12)	507.32 60d/s (12)	474.11 60d/s (12)	455.96 60d/s (12)
1817	451.78 60d/s (12)	455.84 60d/s (12)	451.03 60d/s (12)	447.80 60d/s (12)
1818	446.36 60d/s (12)	447.20 60d/s (12)	444.28 60d/s (12)	445.79 60d/s (12)
1819	445.76 60d/s (12)	447.70 60d/s (12)	446.79 60d/s (12)	447.98 60d/s (12)
1820	449.78 60d/s (12)	448.72 60d/s (12)	449.28 60d/s (12)	478.28 60d/s (12)
1821	479.43 60d/s (12)	480.54 60d/s (12)	478.55 60d/s (12)	497.04 60d/s (12)
1822	494.51 60d/s (12)	495.62 60d/s (12)	492.06 60d/s (12)	479.63 60d/s (12)
1823	477.67 60d/s (12)	477.35 60d/s (12)	477.70 60d/s (12)	485.00 60d/s (12)
1824	484.94 60d/s (12)	483.78 60d/s (12)	484.06 60d/s (12)	480.93 60d/s (12)
1825	480.54 60d/s (12)	480.26 60d/s (12)	480.03 60d/s (12)	489.45 60d/s (12)
1826	488.03 60d/s (12)	488.31 60d/s (12)	488.85 60d/s (12)	492.04 60d/s (12)
1827	491.27 60d/s (12)	491.87 60d/s (12)	491.45 60d/s (12)	491.48 60d/s (12)
1828	491.18 60d/s (12)	491.23 60d/s (12)	490.75 60d/s (12)	485.67 60d/s (10)
1829	484.24 60d/s (12)	484.84 60d/s (12)	483.31 60d/s (12)	
1830	475.91 60d/s (12)	476.66 60d/s (12)	475.90 60d/s (12)	
1831	482.85 60d/s (12)	482.76 60d/s (12)	482.88 60d/s (12)	
1832	483.96 60d/s (12)	483.83 60d/s (12)	484.38 60d/s (12)	
1833	479.06 60d/s (12)	478.36 60d/s (11)	478.59 60d/s (12)	
1834	460.47 60d/s (12)	463.66 60d/s (12)	461.26 60d/s (12)	

	PHILADEL-PHIA on:	NEW YORK on:
	London	London
	per 100 pounds sterling [d]	
	in US dollars	
1835	482.50 60d/s (12)	482.34 60d/s (12)
1836	479.91 60d/s (12)	478.74 60d/s (12)
1837	507.32 60d/s (12)	506.44 60d/s (12)
1838	483.65 60d/s (12)	481.40 60d/s (12)
1839	483.65 60d/s (12)	485.13 60d/s (12)
1840	496.49 60d/s (12)	478.85 60d/s (12)
1841		481.88 60d/s (12)
1842		476.03 60d/s (12)
1843		477.81 60d/s (12)
1844		485.03 60d/s (12)
1845		486.46 60d/s (12)
1846		480.87 60d/s (12)
1847		474.71 60d/s (12)
1848		487.00 60d/s (12)
1849		482.62 60d/s (12)
1850		483.36 60d/s (12)
1851		489.70 60d/s (12)
1852		489.14 60d/s (12)
1853		486.22 60d/s (12)
1854		484.98 60d/s (12)
1855		485.58 60d/s (12)
1856		486.23 60d/s (12)
1857		482.55 60d/s (12)
1858		486.36 60d/s (12)
1859		487.91 60d/s (12)
1860		481.70 60d/s (12)
1861		473.93 60d/s (12)
1862		548.85 60d/s (12)
1863		711.51 60d/s (12)
1864		934.90 60d/s (12)
1865		484.28 60d/s (12)
1866		476.24 60d/s (12)
1867		486.02 60d/s (12)
1868		487.53 60d/s (12)
1869		484.75 60d/s (12)
1870		484.63 60d/s (12)
1871		485.84 60d/s (12)

	NEW YORK on: London per 100 pounds sterling [d] in US dollars				NEW YORK on: London per 100 pounds sterling [d] in US dollars		
1872	484.20	60d/s	(12)	1894	488.05	t.t.	(12)
1873	481.67	60d/s	(12)	1895	489.32	t.t.	(12)
1874	485.74	60d/s	(12)	1896	487.74	t.t.	(12)
1875	484.97	60d/s	(12)	1897	486.80	t.t.	(12)
1876	485.70	60d/s	(12)	1898	485.37	t.t.	(12)
1877	484.35	60d/s	(12)	1899	487.02	t.t.	(12)
1878	483.30	60d/s	(12)	1900	487.28	t.t.	(12)
1879	484.24	60d/s	(12)	1901	487.89	t.t.	(12)
1880	484.85	t.t.	(10)	1902	487.79	t.t.	(12)
1881	486.25	t.t.	(12)	1903	486.85	t.t.	(12)
1882	488.97	t.t.	(11)	1904	486.92	t.t.	(12)
1883	486.46	t.t.	(12)	1905	486.93	t.t.	(12)
1884	487.10	t.t.	(12)	1906	485.68	t.t.	(11)
1885	486.54	t.t.	(12)	1907	486.58	t.t.	(10)
1886	487.74	t.t.	(12)	1908	486.79	t.t.	(12)
1887	486.40	t.t.	(12)	1909	487.59	t.t.	(12)
1888	488.14	t.t.	(12)	1910	486.70	t.t.	(12)
1889	488.27	t.t.	(12)	1911	486.56	t.t.	(12)
1890	486.82	t.t.	(12)	1912	487.00	t.t.	(12)
1891	486.72	t.t.	(12)	1913	487.01	t.t.	(12)
1892	487.68	t.t.	(12)	1914	487.07	t.t.	(6)
1893	487.18	t.t.	(12)				

[a] In the colonial era no usance is given.

[b] In the colonial era bills on London were regularly drawn at 30 or 40 days' sight (MCCUSKER [1978], p. 177).

[c] Usances in the colonial era: "Most bills were drawn at thirty or forty days' sight", but also bills at 60 days' sight can be found (ibid., p. 158).

[d] Concerning the British currency, see pp. 3–5.

14.1.2 Of New Orleans and San Francisco

	NEW ORLEANS on:			NEW ORLEANS on:	SAN FRAN- CISCO on: [b]
	London			London	London
	per 100 pounds sterling [a]			per 100 pounds sterling [a]	
	in US dollars			in US dollars	
1804	444.44 60d/s (2)		1840	492.20 60d/s (12)	
1805	441.23 60d/s (12)		1841	493.00 60d/s (9)	
1806	432.90 60d/s (12)		1842	449.55 60d/s (4)	
1807	441.23 60d/s (12)		1843	469.07 60d/s (12)	
1808	444.44 60d/s (12)		1844	480.17 60d/s (12)	
1809	444.44 60d/s (12)		1845	481.84 60d/s (12)	
1810	444.44 60d/s (12)		1846	476.19 60d/s (12)	
1811	444.44 60d/s (12)		1847	464.63 60d/s (12)	
1812	444.44 60d/s (1)		1848	477.77 60d/s (12)	
1813			1849	478.51 60d/s (12)	
1814			1850	482.14 60d/s (12)	473.97 60d/s (2)
1815			1851	484.80 60d/s (12)	486.32 60d/s (8)
1816	470.64 60d/s (1)		1852	484.80 60d/s (12)	509.86 60d/s (12)
1817			1853	484.06 60d/s (12)	509.29 60d/s (12)
1818			1854	482.72 60d/s (12)	509.29 60d/s (2)
1819	435.12 60d/s (1)		1855	481.93 60d/s (12)	505.27 60d/s (7)
1820	439.56 60d/s (1)		1856	481.05 60d/s (12)	505.27 60d/s (8)
1821	467.03 60d/s (4)		1857	477.95 60d/s (12)	503.94 60d/s (1)
1822	498.39 60d/s (2)		1858	478.28 60d/s (12)	505.27 60d/s (12)
1823	470.64 60d/s (4)		1859	485.00 60d/s (12)	505.27 60d/s (12)
1824	479.02 60d/s (12)		1860	478.46 60d/s (12)	502.21 60d/s (12)
1825	471.52 60d/s (12)		1861	480.56 60d/s (12)	
1826	472.40 60d/s (12)		1862	596.74 60d/s (5)	507.95 60d/s (2)
1827	479.25 60d/s (12)		1863		496.77 60d/s (3)
1828	481.37 60d/s (12)		1864	1,112.78 60d/s (4)	496.46 60d/s (12)
1829	476.19 60d/s (12)		1865	761.28 60d/s (12)	494.64 60d/s (12)
1830	470.09 60d/s (9)		1866	665.36 60d/s (12)	494.34 60d/s (11)
1831	466.76 60d/s (6)		1867	658.28 60d/s (12)	494.85 60d/s (9)
1832	476.19 60d/s (4)		1868	676.29 60d/s (12)	488.55 60d/s (1)
1833	472.78 60d/s (7)		1869	640.01 60d/s (12)	
1834	456.77 60d/s (2)		1870	551.97 60d/s (12)	
1835			1871	533.36 60d/s (3)	
1836	482.85 60d/s (6)		1872	540.30 60d/s (1)	
1837	487.85 60d/s (6)		1873		
1838	493.21 60d/s (3)		1874	539.46 60d/s (1)	
1839	488.88 60d/s (7)				

[a]   Concerning the British currency, see pp. 3–5.

[b]   From August 1860 for bankers' bills.

14.2 Philadelphia exchange rates (except on London)

14.2.1 On Amsterdam, Paris and Hamburg

	PHILADELPHIA on:		
	Amsterdam	**Paris** [a]	**Hamburg**
	per 100 guilders Flemish current [b]	per 100 livres tournois [c]	per 100 mark banco [d]
	in pounds Pennsylvania currency		
1783	15.17 60d/s (5)	7.30 60d/s (5)	
1784	15.70 60d/s (12)	7.34 60d/s (12)	
1785	15.84 60d/s (12)	7.50 60d/s (12)	
1786	15.84 60d/s (9)	7.50 60d/s (9)	
1787	15.42 60d/s (10)	7.25 60d/s (10)	
1788	15.42 60d/s (12)	7.42 60d/s (12)	
1789	15.42 60d/s (12)	7.47 60d/s (12)	
1790	15.28 60d/s (12)	7.32 60d/s (12)	
1791	14.86 60d/s (12)	6.74 60d/s (12)	
	in US dollars		
1792	38.80 60d/s (12)	15.60 60d/s (12)	
1793	39.58 60d/s (12)	10.00 60d/s (1)	
1794	41.75 60d/s (12)	18.50 60d/s (1)	33.50 60d/s (1)
1795	40.99 60d/s (12)		34.00 60d/s (1)
1796	40.21 60d/s (10)		34.63 60d/s (4)
1797	40.00 60d/s (12)		34.50 60d/s (1)
1798	39.00 60d/s (12)		
1799	36.36 60d/s (12)		31.63 60d/s (12)
1800	38.36 60d/s (11)		33.30 60d/s (10)
1801			
1802	40.66 60d/s (12)		34.78 60d/s (6)
1803	41.59 60d/s (12)		35.17 60d/s (12)
1804	40.25 60d/s (12)		35.50 60d/s (12)
1805	38.11 60d/s (12)		33.48 60d/s (11)
1806	39.17 60d/s (12)		33.67 60d/s (11)
1807	39.13 60d/s (12)		33.73 60d/s (12)
1808	40.09 60d/s (12)		34.88 60d/s (12)
1809	42.40 60d/s (10)		35.00 60d/s (10)
1810			36.36 60d/s (1)
1811			
1812			
1813			
1814			

	PHILADELPHIA on:		
	Amsterdam	**Paris** [a]	**Hamburg**
	per 100 guilders Flemish current, from 1816 (10) per 100 Dutch guilders [b]	per 100 francs [c]	per 100 mark banco [d]
		in US dollars	
1815	47.86 60d/s (6)	22.82 60d/s (6)	
1816	46.88 60d/s (12)	22.47 60d/s (12)	38.09 60d/s (4)
1817	40.84 60d/s (12)	19.53 60d/s (12)	36.00 60d/s (6)
1818	39.79 60d/s (12)	18.87 60d/s (12)	
1819	39.84 60d/s (12)	18.76 60d/s (12)	36.20 60d/s (10)
1820	38.33 60d/s (12)	18.11 60d/s (12)	34.25 60d/s (2)
1821	39.25 60d/s (12)	18.49 60d/s (12)	34.58 60d/s (12)
1822	40.19 60d/s (12)	19.41 60d/s (12)	
1823	39.92 60d/s (12)	18.92 60d/s (12)	
1824	40.50 60d/s (12)	19.04 60d/s (12)	
1825	40.71 60d/s (12)	19.28 60d/s (12)	
1826	40.13 60d/s (12)	18.82 60d/s (12)	35.25 60d/s (5)
1827	40.30 60d/s (12)	19.19 60d/s (12)	
1828	40.50 60d/s (12)	19.43 60d/s (12)	
1829	40.50 60d/s (12)	19.14 60d/s (12)	
1830	39.92 60d/s (10)	18.76 60d/s (12)	
1831	40.04 60d/s (12)	19.33 60d/s (12)	
1832	40.69 60d/s (12)	19.04 60d/s (12)	
1833	40.30 60d/s (12)	18.66 60d/s (12)	34.50 60d/s (4)
1834	39.19 60d/s (11)	18.45 60d/s (11)	34.29 60d/s (11)
1835			
1836			
1837		19.96 60d/s (5)	36.50 60d/s (1)
1838		19.26 60d/s (4)	
1839	41.00 60d/s (1)	19.27 60d/s (2)	
1840	40.98 60d/s (6)	19.77 60d/s (8)	37.25 60d/s (6)

[a]   1789/90 and 1817–1820 quoted under "France".

[b]   Concerning the French currency, see pp. 279f.

[c]   Concerning the Dutch currency, see pp. 57–59.

[d]   Concerning the Hamburg currency, see pp. 191–193.

14.3 New York exchange rates (except on London)

14.3.1 On Amsterdam, Paris, Hamburg and Bremen/Germany

	NEW YORK on:		
	Amsterdam	Paris	Hamburg
	per 100 guilders Flemish current, from 1816 (10) per 100 Dutch guilders [a]	per 100 livres tournois, from 1815 per 100 francs [b]	per 100 mark banco [c]
	in US dollars		
1796	40.00 60d/s (10)		39.02 60d/s (1)
1797	39.50 60d/s (12)		
1798	37.50 60d/s (12)		
1799	36.12 60d/s (9)		36.50 60d/s (2)
1800			
1801			
1802			
1803	40.59 60d/s (12)		36.00 60d/s (12)
1804	39.25 60d/s (12)		36.50 60d/s (12)
1805	37.07 60d/s (12)		33.79 60d/s (12)
1806	38.59 60d/s (12)		33.34 60d/s (12)
1807	38.21 60d/s (12)		33.57 60d/s (12)
1808	40.09 60d/s (12)		34.80 60d/s (12)
1809	41.36 60d/s (11)		34.29 60d/s (12)
1810			
1811			
1812			
1813			
1814			
1815	44.53 60d/s (9)	21.48 60d/s (8)	
1816	41.83 60d/s (12)	19.80 60d/s (12)	35.25 60d/s (1)
1817	39.11 60d/s (12)	18.60 60d/s (12)	
1818	39.47 60d/s (12)	18.58 60d/s (12)	
1819	39.55 60d/s (12)	18.55 60d/s (12)	
1820	38.09 60d/s (12)	18.04 60d/s (12)	
1821	38.89 60d/s (12)	18.56 60d/s (12)	
1822	40.12 60d/s (12)	19.26 60d/s (12)	
1823	39.57 60d/s (12)	18.82 60d/s (12)	
1824	40.66 60d/s (12)	19.06 60d/s (12)	
1825	40.63 60d/s (12)	19.20 60d/s (12)	
1826	40.04 60d/s (12)	18.83 60d/s (12)	
1827	40.82 60d/s (12)	19.34 60d/s (12)	
1828	41.00 60d/s (12)	19.43 60d/s (12)	

	NEW YORK on:			
	Amsterdam	**Paris**	**Hamburg**	**Bremen**
	per 100 Dutch guilders [a]	per 100 francs [b]	per 100 mark banco [c]	per 100 rixdollars gold [c]
	in US dollars			
1829	40.48 60d/s (12)	19.18 60d/s (12)		
1830	39.04 60d/s (10)	18.74 60d/s (12)		
1831	39.94 60d/s (7)	19.39 60d/s (12)		
1832	40.69 60d/s (12)	19.01 60d/s (12)	34.99 60d/s (7)	77.34 60d/s (6)
1833	40.12 60d/s (8)	18.65 60d/s (12)	34.87 60d/s (12)	77.00 60d/s (3)
1834	38.30 60d/s (12)	18.26 60d/s (12)	33.91 60d/s (12)	
1835	39.66 60d/s (12)	19.03 60d/s (12)	35.60 60d/s (12)	
1836	39.61 60d/s (12)	18.89 60d/s (12)	35.38 60d/s (12)	
1837	42.01 60d/s (12)	19.79 60d/s (12)	36.92 60d/s (12)	83.22 60d/s (12)
1838	39.99 60d/s (12)	19.03 60d/s (12)	35.67 60d/s (12)	79.47 60d/s (12)
1839	40.49 60d/s (12)	19.25 60d/s (12)	36.42 60d/s (12)	80.42 60d/s (12)
1840	39.80 60d/s (12)	19.13 60d/s (12)	35.92 60d/s (9)	78.01 60d/s (12)
1841	40.03 60d/s (12)	19.08 60d/s (12)	36.07 60d/s (12)	77.32 60d/s (12)
1842	39.10 60d/s (12)	18.67 60d/s (12)	35.12 60d/s (12)	75.89 60d/s (12)
1843	39.31 60d/s (11)	18.75 60d/s (12)	34.96 60d/s (12)	76.77 60d/s (12)
1844	40.02 60d/s (12)	19.03 60d/s (12)	35.63 60d/s (12)	78.93 60d/s (12)
1845	39.70 60d/s (10)	19.04 60d/s (12)	35.47 60d/s (12)	78.82 60d/s (12)
1846	39.10 60d/s (12)	18.83 60d/s (12)	35.27 60d/s (12)	78.12 60d/s (12)
1847	39.42 60d/s (12)	18.79 60d/s (12)	35.39 60d/s (12)	78.12 60d/s (12)
1848	40.20 60d/s (5)	19.08 60d/s (7)	35.58 60d/s (5)	78.43 60d/s (5)
1849	39.98 60d/s (12)	18.93 60d/s (12)	35.16 60d/s (12)	78.11 60d/s (12)
1850	38.51 60d/s (12)	19.10 60d/s (12)	35.59 60d/s (12)	79.20 60d/s (12)
1851	41.54 60d/s (12)	19.61 60d/s (12)	36.71 60d/s (12)	79.32 60d/s (12)
1852	41.02 60d/s (12)	19.38 60d/s (12)	36.36 60d/s (12)	78.69 60d/s (12)
1853	41.40 60d/s (6)	19.47 60d/s (12)	36.38 60d/s (12)	80.23 60d/s (6)
1854	41.56 60d/s (7)	19.47 60d/s (12)	36.71 60d/s (7)	79.01 60d/s (8)
1855		19.44 60d/s (12)	36.60 60d/s (12)	79.16 60d/s (12)
1856	41.41 60d/s (12)	19.37 60d/s (12)	36.68 60d/s (12)	
1857	41.02 60d/s (12)	19.23 60d/s (12)	36.40 60d/s (9)	78.50 60d/s (2)
1858	41.66 60d/s (11)	19.46 60d/s (12)	36.81 60d/s (11)	79.46 60d/s (11)
1859	41.98 60d/s (11)	19.50 60d/s (12)	37.02 60d/s (11)	79.62 60d/s (11)
1860	41.43 60d/s (12)	19.32 60d/s (12)	36.86 60d/s (12)	78.55 60d/s (12)
1861	40.48 60d/s (12)		35.74 60d/s (12)	77.23 60d/s (12)
1862	47.20 60d/s (12)	21.95 60d/s (12)	41.34 60d/s (12)	89.72 60d/s (12)
1863	61.30 60d/s (11)	28.54 60d/s (12)	53.65 60d/s (11)	122.25 60d/s (6)
1864	77.99 60d/s (7)	38.40 60d/s (8)	71.79 60d/s (8)	154.80 60d/s (8)
1865	40.93 60d/s (10)	20.07 s (7)	36.55 60d/s (10)	78.45 60d/s (10)
1866	40.99 60d/s (12)	19.36 s (12)	36.40 60d/s (12)	78.56 60d/s (12)

	NEW YORK on:			
	Amsterdam	**Paris**	**Hamburg, from 1881 Germany** [d]	**Bremen** [e]
	per 100 Dutch guilders [a]	per 100 francs [b]	per 100 mark banco, from 1872 (12) per 100 mark [c]	per 100 rixdollars gold, from 1872 (7) per 100 mark [c]
			in US dollars	
1867	41.22 60d/s (12)	19.49 s (12)	36.24 60d/s (12)	78.93 60d/s (12)
1868	41.16 60d/s (12)	19.50 s (12)	36.09 60d/s (12)	79.41 60d/s (12)
1869	40.56 60d/s (12)	19.42 s (12)	35.85 60d/s (12)	78.70 60d/s (12)
1870	41.00 60d/s (12)	19.47 s (9)	36.13 60d/s (12)	79.16 60d/s (12)
1871	40.88 60d/s (11)	19.12 s (6)	36.37 s (11)	79.64 s (10)
1872	40.49 60d/s (12)	19.23 s (12)	36.31/24.13 s (11+1)	78.71/24.15 s (6+6)
1873	40.20 60d/s (12)	19.18 s (12)	24.12 s (12)	24.12 s (12)
1874	40.97 60d/s (12)	19.49 s (12)	24.11 s (12)	24.09 s (11)
1875	40.94 60d/s (12)	19.42 s (12)	23.91 s (12)	23.93 s (11)
1876	40.21 60d/s (11)	19.40 s (10)	23.94 s (10)	23.94 s (10)
1877	40.15 60d/s (12)	19.40 s (11)	23.84 s (11)	23.83 s (11)
1878	39.98 60d/s (12)	19.34 s (12)	23.83 s (12)	23.83 s (12)
1879	40.04 60d/s (12)	19.29 s (12)	23.82 s (12)	23.81 s (12)
1880	40.13 s/dem (12)	19.22 s/dem (12)	23.76 s/dem (12)	23.76 s/dem (12)
1881	40.06 s/dem (12)	19.19 s/dem (12)	23.70 s/dem (12)	
1882	40.35 s/dem (11)	19.40 s/dem (12)	23.91 s/dem (11)	
1883	40.19 s/dem (12)	19.27 s/dem (12)	23.79 s/dem (12)	
1884	40.38 s/dem (11)	19.33 s/dem (11)	23.86 s/dem (11)	
1885	40.37 s/dem (12)	19.26 s/dem (12)	23.86 s/dem (12)	
1886	40.33 s/dem (12)	19.31 s/dem (12)	23.90 s/dem (12)	
1887	40.22 s/dem (11)	19.20 s/dem (11)	23.82 s/dem (11)	
1888	40.40 s/dem (12)	19.28 s/dem (12)	23.90 s/dem (12)	
1889	40.37 s/dem (12)	19.33 s/dem (12)	23.86 s/dem (12)	
1890	40.25 s/dem (12)	19.29 s/dem (12)	23.86 s/dem (12)	
1891	40.27 s/dem (12)	19.29 s/dem (12)	23.86 s/dem (12)	
1892	40.35 s/dem (12)	19.37 s/dem (12)	23.90 s/dem (12)	
1893	40.23 s/dem (12)	19.32 s/dem (12)	23.85 s/dem (12)	
1894	40.39 s/dem (12)	19.39 s/dem (12)	23.89 s/dem (12)	
1895	40.40 s/dem (12)	19.40 s/dem (12)	23.92 s/dem (12)	
1896	40.26 s/dem (12)	19.36 s/dem (12)	23.86 s/dem (12)	
1897	40.28 s/dem (12)	19.35 s/dem (12)	23.86 s/dem (12)	
1898	40.15 s/dem (12)	19.20 s/dem (12)	23.73 s/dem (12)	
1899	40.18 s/dem (12)	19.30 s/dem (12)	23.80 s/dem (12)	
1900	40.24 s/dem (12)	19.35 s/dem (12)	23.79 s/dem (12)	
1901	40.30 s/dem (12)	19.36 s/dem (12)	23.83 s/dem (12)	
1902	40.21 s/dem (12)	19.37 s/dem (12)	23.82 s/dem (12)	

	NEW YORK on:					
	Amsterdam			**Paris**		**Germany** [d]
	per 100 Dutch guilders [a]			per 100 francs [b]		per 100 mark [c]
	in US dollars					
1903	40.21	s/dem	(11)	19.34 s/dem (12)		23.77 s/dem (12)
1904	40.27	s/dem	(11)	19.34 s/dem (12)		23.82 s/dem (12)
1905	40.24	s/dem	(12)	19.35 s/dem (12)		23.79 s/dem (12)
1906	40.03	s/dem	(11)	19.29 s/dem (11)		23.69 s/dem (11)
1907	40.14	s/dem	(10)	19.31 s/dem (10)		23.71 s/dem (10)
1908	40.24	s/dem	(12)	19.36 s/dem (12)		23.80 s/dem (12)
1909	40.37	t.t.	(11)	19.37 t.t. (12)		23.36 t.t. (12)
1910	40.26	t.t.	(12)	19.31 t.t. (12)		23.79 t.t. (12)
1911	40.28	t.t.	(12)	19.28 t.t. (12)		23.78 t.t. (12)
1912	40.36	t.t.	(11)	19.32 t.t. (12)		23.79 t.t. (12)
1913	40.22	t.t.	(12)	19.30 t.t. (12)		23.81 t.t. (12)
1914	40.41	t.t.	(5)	19.34 t.t. (6)		23.80 t.t. (6)

[a]   Concerning the Dutch currency, see pp. 57–59.

[b]   Concerning the French currency, see pp. 279f.

[c]   Concerning the German currencies, see pp. 171–173, 179. The quotations on Bremen were effected in rixdollars or thaler gold of 72 grote at 5 schwaren. This thaler gold was equal to one-fifth part of the "louis d'or", meaning the different pistoles of the North German territories and of Denmark (from 1828). In Bremen the new mark Reichswährung was introduced on July 1st 1872 (by Act of April 30th 1872), whereby 28 thaler gold were equal to 93 mark (cf. *WdW XI*, pp. 108f.).

[d]   Common quotations on Hamburg, Bremen, Frankfurt am Main and Berlin.

[e]   Further quotations on Bremen: see the column "Germany".

14.3.2 On Frankfurt am Main, Berlin, Antwerp and Switzerland

	NEW YORK on:										
	Frankfurt [a]			**Berlin** [a]			**Antwerp**			**Zurich & Basle**		
	per 100 guilders South German current, from 1874 (11) per 100 mark [b]			per 100 thalers Prussian current, from 1874 (11) per 100 mark [b]			per 100 Belgian francs [c]			per 100 franken [d]		
	in US dollars											
1853	41.35	60d/s	(2)									
1854	41.54	60d/s	(7)				19.43	60d/s	(6)			
1855	41.63	60d/s	(12)	73.69	60d/s	(12)	19.39	60d/s	(12)			
1856												
1857	41.19	60d/s	(2)	72.63	60d/s	(2)	19.14	60d/s	(2)	19.17	60d/s	(2)
1858	41.63	60d/s	(5)	73.25	60d/s	(5)	19.46	60d/s	(9)	19.41	60d/s	(5)
1859							19.54	60d/s	(5)			
1860												
1861	41.88	60d/s	(1)									
1862	47.55	60d/s	(12)	92.83	60d/s	(3)	22.55	60d/s	(7)	23.92	60d/s	(3)
1863	65.96	60d/s	(6)	110.75	60d/s	(4)	28.30	60d/s	(4)	28.17	60d/s	(2)
1864	41.19	60d/s	(1)	71.75	60d/s	(1)	19.35	60d/s	(1)	19.38	60d/s	(1)
1865	40.84	60d/s	(9)	71.57	60d/s	(9)	19.31	60d/s	(10)	19.37	60d/s	(12)
1866	41.06	60d/s	(11)	72.21	60d/s	(12)	19.14	60d/s	(12)	19.19	60d/s	(12)
1867	41.11	60d/s	(12)	72.16	60d/s	(12)	19.32	60d/s	(12)	19.32	60d/s	(12)
1868	41.01	60d/s	(12)	71.80	60d/s	(12)	19.34	60d/s	(12)	19.34	60d/s	(12)
1869	40.69	60d/s	(12)	71.19	60d/s	(12)	19.28	60d/s	(12)	19.28	60d/s	(12)
1870	41.08	60d/s	(12)	71.93	60d/s	(12)	19.34	60d/s	(12)	19.35	60d/s	(10)
1871	41.37	s	(11)	72.51	s	(11)	19.44	s	(11)	19.50	s	(10)
1872	41.44	s	(12)	72.54	s	(12)	19.31	s	(11)	19.37	s	(11)
1873	41.43	s	(12)	72.41	s	(12)	19.27	s	(12)	19.30	s	(10)
1874	41.39/24.06	s	(10+2)	71.72/23.77	60d/s	(8+2)	19.48	s	(12)	19.47	s	(11)
1875	23.93	s	(12)	23.71	60d/s	(11)	19.42	s	(12)	19.42	s	(12)
1876	23.94	s	(12)	23.93	s	(10)	19.40	s	(10)	19.42	s	(10)
1877	23.83	s	(12)	23.83	s	(11)	19.39	s	(11)	19.39	s	(11)
1878	23.83	s	(12)	23.83	s	(12)	19.34	s	(12)	19.34	s	(12)
1879	23.82	s	(12)	23.81	s	(12)	19.29	s	(12)	19.30	s	(12)
1880	23.76	s/dem	(12)	23.84	s/dem	(7)	19.27	s/dem	(7)	19.30	s/dem	(7)

[a]   Further quotations on Frankfurt and Berlin: see the column "Germany" in the table above.

[b]   Concerning the German currencies, see pp. 195–197.

[c]   The Belgian franc was equal to the French franc.

[d]   Concerning the Swiss currency, see p. 313.

14.4 Domestic exchange on New York

14.4.1 Of Boston, New Orleans and San Francisco

	BOSTON on:			NEW ORLEANS on:		
	New York			New York		
	per 100 US dollars					
	in US dollars					
1797	97.23	30d/s	(12)			
1798	97.89	30d/s	(12)			
1799	97.75	30d/s	(12)			
1800	98.27	30d/s	(12)			
1801	99.00	30d/s	(12)			
1802	99.00	30d/s	(12)			
1803	99.25	30d/s	(12)			
1804	99.25	30d/s	(12)	100.00	60d/s	(2)
1805	99.25	30d/s	(12)	100.00	60d/s	(12)
1806	99.36	30d/s	(12)	101.00	60d/s	(12)
1807	98.75	30d/s	(12)	102.00	60d/s	(12)
1808				100.50	60d/s	(12)
1809	99.25	30d/s	(9)	100.00	60d/s	(12)
1810	99.25	30d/s	(12)	100.00	60d/s	(12)
1811	99.25	30d/s	(12)	100.00	60d/s	(12)
1812	99.25	30d/s	(12)	100.00	60d/s	(1)
1813	99.25	30d/s	(12)			
1814	95.07	s	(12)			
1815	89.36	s	(12)			
1816	93.07	s	(11)	100.00	60d/s	(8)
1817	99.63	s	(9)			
1818	99.51	s	(12)			
1819	99.50	s	(12)	107.50	60d/s	(1)
1820	99.75	s	(12)	97.50	60d/s	(1)
1821	99.88	s	(12)	97.50	60d/s	(1)
1822	99.88	s	(12)	99.75	60d/s	(2)
1823	99.87	s	(12)	98.63	60d/s	(4)
1824	99.88	s	(12)	99.00	60d/s	(12)
1825	99.88	s	(12)	97.90	60d/s	(12)
1826	99.63	s	(12)	97.34	60d/s	(12)
1827	99.88	s	(12)	97.40	60d/s	(12)
1828	99.88	s	(12)	97.98	60d/s	(12)
1829	99.94	s	(12)	97.91	60d/s	(12)
1830	99.88	s	(12)	97.93	60d/s	(9)

	BOSTON on:			NEW ORLEANS on:			SAN FRAN-CISCO on: [a]		
	New York			New York			New York		
	per 100 US dollars								
	in US dollars								
1831	99.88	s	(12)	98.52	60d/s	(6)			
1832	100.00	s	(12)	98.53	60d/s	(11)			
1833	100.00	s	(12)	98.61	60d/s	(8)			
1834	99.63	s	(12)	98.75	60d/s	(2)			
1835									
1836				99.65	60d/s	(6)			
1837				98.84	60d/s	(6)			
1838				103.00	60d/s	(3)			
1839				101.47	60d/s	(8)			
1840				97.93	60d/s	(12)			
1841				97.49	60d/s	(9)			
1842				96.07	60d/s	(4)			
1843				98.19	60d/s	(12)			
1844				98.58	60d/s	(12)			
1845				98.56	60d/s	(12)			
1846				97.99	60d/s	(11)			
1847				97.68	60d/s	(12)			
1848				98.02	60d/s	(12)			
1849				98.87	60d/s	(12)	102.75	60d/s	(1)
1850				98.52	60d/s	(12)	99.75	60d/s	(12)
1851				98.12	60d/s	(12)	101.46	60d/s	(12)
1852				98.06	60d/s	(12)	102.42	60d/s	(12)
1853				98.15	60d/s	(12)	101.89	60d/s	(9)
1854				98.04	60d/s	(12)	102.84	60d/s	(8)
1855				98.07	60d/s	(12)	101.69	60d/s	(8)
1856				98.12	60d/s	(12)	101.50	60d/s	(12)
1857				97.54	60d/s	(11)	101.50	60d/s	(12)
1858				97.95	60d/s	(12)	101.50	60d/s	(12)
1859				98.52	60d/s	(12)	101.17	60d/s	(12)
1860				98.16	60d/s	(12)	101.69	60d/s	(12)
1861				97.72	60d/s	(4)			
1862				[b]					
1863				[b]			137.84	60d/s	(3)
1864				100.08	s	(4)	180.09	t.t.	(12)
1865				99.10	s	(12)	170.00	t.t.	(6)
1866				99.79	s	(12)	133.95	t.t.	(10)
1867				99.75	s	(12)	131.62	t.t.	(9)

	BOSTON on:	NEW ORLEANS on:	SAN FRAN-CISCO on: [a]
	New York	New York	New York
		per 100 US dollars	
		in US dollars	
1868		99.64 s (12)	*136.50* t.t. (1)
1869		99.73 s (12)	
1870		100.01 s (12)	
1871		99.58 s (3)	
1872		99.85 s (1)	

[a] From 1863 per 100 US dollars in gold (in *italics*).

[b] From September 1861 until July 1862 the quotation on New York was replaced by the one on Richmond, at sight: 98.75 US dollars per 100 US dollars (1861) and 99.35 US dollars per 100 US dollars (1862) respectively.

15
Canada (1757–1914)

Exchange markets: Quebec (1762–1899), Montreal (1762–1914) and Halifax (1757–1879)

Sources: MCCULLOUGH [1984], pp. 266–281

Concordance: *WdW I/I*, p. 473

Currency: With Britain gradually taking over French Canada (Nouvelle France), the French currency nominally valid hitherto was eliminated, even if French coins were still in circulation for decades. In Lower Canada, they were circulating in signifiucant amounts even up to the 1830s. In the New England Colonies, the pound of 20 shillings at 12 pence became the unit of account, as was common in the mother country. One of the most important coins in circulation, if not the most important one, was the Spanish dollar, i.e. the peso de ocho reales or the piece of eight (at 24.43 grammes of fine silver). The variations between the currencies of the different colonies "were determined by the different legal valuation each colony gave to that coin" (MCCUSKER [1978], p. 132), which was similar to the practice of the colonies forming the future USA.

In Nova Scotia, held by the British since 1713, the currency was *de facto* identical with New England currency, "which for practical purposes may be identified with Massachusetts currency" (MCCUL-LOUGH [1984], p. 126), although the so-called 'Boston money' was the dominant currency (see pp. 399, 404). After 1749, "Nova Scotia began to break away from the New England currency bloc" (ibid., p. 130), especially since Massachusetts retired its paper bills and returned to the silver standard in 1750 with a rating of the Spanish silver dollar at 6 shillings Massachusetts currency. In contrast to this, it was generally equal to 5 shillings Halifax currency at Halifax as well as in the whole of Nova Scotia, which was regulated by law in 1758. Referring to its silver content, the Spanish dollar corresponded to only 4 shillings 6 pence. So, it was overvalued by one-ninth in Halifax, and a bill of exchange for 100 pounds sterling at par cost 111.11 pounds Halifax currency. This relation of 1 dollar = 5 shillings Halifax currency was the basis for the so-called Halifax currency system until the 1850s, when the original silver value relation of 1 dollar = 4 shillings 6 pence had already been invalid for a long time, because of the decreasing silver content of the Spanish dollar. So "the use of the 9:10 ratio became increasingly unrealistic and in commercial exchange it was compensated for by large premiums on sterling exchange" (ibid., pp. 130f.). The home government, however, outlawed the 1758 Currency Act in 1762, for it was contrary to the colonial Currency Act of 1707. As a result, Nova Scotia had actually no legal tender. From 1763 to 1777 provincial treasury notes were issued, which rapidly decreased in value. Thereupon, they were replaced by new Treasury notes, which again declined in value from the late 1780s (May 1792: 40% discount), because of the increasing debts of the colony (ibid., pp. 132., 135). With the Currency Act of 1787, a legal rating system for British silver coins based on the Halifax currency was introduced, but the (Spanish) dollar remained the most common coin in circulation. This status ended for two reasons. First, the Treasury notes were again withdrawn from circulation during the 1790s. Second, the doubloon as the most important coin of the West Indies, Nova Scotia's most important North American trading partner, became overvalued by a rate of 4 pounds Halifax currency (March 8th 1819), thus demonetizing the dollar. Treasury notes, which recirculated after the War of 1812, provincial paper money as well as banknotes (from 1825) were of similar significance as means of payment, all of them were often provided with a changing discount depending on their respective redeemability. When the doubloon was rated at c. 24% above its sterling value in 1819, however, the currency par should have been 124 pounds Halifax currency per 100 pounds sterling after 1819, but instead of this, the traditional par of 111.11 pounds Halifax currency per 100 pounds sterling remained valid. As a result, exchange rates had to be quoted with a permanent premium of 10 to 12% (ibid., p. 144). It was only with the 1834 Customs Act that a new official par of 25% was fixed and the doubloon became equal to 80 shillings Halifax currency or 64 shillings sterling respectively. In 1836, the sovereign was fixed at 25 shillings Halifax currency. Both coins became legal tender in 1842 just as the Spanish, Mexican and Patriot (South American) dollars, which were South American dollars but not US dollars, and which were theoretically equal to 5 shillings 2.5 pence Halifax currency but it was customary to equate them with only 5 shillings. "In keeping with this change the practice of converting sterling money of account to currency money by adding one-ninth to the sterling value was gradually abandoned in the 1830s and the more realistic system of adding one-quarter to sterling value was adopted. In the Blue Books the change was made in 1836. Commercial exchange rates continued in most cases to be quoted on the basis of the old par until after Confederation with the result that sterling exchange was always a nominal premium of from 12% to 15%" (ibid., p. 151). The Decimal Currency Bill was introduced in 1859 and became effective on January 1st 1860, determining that all government accounts had to be kept in dollars and cents. Although this action did not question the legal tender ratings of 1842, dollar rates were fixed for British coins for the first time in Nova Scotia. The sovereign, however, continued to be fixed there at 5 (Nova Scotia) dollars in contrast to Canada and New Brunswick, where it was equal to 4.8667 dollars. Because of this, Nova Scotia's sterling exchange rates were clearly at a higher level than the Canadian ones in the 1860s. Only the extension of the Canadian currency system on Nova Scotia on July 1st 1871 removed the distinction between currencies, fixing the sovereign at 4.8667 Canadian dollars in Nova Scotia so that 75 Nova Scotia cents were then equal to 73 Canadian cents (ibid., pp. 156f.).

In the Province of Quebec, which was divided into Upper Canada (today: Ontario) and Lower Canada (today: Quebec) in 1791, there were two systems of accounting that competed against one another during the first decades of British rule. At Quebec and in most parts of Lower Canada (as well as on Prince Edward Island and at New Brunswick), both accounts were kept and payments were transacted in Halifax currency, which was based on the rate of the Spanish dollar with 5 shillings Halifax currency, i.e. 11.11% above its sterling value of 4 shillings 6 pence sterling. In contrast to this, the payments in Montreal and in Upper Canada were based on the New York system, with a rate of 8 shillings sterling per Spanish dollar (77.7% premium against sterling), because New York merchants, who had brought their system with them, dominated Montreal's trade since the British had taken over the town (ibid., p. 67). In order to balance the different systems, the traditional New England standard was introduced on January 1st 1765 (Ordinance of September 14th 1764) with a rate of 6 shillings per Spanish dollar. It corresponded to the maximum rate authorized by Queen Anne's proclamation of 1704 and was called the New England or Quebec rating, but it was still valid in Halifax or New York (or short: York) currency (ibid, pp. 69–73). During the American Revolutionary War, the unpopular New England standard was abandoned in the Province of Canada and the Halifax standard was introduced in the whole colony in 1777. The most important coins in Canada then became French silver coins and piastreens (ibid., pp. 74s.), notes or bons issued by the merchants, government 'army bills' from July 1812 to 1817 (ibid., pp. 83–85) and, finally, US banknotes from the 1790s and especially after the War of 1812. In addition to this, there were notes of banks founded since 1817, which very rapidly became the dominant means of payment in Canada (ibid., p. 88). According to the Ordinance of 1777, gold coins were undervalued in Canada, and therefore they disappeared. Because of this, the Currency Acts of 1796 and 1808 for Lower Canada and that of 1809 for Upper Canada enhanced their value insofar as these rates persisted in Upper Canada until 1836 and in Lower Canada until 1842 (ibid., p. 81). In the 1820s, the British government tried to introduce British currency in Canada as well as in most of the other colonies of its empire, but this attempt failed, for three reasons. First, the British silver money was undervalued against the dollar; second, British silver was spent for buying bills on England from the government; and, third, "the extensive issue of paper money drove coins out of circulation" (ibid., p. 94).

After reuniting both Canadas to the Province of Canada in 1840, the traditional Halifax standard became the common currency standard of the whole Province by the Currency Act of 1841, establishing new ratings for the circulating coins after April 27th 1842. All Spanish and American dollars were then equal to 5 shillings 1 penny until the 1850s. Since the dollar functioned as the basis for the Halifax currency, the nominal currency par developed as follows:

- traditional par   111.11 pounds Halifax currency per 100 pounds sterling
- from 1825   115.38 pounds Halifax currency per 100 pounds sterling
- from 1838   120.00 pounds Halifax currency per 100 pounds sterling
- from 1842   122.00 pounds Halifax currency per 100 pounds sterling,

whereas the true par had risen to 120 or 121.67 pounds Halifax currency per 100 pounds sterling in Montreal and 125 pounds Halifax currency per 100 pounds sterling in Halifax after the 1820s. It was only after 1842 that the sovereign was officially fixed at 1 pound 4 shillings 4 pence sterling, resulting in a true par of 121.67 pounds Halifax currency per 100 pounds sterling with a 9.5% premium on the traditional nominal par. Unfortunately, only the army and some Canadian merchants adopted this true par. "However, newspaper exchange rate quotations continued to be based on a par of £111.11 to £100 and the provincial accounts continued to be kept in the old currency except in cases where actual foreign exchange dealings were involved such as payments of the provincial debt in Britain. In such cases the new par of £121.67 per £100 was usually used. As a result of the failure of the government to adopt the new par, exchange dealers and perhaps the merchant community returned to the old system, which was generally accepted in Canada until the decimal currency was adopted in 1858" (ibid., p. 106). After the provinces of Canada, Nova Scotia and New Brunswick had agreed to establish a common currency based on the decimal standard, pound and dollar were both declared units of Canadian currency by the proclamation of August 1st 1854. Thus the sovereign was made legal tender at 1 pound 4 shillings 4 pence currency or 4.8667 dollars and, similarly, the new Eagle, a gold coin of 10 US dollars issued from 1834, at 2 pounds currency or 10 dollars (according to CHALMERS [1893], p. 206, the so-called "Halifax-sterling"). "The act did not have any immediate practical effect but it proved legal authority for later changes. British gold and silver coins and American gold coins continued to be acceptable at the same rates they had since 1841" (McCULLOUGH [1984], p. 110). In 1857, a law regulated that in the future all government accounts of the Province of Canada were to be kept solely in dollars and cents. There was a transitional period where a second column was provided for the sterling notation, finally eliminated by 1871. According to the 1857 Act, Canada introduced its own low-value coins on December 10th 1858, which were lighter minted than the respective US coins. With the 1857/58 legislation, the Province of Canada definitely changed to the decimal dollar currency, in which the Canadian dollar was equal to the US one. As a result of the financial crisis of 1857–59, the banks lost their right to issue banknotes in 1866. Instead of this, they had to issue 'provincial notes', i.e. government notes, which were legal tender in the whole province. After the provinces of Canada, Halifax and New Brunswick had become the Dominion of Canada on July 1st 1867, these notes were called 'dominion notes', becoming legal tender in the Dominion. In 1871, the Currency Act of the Province of Canada of 1857 was extended to Nova Scotia and Manitoba, and this so-called Uniform Currency Act of 1871 was further extended to the Northwest Territories in 1875 and to Prince Edward Island and British Columbia in 1881. The Uniform Currency Act of 1871 confirmed US gold coins as well as the British sovereign (at 4.8667 Canadian dollars) as legal tender, and allowed these territories to mint their own gold coins, which did not begin until 1908 (ibid., pp. 112–114).

Original quotations at Halifax, Quebec and Montreal

on:	in:	per:
London	pounds Halifax currency or	100 pounds sterling
	per cent premium or discount on the par of 1	1 pound sterling
	pound sterling = 4.44 dollars Halifax currency	
	or	
	shillings and pence	1 Spanish or US dollar
	from 1858/61 Canadian/Nova Scotia dollars or	100 pound sterling
	per cent premium on the par of 1 pound sterling	1 pound sterling
	= 4.8667 Canadian dollars or	

on:	in:	per:
(at Halifax up to 1871)	per cent premium on the par of 1 pound sterling = 5 Nova Scotia dollars	1 pound sterling
New York	per cent premium or discount	100 US dollars

In the area later called Canada, exchange transactions were common from at least the 1730s. On an annual average, bills of exchange equal to approximately 250,000 livres were drawn on the general treasury of the Marine from the French colony of Nouvelle France during this period (MCCULLOUGH [1984], pp. 46f.). At first, exchange business with Britain was transacted from Nova Scotia, the former French Acadia, which became a British colony with the Treaty of Utrecht of 1713. While the British were primarily present in Nova Scotia with their armed forces and their merchants, close relations between the colony and Britain developed when the Acadians, originally French settlers, were deported between 1749 and 1755 and large settlements of English colonists at Halifax were established from 1759. In only a few years, Halifax became the first 'British' exchange market on the territory of the later Canada with quite regular exchange rate quotations on London from 1757. Before this, the Boston exchange rate quotations were also relevant for Nova Scotia (see p. 404).

With Britain taking over the former French Province of Quebec by the Treaty of Paris in 1763, the exchange markets of Montreal and Quebec were then British territory. Quebec, the seat of the British government, was certainly the exchange market of more importance during the first decades of British rule, because the British government "was probably the largest seller of sterling bills in Canada" until c. 1850 (MCCULLOGH [1984], p. 254). They preferred to finance their expenditures by drawing bills of exchange from Quebec on London and selling them on the spot to the merchants for cash. These government bills negotiated in Quebec were of great significance within the Canadian exchange business, which was, finally but importantly, based on the fact that Canada was mainly buying bills of exchange to settle debts in Britain, although exchange rates were falling because of the rise of both the volume of Canadian exports and the demand for bills of exchange. So "bills on the British government departments were considered the highest quality bills and sold for a higher price than bills on merchants" (ibid., p. 253). Together with the rising government duties, the exchange business in both Canadas increased considerably from the 1790s; it had been of comparatively small even during the 1780s. Because of the frequent oversupply of bills of exchange in Quebec, they were often negotiated with a discount of up to 10% before the War of 1812. During the war, the discount rose as high as 25% before it sank down to 2.5% after the war in December 1814. This discount resulted not only from the excess supply on the Quebec exchange market, but also from the fact that the Bank of England had suspended the convertibility of the pound sterling in specie between 1797 and 1821 (see pp. 3f.). So the prices for sterling bills were often lower in Quebec than in New York or Boston in the first decade of the 19th century, and in some years (e.g. 1807) it could be profitable to bring bills from Quebec to New York or Boston to be cashed in (MCCULLOUGH [1984], pp. 81–85, 225).

It was only after the War of 1812 that fundamental changes of the Canadian exchange business took place, namely the establishment of the first Canadian banks, the Montreal Bank (1817, later Bank of Montreal), the Quebec Bank (1818) and the Bank of Canada (1819, in Montreal as well) (ibid., p. 86). "After Canadian banks became active in the exchange business, their bills formed a third quality of bill. ... Up to the end of the War of 1812 spreads of up to 5% between government bills and private bills were not unknown. After the war the spread seems to have been much smaller. ... bank and government bills were almost equal in quality and good merchant bills were discounted from 0.5% to 1.5% below bank and government bills" (MCCULLOGH [1984], pp. 253s.). With the emergence of bank bills, the terms of the bills were changing in the long run as well: "Until the 1840s, British government 30-day bills were taken as the standard in quoting rates. By 1846, 60-day bank bills had become the standard and government bills were dropped from price quotations. Merchant bills typically had a term of 60 or 90 days; after bank bills became the standard of exchange, 90-day merchant bills were quoted more frequently than were the 60-days variety" (ibid.). At the same time, this fact indicates the shifting importance among the exchange markets of Canada between 1791 and 1840. Quebec dominated with its typical government bills until shortly before the mid-19th century. Thereafter, bank bills controlled the market: they were primarily negotiated in Montreal, which became more important than Quebec. Like Quebec, Montreal was situated in Lower Canada, intensively orientating itself towards Upper Canada and, above all, the adjacent states of the USA and their financial markets of New York and Boston. After the Confederation of the 1840s had reunited the Provinces of Canada, Nova Scotia and New Brunswick to form the Dominion of Canada on July 1st 1867, Montreal was the dominating and, soon, the only Canadian exchange market of international relevance. Similar to European developments (e.g. in Germany or Italy), the unification of the different currencies of the Canadian provinces had considerably supported this process. Montreal kept this prominent position without challenge until World War I.

As an exchange market within the international cashless payment system, Halifax was clearly of marginal and, at best, regional relevance to Nova Scotia and, thus, the adjacent colonies in comparison to both Quebec and Montreal. Nonetheless, the Halifax exchange rates will be documented in the following tables just as those of Quebec and Montreal, because, first, the Halifax currency was the decisive reference currency for all Canadian exchange rate quotations until after the mid-19th century and, second, Halifax itself was able to maintain a certain autonomy as an exchange market until some years after the Confederation of 1867 with its Nova Scotia dollar. It was with the discontinuance of the autonomous exchange rate quotations at Halifax at the end of the 1870s that the importance of Nova Scotia's capital as an independent exchange market definitely ceased.

London was the main exchange partner of all Canadian exchange markets from the 18th century up to World War I. "Most bills of exchange on London were not paid until 30, 60, 90, or occasionally 120 days after the payee presented them to the drawee. Sight bills ... and three-day bills were uncommon in the early nineteenth century but became more common after the completion of the Atlantic cable in 1866" (MC-CULLOUGH [1984], pp. 253), which also holds for the USA. The sterling exchange of the Canadian exchange markets was effected either directly or via mediation by US markets, especially New York and Boston, which more or less regularly maintained exchange transactions with Canadian exchange markets. "From before the American Revolution, Canadian sterling exchange markets were linked with American sterling exchange markets" (ibid., p. 255). "Although exchange on the United States, specifically New York, was an important element in Canadian exchange business and often was a major factor in determining exchange rates on Britain, no attempt has been made to prepare Canadian–American exchange rate runs because of a problem in locating adequate sources. Although sources for sterling exchange on London are more common than sources for rates on New York they are far from complete" (ibid., p. 251), as the data series documented here show. Data series with exchange rate quotations on New York or Boston cannot be presented here at all and there is only scant reference in contemporary merchant manuals. Bills of exchange on New York, for instance, were quoted with 3 to 60 days after sight and with a premium or discount of 1½% to 3% in around 1840, of ½% in the 1850s and 1% in around 1870 (NOBACK [1851], p. 984; NOBACK [1858], p. 610; NOBACK [1877], p. 621). According to contemporary merchant manuals, Paris and Germany are said to have been quoted as well as London and New York in Montreal during the late 19th and early 20th centuries, which is a similar development to that in New York. Montreal's exchange trade was handled exclusively in brokers' offices (SWOBODA [1913], p. 702).

References: CHALMERS [1893], pp. 175–206; Alan Bruce MCCULLOUGH, *Money and Exchange in Canada to 1900*, Toronto – Charlottetown 1984.

15.1 Exchange rates of Canadian places

15.1.1 On London

	QUEBEC & MONTREAL on:			HALIFAX on:		
	London [a]			London [b]		
	per 100 pounds sterling [c]					
	in pounds Halifax currency					
1757				105.00	30-40d/s	(2)
1758				103.65	30-40d/s	(4)
1759				102.56	30-40d/s	(5)
1760				105.00	30-40d/s	(4)
1761				109.50	30-40d/s	(4)
1762	111.99	40d/s	(1)	113.13	30-40d/s	(2)
1763	117.93	40d/s	(1)	110.91	30-40d/s	(4)
1764				108.94	30-40d/s	(4)
1765				110.33	30-40d/s	(5)
1766	99.99	40d/s	(1)	110.02	30-40d/s	(5)
1767	111.79	40d/s	(9)	110.53	30-40d/s	(3)
1768	112.65	40d/s	(12)	109.63	30-40d/s	(5)
1769	111.93	40d/s	(12)	108.70	30-40d/s	(6)
1770	107.76	40d/s	(10)	107.37	30-40d/s	(11)
1771	108.76	40d/s	(7)	110.29	30-40d/s	(5)
1772	108.21	40d/s	(7)	111.09	30-40d/s	(2)
1773	109.24	40d/s	(8)			
1774	111.42	40d/s	(5)			
1775	106.61	40d/s	(10)	100.00	30-40d/s	(1)
1776	111.43	40d/s	(6)	112.57	30-40d/s	(3)
1777	111.98	40d/s	(8)	111.82	30-40d/s	(4)
1778	111.33	40d/s	(7)	111.81	30-40d/s	(2)
1779	110.06	40d/s	(6)	107.28	30-40d/s	(12)
1780	111.11	40d/s	(11)	105.05	30-40d/s	(11)
1781	111.11	40d/s	(12)	113.82	30-40d/s	(8)
1782	111.11	40d/s	(10)	106.02	30-40d/s	(3)
1783	111.11	30-40d/s	(1)	100.00	30-40d/s	(8)
1784	112.41	30-40d/s	(5)			
1785	112.12	30-40d/s	(4)	113.89	30d/s	(2)
1786	112.17	30-40d/s	(9)			
1787	111.75	30-40d/s	(9)			
1788	111.11	30-40d/s	(8)			
1789	111.61	30-40d/s	(5)			
1790	111.18	30-40d/s	(5)	112.78	30d/s	(1)

	QUEBEC & MONTREAL on:			HALIFAX on:		
	London [a]			London [b]		
	per 100 pounds sterling [d]					
	in pounds Halifax currency					
1791	111.17	30-40d/s	(5)			
1792	111.76	30-40d/s	(6)			
1793	111.19	30-40d/s	(4)	111.11	30d/s	(1)
1794				113.89	30d/s	(1)
1795	111.11	30-40d/s	(1)			
1796	112.30	30-40d/s	(3)			
1797	111.88	30-40d/s	(3)	113.89	30d/s	(1)
1798	111.98	30-40d/s	(2)	113.89	30d/s	(1)
1799	104.22	30-40d/s	(2)	108.33	30d/s	(1)
1800	108.48	30-40d/s	(10)			
1801	105.54	30-40d/s	(7)	109.72	30d/s	(1)
1802	108.61	30-40d/s	(5)			
1803	111.11	30-40d/s	(4)	109.43	30d/s	(1)
1804	112.41	30-40d/s	(1)	109.58	30d/s	(1)
1805	111.12	30d/s	(9)	108.89	30d/s	(4)
1806	108.24	30d/s	(9)	109.44	30d/s	(1)
1807	107.36	30d/s	(12)	110.46	30d/s	(3)
1808	108.52	30d/s	(12)	111.11	30d/s	(3)
1809	111.14	30d/s	(11)	109.50	30d/s	(3)
1810	104.31	30d/s	(11)	109.76	30d/s	(2)
1811	96.11	30d/s	(9)	100.26	30d/s	(7)
1812	86.82	30d/s	(12)	96.51	30d/s	(6)
1813	88.10	30d/s	(12)	90.30	30d/s	(2)
1814	*95.13*	30d/s	(12)	93.22	30d/s	(7)
1815	*103.16*	30d/s	(11)	104.90	30d/s	(2)
1816	111.11	30d/s	(1)			
1817	116.42	60d/s	(2)			
1818	112.16	60d/s	(5)			
1819	111.98	60d/s	(7)			
1820	113.94	60d/s	(10)	117.78	30d/s	(2)
1821	119.61	60d/s	(9)	123.61	30d/s	(2)
1822	124.54	60d/s	(12)	127.32	30d/s	(6)
1823	120.15	60d/s	(12)			
1824	122.27	60d/s	(12)	122.22	30d/s	(1)
1825	120.13	60d/s	(12)	122.08	30d/s	(4)
1826	121.40	60d/s	(9)			
1827	122.58	60d/s	(11)	125.79	30d/s	(12)
1828	124.00	60d/s	(11)			

	QUEBEC & MONTREAL on:	HALIFAX on:
	London [b]	**London** [b]
	per 100 pounds sterling [d]	
	in pounds Halifax currency	
1829	122.22 60d/s (12)	
1830	119.41 30d/s (12)	
1831	121.36 30d/s (12)	
1832	123.15 30d/s (12)	
1833	122.53 30d/s (9)	
1834	117.51 30d/s (12)	
1835	121.93 30d/s (9)	
1836	122.98 60d/s (12)	124.63 30d/s (3)
1837	126.98 60d/s (12)	130.11 30d/s (7)
1838	124.07 60d/s (12)	126.43 30d/s (12)
1839	124.21 60d/s (12)	126.56 30d/s (10)
1840	123.28 60d/s (12)	126.28 30d/s (10)
1841	123.37 60d/s (10)	126.94 30d/s (8)
1842	122.01 60d/s (8)	
1843	122.04 60d/s (6)	125.40 30d/s (11)
1844	123.53 60d/s (7)	125.74 30d/s (3)
1845	122.00 60d/s (7)	126.87 30d/s (12)
1846	122.53 60d/s (9)	
1847	121.08 60d/s (10)	
1848	124.57 60d/s (11)	126.76 30d/s (6)
1849	122.92 60d/s (12)	125.00 60d/s (7)
1850	123.77 60d/s (11)	124.72 60d/s (2)
1851	123.47 60d/s (3)	
1852	123.17 60d/s (7)	
1853	122.36 60d/s (8)	
1854	122.00 60d/s (11)	
1855	122.78 60d/s (12)	
1856	122.13 60d/s (12)	
1857	122.12 60d/s (11)	
	in Canadian dollars	
1858	491.57 60d/s (12)	
1859	488.93 60d/s (12)	
1860	488.93 60d/s (12)	
1861	480.00 60d/s (12)	
1862	490.76 60d/s (12)	
1863	490.04 60d/s (12)	
1864	486.64 60d/s (12)	

	QUEBEC & MONTREAL on:	HALIFAX on:
	London [a]	London [b]
	per 100 pounds sterling [d]	
	in Canadian dollars	in Nova Scotia dollars (from 1861 [7])
1865	486.64 60d/s (9)	501.11 60d/s (3)
1866	483.15 60d/s (11)	500.74 60d/s (12)
1867	487.19 60d/s (11)	502.41 60d/s (12)
1868	487.98 60d/s (12)	503.42 60d/s (12)
1869	485.09 60d/s (12)	501.57 60d/s (12)
1870	485.27 60d/s (12)	502.22 60d/s (8)
1871	486.13 60d/s (12)	502.22 60d/s (6)
	in Canadian dollars	
1872	485.30 60d/s (12)	486.98 60d/s (9)
1873	482.71 60d/s (12)	484.94 60d/s (10)
1874	485.72 60d/s (12)	485.97 60d/s (12)
1875	484.25 60d/s (10)	486.48 60d/s (12)
1876	485.58 60d/s (12)	486.36 60d/s (12)
1877	483.95 60d/s (12)	484.76 60d/s (12)
1878	482.94 60d/s (12)	484.53 60d/s (12)
1879	483.65 60d/s (12)	484.53 60d/s (12)
1880	483.60 60d/s (12)	
1881	482.33 60d/s (12)	
1882	484.42 60d/s (12)	
1883	482.94 60d/s (12)	
1884	483.48 60d/s (11)	
1885	483.84 60d/s (12)	
1886	484.86 60d/s (12)	
1887	483.10 60d/s (12)	
1888	485.23 60d/s (12)	
1889	484.86 60d/s (12)	
1890	482.37 60d/s (12)	
1891	483.59 60d/s (12)	
1892	485.50 60d/s (12)	
1893	483.77 60d/s (12)	
1894	486.32 60d/s (12)	
1895	487.75 60d/s (12)	
1896	485.23 60d/s (12)	
1897	484.21 60d/s (12)	
1898	482.43 60d/s (12)	
1899	483.07 60d/s (12)	

[a] Up to 1783 government bills "for a term of 40 rather than 30 days" after sight; 1783–1804 gov-
     ernment and private bills with various terms, mostly for 30 or 40 days after sight; 1805–1815 gov-
     ernment bills, whereby the quotations during the War of 1812 were officially fixed by a
     commission on the 10th and 24th of each month (such official quotations are here only given for the
     years 1814 and 1815); 1817–1829 bank bills of the Bank of Montreal; 1830–1835 government
     bills; 1836–1899 best bank bills of the Bank of Montreal; MCCULLOGH [1984], pp. 256–259.

[b] Up to 1848 government bills, for 1849 bank bills. "As the rates [for 1757–1783] are either for gov-
     ernment bills or for bills drawn by government contractors it is probably that most were for 30 or
     40 days"; MCCULLOGH [1984], p. 259.

[c] Concerning the British currency, see pp. 3–5.

15.1.2 On New York

	MONTREAL on:		
	New York		
	per 100 US dollars [a]		
	in Canadian dollars		
1909	99.97	s	(1)
1910	99.99	s	(11)
1911	99.99	s	(11)
1912	100.02	s	(11)
1913	100.03	s	(12)
1914	100.04	s	(6)

[a]   Concerning the US currency, see p. 404.

16
Jamaica (1675–1914)

Exchange market: Kingston (1692–1914)

Sources: McCusker [1978], pp. 250–253 (1675–1775); PRO London, CO 147: *Blue Books. Island of Jamaica*, Kingston (1822–1914); *The Economist*, London (1850–1873).
Concordance: *WdW VII*, pp. 341–350

Currency: Similarly to the several British colonies on the North American continent (see pp. 399f.) the relation between the colonial currency – here the pound of 20 shillings at 12 pence Jamaica currency – and sterling resulted from the fact that the most important circulating coin, the so-called 'piece of eight' (peso de ocho reales) or the Spanish dollar, was valued differently in the two currencies. In 1669 the Spanish dollar was still equally valued in Jamaica currency and in sterling (4 shillings 2 pence) – so 100 pounds Jamaica currency were equal to 100 pounds sterling – but in 1672 it had already a value of 5 shillings Jamaica currency (111.11 pounds Jamaica currency for 100 pounds sterling), keeping it legitimately until the end of the 18th century. Unauthorized acts in 1688 and in 1758 as well as mercantile customs raised the value of the Spanish dollar up to 6 2/3 shillings Jamaica currency, so that the par of exchange (by custom) was 133.33 pounds Jamaica currency to 100 pounds sterling from the mid-1680s, 138.89:100 (in practice: 140:100) from the early 1720s and 148.15:100 from 1758. But also after 1758 "bills of exchange negotiated on the island maintained the old level of exchange" (McCusker [1978], p. 247), i.e. 140 pounds Jamaica currency for 100 pounds sterling, based on the internal rate of 6¼ shillings per Spanish dollar. The exchange rate quotations available since 1822 as premium quotations on the relation of 140 pounds Jamaica currency = 100 pounds sterling are a late reference to this kind of reckoning. Bills of exchange of this period were payable in Mexican or Colombian doubloons, the following ratio being common practice in trade: 1 doubloon = 64 shillings sterling or 106.67 shillings Jamaica currency (as officially fixed in 1838). Therefore 166.67 pounds Jamaica currency corresponded to 100 pounds sterling. From December 31st 1840 sterling currency was in force on Jamaica as in the mother country; that is the pound sterling of 20 shillings at 12 pence (see pp. 3–5). However, it still took some time until the coins introduced from the American mainland finally lost their function as legal tender and basic medium of circulation in 1876 and "the shilling [sterling] was finally established as the practical standard of value in Jamaica" (Chalmers [1893], p. 113). The circulating notes – initially called 'island cheques' – issued by the Colonial Bank and the Jamaica Bank from 1828, were exclusively reserved for the "commercial and well-to-do classes" at least until the turn of the century while the coloured population only was using coins (ibid.).

Original quotations on Jamaica

on:	in:	per:
London	per cent premium	100 pounds sterling [a]

[a]   1822–1839 on the relation of 140 pounds Jamaica currency = 100 pounds sterling

Further data available: London, 90d/s (commercial bills, 1823–1843; bank bills, 1893–1914); 30d/s (bank bills, 1837–1868); 60d/s (bank bills, 1845–1868).

Jamaica, a British domain since 1655 and crown colony since 1866, was probably the most important possession of the British Empire in the Caribbean and, at the same time, the bullion centre of the British possessions in the New World until the outbreak of the Mexican Wars of Independence in the 1810s. Exchange transactions had already been important for Jamaica since the second half of the 17th century, but "we know little ... about the drawing of bills on Jamaica" (McCUSKER [1978], p. 249): "Jamaicans drew bills of exchange on credit balances in London at rates of exchange that remained incredibly stable over much of the century ... What did vary was the usance ... Jamaica regularly drew bills payable well beyond the usual thirty- to forty-day period. Fifty, sixty, ninety days, and even longer, was not unusual. And such bills sold at a disadvantage" (ibid., pp. 248s.). From the early 1720s to the end of the 1830s the customary par of exchange at Jamaica was in practice 140 pounds Jamaica currency to 100 pounds sterling (from 1672 to the mid-1680s: 111.11, from then to the early 1720s: 133.33) (cf. ibid., p. 247; CHALMERS [1893], p. 103; cf. KELLY [1835], vol. I, p. 361). According to the data collected by McCusker (until 1775), Jamaica quoted London primarily on or with slight fluctuations around this 'par of exchange' from the mid-1730s. For the period from 1776 to 1821 no data have been available until now.

From 1822 rates for Treasury bills on London were listed in the *Blue Books*. These Treasury bills were payable in Mexican and Colombian doubloons. In 1823 quotations for bills, payable in dollars of the same provenance (nominally equal to 1/16 doubloon), were added, being understood as commercial bills of the merchants of Kingston, the biggest town and financial centre of the island (founded in 1692) (cf. *Blue Book. Island of Jamaica*, 1836). The additional remark "payable in ..." had become necessary, because the assembly of the island issued unsecured paper money (the so-called 'island cheques') on a large scale after 1822 in order to compensate for the ceasing inflow of precious metals (doubloons and dollars) since the outbreak of the Mexican War of Independence and to maintain internal payment transactions. The exchange rates were not meant for this paper money, largely useless in foreign trade, but precisely for the doubloons and dollars that were highly sought after because of their international acceptance, although they were no longer in circulation. For this reason a considerable variable premium expressed as a percentage was put on the 'par of exchange' of 140 pounds Jamaica currency = 100 pounds sterling from 1822. This appeared as the actual quotation in the *Blue Books* of these years: "Bills have been sometimes at a premium of 20 per cent. above the legal exchange [i.e. the 'par of exchange'], and they are seldom under 10" (KELLY [1835], vol. I, p. 361). The quotations for these two sorts of bills ended in the 1840s.

Their place was taken by the bank bills quoted after 1837, primarily by those of the Colonial Bank (cf. NOBACK [1877], p. 386). At first, bank exchanges were given for 30 days' sight, later on also for 90 and 60 days' sight. From 1850 even the London *Economist* quoted the rates of Jamaica on London as the most important of the so-called 'West India Exchanges' (ibid., p. 368) and as the only ones of the British possessions in the whole Atlantic area, among those of other important financial places of the non-European world. It is remarkable that only for Jamaica are rates for three usances (30, 60 and 90 days' sight) listed, whereas considerably fewer fluctuations in value can be noted here. *The Economist* took Jamaican exchange customs into account, which had been common practice from the 17th/18th century and applied varying usances rather than varying rates to express the prices of the bills. *The Economist* stopped publishing the quotations of Jamaica for 30 and 60 days' sight bills in 1868 and for 90 days' sight bills in 1873. The *Blue Books* of the Colony, however, continued listing rates on London (90 days' sight and from 1893 at sight as well). In general, only one quotation per year and usance was given and, from 1887/88, just for the year under review in the *Blue Book*, i.e. the period from April to March of the following year. From time to time there was a note saying that the rate per year was valid for every single month (for example for the year 1887/88), so that we may assume that we are dealing with *de facto* monthly rates, which were listed only once because of their correspondence. On the basis of these data the annual average values have been calculated each time for the period from January until December, and these calculated rates are listed in the table presented below.

As a rule, only London is quoted in the documented sources. Furthermore, a rate on New York is always given at least in the contemporary merchant manuals, though it is rarely recorded in the *Blue Books*, because it was of no importance for the interests of the Colonial Government or for the trade activities of private persons in comparison to the exchange on London. According to the various merchant manuals a small extra charge of ½% to 2%, in individual cases even of up to 4%, was common practice for bills of that kind. Towards the end of the 19th century the New York sterling rates became increasingly relevant for Jamaica as well, and customers wanted to buy bills on New York or Montreal (*Blue Book. Island of Jamaica*, 1891/92, p. T2). On the basis of the documented sources it cannot be demonstrated that in the late 19th century Kingston quoted Calcutta and Hong Kong (SWOBODA [1889], p. 520).

References: Robert CHALMERS, *History of Currency in the British Colonies*, London 1893 [repr. Colchester 1972], pp. 97–113; John J. MCCUSKER, *Money and Exchange in Europe and America, 1600–1775. A Handbook*, London – Basingstoke 1978, pp. 246–253; Sydney W. MINTZ, Currency Problems in Eighteenth Century Jamaica and Gresham's Law, in Robert A. MANNERS (ed.), *Process and Pattern in Culture. Essays in Honor of Julian H. Steward*, Chicago 1964, pp. 248–265; Markus A. DENZEL, Finanzplätze, Wechselkurse und Währungsverhältnisse in Lateinamerika (1808–1914), in *WdW VII*, pp. 1–106, here pp. 65–70.

16.1 Jamaica exchange rates

16.1 On London

	JAMAICA on:				JAMAICA on:		
	London				London		
	per 100 pounds sterling [a]				per 100 pounds sterling [a]		
	in pounds Jamaica currency				in pounds Jamaica currency		
1675	106.50	[b]	(1)	1708	120.00	[b]	(2)
1676	115.00	[b]	(1)	1709	116.00	[b]	(1)
1677				1710	125.00	[b]	(1)
1678				1711	135.00	[b]	(1)
1679	109.72	[b]	(2)	1712			
1680				1713	130.00	[b]	(1)
1681	108.00	[b]	(1)	1714			
1682				1715	135.00	[b]	(1)
1683	114.04	[b]	(4)	1716	135.00	[b]	(1)
1684	120.00	[b]	(1)	1717	135.00	[b]	(1)
1685				1718			
1686	111.91	[b]	(3)	1719			
1687	117.65	[b]	(1)	1720	135.00	[b]	(2)
1688	110.00	[b]	(1)	1721			
1689	120.00	[b]	(1)	1722	130.00	[b]	(5)
1690	120.00	[b]	(3)	1723	130.00	[b]	(4)
1691	125.00	[b]	(1)	1724	134.17	[b]	(5)
1692	125.00	[b]	(1)	1725	135.42	[b]	(4)
1693				1726	135.00	[b]	(2)
1694				1727			
1695				1728	135.00	[b]	(1)
1696				1729	135.00	[b]	(1)
1697				1730	135.00	[b]	(2)
1698				1731			
1699				1732	135.00	[b]	(1)
1700				1733	137.50	[b]	(2)
1701				1734	140.00	[b]	(1)
1702				1735	138.75	[b]	(2)
1703				1736	140.00	[b]	(1)
1704	125.00	[b]	(1)	1737			
1705	127.50	[b]	(2)	1738	140.00	[b]	(2)
1706	122.50	[b]	(6)	1739	140.00	[b]	(2)
1707	118.00	[b]	(2)	1740	135.00	[b]	(1)

	JAMAICA on:				JAMAICA on:		
	London [c]				**London** [c]		
	per 100 pounds sterling [a]				per 100 pounds sterling [a]		
	in pounds Jamaica currency				**in pounds Jamaica currency**		
1741	140.00	[b]	(2)	1822	166.25	90d/s	(12)
1742	138.75	[b]	(3)	1823	164.33	90d/s	(8)
1743	140.00	[b]	(1)	1824	[d]		
1744				1825	163.10	90d/s	(10)
1745	145.00	[b]	(3)	1826	163.34	90d/s	(6)
1746				1827	168.53	90d/s	(4)
1747				1828	*154.00*	90d/s	(y)
1748				1829	170.62	90d/s	(11)
1749				1830	*143.15*	90d/s	(y)
1750				1831	168.87	90d/s	(9)
1751	140.00	[b]	(1)	1832	169.05	90d/s	(12)
1752	140.00	[b]	(1)	1833	169.29	90d/s	(12)
1753	140.00	[b]	(4)	1834	162.74	90d/s	(12)
1754	140.00	[b]	(2)	1835	165.19	90d/s	(12)
1755	140.00	[b]	(1)	1836	163.34	90d/s	(12)
1756	140.00	[b]	(1)	1837	169.89	30d/s	(10)
1757	140.00	[b]	(4)	1838	170.10	30d/s	(12)
1758	140.00	[b]	(2)	1839	171.33	30d/s	(12)
1759	140.00	[b]	(2)	1840	171.09	30d/s	(12)
1760	140.00	[b]	(3)		**in pounds sterling**		
1761	140.00	[b]	(2)	1841	99.21	30d/s	(12)
1762	140.00	[b]	(2)	1842	101.75	30d/s	(10)
1763	140.00	[b]	(2)	1843	98.11	90d/s	(12)
1764				1844	*100.68*	90d/s	(12)
1765				1845	100.50	90d/s	(9)
1766	140.00	[b]	(1)	1846	100.34	90d/s	(12)
1767				1847	98.86	90d/s	(12)
1768	140.00	[b]	(2)	1848	100.59	90d/s	(12)
1769				1849	100.71	90d/s	(12)
1770	140.00	[b]	(3)	1850	100.53	90d/s	(11)
1771	140.00	[b]	(2)	1851	100.25	90d/s	(12)
1772	140.00	[b]	(2)	1852	100.31	90d/s	(11)
1773	140.21	[b]	(4)	1853	100.71	90d/s	(12)
1774	140.00	[b]	(1)	1854	100.23	90d/s	(11)
1775	140.00	[b]	(2)	1855	100.69	90d/s	(11)
...				1856	101.25	90d/s	(12)

	JAMAICA on: **London** [c] per 100 pounds sterling [a] **in pounds sterling**					JAMAICA on: **London** [c] per 100 pounds sterling [a] **in pounds sterling**		
1857	100.59	90d/s	(12)		1886	101.00	90d/s	(12)
1858	100.88	90d/s	(12)		1887	101.00	90d/s	(12)
1859	100.25	90d/s	(12)		1888	100.63	90d/s	(12)
1860	100.55	90d/s	(12)		1889	100.00	90d/s	(12)
1861	100.55	90d/s	(12)		1890	100.00	90d/s	(12)
1862	100.69	90d/s	(11)		1891	100.00	90d/s	(12)
1863	100.91	90d/s	(11)		1892	100.00	90d/s	(12)
1864	100.80	90d/s	(12)		1893	100.47	s	(12)
1865	101.63	90d/s	(12)		1894	100.63	s	(12)
1866	101.92	90d/s	(12)		1895	100.63	s	(12)
1867	100.88	90d/s	(12)		1896	100.63	s	(12)
1868	100.91	90d/s	(11)		1897	100.63	s	(12)
1869	100.87	90d/s	(11)		1898	100.63	s	(12)
1870	101.00	90d/s	(12)		1899	100.63	s	(12)
1871	101.00	90d/s	(12)		1900	100.63	s	(12)
1872	101.00	90d/s	(12)		1901	100.63	s	(12)
1873	101.00	90d/s	(12)		1902	100.51	s	(12)
1874	101.00	90d/s	(12)		1903	100.54	s	(12)
1875	101.00	90d/s	(12)		1904	100.66	s	(12)
1876	101.00	90d/s	(12)		1905	100.69	s	(12)
1877	101.00	90d/s	(12)		1906	100.83	s	(12)
1878	101.00	90d/s	(12)		1907	101.21	s	(12)
1879	101.00	90d/s	(12)		1908	100.89	s	(12)
1880	101.00	90d/s	(12)		1909	100.75	s	(12)
1881	101.00	90d/s	(12)		1910	100.75	s	(12)
1882	101.00	90d/s	(12)		1911	100.75	s	(12)
1883	101.00	90d/s	(12)		1912	100.19	s	(12)
1884	101.00	90d/s	(12)		1913	100.75	s	(12)
1885	101.00	90d/s	(12)		1914	101.22	s	(7)

[a]   Concerning the British currency, see pp. 3–5.

[b]   Until 1775 no usance is given in the documented sources.

[c]   1822–1836 government bills, from 1837 bank bills, whereby the quotations of the Colonial Bank were recorded in the *Blue Books*, with the exception of the quotations of the Jamaica Bank, which were listed in the *Blue Book* of 1848.

[d]   In 1824 there was no quotation, but the following remark: "That premium is regulated by the Rate at which either are disposed to poss. Bills, under the real Exchange of the precious metals" (*Blue Book. Island of Jamaica*, 1824, p. 177).

17

Brazil (1808–1914)

Exchange markets: Rio de Janeiro (1808–1914), Bahia (1847–1882) and Pernambuco (1847–1881)

Sources: <u>Rio de Janeiro</u>: SAY [1839], pp. 297–300 (1808–1837); *Jornal de Commercio*, Rio de Janeiro (1821–1897); Camara Syndical dos Corretores de Fundos Públicos da Capital Federal (ed.), *Relatorio da Camara Syndical dos Corretores de Fundos Públicos da Capital Federal ...*, vols. 1897/98–1914/15, Rio de Janeiro 1898–1915 (1898–1914). <u>Bahia and Pernambuco</u>: *The Course of Exchange*, London (1847–1849); *The Economist*, London (1850–1881/82).
Concordance: *WdW VII*, pp. 129–194, 203–209

Currency: Brazil's unit of payment and account was the milréis at 1,000 réis, which was meant to correspond to 25.50 grammes of fine silver or 10/11 of the Portuguese milréis silver according to the Portuguese decree of August 7th 1747, but it was not actually minted (cf. MCCUSKER [1978], p. 301). In contrast to colonial times, the money circulation within Brazil was determined by gold coins to a great extent as this precious metal did not have to be imported from Peru, as did silver. After the Portuguese court had moved to Brazil in 1807, the resulting financial distress of the government brought about the issue of paper money by a newly founded bank in Rio de Janeiro in 1808 and the debasement of the copper coins as well as the issue of undervalued silver coins in 1811. These coins, the so-called patacãos, Spanish pesos bought in Peru, had a value of about 750–800 réis but were reminted and fixed at 960 réis so that they corresponded to 2 new silver crusados at 480 réis or 3 patacas at 320 réis. From 1818/19 the currency devaluation became generally more and more noticeable, but effects on the exchange rate arose only with a certain delay (SCHNEIDER [1975], p. 480). This development was dramatically intensified when new financial gaps arose in the 1820s, owing to political implications such as the imminent war with Portugal, revolts in the northern provinces and the war with Buenos Aires concerning Uruguay. The aim was to get these financial gaps under control by constantly new issues of paper money and undervalued copper coins. When the government changed the unredeemed notes of the bank of Rio de Janeiro into irredeemable government notes in 1829, the paper money, already exposed to high fluctuations against hard coins since 1818, became the main currency of the country. After 1829 all exchange rates are given in milréis paper money until the end of the period of documentation.

Brazilian milréis paper money per 100 Brazilian milréis gold

1830	302.82	1833	187.67	1836	183.38	1839	236.00
1831	290.09	1834	179.30	1837	230.63	1840	224.50
1832	206.88	1835	179.46	1838	248.67		

Source: *WdW VII*, p. 202

In the 1830s the rate of paper money continued to fluctuate strongly against gold, although a currency reform had been carried out by the Act of October 8th 1833: the milréis at 12.84 grammes of fine silver became the standard monetary unit, although it was never minted. Additionally, the Act of September 11th 1846 permitted foreign coins on the Brazilian money market, provided that they had been rated beforehand. The rate for sight bills on London as the country's main exchange rate, reduced by an average discount value, functioned as the basis for this rating. In view of the experiences of the past ten years, a rate of 27 pence per milrée was fixed. After 1846 the value of the paper money became more stable so that it was almost at par with that of the coins. Based on the British model and oriented towards Brazil's most important trade and exchange partner, Great Britain, the gold standard (repealing the law of rating foreign coins from 1846) was introduced into Brazil by the Act of July 28th 1849. On the basis of the parity of 27 pence per milrée, which had already been introduced in 1846, the gold milrée of 0.8218 grammes of fine gold became the standard currency unit of Brazil, whereas silver coins were issued according to the decrees of the Latin Monetary Union after the Act of September 26th 1867 (see p. 280) (2 milréis silver = 5 francs). However, paper money – government notes and notes of the different banks – remained the prevailing currency of Brazil even after 1849, while only some gold and silver coins were circulating. In September 1866 the repeated devaluation of the paper money during the Triple Alliance War against Paraguay (1864–1870) led to the suspension of the obligatory redeeming of the Banco do Brazil, whose notes consequently became the obligatory legal tender. Because the paper money circulation was reduced significantly in the following years, values of about 3% discount against gold and British currency were reached again in the mid-1870s. Owing to the internal conflicts of the time after 1888/89, the issuing of banknotes was intensified, followed again by dramatically rising exchange rates in comparison to the foreign gold currencies. A stabilization with values of about 44½% of the gold parity did not set in until the period between 1901 and 1904. A loan from Europe (1905) supplied the republic with a gold reserve so that the exchange rate rose to about 67% of the gold parity. With the Act of December 6th 1906 the Caixa de Conversão (conversion bank) was established which succeeded in stabilizing the exchange rate on London at 55 2/3% of the gold parity (i.e. 15 pence per milrée) by amassing gold coins at this price for the issue of conversion notes and afterwards cashing them in at the same rate. As early as 1910 the conversion rate could be raised to 16 pence per milréis as the conversion fund, supplied by the budget surplus, had reached the statutory minimum amount of 20 million pounds sterling. Together with the government notes circulating at a compulsory rate, the notes of the conversion bank also functioned as legal tender and circulated as paper money after 1906.

Original quotations at Rio de Janeiro

on:	in:	per:
Buenos Aires	Brazilian milréis	100 pesos gold
Hamburg	Brazilian milréis	100 mark banco
	from 1873 Brazilian milréis	100 mark
Italy	Brazilian milréis	100 Italian lire
Lisbon / Portugal	per cent premium	100 Portuguese milréis
	from 1875 Brazilian milréis	100 Portuguese milréis
London	pence sterling	1 Brazilian milrée
New York	Brazilian milréis	100 US dollars
Paris	Brazilian milréis	100 francs

Original quotations at Bahia and Pernambuco

on:	in:	per:
London	pence sterling	1 Brazilian milrée

Further data from Rio de Janeiro available: Hamburg, 90d/s (1893–1914) – London, 90d/s (1893–1914) – Paris, 90d/s (1893–1914).

For Brazil and its financial centre Rio de Janeiro, sources with exchange rate quotations have been available from 1808, when the Portuguese court moved to Brazil in 1807, fleeing from Napoleon's troops, and when the Brazilian ports were opened for non-Portuguese trade. There are no great gaps in the source material to be noted, so that the quotations of Rio de Janeiro are the only ones in Latin America available throughout the early 19th century. By this time, quotations of other Brazilian exchange markets of more or less regional importance are available only to a limited extent and with greater quotation gaps, as for example those of Bahia (Salvador) and Pernambuco (Recife) on London between 1849 and the early 1880s.

In Rio de Janeiro as well as in the other Brazilian exchange places, the exchange rate on London was always of the utmost importance, because these exchange transactions with London were the basis of the exchange trade in Brazil during the whole period of investigation (cf. NOBACK [1877], p. 706). In the late 1840s, around nine out of ten operations were transacted via the London market, and only the minority were done via Paris and Hamburg (SCHNEIDER [1975], p. 480). The rate fluctuations concerning the pound sterling, some of them immense, resulted from the frequent change of the currency policy in Brazil in the wake of the various involvements of home and foreign affairs, but also – and especially in the first half of the 19th century – in the irregularities of the overseas trade: "L'état d'approvisionnement qui résulte pour les marchés nationaux de l'irrégularité des arrivages d'une navigation au long cours, soumises à toutes les éventualités des choses de l'univers qu'elle embrasse dans ses ports de départ; viennent ensuite la récolte du café, le taux de la demande des produits brésiliens dans les divers pays, la situation très-mobile des rapports de l'Angleterre et de l'Amérique du Nord, le crédit anglais servant d'intermédiaire aux transactions du Brésil et des États-Unis" (VAN DER STRATEN-PONTHOZ [1854], vol. I, p. 10). Fluctuations of the milréis–sterling exchange rates of up to 10% within a few days and weeks were common for most of the documented period. Phases of relative stability in currency policy alternated with years of uncontrollable currency devaluation or issues of paper money. This situation emerged for the first time in the late 1810s and 1820s. During the Triple Alliance War against Paraguay (1864–1870), the discount of paper against gold amounted to 80% in February 1868. After the overthrow of the monarchy and the proclamation of the republic (on November 15th 1889) the exchange rates dropped from 89% in November 1889 to less than 40% of the gold parity at the end of the year 1890 and even to just 32% until December 1896 (cf. CARDOSO DE MELLO / DA CONCEIÇÃO TAVARES [1985], pp. 98–103), so that the European exporters doing business with Brazil invoiced in their European currencies (SONNDORFER [1900], p. 229). Stabilizations of the Brazilian currency succeeded only in accordance with the pound sterling, as is obvious with the introduction of the gold currency in 1849.

Original quotations of the exchange rates of Rio de Janeiro on Paris can only be furnished quite irregularly for the period after the mid-1820s and regularly for the period from the 1830s on. This can be put down to the French–Brazilian trade agreement, which was concluded in 1826. For the previous time Say has calculated a cross exchange rate from the data of Rio de Janeiro on London and of London on Paris (see the quotations in *italics* in the table), which is why the first dramatic rate fluctuations between 1812 and 1814 can be attributed to the devaluation of the pound sterling. In explanation of the lacking direct quotation of Rio de Janeiro on Paris, Say said that during the first years after the opening of the ports there was no trading between Brazil and France (SAY [1839], p. 302).

Further places quoted in the first half of the 19th century were Hamburg, quoted from 1829/36 and Lisbon, being quoted regularly from 1852 after a few years in the 1830s. Occasionally other European ports were listed as well, even though each time only for a few months, as for example Antwerp (in 1855–1857 and 1868) and Le Havre (in 1859/60 and 1868), as well as Marseilles and Oporto (both in 1868). According to several merchant manuals, bills of exchange were also drawn from Rio de Janeiro on Amsterdam and Rotterdam, but this is just as little indicated in the documented sources as the exchange operations within Brazil, although they did certainly exist. Changes on the exchange rate currents of Rio de Janeiro were not noted until towards the end of the 19th century: in 1885 the regular quotations on Italy and on New York started. From 1893 the quotations in the exchange rate lists given for London, Paris, Hamburg and Italy not only included rates for 90 days' sight but also for sight bills. Buenos Aires was the last to join, shortly before World War I and it simultaneously became the first regularly quoted foreign exchange partner on the Latin American continent (from April 1914).

Apart from this, contemporary merchant manuals report some quotations on Spain, Uruguay, Austria and the Ottoman Empire (SWOBODA [1913], p. 766). Bremen was also mentioned relatively rarely, most often together with Hamburg (NOBACK [1877], p. 767). For the beginning of the 20th century there are several exchange rate currents, which gave reason for such statements which can be put down to the fact that in Rio de Janeiro there was no official quotation up to the 1890s, because the bills were traded either directly between banks and merchants or via brokers (SWOBODA [1913], p. 766). Only by a decree of March 13th 1897 was an official exchange rate fixing introduced, which was effected by the Câmara Sindical (LEVY [1974], p. 1908); these rates are presented in the documentation from 1897 onwards.

References: Horace E. SAY, *Histoire des relations commerciales entre la France et le Brésil*, Paris 1839; Gabriel-Auguste VAN DER STRATEN-PONTHOZ, *Le budget du Brésil ou recherches sur les resources de cet Empire dans leurs rapports avec les intérêts européens du commerce et de l'émigration*, 3 vols., Bruxelles 1854; J.P. WILEMAN, *Brazilian Exchange. The Study of an Inconvertible Currency*, Buenos Aires 1896, pp. 159–178; Eduard DETTMANN, *Das moderne Brasilien in seiner neuesten wirtschaftlichen Entwicklung*, Berlin 1912, pp. 347–387; Oliver ONODY, *A inflação brasiliera, 1820–1958*, Rio de Janeiro 1960; Mircea BUESCU, *300 anos de inflação*, Rio de Janeiro 1973; Maria Bárbara LEVY et al., Arrolamento das fontes primárias do arquivo histórico da bolsa de valores do Rio de Janeiro (GB), in *Anais do VII Simpósio Nacional da ANPUH*, São Paolo 1974, pp. 1873–1916; Jürgen SCHNEIDER, *Handel und Unternehmer im französischen Brasiliengeschäft 1815–1848. Versuch einer quantitativen Strukturanalyse*, Köln – Wien 1975, pp. 477–484; Maria Bárbara LEVY, *História da bolsa de valores do Rio de Janeiro*, Rio de Janeiro 1977; Jürgen SCHNEIDER, Les relations commerciales de la France avec le Brésil et les capiteaux français au Brésil 1815–1865, *Lateinamerika-Studien* 3 (1977), pp. 183–202; Carlos Manuel PELÁEZ / Wilson SUZIGAN, *Historía monetária do Brasil*, Brasilia ²1981, pp. 38–155; Manoel CARDOSO DE MELLO / Maria DA CONCEIÇÃO TAVARES, The Capitalist Export Economy in Brazil, 1884–1930, in Roberto CORTÉS CONDE / Shane J. HUNT (eds.), *The Latin American Economies. Growth and Export Sector 1880–1930*, New York – London 1985, pp. 82–136, here pp. 95–105; Markus A. DENZEL, Finanzplätze, Wechselkurse und Währungsverhältnisse in Lateinamerika (1808–1914), in *WdW VII*, pp. 1–106, here pp. 9–18.

17.1 Rio de Janeiro exchange rates

17.1.1 On London, Paris, Hamburg and Lisbon

	RIO DE JANEIRO on:			
	London	**Paris** [a]	**Hamburg**	**Lisbon**
	per 10 pounds sterling [b]	per 100 francs [c]	per 100 mark banco [d]	per 100 milréis [e]
	in Brazilian milréis			
1808	34.29 90d/s (1)	*15.20* 90d/s (1)		
1809	32.89 90d/s (2)	*16.50* 90d/s (2)		
1810	32.88 90d/s (3)	*16.20* 90d/s (3)		
1811	33.57 90d/s (2)	*17.20* 90d/s (2)		
1812	32.11 90d/s (2)	*17.10* 90d/s (2)		
1813	30.79 90d/s (3)	*16.07* 90d/s (3)		
1814	26.51 90d/s (5)	*13.48* 90d/s (5)		
1815	32.77 90d/s (3)	*14.70* 90d/s (3)		
1816	38.27 90d/s (4)	*15.43* 90d/s (4)		
1817	38.92 90d/s (2)	*15.80* 90d/s (2)		
1818	33.73 90d/s (3)	*14.10* 90d/s (2)		
1819	38.38 90d/s (3)	*15.67* 90d/s (3)		
1820	42.09 90d/s (4)	*16.60* 90d/s (4)		
1821	46.76 90d/s (11)	*18.88* 90d/s (3)		
1822	49.00 90d/s (11)	18.98 90d/s (7)		
1823	47.96 90d/s (12)	18.37 90d/s (3)		
1824	50.03 90d/s (12)	*19.90* 90d/s (1)		
1825	47.08 90d/s (12)	*19.17* 90d/s (3)		
1826	51.05 90d/s (4)	*20.00* 90d/s (4)		
1827	66.77 90d/s (5)	*26.28* 90d/s (5)		
1828	75.90 90d/s (11)	29.70 90d/s (11)		
1829	93.84 90d/s (11)	36.57 90d/s (11)	66.25 90d/s (1)	
1830	104.36 90d/s (12)	40.27 90d/s (12)	74.54 90d/s (12)	193.88 90d/s (12)
1831	100.24 90d/s (12)	39.34 90d/s (12)	76.23 90d/s (10)	200.40 90d/s (10)
1832	72.37 90d/s (12)	27.71 90d/s (10)	48.25 90d/s (4)	155.00 90d/s (6)
1833	65.04 90d/s (12)	24.23 90d/s (11)		
1834	60.40 90d/s (12)	24.12 90d/s (12)		
1835	61.62 90d/s (12)	24.41 90d/s (12)		150.00 90d/s (1)
1836	61.57 90d/s (12)	24.38 90d/s (12)	45.23 90d/s (12)	
1837	79.11 90d/s (12)	31.05 90d/s (12)	54.65 90d/s (7)	
1838	83.44 90d/s (12)	33.40 90d/s (12)	60.51 90d/s (10)	
1839	77.09 90d/s (12)	30.86 90d/s (12)	58.13 90d/s (9)	
1840	77.88 90d/s (12)	31.30 90d/s (12)	57.95 90d/s (12)	
1841	78.52 90d/s (12)	31.41 90d/s (12)	58.18 90d/s (12)	

	RIO DE JANEIRO on:			
	London	**Paris**	**Hamburg**	**Lisbon** [f]
	per 10 pounds sterling [b]	per 100 francs [c]	per 100 mark banco, from 1873 per 100 mark [d]	per 100 milréis [e]
	in Brazilian milréis			
1842	88.20 90d/s (12)	34.92 90d/s (12)	64.94 90d/s (12)	
1843	93.56 90d/s (12)	37.00 90d/s (12)	68.36 90d/s (12)	
1844	97.52 90d/s (12)	37.45 90d/s (12)	69.75 90d/s (12)	
1845	95.05 90d/s (12)	37.19 90d/s (12)	69.21 90d/s (12)	
1846	88.99 90d/s (12)	34.82 90d/s (12)	64.56 90d/s (12)	
1847	86.58 90d/s (12)	34.03 90d/s (12)	63.21 90d/s (12)	
1848	97.16 90d/s (12)	37.32 90d/s (10)	68.54 90d/s (9)	
1849	93.40 90d/s (12)	35.95 90d/s (11)	67.97 90d/s (12)	
1850	84.41 90d/s (12)	33.46 90d/s (12)	61.24 90d/s (12)	191.00 90d/s (11)
1851	81.97 90d/s (12)	32.63 90d/s (12)	60.63 90d/s (12)	
1852	88.17 90d/s (11)	35.22 90d/s (11)	65.11 90d/s (11)	197.28 90d/s (11)
1853	85.21 90d/s (12)	34.23 90d/s (12)	63.65 90d/s (12)	193.84 90d/s (12)
1854	86.80 90d/s (12)	35.12 90d/s (12)	65.38 90d/s (12)	197.50 90d/s (8)
1855	87.02 90d/s (12)	35.53 90d/s (12)	65.23 90d/s (12)	198.20 90d/s (5)
1856	87.32 90d/s (12)	34.96 90d/s (12)	65.32 90d/s (12)	199.05 90d/s (11)
1857	87.15 90d/s (12)	34.90 90d/s (11)	65.39 90d/s (11)	200.50 90d/s (2)
1858	93.50 90d/s (12)	37.13 90d/s (11)	69.54 90d/s (7)	204.50 90d/s (2)
1859	95.90 90d/s (12)	38.79 90d/s (12)	73.70 90d/s (10)	217.20 90d/s (6)
1860	93.20 90d/s (12)	38.83 90d/s (12)	70.84 90d/s (12)	213.09 90d/s (11)
1861	93.49 90d/s (12)	37.25 90d/s (12)	69.79 90d/s (12)	213.34 90d/s (12)
1862	92.33 90d/s (12)	36.67 90d/s (12)	68.83 90d/s (12)	210.00 90d/s (12)
1863	87.98 90d/s (12)	34.81 90d/s (12)	65.67 90d/s (12)	202.05 90d/s (12)
1864	88.26 90d/s (12)	34.93 90d/s (12)	66.30 90d/s (12)	202.00 90d/s (12)
1865	96.35 90d/s (12)	38.16 90d/s (12)	70.99 90d/s (11)	216.12 90d/s (9)
1866	98.71 90d/s (12)	39.20 90d/s (12)	74.60 90d/s (12)	228.19 90d/s (11)
1867	108.48 90d/s (12)	42.98 90d/s (12)	80.63 90d/s (12)	237.12 90d/s (9)
1868	143.03 90d/s (12)	51.44 90d/s (12)	95.84 90d/s (6)	*290.00* 90d/s (1)
1869	127.96 90d/s (12)	50.68 90d/s (12)	93.61 90d/s (12)	289.17 90d/s (12)
1870	111.58 90d/s (12)	44.15 90d/s (12)	83.04 90d/s (11)	255.84 90d/s (12)
1871	99.12 90d/s (12)	39.15 90d/s (11)	73.10 90d/s (12)	225.00 90d/s (12)
1872	96.72 90d/s (12)	37.88 90d/s (12)	70.94 90d/s (11)	219.00 90d/s (11)
1873	92.19 90d/s (12)	36.26 90d/s (12)	45.35 90d/s (11)	208.59 90d/s (12)
1874	92.71 90d/s (12)	36.72 90d/s (12)	45.45 90d/s (12)	228.84 90d/s (12)
1875	88.81 90d/s (12)	35.16 90d/s (11)	43.61 90d/s (10)	200.46 90d/s (11)
1876	94.78 90d/s (12)	37.60 90d/s (12)	46.08 90d/s (9)	211.65 90d/s (10)
1877	98.01 90d/s (12)	39.16 90d/s (11)	47.88 90d/s (11)	218.69 90d/s (11)
1878	102.90 90d/s (12)	41.58 90d/s (12)	50.83 90d/s (8)	231.65 90d/s (7)

	RIO DE JANEIRO on:			
	London	**Paris**	**Hamburg**	**Lisbon, from 1891 Portugal**
	per 10 pounds sterling [b]	per 100 francs [c]	per 100 mark [d]	per 100 milréis [e]
	in Brazilian milréis			
1879	114.86 90d/s (12)	45.56 90d/s (12)	56.20 90d/s (12)	254.71 90d/s (12)
1880	107.59 90d/s (12)	41.32 90d/s (12)	51.32 90d/s (11)	240.38 90d/s (12)
1881	110.04 90d/s (12)	42.98 90d/s (12)	53.68 90d/s (12)	145.84 90d/s (12)
1882	112.03 90d/s (12)	44.61 90d/s (12)	55.32 90d/s (12)	150.80 90d/s (12)
1883	112.35 90d/s (12)	44.34 90d/s (12)	54.91 90d/s (12)	148.96 90d/s (12)
1884	117.55 90d/s (12)	46.71 90d/s (12)	56.97 90d/s (12)	162.88 90d/s (12)
1885	131.07 90d/s (12)	51.91 90d/s (12)	63.95 90d/s (12)	193.80 90d/s (12)
1886	116.94 90d/s (12)	46.47 90d/s (12)	57.90 90d/s (12)	262.50 90d/s (12)
1887	107.44 90d/s (12)	42.55 90d/s (12)	52.71 90d/s (12)	242.30 90d/s (12)
1888	95.25 90d/s (12)	37.70 90d/s (12)	46.75 90d/s (12)	213.92 90d/s (12)
1889	88.37 90d/s (12)	35.10 90d/s (12)	43.38 90d/s (12)	198.96 90d/s (12)
1890	105.80 90d/s (12)	42.47 90d/s (12)	52.08 90d/s (12)	241.05 90d/s (12)
1891	150.91 90d/s (12)	60.20 90d/s (12)	74.35 90d/s (12)	336.50 s (12)
1892	203.46 90d/s (12)	80.98 90d/s (12)	99.02 90d/s (12)	385.05 s (12)
1893	220.04 s (9)	87.68 s (9)	107.47 s (9)	404.25 s (12)
1894	242.41 s (12)	97.00 s (12)	119.68 s (12)	429.17 s (12)
1895	244.39 s (10)	97.52 s (10)	120.68 s (10)	436.10 s (10)
1896	270.49 s (12)	107.85 s (12)	133.10 s (12)	475.84 s (12)
1897	309.48 s (12)	123.01 s (12)	151.88 s (12)	472.34 s (3)
1898	335.91 s (12)	134.20 s (12)	165.70 s (12)	436.34 s (6)
1899	323.44 s (12)	128.49 s (12)	158.64 s (12)	517.00 s (12)
1900	263.85 s (12)	107.30 s (12)	131.92 s (12)	427.92 s (12)
1901	213.42 s (12)	84.71 s (12)	104.57 s (12)	349.50 s (12)
1902	201.07 s (12)	79.84 s (12)	98.48 s (12)	359.50 s (12)
1903	198.46 s (12)	79.90 s (12)	98.69 s (12)	370.75 s (12)
1904	201.78 s (12)	79.36 s (12)	97.77 s (12)	372.34 s (12)
1905	154.92 s (12)	61.83 s (12)	76.12 s (12)	326.67 s (12)
1906	150.16 s (12)	59.82 s (12)	73.71 s (12)	330.59 s (12)
1907	159.00 s (12)	63.65 s (12)	78.46 s (12)	349.42 s (12)
1908	159.84 s (12)	63.78 s (12)	78.56 s (12)	319.59 s (12)
1909	159.96 s (12)	63.69 s (12)	78.50 s (12)	317.84 s (12)
1910	150.48 s (12)	60.12 s (12)	74.19 s (12)	323.00 s (12)
1911	147.99 s (12)	59.84 s (12)	73.77 s (12)	320.84 s (12)
1912	148.43 s (12)	59.78 s (12)	73.57 s (12)	312.59 s (12)
1913	150.31 s (12)	59.95 s (12)	73.93 s (12)	300.10 s (12)
1914	151.62 s (7)	60.36 s (7)	74.47 s (7)	295.36 s (7)

[a] From 1808 to 1821 and from 1824 to 1827, only calculated cross rates from the data of Rio de Janeiro on London and of London on Paris can be presented (SAY [1839], p. 302).

[b] Concerning the British currency, see pp. 3–5.

[c] Concerning the French currency, see pp. 279f.

[d] Concerning the Hamburg and German currencies, see pp. 191–193, 197.

[e] In the Portuguese currency system one reckoned in réis respectively in milréis (= 1,000 réis). Since the Coin Act of July 29th 1854 the Portuguese silver standard with the milréis at 27.15 grammes of fine silver (since July 1st 1835 according to the Coin Act of April 24th 1835) was succeeded by the gold standard – on the model of Great Britain – with the milréis at 1.6257 grammes of fine gold. From July 1891 Portugal had the paper standard with a premium for gold coins up to 53% (in May 1897). In 1912 the milréis was succeeded by the escudo of 100 centavos (1 escudo = 1 milrée). It had to be officially reckoned in this new currency from the beginning of 1913, but for all commercial transactions the term 'milréis' continued to be usual (cf. NOBACK [1877], pp. 507f.; SWOBODA [1913], pp. 518f.).

[f] 1868: quotation on Porto, because no quotation on Lisbon is available.

17.1.2 On Italy, New York and Buenos Aires

	RIO DE JANEIRO on:		
	Italy	**New York** [a]	**Buenos Aires**
	per 100 Italian lire [b]	per 100 US dollars [c]	per 100 pesos gold [d]
	in Brazilian milréis		
1879		23.50 s (1)	
1880			
1881		23.12 s (9)	
1882			
1883			
1884			
1885	52.62 s (12)	27.75 s (12)	
1886	46.96 s (12)	24.69 s (12)	
1887	42.92 s (12)	22.42 s (12)	
1888	37.85 s (12)	19.79 s (12)	
1889	35.25 s (12)	18.46 s (12)	
1890	42.25 s (12)	22.65 s (12)	
1891	61.10 s (12)	31.82 s (12)	
1892	80.32 s (12)	41.98 s (12)	
1893	82.83 s (11)	44.19 s (10)	
1894	89.79 s (12)	51.14 s (12)	
1895	91.86 s (10)	51.29 s (10)	
1896	102.57 s (12)	55.84 s (12)	
1897	125.89 s (12)	63.27 s (12)	
1898	128.37 s (12)	69.58 s (12)	
1899	126.98 s (12)	67.03 s (12)	
1900	98.24 s (12)	54.77 s (12)	
1901	78.90 s (12)	43.91 s (12)	
1902	73.93 s (12)	41.64 s (12)	
1903	74.10 s (12)	41.43 s (12)	
1904	76.55 s (12)	41.05 s (12)	
1905	62.25 s (12)	31.96 s (12)	
1906	60.15 s (12)	30.96 s (12)	
1907	63.55 s (12)	32.96 s (12)	
1908	63.90 s (12)	32.99 s (12)	
1909	63.66 s (12)	32.94 s (12)	
1910	60.30 s (12)	31.17 s (12)	
1911	59.77 s (12)	31.00 s (12)	
1912	59.72 s (12)	30.90 s (12)	
1913	59.55 s (12)	31.08 s (12)	
1914	60.33 s (7)	31.30 s (7)	304.38 s (4)

[a] The earliest quotation on New York is available for 1831: 20.86 Brazilian milréis per 100 US dollars at 90 days' sight.

[b] Concerning the Italian currency, see pp. 108f.

[c] Concerning the US currency, see p. 404.

[d] Concerning the Argentinian currency, see pp. 449f.

17.2 Bahia and Pernambuco exchange rates

17.2.1 On London

	BAHIA on:	PERNAMBUCO on:
	London	London
	per 10 pounds sterling [a]	
	in Brazilian milréis	
1847	88.72 60d/s (6)	88.48 60d/s (4)
1848	93.20 60d/s (12)	94.53 60d/s (10)
1849	93.77 60d/s (12)	92.09 60d/s (12)
1850	85.27 60d/s (12)	86.26 60d/s (11)
1851	82.86 60d/s (12)	83.49 60d/s (10)
1852	87.73 60d/s (9)	87.55 60d/s (12)
1853	84.64 60d/s (11)	85.24 60d/s (12)
1854	86.89 60d/s (10)	87.56 60d/s (12)
1855	86.39 60d/s (11)	87.15 60d/s (12)
1856	86.79 60d/s (9)	86.48 60d/s (10)
1857	86.88 60d/s (10)	86.61 60d/s (11)
1858	95.64 60d/s (9)	96.60 60d/s (10)
1859	94.49 60d/s (9)	93.07 60d/s (8)
1860	92.41 60d/s (8)	93.85 60d/s (7)
1861	92.45 60d/s (11)	93.08 60d/s (10)
1862	91.26 60d/s (12)	90.86 60d/s (12)
1863	87.05 60d/s (12)	86.81 60d/s (12)
1864	87.33 60d/s (12)	86.75 60d/s (12)
1865	93.58 60d/s (12)	91.68 60d/s (12)
1866	93.66 60d/s (12)	92.42 60d/s (12)
1867	107.02 60d/s (12)	107.55 60d/s (12)
1868	127.25 60d/s (11)	127.86 60d/s (11)
1869	126.81 90d/s (12)	127.00 90d/s (12)
1870	112.81 90d/s (8)	113.18 90d/s (11)
1871	99.32 90d/s (8)	100.43 90d/s (6)
1872	97.35 90d/s (8)	96.68 90d/s (8)
1873	93.45 90d/s (6)	92.46 90d/s (9)
1874	93.25 90d/s (3)	95.09 90d/s (5)
1875		88.31 90d/s (5)
1876		
1877		
1878		
1879		117.15 90d/s (2)
1880		107.66 90d/s (3)

	BAHIA on:	PERNAMBUCO on:
	London	London
	per 10 pounds sterling [a]	
	in Brazilian milréis	
1881		109.09 90d/s (1)
1882	114.29 90d/s (1)	

[a]   Concerning the British currency, see pp. 3–5.

18
Argentina (1824–1914)

Exchange market: Buenos Aires (1824–1914)

Sources: *Mensagero Argentino*, Buenos Aires (1824–1826); *British Packet and Argentine News*, Buenos Aires (1827–1858); *The Economist*, London (1859–1869); *Weekly Standard*, Buenos Aires (1870–1874); *The Standard & River Plate News*, Buenos Aires (1870–1914).
Concordance: *WdW VII*, pp. 211–287

Currency: As during the colonial era, the basis of the currency in Buenos Aires was the peso of 8 reales de plata or of 100 centavos respectively in international trade and exchange operations from the mid-19th century. Within this system the Spanish and Patriot peso fuerte or hard peso (at 24.43 grammes of fine silver) has to be distinguished from the underweighted peso corriente, peso sencillo or peso macuquina, which were also in circulation. However, the paper money, the peso papel or moneda corriente, became the most important money in circulation from the 1820s. As early as 1826 the lack of precious metals and the extensive issue of paper money, both starting in 1817, led to the abolition of the need to convert banknotes into metallic currency. During the following decades there were several waves of inflation, which resulted from the immense issues of paper money of the province of Buenos Aires, intended to finance the crisis in foreign affairs (War of Independence against Spain, war with Brazil concerning the province of Montevideo from 1826 to 1828; trade blockades of the French fleet from 1837/38 to 1840 and from 1845 to 1848 as well as of the British fleet from 1845 to 1847) and in home affairs (breakdown of the Unitarian republic from 1827; fight against the Argentine confederacy from 1853 to 1861), and the budget deficits (above all in the years between 1835 and 1852). These waves of depreciation of the moneda corriente can be seen not only from the perspective of the exchange rate quotation on London as the determining barometer of the external value of the peso, but also from the quotation of the money rates of the most important circulating coins, the Spanish and Patriot onza de oro (doubloon of 23.4219 grammes of fine gold) and peso fuerte (dollar) (see Table 1). For many decades the attempts to stabilize the paper currency had not been effective in the longer term; only after the political stabilization of the 1860s could a successful reform be carried out. In 1863 the onza de oro was replaced by the peso fuerte as the basis of the peso moneda corriente. In 1864 the parity of the onza de oro in the province of Buenos Aires was fixed on the basis of the gold–silver relation of 1:16, having already been introduced in 1857 at 400 pesos moneda corriente, and that of the peso fuerte at 25 pesos moneda corriente. On this basis, the free convertibility was restored in the province of Buenos Aires in 1867 (valid until 1876) after the paper money had partly been destroyed and, as a consequence, the rate of the peso fuerte had even fallen under the parity mentioned above. Generous grants of credits by the Banco Nacional and the repeated issue of banknotes not covered by precious metal as a result of the economic upturn in the 1860s and the early 1870s once more initiated a wave of inflation (1876–1881), which coincided with the economic crisis in Europe. Even the introduction of the (at first limping) gold standard on November 5th 1881 could only stabilize the currency conditions for a few years in this period of renewed convertibility. Now the peso gold (1.4516 grammes of fine gold) of 100 centavos became the basis of the currency, and the exchange rates were both fixed in pesos (de) oro (or en oro effectivo) and pesos moneda nacional (de curso legal). After a further phase of inconvertibility and inflation from 1885 (see Table 2) the agreement of 1891 with the London creditors (especially Baring Brothers & Co.) on strict monetary discipline, the foundation of the Banco de la Nación Argentina as a trading bank for the development of private industry, the centralization of the issuing of banknotes in the Caja de Conversion, the replacing of the public finances on an even keel by introducing internal taxes, the improvement in balance of payments from 1896 as a result of the worldwide economic upturn and the renewal of the circulation of banknotes in 1894 and 1897 with the returns on investments of the 1880s helped to effect a change to the gold standard on November 4th 1899 on the basis of a new parity of 100 pesos gold = 227.27 pesos moneda nacional or 44 centavos gold = 1 peso moneda nacional respectively (Conversion Law). The rate of the peso moneda nacional, decisive for payment transactions, levelled off in October 1902 on the legal parity, which did not change until the outbreak of World War I. Therefore Argentina actually had paper currency (SWOBODA [1913], p. 746).

Table 1: Pesos moneda corriente per Spanish and Patriot onza de oro and peso fuerte

	Spanish	Patriot	Spanish	Patriot		Spanish	Patriot	Spanish	Patriot
	onza de oro		peso fuerte			onza de oro		peso fuerte	
	(doubloon)		(dollar)			(doubloon)		(dollar)	
1824	19.50		1.14	1.08	1854	326.75	323.25	21.54	18.89
1825					1855	347.34	342.80	24.00	19.97
1826	30.00	30.00	1.69	1.69	1856	350.50	345.46	23.96	20.41
1827	61.32	56.00	3.44	2.95	1857	342.80	336.25	23.92	19.80
1828	50.96	50.00	3.15	2.75	1858	374.10	362.60	25.55	21.39
1829	80.80	87.41	5.06	4.93	1859	351.00	351.00	20.73	20.73
1830	118.00	117.75	7.00	6.75	1860	344.00	344.00	20.09	20.09
1831	113.51	111.51	6.96	6.77	1861	386.00	386.00	22.70	22.70
1832	112.18	111.12	6.87	6.68	1862	409.00	409.00	23.98	23.98
1833	123.98	120.62	7.51	7.37	1863	427.00	427.00	27.60	27.60
1834	121.67	118.44	7.46	7.34	1864			28.81	28.81
1835	121.42	118.52	7.56	7.44	1865			27.41	27.51
1836	123.44	118.80	7.69	7.49	1866			24.35	24.35
1837	131.32	128.84	7.89	7.88	1867			24.25	24.25
1838	149.57	147.19	9.07	8.79	1868			25.00	25.00
1839	252.96	252.17	15.20	14.91	1869			25.00	25.00
1840	344.22	344.22	20.99	20.83	1870			25.00	25.00
1841	353.00	353.00	18.12	18.12	1871			25.00	25.00
1842	284.50	283.50	18.13	17.69	1872			25.00	25.00
1843	267.17	266.42	16.79	16.50	1873			25.00	25.00
1844	226.34	225.09	13.70	13.59	1874			25.00	25.00
1845	240.13	232.09	14.49	14.36	1875			25.00	25.00
1846	362.34	359.92	21.33	21.01	1876			28.60	28.60
1847	356.38	354.88	21.77	21.40	1877			29.50	29.50
1848	354.07	352.75	22.07	21.68	1878			31.97	31.97
1849	308.26	305.99	19.54	19.26	1879			32.30	32.30
1850	248.20	246.10	15.77	15.57	1880			30.55	30.55
1851	164.05	302.77	18.56	17.60	1881			26.95	26.95
1852	273.41	272.69	17.22	16.13	1882			25.05	25.05
1853	316.89	314.24	20.09	18.31					

Source: WdW VII, pp. 288–295; ALVAREZ [1929], pp. 99f., 113

The term 'Spanish' here means 'minted in the colonial times'; the term 'Patriot' here means 'minted by the South American Republics after their independence'.

Table 2: Pesos moneda nacional (de curso legal) per peso gold

1883	1.00	1888	1.48	1893	3.24	1898	2.57
1884	1.00	1889	1.80	1894	3.58	1899	2.25
1885	1.37	1890	2.58	1895	3.44	1900–1914	2.27
1886	1.39	1891	3.74	1896	2.96		
1887	1.35	1892	3.29	1897	2.91		

Source: ALVAREZ [1929], pp. 122f.; cf. *WdW VII*, p. 296

Original quotations at Buenos Aires

on:	in:	per:
Antwerp	centimes	1 peso gold
Asunción	pesos gold	100 gold pesos in Asuncion
Genoa	centesimi	1 peso gold
Hamburg & Berlin	pfennige	1 peso gold
London	pence sterling	1 peso fuerte
in notes:	from 1827 pence sterling	1 peso moneda corriente
	from 1885 pence sterling	1 peso moneda nacional
in gold:	from 1846 shillings and pence sterling	1 onza de oro
	from 1864 (4) pence sterling	1 peso gold
Montevideo	Brazilian réis	1 peso moneda corriente
	from 1827 (11) per cent premium or discount	1 peso fuerte in Montevideo
	from 1831 (9) pesos moneda corriente	1 peso fuerte in Montevideo
	from 1845 (12) per cent premium or discount	1 peso fuerte in Montevideo
	from 1871 per cent premium or discount	1 peso gold in Montevideo
New York	US cents	1 peso moneda corriente
	from 1848 (9) per cent premium or discount	1 US dollar
	from 1879 pesos gold	100 US dollars
Paris, *in notes:*	centimes	1 peso moneda corriente
	from 1885 centimes	1 peso moneda nacional
in gold:	from 1846 centimes	1 onza de oro
	from 1870 centimes	1 peso gold
Rio de Janeiro	per cent discount	1 peso fuerte in Rio de Janeiro
	from 1827 (6) Brazilian réis	1 peso moneda corriente
	from 1828 per cent premium	1 Brazilian milréis
	from 1841 pesos moneda corriente	1 peso fuerte in Rio de Janeiro
	from 1845 (12) per cent premium or discount	1 peso fuerte in Rio de Janeiro
	from 1873 Brazilian milréis	1 pound sterling in Buenos Aires
Spain	centavos	1 peso gold
Valparaiso	pesos gold	100 pesos in Valparaiso

Further data available: Antwerp, 90d/s (1898–1914, in gold; 1876–1914, in paper currency); s (1898–1914, in paper currency); t.t. (1898–1902, in gold) – Genoa, 90d/s (1894–1914, in gold and in paper currency); s (1894–1914, in paper currency); t.t. (1898–1901, in gold) – Hamburg and Berlin, 90d/s (1894–1914, in gold and in paper currency); s (1894–1914, in paper currency); t.t. (1898–1902, in gold) – London, 90d/s (1894–1914, in gold and in paper currency) – Paris, 90d/s (1894–1914, in gold and in paper currency) – Spain, 90d/s (1894–1914, in gold and paper currency); s (1894–1914, in paper currency) – Switzerland, 90d/s (1913/14). *Domestic exchange*: Bahia Blanca (1897–1905); Concordia (1903–1905); Mendoza, s (1897–1905); Porto Gallego (1902–1905); Rosario (1896–1905).

With regard to the international cashless payment system, Argentina with its financial centre Buenos Aires turned out to be the most important country of South America apart from Brazil, and one of the most important countries outside Europe in the 19th and early 20th centuries, though exchange rate currents that are more or less complete can only be found in relevant Argentine newspapers for the period from 1824 to 1858 and from 1871. Furthermore, these newspapers did not always list the rates for all places with which Buenos Aires maintained exchange transactions. For the period between 1858 and 1871 only the rate on London is available up to now.

The exchange rate quotations of Buenos Aires, independent from Spain after 1816, which started in 1824 during the first months of the consolidation of the United Provinces of the Río de la Plata, began with quotations on London and Rio de Janeiro as the financial centres of the most important trading partners of the country. Because of the dominating position of Great Britain in Argentine foreign trade, the quotation on London became the barometer of the external value of the peso when the compulsory conversion of banknotes into effective currency was started in 1826 and exchange rate quotations on London were then done in paper money, the so-called moneda corriente. As the exchange rates of the peso were fluctuating greatly as a consequence of inflationary tendencies, its value had to be settled daily. The various waves of inflation of the following decades – only interrupted by short phases of half-hearted attempts at stabilizing the currency – are reflected especially in the quotations on London.

In 1827, quotations on Paris, New York and Montevideo started, although the one on Paris ended in 1829 and was not listed again until 1841, after French warships had blockaded the port of Buenos Aires from 1838 to 1840. Quotations on Amsterdam or Hamburg can only be found in merchant manuals but not in contemporary newspapers, exchange operations with both places not being important and mostly being done via London (NOBACK [1855], p. 141). According to the sources, all quotations – apart from those on London – ended in 1858 and were restarted in the 1870s. Paris and France respectively were quoted relatively regularly from 1870, whereas there are only incomplete quotations on Antwerp and Belgium respectively, as well as on Montevideo (from 1871). Only occasional quotations are available on Genoa and on Italy respectively (from 1872), and on Rio de Janeiro (from 1873), and there are very irregular quotations on Hamburg, Berlin and the German Empire exchange operations, not effected directly until the introduction of the gold standard in 1881 (NOBACK [1877], p. 207). On the contrary, New York was only quoted in 1879/80 and 1885. Obviously, there is a correlation between the expansion of the range initiated by the European exchange partners of Buenos Aires and which can be noted from 1870, and European immigration to Argentine – especially from Italy and Spain – from the second half of the 1870s. Regular quotations on the European financial places, which had been carried out somewhat irregularly in the former period, can again be found from the 1890s. Last but not least, this development was caused by the rising stabilization of the currency system (official introduction of the at first limping gold standard on November 5th 1881; actual conversion to the gold standard on November 4th 1899) and the economic upturn in the country. These quotations were given in gold as well as in paper currency and each time in two usances (90 days' sight and at sight). From then on, London, Paris/France, Hamburg and Berlin/Germany, Genoa/Italy, Spain (between 1894 and 1912) and Antwerp/Belgium (since 1898) were regularly provided with these four quotations. For the period around the turn of the century there is evidence of quotations for telegraphic transfers, although – owing to a lack of sources – only for a few years and only quoted in gold currency, such as transfers on London and Paris/France in 1894/95 and from 1898 to 1902, on Antwerp/Belgium and Hamburg/Berlin and Germany respectively from 1898 to 1902 as well as on Genoa/Italy from 1898 to 1901. New York, Montevideo and Rio de Janeiro can again be found regularly on the exchange rate currents of Buenos Aires for the period from 1895 to 1905, although telegraphic transfer to New York was only carried out in 1901. In 1897 Valparaiso/Chile, Paysandú (situated at the border between Uruguay and Argentine) and Asunción (all of them only until 1905) as well as some places in Argentina (Rosario, Bahia Blanca, Mendoza, Porto Gallego and Concordia) joined the group. Before World War I, Switzerland was the only other European exchange partner to be newly listed in the exchange rate currents (1913). According to the sources documented here, the circle of exchange partners was restricted to the most important European financial markets (from 1905), whereas all American quotations (even New York) were dropped and were not listed again until World War I or shortly after it. However, private exchange rate currents were still listing a large part of these quotations (cf. SWOBODA [1913], p. 752).

In Buenos Aires the exchange trade was done by brokers at the stock exchange as well as outside this institution. So the quotations officially issued by the stock market actually appeared to be the prices the banks paid for export drafts and which for the European places were given as retail quotations (SCHMIDT [1909], p. 55). For North and South American places, price quotations had been common practice since the beginning of the quotations. Simultaneously, hard gold or silver coins were frequently used as the medium of quoting, which meant that quotations, especially in times of inflation, became largely independent of depreciations of the paper money. So the quotations on Rio de Janeiro or on Montevideo were partly given in (Spanish) pesos fuertes, or those on London or Paris partly even in British or French currency per onza de oro.

References: Jorge PILLADO, *El papel moneda argentino*, Buenos Aires 1901; Fritz SCHMIDT, Die Wechselkurse Argentiniens, in *Zeitschrift für Handelswissenschaft und Handelspraxis* 2 (1909), pp. 54–56, 92–96, 147–151; John H. WILLIAMS, *Argentine International Trade under Inconvertible Paper Money 1880–1900*, Cambridge (Mass.) 1920, pp. 49–53, 109–113, 153–155; Juan ALVAREZ, *Temas de historia económica argentina*, Buenos Aires 1929; A. G. FORD, *The Gold Standard 1880–1914. Britain and Argentina*, Oxford 1962; Roberto T. ALEMANN, *Goldunze, Silberpeso und Papiergeld. 150 Jahre argentinische Währungen* (= *Sonderdruck aus der Beilage vom 9. Juli 1966 des 'Argentinischen Tageblattes' zum 150. Jahrestag der argentinischen Unabhängigkeitserklärung*), Buenos Aires 1966; Roberto CORTÉS CONDE, The Export Economy of Argentina, 1880–1920, in idem / Shane J. HUNT (eds.), *The Latin American Economies. Growth and the Export Sector 1880–1930*, New York – London 1985, pp. 319–381, here pp. 329–351; Markus A. DENZEL, Finanzplätze, Wechselkurse und Währungsverhältnisse in Lateinamerika (1808–1914), in *WdW VII*, pp. 1–106, here pp. 18–28; Roberto CORTÉS CONDE, Regímenes, experiencias monetarias y fluctuationes económicas. De la organización nacional al patrón oro (1862–1899), *Económica* (La Plata) 45/4 (1998), pp. 269–293; idem, The Origins of Banking in Argentina, in Richard SYLLA / Richard TILLY / Gabriel TORTELLA (eds.), *The State, the Financial System and Economic Modernization*, Cambridge 1999, pp. 224–248; Gerardo della PAOLERA / Alan M. TAYLOR, *Straining at the Anchor. The Argentine Currency Board and the Search for Macroeconomic Stability, 1880–1935*, Chicago – London 2001, pp. 37–136.

18.1 Buenos Aires exchange rates

18.1.1 On London and Paris

	BUENOS AIRES on:			
	London		**Paris**	
	per 100 pounds sterling [a]		per 100 francs [b]	
		in pesos fuertes		**in pesos fuertes**
1824		58.67 60d/s (2)		
1825		53.04 60d/s (1)		
1826		53.33 60d/s (1)		
	in pesos moneda corriente	**in onzas de oro**	**in pesos moneda corriente**	**in onzas de oro**
1827	179.82 60d/s (9)		380.00 60d/s (2)	
1828	150.16 60d/s (11)		217.00 60d/s (1)	
1829	253.29 60d/s (12)		240.00 60d/s (2)	
1830	355.56 60d/s (2)			
1831	340.11 60d/s (12)			
1832	336.03 60d/s (12)			
1833	350.27 60d/s (12)			
1834	337.53 60d/s (12)			
1835	350.36 60d/s (12)			
1836	342.93 60d/s (12)			
1837	384.33 60d/s (12)			
1838	425.48 60d/s (12)			
1839	665.71 60d/s (12)			
1840	1002.79 60d/s (11)			
1841	895.47 60d/s (12)		338.59 60d/s (9)	
1842	817.03 60d/s (2)		325.21 60d/s (1)	
1843	789.56 60d/s (12)		310.63 60d/s (12)	
1844	646.94 60d/s (12)		260.52 60d/s (12)	
1845	736.93 60d/s (12)		254.81 60d/s (12)	
1846	1009.83 60d/s (12)	27.78 60d/s (1)	384.06 60d/s (12)	
1847	992.10 60d/s (11)	28.61 60d/s (7)	377.54 60d/s (5)	111.19 60d/s (7)
1848	1181.82 60d/s (2)	31.52 60d/s (12)		123.75 60d/s (10)
1849	895.62 60d/s (6)	30.66 60d/s (12)		119.20 60d/s (12)
1850	703.84 60d/s (12)	28.59 60d/s (12)		114.39 60d/s (12)
1851	785.07 60d/s (12)	27.58 60d/s (12)		110.59 60d/s (12)
1852	836.52 60d/s (11)	30.30 60d/s (11)		119.27 60d/s (11)
1853	1010.19 60d/s (11)	29.74 60d/s (11)		119.32 60d/s (11)
1854	990.09 60d/s (12)	30.77 60d/s (12)		122.92 60d/s (12)
1855	1060.68 60d/s (12)	30.37 60d/s (12)		121.44 60d/s (12)
1856	1030.75 60d/s (12)	29.38 60d/s (12)		116.99 60d/s (12)

	BUENOS AIRES on:			
	London		**Paris** [c]	
	per 100 pounds sterling [a]		per 100 francs [b]	
	in pesos moneda corriente	**in onzas de oro**	**in pesos moneda corriente**	**in onzas de oro**
1857	967.13 60d/s (12)	28.69 60d/s (12)		113.63 60d/s (12)
1858	1174.29 60d/s (4)	30.69 60d/s (12)		124.27 60d/s (2)
1859		29.14 60d/s (9)		
1860		29.99 60d/s (10)		
1861		30.99 60d/s (11)		
1862		30.70 60d/s (12)		
1863		29.91 60d/s (12)		
1864		29.85 60d/s (2)		
	in pesos moneda corriente	**in pesos gold**	**in pesos moneda corriente**	**in pesos gold**
1864		48.44 60d/s (9)		
1865		48.88 60d/s (12)		
1866		48.07 60d/s (12)		
1867		49.42 60d/s (12)		
1868		49.05 60d/s (11)		
1869		48.98 90d/s (10)		
1870		48.70 90d/s (12)		19.23 90d/s (5)
1871		47.67 90d/s (11)		18.67 90d/s (2)
1872		47.77 90d/s (12)		19.09 90d/s (1)
1873		49.01 90d/s (12)		19.08 90d/s (8)
1874		48.51 90d/s (12)		19.22 90d/s (9)
1875		48.37 90d/s (12)		19.16 90d/s (11)
1876	58.82 90d/s (8)	48.54 90d/s (10)	23.82 90d/s (7)	19.26 90d/s (8)
1877	55.48 90d/s (5)	48.57 90d/s (12)	22.45 90d/s (5)	19.32 90d/s (10)
1878		48.58 90d/s (12)		19.11 90d/s (10)
1879	63.58 90d/s (1)	48.61 90d/s (12)		19.31 90d/s (11)
1880	51.91 90d/s (5)	48.24 90d/s (12)		19.01 90d/s (12)
1881		48.48 90d/s (12)		*19.11* 90d/s (11)
1882		48.47 90d/s (12)		19.19 90d/s (10)
1883		48.76 90d/s (12)		19.26 90d/s (7)
1884		51.11 90d/s (12)		*20.19* 90d/s (6)
1885	72.32 90d/s (3)	53.10 90d/s (12)	28.65 90d/s (4)	21.18 90d/s (11)
1886		50.62 90d/s (12)		20.05 90d/s (12)
1887		50.66 90d/s (12)		19.95 90d/s (10)
1888		50.34 90d/s (12)		19.88 90d/s (10)
1889		50.30 90d/s (12)		19.94 90d/s (12)
1890		49.92 90d/s (11)		19.83 90d/s (11)
1891		49.54 90d/s (12)		19.68 90d/s (10)

	BUENOS AIRES on:											
	London [d]						**Paris** [c]					
	per 100 pounds sterling [a]						per 100 francs [b]					
	in pesos moneda corriente			in pesos gold			in pesos moneda corriente			in pesos gold		
1892				*50.11*	90d/s	(12)				19.87	90d/s	(12)
1893				*50.29*	90d/s	(12)				19.95	90d/s	(12)
1894	180.61	s	(6)	50.21	s	(12)	71.84	s	(6)	19.95	s	(12)
1895	177.20	s	(12)	50.46	s	(12)	70.32	s	(12)	20.00	s	(12)
1896	151.05	s	(12)	50.65	s	(12)	60.31	s	(12)	20.13	s	(12)
1897	148.17	s	(12)	50.75	s	(12)	59.09	s	(12)	20.17	s	(12)
1898	131.57	s	(12)	50.47	s	(12)	52.32	s	(12)	19.95	s	(12)
1899	113.50	s	(12)	50.23	s	(12)	45.01	s	(12)	19.92	s	(12)
1900	117.18	s	(12)	50.53	s	(12)	46.51	s	(12)	20.09	s	(12)
1901	115.14	s	(12)	50.54	s	(12)	46.96	s	(12)	20.05	s	(12)
1902	118.22	s	(12)	50.39	s	(12)	46.95	s	(12)	20.02	s	(12)
1903	114.32	s	(12)	50.25	s	(12)	45.40	s	(12)	19.97	s	(12)
1904	114.34	s	(12)	50.26	s	(12)	45.43	s	(12)	19.97	s	(12)
1905	114.32	s	(12)	50.27	s	(12)	45.37	s	(12)	19.96	s	(12)
1906	114.72	s	(12)	50.45	s	(12)	45.55	s	(12)	20.02	s	(12)
1907	114.95	s	(10)	50.28	s	(12)	45.50	s	(10)	20.00	s	(12)
1908	114.52	s	(12)	50.38	s	(12)	45.48	s	(12)	20.00	s	(12)
1909	114.50	s	(12)	50.35	s	(12)	45.43	s	(12)	19.98	s	(12)
1910	114.23	s	(12)	50.41	s	(12)	45.52	s	(12)	20.01	s	(12)
1911	114.71	s	(12)	50.43	s	(12)	45.36	s	(12)	19.97	s	(12)
1912	114.80	s	(12)	50.37	s	(12)	45.43	s	(12)	19.97	s	(12)
1913	115.40	s	(12)	50.38	s	(12)	45.24	s	(12)	19.95	s	(12)
1914	115.42	s	(7)	50.69	s	(7)	45.74	s	(7)	20.07	s	(7)

[a]   Concerning the British currency, see pp. 3–5.
[b]   Concerning the French currency, see pp. 279f.
[c]   1881/84: quotations partially on Le Havre.
[d]   1892/93: quotations for bank bills.

18.1.2 On New York, Rio de Janeiro and Montevideo

	BUENOS AIRES on:										
	New York			Rio de Janeiro						Montevideo		
	per 100 US dollars [a]			per 100 Brazilian milréis [b]			per 100 pesos fuertes [c]			per 100 pesos fuertes [c]		
	in pesos moneda corriente, from 1848 (9) in pesos fuertes						in pesos fuertes			in pesos moneda corriente, from 1845 (12) in pesos fuertes		
1824							89.00	s	(1)			
1825												
1826							89.00	s	(1)			
1827	400.00	s	(2)	286.84	s	(7)	88.50	s	(2)	361,00	s	(2)
1828	500.00	s	(3)	176.69	s	(8)				257.50	s	(9)
1829	588.89	s	(4)	227.05	s	(11)				361.75	s	(12)
1830	770.50	s	(2)	275.00	s	(2)				545.50	s	(2)
1831	670.00	s	(12)	264.50	s	(12)				510.00	s	(11)
1832	665.00	s	(12)	375.33	s	(12)				659.93	s	(5)
1833	718.00	s	(12)	462.29	s	(12)				755.50	s	(11)
1834	720.00	s	(12)	447.92	s	(12)				742.50	s	(12)
1835	725.00	s	(12)	455.60	s	(10)				747.50	s	(12)
1836	724.00	s	(12)	447.50	s	(12)				752.50	s	(12)
1837	775.00	s	(12)	420.50	s	(11)				795.93	s	(12)
1838	886.00	s	(9)	440.23	s	(11)				949.38	s	(12)
1839	1273.25	s	(11)	589.64	s	(7)				1569.75	s	(12)
1840	1717.85	s	(3)							2424.50	s	(11)
1841	1950.00	s	(1)	1863.33	s	(4)	101.00	s	(5)	1902.50	s	(12)
1842				1860.00	s	(2)				1869.38	s	(1)
1843	1600.00	s	(2)	1727.75	s	(12)				1694.25	s	(12)
1844	1356.25	s	(12)	1403.80	s	(12)				1358.75	s	(12)
1845	1393.75	s	(12)	1405.25	s	(11)	102.50	s	(1)	1365.50/102.50	s	(11+1)
1846	1880.00	s	(11)	2196.00	s	(2)	102.44	s	(9)	102.54	s	(12)
1847	1987.50	s	(12)				101.23	s	(12)	101.31	s	(12)
1848	2131.25/100.00	s	(8+4)				103.36	s	(12)	101.72	s	(12)
1849	98.11	s	(12)				101.10	s	(12)	100.76	s	(12)
1850	93.96	s	(12)				101.08	s	(11)	100.16	s	(12)
1851	91.50	s	(12)				100.26	s	(11)	100.20	s	(12)
1852	97.14	s	(11)				100.73	s	(11)	100.04	s	(11)
1853	98.32	s	(11)				101.14	s	(11)	100.50	s	(11)
1854	98.75	s	(12)				101.14	s	(12)	99.93	s	(12)
1855	100.05	s	(12)				100.54	s	(12)	100.00	s	(12)
1856	97.67	s	(12)				100.48	s	(12)	99.99	s	(12)
1857	94.46	s	(12)				100.57	s	(12)	99.92	s	(12)
1858	100.00	s	(2)				100.50	s	(4)	99.82	s	(2)

	BUENOS AIRES on:								
	New York			Rio de Janeiro			Montevideo		
	per 100 US dollars [a]			per 100 Brazilian milreís [b]			per 100 Uruguayan pesos gold [d]		
	in pesos gold			in pounds sterling			in pesos gold		
...									
1871							100.13	s	(1)
1872							100.50	s	(1)
1873				106.39	s	(1)	100.08	s	(4)
1874				92.60	s	(1)	99.91	s	(3)
1875							100.63	s	(2)
1876							100.92	s	(3)
1877							100.25	s	(1)
1878							99.86	s	(6)
1879	104.98	s	(1)	86.21	s	(1)	100.85	s	(5)
1880	104.84	s	(1)	92.45	s	(5)	100.92	s	(6)
1881				91.75	s	(1)	100.57	s	(1)
1882				89.59	s	(2)	100.10	s	(2)
1883				88.89	s	(1)	101.75	s	(3)
1884							102.83	s	(7)
1885	103.25	s	(1)				101.68	s	(5)
1886							100.50	s	(2)
1887				94.79	s	(1)	100.38	s	(2)
1888							103.50	s	(1)
1889									
1890				90.91	s	(1)			
1891									
1892									
1893									
1894									
1895	103.50	s	(2)	38.99	s	(2)	100.13	s	(2)
1896	104.60	s	(12)	38.51	s	(12)	100.79	s	(12)
1897	105.62	s	(12)	32.81	s	(12)	100.20	s	(12)
1898	104.90	s	(12)	30.32	s	(12)	100.31	s	(12)
1899	104.42	s	(12)	31.25	s	(12)	100.22	s	(12)
1900	105.00	s	(12)	38.96	s	(12)	100.20	s	(12)
1901	104.25	s	(12)	47.08	s	(12)	100.25	s	(12)
1902	104.02	s	(12)	50.18	s	(12)	100.43	s	(12)
1903	103.63	s	(12)	50.21	s	(11)	100.64	s	(12)
1904	103.56	s	(12)	50.77	s	(10)	101.58	s	(12)
1905	103.50	s	(6)	62.14	s	(6)	100.70	s	(6)

[a] Concerning the US currency, see p. 404.

[b] Concerning the Brazilian currency, see pp. 451f.

[c] The Spanish peso fuerte or dollar of 8 reales de plata of 24.43 grammes of fine silver functioned as legal tender of the province of Montevideo (NOBACK [1851], 1ˢᵗ part, p. 683).

[d] Concerning the Uruguayan currency, see p. 483.

18.1.3 On Antwerp, Genoa, Hamburg & Berlin and Spain

	BUENOS AIRES on:			
	Antwerp	**Genoa**	**Hamburg & Berlin**	**Spain**
	per 100 Belgian francs [a]	per 100 Italian lire [b]	per 100 mark [c]	per 100 pesetas [d]
	in pesos gold			
1870	19.12 90d/s (3)			
1871	18.72 90d/s (5)			
1872	18.73 90d/s (5)	18.89 90d/s (2)		
1873	19.06 90d/s (9)	18.91 90d/s (1)	23.53 90d/s (1)	
1874	19.19 90d/s (11)	19.16 90d/s (1)	24.28 90d/s (1)	
1875	19.02 90d/s (9)	19.37 90d/s (1)		
1876	19.25 90d/s (8)			
1877	19.26 90d/s (10)	21.17 90d/s (3)		
1878	19.05 90d/s (4)			
1879	19.27 90d/s (12)		23.98 90d/s (3)	
1880	18.99 90d/s (12)	18.98 90d/s (1)	21.19 90d/s (1)	
1881	19.11 90d/s (7)	19.05 90d/s (1)		
1882	19.06 90d/s (6)	19.31 90d/s (2)	23.48 90d/s (4)	
1883	19.24 90d/s (6)	19.35 90d/s (2)	23.86 90d/s (5)	
1884	19.91 90d/s (4)			
1885	21.24 90d/s (10)		23.70 90d/s (1)	
1886	20.00 90d/s (11)			
1887	19.93 90d/s (8)	19.89 90d/s (2)	24.84 90d/s (5)	
1888	19.83 90d/s (9)		23.07 90d/s (3)	
1889	19.92 90d/s (10)	19.69 90d/s (1)	24.88 90d/s (3)	
1890	19.74 90d/s (10)		24.62 90d/s (3)	
1891	19.65 90d/s (5)		24.32 90d/s (4)	
1892	19.89 90d/s (9)		24.42 90d/s (1)	
1893	19.99 90d/s (9)		24.65 90d/s (7)	
1894	19.72 90d/s (7)	18.51 s (6)	24.62 s (12)	17.08 s (6)
1895		19.13 s (12)	24.83 s (12)	17.70 s (12)
1896		18.73 s (12)	24.90 s (12)	16.99 s (12)
1897		19.29 s (12)	24.90 s (12)	15.69 s (12)
1898	19.99 s (10)	18.83 s (12)	24.76 s (12)	13.61 s (12)
1899	19.83 s (12)	18.63 s (12)	24.61 s (12)	16.33 s (11)
1900	20.06 s (12)	18.91 s (12)	24.76 s (12)	15.83 s (12)
1901	20.04 s (12)	19.22 s (12)	24.62 s (12)	14.79 s (12)
1902	20.04 s (10)	19.78 s (12)	24.65 s (12)	17.48 s (10)
1903	20.05 s (4)	20.00 s (12)	24.57 s (12)	14.92 s (10)
1904		19.94 s (12)	24.59 s (12)	14.66 s (9)

	BUENOS AIRES on:										
	Antwerp			Genoa			Hamburg & Berlin			Spain		
	per 100 Belgian francs [a]			per 100 Italian lire [b]			per 100 mark [c]			per 100 pesetas [d]		
	in pesos gold											
1905				19.98	s	(12)	24.57	s	(12)	15.30	s	(12)
1906				20.04	s	(12)	24.66	s	(12)	17.79	s	(12)
1907	19.96	s	(12)	19.99	s	(12)	24.59	s	(12)	18.03	s	(12)
1908	19.71	s	(6)	20.03	s	(12)	24.66	s	(12)	17.80	s	(12)
1909	19.94	s	(12)	19.77	s	(12)	24.59	s	(12)	18.06	s	(12)
1910	19.89	s	(10)	19.94	s	(12)	24.68	s	(12)	18.76	s	(12)
1911	19.93	s	(12)	19.88	s	(12)	24.64	s	(12)	18.43	s	(12)
1912	19.83	s	(12)	19.89	s	(12)	24.64	s	(12)	18.83	s	(12)
1913	19.85	s	(12)	19.77	s	(12)	24.61	s	(12)	18.63	s	(12)
1914	19.97	s	(7)	20.12	s	(7)	24.84	s	(7)	19.24	s	(7)

[a]   The Belgian franc was equal to the the French franc (see p. 280).

[b]   Concerning the Italian currency, see pp. 108f.

[c]   Concerning the German currency, see p. 197.

[d]   Concerning the Spanish currency, see p. 307.

18.1.4 On Asunción and Valparaiso

	BUENOS AIRES on:					
	Asunción			Valparaiso		
	per 100 pesos gold [a]			per 100 pesos gold [b]		
	in pesos gold					
1894	100.50	[c]	(12)	50.37	s	(11)
1895				50.24	s	(12)
1896	100.25	[c]	(12)	49.85	s	(12)
1897	100.25	[c]	(12)	49.52	s	(12)
1898	100.25	[c]	(12)	49.96	s	(12)
1899	100.25	[c]	(12)	50.20	s	(12)
1900	100.25	[c]	(12)	49.94	s	(12)
1901	100.25	[c]	(12)	49.89	s	(12)
1902	100.25	[c]	(6)	49.95	s	(6)

[a] In Paraguay the peso gold was an imaginary unit of account, payable in old Spanish, Mexican or Patriot onzas de oro or in paper money (peso fuerte de curso legal of 100 centavos) with an immense discount against gold. In 1912 the rate fluctuated between 13.78 and 17.13 paper pesos to 1 peso gold. As a fixed ratio, 100 pesos gold were equal to 20 pounds sterling (SWOBODA [1913], pp. 774f.).

[b] Concerning the Chilean currency, see p. 477.

[c] No usance given.

19
Chile (1827–1914)

Exchange market: Valparaiso (1827–1914)

Sources: *El Mercurio de Valparaiso* (1827); *Estadística Minera* [1911], p. 101 (1830–1890); *The Course of Exchange*, London (1847/48); *The Economist*, London (1849–1887, 1911–1914); WAGE-MANN [1913], pp. 113, 115 (1874–1879, 1885, 1888–1891); FETTER [1931], pp. 13–76n (1878–1892); *Le Temps*, Paris (1892–1893, 1896–1897); *Journal des débats politiques et littéraires*, Paris (1894–1910).
Concordance: *WdW VII*, pp. 303–312

Currency: During the first decades of the documented period the exchange rate quotations were recorded for pesos corrientes, the unit of account based on the Spanish peso duro (24.43 grammes of fine silver) of 8 reales of 1772. From 1817 the peso duro was minted with a republican strike, but only a small amount was issued. As gold coins were the main currency of Chile, the gold standard predominated in the country, the onza de oro or the doblón (23.4219 grammes of fine gold) of 16 Spanish pesos duros being fixed at 17¼ Chilean pesos corrientes (NOBACK [1858], p. 650). The term peso corriente helped to mark the Chilean pesos off from the old Spanish, Mexican and other South American (Patriot) pesos (NOBACK [1877], p. 799).

While the Coin Act of 1835 had still prescribed the full-weighted minting of pesos following the Spanish example, the currency reform of January 9th 1851 introduced bimetallism following the French example on the basis of the peso corriente (22.50 grammes of fine silver or 1.3728 grammes of fine gold) of 100 centavos (or – in everyday life – of 8 reales). Therefore the previous gold standard was not much changed by the new laws, but the long-standing unit of account, the peso corriente, became the monetary unit (cf. ibid., p. 800), corresponding to the French 5-francs piece. With the minting of the 1-peso piece in gold (1.3725 grammes of fine gold), which began in 1860, the gold standard was simultaneously introduced and used for all bigger payments and all quotations in the exchange rate currents (cf. ibid.). Notes of private banks were not accepted until a military conflict between Chile and Spain broke out in 1865 and the treasury vouched for the validity of the notes. As a result of the worldwide devaluation of silver which became noticeable in Chile in the 1870s, the new gold coins disappeared quickly, so that Chile had the silver standard from 1875. Owing to their manageability, banknotes were more popular in those years, their circulation amounting to approximately 20 million pesos around 1877 and, in consequence, the rate of the pound sterling was falling. After its dramatic depreciation in 1892/93, the paper currency was abolished (a compulsory rate had been imposed on it on July 23rd 1878). When the gold standard was reintroduced in 1895 and the government paper money was cashed in gold, the peso gold was based on a parity of 18 pence sterling since the (imaginary) peso gold (peso de oro) corresponded to 0.5492 grammes of fine gold (1 pound sterling = 13 1/3 pesos). Only three years later the gold standard collapsed again because of a crisis in the saltpetre industry, in agriculture and in copper mining, as well as because of the need to produce armaments for fear of a war with Argentina. On July 31st 1898 government notes (billetes fiscales) were reintroduced as paper currency with a temporary compulsory rate of three years being prolonged repeatedly until 1915.

Original quotations at Valparaiso

on:	in:	per:
London	pence sterling	1 peso corriente
	from 1861 pence sterling	1 peso gold [a] or in notes [b]

[a] From 1895 on the basis of 1 pound sterling = 13 1/3 pesos.

[b] In banknotes (1878–1893/95) or government notes (billetes fiscales, from 1898).

The earliest exchange rates handed down from independent Chile, a Republic from 1818, date from around 1830. From 1849 the London *Economist* recorded quite regularly the exchange rates of Valparaiso, the main port and by far the most important exchange market of the country, last but not least because of its relative geographical proximity to the capital Santiago de Chile.

Whereas precious metals – especially foreign gold coins – had been the predominant means of payment during the first half of the 19th century, mostly 60, later on 90 days' sight bills were used for transactions with Europe from the mid-century. Apart from some insignificant exceptions these transactions were made in the form of sterling bills on London and partly on Liverpool. So payment transactions with other South American trading centres (above all Rio de Janeiro and Montevideo) continued to be settled with non-Chilean gold coins in particular, as no evidence of exchange operations with these markets can be provided (NOBACK [1858], p. 651). This British predominance in Chilean exchange transactions was caused by the important position British merchant bankers occupied in Chilean business life; British traders mostly granted Chilean merchants a half-year credit whereas merchant bankers from Hamburg, for instance, were not willing to do so. The particular importance of the exchange rate on London is shown in the different rate levels of the quotations for different degrees of creditworthiness. So Valparaiso's exchange rate quotations on London were usually subdivided into, first, Letras de primera clase (first-class commercial or London bills), the highest quotation of the five financially strongest bankers in town on their oldest English business partners and bankers of worldwide reputation – i.e. in particular the company Gibbs & Huth – second, Muy Buen Londres for other great merchants and bankers and, finally, Buen Londres, quotations that were just drafts on London banks, because sterling bills were honoured with lower expenses than other bills. The distinction between the different degrees of creditworthiness is not reflected in the diverse exchange rate currents documented in the following. To be exact, the quoted 'base rate' was the point of reference in Valparaiso and when the creditworthiness declined, a small premium was added to the rate charged in pence per peso (1/64%–1/16% per penny).

This quotation on London was the barometer of Chilean financial and economic development. Owing to the Chilean policy with its extensive issues of paper money and the resulting attempts at stabilizing the currency, the rate on London was also subject to multiple and frequently even drastic fluctuations. Thus the extensive issues of paper money during the last quarter of the 19th century (as a result of the economic crisis in 1878, the war with Bolivia and Peru in 1879, the revolution of the congress and the civil war in 1891, and finally the armaments crisis mentioned above) intensified by the further fall in silver prices and the important outflow of gold, made the rate on London subject to extreme fluctuations and repeatedly caused a dramatic slide.

The reintroduction of the paper currency in 1898 was followed by an important export of gold and a falling exchange rate on London to 11 9/16 pence per peso until the end of January 1899. As a result of the economic upturn in 1900/01 and in 1904, there were new issues of paper money until 1907, which tripled the circulation of banknotes in Chile so that the crisis of 1907/08 again resulted in extreme rate fluctuations and a rate loss (with a low of 7 11/16 pence sterling per peso at the end of June 1908). Within a few hours there were fluctuations of half a penny, i.e. of about 5%, and turn-overs of only 500 pounds sterling are said to have depressed the rate by a quarter of a penny (WAGEMANN [1913], p. 129).

Despite the great importance of the London exchange for the payment transactions of Valparaiso, this rate was quoted quite irregularly and sometimes with changing usances (60 and 90 days' sight) in London as well. Only when Chilean banks, above all the Banco de Valparaiso, gained greater importance and branches of European overseas banks set up in business in the 1870s, were quotations carried out more regularly and with a fixed usance (90 days' sight from 1868). From 1887 to 1911, however, the Chilean quotation in the London *Economist* was given up, but French sources for the interim period (1892–1910) recorded Valparaiso's rates on London, but not on other exchange markets.

Until the end of the documented period, the rate on London remained the only decisive one, also used for clearing rates on other international financial markets. Still around the turn of the century, all payment transactions between Chile and, for example, Germany were carried out via London, so that in Hamburg Chilean bills drawn on London were only discounted, although German banks, especially the Deutsche Überseeische Bank, had already opened branches in Valparaiso and other Chilean towns. If additional exchange rates were quoted in private exchange rate currents as different merchant manuals of the 19th century show, for instance on Paris, Hamburg, New York (5% premium in 1827) or Lima (1% premium in 1827), also on Antwerp (e.g. NOBACK [1858], p. 725; NOBACK [1877], p. 891; SWOBODA [1889], p. 385), then they were scarcely significant for the financial place and "Entrepôt de la mer du Sud", Valparaiso (BARBANCE [1969], p. 53).

References: *Estadística Minera de Chile en 1910*, Santiago 1911; Ernst WAGEMANN, *Die Wirtschaftsverfassung der Republik Chile. Zur Entwicklungsgeschichte der Geldwirtschaft und der Papierwährung*, München – Leipzig 1913; Frank Wh. FETTER, *Monetary Inflation in Chile*, Princeton 1931; Marthe BARBANCE, *Vie commerciale de la route du Cap Horn au XIXᵉ siècle. L'armement A.-D. Bordes et fils*, Paris 1969; Markus A. DENZEL, Finanzplätze, Wechselkurse und Währungsverhältnisse in Lateinamerika (1808–1914), in *WdW VII*, pp. 1–106, here pp. 33–38.

19.1 Valparaiso exchange rates

19.1.1 On London

	VALPARAISO on:				VALPARAISO on:		
	London				**London**		
	per 10 pounds sterling [a]				per 10 pounds sterling [a]		
	in pesos corrientes				**in pesos corrientes, from 1861 in pesos gold or in notes** [b]		
1827	52.56	90d/s	(3)	1859	52.35	60d/s	(12)
1828				1860	54.82	60d/s	(10)
1829				1861	53.95	60d/s	(8)
1830	54.55	90d/s	(y)	1862	52.80	60d/s	(11)
1831	53.93	90d/s	(y)	1863	54.01	60d/s	(11)
1832	53.33	90d/s	(y)	1864	53.96	60d/s	(10)
1833	53.78	90d/s	(y)	1865	52.44	60d/s	(12)
1834	52.46	90d/s	(y)	1866	52.08	60d/s	(12)
1835	53.63	90d/s	(y)	1867	52.20	60d/s	(12)
1836	53.63	90d/s	(y)	1868	55.90	60d/s	(11)
1837	53.71	90d/s	(y)	1868	52.10	90d/s	(y)
1838	53.33	90d/s	(y)	1869	52.13	90d/s	(9)
1839	52.75	90d/s	(y)	1870	52.56	90d/s	(5)
1840	53.04	90d/s	(y)	1871	53.35	90d/s	(4)
1841	52.75	90d/s	(y)	1872	52.49	90d/s	(4)
1842	52.46	90d/s	(y)	1873	53.94	90d/s	(6)
1843	52.75	90d/s	(y)	1874	53.78	90d/s	(y)
1844	53.71	90d/s	(y)	1875	54.78	90d/s	(y)
1845	53.93	90d/s	(y)	1876	59.17	90d/s	(y)
1846	54.01	90d/s	(y)	1877	57.06	90d/s	(y)
1847	54.55	90d/s	(y)	1878	*60.33*	90d/s	(12)
1848	55.17	90d/s	(10)	1879	*73.70*	90d/s	(12)
1849	53.93	90d/s	(8)	1880	*78.82*	90d/s	(12)
1850	52.15	60d/s	(12)	1881	*71.66*	90d/s	(3)
1851	52.34	60d/s	(11)	1882	*67.99*	90d/s	(9)
1852	52.25	60d/s	(10)	1883	*68.58*	90d/s	(2)
1853	50.86	60d/s	(5)	1884	*77.42*	90d/s	(3)
1854	51.54	60d/s	(7)	1885	*94.35*	90d/s	(y)
1855	52.46	60d/s	(y)	1886	*109.64*	90d/s	(3)
1856	52.60	60d/s	(y)	1887	*100.36*	90d/s	(3)
1857	52.60	60d/s	(11)	1888	*91.43*	90d/s	(y)
1858	52.75	60d/s	(12)	1889	*90.35*	90d/s	(y)

	VALPARAISO on:		VALPARAISO on:
	London		**London**
	per 10 pounds sterling [a]		per 10 pound sterling [a]
	in pesos gold or in notes [b]		in pesos in notes [b]
1890	*99.74* 90d/s (y)	1903	*143.65* 90d/s (6)
1891	*132.26* 90d/s (6)	1904	*144.67* 90d/s (12)
1892	*130.12* 90d/s (3)	1905	*152.69* 90d/s (12)
1893	*160.80* 90d/s (12)	1906	*168.93* 90d/s (12)
1894	*194.68* 90d/s (12)	1907	*198.87* 90d/s (12)
1895	144.58 90d/s (12)	1908	*255.58* 90d/s (12)
1896	137.40 90d/s (6)	1909	*224.02* 90d/s (12)
1897	136.87 90d/s (12)	1910	*221.15* 90d/s (12)
1898	*153.52* 90d/s (12)	1911	*224.31* 90d/s (12)
1899	*170.36* 90d/s (12)	1912	*236.56* 90d/s (12)
1900	*142.53* 90d/s (12)	1913	*245.21* 90d/s (12)
1901	*150.41* 90d/s (12)	1914	*256.27* 90d/s (7)
1902	*159.26* 90d/s (12)		

[a]   Concerning the British currency, see pp. 3–5.

[b]   Quotations *in italics*: quotation in banknotes (1878–1893/95) or government notes (billetes fiscales, from 1898).

20
Uruguay (1871–1914)

Exchange market: Montevideo (1871–1914)

Sources: *Weekly Standard*, Buenos Aires (1871–1874); *The Economist*, London (1873/74, 1886–1914); *The Standard & River Plate News*, Buenos Aires (1886).
Concordance: *WdW VII*, pp. 299–302

Currency: Until 1863 Uruguayan payments were made in pesos corrientes of 8 reales at 16 cuartos or at 100 centavos. Since the coinage of Uruguay was insignificant during the first half of the 19th century, mainly Spanish, Mexican and South American silver pesos (at 24.43 grammes of fine silver) and Portuguese and Brazilian patacones at 960 centavos were in circulation (5 pesos de plata or patacones = 6 pesos corrientes). In 1854 the circulating pesos were devalued by 1/24 so that they corresponded to 100 centavos from then on (4 pesos de plata or patacones = 5 pesos corrientes). By the Coin Act of June 23rd 1862 the bimetallism with the silver peso (peso de plata; 23.37 grammes of fine silver) and the doubloon (doblón de oro; 15.56 grammes of fine gold) of 10 pesos was introduced at the beginning of 1863. Payments were made either in gold coins (in the early 1870s primarily still in British sovereigns) or in different kinds of paper money. However, when this paper money was withdrawn from circulation until 1874 and then again from the late 1880s, because its value was fluctuating more or less in comparison with gold, and payments in effective currency were mostly made in gold, the gold standard prevailed (cf. NOBACK [1877], p. 1160; SWOBODA [1889], p. 627; SONNDORFER [1900], p. 234). At the same time, calculations were no longer made on the basis of the silver peso of 1862 but according to the unminted peso gold at 100 centavos, which corresponded to one-tenth part of the doubloon of 1862.

Original quotations at Montevideo

on:	in:	per:
London	pence sterling	1 peso gold

As far as the Uruguayan exchange place Montevideo is concerned, only the quotations on London listed in Argentine and English newspapers in the period from 1871 to 1874 and from 1886 to 1914 can be documented without analysing Uruguayan sources. Earlier quotations of Montevideo could be found only in the London *Course of Exchange*, where rates of Montevideo on London were quoted quite irregularly in the late 1840s (at about 585 pesos per 100 pounds sterling).

In Montevideo – as in nearly all Latin American markets – the quotation on London was considered to be the main exchange rate; so, for example, almost all cashless payment transactions from Uruguay to Germany were effected via London, which is why Hamburg was quoted only in rare cases (NOBACK [1858], p. 492). Despite this, further quotations can be found in contemporary merchant manuals, for example on

Paris, Rio de Janeiro and Hamburg from the 1840s, even on Antwerp, Genoa, other French places (Bordeaux, Le Havre) and Buenos Aires from the 1870s, and additionally on Spain and New York during the early 20th century (ibid.; NOBACK [1851], 2nd part, p. 1793; NOBACK [1877], p. 615; NELKENBRECHER [1890], p. 630; SONNDORFER [1900], p. 235; SWOBODA, Arbitrage [1913], p. 781).

References: Markus A. DENZEL, Finanzplätze, Wechselkurse und Währungsverhältnisse in Lateinamerika (1808–1914), in *WdW VII*, pp. 1–106, here pp. 28–31.

20.1 Montevideo exchange rates

20.1.1 On London

	MONTEVIDEO on:					MONTEVIDEO on:		
	London					London		
	per 100 pounds sterling [a]					per 100 pounds sterling [a]		
	in pesos gold					in pesos gold		
1871	444.44	90d/s	(2)		1893	466.64	90d/s	(12)
1872	461.54	90d/s	(5)		1894	464.54	90d/s	(12)
1873	448.09	90d/s	(5)		1895	463.69	90d/s	(12)
1874	469.45	90d/s	(7)		1896	465.00	90d/s	(12)
1875	[b]				1897	465.56	90d/s	(12)
1876	[b]				1898	464.26	90d/s	(12)
1877	[b]				1899	460.87	90d/s	(12)
1878	[b]				1900	461.58	90d/s	(12)
1879	[b]				1901	462.53	90d/s	(12)
1880	[b]				1902	463.00	90d/s	(12)
1881	[b]				1903	462.06	90d/s	(12)
1882	[b]				1904	463.36	90d/s	(12)
1883	[b]				1905	462.73	90d/s	(12)
1884	[b]				1906	463.32	90d/s	(12)
1885	[b]				1907	461.22	90d/s	(12)
1886	470.51	90d/s	(11)		1908	464.52	90d/s	(12)
1887	472.40	90d/s	(11)		1909	464.00	90d/s	(12)
1888	467.58	90d/s	(12)		1910	464.90	90d/s	(12)
1889	469.24	90d/s	(12)		1911	463.37	90d/s	(11)
1890	466.42	90d/s	(12)		1912	463.03	90d/s	(7)
1891	462.81	90d/s	(12)		1913	463.16	90d/s	(11)
1892	465.43	90d/s	(12)		1914	466.22	90d/s	(6)

[a] Concerning the British currency, see pp. 3–5.

[b] No data could be found for the years between 1875 and 1885. In this period Uruguay had the paper standard with very high premiums on gold coins, for example of 311% in February 1876 (1 peso in notes = 24 1/3 centavos gold) (NOBACK [1877], p. 1160).

21
Mexico (1886–1914)

Exchange market: Mexico City (1886–1914)

Sources: *The Economist*, London (1886/87); SONNDORFER [1900], pp. 220f. (1899); *Boletín Financiero y Minero de México. Diario Consagrado a los Asuntos Financieros y Mineros del País* (1900–1914).
Concordance: *WdW VII*, pp. 315–336

Currency: The Mexican currency system of the 19th century was based on the system of colonial times, i.e. on the Spanish Coin Acts of 1772 and 1786 (see p. 307). The main means of payment was the silver peso (peso de plata) or Mexican dollar (24.43 grammes of fine silver) of 8 reales at 12 granos. Its minting was confirmed by the Coin Act of March 15th 1864, which changed only slightly in 1867. In wholesale trade and customs procedures it had already been common practice to divide the peso into 100 centavos, which became obligatory for the retail trade in 1864 as well. Maintaining the free silver strike, the silver standard was effective until 1905 although the global decline in silver prices became especially noticeable in Mexico, the 'classic' country of silver, from the second half of the 1870s:

Mexican pesos silver per 100 Mexican pesos gold

Year	Value	Year	Value	Year	Value	Year	Value
1820	95.00	1840	95.00	1860	92.90	1880	109.70
1821	97.00	1841	95.50	1861	94.30	1881	110.00
1822	96.10	1842	96.40	1862	93.30	1882	110.60
1823	96.40	1843	96.90	1863	93.40	1883	113.30
1824	96.20	1844	96.30	1864	93.40	1884	113.10
1825	95.50	1845	96.80	1865	93.90	1885	117.90
1826	95.90	1846	96.60	1866	93.80	1886	126.30
1827	95.80	1847	96.10	1867	94.60	1887	128.20
1828	96.00	1848	96.30	1868	96.00	1888	133.70
1829	96.00	1849	96.00	1869	96.10	1889	134.40
1830	96.20	1850	95.50	1870	95.80	1890	120.00
1831	95.60	1851	94.00	1871	96.00	1891	127.20
1832	95.70	1852	94.70	1872	96.30	1892	144.20
1833	96.90	1853	93.20	1873	96.80	1893	161.00
1834	95.70	1854	93.20	1874	98.20	1894	197.90
1835	96.10	1855	93.50	1875	101.10	1895	192.00
1836	95.50	1856	93.50	1876	107.90	1896	190.80
1837	96.30	1857	92.90	1877	104.50	1897	213.70
1838	96.30	1858	93.50	1878	108.90	1898	216.90
1839	95.00	1859	92.40	1879	111.80	1899	207.50

Source: Almanaques "Prevision y Seguridad", Monterrey, N.L. Thus 'pesos in gold' means payable in Mexican onzas de oro or doubloons (23.4219 grammes of fine gold) at 16 pesos, in other South American currencies ('Patriot', especially Colombian) onzas de oro or doubloons at 15 to 15¼ pesos or – from the 1860s – in hidalgos (14.8059 grammes of fine gold) of 10 pesos.

From April 4th 1905 a limping gold standard (Act of March 25th 1905) on the basis of a new peso gold (peso de oro; 0.75 grammes of fine gold) of 100 centavos predominated in Mexico, whereas the silver peso continued to be minted without any change and was legal tender for unlimited amounts of money according to the Act of 1867. The currency changeover, which had brought about the independence of the peso from the silver price fluctuations on the international markets of precious metals, provided the stability of the exchange rates to a large extent; and these were maintained with international assistance during the months of crisis at the European and North American financial markets (1907/08). Characteristic evidence of the confidence in the Mexican currency is the fact that within the postal giro transfer with the USA the Mexican peso was accepted as being of the same value as half a US dollar (SWOBODA [1913], p. 739).

Original quotations at Mexico City

on:	in:	per:
Hamburg	mark	1 peso silver or gold
Havana	% premium	1 peso silver
	from 1906 pesos gold in Havana	100 pesos gold in Mexico
Italy	Italian lire	1 peso gold
London	pence sterling	1 peso silver or gold
Madrid	pesos duros	100 pesos silver or gold
	from 1905 (7) pesetas	1 peso gold
New York	% premium on silver pesos	1 US dollar
	from 1903 US dollars	100 pesos silver or gold
Paris	francs	1 peso silver or gold

All data in or for pesos in Mexico are quoted in or for pesos silver until March 1905 and after April 1905 in or for pesos gold.

Other data available: Vienna, s (1906)

In the 19th century as well as during the colonial era, the importance of Mexico within international payment transactions was based primarily on the export of silver pesos, the so-called Mexican dollars. Until the end of the 19th century the Mexican dollar was one of the most important trade coins in the whole world. As various money rates show, it was spread over both parts of America, over South and East Asia and even over parts of Africa, representing the 'model' for several imitations, like the US trade dollar, the Japanese yen, the British Hong Kong dollar, the Straits Settlements dollar or later the Chinese yuan. The outstanding importance of the Mexican dollar as a trade coin and an export article, and the extremely extensive cash remittances into foreign countries resulting from this were without doubt an indication of the relative unimportance of cashless payment for Mexico in comparison with the other Latin American states. Perhaps this may explain why exchange rate quotations from Mexico are available on a larger scale only for the early 20th century but not for the 19th century. Even in the London *Economist*, which recorded quotations on London for all important Latin American exchange markets in the second half of the 19th century, quotations of Mexico City only for the years 1886 and 1887 can be found.

When payments from Mexico were settled cashlessly, London was the most important foreign financial market and partner – as it was in almost all Latin American countries (cf. NOBACK [1858], p. 484) – especially because London had been a central market for the trade with Mexican dollars since the 18th century which is why the buying rates for this coin are quoted here (*WdW VII*, pp. 365–367). Exchange rate quotations on London were already listed in a British consular report from Vera Cruz in 1824: "The exchange on the coast was about 48d. per hard dollar, while at Mexico it was only 46d., until this year, when the effect of the bills drawn on account of the loans negotiated with British capitalists has been to raise the exchange at Mexico to 50d. and 52d. per dollar. The exchange on the coast ought to be always 4 per cent higher" (HUMPHREYS [ed.] [1940], pp. 325f.).

In addition to this, contemporary merchant manuals also quoted exchange rates of Mexico City on other European places (Hamburg and occasionally Paris and Amsterdam as well), on New York and several Mexican ports and trading cities (especially Tampico and Vera Cruz) from the 1840s (e.g. NELKENBRECHER [1842], p. 284; NOBACK [1858], p. 484). Later on it is to be expected that Havana, New Orleans and Bordeaux also joined this group (e.g. NOBACK [1877], p. 605). During the late 19th and the early 20th centuries Mexico City maintained exchange relations with London, Paris, Germany, Antwerp, New York, Havana and – as a new partner – Spain (cf. SWOBODA [1889], p. 626; SWOBODA [1913], p. 744). These statements are confirmed by the exchange rate quotations on London, Paris, Hamburg, Madrid, New York and Havana (quoted only in 1900 and in 1906) presented here, which were completed by quotations on Italy (since 1906) and even some quotations on Vienna (in the summer and autumn of 1906).

Bills on London and New York were traded most often, whereas bills from abroad on Mexico were drawn rather seldom (SONNDORFER [1900], p. 221). In addition to this, 31 domestic places were quoted in per cent premium or discount in Mexico City – as it was usual in Madrid (see p. 308). Among these domestic places only Vera Cruz, Colima, Guaymas and Guadalajara were probably also of a certain relevance as exchange places with some international quotations (NOBACK [1877], p. 605; NELKENBRECHER [1890], pp. 211, 433, 624). Thus both Vera Cruz as the country's most important port and Mexico City have been relevant to all cashless payment transactions with Europe for large parts of the 19th century. From the end of the 19th century exchange transactions were increasingly focused on the capital, whereas Vera Cruz became gradually less important and finally even completely adopted the quotations of the capital (SONNDORFER [1900], pp. 220f.).

References: A. P. ANDREW, The End of the Mexican Dollar, *Quarterly Journal of Economics* 18 (1904), pp. 321–353; R. A. HUMPHREYS (ed.), *British Consular Reports on the Trade and Politics of Latin America 1824–1826*, London 1940; John MCMASTER, Aventuras asiáticas del peso mexicano, *Historia Mexicana* 8.3 (31) (1959), pp. 372–399; Richard J. SALVUCCI, The Real Exchange Rate of the Mexican Peso, 1762–1812: A Research Note and Estimates, *Journal of European Economic History* 23 (1994), pp. 131–140; Markus A. DENZEL, Finanzplätze, Wechselkurse und Währungsverhältnisse in Lateinamerika (1808–1914), in *WdW VII*, pp. 1–106, here pp. 55–60.

21.1 Exchange rates of Mexico City

21.1.1 On London, Paris, Hamburg and Madrid

	MEXICO CITY on:			
	London	**Paris**	**Hamburg**	**Madrid**
	per 10 pounds sterling [a]	per 100 francs [b]	per 100 mark [c]	per 100 pesos duros, from 1905 (7) per 100 pesetas [d]
	in Mexican pesos silver, from 1905 (4) in Mexican pesos gold			
1886	64.64 60d/s (6)			
1887	63.78 60d/s (10)			
...				
1899	100.00 3d/s (1)	39.76 3d/s (1)	49.14 3d/s (1)	
1900	100.16 s (12)	39.87 s (12)	49.10 s (12)	140.24 s (12)
1901	103.45 s (12)	41.15 s (12)	50.70 s (12)	125.05 s (12)
1902	114.40 s (9)	45.46 s (9)	55.96 s (9)	161.10 s (9)
1903	122.48 s (6)	48.76 s (6)	59.96 s (6)	182.51 s (6)
1904	105.33 s (12)	41.72 s (12)	51.40 s (12)	151.57 s (12)
1905	98.17 s (12)	39.05 s (12)	48.01 s (12)	149.26/32.21 s (7+5)
1906	96.67 s (12)	38.46 s (12)	47.28 s (12)	34.33 s (12)
1907	97.65 s (12)	38.81 s (12)	47.67 s (12)	34.78 s (12)
1908	97.99 s (12)	39.01 s (12)	47.97 s (12)	34.71 s (12)
1909	98.16 s (12)	38.98 s (12)	47.99 s (12)	35.61 s (12)
1910	97.86 s (12)	38.79 s (12)	47.85 s (12)	36.41 s (12)
1911	97.94 s (12)	38.80 s (12)	47.90 s (12)	36.02 s (12)
1912	98.04 s (12)	38.86 s (12)	47.89 s (12)	36.57 s (12)
1913	115.63 s (12)	45.79 s (12)	56.53 s (12)	42.94 s (12)
1914	152.30 s (7)	60.50 s (7)	74.49 s (7)	57.67 s (7)

[a] Concerning the British currency, see pp. 3–5.
[b] Concerning the French currency, see p. 280.
[c] Concerning the German currency, see p. 197.
[d] Concerning the Spanish currency, see p. 307. 1 peso duro = 5 pesetas.

21.1.2 On Italy, New York and Havana

	MEXICO CITY on:							
	Italy			New York			Havana		
	per 100 Italian lire [a]			per 100 US dollars [b]			per 100 Cuban pesos gold [c]		
	in Mexican pesos silver, from 1905 (4) in Mexican pesos gold								
1900				205.48	s	(12)	199.60	s	(5)
1901				211.77	s	(12)			
1902				234.09	s	(9)			
1903				250.71	s	(6)			
1904				215.17	s	(12)			
1905				201.63	s	(12)			
1906	38.60	s	(12)	199.26	s	(12)	181.45	s	(5)
1907	38.91	s	(12)	200.94	s	(12)			
1908	39.07	s	(12)	201.19	s	(12)			
1909	39.07	s	(12)	201.25	s	(12)			
1910	38.88	s	(12)	201.03	s	(12)			
1911	38.89	s	(12)	201.30	s	(12)			
1912	38.93	s	(12)	201.27	s	(12)			
1913	45.26	s	(12)	237.34	s	(12)			
1914	58.03	s	(7)	311.35	s	(7)			

[a] Concerning the Italian currency, see pp. 108f.

[b] Concerning the US currency, see p. 404.

[c] The Cuban peso gold of 100 centavos was an imaginary unit of account, nominally equal to the old Spansih silver peso, but payable in Spanish onzas de oro, which are fixed here at 17 pesos. So the peso gold was nominally equal to 1.3897 grammes of fine gold (NOBACK [1877], p. 377). The decrease of the exchange rate between 1900 and 1906 was the result of the devaluation of the most important gold coins on Cuba (the so-called 'alfonsino' of 25 pesetas and the 20-francs piece), in which the bills of exchange had to be paid, for about 9% by the US government after the American occupation of the island in 1898 (SWOBODA [1902], p. 267).

ASIA

22
British India (1819–1914)

Exchange markets: Calcutta (1819–1914) and Bombay (1823–1914)

Sources: Calcutta: CHEONG [1973], p. 65 (1819–1821); *Calcutta Gazette or Oriental Advertiser* (1791); *Bombay Courier* (1822–1829); *The Bengal Weekly Messenger*, Calcutta (1825); *Oriental Observer*, Calcutta (1828–1833); *Calcutta Courier* (1832–1839); *Calcutta Weekly Gazette or Civil, Military and Commercial Register* (1840–1843); *Calcutta Courier and Civil, Military and Naval Gazette* (1842); *The Economist*, London (1849–1874, 1885–1896, 1901–1914); *China Mail*, Hong Kong (1857); *Indian Daily News / The Overland Summary of the Indian Daily News, Bengal Hurkarn and Indian Gazette* (1875–1885, 1897–1901) Bombay: *Bombay Courier* (1823–1843); *Bombay Gazette* (1843–1846, 1848–1869; quotations of the Oriental Bank Corporation); *Bombay Times* (1847/48; 1870–1872); *The Economist*, London (1873–1914).

Concordance: *WdW IV*, pp. 233–273

Currency in British India: In the three British presidencies there were three major sorts of silver rupees among the several hundred coins circulating on the Indian subcontinent during the 18th century: the Sicca rupee in Bengal, the Surat or older Bombay rupee in Bombay and the Arcot rupee in Madras. In order to standardize the monetary system in its presidencies, the London directorate of the East India Company fixed the Sicca rupee with a weight of 10.69 grammes of fine silver as the standard monetary unit for all its Indian possessions on April 25th 1806, but for the time being the directorate could not realize this plan. It was not until 1818 that a rupee of the same value as the Sicca rupee of 1806 was introduced, namely the Madras rupee of 16 annas at 12 pies. Additionally, a Bombay rupee of the same value was established in 1824. In contrast to this, the Sicca rupee of 11.40 grammes of fine silver, also of 16 annas at 12 pies, was used as currency unit in Bengal from 1818.

By means of the Act XVII of August 17th 1835 the previous Madras or Bombay rupee was declared the only legal tender in British India from September 1st 1835 as 'Company's rupee' (10.69 grammes of fine silver) of 16 annas at 12 pies. On September 26th 1836 it was officially introduced in Ceylon (confirmed by the Order in Council and Proclamation of June 18th 1869) and on Mauritius (see p. 541) on August 12th 1876 as well; apart from this, its area of circulation gradually also covered British Beludshistan, the mountain districts of Arakan, Northern and Southern Burma and the various semi-autonomous states of Indian rajas, as well as large parts of Eastern Africa. By means of the Act XIII of 1862 the company's rupee – keeping its weight of fine silver – was renamed 'Government rupee', and government paper money was established.

When in the 1870s the fall in silver prices began and the resulting speculations in the 1880s had negative effects on the exchange rate stability, the Government rupee was fixed at the value of 16 pence sterling or the sovereign or pound sterling in gold at the value of 15 Government rupees by means of the Indian Coinage and Paper Currency Act of June 26th 1893. So, the Government rupee was linked to the pound sterling. By the Currency Act of September 15th 1899 the sovereign was declared legal tender in British India. From that time the exchange rate on London was entirely stable. After that, the place of the previous silver standard of India was taken over by a system that combined particular characteristic features of the gold standard (in foreign trade) with the silver standard and bimetallism (in all domestic affairs; MAHLBERG [1920], p. 38; SONNDORFER [1910], p. 338). The official introduction of the gold standard in India in 1910 was then of no further importance for exchange rate movement.

Original quotations at Calcutta and Bombay:

on:	in:	per:
China	shillings and pence sterling	1 Spanish dollar [a]
	from 1837 Company's rupees	100 Spanish or Mexican dollars
	from 1862 Government rupees	100 Spanish or Mexican dollars
Hong Kong	Government rupees	100 Hong Kong dollars
Indian places (Calcutta, Bombay,	per cent premium or discount	100 rupees [b]
Madras)	or annas premium or discount	1 rupee [b]
London	shillings and pence sterling	1 Sicca or Bombay rupee
	from 1835 (9) shillings and pence sterling	1 Company's rupee
	from 1862 shillings and pence sterling	1 Government rupee

[a]   On the basis of the Bombay–London quotation, these rates have been converted for the documentation into rupees per 100 dollars.

[b]   The quotation was always effected on the basis of the rupee, which was customary in the trade of the given financial market at the time of quotation (see table).

Other data from Calcutta available: Bombay, 30d/s (1880–1885); 60d/s (1875–1885) – France, s (1840/41); 6m/s (1875–1879, 1897–1900); 3m/s (1875–1879) – London, 3m/s (1843, 1875–1885, 1897–1900); s (1875–1885, 1897–1900); 6m/s (1878–1882, 1893, 1897–1900); 4m/s (1879–1885) – Réunion, 60d/s (1875/76) – **from Bombay:** Calcutta, 60d/s (1842–1872); s (1844–1847); 30d/s (1848–1872) – London, 1m/s (1837–1864); s (1844–1872); 3m/s (1847–1864) – Madras, s (1844–1872).

Since the 17th century the bill of exchange had been used in the intercontinental cashless payment system between the Indian possessions of the East India Company (EIC) and England, as well as for payment transactions between the presidencies of Bengal (Calcutta), Madras and Bombay itself. Although the quotations for the so-called Company's bills resulting from these transactions can be found in the India Office Records, they have not yet been evaluated because of the great amount of data they cover. Provable since the end of the 18th century, bills on London were supplied and demanded by private persons in the relevant commercial newspapers of Calcutta. For example, bills of exchange with usances between one and 12 months were offered in advertisements of the Bengal Bank and of private brokers in Calcutta for about 9¼ to 10 1/8 Sicca rupees per pound sterling (after conversion) in 1791. Additionally, an exchange relation with the South Chinese port Canton had been developing in connection with the Canton System and the Country Trade in the scope of the EIC since the 1760s, with Calcutta playing the central role on the Indian part of that trading system. So Calcutta became the most important exchange market of the Europeans in India and in Asia as a whole in these decades. In 1811 Kelly wrote that "the business of exchange in India is chiefly carried on between the three Presidencies – namely, Bengal, Madras, and Bombay – which draw on each other at various dates, and mostly in the denomination of money of the place where the bill is to be paid; but as there is always the greatest demand for bills on Bengal, being considered the capital of the English possessions in India, the course of exchange is mostly in favour of that place" (KELLY [1811], p. 136).

When after 1820 the quotation of exchange rates of the metropolises of British India started in English-language newspapers, only the two other capitals of the presidencies were quoted apart from London because the exchange operations within India remained limited to the payment transactions between Calcutta, Bombay and Madras as a matter of priority (KELLY [1821, repr. 1835], vol. II, p. 103). Such quotation lists were not published in English-language newspapers until the 1820s, e.g. those of Madras in the *Bombay Courier* in 1821 (published from the 1790s), those of Calcutta from 1822 and those of Bombay itself from 1823. This result may be regarded as evidence of the fact that exchange operations in these towns also gained importance outside the EIC from this decade onwards, so that the publication of quotation lists became important to merchants and brokers. In around 1820 the pure annual turnover of Company's bills amounted to about 10 million rupees.

Although Calcutta did not have an extensive network of exchange partners during the whole documented period, it remained the most important centre of cashless payment transactions in the whole of British India and, furthermore, in the whole of South Asia. This position was based last but not least on Calcutta's close commercial links with Bengal and Hindustan. During the the first half of the 19th century these transactions were often made cashlessly by means of hoondees (see p. xxiii) and either on British merchants' disposition or in coororation with them. So Calcutta was not only the centre of the cashless payment system of the Europeans in India, but also that of the Bengali merchants, whose network of cashless payment contacts based on hoondees covered Hindustan up to the borders of the Punjab and some towns from the neighbouring Rajputana states and Madhya Pradesh as well as the metropolises of British India in around 1840 (DENZEL [2001], p. 245). Nevertheless, the most important international quotation of Calcutta was that on London, which was simply the most important Asian quotation on a European place around the mid-19th century.

At this time, Madras had already lost much of its former importance; contemporary merchant manuals report that exchange operations in Madras were settled according to quotations of Calcutta, so that Madras no longer showed itself as an independent exchange place of international relevance (cf. e.g. NOBACK [1851], p. 1122).

On the other hand, from the 1830s Bombay advanced to become the second internationally most relevant Indian exchange market: the decline of Poona after 1818 and above all the opening of the overland route in 1835 and, finally, the cotton boom during the American Civil War strengthened its economic position in the western part of India, thereby gaining relevance within the international cashless payment system. The quotations in Bombay were given in the same way and for approximately the same exchange partners as in Calcutta, although this can only be found out by means of merchant manuals due to a lack of other sources. A fundamental difference only arose from and concerned the very early quotations on China (Canton) in Bombay (from 1834 onwards), which did not seem to be necessary for the financial market of Calcutta (before 1875) because of its strong position within Indian–Chinese payment transactions.

According to contemporary merchant manuals, both Indian exchange markets of international importance noted a far higher number of exchange partners during the second part of the 19th century than documented here. Quotations of Calcutta on Paris are given only for the period around 1840 and from the 1870s. Evidence of Mauritius and Réunion as exchange partners of Calcutta can also only be furnished for a short period in the 1870s. On the contrary, in Bombay there are no quotations on Paris available at all (cf. NOBACK [1858], pp. 139, 219). Australia and Berlin/Germany can be documented from Bombay just as infrequently as Shanghai, Japan or Singapore (NOBACK [1877], pp. 170, 387; SWOBODA [1889], p. 666; SWOBODA [1902], p. 440; SPALDING [1918], p. 77; SONNDORFER [1900], p. 244). Especially during the late 19th and the early 20th centuries great Indian newspapers often listed quotations exclusively on London, which, of course, were the most important of all Indian connections in international cashless payment transactions. Other places are frequently recorded only in the quotation lists of brokers or exchange banks, i.e. "branches of the largest Colonial and foreign banks" (SPALDING [1918], pp. 65f.); so, for the period after 1910 there are lists from Calcutta with quotations on London, France, Germany, Hong Kong, Shanghai, Mauritius, Melbourne, Natal and Bombay (MAHLBERG [1920], fig. between p. 48 and p. 49; SWOBODA [1913], p. 667).

In most of the newspapers the central quotation on London was given in a subtly differentiated way in the order of usances and qualities of bills of exchange. Up to 13 different quotations on London were given in Calcutta around 1910, the relatively small differences in their quotation resulting from the variable degree of security of the various categories (cf. NOBACK [1877], pp. 219f.). As a usance there could be given: 'demand' (i.e. payable on demand), (at) sight, 15, 30, 60 and 90 days' or three months', four and six months' sight, and cable transfer (or bank wire) after 1878. After the opening of the Suez Canal in November 1869, the standard usance for bills drawn from India on London had been reduced from six months' sight to four months' sight or six months' date, and this reduction "seems to have come about after 1873" (NISHIMURA [1971], p. 39), although in the documented newspapers quotations for four months sight bills are available only for a few years; Calcutta quoted such exchange rates from July 1879 to July 1885, and Bombay did so from December 1879 to July 1883. The most important sorts of bills in circulation were bank bills, first-class credits or credit bills and documents. The last were meant to be commercial and agency bills, drawn when exporting goods, adding one specimen of the bill of lading and the insurance policy for attestation (SONNDORFER [1918], p. 244; SPALDING [1918], pp. 77–79; NOBACK [1877], pp. 219f.). "Bills on London drawn under first-class bank credits and D/A bills (bills bearing the clause 'documents on acceptance') are usually quoted at about the same rate ... But for D/P paper (bills against which the documents will only be given up on payment), the rate is usually 1/32d. better for three and four months' bills, and 1/16d. better for six months' bills" (SPALDING [1918], p. 79). Treasury bills and navy drafts drawn on the Treasury or on the Admiralty in London were in general not quoted.

Despite its outstanding importance as a trading centre, Bombay was not listed in contemporary merchant manuals as an independent exchange market after the late 19th and the early 20th centuries, although it was still quoted by other Asian financial places. However, the quotations of Bombay and Calcutta as well as the quotations on these financial places only differ marginally from one another, so that both places were increasingly quoted together as 'Calcutta and Bombay' or as 'India': "There is rarely a difference of more than 1 per cent between the Bombay and Bengal rates, but the Bank of Madras rate is often a good deal higher than those of the other Presidency banks" (SPALDING [1918], p. 81). Owing to the standardization of the currencies by the introduction of the company's rupee on September 1ˢᵗ 1835 and the continuing integration of the Indian market, India had gradually consolidated into one money and exchange market in the course of the 19ᵗʰ century. Although Calcutta is mentioned as the more important and greater money and exchange market in general, Bombay could be more important due to seasonal influences, especially in the period when seeds and wheat were exported (MAHLBERG [1920], p. 49). Until World War I Bombay did not just take over or copy the quotations of Calcutta on London. This fact is important because it provides firm evidence of the (limited) independent role of the Bombay exchange market. By the Indian Coinage and Paper Currency Act of June 26ᵗʰ 1893, which linked the (silver) rupee closely to the world reserve currency, the pound sterling (gold), and thus eliminated the consequences of the fluctuations of the silver price in the long term, internal Indian quotations, as can be shown for Calcutta on Bombay and Madras up to the mid-1880s, became obsolete. As the sovereign was declared legal tender in British India in 1899, the London exchange rate was entirely stabilized. Therefore "the rupee–sterling exchange was … the dominating factor in the Bombay or Calcutta exchange with all foreign commercial and financial centres, and was therefore the only exchange in which practical business men felt themselves interested" before World War I (CHABLANI [1932], p. 64).

References: Karl ELLSTÄTTER, *Indiens Silberwährung. Eine wirtschaftsgeschichtliche Studie*, Stuttgart 1894, pp. 1–4, 88–114; Anton ARNOLD, *Das indische Geldwesen unter besonderer Berücksichtigung seiner Reformen seit 1893*, Jena 1906; Robert CHALMERS, *History of Currency in the British Colonies*, London 1893 [repr. Colchester 1972], pp. 336–348; Rudolf SONNDORFER, Die Währungsreformen in Ostasien und Ostafrika, *Zeitschrift für Handelswissenschaft und Handelspraxis* 2/10 (1910), pp. 337–343; William F. SPALDING, *Eastern Exchange, Currency and Finance*, London ²1918, pp. 15–85; Walter MAHLBERG, *Über asiatische Wechselkurse*, Leipzig ²1920, pp. 38–57; Brij NARAIN, Exchange and Prices in India 1873–1924, *Weltwirtschaftliches Archiv (Chronik und Archivalien)* 23 (1926), pp. 247*–272*; Hashmat-Rai Lekharaja CHABLANI, *Indian Currency, Banking and Exchange*, London 1932; Dietmar ROTHERMUND, The Monetary Policy of British Imperialism, *Indian Economic and Social History Review* 7 (1963), pp. 91–107; Shizuya NISHIMURA, *The Decline of Inland Bills of Exchange in the London Money Market 1855–1913*, Cambridge 1971; W. E. CHEONG, China Houses and the Bank of England Crisis of 1825, *Business History* 15 (1973), pp. 56–73; John ADAMS / Robert Craig WEST, Money, Prices, and Economic Development in India, 1861–1895, *Journal of Economic History* 39 (1979), pp. 55–68; Om PRAKASH, The Dutch East India Company and the Economy of Bengal, 1630–1720, Princeton (NJ) 1985; Oskar SCHWARZER / Markus A. DENZEL / Friedrich ZELLFELDER, Ostasiatische, indische und australische Wechselkurse (1800–1914), in *WdW IV*, pp. 1–65, here pp. 42–51; Markus A. DENZEL, Kolonialstädte als Finanzplätze vom 18. Jahrhundert bis 1914. Das asiatische Wechselnetz und seine Anbindung an das europäisch-internationale Zahlungsverkehrssystem, in Horst GRÜNDER / Peter JOHANEK (eds.), *Kolonialstädte – Europäische Enklaven oder Schmelztigel der Kulturen?*, Münster 2001, pp. 225–259.

22.1 Calcutta and Bombay foreign exchange rates

22.1.1 On London, China, Hong Kong and Mauritius

	CALCUTTA on:	BOMBAY on:	
	London [a, b]	London [a, c]	China [d]
	per 10 pounds sterling [e]	per 10 pounds sterling [e]	per 100 Spanish or Mexican dollars [f]
	in Sicca rupees	in Bombay rupees	
1819	*125.00* 6m/s (y)		
1820	*112.50* 6m/s (y)		
1821	*100.00* 6m/s (y)		
1822	94.65 6m/s (4)		
1823	101.48 6m/s (12)	*114.65* 6m/s (8)	
1824	104.55 6m/s (12)	118.21 6m/s (12)	
1825	101.60 6m/s (12)	111.66 6m/s (12)	
1826	98.24 6m/s (12)	110.02 6m/s (12)	
1827	103.12 6m/s (12)	115.22 6m/s (12)	
1828	103.89 6m/s (12)	117.08 6m/s (12)	
1829	104.69 6m/s (11)	117.08 6m/s (12)	
1830	104.27 6m/s (12)	116.96 6m/s (12)	
1831	105.22 6m/s (11)	114.40 6m/s (12)	
1832	106.43 6m/s (11)	114.29 6m/s (12)	
1833	105.95 6m/s (12)	113.62 6m/s (12)	
1834	91.85 6m/s (12)	107.98 6m/s (12)	202.09 60d/s (2)
1835	93.81 6m/s (12)	102.51 6m/s (12)	200.00 60d/s (4)
		in Company's rupees [g]	
1836	91.33 6m/s (12)	98.22 6m/s (12)	
1837	90.67 6m/s (12)	98.58 6m/s (10)	218.25 60d/s (3)
1838	94.22 6m/s (12)	98.47 6m/s (1)	
1839	97.48 6m/s (12)	95.92 6m/s (10)	207.80 60d/s (10)
1840	99.94 6m/s (12)	97.02 6m/s (11)	207.46 60d/s (11)
1841	96.52 6m/s (12)	97.90 6m/s (12)	208.00 60d/s (12)
1842	92.31 6m/s (2)	96.86 6m/s (12)	207.96 60d/s (12)
1843	103.24 6m/s (11)	101.23 6m/s (10)	211.12 60d/s (9)
1844		106.19 6m/s (12)	216.37 60d/s (11)
1845		107.66 6m/s (10)	219.13 60d/s (4)
1846		100.60 6m/s (12)	208.80 60d/s (5)
1847	101.27 6m/s (6)	102.37 6m/s (11)	209.34 60d/s (9)
1848	106.37 6m/s (8)	109.16 6m/s (12)	207.52 60d/s (12)
1849	107.99 6m/s (5)	107.21 6m/s (12)	209.30 60d/s (12)
1850	97.69 6m/s (12)	98.67 6m/s (12)	213.46 60d/s (12)
1851	94.08 6m/s (12)	95.70 6m/s (12)	218.13 60d/s (12)

	CALCUTTA on:	BOMBAY on:			CALCUTTA on:
	London [h]	London [h]	China		Mauritius
	per 10 pounds sterling [e]	per 10 pounds sterling [e]	per 100 Mexican dollar, from 1875 per 100 Hong Kong dollars [f]		per 100 Government rupees [i]
	in Company's rupees, from 1862 in Government rupees				
1852	97.65 6m/s (12)	98.89 6m/s (12)	218.80 60d/s (12)		
1853	95.72 6m/s (12)	97.07 6m/s (12)	231.34 60d/s (12)		
1854	99.46 6m/s (11)	100.06 6m/s (12)	233.92 60d/s (12)		
1855	94.49 6m/s (12)	96.28 6m/s (12)	222.21 60d/s (12)		
1856	93.08 6m/s (12)	94.92 6m/s (12)	221.92 60d/s (12)		
1857	91.55 6m/s (12)	93.63 6m/s (12)	219.09 60d/s (12)		
1858	96.64 6m/s (12)	97.55 6m/s (12)	217.50 60d/s (12)		
1859	96.63 6m/s (12)	95.09 6m/s (12)			
1860	96.78 6m/s (12)	97.17 6m/s (12)	223.57 60d/s (12)		
1861	96.52 6m/s (12)	96.49 6m/s (12)	215.59 60d/s (12)		
1862	97.83 6m/s (12)	98.03 6m/s (12)	217.86 60d/s (12)		
1863	97.13 6m/s (12)	97.26 6m/s (12)	223.92 60d/s (12)		
1864	94.26 6m/s (12)	95.51 6m/s (12)	224.00 60d/s (12)		
1865	96.78 6m/s (12)	97.48 6m/s (12)	214.00 60d/s (12)		
1866	96.50 6m/s (12)	97.05 6m/s (12)	213.50 60d/s (12)		
1867	101.43 6m/s (12)	101.93 6m/s (12)	218.17 60d/s (12)		
1868	102.32 6m/s (12)	102.82 6m/s (12)	217.80 60d/s (12)		
1869	100.54 6m/s (12)	100.42 6m/s (12)	221.75 60d/s (12)		
1870	103.44 6m/s (11)	103.31 6m/s (12)	224.86 60d/s (12)		
1871	102.61 6m/s (10)	103.96 6m/s (12)	223.59 60d/s (12)		
1872	102.32 6m/s (11)	101.84 6m/s (12)	222.67 60d/s (9)		
1873	104.93 6m/s (12)	104.64 6m/s (12)	CALCUTTA on:		
1874	105.32 6m/s (12)	104.76 6m/s (12)	Hong Kong		
1875	108.54 6m/s (12)	107.68 6m/s (9)	219.63 60d/s (6)	95.84 60d/s (6)	
1876	115.86 6m/s (12)	115.61 6m/s (10)	223.85 60d/s (10)	95.42 60d/s (12)	
1877	111.99 6m/s (12)	112.39 6m/s (12)	223.44 60d/s (12)	94.71 60d/s (12)	
1878	119.55 t.t. (10)	116.61 t.t. (12)	222.42 60d/s (12)	97.34 60d/s (11)	
1879	125.72 t.t. (6)	119.87 t.t. (11)	218.98 60d/s (10)	96.85 60d/s (12)	
1880	120.50 t.t. (11)	118.53 4m/s (10)	222.89 60d/s (12)		
1881	121.59 t.t. (12)	120.67 4m/s (12)	222.80 60d/s (12)		
1882	120.17 t.t. (12)	120.13 4m/s (12)	221.00 60d/s (12)		
1883	124.39 t.t. (12)	123.38 t.t. (8)	223.34 60d/s (12)		
1884	123.30 t.t. (12)	122.86 t.t. (12)	222.00 60d/s (12)		
1885	128.47 t.t. (12)	128.39 t.t. (12)	222.15 60d/s (7)		
1886	138.31 t.t. (12)	138.34 t.t. (12)			
1887	140.26 t.t. (12)	140.41 t.t. (12)			
1888	146.39 t.t. (12)	146.30 t.t. (12)			

	CALCUTTA on:			BOMBAY on:			CALCUTTA on:		
	London [h]			**London** [h]			**Hong Kong**		
	per 10 pounds sterling [e]			per 10 pounds sterling [e]			per 100 Hong Kong dollars [f]		
	in Government rupees								
1889	145.98	t.t.	(12)	146.10	t.t.	(12)			
1890	132.42	t.t.	(12)	132.40	t.t.	(12)			
1891	139.60	t.t.	(12)	140.35	t.t.	(11)			
1892	157.20	t.t.	(12)	158.01	t.t.	(12)			
1893	160.29	t.t.	(12)	160.44	t.t.	(12)			
1894	178.75	t.t.	(12)	177.74	t.t.	(12)			
1895	181.16	t.t.	(12)	180.94	t.t.	(12)			
1896	168.20	t.t.	(12)	168.20	t.t.	(12)			
1897	156.42	t.t.	(12)	158.81	t.t.	(12)	146.93	60d/s	(7)
1898	151.02	t.t.	(12)	151.52	t.t.	(12)	141.38	60d/s	(8)
1899	150.13	t.t.	(12)	149.82	t.t.	(12)	144.42	60d/s	(12)
1900	150.50	t.t.	(12)	150.16	t.t.	(12)	142.82	60d/s	(4)
1901	150.45	t.t.	(12)	150.45	t.t.	(12)			
1902	150.33	t.t.	(12)	150.30	t.t.	(12)			
1903	149.10	t.t.	(12)	149.80	t.t.	(12)			
1904	149.60	t.t.	(12)	149.64	t.t.	(12)			
1905	149.72	t.t.	(12)	149.79	t.t.	(12)			
1906	149.60	t.t.	(12)	149.62	t.t.	(12)			
1907	149.52	t.t.	(12)	149.57	t.t.	(12)			
1908	151.91	t.t.	(11)	151.24	t.t.	(12)			
1909	150.40	t.t.	(12)	150.48	t.t.	(12)			
1910	149.74	t.t.	(11)	149.72	t.t.	(11)			
1911	149.55	t.t.	(12)	149.60	t.t.	(12)			
1912	149.45	t.t.	(12)	149.47	t.t.	(12)			
1913	149.69	t.t.	(12)	149.74	t.t.	(12)			
1914	149.76	t.t.	(7)	149.80	t.t.	(7)			

[a] "Imports from India had been drawn for by 10 months' date bills before 1847; since then the usance had been reduced to six months' sight (equal to eight months' date)"; Nishimura [1971], p. 36.

[b] 1819–1821 purchasing rates of Bengal bills on London.

[c] In 1823 Bombay quoted London in older Bombay or Surat rupees.

[d] 1834–1843 quotation for Canton, afterwards for 'China'.

[e] Concerning the British currency, see pp. 3–5.

[f] Concerning the Chinese currencies, see pp. 507f.

[g] Although the Company's rupee was introduced on September 1st 1835, the change in currency is not noticeable in the quotations before the beginning of 1836.

[h] In the quotations from the London *Economist* (Calcutta on London: 1885–1896 and 1901–1914; Bombay on London: 1873–1914) we can find the following remark: "Exchange banks in London

all quote cash rates for telegraphic transfers based on the daily cable quotations received from their Indian branches, and as a rule the London price will be from 1/32d. to 1/8d. over the Indian rates" (SPALDING [1918], p. 80). In February 1895 the Government rupee reached its low at 18.96 rupees per pound sterling.

[i] Concerning the currency on Mauritius, see p. 555.

22.2 Calcutta and Bombay domestic exchange rates

	BOMBAY on:		CALCUTTA on:	
	Calcutta [a]	**Madras** [a]	**Bombay** [b]	**Madras**
	per 100 Sicca rupees, from 1837 (5) per 100 Company's rupees	per 100 Madras rupees, from 1835 (12) per 100 Company's rupees	per 100 Bombay rupees, from 1836 per 100 Company's rupees	per 100 Madras rupees, from 1836 per 100 Company's rupees
	in Bombay rupees		**in Sicca rupees**	
1822			*92.00* 30d/s (4)	96.75 30d/s (4)
1823	*105.00* 30d/s (8)	*99.00* 30d/s (8)	92.00 30d/s (12)	96.00 30d/s (12)
1824	103.50 30d/s (12)	99.09 30d/s (12)	92.14 30d/s (11)	96.00 30d/s (11)
1825	102.46 30d/s (12)	98.00 30d/s (12)	95.37 30d/s (11)	95.55 30d/s (11)
1826	103.00 30d/s (12)	98.50 30d/s (12)	98.00 30d/s (12)	94.00 30d/s (12)
1827	105.48 30d/s (12)	99.47 30d/s (12)	98.00 30d/s (12)	93.67 30d/s (12)
1828	105.58 30d/s (12)	99.17 30d/s (12)	97.47 30d/s (9)	91.50 30d/s (9)
1829	108.35 30d/s (12)	100.73 30d/s (12)	98.00 30d/s (4)	88.63 30d/s (4)
1830	108.15 30d/s (12)	101.09 30d/s (12)	93.05 30d/s (12)	91.17 30d/s (12)
1831	106.46 30d/s (12)	101.00 30d/s (12)	94.59 30d/s (11)	94.59 30d/s (11)
1832	105.85 30d/s (12)	100.27 30d/s (12)	94.50 30d/s (10)	94.50 30d/s (10)
1833	106.25 30d/s (12)	101.38 30d/s (12)	94.50 30d/s (2)	94.50 30d/s (2)
1834	106.61 30d/s (12)	101.73 30d/s (12)		
1835	108.17 30d/s (12)	103.10/102.75 30d/s (11+1)		
	in Company's rupees			
1836	107.71 30d/s (12)	102.50 30d/s (12)		
1837	105.81/101.47 30d/s (4+8)	99.58 30d/s (12)		
1838	102.18 30d/s (12)	99.82 30d/s (12)		
1839	101.69 30d/s (12)	100.52 30d/s (12)		
1840	99.56 30d/s (12)	99.63 30d/s (11)	98.93 30d/s (11)	99.83 30d/s (11)
1841	99.30 30d/s (12)	99.33 30d/s (12)	98.68 30d/s (7)	99.72 30d/s (7)
1842	98.22 30d/s (12)	99.00 30d/s (12)		
1843	99.81 30d/s (8)	99.67 30d/s (10)		
1844	100.89 30d/s (10)	100.52 30d/s (10)		
1845	99.84 30d/s (3)	99.64 30d/s (9)		
1846	99.01 30d/s (8)	98.88 30d/s (4)		
1847	99.56 30d/s (7)	99.38 30d/s (9)		
1848	100.43 s (12)	98.84 30d/s (12)		
1849	100.50 s (12)	99.84 30d/s (12)		
1850	99.59 s (12)	99.52 30d/s (11)		
1851	100.34 s (12)	99.56 30d/s (7)		
1852	100.81 s (12)	100.17 30d/s (12)		
1853	99.81 s (12)	99.87 30d/s (12)		
1854	99.66 s (12)	99.23 30d/s (9)		
1855	100.00 s (12)	99.32 30d/s (10)		

	BOMBAY on:		CALCUTTA on:	
	Calcutta	**Madras**	**Bombay**	**Madras**
	per 100 Company's rupees, from 1862 per 100 Government rupees			
	in Company's rupees, from 1862 in Government rupees			
1856	99.95 s (12)	99.21 30d/s (11)		
1857	100.04 s (12)	99.59 30d/s (11)		
1858	101.06 s (12)	99.36 30d/s (12)		
1859				
1860	100.99 s (11)	99.45 30d/s (12)		
1861	100.07 s (12)	99.19 30d/s (12)		
1862	100.22 s (12)	99.63 30d/s (12)		
1863	99.37 s (12)	99.11 30d/s (12)		
1864	100.75 s (12)	99.74 30d/s (12)		
1865	100.87 s (12)	99.81 30d/s (12)		
1866	100.33 s (12)	99.00 30d/s (12)		
1867	100.39 s (12)	99.00 30d/s (12)		
1868	99.54 s (12)	99.17 30d/s (3)		
1869	100.09 s (12)	98.98 30d/s (12)		
1870	100.14 s (12)	99.30 30d/s (11)		
1871	100.29 s (12)	99.57 30d/s (12)		
1872	100.16 s (9)	99.25 30d/s (9)		
1873				
1874				
1875			100.12 s (6)	
1876			100.04 s (12)	
1877			99.69 s (11)	99.38 s (2)
1878			99.85 s (10)	99.39 s (2)
1879			99.91 s (10)	100.00 s (1)
1880			100.01 s (12)	100.01 s (12)
1881			100.06 s (12)	100.05 s (12)
1882			100.04 s (12)	100.00 s (12)
1883			99.97 s (12)	100.00 s (7)
1884			99.99 s (12)	
1885			100.00 s (7)	100.00 s (6)

[a] In 1823 Bombay quoted Calcutta and Madras in older Bombay or Surat rupees.

[b] In 1822 and 1823 Calcutta quoted Bombay per older Bombay or Surat rupees.

23
China (1764–1914)

Exchange market: Canton (1764–1856)

Sources: MORSE [1926], vol. II–V (1764–1824); CHEONG [1979], pp. 96, 102 (1811, 1813, 1819–1827); *Canton General Price Current* (1827–1839); *Commercial Price Current*, Canton (1835–1836); *The Course of Exchange*, London (1847); *Overland Register and Price Current*, Hong Kong (1848–1856); *China Mail*, Hong Kong (1848–1856).
Concordance (from 1819): *WdW IV*, pp. 89–95

Currency at Canton: Since the beginning of the Chinese–European trade in Canton, the Spanish dollar, which had been known on the Chinese coast since the early 16th century, functioned as the most important means of payment and clearing unit. Therefore the Spanish dollar was the basis for all exchange rate quotations in Canton in the 18th and early 19th centuries. At the beginning of the 19th century Chinese traders particularly liked to accept the Spanish dollars of Charles III (King of Spain 1759–1788) and Charles IV (King of Spain 1788–1808), the so-called Carolus dollar (minted until 1808), and paid a premium of 4% to 15% for it, sometimes even 30% (SPALDING [1918], pp. 329f.). In contrast to this, the dollar of Ferdinand VII (King of Spain 1808 and 1813–1833) was traded at par whereas the Mexican and 'Republican' (South American) dollars, minted since the 1820s, were quoted with a discount of 3% to 7%. As in Hong Kong the Mexican dollar became the standard dollar coin in Canton in around 1853/54 (see p. 494).

Original quotations at Canton

on:	in:	per:
Bombay	Bombay rupees	1 Spanish (or Mexican) dollar
	from 1835 (9) Company's rupees	1 Spanish (or Mexican) dollar
Calcutta	current rupees [a]	1 Spanish dollar
	from 1816 Sicca rupees	1 Spanish dollar
	from 1835 (9) Company's rupees	1 Spanish (or Mexican) dollar
London	shillings and pence sterling	1 Spanish (or Mexican) dollar
Madras	shillings and pence sterling	1 Spanish (or Mexican) dollar

[a] 10 current rupees = 9 Sicca rupees

Exchange market: Hong Kong (1844–1914)

Sources: PRO London, CO 133: *Books of the Colony of Hong Kong*, vols. 2–4 (1844–1846); *Overland Register and Price Current*, Hong Kong (1846–1861); *China Mail*, Hong Kong (1848–1858, 1863–1888, 1901–1904); *China Overland Trade Reporter*, Hong Kong (1858–1871, 1878–1888); *Hong Kong Daily Press* (1889–1896, 1908–1912); *Hong Kong Telegraph* (1897–1908, 1912–1914).
Concordance: *WdW IV*, pp. 97–147

Currency at Hong Kong: Based on the model of Canton, the Spanish, Mexican and other Republican dollars were introduced as the "standard in all Government and mercantile transactions at Hong Kong" (SPALDING [1918], p. 293) on April 27th 1842. So the dollar and not the pound sterling became the standard coin unit of the British possession as well as of the merchants in its Chinese hinterland. "For all practical purposes the currency of Hong Kong from 1845 to 1863 was de facto identical to that of Canton" (KING [1965], p. 138), 717 Canton taels being equal to 1,000 dollars. This decree from 1842 was withdrawn on November 28th 1844 by means of a Royal Proclamation, and British silver tokens were introduced as nominal standard, the rate of the circulating dollars being fixed at 4 shillings 2 pence sterling. Nevertheless, all payments apart from those of the government continued to be made in dollars. "In course of time the Mexican dollar became the recognised standard coin of the Colony" (SPALDING [1918], p. 294) and "the sole instrument and medium of exchange" (CHALMERS [1893], p. 373) in Hong Kong as well as in the other treaty ports (except Shanghai), particularly because the Royal Proclamation of 1844 was actually cancelled by a decision of the Colonial Chief Justice in 1854.

When in the early 1850s the number of Spanish dollars was insufficient to fit the needs of the quickly growing trade, the Mexican dollar became the predominant coin of the colony in around 1853/54. After the gold discoveries in Australia (1852), the gold standard on the basis of the British sovereign was established on April 27th 1853 for October 1st 1853, but only nominally because the silver coins remained the currency in the colony. On January 9th 1863 a further Royal Proclamation (published on May 2nd 1863) fixed the Mexican dollar and every other dollar of equal value as the colony's legal tender at an unlimited level. "Thus, Hong Kong was finally and formally recognized as being outside the currency area of Great Britain" (ibid., p. 374). But Hong Kong did not belong to the Chinese currency area, either. Although it used the precious metal silver, the means of payment used in China, it did not use it in the 'tael' unit of weight, but in the dollar unit. "As local feeling, especially among bankers, was strongly in favour of the policy of having a British dollar, and as the establishment of Branch Mints in the colonies had already been agreed to by the Imperial Government in the case of New South Wales, the Colony of Hong Kong decided to establish a local Mint to coin a British dollar" (ibid., p. 375). On September 14th 1866 this Hong Kong dollar of 100 cents became legal tender in addition to the Mexican dollar, and on October 20th 1866 its weight and its fineness were fixed in accordance with the Mexican dollar (24.26 grammes of fine silver). Nevertheless, the Mexican dollar was quoted with a premium in comparison with the new Hong Kong dollar during the following decades until the merchants on the Chinese mainland had accustomed themselves to the new coin and accepted it as equal to the Mexican dollar:

Hong Kong dollars per 100 Mexican dollars

1867	101.95	1871	no data	1875	100.75	1879	100.75
1868	101.02	1872	104.13	1876	104.00		
1869	100.36	1873	101.99	1877	101.55		
1870	100.29	1874	101.07	1878	101.11		

Source: WdW IV, pp. 144f.

On October 21st 1866 the Chinese practice of 'chopping' ('sealing') the dollar was officially accepted, because "no Chinaman will take back a dollar on which his stamp cannot be pointed out, though by the multitude of successive stamps a chopped dollar not only looses its 'ring', but gradually becomes so obliterated that any individual stamp cannot be distinguished in one case out of a hundred" (CHALMERS [1893], p. 378). With the Coin Act of February 2nd 1895 the silver standard with the Mexican dollar and the Hong Kong dollar (now also called the 'New British dollar') was fixed in Hong Kong as the standard coin unit. This New British dollar was nothing other than a remake of the Hong Kong dollar of 1866.

Original quotations at Hong Kong

on:	in:	per:
Bangkok	Hong Kong dollars	100 ticals
Batavia	Dutch guilders	100 Hong Kong dollars
Berlin	mark	100 Hong Kong dollars
Calcutta & Bombay	Company's rupees	100 Spanish or Mexican dollars
from 1863	Government rupees	100 Mexican dollars
from 1866 (10)	Government rupees	100 Hong Kong dollars
Hankow	per cent premium on 100 Mexican dollars	100 Hong Kong dollars
London	shillings and pence sterling	1 Spanish (or Mexican) dollar
from 1866 (10)	shillings and pence sterling	1 Hong Kong dollar
Manila	% premium	1 Spanish peso (gold)
from 1908 (9)	Philippine pesos gold	100 Hong Kong dollars
New York	US dollars	100 Hong Kong dollars
Paris	francs	100 Hong Kong dollars
Saigon	piastres trésor	100 Hong Kong dollars
Shanghai	Shanghai taels	100 Hong Kong dollars
Singapore	per cent premium or discount	1 Mexican dollar in Singapore
from 1905	per cent premium	1 Straits Settlements dollar
from 1908 (8)	Straits Settlements dollars	100 Hong Kong dollars
Sydney & Melbourne	shillings and pence sterling	1 Hong Kong dollar
from 1911	shillings and pence of Australia	1 Hong Kong dollar
Yokohama	per cent premium or discount	1 Mexican dollar or yen
from 1903	yen	100 Hong Kong dollars

For a detailed explanation of the Hong Kong exchange rate currents see SPALDING [1918], pp. 302–304.

Other data available: Berlin, 4m/s (1904–1914) – Calcutta and Bombay, s (1879–1914) – London, 6m/s (1904–1908; 1912–1914, credit bills); 4m/s (1879–1914; 1908–1914, credit bills as well as documentary bills); 30d/s (1876–1914); 60 d/s (1912–1914); s (1876–1914) – New York, 60d/s (1886–1908); 4m/s (1887–1908); 30d/s (1904–1908); s (1912–1914) – Paris, 4m/s (1886–1914, credit bills and partially bank bills); 6m/s (1904–1908); dem (1912–1914) – Shanghai, 30d/s (1875–1914).

Exchange market: Shanghai (1848–1914)

Sources: *China Mail*, Hong Kong (1848–1857, 1863–1866); *Overland Register and Price Current*, Hong Kong (1849–1861); *China Overland Trade Reporter*, Hong Kong (1860–1861); *Daily Shipping and Commercial News*, Shanghai (1862); *North China Daily News*, Shanghai (1869–1879, 1889–1893); *The Economist*, London (1869–1914).

Concordance: *WdW IV*, pp. 149–166

Currency at Shanghai: Unlike in Hong Kong or in other Treaty Ports, all merchants – even the European ones – used a money of account in Shanghai, as in large parts of China during the whole period of documentation. The standard unit of account of the local silver currency was the Shanghai tael or liang. Its fine weight (33.92 grammes of fine silver) resulted from the so-called Haikwan tael (37.783 grammes of fine silver) (cf. SWOBODA [1902], p. 234: c. 35.82 grammes of fine silver). By the treaties of 1858 this Haikwan tael, which was used in the maritime customs office, became a kind of official 'Government tael', 100 Haikwan taels being equal to 111.40 Shanghai taels (in around 1910: 100 Shanghai taels = 97 Haikwan taels; SWOBODA [1913], p. 671). "In the course of time, principally with the development of modern-style Chinese banks in the twentieth century, the tael system in Shanghai was modified in practice until it became similar to that of the modern European bullion standard" (KING [1965], p. 174). Every single exchange rate quotation at Shanghai was made on the basis of the tael, whereas the circulating currency consisted mainly of Mexican dollars and sycee silver – silver bars in the form of shoes – during the whole period of documentation (SWOBODA [1902], p. 234).

Haikwan taels per 100 pounds sterling

1871	307.69	1882	350.37	1893	507.94	1904	697.67
1872	300.94	1883	356.88	1894	625.41	1905	665.51
1873	311.69	1884	358.21	1895	611.47	1906	607.60
1874	315.27	1885	377.95	1896	600.00	1907	615.38
1875	323.45	1886	399.17	1897	671.33	1908	750.00
1876	336.13	1887	412.02	1898	693.14	1909	769.54
1877	333.33	1888	425.72	1899	664.34	1910	742.75
1878	334.49	1889	422.91	1900	644.30	1911	744.19
1879	356.44	1890	385.54	1901	674.87	1912	655.29
1880	344.70	1891	406.78	1902	769.23	1913	662.07
1881	360.90	1892	459.33	1903	757.89	1914	732.83

Source: REMER [1967], p. 250 (table 6)

Original quotations at Shanghai

on:	in:	per:
Calcutta	Company's rupees	100 Shanghai taels
	from 1862 Government rupees	100 Shanghai taels
Canton	Shanghai taels	100 Spanish or Mexican dollars
Hong Kong	Shanghai taels	100 Mexican dollars
	from 1866 (10) Shanghai taels	100 Hong Kong dollars
London	shillings and pence sterling	1 Shanghai tael
Paris	francs	1 Shanghai tael

For a detailed explanation of the Shanghai exchange rate currents see SPALDING [1918], pp. 353–355.

Other data available: Bombay, 3d/s (1855–1879) – Germany, 4m/s (1889–1893); s (1889–1893); t.t. (1890–1893) – London, s (1862–1893); t.t. (1878–1893) – Paris, s (1890–1893) – New York, 4m/s (1889–1893); s (1890–1893).

Exchange market: Tientsin (1898–1914)

Source: HO [1928], pp. 5–19

Concordance: *WdW V*, pp. 209–216

Currency at Tientsin: In Tientsin the exchange rate quotations were based on the local tael, the Tientsin tael (nominally 35.29 grammes of fine silver). According to the Russian–Chinese Bank the Tientsin tael corresponded to 0.9786 Shanghai taels whereas the Chinese Bureau of Economic Information fixed the Tientsin tael at 1.0530 Shanghai taels in its *Weekly Bulletin* of 1924. All available data about the value of the Tientsin tael are guidelines, which did not claim to be absolutely reliable even at that time (KANN [1928], pp. 84–86).

Original quotations at Tientsin

on:	in:	per:
Japan	Tientsin taels	100 yen
London	shillings and pence sterling	1 Tientsin tael
New York	Tientsin taels	100 US dollars
Paris	francs	1 Tientsin tael

The exchange transactions of European merchants in China developed together with the Canton System and the Country Trade in interrelation with the triangular trade between India, Canton and England of the East India Company, their partners and competitors. After the East India Company in Canton had, for the first time, drawn a bill on London in November 1761, Canton, the only treaty port for the Chinese–European trade until the first half of the 19th century, also became the only exchange market in China for the time being (DERMIGNY [1964], vol. II, p. 762). Since the 1760s the bills issued by the East India Company, the so-called Company's bills, gained increasing importance with regard to the payment transactions between China on the one hand and London or India on the other. This importance was intensified when the silver deliveries from Europe to Asia stopped, owing to the independence of the Spanish colonies in America (ibid., vol. II, pp. 692–694, 763–767). At the same time, there was a constantly growing need for means of payment in the course of the rapidly increasing trade in opium. The "sale of bills seems to have been the most important source of silver after it was once established" (REMER [1967], p. 23), but "the terms on which the Company's Bills were issued were often disadvantageous in point of 'sight' and rate of exchange" (GREENBERG [1951], p. 157) because the usance was regularly two years after sight.

Annual exchange rates of Canton on London are already available for the years 1764/65 and regularly from the 1770s, as well as on Bengal occasionally from 1773 and regularly from 1796. While Calcutta later appeared to be the central contact place between Canton and India, regular quotations of Canton on Bombay do not start until 1827/31, while those on Madras are limited to the years from 1834 to 1837. Above all, US bills on London began to complete the constantly restricted means of payment of the East India Company from 1826 (CHEONG [1965], pp. 39–45). So "the bills of J.J. Astor and Stephen Girard of Philadelphia, or those drawn under letter of credit from Baring Bros. and half-a-dozen other London houses, were always negotiable in Canton" (GREENBERG [1951], p. 163). Simultaneously, the growing European trade via Singapore had an influence on the exchange rates; in particular the company constantly limited the issuing of bills on London. Between the credit crisis in Calcutta (1829–1834) and the breakdown of important US firms during the American financial crisis of 1837, US bills on London, in turn guaranteed primarily by Baring Brothers, were used on a large scale in Canton (ibid., pp. 160–164).

The central part Canton played in the cashless payment transactions between China on the one hand and Europe (London) and India on the other was gradually superseded by the colony of Victoria on the Island of Hong Kong off Canton, British since the Treaty of Nanking (1842), which became the most important trading centre of South China and the main store for opium in the second half of the 19th century. As early as 1844 Hong Kong quoted exchange rates on London and Calcutta as well as on Bombay from 1846, whereas Canton exchange rate currents were no longer published in the English-language newspapers of the region after 1856 – probably in the wake of the Taiping Revolt (1850–1864) and of the shift of the European trade with China to Shanghai. In this process of separation Hong Kong adopted Canton's way of quoting and took over its network of exchange partners.

In Hong Kong the exchange rate currents were completed in the 1860s by Shanghai (from 1863) and above all in the 1880s and the 1890s by Paris and New York (from 1886), Hamburg (1889) and Berlin (from 1889), Singapore, Yokohama and Manila (from 1893). In 1863 one can also find single quotations on Paris, Amsterdam and Australia. According to contemporary merchant manuals, direct exchange relations are, however, supposed to have already existed (e.g. NOBACK [1877], pp. 383f.). In the first decade of the 20th century this tendency towards constantly closer interconnections within the Asian-Pacific area was intensified by the admission of the 'new' exchange places San Francisco, Batavia, Sydney and Melbourne (from 1904), Saigon, Bangkok and Hankow (from 1908) to the exchange rate currents of Hong Kong. This might have been a reaction to the fact that the branch network of the Hongkong Bank and the Hongkong & Shanghai Banking Corporation respectively, the fourth biggest bank in the world which had attracted a large part of the East Asian business, had expanded into the Asian, European and North American area. Especially when the quotation on the German Empire started in 1889, there was an unmistakably direct temporal connection with the opening of a branch of the bank in Hamburg in the same year (KING [1983], pp. 522f.). So, in the years before World War I Hong Kong maintained relationships with the most important financial places of Europe, India, the USA and the up-and-coming exchange places of the East Asian area. It had by far the largest network of exchange contacts among all places of East and South East Asia, and could therefore be regarded as the most important exchange market of China and the whole East Asia.

A few years after the opening of the treaty port of Shanghai, according to contemporary merchant manuals, the most important Chinese trading city after the Taiping Revolt became the centre of new trade with Japan and the Yangtze ports as far as Hankow after 1860. Quotations on European and Asian exchange places started at Shanghai as well, for instance that on London as early as 1848, followed by that on Canton in 1849/52 and on Hong Kong in 1856, on Calcutta in 1850 and on Bombay in 1855. Among the European markets, Paris joined the network at the end of the 1860s and Germany did so a little bit later. Apart from this, the quotation on New York started in the late 1880s. The fact that Shanghai's quotations are available only fragmentarily from the 1880s (except those on London), and that they even discontinue after 1893, can be put down to the fact that relevant sources for these periods have not yet been found. Only the quotation on London is (almost) completely available until World War I because it was published regularly in the London *Economist* after 1869. According to the exchange rate currents published in the merchant manuals, Shanghai, which was called the main trading centre of China, quoted London, France,

Germany, Hong Kong, India (Calcutta and Bombay), New York, Japan und Batavia until 1914. "Most of the banks in Shanghai also quote rates for demand bills drawn on Hankow, Peking, Tientsin, and places in Manchuria, Dalny (Dairen), Harbin, etc., the quotations in each case being given in dollars local currency in exchange for taels Shanghai currency" (SPALDING [1918], p. 355). Altogether, Shanghai had clearly fewer quotations, especially for the Asian–Pacific area, than Hong Kong, although it had been not only the financial centre of Middle China with the Yangtze valley and the territories north of it (until Tientsin became important in around 1910). This is why Shanghai was regarded as an internationally important exchange market, but it was also the most important one with regard to transactions with Japan, as the geographically closest place to China and to the whole of East Asia (BASTER [1934], p. 145).

In the last decades of the 19th century the north of China had become increasingly important for international trade and finance as well. The treaty port Tientsin near the capital Peking (now Beijing) became the economic centre and financial place of this area, and at the beginning of the 20th century it became the third internationally important exchange place after Hong Kong and Shanghai (MAHLBERG [1920], p. 93). The exchange rates on London, Paris, Japan and New York quoted there by the Hongkong & Shanghai Banking Corporation are available from 1898. In addition to this, Germany is supposed to have been quoted before World War I, and the Russian chervonets (gold bullion coins) had entered the market shortly before, but the volume of transaction was too insignificant (HO [1928], p. 2). Apart from that, private exchange rate currents, published in contemporary merchant manuals, list quotations on Shanghai and Hong Kong (cf. SWOBODA [1913], p. 683).

That Hong Kong occupied the highest position among the three Chinese exchange markets of international importance before World War I was owing to the different currency systems serving as the basis for quoting: all Chinese exchange places had the silver standard, which is why the price of silver at London as the world's most important market for precious metals had an outstanding and fundamental importance for all quotations, and the exchange rates at the Chinese financial places perfectly reflect the trend of the silver prices (MAHLBERG [1920], pp. 104ss.; SPALDING [1918], pp. 348ss.). Nevertheless, compared to the price of silver, the quotation of the telegraphic transfer in Hong Kong was without exception much higher than in Shanghai (or in Tientsin). So, for European merchants, bills of exchange in Hong Kong were significantly cheaper than those in Shanghai, so that in order to get 100 pounds sterling in London, one needed comparatively more units of silver bullion in Shanghai than one needed silver dollars in Hong Kong. So the minted dollar coin in Hong Kong had a certain advantage – or certain premium – over silver bullion used for transactions in Shanghai and in Tientsin (MAHLBERG [1920], p. 101).

From the 1880s the telegraphic transfer had gained acceptance, when, despite the continuous resistance of the banks (VINNAI [1971], p. 177), the fixing of the rates at all Chinese exchange markets was done by the local banks on the basis of the silver prices at London transmitted via cable and then communicated to the business firms by brokers (SWOBODA [1913], p. 681): "The unit of exchange … is, by common consent, the rate for telegraphic transfers on London, and upon this rate all other rates are based" (SPALDING [1918], p. 348). Consequently, it was not the sterling bill at six months' sight that functioned as the basis for exchange calculations but the sterling bill at sight (VINNAI [1971], p. 178). Moreover, Hong Kong distinguished between bank selling rates and bank buying rates from August 1904: as a rule, selling rates refer to telegraphic transfers, although they could also refer to bills at 30 days', 60 days' or four months' sight, as was the case with the quotation on London. However, buying rates were usually only given for bills with a usance of at least 30 days' sight (cf. MAHLBERG [1920], pp. 98f.; SPALDING [1918], p. 302). The price difference between private bills and the first-class bankers' bills quoted in the exchange rate currents and documented here amounted to 0.25% to 1% (NOBACK [1877], p. 383; cf. SPALDING [1918], p. 304).

In Shanghai a distinction was made between bank buying rates and bank selling rates, the first including telegraphic transfers on all the places mentioned as well as drafts on demand and four months' sight bills on London, while the latter referred only to four months' sight bills on the European places and New York as well as six months' sight bills on London (SWOBODA [1913], p. 682; cf. MAHLBERG [1920], pp. 96f.). So the difference between the quotations of the various usances resulted not only from the allowance of interest for the later maturity of the longer sights but also from the margin between selling rate and buying rate, which usually amounted to about 1/8% (ibid., p. 131). Bills of exchange on China in Chinese money hardly occurred at all (FRIEDRICH [1910], p. 350).

References: James PENNINGTON, *The Currency of the British Colonies*, London 1848 [repr. New York 1967]; Robert CHALMERS, *History of Currency in the British Colonies*, London 1893 [repr. Colchester 1972], pp. 371–380; A. PIATT ANDREW, The End of the Mexican Dollar, *Quarterly Journal of Economics* 18 (1904), pp. 321–356; Rudolf SONNDORFER, Die Währungsreformen in Ostasien und Ostafrika, *Zeitschrift für Handelswissenschaft und Handelspraxis* 2/10 (1910), pp. 337–343; Wilhelm FRIEDRICH, Die Technik des Zahlungs-Verkehrs im Export mit China, *Zeitschrift für handelswissenschaftliche Forschung* 4 (1910), pp. 340–350; William F. SPALDING, *Eastern Exchange, Currency and Finance*, London ²1918, pp. 291–360; Walter MAHLBERG, *Über asiatische Wechselkurse*, Leipzig ²1920, pp. 88–126; Charles F. REMER, *The Foreign Trade of China*, Shanghai 1926 (repr. Taipei 1967); F.L. HO, An Index of Foreign Exchange Rates, 1898–1926, *Chinese Economic Journal* 1928, pp. 1–40; Eduard KANN, *The Currencies of China. An Investigation of Silver & Gold Transactions Affecting China. With a Section on Copper*, Shanghai 1928; Hosea Ballou MORSE, *The Chronicles of the East India Company Trading to China 1635–1834*, Oxford 1926; A.S.J. BASTER, The Origins of the British Exchange Banks in China, *Economic History* 1934, pp. 140–151; Michael GREENBERG, *British Trade and the Opening of China 1800–1842*, New York – London 1951; Louis DERMIGNY, *La Chine et l'Occident. Le commerce à Canton au XVIIIᵉ siècle 1719–1833*, Paris 1964; Weng E. CHEONG, Trade and Finance in China: 1784–1834. A Reappraisal, *Business History* 7/1 (1965), pp. 34–56; Frank H.H. KING, *Money and Monetary Policy in China 1845–1895*, Cambridge (Mass.) 1965; Volker VINNAI, *Die Entstehung der Überseebanken und die Technik des Zahlungsverkehrs im Asienhandel von 1850 bis 1875*, Frankfurt am Main 1971; Weng E. CHEONG, China Houses and the Bank of England Crisis of 1825, *Business History* 15 (1973), pp. 56–73; idem, *Mandarins and Merchants. Jardine Matheson & Co. A China Agency in the Early Nineteenth Century*, London – Malmö 1979; David S.J. KING, The Hamburg Branch: The German Period, 1889–1920, in Frank H.H. KING (ed.), *Eastern Banking. Essays in the History of the Hong Kong and Shanghai Banking Corporation*, London 1983, pp. 517–544; idem et al., *The History of the Hong Kong and Shanghai Banking Corporation, vol. I: The Hong Kong Bank in Late Imperial China, 1864–1902. On an Even Keel. Wayfoong, the Focus of Wealth*, Cambridge 1987; *vol. II: The Hong Kong Bank in the Period of Imperialism and War, 1895–1918. Wayfoong, the Focus of Wealth*, Cambridge 1988; C.F. Joseph TOM, *Monetary Problems of an Entrepot: The Hong Kong Experience*, New York et al. 1989; Markus A. DENZEL /

Oskar SCHWARZER / Friedrich ZELLFELDER, Ostasiatische, indische und australische Wechselkurse (1800–1914), in *WdW IV*, pp. 1–65; Markus A. DENZEL, Die Adaption 'europäischer Währungssysteme' in China und Japan im 19. und beginnenden 20. Jahrhundert. Zur Durchsetzung des Dollar-Systems im ostasiatischen Raum, in Harald WITTHÖFT (ed.) in cooperation with Karl Jürgen ROTH, *Acta Metrologiae Historicae V: 7. Internationaler Kongreß des Internationalen Komitees für Historische Metrologie 25.–27. September 1997 in Siegen 1997)*, St Katharinen 1999, pp. 227–254.

23.1 Canton exchange rates

23.1.1 On London and India

	CANTON on:		
	London	Calcutta	
	per 100 pounds sterling [a]	per 100 current rupees [b]	
	in Spanish dollars		
1764	363.64 12m/s (y)		
1765	363.64 12m/s (y)		
1766			
1767			
1768			
1769			
1770			
1771	363.64 12m/s (y)		
1772	363.64 12m/s (y)		
1773		41.00 30d/s (y)	
1774		41.00 30d/s (y)	
1775			
1776			
1777	386.85 12m/s (y)		
1778	363.64 12m/s (y)	40.50 30d/s (y)	
1779	380.95 12m/s (y)		
1780	393.70 12m/s (y)		
1781	363.64 12m/s (y)		
1782	363.64 12m/s (y)	46.75 30d/s (y)	
1783	363.64 12m/s (y)		
1784			
1785	363.64 12m/s (y)		
1786	363.64 12m/s (y)	39.00 30d/s (y)	
1787	363.64 12m/s (y)		
1788	375.23 12m/s (y)		
1789	380.95 12m/s (y)	37.50 30d/s (y)	
1790	380.95 12m/s (y)		
1791	380.95 12m/s (y)	33.00 30d/s (y)	
1792	375.23 12m/s (y)	34.00 30d/s (y)	
1793	386.85 12m/s (y)		
1794	393.70 12m/s (y)		
1795	380.95 12m/s (y)		
1796	369.00 12m/s (y)	41.00 30d/s (y)	
1797	363.64 12m/s (y)	38.50 30d/s (y)	

	CANTON on:			
	London [c]	**Calcutta** [c]	**Bombay**	**Madras**
	per 100 pounds sterling [a]	per 100 current rupees, from 1816 per 100 Sicca rupees [b]	per 100 Bombay rupees [b]	per 100 Sicca rupees [b]
	in Spanish dollars			
1798	363.64 12m/s (y)	39.00 30d/s (y)		
1799	363.64 12m/s (y)	39.00 30d/s (y)		
1800	363.64 12m/s (y)	42.00 30d/s (y)		
1801	363.64 12m/s (y)	43.00 30d/s (y)		
1802	363.64 12m/s (y)	42.00 30d/s (y)		
1803	363.64 12m/s (y)	42.00 30d/s (y)		
1804	363.64 12m/s (y)	43.00 30d/s (y)		
1805	363.64 12m/s (y)	43.00 30d/s (y)		
1806	363.64 12m/s (y)	43.00 30d/s (y)		
1807	380.95 12m/s (y)	43.00 30d/s (y)		
1808	386.85 12m/s (y)	45.00 30d/s (y)		
1809	386.85 12m/s (y)	45.00 30d/s (y)		
1810	393.70 12m/s (y)	44.00 30d/s (y)		
1811	*390.48* 12m/s (y)	44.00 30d/s (y)		
1812	380.95 12m/s (y)	42.00 30d/s (y)		
1813	*372.30* 12m/s (y)	*42.25* 30d/s (y)		
1814	363.64 12m/s (y)	42.00 30d/s (y)		
1815	347.83 12m/s (y)	41.00 30d/s (y)		
1816	386.85 12m/s (y)	48.08 30d/s (y)		
1817	386.85 12m/s (y)	48.78 30d/s (y)		
1818	400.00 12m/s (y)			
1819	369.23 6m/s (1)	50.00 30d/s (1)		
1820		49.02 30d/s (1)		
1821	428.57 6m/s (1)	49.34 30d/s (3)		
1822		49.26 30d/s (2)		
1823	444.44 6m/s (y)	49.02 30d/s (3)		
1824	444.44 6m/s (y)	47.96 30d/s (2)		
1825	444.44 6m/s (1)	48.79 30d/s (3)		
1826	457.51 6m/s (2)	49.26 30d/s (1)		
1827	486.50 6m/s (3)	49.67 30d/s (3)	47.29 30d/s (1)	
1828	499.44 6m/s (7)	49.02 30d/s (4)	47.26 30d/s (4)	
1829	497.54 6m/s (12)	50.00 30d/s (10)		
1830	501.59 6m/s (12)	49.80 30d/s (12)		
1831	500.10 6m/s (12)	49.09 30d/s (12)	46.87 30d/s (8)	
1832	480.17 6m/s (12)	48.79 30d/s (12)	46.19 30d/s (12)	
1833	458.20 6m/s (11)	48.31 30d/s (11)	46.11 30d/s (11)	
1834	406.78 6m/s (1)	49.02 30d/s (1)	46.09 30d/s (1)	48.31 30d/s (1)

	CANTON on:			
	London	**Calcutta**	**Bombay**	**Madras**
	per 100 pounds sterling [a]	per 100 Sicca rupees, from 1837 per 100 Company's rupees [b]	per 100 Bombay rupees, from 1835 (7) per 100 Company's rupees [b]	per 100 Madras rupees, from 1835 (9) per 100 Company's rupees [b]
	in Spanish dollars			
1835	416.79 6m/s (12)	48.08 30d/s (12)	45.83 30d/s (12)	44.06 30d/s (12)
1836	412.44 6m/s (12)	48.59 30d/s (12)	45.97 30d/s (12)	44.06 30d/s (12)
1837	412.79 6m/s (12)	45.79 30d/s (10)	45.50 30d/s (12)	45.25 30d/s (5)
1838	445.96 6m/s (12)	47.45 60d/s (12)	46.95 30d/s (8)	
1839	408.55 6m/s (7)	45.68 60d/s (5)	45.67 30d/s (2)	
1840				
1841				
1842				
1843				
1844				
1845				
1846				
1847	466.39 6m/s (6)			
1848	486.22 6m/s (12)	46.89 60d/s (12)	46.52 30d/s (1)	
1849	482.59 6m/s (12)	46.39 60d/s (12)	45.94 30d/s (9)	
1850	426.07 6m/s (12)	44.03 60d/s (12)	43.97 30d/s (12)	
1851	405.48 6m/s (12)	43.69 60d/s (12)	43.45 30d/s (5)	
1852	427.28 6m/s (12)	43.88 60d/s (12)	43.48 30d/s (1)	
1853	385.02 6m/s (12)	40.91 60d/s (12)		
1854	406.25 6m/s (11)	41.47 60d/s (11)		
1855	418.69 6m/s (12)	44.57 60d/s (12)	44.87 30d/s (5)	
1856	408.76 6m/s (12)	44.05 60d/s (12)	44.02 30d/s (12)	

[a]   Concerning the British currency, see pp. 3–5.

[b]   Concerning the currencies of the Indian exchange markets, see p. 495.

[c]   The exchange rates given here on London 1811 and 1813 and on Calcutta 1813 are average values of the data of CHEONG ([1965], p. 36) for the years 1811/12 and 1812/13 respectively 1812/13 and 1813/14. The exchange rates on London and Calcutta from 1819 to September 1827 are for bills of the East India Company.

23.2 Hong Kong exchanges rates

23.2.1 On London, India and Shanghai

	HONG KONG on:			
	London	**Calcutta**	**Bombay**	**Shanghai**
	per 100 pounds sterling [a]	per 100 Company's rupees, from 1863 per 100 Government rupees [b]		per 100 Shanghai taels [c]
	in Spanish or Mexican dollars, from 1866 (10) in Hong Kong dollars			
1844	463.03 6m/s (12)	44.93 30d/s (6)		
1845	479.24 6m/s (5)	46.30 30d/s (3)		
1846	466.66 6m/s (8)	46.37 30d/s (8)	46.13 30d/s (7)	
1847	460.49 6m/s (12)	46.40 30d/s (12)	46.38 30d/s (12)	
1848	490.38 6m/s (12)	46.61 30d/s (12)	46.53 30d/s (12)	
1849	483.20 6m/s (11)	46.34 30d/s (11)	46.22 30d/s (11)	
1850	438.37 6m/s (12)	44.54 3d/s (12)	44.66 3d/s (12)	
1851	416.62 6m/s (12)	43.78 3d/s (12)	44.02 3d/s (12)	
1852	432.54 6m/s (12)	44.41 3d/s (12)	44.37 3d/s (12)	
1853	395.75 6m/s (12)	41.28 3d/s (12)	41.34 3d/s (12)	
1854	410.10 6m/s (12)	41.63 3d/s (11)	41.72 3d/s (11)	
1855	423.94 6m/s (12)	45.09 3d/s (10)	44.99 3d/s (12)	
1856	388.20 6m/s (12)	44.31 3d/s (11)	44.23 3d/s (10)	
1857	414.06 6m/s (12)	44.79 3d/s (12)	44.47 3d/s (12)	
1858	437.24 6m/s (12)	45.68 3d/s (12)	45.64 3d/s (12)	
1859	421.58 6m/s (12)	44.35 3d/s (12)	44.32 3d/s (12)	
1860	420.11 6m/s (12)	43.89 3d/s (11)	43.94 3d/s (11)	
1861	441.98 6m/s (12)	46.14 3d/s (12)	46.12 3d/s (12)	
1862	441.18 6m/s (12)			
1863	413.12 6m/s (12)	42.65 3d/s (6)	43.08 3d/s (5)	129.13 15d/s (4)
1864	415.72 6m/s (12)	43.94 3d/s (10)	43.85 3d/s (10)	
1865	441.81 6m/s (12)			
1866	439.31 6m/s (12)	45.79 3d/s (4)	45.06 3d/s (4)	133.78 3d/s (2)
1867	455.46 6m/s (12)	45.65 3d/s (11)	45.64 3d/s (11)	137.99 3d/s (11)
1868	455.54 6m/s (12)	44.74 3d/s (12)	44.91 3d/s (12)	136.81 3d/s (12)
1869	444.19 6m/s (12)	44.29 3d/s (12)	44.32 3d/s (12)	133.23 3d/s (12)
1870	449.50 6m/s (12)	44.09 3d/s (12)	44.09 3d/s (12)	134.31 3d/s (12)
1871	457.41 6m/s (12)	44.29 3d/s (12)	44.28 3d/s (12)	136.37 3d/s (12)
1872	446.60 6m/s (12)	43.98 3d/s (12)	43.97 3d/s (12)	137.01 3d/s (12)
1873	456.74 6m/s (12)	43.88 3d/s (12)	43.88 3d/s (12)	135.04 3d/s (12)
1874	470.07 6m/s (12)	44.82 3d/s (12)	44.82 3d/s (12)	137.42 dem (12)
1875	481.19 6m/s (12)	44.87 3d/s (12)	44.91 3d/s (12)	138.20 dem (12)
1876	506.22 6m/s (12)	43.66 3d/s (12)	43.66 3d/s (12)	136.86 dem (12)
1877	504.08 6m/s (12)	44.29 3d/s (12)	44.29 3d/s (12)	136.47 dem (12)

	HONG KONG on:			
	London [d]	**Calcutta, from 1879 India** [e]	**Bombay**	**Shanghai** [f]
	per 100 pounds sterling [a]	per 100 Government rupees [b]		per 100 Shanghai taels [c]
		in Hong Kong dollars		
1878	528.00 6m/s (12)	44.70 3d/s (12)	44.70 3d/s (12)	138.46 dem (12)
1879	550.67 6m/s (12)	44.97 t.t. (12)		137.10 dem (12)
1880	534.64 t.t. (11)	44.52 t.t. (12)		137.35 dem (12)
1881	540.88 t.t. (12)	44.65 t.t. (12)		137.80 dem (12)
1882	539.79 t.t. (12)	44.94 t.t. (12)		137.64 dem (12)
1883	551.23 t.t. (12)	44.67 t.t. (12)		138.24 dem (12)
1884	548.15 t.t. (12)	44.54 t.t. (12)		137.61 dem (12)
1885	571.27 t.t. (9)	44.77 t.t. (8)		137.49 dem (9)
1886	620.43 t.t. (12)	44.90 t.t. (12)		139.22 dem (12)
1887	633.93 t.t. (12)	45.16 t.t. (12)		138.82 dem (12)
1888	659.21 t.t. (12)	44.96 t.t. (12)		138.59 dem (12)
1889	657.93 t.t. (12)	44.80 t.t. (12)		138.91 s (12)
1890	601.00 t.t. (12)	45.38 t.t. (12)		138.88 s (12)
1891	629.93 t.t. (12)	45.21 t.t. (12)		139.18 s (12)
1892	705.52 t.t. (12)	45.05 t.t. (12)		138.81 s (12)
1893	784.19 t.t. (12)	49.07 t.t. (12)		138.74 s (12)
1894	952.91 t.t. (12)	53.56 t.t. (12)		136.96 s (12)
1895	948.87 t.t. (12)	52.29 t.t. (12)		138.30 s (12)
1896	925.96 t.t. (12)	55.30 t.t. (12)		138.60 s (12)
1897	1016.18 t.t. (12)	64.28 t.t. (12)		135.96 t.t. (10)
1898	1047.74 t.t. (12)	69.78 t.t. (12)		136.23 t.t. (9)
1899	1031.30 t.t. (12)	68.63 t.t. (12)		138.49 t.t. (12)
1900	1001.09 t.t. (12)	66.89 t.t. (12)		139.64 t.t. (10)
1901	1028.43 t.t. (12)	68.56 t.t. (12)		137.43 dem/t.t. (12)
1902	1177.48 t.t. (12)	77.36 t.t. (12)		136.36 dem/t.t. (12)
1903	1182.52 t.t. (12)	79.00 t.t. (12)		138.54 dem/t.t. (12)
1904	1100.86 t.t. (11)	73.76 t.t. (11)		139.75 dem/t.t. (10)
1905	1054.62 t.t. (10)	70.55 t.t. (10)		139.90 t.t. (9)
1906	935.10 t.t. (10)	62.72 t.t. (11)		138.47 t.t. (10)
1907	926.99 t.t. (12)	62.17 t.t. (12)		136.69 t.t. (12)
1908	1104.69 t.t. (11)	73.73 t.t. (12)		133.80 t.t. (12)
1909	1144.49 t.t. (12)	76.02 t.t. (11)		133.62 t.t. (12)
1910	1114.98 t.t. (11)	74.53 t.t. (9)		134.69 t.t. (10)
1911	1110.51 t.t. (11)	74.11 t.t. (12)		133.86 t.t. (12)
1912	1009.02 t.t. (11)	67.91 t.t. (10)		137.57 t.t. (11)
1913	1010.75 t.t. (11)	67.82 t.t. (10)		137.10 t.t. (11)
1914	1043.18 t.t. (7)	69.59 t.t. (6)		135.46 t.t. (5)

[a] Concerning the British currency, see pp. 3–5.

[b] Concerning the Indian currency, see pp. 495f.

[c] Concerning the Shanghai currency, see pp. 509f.

[d] From August 1904 bank selling rate.

[e] From February 1879 Calcutta and Bombay were recorded with a joint quotation. From August 1904 bank selling rate.

[f] The comparatively frequent change of the usances is caused by the sources listing first one usance and then another. From August 1904 bank selling rate.

23.2.2 On Paris, Berlin and New York

	HONG KONG on:		
	Paris [a]	**Berlin** [c]	**New York** [d]
	per 100 francs [b]	per 100 mark [e]	per 100 US dollars [f]
	in Hong Kong dollars		
1886	24.22 dem (3)		125.42 dem (3)
1887	25.07 dem (12)		129.91 dem (12)
1888	26.01 dem (12)		134.64 dem (12)
1889	25.93 dem (12)	*32.38* dem (7)	133.63 dem (12)
1890	23.66 dem (12)	29.11 dem (10)	122.38 dem (12)
1891	24.80 dem (12)	30.89 dem (12)	128.20 dem (12)
1892	27.87 dem (12)	34.57 dem (12)	143.76 dem (12)
1893	31.11 dem (12)	38.50 dem (12)	159.74 dem (12)
1894	37.74 dem (12)	46.62 dem (12)	194.16 dem (12)
1895	37.66 dem (12)	46.65 dem (12)	194.11 dem (12)
1896	36.71 dem (12)	45.37 dem (12)	189.66 dem (9)
1897	40.31 dem (12)	50.51 dem (2)	207.17 dem (12)
1898	41.63 dem (12)	51.41 dem (12)	215.55 dem (12)
1899	40.53 dem (12)	50.02 dem (12)	210.00 dem (12)
1900	39.67 dem (12)	48.77 dem (12)	204.78 dem (12)
1901	40.33 dem (10)	50.17 dem (12)	209.97 dem (11)
1902	45.99 dem (12)	56.52 dem (12)	236.86 dem (12)
1903	46.89 dem (12)	57.63 dem (12)	241.94 dem (12)
1904	43.71 dem/t.t. (11)	53.75 dem/t.t. (11)	225.88 dem/t.t. (11)
1905	41.81 t.t. (9)	51.55 t.t. (10)	216.12 t.t. (9)
1906	37.19 t.t. (11)	45.56 t.t. (11)	192.71 t.t. (11)
1907	36.56 t.t. (12)	45.31 t.t. (12)	190.92 t.t. (12)
1908	43.63 t.t. (7)	53.30 t.t. (8)	225.08 t.t. (7)
1909	45.42 dem (11)	*55.74* t.t. (11)	234.09 dem (11)
1910	44.08 dem (11)	*54.35* t.t. (11)	227.96 dem (11)
1911	43.74 dem (12)	*53.98* t.t. (12)	226.69 dem (12)
1912	38.32 t.t. (2)	47.17 t.t. (2)	199.51 t.t. (2)
1913	40.10 t.t. (11)	49.54 t.t. (11)	208.50 t.t. (11)
1914	41.24 t.t. (6)	50.79 t.t. (6)	213.73 t.t. (6)

[a] From August 1904 bank selling rate.   [b] Concerning the French currency, see p. 280.

[c] For exchanges on Germany there was no independent price fixing either in Hong Kong or in Shanghai. To determine the rates on Berlin one converted the rates of London on Berlin, which were daily transmitted from London (MAHLBERG [1920], p. 94). 1889, June and July: quotations on Hamburg. From August 1904 bank selling rate.

[d] From August 1904 to August 1908 and from November 1912 the quotation for telegraphic transfer on San Francisco was equal to that on New York. From August 1904 bank selling rate.

[e] Concerning the German currency, see p. 197.   [f] Concerning the US currency, see p. 404.

23.2.3 On Singapore, Yokohama, Manila and Batavia

	HONG KONG on:			
	Singapore [a]	**Yokohama** [b]	**Manila** [c]	**Batavia** [d]
	per 100 Mexican dollars, from 1905 per 100 Straits Settlements dollars [e]	per 100 yen [f]	per 100 Spanish pesos (gold), from 1908 (8) per 100 Philippine pesos gold [g]	per 100 Dutch guilders [h]
	in Hong Kong dollars			
1893	101.00 dem (4)	100.63 dem (4)	90.09 dem (4)	
1894	100.96 dem (12)	99.52 dem (21)	85.60 dem (8)	
1895	100.00 dem (12)	99.92 dem (12)	93.09 dem (12)	
1896	99.56 dem (12)	99.54 dem (12)	88.23 dem (12)	
1897	100.70 t.t. (12)	101.88 t.t. (12)	94.30 dem (12)	
1898	101.15 t.t. (7)	106.04 t.t. (12)	94.79 dem (5)	
1899		95.37 t.t. (12)		
1900		97.26 t.t. (12)		
1901	100.00 dem/t.t. (1)	104.62 dem/t.t. (12)	96.62 dem (2)	
1902	99.59 dem/t.t. (8)	118.31 dem/t.t. (12)	98.63 dem/t.t. (12)	
1903	100.75 dem/t.t. (2)	121.08 dem/t.t. (12)	99.30 dem (7)	
1904		112.01 dem/t.t. (10)		89.76 t.t. (5)
1905	108.30 t.t. (4)	107.39 t.t. (10)		87.73 t.t. (10)
1906	109.95 t.t. (10)	96.08 t.t. (10)		77.59 t.t. (11)
1907	108.50 t.t. (11)	95.21 t.t. (11)		76.21 t.t. (12)
1908	128.60 t.t. (12)	113.47 t.t. (12)	117.36 dem (4)	92.35 t.t./s (12)
1909	133.35 t.t. (12)	117.18 t.t. (12)	116.34 dem (12)	94.90 s (12)
1910	130.67 t.t. (10)	113.09 t.t. (8)	110.09 dem (10)	92.49 s (10)
1911	129.45 t.t. (12)	112.88 t.t. (12)	120.70 dem (12)	92.02 s (12)
1912	117.62 t.t. (11)	103.15 t.t. (11)	103.05 dem (10)	83.85 s (11)
1913	118.19 t.t. (11)	103.40 t.t. (11)	102.90 dem (7)	83.74 t.t. (11)
1914	121.30 t.t. (6)	106.06 t.t. (6)	105.65 dem (6)	85.95 t.t. (6)

[a] The comparatively frequent change of the usances is caused by the sources listing first one usance and then another.

[b] The comparatively frequent change of the usances is caused by the sources listing first one usance and then another. From November 1912 bank selling rate.

[c] From November 1912 selling rate.

[d] From August 1904 to August 1908 and from November 1912: quotations on Java; from August 1904 bank selling rate.

[e] Concerning the Straits Settlements currency, see p. 537.

[f] Concerning the Japanese currency, see pp. 529f.

[g] The silver peso (duro or fuerte) was the legal standard unit of account on the Philippines in the Spanish era (see p. 307), but in practice the Philippines had a gold currency on the basis of the Spanish onza de oro (at 23.4219 grammes of fine gold), which was minted until 1848 and fixed at 16 pesos (fuertes) (NOBACK [1877], p. 726). From the second half of 1903 the Philippines had a new currency following the model of the USA which had occupied the islands in 1898/99: 2

Philippine pesos gold = 1 US dollar (gold). Therefore 1 peso gold of 100 centavos was equal to 0.75 grammes of fine gold. Although the Philippines were part of the gold standard area from 1903, new silver pesos (16.00 grammes of fine silver) were minted for domestic transactions; SONNDORFER [1910], pp. 340s.; SPALDING [1918], pp. 238–258.

[h] Concerning the Netherlands Indian currency, see pp. 545f.

23.2.4 On Bangkok, Saigon, Hankow and Australia

	HONG KONG on:			
	Bangkok	**Saigon**	**Hankow** [a]	**Australia** [b]
	per 100 ticals [c]	per 100 piastres trésor [d]	per 100 Mexican dollars [e]	per 100 pounds sterling, from 1911 per 100 pounds of Australia [f]
	in Hong Kong dollars			
1904				1052.95 30d/s (5)
1905				1027.69 30d/s (9)
1906				909.20 30d/s (11)
1907				898.96 30d/s (12)
1908	87.38 dem (4)	101.38 dem (4)	89.58 dem (4)	1062.63 30d/s (8)
1909	87.09 dem (12)	109.52 dem (12)	91.10 dem (12)	
1910	86.31 dem (11)	104.60 dem (10)	95.37 dem (10)	
1911	84.59 dem (11)	100.84 dem (12)	98.92 dem (12)	
1912	77.48 dem (9)	100.22 dem (9)	99.36 dem (9)	934.33 30d/s (2)
1913	77.92 dem (3)	100.75 dem (3)	99.01 dem (3)	977.21 30d/s (11)
1914	80.11 dem (6)	102.25 dem (4)	97.68 dem (4)	1009.28 30d/s (6)

[a] Hankow (today Wuhan), the most landward port of the Yangtze for big overseas ships, was opened to foreign trade in 1860. From November 1912 bank selling rate.

[b] Quotations on Sydney and Melbourne, from August 1904 bank buying rate.

[c] From November 11th 1908 the Kingdom of Siam had the gold standard based on the tical (0.558 grammes of fine gold or 13.5 grammes of fine silver) of 100 salung as the standard monetary unit. This (new) tical was equal to the former tical (15.50 grammes of fine silver) of 4 salung or 64 atts, so there is no great change in the exchange rate quotation. The most important medium of circulation, however, was paper money, emitted by the government from 1902; SONNDORFER [1910], p. 341; SWOBODA [1913], p. 698.

[d] Concerning the currency in the Indochinese Union, see p. 567.

[e] Although in Hankow the standard unit of account was the Hankow tael (96.50 Hankow taels = 100 Shanghai taels; KANN [1928], pp. 84f.), the exchange rate quotations were effected in Mexican dollars.

[f] Concerning the Australian currency, see pp. 581f.

23.3 Shanghai exchange rates

23.3.1 On London, Paris, China and India

	SHANGHAI on:			
	London	**Paris**	**Canton, from 1857** **Hong Kong** [a]	**Calcutta, from** **1871 also Bombay**
	per 10 pounds sterling [b]	per 100 francs [c]	per 100 Spanish or Mexican dollars, from 1866 (10) per 100 Hong Kong dollars [d]	per 100 Company's rupees, from 1862 per 100 Government rupees [e]
	in Shanghai taels			
1848	45.71 6m/s (9)			
1849	46.17 6m/s (12)	97.84 15d/s (3)		
1850	42.59 6m/s (12)			43.34 3d/s (8)
1851	40.88 6m/s (10)			43.76 3d/s (9)
1852	41.08 6m/s (12)		93.46 15d/s (1)	43.04 3d/s (12)
1853	33.43 6m/s (10)		82.27 15d/s (5)	35.68 3d/s (10)
1854	32.07 6m/s (12)		78.19 15d/s (9)	33.00 3d/s (12)
1855	31.21 6m/s (10)		74.10 15d/s (10)	33.18 3d/s (10)
1856	30.12 6m/s (11)		71.25 15d/s (11)	32.31 3d/s (11)
1857	29.52 6m/s (10)		73.29 15d/s (8)	31.96 3d/s (8)
1858	32.69 6m/s (11)		74.66 15d/s (8)	33.69 3d/s (8)
1859	30.94 6m/s (12)		73.46 15d/s (12)	32.37 3d/s (12)
1860	30.75 6m/s (12)		73.34 15d/s (12)	32.07 3d/s (8)
1861	32.51 6m/s (12)		73.85 3d/s (12)	33.52 3d/s (11)
1862	32.54 6m/s (8)		73.74 3d/s (8)	33.40 3d/s (7)
1863	31.67 6m/s (6)		75.88 3d/s (6)	32.52 3d/s (6)
1864	30.57 6m/s (10)		71.95 3d/s (5)	32.05 3d/s (10)
1865	32.00 6m/s (1)		73.25 3d/s (1)	33.56 3d/s (1)
1866	31.96 6m/s (4)	12.75 6m/s (2)	72.90 3d/s (5)	33.42 3d/s (5)
1867				
1868				
1869	33.43 6m/s (12)	13.27 6m/s (11)	75.48 3d/s (11)	33.12 3d/s (11)
1870	33.78 6m/s (11)			
1871	33.64 6m/s (12)	13.08 6m/s (2)	73.46 3d/s (12)	32.55 3d/s (12)
1872	32.86 6m/s (12)	12.91 6m/s (6)	73.92 dem (6)	32.07 3d/s (6)
1873	33.88 6m/s (12)	13.22 6m/s (12)	74.49 dem (12)	32.63 3d/s (12)
1874	34.27 6m/s (12)	13.54 6m/s (12)	73.06 dem (12)	32.72 3d/s (12)
1875	35.11 6m/s (11)	13.93 6m/s (6)	72.46 dem (6)	32.69 3d/s (6)
1876	37.10 6m/s (12)	14.67 6m/s (12)	73.30 dem (12)	31.88 3d/s (12)
1877	36.29 6m/s (11)	14.30 6m/s (6)	73.77 dem (6)	32.37 3d/s (6)
1878	37.50 6m/s (12)	14.91 6m/s (12)	72.38 dem (12)	32.34 3d/s (12)
1879	39.23 6m/s (12)	16.01 6m/s (6)	72.69 dem (6)	32.84 3d/s (6)

	SHANGHAI on:			
	London [f]	**Paris**	**Hong Kong** [a]	**Calcutta & Bombay**
	per 10 pounds sterling [b]	per 100 francs [c]	per 100 Hong Kong dollars [d]	per 100 Government rupees [e]
	in Shanghai taels			
1880	38.37 4m/s (10)		*73.15* (y)	
1881	38.82 4m/s (11)		*74.44* (y)	
1882	38.54 4m/s (12)		*71.15* (y)	
1883	38.93 4m/s (12)		*72.68* (y)	
1884	39.23 4m/s (12)	15.32 4m/s (1)	72.88 dem (1)	32.68 t.t. (1)
1885	41.29 4m/s (12)		*72.59* (y)	
1886	43.98 4m/s (12)		*70.64* (y)	
1887	45.15 4m/s (12)		*73.39* (y)	
1888	46.98 4m/s (12)		*72.13* (y)	
1889	46.75 4m/s (12)	18.34 4m/s (12)	72.51 dem (12)	32.42 t.t. (12)
1890	39.80 4m/s (12)	15.96 4m/s (6)	72.40 dem (6)	32.81 t.t. (6)
1891	44.67 4m/s (12)	17.50 4m/s (12)	72.25 dem (12)	32.66 t.t. (12)
1892	50.58 4m/s (12)	19.82 4m/s (12)	72.40 dem (12)	32.57 t.t. (12)
1893	55.75 4m/s (12)	20.60 4m/s (6)	71.92 dem (6)	32.55 t.t. (6)
1894	68.54 4m/s (12)		*72.93* (y)	
1895	67.75 4m/s (12)		*72.99* (y)	
1896	66.55 4m/s (12)		*72.24* (y)	
1897	74.98 4m/s (12)		*71.28* (y)	
1898	77.12 4m/s (12)		*72.99* (y)	
1899	74.10 4m/s (12)		*71.69* (y)	
1900	72.17 4m/s (12)		*72.52* (y)	
1901	74.94 4m/s (12)		*73.29* (y)	
1902	85.63 4m/s (12)		*73.91* (y)	
1903	85.42 4m/s (12)		*72.12* (y)	
1904	78.64 4m/s (12)		*71.57* (y)	
1905	74.59 4m/s (12)		*71.59* (y)	
1906	67.93 4m/s (12)		*73.04* (y)	
1907	67.61 4m/s (12)		*73.55* (y)	
1908	83.57 4m/s (12)		*72.24* (y)	
1909	86.35 4m/s (11)		*72.04* (y)	
1910	82.89 4m/s (11)		*72.39* (y)	
1911	82.70 4m/s (12)		*71.68* (y)	
1912	73.37 4m/s (12)		*72.62* (y)	
1913	73.86 4m/s (12)		*72.22* (y)	
1914	77.69 t.t. (5)		*73.13* (y)	

[a] Shanghai exchange rates on Hong Kong in *italics*: Cross-rates of the Hong Kong dollar–sterling rate and the Shanghai tael–sterling rate, calculated by TOM (1989), pp. 43f.

[b] Concerning the British currency, see pp. 3–5.

[c] Concerning the French currency, see p. 280.

[d] Concerning the Hong Kong currency, see p. 508.

[e] Concerning the Indian currency, see pp. 495f.

[f] Although the quotation for telegraphic transfer, which was called 'bank wire' at Shanghai, had become the decisive one within Asian–European exchange transactions since the 1880s, the source on hand lists bank bills at four months' sight because only quotations for this usance are recorded in the London *Economist*.

23.4 Tientsin exchange rates

23.4.1 On London, Paris, Japan and New York

	TIENTSIN on:			
	London [a]	**Paris** [a]	**Japan** [a]	**New York** [a]
	per 10 pounds sterling [b]	per 100 francs [c]	per 100 yen [d]	per 100 US dollars [d]
	in Tientsin taels			
1898	74.18 t.t. (12)	29.48 t.t. (12)	75.58 t.t. (12)	151.92 t.t. (12)
1899	71.35 t.t. (12)	28.27 t.t. (12)	73.13 t.t. (12)	146.42 t.t. (12)
1900	70.02 t.t. (12)	27.80 t.t. (12)	71.35 t.t. (12)	143.25 t.t. (12)
1901	72.28 t.t. (12)	28.69 t.t. (12)	73.17 t.t. (12)	147.25 t.t. (12)
1902	82.50 t.t. (12)	32.79 t.t. (12)	84.44 t.t. (12)	167.92 t.t. (12)
1903	82.55 t.t. (12)	33.94 t.t. (12)	84.45 t.t. (12)	168.34 t.t. (12)
1904	75.28 t.t. (12)	29.85 t.t. (12)	76.82 t.t. (12)	153.92 t.t. (12)
1905	71.43 t.t. (12)	28.16 t.t. (12)	72.25 t.t. (12)	145.17 t.t. (12)
1906	64.99 t.t. (12)	25.69 t.t. (12)	66.19 t.t. (12)	132.50 t.t. (12)
1907	66.90 t.t. (12)	26.42 t.t. (12)	68.01 t.t. (12)	136.09 t.t. (12)
1908	80.40 t.t. (12)	31.80 t.t. (12)	81.90 t.t. (12)	163.59 t.t. (12)
1909	81.23 t.t. (12)	32.22 t.t. (12)	83.14 t.t. (12)	165.92 t.t. (12)
1910	78.75 t.t. (12)	31.24 t.t. (12)	80.08 t.t. (12)	161.34 t.t. (12)
1911	77.89 t.t. (12)	31.28 t.t. (12)	80.09 t.t. (12)	160.92 t.t. (12)
1912	69.02 t.t. (12)	27.58 t.t. (12)	70.92 t.t. (12)	142.25 t.t. (12)
1913	69.97 t.t. (12)	27.92 t.t. (12)	71.67 t.t. (12)	144.09 t.t. (12)
1914	73.72 t.t. (7)	29.41 t.t. (7)	75.71 t.t. (7)	152.00 t.t. (7)

[a]   All exchange rates given here are selling rates.
[b]   Concerning the British currency, see pp. 3–5.
[c]   Concerning the French currency, see p. 280.
[d]   Concerning the Japanese currency, see pp. 529f.
[e]   Concerning the US currency, see p. 404.

24
Japan (1861–1914)

Exchange market: Yokohama (1861–1914)

Sources: *The Nagasaki Shipping List and Advertiser* (1861/62); *The Japan Herald*, Yokohama (1861–1865); *China Overland Trade Report*, Hong Kong (1861, 1863); *The China Mail*, Hong Kong (1864); *The Japan Times*, Yokohama (1865–1866); *The Daily Japan Herald*, Yokohama (1866–1867); *The Japan Times' Overland Mail*, Yokohama (1868–1869); *The Japan Weekly Mail*, Yokohama (1870–1914); *The Japan Weekly Chronicle, Commercial Supplement*, Kobe (1897–1900, 1904–1910).

Concordance: *WdW IV*, pp. 169–206; *WdW V*, p. 206

Currency: In Japan the exchange rate quotations on foreign places were given in Mexican dollars as the most important internationally accepted coins in circulation in the East Asian area. During the Meiji era (1868–1912) the Japanese government intended to create an efficient medium of exchange for trade and payment transactions that was supposed to be greatly appreciated in contrast to the previous Japanese currency, and easily and economically transferable. As a result, a currency reform was carried out in 1871. Following the system of the Mexican dollar already in common practice in foreign trade, the previous traditional and complicated Japanese currency system was superseded by the yen at 100 sen as the new standard coin. Thus the gold yen was treated as equal to the former río (cf. DENZEL [1999], pp. 238–243). Nominally the gold standard was established (1 yen at 1.50 grammes of fine gold), whereas the silver yen at 24.26 grammes of fine silver was introduced based on the model of the Mexican dollar. Until 1877/78 the silver yen was only valid in the ports that were opened for foreign trade. This silver yen was supposed to have (almost) the same value as the gold yen, to be slightly lighter than the Mexican dollar and to be exactly the same as the Hong Kong dollar of 1866 (see p. 494). When the silver yen was no longer struck after 1872, the value of the gold yen began to drop in comparison to the Mexican dollar.

Mexican dollars per 100 gold yen in Hiogo-Osaka 1872/73

1872, July:	104.00	1872, October:	99.00	1873, January:	93.25
1872, August:	102.63	1872, November:	95.75	1873, June:	96.63
1872, September:	99.38	1872, December:	93.50	1873, December:	97.25

Source: NOBACK [1877], p. 388; cf. *WdW IV*, p. 24

From 1877 the silver yen was minted again, but henceforth with exactly the same fine weight as the Mexican and the US trade dollar, which became legal tender in Japan in May 1878. In 1879 this (new) silver yen (24.43 grammes of fine silver; 101 gold yen = 100 silver yen = 100 Mexican dollars) was declared the standard currency unit, although there was a return to the (older) silver yen of 1871 with regard to the strike of the coins. In the coin circulation of Japan and consequently in the trade as well, Japanese silver coins played an insignificant role, because payment transactions were usually concluded in Mexican dollars, as far as foreign countries were concerned, and in government paper money, the so-called 'kinsatsu', in domestic affairs.

Japanese bu in kinsatsu per 100 Mexican dollars

1861	234.25	1867	323.59	1873	414.89	1879	502.79
1862	230.11	1868	no data	1874	414.59	1880	512.80
1863	239.67	1869	339.50	1875	411.80	1881	684.90
1864	237.36	1870	339.50	1876	394.50	1882	700.00
1865	238.50	1871	386.50	1877	413.88		
1866	281.00	1872	no data	1878	436.17		

Source: *WdW IV*, pp. 207f.

The bu or itsibu was a traditional Japanese currency unit and minted in the form of a rectangular plate of silver which contained nominally 8.6418 grammes of fine silver (the so-called 'old bu') or 7.7920 grammes of fine silver respectively (the so-called 'new bu'). The table shows the inflationary tendencies of the Japanese government paper money.

Between 1878 and 1881 the excessively increasing amount of paper money issued led to inflation, especially after the Satsuma Revolt in 1877. In 1886 the nominal bimetallism and real paper currency were converted into a nominal silver standard. After the continuing fall in the world silver price, the gold standard was introduced on October 1ˢᵗ 1897 on the basis of a new gold yen (0.75 grammes of fine gold) of 10 rin or 100 sen. This was possible because the reparations of China, agreed in the Peace of Shimonoseki in 1895 after the war between Japan and China, were available as sterling credit bills in London. Therefore one can speak of a gold exchange standard. However, the banknotes issued by the National Bank (Nippon Ginko) constituted the real means of payment, while Japan was successful in stabilizing the exchange rates on foreign places, with the gold standard (cf. MAHLBERG [1920], p. 73) henceforth quoted on the basis of the gold yen. So "one of the most important effects of the adoption of the new system is that [the Japanese] money market has been brought into closer relation with the European markets" (Bank of Japan (ed.) [1915], p. 276).

Original quotations at Yokohama: Even after the introduction of the yen in 1871, the Japanese quotations continued to be given for the Mexican dollar, which was approximately equal in value to the yen. The Mexican dollar predominated in foreign trade until at least 1885. If at all, the merchant manuals give only inconsistent information about when the quotation was changed over from Mexican dollars to yen. When the gold standard was introduced in 1897, the quotation was given for 1 or 100 yen.

on:	in:	per:
Australia	shillings and pence sterling	1 yen
	from 1911 shillings and pence of Australia	1 yen
Germany	mark and pfennig	1 Mexican dollar / yen
Hong Kong	Mexican dollars	100 Mexican dollars
	from 1866 (10) Hong Kong dollars	100 Mexican dollars / yen
India	Government rupees	100 Mexican dollars / yen
London	shillings and pence sterling	1 Mexican dollar / yen
Paris & Lyons	francs and centimes	1 Mexican dollar / yen
San Francisco & New York	US dollars	100 Mexican dollars / yen
Shanghai	Shanghai taels	100 Mexican dollars / yen

For an explanation of the Yokohama exchange rate currents, see also SPALDING [1918], pp. 170–172.

Further data available: Berlin, 4m/s (1894–1914) – Hong Kong, 10d/s (private credits, 1863–1914) – India, 30d/s (private credits, 1894–1914) – London, 6m/s (documents, 1870/73; private credits, 1864–1908); 4m/s (bank bills, 1867–1879; private credits, 1867–1908); 60d/s (bank bills, 1910–1914); s (1894–1910) – Lyons, 4m/s (private credits, 1894–1900) – Paris, 6m/s (bank bills, 1877–1906; private credits 1870–1906); 4m/s (bank bills and private credits, 1868–1906) – Paris & Lyons, 6m/s (private credits, 1907–1914); 4m/s (private credits, 1907–1914) – New York, 30d/s (private credits, 1873–1892) – San Francisco, 30d/s (private credits, 1873–1892) – New York & San Francisco, 4m/s (private credits, 1892–1914); 30d/s (private credits, 1893–1896, 1902–1914).

With the expansion of the European and the North American trade in Japan from the 1850s, exchange rates were published more or less regularly in English-language newspapers of Japanese ports from the 1860s onwards (e.g. in Yokohama, Hiogo-Osaka or Kobe). The earliest quotation at Yokohama, which had quickly become the leading financial centre of Japan, was that on Shanghai (from 1861 on), the neighbouring place on the Chinese coast, followed by those on London and Hong Kong one year later. In 1869 the first transpacific quotation was effected on San Francisco, which was the consequence of financial relations with the USA becoming ever closer. So, in 1873, another one on New York was added, and from 1893 the rates on San Francisco and on New York were equal. Besides London, Yokohama quoted the following European places: Paris from 1868, Lyons from 1894 (and from 1907 both together) and – apart from a few quotations on Hamburg at the beginning of the 1870s – German bank places from 1894. The quotation on Lyons, which is comparatively unusual in the context of intercontinental exchange rates at the end of the 19th and in the early 20th centuries, can be put down to the fact that great parts of the Japanese raw silk exports of that time went to the traditional French centre of this industry, Lyons (cf. BRÖTEL [2002], p. 142), so that there were considerable exchange operations between Yokohama and Lyons. Further quotations inside Asia can be noted on India after 1893, but according to the documented sources there were no quotations on the places of South East Asia. Finally, Yokohama obtained exchange contact with Australia in 1910, which had already been quoted from Kobe from 1897. Beyond that, "the Exchange Banks in Japan quote rates of exchange on most foreign centres, but their principal business is with London, Paris, New York and San Francisco, Berlin, Hong-Kong, Shanghai, and India" (SPALDING [1918], p. 170). It was not until World War I that official quotations on further Chinese (Tientsin, Peking [now Beijing], Harbin, Dairen, Tsingtao and Hankow since 1915) and South East Asian places (Singapore from 1916, Manila, Batavia and Sourabaya from 1918) were noted (*WdW V*, pp. 112–136).

   In Yokohama exchange operations were either effected by a few merchants and most of all by the foreign banks established there or – even after the formation of the Bank of Japan in October 1882 – by the most important local institution for exchange operations, the Yokohama Specie Bank (Shokin Ginko). Among the foreign banks the Hong Kong & Shanghai Banking Corporation, the Chartered Bank of India, Australia, and China, the Mercantile Bank of India, the Russo-Asiatic Bank, the Banque de l'Indo-Chine, and the International Banking Corporation were the most important ones. "These banks, together with their Japanese *confrères*, are responsible for an enormous bill business" at the Japanese financial markets (SPALDING [1918], p. 163).

   The bills of exchange were drawn as documents on acceptance, documents on payment and as clean bills (ibid., p. 166), but distinctions were regularly made between bank bills and private bills or private credits in the exchange rate currents; documents had been quoted on London only for a few years (1870 and 1873). The principal usance for long-dated papers was first six, later on three to four months' sight for European and American places. During the early 20th century six months' bills were "also occasionally drawn, but … Eastern bankers do not like this long-dated paper" (ibid.). From the 1870s, bank demands (bank bills payable on demand) became common paper, and telegraphic transfers on London were also accepted from 1894 (see Chapters 22 and 23). In general, these quotations for bank bills "are the prices for which the banks will *sell* the various classes of remittance. The Private Credits, on the other hand, are the banks' *buying* rates for first-class commercial bills" (ibid., p. 171). Only these buying rates for such private credits are available on Shanghai and Australia up to 1914 in the sources documented here (cf. MAHLBERG [1920], p. 72).

References: Bank of Japan (ed.), *The Recent Economic Development of Japan*, Tokyo 1915; William F. SPALDING, *Eastern Exchange, Currency and Finance*, London ²1918, pp. 163–178; Walter MAHLBERG, *Über asiatische Wechselkurse*, Leipzig ²1920, pp. 69–76; Junnosuke INOUYE, *Problems of the Japanese Exchange 1914–1926*, London 1931, pp. 241–244; Hiroshi SHINJO, *History of the Yen – 100 Years of Japanese Money-Economy*, Tokyo 1962; Hugh T. PATRICK, External Equilibrium and Internal Convertibility: Financial Policy in Meiji Japan, *Journal of Economic History* 25 (1965), pp. 187–213; Norio TAMAKI, The Yokohama Specie Bank: A Multinational in the Japanese Interest 1879–1931, in Geoffrey JONES (ed.), *Banks as Multinationals*, London 1990, pp. 191–216; Markus A. DENZEL, Die Adaption 'europäischer Währungssysteme' in China und Japan im 19. und beginnenden 20. Jahrhundert. Zur Durchsetzung des Dollar-Systems im ostasiatischen Raum, in Harald WITTHÖFT (ed.) in cooperation with Karl Jürgen ROTH, *Acta Metrologiae Historicae V: 7. Internationaler Kongreß des Internationalen Komitees für Historische Metrologie 25.–27. September 1997 in Siegen 1997)*, St Katharinen 1999, pp. 227-254; Dieter BRÖTEL, Die europäische und die asiatische Seidenindustrie 1860–1930. Modernisierung und Weltmarkteinbindung der Rohseideproduzenten China und Japan im Vergleich, *Geschichte und Gesellschaft* 28/1 (2002), pp. 109–144.

24.1 Yokohama exchange rates

24.1.1 On London, France, Germany and the United States

	YOKOHAMA on:			
	London	**Paris**	**Hamburg**	**San Francisco** [a], from 1892 also **New York**
	per 100 pounds sterling [b]	per 100 francs [c]	per 100 mark [d]	per 100 US dollars [e]
	in Mexican dollars, latest from 1897 in yen			
1862	383.00 6m/s (3)			
1863	400.37 6m/s (4)			
1864	400.25 6m/s (12)			
1865	439.27 6m/s (12)			
1866	431.50 6m/s (11)			
1867	441.85 6m/s (9)			
1868	447.51 6m/s (12)	17.56 6m/s (9)		
1869	444.52 6m/s (12)	17.54 6m/s (10)		*106.67* 30d/s (1)
1870	444.48 6m/s (5)	17.70 6m/s (1)		*106.96* 30d/s (1)
1871	450.73 6m/s (9)			
1872				
1873	465.54 dem (10)	17.75 6m/s (12)	23.25 3d/s (4)	95.39 dem (7)
1874	478.64 dem (12)	18.59 6m/s (12)		98.24 dem (12)
1875	490.99 dem (12)	18.97 6m/s (12)		100.30 dem (12)
1876	504.42 dem (12)	19.54 6m/s (12)	25.32 3d/s (2)	104.40 dem (12)
1877	499.69 dem (12)	19.89 dem (12)		103.08 dem (12)
1878	525.67 dem (12)	20.95 dem (12)		108.01 dem (12)
1879	545.75 dem (12)	21.74 dem (12)		112.15 dem (12)
1880	533.66 dem (12)	21.14 dem (12)		109.71 dem (12)
1881	540.32 dem (12)	21.34 dem (12)		111.09 dem (12)
1882	533.48 dem (12)	21.17 dem (12)		109.91 dem (12)
1883	548.23 dem (11)	21.58 dem (9)		112.80 dem (11)
1884	543.50 dem (12)	21.61 dem (12)		112.47 dem (12)
1885	572.17 dem (12)	22.64 dem (12)		117.86 dem (12)
1886	616.48 dem (12)	24.39 dem (12)		126.71 dem (12)
1887	631.59 dem (12)	25.01 dem (12)		131.08 dem (12)
1888	654.32 dem (12)	25.88 dem (12)		134.82 dem (12)
1889	647.26 dem (12)	25.63 dem (12)		132.87 dem (12)
1890	598.24 dem (12)	23.71 dem (12)		122.90 dem (12)
1891	619.46 dem (12)	24.50 dem (12)		127.58 dem (12)
1892	692.58 dem (12)	27.42 dem (12)		142.33 dem (12)
1893	782.14 dem (12)	30.97 dem (12)		160.85 dem (12)

	YOKOHAMA on:										
	London [f]			**Paris, from 1907 also Lyons**			**Germany**			**San Francisco & New York**		
	per 100 pounds sterling [b]			per 100 francs [c]			per 100 mark [d]			per 100 US dollars [e]		
	in Mexican dollars, latest from 1897 in yen											
1894	961.28	t.t.	(11)	37.87	dem	(12)	47.10	dem	(11)	196.29	dem	(12)
1895	958.58	t.t.	(12)	37.85	dem	(12)	47.06	dem	(12)	196.42	dem	(12)
1896	924.88	t.t.	(12)	36.62	dem	(12)	45.28	dem	(12)	189.49	dem	(12)
1897	986.28	t.t.	(12)	39.14	dem	(12)	48.31	dem	(12)	202.43	dem	(12)
1898	990.57	t.t.	(12)	39.18	dem	(12)	48.46	dem	(12)	203.68	dem	(12)
1899	975.89	t.t.	(12)	38.71	dem	(12)	47.77	dem	(12)	200.89	dem	(12)
1900	986.76	dem	(12)	39.22	dem	(12)	48.29	dem	(12)	196.71	dem	(12)
1901	985.93	dem	(12)	39.17	dem	(12)	48.23	dem	(12)	196.23	dem	(12)
1902	976.33	dem	(12)	38.92	dem	(12)	47.91	dem	(12)	200.74	dem	(12)
1903	977.12	dem	(12)	38.89	dem	(12)	47.80	dem	(12)	200.76	dem	(12)
1904	989.72	dem	(12)	39.35	dem	(12)	48.46	dem	(12)	203.27	dem	(12)
1905	*978.34*	4m/s	(12)	38.97	dem	(10)	48.25	dem	(12)	200.34	dem	(12)
1906	*972.36*	4m/s	(12)	39.12	dem	(10)	47.97	dem	(12)	199.86	dem	(12)
1907	984.21	t.t.	(12)	38.97	dem	(12)	47.95	dem	(12)	195.92	dem	(12)
1908	983.49	t.t.	(11)	39.09	dem	(11)	48.17	dem	(11)	195.65	dem	(11)
1909	978.65	t.t.	(12)	38.88	dem	(12)	47.87	dem	(12)	195.58	dem	(12)
1910	985.28	t.t.	(12)	39.01	dem	(12)	48.09	dem	(12)	196.16	dem	(12)
1911	984.32	t.t.	(12)	38.95	dem	(12)	48.14	dem	(12)	196.12	dem	(12)
1912	982.22	t.t.	(12)	38.89	dem	(12)	48.02	dem	(12)	195.75	dem	(12)
1913	985.66	t.t.	(12)	38.97	dem	(12)	48.08	dem	(12)	195.69	dem	(12)
1914	986.09	t.t.	(7)	39.05	dem	(7)	48.15	dem	(7)	195.67	dem	(7)

[a]   1869/70: private credits, buying rate.

[b]   Concerning the British currency, see pp. 3–5.

[c]   Concerning the French currency, see p. 280.

[d]   Concerning the Hamburg and the German currencies, see pp. 191–193, 197.

[e]   Concerning the US currency, see p. 404.

[f]   1905/06: bank bills, selling rate.

24.1.2 On China, India and Australia

	YOKOHAMA on:		
	Hong Kong [a]	**Shanghai** [b]	**India**
	per 100 Mexican dollars, from 1866 (10) per 100 Hong Kong dollars [c]	per 100 Shanghai taels [c]	per 100 Government rupees [d]
	in Mexican dollars, latest from 1897 in yen		
1861		101.42 10d/s (4)	
1862	94.00 10d/s (1)	104.08 10d/s (10)	
1863	94.75 10d/s (3)	125.64 10d/s (4)	
1864	95.10 10d/s (10)	133.59 10d/s (12)	
1865	100.71 10d/s (3)	136.37 10d/s (12)	
1866	99.64 10d/s (9)	135.17 10d/s (9)	
1867	99.09 10d/s (9)	135.81 10d/s (8)	
1868	98.70 10d/s (12)	133.66 10d/s (11)	
1869	99.53 10d/s (12)	131.83 10d/s (9)	
1870	99.67 10d/s (5)	132.64 10d/s (5)	
1871	98.81 10d/s (9)	134.08 10d/s (3)	
1872			
1873	99.72 dem (12)	133.37 10d/s (12)	
1874	99.89 dem (12)	136.14 10d/s (12)	
1875	99.99 dem (12)	137.11 10d/s (12)	
1876	98.67 dem (12)	132.81 10d/s (12)	
1877	99.25 dem (12)	133.99 10d/s (12)	
1878	99.33 dem (12)	136.53 10d/s (9)	
1879	100.23 dem (12)	137.11 10d/s (9)	
1880	100.52 dem (12)	137.29 10d/s (12)	
1881	99.89 dem (12)	136.35 10d/s (12)	
1882	99.73 dem (12)	135.81 10d/s (12)	
1883	99.77 dem (11)	136.49 10d/s (12)	
1884	100.01 dem (12)	136.70 10d/s (12)	
1885	99.76 dem (12)	135.66 10d/s (12)	
1886	99.59 dem (12)	137.17 10d/s (12)	
1887	99.98 dem (12)	136.69 10d/s (12)	
1888	99.65 dem (12)	137.19 10d/s (12)	
1889	99.39 dem (12)	136.22 10d/s (12)	
1890	99.75 dem (12)	136.88 10d/s (12)	
1891	99.08 dem (12)	136.53 10d/s (12)	
1892	98.79 dem (12)	135.68 10d/s (12)	
1893	99.85 dem (12)	137.19 10d/s (12)	52.18 dem (4)
1894	100.27 dem (12)	135.80 10d/s (12)	53.29 dem (11)
1895	100.74 dem (12)	137.78 10d/s (12)	52.46 dem (12)

	YOKOHAMA on:			
	Hong Kong [a]	**Shanghai** [b]	**India**	**Australia** [e]
	per 100 Hong Kong dollars [c]	per 100 Shanghai taels [c]	per 100 Government rupees [d]	per 100 pounds sterling, from 1911 per 100 pounds of Australia [f]
	in Mexican dollars, latest from 1897 in yen			
1896	100.31 dem (12)	136.96 10d/s (12)	55.19 dem (12)	
1897	97.39 dem (12)	130.91 10d/s (12)	62.58 dem (12)	*974.74* 30d/s (6)
1898	95.37 dem (12)	126.29 10d/s (12)	65.98 dem (12)	*965.69* 30d/s (12)
1899	104.02 dem (12)	130.26 10d/s (12)	65.49 dem (12)	*950.90* 30d/s (12)
1900	102.75 dem (11)	135.47 10d/s (12)	66.10 dem (12)	*957.04* 30d/s (8)
1901	96.62 dem (12)	130.56 10d/s (12)	66.14 dem (12)	
1902	85.56 dem (11)	114.04 10d/s (12)	65.53 dem (12)	
1903	83.82 dem (12)	113.29 10d/s (12)	65.56 dem (12)	
1904	91.55 dem (11)	123.85 10d/s (12)	66.41 dem (12)	
1905	93.63 10d/s (12)	130.42 10d/s (12)	66.15 dem (12)	*964.93* 30d/s (11)
1906	103.18 10d/s (12)	141.50 10d/s (12)	65.92 dem (12)	*956.71* 30d/s (12)
1907	107.58 dem (12)	142.58 10d/s (12)	65.82 dem (11)	*953.29* 30d/s (12)
1908	88.74 dem (12)	117.07 10d/s (11)	65.39 dem (11)	*961.05* 30d/s (12)
1909	86.21 dem (12)	113.04 10d/s (12)	65.28 dem (12)	*954.61* 30d/s (11)
1910	89.00 dem (12)	117.11 10d/s (12)	65.80 dem (12)	*957.83* 30d/s (12)
1911	89.57 dem (12)	117.66 10d/s (12)	65.87 dem (12)	957.93 30d/s (12)
1912	98.46 dem (12)	132.22 10d/s (12)	65.75 dem (12)	951.75 30d/s (12)
1913	98.59 dem (12)	132.17 10d/s (12)	65.76 dem (12)	948.38 30d/s (11)
1914	94.93 dem (7)	125.93 10d/s (7)	65.76 dem (7)	957.46 30d/s (7)

[a] Up to 1871 and 1905/06: private credits, buying rate.

[b] Private credits, buying rate.

[c] Concerning the Chinese currencies, see pp. 508–510.

[d] Concerning the Indian currency, see pp. 495f.

[e] Private credits, buying rate. 1897 to 1910 quotations of Kobe on Australia (in *italics*).

[f] Concerning the Australian currency, see pp. 581f.

25
Straits Settlements (1834–1914)

Exchange market: Singapore (1834–1914)

Sources: *Singapore Chronicle and Commercial Register* (1834–1837); NOBACK [1851], p. 1121 (1845/46); *The Course of Exchange*, London (1847–1849); *The Economist*, London (1850–1870); PRO London, CO 277: *Blue Books of the Straits Settlements* (1868–1914).
Concordance: *WdW IV*, pp. 209–230

Currency: In the Straits Settlements merchants and bankers did their calculations and their exchange business using the Spanish and the Mexican dollar respectively (24.43 grammes of fine silver) of 100 cents, although the Company's rupee (see p. 481) had been introduced as legal tender in 1835. Additionally, various dollar strikes were declared legal tender in the Straits Settlement in 1867 as well as the US trade dollar and the yen in 1874. On October 21ˢᵗ 1890 the Mexican dollar was raised as the standard currency unit apart from which only the yen (until 1898), the US trade dollar (until 1895) and the Hong Kong dollar kept the status of legal tender. With the Straits Settlements Coinage Order of June 25ᵗʰ 1903, the striking of a Straits Settlements dollar (24.26 grammes of fine silver) at 100 cents started, and became legal tender from October 3ʳᵈ 1903 and the only legal tender of the Straits Settlements from September 1ˢᵗ 1904 (Straits Settlements Order in Council of August 24ᵗʰ 1904). The coins were changed gradually in 1903/04 as at that time the Mexican as well as the Straits Settlements dollar (and also the British trade dollar and the Hong Kong dollar) were accepted as legal tender and the quoting of the exchange rates was simply done in or for "dollars". On January 29ᵗʰ 1906 the gold value of the Straits Settlements dollar was fixed according to its actual price at 2 shillings 4 pence sterling. On this basis a fixed relation between the Straits Settlements dollar and the pound sterling (legal tender since November 1906) was laid down by the Straits Settlements Order in Council of October 22ⁿᵈ 1906: 7 pounds sterling = 60 Straits Settlements dollars or 2 shillings 4 pence sterling = 1 Straits Settlements dollar. So, the gold standard was introduced officially whereas the circulation of money in the Straits Settlements continued to be determined by silver dollars, i.e. new Straits Settlements dollars at 18.20 grammes of fine silver (since March 4ᵗʰ 1907), and by government notes (issued from 1906).

Original quotations at Singapore

on:	in:	per:
Batavia	Dutch guilders	100 Spanish or Mexican dollars
from 1904 (9)	Dutch guilders	100 Straits Settlements dollars
Calcutta	Sicca rupees	100 Spanish or Mexican dollars
from 1868	Government rupees	100 Mexican dollars
from 1904 (9)	Government rupees	100 Straits Settlements dollars
China (Canton)	per cent premium or discount	1 Spanish or Mexican dollar
Hong Kong	per cent premium or discount	1 Hong Kong dollar

on:	in:	per:
London	shillings and pence sterling	1 Spanish or Mexican dollar
	from 1876 pence sterling	1 Mexican dollar
	from 1904 (9) pence sterling	1 Straits Settlements dollar
	from 1911 shillings and pence sterling	1 Straits Settlements dollar
Paris	francs	1 Mexican dollar
	from 1904 (9) francs	1 Straits Settlements dollar
Shanghai	Mexican dollars	100 Shanghai taels
	from 1904 (9) Straits Settlements dollars	100 Shanghai taels

Other data available: Bombay, s (1836/37, 1870–1875) – Madras, s (1836/37, 1874/75) – Rangoon, 3 d/s (1870–1872).

Being a British possession since 1819, Singapore was a main source of Indian and Chinese trade during the period documented and, at the same time, the most important trading centre of the Malay Archipelago. In Singapore there was mainly trade in goods. In the early 20th century there were still no capital transactions on a larger scale, because there was no corresponding demand for investments of that kind, neither on the spot nor in the hinterland. At that time the exchange market of Singapore was still regarded as having been developed very modestly, and among all Asian exchange places of international relevance it was the one that was mostly characterized by private bills. Exchange turnovers resulted mainly from the actual demand for the trade in goods, whereas arbitrage transactions were concluded only in exceptional cases, especially as no remittances were generally granted on credit for that. Until the price deterioration of silver in 1907 only the Chinese living in the Federated and Protected Malay States and in Dutch East India used the rate fluctuations in Singapore for extensive speculation in bills on Hong Kong and Shanghai when transferring their money to their homeland (MAHLBERG [1920], pp. 58–68).

Exchange rates at Singapore are available on London, Calcutta and Batavia from 1834 on as well as on China (Canton) from 1835 onwards and on Bombay and Madras from 1836 onwards. Among them, the most important ones were those on London and Calcutta, the former for transactions with Europe and the USA, the latter for those with India and China (cf. NOBACK [1851], p. 1121). After Singapore had been released from the Bengal Presidency in 1867, the official quotations were listed in the *Blue Books of the Straits Settlements* from 1868 onwards. London and Calcutta were quoted as well as Bombay from 1870 on (from 1876 onwards with the same quotation as Calcutta), Batavia, Hong Kong, Shanghai and Paris and, for some years, Rangoon (1871/72) and Madras (1874/75). In addition to this, contemporary merchant manuals also mention other places of the Far Eastern region (Yokohama, Canton, Amoy) and Australia as exchange partners of Singapore (NOBACK [1858], pp. 664f.; NOBACK [1877], p. 822; SWOBODA [1889], p. 822). The quotations of the banks and brokers of around 1910 also applied to a much greater network of exchange places than the official quotations. In such private exchange rate currents one can find quotations on Lyons, Marseilles, Hamburg, New York, Sourabaya, Samarang, Penang, Rangoon, Madras, Colombo, Saigon, Amoy, Manila, Bangkok, Yokohama, Sydney and Melbourne as well.

Usually, the basis of such quotations was probably the calculations of cross-rates via London for the European places or via Hong Kong for the Asian and Australian markets (cf. MAHLBERG [1920], p. 65; SWOBODA [1913], pp. 669f.). The Deutsch–Asiatische Bank, for example, which had a branch in Singapore from 1906, documented cable transfers for London and Hamburg which it telegrammed daily to the head office in Berlin (SONNDORFER [1910], p. 340). Because of the close linking of the Straits Settlements dollar to the pound sterling, Singapore lost its position as intermediary for cashless payment transactions from Siam, Sumatra and Dutch East India to Europe in 1906. Since London was, as the only European place, an exchange partner of greater importance for Singapore, the exchange rate of Singapore on London could be regarded as a barometer for the payment obligations of the Straits Settlements and the Federated and Protected Malay States to Europe in around 1910 (MAHLBERG [1920], p. 61, 64).

The slow progress and a certain backwardness of the exchange market of Singapore until World War I is not only proved by the generally very high rate fluctuations before 1907 (cf. NOBACK [1877], p. 822), but also by the fact that the usances varied enormously. The most frequent bank's and merchant's usances were, for example, from demand to four months' sight, three months' sight and from time to time also six months' sight. Yet these long-term bills were unpopular with the banks, because they were often very difficult to discount on the London market (SPALDING [1918], pp. 129f.; MAHLBERG [1920], p. 64). That is why there were up to six different quotations on London in the exchange rate currents of the banks and brokers, whereas the official quotations in the *Blue Books of the Straits Settlements* referred only to six months' sight. Among them also telegraphic transfer was quoted, but this rate was of much less importance than at other Asiatic exchange markets (cf. ibid., p. 65; SWOBODA [1913], pp. 669s.). The other exchange places (except Batavia) were officially quoted at sight, whereas the exchange rate currents of the banks and brokers listed the rates on demand.

References: Rudolf SONNDORFER, Die Währungsreformen in Ostasien und Ostafrika, *Zeitschrift für Handelswissenschaft und Handelspraxis* 2/10 (1910), pp. 337–343, here pp. 339f.; William F. SPALDING, *Eastern Exchange, Currency and Finance*, London ²1918, pp. 115–134; Walter MAHLBERG, *Über asiatische Wechselkurse*, Leipzig ²1920, pp. 58–69; W. Evan NELSON, The Gold Standard in Mauritius and the Straits Settlements between 1850 and 1914, *Journal of Imperial and Commonwealth History* 16 (1987), pp. 48–76; Oskar SCHWARZER / Markus A. DENZEL / Friedrich ZELLFELDER, Ostasiatische, indische und australische Wechselkurse (1800–1914), in *WdW IV*, pp. 1–65, here pp. 28–33.

25.1 Singapore exchange rates

25.1.1 On London, India, China and Java

	SINGAPORE on:			
	London	**Calcutta**	**China (Canton)**	**Batavia**
	per 100 pounds sterling [a]	per 100 Sicca rupees [b]	per 100 Spanish dollars [c]	per 100 Dutch guilders [d]
	in Spanish or Mexican dollars			
1834	449.28 3m/s (7)	47.51 30d/s (7)		38.47 30d/s (7)
1835	454.01 3m/s (11)	47.80 30d/s (11)	99.60 30d/s (5)	38.47 30d/s (11)
1836	445.67 3m/s (12)	48.33 30d/s (12)	100.00 30d/s (12)	38.47 30d/s (12)
1837	436.40 3m/s (10)	47.71 30d/s (10)	100.00 30d/s (10)	37.68 30d/s (10)
1838				
1839				
1840				
1841				
1842				
1843				
1844				
1845	468.29 6m/s (1)			
1846	466.02 6m/s (2)			
1847	454.63 6m/s (6)			
1848	465.40 6m/s (11)			
1849	470.28 6m/s (10)			
1850	432.65 6m/s (12)			
1851	424.04 6m/s (10)			
1852	438.62 6m/s (11)			
1853	414.27 6m/s (12)			
1854	408.51 6m/s (11)			
1855	420.45 6m/s (9)			
1856	416.12 6m/s (8)			
1857	406.70 6m/s (7)			
1858	437.16 6m/s (9)			
1859	423.77 6m/s (11)			
1860	412.33 6m/s (12)			
1861	430.15 6m/s (12)			
1862	433.78 6m/s (10)			
1863	410.18 6m/s (11)			
1864	409.92 6m/s (10)			
1865	434.09 6m/s (9)			
1866	437.27 6m/s (8)			

	SINGAPORE on:			
	London	**Calcutta, from 1876 also Bombay**	**Hong Kong**	**Batavia**
	per 100 pounds sterling [a]	per 100 Government rupees [b]	per 100 Hong Kong dollars [c]	per 100 Dutch guilders [d]
	in Mexican dollars			
1867	450.06 6m/s (9)			
1868	456.34 6m/s (8)	44.84 3d/s (y)		
1869	443.81 6m/s (10)	43.67 3d/s (y)		
1870	447.85 6m/s (12)	43.75 3d/s (12)	99.08 3d/s (12)	37.77 10d/s (12)
1871	453.56 6m/s (12)	44.03 3d/s (12)	98.98 3d/s (12)	38.73 10d/s (12)
1872	441.79 6m/s (12)	44.03 3d/s (12)	99.46 3d/s (12)	38.29 10d/s (12)
1873	456.26 6m/s (12)	44.22 3d/s (12)	100.11 3d/s (12)	38.33 10d/s (8)
1874	469.21 6m/s (12)	45.09 s (12)	99.98 s (12)	40.23 10d/s (7)
1875	480.61 6m/s (12)	44.90 s (11)	99.89 s (12)	40.79 10d/s (7)
1876	499.96 6m/s (12)	43.32 s (12)	99.34 s (8)	41.53 10d/s (12)
1877	491.82 6m/s (12)	44.14 s (12)	99.45 s (12)	40.81 10d/s (12)
1878	515.55 6m/s (12)	44.48 s (12)	99.28 s (12)	42.83 10d/s (12)
1879	532.12 6m/s (12)	44.84 s (12)	99.80 s (12)	44.18 10d/s (12)
1880	526.45 6m/s (12)	44.30 s (12)	99.96 s (12)	43.49 10d/s (12)
1881	528.22 6m/s (12)	44.27 s (12)	99.49 s (12)	43.79 10d/s (12)
1882	528.04 6m/s (12)	44.60 s (12)	99.83 s (12)	43.51 10d/s (12)
1883	541.51 6m/s (12)	44.52 s (12)	100.03 s (12)	44.64 10d/s (12)
1884	539.91 6m/s (12)	44.43 s (12)	99.89 s (12)	44.23 10d/s (12)
1885	563.73 6m/s (12)	44.42 s (12)	99.74 s (12)	46.62 10d/s (12)
1886	605.05 6m/s (12)	44.43 s (12)	99.23 s (12)	49.93 10d/s (12)
1887	619.77 6m/s (12)	44.87 s (12)	99.69 s (12)	51.80 10d/s (12)
1888	644.08 6m/s (12)	44.65 s (12)	99.50 s (12)	54.18 10d/s (12)
1889	639.19 6m/s (12)	44.47 s (12)	99.35 s (12)	53.10 10d/s (12)
1890	584.73 6m/s (12)	45.14 s (12)	99.72 s (12)	48.33 10d/s (12)
1891	612.83 6m/s (12)	44.73 s (12)	99.58 s (12)	50.40 10d/s (12)
1892	694.46 6m/s (12)	44.67 s (12)	99.55 s (12)	56.54 10d/s (12)
1893	775.18 6m/s (12)	48.71 s (12)	99.55 s (12)	62.54 10d/s (12)
1894	932.11 6m/s (12)	53.08 s (12)	99.89 s (12)	76.67 10d/s (12)
1895	940.41 6m/s (12)	52.46 s (12)	100.59 s (12)	76.59 10d/s (12)
1896	917.82 6m/s (12)	55.30 s (12)	100.24 s (12)	74.62 10d/s (12)
1897	1005.87 6m/s (12)	64.12 s (12)	100.08 s (12)	81.70 10d/s (12)
1898	1030.51 6m/s (12)	69.27 s (12)	99.80 s (12)	83.68 10d/s (12)
1899	1003.17 6m/s (12)	68.02 s (12)	99.67 s (12)	82.65 10d/s (12)
1900	978.07 6m/s (12)	66.38 s (12)	99.81 s (12)	81.08 10d/s (12)
1901	1012.62 6m/s (12)	68.31 s (12)	100.06 s (12)	84.14 10d/s (12)
1902	1141.16 6m/s (12)	77.10 s (12)	100.27 s (12)	95.71 10d/s (12)
1903	1123.57 6m/s (12)	76.40 s (12)	97.70 s (12)	94.66 10d/s (12)

	SINGAPORE on:			
	London	**Calcutta, up to 1906 also Bombay**	**Hong Kong**	**Batavia**
	per 100 pounds sterling [a]	per 100 Government rupees [b]	per 100 Hong Kong dollars [c]	per 100 Dutch guilders [d]
	in Mexican dollars			
1904	1035.37 6m/s (12)	70.42 s (12)	96.33 s (12)	86.43 10d/s (12)
	in Straits Settlement dollars			
1905	973.06 6m/s (12)	65.97 s (12)	95.45 s (12)	81.61 10d/s (12)
1906	850.38 6m/s (12)	57.48 s (12)	92.17 s (12)	71.02 10d/s (12)
1907	842.81 6m/s (12)	57.54 s (12)	92.91 s (12)	71.25 10d/s (12)
1908	851.57 6m/s (12)	57.28 s (12)	78.64 s (12)	71.70 10d/s (12)
1909	851.30 6m/s (12)	57.16 s (12)	75.89 s (12)	71.30 10d/s (12)
1910	844.16 6m/s (12)	57.21 s (12)	77.29 s (12)	71.04 10d/s (12)
1911	848.88 6m/s (12)	57.31 s (12)	78.20 s (12)	71.12 10d/s (12)
1912	855.11 6m/s (12)	57.35 s (12)	86.05 s (12)	71.14 10d/s (12)
1913	843.58 6m/s (12)	57.30 s (12)	85.47 s (12)	70.92 10d/s (12)
1914	846.90 6m/s (7)	57.35 s (7)	82.15 s (7)	70.81 10d/s (7)

[a]   Concerning the British currency, see pp. 3–5.

[b]   Concerning the Indian currencies, see pp. 495f.

[c]   Concerning the currencies in South China, see pp. 507f.

[d]   Concerning the Netherlands Indian currency, see pp. 545f.

25.1.2 On Paris and Shanghai

	SINGAPORE on:				
	Paris		**Shanghai**		
	per 100 francs [a]		per 100 Shanghai taels [b]		
	in Mexican dollars				
1870	18.08	3d/s	(9)	133.81	3d/s	(12)
1871	18.70	3d/s	(4)	134.73	3d/s	(12)
1872	18.36	3d/s	(12)	135.03	3d/s	(7)
1873	18.75	s	(12)	135.16	3d/s	(3)
1874	19.11	s	(12)	136.31	s	(12)
1875	19.80	s	(8)	137.82	s	(8)
1876	20.23	s	(12)	136.45	s	(12)
1877	19.96	s	(12)	135.79	s	(12)
1878	20.87	s	(12)	137.78	s	(9)
1879	21.45	s	(12)	137.46	s	(3)
1880	21.10	s	(12)	136.99	s	(8)
1881	21.26	s	(12)	136.80	s	(12)
1882	21.30	s	(12)	136.55	s	(12)
1883	21.83	s	(12)	138.14	s	(7)
1884	21.71	s	(12)	137.84	s	(12)
1885	22.72	s	(12)	136.76	s	(7)
1886	24.29	s	(12)	138.42	s	(12)
1887	25.07	s	(12)	138.80	s	(12)
1888	25.97	s	(12)	137.86	s	(12)
1889	25.74	s	(12)	137.61	s	(12)
1890	23.63	s	(12)	139.56	s	(12)
1891	24.94	s	(12)	138.68	s	(12)
1892	27.85	s	(12)	138.53	s	(12)
1893	31.03	s	(12)	137.96	s	(12)
1894	37.77	s	(12)	136.41	s	(12)
1895	37.68	s	(12)	138.97	s	(12)
1896	36.71	s	(12)	138.47	s	(12)
1897	40.41	s	(12)	137.90	s	(12)
1898	41.14	s	(12)	136.33	s	(12)
1899	40.38	s	(12)	138.01	s	(12)
1900	39.46	s	(12)	139.28	s	(12)
1901	40.81	s	(12)	137.37	s	(12)
1902	46.05	s	(12)	136.45	s	(12)
1903	45.23	s	(12)	134.99	s	(12)
	in Straits Settlements dollars				
1904	41.49	s	(12)	135.61	s	(12)

	SINGAPORE on:					
	Paris			Shanghai		
	per 100 francs [a]			per 100 Shanghai taels [b]		
	in Straits Settlements dollars					
1905	39.15	s	(12)	133.34	s	(12)
1906	34.17	s	(12)	127.19	s	(12)
1907	34.03	s	(12)	125.88	s	(12)
1908	34.31	s	(12)	104.78	s	(12)
1909	34.10	s	(12)	101.05	s	(12)
1910	33.93	s	(12)	103.88	s	(12)
1911	33.92	s	(12)	103.86	s	(12)
1912	33.90	s	(12)	118.24	s	(12)
1913	33.88	s	(12)	116.52	s	(12)
1914	33.96	s	(7)	110.29	s	(7)

[a]   Concerning the French currency, see p. 280.

[b]   Concerning the Shanghai currency, see pp. 509f.

26
Netherlands India (1818–1914)

Exchange market: Batavia (1818–1914)

Sources: *Staat van de wisselkoers* [1852], pp. 65–69 (1818–1850); VAN LAANEN [1980], pp. 123–126 (1850–1914); Departement van economische zaken (ed.), *Prijzen* [1938], p. 65 (Tabel XIX) (1913/14).
Concordance: *WdW IV*, pp. 373–378; *WdW V*, pp. 247f.

Currency: From the 17th century the Vereenigde Oost-Indische Compagnie (VOC) imported Dutch trade coins made of silver as a "remittance-medium for foreign payments". Moreover, "the higher value assigned to silver money imported from the Netherlands was based on the argument that, partly because of the cost of transport, silver was worth approximately 20% more than it was in the Netherlands" (VAN LAANEN [1980], pp. 15, 43). When the supply of silver from the Netherlands diminished because of the numerous wars with England (above all from 1780 to 1784), several sorts of paper money were issued from 1782. For the trade with the Asian inhabitants, loads of copper coins, the most appreciated means of payment and exchange, were imported. By the mid-18th century "the Asian monetary system of the Company … [was] in a state of great chaos and confusion" (KLEIN [1991], p. 427), which did not even change when the colony of the VOC was taken over by the Batavian Republic in 1799.

During the British Interregnum (1811–1816) a new standard currency unit, the Java rupee, was introduced (according to the proclamation of November 1st 1813) with 10.37 grammes of fine silver, which was meant to be subdivided into 30 stivers (stuivers of 1767) or 120 doits (duiten). After the restoration of Dutch rule in 1816, this standard monetary unit was renamed the Netherlands Indian guilder in 1817. This guilder corresponded to 24 Dutch stivers or 1.2 Dutch guilders of 20 stuivers, whereas the Dutch guilder was fixed vice versa at 25 Netherlands Indian stivers and the Spanish dollar (peso; at 24.43 grammes of fine silver) at 66 Netherlands Indian stuivers. As the Dutch and the Netherlands Indian guilder had the same intrinsic value, "a coin, therefore, issued at 20% above this value, was designated as the standard coin!" (VAN LAANEN [1980], p. 16). The significant issues of paper money of the time before 1811 were taken up again in 1817 and, additionally, great amounts of copper coins were put into circulation. Since paper and copper money were legal tender of the same value as silver money, the latter gradually disappeared from circulation so that the exchange rates for silver money were dropping constantly. Consequently, the Dutch Currency Law of 1816 (see p. 59) was extended to Netherlands India on March 22nd 1826 (based on the confidential Orders in Council of September 12th 1825 and February 11th 1826). The Dutch guilder at 100 cents was declared the standard monetary unit, and so a currency union between the Netherlands and Netherlands India was established. Because of that, the Netherlands Indian guilder was *de facto* devalued by 16.67% compared to its value in 1817. It was theoretically treated as equal to the Dutch guilder, but it kept its legal value of 24 Dutch stivers or 120 doits whereas the exchange rate was fixed at 20 Dutch stivers or 100 doits. Although it was the aim of the reform of 1826 to eliminate copper coins from circulation, the government reintroduced large amounts of doits in connection with the Culture System and the Consignment System in the 1830s. It fixed the prices for 'cultivated products' exclusively in copper coins and settled their payments mainly in copper coins from 1827 because not enough silver money was available. That is why silver money was quoted with a marked premium (12% to 32%) in relation to copper money between 1827 and 1834. In contrast to this, payments of the commercial sphere were even after 1826 often settled in silver or the temporarily trustworthy notes of the private Java Bank, founded in 1827, which were redeemable until 1839. Therefore, the term 'Netherlands Indian guilder' had a fourfold meaning in the 1830s: [1] payable in silver (or gold) coins according to the legal value (gulden zilver); [2] payable in notes of the Java Bank (after 1839 the 'zoge-naamd zilver'); [3] payable in copper coins according to the legal value (gulden koper); [4] payable in government copper notes (the koper-certificaten). From 1832 these last were issued by the Java Bank by order of the government. The intention was to reduce the copper circulation and the premium on silver, but the premium increased so much that the government ordered the depreciation of copper on January 4th 1834. Although payments could henceforth be settled to a limited extent in silver as well as in copper – which was the basis of the 'copper standard' – 6 guilders copper were meant to be of the same value as 5 guilders silver (120 doits for 1 silver or Java Bank guilder). In 1839 the monetary union between the Netherlands and its colony was renewed, designating the Dutch guilder as the standard coin, but "it will be evident that in practical terms this regulation was of little importance, for silver money was virtually out of circulation until the reform of the coinage system in 1854" (ibid., p. 20). When in 1842 the government continued to issue copper notes without the participation of the Java Bank, there was hardly any copper left – even to cover the first issue of 1832. In 1830, because the silver had also left the country to a great extent because of private imports or because it had been hoarded for this purpose, there was inflation due to increased issuings of copper. The rate for 1 silver guilder rose to 140 to 180 doits and even to 200 doits in the interior of Java.

A drastic reform was started in 1846 when the copper coins could be redeemed for 'recepissen' representing the Dutch silver gulden as the new kind of national paper money. In this scrip system (recepissenstelsel) the recepis guilder of 120 doits became temporarily the standard money. At the same time, the copper notes were withdrawn and 6 guilders copper money were changed into 5 recepis guilders. The recepissen were accepted at all administrative offices at a ratio of 1:1 to the silver guilder as well as in connection with the purchase of bills of exchange drawn by the Governor-General of the Ministry of the Colonies in The Hague. Simultaneously the notes of the Java Bank were changed into recepissen at a ratio of 1:1. As early as the end of 1847 the total amount of money circulating in Netherlands India could be redeemed for silver or recepissen. "In practice, the international value of the Netherlands-Indian guilder was maintained by sustaining claims (bills of exchange) on other countries with a silver standard, especially the Netherlands" (ibid.). Due to the introduction of the silver standard (until 1877), the recepis system could be abandoned in 1854 in accordance with the Netherlands Coinage Act of 1847 establishing the free minting of silver standard coins, the recognition of the Dutch coins as unlimited legal tender even in Netherlands India and the introduction of small subsidiary coins in silver. The recepissen were gradually changed partly into silver, partly into banknotes, and were finally withdrawn from circulation. In 1858/59 the old copper doits lost their status as legal means of payment but continued to be used, above all in the interior.

After the Netherlands had introduced the gold standard (to be exact: the gold exchange standard) on June 6th 1875, Netherlands India followed formally on March 28th 1877, but in practice it had already been implemented in 1875 because of the currency union with the Netherlands (1 guilder being equal to 0.6048 grammes of fine gold; see p. 59). Neither some modifying acts concerning small coins (in 1882, 1900 and 1901) nor the Coin Act of 1912 combining the active legislation were of any account for the development of the cashless payment system of Netherlands India.

Original quotations at Batavia

on:	in:	per:
Amsterdam	Dutch stuivers (= 1/20 Dutch guilder)	1 Spanish dollar
from 1826	Dutch cents or guilders	1 or 100 Dutch guilders (NIC)
Japan	Dutch guilders (NIC)	100 yen
London	shillings and pence sterling	1 Spanish dollar
from 1826	shillings and pence sterling	1 Dutch guilder (NIC)
Singapore	Dutch guilders (NIC)	100 Mexican dollars
from 1906	Dutch guilders (NIC)	100 Straits Settlements dollars

NIC = Netherlands Indian current

Other data available: Amsterdam, 3m/s (1818–1827); 4m/s (1821–1826) – London, 3m/s (1818–1827); 4m/s (1824–1835); 30d/s (1821–1823).

Since the 17th century Batavia had been the central trading and financial centre of the Dutch possessions in East India. Within the Vereenigde Oost-Indische Compagnie (VOC; United East India Company) it had been common practice since the 1620s to transfer money cashlessly from the East Indian estates to the mother country. Similar to the internal Dutch transactions, this process took place by means of a special form of the three-person bill of exchange, the 'assignatië' (see p. xlviii). Its quotations resulted from the different valuations of the silver money in the Netherlands and in Netherlands India plus a payment of interest on the sum transferred at a rate of 4% (1664–1735). Therefore their quotations varied by 24% at the beginning of the 18th century. After 1680 a considerable part of all payment transactions between Batavia and the Netherlands were concluded in this way, and since the 1760s more than 40% of the precious metals flowing from the mother country into Netherlands India were subsituted by assignatiës (GAASTRA [1994], pp. 66–68; PRAKASH [1998], pp. 337f.; DENZEL [1999], pp. 53–58).

Batavia could already look back on a 200-year tradition as a 'coordinating point' within the intercontinental cashless payment system, when the earliest exchange transactions after the period of the British occupation (1811–1816) found their expression in the exchange rate quotations (from 1818 onwards). As a result, the cash-less payment transactions from Netherlands India to Europe – i.e. above all to Amsterdam – and other Asian places were almost exclusively dominated by the government during the following decades of the 19th century, in which export production (Culture System; 1830–1870) and foreign trade (Consignment System) were concentrated in the hands of the government. Due to the close connection between the official exchange rate policy and the economic and monetary policy of the government, the government rate on Amsterdam has been the most important quotation in Batavia and has therefore set the standard for most transactions for large parts of the 19th century. It was not until the 1890s that the government gradually withdrew from the exchange market which becomes evident from the quotation on Amsterdam becoming increasingly irregular and, finally, ending in 1898. Since 1901 the government increasingly used the Java Bank for its financial transactions with the mother country. This private bank, founded in 1827, could only buy or discount foreign bills in Netherlands India until 1891, but it could not take an active part in the exchange transactions. It was not until that year that the Java Bank was authorized to trade bills on Amsterdam and London in Amsterdam with the help of an agency set up especially for this purpose. From 1909 the Java Bank could concentrate increasingly on the exchange policy as 'financier' of the government (VAN LAANEN [1980], pp. 43–50, 118–121).

However, private exchange transactions remained modest in their extent even after the mid-19thcentury. From the 1830s they resulted especially from the necessities of the trade in goods of local English or American carriers, who effected their payment transactions primarily via London. "A private exchange market was still in its infancy" (ibid., p. 46), particularly as its growth was hindered by the Consignment System. Banks and bill brokers did not take up their activities in Netherlands India until the early 1860s, when private exports became possible to a far greater extent than ever before and, consequently, payment transactions of private individuals became necessary to a greater extent as well. When brokers and banks, among them the subsidiary company of the Chartered Bank of India, Australia, and China, which could record the highest exchange turnover in Batavia (NOBACK [1877], p. 114), became increasingly involved in the exchange business, the trading houses became more independent of the current supply and demand on the exchange market, because they did not have to provide for their exchange transactions themselves but could employ professional financial services for this. In 1876 the first D/P (documents against payment) and D/A (documents against acceptance) bills were traded. The exchange transactions of merchants and banks were principally based on the financial execution of Javanese sugar exports: "The Netherlands-Indian foreign exchange market largely owed its existence to this outflow of sugar money" (VAN LAANEN [1980], p. 119). So the exporters drew bills on credit accounts which the importers had conceded them at commercial banks in London where these bills were then discounted. Thus London became a central intermediary in the cashless payment system between Netherlands India and the mother country itself from the sugar crisis in 1884, Batavia's exchange rate on London matching at least that on Amsterdam in relevance.

Apart from these two central exchange rate quotations on Amsterdam and on London, which were the most important for the exchange market of Batavia, the 'neighbouring' financial market of Singapore was also quoted from 1855 as extensive transfers of precious metal were completed via this entrepôt. Despite the clearly increasing trade with India during the second half of the 19th century, evidence of quotations on Calcutta, as mentioned in contemporary merchant manuals, is just as rare at this date as that of quotations on Hamburg, China or Paris (NOBACK [1851], p. 95; NOBACK [1877], p. 114). References for New York and Japan as further exchange partners of Batavia are unavailable until 1913.

References: *Staat van de wisselkoers van Java op Nederland en Engeland. Handelingen van de Tweed Kamer der Staaten General 1851/52 II, Annex VIII, B6*, The Hague 1852; William F. SPALDING, *Eastern Exchange, Currency and Finance*, London ²1918, pp. 204–223; Keng Liem KHOUW, *De wisselkoers tusschen Indië en Nederland 1854–1925*, The Hague 1929; Departement van economische zaken (ed.), *Prijzen, indexcijfers en wisselkoersen op Java 1913–1937* (= *Mededeelingen van het centraal kantoor voor de statistiek*, No. 146), Batavia 1938; J. T. M. VAN LAANEN, *Money and Banking 1816–1940* (= P. CREUTZBERG / J. T. M. VAN LAANEN (eds.), *Changing Economy in Indonesia. A Selection of Statistical Source Material from the Early 19th Century up to 1940*, vol. 6), The Hague 1980; Peter W. KLEIN, Dutch Monetary Policy in the East Indies. 1602–1942: A Case of Changing Continuity, in Eddy H. G. VAN CAUWENBERGHE (ed.), *Money, Coins, and Commerce:*

Essays in the Monetary History of Asia and Europe (From Antiquity to Modern Times), Leuven 1991, pp. 419–453; Femme S. GAASTRA, Private Money for Company Trade. The Role of the Bills of Exchange in Financing the Return Cargoes of the VOC, *Itinerario. European Journal of Overseas History* 18 (1994), pp. 65–76; Om PRAKASH, Financing the European Trade with Asia in the Early Modern Period: Dutch Initiatives and Innovations, *Journal of European Economic History* 27 (1998), pp. 331–356; Markus A. DENZEL, Zur Finanzierung des europäischen Asienhandels in der Frühen Neuzeit: Vom Zahlungsausgleich im Gewürzhandel zum bargeldlosen Zahlungsverkehr, in idem (ed.), *Gewürze in der Frühen Neuzeit: Produktion, Handel und Konsum*, St Katharinen 1999, pp. 37–69.

26.1 Batavia exchange rates

The annual average values (y) presented here are based on monthly rates (VAN LAANEN [1980]).

26.1.1 On Amsterdam, London, Singapore and Japan

	BATAVIA on:	
	Amsterdam [a]	**London** [b]
	per 100 Dutch guilders [c]	per 10 pounds sterling [d]
	in Spanish dollars	
1818	35.88 6m/s (2)	38.40 6m/s (2)
1819	36.04 6m/s (12)	37.61 6m/s (12)
1820	*37.74* 6m/s (12)	*40.00* 6m/s (12)
1821	*38.10* 6m/s (4)	40.98 6m/s (5)
1822		
1823	39.88 6m/s (3)	*49.83* 6m/s (6)
1824	*47.35* 6m/s (6)	*54.35* 6m/s (3)
1825	48.78 6m/s (2)	*57.15* 6m/s (2)
	in Dutch guilders (Netherlands Indian current)	
1826	*106.19* 6m/s (3)	*118.39* 6m/s (10)
1827	*99.50* 6m/s (1)	*114.29* 6m/s (1)
1828		
1829		
1830		
1831		
1832		
1833	102.21 6m/s (6)	*119.59* 6m/s (6)
1834	99.70 6m/s (10)	*118.33* 6m/s (10)
1835	101.83 6m/s (5)	*120.94* 6m/s (4)
1836	100.25 6m/s (8)	119.46 6m/s (8)
1837	100.66 6m/s (12)	122.19 6m/s (12)
1838	106.10 6m/s (10)	126.75 6m/s (10)
1839	103.31 6m/s (10)	124.63 6m/s (10)
1840	*105.66* 6m/s (11)	*126.37* 6m/s (11)
1841	105.26 6m/s (11)	125.00 6m/s (11)
1842	107.53 6m/s (6)	128.54 6m/s (6)
1843	127.31 6m/s (11)	151.88 6m/s (10)
1844	126.74 6m/s (10)	153.89 6m/s (9)
1845	125.00/<u>105.26</u> 6m/s (9+1)	151.88 6m/s (10)
1846	<u>105.26</u> 10m/d (11)	127.39 6m/s (11)
1847	<u>105.26</u> 10m/d (9)	129.73 6m/s (9)
1848	<u>105.26</u> 10m/d (12)	130.00 6m/s (12)

	BATAVIA on:		
	Amsterdam [a]	**London** [b]	**Singapore** [e]
	per 100 Dutch guilders [c]	per 10 pounds sterling [d]	per 100 Mexican dollars [f]
	in Dutch guilders (Netherlands Indian current)		
1849	*105.26* 10m/d (9)	130.00 6m/s (9)	
1850	*105.26* 10m/d (9)	130.00 6m/s (9)	
1851	112.30 6m/s (y)	132.00 6m/s (y)	
1852	112.30 6m/s (y)	132.00 6m/s (y)	
1853	106.60 6m/s (y)	124.00 6m/s (y)	
1854	101.00 6m/s (y)	119.00 6m/s (y)	
1855	102.60 6m/s (y)	123.00 6m/s (y)	290.00 s (y)
1856	98.80 6m/s (y)	122.00 6m/s (y)	283.00 s (y)
1857	99.90 6m/s (y)	117.00 6m/s (y)	
1858	103.20 6m/s (y)	121.10 6m/s (y)	267.00 s (y)
1859	102.10 6m/s (y)	120.90 6m/s (y)	271.00 s (y)
1860	103.50 6m/s (y)	120.80 6m/s (y)	279.00 s (y)
1861	103.10 6m/s (y)	124.30 6m/s (y)	270.00 s (y)
1862	105.50 6m/s (y)	123.60 6m/s (y)	273.00 s (y)
1863	102.10 6m/s (y)	121.00 6m/s (y)	280.00 s (y)
1864	101.20 6m/s (y)	118.70 6m/s (y)	277.00 s (y)
1865	101.20 6m/s (y)	120.10 6m/s (y)	263.00 s (y)
1866	101.20 6m/s (y)	121.80 6m/s (y)	
1867	102.60 6m/s (y)	123.40 6m/s (y)	
1868	102.10 6m/s (y)	123.00 6m/s (y)	
1869	99.90 6m/s (y)	122.10 6m/s (y)	268.00 s (y)
1870	101.70 6m/s (y)	122.60 6m/s (y)	269.00 s (y)
1871	100.80 6m/s (y)	121.60 6m/s (y)	262.00 s (y)
1872	100.50 6m/s (y)	119.50 6m/s (y)	262.00 s (y)
1873	100.30 6m/s (y)	122.30 6m/s (y)	262.00 s (y)
1874	99.90 6m/s (y)	122.70 6m/s (y)	254.00 s (y)
1875	101.00 6m/s (y)	123.10 6m/s (y)	249.00 s (y)
1876	100.10 6m/s (y)	124.80 6m/s (y)	245.00 s (y)
1877	99.60 6m/s (y)	123.80 6m/s (y)	244.00 s (y)
1878	101.80 6m/s (y)	124.20 6m/s (y)	237.00 s (y)
1879	102.00 6m/s (y)	124.00 6m/s (y)	229.00 s (y)
1880	100.30 6m/s (y)	122.70 6m/s (y)	233.00 s (y)
1881	99.80 6m/s (y)	123.40 6m/s (y)	229.00 s (y)
1882	99.80 6m/s (y)	123.80 6m/s (y)	227.00 s (y)
1883	100.70 6m/s (y)	124.10 6m/s (y)	
1884	101.40 6m/s (y)	123.20 6m/s (y)	227.00 s (y)
1885	101.30 6m/s (y)	122.70 6m/s (y)	216.00 s (y)
1886	101.40 6m/s (y)	122.30 6m/s (y)	200.00 s (y)

	BATAVIA on:			
	Amsterdam [a]	**London** [b]	**Singapore** [e]	**Japan** [g]
	per 100 Dutch guilders [c]	per 10 pounds sterling [d]	per 100 Mexican dollars, from 1906 per 100 Straits Settlements dollars [f]	per 100 yen [h]
	in Dutch guilders (Netherlands Indian current)			
1887	101.30 6m/s (y)	121.20 6m/s (y)	193.00 s (y)	
1888	99.90 6m/s (y)	120.40 6m/s (y)	185.00 s (y)	
1889	*100.30* 6m/s (y)	119.70 6m/s (y)	188.00 s (y)	
1890	101.00 6m/s (y)	121.00 6m/s (y)	208.00 s (y)	
1891	*101.00* 6m/s (y)	121.90 6m/s (y)	199.00 s (y)	
1892	*101.80* 6m/s (y)	121.80 6m/s (y)	177.00 s (y)	
1893	*101.10* 6m/s (y)	121.00 6m/s (y)	160.00 s (y)	
1894	100.90 6m/s (y)	121.20 6m/s (y)	132.00 s (y)	
1895	100.80 6m/s (y)	122.10 6m/s (y)	131.00 s (y)	
1896	100.20 6m/s (y)	122.30 6m/s (y)	134.00 s (y)	
1897	100.10 6m/s (y)	121.30 6m/s (y)	122.00 s (y)	
1898	100.00 6m/s (y)	121.20 6m/s (y)	118.00 s (y)	
1899	99.50 6m/s (y)	120.40 6m/s (y)	120.00 s (y)	
1900	99.30 6m/s (y)	120.00 6m/s (y)	123.00 s (y)	
1901	100.20 6m/s (y)	120.90 6m/s (y)	120.00 s (y)	
1902	100.80 6m/s (y)	122.60 6m/s (y)	106.00 s (y)	
1903	100.20 6m/s (y)	121.80 6m/s (y)	108.00 s (y)	
1904	100.60 t.t. (y)	121.70 6m/s (y)	117.00 s (y)	
1905	100.30 t.t. (y)	120.80 6m/s (y)	123.00 s (y)	
1906	99.80 t.t. (y)	121.30 6m/s (y)	141.00 s (y)	
1907	99.90 t.t. (y)	121.40 6m/s (y)	141.00 s (y)	
1908	99.80 t.t. (y)	121.40 6m/s (y)	140.00 s (y)	
1909	100.00 t.t. (y)	121.00 6m/s (y)	141.00 s (y)	
1910	99.80 t.t. (y)	120.70 6m/s (y)	142.00 s (y)	
1911	99.80 t.t. (y)	120.60 6m/s (y)	141.00 s (y)	
1912	99.80 t.t. (y)	120.20 6m/s (y)	141.00 s (y)	
1913	100.00 t.t. (y)	120.30 t.t. (y)	142.00 s (y)	124.00 t.t. (y)
1914	100.40 t.t. (y)	120.60 t.t. (y)	143.00 s (y)	125.00 t.t. (y)

[a]   Until 1827 the usance changed very often between three, four and six months' sight. In the 1830s usances deviating from six months' sight are given only in exceptional cases. Annual average values including rates for usances other than on six months are printed *in italics*.
From December 3ʳᵈ 1845 until the end of 1850 fixed rates are given (<u>underlined</u>; 95.00 silver guilders in the Netherlands for 100 recepis guilders in Batavia at the usance of ten months after date) (VAN LAANEN [1980], p. 20).
From 1851 onwards, government rates; in 1889, from 1891 to 1893 and from 1899 onwards bank and private rates. In the case of bank bills on the Netherlands there was still a distinction between 'Dutch bank bills' on the one hand, i.e. bills on the Dutch bank in Amsterdam, and 'particulare bank bills' on the other, i.e. bills on other Dutch bankers (NOBACK [1877], p. 114). "During the

1860s the Government's selling rates were higher than private rates, while thereafter, up to 1884, they were somewhat lower" (VAN LAANEN [1980], p. 120). Detailed notes to the compiling of this rate series in ibid., pp. 118f.

[b] Until 1835 the usance changed very often between 30 days', 90 days', four and six months' sight. Around 1840 usances differing from six months sight were exceptional. Annual average values that contain rates for usances other than six months are printed *in italics*.
Until 1862 private and bank rates, from 1863 bank rates. "Because of their greater financial strength, the banks could offer rates that were generally around 1% higher than private rates (probably trading houses)"; ibid., p. 120.

[c] Concerning the Dutch currency, see pp. 58f.

[d] Concerning the British currency, see pp. 3–5.

[e] The duration of a journey from Batavia to Singapore is irrelevant to the usance; VAN LAANEN [1980], p. 120.

[f] Concerning the Straits Settlements currency, see p. 537.

[g] Quotations of the Factorij of the Nederlandsche Handel-Maatschappij in Batavia.

[h] Concerning the Japanese currency, see pp. 529f.

27
Mauritius (1825–1914)

Exchange market: Port Louis (1825–1914)

Sources: PRO London, CO 172: *Blue Books of the Colony of Mauritius* (1825–1846, 1853–1864); *Mauritius Price Current and Shipping List* (1847–1853); *The Economist*, London (1853–1864); *The Commercial Gazette*, Port Louis (1864–1869, 1893–1897); *Overland Commercial Gazette*, Port Louis (1864–1878); *Mercantile Record Overland Edition*, Port Louis (1877–1887); *Bulletin Commercial du Carnéen*, Port Louis (1888–1892); *The Merchants and Planters Gazette (Overland Mail Edition)*, Port Louis (1897–1914).

Concordance: *WdW IV*, pp. 275–312

Currency: Originally Mauritius had been part of the Indian currency area, but British authorities were trying to introduce the pound sterling as the standard currency unit on Mauritius for large parts of the 19th century. Nevertheless, 'local' silver money, above all Spanish dollars and rupees, continued to be dominant in internal payment transactions, similar to the French colonial era (up to 1810). Because silver was also used for paying bills, the fall in silver prices from the 1860s found its explicit expression in the quotations on those countries, which had the gold standard as well. The former French colonial currency of account piastre coloniale or courante (of 10 livres colonials; approximately equal to 1 Spanish dollar), i.e. in English: 'current dollar' or 'colonial dollar' (of 100 cents), was used for the quotations as well. After the British conquest of Mauritius in 1810, the Spanish or current dollar was valued at 2 (Sicca) rupees on December 6th 1810, which became the basis of the ratio common in trade during the following decades. The Sicca rupee of 1818 was traded at 2 shillings (officially fixed with 1 shilling 10 pence sterling) and the current dollar at 4 shillings since the introduction of sterling as the only means of payment for public spending by Governor Ordinance of November 25th 1825, effective from January 1st 1826. Apart from the quoting in current dollars, the exchange rate quotations at Mauritius were carried out – with premium and discount – in different currencies depending on the quoted countries:

- on Great Britain, Australia and New Zealand in pounds sterling of 20 shillings at 12 pence (according to Governor-Ordinance of November 25th 1825) (see pp. 3–5);
- on France and Bourbon/Réunion in francs (see p. 280);
- on India, Ceylon and Aden in the different rupees (see pp. 481f.).

The different valuation of the rupee which had been dominating (again) internal payment transactions since the end of the 1860s and the fall in silver prices in the 1870s led to the introduction of the Government rupee of 100 cents as the only means of payment on the island (Order in Council and Proclamation of August 12th 1876), which was also used for quoting all exchange rates from the beginning of 1877 but now in a standardized manner. Thus Mauritius became finally and officially part of the Indian currency area (see p. 482) (CHALMERS [1893], pp. 360–368).

Original quotations on Mauritus: All quotations found in current dollars are converted into pound sterling, francs or rupees on the basis of the following commercial relations between the different currencies:

- 1 current dollar = 4 shillings, therefore: 1 pound sterling = 5 current dollars
- 1 current dollar = 5 francs, therefore: 100 francs = 20 current dollars [a]
- 1 current dollar = 2 rupees, therefore: 100 rupees = 50 current dollars

on:	in:	per:
Aden	per cent premium or discount	1 Government rupee
Bourbon/Réunion	current dollars	1 pound sterling [a]
from 1829	per cent premium or discount	100 francs
from 1877	per cent premium or discount	1 pound sterling [a]
Calcutta	per cent premium or discount	1 Sicca rupee
from 1835 (9)	per cent premium or discount	1 Company's rupee
from 1843	current dollars	100 Company's rupees
from 1862	current dollars	100 Government rupees
from 1877	per cent premium or discount	1 Government rupee
Ceylon	current dollars	100 Government rupees
from 1877	per cent premium or discount	1 Government rupee
France	current dollars	1 pound sterling [a]
from 1829	per cent premium or discount	100 francs
from 1877	per cent premium or discount	1 pound sterling [a]
London	current dollars	1 pound sterling
from 1826	per cent premium or discount [b]	1 pound sterling
New Zealand	per cent premium or discount [b]	1 pound sterling
Sydney & Melbourne	per cent premium or discount [b]	1 pound sterling

[a]   1 pound sterling = 25 francs (cf. NOBACK [1877], p. 595)

[b]   "The old habit of treating the rupee as 2 s. [shillings] sterling survives in the local method of quoting the exchanges on London on the basis of a nominal par of 100 rupees = 10 l. [pounds], and adding the requisite number of rupees 'per cent premium'" (CHALMERS [1893], p. 368; cf. ibid., p. 361; SWOBODA [1889], p. 432).

Other data available: Australia, s (1888–1891) – Bombay, 30d/s (1864–1895); 60d/s (1877–1884); s (1864–1897) – Calcutta, 30d/s (1864–1895) – Ceylon, s (1879–1895) – Hong Kong, 90d/s (1885/86); s (1889/90) – London, 6m/s (1829; 1841–1847); 60d/s (1864–1897); 30d/s (1829–1853, 1864–1897); s (1864–1897) – Madras, 60d/s (1841–1879); 30d/s (1847/48, 1864–1895); s (1864–1897) – Melbourne, 60d/s (1864–1891) – Seychelles, s (1888–1890) – Singapore (1889/90) – Sydney, 30d/s (1879–1887); s (1879–1891) – Tamatave, s (1888–1890).

Belonging to Great Britain from 1815, Mauritius was – with Port Louis as the best port in the southern Indian Ocean area – the most important traffic junction as well as an important producer of sugar in that region: "Lying on the highway round the Cape to India, and ruled successively by the two European powers who have built up an Indian Empire, Mauritius necessarily formed its chief trading relations with India. With the opening up of Australia, Mauritius grew to be a great entrepôt for the East and the rising Australian Colonies …, but the opening of the Suez Canal in 1869 … [dealt] a heavy blow at the commerce of the Colony" (CHALMERS [1893], p. 360). Because of these trade and transport relations, the cashless payment transactions of Mauritius were primarily oriented towards Europe, India and, in the second half of the 19th century, increasingly towards Australia as well, but not towards South East and East Asia or the African coasts.

Therefore London, France – as the former colonial powers –, India (Calcutta, Bombay and Madras as well as Ceylon) and the Île de Bourbon or Réunion respectively (since 1848) were the most important exchange partners of Mauritius in the 19th century. The greatest number of all exchange operations of Mauritius were carried out with London. Mauritius' quotations on this financial market were divided into Treasury bills (30 days' sight) and private bills (90 days' sight, later 60 days' sight as well) (cf. NOBACK [1858], p. 478), only the last being available throughout the whole period of documentation (excluding from the years 1825 and 1827) and being therefore presented here. Until around the mid-century Treasury bills were generally quoted 3–6%, in certain years (in around 1845/46) even 10–12% higher than private bills, because British coins, being undervalued on Mauritius with regard to the Spanish dollar and the rupee, were accepted as Treasury bills at full par. The (relatively) high importance of Mauritius as exchange partner of London at that time resulted from the fact that the exchange rates of Mauritius on London were quoted regularly in the London *Economist* in the third quarter of the 19th century.

Up to 1840 all quotations on "India" referred equally to Calcutta, Bombay and Madras. When a distinction was made between Calcutta and Madras (with only slight differences) from 1841, the quotations on Calcutta were of an evidently higher number and regularity so that these figures were chosen for presentation here; Bombay does not seem to appear again on the exchange rate currents until 1864. Quotations on New South Wales were given for the first time in 1839/40, on Sydney and Melbourne with generally equal rates from the 1860s, and there are occasionally even rates on New Zealand. In the wake of the Australian gold fever during the 1850s and the inflow of Australian sovereigns to Mauritius, the cashless payment transactions from Mauritius to the Australian colonies became increasingly important.

In the case of Mauritius the quotations on 'neighbouring' places in the Indian Ocean area are of special interest. Apart from Réunion these were mainly Aden as well as – significantly less relevant – Tamatave, the main trading centre of Madagascar, and the Seychelles (in around 1890). The opening of the Suez Canal in 1869 marked particularly the fall of Mauritius as an important emporium within the trade with India and the rise of the Arabian port Aden (cf. CHALMERS [1893], p. 360; NELKENBRECHER [1890], p. 7). Exchange operations with the latter seem to have become interesting in Port Louis for some years. Hong Kong and Singapore, however, had been quoted only for a few months during the 1880s.

After 1890 the network of quoted exchange partners was reduced by the exit of Australia, so that London remained the only city to be quoted from 1897 on (90 days' sight), presumably owing to a lack of sources. It can be assumed that Mauritius had lost its formerly international, but from 1869 already declining, importance as exchange place to a great extent by that time. In addition, the drop in local sugar production at around the turn of the century supports this assumption (cf. TOUSSAINT [1977], p. 96).

The obvious gaps in the quotations on Mauritius can be put down primarily to a lack of sources. The newspapers of Port Louis, though not constantly available, give, in general, exchange rate currents of the three most important banks of the island: the local Commercial Bank, the branches of the Oriental Bank and of the Chartered Bank of India, Australia, and China (cf. NOBACK [1877], p. 596). From those banks the rates of the Oriental Bank Corporation are almost exclusively documented because they record the greatest variety of quoted places. Nevertheless, even these data are somewhat incomplete, which indicates, together with the non-standardized manner of quotation up to 1876, that the exchange market in Port Louis was comparatively underdeveloped throughout large parts of the 19th century.

References: James PENNINGTON, *The Currency of the British Colonies*, London 1848 [repr. New York 1967], pp. 154–169; Robert CHALMERS, *History of Currency in the British Colonies*, London 1893 [repr. Colchester 1972], pp. 360–370; Auguste TOUSSAINT, *History of Mauritius*, London – Basingstoke 1977 (1971); W. Evan NELSON, The Gold Standard in Mauritius and the Straits Settlements between 1850 and 1914, *Journal of Imperial and Commonwealth History* 16 (1987), pp. 48–76; Markus A. DENZEL, Kolonialstädte als Finanzplätze vom 18. Jahrhundert bis 1914. Das asiatische Wechselnetz und seine Anbindung an das europäisch-internationale Zahlungsverkehrssystem, in Horst GRÜNDER / Peter JOHANEK (eds.), *Kolonialstädte – Europäische Enklaven oder Schmelztigel der Kulturen?*, Münster 2001, pp. 225–259.

27.1 Mauritus exchange rates

27.1.1 On places in the sterling currency area (London, Australia, New Zealand)

	MAURITIUS on:	
	London [a]	**New South Wales** [b]
	per 100 pounds sterling [c]	
	in pounds sterling	
1825	103.24 30d/s (8)	
1826	98.96 90d/s (12)	
1827	101.58 30d/s (11)	
1828		
1829	99.20 90d/s (12)	
1830	99.89 90d/s (10)	
1831	102.48 90d/s (12)	
1832	100.84 90d/s (12)	
1833	99.28 90d/s (10)	
1834	98.13 90d/s (12)	
1835	97.77 90d/s (12)	
1836	96.22 90d/s (9)	
1837	94.90 90d/s (11)	
1838	98.81 90d/s (12)	
1839	96.07 90d/s (12)	102.12 30d/s (12)
1840	95.57 90d/s (12)	102.18 30d/s (7)
1841	100.00 90d/s (3)	
1842	103.84 90d/s (6)	
1843	105.48 90d/s (11)	
1844	97.30 90d/s (12)	
1845	95.22 90d/s (11)	
1846	93.84 90d/s (12)	
1847	98.11 90d/s (12)	
1848	100.92 90d/s (12)	
1849	100.38 90d/s (12)	
1850	99.05 90d/s (12)	
1851	95.65 90d/s (12)	
1852	97.58 90d/s (10)	
1853	96.84 90d/s (11)	
1854	97.77 90d/s (12)	
1855	98.25 90d/s (12)	
1856	95.02 90d/s (12)	
1857	97.25 90d/s (12)	
1858	96.84 90d/s (12)	

	MAURITIUS on:		
	London [a]	**Sydney & Melbourne** [d]	**New Zealand**
	per 100 pounds sterling, from 1877 per 10 pounds sterling [c]		
	in pounds sterling		
1859	99.32 90d/s (12)		
1860	98.11 90d/s (12)		
1861	99.07 90d/s (12)		
1862	98.77 90d/s (12)		
1863	99.61 90d/s (12)		
1864	99.98 90d/s (8)	94.71 60d/s (6)	
1865	100.37 90d/s (11)	*100.93* 60d/s (10)	
1866	101.72 90d/s (7)	95.00 60d/s (1)	
1867	102.50 90d/s (12)	95.25 60d/s (4)	94.50 60d/s (2)
1868	101.89 90d/s (4)	97.00 60d/s (1)	95.00 60d/s (1)
1869	103.43 90d/s (7)		
1870	101.40 90d/s (10)	95.00 60d/s (2)	
1871	103.64 90d/s (11)	99.69 60d/s (4)	
1872	101.69 90d/s (12)	99.71 60d/s (6)	
1873	103.46 90d/s (12)	100.01 60d/s (11)	100.00 60d/s (3)
1874	106.87 90d/s (9)	102.48 60d/s (7)	101.50 60d/s (6)
1875	109.50 90d/s (8)	104.92 60d/s (9)	104.00 60d/s (1)
1876	113.15 90d/s (9)	108.36 60d/s (9)	
	in Government rupees		
1877	113.94 90d/s (12)	111.07 60d/s (4)	
1878	113.85 90d/s (12)	*114.07* 60d/s (4)	
1879	122.22 90d/s (12)	115.70 60d/s (4)	117.50 60d/s (2)
1880	120.03 90d/s (12)		
1881	118.50 90d/s (12)	115.79 60d/s (6)	114.50 60d/s (2)
1882	120.52 90d/s (11)	119.52 60d/s (10)	
1883	121.56 90d/s (11)	120.40 60d/s (9)	
1884	121.10 90d/s (12)	118.40 60d/s (5)	
1885	127.14 90d/s (11)	127.25 60d/s (4)	125.50 60d/s (2)
1886	138.75 90d/s (12)	138.75 60d/s (12)	
1887	141.34 90d/s (12)	141.34 60d/s (12)	
1888	145.67 90d/s (12)	145.67 60d/s (12)	
1889	146.17 90d/s (12)	145.92 60d/s (12)	
1890	135.52 90d/s (11)	135.96 60d/s (11)	
1891	138.45 90d/s (9)	139.65 60d/s (9)	
1892	163.50 90d/s (2)		
1893	164.25 90d/s (12)		
1894	178.34 90d/s (12)		
1895	185.34 90d/s (9)		

	MAURITIUS on:
	London [a]
	per 10 pounds sterling [c]
	in Government rupees
1896	169.25 90d/s (6)
1897	162.34 90d/s (3)
1898	153.55 90d/s (12)
1899	150.15 90d/s (12)
1900	150.09 90d/s (12)
1901	151.32 90d/s (12)
1902	152.88 90d/s (12)
1903	151.17 90d/s (12)
1904	150.88 90d/s (12)
1905	150.42 90d/s (12)
1906	150.63 90d/s (12)
1907	151.84 90d/s (12)
1908	152.38 90d/s (12)
1909	151.42 90d/s (12)
1910	151.00 90d/s (12)
1911	150.90 90d/s (12)
1912	150.96 90d/s (12)
1913	150.77 90d/s (12)
1914	151.00 90d/s (7)

[a] From 1829 to 1865 the quotations were done for private bills, and from 1854 also for documentary bills. Until the end of the documented period, the usance of 90 days' sight was the most important one, although much shorter ones were quoted as well.

[b] In 1839 the quotations were for Treasury bills, in 1840 for private bills.

[c] Concerning the sterling currencies in Great Britain, Australia and New Zealand, see pp. 3–5, 581f., 591.

[d] From 1864 the quotations on Sydney are generally equal to those on Melbourne. In rare cases when the quotations on both places differ from one another, those on Sydney were preferred. In 1865 and 1878 the quotation on Sydney was effected for 10 pounds sterling in Australian sovereigns.

27.1.2 On places in the franc currency area (France, Bourbon/Réunion)

	MAURITIUS on:				
	France		Bourbon/Réunion [a]		
	per 100 francs [b]				
	in francs				
1825	98.58	90d/s	(6)	102.84	15d/s	(6)
1826				103.09	15d/s	(12)
1827				96.70	15d/s	(10)
1828						
1829	100.20	90d/s	(10)	96.33	15d/s	(10)
1830	100.48	90d/s	(11)	95.46	15d/s	(11)
1831	101.37	90d/s	(9)	95.75	15d/s	(12)
1832	101.50	90d/s	(11)	96.00	15d/s	(10)
1833	100.14	90d/s	(11)	97.59	15d/s	(11)
1834	99.40	90d/s	(10)	99.08	15d/s	(12)
1835	97.92	90d/s	(12)	99.91	15d/s	(11)
1836	96.93	90d/s	(10)	98.76	15d/s	(12)
1837	94.92	90d/s	(12)	98.00	15d/s	(12)
1838	98.89	90d/s	(12)	97.21	15d/s	(11)
1839	96.33	90d/s	(12)	97.19	15d/s	(12)
1840	97.05	90d/s	(12)	98.42	15d/s	(6)
1841	100.00	90d/s	(3)			
1842	104.17	90d/s	(9)			
1843	105.55	90d/s	(12)			
1844	95.88	90d/s	(8)			
1845	95.95	90d/s	(5)			
1846	95.22	90d/s	(3)			
1847	93.84	90d/s	(12)			
1848	98.11	90d/s	(12)			
1849	100.92	90d/s	(12)			
1850	100.38	90d/s	(12)			
1851	99.05	90d/s	(12)			
1852	95.65	90d/s	(10)			
1853	97.58	90d/s	(11)			
...						
1864	100.62	90d/s	(12)	96.25	15d/s	(6)
1865	101.05	90d/s	(11)			
1866	102.22	90d/s	(7)			
1867	103.00	90d/s	(12)			
1868	102.39	90d/s	(9)			
1869	103.93	90d/s	(8)			

	MAURITIUS on:	
	France	**Réunion** [a]
	per 100 francs [b]	
	in francs	
1870	101.95 90d/s (10)	
1871	104.09 90d/s (11)	
1872	102.15 90d/s (12)	
1873	103.94 90d/s (12)	
1874	107.37 90d/s (9)	
1875	110.00 90d/s (8)	
1876	113.64 90d/s (9)	
	in Government rupees	
1877	45.77 90d/s (12)	
1878	45.73 90d/s (12)	
1879	48.98 90d/s (12)	
1880	48.22 90d/s (12)	
1881	47.61 90d/s (12)	
1882	48.38 90d/s (11)	
1883	48.86 90d/s (11)	48.00 s (1)
1884	48.63 90d/s (12)	46.98 s (9)
1885	51.06 90d/s (11)	45.96 s (10)
1886	55.70 90d/s (12)	54.57 s (12)
1887	56.74 90d/s (12)	55.80 s (12)
1888	58.47 90d/s (12)	57.17 s (11)
1889	58.67 90d/s (12)	57.20 s (12)
1890	54.34 90d/s (11)	53.46 s (8)
1891	55.58 90d/s (9)	
1892	65.60 90d/s (2)	
1893	65.94 90d/s (12)	60.94 s (3)
1894	71.54 90d/s (12)	67.34 s (12)
1895	74.34 90d/s (9)	70.27 s (9)
1896	67.90 90d/s (6)	67.60 s (6)
1897	65.14 90d/s (3)	64.80 s (3)

[a]   After 1848 the Île de Bourbon was called Réunion.

[b]   Concerning the franc currency in France and on Réunion, where the French currency was legal tender as well, see p. 280.

27.1.3 On places in the rupee currency area (Calcutta, Ceylon, Aden)

	MAURITIUS on:
	Calcutta [a]
	per 100 Sicca rupees, from 1835 per 100 Company's rupees [b]
	in Sicca rupees
1825	102.20 30d/s (5)
1826	
1827	100.45 30d/s (9)
1828	
1829	100.68 30d/s (11)
1830	100.11 30d/s (11)
1831	100.14 30d/s (11)
1832	98.19 30d/s (11)
1833	98.67 30d/s (6)
1834	100.00 30d/s (6)
	in Company's rupees
1835	99.26 30d/s (6)
1836	101.44 30d/s (7)
1837	100.88 30d/s (10)
1838	105.58 30d/s (12)
1839	102.00 30d/s (10)
1840	100.26 30d/s (12)
1841	101.00 60d/s (3)
1842	104.78 60d/s (9)
1843	108.62 60d/s (9)
1844	99.50 60d/s (4)
1845	102.00 60d/s (5)
1846	102.34 60d/s (6)
1847	99.88 60d/s (8)
1848	101.18 60d/s (12)
1849	97.00 60d/s (12)
1850	101.04 60d/s (12)
1851	102.18 60d/s (12)
1852	101.44 60d/s (10)
1853	101.14 60d/s (4)
1854	
1855	
1856	
1857	
1858	

	MAURITIUS on:							
	Calcutta			Ceylon [c]			Aden [d]		
	per 100 Company's rupees, from 1862 per 100 Government rupees [b]								
	in Company's rupees, from 1862 in Government rupees								
1859									
1860									
1861									
1862									
1863									
1864	101.38	s	(11)	104.50	3d/s	(6)			
1865	101.60	s	(11)						
1866	102.76	s	(6)						
1867	103.54	s	(12)						
1868	100.66	s	(9)						
1869	105.44	s	(7)						
1870	101.00	s	(10)						
1871	100.46	s	(11)						
1872	100.92	s	(12)						
1873	101.00	s	(12)				100.75	60d/s	(2)
1874	102.80	s	(7)				101.84	60d/s	(6)
1875	103.26	s	(6)	102.00	30d/s	(2)	104.50	60d/s	(1)
1876	101.00	s	(9)	102.00	30d/s	(9)			
1877	101.13	s	(12)	101.88	30d/s	(12)			
1878	100.41	s	(12)	100.34	30d/s	(9)			
1879	101.33	s	(10)	101.44	30d/s	(8)			
1880	102.96	s	(12)	103.13	30d/s	(12)			
1881	100.38	s	(12)	101.38	30d/s	(12)			
1882	101.14	s	(11)	101.23	30d/s	(9)			
1883	101.14	s	(11)	101.14	30d/s	(11)			
1884	100.92	s	(6)	100.92	30d/s	(6)			
1885	101.00	s	(11)	100.69	30d/s	(11)			
1886	101.50	s	(12)	101.00	30d/s	(11)			
1887	100.88	s	(12)	100.28	30d/s	(11)			
1888	100.30	s	(10)	99.84	30d/s	(12)	100.50	s	(6)
1889	100.25	s	(12)	100.00	30d/s	(12)	100.42	s	(12)
1890	100.29	s	(8)	99.72	30d/s	(8)	101.00	s	(8)
1891									
1892	101.00	s	(2)						
1893	101.34	s	(9)	101.92	30d/s	(3)			
1894	101.53	30d/s	(12)	101.79	30d/s	(12)			
1895	101.50	30d/s	(9)	101.75	30d/s	(9)			
1896	101.50	s	(6)	101.75	s	(6)			
1897	101.50	s	(3)	101.75	s	(3)			

[a]   Until August 1835 Bombay and Madras are listed with the same quotation, though in Bombay or
      Madras rupees respectively per 100 Bombay or Madras rupees respectively. From September un-
      til the end of 1835 there is no evidence of any quotation. From 1836 until 1840 Calcutta, Bombay
      and Madras are quoted with the same rates per 100 Company's rupees.

[b]   Concerning the rupees currencies, see pp. 495f.

[c]   Although the official currency of Ceylon was the pound sterling of 20 shillings at 12 pence, all
      transactions in trade and exchange business were done in rupees, but here – and on Mauritius as
      well – at 100 cents (PENNINGTON [1848], pp. 164–169; NOBACK [1877], p. 238; SONNDORFER
      [1910], p. 339).

[d]   Exchange rates on Aden were quoted per rupees, which functionned as the common currency in
      the whole Indian Ocean area.

28
Indochinese Union (1888–1914)

Exchange market: Saigon (1888–1914)

Source: *Administration des monnaies* [1916], pp. 138–145 (1888–1914); *Le Temps*, Paris (1910–1913).

Concordance: *WdW V*, pp. 255–259

Currency: The French Treasury in Saigon sold bills of exchange in piastres trésor, which were equal to the Spanish or Mexican dollar.

Original quotations at Saigon

on:	in:	per:
Paris	francs	1 piastre trésor
London	shillings and pence sterling	1 piastre trésor

Saigon, which had been in the possession of France since 1859, was the most important trading centre and the only exchange place of international relevance in French Indochina and in the Indochinese Union from 1887 respectively. There are references to exchange operations of Saigon with Paris from the end of the 1860s, when the French Treasury (Trésor) sold a bill of 100 francs for 18 to 18½ piastres trésor (cf. NOBACK [1877], p. 53), whereas local banks generally sold them for almost 17 piastres. Nevertheless, longer exchange rate series are not available until 1888, and there are exclusively government quotations on Paris and London. According to the decree of December 30th 1886, the governor-general could fix the official quotations for the franc for government purposes, although this rate should have been fixed as close to the commercial rate as possible. When the commercial rate fluctuated noticeably, the governor-general also changed the official rate (SPALDING [1918], p. 228), so that the documented quotations perfectly describe the changes on the Saigon exchange market. Apart from the quotations on Paris and London, the three most important banks of Saigon – the Banque de l'Indo-Chine, the Chartered Bank of India, Australia, and China, and the Hongkong & Shanghai Banking Corporation – also listed the quotations on Hong Kong and Singapore as well as on Manila from the end of the 1860s. In any case, the main business of these banks in Saigon consisted in buying up the drafts of the export business, above all those on Hong Kong and partly those on other places on the Chinese coast (NOBACK [1877], p. 53). While the source mentioned above does not list any usances at all, the information given in contemporary merchant manuals and in the literature is contradictory: on Paris and Asian places mainly 30 days' sight bills seem to have been drawn, on London those with terms between three and six months' sight. At the beginning of the 20th century the two European places have probably been quoted at sight and three months' sight (ibid.; SWOBODA [1889], p. 472; SPALDING [1918], p. 231).

References: Administration des monnaies et des médailles, *Rapport au Ministre des Finances*, Paris 1916; William F. SPALDING, *Eastern Exchange, Currency and Finance*, London ²1918, pp. 227–236.

28.1 Saigon exchange rates

28.1.1 On Paris and London

	SAIGON on:				
	Paris		London		
	per 100 francs [a]		per 10 pounds sterling [b]		
	in piastres trésor				
1888	26.10	[c]	(12)	65.83	[c]	(12)
1889	26.21	[c]	(12)	65.91	[c]	(12)
1890	23.95	[c]	(12)	60.05	[c]	(12)
1891	24.62	[c]	(12)	62.33	[c]	(12)
1892	27.65	[c]	(12)	69.78	[c]	(12)
1893	30.69	[c]	(12)	77.58	[c]	(12)
1894	37.32	[c]	(12)	94.02	[c]	(12)
1895	37.32	[c]	(12)	95.05	[c]	(12)
1896	36.64	[c]	(12)	92.86	[c]	(12)
1897	40.50	[c]	(12)	99.27	[c]	(12)
1898	41.50	[c]	(12)	105.09	[c]	(12)
1899	40.27	[c]	(12)	101.52	[c]	(12)
1900	39.16	[c]	(12)	98.85	[c]	(12)
1901	40.07	[c]	(12)	101.59	[c]	(12)
1902	45.69	[c]	(12)	114.99	[c]	(12)
1903	46.84	[c]	(12)	116.09	[c]	(12)
1904	43.44	[c]	(12)	109.18	[c]	(12)
1905	41.79	[c]	(12)	105.59	[c]	(12)
1906	36.89	[c]	(12)	93.13	[c]	(12)
1907	35.66	[c]	(12)	90.05	[c]	(12)
1908	40.84	[c]	(12)	102.89	[c]	(12)
1909	41.57	[c]	(12)	105.89	[c]	(12)
1910	43.07	[c]	(12)	109.93	[c]	(12)
1911	43.76	[c]	(12)	111.63	[c]	(12)
1912	40.08	[c]	(12)	101.18	[c]	(12)
1913	39.91	[c]	(12)	100.67	[c]	(12)
1914	40.62	[c]	(7)	102.30	[c]	(7)

[a]   Concerning the French currency, see pp. 279f.

[b]   Concerning the British currency, see pp. 3–5.

[c]   In the documented sources no usances could be found (see above).

29
Persia (1809–1914)

Exchange markets: Tehran (1814–1914), Tabriz (1809–1814), Rasht (1869/70–1914), Mashhad (1889/90–1914) and Bushire (1900/01–1914)

Sources: ISSAWI (ed.) [1971], pp. 343–345 (1814–1914); RABINO [1892], p. 31 (1863–1889).

Currency: In Persia foreign exchange rates were fixed in krans of 20 shâhîs at 50 dînârs. During the early 19th century, this kran (or qirân), which was equal to one-tenth of a tûmân (1 tûmân = 10,000 dînârs), contained 8.72 grammes of fine silver. "The history of Iran's currency in the nineteenth century is one of continuous depreciation …, due at first mainly to debasement and later to the sharp drop in the price of silver" (ISSAWI [ed.] [1971], p. 388). Just to mention only a few important steps the legal fine weight of the krân was 5.14 grammes of fine silver from 1834, 4.59 grammes of fine silver from c. 1857 and 4.14 grammes of fine silver from 1879. Although the gold standard was nominally introduced in 1857, the banknotes issued by the Imperial Bank of Persia were convertible only in silver. So the decline of the price of silver (from the 1860s, but above all from 1871 to 1898) reduced the value of Persia's silver currency against the foreign gold currencies, although the debasement was still continuing and the Imperial Bank of Persia was issuing banknotes. So Persia "had to wait till after the First World War for a sound and flexible currency" (ibid., p. 389; cf. SWOBODA [1909], p. 770).

Original quotations at the Persian exchange markets:

on:	in:	per:
London	krâns	1 pound sterling

All quotations documented in the following have already been calculated in this way by ISSAWI and RABINO.

Concerning the Middle Asian region, there are only a few exchange rate quotations from Persia, which Issawi has already compiled: "In the first half of the period, the source was usually a statement of expenses incurred in Iranian money, with the equivalent amount given in either sterling or sicca or Bombay rupees. In the latter half, the consular reports give either the average rate prevailing in their district during the year under review, or the range of such rates" (ISSAWI [ed.] [1971], p. 339). In that case we are dealing with quotations exclusively on London, which were noted down in several Persian trading places, although a constant, long series cannot be drawn up for any of the towns and for many years no quotation was available at all. For the years before 1870 the quotations come almost exclusively from Tabriz and Tehran, by far – and in this order – the two most important trading centres of Persia (NOBACK [1851], p. 885; NOBACK [1877], p. 869; RABINO [1892], pp. 33). For the following decades, rates are increasingly available from other places as well, especially from Rasht at the Caspian Sea, from Mashhad in Khorasan and Bushire at the Persian Gulf. However, since there was no market for bills of exchange on Persia in London, the relevant financial journals – e.g. the London *Economist* – did not publish any quotations from Persia, as was the case for other Asian markets. If any exchanges were drawn on Persia at all, this was done similarly to the cashless payment transactions from Europe, that is, from London on India: "The financial status and responsibility of the drawer and the drawee being usually the deciding factors as to which class of bill shall be negotiated" (SPALDING [1918], p. 105).

The geographic situation of Persia between the Russian Empire, the Ottoman Empire and British India, and far from the big intercontinental trade flows of the 19th century, resulted in "the comparative neglect of Iran by European capital and enterprise" (ISSAWI [ed.] [1971], p. 16). Immediately before World War I only a few European merchants and entrepreneurs were residing in Persia, so that the need for cashless payment transactions in the European manner, and the institutions necessary for this, was comparatively small. Not only the Persian exchange market(s), but also the banking system was developed only rudimentarily. In 1888 the New Oriental Banking Corporation was established as the first European bank in Persia, but as early as 1890 it was transformed into the Imperial Bank of Persia. Besides that, only the Russian Banque d'Escompte was of greater international relevance, especially for the transactions between Persia and Russia. Since the banks in Persia did not align the rates individually with the respective quality of the exchanges, but rather negotiated bills of all qualities at a regular rate without any exception, exporters frequently sold their bills at a more favourable price in the bazaars, from where they were directly remitted to London for acceptance, so that the banks missed a considerable part of their profit in exchange transactions (SPALDING [1918], p. 106).

Nevertheless, extensive exchange transactions among different Persian towns and with London, Odessa or Bombay, for example, in connection with greater arbitrage dealings with these precious metal markets remained rare in Persia, because "markets are so small in Persia, that such operations are few and far between, and the slightest miscalculation or unforeseen accident may change a profit into a loss" (RABINO [1892], p. 36). At the beginning of the 20th century money transfer with caravans – for instance to the great Russian fairs or to India – was still common practice. Although in Isfahan and Yezd there was a market for rupee bills on Bombay and the rouble was quoted in Tabriz as well as in Khorasan (Mashhad) (thus in 1914, April to July, with 578 krans per 100 roubles; SPALDING [1918], p. 105), the Persian exchange transactions with London were of greater international importance according to the sources known so far. Nonetheless, Tehran is supposed to have quoted London, Odessa, Constantinople, Bombay and Paris before World War I (SWOBODA [1913], p. 697). Exchanges from Persia on London were drawn mostly in pounds sterling, the usance varying between 30 and 90 days after sight (but no precise data are given by Issawi or Rabino).

"Exchange in Persia on London is governed chiefly by the course of exports and imports" (SPALDING [1918], p. 101). As the economically more important northern provinces, in particular Khorasan, orientated themselves mainly towards the Russian Empire, payments resulting from these exports were often settled from Saint Petersburg on London, if they were paid cashlessly at all. Thus "the exchange of Persia on London is specially affected in the north by the value of the rouble, in the south, by that of the rupee. Of these two influences, that of the rouble is the more important and the more constant, Tabriz, the Persian centre of the Russian exchange, approaching much nearer to a regular market than any other place in the country" (RABINO [1892], p. 36). The great importance that the currencies of the neighbouring countries of Russia and India still had in the international trade of Persia at the beginning of the 20th century not only resulted from the increasing political and economic influence of the great powers Russia and Great Britain – especially after the Anglo–Russian Agreement of 1907 in the Treaty of St Petersburg – but above all from the exchange value of the kran, which declined dramatically in the course of the 19th century (see above).

References: Joseph RABINO, Banking in Persia, *Journal of the Institute of Bankers* 13 (1892), pp. 1–54; William F. SPALDING, *Eastern Exchange, Currency and Finance*, London ²1918, pp. 100–106; Charles ISSAWI (ed.), *The Economic History of Iran 1800–1914*, Chicago – London 1971; Hyacinth L. RABINO DI BORGOMALE, *Coins, Medals, and Seals of the Shâhs of Îrân, 1500–1941*, [Tehran] 1971.

29.1 Persian exchange rates

Usances: There is no information available concerning the usances.

29.1.1 On London (from various Persian exchange markets)

	TEHRAN on:		TABRIZ on:	
	London		London	
	per 1 pound sterling [a]			
	in krans			
1809			11.00	(1)
1810				
1811				
1812			11.40	(1)
1813				
1814	12.70	(2)		
1815	13.10	(2)		
1816	12.90	(4)		
1817	12.93	(12)		
1818				
1819				
1820	11.30	(1)		
1821				
1822				
1823				
1824	13.55	(2)		
1825	17.60	(3)	17.60	(3)
1826	17.20	(10)		
1827				
1828				
1829				
1830				
1831				
1832				
1833				
1834	20.00	(1)		
1835				
1836				
1837				
1838				
1839				
1840				

	TEHRAN on:		TABRIZ on:		RASHT on:	
	London		London		London	
	per 1 pound sterling [a]					
	in krans					
1841						
1842	20.00	(1)				
1843						
1844	20.40	(2)				
1845	21.85	(3)				
1846			21.60	(2)		
1847	21.80	(1)	21.25	(2)		
1848	22.20	(5)	21.00	(y)		
1849						
1850						
1851			22.10	(y)		
1852			21.50	(y)		
1853			21.50	(y)		
1854			22.30	(1)		
1855						
1856			22.00	(1)		
1857			22.80	(y)		
1858			22.80	(1)		
1859			22.00	(y)		
1860			22.40	(y)		
1861			22.45	(2)		
1862			22.55	(2)		
1863			22.50	(1)		
1864			22.50	(1)		
1865						
1866			23.92	(9)		
1867			25.00	(9)		
1868	25.00	(1)				
1869/70	26.00	(y)			26.00	(y)
1870/71	25.00	(y)			26.00	(y)
1871/72	23.50	(y)			23.50	(y)
1872/73			24.00	(y)	22.00	(y)
1873/74			24.00	(y)	23.50	(y)
1873/74					23.50	(y)
1875					25.00	(y)
1876			27.00	(1)	26.00	(y)
1876/77	26.00	(y)			25.75	(12)

	TEHRAN on:		TABRIZ on:		RASHT on:		MASHHAD on:		BUSHIRE on:	
	London		London		London		London		London	
	per 1 pound sterling [a]									
	in krans									
1877/78			29.00	(y)							
1878/79	27.00	(y)	27.50	(y)	26.00	(y)					
1879/80	27.00	(y)	27.00	(y)							
1880/81	27.00	(y)									
1881/82	26.80	(y)									
1882/83	28.60	(y)									
1883/84	29.00	(y)			28.00	(y)					
1884/85	31.00	(y)									
1885/86											
1886/87											
1887/88											
1888/89											
1889/90							35.10	(y)			
1890/91							34.00	(y)			
1892					36.00	(y)					
1893											
1894			50.00	(1)	50.00	(y)					
1895											
1896											
1897	51.20	(y)									
1898	50.90	(y)			49.50	(y)					
1899	52.00	(y)			51.80	(y)					
1900	51.10	(y)			50.40	(y)					
1900/01									52.80	(y)
1901	52.50	(y)			52.50	(y)					
1901/02									54.40	(y)
1902	55.50	(y)			55.00	(y)					
1902/03									57.50	(y)
1903	55.70	(y)			53.25	(y)					
1903/04									57.30	(y)
1904/05							59.50	(y)	60.20	(y)
1905/06							61.25	(y)	60.10	(y)
1906/07							54.00	(y)	55.50	(y)
1907/08							48.00	(y)	51.30	(y)
1908/09					53.50	(y)			54.50	(y)
1909/10					54.25	(y)	54.00	(y)	56.55	(y)
1910/11					54.00	(y)					
1911/12	54.50	(y)	54.75	(y)			55.00	(y)	53.65	(y)

	TEHRAN on:	TABRIZ on:	RASHT on:	MASHHAD on:	BUSHIRE on:
	London	London	London	London	London
	per 1 pound sterling [a]				
	in krans				
1912/13					
1913/14	55.00 (y)			55.00 (y)	56.80 (y)

[a]   Concerning the British currency, see pp. 3–5.

29.1.2 On London (yearly average)

	PERSIA on:	
	London	
	per 1 pound sterling [a]	
	in krans	
1863	21.20	(y)
1864	21.20	(y)
1865	21.95	(y)
1866	24.70	(y)
1867	25.00	(y)
1868	25.00	(y)
1869	25.00	(y)
1870	25.00	(y)
1871	22.65	(y)
1872	23.00	(y)
1873	24.50	(y)
1874	25.00	(y)
1875	26.50	(y)
1876	27.00	(y)
1877	27.80	(y)
1878	28.00	(y)
1879	28.00	(y)
1880	27.75	(y)
1881	28.00	(y)
1882	28.00	(y)
1883	29.00	(y)
1884	30.75	(y)
1885	32.10	(y)
1886	33.00	(y)
1887	32.75	(y)
1888	34.75	(y)
1889	36.25	(y)

[a]   Concerning the British currency, see pp. 3–5.

AUSTRALIA/
OCEANIA

30
Australia (1822–1914)

Exchange Markets: Sydney (1822–1914), Melbourne (1851–1914) and Adelaide (1838–1914)

Sources: Sydney: PRO London, CO 206: *Blue Books of the Colony of New South Wales* (1822–1845); BUTLIN [1953], pp. 623–626 (1826–1851); BUTLIN / GINSWICK / STATHAM [1986], p. 58 (1835–1850); *The Course of Exchange*, London (1849); BUTLIN [1986], pp. 333–337 (1851–1875); *Sydney Herald* (*Sydney Morning Herald*) (1846–1849); *The Economist*, London (1849–1894, 1908–1914); *Statistical Register of New South Wales for the Year 1871*, Sydney 1872, p. 189 (1871); *The Sydney Trade Review* (1894–1911). Melbourne: PRO London, CO 313: *Blue Books of the Colony of Victoria* (1851–1854, 1860–1863); BUTLIN [1986], pp. 338–341 (1851–1875); *The Economist*, London (1855–1914); *Statistics of the Colony of Victoria for the Year 1872. Compiled from the Official Records in the Registrar-General's Office*, Melbourne 1873, Part IV: Accumulation (1872). Adelaide: BUTLIN [1953], pp. 696f. (1838–1851); PRO London, CO 17: *Blue Books of the Colony of South Australia*, vol. 13-31 (1841–1858); BUTLIN [1986], pp. 343–345 (1851–1875); *The Economist*, London (1881–1914).

Concordance: *WdW IV*, pp. 321–335

Currency at Sydney: After the setting up of New South Wales in 1788 there were neither coins nor any other kind of transactions with money in the first British colony on the Australian continent. Until 1822, in the "age of barter and tokens" (CHALMERS [1893], p. 242), a few imported coins (above all Spanish dollars), sales receipts, which "passed from hand to hand and constituted a paper currency which could be at any time exchanged for a sterling bill" (ibid., p. 243) on the London Treasury, and several other promissory notes served as means of payment. "Within this miscellany, sterling was frequently employed as a unit of account despite its limited availability as a medium of exchange" (BUTLIN [1994], p. 132), but "in the early nineteenth century 'sterling' very rarely means English money. Occasionally it means pounds, shillings and pence, as opposed to reckoning in, say, dollars or rupees. But in general it referred to Australian money, expressed in £ s. d. of a kind distinguished from 'currency'. 'Colonial currency', which by an easy transition became simply 'currency', meant media of exchange having a purely local circulation and often a very limited acceptability. Before 1810 it meant primarily copper coin, promissory notes and at times wheat" (BUTLIN [1953], p. 65), later on also dollars. The premium on sterling in 'currency' was 20% in 1811, 33.75% in 1812, 43.75% in 1813, 25% in 1814, and 43.75% in 1815 (average values of quarterly rates; ibid., p. 99). Although it was officially laid down in 1816 that in the case of a reorganization of the colony's monetary system the sterling with the pound of 20 shillings or 240 pence (see pp. 3–5) was meant to be the only currency, Spanish dollars were imported on a large scale during the 1810s and in the first half of the 1820s, and dominated the coin circulation of the following years, although they were overvalued. The era of the "supremacy of the Spanish Dollar as the actual standard and measure of value" (1822–1829; CHALMERS [1893], p. 242) was on the one hand characterized by the fact that payments within New South Wales and abroad were generally settled in Spanish dollars until 1829 – either in bills of exchanges (with London) or in cash (with China) – while on the other hand this coin was officially valued differently (since 1823): the same dollar – according to its silver content equal to 4 shillings 2 pence – was paid out by the colonial government at 5 shillings for purchases, at 4 shillings 8 pence to the troops, and at 4 shillings for salaries, but was accepted by the government at a fluctuating exchange rate. On November 23rd 1829 the merchants of Sydney decided to accept from then on the dollar only at 4 shillings 2 pence. With this "popular revolution in the local currency" (ibid, p. 249) the "substitution of a sterling standard" (1829–1851; ibid., p. 242) began. After the second half of the 1820s such large quantities of sterling currency were imported that "a dual dollar–sterling system existed" (BUTLIN [1994], p. 134). "By the early 1830s, Australia was established as part of the sterling area" (ibid.) despite the financial crisis of 1834 and inflation from 1839 to 1841. As early as 1832 the Spanish dollar was everywhere accepted at 4 shillings only. When gold was found in New South Wales in 1851, "a sudden and revolutionary change in the internal trade" (CHALMERS [1893], p. 251) was the result. So, gold dust was a common means of payment for buying bills of exchange by the 1850s (NOBACK [1877], p. 861). In 1853 a mint was established in Sydney, in 1855 British gold was declared to be legal tender and Australian sovereigns were issued and became legal tender in the whole British Empire in 1866. "So the gold discoveries in 1851 finally ended the colonial dependence on British specie supply and, indeed, Australia quickly became not merely a source of gold for minting but in fact became a source of coinage for other parts of the empire, particularly in India" (BUTLIN [1994], p. 91). In 1871 it was determined that all coins minted in Sydney should have the same weight and fineness as those issued in London.

Currency at Melbourne: In the 19th century in the colony of Victoria, separated from New South Wales in 1851, with its capital Melbourne, the currency developed, i.e. the pound sterling of 20 shillings or 240 pence (see pp. 3–5), largely in the same way as that of New South Wales (see above; CHALMERS [1893], p. 263), although the setting up of a mint in Melbourne lasted until 1869. The coins minted there became legal tender in the whole British Empire as well.

Currency at Adelaide: In South Australia, constituted in 1837, exchange transactions were also carried out in pounds sterling of 20 shillings or 240 pence (see pp. 3–5). "The currency of South Australia has little or no history" (CHALMERS [1893], p. 275).

Currency in the Commonwealth of Australia: When in 1901 the Commonwealth of Australia was constituted, the sterling currency was kept as legal tender in Australia. In 1911 the pound of Australia was introduced, which was equal to the former pound sterling.

Original quotations at Sydney, Melbourne and Adelaide

on:	in:	per:
London	% premium or discount or	1 pound sterling
	shillings and pence premium or discount	100 pounds sterling

Other data available from Sydney: London, 30d/s (1831–1845, 1895–1907); 60d/s (1895–1907); 90d/s (1895–1907); 120d/s (1897/98, 1907); dem (1895–1907) – **from Australia:** London, dem (1908–1914); 30d/s (1908–1914); 60d/s (1908–1914); 90d/s (1908–1911); 120d/s (1908–1911).

Regarding the Australian colonies, which were combined in the Commonwealth of Australia on January 1st 1901, three exchange markets with quotations on London were listed in the London *Economist* in the second half of the 19th century: Sydney, Melbourne and Adelaide. From an intercontinental point of view, the quotations of the other Australian colonies (Western Australia, Van Diemen's Land or Tasmania respectively, and Queensland; cf. BUTLIN [1953], passim) were of clearly less relevance which was why they did not receive any further attention in the London financial journals. Because of that the following exposition and the documentation of the Australian exchange rates are limited to the exchange markets of Sydney, Melbourne and Adelaide.

Among these towns Sydney, the capital of New South Wales, is not only the oldest but has also been the most important Australian exchange market for a long period of the 19th century. "The basic source of foreign exchange was in the form of Treasury bills and bills from the military" (BUTLIN [1994], p. 132). These Treasury bills, chargeable to the British government in London, were issued in large numbers (cf. ibid., p. 90) by the Commissariat, "a dominant government store", importer and bank up to 1810, and brought about a "vital foreign exchange" of the colony (ibid.). It was not until the 1810s that private institutions – first the Bank of New South Wales, founded in 1817 – and private transactions in exchange business became increasingly important while the role of the Commissariat was fading so quickly, above all in the 1830s, that it was finally insignificant in around 1840. (Incidentally: "Bills drawn in England on Sydney were even rarer but not entirely absent"; BUTLIN [1953], p. 57.)

After 1822 quotations for such Treasury bills on London were noted in the *Blue Books* of the colony, the rate being fixed as follows: "The Rates of Exchange for Bills on the British Treasury were established from time to time by public competition, the Officer at the Head of the Commissariat Department advertising for Tenders at such periods as the Public Service required, and accepting those of the highest Bidders" (*Blue Book ... New South Wales*, 1825, p. 161), but "there is no uniform principle or mode of fixing the Rate of Exchange for Private Bills" (ibid. 1828, p. 162). The premium of the Treasury bills, with an extreme between 1822 and 1825 and even rising up to 25% for a short time in May 1823 resulted from the fact that the government put a considerable number of imported Spanish dollars in circulation and, therefore, largely stopped the selling of the Government or Commissariat bills on the Treasury. Bills of that kind, which were urgently needed for imports because of the negative balance of payments with England were therefore offered and traded on the 'free market' with a comparatively high premium provided that they were available at all. In 1824 it became legal to draw bills of exchange in Spanish dollars as well, but this was prohibited again after only a few months. In 1826 and 1827 the rate of 103 pounds for a bill of 100 pounds sterling, fixed by the Treasury, was "based upon an estimate of 'the expense and risk' of re-export of coin to Britain" (BUTLIN [1953], p. 162). As this premium was clearly overrated, it was halved on May 8th/24th 1828 and was modified only twice during the ten following years (on February 28th 1835 and on August 13th 1838). "The fixed rate was designed to establish and maintain, in effect, a sterling exchange standard" (ibid., pp. 473f.). In 1839 this official quotation was stopped in the *Blue Books* as the Commissariat and its Treasury bills had lost their relevance for the cashless payment transactions of the colony (BUTLIN [1994], p. 132).

In the 1830s the current situation on the exchange market in Sydney, which emerged as a market outside the Commissariat only in the second half of the 1820s, is reflected in the quotations for private bills (since 1831) and for the bills of different banks (Bank of Australasia, Union Bank of Australia, Commercial Bank; from 1837), which partly had a clearly lower price (with considerable discounts of up to 5%) than the Treasury bills (cf. NOBACK [1855], II, p. 1209). However, owing to the wool exports from Australia, being of sole importance until 1851 and being carried out during the four months between November and February, the yearly exchange rate was subject to intense fluctuations.

During the whole period of documentation London was the only foreign place to be quoted regularly in Sydney (and in the two other Australian exchange markets as well) (cf. ibid.). In the *Blue Book* of New South Wales of 1839, one can find the following reference: "So few Bills of Exchange on Foreign Countries are negociated that it is impossible to give with any precision the rates at which [they] are issued" (*Blue Book ... New South Wales*, 1839, p. 318). Even during the early 20th century, too much had to be paid for bills of exchange on France and Germany, which is why they were not quoted (SONNDORFER [1900], p. 302). In addition to this, China (Canton) or India were only rarely listed; for example, there is a quotation of Sydney on Paris for the year 1843 with 25 francs per 1 pound sterling and on Calcutta with 1 shilling 8 pence per Company's rupee, although "certainly after the early 1820s, the trend of trade connections was set strongly away from India and China and towards Britain" (BUTLIN [1994], p. 164). Nonetheless, merchant manuals of the end of the 19th century also list Scotland, Ireland, Colombo, Singapore, Calcutta, Bombay, Madras, Hong Kong, Canton and Port Louis (Mauritius) as exchange partners of Sydney, whereas the USA – above all New York – was only rarely quoted (NOBACK [1877], p. 861). However, in the sources documented here, no evidence can be furnished of such quotations, although yearly rates for New Zealand as well as for other Australian colonies or places respectively were quoted in some years, e.g. Broken Hill and Wilcannia in New South Wales, Coolgardie, Kalgoorlie, Kanowna, Day Drawn, Roeburne, Perth and Fremantle in Western Australia, Rockhampton and Townsland in Queensland as well as Victoria, South Australia and Tasmania with rates between 98.50 to 99.75 pounds sterling for 100 pounds sterling at the quoted place from 1897 to 1899.

Since 1851, when the exchange rates of the colony of Victoria began, Melbourne quoted only London as well. In 1852 exchange rates on India were listed by the Bank of New South Wales in the colony of Victoria with 1% "in Excess of the Rate on England" (*Blue Book ... Victoria*, 1852). In Melbourne the rupee constantly cost 2 shillings 1 penny at exchange transactions of the Oriental Bank Corporation between 1860 and 1872 and of the Bank of Victoria between 1862 and 1872. Tasmania, South Australia, New Zealand, Queensland and New South Wales were quoted in Melbourne occasionally during the 1860s and 1870s as well, whereas no evidence can be furnished for the quotation on British India, which is listed in the merchant manuals (cf. NOBACK [1877], p. 601).

Exchange rate quotations of the colony of South Australia, founded in 1837 are available from 1838, although the quotations of Adelaide differ significantly from the quotations of, for example, Victoria or New South Wales at least during the first decades (cf. CHALMERS [1893], p. 275). The fact that places of the Asian or Indian area recording Australian exchange markets solely quoted on Sydney and/or Melbourne shows that among the three exchange markets documented here Adelaide had by far the least international importance. All in all, it can be assumed that the exchange markets of Sydney and Melbourne were more or less of the same international importance within the cashless payment system, whereas Adelaide was at most of regional relevance during the early 20th century.

When the quotations of Sydney, Melbourne and Adelaide approximated to each other in the London *Economist* from the turn of the century, they were subsumed under the term 'Australia' after 1908. By the second half of the 1890s the quotations had been split up into several usances (30, 60 and 90 days after sight, drafts on demand), joined by the "telegraphic transfer on London" in Sydney from August 1906 as a further usance, which became the most important quotation of Australia on London. In contrast to this, another usance had prevailed on all Australian exchange markets during the 19th century, namely "until 1857 the normal usance of bills of exchange [was] ... thirty days after sight, after which standard usance became sixty days after sight in recognition of the fact that, with mails carried by steamship, bills could reach London long before the goods with which they were associated" (BUTLIN / GINSWICK / STATHAM [1986], p. 318).

References: Robert CHALMERS, *History of Currency in the British Colonies*, London 1893 [repr. Colchester 1972], pp. 242–268, 273–278; Sydney J. BUTLIN, *Foundations of the Australian Monetary System 1788–1851*, Melbourne 1953 (Sydney ²1968); Noel G. BUTLIN / J. GINSWICK / P. STATHAM, Colonial Statistics before 1850, *Australian National University, Source Papers in Economic History* No. 12, June 1986; Sydney J. BUTLIN, *The Australian Monetary System 1851 to 1914*, [Sydney] 1986; Noel G. BUTLIN, *Forming a Colonial Economy, Australia 1810–1850*, Cambridge 1994.

30.1 Exchange rates of Sydney, Melbourne and Adelaide

30.1.1 On London

	SYDNEY on:			MELBOURNE on:			ADELAIDE on:		
	London [a]			London [b]			London [c]		
	per 100 pounds sterling [d]								
	in pounds sterling								
1822	105.29	30d/s	(7)						
1823	119.17	30d/s	(y)						
1824									
1825	114.50	30d/s	(y)						
1826	*103.00*	30d/s	(y)						
1827	*103.00*	30d/s	(y)						
1828	*101.50*	30d/s	(y)						
1829	*101.50*	30d/s	(y)						
1830	*101.50*	30d/s	(y)						
1831	*101.50*	30d/s	(y)						
1832	*101.50*	30d/s	(y)						
1833	*101.50*	30d/s	(y)						
1834	*101.50*	30d/s	(y)						
1835	*100.00*	30d/s	(y)						
1836	*100.00*	30d/s	(y)						
1837	*100.00*	30d/s	(y)						
1838	*101.50*	30d/s	(y)				98.67	30d/s	(3)
1839	104.00	30d/s	(y)				103.25	30d/s	(2)
1840	103.00	30d/s	(y)				101.31	30d/s	(4)
1841	101.25	30d/s	(y)				101.50	30d/s	(12)
1842	102.50	30d/s	(y)				100.38	30d/s	(12)
1843	100.25	30d/s	(y)				100.75	30d/s	(10)
1844	97.75	30d/s	(y)				101.50	30d/s	(4)
1845	97.00	30d/s	(y)				100.50	30d/s	(12)
1846	98.50	30d/s	(2)				100.00	30d/s	(12)
1847	100.67	30d/s	(6)				100.50	30d/s	(4)
1848	100.63	30d/s	(4)				102.00	30d/s	(1)
1849	102.77	30d/s	(11)				100.83	30d/s	(3)
1850	100.05	30d/s	(12)				100.17	30d/s	(3)
1851	98.25	30d/s	(12)	97.07	30d/s	(7)	99.38	30d/s	(2)
1852	92.28	30d/s	(9)	91.32	30d/s	(7)	95.42	30d/s	(6)
1853	100.23	30d/s	(12)	97.70	30d/s	(5)	99.96	30d/s	(7)
1854	103.82	30d/s	(11)	102.40	30d/s	(5)	102.00	30d/s	(2)
1855	102.07	30d/s	(8)	100.38	30d/s	(8)	101.80	30d/s	(5)

	SYDNEY on:			MELBOURNE on:			ADELAIDE on:		
	London			London [b]			London		
	per 100 pounds sterling [d]								
	in pounds sterling								
1856	101.50	30d/s	(9)	100.30	30d/s	(4)	100.10	30d/s	(5)
1857	101.54	30d/s	(7)	102.00	30d/s	(2)	101.25	30d/s	(2)
1858	100.59	30d/s	(9)	100.25	60d/s	(4)	100.96	60d/s	(6)
1859	101.08	30d/s	(7)	101.40	60d/s	(5)	101.29	60d/s	(7)
1860	100.84	30d/s	(12)	99.75	60d/s	(2)			
1861	101.00	30d/s	(12)	100.63	60d/s	(4)	101.00	60d/s	(5)
1862	101.23	30d/s	(12)	100.60	60d/s	(5)	101.19	60d/s	(4)
1863	100.92	30d/s	(12)	100.45	60d/s	(5)	100.50	60d/s	(2)
1864	100.38	30d/s	(12)	99.88	60d/s	(10)	99.75	60d/s	(1)
1865	100.63	30d/s	(12)	100.38	60d/s	(5)	100.18	60d/s	(5)
1866	101.19	30d/s	(12)	100.53	60d/s	(9)	101.25	60d/s	(3)
1867	101.40	30d/s	(12)	100.50	60d/s	(4)	99.75	60d/s	(4)
1868	100.77	60d/s	(12)	100.58	60d/s	(3)	100.25	60d/s	(2)
1869	101.00	60d/s	(9)	100.48	60d/s	(9)	100.25	60d/s	(2)
1870	100.39	60d/s	(8)	100.87	60d/s	(9)	100.52	60d/s	(7)
1871	99.94	60d/s	(y)	100.17	60d/s	(3)	100.00	60d/s	(2)
1872	100.33	60d/s	(7)	100.10	60d/s	(5)	99.95	60d/s	(5)
1873	100.13	60d/s	(7)	99.38	60d/s	(8)	100.06	60d/s	(2)
1874	100.25	60d/s	(9)	99.67	60d/s	(5)	100.13	60d/s	(2)
1875	100.52	60d/s	(8)	100.30	60d/s	(5)	100.06	60d/s	(2)
1876	100.60	60d/s	(4)	99.50	60d/s	(6)			
1877	100.65	60d/s	(5)	100.02	60d/s	(4)			
1878									
1879				99.75	60d/s	(1)			
1880				99.00	60d/s	(1)			
1881				99.47	60d/s	(4)	99.88	60d/s	(1)
1882	100.00	60d/s	(2)	100.05	60d/s	(3)			
1883	100.00	60d/s	(1)	99.25	60d/s	(2)			
1884	99.96	60d/s	(6)	100.00	60d/s	(5)	99.88	60d/s	(3)
1885	100.23	60d/s	(11)	100.21	60d/s	(7)	100.35	60d/s	(6)
1886	100.32	60d/s	(12)	100.30	60d/s	(12)	100.32	60d/s	(12)
1887	99.94	60d/s	(12)	99.99	60d/s	(12)	99.99	60d/s	(11)
1888	100.25	60d/s	(12)	100.25	60d/s	(11)	100.25	60d/s	(11)
1889	100.28	60d/s	(12)	100.21	60d/s	(11)	100.28	60d/s	(11)
1890	100.16	60d/s	(12)	100.13	60d/s	(11)	100.13	60d/s	(11)
1891	100.21	60d/s	(12)	100.10	60d/s	(12)	100.10	60d/s	(12)
1892	100.17	60d/s	(12)	100.15	60d/s	(12)	100.15	60d/s	(12)
1893	100.05	60d/s	(12)	100.04	60d/s	(11)	100.04	60d/s	(11)

	SYDNEY on:	MELBOURNE on:	ADELAIDE on:
	London	London	London
	per 100 pounds sterling [d]		
	in pounds sterling		
1894	100.13 60d/s (11)	100.12 60d/s (10)	100.12 60d/s (10)
1895	100.11 60d/s (10)	100.35 60d/s (8)	100.30 60d/s (8)
1896	100.20 60d/s (12)	100.20 60d/s (10)	100.25 60d/s (10)
1897	100.35 60d/s (12)	100.32 60d/s (11)	100.32 60d/s (11)
1898	100.33 60d/s (12)	100.01 60d/s (8)	99.91 60d/s (8)
1899	100.09 60d/s (12)	100.05 60d/s (9)	100.05 60d/s (9)
1900	99.91 60d/s (12)	100.06 60d/s (7)	100.06 60d/s (7)
1901	99.99 60d/s (12)	100.19 60d/s (10)	100.19 60d/s (10)
1902	99.91 60d/s (12)	99.87 60d/s (9)	99.87 60d/s (9)
1903	99.99 60d/s (12)	100.00 60d/s (7)	100.02 60d/s (8)
1904	99.78 60d/s (12)	99.73 60d/s (8)	99.73 60d/s (8)
1905	99.85 60d/s (12)	99.75 60d/s (9)	99.75 60d/s (9)
1906	99.77 60d/s (12)	99.69 60d/s (10)	99.69 60d/s (10)
1907	99.18 60d/s (12)	99.39 60d/s (2)	99.39 60d/s (10)

[a]   1822–1838: Treasury bills.
       1839–1845: bank bills of the Union Bank of Australia.
       "No course of Exchange existed during the first half of the Year 1822" (*Blue Books ... New South Wales*, 1825, p. 161).
       For the period between 1826 and 1838 officially fixed rates are given here only. The quotation of 1828 covers the period after May 8th and 24th 1828 respectively.
       The quotation of 1835 corresponds to the quotation after February 28th 1835. Before that date there had been an exchange rate of 98.50 pounds sterling. "Few, if any, Bills of Exchange are negociated on Foreign Countries, and no Rate of Exchange on such Bills can therefore be quoted" (*Blue Books ... New South Wales*, 1835, p. 174).
       The quotation of 1838 covers the period after August 13th 1838. Before that date there had been an exchange rate of 100.00 pounds sterling.

[b]   1851: quotation of the Bank of Australasia and the Union Bank of Australia.
       1852: quotation of the Bank of Australasia.
       1853: quotation of the Bank of Australasia, the Bank of Victoria and the Bank of New South Wales.
       1854, 1860 to 1863 and 1872: quotations of the Bank of Victoria.

[c]   Up to 1851: quotations of the Bank of South Australia.

[d]   Concerning the British currency, see pp. 3–5.

30.2 Exchange rates of Australia

30.2.1 On London

	AUSTRALIA [a] on:
	London
	per 100 pounds sterling [b]
	in pounds sterling, from 1911 in pounds of Australia
1906	*100.88* t.t. (5)
1907	*100.90* t.t. (12)
1908	101.11 t.t. (12)
1909	100.97 t.t. (12)
1910	100.84 t.t. (12)
1911	100.75 t.t. (12)
1912	100.87 t.t. (12)
1913	100.87 t.t. (12)
1914	100.75 t.t. (7)

[a]   1906 and 1907: quotations of Sydney.
      From 1908 on: quotations of Sydney, Melbourne and Adelaide.

[b]   Concerning the British currency, see pp. 3–5.

31

New Zealand (1841–1914)

Exchange markets: Auckland (1841–1852) and Wellington (1892–1914)

Sources: <u>Auckland</u>: PRO London, CO 213: *Blue Books of the Colony of the Province of New Munster*, vols. 27–39 (1841–1853). <u>Wellington</u>: *New Zealand Trade Review and Wellington Price Current* (1892–1914).

Concordance: *WdW V*, pp. 44, 269–279

Currency at Auckland and Wellington: From the beginning of British rule the pound sterling of 20 shillings at 12 pence (see pp. 3–5) was the common currency used for all transactions in New Zealand. In 1858 sterling also became officially the legal tender of New Zealand.

Original quotations at Auckland and Wellington

on:	in:	per:
Australia	% premium or discount	100 pounds sterling
	from 1911 % premium or discount	100 Australian pounds
London	% premium or discount	100 pounds sterling

Other data available from Wellington: London, 30d/s (1892–1914); 60d/s (1892–1914); 90d/s (1892–1904).

Exchange rate quotations from New Zealand are available only for two short periods, first for 1841 to 1852 and then from 1892 onwards. That the reports of the colonial government to the government in London – the *Blue Books* – do not list any exchange rate quotations for all the other years can be put down to the colonial administration in New Zealand, which was quite disorganized compared to those of other colonies.

Around the mid-19th century five towns are mentioned in the *Blue Books*, which quoted exchange rates, each one covering different periods:

Exchange places of New Zealand and their quotations in the mid-19th century

	Quotations on London	Quotations on Australia
Auckland	1841–1852	1842–1852
Wellington	1841–1847	1842–1848
Nelson	1842–1847	1842 and 1847
New Plymouth	1843–1851	1843 and 1847–1850
Russell	1843–1848	1847–1848

In the context of payment transactions, Wellington, Russell, New Plymouth and Nelson fulfilled rather local functions, limited to a few years of the early days of the colony. In comparison to this the capital Auckland was the most important exchange place about the mid-19th century, which can be inferred from the temporal continuity within the source.

The bills of exchange were classified in the *Blue Books* according to their quotation from 1842: the bank bills were drawn by a bank on demand on a corresponding bank in London (or Sydney) and sold to the prospective customer. Such bills were quoted in Auckland, Wellington and Nelson. Then there were private bills merchants who drew on a correspondent in England or Australia. Exchange rates are given for them in all five towns mentioned above. Thus the most important competitors of the banks concerning the exchange operations of these years were those "various missonary societies, who drew bills on their headquarters in London" (BUTLIN [1961], p. 158), and the Commissariat, which drew the so-called Commissiory bills on Sydney on behalf of the natives as well as for the pay of the troops, as well as the navy, which drew navy bills on London. Then both kinds of bills were sold to merchants on the spot. These bills were quoted in the *Blue Books* for the first time in 1847 in Auckland, Wellington and Russell instead of the bank bills listed up to now. Bank bills were listed in general on the parity or with a premium between ¼% and 3%, whereas private bills were listed with a discount of up to 5% and even 10% in Russell in 1848.

Generally speaking the different banks, from the late 1840s, had a determining influence on the exchange market. So, the *Blue Book* of 1854 noted that the official exchange rates were regulated by the Union Bank of Australia, which had been based in Auckland since January 1848 and which had branches in the Provinces of Auckland, Wellington, Nelson and Canterbury, its main part of the work consisting of exchange transactions (*Blue Book ... New Munster*, 1854, p. 224). Its most important competitor in exchange business became the Oriental Bank Corporation when it opened a branch in Auckland in August 1847. "Unable to secure discount business of a normal type, the Oriental took twelve-months bills secured by mortgages, 'a system ... unwise, unsafe, and in direct violation of every sound principle of banking'" (BUTLIN [1961], p. 162). Because of that, as John McMullen, Inspector of the Union Bank in New Zealand, emphasized in 1858, New Zealand was not comparable with Australia; "it is not in fact an open exchange market in which they can operate as they do here [in Melbourne]" (ibid., p. 163).

From November 1892 on there are quotations on London and Australia from Wellington, as probably the most important financial place of New Zealand from this time onwards, i.e. current rates were given for the first time. Apart from the various usances quoted, buying and selling rates were also distinguished, which were averaged for the statistical series at hand. The sum of the premium, respectively the discount, could be quite different in the individual months of a year. Because of many remittances to New Zealand, it was often possible, above all during the wool season, to buy bills on London at the rate of the parity as an equivalent to the wool delivered to England. Telegraphic transfers were not quoted in New Zealand until 1913, which is comparatively late. In 1914 telegraphic transfers were more expensive by 1.84% than the bills, which had the longest period of currency at that time, namely 60 days' sight. Australia was quoted in Wellington in the same way as London, but without the usance being given.

References: Robert CHALMERS, *History of Currency in the British Colonies*, London 1893 [repr. Colchester 1972], pp. 286–291; Sydney J. BUTLIN, *Australia and New Zealand Bank. The Bank of Australasia and the Union Bank of Australia Limited, 1828–1951*, London 1961; Markus A. DENZEL, Neuseeländisch-europäischer Zahlungsverkehr: Neuseeländische Wechselkurse vor 1914, in *WdW V*, pp. 28–46.

31.1 Auckland exchange rates

31.1.1 On London and Australia

	AUCKLAND on:					
	London [a]			Australia (Sydney) [b]		
	per 100 pounds sterling [c]			per 100 pounds sterling [d]		
	in pounds sterling					
1841	100.00	[e]	(y)			
1842	100.00	[e]	(y)	101.00	[e]	(y)
1843	98.50	[e]	(y)			
1844	100.25	[e]	(y)	101.50	[e]	(y)
1845						
1846						
1847	102.50	[e]	(y)	102.50	[e]	(y)
1848	100.00	[e]	(y)	100.00	[e]	(y)
1849	100.00	[e]	(y)	100.00	[e]	(y)
1850	100.00	[e]	(y)	100.00	[e]	(y)
1851	97.50	[e]	(y)	99.50	[e]	(y)
1852	97.50	[e]	(y)	97.50	[e]	(y)

[a]   1842 to 1847 bank bills, 1843 private bills, 1848 to 1852 Commissionary and navy bills.

[b]   1842 to 1847 bank bills, 1848 to 1850 Commissionary and navy bills, 1851 private bills, 1852 Commissionary and navy bills.

[c]   Concerning the British currency, see pp. 3–5.

[d]   Concerning the currency of New South Wales, see pp. 581f.

[e]   No usances were given in the documented sources.

31.2 Wellington exchange rates

31.2.1 On London and Australia

	WELLINGTON on:				
	London		**Australia (Sydney)**		
	per 100 pounds sterling [a]		per 100 pounds sterling, from 1911 per 100 Australian pounds [b]		
	in pounds sterling				
1892	101.75	dem	(2)	100.50	[c]	(2)
1893	100.76	dem	(12)	100.08	[c]	(7)
1894	100.75	dem	(12)	100.00	[c]	(7)
1895	100.75	dem	(12)	100.00	[c]	(12)
1896	100.75	dem	(12)	100.00	[c]	(12)
1897	100.75	dem	(12)	100.00	[c]	(12)
1898	100.75	dem	(12)	100.00	[c]	(12)
1899	100.75	dem	(12)	100.00	[c]	(12)
1900	100.55	dem	(12)	100.00	[c]	(12)
1901	100.57	dem	(12)	100.00	[c]	(12)
1902	100.57	dem	(12)	100.00	[c]	(12)
1903	100.45	dem	(12)	100.00	[c]	(12)
1904	100.41	dem	(12)	100.00	[c]	(12)
1905	100.32	dem	(12)	100.00	[c]	(12)
1906	100.13	dem	(12)	100.00	[c]	(12)
1907	100.05	dem	(12)	100.00	[c]	(12)
1908	99.98	dem	(12)	100.00	[c]	(12)
1909	99.97	dem	(12)	100.00	[c]	(12)
1910	99.82	dem	(12)	100.00	[c]	(12)
1911	99.82	dem	(12)	100.00	[c]	(12)
1912	99.82	dem	(12)	100.00	[c]	(12)
1913	100.88	t.t.	(12)	100.00	[c]	(12)
1914	101.07	t.t.	(7)	100.00	[c]	(7)

[a]   Concerning the British currency, see pp. 3–5.

[b]   Concerning the Australian currency, see pp. 581f.

[c]   No usances were given in the documented sources.

AFRICA

32
Egypt (1869–1914)

Exchange market: Alexandria (1869–1914)

Sources: *The Economist*, London (1869–1890); *Egyptian Gazette*, Alexandria & Cairo (1884, 1893–1914).

Concordance: *WdW VIII*, pp. 135–167

Currency: The basis of the Egyptian currency in the 19th century was the piastre (kurus) of 40 para. After the Turkish–Egyptian treaty of 1840, the piastre of both Turkish and Egyptian strikes should be equal by value, but the piastre of the Egyptian currency was commonly regarded as being of higher value than the Turkish one (see Chapter 13). Therefore 10 Egyptian piastres were equal to 11 Turkish piastres in Alexandria around the mid-19th century, whereas 10 Egyptian piastres were equal to 11.71 (since 1839) and later on to 11.27 Turkish piastres.

In 1834 Egypt adopted the bimetallic standard on the basis of the Marie Theresa thaler, the famous Austrian trade coin for the Levant which was called abu taqa in Egypt, as the main coin unit equal to 20 piastre (confirmed by the Coin Act of 1842 and the government tariff of February 15th 1859). The piastre of 1839 contained 1.146 grammes of fine silver, the piastre of 1801 approximately 4.6 grammes of fine silver. The most important Egyptian coins, the bedidlik in gold (= 100 piastres; 7.487 grammes of fine gold) and the rial in silver (20 piastres; 23.294 grammes of fine silver), were minted since 1836/39 in the wake of the currency reform of December 1835, in force from May 1836. In addition, official money rates were fixed for these foreign coins whose circulation was allowed, but all these coins were undervalued, such as the British sovereign with 97½ piastres. This reform brought little improvement, because "foreign coins circulated much above the tariff rate, their value often fluctuating greatly from one part of the country to another" (OWEN [1969], p. 384). To make the quoting of the exchange rates independent of the devaluations of the Egyptian government, during this decade and those that followed the quotation was either done in Marie Theresa thalers or in piastres Egyptian money, as Egyptian money, both the actually minted Egyptian silver coins and the internationally accepted trade coins were understood, each at their daily price.

Due to the pressure imposed by the British occupying power, the fall in silver prices from the end of the 1860s and the unsuccessful coin policy of the Egyptian government led to a currency reform in 1885. So bimetallism was superseded by the gold standard. Based on the model of the British sovereign and the Turkish lira, the Egyptian pound or lira (guinée el maes; 7.4375 grammes of fine gold) of 100 piastres became the basic monetary unit. Pieces of 10 piastres, the so-called Parisi, were minted in silver (11.25 grammes of fine silver) and 20 Egyptian piastres were equal to the 5-francs piece (the so-called real franca) or 1 piastre (1 1/8 grammes of fine silver) was equal to ¼ franc. Therefore the Marie Theresa thaler was fixed at 21 piastres and the sovereign at 97½ piastres as was done since 1835 (cf. ISSAWI [ed.] [1966], p. 523). This decree of November 14th 1885 remained in force even after the period documented here: "On the outbreak of the First World War Egypt shifted to a sterling exchange standard, and the link between the Egyptian pound and sterling was maintained until 1947" (ibid., p. 524).

Original quotations at Alexandria until 1885

on:	in:	per:
London	piastres Egyptian money	1 pound sterling
Paris	centimes	20 piastres Egyptian money or 1 Marie Theresa thaler
Switzerland	centimes/rappen	20 piastres Egyptian money or 1 Marie Theresa thaler

From 1885 all quotations were effected in piastre per 1 (on London and partially on Vienna and Trieste) or 100 units of foreign currency.

Other data available: Germany, 3m/d (1900–1914, bank bills) – London, 3m/d (1893–1914, bank bills and commercial bills); ch (1884) – Paris, 3m/d (1884, 1893–1914, bank bills and commercial bills).

Although exchange operations in Egypt were already listed in merchant manuals and travel reports of the first quarter of the 19th century (e.g. ISSAWI [ed.] [1966], p. 389), relatively regular exchange rate quotations of Alexandria can be found only comparatively late. Alexandria had became the country's most important town of maritime trade, the centre of export of Egyptian cotton and the leading Egyptian financial place for cashless payment transactions during the 19th century. Before the increasing business engagement of European merchants in Alexandria in the second half of the century, it had not been bills of exchange but internationally accepted trade coins like the Spanish peso (usually called 'colonnato') or Marie Theresa thalers that were generally the common means of payment in international trade on the "primitive money markets" of Egypt (ibid., p. 398), especially as the Egyptian silver coins were noticeably falling in value from the end of the 18th century as a result of the economic and monetary policy of the government. In contrast, a description of Egypt in 1843 contains the instruction that for payments "it is also necessary to have bills on London. They may be drawn either at Alexandria or Cairo" (WILKINSON [1843], p. 104).

Around 1848 there were only seven British private bankers in Alexandria, but from the 1850s and especially after the building of the Suez Canal (from 1859 on) the banks became significantly more important for the Egyptian economy as the foundation of incorporated banks (Bank of Egypt 1855, Anglo–Egyptian Bank 1864) shows (ISSAWI [ed.] [1966], pp. 10f.) At around that time first evidence of exchange rate quotations of Alexandria on London, Marseilles, Leghorn and Trieste can be found in contemporary merchant manuals (cf. NOBACK [1858], p. 6). But the London *Economist* did not report the quotation of Alexandria on London until the beginning of 1869, when two facts were obvious: first, a huge increase in international traffic via Egypt after the opening of the Suez Canal and, second, an extension of the international economic relations of the country, already evident from the Cotton Boom during the American Civil War (1861–1865) (OWEN [1969], passim). Additionally, "having abandoned debasement as a means of raising fiscal revenue, the Egyptian government began borrowing in the European financial markets in the 1860s for its budgetary and investment needs" (PAMUK [2000], p. 178; cf. LANDES [1958], passim). As one consequence of that process, branches of European banks were established, and Egypt became increasingly dependent on the European financial markets and powers (ISSAWI [ed.] [1966], p. 11). Thus relatively regular quotations at Alexandria on the European financial markets had become essential. According to contemporary merchant manuals Alexandria regularly quoted London, Paris and Leghorn, and, apart from this, occasionally Amsterdam, Marseilles, Genoa, Cairo and Malta during the 1870s, whereas the rate on Trieste had been cancelled because of the fluctuating value of the Austrian paper currency (e.g. NOBACK [1877], pp. 13f.; see Chapter 5). "By 1877 eight banks were providing telegraphic exchanges on Paris and London" (ISSAWI [1961], p. 10), although evidence of telegraphic transfers of this kind can not be furnished in the sources documented here.

Nevertheless, the rates of Alexandria on London documented here do not reflect the fall in silver prices because they are quoted in the so-called Egyptian money, which guaranteed relatively stable exchange rates because it was based on the actual minted, full-weighted Egyptian coins as well as on the internationally accepted trade coins.

The quotations of Alexandria on London in the *Economist* end with the British occupation of Egypt in 1882 (apart from a few quotations in 1890), but quotations on a greater network of exchange places are available in the *Egyptian Gazette* for the first time from 1884/93. London and Paris continued to be the most important exchange partners for Alexandria – in this order. Apart from this, Swiss bank places were quoted (probably already from the 1880s), which can be put down to the comparatively important role of Swiss merchants in the cotton trade (cf. WITSCHI [1987], p. 96). Since 1900, German and Italian bank places, Vienna and Trieste as well as Constantinople (the latter only until 1906), joined this group as well. Before World War I the rate overviews of single banks could also mention other places and countries as exchange partners of Alexandria, such as Belgium (e.g. SWOBODA [1913], p. 644).

In general, the quotations were made for three months' dato and cheque. Only cheques were quoted for Italian places and probably for Constantinople as well (cf. ibid.), whereas at first eight days' dato bills (1900/01) and later on cheques (1902–1906) were quoted for Austrian places. Each time the distinction was made between Banque sur Banque, Commerce sur Banque and Commerce sur Commerce which were quoted in this order and with a decreasing rate level (SWOBODA [1902], p. 28). However, the *Egyptian Gazette* differentiated only in the case of the three months' dato bills on London between bank bills and commercial bills, which obviously have to be interpreted as Banque sur Banque and Commerce sur Banque.

British dominance can be established on the Egyptian exchange market until World War I, resulting from three facts: first, Egypt gave up its bimetallism, which had been pursued since 1834; second, the gold standard was introduced in Egypt in 1885 based on the model of Great Britain, and this introduction was a result of the outstanding importance of the undervalued British gold coins for the Egyptian payment transactions, "which came to account for practically the whole monetary gold stock of Egypt" (ISSAWI [ed.] [1966], p. 524); and last but not least the intense economic and political involvement of Great Britain in the country. That is why "at the outbreak of the First World War, a shift to a sterling exchange occurred so that to all intents and purposes, Egypt became an extension of the London money market, with large movements of funds to and from London each year" (ISSAWI [1961], p. 10).

References: Gardner WILKINSON, *Modern Egypt and Thebes: Being a Description of Egypt; Including the Information Required for Travellers in that Country*, vol. I, London 1843; David S. LANDES,

Bankers and Pashas. International Finance and Economic Imperialism in Egypt, London 1958; Charles ISSAWI, Egypt since 1800: A Study in Lopsided Development, *Journal of Economic History* 21 (1961), pp. 1–25; idem. (ed.), *The Economic History of the Middle East 1800–1914. A Book of Readings*, Chicago – London 1966, esp. pp. 522–524; Edward R. J. OWEN, *Cotton and the Egyptian Economy 1820–1914. A Study in Trade and Development*, Oxford 1969, pp. 383–385; Beat WITSCHI, *Schweizer auf imperialistischen Pfaden. Die schweizerischen Handelsbeziehungen mit der Levante 1848–1914*, Stuttgart 1987; Kenneth M. CUNO, *The Pasha's Peasants. Land, Society, and Economy in Lower Egypt, 1740–1858*, Cambridge 1992, pp. 211–215; Markus A. DENZEL, Finanzplätze in der Levante und Nordafrika im 19. und 20. Jahrhundert, in: *WdW VIII*, pp. 30–70, here pp. 47–57; Sevket PAMUK, *A Monetary History of the Ottoman Empire*, Cambridge 2000, pp. 172–178.

32.1 Alexandria exchange rates

32.1.1 On London, Paris, Switzerland and Germany

	ALEXANDRIA on:			
	London [a]	**Paris**	**Switzerland** [b]	**Germany**
	per 1 pound sterling [c]	per 100 francs [d]	per 100 franken [e]	per 100 mark [f]
	in piastres Egyptian money			
1869	96.54 3m/d (12)			
1870	96.42 3m/d (11)			
1871	95.91 3m/d (11)			
1872	96.13 3m/d (8)			
1873	96.78 3m/d (9)			
1874	96.07 3m/d (10)			
1875	95.80 3m/d (10)			
1876	96.34 3m/d (9)			
1877	95.40 3m/d (5)			
1878	95.00 3m/d (1)			
1879	95.67 3m/d (3)			
1880	96.50 3m/d (4)			
1881	96.86 3m/d (7)			
1882				
1883				
1884	97.25 3m/d (1)	388.54 ch (1)	384.25 3m/d (1)	
1885				
	in Egyptian piastres			
1886				
1887				
1888				
1889				
1890	97.13 3m/d (2)			
1891				
1892				
1893	97.61 ch (12)	388.10 ch (12)	382.85 3m/d (12)	
1894	97.31 ch (4)	383.66 ch (4)	383.66 3m/d (4)	
1895	97.43 ch (8)	386.99 ch (8)	384.25 3m/d (4)	
1896	97.50 ch (12)	387.27 ch (12)	381.95 3m/d (9)	
1897	97.52 ch (12)	387.64 ch (12)	381.75 3m/d (12)	
1898	97.58 ch (12)	385.81 ch (12)	379.92 3m/d (12)	
1899	97.61 ch (12)	387.35 ch (12)	387.35 3m/d (12)	
1900	97.49 ch (12)	387.21 ch (12)	380.18 3m/d (12)	475.94 ch (12)
1901	97.37 ch (12)	387.52 ch (12)	382.33 3m/d (12)	476.95 ch (11)
1902	97.51 ch (12)	387.48 ch (12)	381.84 3m/d (12)	476.59 ch (12)

	ALEXANDRIA on:										
	London			**Paris**			**Switzerland** [b]			**Germany**	
	per 1 pound sterling [c]			per 100 francs [d]			per 100 franken [e]			per 100 mark [f]	
	in Egyptian piastres										
1903	97.53	ch	(1)	387.30	ch	(1)	382.56	3m/d	(8)	476.74	ch	(1)
1904	97.54	ch	(11)	387.58	ch	(11)	382.38	3m/d	(12)	477.21	ch	(11)
1905	97.50	ch	(12)	387.07	ch	(12)	386.63	ch	(1)	476.23	ch	(12)
1906	97.46	ch	(12)	387.38	ch	(12)	386.91	ch	(12)	476.01	ch	(12)
1907	97.30	ch	(1)	385.75	ch	(1)	385.17	ch	(1)	474.38	ch	(1)
1908	97.60	ch	(12)	388.11	ch	(12)	387.74	ch	(12)	477.61	ch	(12)
1909	97.58	ch	(12)	387.50	ch	(12)	387.08	ch	(12)	476.52	ch	(12)
1910	97.47	ch	(12)	386.42	ch	(12)	385.77	ch	(12)	476.19	ch	(12)
1911	97.41	ch	(12)	385.66	ch	(12)	385.31	ch	(12)	475.74	ch	(12)
1912	97.39	ch	(12)	385.72	ch	(12)	384.83	ch	(12)	475.48	ch	(12)
1913	97.57	ch	(12)	386.43	ch	(12)	385.43	ch	(12)	476.52	ch	(12)
1914	97.58	ch	(7)	387.65	ch	(7)	387.15	ch	(7)	476.72	ch	(7)

[a]   1869–1881 and 1890 bank bills.

[b]   Until 1904 bank and commercial bills.

[c]   Concerning the British currency, see pp. 3–5.

[d]   Concerning the French currency, see pp. 279f.

[e]   Concerning the Swiss currency, see p. 313.

[f]   Concerning the German currency, see p. 197.

32.1.2 On Italy, the Habsburg Monarchy and Constantinople

	ALEXANDRIA on:		
	Italy	**Vienna & Trieste**	**Constantinople**
	per 100 Italian lire [a]	per 1 Marie Theresa thaler, from 1901 (5) per 100 Austrian crowns [b]	per 100 (Turkish) piastres [c]
		in Egyptian piastres	
1900	363.38 ch (12)	19.53 8d/d (12)	88.45 [d] (12)
1901	369.71 ch (12)	19.04/407.08 8d/d (4+8)	88.49 [d] (12)
1902	382.71 ch (12)	406.58 ch (12)	88.60 [d] (11)
1903	387.64 ch (9)	406.18 ch (9)	88.75 [d] (9)
1904	386.95 ch (11)	406.62 ch (11)	88.68 [d] (11)
1905	387.40 ch (12)	405.72 ch (12)	88.73 [d] (12)
1906	387.42 ch (12)	406.25 ch (7)	88.78 [d] (11)
1907	384.74 ch (9)		
1908	388.10 ch (12)		
1909	386.26 ch (12)		
1910	384.41 ch (12)		
1911	383.79 ch (12)		
1912	382.49 ch (12)		
1913	380.80 ch (12)		
1914	385.98 ch (7)		

[a]   Concerning the Italian currency, see pp. 108f.

[b]   Concerning the Austrian currency, see p. 256.

[c]   Concerning the Turkish currency, see pp. 387f.

[d]   No usance given.

33

Cape Colony/South African Union (1811–1914)

Exchange market: Cape Town (1811–1914)

Sources: CHALMERS [1893], p. 233 (1811–1814); PRO London, CO 53: *Blue Books of the Colony of the Cape of Good Hope*, vols. 60–62, 93–144 (1822/24, 1856–1907); *Cape of Good Hope and Port Natal Shipping and Mercantile Gazette* (1844–1855); *The Economist*, London (1908–1914).
Concordance: *WdW VIII*, pp. 75–95

Currency at Cape Town: Until the British conquest of the Cape Colony, the Dutch monetary system had been a determining influence in Southern Africa because of the government of the Dutch East India Company (VOC). The rixdollar (rijksdaalder) of 8 shillings or 48 stuivers and the guilder of 20 stuivers were the units of account, although the VOC had been issuing rixdollar paper currency, the so-called Cape–Dutch current, for the Cape Colony since 1781/82. In 1795, when the British conquered the Cape Colony for the first time, this paper money was quoted at 20–30% discount (CHALMERS [1893], p. 231). Under the British administration the issuing of paper money following the Dutch example continued, although the pound sterling of 20 shillings at 12 pence was introduced as official unit of payment and account (see pp. 3–5). Since the renewed Dutch occupation of the colony (from 1803 to 1806), the monetary system of the colony was destroyed: bills on Holland were quoted with a premium of 160%, the rixdollar Cape-Dutch current dropped from 4 shillings (in 1795) down to 1½ shillings. Despite the attempts at stabilizing the monetary system when Great Britain finally reconquered the Cape Colony after 1806, there was a further drastic devaluation of the currency after 1810, caused by additional extensive issues of paper money the Government Bank had carried out (PENNINGTON [1848], pp. 148f.; CHALMERS [1893], pp. 231–234).

Shillings sterling per rixdollar Cape–Dutch current (average)

1795	4	1806–1810	3½	1816–1820	1 5/6	1825	1 5/12
1803	1½	1811–1815	2½	1821–1825	1½		

Source: CHALMERS [1893], p. 234

A stabilization of the paper currency's value did not happen until the setting of the rixdollar's value at 1½ shillings (on June 6th 1825) and "the Course of the Exchange became thereby, in a manner, settled at that rate, with slight variations, depending upon the demand for bills" (*Blue Book ... Cape of Good Hope*, 1838, p. 222): "A new era had now begun for the paper rix-dollar. It had received a sterling rating at which it was readily exchangeable into sterling bills" (CHALMERS [1893], p. 235). On January 1st 1826 the British accounting in pounds sterling of 20 shillings at 12 pence was introduced as the legal one whereas the merchants often carried on calculating with the old Dutch units (*Blue Book ... Cape of Good Hope*, 1825, p. 329; ibid., 1838, p. 225). Although British money dominated the coinage system of the Cape Colony after 1825, all existing rixdollars Cape-Dutch current were withdrawn from circulation in the 1830s (until March 31st 1841): "After nearly 60 years, the currency of the Cape of Good Hope was finally purged of the paper rix-dollar" (CHALMERS [1893], p. 236). Since that time the notes issued by the eleven existing joint-stock banks were the only valid paper money of the Colony.

During the later 19th century there was only one more relevant change in the legislation concerning the currency system of the Cape Colony: on November 29th 1881 the British Coinage Act of 1870 was declared valid for the Cape Colony from February 3rd 1882 on: "By this important measure the currency of the Cape was placed on the sterling basis of gold" (ibid., p. 236). Although the South African Union was founded as a dominion of the British Empire in 1910, South African coins did not exist before 1923.

Original quotations at Cape Town

on:	in:	per:
Amsterdam	pence sterling	1 Dutch guilder
Calcutta & Madras	shillings and pence sterling	1 Company's rupee
London	shillings and pence sterling	1 pound sterling
	from 1844 per cent premium or discount	100 pounds sterling

Other data available: Bombay, 30d/s (1844–1848) – France, 30d/s (1844–1848) – London, 30d/s (government and marine bills, 1868–1870; private and mercantile bills, 1868–1880; bank bills, 1906–1914); 60d/s (bank bills, 1868–1914; private and mercantile bills, 1868–1880); 90d/s (bank bills, 1868–1914; private and mercantile bills, 1868–1880).

Exchange rate quotations of the Cape Colony or Cape Town respectively, its by far the most important exchange market, are available in the *Blue Books of the Colony of the Cape of Good Hope* for most parts of the documented period, also recording quotations from Port Elizabeth, the port for Transvaal, for the period from 1872 to 1906 (cf. *WdW VIII*, pp. 97–104). From 1906 onwards exchange rates were recorded only for the whole Cape Colony or, as the London financial publication, *The Economist*, has it, for "South Africa" (from 1910 on the South African Union).

In both sources London was the only mentioned exchange partner of the Cape. The corresponding bills of exchange were drawn by the Commissariat in Cape Town on the London Treasury. In addition, the Naval Office issued Navy bills on Amsterdam. Furthermore, Government bills were quoted on France as well as on the Indian places of Calcutta, Madras and Bombay. The corresponding quotations were published in the local *Shipping and Mercantile Gazette* (only available for a short time), but not in the *Blue Books*, since they were of no interest to the government. In the 1870s and the 1880s there were six different quotations on London from Cape Town as well as from Port Elizabeth. Usually 90 days' sight bills were used, whereas six months' sight bills were traded only in exceptional cases and were, therefore, not listed in the quotations (*Blue Book ... Cape of Good Hope*, 1869, Z2), because "banks in this Colony never draw at six months, the longest term is 120 days sight" (ibid., 1875, Z2). In contrast to this, 30 and 60 days' sight bills were also quoted for bank bills as well as for private and mercantile bills in the *Blue Books* in 1856 and from 1868 to 1880. Private bills of all usances "have, on an average, been at a small premium, but liable to very irregular fluctuations. ... Premiums on first-class Private Bills vary in a very trifling degree, if at all, from those obtained by the Commissariat for Drafts on the Treasury" (ibid., 1857, U6). Sight drafts have been recorded since 1906, while telegraphic transfer was not mentioned until 1915.

Apart from that, private exchange rate currents listed quotations on Calcutta, Madras and Bombay, Hong Kong, France and Holland. Quotations on further places of the British Empire were given in the same way as those on London, probably showing only a few rate divergences. As early as in the 1870s the rate on Paris was usually not quoted. Business transactions with Germany were done via London (NO-BACK [1877], p. 436).

No official quotation was carried out in any of the British possessions in South Africa until the period between the world wars. Exchange operations were almost exclusively processed in the banks' offices (SWOBODA [1925], p. 731).

From the second quarter of the 19th century onwards exchange rates at the Cape showed a relatively high stability, particularly when "the currency of the Cape was placed on the sterling basis of gold" on November 29th 1881 for February 3rd 1882 (CHALMERS [1893], p. 236). In contrast, the quotations of the first quarter of the 19th century had been subject to the negative influences of an unsuccessful currency policy: during the first decades after the conquest (for the first time in 1795, certainly in 1806) the British colonial power had the problem of removing the paper money of the Dutch VOC as well as that of the British administration. Simultaneously with the beginning of the stabilization of the paper currency (see above) in 1825/26, the procedures of the exchange operations in the Cape Colony changed: "Prior to the 6th June 1825, the Exchange between this Colony and Great Britain was chiefly regulated by the average rate at which the Commissariat Department disposed of its Bills (by public tender) on the Lords Commissioners of the British Treasury. … [After June 6th 1825] by the Treasury Instructions to the Commissariat, Bills drawn by that Department are issued at £101:10, for every £100, being at that rate of one and a half per cent against the Colony or remitter; and this … regulates the premium on private bills. The latter, however, are mostly sold at a discount, even of 5 per cent, although some are occasionally sold at par, i.e. a bill of £100 for the same amount in specie: but this depends upon the credit attached to the parties whose bills or endorsements are in the market, as also upon the number to be disposed of at any one time, and upon the amount which it may then be necessary to remit" (*Blue Book … Cape of Good Hope*, 1838, p. 222).

References: James PENNINGTON, *The Currency of the British Colonies*, London 1848 [repr. New York 1967], pp. 148–153; Robert CHALMERS, *History of Currency in the British Colonies*, London 1893 [repr. Colchester 1972], pp. 230–241; Ernst H. D. ARNDT, *Banking and Currency Development in South Africa, 1652–1927*, Cape Town et al. 1928; Markus A. DENZEL, Zahlungsverkehr, Wechselkurse und Währungsverhältnisse von Britischen Besitzungen in Afrika (1822–1931), in *WdW VIII*, pp. 1–29, here pp. 19–28.

33.1 Cape Town exchange rates

33.1.1 On London, Amsterdam and India

	CAPE TOWN on:
	London [a]
	per 100 pounds sterling [b]
	in pounds sterling payable in rixdollars Cape–Dutch current, from 1825 payable in sterling
1811	145.00 (y)
1812	160.00 (y)
1813	165.00 (y)
1814	180.00 (y)
1815	
1816	
1817	
1818	
1819	
1820	
1821	
1822	178.16 (9)
1823	175.25 (y)
1824	167.62 (8)
1825	*103.00* (y)
1826	*103.00* (y)
1827	*103.00* (y)
1828	*103.00* (y)
1829	*103.00* (y)
1830	*103.00* (y)
1831	*103.00* (y)
1832	*103.00* (y)
1833	*103.00* (y)
1834	*103.00* (y)
1835	*103.00* (y)
1836	*103.00* (y)
1837	*103.00* (y)
1838	*103.00* (y)
1839	*103.00* (y)
1840	*103.00* (y)

	CAPE TOWN on:		
	London [a]	**Amsterdam** [c]	**Calcutta & Madras** [d]
	per 100 pounds sterling [b]	per 1,000 Dutch guilders [e]	per 1,000 Company's rupees [f]
	in pounds sterling		
1841	*103.00* (y)		
1842	*103.00* (y)		
1843	*103.00* (y)		
1844	102.34 30d/s (12)	79.69 30d/s (1)	92.80 30d/s (12)
1845	100.10 30d/s (2)	79.34 30d/s (12)	88.37 30d/s (12)
1846	100.00 30d/s (8)	76.57 30d/s (8)	87.89 30d/s (8)
1847	100.00 30d/s (11)	75.00 30d/s (11)	88.54 30d/s (11)
1848	102.60 30d/s (12)	77.43 30d/s (12)	86.46 30d/s (12)
1849	102.86 30d/s (10)	82.47 30d/s (12)	85.42 30d/s (12)
1850	101.75 30d/s (10)	79.78 30d/s (12)	87.24 30d/s (12)
1851	100.00 30d/s (8)	78.09 30d/s (12)	95.92 30d/s (12)
1852	100.23 30d/s (12)	78.13 30d/s (12)	93.75 30d/s (12)
1853	100.48 30d/s (11)	78.13 30d/s (11)	93.37 30d/s (11)
1854	101.07 30d/s (12)	78.52 30d/s (12)	94.79 30d/s (12)
1855	102.00 30d/s (12)	78.91 30d/s (12)	93.93 30d/s (12)
1856	101.76 30d/s (12)		
1857	100.01 30d/s (12)		
1858	100.47 30d/s (12)		
1859	101.00 30d/s (10)		
1860	100.88 30d/s (12)		
1861	100.09 30d/s (12)		
1862	101.61 30d/s (12)		
1863	99.91 30d/s (12)		
1864	99.55 30d/s (12)		
1865	100.37 30d/s (8)		
1866	100.46 30d/s (12)		
1867	100.34 30d/s (12)		
1868	100.00 30d/s (y)		
1869	100.00 30d/s (y)		
1870	99.34 90d/s (12)		
1871	97.94 90d/s (12)		
1872	98.56 90d/s (11)		
1873	99.45 90d/s (12)		
1874	100.34 90d/s (12)		
1875	100.40 90d/s (12)		
1876	100.40 90d/s (12)		
1877	99.17 90d/s (12)		

	CAPE TOWN on:
	London [a]
	per 100 pounds sterling [b]
	in pounds sterling
1878	98.96 90d/s (12)
1879	99.05 90d/s (12)
1880	99.88 90d/s (12)
1881	99.29 90d/s (12)
1882	100.02 90d/s (12)
1883	100.22 90d/s (12)
1884	99.39 90d/s (12)
1885	99.96 90d/s (12)
1886	99.54 90d/s (12)
1887	98.95 90d/s (12)
1888	98.93 90d/s (12)
1889	98.49 90d/s (12)
1890	98.90 90d/s (12)
1891	99.78 30d/s (12)
1892	100.36 30d/s (12)
1893	99.58 30d/s (12)
1894	99.48 30d/s (12)
1895	99.06 30d/s (12)
1896	99.88 30d/s (12)
1897	100.25 30d/s (12)
1898	100.11 30d/s (12)
1899	99.43 30d/s (12)
1900	99.67 30d/s (12)
1901	99.79 30d/s (12)
1902	99.78 30d/s (12)
1903	99.84 30d/s (12)
1904	99.86 30d/s (12)
1905	99.68 30d/s (12)
1906	*100.22* s (12)
1907	*100.12* s (12)
1908	99.51 s (8)
1909	99.39 s (12)
1910	99.43 s (12)
1911	99.61 s (12)
1912	99.61 s (12)
1913	99.48 s (12)
1914	99.52 s (7)

[a] From 1825 to 1843 official rates are presented. Up to 1843 no data for the usance can be given. From 1825 up to 1869 the quotations are for Government bills and for Navy bills, from 1870 for bank bills. Since 1906 quotations of South Africa, i.e. of Cape Town and Port Elizabeth, are documented. 1906/07 selling rates.

[b] Concerning the British currency, see pp. 3–5.

[c] Navy bills.

[d] Government bills.

[e] Concerning the Dutch currency, see p. 59.

[f] Concerning the Indian currency, see pp. 495f.